FOURTH EDITION

The Earth and Its Peoples

A Global History

Volume II:

Since 1500

Richard W. Bulliet
Columbia University

Pamela Kyle Crossley
Dartmouth College

Daniel R. Headrick
Roosevelt University

Steven W. Hirsch
Tufts University

Lyman L. Johnson
University of North Carolina –Charlotte

David Northrup
Boston College

Houghton Mifflin Company

Boston   New York

Publisher for History and Political Science: Suzanne Jeans
Senior Sponsoring Editor: Nancy Blaine
Senior Marketing Manager: Katherine Bates
Marketing Assistant: Lauren Bussard
Senior Development Editor: Katie White
Editorial Assistant: Adrienne Zicht
Senior Project Editor: Carol Newman
Editorial Assistant: Paola Moll
Senior Art and Design Coordinator: Jill Haber
Cover Design Director: Tony Saizon
Senior Photo Editor: Jennifer Meyer Dare
Composition Buyer: Chuck Dutton
New Title Project Manager: James Lonergan

Cover image: Diego Rivera (1866-1957). *The Canoe with Flowers*, 1939. Fundacion Dolores Olmedo, Mexico City, D. F. Mexico © Banco de Mexico Trsut/Schalkwijk/Art Resource, NY.

Printed in the U.S.A.

Library of Congress Catalog Card Number: 2006938351

Instructor's exam copy:
ISBN 13: 978-0-618-83432-7
ISBN 10: 0-618-83432-X

For orders, use student text ISBNs:
ISBN 13: 978-0-618-77151-6
ISBN 10: 0-618-77151-4

2 3 4 5 6 7 8 9—VH—10 09 08 07

BRIEF CONTENTS

INTRODUCTION: THE WORLD BEFORE 1500   *xxi*

16 The Maritime Revolution, to 1550 *458*

PART FIVE
THE GLOBE ENCOMPASSED, 1500–1750   **488**

17 Transformations in Europe, 1500–1750 *490*
18 The Diversity of American Colonial Societies, 1530–1770 *518*
19 The Atlantic System and Africa, 1550–1800 *548*
20 Southwest Asia and the Indian Ocean, 1500–1750 *576*
21 Northern Eurasia, 1500–1800 *604*

PART SIX
REVOLUTIONS RESHAPE THE WORLD, 1750–1870   **634**

22 Revolutionary Changes in the Atlantic World, 1750–1850 *636*
23 The Early Industrial Revolution, 1760–1851 *666*
24 Nation Building and Economic Transformation in the Americas, 1800–1890 *692*

25 Land Empires in the Age of Imperialism, 1800–1870 *726*
26 Africa, India, and the New British Empire, 1750–1870 *754*

PART SEVEN
GLOBAL DIVERSITY AND DOMINANCE, 1850–1945   **784**

27 The New Power Balance, 1850–1900 *786*
28 The New Imperialism, 1869–1914 *816*
29 The Crisis of the Imperial Order, 1900–1929 *844*
30 The Collapse of the Old Order, 1929–1949 *876*
31 Striving for Independence: India, Africa, and Latin America, 1900–1949 *906*

PART EIGHT
PERILS AND PROMISES OF A GLOBAL COMMUNITY, 1945 TO THE PRESENT   **932**

32 The Cold War and Decolonization, 1945–1975 *934*
33 The End of the Cold War and the Challenge of Economic Development and Immigration, 1975–2000 *964*
34 Globalization in the New Millennium *996*

CONTENTS

Maps *xi*
Environment and Technology *xii*
Diversity and Dominance *xii*
Material Culture *xii*
Issues in World History *xii*
Preface *xiii*
About the Authors *xviii*
Note on Spelling and Usage *xix*

INTRODUCTION: THE WORLD BEFORE 1500 *xxi*

16 THE MARITIME REVOLUTION, TO 1550 458

Global Maritime Expansion Before 1450 *460*
  The Pacific Ocean *460* • The Indian Ocean *462*
  • The Atlantic Ocean *465*
European Expansion, 1400–1550 *465*
  • Motives for Exploration *466* • Portuguese
  Voyages *467* • Spanish Voyages *470*
Encounters with Europe, 1450–1550 *473*
  Western Africa *473* • Eastern Africa *474*
  • Indian Ocean States *475* • The Americas *479*
Comparative Perspectives *482*

Summary *483* • Key Terms *484*

Suggested Reading *484* • Notes *485*

ENVIRONMENT AND TECHNOLOGY: Vasco da Gama's Fleet *471*
DIVERSITY AND DOMINANCE: Kongo's Christian King *476*
ISSUES IN WORLD HISTORY: Climate and Population, to 1500 *486*

PART FIVE

The Globe Encompassed, 1500–1750 488

17 TRANSFORMATIONS IN EUROPE, 1500–1750 490

Culture and Ideas *492*
  Religious Reformation *492* • Traditional Thinking
  and Witch-Hunts *496* • The Scientific Revolution *497*
  • The Early Enlightenment *498*
Social and Economic Life *499*
  The Bourgeoisie *499* • Peasants and Laborers *502*
  • Women and the Family *504*

Political Innovations *505*
  State Development *505* • Religious Policies *507*
  • Monarchies in England and France *507* • Warfare
  and Diplomacy *511* • Paying the Piper *512*
Comparative Perspectives *515*

Summary *515* • Key Terms *516*

Suggested Reading *517* • Notes *517*

ENVIRONMENT AND TECHNOLOGY: Mapping the World *501*
DIVERSITY AND DOMINANCE: Political Craft and Craftiness *508*

18 THE DIVERSITY OF AMERICAN COLONIAL SOCIETIES, 1530–1770 518

The Columbian Exchange *520*
  Demographic Changes *520* • Transfer of Plants and
  Animals *522*
Spanish America and Brazil *523*
  State and Church *523* • Colonial Economies *526*
  • Society in Colonial Latin America *529*
English and French Colonies in North America *534*
  Early English Experiments *534* • The South *534*
  • New England *536* • The Middle Atlantic
  Region *537* • French America *538*
Colonial Expansion and Conflict *541*
  Imperial Reform in Spanish America and Brazil *541*
  • Reform and Reorganization in British America *543*
Comparative Perspectives *544*

Summary *544* • Key Terms *546*

Suggested Reading *546* • Notes *547*

ENVIRONMENT AND TECHNOLOGY: A Silver Refinery at
  Potosí, Bolivia, 1700 *527*
DIVERSITY AND DOMINANCE: Race and Ethnicity
  in the Spanish Colonies: Negotiating Hierarchy *530*

19 THE ATLANTIC SYSTEM AND AFRICA, 1550–1800 548

Plantations in the West Indies *550*
  Colonization Before 1650 *550* • Sugar and Slaves *552*
Plantation Life in the Eighteenth Century *553*
  Technology and Environment *553* • Slaves' Lives *555*
  • Free Whites and Free Blacks *558*
Creating the Atlantic Economy *559*
  Capitalism and Mercantilism *559* • The Atlantic
  Circuit *561*
Africa, the Atlantic, and Islam *565*

The Gold Coast and the Slave Coast *565* • The Bight of Biafra and Angola *567* • Africa's European and Islamic Contacts *568*

Comparative Perspectives *573*

Summary *574* • Key Terms *574*

Suggested Reading *575* • Notes *575*

ENVIRONMENT AND TECHNOLOGY: Amerindian Foods in Africa *555*

DIVERSITY AND DOMINANCE: Slavery in West Africa and the Americas *571*

20 SOUTHWEST ASIA AND THE INDIAN OCEAN, 1500–1750   576

The Ottoman Empire, to 1750 *578*
Expansion and Frontiers *578* • Central Institutions *582* • Crisis of the Military State, 1585–1650 *586* • Economic Change and Growing Weakness, 1650–1750 *586*

The Safavid Empire, 1502–1722 *589*
The Rise of the Safavids *589* • Society and Religion *589* • A Tale of Two Cities: Isfahan and Istanbul *591* • Economic Crisis and Political Collapse *593*

The Mughal Empire, 1526–1761 *594*
Political Foundations *594* • Hindus and Muslims *596* • Central Decay and Regional Challenges, 1707–1761 *597*

The Maritime Worlds of Islam, 1500-1750 *597*
Muslims in Southeast Asia *598* • Muslims in Coastal Africa *600* • European Powers in Southern Seas *601*

Summary *602* • Key Terms *602*

Suggested Reading *603* • Notes *603*

DIVERSITY AND DOMINANCE: Islamic Law and Ottoman Rule *584*

ENVIRONMENT AND TECHNOLOGY: Tobacco and Waterpipes *588*

21 NORTHERN EURASIA, 1500–1800   604

Japanese Reunification *606*
Civil War and the Invasion of Korea, 1500–1603 *606* • The Tokugawa Shogunate, to 1800 *607* • Japan and the Europeans *610* • Elite Decline and Social Crisis *611*

The Later Ming and Early Qing Empires *612*
The Ming Empire, 1500–1644 *612* • Ming Collapse and the Rise of the Qing *613* • Trading Companies and Missionaries *615* • Emperor Kangxi (r. 1662–1722) *615* • Chinese Influences on Europe *619* • Tea and Diplomacy *620* • Population and Social Stress *621*

The Russian Empire *622*
The Drive Across Northern Asia *622* • Russian Society and Politics to 1725 *623* • Peter the Great *625* • Consolidation of the Empire *627*

Comparative Perspectives *628*

Summary *629* • Key Terms *630*

Suggested Reading *630* • Notes *631*

ENVIRONMENT AND TECHNOLOGY: East Asian Porcelain *609*

DIVERSITY AND DOMINANCE: Gendered Violence: The Yangzhou Massacre *616*

ISSUES IN WORLD HISTORY: The Little Ice Age *632*

PART SIX

Revolutions Reshape the World, 1750–1870   634

22 REVOLUTIONARY CHANGES IN THE ATLANTIC WORLD, 1750–1850   636

Prelude to Revolution: The Eighteenth-Century Crisis *638*
Colonial Wars and Fiscal Crises *638* • The Enlightenment and the Old Order *640* • Folk Cultures and Popular Protest *642*

The American Revolution, 1775–1800 *643*
Frontiers and Taxes *643* • The Course of Revolution, 1775–1783 *644* • The Construction of Republican Institutions, to 1800 *646*

The French Revolution, 1789–1815 *647*
French Society and Fiscal Crisis *648* • Protest Turns to Revolution, 1789–1792 *649* • The Terror, 1793–1794 *651* • Reaction and the Rise of Napoleon, 1795–1815 *653*

Revolution Spreads, Conservatives Respond, 1789–1850 *656*
The Haitian Revolution, 1789–1804 *658* • The Congress of Vienna and Conservative Retrenchment, 1815–1820 *660* • Nationalism, Reform, and Revolution, 1821–1850 *660*

Comparative Perspectives *662*

Summary *663* • Key Terms *664*

Suggested Reading *665* • Notes *665*

ENVIRONMENT AND TECHNOLOGY: The Guillotine *652*

DIVERSITY AND DOMINANCE: Robespierre and Wollstonecraft Defend and Explain the Terror *654*

23 THE EARLY INDUSTRIAL REVOLUTION, 1760–1851 666

Causes of the Industrial Revolution 668
Population Growth 668 • The Agricultural Revolution 669 • Trade and Inventiveness 670 • Britain and Continental Europe 670

The Technological Revolution 674
Mass Production: Pottery 674 • Mechanization: The Cotton Industry 675 • The Iron Industry 676 • The Steam Engine 677 • Railroads 678 • Communication over Wires 679

The Impact of the Early Industrial Revolution 680
The New Industrial Cities 680 • Rural Environments 681 • Working Conditions 682 • Changes in Society 685

New Economic and Political Ideas 686
Laissez Faire and Its Critics 686 • Positivists and Utopian Socialists 687 • Protests and Reforms 687

The Limits of Industrialization Outside the West 688

Summary 690 • Key Terms 690

Suggested Reading 691 • Notes 691

DIVERSITY AND DOMINANCE: Adam Smith and the Division of Labor 672

ENVIRONMENT AND TECHNOLOGY: Gas Lighting 683

24 NATION BUILDING AND ECONOMIC TRANSFORMATION IN THE AMERICAS, 1800–1890 692

Independence in Latin America, 1800–1830 694
Roots of Revolution, to 1810 694 • Spanish South America, 1810–1825 696 • Mexico, 1810–1823 698 • Brazil, to 1831 699

The Problem of Order, 1825–1890 702
Constitutional Experiments 702 • Personalist Leaders 703 • The Threat of Regionalism 705 • Foreign Interventions and Regional Wars 707 • Native Peoples and the Nation-State 708

The Challenge of Social and Economic Change 711
The Abolition of Slavery 711 • Immigration 713 • American Cultures 715 • Women's Rights and the Struggle for Social Justice 716 • Development and Underdevelopment 717 • Altered Environments 720

Comparative Perspectives 722

Summary 723 • Key Terms 724

Suggested Reading 724 • Notes 725

DIVERSITY AND DOMINANCE: The Afro-Brazilian Experience, 1828 700

ENVIRONMENT AND TECHNOLOGY: Constructing the Port of Buenos Aires, Argentina 718

25 LAND EMPIRES IN THE AGE OF IMPERIALISM, 1800–1870 726

The Ottoman Empire 728
Egypt and the Napoleonic Example, 1798–1840 728 • Ottoman Reform and the European Model, 1807–1853 730 • The Crimean War and Its Aftermath, 1853–1877 734

The Russian Empire 738
Russia and Europe 738 • Russia and Asia 739 • Cultural Trends 740

The Qing Empire 741
Economic and Social Disorder, 1800–1839 742 • The Opium War and Its Aftermath, 1839–1850 742 • The Taiping Rebellion, 1851–1864 744 • Decentralization at the End of the Qing Empire, 1864–1875 747

Comparative Perspectives 751

Summary 752 • Key Terms 752

Suggested Reading 753

ENVIRONMENT AND TECHNOLOGY: The Web of War 735

DIVERSITY AND DOMINANCE: Chinese Responses to Imperialism 749

26 AFRICA, INDIA, AND THE NEW BRITISH EMPIRE, 1750–1870 754

Changes and Exchanges in Africa 756
New African States 756 • Modernization in Egypt and Ethiopia 759 • European Penetration 761 • Abolition and Legitimate Trade 761 • Secondary Empires in Eastern Africa 763

India Under British Rule 764
Company Men 764 • Raj and Rebellion, 1818–1857 766 • Political Reform and Industrial Impact 767 • Rising Indian Nationalism 771

Britain's Eastern Empire 772
Colonies and Commerce 772 • Imperial Policies and Shipping 775 • Colonization of Australia and New Zealand 775 • New Labor Migrations 778

Comparative Perspectives 779

Summary 780 • Key Terms 781

Suggested Reading 781 • Notes 781

DIVERSITY AND DOMINANCE: Ceremonials of Imperial Domination 768

ENVIRONMENT AND TECHNOLOGY: Whaling 777

ISSUES IN WORLD HISTORY: State Power, the Census, and the Question of Identity 782

PART SEVEN

Global Diversity and Dominance, 1850–1945   **784**

27 THE NEW POWER BALANCE, 1850–1900   **786**

New Technologies and the World Economy *788*
Railroads *788* • Steamships and Telegraph Cables *789* • The Steel and Chemical Industries *790* • Electricity *791* • World Trade and Finance *792*

Social Changes *792*
Population and Migrations *792* • Urbanization and Urban Environments *794* • Middle-Class Women's "Separate Sphere" *795* • Working-Class Women *797*

Socialism and Labor Movements *797*
Marx and Socialism *797* • Labor Movements *799*

Nationalism and the Rise of Italy, Germany, and Japan *802*
Language and National Identity in Europe Before 1871 *802* • The Unification of Italy, 1860–1870 *802* • The Unification of Germany, 1866–1871 *804* • The West Challenges Japan *804* • The Meiji Restoration and the Modernization of Japan, 1868–1894 *806* • Nationalism and Social Darwinism *808*

The Great Powers of Europe, 1871–1900 *809*
Germany at the Center of Europe *809* • The Liberal Powers: France and Great Britain *809* • The Conservative Powers: Russia and Austria-Hungary *810*

China, Japan, and the Western Powers *811*
China in Turmoil *812* • Japan Confronts China *812*

Summary *813* • Key Terms *814*

Suggested Reading *815* • Notes *815*

ENVIRONMENT AND TECHNOLOGY: Railroads and Immigration *793*

MATERIAL CULTURE: Cotton Clothing *798*

DIVERSITY AND DOMINANCE: Marx and Engels on Global Trade and the Bourgeoisie *800*

28 THE NEW IMPERIALISM, 1869–1914   **816**

The New Imperialism: Motives and Methods *818*
Political Motives *818* • Cultural Motives *820* • Economic Motives *820* • The Tools of the Imperialists *821* • Colonial Agents and Administration *821*

The Scramble for Africa *823*

Egypt *823* • Western and Equatorial Africa *825* • Southern Africa *827* • Political and Social Consequences *828* • Cultural Responses *829*

Imperialism in Asia and the Pacific *832*
Central Asia *832* • Southeast Asia and Indonesia *832* • Hawaii and the Philippines, 1878–1902 *836*

Imperialism in Latin America *837*
Railroads and the Imperialism of Free Trade *837* • American Expansionism and the Spanish-American War, 1898 *838* • American Intervention in the Caribbean and Central America, 1901–1914 *838*

The World Economy and the Global Environment *839*
Expansion of the World Economy *839* • Transformation of the Global Environment *839*

Summary *841* • Key Terms *842*

Suggested Reading *843* • Notes *843*

DIVERSITY AND DOMINANCE: Two Africans Recall the Arrival of the Europeans *830*

ENVIRONMENT AND TECHNOLOGY: Imperialism and Tropical Ecology *835*

29 THE CRISIS OF THE IMPERIAL ORDER, 1900–1929   **844**

Origins of the Crisis in Europe and the Middle East *846*
The Ottoman Empire and the Balkans *846* • Nationalism, Alliances, and Military Strategy *846*

The "Great War" and the Russian Revolutions, 1914–1918 *848*
Stalemate, 1914–1917 *848* • The Home Front and the War Economy *850* • The Ottoman Empire at War *853* • Double Revolution in Russia *854* • The End of the War in Western Europe, 1917–1918 *854*

Peace and Dislocation in Europe, 1919–1929 *855*
The Impact of the War *855* • The Peace Treaties *856* • Russian Civil War and the New Economic Policy *856* • An Ephemeral Peace *859*

China and Japan: Contrasting Destinies *859*
Social and Economic Change *860* • Revolution and War, 1900–1918 *861* • Chinese Warlords and the Guomindang, 1919–1929 *862*

The New Middle East *862*
The Mandate System *862* • The Rise of Modern Turkey *863* • Arab Lands and the Question of Palestine *863*

Society, Culture, and Technology in the Industrialized World *868*
Class and Gender *868* • Revolution in the Sciences *869* • The New Technologies of Modernity *869* • Technology and the Environment *872*

Comparative Perspectives *873*

Summary *874* • Key Terms *875*

Suggested Reading *875*

DIVERSITY AND DOMINANCE: The Middle East After
World War I *866*

ENVIRONMENT AND TECHNOLOGY: The Birth of Civil
Aviation *871*

30 THE COLLAPSE OF THE OLD ORDER, 1929–1949   876

The Stalin Revolution *878*
Five-Year Plans *878* • Collectivization of
Agriculture *879* • Terror and Opportunities *880*

The Depression *881*
Economic Crisis *881* • Depression in Industrial
Nations *881* • Depression in Nonindustrial
Regions *884*

The Rise of Fascism *885*
Mussolini's Italy *885* • Hitler's Germany *886*
• The Road to War, 1933–1939 *886*

East Asia, 1931–1945 *888*
The Manchurian Incident of 1931 *888* • The Chinese
and the Long March *888* • The Sino-Japanese
War, 1937–1945 *889*

The Second World War *891*
The War of Movement *891* • War in Europe and
North Africa *892* • War in Asia and the Pacific *894*
• The End of the War *894* • Chinese Civil
War and Communist Victory *897*

The Character of Warfare *898*
The Science and Technology of War *899* • Bombing
Raids *899* • The Holocaust *899* • The
Home Front in Europe and Asia *901*
• The Home Front in the United States *902*
• War and the Environment *902*

Summary *903* • Key Terms *904*

Suggested Reading *905* • Notes *905*

DIVERSITY AND DOMINANCE: Women, Family Values,
and the Russian Revolution *882*

ENVIRONMENT AND TECHNOLOGY: The Enigma
Machine *900*

31 STRIVING FOR INDEPENDENCE: INDIA, AFRICA, AND LATIN AMERICA, 1900–1949   906

**The Indian Independence Movement,
1905–1947** *908*
The Land and the People *908* • British Rule and
Indian Nationalism *909* • Mahatma Gandhi and

Militant Nonviolence *912* • India Moves Toward
Independence *912* • Partition and Independence *914*

Sub-Saharan Africa, 1900–1945 *915*
Colonial Africa: Economic and Social Changes *915*
• Religious and Political Changes *919*

Mexico, Argentina, and Brazil, 1900–1949 *920*
Background to Revolution: Mexico in 1910 *920*
• Revolution and Civil War in Mexico *921* • The
Transformation of Argentina *924* • Brazil and
Argentina, to 1929 *924* • The Depression and the Vargas
Regime in Brazil *925* • Argentina After 1930 *926*

Comparative Perspectives *927*

Summary *928* • Key Terms *928*

Suggested Reading *929* • Notes *929*

ENVIRONMENT AND TECHNOLOGY: Gandhi and Technology *913*

DIVERSITY AND DOMINANCE: A Vietnamese Nationalist
Denounces French Colonialism *916*

ISSUES IN WORLD HISTORY: Famines and Politics *930*

PART EIGHT

*Perils and Promises of a Global
Community, 1945 to the Present* **932**

32 THE COLD WAR AND DECOLONIZATION, 1945–1975   934

The Cold War *936*
The United Nations *937* • Capitalism and
Communism *939* • West Versus East in Europe and
Korea *941* • United States Defeat in Vietnam *943*
• The Race for Nuclear Supremacy *944*

Decolonization and Nation Building *945*
New Nations in South and Southeast Asia *945* • The
Struggle for Independence in Africa *947* • The Quest
for Economic Freedom in Latin America *950*
• Challenges of Nation Building *954*

Beyond a Bipolar World *954*
The Third World *954* • Japan and China *956* • The
Middle East *957* • The Emergence of Environmental
Concerns *960*

Comparative Perspectives *960*

Summary *961* • Key Terms *962*

Suggested Reading *962* • Notes *963*

ENVIRONMENT AND TECHNOLOGY: The Green
Revolution *938*

DIVERSITY AND DOMINANCE: Race and the Struggle for
Justice in South Africa *952*

33 The End of the Cold War and the Challenge of Economic Development and Immigration, 1975–2000   964

Postcolonial Crises and Asian Economic Expansion   *966*
Revolutions, Repression, and Democratic Reform in Latin America   *966* • Islamic Revolutions in Iran and Afghanistan   *969* • Asian Transformation   *973* • China Rejoins the World Economy   *974*

The End of the Bipolar World   *975*
Crisis in the Soviet Union   *975* • The Collapse of the Socialist Bloc   *976* • Progress and Conflict in Africa   *978* • The Persian Gulf War   *978*

The Challenge of Population Growth   *979*
Demographic Transition   *979* • The Industrialized Nations   *980* • The Developing Nations   *982* • Old and Young Populations   *982*

Unequal Development and the Movement of Peoples   *984*
The Problem of Growing Inequality   *984* • Internal Migration: The Growth of Cities   *986* • Global Migration   *986*

Technological and Environmental Change   *987*
New Technologies and the World Economy   *987* • Conserving and Sharing Resources   *989* • Responding to Environmental Threats   *992*

Comparative Perspectives   *993*

Summary   *993* • Key Terms   *994*

Suggested Reading   *995* • Notes   *995*

DIVERSITY AND DOMINANCE: The Struggle for Women's Rights in an Era of Global Political and Economic Change   *970*
ENVIRONMENT AND TECHNOLOGY: The Personal Computer   *988*
MATERIAL CULTURE: Fast Food   *990*

34 Globalization in the New Millennium   996

Global Economic and Political Currents   *998*
An Interconnected Economy   *999* • Globalization and Democracy   *1003* • Regime Change in Iraq and Afghanistan   *1004*

Trends and Visions   *1006*
Faith and Politics   *1006* • Universal Rights and Values   *1009* • Women's Rights   *1010*

Global Culture   *1012*
The Media and the Message   *1013* • The Spread of Pop Culture   *1014* • Emerging Global Culture   *1015* • Enduring Cultural Diversity   *1016*

Conclusion   *1019*

Key Terms   *1020* • Suggested Reading   *1020* • Notes   *1020*

ENVIRONMENT AND TECHNOLOGY: Global Warming   *1011*

DIVERSITY AND DOMINANCE: World Literature in English   *1017*

Glossary   *G-1*

Index   *I-1*

Maps

16.1 Exploration and Settlement in the Indian and Pacific Oceans Before 1500 *462*

16.2 Middle America to 1533 *466*

16.3 European Exploration, 1420–1542 *469*

17.1 Religious Reformation in Europe *495*

17.2 The European Empire of Charles V *506*

17.3 Europe in 1740 *513*

18.1 Colonial Latin America in the Eighteenth Century *524*

18.2 European Claims in North America, 1755–1763 *540*

19.1 The Atlantic Economy *562*

19.2 The African Slave Trade, 1500–1800 *563*

19.3 West African States and Trade, 1500–1800 *566*

20.1 Muslim Empires in the Sixteenth and Seventeenth Centuries *580*

20.2 European Colonization in the Indian Ocean, to 1750 *599*

21.1 The Qing Empire, 1644–1783 *614*

21.2 Climate and Diversity in the Qing Empire *622*

21.3 The Expansion of Russia, 1500–1800 *624*

22.1 The American Revolutionary War *646*

22.2 Napoleon's Europe, 1810 *657*

22.3 The Haitian Revolution *659*

23.1 The Industrial Revolution in Britain, ca. 1850 *671*

23.2 Industrialization in Europe, ca. 1850 *679*

24.1 Latin America by 1830 *697*

24.2 Dominion of Canada, 1873 *703*

24.3 Territorial Growth of the United States, 1783–1853 *706*

24.4 The Expansion of the United States, 1850–1920 *720*

25.1 The Ottoman and Russian Empires, 1829–1914 *731*

25.2 Conflicts in the Qing Empire, 1839–1870 *744*

26.1 Africa in the Nineteenth Century *758*

26.2 India, 1707–1805 *765*

26.3 European Possessions in the Indian Ocean and South Pacific, 1870 *773*

27.1 The Unification of Italy, 1859–1870 *803*

27.2 Unification of Germany, 1866–1871 *805*

27.3 Expansion and Modernization of Japan, 1868–1918 *807*

28.1 Africa in 1878 and 1914 *824*

28.2 Asia in 1914 *833*

28.3 The Great Powers and Their Colonial Possessions in 1913 *840*

29.1 Europe in 1913 *849*

29.2 The First World War in Europe *851*

29.3 Territorial Changes in Europe After World War I *857*

29.4 Territorial Changes in the Middle East After World War I *864*

30.1 Chinese Communist Movement and the Sino-Japanese War, to 1938 *890*

30.2 World War II in Europe and North Africa *893*

30.3 World War II in Asia and the Pacific *895*

31.1 The Partition of India, 1947 *910*

31.2 The Mexican Revolution *922*

32.1 Cold War Confrontation *942*

32.2 Decolonization, 1947–1990 *946*

32.3 Middle East Oil and the Arab-Israeli Conflict, 1947–1973 *959*

33.1 The End of the Soviet Union *977*

33.2 World Population Growth *983*

33.3 Fresh Water Resources *991*

34.1 Global Distribution of Wealth *1000*

34.2 Regional Trade Associations, 2004 *1002*

34.3 World Religions *1007*

FEATURES

ENVIRONMENT AND TECHNOLOGY

Vasco da Gama's Fleet   *471*
Mapping the World   *501*
A Silver Refinery at Potosí, Bolivia, 1700   *527*
Amerindian Foods in Africa   *555*
Tobacco and Waterpipes   *588*
East Asian Porcelain   *609*
The Guillotine   *652*
Gas Lighting   *683*
Constructing the Port of Buenos Aires, Argentina   *718*
The Web of War   *735*
Whaling   *777*
Railroads and Immigration   *793*
Imperialism and Tropical Ecology   *835*
The Birth of Civil Aviation   *871*
The Enigma Machine   *900*
Gandhi and Technology   *913*
The Green Revolution   *938*
The Personal Computer   *988*
Global Warming   *1011*

DIVERSITY AND DOMINANCE

Kongo's Christian King   *476*
Political Craft and Craftiness   *508*
Race and Ethnicity in the Spanish Colonies: Negotiating Hierarchy   *530*
Slavery in West Africa and the Americas   *571*
Islamic Law and Ottoman Rule   *584*
Gendered Violence: The Yangzhou Massacre   *616*
Robespierre and Wollstonecraft Defend and Explain the Terror   *654*
Adam Smith and the Division of Labor   *672*

The Afro-Brazilian Experience, 1828   *700*
Chinese Responses to Imperialism   *749*
Ceremonials of Imperial Domination   *768*
Marx and Engels on Global Trade and the Bourgeoisie   *800*
Two Africans Recall the Arrival of the Europeans   *830*
The Middle East After World War I   *866*
Women, Family Values, and the Russian Revolution   *882*
A Vietnamese Nationalist Denounces French Colonialism   *916*
Race and the Struggle for Justice in South Africa   *952*
The Struggle for Women's Rights in an Era of Global Political and Economic Change   *970*
World Literature in English   *1017*

MATERIAL CULTURE

Cotton Clothing   *798*
Fast Food   *990*

ISSUES IN WORLD HISTORY

Climate and Population, to 1500   *486*
The Little Ice Age   *632*
State Power, the Census, and the Question of Identity   *782*
Famines and Politics   *930*

When a textbook reaches its fourth edition, the authors feel justified in assessing their work a success. The first edition contained a basic concept. The second used the myriad valuable comments made by teachers and reviewers to make major adjustments in the presentation of that concept. The third edition incorporated a further round of comments and suggestions aimed at filling lacunae and improving the flow of the exposition. At the same time, pedagogical aids were steadily improved to make the text more accessible to both students and teachers.

In the fourth edition the authors have focused on refining their work, updating bibliographies, and incorporating the most recent scholarship. Refinement consists of scrutinizing the text closely for clarity, logical consistency, reading comfort, and adequacy of coverage. In a few cases, chapters have been substantially rewritten, and in one instance the sequence of chapters has been altered. The authors are confident that by making hundreds of relatively small changes and adding new pedagogical aids, they have produced a text that retains the vision and values of the earlier editions but that will be easier to teach and easier for students to study.

Our overall goal remains unchanged: to produce a textbook that speaks not only for the past but also to today's student and teacher. Students and instructors alike should take away from this text a broad vision of human societies beginning as sparse and disconnected communities reacting creatively to local circumstances; experiencing ever more intensive stages of contact, interpenetration, and cultural expansion and amalgamation; and arriving at a twenty-first-century world in which people increasingly visualize a single global community.

Process, not progress, is the keynote of this book: a steady process of change over time, at first differently experienced in various regions, but eventually connecting peoples and traditions from all parts of the globe. Students should come away from this book with a sense that the problems and promises of their world are rooted in a past in which people of every sort, in every part of the world, confronted problems of a similar character and coped with them as best they could. We believe that our efforts will help students see where their world has come from and learn thereby something useful for their own lives.

Central Themes

We subtitled *The Earth and Its Peoples* "A Global History" because the book explores the common challenges and experiences that unite the human past. Although the dispersal of early humans to every livable environment resulted in a myriad of different economic, social, political, and cultural systems, all societies displayed analogous patterns in meeting their needs and exploiting their environments. Our challenge was to select the particular data and episodes that would best illuminate these global patterns of human experience.

To meet this challenge, we adopted two themes for our history: "technology and the environment" and "diversity and dominance." The first theme represents the commonplace material bases of all human societies at all times. It grants no special favor to any cultural group even as it embraces subjects of the broadest topical, chronological, and geographical range. The second theme expresses the reality that every human society has constructed or inherited structures of domination. We examine practices and institutions of many sorts: military, economic, social, political, religious, and cultural, as well as those based on kinship, gender, and literacy. Simultaneously we recognize that alternative ways of life and visions of societal organization continually manifest themselves both within and in dialogue with every structure of domination.

With respect to the first theme, it is vital for students to understand that technology, in the broad sense of experience-based knowledge of the physical world, underlies all human activity. Writing is a technology, but so is oral transmission from generation to generation of lore about medicinal or poisonous plants. The magnetic compass is a navigational technology, but so is Polynesian mariners' hard-won knowledge of winds, currents, and tides that made possible the settlement of the Pacific islands.

All technological development has come about in interaction with environments, both physical and human, and has, in turn, affected those environments. The story of how humanity has changed the face of the globe is an integral part of our first theme. Yet technology and the environment do not explain or underlie all important episodes of human experience. The theme of "diversity and dominance" informs all our discussions of politics, culture, and society. Thus when narrating the histories of empires, we describe a range of human experiences within and beyond the imperial frontiers without assuming that imperial institutions are a more fit topic for discussion than the economic and social organization of pastoral nomads or the lives of peasant women. When religion and culture occupy our narrative, we focus not only on the dominant tradition but also on the diversity of alternative beliefs and practices.

Changes in the Fourth Edition

The most visible structural change between the third and fourth editions is the addition of one new category of historical essays and three new pedagogical aids. The new essays, one for each of the book's eight parts, expand the scope of one of the improvements in the third edition, the essays on *Issues in World History*. While those essays were designed to alert students to broad and recurring conceptual issues that are of great interest to contemporary historians, the new essays on *Material Culture* call particular attention to the many ways in which objects and processes of everyday life can play a role in understanding human history on a broad scale. Thus essays like "Wine and Beer in the Ancient World" and "Fast Food" are not only interesting in and of themselves but also suggestive of how today's world historians find meaning in the ordinary dimensions of human life.

The pedagogical aids added to the fourth edition include the following:

Chapter Opening Focus Questions   These questions are keyed to every major subdivision of the chapter and are repeated and summarized in the completely revised summaries found at the end of each chapter.

Comparative Perspectives   Though interregional comparison has always been a strong point of *The Earth and Its Peoples*, new sections added at the end of many chapters specifically focus on comparison in order to highlight comparative lessons and ease the transition to the next chapter.

Icons   Throughout the text, icons direct students to online interactive maps and primary sources corresponding to discussions in the text and to the Online Study Center.

Though chapter-by-chapter changes, including new illustrations, new maps, and text changes in many of the boxed feature essays, are too numerous to mention, a few may be highlighted:

- Material on the Western Hemisphere in Chapters 12 and 16 has been significantly updated and revised.
- Coverage of Japan and Korea has been expanded in Chapters 11 and 13, and Chapter 27 contains new materials on Japan.

- The sequence of Chapters 25 and 26 has been reversed to avoid divided coverage of Egypt and to improve the transition from topic to topic.
- Chapter 34 has been thoroughly revised and updated to cover the war in Iraq and other contemporary problems.
- Suggested Reading lists have been updated with important recent scholarship.

Organization

The Earth and Its Peoples uses eight broad chronological divisions to define its conceptual scheme of global historical development. In **Part One: The Emergence of Human Communities, to 500 B.C.E.**, we examine important patterns of human communal organization in both the Eastern and Western Hemispheres. Small, dispersed human communities living by foraging spread to most parts of the world over tens of thousands of years. They responded to enormously diverse environmental conditions, at different times in different ways, discovering how to cultivate plants and utilize the products of domestic animals. On the basis of these new modes of sustenance, population grew, permanent towns appeared, and political and religious authority, based on collection and control of agricultural surpluses, spread over extensive areas.

Part Two: The Formation of New Cultural Communities, 1000 B.C.E.–400 C.E., introduces the concept of a "cultural community," in the sense of a coherent pattern of activities and symbols pertaining to a specific human community. While all human communities develop distinctive cultures, including those discussed in Part One, historical development in this stage of global history prolonged and magnified the impact of some cultures more than others. In the geographically contiguous African-Eurasian landmass, the cultures that proved to have the most enduring influence traced their roots to the second and first millennia B.C.E.

Part Three: Growth and Interaction of Cultural Communities, 300 B.C.E.–1200 C.E., deals with early episodes of technological, social, and cultural exchange and interaction on a continental scale both within and beyond the framework of imperial expansion. These are so different from earlier interactions arising from more limited conquests or extensions of political boundaries that they constitute a distinct era in world history, an era that set the world on the path of increasing global interaction and interdependence that it has been following ever since.

In **Part Four: Interregional Patterns of Culture and Contact, 1200–1550**, we look at the world during the three and a half centuries that saw both intensified cultural and commercial contact and increasingly confident self-definition of cultural communities in Europe, Asia, and Africa. The Mongol conquest of a vast empire extending from the Pacific Ocean to eastern Europe greatly stimulated trade and interaction. In the West, strengthened European kingdoms began maritime expansion in the Atlantic, forging direct ties with sub-Saharan Africa and beginning the conquest of the civilizations of the Western Hemisphere.

Part Five: The Globe Encompassed, 1500–1750, treats a period dominated by the global effects of European expansion and continued economic growth. European ships took over, expanded, and extended the maritime trade of the Indian Ocean, coastal Africa, and the Asian rim of the Pacific Ocean. This maritime commercial enterprise had its counterpart in European colonial empires in the Americas and a new Atlantic trading system. The contrasting capacities and fortunes of traditional land empires and new maritime empires, along with the exchange of domestic plants and animals between the hemispheres, underline the technological and environmental dimensions of this first era of complete global interaction.

In **Part Six: Revolutions Reshape the World, 1750–1870,** the word *revolution* is used in several senses: in the political sense of governmental overthrow, as in France and the Americas; in the metaphorical sense of radical transformative change, as in the Industrial Revolution; and in the broadest sense of a perception of a profound change in circumstances and world-view. Technology and environment lie at the core of these developments. With the rapid ascendancy of the Western belief that science and technology could overcome all challenges—environmental or otherwise—technology became an instrument not only of transformation but also of domination, to the point of threatening the integrity and autonomy of cultural traditions in nonindustrial lands.

Part Seven: Global Diversity and Dominance, 1850–1945, examines the development of a world arena in which people conceived of events on a global scale. Imperialism, world war, international economic connections, and world-encompassing ideological tendencies, such as nationalism and socialism, present the picture of a globe becoming increasingly interconnected. European dominance took on a worldwide dimension, seeming at times to threaten the diversity of human cultural experience with permanent subordination to European values and philosophies, while at other times triggering strong political or cultural resistance.

For **Part Eight: Perils and Promises of a Global Community, 1945 to the Present**, we divided the last half of the twentieth century into three time periods: 1945–1975, 1975–1991, and 1991 to the present. The challenges of the Cold War and postcolonial nation building dominated most of the period and unleashed global economic, technological, and political forces that became increasingly important in all aspects of human life. Technology is a key topic in Part Eight because of its integral role in the growth of a global community and because its many benefits in improving the quality of life seem clouded by real and potential negative impacts on the environment.

Formats

To accommodate different academic calendars and approaches to the course, *The Earth and Its Peoples* is available in three formats. There is a one-volume hardcover version containing all 34 chapters, along with a two-volume paperback edition: Volume I: To 1550 (Chapters 1–16) and Volume II: Since 1500 (Chapters 16–34). For readers at institutions with the quarter system, we offer a three-volume paperback version: Volume A: To 1200 (Chapters 1–12), Volume B: From 1200 to 1870 (Chapters 12–26), Volume C: Since 1750 (Chapters 22–34). Volume II includes an Introduction that surveys the main developments set out in Volume I and provides a groundwork for students studying only the period since 1500.

Ancillaries

A wide array of supplements accompany this text to help students better master the material and to help instructors teach from the book:

- Online Study Center student website
- Online Teaching Center instructor website
- Online Instructor's Resource Manual
- HM Testing CD-ROM (powered by Diploma®)
- PowerPoint® maps, images, and lecture outlines
- PowerPoint® questions for personal response systems
- Blackboard® and WebCT® course cartridges
- Eduspace® (powered by Blackboard Æ)
- Interactive eBook

Online Study Center

Online Teaching Center

The *Online Study Center* is a companion website for students that features a wide array of resources to help students master the subject matter. The website, prepared by John Reisbord of Vassar College, is divided into three major sections:

- "Prepare for Class" includes material such as learning objectives, chapter outlines, and preclass quizzes for a student to consult before going to class.
- "Improve Your Grade" includes practice review material like interactive flashcards, chronological ordering exercises, primary sources, and interactive map exercises.
- "ACE the Test" features our successful ACE brand of practice tests as well as other self-testing materials.

Students can find additional text resources in the "General Resources" section, such as an online glossary, audio mp3 files of chapter summaries, and material on how to study more effectively. Throughout the text, icons direct students to relevant exercises and self-testing material located on the *Online Study Center*. Access the *Online Study Center* for this text by visiting **college.hmco.com/pic/bulliet4e.**

The *Online Teaching Center* is a companion website for instructors. It features all of the material on the student site plus additional password-protected resources that help instructors teach the course, such as the *Instructor's Resource Manual* and *PowerPoint*® slides. Access the *Online Teaching Center* for this text by visiting **college.hmco.com/pic/bulliet4e.**

The *Online Instructor's Resource Manual*, thoroughly revised by Sheila Phipps of Appalachian State University, provides useful teaching strategies for the world history course and tips for getting the most out of the text. Each chapter contains instructional objectives, a detailed chapter outline, discussion questions, lecture topics, paper topics, and Internet resources.

HM Testing (powered by Diploma™) offers instructors a flexible and powerful tool for test generation and test management. Now supported by the Brownstone Research Group's market-leading Diploma™ software, this new version of *HM Testing* significantly improves on functionality and ease of use by offering all the tools needed to create, author, deliver, and customize multiple types of tests. Diploma™ is currently used by thousands of college and university campuses throughout the United States and Canada. The *HM Testing* content for this text was developed by Kathleen Addison of California State University, Northridge, and offers 15 to 25 key term identifications, 5 to 10 essay questions with answer guidelines, 35 to 40 multiple-choice questions, and 2 to 8 history and geography exercises for each chapter.

We are pleased to offer a collection of world history Power Point® lecture outlines, maps, and images for use in classroom presentations. Detailed lecture outlines correspond to the book's chapters and make it easier for instructors to cover the major topics in class. The art collection includes all of the photos and maps in the text, as well as numerous other images from our other world history titles. Power Point® questions and answers for use with personal response system software are also offered to adopters free of charge.

A variety of assignable homework and testing material has been developed to work with the Blackboard® and WebCT® course management systems, as well as with Eduspace®: Houghton Mifflin's Online Learning Tool (Powered by Blackboard®). Eduspace® is a web-based online learning environment that provides instructors with a gradebook and communication capabilities, such as synchronous and asynchronous chats and announcement postings. It offers access to assignments such as over 650 gradable homework exercises, writing assignments, interactive maps with questions, primary sources, discussion questions for online discussion boards, and tests, which all come ready to use. Instructors can choose to use the content as is, modify it, or even add their own. Eduspace® also contains an interactive eBook, which contains in-text links to interactive maps, primary sources, and audio pronunciation files, as well as review and self-testing material for students.

Acknowledgments

In preparing the fourth edition, we benefited from the critical readings of many colleagues. Our sincere thanks go in particular to the following instructors: Kathleen Addison, California State University, Northridge; Bruce A. Castleman, San Diego State University; Lynne M. Getz, Appalachian State University; Jane Hathaway, Ohio State University; Emmanuel Konde, Albany State University; Patrick M. Patterson, Honolulu Community College; Stephen H. Rapp, Jr., Georgia State University; Eric C. Rust, Baylor University; Sara W. Tucker, Washburn University; David J. Ulbrich, Ball State University; and Michael C. Weber, Salem State College.

When textbook authors set out on a project, they are inclined to believe that 90 percent of the effort will be theirs and 10 percent that of various editors and production specialists employed by their publisher. How very naïve. This book would never have seen the light of day had it not been for the unstinting labors of the great team of professionals who turned the authors' words into beautifully presented print. Our debt to the staff of Houghton Mifflin remains undiminished in the fourth edition. Nancy Blaine, Senior Sponsoring Editor, has offered us firm but sympathetic guidance throughout the revision process. Julie Swasey offered astute and sympathetic assistance as the authors worked to incorporate many new ideas and subjects into the text.

Carol Newman, Senior Project Editor, moved the work through the production stages to meet what had initially seemed like an unachievable schedule. Carole Frohlich did an outstanding job of photo research. And Susan Zorn again lent her considerable copyediting skills to the text.

We thank also the many students whose questions and concerns, expressed directly or through their instructors, shaped much of this revision. We continue to welcome all readers' suggestions, queries, and criticisms. Please contact us at our respective institutions or at this e-mail address: **history@hmco.com.**

ABOUT THE AUTHORS

RICHARD W. BULLIET   Professor of Middle Eastern History at Columbia University, Richard W. Bulliet received his Ph.D. from Harvard University. He has written scholarly works on a number of topics: the social history of medieval Iran *(The Patricians of Nishapur)*, the history of human-animal relations *(The Camel and the Wheel* and *Hunters, Herders, and Hamburgers)*, the process of conversion to Islam *(Conversion to Islam in the Medieval Period)*, and the overall course of Islamic social history *(Islam: The View from the Edge* and *The Case for Islamo-Christian Civilization)*. He is the editor of the *Columbia History of the Twentieth Century*. He has published four novels, coedited *The Encyclopedia of the Modern Middle East*, and hosted an educational television series on the Middle East. He was awarded a fellowship by the John Simon Guggenheim Memorial Foundation.

PAMELA KYLE CROSSLEY   Pamela Kyle Crossley received her Ph.D. in Modern Chinese History from Yale University. She is Professor of History and Rosenwald Research Professor in the Arts and Sciences at Dartmouth College. Her books include *A Translucent Mirror: History and Identity in Qing Imperial Ideology; The Manchus; Orphan Warriors: Three Manchu Generations and the End of the Qing World;* and (with Lynn Hollen Lees and John W. Servos) *Global Society: The World Since 1900*. Her research, which concentrates on the cultural history of China, Inner Asia, and Central Asia, has been supported by the John Simon Guggenheim Memorial Foundation and the National Endowment for the Humanities.

DANIEL R. HEADRICK   Daniel R. Headrick received his Ph.D. in History from Princeton University. Professor of History and Social Science at Roosevelt University in Chicago, he is the author of several books on the history of technology, imperialism, and international relations, including *The Tools of Empire: Technology and European Imperialism in the Nineteenth Century; The Tentacles of Progress: Technology Transfer in the Age of Imperialism; The Invisible Weapon: Telecommunications and International Politics;* and *When Information Came of Age: Technologies of Knowledge in the Age of Reason and Revolution, 1700–1850*. His articles have appeared in the *Journal of World History* and the *Journal of Modern History*, and he has been awarded fellowships by the National Endowment for the Humanities, the John Simon Guggenheim Memorial Foundation, and the Alfred P. Sloan Foundation.

STEVEN W. HIRSCH   Steven W. Hirsch holds a Ph.D. in Classics from Stanford University and is currently Associate Professor of Classics and History at Tufts University. He has received grants from the National Endowment for the Humanities and the Massachusetts Foundation for Humanities and Public Policy. His research and publications include *The Friendship of the Barbarians: Xenophon and the Persian Empire*, as well as articles and reviews in the *Classical Journal*, the *American Journal of Philology*, and the *Journal of Interdisciplinary History*. He is currently working on a comparative study of ancient Mediterranean and Chinese civilizations.

LYMAN L. JOHNSON   Professor of History at the University of North Carolina at Charlotte, Lyman L. Johnson earned his Ph.D. in Latin American History from the University of Connecticut. A two-time Senior Fulbright-Hays Lecturer, he also has received fellowships from the Tinker Foundation, the Social Science Research Council, the National Endowment for the Humanities, and the American Philosophical Society. His recent books include *Death, Dismemberment, and Memory; The Faces of Honor* (with Sonya Lipsett-Rivera); *The Problem of Order in Changing Societies; Essays on the Price History of Eighteenth-Century Latin America* (with Enrique Tandeter); and *Colonial Latin America* (with Mark A. Burkholder). He also has published in journals, including the *Hispanic American Historical Review*, the *Journal of Latin American Studies*, the *International Review of Social History, Social History*, and *Desarrollo Económico*. He recently served as president of the Conference on Latin American History.

DAVID NORTHRUP   Professor of History at Boston College, David Northrup earned his Ph.D. in African and European History from the University of California at Los Angeles. He earlier taught in Nigeria with the Peace Corps and at Tuskegee Institute. Research supported by the Fulbright-Hays Commission, the National Endowment for the Humanities, and the Social Science Research Council led to publications concerning precolonial Nigeria, the Congo (1870–1940), the Atlantic slave trade, and Asian, African, and Pacific islander indentured labor in the nineteenth century. A contributor to the *Oxford History of the British Empire* and *Blacks in the British Empire*, his latest book is *Africa's Discovery of Europe, 1450–1850*. In 2004 and 2005 he served as president of the World History Association.

Note on Spelling and Usage

Where necessary for clarity, dates are followed by the letters C.E. or B.C.E. The abbreviation C.E. stands for "Common Era" and is equivalent to A.D. (*anno Domini,* Latin for "in the year of the Lord"). The abbreviation B.C.E. stands for "before the Common Era" and means the same as B.C. ("before Christ"). In keeping with our goal of approaching world history without special concentration on one culture or another, we chose these neutral abbreviations as appropriate to our enterprise. Because many readers will be more familiar with English than with metric measurements, however, units of measure are generally given in the English system, with metric equivalents following in parentheses.

In general, Chinese has been Romanized according to the *pinyin* method. Exceptions include proper names well established in English (e.g., *Canton, Chiang Kai-shek*) and a few English words borrowed from Chinese (e.g., *kowtow*). Spellings of Arabic, Ottoman Turkish, Persian, Mongolian, Manchu, Japanese, and Korean names and terms avoid special diacritical marks for letters that are pronounced only slightly differently in English. An apostrophe is used to indicate when two Chinese syllables are pronounced separately (e.g., *Chang'an*).

For words transliterated from languages that use the Arabic script—Arabic, Ottoman Turkish, Persian, Urdu—the apostrophe indicating separately pronounced syllables may represent either of two special consonants, the *hamza* or the *ain*. Because most English-speakers do not hear the distinction between these two, they have not been distinguished in transliteration and are not indicated when they occur at the beginning or end of a word. As with Chinese, some words and commonly used place-names from these languages are given familiar English spellings (e.g., *Quran* instead of *Qur'an, Cairo* instead of *al-Qahira*). Arabic romanization has normally been used for terms relating to Islam, even where the context justifies slightly different Turkish or Persian forms, again for ease of comprehension.

Before 1492 the inhabitants of the Western Hemisphere had no single name for themselves. They had neither a racial consciousness nor a racial identity. Identity was derived from kin groups, language, cultural practices, and political structures. There was no sense that physical similarities created a shared identity. America's original inhabitants had racial consciousness and racial identity imposed on them by conquest and the occupation of their lands by Europeans after 1492. All of the collective terms for these first American peoples are tainted by this history. *Indians, Native Americans, Amerindians, First Peoples,* and *Indigenous Peoples* are among the terms in common usage. In this book the names of individual cultures and states are used wherever possible. *Amerindian* and other terms that suggest transcultural identity and experience are used most commonly for the period after 1492.

There is an ongoing debate about how best to render Amerindian words in English. It has been common for authors writing in English to follow Mexican usage for Nahuatl and Yucatec Maya words and place-names. In this style, for example, the capital of the Aztec state is spelled Tenochtitlán, and the important late Maya city-state is spelled Chichén Itzá. Although these forms are still common even in the specialist literature, we have chosen to follow the scholarship that sees these accents as unnecessary. The exceptions are modern place-names, such as Mérida and Yucatán, which are accented. A similar problem exists for the spelling of Quechua and Aymara words from the Andean region of South America. Although there is significant disagreement among scholars, we follow the emerging consensus and use the spellings *khipu* (not *quipu*), *Tiwanaku* (not *Tiahuanaco*), and *Wari* (not *Huari*). However, we keep *Inca* (not *Inka*) and *Cuzco* (not *Cusco*), since these spellings are expected by most of our potential readers and we hope to avoid confusion.

THE WORLD BEFORE 1500

ANTIQUITY: HUMANS, CULTURES, AND CONQUESTS, TO 400 C.E.

GROWTH AND INTERACTION, 400–1200

INTERREGIONAL CONQUESTS AND EXCHANGES, 1200–1500

History occurs in a continuous stream. Because new events are the products of their past, each historical period is intimately linked to what preceded it. As a Roman historian put it, "History doesn't make leaps." Nevertheless, modern historians find it useful to divide the past into eras or ages to make sense of the sweep of history. The longest historical eras are antiquity, the Middle Ages, and modern times. Volume II of *The Earth and Its Peoples* is devoted to the third of these—modern world history, the five centuries since about 1500.

World historians largely agree that the intensity of interaction around the world during the modern period distinguishes it from all earlier times. European maritime exploration opened up or intensified these contacts. The modern era is also characterized by the steady expansion of European political, economic, and cultural leadership in every part of the world.

How and when different parts of the world felt the impact of the West varied. By 1500 parts of the Americas were already reeling under the impact of their first contacts with Europeans, but in most other parts of the world the West did not make a big difference until the century after 1750 or even later. Thus, while in hindsight Western ascendancy seems to be a defining theme of modern history, for the people of Asia, Africa, and elsewhere the modern era was a time in which the internal patterns of historical change only gradually became altered by the growing influence of Westerners and by their own reactions to these influences.

In order to explain how the modern era came into being, the first chapter of Volume II of *The Earth and Its Peoples* (Chapter 16) begins in about 1450. To help the reader understand the broader sweep of history, this Introduction provides an overview of earlier eras. The Introduction reviews three periods of decreasing temporal length. The first is the very long period from human origins until the end of ancient history in about 400 C.E. Next comes the early medieval period down to about 1200; and, finally, the three hundred years immediately preceding 1500. Because the centuries after 1200 were most important for shaping the transition to the modern era, they receive the most detailed treatment.

ANTIQUITY: HUMANS, CULTURES, AND CONQUESTS, TO 400 C.E.

All historical periods were shaped by natural environment and human technology (whether simple tools, techniques, or complex machines). The paramount role played by environmental forces is apparent when historians seek to explain how human beings—and thus history—began. Like all other living creatures, early humans were products of biological adjustments to changing environments. Over millions of years, our ancestors in eastern and southern Africa evolved biologically to enhance their chances for survival. The evolution of an upright posture enabled early people to walk and run on two legs, thereby freeing their hands for tool making. The evolution of larger brains gave them the capacity to learn and understand all sorts of new things and devise techniques for putting them to use. Finally, evolutionary changes in the throat gave humans the capacity for speech, which, as language developed, had the dual effect of making complex social relations easier and fostering the development of intellectual culture.

With these physical traits in place, humans were able to develop in a direction taken by no other creature. Instead of relying on the glacially slow process of biological evolution to adapt their bodies to new environments, our ancestors used their minds to devise technologies for transforming nature to suit their needs. By the standards of today, these early technologies may seem crude—stone tools for cutting and chopping, clothing made from plants and animal skins, shelters in caves and huts—but they were sufficient to enable humans to survive environmental changes in their homelands. They also enabled bands of humans to migrate to new environments in every part of the world. Through trial and error Stone Age people learned what could safely be eaten in new environments. Other primates acted primarily by instinct; humans acted according to the dictates of culture. The capacity to create and change material and intellectual culture marked the beginning of human history.

Agricultural Civilizations

Beginning about 10,000 years ago, the transition from food gathering to food production marked a major turning point in history. Human communities in many different parts of the world learned to alter the natural food supply. Some people promoted the growth of foods they liked by scattering seeds on good soils and restricting the growth of competing plants. In time some people became full-time farmers. Other communities tamed wild animals whose meat, milk, fur, and hides they desired, and they controlled their breeding to produce animals with the most desired characteristics. Promoted by a warmer world climate, these agricultural revolutions slowly spread from the Middle East around the Mediterranean. People in South and East Asia, Africa, and the Americas domesticated other wild plants and animals for their use. Just as humans had ceased to rely on evolution to enable them to adjust to new surroundings, so too they had bypassed evolution in bringing new species of plants and animals into existence (see Map I.1).

The agricultural revolutions greatly enhanced people's chances for survival in two ways. One was a rapid increase in population fostered by the ability to grow and store more food (see Issues in World History: Climate and Population, to 1500). A second change was taking place in the composition of human communities. The earliest communities consisted of small bands of biologically related people and their spouses from other bands. However, more complex societies made their first appearances as more and more unrelated people concentrated in lush river valleys, where the soils, temperatures, and potential to irrigate with river water produced conditions suitable for farming.

In the Fertile Crescent of the Middle East, Egypt, India, and China the existence of a regular food surplus enabled a few people to develop highly specialized talents and tools that were not tied to food production. Some talented military leaders became rulers of large areas and headed government with specialized administrators. Specialists constructed elaborate irrigation systems, monumental palaces, and temples. Others made special metal tools and weapons, first of bronze, then of iron. Because of the value of their talents these specialists acquired privileges. It was grandest to be a king, queen, or head priest. For the average person, life was harder in complex societies than in parts of the world where such specialization had not yet occurred.

Culture and Civilization

Complex and populous agricultural societies developed specialists who dealt with abstract and unseen forces. This development was not entirely new. For tens of thousands of years before the first settled societies, humans had used their minds to think about the meaning of life. The remains of elaborate burials and sites of worship suggest that some early societies had clear beliefs in an afterlife and in spiritual forces that controlled their lives. Many cultures believed the sun, moon, and nature had supernatural powers.

Another form of intellectual activity was the collection of technical knowledge about the environment. Cultural communities learned what plants were best for food, clothing, or building materials and passed this knowledge along to later generations. Most specialized was the knowledge of how to make medicines and poisons. Assigning names for all these facilitated the transmission of this knowledge. In the absence of written records, very little specific information about these early treasuries of knowledge exists, but the elaborate and beautiful paintings in caves dating to tens of thousands of years before the emergence of early agricultural societies provide the clearest evidence of the cultural sophistication of early humans.

Cultural change surged as settled agricultural communities became more specialized. Temple priests devised elaborate rituals and prayers for the gods who protected the community, and they studied the movements of stars, planets, and the moon for signs of the progress of the seasons or the will of the gods. In Mesopotamia, Egypt, and elsewhere a new class of scribes used written symbols to preserve administrative and commercial records, laws, and bodies of specialized knowledge. Thoughtful people recorded the myths and legends passed down orally from earlier days, systematizing them and often adapting them to new social conditions, as well as creating new literary forms. Communications could now be sent unchanged over long distances. Some of these works were lost for millennia only to be rediscovered in recent times, allowing us to know much more about the lives, thoughts, and values of ancient peoples.

Scene from the Egyptian Book of the Dead, ca. 1300 B.C.E. The mummy of a royal scribe named Hunefar is approached by members of his household before being placed in the tomb. Behind Hunefar is jackel-headed Anubis, the god who will conduct the spirit of the deceased to the afterlife. The Book of the Dead provided Egyptians with the instructions they needed to complete this arduous journey and gain a blessed existence in the afterlife. (Courtesy of the Trustees of the British Museum)

Empires and Regional

In time governments weakened or fell victim to conquest. Egypt, for example, fell to Nubians from up the Nile then to the Assyrians from Mesopotamia. Some conquerors created vast new empires. Late in the fourth century B.C.E., Alexander the Great brought everything from the eastern Mediterranean to India and Egypt under his sway, spreading Greek culture and language. After the collapse of Alexander's empire, the first of a series of Indian empires arose. In the second and first centuries B.C.E., Latin-speakers spread their rule, language, and culture throughout the Roman Empire, which encompassed the Mediterranean and reached across the Alps into Gaul (France) and Britain. At much the same time, the Han consolidated control over the densely populated lands of China, and successive rulers extended the sway of imperial China over much of East Asia. In the isolated continents of the Americas, advanced agricultural societies were also building larger states in late antiquity.

Essential to empire formation was the significant enhancement of old technologies and the development of new ones. In many parts of the world iron replaced bronze as the preferred metal for tools and weapons. In the Middle East and China soldiers on horseback played important military roles. In most places there were advances in the fighting techniques and in defensive strategies and fortifications.

Empires encouraged the growth of cities to serve as administrative, economic, and cultural centers. Temples, palaces, monuments, markets, and public amenities advertised the glory of these imperial centers. Large states regularly mobilized large pools of labor for massive

Map I.1 Early Centers of Plant and Animal Domestication Many different parts of the world made original contributions to domestication during the Agricultural Revolutions that began about 10,000 years ago. Later interactions helped spread these domesticated animals and plants to new locations. In lands less suitable for crop cultivation, pastoralism and hunting remained more important for supplying food.

construction projects. By late antiquity, a few cities had populations in the hundreds of thousands—Alexandria in Egypt, Rome in Italy, Chang'an in China, Pataliputra in India—though such large numbers strained cities' capacities to supply food and water and dispose of waste. Such architectural monuments established "classical" styles that were frequently imitated and affected wide areas even after the empires were gone.

Other imperial building projects were more practical. The Roman and Chinese governments built thousands of miles of paved roads for moving troops and communication; long barrier walls and strings of forts defended frontier areas from invasion. Trade often flourished on these political frontiers, and good roads further encouraged trade. Improvements in shipping also encouraged the movement of goods over long distances and allowed transport of bulkier goods. Much long-distance trade in antiquity was in luxury goods for the privileged classes in urban civilizations. The search for exotic items tied remote parts of the world together and gave rise to new specialists both within the urban civilizations and in less stratified parts of the world. Gold, ivory, animal pelts, and exotic feathers from inner Africa reached Egypt. Phoenician mariners marketed lumber, papyrus (for paper), wine, and fish around the Mediterranean Sea. Other merchants carried silk from China across arid Central Asia to the Middle East and lands to the west. The advent of coinage in the first millennium B.C.E. stimulated local and regional economies.

The routes that carried goods also helped spread religions, inventions, and ideas. The Zoroastrian religion of the Persians became one of the great ethical creeds of antiquity. The diaspora of Jews from Palestine after their southern kingdom was destroyed by the Neo-Babylonian Empire in the seventh century B.C.E. also helped spread monotheistic beliefs. The beliefs and culture of the Greeks and Romans spread throughout their empires, largely because many of their subjects saw the advantages in adopting the ways of the ruling elite. Similarly, Indian traders introduced Hinduism and Buddhism to Southeast Asia.

GROWTH AND INTERACTION, 400–1200

During the Early Middle Ages expanding political and commercial links drew regions closer together. In addition, the growth of interregional trade and the spread of new world religions helped unite and redefine the boundaries of cultural regions, though divisions within religions undercut some of this cultural unity. All of these factors were interrelated, but let's begin with the one that left the most enduring impression on the course of history: the spread of world religions.

World Religions

The first religious tradition to experience widespread growth in this period was Buddhism, which spread from the Indian homeland where it had arisen around 500 B.C.E. One direction of growth was eastward into Southeast Asia. After 500 C.E. there were particular strongholds of the faith on the large islands of Ceylon, Sumatra, and Java, whose kings supported the growth of schools and monasteries and constructed temple complexes. Traders also carried Buddhism to China and from there to Korea, Japan, and Tibet. In some places Buddhism's growing strength led to political reactions. In China the Tang emperors reduced the influence of the monasteries in 840 by taking away their tax exemption and by promoting traditional Confucian values. A similar effort by the Tibetan royal family to curtail Buddhism failed, and Buddhist monks established their political dominance in mountainous Tibet. In India, however, Buddhism gradually lost support during this period and by 1200 had practically disappeared from the land of its origin.

Meanwhile, people in western Eurasia were embracing two newer religious systems. In the fourth century, Christianity became the official religion of the Roman Empire, adding new followers all around the Mediterranean to this once persecuted faith. But when the western half of the empire collapsed under the onslaught of "barbarian" invasions in the late fifth century, the Latin Church had to shoulder alone the tasks of converting these peoples to Christianity and preserving the intellectual, political, and cultural heritage of Roman antiquity. In its religious mission the Latin Church was quite successful. One by one Frankish, German, English, Irish, Hungarian, and other leaders were converted, and their subjects gradually followed suit. Preserving other Roman achievements was more difficult. The church continued to use the Latin language and Roman law, and Christian monasteries preserved manuscripts of many ancient works. But the trading economy and urban life that had been the heart blood of ancient Rome became only a memory in most of the Latin West.

In the eastern Mediterranean, Byzantine Roman emperors continued to rule, and the Greek-speaking Christian church continued to enjoy political protection. Greek monks were also active Christian missionaries among the Slavic peoples of eastern Europe. The

Armored Knights in Battle   This painting from around 1135 shows the armament of knights at the time of the Crusades. Chain mail, a helmet, and a shield carried on the left side protect the rider. The lance carried underarm and the sword are the primary weapons. Notice that riders about to make contact with lances have their legs straight and braced in the stirrups, while riders with swords and in flight have bent legs.   (Pierpont Morgan Library/ Art Resource, NY)

armies introduced Islam and an accompanying state system into the Middle East, across North Africa, and into the Iberian Peninsula. Over time most Middle Eastern and African Christians and members of other religions chose to adopt the new faith. Muslim merchants helped spread the faith along trade routes into sub-Saharan Africa and across southern Asia. Like Christianity, Islam eventually split along cultural, theological, and political lines as it expanded. Beginning in 1095, Latin Christians launched military Crusades against Muslim dominance of Christian holy places in Palestine. In later Crusades, political and commercial ends became more important than religious goals, and the boundaries between Christianity and Islam changed little.

Commercial and Political Contacts

In many other parts of the world empires played a fundamental role in defining and unifying cultural areas. Under the Tang and Song dynasties (618–1279) China continued to have stability and exhibited periods of remarkable economic growth and technological creativity. Ghana, the first notable empire in sub-Saharan Africa, emerged to control one end of the trans-Saharan trade. In the isolated continents of the Americas a series of cultural complexes formed in the Andes, among the Maya of the Yucatán, along the Mississippi, and in the arid North American southwest. But despite efforts by Christian northern Europeans to create a loosely centralized "Holy Roman Empire," a very decentralized political system prevailed in most of western Europe. In Japan development was moving in a similar direction.

Political and religious expansion helped stimulate regional and long-distance trade. The challenge of moving growing quantities of goods over long distances produced some important innovations in land and sea travel. Two of the most important land-based, long-distance routes in this period depended on pack animals, especially the camel. One was the Silk Road, a caravan route across Central Asia. On the other trade route, between sub-Saharan Africa and North Africa, camels carried goods across the Sahara, the world's largest desert.

The Silk Road took its name from the silk textiles that were carried from eastern China to the Mediterranean Sea. In return, the Chinese received horses and other goods from the West. In existence since about 250 B.C.E., this series of roads nearly 6,000-miles (9,000-kilometers) in length passed through arid lands whose pastoral populations provided guides, food, and fresh camels (specially bred for caravan work).

conversion of the Russian rulers in the tenth century was a notable achievement. However, by the middle of the next century, cultural, linguistic, and theological differences led to a deep rift between Greek and Russian Christians in the east and Latin Christians in the west.

Meanwhile, prophetic religion founded by Muhammad in the seventh century was spreading like a whirlwind out of its Arabian homeland. With great fervor Arab

After 900 C.E. the Silk Road declined for a time. By coincidence, the trans-Saharan caravan routes were growing more important during the period from 700 to 1200. Here, too, horses were an important trade purchased by African rulers to the south in return for gold, slaves, and other goods. The pastoralists who controlled the Saharan oases became essential guides for the camel caravans.

Since ancient times sea travel had been important in moving goods over relatively short distances, usually within sight of land, as around the Mediterranean Sea, the Red Sea, the Persian Gulf, and among the islands of the East Indies. During this period the water links around and through the Indian Ocean were increasing enough to make it an alternative to moving goods from China to the Middle East. Shipments went from port to port and were exchanged many times. Special ships known as dhows made use of the seasonal shifts in the winds across the Indian Ocean to plan their voyages in each direction. These centuries also saw remarkable maritime voyages in the Pacific (see Chapter 16).

INTERREGIONAL CONQUESTS AND EXCHANGES, 1200–1500

Between 1200 and 1500, cultural and commercial contacts grew rapidly across wide expanses of Eurasia, Africa, the Americas, and the Indian Ocean. In part, the increased contacts were the product of an unprecedented era of empire building around the world. The Mongols conquered a vast empire spanning Eurasia from the Pacific to eastern Europe. Muslim peoples created new empires in India, the Middle East, and sub-Saharan Africa. Amerindian empires united extensive regions of the Americas. Most of Europe continued to lack political unity, but unusually powerful European kingdoms were expanding their frontiers.

Empires stimulated commercial exchanges. The Mongol conquests revived the Silk Road across Central Asia, while a complex maritime network centered on the Indian Ocean stretched around southern Eurasia from the South China Sea to the North Atlantic, with overland connections in all directions (see Map I.2). Trade in the Americas and Africa also expanded. In the fifteenth century, Portuguese and Spanish explorers began an expansion southward along the Atlantic coast of Africa that by 1500 had opened a new all-water route to the riches of the Indian Ocean and set the stage for transoceanic routes that for the first time were to span the globe.

Mongol, Muslim, and European expansion promoted the spread of technologies. Printing, compasses, crossbows, gunpowder, and firearms—all East Asian inventions found broader applications and new uses in western Eurasia. Both the Ottomans and the kingdoms of western Europe made extensive use of gunpowder technologies. However, the highly competitive and increasingly literate peoples of the Latin West surpassed all others of this period in their use of technologies that they borrowed from elsewhere or devised themselves. Europeans mined and refined more metals, produced more books, built more kinds of ships, and made more weapons than did people in any other comparable place on earth.

Why was so much change taking place all at once? Historians attribute many of the changes in South and Central Asia directly or indirectly to the empire building of the Mongols. But other changes took place far from that area. The role of simple coincidence, of course, should never be overlooked in history. And some historians believe that larger environmental factors were also at work—changes in climate that promoted population growth, trade, and empire building.

Mongols and Turks

The earliest and largest of the new empires was the work of the Mongols of northeastern Asia. Using their extraordinary command of horses and refinements in traditional forms of military and social organization, Mongols and allied groups united under Genghis Khan overran northern China in the early thirteenth century and spread their control westward across Central Asia to eastern Europe. By the later part of the century, the Mongol Empire stretched from Korea to Poland. It was ruled initially in four separate khanates: one in Russia, one in Iran, one in Central Asia, and one in China.

By ensuring traders protection from robbers and excessive tolls, the Mongol Empire revitalized the Silk Road. Never before had there been such a volume of commercial exchanges between eastern and western Eurasia. Easier travel also helped Islam and Buddhism spread to new parts of Central Asia.

The strains of holding such vast territories together caused the Mongol Empire to disintegrate over the course of the fourteenth and early fifteenth centuries. The Ming rulers of China overthrew Mongol rule in 1368 and began an expansionist foreign policy to reestablish China's predominance and prestige. Their armies repeatedly

Map I.2   Arteries of Trade and Travel in the Islamic World, to 1500   Ibn Battuta's journeys across Africa and Asia made use of land and sea routes along which Muslim traders and the Islamic faith had long traveled.

invaded Mongolia, reestablished dominion over Korea, and occupied northern Vietnam (Annam). One by one the other khanates collapsed.

The Mongols left a formidable legacy, but it was not Mongolian. Instead, Mongol rulers tended to adopt and promote the political systems, agricultural practices, and local customs of the peoples they ruled. Their encouragement of local languages helped later literary movements to flower. The political influence of the administrations the Mongols established in China, Iran, and Russia lingered even after locals had overthrown their rule, creating the basis for new national regimes.

At about the same time as the early Mongol expansion, Turkic war leaders from what is now Afghanistan were surging through the Khyber Pass and established a Muslim empire centered at Delhi. In short order, they overwhelmed the several Hindu states of north and central India and established a large empire ruled from the city of Delhi. The subsequent migration of large numbers of Muslims into India

and the prestige and power of the Muslim ruling class brought India into the Islamic world. After their conquests in the Middle East, Mongols had recruited other Turkic-speaking Muslims from Central Asia to serve as their agents. In the decades after 1250, a large Turkic community in Anatolia (now Turkey) known as Ottomans took advantage of the weakness of the Byzantine Empire to extend their base in Anatolia. They then crossed into the Balkan Peninsula of southeastern Europe.

In the late 1300s, the Central Asian conqueror Timur (Tamerlane) shattered the Delhi Sultanate and stopped the expansion of the Ottoman Empire. The conquest and pillage of Timur's armies left the Delhi Sultanate a shadow of its former self, but the Ottoman Turks were able to reconstitute their empire in the fifteenth century. Ottoman conquerors swept deep into southeastern Europe (taking Constantinople, the last surviving remnant of the Byzantine Empire, in 1453) and southward into the Middle East, establishing a stable presence that was to endure into the twentieth century.

Indian Ocean Exchanges

In the wake of the Mongol Empire's collapse, the Indian Ocean assumed greater importance in the movement of goods across Eurasia. Alliances among Muslim merchants of many nationalities made these routes the world's richest trading area. Merchant dhows sailed among the trading ports, carrying cotton textiles, leather goods, grains, pepper, jewelry, carpets, horses, ivory, and many other goods. Chinese silk and porcelain and Indonesian spices entered from the east, meeting Middle Eastern and European goods from the west. It is important to note that Muslim merchant networks were almost completely independent of the giant Muslim land empires.

As a consequence of the Islamic world's political and commercial expansion, the number of adherents to the Muslim faith also grew. By 1500 Islam had replaced Buddhism as the second most important faith in India and was on its way to displacing Hinduism and Buddhism in Southeast Asia. The faith was also spreading in the Balkans. Meanwhile, raids by Arab pastoralists undermined ancient Christian states along Africa's upper Nile, leaving Ethiopia as the only Christian-ruled state in Africa. In the trading cities below the Sahara and along the Indian Ocean coast where Islam had established itself well before 1200, the strength and sophistication of Islamic religious practice was growing.

Mediterranean Exchanges

The Mediterranean Sea, which since antiquity had been a focus of commerce and cultural exchange for the peoples of Europe, the Middle East, and Africa, saw increased activity in the later Middle Ages. Part of the Mediterranean's importance derived from its trading links to the Indian Ocean by land and water routes. Another area that contributed to expanded trade was northern Africa. Camel caravans brought great quantities of gold and large numbers of slaves to the Mediterranean from the lands below the Sahara. This trade facilitated the growth of the powerful empire of Mali, which controlled some of the main gold-producing regions of West Africa. The rulers of Mali became rich and Muslim. Their wars and those of other states produced the captives that were sold north. In the fourteenth century the disruption of supplies of slaves from the eastern Mediterranean led to more slaves being purchased in southern Europe.

Another part of the expansion of Mediterranean trade was tied to the revival of western Europe. In 1204 the Italian city-state of Venice had shown its determination to be a

Silk Painting Depicting Khitan Hunters Resting Their Horses The artist shows the Khitans' soft riding boots, leggings, and robes (much like those used by the Mongols) and the Khitans' patterned hairstyle, with part of the skull shaved and some of the hair worn long. Men in Central and North Asia (including Japan) used patterned hairstyles to indicate their political allegiance. The custom was documented in the 400s (but is certainly much older) and continued up to the twentieth century.   (National Palace Museum, Taipai, Taiwan, Republic of China)

dominant player in the eastern Mediterranean by attacking the Greek city of Constantinople and ensuring access to the Black Sea. Trade routes from the Mediterranean spread northward to the Netherlands and connected by sea to the British Isles, the Baltic Sea, and the Atlantic. The growth of trade in Europe accompanied a revival of urban life and culture. Both the cities and the countryside saw increased use of energy, minerals, and technologies from printing to gunpowder. Despite a high level of warfare among European states and devastating population losses in the fourteenth century, much of Europe was exhibiting cultural and economic vitality that was to have great consequences for the entire world in the centuries that followed.

The Aztecs and Inca

In the continents of the Western Hemisphere, American peoples were also creating important empires in the period from 1200 to 1500, although they had more limited resources with which to do so. For thousands of years their cultures had developed in isolation from the rest of humanity and thus had been unable to borrow any plants, animals, or technologies. Amerindian conquests were made without the aid of riding animals like the Mongols' horses, without the iron weapons all Old World empire builders had been using for many centuries, and without the new gunpowder weaponry that some Eurasians were employing in their conquests in this period.

In the wake of the collapse of the Toltec Empire, a martial people known as the Aztecs pushed southward into the rich agricultural lands of central Mexico. At first the Aztecs placed themselves at the service of strong indigenous residents, but after 1300 they began to build their own empire. Relying on their military skills, members of the Aztec warrior elite were able to conquer territories and reduce peasants to their service. The growth of a servile class at the bottom of society was paralleled by the growth of a powerful ruling class housed in well-constructed two-story dwellings in the Aztec capital cities. The servile laborers supplied the food needs of the growing cities and were impressed into building elaborate canals and land reclamation projects. Underpinning the power of the Aztec rulers were religious rituals that emphasized human sacrifice, mostly captives of the armies. By 1500 the Aztecs ruled a densely populated empire of subject and allied peoples.

Meanwhile, in the Andean highlands of western South America another powerful Amerindian empire was forming. Like central Mexico this region already had a rich agricultural base and a dense population when, in the fifteenth century, the Inca began using military skills to expand from a chiefdom into an empire. The Inca rulers, like the Aztecs, built impressive cities, promoted irrigation projects, and relied on religious rituals to bolster their authority. Tribute in goods and labor from their subject peoples supported their projects, and a network of mountain roads tied together the pieces of an empire that stretched for more than 3,000 miles (nearly 5,000 kilometers) north to south.

Both empires were cultural and commercial centers as well as political ones. In the Aztec Empire, well-armed private merchants controlled a long-distance trade in luxuries for the elites, including gold, jewels, feathered garments, and animal skins. There was also a network of local markets, large and small, that supplied the needs of more ordinary folks. State direction featured more prominently in Inca-ruled areas and promoted a vast exchange of specialized goods and a huge variety of foodstuffs grown at different altitudes.

The Mesoamerican Ball Game From Guatemala to Arizona, archaeologists have found evidence of an ancient ball game played with a solid rubber ball on slope-sided courts shaped like a capital T. Among the Maya the game was associated with a creation myth and thus had deep religious meaning. There is evidence that some players were sacrificed. In this scene from a ceramic jar, players wearing elaborate ritual clothing—which includes heavy, protective pads around the chest and waist—play with a ball much larger than the ball actually used in such games. Some representations show balls drawn to suggest a human head. (Chrysler Museum of Art/Justin Kerr)

SUGGESTED READING

A fuller treatment of all these topics can be found in the first volume of *The Earth and Its Peoples*. Richard Bulliet provides a brief overview of world history both before and after 1500 in "Themes, Conquerors, and Commerce," in Heidi Roupp, ed., *World History: A Resource Book* (1997).

For summaries of the latest scholarship on some select topics see these pamphlets in the American Historical Association's series "Essays in Global and Comparative History": John A. Mears, *Agricultural Origins in Global Perspective* (2003); Christopher Ehret, *Sudanic Civilization* (2003); Stanley M. Burstein, *The Hellenistic Period in World History* (1996); Richard M. Eaton, *Islamic History as World History* (1990); John E. Kicza, *The Peoples and Civilizations of the Americas Before Contact* (1998); Xinru Liu, *The Silk Road: Overland Trade and Cultural Interactions in Eurasia* (1998); Sarah Shaver Hughes and Brady Hughes, *Women in Ancient Civilizations* (1998); Jonathan S. Walters, *Finding Buddhists in Global History* (1998); Peter B. Golden, *Nomads and Sedentary Societies in Medieval Eurasia* (1998); and Janet Lippman Abu-Lughod, *The World System in the Thirteenth Century: Dead-End or Precursor?* (1993). Sarah Hughes and Brady Hughes have also edited a useful work correcting the dominance of patriarchal themes: *Women in World History*, vol. 1 (1995).

The Earth and Its Peoples

A GLOBAL HISTORY

Ferdinand Magellan Navigating the Straits Connecting the Atlantic and Pacific Oceans
This late sixteenth-century print embellishes the first circumnavigation of the globe voyage with fanciful representations of native peoples and creatures as residents of South America. (The Granger Collection, New York)

What were the objectives and major accomplishments of the voyages of exploration undertaken by Chinese, Polynesians, and other non-Western peoples?

In this era of long-distance exploration, did Europeans have any special advantages over other cultural regions?

What were the different outcomes of European interactions with Africa, India, and the Americas?

16

THE MARITIME REVOLUTION, TO 1550

CHAPTER OUTLINE

Global Maritime Expansion Before 1450

European Expansion, 1400–1550

Encounters with Europe, 1450–1550

Comparative Perspectives

ENVIRONMENT AND TECHNOLOGY: Vasco da Gama's Fleet

DIVERSITY AND DOMINANCE: Kongo's Christian King

In 1511 young Ferdinand Magellan sailed from Europe around the southern tip of Africa and eastward across the Indian Ocean as a member of the first Portuguese expedition to explore the East Indies (maritime Southeast Asia). Eight years later, this time in the service of Spain, he headed an expedition that sought to demonstrate the feasibility of reaching the East Indies by sailing westward from Europe. By the middle of 1521 Magellan's expedition had achieved its goal by sailing across the Atlantic, rounding the southern tip of South America, and crossing the Pacific Ocean—but at a high price.

One of the five ships that had set out from Spain in 1519 was wrecked on a reef, and the captain of another deserted and sailed back to Spain. The passage across the vast Pacific took much longer than anticipated, resulting in the deaths of dozens of sailors due to starvation and disease. In the Philippines, Magellan himself was killed in battle on April 27, 1521, while aiding a local ruler who had

Online Study Center

This icon will direct you to interactive activities and study materials on the website: *college.hmco.com/pic/bulliet4e.*

promised to become a Christian. Magellan's successor met the same fate a few days later.

To consolidate their dwindling resources, the expedition's survivors burned the least seaworthy of their remaining three ships and transferred the men and supplies from that ship to the smaller *Victoria*, which continued westward across the Indian Ocean, around Africa, and back to Europe. Magellan's flagship, the *Trinidad*, tried unsuccessfully to recross the Pacific to Central America. The *Victoria*'s return to Spain on September 8, 1522, was a crowning example of Europeans' new ability and determination to make themselves masters of the oceans. A century of daring and dangerous voyages backed by the Portuguese crown had opened new routes through the South Atlantic to Africa, Brazil, and the rich trade of the Indian Ocean. Rival voyages sponsored by Spain since 1492 had opened new contacts with the American continents. Now the unexpectedly broad Pacific Ocean had been crossed as well. A maritime revolution was under way that would change the course of history.

This new maritime era marked the end of a long period in which the flow of historical influences tended to move from east to west. Before 1500 most overland and maritime expansion had come from Asia, as had the most useful technologies and the most influential systems of belief. Asia also had been home to the most powerful states and the richest trading networks. The Iberians set out on their voyages of exploration to reach Eastern markets. Their successes in the following century redirected the world's center of power, wealth, and innovation to the West.

The maritime revolution broadened and deepened contacts, alliances, and conflicts across ancient cultural boundaries. Some of these contacts ended tragically for individuals like Magellan. Some proved disastrous for entire populations: Amerindians, for instance, suffered conquest, colonization, and a rapid decline in numbers. And sometimes the results were mixed: Asians and Africans found both risks and opportunities in their new relations with the visitors from Europe.

Since ancient times travel across the world's seas and oceans had been one of the great challenges to technological ingenuity. Ships had to be sturdy enough to survive heavy winds and waves, and pilots had to learn how to cross featureless expanses of water to reach their destinations. In time ships, sails, and navigational techniques perfected in the more protected seas were tried on the vast, open oceans.

However complex the solutions and dangerous the voyages, the rewards of sea travel made them worthwhile. Ships could move goods and people more quickly and cheaply than any form of overland travel then possible. Because of its challenges and rewards, sea travel attracted adventurers. To cross the unknown waters, find new lands, and open up new trade or settlements was an exciting prospect. For these reasons, some men on every continent had long turned their attention to the sea.

By 1450 much had been accomplished, and much remained undone. Daring mariners had discovered and settled most of the islands of the Pacific, the Atlantic, and the Indian Ocean. The greatest success was the trading system that united the peoples around the Indian Ocean. But no individual had yet crossed the Pacific in either direction. Even the smaller Atlantic was a barrier that kept the peoples of the Americas, Europe, and Africa in ignorance of each other's existence. The inhabitants of Australia were likewise completely cut off from contact with the rest of humanity. All this was about to change.

The Pacific Ocean

The voyages of Polynesian peoples over vast distances across the Pacific Ocean were some of the most impressive feats in maritime history before 1450 (see Map 16.1). Though they left no written records, over several thousand years intrepid mariners from the Malay° Peninsula of Southeast Asia had explored and settled the island chains of the East Indies and moved onto New Guinea and the smaller islands of Melanesia°. Beginning sometime before the Common Era (C.E.), a new wave of expansion from the area of Fiji brought the first humans to the islands of the central Pacific known as Polynesia. The easternmost of the Marquesas° Islands were reached

Malay (may-LAY) **Melanesia** (mel-uh-NEE-zhuh)
Marquesas (mar-KAY-suhs)

CHRONOLOGY

Pacific Ocean	Atlantic Ocean	Indian Ocean
400–1300 Polynesian settlement of Pacific islands	**770–1200** Viking voyages **1300s** Settlement of Madeira, Azores, Canaries **Early 1300s** Mali voyages **1418–1460** Voyages of Henry the Navigator **1440s** First slaves from West Africa sent to Europe **1482** Portuguese at Gold Coast and Kongo **1486** Portuguese at Benin **1488** Bartolomeu Dias reaches Indian Ocean **1492** Columbus reaches Caribbean **1492–1500** Spanish conquer Hispaniola **1493** Columbus returns to Caribbean (second voyage) **1498** Columbus reaches mainland of South America (third voyage) **1500** Cabral reaches Brazil	**1405–1433** Voyages of Zheng He
		1497–1498 Vasco da Gama reaches India
		1505 Portuguese bombard Swahili Coast cities **1510** Portuguese take Goa **1511** Portuguese take Malacca **1515** Portuguese take Hormuz
1519–1522 Magellan expedition	**1513** Ponce de León explores Florida **1519–1521** Cortés conquers Aztec Empire **1531–1533** Pizarro conquers Inca Empire **1536** Rebellion of Maco Inca in Peru	**1535** Portuguese take Diu **1538** Portuguese defeat Ottoman fleet **1539** Portuguese aid Ethiopia

(Row labels on left margin: **1400**, **1500**)

about 400 C.E. From the Marquesas, Polynesian sailors first reached the Hawaiian Islands as early as 500 C.E. Then, between 1100 and 1300, new voyages northward from Tahiti brought Polynesian settlers across more than 2,000 nautical miles (4,000 kilometers) to Hawaii. New Zealand was settled about 1200. Easter Island, 2,200 miles (3,540 kilometers) off the coast of South America, became the easternmost outpost of Polynesian culture a century later. The fact that the sweet potato, domesticated in South America, became a staple in the Polynesian diet suggests that this thrust to the east had enabled Polynesians to reach the mainland of the Americas as well.

Until recent decades some historians argued that Polynesians could have reached the eastern Pacific islands only by accident because they lacked navigational devices to plot their way. Others wondered how Polynesians could have overcome the difficulties, illustrated by Magellan's flagship, *Trinidad*, of sailing eastward across

Map 16.1   Exploration and Settlement in the Indian and Pacific Oceans Before 1500
Over many centuries, mariners originating in Southeast Asia gradually colonized the islands of the Pacific and Indian Oceans. The Chinese voyages led by Zheng He in the fifteenth century were lavish official expeditions.

Online Study Center
Improve Your Grade
Interactive Map: Exploration and Settlement in the Indian and Pacific Oceans Before 1500

the Pacific. In 1947 one energetic amateur historian of the sea, Thor Heyerdahl°, argued that Easter Island and Hawaii were actually settled from the Americas. He sought to prove his theory by sailing his balsawood raft, *Kon Tiki*, westward from Peru.

Scholars have found evidence that suggests limited Amerindian maritime contacts from what is now Ecuador and Colombia northward to Mesoamerica in the period 300–900 C.E., but evidence for ongoing maritime contacts between these culture zones is unclear. Evidence that the settlement of the islands of the eastern Pacific was the result of planned expansion by Polynesian mariners is much more compelling. The first piece of evidence is the fact that the languages of these islanders are all closely related to the languages of the western Pacific and ultimately to those of Malaya. The second is the finding that accidental voyages could not have brought sufficient numbers of men and women for founding a new colony along with all the plants and domesticated animals that were basic to other Polynesian islands.

In 1976 a Polynesian crew led by Ben Finney used traditional navigational methods to sail an ocean canoe from Hawaii south to Tahiti. The *Hokulea* was a 62-foot-long (19-meter-long) double canoe patterned after old ocean-going canoes, which sometimes were as long as 120 feet (37 meters). Not only did the *Hokulea* prove seaworthy, but, powered by an inverted triangular sail and steered by paddles (not by a rudder), it was able to sail across the winds at a sharp enough angle to make the difficult voyage, just as ancient mariners must have done. Perhaps even more remarkable, the *Hokulea*'s crew was able to navigate to their destination using only their observation of the currents, stars, and evidence of land.

The Indian Ocean

While Polynesian mariners were settling Pacific islands, other Malayo-Indonesians were sailing westward across the Indian Ocean and colonizing the large island of Madagascar off the southeastern coast of Africa. These voyages continued through the fifteenth century. To this day the inhabitants of Madagascar speak Malayo-Polynesian languages. However, part of the island's

---

Heyerdahl (HIGH-uhr-dahl)

Polynesian Canoes   Pacific Ocean mariners sailing canoes such as these, shown in an eighteenth-century painting, made epic voyages of exploration and settlement. A large platform connects two canoes at the left, providing more room for the members of the expedition, and a sail supplements the paddlers.   ("Tereoboo, King of Owyhee, bringing presents to Captain Cook," D. L. Ref. p. xx 2f. 35. Courtesy, The Dixon Library, State Library of New South Wales)

population is descended from Africans who had crossed the 300 miles (500 kilometers) from the mainland to Madagascar, most likely in the centuries leading up to 1500.

Other peoples had been using the Indian Ocean for trade since ancient times. The landmasses of Southeast Asia and eastern Africa that enclose the Indian Ocean on each side, and the Indian subcontinent that juts into its middle, provided coasts that seafarers might safely follow and coves for protection. Moreover, seasonal winds known as monsoons are so predictable and steady that navigation in these waters using sailing vessels called dhows° was less difficult and dangerous than elsewhere.

The rise of medieval Islam gave Indian Ocean trade an important boost. The great Muslim cities of the Middle East provided a demand for valuable commodities. Even more important were the networks of Muslim traders that tied the region together. Muslim traders shared a common language, ethic, and law and actively spread their religion to distant trading cities. By 1400 there were Muslim trading communities all around the Indian Ocean.

---

dhow (dow)

The Indian Ocean traders operated largely independently of the empires and states they served, but in East Asia imperial China's rulers were growing more and more interested in these wealthy ports of trade. In 1368 the Ming dynasty overthrew Mongol rule and began expansionist policies to reestablish China's predominance and prestige abroad.

Having restored Chinese dominance in East Asia, the Ming next moved to establish direct contacts with the peoples around the Indian Ocean. In choosing to send out seven imperial fleets between 1405 and 1433, the Ming may have been motivated partly by curiosity. The fact that most of the ports the fleets visited were important in the Indian Ocean trade suggests that enhancing China's commerce was also a motive. Yet because the expeditions were far larger than needed for exploration or promoting trade, their main purpose probably was to inspire awe of Ming power and achievements.

The Ming expeditions into the Indian Ocean Basin were launched on a scale that reflected imperial China's resources and importance. The first consisted of sixty-two specially built "treasure ships," large Chinese junks each about 300 feet long by 150 feet wide (90 by 45 meters).

Chinese Junk This modern drawing shows how much larger one of Zheng He's ships was than one of Vasco da Gama's vessels. Watertight interior bulkheads made junks the most seaworthy large ships of the fifteenth century. Sails made of pleated bamboo matting hung from the junk's masts, and a stern rudder provided steering. European ships of exploration, though smaller, were faster and more maneuverable. (Dugald Stermer)

There were also at least a hundred smaller vessels, most of which were larger than the flagship in which Columbus later sailed across the Atlantic. Each treasure ship had nine masts, twelve sails, many decks, and a carrying capacity of 3,000 tons (six times the capacity of Columbus's entire fleet). One expedition carried over 27,000 individuals, including infantry and cavalry troops. The ships would have been armed with small cannon, but in most Chinese sea battles arrows from highly accurate crossbows dominated the fighting.

At the command of the expeditions was Admiral **Zheng He°** (1371–1435). A Chinese Muslim with ancestral connections to the Persian Gulf, Zheng was a fitting emissary to the increasingly Muslim-dominated Indian Ocean Basin. The expeditions carried other Arabic-speaking Chinese as interpreters.

One of these interpreters kept a journal recording the customs, dress, and beliefs of the people visited, along with the trade, towns, and animals of their countries. He observed exotic animals such as the black panther of Malaya and the tapir of Sumatra and encountered local legends such as that of the "corpse-headed barbarians" whose heads left their bodies at night and

caused infants to die. In India he noted the division of the coastal population into five classes, which correspond to the four Hindu varna and a separate Muslim class, and passed on the fact that traders in the rich Indian trading port of Calicut° could perform error-free calculations by counting on their fingers and toes rather than using the Chinese abacus. After his return, the interpreter went on tour in China, telling of these exotic places and "how far the majestic virtue of [China's] imperial dynasty extended."[1]

The Chinese "treasure ships" carried rich silks, precious metals, and other valuable goods intended as gifts for distant rulers. In return those rulers sent back gifts of equal or greater value to the Chinese emperor. Although the main purpose of these exchanges was diplomatic, they also stimulated trade between China and its southern neighbors. For that reason they were welcomed by Chinese merchants and manufacturers. Yet commercial profits could not have offset the huge cost of the fleets.

Interest in new contacts was not confined to the Chinese side. In 1415–1416 at least three trading cities on the Swahili° Coast of East Africa sent delegations to China. The delegates from one of them, Malindi, presented the

Zheng He (jung huh)

Calicut (KAL-ih-kut)   **Swahili** (swah-HEE-lee)

emperor of China with a giraffe, creating quite a stir among the normally reserved imperial officials. Such African delegations may have encouraged more contacts, for the next three of Zheng's voyages were extended to the African coast. Unfortunately, no documents record how Africans and Chinese reacted to each other during these historic meetings between 1417 and 1433, but it appears that China's lavish gifts stimulated the Swahili market for silk and porcelain. An increase in Chinese imports of pepper from southern Asian lands also resulted from these expeditions.

Had the Ming court wished to promote trade for the profit of its merchants, Chinese fleets might have continued to play a dominant role in Indian Ocean trade. But some high Chinese officials opposed increased contact with peoples whom they regarded as barbarians with no real contribution to make to China. Such opposition caused a suspension in the voyages from 1424 to 1431, and after the final expedition of 1432 to 1433, no new fleets were sent out. Later Ming emperors focused their attention on internal matters in their vast empire. China's withdrawal left a power vacuum in the Indian Ocean.

The Atlantic Ocean

The greatest mariners of the Atlantic in the early Middle Ages were the Vikings. These northern European raiders and pirates used their small, open ships to attack coastal European settlements for several centuries. They also discovered and settled one island after another in the North Atlantic during these warmer-than-usual centuries. Like the Polynesians, the Vikings had neither maps nor navigational devices, but they managed to find their way wonderfully well using their knowledge of the heavens and the seas.

The Vikings first settled Iceland in 770. From there some moved to Greenland in 982, and by accident one group sighted North America in 986. Fifteen years later Leif Ericsson established a short-lived Viking settlement on the island of Newfoundland, which he called Vinland. When a colder climate returned after 1200, the northern settlements in Greenland went into decline, and Vinland was abandoned, becoming a mysterious place mentioned only in Norse sagas.

Some southern Europeans applied maritime skills acquired in the Mediterranean and along the Atlantic coastal regions to explore the Atlantic. In 1291 the two Vivaldo brothers from Genoa set out to sail through the South Atlantic and around Africa to India. They were never heard of again. Other Genoese and Portuguese expeditions into the Atlantic in the fourteenth century discovered (and settled) the islands of Madeira°, the Azores°, and the Canaries.

There is also written evidence of African voyages of exploration in the Atlantic in this period. The celebrated Syrian geographer al-Umari (1301–1349) relates that when Mansa Kankan Musa°, the ruler of the West African empire of Mali, passed through Egypt on his lavish pilgrimage to Mecca in 1324, he told of voyages to cross the Atlantic undertaken by his predecessor, Mansa Muhammad. According to this source, Muhammad had sent out four hundred vessels with men and supplies, telling them, "Do not return until you have reached the other side of the ocean or if you have exhausted your food or water." After a long time one canoe returned, reporting that the others had been swept away by a "violent current in the middle of the sea." Muhammad himself then set out at the head of a second, even larger, expedition, from which no one returned.

In the Americas, limited maritime contacts were made between coastal populations in northern South America and Central America, and early Amerindian voyagers from South America also colonized the West Indies. By the year 1000 Amerindians known as the **Arawak**° (also called Taino) had moved up from the small islands of the Lesser Antilles (Barbados, Martinique, and Guadeloupe) into the Greater Antilles (Cuba, Hispaniola, Jamaica, and Puerto Rico) as well as into the Bahamas (see Map 16.2). The Carib followed the same route in later centuries and by the late fifteenth century had overrun most Arawak settlements in the Lesser Antilles and were raiding parts of the Greater Antilles. From the West Indies Arawak and Carib also undertook voyages to the North American mainland.

EUROPEAN EXPANSION, 1400–1550

The preceding survey shows that maritime expansion occurred in many parts of the world before 1450. Nevertheless, the epic sea voyages sponsored by the Iberian kingdoms of Portugal and Spain are of special interest because they began a maritime revolution that profoundly altered the course of world history. The Portuguese and Spanish expeditions ended the isolation of the Americas and increased the volume of global interaction. The influence in world affairs of the Iberians and other Europeans

Madeira (muh-DEER-uh) **Azores** (A-zorz)
Mansa Kankan Musa (MAHN-suh KAHN-kahn MOO-suh)
Arawak (AR-uh-wahk)

Map 16.2 Middle America to 1533 Early Amerindian voyages from South America brought new settlers to the West Indies and western Mexico. The arrival of Europeans in 1492 soon led to the conquest and depopulation of Amerindians.

who followed them overseas rose steadily in the centuries after 1500.

Iberian overseas expansion was the product of two related phenomena. First, Iberian rulers had strong economic, religious, and political motives to expand their contacts and increase their dominance. Second, improvements in their maritime and military technologies gave them the means to master treacherous and unfamiliar ocean environments, seize control of existing maritime trade routes, and conquer new lands.

Online Study Center
Improve Your Grade
Interactive Map: Europe's Overseas Expansion in the Fifteenth and Sixteenth Centuries

Motives for Exploration

Why did Iberian kingdoms decide to sponsor voyages of exploration in the fifteenth century? Part of the answer lies in the individual ambitions and adventurous personalities of the rulers. Another part of the answer can be found in long-term tendencies in Europe and the Mediterranean. In many ways these voyages continued four trends evident in the Latin West since about the year 1000: (1) the revival of urban life and trade, (2) a peculiarly European alliance between merchants and rulers, (3) a struggle with Islamic powers for dominance of the Mediterranean that mixed religious motives with the desire for trade with distant lands, and (4) growing intellectual curiosity about the outside world.

The city-states of northern Italy took the lead in all these developments. By 1450 they had well-established trade links to northern Europe, the Indian Ocean, and the Black Sea, and their merchant princes had also sponsored an intellectual and artistic Renaissance. But the trading states of Venice and Genoa continued to maintain profitable commercial ties in the Mediterranean and preferred to continue the system of alliances with the Muslims that had given their merchants privileged access to the lucrative trade from the East. Even after the expansion of the Ottoman Empire disrupted their trade to the East, they did not take the lead in exploring the Atlantic. Also, the ships of the Mediterranean were ill suited to the more violent weather of the Atlantic. However, many individual Italians played leading roles in the Atlantic explorations.

In contrast, the special history and geography of the Iberian kingdoms led them in a different direction. Part of that special history was centuries of warfare with Muslim kingdoms that were established in the eighth century, when most of Iberia was occupied by invaders from North Africa. By about 1250 the Iberian kingdoms of Portugal, Castile, and Aragon had conquered all the Muslim lands in Iberia except the southern kingdom of Granada. United by a dynastic marriage in 1469, Castile and Aragon conquered Granada in 1492. These separate kingdoms were gradually amalgamated into Spain, sixteenth-century Europe's most powerful state.

Christian militancy continued to be an important motive for both Portugal and Spain in their overseas ventures. But the Iberian rulers and their adventurous subjects also sought material returns. With only a modest share of the Mediterranean trade, they were much more willing than the Italians to take risks to find new routes through the Atlantic to the rich trade of Africa and Asia. Moreover, both were participants in the shipbuilding changes and the gunpowder revolution that were under way in Atlantic Europe. Though not centers of Renaissance learning, both were especially open to new geographical knowledge. Finally, both states were blessed with exceptional leaders.

Portuguese Voyages

Portugal's decision to invest significant resources in new exploration rested on an already well-established Atlantic fishing industry and a history of anti-Muslim warfare. When the Muslim government of Morocco in northwestern Africa showed weakness in the fifteenth century, the Portuguese went on the attack, beginning with the city of Ceuta° conquered in 1415. This assault combined aspects of a religious crusade, a plundering expedition, and a military tournament in which young Portuguese knights displayed their bravery. The capture of the rich North African city made the Portuguese better informed about the caravans that brought gold and slaves to Ceuta from the African states south of the Sahara. Despite the capture of several more ports along Morocco's Atlantic coast, the Portuguese were unable to push inland and gain access to the gold trade. So they sought more direct contact with the gold producers by sailing down the African coast.

The attack on Ceuta was led by young Prince Henry (1394–1460), third son of the king of Portugal. Because he devoted the rest of his life to promoting exploration of the South Atlantic, he is known as **Henry the Navigator**. His official biographer emphasized Henry's mixed motives for exploration—converting Africans to Christianity, making contact with existing Christian rulers in Africa, and launching joint crusades with them against the Ottomans. Prince Henry also wished to discover new places and hoped that such new contacts would be profitable. His initial explorations were concerned with Africa. Only later did reaching India become an explicit goal of Portuguese explorers. Despite being called "the Navigator," Prince Henry himself never ventured far from home. Instead, he founded a sort of research institute at Sagres° for studying navigation that drew on the pioneering efforts of Italian merchants, especially the Genoese, as well as fourteenth-century Jewish cartographers who used information from Arab and European sources to produce remarkably accurate charts and maps. Henry both oversaw the collection of geographical information from sailors and travelers and sponsored new expeditions to explore the Atlantic. His ships established permanent contact with the islands of Madeira in 1418 and the Azores in 1439.

Henry's staff studied and improved navigational instruments that had come into Europe from China and the Islamic world. These instruments included the magnetic compass, first developed in China, and the astrolabe, an instrument of Arab or Greek invention that enabled mariners to determine their location at sea by measuring the position of the sun or the stars in the night sky. Even with such instruments, however, voyages still depended on the skill and experience of the navigators.

Another achievement of Portuguese mariners was the design of vessels appropriate for the voyages of exploration. Neither the galleys in use in the Mediterranean, which were powered by large numbers of oarsmen, nor

---

Ceuta (say-OO-tuh)   **Sagres** (SAH-gresh)

Portuguese Map of Western Africa, 1502 This map shows in great detail a section of African coastline that Portuguese explorers charted and named in the fifteenth century. The cartographer illustrated the African interior, which was almost completely unknown to Europeans, with drawings of birds and views of coastal sights: Sierra Leone (Serra lioa), named for a mountain shaped like a lion, and the Portuguese Castle of the Mine (Castello damina) on the Gold Coast. (akg-images)

the three-masted ships of northern Europe with their square sails proved adequate for the Atlantic. The large crews of the galleys could not carry supplies adequate to long voyages far from shore and the square-rigged northern vessels had trouble sailing at an angle to the wind. Instead, the voyages of exploration made use of a new vessel, the **caravel**°. Caravels were much smaller than the largest European ships and the Chinese junks Zheng He had used to explore the Indian Ocean early in the fifteenth century. Their size permitted them to enter shallow coastal waters and explore upriver, but they were strong enough to weather ocean storms. When equipped with the triangular lateen sails that could take the wind on either side, caravels had great maneuverability and, alternately, when sporting square Atlantic sails and with a following wind, they had great speed. The addition of

small cannon made them good fighting ships as well. The caravels' economy, speed, agility, and power justified a contemporary's claim that they were "the best ships that sailed the seas."[2]

To conquer the seas, pioneering captains had to overcome the common fear that South Atlantic waters were boiling hot or contained ocean currents that would prevent any ship entering them from ever returning home. It took Prince Henry fourteen years—from 1420 to 1434—to coax an expedition to venture beyond southern Morocco (see Map 16.3). The crew's fears proved unfounded, but the next stretch of coast, 800 miles (1,300 kilometers) of desert, offered little of interest to the explorers. It would take the Portuguese four decades to cover the 1,500 miles (2,400 kilometers) from Lisbon to Sierra Leone°; it then took only three decades to explore

---

caravel (KAR-uh-vel)

Sierra Leone (see-ER-uh lee-OWN)

Map 16.3   European Exploration, 1420–1542   Portuguese and Spanish explorers showed the possibility and practicality of intercontinental maritime trade. Before 1540 European trade with Africa and Asia was much more important than that with the Americas, but after the Spanish conquest of the Aztec and Inca Empires transatlantic trade began to increase. Notice the Tordesillas line, which in theory separated the Spanish and Portuguese spheres of activity.

the remaining 4,000 miles (6,400 kilometers) to the southern tip of the African continent.

In the years that followed, Henry's explorers made an important contribution to the maritime revolution by learning how to return speedily to Portugal. Instead of battling the prevailing northeast trade winds and currents back up the coast, they discovered that by sailing northwest into the Atlantic to the latitude of the Azores, ships could pick up prevailing westerly winds that would blow them back to Portugal. The knowledge that ocean winds tend to form large circular patterns helped explorers discover many other ocean routes.

To pay for the research, the ships, and the expeditions during the many decades before voyages became profitable, Prince Henry drew partly on the income of the Order of Christ, a religious military order of which he was governor. The Order of Christ had inherited the properties and crusading traditions of the Order of Knights Templar, which had disbanded in 1314. The Order of Christ received the exclusive right to promote Christianity in all the lands that were discovered, and the Portuguese emblazoned their ships' sails with the crusaders' red cross.

The profits from these voyages came from selling into slavery Africans captured by the Portuguese in raids on the northwest coast of Africa and the Canary Islands during the 1440s. The total number of Africans captured or purchased on voyages exceeded eighty thousand by the end of the century and rose steadily thereafter. However, the gold trade quickly became more important than the slave trade as the Portuguese made contact with the trading networks that flourished in West Africa and reached across the Sahara. By 1457 enough African gold was coming back to Portugal for the kingdom to issue a new gold coin called the *cruzado* (crusader), another reminder of how deeply the Portuguese entwined religious and secular motives.

The Portuguese crown continued to sponsor voyages of exploration, but speedier progress resulted from the growing participation of private commercial interests. In 1469 a prominent Lisbon merchant named Fernão Gomes purchased from the Crown the privilege of exploring 350 miles (550 kilometers) of African coast in return for a monopoly on trade. He discovered the uninhabited island of São Tomé° located on the equator. In the next century it became a major source of sugar produced by slave laborers imported from the African mainland, serving as a model for the sugar plantations later developed in Brazil and the Caribbean. Gomes also explored the **Gold Coast**, which became the headquarters of Portugal's West African trade.

The final thrust down the African coast was spurred by the expectation of finding a passage around Africa to the rich trade of the Indian Ocean. In 1488 **Bartolomeu Dias** was the first Portuguese explorer to round the southern tip of Africa and enter the Indian Ocean. Then in 1497–1498 a Portuguese expedition led by **Vasco da Gama** sailed around Africa and reached India (see Environment and Technology: Vasco da Gama's Fleet). In 1500, ships on the way to India under the command of Pedro Alvares Cabral° sailed too far west and reached the South American mainland. This discovery established Portugal's claim to Brazil, which would become one of the Western Hemisphere's richest colonies. The gamble that Prince Henry had begun eight decades earlier was about to pay off handsomely.

Spanish Voyages

In contrast to the persistence and planning behind Portugal's century-long exploration of the South Atlantic, haste and blind luck lay behind Spain's early discoveries. Throughout most of the fifteenth century, the Spanish kingdoms had been preoccupied with internal affairs: completion of the reconquest of southern Iberia from the Muslims; amalgamation of the various dynasties; and the conversion or expulsion of religious minorities. Only in the last decade of the century were Spanish monarchs ready to turn to overseas exploration, by which time the Portuguese had already found a new route to the Indian Ocean.

The leader of the Spanish overseas mission was **Christopher Columbus** (1451–1506), a Genoese mariner. His four voyages between 1492 and 1502 established the existence of a vast new world across the Atlantic, whose existence few in "old world" Eurasia and Africa had ever suspected. But Columbus refused to accept that he had found unknown continents and peoples, insisting that he had succeeded in his goal of finding a shorter route to the Indian Ocean than the one the Portuguese had found.

As a younger man Columbus had gained considerable experience of the South Atlantic while participating in Portuguese explorations along the African coast, but he had become convinced there was a shorter way to reach the riches of the East than the route around Africa. By his reckoning (based on a serious misreading of a ninth-century Arab authority), the Canaries were a mere 2,400 nautical miles (4,450 kilometers) from Japan. The actual distance was five times as far.

It was not easy for Columbus to find a sponsor willing to underwrite the costs of testing his theory that one could reach Asia by sailing west. Portuguese authorities

---

São Tomé (sow toh-MAY)

Cabral (kah-BRAHL)

Vasco da Gama's Fleet

The four small ships that sailed for India from Lisbon in June 1497 may seem a puny fleet compared to the sixty-two Chinese vessels that Zheng He had led into the Indian Ocean ninety-five years earlier. But given the fact that China had a hundred times as many people as Portugal, Vasco da Gama's fleet represented at least as great a commitment of resources. In any event, the Portuguese expedition had a far greater impact on the course of history. Having achieved its aim of inspiring awe at China's greatness, the Chinese throne sent out no more expeditions after 1432. Although da Gama's ships seemed more odd than awesome to Indian Ocean observers, that modest fleet began a revolution in global relations.

Portugal spared no expense in ensuring that the fleet would make it to India and back. Craftsmen built extra strength into the hulls to withstand the powerful storms that Dias had encountered in 1488 at the tip of Africa. Small enough to be able to navigate any shallow harbors and rivers they might encounter, the ships were crammed with specially strengthened casks and barrels of water, wine, oil, flour, meat, and vegetables far in excess of what was required even on a voyage that would take the better part of a year. Arms and ammunition were also in abundance.

Three of da Gama's ships were rigged with square sails on two masts for speed and a lateen sail on the third mast. The fourth vessel was a caravel with lateen sails. Each ship carried three sets of sails and plenty of extra rigging so as to be able to repair any damages due to storms. The crusaders' red crosses on the sails signaled one of the expedition's motives.

The captains and crew—Portugal's most talented and experienced—received extra pay and other rewards for their service. Yet there was no expectation that the unprecedented

Vasco da Gama's Flagship This vessel carried the Portuguese captain on his second expedition to India in 1505. (The Pierpont Morgan Library/Art Resource, NY)

sums spent on this expedition would bring any immediate return. According to a contemporary chronicle, the only immediate return the Portuguese monarch received was "the knowledge that some part of Ethiopia and the beginning of Lower India had been discovered." However, the scale and care of the preparations suggest that the Portuguese expected the expedition to open up profitable trade to the Indian Ocean. And so it did.

twice rejected his plan, first in 1485 following a careful study and again in 1488 after Dias had established the feasibility of a route around Africa. Columbus received a more sympathetic hearing in 1486 from Castile's able ruler, Queen Isabella, but no commitment of support. After a four-year study a Castilian commission appointed by Isabella concluded that a westward sea route to the Indies rested on many questionable geographical assumptions, but Columbus's persistence finally won over the queen and her husband, King Ferdinand of Aragon. In 1492 they agreed to fund a modest expedition. Their elation at defeating Granada, the last independent Muslim kingdom in Iberia, may have put them in a favorable mood.

Online Study Center

Improve Your Grade

Primary Source: Agreement with Columbus
on April 17 and April 30, 1492

Columbus recorded in his log that he and his mostly Spanish crew of ninety men "departed Friday the third day of August of the year 1492" toward "the regions of India." Their mission, the royal contract stated, was "to discover and acquire certain islands and mainland in the Ocean Sea." He carried letters of introduction from the Spanish sovereigns to Eastern rulers, including one to the "Grand Khan" (meaning the Chinese emperor). Also on board was a Jewish convert to Christianity whose knowledge of Arabic was expected to facilitate communication with the peoples of eastern Asia. The expedition traveled in three small ships, the *Santa María*, the *Santa Clara* (nicknamed the *Niña*), and a third vessel now known only by its nickname, the *Pinta*. The *Niña* and the *Pinta* were caravels.

The expedition began well. Other attempts to explore the Atlantic west of the Azores had been impeded by unfavorable headwinds. But on earlier voyages along the African coast, Columbus had learned that he could find west-blowing winds in the latitudes of the Canaries, which is why he chose that southern route. After reaching the Canaries, he had the *Niña*'s lateen sails replaced with square sails, for he knew that from then on speed would be more important than maneuverability.

In October 1492 the expedition reached the islands of the Caribbean. Columbus insisted on calling the inhabitants "Indians" because he believed that the islands were part of the East Indies. A second voyage to the Caribbean in 1493 did nothing to change his mind. Even when, two months after Vasco da Gama reached India in 1498, Columbus first sighted the mainland of South America on a third voyage, he stubbornly insisted it was part of Asia. But by then other Europeans were convinced that he had discovered islands and continents previously unknown to the Old World. Amerigo Vespucci's explorations, first on behalf of Spain and then for Portugal, led mapmakers to name the new continents "America" after him, rather than "Columbia" after Columbus.

To prevent disputes arising from their efforts to exploit their new discoveries and to spread Christianity among the people there, Spain and Portugal agreed to split the world between them. The Treaty of Tordesillas°, negotiated by the pope in 1494, drew an imaginary line down the middle of the North Atlantic Ocean. Lands east

of the line in Africa and southern Asia could be claimed by Portugal; lands to the west in the Americas were reserved for Spain. Cabral's discovery of Brazil, however, gave Portugal a valid claim to the part of South America located east of the line.

But if the Tordesillas line were extended around the earth, where would Spain's and Portugal's spheres of influence divide in the East? Given Europeans' ignorance of the earth's true size in 1494, it was not clear whether the Moluccas°, whose valuable spices had been a goal of the Iberian voyages, were on Portugal's or Spain's side of the line. The missing information concerned the size of the Pacific Ocean. By chance, in 1513 a Spanish adventurer named Vasco Núñez de Balboa° crossed the Isthmus (a narrow neck of land) of Panama from the east and sighted the Pacific Ocean on the other side. And the 1519 expedition of **Ferdinand Magellan** (ca. 1480–1521) was designed to complete Columbus's interrupted westward voyage by sailing around the Americas and across the Pacific, whose vast size no European then guessed. The Moluccas turned out to lie well within Portugal's sphere, as Spain formally acknowledged in 1529.

Magellan's voyage established the basis for Spanish colonization of the Philippine Islands after 1564. Nor did Magellan's death prevent him from being considered the first person to encircle the globe, for a decade earlier he had sailed from Europe to the East Indies as part of an expedition sponsored by his native Portugal. His two voyages took him across the Tordesillas line, through the separate spheres claimed by Portugal and Spain—at least until other Europeans began demanding a share. Of course, in 1500 European claims were largely theoretical. Portugal and Spain had only modest settlements overseas.

Although Columbus failed to find a new route to the East, the consequences of his voyages for European expansion were momentous. Those who followed in his wake laid the basis for Spain's large colonial empires in the Americas and for the empires of other European nations. In turn, these empires promoted, among the four Atlantic continents, the growth of a major new trading network whose importance rivaled and eventually surpassed that of the Indian Ocean network. The more immediately important consequence was Portugal's entry into the Indian Ocean, which quickly led to a major European presence and profit. Both the eastward and the westward voyages of exploration marked a tremendous expansion of Europe's role in world history.

Tordesillas (tor-duh-SEE-yuhs)

Moluccas (muh-LOO-kuhz)   **Balboa** (bal-BOH-uh)

ENCOUNTERS WITH EUROPE, 1450–1550

European actions alone did not determine the global consequences of the new contacts that Iberian mariners had opened. The ways in which Africans, Asians, and Amerindians perceived their new visitors and interacted with them also influenced future developments. Everywhere indigenous peoples evaluated the Europeans as potential allies or enemies, and everywhere Europeans attempted to insert themselves into existing commercial and geopolitical arrangements. In general, Europeans made slow progress in establishing colonies and asserting political influence in Africa and Asia, even while profiting from new commercial ties. In the Americas, however, Spain, Portugal, and later other European powers moved rapidly to create colonial empires. In this case the long isolation of the Amerindians from the rest of the world made them more vulnerable to the diseases that these explorers introduced, limiting their potential for resistance and facilitating European settlement.

Western Africa

Many Africans along the West African coast were eager for trade with the Portuguese. It would give them new markets for their exports and access to imports cheaper than those that reached them through the middlemen of the overland routes to the Mediterranean. This reaction was evident along the Gold Coast of West Africa, first visited by the Portuguese in 1471. Miners in the hinterland had long sold their gold to African traders, who took it to the trading cities along the southern edge of the Sahara, where it was sold to traders who had crossed the desert from North Africa. Recognizing that they might get more favorable terms from the new visitors from the sea, coastal Africans were ready to negotiate with the royal representative of Portugal who arrived in 1482 seeking permission to erect a trading fort.

The Portuguese noble in charge and his officers (likely including the young Christopher Columbus, who had entered Portuguese service in 1476) were eager to make a proper impression. They dressed in their best clothes, erected and decorated a reception platform, celebrated a Catholic Mass, and signaled the start of negotiations with trumpets, tambourines, and drums. The African king, Caramansa, staged his entrance with equal ceremony, arriving with a large retinue of attendants and musicians. Through an African interpreter, the two leaders exchanged flowery speeches pledging goodwill and mutual benefit. Caramansa then gave his permission for a small trading fort to be built, assured, he said, by the appearance of these royal delegates that they were honorable persons, unlike the "few, foul, and vile" Portuguese visitors of the previous decade.

Neither side made a show of force, but the Africans' upper hand was evident in Caramansa's warning that if the Portuguese failed to be peaceful and honest traders, he and his people would simply move away, depriving their post of food and trade. Trade at the post of Saint George of the Mine (later called Elmina) enriched both sides. From there the Portuguese crown was soon purchasing gold equal to one-tenth of the world's production at the time. In return, Africans received large quantities of goods that Portuguese ships brought from Asia, Europe, and other parts of Africa.

After a century of aggressive expansion, the kingdom of Benin in the Niger Delta was near the peak of its power when it first encountered the Portuguese. Its oba (king) presided over an elaborate bureaucracy from a spacious palace in his large capital city, also known as Benin. In response to a Portuguese visit in 1486, the oba sent an ambassador to Portugal to learn more about the homeland of these strangers. He then established a royal monopoly on trade with the Portuguese, selling pepper

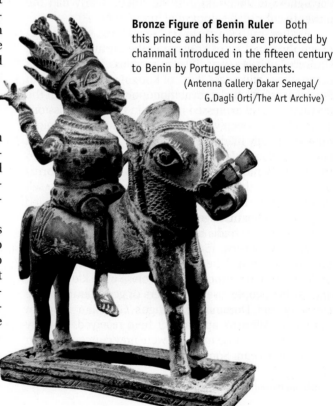

Bronze Figure of Benin Ruler   Both this prince and his horse are protected by chainmail introduced in the fifteen century to Benin by Portuguese merchants. (Antenna Gallery Dakar Senegal/ G.Dagli Orti/The Art Archive)

and ivory tusks (to be taken back to Portugal) as well as stone beads, textiles, and prisoners of war (to be resold at Elmina). In return, Portuguese merchants provided Benin with copper and brass, fine textiles, glass beads, and a horse for the king's royal procession. In the early sixteenth century, as the demand for slaves for the Portuguese sugar plantations on the nearby island of São Tomé grew, the oba first raised the price of slaves and then imposed restrictions that limited their sale.

Early contacts generally involved a mixture of commercial, military, and religious interests. Some African rulers were quick to appreciate that European firearms could be a useful addition to their spears and arrows in conflicts with their enemies. Because African religions did not presume to have a monopoly on religious knowledge, coastal rulers were also willing to test the value of Christian practices, which the Portuguese eagerly promoted. The rulers of Benin and Kongo, the two largest coastal kingdoms, invited Portuguese missionaries and soldiers to accompany them into battle to test the Christians' religion along with their muskets.

Portuguese efforts to persuade the king and nobles of Benin to accept the Catholic faith ultimately failed. Early kings showed some interest, but after 1538 the rulers declined to receive more missionaries. They also closed the market in male slaves for the rest of the sixteenth century. Exactly why Benin chose to limit its contacts with the Portuguese is uncertain, but the rulers clearly had the power to control the amount of interaction.

Farther south, on the lower Congo River, relations between the kingdom of Kongo and the Portuguese began similarly but had a very different outcome. Like the oba of Benin, the manikongo° (king of Kongo) sent delegates to Portugal, established a royal monopoly on trade with the Portuguese, and expressed interest in Christian missionary teachings. Deeply impressed with the new religion, the royal family made Catholicism the kingdom's official faith. But Kongo, lacking ivory and pepper, had less to trade than Benin. To acquire the goods brought by Portugal and to pay the costs of the missionaries, it had to sell more and more slaves.

Soon the manikongo began to lose his royal monopoly over the slave trade. In 1526 the Christian manikongo, Afonso I (r. 1506–ca. 1540), wrote to his royal "brother," the king of Portugal, begging for his help in stopping the trade because unauthorized Kongolese were kidnapping and selling people, even members of good families (see Diversity and Dominance: Kongo's Christian King on page 476). Alfonso's appeals for help received no reply from Portugal, whose interests were now concentrated in the Indian Ocean. Some subjects took advantage of the

manikongo (mah-NEE-KONG-goh)

manikongo's weakness to rebel against his authority. After 1540 the major part of the slave trade from this part of Africa moved farther south.

Eastern Africa

Different still were the reactions of the Muslim rulers of the trading coastal states of eastern Africa. As Vasco da Gama's fleet sailed up the coast in 1498, most rulers gave the Portuguese a cool reception, suspicious of the intentions of these visitors who painted crusaders' crosses on their sails. But the ruler of one of the ports, Malindi, saw in the Portuguese an ally who could help him expand the city's trading position and provided da Gama with a pilot to guide him to India. The initial suspicions of most rulers were justified seven years later when a Portuguese war fleet bombarded and looted most of the coastal cities of eastern Africa in the name of Christianity and commerce, though they spared Malindi.

Another eastern African state that saw potential benefit in an alliance with the Portuguese was Christian Ethiopia. In the fourteenth and early fifteenth centuries, Ethiopia faced increasing conflicts with Muslim states along the Red Sea. Emboldened by the rise of the Ottoman Turks, who had conquered Egypt in 1517 and launched a major fleet in the Indian Ocean to counter the Portuguese, the talented warlord of the Muslim state of Adal launched a furious assault on Ethiopia. Adal's decisive victory in 1529 reduced the Christian kingdom to a precarious state. At that point Ethiopia's contacts with the Portuguese became crucial.

For decades, delegations from Portugal and Ethiopia had been exploring a possible alliance between their states based on their mutual adherence to Christianity. A key figure was Queen Helena of Ethiopia, who acted as regent for her young sons after her husband's death in 1478. In 1509 Helena sent a letter to "our very dear and well-beloved brother," the king of Portugal, along with a gift of two tiny crucifixes said to be made of wood from the cross on which Christ had died in Jerusalem. In her letter she proposed an alliance of her land army and Portugal's fleet against the Turks. No such alliance was completed by the time Helena died in 1522. But as Ethiopia's situation grew increasingly desperate, renewed appeals for help were made.

Finally, a small Portuguese force commanded by Vasco da Gama's son Christopher reached Ethiopia in 1539, at a time when what was left of the empire was being held together by another woman ruler. With Portuguese help, the queen rallied the Ethiopians to renew their struggle. Christopher da Gama was captured and tortured to death, but Muslim forces lost heart when their leader was mortally wounded in a later battle.

Portuguese aid helped the Ethiopian kingdom save itself from extinction, but a permanent alliance faltered because Ethiopian rulers refused to transfer their Christian affiliation from the patriarch of Alexandria to the Latin patriarch of Rome (the pope) as the Portuguese wanted.

Online Study Center
Improve Your Grade
Interactive Map: East Africa
in the Sixteenth Century

As these examples illustrate, African encounters with the Portuguese before 1550 varied considerably, as much because of the strategies and leadership of particular African states as because of Portuguese policies. Africans and Portuguese might become royal brothers, bitter opponents, or partners in a mutually profitable trade, but Europeans remained a minor presence in most of Africa in 1550. By then the Portuguese had become far more interested in the Indian Ocean trade.

Indian Ocean States

Vasco da Gama's arrival on the Malabar Coast of India in May 1498 did not make a great impression on the citizens of Calicut. After more than ten months at sea, many members of the crew were in ill health. Da Gama's four small ships were far less imposing than the Chinese fleets of gigantic junks that had called at Calicut sixty-five years earlier and no larger than many of the dhows that filled the harbor of this rich and important trading city. The samorin (ruler) of Calicut and his Muslim officials showed mild interest in the Portuguese as new trading partners, but the gifts da Gama had brought for the samorin evoked derisive laughter. Twelve pieces of fairly ordinary striped cloth, four scarlet hoods, six hats, and six wash basins seemed inferior goods to those accustomed to the luxuries of the Indian Ocean trade. When da Gama tried to defend his gifts as those of an explorer, not a rich merchant, the samorin cut him short, asking whether he had come to discover men or stones: "If he had come to discover men, as he said, why had he brought nothing?"

Coastal rulers soon discovered that the Portuguese had no intention of remaining poor competitors in the rich trade of the Indian Ocean. Upon da Gama's return to Portugal in 1499, the jubilant King Manuel styled himself "Lord of the Conquest, Navigation, and Commerce of Ethiopia, Arabia, Persia, and India," setting forth the ambitious scope of his plans. Previously the Indian Ocean had been an open sea, used by merchants (and pirates) of all the surrounding coasts. Now the Portuguese crown intended to make it a Portuguese sea, the private property of Portugal alone.

The ability of little Portugal to assert control over the Indian Ocean stemmed from the superiority of its ships and weapons over those of the regional powers, especially the lightly armed merchant dhows. In 1505 a Portuguese fleet of eighty-one ships and some seven thousand men bombarded Swahili Coast cities. Next on the list were Indian ports. Goa, on the west coast of India, fell to a well-armed fleet in 1510, becoming the base from which the Portuguese menaced the trading cities of Gujarat° to the north and Calicut and other Malabar Coast cities to the south. The port of Hormuz, controlling entry to the Persian Gulf, was taken in 1515, but Aden, at the entrance to the Red Sea, used its intricate natural defenses to preserve its independence. The addition of the Gujarati port of Diu in 1535 consolidated Portuguese dominance of the western Indian Ocean.

Meanwhile, Portuguese explorers had been reconnoitering the Bay of Bengal and the waters farther east. The independent city of Malacca° on the strait between the Malay Peninsula and Sumatra became the focus of their attention. During the fifteenth century Malacca had become the main entrepôt° (a place where goods are stored or deposited and from which they are distributed) for the trade from China, Japan, India, the Southeast Asian mainland, and the Moluccas. Among the city's more than 100,000 residents an early Portuguese visitor counted eighty-four different languages, including those of merchants from as far west as Cairo, Ethiopia, and the Swahili Coast of East Africa. Many non-Muslim residents of the city supported letting the Portuguese join its cosmopolitan trading community, perhaps hoping to offset the growing solidarity of Muslim traders. In 1511, however, the Portuguese seized this strategic trading center outright with a force of a thousand fighting men, including three hundred recruited in southern India.

Force was not always necessary. On the China coast, local officials and merchants interested in profitable new trade with the Portuguese persuaded the imperial government to allow the Portuguese to establish a trading post at Macao° in 1557. Operating from Macao, Portuguese ships came to nearly monopolize trade between China and Japan.

In the Indian Ocean, the Portuguese used their control of major port cities to enforce an even larger trading monopoly. As their power grew, they required all spices, as well as all goods on the major ocean routes such as between Goa and Macao, to be carried in Portuguese ships. In addition, the Portuguese tried to control and tax other Indian Ocean trade by requiring all merchant ships entering and leaving one of their ports to carry a Portuguese

---

Gujarat (goo-juh-RAHT)   **Malacca** (muh-LAH-kuh)
entrepôt (ON-truh-poh)   **Macao** (muh-COW)

Kongo's Christian King

The new overseas voyages brought conquest to some and opportunities for fruitful borrowings and exchanges to others. The decision of the ruler of the kingdom of Kongo to adopt Christianity in 1491 added cultural diversity to Kongolese society and in some ways strengthened the hand of the king. From then on Kongolese rulers sought to introduce Christian beliefs and rituals while at the same time Africanizing Christianity to make it more intelligible to their subjects. In addition, the kings of Kongo sought a variety of more secular aid from Portugal, including schools and medicine. Trade with the Portuguese introduced new social and political tensions, especially in the case of the export trade in slaves for the Portuguese sugar plantations on the island of São Tomé to the north.

Two letters sent to King João (zhwao) III of Portugal in 1526 illustrate how King Afonso of Kongo saw his kingdom's new relationship with Portugal and the problems that resulted from it. (Afonso adopted that name when he was baptized as a young prince.) After the death of his father in 1506, Afonso successfully claimed the throne and ruled until 1542. His son Henrique became the first Catholic bishop of the Kongo in 1521.

These letters were written in Portuguese and penned by the king's secretary João Teixera (tay-SHER-uh), a Kongo Christian, who, like Afonso, had been educated by Portuguese missionaries.

6 July 1526

To the very powerful and excellent prince Dom João, our brother:

On the 20th of June just past, we received word that a trading ship from your highness had just come to our port of Sonyo. We were greatly pleased by that arrival for it had been many days since a ship had come to our kingdom, for by it we would get news of your highness, which many times we had desired to know, . . . and likewise as there was a great and dire need for wine and flour for the holy sacrament; and of this we had had no great hope for we have the same need frequently. And that, sir, arises from the great negligence of your highness's officials toward us and toward shipping us those things. . . .

Sir, your highness should know how our kingdom is being lost in so many ways that we will need to provide the needed cure, since this is caused by the excessive license given by your agents and officials to the men and merchants who come to this kingdom to set up shops with goods and many things which have been prohibited by us, and which they spread throughout our kingdoms and domains in such abundance that many of our vassals, whose submission we could once rely on, now act independently so as to get the things in greater abundance than we ourselves; whom we had formerly held content and submissive and under our vassalage and jurisdiction, so it is doing a great harm not only to the service of God, but also to the security and peace of our kingdoms and state.

And we cannot reckon how great the damage is, since every day the mentioned merchants are taking our people, sons of the land and the sons of our noblemen and vassals and our relatives, because the thieves and men of bad conscience grab them so as to have the things and wares of this kingdom that they crave; they grab them and bring them to be sold. In such a manner, sir, has been the corruption and deprivation that our land is becoming completely depopulated, and your highness should not deem this good nor in your service. And to avoid this we need from these kingdoms [of yours] no more than priests and a few people to teach in schools, and no other goods except wine and flour for the holy sacrament, which is why we beg of your highness to help and assist us in this matter. Order your agents to send here neither merchants nor wares, because it is our will that in these kingdoms there should not be any dealing in slaves nor outlet for them, for the reasons stated above. Again we beg your highness's agreement, since otherwise we cannot cure such manifest harm. May Our Lord in His mercy have your highness always under His protection and may you always do the things of His holy service. I kiss your hands many times.

From our city of Kongo. . . .

The King, Dom Afonso

18 October 1526

Very high and very powerful prince King of Portugal, our brother,

Sir, your highness has been so good as to promise us that anything we need we should ask for in our letters, and that everything will be provided. And so that there may be peace and health of our kingdoms, by God's will, in our lifetime. And as there are among us old folks and people who have lived for many days, many and different diseases happen so often that we are pushed to the ultimate extremes. And the same happens to our children, relatives, and people, because this country lacks physicians and surgeons who might know the proper cures for such diseases, as well as pharmacies and drugs to make them better. And for this reason many of those who had been already confirmed and instructed in the things of the holy faith of Our Lord Jesus Christ perish and die. And the rest of the people for the most part cure themselves with herbs and sticks and other ancient methods, so that they live putting all their faith in these herbs and ceremonies, and die believing that they are saved; and this serves God poorly.

And to avoid such a great error, I think, and inconvenience, since it is from God and from your highness that all the good and the drugs and medicines have come to us for our salvation, we ask your merciful highness to send us two physicians and two pharmacists and one surgeon, so that they may come with their pharmacies and necessary things to be in our kingdoms, for we have extreme need of each and every one of them. We will be very good and merciful to them, since sent by your highness, their work and coming should be for good. We ask your highness as a great favor to do this for us, because besides being good in itself it is in the service of God as we have said above.

Moreover, sir, in our kingdoms there is another great inconvenience which is of little service to God, and this is that many of our people, out of great desire for the wares and things of your kingdoms, which are brought here by your people, and in order to satisfy their disordered appetite, seize many of our people, freed and exempt men. And many times noblemen and the sons of noblemen, and our relatives are stolen, and they take them to be sold to the white men who are in our kingdoms and take them hidden or by night, so that they are not recognized. And as soon as they are taken by the white men, they are immediately ironed and branded with fire. And when they are carried off to be embarked, if they are caught by our guards, the whites allege that they have bought them and cannot say from whom, so that it is our duty to do justice and to restore to the free their freedom. And so they went away offended.

And to avoid such a great evil we passed a law so that every white man living in our kingdoms and wanting to purchase slaves by whatever means should first inform three of our noblemen and officials of our court on whom we rely in this matter, namely Dom Pedro Manipunzo and Dom Manuel Manissaba, our head bailiff, and Gonçalo Pires, our chief supplier, who should investigate if the said slaves are captives or free men, and, if cleared with them, there will be no further doubt nor embargo and they can be taken and embarked. And if they reach the opposite conclusion, they will lose the aforementioned slaves. Whatever favor and license we give them [the white men] for the sake of your highness in this case is because we know that it is in your service too that these slaves are taken from our kingdom; otherwise we should not consent to this for the reasons stated above that we make known completely to your highness so that no one could say the contrary, as they said in many other cases to your highness, so that the care and remembrance that we and this kingdom have should not be withdrawn. . . .

We kiss your hands of your highness many times.

From our city of Kongo, the 18th day of October,

The King, Dom Afonso

QUESTIONS FOR ANALYSIS

1. What sorts of things does King Afonso desire from the Portuguese?

2. What is he willing and unwilling to do in return?

3. What problem with his own people has the slave trade created, and what has King Afonso done about it?

4. Does King Afonso see himself as an equal to King João or his subordinate? Do you agree with that analysis?

Source: From António Brásio, ed., *Monumenta Missionaria Africana: Africa Ocidental (1471-1531)* (Lisbon: Agência Geral do Ultramar, 1952), I: 468, 470-471, 488-491. Translated by David Northrup.

Portuguese in India
In the sixteenth century Portuguese men moved to the Indian Ocean Basin to work as administrators and traders. This Indo-Portuguese drawing from about 1540 shows a Portuguese man speaking to an Indian woman, perhaps making a proposal of marriage.　(Ms. 1889, c. 97, Biblioteca Casanate-unse Rome. Photo: Humberto Nicoletti Serra)

passport and to pay customs duties. Portuguese patrols seized vessels that attempted to avoid these monopolies, confiscated their cargoes, and either killed the captain and crew or sentenced them to forced labor.

Reactions to this power grab varied. Like the emperors of China, the Mughal° emperors of India largely ignored Portugal's maritime intrusions, seeing their interests as maintaining control over their vast land possessions. The Ottomans responded more aggressively, supporting Egypt against the Christian intruders with a large fleet and fifteen thousand men between 1501 and 1509. Then, having absorbed Egypt into their empire, the Ottomans sent another large expedition against the Portuguese in 1538. Both expeditions failed because Ottoman galleys were no match for the faster, better-armed Portuguese vessels in the open ocean. However, the Ottomans retained the advantage in the Red Sea and Persian Gulf, where they had many ports of supply.

The smaller trading states of the region were less capable of challenging Portuguese domination head on, since rivalries among them impeded the formation of any common front. Some chose to cooperate with the Portuguese to maintain their prosperity and security. Others engaged in evasion and resistance. Two examples illustrate the range of responses among Indian Ocean peoples.

Mughal (MOO-gahl)

The merchants of Calicut put up some of the most sustained local resistance. In retaliation, the Portuguese embargoed all trade with Aden, Calicut's principal trading partner, and centered their trade on the port of Cochin, which had once been a dependency of Calicut. Some Calicut merchants became adept at evading these patrols, but the price of resistance was the shrinking of Calicut's commercial importance as Cochin gradually became the major pepper-exporting port on the Malabar Coast.

The traders and rulers of the state of Gujarat farther north had less success in keeping the Portuguese at bay. At first they resisted Portuguese attempts at monopoly and in 1509 joined Egypt's failed effort to sweep the Portuguese from the Arabian Sea. But in 1535, finding his state at a military disadvantage due to Mughal attacks, the ruler of Gujarat made the fateful decision to allow the Portuguese to build a fort at Diu in return for their support. Once established, the Portuguese gradually extended their control, so that by midcentury they were licensing and taxing all Gujarati ships. Even after the Mughals (who were Muslims) took control of Gujarat in 1572, the Mughal emperor Akbar permitted the Portuguese to continue their maritime monopoly in return for allowing one ship a year to carry pilgrims to Mecca without paying the Portuguese any fee.

The Portuguese never gained complete control of the Indian Ocean trade, but their naval supremacy allowed them to dominate key ports and trade routes during the sixteenth century. The resulting profits were sent back to Europe in the form of spices and other luxury goods. The effects were dramatic. The Portuguese were now able to break the pepper monopoly long held by Venice and Genoa, who both depended on Egyptian middlemen, by selling at much lower prices. They were also able to fund a more aggressive colonization of Brazil.

In both Asia and Africa the consequences flowing from these events were startling. Asian and East African traders were now at the mercy of Portuguese warships, but their individual responses affected their fates. Some were devastated. Others prospered by meeting Portuguese demands or evading their patrols. Because Portuguese power was based on the control of trade routes, not the occupation of large territories, Portugal had little impact on the Asian and African mainlands, in sharp contrast to what was occurring in the Americas.

The Americas

In the Americas the Spanish established a vast territorial empire, in contrast to the trading empires the Portuguese created in Africa and Asia. This outcome had little to do with differences between the two Iberian kingdoms, except for the fact that the Spanish kingdoms had a much larger population and greater resources to draw on. The Spanish and Portuguese monarchies had similar motives for expansion and used identical ships and weapons. Rather, the isolation of the Amerindian peoples made their responses to outside contacts different from the responses of peoples in Africa and the Indian Ocean cities. In dealing with the relatively small indigenous populations on the Caribbean islands, the first Spanish settlers resorted to conquest and plunder rather than trade. This practice was later extended to the more powerful Amerindian kingdoms on the American mainland. The spread of deadly new diseases, especially smallpox, among Amerindians after 1518 weakened their ability to resist.

The first Amerindians to encounter Columbus were the Arawak of Hispaniola (modern Haiti and the Dominican Republic) in the Greater Antilles and the Bahamas to the north (see Map 16.2). They cultivated maize (corn), cassava (a tuber), sweet potatoes, and hot peppers, as well as cotton and tobacco. They met their other material needs from the sea and from wild plants. Although they had no hard metals such as bronze or iron, they were skilled at working gold. However, these islands did not have large gold deposits, and, unlike West Africans, the Arawak did not trade gold over long distances. The Arawak at first extended a cautious welcome

to the Spanish but soon learned to tell exaggerated stories about gold in other places to persuade them to move on.

When Columbus made his second trip to Hispaniola in 1493, he brought several hundred settlers from southern Iberia who hoped to make their fortune, as well as missionaries who were eager to persuade the Amerindians to accept Christianity. The settlers demanded indigenous labor to look for gold, stole gold ornaments, confiscated food, and sexually assaulted native women, provoking the Arawak to rebel in 1495. In this and later conflicts, steel swords, horses, and body armor gave the Spaniards a great advantage, and thousands of Arawak were slaughtered and captives forced into bondage. Those who survived were forced to pay a heavy tax in gold, spun cotton, and food. Any who failed to meet the quotas were condemned to forced labor. Meanwhile, the cattle, pigs, and goats introduced by the settlers devoured the Arawak's food crops, causing deaths from famine and disease. A governor appointed by the Spanish crown in 1502 institutionalized these demands by dividing the surviving Arawak on Hispaniola among his political allies as laborers.

Online Study Center
Improve Your Grade
Primary Source: A Dominican Voice in the Wilderness: Preaching Against Tyranny in Hispaniola

The actions of the Spanish in the Antilles were reflections of Spanish actions and motives during the wars against the Muslims in Spain in the previous centuries: they sought to serve God by defeating nonbelievers and placing them under Christian control—and to become rich in the process. Individual **conquistadors**° (conquerors) extended that pattern around the Caribbean. As gold and indigenous labor became scarce on Hispaniola, Spanish expeditions looked for new opportunities. The search for gold and the Spanish need to replace the rapidly declining Amerindian population of Hispaniola led to the forced removal of most of the Arawaks from the Bahamas, taken to Hispaniola as slaves. Juan Ponce de León (1460–1521), who had participated in the conquest of Muslim Spain and the seizure of Hispaniola, conquered the island of Borinquen (Puerto Rico) in 1508 and then initiated the exploration of southeastern Florida in 1513. Cuba was conquered by forces led by Diego Velázquez between 1510 and 1511.

Following two failed expeditions to Mexico, the governor of Cuba appointed an ambitious and ruthless nobleman, **Hernán Cortés**° (1485–1547) to undertake a

---

conquistador (kon-KEY-stuh-dor)   **Cortés** (kor-TEZ)

Coronation of Emperor Moctezuma This painting by an unnamed Aztec artist depicts the Aztec ruler's coronation. Moctezuma, his nose pierced by a bone, receives the crown from a prince in the palace at Tenochtitlan. (Oronoz)

new effort. Cortés left Cuba in 1519 with six hundred fighting men, including many who had sailed with the earlier expeditions, and most of the island's stock of weapons and horses. After demonstrating his military skills in a series of battles with the Maya, Cortés learned of the rich Aztec Empire in central Mexico. Cortés brought to the American mainland the military tactics, political skills, and institutions that had been developed earlier in the reconquest of Muslim Iberia and the settlement of the Greater Antilles.

The Aztecs themselves had conquered their vast empire only during the previous century, and many of the subjugated Amerindian peoples were far from loyal subjects. Many resented the tribute they had to pay the Aztecs, the forced labor, and the large-scale human sacrifices to the Aztec gods. The Aztecs also had powerful enemies, including the Tlaxcalans°, who would become crucial supporters of Cortés's military campaign. After fierce battles with the Spanish, who believed they were allies of the Aztecs, the Tlaxcalans forged a lasting military alliance with Cortés. Like the peoples of Africa and Asia when confronted by Europeans, the Amerindian peoples of Mexico calculated as best they could the benefits and threats represented by these strange visitors.

Individuals were forced to make these kinds of choices as well. Malintzin° (Malinche), a native woman who was given to Cortés shortly after his arrival in the Maya region, became his translator, key source of intelligence, and mistress. As peoples and as individuals, native allies were crucial to the Spanish campaign.

While Cortés proved decisive, directing his force toward the center of the Aztec Empire, the Aztec emperor **Moctezuma**° II (r. 1502–1520) hesitated to use force and attempted diplomacy instead. Cortés pushed toward the glorious capital city of Tenochtitlan°. Along his route he demonstrated the technological advantages enjoyed by the Spanish on the battlefield, using his firearms, cavalry tactics, and steel swords to great effect. In the end Moctezuma agreed to welcome the Spaniards. As they approached the island city, the emperor went out in a great procession, dressed in all his finery, to welcome Cortés with gifts and flower garlands.

Despite Cortés's initial promise that he came in friendship, Moctezuma quickly found himself a prisoner in his own palace. The Spanish looted his treasury, interfered with the city's religious rituals, and eventually massacred hundreds during a festival. The Aztecs then rose in mass rebellion, forcing the Spanish to attempt a desperate nighttime

---

Tlaxcalans (thlash-KAH-lans)

Malintzin (mah-LEENT-zeen) **Moctezuma** (mock-teh-ZOO-ma)
Tenochtitlan (teh-noch-TIT-lan)

escape. Briefly the Aztecs gained the upper hand. They destroyed half of the Spanish force and four thousand of the Spaniards' Amerindian allies, sacrificing fifty-three Spanish prisoners and four horses to their gods and displaying their severed heads on pikes. In the battle Moctezuma was killed.

The Spanish survivors retreated from the city and rebuilt their strength with the help of the Tlaxcalans. Their successful capture of Tenochtitlan in 1521 was greatly facilitated by the spread of smallpox, which weakened and killed more of the city's defenders than died in the fighting. One source remembered that the disease "spread over the people as a great destruction." The bodies of the afflicted were covered with oozing sores, and large numbers soon died. It is likely that many Amerindians as well as Europeans blamed the devastating spread of this disease on supernatural forces. After the Aztec capital fell, Cortés and other Spanish leaders led expeditions to the north and south accompanied by indigenous allies including the Tlaxcalans and others. Everywhere epidemic disease, especially smallpox, helped crush indigenous resistance.

Before these events, Spanish settlements had been established in Panama, and settlers there had heard tales of rich and powerful civilizations to the south, although they did not have specific intelligence of the Inca Empire (see Chapter 12). During the previous century the Inca had built a vast empire along the Pacific coast of South America, stretching nearly 3,000 miles (5,000 kilometers) from southern Colombia to Chile. As the empire expanded through conquest, the Inca enforced new labor demands and taxes and even exiled rebellious populations from their lands.

The Inca Empire was a great empire with highly productive agriculture, exquisite stone cities (such as the capital, Cuzco), complex trading networks, and rich gold and silver mines. The power of the Inca emperor was sustained by the belief that he was descended from the Sun God, as well as by a professional military and an efficient system of roads and messengers that kept him informed about major events in the empire. Yet all was not well.

The Execution of Inca Ruler Atahualpa This representation of the execution was drawn by Felipe Guaman Poma de Ayala, a native Andean from the area of Huamanga in Peru. While Atahualpa was strangled, not beheaded, by Pizarro, Guaman Poma's illustration helped make the case that the conquest had imposed a corrupt and violent government on the Andean people. (Courtesy, Musée du Quai Branly, Paris)

About 1525 the Inca ruler Huayna Capac° died in Quito, where he had led a successful military campaign. His death set off a contested succession between two of his sons that led to civil war. In the end Atahualpa, the candidate of the northern army, defeated Huascar, the candidate of the royal court at Cuzco. The military and political leadership were decimated, and the surviving supporters of Huascar were embittered. Even more devastating was the threat awaiting the empire from **Francisco Pizarro°** (ca. 1478–1541) and his force of 180 men, 37 horses, and two cannon.

With limited education and some military experience, Pizarro had come to the Americas in 1502 at the age of twenty-five to seek his fortune. He had participated in the conquest of Hispaniola and in Balboa's expedition across the Isthmus of Panama. By 1520 Pizarro was a wealthy landowner and official in Panama, yet he gambled his fortune on more adventures, exploring the Pacific coast to a point south of the equator, where he learned of the riches of the Inca. With a license from the king of Spain, he set out from Panama in 1531 to conquer them.

Huayna Capac (WHY-nah KAH-pak)   **Pizarro** (pih-ZAHR-oh)

Having seen signs of the civil war after landing, Pizarro arranged to meet the Inca emperor, **Atahualpa°** (r. 1531–1533) near the Andean city of Cajamarca° in November 1532. With supreme boldness and brutality, Pizarro's small band of armed men seized Atahualpa from a rich litter borne by eighty nobles as it passed through an enclosed courtyard. Though surrounded by an Inca army of at least forty thousand, the Spaniards were able to use their cannon to create confusion while their swords brought down thousands of the emperor's lightly armed retainers and servants. The strategy to replicate the earlier Spanish conquest of Mexico was working.

Atahualpa, seeking to guard his authority even as a captive, ordered the execution of his imprisoned brother Huascar. He also attempted to gain his freedom. Having noted the glee with which the Spaniards seized gold, silver, and emeralds, Atahualpa offered a ransom he thought would satisfy even the greediest among them: rooms filled to shoulder height with gold and silver. But when the ransom of 13,400 pounds (6,000 kilograms) of

gold and 26,000 pounds (12,000 kilograms) of silver was paid, the Spaniards gave Atahualpa a choice: he could be burned at the stake as a heathen or baptized as a Christian and then strangled. He chose the latter. The unity of the Inca Empire, already battered by the civil war and Atahualpa's decision to execute his brother Huascar, was further undermined by the Spanish occupation of Cuzco, the capital city.

Nevertheless, a massive native rebellion was led in 1536 by Manco Inca, whom the Spanish had placed on the throne following the execution of his brother Atahualpa. Although defeated by the Spanish, Manco Inca and his heirs retreated to the interior and created a much-reduced independent kingdom that survived until 1572. The victorious Spaniards, now determined to settle their own rivalries, initiated a bloody civil war fueled by greed and jealousy. Before peace was established, this struggle took the lives of Francisco Pizarro and most of the other prominent conquistadors. But the conquest of the mainland continued. Incited by the fabulous wealth of the Aztecs and Inca, conquistadors extended Spanish conquest and exploration in South and North America, dreaming of new treasuries to loot.

Atahualpa (ah-tuh-WAHL-puh)   **Cajamarca** (kah-hah-MAHR-kah)

COMPARATIVE PERSPECTIVES

The rapid expansion of European empires and the projection of European military power around the world is one of the most important topics in world history, but it would have seemed unlikely in 1492. No European power matched the military and economic strength of China and few could rival the Ottomans. Spain lacked strong national institutions and Portugal had a small population, both had limited economic resources. Because of these limitations the monarchs of Spain and Portugal allowed their subjects greater initiative. While royal sponsorship was often crucial in, for example, the Portuguese contacts with Africa and the first voyages to Asia, many of the commercial and military expeditions were effectively organized and financed as private companies. Very often the kings of Spain and Portugal struggled to catch up with their restless and ambitious subjects, sometimes taking decades to establish royal control in new colonies.

The pace and character of European expansion was different in Africa and Asia than in the Americas. In Africa local rulers were generally able to limit European military power to coastal

outposts and to control European trade. Only in the Kongo were the Portuguese able to project their power inland. In the Indian Ocean there were mature markets and specialized production for distant consumers when Europeans arrived. Here Portuguese (and later Dutch and British) naval power allowed Europeans to harvest large profits and influence local commercial patterns, but most native populations continued to enjoy autonomy for centuries.

In the Americas the terrible effects of epidemic disease and the destructiveness of the conquest led to the rapid creation of European settlements and the subordination of the surviving indigenous population. The Spanish and Portuguese found few long-distance markets and little large scale production of goods that could be exported profitably to Europe. The Americas would eventually produce great amounts of wealth, but the production of the gold, silver, and sugar resulted from the introduction of new technologies, the imposition of oppressive new forms of labor, such as slavery, as well as the development of new roads and ports.

SUMMARY

— What were the objectives and major accomplishments of the voyages of exploration undertaken by Chinese, Polynesians, and other non-Western peoples?

— In this era of long-distance exploration, did Europeans have any special advantages over other cultural regions?

— What were the different outcomes of European interactions with Africa, India, and the Americas?

Online Study Center
ACE the Test

The voyages of exploration undertaken by the Chinese and Polynesians pursued diverse objectives. In the Chinese case, the great voyages of the early fifteenth century were made out of interest in trade, curiosity, and the projection of imperial power. For the Polynesians, exploration opened the opportunity to both project power and demonstrate expertise while at the same settling satellite populations that would relieve population pressures on limited resources. In both cases new connections were made and societies were invigorated. The Vikings had similarly explored new lands in the North Atlantic, using their knowledge of the heavens and seas to establish settlements. There is also written evidence of African voyages in the Atlantic during this same period, although their purpose is less clear.

The projection of European influence between 1450 and 1550 was in some ways similar to that of other cultural regions in that it expanded commercial linkages, increased cross-cultural contacts, and served the ambitions of political leaders. But the result was a major turning point in world history. During those years European explorers opened new long-distance trade routes across the world's three major oceans, for the first time establishing regular contact among all the continents. As a result, a new balance of power arose in parts of Atlantic Africa, the Indian Ocean, and the Americas.

Europeans created colonial empires in the Americas quite rapidly, while their progress in Africa and Asia was much slower. Many Amerindians welcomed the Spanish settlers at first, only to have them tax their labors, steal their food, introduce disease and warfare, and eventually subjugate them. In contrast, Portuguese visitors to

Africa remained a minor presence in 1550. In some regions, the Portuguese were welcomed as trading partners; in others they were regarded as potential political and military allies. The real focus of the Portuguese was to capture the rich trade of the Indian Ocean. While they never gained complete control, they used their superior military strength to dominate key ports and major trade routes.

As dramatic and momentous as these events were, they were not completely unprecedented. The riches of the Indian Ocean trade that brought a gleam to the eye of many Europeans had been developed over many centuries by the trading peoples who inhabited the surrounding lands. While rapid, the European conquest of the Americas was no more rapid or brutal than the earlier Mongol conquests of Eurasia. Even the crossing of the Pacific had been done before, though in stages, by Polynesians.

What gave this maritime revolution unprecedented importance had more to do with what happened after 1550 than with what happened earlier. The overseas empires of the Europeans would endure longer than the Mongols' and would continue to expand for three and a half centuries after 1550. Unlike the Chinese, the Europeans did not turn their backs on the world after an initial burst of exploration. Not content with dominance in the Indian Ocean trade, Europeans opened an Atlantic maritime network that grew to rival the Indian Ocean network in the wealth of its trade; they also pioneered trade across the Pacific. The maritime expansion begun in the period from 1450 to 1550 marked the beginning of a new age of growing global interaction.

KEY TERMS

Zheng He   *p. 464*

Arawak   *p. 465*

Henry the Navigator   *p. 467*

caravel   *p. 468*

Gold Coast   *p. 470*

Bartolomeu Dias   *p. 470*

Vasco da Gama   *p. 470*

Christopher Columbus
   p. 470

Ferdinand Magellan   *p. 472*

Conquistadors   *p. 479*

Hernán Cortés   *p. 479*

Moctezuma II   *p. 480*

Francisco Pizarro   *p. 481*

Atahualpa   *p. 482*

Online Study Center
Improve Your Grade
Flashcards

SUGGESTED READING

There is no single survey of the different expansions covered by this chapter, but the selections edited by Joseph R. Levenson, *European Expansion and the Counter Example of Asia, 1300–1600* (1967), remain a good introduction to Chinese expansion and Western impressions of China. Janet Abu-Lughod, *Before European Hegemony: The World System,* A.D. *1250–1350* (1989), provides a stimulating speculative reassessment of the importance of the Mongols and the Indian Ocean trade in the creation of the modern world system; she summarizes her thesis in the American Historical Association booklet *The World System in the Thirteenth Century: Dead-End or Precursor?* (1993).

The Chinese account of Zheng He's voyages is Ma Huan, *Ying-yai Sheng-lan: "The Overall Survey of the Ocean's Shores"* [1433], ed. Feng Ch'end Chun and trans. J. V. G. Mills (1970). A reliable guide to Polynesian expansion is Jesse D. Jennings, ed., *The Prehistory of Polynesia* (1979), especially the excellent chapter "Voyaging" by Ben R. Finney, which encapsulates his *Voyage of Rediscovery: A Cultural Odyssey Through Polynesia* (1994). The medieval background to European intercontinental voyages is summarized by Felipe Fernandez-Armesto, *Before Columbus: Exploration and Colonization from the Mediterranean to the Atlantic, 1229–1492* (1987). Tim Severin, *The Brendan Voyage* (2000), vividly recounts a modern retracing of even earlier Irish voyages.

A simple introduction to the technologies of European expansion is Carlo M. Cipolla, *Guns, Sails, and Empires: Technological Innovation and the Early Phases of European Expansion, 1400–1700* (1965; reprint, 1985). More advanced is Roger C. Smith, *Vanguard of Empire: Ships of Exploration in the Age of Columbus* (1993).

The European exploration is well documented and the subject of intense historical investigation. Clear general accounts based on the contemporary records are Boies Penrose, *Travel and Discovery in the Age of the Renaissance, 1420–1620* (1952); J. H. Parry, *The Age of Reconnaissance: Discovery, Exploration, and Settlement, 1450–1650* (1963); and G. V. Scammell, *The World Encompassed: The First European Maritime Empires, c. 800–1650* (1981).

An excellent general introduction to Portuguese exploration is C. R. Boxer, *The Portuguese Seaborne Empire, 1415–1825* (1969). More detail can be found in Bailey W. Diffie and George D. Winius, *Foundations of the Portuguese Empire, 1415–1580* (1977); A. J. R. Russell-Wood, *The Portuguese Empire: A World on the Move* (1998); and Luc Cuyvers, *Into the Rising Sun: The Journey of Vasco da Gama and the Discovery of the Modern World* (1998). John William Blake, ed., *Europeans in West Africa, 1450–1560* (1942), is an excellent two-volume collection of contemporary Portuguese, Castilian, and English sources. The *Summa Oriental of Tomé Pires: An Account of the East, from the Red Sea to Japan, Written in Malacca and India in 1512–1515*, trans. Armando Cortesão (1944), provides a detailed firsthand account of the Indian Ocean during the Portuguese's first two decades there.

The other Iberian kingdoms' expansion is well summarized by Henry Kamen, *Spain, 1469–1714: A Society of Conflict*, 2nd ed. (1991); and John Lynch, *Spain 1516–1598: From Nation State to World Empire* (1991). Miles H. Davidson, *Columbus Then and Now: A Life Reexamined* (1997), is a useful modern treatment. More focused on the shortcomings of Columbus and his Spanish peers is Tzvetan Todorov, *The Conquest of America*, trans. Richard Howard (1985). William D. Phillips and Carla Rhan Phillips, *The Worlds of Christopher Columbus* (1992), examines the mariner and his times in terms of modern concerns. Peggy K. Liss, *Isabel the Queen: Life and Times* (1992), is a sympathetic examination of Queen Isabella of Castile. For the conquest period see Matthew Restall, *Seven Myths of the Spanish Conquest* (2003); Rafael Varón Gabai, *Francisco Pizarro and His Brothers* (1997); and Kenneth J. Adrien and Roena Adorno, eds., *Transatlantic Encounters* (1991). Detailed individual biographies of all of the individuals in Pizarro's band are also the subject of James Lockhart's *Men of Cajamarca: A Social and Biographical Study of the First Conquerors of Peru* (1972). A firsthand account of Magellan's expedition is Antonio Pigafetta, *Magellan's Voyage: A Narrative Account of the First Circumnavigation*, available in a two-volume edition (1969).

The perceptions of the peoples European explorers encountered are not as well documented. David Northrup, *Africa's Discovery of Europe, 1450–1850* (2002), and John Thornton, *Africa and Africans in the Making of the Atlantic World, 1400–1800,* 2nd ed. (1998), examine Africans' encounters with Europeans and their involvement in the Atlantic economy. *The Broken Spears: The Aztec Account of the Conquest of Mexico,* ed. Miguel Leon-Portilla

(1962), presents Amerindian chronicles in a readable package, as does Nathan Wachtel, *The Vision of the Vanquished: The Spanish Conquest of Peru Through Indian Eyes* (1977). Anthony Reid, *Southeast Asia in the Age of Commerce, 1450–1680,* 2 vols. (1988, 1993), deals with events in that region.

NOTES

1. Ma Huan, *Ying-yai Sheng-lan: "The Overall Survey of the Ocean's Shores,"* ed. Feng Ch'eng-Chün, trans. J. V. G. Mills (Cambridge, England: Cambridge University Press, 1970), 180.

2. Alvise da Cadamosto in *The Voyages of Cadamosto and Other Documents,* ed. and trans. G. R. Crone (London: Hakluyt Society, 1937), 2.

Climate and Population to 1500

During the millennia before 1500, human populations expanded in three momentous surges. The first occurred after 50,000 B.C.E. when humans emigrated from their African homeland to all of the inhabitable continents. After that, the global population remained steady for several millennia. During the second expansion, between about 5000 and 500 B.C.E., population rose from about 5 million to 100 million as agricultural societies spread around the world (see Figure 1). Again population growth then slowed for several centuries before a third surge took world population to over 350 million by 1200 C.E. (see Figure 2).

For a long time historians tended to attribute these population surges to cultural and technological advances. Indeed, a great many changes in culture and technology are associated with adaptation to different climates and food supplies in the first surge and with the domestication of plants and animals in the second. However, historians have not found a cultural or technological change to explain the third surge, nor can they explain why creativity would have stagnated for

long periods between the surges. Something else must have been at work.

Recently historians have begun to pay more attention to the impact of long-term variations in global climate. By examining ice cores drilled out of glaciers, scientists have been able to compile records of thousands of years of climate change. The comparative width of tree rings from ancient forests has provided additional data on periods of favorable and unfavorable growth. Such evidence shows that cycles of population growth and stagnation followed changes in global climate.

Historians now believe that global temperatures were above normal for extended periods from the late 1100s to the late 1200s C.E. In the temperate lands where most of the world's people lived, above-normal temperatures meant a longer growing season, more bountiful harvests, and thus a more adequate and reliable food supply. The ways in which societies responded to the medieval warm period are as important as the climate change, but it is unlikely that human agency alone would have produced the me-

Figure 1   World Population, 5000–1 B.C.E.

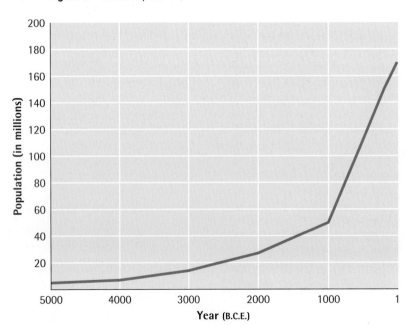

dieval surge. One notable response was that of the Vikings, who increased the size and range of their settlements in the North Atlantic, although their raids also caused death and destruction.

Some of the complexities involved in the interaction of human agency, climate, and other natural factors are also evident in the demographic changes that followed the medieval warm period. During the 1200s the Mongol invasions caused death and disruption of agriculture across Eurasia. China's population, which had been over 100 million in 1200, declined by a third or more by 1300. The Mongol invasions did not cause harm west of Russia, but climate changes in the 1300s resulted in population losses in Europe. Unusually heavy rains caused crop failures and a prolonged famine in northern Europe from 1315 to 1319.

The freer movement of merchants within the Mongol Empire also facilitated the spread of disease across Eurasia, culminating in the great pandemic known as the Black Death in Europe. The demographic recovery under way in China was reversed. The even larger population losses in Europe may have been affected by the decrease in global temperatures to their lowest point in many millennia between 1350 and 1375. Improving economic conditions enabled population to recover more rapidly in Europe after 1400 than in China, where the conditions of rural life remained harsh.

Because many other historical circumstances interact with changing weather patterns, historians have a long way to go in deciphering the role of climate in history. Nevertheless, it is a factor that can no longer be ignored.

Figure 2   Population in China and Europe, 1–1500 C.E.

PART FIVE

THE GLOBE ENCOMPASSED, 1500–1750

CHAPTER 17
Transformations in Europe, 1500–1750

CHAPTER 18
The Diversity of American Colonial Societies, 1530–1770

CHAPTER 19
The Atlantic System and Africa, 1550–1800

CHAPTER 20
Southwest Asia and the Indian Ocean, 1500–1750

CHAPTER 21
Northern Eurasia, 1500–1800

The decades between 1500 and 1750 witnessed a tremendous expansion of commercial, cultural, and biological exchanges around the world. New long-distance sea routes linked Europe with sub-Saharan Africa and the existing maritime networks of the Indian Ocean and East Asia. Spanish and Portuguese voyages ended the isolation of the Americas and created new webs of exchange in the Atlantic and Pacific. Overland expansion of Muslim, Russian, and Chinese empires also increased global interaction.

These expanding contacts had major demographic and cultural consequences. Domesticated animals and crops from the Old World transformed agriculture in the Americas, while Amerindian foods such as the potato became staples of the diet of the Old World. European diseases, meanwhile, devastated the Amerindian population, facilitating the establishment of large Spanish, Portuguese, French, and British empires. Europeans introduced enslaved Africans to relieve the labor shortage. Immigrant Africans and Europeans brought new languages, religious practices, music, and forms of personal adornment.

Map of the World, ca. 1595 After Ferdinand Magellan, the next explorer to circumnavigate the world was Sir Francis Drake (ca. 1540-1596). Departing with five ships in 1577, Drake nonetheless completed the majority of his voyage in a single ship, the *Golden Hind*, returning to England in 1580. This hand-colored engraving by Jodocus Hondius shows his route. Supported by Queen Elizabeth and other investors, Drake raided Spanish ships and ports and returned with great riches. Unlike Magellan, he traveled far northward before crossing the Pacific, harboring for several weeks near San Francisco Bay and making friendly contact with the native peoples there. Drake played a decisive role in England's victory against the Spanish Armada in 1587. (Library of Congress)

In Asia and Africa, by contrast, the most important changes owed more to internal forces than to European actions. The Portuguese seized control of some important trading ports and networks in the Indian Ocean and pioneered new contacts with China and Japan. In time, the Dutch, French, and English expanded these profitable connections, but in 1750 Europeans were still primarily a maritime force. Asians and Africans generally retained control of their lands and participated freely in overseas trade.

The Islamic world saw the dramatic expansion of the Ottoman Empire in the Middle East and the establishment of the Safavid Empire in Iran and the Mughal Empire in South Asia. In northern Eurasia, Russia and China acquired vast new territories and populations, while a new national government in Japan promoted economic development and stemmed foreign influence.

Hunters in the Snow, 1565 This January scene by the Flemish artist Pieter Bruegel the Elder, shows many everyday activities. (Kunsthistorisches Museum, Vienna/The Bridgeman Art Library)

- How was the cultural history of early modern Europe determined by the interplay of traditional beliefs and revolutionary ideas?

- What factors contributed to the wealth of some Europeans and the great poverty of others in this period?

- How was the history of early modern European states determined by differing policies in the areas of religion, foreign relations, and economics?

17

TRANSFORMATIONS IN EUROPE, 1500–1750

CHAPTER OUTLINE

Culture and Ideas

Social and Economic Life

Political Innovations

Comparative Perspectives

ENVIRONMENT AND TECHNOLOGY: Mapping the World

DIVERSITY AND DOMINANCE: Political Craft and Craftiness

Four years before his death, the Flemish artist Pieter Bruegel the Elder (ca. 1525–1569) painted *Hunters in the Snow*, a masterpiece of the cultural revival that later ages would call the European **Renaissance**. After a period of apprenticeship, Bruegel was accepted as a Master in the Antwerp Painters Guild in 1551. Though he also painted biblical and allegorical subjects, Bruegel is known especially for the technical skill and powers of observation he used to depict the scenes of natural and social life that surrounded him in his homeland. Art flourished in early modern Europe to an extent that can scarcely be overestimated, as exemplified by the musical compositions of Johann Sebastian Bach (1685–1750) in Germany and Antonio Vivaldi (ca. 1675–1741) in Italy, and by the literature of William Shakespeare (1564–1616) in England and Miguel de Cervantes (1547–1616) in Spain.

Online Study Center

This icon will direct you to interactive activities and study materials on the website: *college.hmco.com/pic/bulliet4e.*

From a political perspective, Europe in this period was marked by powerful and efficient armies, economies, and governments, which larger states elsewhere in the world feared, envied, and sometimes imitated. Globally, the balance of power was shifting slowly, but inexorably, in the Europeans' favor. In 1500 the Ottomans threatened Europe. By 1750, as the remaining chapters of Part Five detail, Europeans had brought the world's seas and a growing part of its land and people under their control. No single group of Europeans accomplished this. The Dutch eclipsed the pioneering Portuguese and Spanish; then the English and French bested the Dutch. Moreover, an increasing subordination of religious to political and economic interests helped Christian Europe to make the first successful achievements in international peacekeeping.

Yet the years from 1500 to 1750 were not simply—perhaps not even primarily—an age of progress for Europe. For many, the ferocious competition of European armies, merchants, and ideas was a wrenching experience. The growth of powerful states extracted a terrible price in death and destruction. The Reformation brought greater individual choice in religion but widespread religious persecution as well. Women's fortunes were closely tied to their social class, and few gained equality with men. The expanding economy benefited members of the emerging merchant elite and their political allies, but most Europeans became worse off as prices rose faster than wages.

CULTURE AND IDEAS

One place to observe the conflict and continuity of early modern Europe is in the world of ideas. Theological controversies broke the religious unity of the Latin Church and contributed to violent wars. A huge witch scare showed the power of Christian beliefs about the Devil and of traditional folklore about malevolent powers. The influence of classical ideas from Greco-Roman antiquity increased among better-educated people, but some thinkers challenged the authority of the ancients. Their new models of the motion of the planets encouraged others to challenge traditional social

and political systems, with important implications for the period after 1750. Each of these events has its own causes, but the technology of the printing press enhanced the impact of all.

Religious Reformation

In 1500 the **papacy**, the central government of Latin Christianity, was simultaneously gaining stature and suffering from corruption and dissent. Larger donations and tax receipts let popes fund ambitious construction projects in Rome, their capital city. During the sixteenth century Rome gained fifty-four new churches and other buildings, which showcased the artistic Renaissance then under way. However, the church's wealth and power also attracted ambitious men, some of whose personal lives became the source of scandal.

The jewel of the building projects was the magnificent new Saint Peter's Basilica in Rome. The unprecedented size and splendor of this church were intended to glorify God, display the skill of Renaissance artists and builders, and enhance the standing of the papacy. Such a project required refined tastes and vast sums of money.

The skillful overseer of the design and financing of the new Saint Peter's was Pope Leo X (r. 1513–1521), a member of the wealthy Medici° family of Florence, famous for its patronage of the arts. Pope Leo's artistic taste was superb and his personal life free from scandal, but he was more a man of action than a spiritual leader. One technique that he used to raise funds for the basilica was to authorize an **indulgence**—a forgiveness of the punishment due for past sins, granted by church authorities as a reward for a pious act such as making a pilgrimage, saying a particular prayer, or making a donation to a religious cause.

A young professor of sacred scripture, Martin Luther (1483–1546), objected to the way the new indulgence was preached. As the result of a powerful religious experience, Luther had forsaken money and marriage for a monastic life of prayer, self-denial, and study. In his religious quest, he found personal consolation in a passage in Saint Paul's Epistle to the Romans that argued that salvation came not from "doing certain things" but from religious faith. That passage also led Luther to object to the way the indulgence preachers appeared to emphasize giving money more than the faith behind the act. He wrote to Pope Leo, asking him to stop this abuse, and challenged the preachers to a debate on the theology of indulgences.

Medici (MED-ih-chee)

CHRONOLOGY

	Politics and Culture	Environment and Technology	Warfare
1500	**1500s** Spain's golden century		
	1519 Protestant Reformation begins		**1526–1571** Ottoman wars
	1540s Scientific Revolution begins		**1546–1555** German Wars of Religion
	1545 Catholic Reformation begins		**1562–1598** French Wars of Religion
			1566–1648 Netherlands Revolt
	Late 1500s Witch-hunts increase	**1590s** Dutch develop flyboats; Little Ice Age begins	
1600	**1600s** Holland's golden century	**1600s** Depletion of forests growing	
		1609 Galileo's astronomical telescope	**1618–1648** Thirty Years War
			1642–1648 English Civil War
			1652–1678 Anglo-Dutch Wars
		1682 Canal du Midi completed	**1667–1697** Wars of Louis XIV
			1683–1697 Ottoman wars
1700	**1700s** The Enlightenment begins		**1700–1721** Great Northern War
			1701–1714 War of the Spanish Succession
		1750 English mine nearly 5 million tons of coal a year	
		1755 Lisbon earthquake	

This theological dispute quickly escalated into a contest between two strong-minded men. Largely ignoring Luther's theological objections, Pope Leo regarded his letter as a challenge to papal power and moved to silence the German monk. During a debate in 1519, a papal representative led Luther into open disagreement with some church doctrines, for which the papacy condemned him. Blocked in his effort to reform the church from within, Luther burned the papal bull (document) of condemnation, rejecting the pope's authority and beginning the movement known as the **Protestant Reformation**.

Online Study Center
Improve Your Grade
Primary Source: Table Talk

Accusing those whom he called "Romanists" (Roman Catholics) of relying on "good works," Luther insisted that the only way to salvation was through faith in Jesus Christ. He further declared that Christian belief must be based on the word of God in the Bible and on Christian tradition, not on the authority of the pope, as Catholics held. Eventually his conclusions led him to abandon his monastic prayers and penances and to marry a former nun.

Today Roman Catholics and Lutherans have resolved many of their theological differences, but in the sixteenth century stubbornness on both sides made reconciliation impossible. Moreover, Luther's use of the printing press to promote his ideas won him the support of powerful Germans, who responded to his nationalist portrayal of the dispute as an effort of an Italian pope to beautify his city with German funds.

Inspired by Luther's denunciation of the ostentation and corruption of church leaders, other leaders called for a return to authentic Christian practices and beliefs. John Calvin (1509–1564), a well-educated Frenchman who turned from the study of law to theology after experiencing a religious conversion, became a highly

Luther and the Reformation
This sixteenth-century woodcut of Martin Luther shows him writing his demands for religious reform with a symbolically oversized quill pen on the door of All Saints Church in Wittenberg, Germany. (Private Collection/The Bridgeman Art Library)

influential Protestant leader. As a young man, Calvin published *The Institutes of the Christian Religion,* a masterful synthesis of Christian teachings, in 1535. Much of the *Institutes* was traditional medieval theology, but Calvin's teaching differed from that of Roman Catholics and Lutherans in two respects. First, while agreeing with Luther's emphasis on faith over works, Calvin denied that even human faith could merit salvation. Salvation, said Calvin, was a gift God gave to those He "predestined" for salvation. Second, Calvin went farther than Luther in curtailing the power of a clerical hierarchy and in simplifying religious rituals. Calvinist congregations elected their own governing committees and in time created regional and national synods (councils) to regulate doctrinal issues. Calvinists also displayed simplicity in dress, life, and worship. In an age of ornate garments, they wore simple black clothes, avoided ostentatious living, and worshiped in churches devoid of statues, most musical instruments, stained-glass windows, incense, and vestments.

The Reformers appealed to genuine religious sentiments, but their successes and failures were also due to political circumstances (discussed below) and the social agendas that motivated people to join them. It was no coincidence that Lutheranism had its greatest appeal to German speakers and linguistically related Scandinavians. Peasants and urban laborers sometimes defied their masters by adopting a different faith. Protestants were no more inclined than Roman Catholics to question male dominance in the church and the family, but most Protestants rejected the medieval tradition of celibate priests and nuns and advocated Christian marriage for all adults.

Shaken by the intensity of the Protestant Reformers' appeal, the Catholic Church undertook its own reforms. A council that met at the city of Trent, in northern Italy, in three sessions between 1545 and 1563 painstakingly distinguished proper Catholic doctrines from Protestant "errors." The council also reaffirmed the supremacy of the pope and called for a number of reforms, including requiring each bishop to reside in his diocese and each diocese to have a theological seminary to train priests. Also important to this **Catholic Reformation** were the activities of a new religious order—the Society of Jesus, or "Jesuits," that Ignatius of Loyola (1491–1556), a Spanish nobleman, founded in 1540. Well-educated Jesuits helped stem the Protestant tide and win back some adherents by their teaching and preaching (see Map 17.1). Other Jesuits became important missionaries overseas (see Chapters 18 and 21).

Given the complexity of the issues and the intensity of the emotions that the Protestant Reformation stirred, it is not surprising that violence often flared up. Both sides persecuted and sometimes executed those of differing views. Bitter "wars of religion," fought over a mixture of religious and secular issues, continued in parts of western Europe until 1648.

Online Study Center
Improve Your Grade
Interactive Map: The Protestant and Catholic Reformations

Map 17.1 Religious Reformation in Europe The Reformation brought greater religious freedom but also led to religious conflict and persecution. In many places the Reformation accelerated the trend toward state control of religion and added religious differences to the motives for wars among Europeans.

Predominant Religion in 1555
- Lutheran
- Calvinist (Reformed)
- Church of England
- Roman Catholic
- ▲ Huguenot centers
- → Spread of Calvinism

0   150   300 Km.
0   150   300 Mi.

Helsinki
Riga
LITHUANIA
Warsaw
PRUSSIA
POLAND
TRANSYLVANIA
OTTOMAN EMPIRE
Black Sea
Bergen
NORWAY 1536/1607
Stockholm
Baltic Sea
BRANDENBURG
Wittenberg
Birthplace of Martin Luther
Prague
John Hus, 1369–1415
BOHEMIA
MORAVIA
Pest
Buda
Vienna
HUNGARY
DENMARK
Copenhagen
Hamburg
SAXONY
Eisleben
Martin Luther, 1483–1546
Erfurt
Leipzig
Nuremburg
HOLY ROMAN EMPIRE
Speyer
Stuttgart
Augsburg
Munich
AUSTRIA
Council of Trent, 1545–1563
Trent
Venice
Adriatic Sea
Bari
Naples
Roman Inquisition established, 1542
Rome
ITALY
Florence
Pisa
Milan
Pavia
Genoa
Corsica
Sardinia
Sicily
Mediterranean Sea
North Sea
Münster
Amsterdam
Antwerp
Brussels
NETHERLANDS
Birthplace of John Calvin, 1509–1564
Worms
Edict of Worms, 1521
Strasbourg
Basel
Zurich
Ulrich Zwingli, 1484–1531
Geneva
John Calvin
Marseille
Avignon
Penetration of Calvinism to England after 1558
Edinburgh
John Knox, 1505–1572
SCOTLAND 1560
IRELAND
Dublin
ENGLAND 1536
Oxford
John Wyclif, 1320–1384
London
Plymouth
Rennes
Orléans
Paris
Noyon
Birthplace of John Calvin, 1509–1564
FRANCE
Toulouse
Nantes
Edict of Nantes, 1598
La Rochelle
Bordeaux
Loyola
Birthplace of Ignatius Loyola, 1491
Barcelona
Valencia
Balearic Is.
Madrid
Toledo
Granada
Seville
SPAIN
PORTUGAL
Lisbon
MUSLIM STATES
ATLANTIC OCEAN

Traditional Thinking and Witch-Hunts

Religious differences among Protestants and between them and Catholics continued to generate animosity long after the first generation of reformers, but from a global perspective European Christians still had much in common both in their theology and in the local folk customs and pre-Christian beliefs that remained powerful everywhere in Europe. The widespread **witch-hunts** that Protestants and Catholics undertook in early modern Europe are a dramatic illustration of those common beliefs and cultural heritage.

Prevailing European ideas about the natural world blended two distinct traditions. One was the folklore about magic and forest spirits passed down orally from pre-Christian times. The second was the biblical teachings of the Christian and Jewish scriptures, heard by all in church and read by growing numbers in vernacular translations. In the minds of most people, Christian teachings about miracles, saints, and devils mixed with folklore.

Like people in other parts of the world, most early modern Europeans believed that natural events could have supernatural causes. When crops failed or domestic animals died unexpectedly, many people blamed un-

seen spirits. People also attributed human triumphs and tragedies to supernatural causes. When an earthquake destroyed much of Lisbon, Portugal's capital city, in November 1755, for example, both educated and uneducated people saw the event as a punishment sent by God. A Jesuit charged it "scandalous to pretend that the earthquake was just a natural event." An English Protestant leader agreed, comparing Lisbon's fate with that of Sodom, the city that God destroyed because of the sinfulness of its citizens, according to the Hebrew Bible.

The extraordinary fear of the power of witches that swept across northern Europe in the late sixteenth and seventeenth centuries was powerful testimony to belief in the spiritual causes of natural events. It is estimated that secular and church authorities tried over a hundred thousand people—some three-fourths of them women—for practicing witchcraft. Some were acquitted; some recanted; but more than half were executed—most in Protestant lands. Torture and badgering questions persuaded many accused witches to confess to casting spells and to describe in vivid detail their encounters with the Devil and their attendance at nighttime assemblies of witches.

The trial records make it clear that both the accusers and the accused believed that it was possible for angry and jealous individuals to use evil magic and the power of the Devil to cause people and domestic animals to sicken and die or to cause crops to wither in the fields. Researchers think that at least some of those accused in early modern Europe may really have tried to use witchcraft to harm their enemies. However, it was the Reformation's focus on the Devil—the enemy of God—as the source of evil that made such malevolence so serious a crime and may have helped revive older fears of witchcraft.

Modern historians also argue that many accusations against widows and independent-minded women drew on the widespread belief that women not directly under the control of fathers or husbands were likely to turn to evil. The fact that such women had important roles in tending animals and the sick and in childbirth also made them suspects if death occurred. In parts of the world where belief in witchcraft is still strong, witch-hunts arise at times of social stress, and people who are marginalized by poverty and by the suspicions of others often relish the celebrity that public confession brings. Self-confessed "witches" may even find release from the guilt they feel for wishing evil on their neighbors.

No single reason can explain the rise in witchcraft accusations and fears in early modern Europe, but, for both the accusers and the accused, there are plausible connections between the witch-hunts and rising social tensions, rural poverty, and environmental strains. Far from being a bizarre aberration, witch-hunts reflected the larger social climate of early modern Europe.

Death to Witches This woodcut from 1574 depicts three women convicted of witchcraft being burned alive in Baden, Switzerland. The well-dressed townsmen look on stolidly. (Zentralbibliothek Zurich, Ms. F. 23, p. 56)

The Scientific Revolution

Among the educated, the writings of Greco-Roman antiquity and the Bible were more trusted guides to the natural world than was folklore. The Renaissance had recovered many manuscripts of ancient writers, some of which were printed and widely circulated. The greatest authority on physics was Aristotle, a Greek philosopher who taught that everything on earth was reducible to four elements. The surface of the earth was composed of the two heavy elements, earth and water. The atmosphere was made up of two lighter elements, air and fire, which floated above the ground. Higher still were the sun, moon, planets, and stars, which, according to Aristotelian physics, were so light and pure that they floated in crystalline spheres. This division between the ponderous, heavy earth and the airy, celestial bodies accorded perfectly with the commonsense perception that all heavenly bodies revolved around the earth.

The prevailing conception of the universe was also influenced by the tradition derived from the ancient Greek mathematician Pythagoras, who proved the validity of the famous theorem that still bears his name: in a right triangle, the square of the hypotenuse is equal to the sum of the squares of the other two sides ($a^2 + b^2 = c^2$). Pythagoreans attributed to mystical properties the ability of simple mathematical equations to describe physical objects. They attached special significance to the simplest (to them perfect) geometrical shapes: the circle (a point rotated around another point) and the sphere (a circle rotated on its axis). They believed that celestial objects were perfect spheres orbiting the earth in perfectly circular orbits.

In the sixteenth century, however, the careful observations and mathematical calculations of some daring and imaginative European investigators began to challenge these prevailing conceptions of the physical world. These pioneers of the **Scientific Revolution** demonstrated that the workings of the universe could be explained by natural causes.

Over the centuries, observers of the nighttime skies had plotted the movements of the heavenly bodies, and mathematicians had worked to fit these observations into the prevailing theories of circular orbits. To make all the evidence fit, they had come up with eighty different spheres and some ingenious theories to explain the many seemingly irregular movements. Pondering these complications, a Polish monk and mathematician named Nicholas Copernicus (1473–1543) came up with a mathematically simpler solution: switching the center of the different orbits from the earth to the sun would reduce the number of spheres that were needed.

Copernicus did not challenge the idea that the sun, moon, and planets were light, perfect spheres or that

Tycho Brahe at Work Between 1576 and 1597, on the island of Ven between Denmark and Sweden, Tycho built the best observatory in Europe and set a new standard for accurate celestial observations before the invention of the telescope. This contemporary hand-colored engraving shows the Danish astronomer at work. (Maritime Museum Kronberg Castle Denmark/ G.Dagli Orti/The Art Archive)

they moved in circular orbits. But his placement of the sun, not the earth, at the center of things began a revolution in understanding about the structure of the heavens and about the central place of humans in the universe. To escape the anticipated controversies, Copernicus delayed the publication of his heliocentric (sun-centered) theory until the end of his life.

Other astronomers, including the Danish Tycho Brahe (1546–1601) and his German assistant Johannes Kepler (1571–1630), strengthened and improved on Copernicus's model, showing that planets actually move in elliptical, not circular orbits. The most brilliant of the

Copernicans was the Italian Galileo Galilei° (1564–1642). In 1609 Galileo built a telescope through which he took a closer look at the heavens. Able to magnify distant objects thirty times beyond the power of the naked eye, Galileo saw that heavenly bodies were not the perfectly smooth spheres of the Aristotelians. The moon, he reported in *The Starry Messenger* (1610), had mountains and valleys; the sun had spots; other planets had their own moons. In other words, the earth was not alone in being heavy and changeable.

At first, the Copernican universe found more critics than supporters because it so directly challenged not just popular ideas but also the intellectual synthesis of classical and biblical authorities. How, demanded Aristotle's defenders, could the heavy earth move without producing vibrations that would shake the planet apart? Is the Bible wrong, asked the theologians, when the Book of Joshua says that, by God's command, "the sun [not the earth] stood still . . . for about a whole day" to give the ancient Israelites victory in their conquest of Palestine? If Aristotle's physics was wrong, worried other traditionalists, would not the theological synthesis built on other parts of his philosophy be open to question?

Intellectual and religious leaders encouraged political authorities to suppress the new ideas. Most Protestant leaders, following the lead of Martin Luther, condemned the heliocentric universe as contrary to the Bible. Catholic authorities waited longer to act. After all, both Copernicus and Galileo were Roman Catholics. Copernicus had dedicated his book to the pope, and in 1582 another pope, Gregory XIII, had used the latest astronomical findings to issue a new and more accurate calendar (still used today). Galileo ingeniously argued that the conflict between scripture and science was only apparent: the word of God revealed in the Bible was expressed in the imperfect language of ordinary people, but in nature God's truth was revealed more perfectly in a language that could be learned by careful observation and scientific reasoning.

Online Study Center
Improve Your Grade
Primary Source: Letter to the
Grand Duchess Christina

Unfortunately, Galileo also ridiculed those who were slow to accept his findings, charging that Copernican ideas were "mocked and hooted at by an infinite multitude . . . of fools." Smarting under Galileo's stinging sarcasm, some Jesuits and other critics got his ideas condemned by the Roman Inquisition in 1616, which

Galileo Galilei (gal-uh-LAY-oh gal-uh-LAY-ee)

put *The Starry Messenger* on the Index of Forbidden Books and prohibited Galileo from publishing further on the subject. (In 1992 the Catholic Church officially retracted its condemnation of Galileo.)

Despite official opposition, printed books spread the new scientific ideas among scholars across Europe. In England, Robert Boyle (1627–1691) used experimental methods and a trial-and-error approach to examine the inner workings of chemistry. Through the Royal Society, chartered in London in 1662 to promote knowledge of the natural world, Boyle and others became enthusiastic missionaries of mechanical science and fierce opponents of the Aristotelians.

Meanwhile, English mathematician Isaac Newton (1642–1727) was carrying Galileo's demonstration that the heavens and earth share a common physics to its logical conclusion. Newton formulated a set of mathematical laws that all physical objects obeyed. It was the force of gravity—not angels—that governed the elliptical orbits of heavenly bodies. It was gravitation (and the resistance of air) that caused cannonballs to fall back to earth. From 1703 until his death Newton served as president of the Royal Society, using his prestige to promote the new science that came to bear his name.

As the condemnation of Galileo demonstrates, in 1700 most religious and intellectual leaders viewed the new science with suspicion or outright hostility because of the unwanted challenge it posed to established ways of thought. Yet all the principal pioneers of the Scientific Revolution were convinced that scientific discoveries and revealed religion were not in conflict. At the peak of his fame Newton promoted a series of lectures devoted to proving the validity of Christianity. However, by showing that the Aristotelians and biblical writers held ideas about the natural world that were naive and unfactual, these pioneers opened the door to others who used reason to challenge a broader range of unquestioned traditions and superstitions. The world of ideas was forever changed.

The Early Enlightenment

The advances in scientific thought inspired a few brave souls to question the reasonableness of everything from agricultural methods to laws, religion, and social hierarchies. The belief that human reason could discover the laws that governed social behavior and that those laws were just as scientific as the laws that governed physics energized a movement known as the **Enlightenment**. Like the Scientific Revolution, this movement was the work of a few "enlightened" individuals, who often faced bitter opposition from the political, intellectual, and religious establishment. Leading Enlightenment thinkers became accustomed to having their books burned or banned and spent long periods in exile to escape being imprisoned.

Influences besides the Scientific Revolution affected the Enlightenment. The Reformation had aroused many to champion one creed or another, but partisan bickering and bloodshed led others to doubt the superiority of any theological position and to recommend toleration of all religions. The killing of suspected witches also shocked many thoughtful people. The leading French thinker Voltaire (1694–1778) declared: "No opinion is worth burning your neighbor for."

Online Study Center
Improve Your Grade
Primary Source:
Treatise on Toleration

Accounts of cultures in other parts of the world also led some European thinkers to question assumptions about the superiority of European political institutions, moral standards, and religious beliefs. Reports of Amerindian life, though romanticized, led some to conclude that those whom they had called savages were in many ways nobler than European Christians. Matteo Ricci, a Jesuit missionary to China whose journals made a strong impression in Europe, contrasted the lack of territorial ambition of the Chinese with the constant warfare in the West and attributed the difference to the fact that China was wisely ruled by educated men whom he called "Philosophers."

Although many circumstances shaped "enlightened" thinking, the new scientific methods and discoveries provided the clearest model for changing European society. Voltaire posed the issues in these terms: "it would be very peculiar that all nature, all the planets, should obey eternal laws" but a human being, "in contempt of these laws, could act as he pleased solely according to his caprice." The English poet Alexander Pope (1688–1774) made a similar point in verse: "Nature and Nature's laws lay hidden in night;/God said, 'Let Newton be' and all was light."

The Enlightenment was more a frame of mind than a coherent movement. Individuals who embraced it drew inspiration from different sources and promoted different agendas. By 1750 its proponents were clearer about what they disliked than about what new institutions should be created. Some "enlightened" thinkers thought society could be made to function with the mechanical orderliness of planets spinning in their orbits. Nearly all were optimistic that—at least in the long run—human beliefs and institutions could be improved. This belief in progress would help foster political and social revolutions after 1750, as Chapter 22 recounts.

Despite the enthusiasm the Enlightenment aroused in some circles, it was decidedly unpopular with many absolutist rulers and with most clergymen. Europe in 1750 was neither enlightened nor scientific. It was a place where political and religious divisions, growing literacy, and the printing press made possible the survival of the new ideas that profoundly changed life in future centuries.

SOCIAL AND ECONOMIC LIFE

From a distance European society seemed quite rigid. At the top of the social pyramid a small number of noble families had privileged access to high offices in the church, government, and military and enjoyed many special privileges, including exemption from taxation. A big step below them were the classes of merchants and professionals, who had acquired wealth but no legal privileges. At the base of the pyramid were the masses, mostly rural peasants and landless laborers, who were exploited by everyone above them. The subordination of women to men seemed equally rigid.

This model of European society is certainly not wrong, but even contemporaries knew that it was too simple. A study of English society in 1688, for example, distinguished twenty-five different social categories and pointed out the shocking inequality among them. It argued that less than half the population contributed to increasing the wealth of the kingdom, while the rest—the majority—were too poor and unskilled to make any substantial contribution.

Some social mobility did occur, particularly in the middle. The principal engine of social change was the economy, and the places where social change occurred most readily were the cities. A secondary means of change was education—for those who could get it.

The Bourgeoisie

Europe's growing cities were the products of a changing economy. In 1500 Paris was the only northern European city with over 100,000 inhabitants. By 1700 both Paris and London had populations over 500,000, and twenty other European cities contained over 60,000 people.

The wealth of the cities came from manufacturing and finance, but especially from trade, both within Europe and overseas. The French called the urban class that dominated these activities the **bourgeoisie°** (burghers, town

bourgeoisie (boor-zwah-ZEE)

dwellers). Members of the bourgeoisie devoted long hours to their businesses and poured much of their profits back into them or into new ventures. Even so, they had enough money to live comfortably in large houses with many servants. In the seventeenth and eighteenth centuries wealthier urban classes could buy exotic luxuries imported from the far corners of the earth—Caribbean and Brazilian sugar and rum, Mexican chocolate, Virginia tobacco, North American furs, East Indian cotton textiles and spices, and Chinese tea.

The Netherlands provided many good examples of bourgeois enterprise in the seventeenth century. Manufacturers and skilled craftsmen turned out a variety of goods in the factories and workshops of many cities and towns in the province of Holland. The highly successful Dutch textile industry concentrated on the profitable weaving, finishing, and printing of cloth, leaving the spinning to low-paid workers elsewhere. Along with fine woolens and linens the Dutch were successfully making cheaper textiles for mass markets. Other factories in Holland refined West Indian sugar, brewed beer from Baltic grain, cut Virginia tobacco, and made imitations of Chinese ceramics (see Environment and Technology: East Asian Porcelain in Chapter 21). Free from the censorship imposed by political and religious authorities in neighboring countries, Holland's printers published books in many languages, including manuals with the latest advances in machinery, metallurgy, agriculture, and other technical areas. For a small province barely above sea level, lacking timber and other natural resources, this was a remarkable achievement.

Burgeoning from a fishing village to a metropolis of some 200,000 by 1700, Amsterdam was Holland's largest city and Europe's major port. The bourgeoisie there and in other cities had developed huge commercial fleets that dominated sea trade in Europe and overseas. Dutch ships carried over 80 percent of the trade between Spain and northern Europe, even while Spain and the Netherlands were at war. By one estimate, the Dutch conducted more than half of all the oceangoing commercial shipping in the world in the seventeenth century (for details see Chapters 20 and 21).

Amsterdam also served as Europe's financial center. Seventeenth-century Dutch banks had such a reputation for security that wealthy individuals and governments from all over western Europe entrusted them with their money. The banks in turn invested these funds in real estate, loaned money to factory owners and governments, and provided capital for big business operations overseas.

The expansion of maritime trade led to new designs for merchant ships. In this, too, the Dutch played a dominant role. Using timber imported from northern

The Fishwife, 1572   Women were essential partners in most Dutch family businesses. This scene by the Dutch artist Adriaen van Ostade shows a woman preparing fish for retail sale. (Rijksmuseum-Amsterdam)

Europe, shipyards in Dutch ports built their own vast fleets and other ships for export. Especially successful was the *fluit,* or "flyboat," a large-capacity cargo ship developed in the 1590s. It was inexpensive to build and required only a small crew. Another successful type of merchant ship, the heavily armed "East Indiaman," helped the Dutch establish their supremacy in the Indian Ocean. The Dutch also excelled at mapmaking (see Environment and Technology: Mapping the World).

Like merchants in the Islamic world, Europe's merchants relied on family and ethnic networks. In addition to families of local origin, many northern European cities contained merchant colonies from Venice, Florence, Genoa, and other Italian cities. In Amsterdam and Hamburg lived Jewish merchants who had fled religious persecution in Iberia. Other Jewish communities expanded out of eastern Europe into the German states, especially after the Thirty Years War. Armenian merchants from Iran were moving into the Mediterranean and became important in Russia in the seventeenth century.

The bourgeoisie sought mutually beneficial alliances with European monarchs, who welcomed economic growth as a means of increasing state revenues. The Dutch government pioneered chartering **joint-stock companies**, giving the Dutch East and West India

ENVIRONMENT + TECHNOLOGY

Mapping the World

In 1602 in China the Jesuit missionary Matteo Ricci printed an elaborate map of the world. Working from maps produced in Europe and incorporating the latest knowledge gathered by European maritime explorers, Ricci introduced two changes to make the map more appealing to his Chinese hosts. He labeled it in Chinese characters, and he split his map down the middle of the Atlantic so that China lay in the center. This version pleased the Chinese elite, who considered China the "Middle Kingdom" surrounded by lesser states. A copy of Ricci's map in six large panels adorned the emperor's Beijing palace.

The stunningly beautiful maps and globes of sixteenth-century Europe were the most complete, detailed, and useful representations of the earth that any society had ever produced. The best mapmaker of the century was Gerhard Kremer, who is remembered as Mercator (the merchant) because his maps were so useful to European ocean traders. By incorporating the latest discoveries and scientific measurements, Mercator could depict the outlines of the major continents in painstaking detail, even if their interiors were still largely unknown to outsiders.

To represent the spherical globe on a flat map, Mercator drew the lines of longitude as parallel lines. Because such lines actually meet at the poles, Mercator's projection greatly exaggerated the size of every landmass and body of water distant from the equator. However, Mercator's rendering offered a very practical advantage: sailors could plot their course by drawing a straight line between their point of departure and their destination. Because of this useful feature, the Mercator projection of the world remained in common use until quite recently. To some extent, its popularity came from the exaggerated size this projection gave to Europe. Like the Chinese, Europeans liked to think of themselves as at the center of things. Europeans also understood their true geographical position better than people in any other part of the world.

Dutch World Map, 1641   It is easy to see why the Chinese would not have liked to see their empire at the far right edge of this widely printed map. Besides the distortions caused by the Mercator projection, geographical ignorance exaggerates the size of North America and Antarctica.   (Courtesy of the Trustees of the British Museum)

Port of Amsterdam   Ships, barges, and boats of all types are visible in this busy seventeenth-century scene. The large building in the center is the Admiralty House, the headquarters of the Dutch East India Company. (Mansell/TimeLife Pictures/Getty Images)

Companies monopolies over trade to the East and West Indies. France and England chartered companies of their own. The companies then sold shares to individuals to raise large sums for overseas enterprises while spreading the risks (and profits) among many investors (see Chapter 19). Investors could buy and sell shares in specialized financial markets called **stock exchanges**, an Italian innovation transferred to the cities of northwestern Europe in the sixteenth century. The greatest stock market in the seventeenth and eighteenth centuries was the Amsterdam Exchange, founded in 1530. Large insurance companies also emerged in this period, and insuring long voyages against loss became a standard practice after 1700.

Governments also undertook large projects to improve water transport. The Dutch built numerous canals for transport and to drain the lowlands for agriculture. Other governments also financed canals, which included elaborate systems of locks to raise barges up over hills. One of the most important was the 150-mile (240-kilometer) Canal du Midi in France, built by the French government between 1661 and 1682 to link the Atlantic and the Mediterranean. By the seventeenth century rulers sought the talents of successful businessmen as administrators. Jean Baptiste Colbert° (1619–1683), Louis XIV's able minister of finance, was a notable example.

Colbert (kohl-BEAR)

After 1650 the Dutch faced growing competition from the English, who were developing their own close association between business and government. With government support, the English merchant fleet doubled between 1660 and 1700, and foreign trade rose by 50 percent. As a result, state revenue from customs duties tripled. In a series of wars (1652–1678) the English government used its naval might to break Dutch dominance in overseas trade and to extend England's colonial empire.

Some successful members of the bourgeoisie in England and France chose to use their wealth to raise their social status. By retiring from their businesses and buying country estates, they could become members of the **gentry**. These landowners affected the lifestyle of the old aristocracy. The gentry loaned money to impoverished peasants and to members of the nobility and in time increased their ownership of land. Some families sought aristocratic husbands for their daughters. The old nobility found such alliances attractive because of the large dowries that the bourgeoisie provided. In France a family could gain the exemption from taxation by living in gentility for three generations or, more quickly, by purchasing a title from the king.

Peasants and Laborers

At the other end of society things were bad, but they had been worse. Serfdom, which bound men and women to land owned by a local lord, had been in deep decline since the great plague of the mid-fourteenth century. The institution did not return in western Europe as the population recovered, but competition for work exerted a downward pressure on wages. However, the development of large estates raising grain for the cities led to the rise of serfdom in eastern Europe for the first time. There was also a decline in slavery, which had briefly expanded in southern Europe around 1500 as the result of the Atlantic slave trade from sub-Saharan Africa. After 1600, however, Europeans shipped nearly all African slaves to the Americas.

There is much truth in the argument that western Europe continued to depend on unfree labor but kept it at a distance rather than at home. In any event, legal freedom did little to make a peasant's life safer and more secure. The techniques and efficiency of European agriculture had improved little since 1300. As a result, bad years brought famine; good ones provided only small surpluses. Indeed, the condition of the average person in western Europe may have worsened between 1500 and 1750 as the result of prolonged warfare, environmental problems, and adverse economic conditions. In addition, Europeans felt the adverse effects of a century of relatively cool climate that began in the 1590s. During this **Little Ice Age** average temperatures fell only a few degrees, but the effects were startling (see Issues in World History: The Little Ice Age).

By 1700 high-yielding new crops from the Americas were helping the rural poor avoid starvation. Once grown only as hedges against famine, potatoes and maize (corn) became staples for the rural poor in the eighteenth century. Potatoes sustained life in northeastern and central Europe and in Ireland, while poor peasants in Italy subsisted on maize. The irony is that all of these lands were major exporters of wheat, but most of those who planted and harvested it could not afford to eat it.

Instead, the grain was put on carts, barges, and ships and carried to the cities of western Europe. Other fleets brought wine from southern to northern Europe. Parisians downed 100,000 barrels of wine a year at the end of the seventeenth century. Some of the grain was made into beer, which the poor drank because it was cheaper than wine. In 1750 Parisian breweries brewed 23 million quarts (22 million liters) of beer for local consumption.

Other rural men made a living as miners, lumberjacks, and charcoal makers. The expanding iron industry in England provided work for all three, but the high consumption of wood fuel for this and other purposes caused serious **deforestation**. One early-seventeenth-century observer lamented: "within man's memory, it was held impossible to have any want of wood in England. But . . . at present, through the great consuming of wood . . . and the neglect of planting of woods, there is a great scarcity of wood throughout the whole kingdom."[1] The managers of the hundreds of ironworks in England tried to meet the shortages by importing timber and charcoal from more heavily forested Scandinavian countries and Russia. Eventually, the high price of wood and charcoal encouraged smelters to use coal as an alternative fuel. England's coal mining increased twelvefold, from 210,000 tons in 1550 to 2,500,000 tons in 1700. From 1709 coke—coal refined to remove impurities—gradually replaced charcoal in the smelting of iron. These new demands drove English coal production to nearly 5 million tons a year by 1750.

France was much more forested than England, but increasing deforestation there prompted Colbert to predict that "France will perish for lack of wood." By the late eighteenth century deforestation had become an issue even in Sweden and Russia, where iron production had become a major industry. New laws in France and England designed to protect the forests were largely inspired by fears of shortages for naval vessels, whose keels required high-quality timbers of exceptional size and particular curvature. Although wood consumption remained high, rising prices encouraged some individuals to plant trees for future harvest.

Everywhere in Europe the rural poor felt the depletion of the forests most strongly. For centuries they had depended on woodlands for abundant supplies of wild nuts and berries, free firewood and building materials, and wild game. Modest improvements in food production in some places were overwhelmed by population growth. Rural women had long supplemented household incomes by spinning yarn. From the mid-1600s rising wages in towns led textile manufacturers to farm more and more textile weaving out to rural areas with high underemployment. This provided men and women with enough to survive on, but the piecework paid very little for long hours of tedious labor.

Throughout this period, many rural poor migrated to the towns and cities in hopes of better jobs, but only some were successful. Even in the prosperous Dutch towns, half of the population lived in acute poverty. Authorities estimated that those permanent city residents who were too poor to tax, the "deserving poor," made up 10 to 20 percent of the population. That calculation did not include the large numbers of "unworthy poor"—recent migrants from impoverished rural areas, peddlers traveling from place to place, and beggars (many with horrible deformities and sores) who tried to survive on charity. Many young women were forced into prostitution to survive. There were also many criminals, usually organized in gangs, ranging from youthful pickpockets to highway robbers.

The pervasive poverty of rural and urban Europe shocked those who were not hardened to it. In about 1580 the mayor of the French city of Bordeaux° asked a group of visiting Amerindian chiefs what impressed them most about European cities. The chiefs are said to have expressed astonishment at the disparity between the fat, well-fed people and the poor, half-starved men and women in rags. Why, the visitors wondered, did the poor not grab the rich by the throat or set fire to their homes?[2]

In fact, misery provoked many rebellions in early modern Europe. For example, in 1525 peasant rebels in the Alps attacked both nobles and clergy as representatives of the privileged and landowning classes. They had no love for merchants either, whom they denounced for lending at interest and charging high prices. Rebellions multiplied as rural conditions worsened. In southwestern France alone some 450 uprisings occurred between 1590 and 1715, many of them set off by food shortages and tax increases. The exemption of the wealthy from taxation was a frequent source of complaint. A rebellion in southern France in 1670 began when a mob of townswomen attacked the tax collector. It quickly spread to the country, where peasant leaders cried, "Death to the people's oppressors!" Authorities dealt severely with such revolts and executed or maimed their leaders.

| Women and the Family |

Women's status and work were closely tied to their husbands' and families'. In lands that allowed it, a woman in a royal family might inherit a throne (see Table 17.1 on page 510 for examples)—in the absence of a male heir. These rare exceptions do not negate the rule that women everywhere ranked below men, but one should also not forget that her class and wealth defined a woman's position in life more than her sex. The wife or daughter of a rich man, for example, had a much better life than any poor man. In special cases, a single woman might be secure and respected, as in the case of women from good families who might head convents of nuns in Catholic countries. But unmarried women and widows were less well off than their married sisters. A good marriage was thus of great importance.

In contrast to the arranged marriages that prevailed in much of the rest of the world, young men and women in early modern Europe most often chose their own spouses. Ironically, privileged families were more inclined to control marriage plans than poor ones. Royal and noble families carefully plotted the suitability of their children's marriages in furthering the family's status. Bourgeois parents were less likely to force their children into arranged marriages, but the fact that nearly all found spouses within their social class strongly suggests that the bourgeoisie promoted marriages that furthered their business alliances.

Europeans also married later than people in other lands. The sons and daughters of craftworkers and the poor had to delay marriage until they could afford to live on their own. Young men had to serve long apprenticeships to learn trades. Young women also had to work—helping their parents, as domestic servants, or in some other capacity—to save money for the dowry they were expected to bring into the marriage. A dowry was the money and household goods—the amount varied by social class—that enabled a young couple to begin marriage independent of their parents. The typical groom in western and central Europe could not hope to marry before his late twenties, and his bride would be a few years younger—in contrast to the rest of the world, where people usually married in their teens. Marriage also came late in bourgeois families, in part to allow young men to complete their education.

Besides enabling young people to be independent of their parents, the late age of marriage in early modern Europe also held down the birthrate and thus limited family size. Even so, about one-tenth of the births in a city were to unmarried women, often servants, who generally left their infants on the doorsteps of churches, convents, or rich families. Despite efforts to raise such abandoned children, many perished. Delayed marriage also had links to the existence of public brothels, where young men could satisfy their lusts in cheap and impersonal encounters with unfortunate young women, often newly arrived from impoverished rural villages. Nevertheless, rape was a common occurrence, usually perpetrated by gangs of young men who attacked young women rumored to be free with their favors. Some historians believe that such gang rapes reflected poor young men's jealousy at older men's easier access to women.

Bourgeois parents were very concerned that their children have the education and training necessary for success. They promoted the establishment of municipal schools to provide a solid education, including Latin and perhaps Greek, for their sons, who were then sent abroad to learn modern languages or to a university to earn a law degree. Legal training was useful for conducting business and was a prerequisite for obtaining government judgeships and treasury positions. Daughters were less likely to be groomed for business careers, but wives often helped their husbands as bookkeepers and sometimes inherited businesses.

Bordeaux (bor-DOH)

The fact that most schools barred female students, as did most guilds and professions, explains why women were not prominent in the cultural Renaissance, the Reformation, the Scientific Revolution, and the Enlightenment. Yet from a global perspective, women in early modern Europe were more prominent in the creation of culture than were women in most other parts of the world. Recent research has brought to light the existence of a number of successful women who were painters, musicians, and writers. Indeed, the spread of learning, the stress on religious reading, and the growth of business likely meant that Europe led the world in female literacy. From the late 1600s some wealthy French women ran intellectual gatherings in their homes. Many more were prominent letter writers. Galileo's daughter, Maria Celeste Galilei, carried on a detailed correspondence with her father from the confinement of her convent, whose walls she had taken a religious vow never to leave. Nevertheless, in a period when most men were illiterate, the number of literate women was small, and only women in wealthier families might have a good education.

POLITICAL
INNOVATIONS

The monarchs of early modern Europe occupied the apex of the social order, were arbitrators of the intellectual and religious conflicts of their day, and had important influences on the economic life of their realms. For these reasons an overview of political life incorporates all the events previously described in this chapter. In addition, monarchs' political agendas introduced new elements of conflict and change.

The effort to create a European empire failed, but monarchs succeeded in achieving a higher degree of political centralization within their separate kingdoms. The frequent civil and international conflicts of this era sometimes promoted cooperation, and they often encouraged innovation. Leadership and success passed from Spain to the Netherlands and then to England and France. It is hard to avoid the conclusion that the key political technology was cannonry.

State Development

Political diversity characterized Europe. City-states and principalities abounded, either independently or bound into loose federations, of which the **Holy Roman Empire** of the German heartland was the most notable example. In western Europe the strong monarchies that had emerged were acquiring national identities. Dreams of a European empire comparable to those of Asia remained strong, although efforts to form one were frustrated.

Dynastic ambitions and historical circumstances combined to favor and then block the creation of a powerful empire in the early sixteenth century. In 1519 electors of the Holy Roman Empire chose Charles V (r. 1519–1556) to be the new emperor. Like his predecessors for three generations, Charles belonged to the powerful **Habsburg**° family of Austria, but he had recently inherited the Spanish thrones of Castile and Aragon. With the vast resources of all these offices behind him (see Map 17.2), Charles hoped to centralize his imperial power and lead a Christian coalition to halt the advance into southeastern Europe of the Ottoman Empire, whose Muslim rulers already controlled most of the Middle East and North Africa.

Charles and his Christian allies eventually halted the Ottomans at the gates of Vienna in 1529, although Ottoman attacks continued on and off until 1697. But Charles's efforts to forge his several possessions into Europe's strongest state failed. King Francis I of France, who had lost to Charles in the election for Holy Roman Emperor, openly supported the Muslim Turks to weaken his rival. In addition, the princes of the Holy Roman Empire's many member states were able to use Luther's religious Reformation to frustrate Charles's efforts to reduce their autonomy. Swayed partly by Luther's appeals to German nationalism, many German princes opposed Charles's defense of Catholic doctrine in the imperial Diet (assembly).

After decades of bitter squabbles turned to open warfare in 1546 (the German Wars of Religion), Charles V finally gave up his efforts at unification, abdicated control of his various possessions to different heirs, and retired to a monastery. By the Peace of Augsburg (1555), he recognized the princes' right to choose whether Catholicism or Lutheranism would prevail in their particular states, and he allowed them to keep the church lands they had seized before 1552. The triumph of religious diversity had derailed Charles's plan for centralizing authority in central Europe and put off German political unification for three centuries.

Meanwhile, the rulers of Spain, France, and England were building a more successful program of political unification based on political centralization and religious unity. The most successful rulers reduced the autonomy of the church and the nobility in their states,

---

Habsburg (HABZ-berg)

Political Craft and Craftiness

*P*olitical power was becoming more highly concentrated in early modern Europe, but absolute dominance was more a goal than a reality. Whether subject to constitutional checks or not, rulers were very concerned with creating and maintaining good relations with their more powerful subjects. Their efforts to manipulate public opinion and perceptions have much in common with the efforts of modern politicians to manage their "image."

A diplomat and civil servant in the rich and powerful Italian city-state of Florence, Niccolò Machiavelli, is best known for his book The Prince *(1532). This influential essay on the proper exercise of political power has been interpreted as cynical by some and as supremely practical and realistic by others. Because Machiavelli did not have a high opinion of the intelligence and character of most people, he urged rulers to achieve obedience by fear and deception. But he also suggested that genuine mercy, honesty, and piety may be superior to feigned virtue.*

Of Cruelty and Clemency, and Whether It Is Better to be Loved Than Feared

. . . It will naturally be answered that it would be desirable to be both the one and the other; but, as it is difficult to be both at the same time, it is much safer to be feared than to be loved, when you have to choose between the two. For it may be said of men in general that they are ungrateful and fickle, dissemblers, avoiders of danger, and greedy of gain. So long as you shower benefits on them, they are all yours; they offer you their blood, their substance, their lives, and their children, provided the necessity for it is far off; but when it is near at hand, then they revolt. And the prince who relies on their words, without having otherwise provided for his security, is ruined; for friendships that are won by rewards, not by greatness and nobility of soul, although deserved, yet are not real, and cannot be depended upon in time of adversity.

Besides, men have less hesitation in offending one who makes himself beloved than one who makes himself feared; for love holds by a bond of obligation which, as mankind is bad, is broken on every occasion whenever it is for the inter-est of the obligated party to break it. But fear holds by the apprehension of punishment, which never leaves men. A prince, however, should make himself feared in such a manner that, if he has not won the affection of his people, he shall at least not incur their hatred. . . .

In What Manner Princes Should Keep Their Faith

It must be evident to every one that it is more praiseworthy for a prince always to maintain good faith, and practice integrity rather than craft and deceit. And yet the experience of our own times has shown those princes have achieved great things who made small account of good faith, and who understood by cunning to circumvent the intelligence of others; and that in the end they got the better of those whose actions were dictated by loyalty and good faith. You must know, therefore, that there are two ways of carrying on a struggle; one by law and the other by force. The first is practiced by men, and the other by animals; and as the first is often insufficient, it becomes necessary to resort to the second.

. . . If men were altogether good, this advice would be wrong; but since they are bad and will not keep faith with you, you need not keep faith with them. Nor will a prince ever be short of legitimate excuses to give color to his breaches of faith. Innumerable modern examples could be given of this; and it could easily be shown how many treaties of peace, and how many engagements, have been made null and void by the faithlessness of princes; and he who has best known how to play the fox has ever been the most successful.

But it is necessary that the prince should know how to color this nature well, and how to be a great hypocrite and dissembler. For men are so simple, and yield so much to immediate necessity, that the deceiver will never lack dupes. I will mention one of the most recent examples. [Pope] Alexander VI never did nor ever thought of anything but to deceive, and always found a reason for doing so . . . and yet he was always successful in his deceits, because he knew the weakness of men in that particular.

It is not necessary, however, for a prince to possess all the above-mentioned qualities; but it is essential that he should at least seem to have them. I will even venture to say, that to have and practice them constantly is pernicious, but to seem to have them is useful. For instance, a prince should seem to be merciful, faithful, humane, religious, and upright, and should even be so in reality; but he should have his mind so trained that, when occasion requires it, he may know how to change to the opposite. And it must be understood that a prince, and especially one who has but recently acquired his state, cannot perform all those things which cause men to be esteemed as good; he being obligated, for the sake of maintaining his state, to act contrary to humanity, charity, and religion. And therefore, it is necessary that he should have a versatile mind, capable of changing readily, according as the winds and changes of fortune bid him; and, as has been said above, not to swerve from the good if possible, but to know how to resort to evil if necessity demands it.

A prince then should be very careful never to allow anything to escape his lips that does not abound in the above-mentioned five qualities, so that to see and to hear him he may seem all charity, integrity, and humanity, all uprightness and all piety. And more than all else is it necessary for a prince to seem to possess the last quality; for mankind in general judge more by what they see than by what they feel, every one being capable of the former, and few of the latter. Everybody sees what you seem to be, but few really feel what you are; and those few dare not oppose the opinion of the many, who are protected by the majority of the state; for the actions of all men, and especially those of princes, are judged by the result, where there is no other judge to whom to appeal.

A prince should look mainly to the successful maintenance of his state. For the means which he employs for this will always be counted honorable, and will be praised by everybody; for the common people are always taken in by appearances and by results, and it is the vulgar mass that constitutes the world.

*B*ecause, as Machiavelli argued, appearances count for as much in the public arena as realities, it is difficult to judge whether rulers' statements expressed their real feelings and beliefs or what may have been the most expedient to say at the moment. An example is this speech Queen Elizabeth of England made at the end of November 1601 to Parliament after a particularly difficult year. One senior noble had led a rebellion and was subsequently executed. Parliament was pressing for extended privileges. Having gained the throne in 1558 after many difficulties (including a time in prison), the sixty-eight-year-old queen had much experience in the language and wiles of politics and was well aware of the importance of public opinion. Reprinted many times, the speech became famous as "The Golden Speech of Queen Elizabeth."

I do assure you, there is no prince that loveth his subjects better, or whose love can countervail our love. There is no jewel, be it of never so rich a price, which I set before this jewel: I mean your love. For I do esteem it more than any treasure or riches; for that we know how to prize, but love and thanks I count invaluable.

And, though God has raised me high, yet this I count the glory of my crown, that I have reigned with your loves. This makes me that I do not so much rejoice that God hath made me to be a Queen, as to be Queen over so thankful a people.

Therefore, I have cause to wish nothing more than to content the subjects; and that is the duty I owe. Neither do I desire to live longer days than I may see your prosperity; and that is my only desire.

And as I am that person that still (yet under God) has delivered you, so I trust, by the almighty power of God, that I shall be His instrument to preserve you from every peril, dishonour, shame, tyranny, and oppression. . . .

Of myself I must say this: I was never any greedy scraping grasper, nor a straight, fast-holding prince, nor yet a waster. My heart was never set on worldly goods, but only for my subjects' good. What you bestow on me, I will not hoard it up, but receive it to bestow on you again. Yea, mine own properties I count yours, and to be expended for your good. . . .

To be a king and wear a crown is a thing more glorious to them that see it, than it is pleasing to them that bear it. For myself, I was never so much enticed with the glorious name of king, or royal authority of a queen, as delighted that God made me his instrument to maintain his truth and glory, and to defend this Kingdom (as I said) from peril, dishonour, tyranny and oppression.

There will never Queen sit in my seat with more zeal to my country, care for my subjects, and that sooner with willingness will venture her life for your good and safety than myself. For it is not my desire to live nor reign longer than my life and reign shall be for your good. And though you have had and may have many more princes more mighty and wise sitting in this state, yet you never had or shall have any that will be more careful and loving. Shall I ascribe anything to myself and my sexly weakness? I were not worthy to live then; and of all, most unworthy of the great mercies I have had from God, who has even yet given me a heart, which never feared foreign or home enemy. I speak to give God the praise . . . That I should speak for any glory, God forbid.

QUESTIONS FOR ANALYSIS

1. Do you find Machiavelli's advice to be cynical or realistic?
2. Describe how a member of Parliament might have responded to Queen Elizabeth's declarations of her concern for the welfare of her people above all else.
3. Can a ruler be sincere and manipulative at the same time?

Source: From *The Historical, Political, and Diplomatic Writings of Niccolo Machiavelli*, trans. Christian E. Detmold (Boston: Houghton Mifflin and Company, 1891), II: 54–59; and Heywood Townshend, *Historical Collections, or an Exact Account of the Proceedings of the Last Four Parliaments of Q. Elizabeth* (London: Basset, Crooke, and Cademan, 1680), 263–266.

TABLE 17.1   Rulers in Early Modern Western Europe

Spain	France	England/Great Britain
Habsburg Dynasty	**Valois Dynasty**	**Tudor Dynasty**
Charles I (1516–1556) (Holy Roman Emperor Charles V)	Francis I (1515–1547)	Henry VIII (1509–1547)
Philip II (1556–1598)	Henry II (1547–1559)	Edward VI (1547–1553)
	Francis II (1559–1560)	Mary I (1553–1558)
	Charles IX (1560–1574)	Elizabeth I (1558–1603)
	Henry III (1574–1589)	
	Bourbon Dynasty	**Stuart Dynasty**
Philip III (1598–1621)	Henry IV (1589–1610)[a]	James I (1603–1625)
Philip IV (1621–1665)	Louis XIII (1610–1643)	Charles I (1625–1649) [a,b]
Charles II (1665–1700)	Louis XIV (1643–1715)	(Puritan Republic, 1649–1660)
		Charles II (1660–1685)
		James II (1685–1688)[b]
		William III (1689–1702)
		and Mary II (1689–1694)
		Anne (1702–1714)
Bourbon Dynasty		
Philip V (1700–1746)	**Hanoverian Dynasty**	
	Louis XV (1715–1774)	
		George I (1714–1727)
Ferdinand VI (1746–1759)		George II (1727–1760)

[a]Died a violent death.   [b]Was overthrown.

be called frequently and had to consent to changes in laws and to the raising of an army in peacetime. Another law reaffirmed the official status of the Church of England but extended religious toleration to the Puritans.

A similar struggle in France produced a different outcome. There the Estates General represented the traditional rights of the clergy, the nobility, and the towns (that is, the bourgeoisie). The Estates General was able to assert its rights during the sixteenth-century French Wars of Religion, when the monarchy was weak. But thereafter the Bourbon monarchs generally ruled without having to call it into session. They avoided financial crises by more efficient tax collection and by selling appointments to high government offices. In justification they claimed that the monarch had absolute authority to rule in God's name on earth.

Louis XIV's gigantic new palace at **Versailles**° symbolized the French monarch's triumph over the traditional rights of the nobility, clergy, and towns. Capable of housing ten thousand people and surrounded by elaborately landscaped grounds and parks, the palace

can be seen as a sort of theme park of royal absolutism. Elaborate ceremonies and banquets centered on the king kept the nobles who lived at Versailles away from plotting rebellion. According to one of them, the duke of Saint-Simon°, "no one was so clever in devising petty distractions" as the king.

The balance of powers in the English model would be widely admired in later times. Until well after 1750 most European rulers admired and imitated the centralized powers and absolutist claims of the French. Some went so far as to build imitations of the Versailles palace. The checks and balances of the English model had a less immediate effect. In his influential *Second Treatise of Civil Government* (1690), the English political philosopher John Locke (1632–1704) disputed monarchial claims to absolute authority by divine right. Rather, he argued, rulers derived their authority from the consent of the governed and, like everyone else, were subject to the law. If monarchs overstepped the law, Locke argued, citizens had not only the right but also the duty to rebel. The later consequences of this idea are considered in Chapter 22.

Versailles (vuhr-SIGH)

Saint-Simon (san see-MON)

Versailles, 1722 This painting by P.-D. Martin shows the east expanse of buildings and courtyards that make up the palace complex built by King Louis XIV. (Giraudon/Art Resource, NY)

Warfare and Diplomacy

In addition to the bitter civil wars that pounded the Holy Roman Empire, France, and England, European states engaged in numerous international conflicts. Warfare was almost constant in early modern Europe (see the Chronology at the beginning of the chapter). In their pursuit of power monarchs expended vast sums of money and caused widespread devastation and death. The worst of the international conflicts, the Thirty Years War (1618–1648), caused long-lasting depopulation and economic decline in much of the Holy Roman Empire.

However, the wars also produced dramatic improvements in the skill of European armed forces and in their weaponry that arguably made them the most powerful in the world. The numbers of men in arms increased steadily throughout the early modern period. French forces, for example, grew from about 150,000 in 1630 to 400,000 by the early eighteenth century. Even smaller European states built up impressive armies. Sweden, with under a million people, had one of the finest and best-armed military forces in seventeenth-century Europe. Though the country had fewer than 2 million inhabitants in 1700, Prussia's splendid army made it one of Europe's major powers.

Larger armies required more effective command structures. In the words of a modern historian, European armies "evolved . . . the equivalent of a central nervous system, capable of activating technologically differentiated claws and teeth."[3] New signaling techniques improved control of battlefield maneuvers. Frequent marching drills trained troops to obey orders instantly and gave them a close sense of comradeship. To defend themselves cities built new fortifications able to withstand cannon bombardments. Each state tried to outdo its rivals by

The Spanish Armada   This drawing for a tapestry shows the great warships of the Spanish fleet lined up to face the smaller but faster vessels of the British navy. The ship with oars in the foreground is a galley.   (Eileen Tweedy/The Art Archive)

improvements in military hardware, but battles between evenly matched armies often ended in stalemates that prolonged the wars. Victory increasingly depended on naval superiority.

Only England did not maintain a standing army in peacetime, but England's rise as a sea power had begun under King Henry VIII, who spent heavily on ships and promoted a domestic iron-smelting industry to supply cannon. The Royal Navy also copied innovative ship designs from the Dutch in the second half of the seventeenth century. By the early eighteenth century the Royal Navy surpassed the rival French fleet in numbers. By then, England had merged with Scotland to become Great Britain, annexed Ireland, and built a North American empire.

Although France was Europe's most powerful state, Louis XIV's efforts to expand its borders and dominance were increasingly frustrated by coalitions of the other great powers. In a series of eighteenth-century wars beginning with the War of the Spanish Succession (1701–1714), the combination of Britain's naval strength and the land armies of its Austrian and Prussian allies was able to block French expansionist efforts and prevent the Bourbons from uniting the thrones of France and Spain.

This defeat of the French monarchy's empire-building efforts illustrated the principle of **balance of power** in international relations: the major European states formed temporary alliances to prevent any one state from becoming too powerful. Russia emerged as a major power in Europe after its modernized armies defeated Sweden in the Great Northern War (1700–1721). During the next two centuries, though adhering to four different branches of Christianity, the great powers of Europe—Catholic France, Anglican Britain, Catholic Austria, Lutheran Prussia, and Orthodox Russia (see Map 17.3)—maintained an effective balance of power in Europe by shifting their alliances for geopolitical rather than religious reasons. These pragmatic alliances were the first successful efforts at international peacekeeping.

Paying the Piper

To pay the extremely heavy military costs of their wars, European rulers had to increase their revenues. The most successful of them after 1600 promoted mutually beneficial alliances with the rising commercial elite. Both sides understood that trade thrived where government taxation and regulation were not excessive, where courts enforced contracts and collected debts, and where military power stood ready to protect overseas expansion by force when necessary.

Map 17.3 Europe in 1740 By the middle of the eighteenth century the great powers of Europe were France, the Austrian Empire, Great Britain, Prussia, Spain, and Russia. Spain, the Holy Roman Empire, and the Ottoman Empire were far weaker in 1740 than they had been two centuries earlier.

Spain, sixteenth-century Europe's mightiest state, illustrates how the financial drains of an aggressive military policy and the failure to promote economic development could lead to decline. Expensive wars against the Ottomans, northern European Protestants, and rebellious Dutch subjects caused the treasury to default on its debts four times during the reign of King Philip II. The Spanish rulers' concerns for religious uniformity and traditional aristocratic privilege further undermined the country's economy. In the name of religious uniformity they expelled Jewish merchants, persecuted Protestant dissenters, and forced tens of thousands of skilled farmers and artisans into exile because of their Muslim ancestry. In the name of aristocratic privilege the 3 percent of the population that controlled 97 percent of the land in 1600 was exempt from taxation, while high sales taxes discouraged manufacturing.

For a time, vast imports of silver and gold bullion from Spain's American colonies filled the government treasury. These bullion shipments also contributed to severe inflation (rising prices), worst in Spain but bad throughout the rest of western Europe as well. A Spanish saying captured the problem: American silver was like rain on the roof—it poured down and washed away. Huge debts for foreign wars drained bullion from Spain to its creditors. More wealth flowed out to purchase manufactured goods and even food in the seventeenth century.

The rise of the Netherlands as an economic power stemmed from opposite policies. The Spanish crown had acquired these resource-poor but commercially successful provinces as part of Charles V's inheritance. But King Philip II's decision to impose Spain's ruinously heavy sales tax and enforce Catholic orthodoxy drove the Dutch to revolt in 1566 and again in 1572. If successful, those measures would have discouraged business and driven away the Calvinists, Jews, and others who were essential to Dutch prosperity. The Dutch fought with skill and ingenuity, raising and training an army and a navy that were among the most effective in Europe. By 1609 Spain was forced to agree to a truce that recognized the autonomy of the northern part of the Netherlands. In 1648, after eight decades of warfare, the independence of these seven United Provinces of the Free Netherlands (their full name) became final.

Rather than being ruined by the long war, the United Netherlands emerged as the dominant commercial power in Europe and the world's greatest trading nation.

During the seventeenth century, the wealth of the Netherlands multiplied. This economic success owed much to a decentralized government. During the long struggle against Spain, the provinces united around the prince of Orange, their sovereign, who served as commander-in-chief of the armed forces. But in economic matters each province was free to pursue its own interests. The maritime province of Holland grew rich by favoring commercial interests.

After 1650 the Dutch faced growing competition from the English, who were developing their own close association of business and government. In a series of wars (1652–1678) England used its naval might to break Dutch dominance in overseas trade and to extend its own colonial empire. With government support, the English merchant fleet doubled between 1660 and 1700, and foreign trade rose by 50 percent. As a result, state revenue from customs duties tripled. During the eighteenth century Britain's trading position strengthened still more.

The debts run up by the Anglo-Dutch Wars helped persuade the English monarchy to greatly enlarge the government's role in managing the economy. The outcome has been called a "financial revolution." The government increased revenues by taxing the formerly exempt landed estates of the aristocrats and by collecting taxes directly. Previously, private individuals known as tax farmers had advanced the government a fixed sum of money; in return they could keep whatever money they were able to collect from taxpayers. To secure cash quickly for warfare and other emergencies and to reduce the burden of debts from earlier wars, England also followed the Dutch lead in creating a central bank, from which the government was able to obtain long-term loans at low rates.

The French government was also developing its national economy, especially under Colbert. He streamlined tax collection, promoted French manufacturing and shipping by imposing taxes on foreign goods, and improved transportation within France itself. Yet the power of the wealthy aristocrats kept the French government from following England's lead in taxing wealthy landowners, collecting taxes directly, and securing low-cost loans. Nor did France succeed in managing its debt as efficiently as England. (The role of governments in promoting overseas trade is further discussed in Chapter 19.)

COMPARATIVE PERSPECTIVES

As he approached the end of his life in 1575, the French scholar and humanist Loys Le Roy° reflected on the world in which he had lived. It was, he believed, a golden age for Europe, and he listed the names of more than 130 scholars and translators, writers and poets, artists and sculptors, and explorers and philosophers whose work over the preceding two centuries had restored the standards of ancient learning. Le Roy singled out three technological innovations that he believed had transformed his age: printing, the marine compass, and cannonry. He put printing first because its rapid spread across Europe had done so much to propagate this cultural revival. The marine compass had made possible the sea voyages that now connected Europe directly to Africa and Asia and that had led to the discovery and conquest of the Americas. He gave third place to firearms because they had transformed warfare. Cannon and more recently devised hand-held weapons had swept before them all older military instruments. His enthusiasm for this transformation was dampened by the capacity of firearms to cause devastation and ruin. Among the other evils of his age Le Roy enumerated syphilis and the spread of religious heresies and sects.

Loys Le Roy (lwa-EES le RWAH)

Reading Le Roy's analysis more than four centuries later, one is struck by the geographical and historical range of his understanding. He credits both ancient and modern Greeks and Italians for their cultural contributions, the Germans for their role in perfecting printing and cannonry, and the Spanish for their overseas voyages. But his frame of reference is not confined to Europe. He cites the mathematical skills of ancient Egyptians; the military conquests of Mongols, Turks, and Persians (Iranians); Arabs' contributions to science and medicine; and China's contributions to the development of printing. Le Roy concluded that he was living at a turning point in world history. For long centuries, the military might of the Mongols and Turks had threatened the peoples of Europe, and Safavid Iran and Mamluk Egypt had surpassed any European land in riches. Now Europeans' military might equaled that of their Middle Eastern neighbors. They were amassing new wealth from Asian trade and American silver. Most of all, the explosion of learning and knowledge had given Europe intellectual equality and perhaps superiority. Le Roy noted perceptively that while printing presses were in use all across Europe by the end of the sixteenth century, the Islamic world had closed itself off to the benefits of this new technology, refusing to allow presses to be set up and even forbidding the entry of Arabic works about their lands printed in Europe.

SUMMARY

— How was the cultural history of early modern Europe determined by the interplay of traditional beliefs and revolutionary ideas?

— What factors contributed to the wealth of some Europeans and the great poverty of others in this period?

— How was the history of early modern European states determined by differing policies in the areas of religion, foreign relations, and economics?

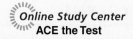

Online Study Center
ACE the Test

Early modern Europe underwent the Scientific Revolution as well as the fragmentation of the Catholic Church and the emergence of the Protestant Reformation. Rejecting the authority of the pope and criticizing the institution of indulgences, Luther insisted on the moral primacy of faith over deeds; Calvin went further, holding that salvation was predestined by God. While accepting male dominance in society, most Protestants rejected the church's requirement that priests and nuns live a life of celibacy. Influenced by traditional antifeminist beliefs, pagan folklore about witchcraft, and Protestant Reformers' focus on the Devil as the source of evil, religious and secular leaders instigated witch-hunts in which thousands of women were tortured and executed. Supporting the belief in witchcraft was a more fundamental belief that human misfortune could be blamed on supernatural forces, but this idea was powerfully challenged by pioneers of the Scientific Revolution such as Copernicus and Newton, who showed that the workings of the physical universe could be explained in natural terms. These scientists did not see any conflict between science and religion, and they paved the way for influential figures of the Enlightenment, who believed that human reason was capable of—and responsible for—discovering the laws that govern social behavior.

Thanks to foreign and domestic trade, European cities in this period experienced rapid growth and the rise of a wealthy commercial class. The Netherlands in particular prospered from expanded manufacturing and trade: with the formation of joint-stock companies and a powerful stock market, Amsterdam became Europe's major port and financial center. For peasants and laborers, however, life did not improve much: serfdom had all but ended in western Europe, only to rise in eastern Europe. Agricultural techniques had not improved much since medieval times, and environmental hardships such as the Little Ice Age and deforestation caused by mining and logging brought great difficulties to the poor. Rural poverty, coupled with the exemption from taxation enjoyed by wealthy landowners, sparked numerous armed rebellions. Women were dependent on their families' and husbands' wealth or lack of it, and they were barred from attending schools or joining guilds and professions.

Differing policies in the areas of religion, foreign relations, and economics led to different outcomes in the histories of early modern European states. Charles V, unable to reconcile the diverse interests of his Catholic and Protestant territories and their powerful local rulers, failed to create a unified Holy Roman Empire. Philip II enforced religious uniformity through the courts of the Spanish Inquisition and the expulsion of Jews and people of Muslim ancestry. Henry VIII, having failed to win an annulment of his marriage to Catherine of Aragon, severed all ties with the Pope and led Parliament to accept him as head of the Church of England. Power struggles in England during this period led to a stronger Parliament, while in France a stronger monarchy emerged, symbolized by Louis XIV's construction of the palace at Versailles. Spain was Europe's mightiest state in the sixteenth century, but it was unable to suppress the Netherlands Revolt, and by the middle of the seventeenth century the United Netherlands had become the dominant commercial power on the continent. The growth of English naval power led to the defeat of the Dutch in the Anglo-Dutch Wars and of France in the early eighteenth century when it attempted to expand its own empire through a union with Spain. Unlike Spain and France, which maintained aristocrats' traditional exemption from taxation, England began to tax their estates, and this policy—together with the establishment of direct taxation and the creation of a central bank from which it could secure low-cost loans—gave England a stronger financial foundation than its rivals enjoyed.

KEY TERMS

Renaissance (European)   *p. 491*

papacy   *p. 492*

indulgence   *p. 492*

Protestant Reformation   *p. 493*

Catholic Reformation   *p. 494*

witch-hunt   *p. 496*

Scientific Revolution   *p. 497*

Enlightenment   *p. 498*

bourgeoisie   *p. 499*

joint-stock company   *p. 502*

stock exchange   *p. 502*

gentry   *p. 502*

Little Ice Age   *p. 503*

deforestation   *p. 503*

Holy Roman Empire
   p. 505

Habsburg   *p. 505*

English Civil War   *p. 507*

Versailles   *p. 510*

balance of power   *p. 512*

Online Study Center
Improve Your Grade
Flashcards

SUGGESTED READING

Overviews of this period include Euan Cameron, ed., *Early Modern Europe* (1999); H. G. Koenigsberger, *Early Modern Europe, 1500-1789* (1987); and Joseph Bergin, *The Short Oxford History of Europe: The Seventeenth Century* (2001). Global perspectives can be found in Fernand Braudel, *Civilization and Capitalism, 15th–18th Century*, trans. Siân Reynolds, 3 vols. (1992), and Immanuel Wallerstein, *The Modern World-System*, vol. 2, *Mercantilism and the Consolidation of the European World-Economy, 1600–1750* (1980).

Technological and environmental changes are the focus of Geoffrey Parker, *Military Revolution: Military Innovation and the Rise of the West, 1500–1800*, 2nd ed. (1996); William H. McNeill, *The Pursuit of Power: Technology, Armed Force, and Society Since A.D. 1000* (1982); Robert Greenhalgh Albion, *Forests and Sea Power: The Timber Problem of the Royal Navy, 1652–1862* (1965); Emmanuel Le Roy Ladurie, *Times of Feast, Times of Famine: A History of Climate Since the Year 1000*, trans. Barbara Bray (1971); and Brian Fagan, *The Little Ice Age: How Climate Made History, 1300–1850* (2000). Robert C. Allen, *Enclosure and the Yeoman: The Agricultural Development of the South Midlands, 1450–1850* (1992), focuses on England.

Steven Shapin, *The Scientific Revolution* (1996), and Hugh Kearney, *Science and Change, 1500–1700* (1971), are accessible introductions. Thomas S. Kuhn, *The Structure of Scientific Revolutions*, 3rd ed. (1996), and A. R. Hall, *The Scientific Revolution, 1500–1800: The Formation of the Modern Scientific Attitude*, 2nd ed. (1962), are classic studies. Carolyn Merchant, *The Death of Nature: Women, Ecology and the Scientific Revolution* (1980), tries to combine several broad perspectives. *The Sciences in Enlightened Europe*, ed. W. Clark, J. Golinski, and S. Schaffer (1999), examines particular topics in a sophisticated way. Dorinda Outram, *The Enlightenment*, 2nd ed. (2005), provides a recent summary of research.

Excellent introductions to social and economic life are George Huppert, *After the Black Death: A Social History of Early Modern Europe*, 2nd ed. (1998), and Carlo M. Cipolla, *Before the Industrial Revolution: European Society and Economy, 1000–1700*, 3rd ed. (1993). Peter Burke, *Popular Culture in Early Modern Europe* (1978), offers a broad treatment of nonelite perspectives, as does Robert Jütte, *Poverty and Deviance in Early Modern Europe* (1994). For more economic detail see Robert S. DuPlessis, *Transitions to Capitalism in Early Modern Europe* (1997); Myron P. Gutmann, *Toward the Modern Economy: Early Industry in Europe, 1500–1800* (1988); and Carlo M. Cipolla, ed., *The Fontana Economic History of Europe*, vol. 2, *The Sixteenth and Seventeenth Centuries* (1976).

Topics of women's history are examined by Merry E. Wiesner, *Women and Gender in Early Modern Europe*, 2nd ed. (2000); Bonnie S. Anderson and Judith P. Zinsser, *A History of Their Own: Women in Europe from Prehistory to the Present*, vol. 2, rev. ed. (2000); and *Ages of Woman, Ages of Man: Sources in European Social History, 1400-1750*, ed. Monica Chojnacka and Merry E. Wiesner-Hanks (2002). An excellent place to begin examining the complex subject of witchcraft is Brian P. Levack, *The Witch-Hunt in Early Modern Europe*, 2nd ed. (1995); other up-to-date perspectives can be found in J. Barry, M. Hester, and G. Roberts, eds., *Witchcraft in Early Modern Europe: Studies in Culture and Belief* (1996), and Carlo Ginzburg, *The Night Battles: Witchcraft and Agrarian Cults in the Sixteenth and Seventeenth Centuries*, trans. John and Anne Tedechi (1983).

Good single-country surveys are J. A. Sharpe, *Early Modern England: A Social History, 1550–1760*, 2nd ed. (1997); Emmanuel Le Roy Ladurie, *The Royal French State, 1460–1610*, trans. Juliet Vale (1994), and *The Ancien Régime: A History of France, 1610–1774*, trans. Mark Greengrass (1996); Jonathan Israel, *The Dutch Republic: Its Rise, Greatness and Fall, 1477–1806* (1995); and James Casey, *Early Modern Spain: A Social History* (1999).

NOTES

1. Quoted by Carlo M. Cipolla, "Introduction," *The Fontana Economic History of Europe*, vol. 2, *The Sixteenth and Seventeenth Centuries* (Glasgow: Collins/Fontana Books, 1976), 11–12.

2. Michel de Montaigne, *Essais* (1588), ch. 31, "Des Cannibales."

3. William H. McNeill, *The Pursuit of Power: Technology, Armed Force, and Society Since A.D. 1000* (Chicago: University of Chicago Press, 1982), 124.

Desseins de Sauvages de Plusieurs Nations, Nlle Orleans 1735

Choctaw Village in Louisiana at Time of French Colonial Rule In this scene of village life we see strong indications of integration in the colonial economy. While natives are shown pursuing traditional tasks, a black slave and European trade goods obtained in exchange for deerskins are arrayed along the river bank. (© 2006 Harvard University Peabody Museum Photo 41-72 10/20 T2377)

○— How did the Columbian Exchange alter the natural environment of the Americas?

○— What role did forced labor play in the main industries of Spanish America and Brazil?

○— What were the main similarities and differences among colonies of Spain, Portugal, England, and France?

○— What were the effects of the colonial reforms and wars among imperial powers that dominated the Americas during the eighteenth century?

18

THE DIVERSITY OF AMERICAN COLONIAL SOCIETIES, 1530 – 1770

CHAPTER OUTLINE

The Columbian Exchange

Spanish America and Brazil

English and French Colonies in North America

Colonial Expansion and Conflict

Comparative Perspectives

ENVIRONMENT AND TECHNOLOGY: A Silver Refinery at Potosí, Bolivia, 1700

DIVERSITY AND DOMINANCE: Race and Ethnicity in the Spanish Colonies: Negotiating Hierarchy

Shulush Homa—an eighteenth-century Choctaw leader called "Red Shoes" by the English—faced a dilemma. For years he had befriended the French who had moved into the lower Mississippi Valley, protecting their outlying settlements from other indigenous groups and producing a steady flow of deerskins for trade. In return he received guns and gifts as well as honors previously given only to chiefs. Though born a commoner, he had parlayed his skillful politicking with the French—and the shrewd distribution of the gifts he received—to enhance his position in Choctaw society. Then his fortunes turned. In the course of yet another war between England and France, the English cut off French shipping. Faced with followers unhappy over his sudden inability to supply French guns, Red Shoes forged a dangerous new arrangement with the English that led his former allies, the French, to put a price on his head. His

Online Study Center

This icon will direct you to interactive activities and study materials on the website: *college.hmco.com/pic/bulliet4e.*

519

murder in 1747 launched a civil war among the Choctaw. By the end of this conflict both the French colonial population and the Choctaw people had suffered greatly.

The story of Red Shoes reveals a number of themes from the period of European colonization of the Americas. First, although the wars, epidemics, and territorial loss associated with European settlement threatened Amerindians, many adapted the new technologies and new political possibilities to their own purposes and thrived—at least for a time. In the end, though, the best that they could achieve was a holding action. The people of the Old World were coming to dominate the people of the New World.

Second, after centuries of isolation, the Americas were being drawn into global events, influenced by the political and economic demands of Europe. The influx of Europeans and Africans resulted in a vast biological and cultural transformation, as the introduction of new plants, animals, diseases, peoples, and technologies fundamentally altered the natural environment of the Western Hemisphere. This was not a one-way transfer, however. The technologies and resources of the New World contributed to profound changes in the Old. Staple crops introduced from the Americas provided highly nutritious foods that helped fuel a population spurt in Europe, Asia, and Africa. As we saw in Chapter 17, riches and products funneled from the Americas changed economic, social, and political relations in Europe.

Third, the fluidity of the Choctaw's political situation reflects the complexity of colonial society, where Amerindians, Europeans, and Africans all contributed to the creation of new cultures. Although similar processes took place throughout the Americas, the particulars varied from place to place, creating a diverse range of cultures. The society that arose in each colony reflected the colony's mix of native peoples, its connections to the slave trade, and the characteristics of the European society establishing the colony. As the colonies matured, new concepts of identity developed, and those living in the Americas began to see themselves as distinct.

THE COLUMBIAN EXCHANGE

The term **Columbian Exchange** refers to the transfer of peoples, animals, plants, and diseases between the New and Old Worlds. The European invasion and settlement of the Western Hemisphere opened a long era of biological and technological transfers that altered American environments. Within a century of first settlement, the domesticated livestock and major agricultural crops of the Old World (the known world before Columbus's voyage) had spread over much of the Americas, and the New World's useful staple crops had enriched the agricultures of Europe, Asia, and Africa. Old World diseases that entered the Americas with European immigrants and African slaves devastated indigenous populations. These dramatic population changes weakened native peoples' capacity for resistance and accelerated the transfer of plants, animals, and related technologies. As a result, the colonies of Spain, Portugal, England, and France became vast arenas of cultural and social experimentation.

Demographic Changes

Because of their long isolation from other continents (see Chapter 16), the peoples of the New World lacked immunity to diseases introduced from the Old World. As a result, death rates among Amerindian peoples during the epidemics of the early colonial period were very high. The lack of reliable estimates of the Amerindian population at the moment of contact has frustrated efforts to measure the deadly impact of these diseases, but scholars agree that Old World diseases had a terrible effect on native peoples. According to one estimate, in the century that followed the triumph of Hernán Cortés in 1521, the indigenous population of central Mexico fell from a high of more than 13 million to approximately 700,000. In this same period the Maya population declined by nearly 75 percent. In the region of the Inca Empire, population fell from about 9 million to approximately 600,000. Brazil's native population was similarly ravaged, falling from 2.5 million to under a million within a century of the arrival of the Portuguese.

Smallpox, which arrived in the Caribbean in 1518, was the most deadly of the early epidemics. In Mexico and Central America, 50 percent or more of the Amerindian population died during the first wave of smallpox epidemics. The disease then spread to South America with equally devastating effects. Measles arrived in the New World in the 1530s and was followed by diphtheria, typhus, influenza, and, perhaps, pulmonary

CHRONOLOGY

	Spanish America	Brazil	British America	French America
1500	**1518** Smallpox arrives in Caribbean	**1530s** Twelve captaincies created to promote development of Brazil		**1534–1542** Jacques Cartier's voyages to explore Newfoundland and Gulf of St. Lawrence
	1535 Creation of Viceroyalty of New Spain	**1540–1600** Era of Amerindian slavery		
	1540s Creation of Viceroyalty of Peru	**After 1540** Sugar begins to dominate the economy		
	1542 New Laws attempt to improve treatment of Amerindians			
	1545 Silver discovered at Potosí, Bolivia			
			1583 Unsuccessful effort to establish Newfoundland colony	
1600			**1607** Jamestown founded	**1608** Quebec founded
	1625 Population of Potosí reaches 120,000	**By 1620** African slave trade provides majority of plantation workers	**1620** Plymouth founded	
		1630s Quilombo of Palmares founded	**1660** Slave population in Virginia begins period of rapid growth	
			1664 English take New York from Dutch	
1700	**1700** Last Habsburg ruler of Spain dies			**1699** Louisiana founded
	1713 First Bourbon ruler of Spain crowned			
		1750–1777 Reforms of marquis de Pombal	**1754–1763** French and Indian War	**1760** English take Canada
	1770s and 1780s Amerindian revolts in Andean region			

plague. Mortality was often greatest when two or more diseases struck at the same time. Between 1520 and 1521 influenza, in combination with other ailments, attacked the Cakchiquel of Guatemala. Their chronicle recalls:

> Great was the stench of the dead. After our fathers and grandfathers succumbed, half the people fled to the fields. The dogs and vultures devoured the bodies . . . . So it was that we became orphans, oh my sons! . . . We were born to die![1]

By the mid-seventeenth century malaria and yellow fever were also present in tropical regions of the Americas. The deadliest form of malaria arrived with the African slave trade, ravaging the already reduced native populations and afflicting European immigrants as well. Most scholars believe that yellow fever was also brought from Africa, but new research suggests that the disease may have been present before the conquest in the tropical low country near present-day Veracruz on the Gulf of Mexico. Whatever its origins, yellow fever killed Europeans in the Caribbean Basin and in other tropical regions nearly as efficiently as smallpox had earlier attacked Amerindian populations.

The development of English and French colonies in North America in the seventeenth century led to similar patterns of contagion and mortality. In 1616 and 1617 epidemics nearly exterminated many of New England's indigenous groups. French fur traders transmitted measles, smallpox, and other diseases as far as Hudson Bay and the Great Lakes. Although there is very little evidence that Europeans consciously used disease as a tool of empire, the deadly results of contact clearly undermined the ability of native peoples to resist settlement.

Transfer of Plants and Animals

Even as epidemics swept through the indigenous population, the New and the Old Worlds were participating in a vast exchange of plants and animals that radically altered diet and lifestyles in both regions. All the staples of southern European agriculture—such as wheat, olives, grapes, and garden vegetables—were being grown in the Americas in a remarkably short time after contact. African and Asian crops—such as rice, bananas, coconuts, breadfruit, and sugar—were soon introduced as well. While native peoples remained loyal to their traditional staples, they added many Old World plants to their diet. Citrus fruits, melons, figs, and sugar as well as onions, radishes, and salad greens all found a place in Amerindian cuisines.

In return the Americas offered the Old World an abundance of useful plants. The New World staples—maize, potatoes, and manioc—revolutionized agriculture and diet in parts of Europe, Africa, and Asia (see Environment and Technology: Amerindian Foods in Africa, in Chapter 19). Many experts assert that the rapid growth of world population after 1700 resulted in large measure from the spread of these useful crops, which provided more calories per acre than did any Old World staples other than rice. Beans, squash, tomatoes, sweet potatoes, peanuts, chilies, and chocolate also gained widespread acceptance in the Old World. In addition, the New World provided the Old with plants that provided dyes, medicine, varieties of cotton, and tobacco.

The introduction of European livestock had a dramatic impact on New World environments and cultures. Faced with few natural predators, cattle, pigs, horses, and sheep, as well as pests like rats and rabbits, multiplied rapidly in the open spaces of the Americas. On the vast plains of present-day southern Brazil, Uruguay, and Argentina, herds of wild cattle and horses exceeded 50

The Columbian Exchange After the conquest, the introduction of plants and animals from the Old World dramatically altered the American environment. Here an Amerindian woman is seen milking a cow. Livestock sometimes destroyed the fields of native peoples, but cattle, sheep, pigs, and goats also provided food, leather, and wool. (From Martinez Compañon, Trujillo del Perú, V.II, E 79. Photo: Imaging services, Harvard College Library).

million by 1700. Large herds of both animals also appeared in northern Mexico and what became the southwest of the United States.

Where Old World livestock spread most rapidly, environmental changes were dramatic. Many priests and colonial officials noted the destructive impact of marauding livestock on Amerindian agriculturists. The first viceroy of Mexico, Antonio de Mendoza, wrote to the Spanish king: "May your Lordship realize that if cattle are allowed, the Indians will be destroyed." Sheep, which grazed grasses close to the ground, were also an environmental threat. Yet the viceroy's stark choice misrepresented the complex response of indigenous peoples to these new animals.

Wild cattle on the plains of South America, northern Mexico, and Texas provided indigenous peoples with abundant supplies of meat and hides. In the present-day southwestern United States, the Navajo became sheepherders and expert weavers of woolen cloth. Even in the centers of European settlement, individual Amerindians turned European animals to their own advantage by becoming muleteers, cowboys, and sheepherders.

No animal had a more striking effect on the cultures of native peoples than the horse, which increased the efficiency of hunters and the military capacity of warriors on the plains. The horse permitted the Apache, Sioux, Blackfoot, Comanche, Assiniboine, and others to more efficiently hunt the vast herds of buffalo in North America. The horse also revolutionized the cultures of the Araucanian (or Mapuche) and Pampas peoples in South America.

SPANISH AMERICA AND BRAZIL

The frontiers of conquest and settlement expanded rapidly. Within one hundred years of Columbus's first voyage to the Western Hemisphere, the Spanish Empire in America included most of the islands of the Caribbean, Mexico, the American southwest, Central America, the Caribbean and Pacific coasts of South America, the Andean highlands, and the vast plains of the Rio de la Plata region (a region that includes the modern nations of Argentina, Uruguay, and Paraguay). Portuguese settlement in the New World developed more slowly. But before the end of the sixteenth century, Portugal occupied most of the Brazilian coast.

Online Study Center
Improve Your Grade
Interactive Map: Latin America
Before Independence

Early settlers from Spain and Portugal sought to create colonial societies based on the institutions and customs of their homelands. They viewed society as a vertical hierarchy of estates (classes of society), as uniformly Catholic, and as an arrangement of patriarchal extended-family networks. They quickly moved to establish the religious, social, and administrative institutions that were familiar to them.

Despite the imposition of foreign institutions and the massive loss of life caused by epidemics in the sixteenth century, indigenous peoples exercised a powerful influence on the development of colonial societies. Aztec and Inca elite families sought to protect their traditional privileges and rights through marriage or less formal alliances with Spanish settlers. They also used colonial courts to defend their claims to land. In Spanish and Portuguese colonies, indigenous military allies and laborers proved crucial to the development of European settlements. Nearly everywhere, Amerindian religious beliefs and practices survived beneath the surface of an imposed Christianity. Amerindian languages, cuisines, medical practices, and agricultural techniques also survived the conquest and influenced the development of Latin American culture.

Online Study Center
Improve Your Grade
Primary Source: General History
of the Things in Spain

The African slave trade added a third cultural stream to colonial Latin American society. At first, African slaves were concentrated in plantation regions of Brazil and the Caribbean (see Chapter 19), but by the end of the colonial era, Africans and their descendants were living throughout Spanish and Portuguese America, enriching colonial societies with their traditional agricultural practices, music, religious beliefs, cuisine, and social customs.

State and Church

The Spanish crown moved quickly to curb the independent power of the conquistadors and to establish royal authority over both the defeated native populations and the rising tide of European settlers. Created in 1524, the **Council of the Indies** in Spain supervised all government, ecclesiastical, and commercial activity in the Spanish colonies. Geography and technology, however, limited the Council's real power. Local officials could not be controlled too closely given that it took a ship more than two hundred days to make a roundtrip voyage from Spain to Veracruz, Mexico. Additional months of travel were required to reach Lima, Peru.

As a result, the highest-ranking Spanish officials in the colonies, the viceroys of New Spain and Peru, enjoyed broad power, but these two officials also faced obstacles to their authority in the vast territories they sought to control. Created in 1535, the Viceroyalty of New Spain, with its capital in Mexico City, included Mexico, the southwest of what is now the United States, Central America, and the islands of the Caribbean. The Viceroyalty of Peru, with its capital in Lima, was formed in the 1540s to govern Spanish South America (see Map 18.1). To overcome the problems of distance and geographic

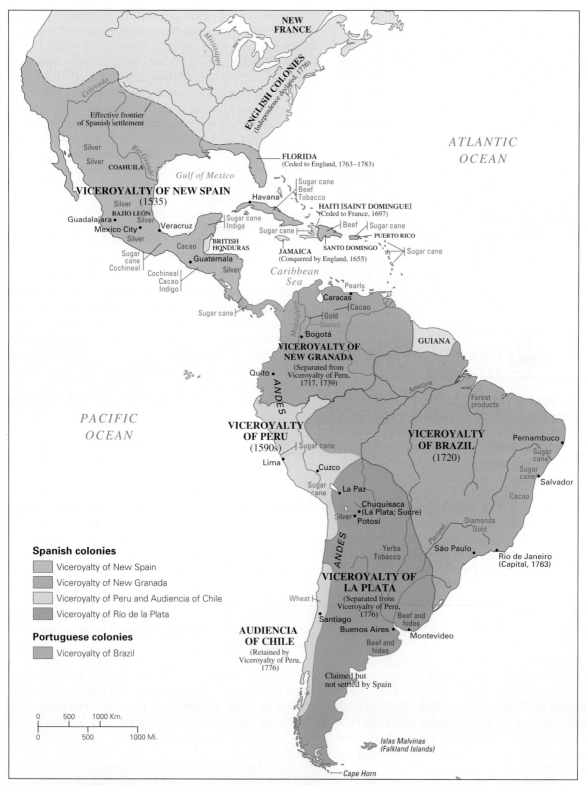

Map 18.1   Colonial Latin America in the Eighteenth Century   Spain and Portugal controlled most of the Western Hemisphere in the eighteenth century. In the sixteenth century they had created new administrative jurisdictions—viceroyalties—to defend their respective colonies against European rivals. Taxes assessed on colonial products helped pay for this extension of governmental authority.

Saint Martín de Porres (1579–1639) Martín de Porres was the illegitimate son of a Spanish nobleman and his black servant. Eventually recognized by his father, he entered the Dominican Order in Lima, Peru. Known for his generosity, he experienced visions and gained the ability to heal the sick. As was common in colonial religious art, the artist celebrates Martín de Porres's spirituality while representing him doing the type of work assumed most suitable for a person of mixed descent. (Private Collection)

New World. Seeking to promote settlement but limit costs, the king granted administrative responsibilities in Brazil to court favorites by creating twelve hereditary captaincies in the 1530s. After mismanagement and inadequate investment doomed this experiment, the king appointed a governor-general in 1549 and made Salvador, in the northern province of Bahia, Brazil's capital. In 1720 the first viceroy of Brazil was named.

The government institutions of the Spanish and Portuguese colonies had a more uniform character and were much more extensive and costly than those later established in North America by France and Great Britain. The enormous wealth produced in Spanish America by silver and gold mines and in Brazil by sugar plantations and, after 1690, gold mines financed these large and intrusive colonial bureaucracies. These institutions made the colonies more responsive to the initiatives of Spanish and Portuguese monarchs, but they also thwarted local economic initiative and political experimentation. More importantly, the heavy tax burden imposed by these colonial states drained capital from the colonies, slowing investment and retarding economic growth.

In both Spanish America and Brazil the Catholic Church became the primary agent for the introduction and transmission of Christian belief as well as European language and culture. The church undertook the conversion of Amerindians, ministered to the spiritual needs of European settlers, and promoted intellectual life through the introduction of the printing press and the founding of schools and universities.

Spain and Portugal justified their American conquests by assuming an obligation to convert native populations to Christianity. This religious objective was sometimes forgotten, and some members of the clergy were themselves exploiters of native populations. Nevertheless, the effort to convert America's native peoples expanded Christianity on a scale similar to its earlier expansion in Europe at the time of Constantine in the fourth century. In New Spain alone hundreds of thousands of conversions and baptisms were achieved within a few years of the conquest. However, both the number of conversions and the quality of indoctrination were undermined by the small numbers of missionaries. One Dominican claimed to the king that the Franciscans "have taken and occupied three fourths of the country, though they do not have enough friars for it. . . . In most places they are content to say a mass once a year; consider what sort of indoctrination they give them!"[2]

The Catholic clergy sought to achieve their evangelical ends by first converting members of the Amerindian elites, in the hope that they could persuade others to follow their example. To pursue this objective, Franciscan

barriers like the Andes Mountains, each viceroyalty was divided into a number of judicial and administrative districts. Until the seventeenth century, almost all colonial officials were born in Spain, but fiscal mismanagement eventually forced the Crown to sell appointments to these positions. As a result, local-born members of the colonial elite gained many offices.

In the sixteenth century Portugal concentrated its resources and energies on Asia and Africa. Because early settlers found neither mineral wealth nor rich native empires in Brazil, the Portuguese king hesitated to set up expensive mechanisms of colonial government in the missionaries in Mexico created a seminary to train members of the indigenous elite to become priests, but these idealistic efforts were dramatically curtailed when church authorities discovered that many converts were secretly observing old beliefs and rituals. The trial and punishment of two converted Aztec nobles for heresy in the 1530s highlighted this problem. Three decades later, Spanish clergy resorted to torture, executions, and the destruction of native manuscripts to eradicate traditional beliefs and rituals among the Maya. Repelled by these events, the church hierarchy ended both the violent repression of native religious practice and the effort to recruit an Amerindian clergy.

Despite its failures, the Catholic clergy did provide native peoples with some protections against the abuse and exploitation of Spanish settlers. The priest **Bartolomé de Las Casas** (1474–1566) was the most influential defender of the Amerindians in the early colonial period. He arrived in Hispaniola in 1502 as a settler and initially lived off the forced labor of Amerindians. Deeply moved by the deaths of so many Amerindians and by the misdeeds of the Spanish, Las Casas gave up this way of life and entered the Dominican Order, later becoming the first bishop of Chiapas, in southern Mexico. For the remainder of his long life Las Casas served as the most important advocate for native peoples, writing a number of books that detailed their mistreatment by the Spanish. His most important achievement was the enactment of the New Laws of 1542—reform legislation that outlawed the enslavement of Amerindians and limited other forms of forced labor.

European clergy had arrived in the Americas with the intention of transmitting Catholic Christian belief and ritual without alteration. This ambition was defeated by the large size and linguistic diversity of Amerindian populations and their geographic dispersal over a vast landscape. These problems frustrated Catholic missionaries and sometimes led to repression and cruelty. But the slow progress and limited success of evangelization led to the appearance of what must be seen as an Amerindian Christianity that blended European Christian beliefs with important elements of traditional native cosmology and ritual. Most commonly, indigenous beliefs and rituals came to be embedded in the celebration of saints' days or Catholic rituals associated with the Virgin Mary. The Catholic clergy and most European settlers viewed this evolving mixture as the work of the Devil or as evidence of Amerindian inferiority. Instead, it was one component of the process of cultural borrowing and innovation that contributed to a distinct and original Latin American culture.

After 1600 the terrible loss of Amerindian population caused by epidemics and growing signs of resistance to conversion led the Catholic Church to redirect most of its resources from native regions in the countryside to growing colonial cities and towns with large European populations. One important outcome of this altered mission was the founding of universities and secondary schools and the stimulation of urban intellectual life. Over time, the church became the richest institution in the Spanish colonies, controlling ranches, plantations, and vineyards as well as serving as the society's banker.

Colonial Economies

The silver mines of Peru and Mexico and the sugar plantations of Brazil dominated the economic development of colonial Latin America. The mineral wealth of the New World fueled the early development of European capitalism and funded Europe's greatly expanded trade with Asia. Profits produced in these economic centers also promoted the growth of colonial cities, concentrated scarce investment capital and labor resources, and stimulated the development of livestock raising and agriculture in neighboring rural areas (see Map 18.1). Once established, this colonial dependence on mineral and agricultural exports left an enduring social and economic legacy in Latin America.

Gold worth millions of pesos was extracted from mines in Latin America, but silver mines in the Spanish colonies generated the most wealth and therefore exercised the greatest economic influence. The first important silver strikes occurred in Mexico in the 1530s and 1540s. In 1545 the single richest silver deposit in the Americas was discovered at **Potosí°** in Alto Peru (what is now Bolivia), and until 1680 the silver production of Alto Peru and Peru dominated the Spanish colonial economy. After this date Mexican silver production greatly surpassed that of the Andean region. At first, silver was extracted from ore by smelting: the ore was crushed in giant stamping mills, then packed with charcoal in a furnace and fired. Within a short time, the wasteful use of forest resources for fuel destroyed forests near the mining centers. Faced with rising fuel costs, Mexican miners developed an efficient method of chemical extraction that relied on mixing mercury with the silver ore (see Environment and Technology: The Silver Refinery at Potosí, Bolivia, 1700). Silver yields and profits increased with the use of mercury amalgamation, but this process, too, had severe environmental costs. Mercury was a poison, and its use contaminated the environment and sickened the Amerindian work force.

Potosí (poh-toh-SEE)

A Silver Refinery at Potosí, Bolivia, 1700

The silver refineries of Spanish America were among the largest and most heavily capitalized industrial enterprises in the Western Hemisphere during the colonial period. By the middle of the seventeenth century the mines of Potosi, Bolivia, had attracted a population of more than 120,000.

The accompanying illustration shows a typical refinery (*ingenio*). Aqueducts carried water from large reservoirs on nearby mountainsides to the refineries. The water wheel shown on the right drove two sets of vertical stamps that crushed ore. Each iron-shod stamp was about the size and weight of a telephone pole. Crushed ore was sorted, dried, and mixed with mercury and other catalysts to extract the silver. The amalgam was then separated by a combination of washing and heating. The end result was a nearly pure ingot of silver that was later assayed and taxed at the mint.

Silver production carried a high environmental cost. Forests were cut to provide fuel and the timbers needed to shore up mine shafts and construct stamping mills and other machinery. Unwanted base metals produced in the refining process poisoned the soil. In addition, the need for tens of thousands of horses, mules, and oxen to drive machinery and transport material led to overgrazing and widespread erosion.

A Bolivian Silver Refinery, 1700
The silver refineries of Spanish America were among the largest industrial establishments in the Western Hemisphere.

Legend
(A) Storage sheds for ore
(B) Two water-driven stamping mills to crush ore
(C) Additional stamping mill
(D) Screen to sort ore
(E) Ore packed in mixing box
(F) Mercury and catalysts added to ore
(G) Amalgamation occurs
(H) Ore dried in furnace
(I) Mercury removed
(J) Refined ore washed
(K) Ore assayed
(L) Poor quality ore remixed with catalysts
(M) Housing
(N) Offices and sheds
(O) Aquaduct
(P) Chapel
(Q) Mill owner's house

From the time of Columbus, indigenous populations had been compelled to provide labor for European settlers in the Americas. Until the 1540s in Spanish colonies, Amerindian peoples were divided among the settlers and were forced to provide them with labor or with textiles, food, or other goods. This form of forced labor was called the **encomienda**°. As epidemics and mistreatment led to the decline in Amerindian population, reforms such as the New Laws sought to eliminate the encomienda. The discovery of silver in both Peru and Mexico, however, led to new forms of compulsory labor. In the mining region of Mexico, Amerindian populations had been greatly reduced by epidemic diseases. Therefore, from early in the colonial period, Mexican silver miners relied on free-wage laborers. Peru's Amerindian population survived in larger numbers, allowing the Spanish to impose a form of labor called the **mita**°. Under this system, one-seventh of adult male Amerindians were compelled to work for two to four months each year in mines, farms, or textile factories. The most dangerous working conditions existed in the silver mines, where workers were forced to carry heavy bags of ore up fragile ladders to the surface.

This colonial institution was a corrupted version of the Inca-era mit'a, which had been both a labor tax that supported elites and a reciprocal labor obligation that allowed kin groups to produce surpluses of essential goods that provided for the elderly and incapacitated. In the Spanish mita, few Amerindian workers could survive on their wages. Wives and children were commonly forced to join the work force to help meet expenses. Even those who remained behind in the village were forced to send food and cash to support mita workers.

As the Amerindian population fell with each new epidemic, some of Peru's villages were forced to shorten the period between mita obligations. Instead of serving every seven years, many men were forced to return to mines after only a year or two. Unwilling to accept mita service and the other tax burdens imposed on Amerindian villages, large numbers of Amerindians abandoned traditional agriculture and moved permanently to Spanish mines and farms as wage laborers. The long-term result of these individual decisions weakened Amerindian village life and promoted the assimilation of Amerindians into Spanish-speaking Catholic colonial society.

Before the settlement of Brazil, the Portuguese had already developed sugar plantations that depended on African slave labor on the Atlantic islands of Madeira, the Azores, the Cape Verdes, and São Tomé. Because of the success of these early experiences, they were able to quickly transfer this profitable form of agriculture to Brazil. After 1540 sugar production expanded rapidly in the northern provinces of Pernambuco and Bahia. By the seventeenth century, sugar dominated the Brazilian economy.

The sugar plantations of colonial Brazil always depended on slave labor. At first the Portuguese sugar planters enslaved Amerindians captured in war or seized from their villages. They used Amerindian men as field hands, although in this indigenous culture women had primary responsibility for agriculture. Any effort to resist or flee led to harsh punishments. Thousands of Amerindian slaves died during the epidemics that raged across Brazil in the sixteenth and seventeenth centuries. This terrible loss of Amerindian life and the rising profits of the sugar planters led to the development of an internal slave trade dominated by settlers from the southern region of São Paulo. To supply the rising labor needs of the sugar plantations of the northeast, slave raiders pushed into the interior, even attacking Amerindian populations in neighboring Spanish colonies. Many of the most prominent slavers were the sons of Portuguese fathers and Amerindian mothers.

Amerindian slaves remained an important source of labor and slave raiding a significant business in frontier regions into the eighteenth century. But sugar planters eventually came to rely more on African than Amerindian slaves. Although African slaves at first cost much more than Amerindian slaves, planters found them to be more productive and more resistant to disease. As profits from the plantations increased, imports of African slaves rose from an average of two thousand per year in the late sixteenth century to approximately seven thousand per year a century later, outstripping the immigration of free Portuguese settlers. Between 1650 and 1750, for example, more than three African slaves arrived in Brazil for every free immigrant from Europe.

Within Spanish America, the mining centers of Mexico and Peru eventually exercised global economic influence. American silver increased the European money supply, promoting commercial expansion and, later, industrialization. Large amounts of silver also flowed across the Pacific to the Spanish colony of the Philippines, where it was exchanged for Asian spices, silks, and pottery. Spain tried to limit this trade, but the desire for Asian goods in the colonies was so strong that there was large-scale trade in contraband goods.

The rich mines of Peru, Bolivia, and Mexico stimulated urban population growth as well as commercial links with distant agricultural and textile producers. The population of the city of Potosí, high in the Andes, reached 120,000 inhabitants by 1625. This rich mining town became the center of a vast regional market that depended on Chilean wheat, Argentine livestock, and Ecuadorian textiles.

---

encomienda (in-co-mee-EN-dah)   **mita** (MEE-tah)

Vista de una Máquina, para cernír Tabáco enla R.¹ Fabrica de Sigarros

VIVA EL REY.

Tobacco Factory Machinery in Colonial Mexico City The tobacco factory in eighteenth-century Mexico City used a horse-driven mechanical shredder to produce snuff and cigarette tobacco. (Archivo General de Indias, Seville, Spain)

The sugar plantations of Brazil played a similar role in integrating the economy of the south Atlantic region. The ports of Salvador and Rio de Janeiro in Brazil exchanged sugar, tobacco, and reexported slaves from Brazil for yerba (Paraguayan tea), hides, livestock, and silver produced in neighboring Spanish colonies. Portugal's increasing openness to British trade also allowed Brazil to become a conduit for an illegal trade between Spanish colonies and Europe. At the end of the seventeenth century the discovery of gold in Brazil helped overcome this large region's currency shortage and promoted further economic integration.

Both Spain and Portugal attempted to control the trade of their American colonies. Spain's efforts were more ambitious, granting monopoly trade rights to merchant guilds. Because ships returning to Spain with silver and gold were often attacked by foreign naval forces and pirates, Spain came to rely on convoys escorted by warships to supply the colonies and return with silver and gold. By 1650 Portugal had instituted a similar system of monopoly trade and fleets. The combination of monopoly commerce and convoy systems protected shipping and facilitated the collection of taxes, but these measures also slowed the flow of European goods to the colonies and kept prices high. Frustrated by these restraints, colonial populations established illegal commercial relations with the English, French, and Dutch. By the middle of the seventeenth century a majority of European imports were arriving in Latin America illegally.

Society in Colonial Latin America

With the exception of some early viceroys, few members of Spain's great noble families came to the New World. *Hidalgos*°— lesser nobles—were well represented, as were Spanish merchants, artisans, miners, priests, and lawyers. Small numbers of criminals, beggars, and prostitutes also found their way to the colonies. This flow of immigrants from Spain was never large, and Spanish settlers were always a tiny minority in a colonial society numerically dominated by Amerindians and rapidly growing populations of Africans, **creoles** (whites born in America to European parents), and people of mixed ancestry (see Diversity and Dominance: Race and Ethnicity in the Spanish Colonies: Negotiating Hierarchy).

The most powerful conquistadors and early settlers were granted the right to extract labor and tribute goods (encomienda) from Amerindian communities. These encomenderos sought to create a hereditary social and political class comparable to the European nobility. But

---

hidalgos (ee-DAHL-goes)

Race and Ethnicity in the Spanish Colonies: Negotiating Hierarchy

Many European visitors to colonial Latin America were interested in the mixing of Europeans, Amerindians, and Africans in the colonies. Many also commented on the treatment of slaves. The passages that follow allow us to examine two colonial societies.

The first selection was written by two young Spanish naval officers and scientists, Jorge Juan and Antonio de Ulloa, who arrived in the colonies in 1735 as members of a scientific expedition. They visited the major cities of the Pacific coast of South America and traveled across some of the most difficult terrain in the hemisphere. In addition to their scientific chores, they described architecture, local customs, and the social order. In this section they describe the ethnic mix in Quito, now the capital of Ecuador.

The second selection was published in Lima under the pseudonym Concolorcorvo around 1776. We now know that the author was Alonso Carrío de la Vandera. Born in Spain, he traveled to the colonies as a young man. He served in many minor bureaucratic positions, one of which was the inspection of the postal route between Buenos Aires and Lima. Carrío turned his long and often uncomfortable trip into an insightful, and sometimes highly critical, examination of colonial society. The selection that follows describes Córdoba, Argentina.

Juan and Ulloa and Carrío seem perplexed by colonial efforts to create and enforce a racial taxonomy that stipulated and named every possible mixture of European, Amerindian, and African, and they commented on the vanity and social presumptions of the dominant white population. We are fortunate to have these contemporary descriptions of the diversity of colonial society, but it is important to remember that these authors were clearly rooted in their time and confident in the superiority of Europe. Although they noted many of the abuses of Amerindian, mixed, and African populations and sometimes punctured the pretensions of colonial elites, they were also quick to assume the inferiority of the nonwhite population.

Quito

This city is very populous, and has, among its inhabitants, some families of high rank and distinction; though their number is but small considering its extent, the poorer class bearing here too great a proportion. The former are the descendants either of the original conquerors, or of presidents, auditors, or other persons of character [high rank], who at different times came over from Spain invested with some lucrative post, and have still preserved their luster, both of wealth and descent, by intermarriages, without intermixing with meaner families though famous for their riches. The commonalty may be divided into four classes; Spaniards or Whites, Mestizos, Indians or Natives, and Negroes, with their progeny. These last are not proportionally so numerous as in the other parts of the Indies; occasioned by it being something inconvenient to bring Negroes to Quito, and the different kinds of agriculture being generally performed by Indians.

The name of Spaniard here has a different meaning from that of Chapitone [sic] or European, as properly signifying a person descended from a Spaniard without a mixture of blood. Many Mestizos, from the advantage of a fresh complexion, appear to be Spaniards more than those who are so in reality; and from only this fortuitous advantage are accounted as such. The Whites, according to this construction of the word, may be considered as one sixth part of the inhabitants.

The Mestizos are the descendants of Spaniards and Indians, and are to be considered here in the same different degrees between the Negroes and Whites, as before at Carthagena [sic]; but with this difference, that at Quito the degrees of Mestizos are not carried so far back; for, even in the second or third generations, when they acquire the European color, they are considered as Spaniards. The complexion of the Mestizos is swarthy and reddish, but not of that red common in the fair Mulattos. This is the first degree, or the immediate issue of a Spaniard and Indian. Some are, however, equally tawny with the Indians themselves, though they are distinguished from them by their beards: while others, on the contrary, have so fine a complexion that they might pass for Whites, were it not for some signs which betray them, when viewed attentively. Among these, the most remarkable is the lowness of the forehead, which often leaves but a small space between their hair and eye-brows; at the same time the hair grows remarkably forward on the temples, extending to the lower part of the ear. Besides, the hair itself is harsh, lank, coarse, and very black; their nose very small, thin, and has a little rising on the middle, from whence it forms a small curve, terminating in a point, bending towards the upper lip. These marks, besides some dark spots on the body, are so constant and invariable, as to make it very difficult to conceal the fallacy of their complexion. The Mestizos may be reckoned a third part of the inhabitants.

The next class is the Indians, who form about another third; and the others, who are about one sixth, are the Castes [mixed]. These four classes, according to the most authentic accounts taken from the parish register, amount to between 50 and 60,000 persons, of all ages, sexes, and ranks. If among these classes the Spaniards, as is natural to think, are the most eminent for riches, rank, and power, it must at the same time be owned, however melancholy the truth may appear, they are in proportion the most poor, miserable and distressed; for they refuse to apply themselves to any mechanic business, considering it as a disgrace to that quality they so highly value themselves upon, which consists in not being black, brown, or of a copper color. The Mestizos, whose pride is regulated by prudence, readily apply themselves to arts and trades, but chose those of the greatest repute, as painting, sculpture, and the like, leaving the meaner sort to the Indians.

Córdoba

There was not a person who would give me even an estimate of the number of residents comprising this city, because neither the secular nor the ecclesiastical council has a register, and I know not how these colonists prove the ancient and distinguished nobility of which they boast; it may be that each family has its genealogical history in reserve. In my computation, there must be within the city and its limited common lands around 500 to 600 residents, but in the principal houses there are a very large number of slaves, most of them Creoles [native born] of all conceivable classes, because in this city and in all of Tucumán there is no leniency about granting freedom to any of them. They are easily supported since the principal aliment, meat, is of such moderate price, and there is a custom of dressing them only in ordinary cloth which is made at home by the slaves themselves, shoes being very rare. They aid their masters in many profitable ways and under this system do not think of freedom, thus exposing themselves to a sorrowful end, as is happening in Lima.

As I was passing through Córdoba, they were selling 2,000 Negroes, all Creoles from Temporalidades [property confiscated from the Jesuit order in 1767], from just the two farms of the [Jesuit] colleges of this city. I have seen the lists, for each one has its own, and they proceed by families numbering from two to eleven, all pure Negroes and Creoles back to the fourth generation, because the priests used to sell all of those born with a mixture of Spanish, mulatto, or Indian blood. Among this multitude of Negroes were many musicians and many of other crafts; they proceeded with the sale by families. I was assured that the nuns of Santa Teresa alone had a group of 300 slaves of both sexes, to whom they give their just ration of meat and dress in the coarse cloth which they make, while these good nuns content themselves with what is left from other ministrations. The number attached to other religious establishments is much smaller, but there is a private home which has 30 or 40, the majority of whom are engaged in various gainful activities. The result is a large number of excellent washerwomen whose accomplishments are valued so highly that they never mend their outer skirts in order that the whiteness of their undergarments may be seen. They do the laundry in the river, in water up to the waist, saying vaingloriously that she who is not soaked cannot wash well. They make ponchos [hand-woven capes], rugs, sashes, and sundries, and especially decorated leather cases which the men sell for 8 reales each, because the hides have no outlet due to the great distance to the port; the same thing happens on the banks of the Tercero and Cuarto rivers, where they are sold at 2 reales and frequently for less.

The principal men of the city wear very expensive clothes, but this is not true of the women, who are an exception in both Americas and even in the entire world, because they dress decorously in clothing of little cost. They are very tenacious in preserving the customs of their ancestors. They do not permit slaves, or even freedmen who have a mixture of Negro blood, to wear any cloth other than that made in this country, which is quite coarse. I was told recently that a certain bedecked mulatto [woman] who appeared in Córdoba was sent word by the ladies of the city that she should dress according to her station, but since she paid no attention to this reproach, they endured her negligence until one of the ladies, summoning her to her home under some other pretext, had the servants undress her, whip her, burn her finery before her eyes, and dress her in the clothes befitting her class; despite the fact that the [victim] was not lacking in persons to defend her, she disappeared lest the tragedy be repeated.

QUESTIONS FOR ANALYSIS

1. What do the authors of these selections seem to think about the white elites of the colonies? Are there similarities in the ways that Juan and Ulloa and Carrío describe the mixed population of Quito and the slave population of Córdoba?

2. How do these depictions of mestizos compare with the image of the mestiza daughter in the painting of castas on page 533?

3. What does the humiliation of the mixed-race woman in Córdoba tell us about ideas of race and class in this Spanish colony?

Sources: Jorge Juan and Antonio de Ulloa, *A Voyage to South America*, The John Adams translation (abridged), Introduction by Irving A. Leonard (New York: Alfred A. Knopf, 1964), 135–137, copyright © 1964 by Alfred A. Knopf, Inc. Used by permission of Alfred A. Knopf, a division of Random House, Inc.; Concolorcorvo, *El Lazarillo, A Guide for Inexperienced Travelers Between Buenos Aires and Lima, 1773*, translated by Walter D. Kline (Bloomington: Indiana University Press, 1965), 78–80. Used with permission of Indiana University Press.

their systematic abuse of Amerindian communities and the catastrophic effects of the epidemics of the sixteenth century undermined their economic position. By the end of the sixteenth century they had lost direct power over native dependents, and their social position was eclipsed by colonial officials. The elite of Spanish America came to include both European immigrants and creoles. Europeans dominated the highest levels of the church and government as well as commerce, while wealthy creoles controlled colonial agriculture and mining. The two groups were held together by the desire of wealthy creole families to increase family prestige by arranging for their daughters to marry successful Spanish merchants and officials. Although tensions between Spaniards and creoles were inevitable, most elite families included members of both groups.

Before the Europeans arrived in the Americas, the native peoples were members of a large number of distinct cultural and linguistic groups. Cultural diversity and class distinctions were present even in the highly centralized Aztec and Inca Empires. The effects of conquest and epidemics undermined this rich social and cultural complexity, as did the imposition of Catholic Christianity. The relocation of Amerindian peoples to promote conversion or to provide labor for Spanish mines further eroded ethnic boundaries among native peoples. Application of the racial label "Indian" by colonial administrators and settlers helped organize the tribute and labor demands imposed on native peoples, but it also registered the cultural costs of colonial rule.

Amerindian elites struggled to survive in the new political and economic environments created by military defeat and European settlement. Crucial to this survival was the maintenance of hereditary land rights and continued authority over indigenous commoners. Some sought to protect their positions by forging marriage or less formal relations with colonists. As a result, some indigenous and settler families were tied together by kinship in the decades after conquest, but these links weakened with the passage of time. Indigenous leaders also quickly gained familiarity with colonial legal systems and established political alliances with judges and other members of the colonial administrative classes. A minority of indigenous elite gained both recognition of their nobility and new hereditary land rights from Spanish authorities. More commonly hereditary native elites gained some security by becoming essential intermediaries between the indigenous masses and colonial administrators, collecting Spanish taxes and organizing the labor of their dependents for colonial enterprises.

Indigenous commoners suffered the heaviest burdens. Tribute payments, forced labor obligations, and the loss of traditional land rights were common. European

domination dramatically changed the indigenous world. The old connections between peoples and places were weakened or, in some cases, lost. Religious life, marriage practices, diet, and material culture were altered profoundly. The survivors of these terrible shocks learned to adapt to the new colonial environment. They embraced some elements of the dominant colonial culture and its technologies. They found ways to enter the market economies of the cities. They learned to produce new products, such as raising sheep and growing wheat. Most importantly, they learned new forms of resistance, like using colonial courts to protect community lands or to resist the abuses of corrupt officials.

Thousands of blacks participated in the conquest and settlement of Spanish America. While some free blacks immigrated voluntarily from Iberia, most black participants in the conquest and settlement of Spanish America and Brazil were slaves. More than four hundred slaves participated in the conquests of Peru and Chile. In the fluid social environment of the conquest era, many were able to gain their freedom. Juan Valiente escaped from his master in Mexico and then participated in Francisco Pizarro's conquest of the Inca Empire. He later became one of the most prominent early settlers of Chile, where he was granted Amerindian laborers in an encomienda.

With the opening of a direct slave trade with Africa (for details, see Chapter 19), the cultural character of the black population of colonial Latin America was altered dramatically. While Afro-Iberians, both slave and free, typically spoke Spanish or Portuguese and were Catholic, African slaves arrived in the colonies with different languages, religious beliefs, and cultural practices. These differences were viewed by European settlers as signs of inferiority and came to serve as a justification for slavery and discrimination. By 1600 free blacks, regardless of ancestry, were barred from positions in church and government as well as from many skilled crafts.

The rich mosaic of African identities was retained in colonial Latin America. Enslaved members of many cultural groups struggled to retain their languages, religious beliefs, and marriage customs. But in regions with large slave majorities, especially the sugar-producing regions of Brazil, these cultural and linguistic barriers often divided slaves and made resistance more difficult. Over time, elements from many African traditions blended and mixed with European (and in some cases Amerindian) language and beliefs to forge distinct local cultures. The rapid growth of an American-born slave population accelerated this process of cultural change.

Slave resistance took many forms, including sabotage, malingering, running away, and rebellion. Although many slave rebellions occurred, colonial authorities were always able to reestablish control. Groups of runaway slaves, however, were sometimes able to defend themselves for years. In both Spanish America and Brazil, communities of runaways (called quilombos° in Brazil and palenques° in Spanish colonies) were common. The largest quilombo was Palmares, where thousands of slaves defended themselves against Brazilian authorities for sixty years until they were finally overrun in 1694.

Slaves served as skilled artisans, musicians, servants, artists, cowboys, and even soldiers. However, the vast majority worked in agriculture. Conditions for slaves were worst on the sugar plantations of Brazil and the Caribbean, where harsh discipline, brutal punishments, and backbreaking labor were common. Because planters preferred to buy male slaves, there was always a gender imbalance on plantations, proving a significant obstacle to the traditional marriage and family patterns of both Africa and Europe. The disease environment of the tropics, as well as the poor housing, diet, hygiene, and medical care offered to slaves, also undermined the formation of slave families because of the high rates of mortality for both infants and adults.

The colonial development of Brazil was distinguished from that of Spanish America by the absence of rich and powerful indigenous civilizations such as those of the Aztecs and Inca and by lower levels of European immigration. Nevertheless, Portuguese immigrants came to exercise the same domination in Brazil as the Spanish exercised in their colonies. The growth of cities and the creation of imperial institutions eventually duplicated in outline the social structures found in Spanish America, but with an important difference. By the early seventeenth century, Africans and their American-born descendants were by far the largest racial group in Brazil. As a result, Brazilian colonial society (unlike Spanish Mexico and Peru) was influenced more by African culture than by Amerindian culture.

Both Spanish and Portuguese law provided for manumission, the granting of freedom to individual slaves, and colonial courts often intervened to protect slaves from the worst physical abuse or to protect married couples from forced separation. The majority of those gaining their liberty had saved money and purchased their own freedom. This was easiest to do in cities, where slave artisans and market women had the opportunity to earn and save money. If an owner refused permission for a slave to purchase his or her own freedom, the courts could intervene to facilitate manumission. Few owners freed slaves without demanding compensation; manumission was more about the capacity of individual slaves and slave families to earn income and save than about the generosity of slave owners. Among the minority of

Painting of Castas This is an example of a common genre of colonial Spanish American painting. In the eighteenth century there was increased interest in ethnic mixing, and wealthy colonials as well as some Europeans commissioned sets of paintings that showed mixed families. The paintings commonly indicated what the artist believed was an appropriate class setting. This richly dressed Spaniard is depicted with his Amerindian wife dressed in European clothing. Notice that the painter has the mestiza child look to her European father for guidance.   (Private Collection. Photographer: Camilo Garza/Fotocam, Monterrey, Mexico)

slaves to be freed without compensation, household servants were the most likely beneficiaries. Despite these legal protections and the resolve of slaves to gain freedom, only about 1 percent of the slave population gained freedom each year through manumission. However, because slave women received the majority of manumissions and because children born subsequently were considered free, the free black population grew rapidly.

Within a century of settlement, groups of mixed descent were in the majority in many regions. There were few marriages between Amerindian women and European men, but less formal relationships were common. Few European or creole fathers recognized their mixed offspring, who were called **mestizos**°. Nevertheless, this

---

quilombos (key-LOM-bos) **palenques** (pah-LEN-kays)

mestizo (mess-TEE-zoh)

rapidly expanding group came to occupy a middle position in colonial society, dominating urban artisan trades and small-scale agriculture and ranching. In frontier regions many members of the elite were mestizos, some proudly asserting their descent from the Amerindian elite. The African slave trade also led to the appearance of new American ethnicities. Individuals of mixed European and African descent—called **mulattos**—came to occupy an intermediate position in the tropics similar to the social position of mestizos in Mesoamerica and the Andean region. In Spanish Mexico and Peru and in Brazil, mixtures of Amerindians and Africans were also common.

All these mixed-descent groups were called castas° in Spanish America. Castas dominated small-scale retailing and construction trades in cities. In the countryside, many small ranchers and farmers as well as wage laborers were castas. Members of mixed groups who gained high status or significant wealth generally spoke Spanish or Portuguese, observed the requirements of Catholicism, and, whenever possible, lived the life of Europeans in their residence, dress, and diet.

ENGLISH AND FRENCH COLONIES IN NORTH AMERICA

The North American colonial empires of England and France and the colonies of Spain and Portugal had many characteristics in common (see Map 18.1). The governments of England and France hoped to find easily extracted forms of wealth or great indigenous empires like those of the Aztecs or Inca. Like the Spanish and Portuguese, English and French settlers responded to native peoples with a mixture of diplomacy and violence. African slaves proved crucial to the development of all four colonial economies.

Important differences, however, distinguished North American colonial development from the Latin American model. The English and French colonies were developed nearly a century after Cortés's conquest of Mexico and initial Portuguese settlement in Brazil. The intervening period witnessed significant economic and demographic growth in Europe. It also witnessed the Protestant Reformation, which helped propel English and French settlement in the Americas. By the time England and France secured a foothold in the Americas, the regions of the world were also more interconnected by trade. Distracted by ventures elsewhere and by increasing military confrontation in Europe, neither England nor France imitated the large and expensive colonial bureaucracies established by Spain and Portugal. As a result, private companies and individual proprietors played a much larger role in the development of English and French colonies. Particularly in the English colonies, this practice led to greater regional variety in economic activity, political institutions and culture, and social structure than was evident in the colonies of Spain and Portugal.

Early English Experiments

England's first efforts to gain a foothold in the Americas produced more failures than successes. The first attempt was made by a group of West Country gentry and merchants led by Sir Humphrey Gilbert. Their effort in 1583 to establish a colony in Newfoundland, off the coast of Canada, quickly failed. After Gilbert's death in 1584, his halfbrother, Sir Walter Raleigh, organized private financing for a new colonization scheme. A year later 108 men attempted a settlement on Roanoke Island, off the coast of present-day North Carolina. Afflicted with poor leadership, undersupplied, and threatened by Amerindian groups, the colony was abandoned within a year. Another effort to settle Roanoke was made in 1587. Because the Spanish Armada was threatening England, no relief expedition was sent to Roanoke until 1590. When help finally arrived, there was no sign of the 117 men, women, and children who had attempted settlement. Raleigh's colonial experiment was abandoned.

In the seventeenth century England renewed its effort to establish colonies in North America. England continued to rely on private capital to finance settlement and continued to hope that the colonies would become sources of high-value products such as silk, citrus, and wine. New efforts to establish American colonies were also influenced by English experience in colonizing Ireland after 1566. In Ireland land had been confiscated, cleared of its native population, and offered for sale to English investors. The city of London, English guilds, and wealthy private investors all purchased Irish "plantations" and then recruited "settlers." By 1650 investors had sent nearly 150,000 English and Scottish immigrants to Ireland. Indeed, Ireland attracted six times as many colonists in the early seventeenth century as did New England.

The South

London investors, organized as the privately funded Virginia Company, took up the challenge of colonizing Virginia in 1606. A year later 144 settlers disembarked at Jamestown, an island 30 miles

---

mestizo (mess-TEE-zoh) **castas** (CAZ-tahs)

(48 kilometers) up the James River in the Chesapeake Bay region. Additional settlers arrived in 1609. The investors and settlers hoped for immediate profits, but these unrealistic dreams were soon dashed. Although the location was easily defended, it was a swampy and unhealthy place; in the first fifteen years nearly 80 percent of all settlers in Jamestown died from disease or Amerindian attacks. There was no mineral wealth, no passage to Asia, and no docile and exploitable native population. By concentrating their energies on the illusion of easy wealth, settlers failed to grow enough food and were saved on more than one occasion by the generosity of neighboring Amerindian peoples.

In 1624 the English crown was forced to dissolve the Virginia Company because of its mismanagement of the colony. Freed from the company's commitment to Jamestown's unhealthy environment, colonists pushed deeper into the interior, developing a sustainable economy based on furs, timber, and, increasingly, tobacco. The profits from tobacco soon attracted new immigrants and new capital. Along the shoreline of Chesapeake Bay and the rivers that fed it, settlers spread out, developing plantations and farms. Colonial Virginia's population remained dispersed. In Latin America large and powerful cities dominated by viceroys and royal courts and networks of secondary towns flourished. In contrast, no city of any significant size developed in colonial Virginia.

Colonists in Latin America had developed systems of forced labor to develop the region's resources. Encomienda, mita, and slavery were all imposed on indigenous peoples, and later the African slave trade compelled the migration of millions of additional forced laborers to the colonies of Spain and Portugal. The English settlement of the Chesapeake Bay region added a new system of compulsory labor to the American landscape: **indentured servants**. Ethnically indistinguishable from free settlers, indentured servants eventually accounted for approximately 80 percent of all English immigrants to Virginia and the neighboring colony of Maryland. A young man or woman unable to pay for transportation to the New World accepted an indenture (contract) that bound him or her to a term ranging from four to seven years of labor in return for passage and, at the end of the contract, a small parcel of land, some tools, and clothes.

During the seventeenth century approximately fifteen hundred indentured servants, mostly male, arrived each year (see Chapter 19 for details on the indentured labor system). Planters were less likely to lose money if they purchased the cheaper limited contracts of indentured servants instead of purchasing African slaves during the period when both groups suffered high mortality rates. As life expectancy in the colony improved, planters

began to purchase more slaves. They calculated that greater profits could be secured by paying the higher initial cost of slaves owned for life than by purchasing the contracts of indentured servants bound for short periods of time. As a result, Virginia's slave population grew rapidly from 950 in 1660 to 120,000 by 1756.

By the 1660s many of the elements of the mature colony were in place in Virginia. Colonial government was administered by a Crown-appointed governor and his council, as well as by representatives of towns meeting together as the **House of Burgesses**. When these representatives began to meet alone as a deliberative body, they initiated a form of democratic representation that distinguished the English colonies of North America from the colonies of other European powers. Ironically, this expansion in colonial liberties and political rights occurred along with the dramatic increase in the colony's slave population. The intertwined evolution of American freedom and American slavery gave England's southern colonies a unique and conflicted political character that endured after independence.

At the same time, the English colonists were expanding settlements in the South. The Carolinas at first prospered from the profits of the fur trade. Fur traders pushed into the interior, eventually threatening the French trading networks based in New Orleans and Mobile. Native peoples eventually provided over 100,000 deerskins annually to this profitable commerce. The environmental and cultural costs of the fur trade were little appreciated at the time. As Amerindian peoples hunted more intensely, the natural balance of animals and plants was disrupted in southern forests. The profits of the fur trade altered Amerindian culture as well, leading villages to place less emphasis on subsistence hunting and fishing and traditional agriculture. Amerindian life was profoundly altered by deepening dependencies on European products, including firearms, metal tools, textiles, and alcohol.

Although increasingly brought into the commerce and culture of the Carolina colony, indigenous peoples were being weakened by epidemics, alcoholism, and a rising tide of ethnic conflicts generated by competition for hunting grounds. Conflicts among indigenous peoples—who now had firearms—became more deadly. Many Amerindians captured in these wars were sold as slaves to local colonists, who used them as agricultural workers or exported them to the sugar plantations of the Caribbean islands. Dissatisfied with the terms of trade imposed by fur traders and angered by this slave trade, Amerindians launched attacks on English settlements in the early 1700s. Their defeat by colonial military forces inevitably led to new seizures of Amerindian land by European settlers.

The northern part of the Carolinas had been settled from Virginia and followed that colony's mixed economy of tobacco and forest products. Slavery expanded slowly in this region. Charleston and the interior of South Carolina followed a different path. Settled first by planters from the Caribbean island of Barbados in 1670, this colony soon developed an economy based on plantations and slavery in imitation of the colonies of the Caribbean and Brazil. In 1729 North and South Carolina became separate colonies.

Despite an unhealthy climate, the prosperous rice and indigo plantations near Charleston attracted a diverse array of immigrants and an increasing flow of African slaves. African slaves were present from the founding of Charleston. They were instrumental in introducing irrigated rice agriculture along the coastal lowlands and in developing indigo (a plant that produced a blue dye) plantations at higher elevations away from the coast. Slaves were often given significant responsibilities. As one planter sending two slaves and their families to a frontier region put it: "[They] are likely young people, well acquainted with Rice & every kind of plantation business, and in short [are] capable of the management of a plantation themselves."[3]

As profits from rice and indigo rose, the importation of African slaves created a black majority in South Carolina. African languages, as well as African religious beliefs and diet, strongly influenced this unique colonial culture. Gullah, a dialect with African and English roots, evolved as the common idiom of the Carolina coast. African slaves were more likely than American-born slaves to rebel or run away. Africans played a major role in South Carolina's largest slave uprising, the Stono Rebellion of 1739. After a group of about twenty slaves, many of them African Catholics who sought to flee south to Spanish Florida, seized firearms, about a hundred slaves from nearby plantations joined them. The colonial militia soon defeated the rebels and executed many of them, but the rebellion shocked slave owners throughout England's southern colonies and led to greater repression.

Colonial South Carolina was the most hierarchical society in British North America. Planters controlled the economy and political life. The richest families maintained impressive households in Charleston, the largest city in the southern colonies, as well as on their plantations in the countryside. Small farmers, cattlemen, artisans, merchants, and fur traders held an intermediate but clearly subordinate social position. Native peoples remained influential participants in colonial society through commercial contacts and alliances, but they were increasingly marginalized. As had occurred in colonial Latin America, the growth of a large mixed population blurred racial and cultural boundaries. On the frontier, the children of white men and Amerindian women held an important place in the fur trade. In the plantation regions and Charleston, the offspring of white men and black women often held preferred positions within the slave work force or, if they had been freed, as carpenters, blacksmiths, or in other skilled trades.

New England

The colonization of New England by two separate groups of Protestant dissenters, Pilgrims and Puritans, put the settlement of this region on a different course. The **Pilgrims**, who came first, wished to break completely with the Church of England, which they believed was still essentially Catholic. Unwilling to confront the power of the established church and the monarch, they sought an opportunity to pursue their spiritual ends in a new land. As a result, in 1620 approximately one hundred settlers—men, women, and children—established the colony of Plymouth on the coast of present-day Massachusetts. Although nearly half of the settlers died during the first winter, the colony survived. Plymouth benefited from strong leadership and the discipline and cooperative nature of the settlers. Nevertheless, this experiment in creating a church-directed community failed. The religious enthusiasm and purpose that at first sustained the Pilgrims was dissipated by new immigrants who did not share the founders' religious beliefs, and by geographic dispersal to new towns. In 1691 Plymouth was absorbed into the larger Massachusetts Bay Colony of the Puritans.

The **Puritans** wished to "purify" the Church of England, not break with it. They wanted to abolish its hierarchy of bishops and priests, free it from governmental interference, and limit membership to people who shared their beliefs. Subjected to increased discrimination in England for their efforts to transform the church, large numbers of Puritans began emigrating from England in 1630.

The Puritan leaders of the Massachusetts Bay Company—the joint-stock company that had received a royal charter to finance the Massachusetts Bay Colony—carried the company charter, which spelled out company rights and obligations as well as the direction of company government, with them from England to Massachusetts. By bringing the charter, they limited Crown efforts to control them; the Crown could revoke but not alter the terms of the charter. By 1643 more than twenty thousand Puritans had settled in the Bay Colony.

Immigration to Massachusetts differed from immigration to the Chesapeake and to South Carolina. Most newcomers to Massachusetts arrived with their families.

Whereas 84 percent of Virginia's white population in 1625 was male, Massachusetts had a normal gender balance in its population almost from the beginning. It was also the healthiest of England's colonies. The result was a rapid natural increase in population. The population of Massachusetts quickly became more "American" than the population of the colonies to the south or in the Caribbean, whose survival depended on a steady flow of new English immigrants to counter high mortality rates. Massachusetts also was more homogeneous and less hierarchical than the southern colonies.

Political institutions evolved out of the terms of the company charter. A governor was elected, along with a council of magistrates drawn from the board of directors of the Massachusetts Bay Company. Disagreements between this council and elected representatives of the towns led, by 1650, to the creation of a lower legislative house that selected its own speaker and began to develop procedures and rules similar to those of the House of Commons in England. The result was greater autonomy and greater local political involvement than in the colonies of Latin America.

Economically, Massachusetts differed dramatically from the southern colonies. Agriculture met basic needs, but poor soils and harsh climate offered no opportunity to develop cash crops like tobacco or rice. To pay for imported tools, textiles, and other essentials, the colonists needed to discover some profit-making niche in the growing Atlantic market. Fur, timber and other forest products, and fish provided the initial economic foundation, but New England's economic well-being soon depended on providing commercial and shipping services in a dynamic and far-flung commercial arena that included the southern colonies, the smaller Caribbean islands, Africa, and Europe.

In Spanish and Portuguese America, heavily capitalized monopolies (companies or individuals given exclusive economic privileges) dominated international trade. In New England, by contrast, merchants survived by discovering smaller but more sustainable profits in diversified trade across the Atlantic. The colony's commercial success rested on market intelligence, flexibility, and streamlined organization. The success of this development strategy is demonstrated by urban population growth. With sixteen thousand inhabitants in 1740, Boston, the capital of Massachusetts Bay Colony, was the largest city in British North America. This coincided with the decline of New England's once-large indigenous population, which had been dramatically reduced by a combination of epidemics and brutal military campaigns.

Lacking a profitable agricultural export like tobacco, New England did not develop the extreme social stratification of the southern plantation colonies. Slaves and indentured servants were present, but in very small numbers. New England was ruled by the richest colonists and shared the racial attitudes of the southern colonies, but it also was the colonial society with fewest differences in wealth and status and with the most uniformly British and Protestant population in the Americas.

The Middle Atlantic Region

Much of the future success of English-speaking America was rooted in the rapid economic development and remarkable cultural diversity that appeared in the Middle Atlantic colonies. In 1624 the Dutch West India Company established the colony of New Netherland and located its capital on Manhattan Island. The colony was poorly managed and underfinanced from the start, but its location commanded the potentially profitable and strategically important Hudson River. Dutch merchants established trading relationships with the **Iroquois Confederacy**—an alliance among the Mohawk, Oneida, Onondaga, Cayuga, and Seneca peoples—and with other native peoples that gave them access to the rich fur trade of Canada. When confronted by an English military expedition in 1664, the Dutch surrendered without a fight. James, duke of York and later King James II of England, became proprietor of the colony, which was renamed New York.

New York was characterized by tumultuous politics and corrupt public administration. The colony's success was guaranteed in large measure by the development of New York City as a commercial and shipping center. Located at the mouth of the Hudson River, the city played an essential role in connecting the region's grain farmers to the booming markets of the Caribbean and southern Europe. By the early eighteenth century New York Colony had a diverse population that included English colonists; Dutch, German, and Swedish settlers; and a large slave community.

Pennsylvania began as a proprietary colony and as a refuge for Quakers, a persecuted religious minority. In 1682 William Penn secured an enormous grant of territory (nearly the size of England) because the English king Charles II was indebted to Penn's father. As proprietor (owner) of the land, Penn had sole right to establish a government, subject only to the requirement that he provide for an assembly of freemen.

Penn quickly lost control of the colony's political life, but the colony enjoyed remarkable success. By 1700 Pennsylvania had a population of more than 21,000, and

The Home of Sir William Johnson, British Superintendent for Indian Affairs, Northern District As the colonial era drew to a close, the British attempted to limit the cost of colonial defense by negotiating land settlements between native peoples and settlers. These agreements were doomed by the growing tide of western migration. William Johnson (1715–1774) maintained a fragile peace along the northern frontier by building strong personal relations with influential leaders of the Mohawk and other members of the Iroquois Confederacy. His home in present-day Johnstown, New York, shows the mixed nature of the frontier—the relative opulence of the main house offset by the two defensive blockhouses built for protection. ("Johnson Hall," by E. L. Henry. Courtesy, Albany Institute of History and Art)

Philadelphia, its capital, soon passed Boston to become the largest city in the British colonies. Healthy climate, excellent land, relatively peaceful relations with native peoples (prompted by Penn's emphasis on negotiation rather than warfare), and access through Philadelphia to good markets led to rapid economic and demographic growth in the colony.

Both Pennsylvania and South Carolina were grain-exporting colonies, but they were very different societies. South Carolina's rice plantations required large numbers of slaves. In Pennsylvania free workers, including a large number of German families, produced the bulk of the colony's grain crops on family farms. As a result, Pennsylvania's economic expansion in the late seventeenth century occurred without reproducing South Carolina's hierarchical and repressive social order. By the early eighteenth century, however, the prosperous city of Philadelphia did have a large population of black slaves and freedmen. Many were servants in the homes of wealthy merchants, but the fast-growing economy offered many opportunities in skilled trades as well.

French America

Patterns of French settlement more closely resembled those of Spain and Portugal than of England. The French were committed to missionary activity among Amerindian peoples and emphasized the extraction of natural resources—furs rather than minerals. The navigator and promoter Jacques Cartier first stirred France's interest in North America. In three voyages between 1534 and 1542, he explored the region of Newfoundland and the Gulf of St. Lawrence. A contemporary of Cortés and Pizarro, Cartier also hoped to find mineral wealth, but the stones he brought back to France turned out to be quartz and iron pyrite, "fool's gold."

The French waited more than fifty years before establishing settlements in North America. Coming to Canada after spending years in the West Indies, Samuel de Champlain founded the colony of **New France** at Quebec°, on the banks of the St. Lawrence River, in 1608. This location provided ready access to Amerindian trade routes, but it also compelled French settlers to take sides in the region's ongoing warfare. Champlain allied New France with the Huron and Algonquin peoples, traditional enemies of the powerful Iroquois Confederacy. Although French firearms and armor at first tipped the balance of power to France's native allies, the Iroquois Confederacy proved to be a resourceful and persistent enemy.

The European market for fur, especially beaver, fueled French settlement. Young Frenchmen were sent to live among native peoples to master their languages and customs. These **coureurs de bois°**, or runners of the woods, often began families with indigenous women, and they and their children, who were called métis°, helped direct the fur trade, guiding French expansion to the west and south. Amerindians actively participated in the trade because they quickly came to depend on the goods they received in exchange for furs—firearms, metal tools and utensils, textiles, and alcohol. This change in the material culture of the native peoples led to overhunting, which rapidly transformed the environment and led to the depletion of beaver and deer populations. It also increased competition among native peoples for hunting grounds, thus promoting warfare.

The proliferation of firearms made indigenous warfare more deadly. The Iroquois Confederacy responded to the increased military strength of France's Algonquin allies by forging commercial and military links with Dutch and later English settlements in the Hudson River Valley. Well armed by the Dutch and English, the Iroquois Confederacy nearly eradicated the Huron in 1649 and inflicted a series of humiliating defeats on the French. At the high point of their power in the early 1680s, Iroquois hunters and military forces gained control of much of the Great Lakes region and the Ohio River Valley. A large French military expedition and a relentless attack focused on Iroquois villages and agriculture finally checked Iroquois power in 1701.

Spain had effectively limited the spread of firearms in its colonies. But the fur trade, together with the growing military rivalry between Algonquin and Iroquois peoples and their respective French and English allies, led to the rapid spread of firearms in North America. Use of firearms in hunting and warfare moved west and south, reaching indigenous plains cultures that had previously

Canadian Fur Traders The fur trade provided the economic foundation of early Canadian settlement. Fur traders were cultural intermediaries. They brought European technologies and products like firearms and machine-made textiles to native peoples and native technologies and products like canoes and furs to European settlers. This canoe with sixteen paddlers was adapted from the native craft by fur traders to transport large cargoes.   (Frances Anne Hopkins, "Shooting the Rapids," Library and Archives Canada, Ref. # C-2774)

Quebec (kwuh-BEC)   **coureurs de bois** (koo-RUHR day BWA)
métis (may-TEES)

adopted the horse introduced by the Spanish. This intersection of horse and gun frontiers in the early eighteenth century dramatically increased the military power and hunting efficiency of the Sioux, Comanche, Cheyenne, and other indigenous peoples and slowed the pace of European settlement in the North American west.

In French Canada, the Jesuits led the effort to convert native peoples to Christianity. Building on earlier evangelical efforts in Brazil and Paraguay, French Catholic missionaries mastered native languages, created boarding schools for young boys and girls, and set up model agricultural communities for converted Amerindians. The Jesuits' greatest successes coincided with a destructive wave of epidemics and renewed warfare among native peoples in the 1630s. Eventually, churches were established throughout Huron and Algonquin territories. Nevertheless, local culture persisted. In 1688 a French nun who had devoted her life to instructing Amerindian girls expressed the frustration of many missionaries with the resilience of indigenous culture:

> We have observed that of a hundred that have passed through our hands we have scarcely civilized one. . . . When we are least expecting it, they clamber over our wall and go off to run with their kinsmen in the woods, finding more to please them there than in all the amenities of our French house.[4]

As epidemics undermined conversion efforts in mission settlements and evidence of indigenous resistance to conversion mounted, the church redirected some of its resources from the evangelical effort to the larger French settlements, founding schools, hospitals, and churches.

Responsibility for finding settlers and supervising the colonial economy was first granted to a monopoly

Map 18.2 European Claims in North America, 1755–1763 The results of the French and Indian War dramatically altered the map of North America. France's losses precipitated conflicts between Amerindian peoples and the rapidly expanding population of the British colonies.

company chartered in France. Even though the fur trade flourished, population growth was slow. Founded at about the same time as French Canada, Virginia had twenty times more European residents by 1627. After the establishment of royal authority in the 1660s, Canada's French population increased but remained at only seven thousand in 1673. Although improved fiscal management and more effective colonial government did promote a limited agricultural expansion, the fur trade remained important. It is clear that Canada's small settler population and the fur trade's dependence on the voluntary participation of Amerindians allowed indigenous peoples to retain greater independence and more control over their traditional lands than was possible in the colonies of Spain, Portugal, or England. Unlike these colonial regimes, which sought to transform ancient ways of life or force the transfer of native lands, the French were compelled to treat indigenous peoples as allies and trading partners. This permitted indigenous peoples to more gradually adapt to new religious, technological, and market realities.

Despite Canada's small population, limited resources, and increasing vulnerability to attack by the English and their indigenous allies, the French aggressively expanded to the west and south. Louisiana was founded in 1699, but by 1708 there were fewer than three hundred soldiers, settlers, and slaves in the territory. Like Canada, Louisiana depended on the fur trade, exporting more than fifty thousand deerskins in 1726. Also as in Canada, Amerindians, driven by a desire for European goods, eagerly embraced this trade. In 1753 a French official reported a Choctaw leader as saying, "[The French] were the first . . . who made [us] subject to the different needs that [we] can no longer now do without."[5]

France's North American colonies were threatened by a series of wars fought by France and England and by the population growth and increasing prosperity of neighboring English colonies. The "French and Indian War" began in 1754 and led to the wider conflict called the Seven Years War, 1756–1763. This would prove to be the final contest for North American empire (see Map 18.2). England committed a larger military force to the struggle and, despite early defeats, took the French capital of Quebec in 1759. Although resistance continued briefly, French forces in Canada surrendered in 1760. The peace agreement forced France to yield Canada to the English and cede Louisiana to Spain. The differences between French and English colonial realities were suggested by the petition of one Canadian indigenous leader to a British officer after the French surrender. "[W]e learn that our lands are to be given away not only to trade thereon but also to them in full title to various [English] individuals. . . . We have always been a free nation, and now we will become slaves, which would be very difficult to accept after having enjoyed our liberty so long."[6] With the loss of Canada the French concentrated their efforts on their sugar-producing colonies in the Caribbean (see Chapter 19).

COLONIAL EXPANSION AND CONFLICT

In the last decades of the seventeenth century, all of the European colonies in the Americas began to experience a long period of economic and demographic expansion. In the next century, the imperial powers responded by strengthening their administrative and economic controls in the colonies. They also sought to force colonial populations to pay a larger share of the costs of administration and defense. These efforts at reform and restructuring coincided with a series of imperial wars fought along Atlantic trade routes and in the Americas. France's loss of its North American colonies in 1763 was one of the most important results of these struggles. Equally significant, colonial populations throughout the Americas became more aware of separate national identities and more aggressive in asserting local interests against the will of distant monarchs.

Imperial Reform in Spanish America and Brazil

Spain's Habsburg dynasty ended when the Spanish king Charles II died without an heir in 1700 (see Table 17.1 on page 510). After thirteen years of conflict involving the major European powers and factions within Spain, Philip of Bourbon, grandson of Louis XIV of France, gained the Spanish throne. Under Philip V and his Bourbon heirs, Spain's colonial administration and tax collection were reorganized. Spain's reliance on convoys protected by naval vessels was abolished; more colonial ports were permitted to trade with Spain; and intercolonial trade was expanded. Spain also created new commercial monopolies to produce tobacco, some alcoholic beverages, and chocolate. The Spanish navy was strengthened, and trade in contraband was more effectively policed.

For most of the Spanish Empire, the eighteenth century was a period of remarkable economic expansion associated with population growth. Amerindian populations

Market in Rio de Janeiro In many of the cities of colonial Latin America female slaves and black free women dominated retail markets. In this scene from late colonial Brazil, Afro-Brazilian women sell a variety of foods and crafts. *(Sir Henry Chamberlain, Views and Costumes of the City and Neighborhoods of Rio de Janeiro, London, 1822)*

began to recover from the early epidemics; the flow of Spanish immigrants increased; and the slave trade to plantation colonies was expanded. Mining, the heart of the Spanish colonial economy, increased as silver production in Mexico and Peru rose steadily into the 1780s. Agricultural exports also expanded: tobacco, dyes, hides, chocolate, cotton, and sugar joined the flow of goods to Europe.

But these reforms carried unforeseen consequences that threatened the survival of the Spanish Empire. Despite expanded silver production, the economic growth of the eighteenth century was led by the previously minor agricultural and grazing economies of Cuba, the Rio de la Plata region, Venezuela, Chile, and Central America. These export economies were less able than the mining economies of Mexico and Peru to weather breaks in trade caused by imperial wars. Each such disruption forced landowning elites in Cuba and the other regions to turn to alternative, often illegal, trade with English, French, or Dutch merchants. By the 1790s the wealthiest and most influential sectors of Spain's colonial society had come to view the Spanish Empire as an impediment to prosperity and growth.

The Spanish and Portuguese kings also sought to reduce the power of the Catholic Church in their colonies while at the same time transferring some church wealth to their treasuries. These efforts led to a succession of confrontations between colonial officials and the church hierarchy. In the Spanish Empire in particular, these disputes began to undermine the clergy's previously reliable support for the colonial state. To the kings of Portugal and Spain, the Jesuits symbolized the independent power of the church. As a result, the order was expelled from the realms of the Portuguese king in 1759 and from the Spanish colonies in 1767. In practice this meant forcing many colonial-born Jesuits from their native lands and shutting the doors of the schools that had educated many members of the colonial elite.

Bourbon political and fiscal reforms also contributed to a growing sense of colonial grievance by limiting creoles' access to colonial offices and by imposing new taxes and monopolies that transferred more colonial wealth to Spain. Consumer and producer resentment in the colonies led to a series of violent confrontations with Spanish administrators when monopolies were imposed on tobacco, cacao (chocolate), and brandy. Because these reforms produced a more intrusive and expensive colonial government, many colonists saw the changes as an abuse of the informal constitution that had long governed the empire. Only in the Bourbon effort to expand colonial militias in the face of English threats did creoles find opportunity for improved status and greater responsibility.

In addition to tax rebellions and urban riots, colonial policies also provoked Amerindian uprisings beginning in the 1770s. Most spectacular was the rebellion initiated in 1780 by the Peruvian Amerindian leader José Gabriel Condorcanqui. He took the name of his Inca ancestor Tupac Amaru°, who had been executed by the Spanish in 1572. **Tupac Amaru II** was well connected in Spanish colonial society. He had been educated by the Jesuits and had close ties to the Bishop of Cuzco and other powerful church authorities. He was also actively involved in trade with the silver mines at Potosí. Despite these connections, he still resented the abuse of Amerindian villagers.

Historians still debate the objectives of this rebellion. Tupac Amaru's own pronouncements did not clearly state whether he sought to end local injustices or overthrow Spanish rule. His bitter dispute with a local Spanish judge who challenged his hereditary rights provided the initial provocation. Tupac Amaru also sought to redress grievances of Amerindian communities suffering under the mita and tribute obligations. His rebellion quickly spread across Alto Peru (Bolivia) and attracted creoles, mestizos, and slaves as well as Amerindians. Tupac Amaru II was captured in 1781 and brutally executed, as were his wife and fifteen other family members and allies. After the execution, Amerindian rebels continued the struggle for more than two years. By the time Spanish authority was firmly reestablished, more than 100,000 lives had been lost and enormous amounts of property destroyed.

Brazil experienced a similar period of expansion and reform after 1700. Portugal created new administrative positions and gave monopoly companies exclusive rights to little-developed regions. As in Spanish America, a more intrusive colonial government that imposed new taxes led to rebellions and plots, including open warfare in 1707 between "sons of the soil" and "outsiders" in São Paulo. The most aggressive period of reform occurred during the ministry of the marquis of Pombal (1750–1777). The Pombal reforms were made possible by an economic expansion fueled by the discovery of gold in the 1690s and diamonds after 1720 as well as by the development of

markets for Brazil's coffee and cotton. The colony's economic expansion depended on an increase in the slave trade: nearly 2 million African slaves were imported in the eighteenth century.

Reform and Reorganization in British America

England's efforts to reform and reorganize its North American colonies began earlier than the Bourbon initiative in Spanish America. After the period of Cromwell's Puritan Republic (see Chapter 17), the restored Stuart king, Charles II, undertook an ambitious campaign to establish greater Crown control over the colonies. Between 1651 and 1673 a series of Navigation Acts sought to severely limit colonial trading and colonial production that competed directly with English manufacturers. James II also attempted to increase royal control over colonial political life. Royal governments replaced original colonial charters as in Massachusetts and proprietorships as in the Carolinas. Because the New England colonies were viewed as centers of smuggling, the king temporarily suspended their elected assemblies. At the same time, he appointed colonial governors and granted them new fiscal and legislative powers.

James II's overthrow in the Glorious Revolution of 1688 ended this confrontation, but not before colonists were provoked to resist and, in some cases, rebel. They overthrew the governors of New York and Massachusetts and removed the Catholic proprietor of Maryland. William and Mary restored relative peace, but these conflicts alerted the colonists to the potential for aggression by the English government. Colonial politics would remain confrontational until the American Revolution.

During the eighteenth century the English colonies experienced renewed economic growth and attracted a new wave of European immigration, but social divisions were increasingly evident. The colonial population in 1770 was more urban, more clearly divided by class and race, and more vulnerable to economic downturns. Crises were provoked when imperial wars with France and Spain disrupted trade in the Atlantic, increased tax burdens, forced military mobilizations, and provoked frontier conflicts with the Amerindians. On the eve of the American Revolution, England defeated France and weakened Spain. The cost, however, was great. Administrative, military, and tax policies imposed to gain empirewide victory alienated much of the American colonial population.

Tupac Amaru (TOO-pack a-MAH-roo)

COMPARATIVE PERSPECTIVES

The New World colonial empires of Spain, Portugal, France, and England had many characteristics in common. All subjugated Amerindian peoples and introduced large numbers of enslaved Africans. Within all four empires forests were cut down, virgin soils were turned by the metal plow for the first time, and Old World animals and plants were introduced. Colonists in all four applied the technologies of the Old World to the resources of the New, producing wealth and exploiting the commercial possibilities of the emerging Atlantic market.

Each of the New World empires also reflected the distinctive cultural and institutional heritages of its colonizing power. Mineral wealth allowed Spain to develop the most centralized empire. Political and economic power was concentrated in the great capital cities of Mexico City and Lima. Portugal and France pursued in their colonies objectives similar to Spain's. However, neither Brazil's agricultural economy, based on sugar, nor France's Canadian fur trade produced the financial resources that would make possible the level of centralized political control achieved by Spain. Nevertheless, unlike Britain, all three of these

Catholic powers were able to impose and enforce significant levels of religious and cultural uniformity.

Greater cultural and religious diversity characterized British North America. Colonists were drawn from throughout the British Isles and included all of Britain's numerous religious traditions. They were joined by German, Swedish, Dutch, and French Protestant immigrants. British colonial government varied somewhat from colony to colony and was more responsive to local interests. Thus colonists in British North America were better able than those in the areas controlled by Spain, Portugal, and France to respond to changing economic and political circumstances and to influence government policies. Most importantly, the British colonies attracted many more European immigrants than did the other New World colonies. Between 1580 and 1760 French colonies received 60,000 immigrants, Brazil 523,000, and the Spanish colonies 678,000. Within a shorter period—between 1600 and 1760—the British settlements welcomed 746,000. Population in British North America—free and slave combined—had reached an extraordinary 2.5 million by 1775.

SUMMARY

○— How did the Columbian Exchange alter the natural environment of the Americas?

○— What role did forced labor play in the main industries in Spanish America and Brazil?

○— What were the main similarities and differences among colonies of Spain, Portugal, England, and France?

○— What were the effects of the colonial reforms and wars among imperial powers that dominated the Americas during the eighteenth century?

Online Study Center
ACE the Test

The creation of colonies in the Western Hemisphere led to the introduction of new plants and animals that affected the environment and forced indigenous peoples to adapt. Europeans also brought over Old World diseases, such as smallpox, that had a devastating effect on the native populations. The exchange of plants and animals altered diets and lifestyles in dramatic ways. In their relentless effort to discover a viable basis for their settlements, European colonists introduced sugar, rice, and coffee. They also took Western Hemisphere domesticates, like indigo, cacao, and tobacco, and spread them to new regions. New animals such as horses, cattle, sheep, and goats faced few predators in the Americas and multiplied rapidly, threatening Amerindian agriculture in some places and making Amerindian peoples elsewhere more efficient hunters and more formidable fighters.

The rapid development of the Spanish colonies was promoted by the discovery of rich gold and silver mines. The concentration of the mines in Mexico and the Andean region allowed Spain to impose taxes that financed a large and intrusive bureaucracy led by viceroys located in Mexico City and Lima. It also concentrated wealth in a network of large colonial cities. The sugar industry was crucial to Brazil, but nearly a century passed before profits permitted a dramatic expansion in Portuguese colonial government that culminated with the appointment of the first viceroy in 1749, more than two centuries after the same office was created in Spanish America. In those parts of the Spanish and Portuguese colonies where Amerindian populations survived in significant numbers, various forms of compulsory labor service were imposed. In the Spanish Empire the encomienda and mita forced tens of thousands of indigenous laborers to work in mines, farms, and factories. In Brazil the Portuguese permitted the enslavement of Amerindians, and slave raiding into neighboring Spanish colonies roiled the border until nearly the end of the colonial era in the nineteenth century. Eventually the sugar plantations of Brazil depended on the African slave trade, importing nearly 2 million slaves in the eighteenth century.

French Canada was founded with the false hope that mineral wealth would be discovered, but it survived because of the modest profits of the fur trade. Population grew slowly, and France relied on alliances with native peoples to exploit the fur trade and protect its colony from European rivals. In the Caribbean, France imitated the plantation model developed by the Portuguese in Brazil and by the Dutch and English on their island possessions. All the Caribbean colonies established by Europeans came to depend on slavery to produce tropical export crops like sugar, tobacco, cacao, and coffee.

The English colonies of North America followed a different path. Settlements were first created by groups of private investors or by religious minorities. England never established the unified, hierarchical model that concentrated power in a single individual, a viceroy. Settlers generally exercised greater political power, and effective local control was a reality in many colonies. The economies of British North America were more diverse and much less profitable in the seventeenth and early eighteenth centuries than were the colonies of Spain and Portugal. With the exception of the southern colonies' rice, tobacco, and indigo regions that came to depend on slave labor, the English-speaking colonies of North America relied on diverse economic activities such as commercial services, shipbuilding, fishing, and food crops. While slavery was important to these colonies, free immigration and indentured laborers were more common than anywhere else in the Western Hemisphere.

The eighteenth century brought economic and population growth across the Americas. The century also witnessed a series of destructive and costly wars among the European colonial powers. In an effort to force the colonies to pay a greater share of the costs of imperial defense, Spain, Portugal, England, and France all introduced new taxes and created more intrusive colonial governments. With these reforms came increased resentment among colonial populations as well as tax rebellions and riots. The failed rebellion led by Tupac Amaru II in the Andean region of Spanish South America was the largest and most costly, but conspiracies and riots afflicted Brazil as well. In British North America, colonists overthrew the governors of New York and Massachusetts, and tensions would remain high until the American Revolution.

KEY TERMS

Columbian Exchange   *p. 520*

Council of the Indies   *p. 523*

Bartolomé de Las Casas
   p. 526

Potosí   *p. 526*

encomienda   *p. 528*

creoles   *p. 529*

mestizo   *p. 533*

mulatto   *p. 534*

indentured servant   *p. 535*

House of Burgesses   *p. 535*

Pilgrims   *p. 536*

Puritans   *p. 536*

Iroquois Confederacy
   p. 537

New France   *p. 539*

coureurs de bois   *p. 538*

Tupac Amaru II   *p. 543*

Online Study Center
Improve Your Grade
Flashcards

SUGGESTED READING

Alfred W. Crosby, Jr., is justifiably the best-known student of the Columbian Exchange. See his *The Columbian Exchange: Biological and Cultural Consequences of 1492* (1972) and *Ecological Imperialism* (1986). William H. McNeill, *Plagues and Peoples* (1976), puts the discussion of the American exchange in a world history context. Elinor G. K. Melville, *A Plague of Sheep: Environmental Consequences of the Spanish Conquest of Mexico* (1994), is the most important recent contribution to this field.

Colonial Latin America, 5th ed. (2005), by Mark A. Burkholder and Lyman L. Johnson, provides a good introduction to colonial Latin American history. *Early Latin America* (1983) by James Lockhart and Stuart B. Schwartz and *Spain and Portugal in the New World, 1492–1700* (1984) by Lyle N. McAlister are both useful introductions as well.

The specialized historical literature on the American colonial empires is extensive and deep. A sampling of useful works follows. For the early colonial period see Inga Clendinnen, *Ambivalent Conquests* (1987); James Lockhart, *The Nahuas After the Conquest* (1992); and John Hemming, *Red Gold: The Conquest of the Brazilian Indians* (1978). Nancy M. Farriss, *Maya Society Under Spanish Rule: The Collective Enterprise of Survival* (1984), is also one of the most important books on colonial Spanish America. For the Catholic Church see William Taylor, *Magistrates of the Sacred: Priests and Parishioners in Eighteenth-Century Mexico* (1996). For the church as experienced by the colonial masses, see Martin Austin Nesvig, *Local Religion in Colonial Mexico* (2006). The social complexities of colonial Ecuadorian society are clearly explored by Kris Lane, *Quito 1599* (2002). Lyman L. Johnson and Sonya Lipsett-Rivera, eds., *The Faces of Honor* (1999), provides a good introduction to the culture of honor. For the place of women see Asunción Lavrin, ed., *Sexuality and Marriage in Colonial Latin America* (1989). On issues of class R. Douglas Cope, *The Limits of Racial Domination* (1994), is recommended. On the slave trade Herbert S. Klein, *The Middle Passage* (1978), and David Eltis, *The Rise of African Slavery in the Americas* (2000), are indispensable. Frederick P. Bowser, *The African Slave in Colonial Peru, 1524–1650* (1973); Mary C. Karasch, *Slave Life and Culture in*

Rio de Janeiro, 1808–1850 (1986); and Stuart B. Schwartz, *Sugar Plantations in the Formation of Brazilian Society: Bahia, 1550–1835* (1985), are excellent introductions to the African experience in two very different Latin American societies. For the eighteenth-century Amerindian rebellions of the Andean region, see Sergio Serulnikov, *Subverting Colonial Authority* (2003).

Among the useful general studies of the British colonies are Charles M. Andrews, *The Colonial Period of American History: The Settlements*, 3 vols. (1934–1937); David Hackett Fischer, *Albion's Seed: Four British Folkways in America* (1989); and Gary B. Nash, *Red, White, and Black: The Peoples of Early America*, 2nd ed. (1982). On the economy see John J. McCusker and Russell R. Menard, *The Economy of British America, 1607–1789* (1979). For slavery see David Brion Davis, *The Problem of Slavery in Western Culture* (1966); Allan Kulikoff, *Tobacco and Slaves: The Development of Southern Cultures in the Chesapeake, 1680–1800* (1986); and Peter H. Wood, *Black Majority: Negroes in Colonial South Carolina from 1670 Through the Stono Rebellion* (1974). Among the best works on the relations between Europeans and Indians are Alan Gallay, *The Indian Slave Trade: The Rise of the English Empire in the American South, 1670–1717* (2002); James Merrill, *The Indians' New World: Catawbas and Their Neighbors from European Contact Through the Era of Removal* (1989); and Daniel H. Usner, Jr., *Indians, Settlers, and Slaves in a Frontier Exchange Economy: The Lower Mississippi Valley Before 1783* (1992).

For late colonial politics see Gary B. Nash, *Urban Crucible: Social Change, Political Consciousness, and the Origins of the American Revolution* (1979); Bernard Bailyn, *The Origins of American Politics* (1986); Jack P. Greene, *The Quest for Power: The Lower Houses of Assembly in the Southern Royal Colonies* (1963); and Richard Bushman, *King and People in Provincial Massachusetts* (1985). On immigration see Bernard Bailyn, *The Peopling of British North America* (1986).

On French North America, William J. Eccles, *France in America*, rev. ed. (1990), is an excellent overview; see also his *The Canadian Frontier, 1534–1760* (1969). G. F. G. Stanley, *New France,*

1701–1760 (1968), is also an important resource. R. Cole Harris, *The Seigneurial System in Canada: A Geographical Study* (1966), provides an excellent analysis of the topic. Harold Innis, *The Fur Trade in Canada: An Introduction to Canadian Economic History* (1927), remains indispensable. Also of value are Cor-

nelius Jaenen, *The Role of the Church in New France* (1976); Carole Blackburn, *Harvest of Souls: The Jesuit Missions and Colonialism in North America, 1632–1650* (2000); and Alison L. Prentice, *Canadian Women: A History* (1988).

NOTES

1. Quoted in Alfred W. Crosby, Jr., *The Columbian Exchange: Biological and Cultural Consequences of 1492* (Westport, CT: Greenwood, 1972), 58.
2. Fray Andés de Moguer, 1554, quoted in James Lockhart and Enrique Otte, eds., *Letters and People of the Spanish Indies Sixteenth Century* (1976), 216.
3. Crosby, *The Columbian Exchange*, 58.
4. Quoted in R. Douglas Francis, Richard Jones, and Donald B. Smith, *Origins: Canadian History to Confederation* (Toronto: Holt, Rinehart, and Winston of Canada, 1992), 52.
5. Quoted in Daniel H. Usner, Jr., *Indians, Settlers and Slaves in a Frontier Exchange Economy: The Lower Mississippi Valley Before 1783*, Institute of Early American History and Culture Series (Chapel Hill: University of North Carolina Press, 1992), 96.
6. Quoted in Cornelius J. Jaenen, "French and Native Peoples in New France," in *Interpreting Canada's Past*, ed. J. M. Bumsted, vol. 1, 2nd ed. (Toronto: Oxford University Press, 1993), 73.

Caribbean Sugar Mill The windmill crushes sugar cane, whose juice is boiled down in the smoking building next door. (From William Clark, *Ten Views in the Islands of Antigua*, 1823. British Library)

How important was sugar production to the European colonies of the West Indies and to the expansion of the African slave trade?

What effect did sugar plantations have on the natural environment and on living conditions?

What was the relationship between private investors and European governments in the development of the Atlantic economy?

How did sub-Saharan Africa's expanding contacts in the Atlantic compare with its contacts with the Islamic world?

19

THE ATLANTIC SYSTEM AND AFRICA, 1550–1800

CHAPTER OUTLINE

Plantations in the West Indies

Plantation Life in the Eighteenth Century

Creating the Atlantic Economy

Africa, the Atlantic, and Islam

Comparative Perspectives

ENVIRONMENT AND TECHNOLOGY: Amerindian Foods in Africa

DIVERSITY AND DOMINANCE: Slavery in West Africa and the Americas

By the eighteenth century, Caribbean colonies had become the largest producers of sugar in the world. Slaves represented about 90 percent of the islands' population and were forced to work in the fields harvesting the crops, as well as in mills where the sugar cane was crushed and processed before being shipped off to Europe.

The profitable expansion of sugar agriculture in the Caribbean in the seventeenth century opened a new era in the African slave trade. As English, French, and Dutch sugar producers competed for slaves with the well-established Portuguese in Brazil, the number of merchants and ships in this cruel trade increased. Larger and faster ships carried slaves from Africa, but the human cost remained high, as the following example demonstrates.

Online Study Center

This icon will direct you to interactive activities and study materials on the website: *college.hmco.com/pic/bulliet4e.*

In 1694 the English ship *Hannibal* called at the West African port of Whydah° to purchase slaves. The king of Whydah invited the ship's captain and officers to his residence, where they negotiated an agreement on the prices for slaves. In all, the *Hannibal* purchased 692 slaves, of whom about a third were women and girls. The ship's doctor then carefully inspected the naked captives to be sure they were of sound body, young, and free of disease. After their purchase, the slaves were branded with an H (for *Hannibal*) to establish ownership. Once they were loaded on the ship, the crew put shackles on the men to prevent their escape.

To keep the slaves healthy, the captain had the crew feed them twice a day on boiled corn meal and beans brought from Europe and flavored with hot peppers and palm oil purchased in Africa. Each slave received a pint (half a liter) of water with every meal. In addition, the slaves were made to "jump and dance for an hour or two to our bagpipe, harp, and fiddle" every evening to keep them fit. Despite the incentives and precautions for keeping the cargo alive, deaths were common among the hundreds of people crammed into every corner of a slave ship. The *Hannibal*'s experience was worse than most, losing 320 slaves and 14 crew members to smallpox and dysentery during the seven-week voyage to Barbados.

As the *Hannibal*'s experience suggests, the Atlantic slave trade took a devastating toll in African lives and was far from a sure-fire money maker for European investors, who in this case lost more than £3,000 on the voyage. Nevertheless, the slave trade and plantation slavery were crucial pieces of a booming new **Atlantic system** that moved goods and wealth, as well as peoples and cultures, around the Atlantic.

PLANTATIONS IN THE WEST INDIES

The West Indies was the first place in the Americas reached by Columbus, and it was also the first region in the Americas where native populations collapsed from epidemics. It took a long time to repopulate these islands from abroad and forge new economic links between them and other parts of the Atlantic. But after 1650 sugar plantations, African slaves, and European capital made these islands a major center of the Atlantic economy.

Colonization Before 1650

Spanish settlers introduced sugar-cane cultivation into the West Indies shortly after 1500, but these colonies soon fell into neglect as attention shifted to colonizing the American mainland. After 1600 the West Indies revived as a focus of colonization, this time by northern Europeans interested in growing tobacco and other crops. In the 1620s and 1630s English colonization societies founded small European settlements on Montserrat°, Barbados°, and other Caribbean islands, while the French colonized Martinique°, Guadeloupe°, and some other islands. Because of greater support from their government, the English colonies prospered first, largely by growing tobacco for export.

This New World leaf, long used by Amerindians for recreation and medicine, was finding a new market among seventeenth-century Europeans. Despite the opposition of individuals like King James I of England, who condemned tobacco smoke as "dangerous to the eye, hateful to the nose, harmful to the brain, and dangerous to the lungs," the habit spread. By 1614 tobacco was reportedly being sold in seven thousand shops in and around London, and some English businessmen were dreaming of a tobacco trade as valuable as Spain's silver fleets.

Turning such pipe dreams into reality was not easy. Diseases, hurricanes, and attacks by the native Carib as well as the Spanish threatened the early French and English West Indies settlements. They also suffered from shortages of supplies from Europe and shortages of labor sufficient to clear and plant virgin land with tobacco. Two changes improved the colonies' prospects. One was the formation of **chartered companies**. To promote national claims without government expense, France and England gave groups of private investors monopolies over trade to their West Indies colonies in exchange for the payment of annual fees. These companies then began to provide passage to the colonies for poor Europeans who paid off their debt for transportation by working three or four years for the established colonists as indentured servants (see Chapter 18). Under this system the French and English population on several tobacco islands grew rapidly in the 1630s and 1640s. By the middle of the century, however, the Caribbean colonies were in crisis

Whydah (WEE-duh)

Montserrat (mont-suh-RAHT)   **Barbados** (bahr-BAY-dohs)
Martinique (mahr-tee-NEEK)   **Guadeloupe** (gwah-duh-LOOP)

C H R O N O L O G Y		
West Indies	**Atlantic**	**Africa**
1500 **ca. 1500** Spanish settlers introduce sugar-cane cultivation	**1530** Amsterdam Exchange opens	**1500–1700** Gold trade predominates **1591** Morocco conquers Songhai
1600 **1620s and 1630s** English and French colonies in Caribbean **1640s** Dutch bring sugar plantation system from Brazil **1655** English take Jamaica **1670s** French occupy western half of Hispaniola (modern Haiti)	**1621** Dutch West India Company chartered **1654** Dutch expelled from Brazil **1660s** English Navigation Acts **1672** Royal African Company chartered **1698** French Exclusif	**1638** Dutch take Elmina **1680s** Rise of Asante
1700 **1700** West Indies surpass Brazil in sugar production **1760** Tacky's rebellion in Jamaica	**1700 to present** Atlantic system flourishing **1713** English receive slave trade monopoly from Spanish Empire	**1700–1830** Slave trade predominates **1720s** Rise of Dahomey **1730** Oyo makes Dahomey pay tribute

because of stiff competition from milder Virginia-grown tobacco, also cultivated by indentured servants.

The English, French, and Dutch colonies of the Caribbean emerged from this crisis richer than before, but the region's economy would be based on the cultivation of sugar cane, not tobacco, and the labor force would be overwhelmingly composed of African slaves, not European indentured laborers and free settlers. The Portuguese had introduced sugar cultivation into Brazil from islands along the African coast after 1550 and had soon introduced enslaved African labor as well (see Chapter 18). By 1600 Brazil was the Atlantic world's greatest sugar producer. Some Dutch merchants invested in Brazilian sugar plantations so that they might profit from transporting the sugar across the Atlantic and distributing it in Europe. However, in the first half of the seventeenth century the Dutch were fighting for their independence from the Spanish crown, which then ruled Portugal and Brazil. As part of that struggle, the Dutch government chartered the **Dutch West India Company** in 1621 to carry the conflict to Spain's overseas possessions.

Not just a disguised form of the Dutch navy, the Dutch West India Company was a private trading company. Its investors expected the company's profits to cover its expenses and pay them dividends. After the capture of a Spanish treasure fleet in 1628, the company used some of the windfall to pay its stockholders a huge dividend and the rest to finance an assault on Brazil's valuable sugar-producing areas. By 1635 the Dutch company controlled 1,000 miles (1,600 kilometers) of northeastern Brazil's coast. Over the next fifteen years the new Dutch owners improved the efficiency of the Brazilian sugar industry, and the company prospered by supplying the plantations with enslaved Africans and European goods and carrying the sugar back to Europe.

Like its assault on Brazil, the Dutch West India Company's entry into the African slave trade combined economic and political motives. It seized the important West African trading station of Elmina from the Portuguese in 1638 and took their port of Luanda° on the Angolan coast in 1641. From these coasts the Dutch shipped slaves to Brazil and the West Indies. Although the Portuguese were able to drive the Dutch out of Angola after a few years, Elmina remained the Dutch

---

Luanda (loo-AHN-duh)

Figure 19.1 Transatlantic Slave Trade from Africa, 1551–1850
Source: Data from David Eltis, "The Volume and Structure of the Transatlantic Slave Trade: A Reassessment," *William and Mary Quarterly,* 3rd Series, 58 (2001), tables II and III.

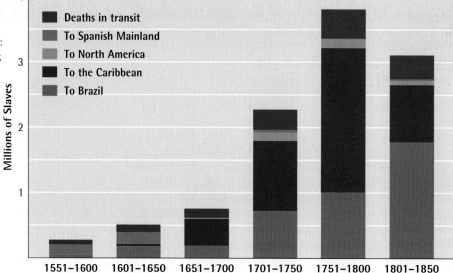

West India Company's headquarters in West Africa.

Once free of Spanish rule in 1640, the Portuguese crown turned its attention to reconquering Brazil. By 1654 Portuguese armies had driven the last of the Dutch sugar planters from Brazil. Some of the expelled planters transplanted their capital and knowledge of sugar production to small Caribbean colonies, which the Dutch had founded earlier as trading bases with Spanish colonies; others introduced the Brazilian system into English and French Caribbean islands. This was a momentous turning point in the history of the Atlantic economy.

Sugar and Slaves

The Dutch infusion of expertise and money revived the French colonies of Guadeloupe and Martinique, but the English colony of Barbados best illustrates the dramatic transformation that sugar brought to the seventeenth-century Caribbean. In 1640 Barbados's economy depended largely on tobacco, mostly grown by European settlers, both free and indentured. By the 1680s sugar had become the colony's principal crop, and enslaved Africans were three times as numerous as Europeans. Exporting up to 15,000 tons of sugar a year, Barbados had become the wealthiest and most populous of England's American colonies. By 1700 the West Indies had surpassed Brazil as the world's principal source of sugar.

The expansion of sugar plantations in the West Indies required a sharp increase in the volume of the slave trade from Africa (see Figure 19.1). During the first half of the seventeenth century about ten thousand slaves a year had arrived from Africa. Most were destined for Brazil and the mainland Spanish colonies. In the second half of the century the trade averaged twenty thousand slaves a year. More than half were intended for the English,

French, and Dutch West Indies and most of the rest for Brazil. A century later, as sugar production increased and the Spanish colony of Cuba became a major importer of slaves, the volume of the Atlantic slave trade became three times larger.

This growing dependence on African slaves was a product of many factors. Recent scholarship has cast doubt on the once-common assertion that Africans were more suited than Europeans to field labor, since newly arrived Africans and Europeans both died in large numbers in the American tropics. Africans' slightly higher survival rate was not decisive because mortality was about the same among later generations of blacks and whites born in the West Indies and acclimated to its diseases.

The West Indian historian Eric Williams also refuted the idea that the rise of African slave labor was primarily motivated by prejudice. Citing the West Indian colonies' prior use of enslaved Amerindians and indentured Europeans, along with European convicts and prisoners of war, he argued that "slavery was not born of racism: rather, racism was the consequence of slavery.[1] Williams suggested that the shift was due to the lower cost of African labor.

Yet African slaves were far from cheap. Cash-short tobacco planters in the seventeenth century preferred indentured Europeans because they cost half as much as African slaves. Poor European men and women were willing to work for little in order to get to the Americas, where they could acquire their own land cheaply at the end of their term of service. However, as the cultivation of sugar spread after 1750, rich speculators drove the price of land in the West Indies so high that end-of-term indentured servants could no longer afford to buy it. As a result, poor Europeans chose to indenture themselves in the mainland North American colonies, where cheap land was still available. Rather than raise wages to attract European laborers, Caribbean sugar planters switched to slaves.

Rising sugar prices helped the West Indian sugar planters afford the higher cost of African slaves. The fact that slaves lived seven years on average after their arrival, while the typical indentured labor contract was for only three or four years, also made slaves a better investment. The planters could rely on the Dutch and other traders to supply them with enough new slaves to meet the demands of the expanding plantations. Rising demand for slaves (see Figure 19.1) drove their sale price up steadily during the eighteenth century. These high labor costs were one more factor favoring large plantations over smaller operations.

PLANTATION LIFE IN THE EIGHTEENTH CENTURY

To find more land for sugar plantations, France and England founded new Caribbean colonies. In 1655 the English had wrested the island of Jamaica from the Spanish (see Map 18.1 on page 524). They seized Havana, Cuba, in 1762 and held the city for a year. By the time the occupation had ended, English merchants had imported large numbers of slaves and Cuba had begun to switch from tobacco to sugar production. The French seized the western half of the large Spanish island of Hispaniola in the 1670s. During the eighteenth century this new French colony of Saint Domingue° (present-day Haiti) became the greatest producer of sugar in the Atlantic world, while Jamaica surpassed Barbados as England's most important sugar colony. The technological, environmental, and social transformation of these island colonies illustrates the power of the new Atlantic system.

Technology and Environment

The cultivation of sugar cane was fairly straightforward. From fourteen to eighteen months after planting, the cane was ready to be cut. The roots continued to produce new shoots that could be harvested about every nine months. Only simple tools were needed: spades for planting, hoes to control the weeds, and sharp machetes to cut the cane. What made the sugar plantation a complex investment was that it had

Saint Domingue (san doh-MANGH)

to be a factory as well as a farm. Freshly cut cane needed to be crushed within a few hours to extract the sugary sap. Thus, for maximum efficiency, each plantation needed its own expensive crushing and processing equipment.

At the heart of the sugar works was the mill where cane was crushed between sets of heavy rollers. Small mills could be turned by animal or human power, but larger, more efficient mills needed more sophisticated sources of power. Eighteenth-century Barbados went in heavily for windmills, and the French sugar islands and Jamaica used costly water-powered mills, often fed by elaborate aqueducts.

From the mill, lead-lined wooden troughs carried the cane juice to a series of large copper kettles in the boiling shed, where the excess water was boiled off, leaving a thick syrup. Workers poured the syrup into conical clay molds in the drying shed. The sugar crystals that formed in the molds were packed in wooden barrels for shipment to Europe. The dark molasses that drained off was made into rum in yet another building or barreled for export.

To make the operation more efficient and profitable, investors sought to utilize the costly crushing and refining machinery intensively. As a result, West Indian plantations expanded from an average of around 100 acres (40 hectares) in the seventeenth century to at least twice that size in the eighteenth century. Some plantations were even larger. In 1774 Jamaica's 680 sugar plantations averaged 441 acres (178 hectares) each; the largest reached over 2,000 acres (800 hectares). Jamaica specialized so heavily in sugar production that the island had to import most of its food. Saint Domingue had a comparable number of plantations of smaller average size but generally higher productivity. The French colony was also more diverse in its economy. Although sugar production was paramount, some planters raised provisions for local consumption and crops such as coffee and cacao for export.

In some ways the mature sugar plantation was environmentally responsible. The crushing mill was powered by water, wind, or animals, not fossil fuels. The boilers were largely fueled by burning the crushed cane, and the fields were fertilized by manure from the cattle. In two respects, however, the plantation was very damaging to the environment: soil exhaustion and deforestation.

Repeated cultivation of a single crop removes more nutrients from the soil than animal fertilizer and fallow periods can restore. Instead of rotating sugar with other crops in order to restore the nutrients naturally, planters found it more profitable to clear new lands when yields declined in the old fields. When land close to the sea was exhausted, planters moved on to new islands. Many of the English who first settled Jamaica were from Barbados, and the pioneer planters on Saint Domingue came from

Plantation Scene, Antigua, British West Indies   The sugar made at the mill in the background was sealed in barrels and loaded on carts that oxen and horses drew to the beach. By means of a succession of vessels the barrels were taken to the ship that hauled the cargo to Europe. The importance of African labor is evident from the fact that only one white person appears in the painting.   (Courtesy of the John Carter Brown Library at Brown University)

older French sugar colonies. In the second half of the eighteenth century, Jamaican sugar production began to fall behind that of Saint Domingue, which still had access to virgin land. Thus the plantations of this period were not a stable form of agriculture but rather gradually laid waste to the landscape in the search for higher yields.

Deforestation, the second form of environmental damage, continued a trend begun in the sixteenth century. The Spanish had cut down some forests in the Caribbean to make pastures for the cattle they introduced. Sugar cultivation rapidly accelerated land clearing. Forests near the coast were the first to disappear, and by the end of the eighteenth century only land in the interior of the islands retained dense forests.

Combined with soil exhaustion and deforestation, other changes profoundly altered the ecological balance of the West Indies. By the eighteenth century nearly all of the domesticated animals and cultivated plants in the Caribbean were those introduced by Europeans. The Spanish had brought cattle, pigs, and horses, all of which multiplied so rapidly that no new imports had been necessary after 1503. They had also introduced new plants.

Of these, bananas and plantain from the Canary Islands were a valuable addition to the food supply, and sugar and rice formed the basis of plantation agriculture, along with native tobacco. Other food crops arrived with the slaves from Africa, including okra, black-eyed peas, yams, grains such as millet and sorghum, and mangoes. Many of these new animals and plants were useful additions to the islands, but they crowded out indigenous species. New World foods also found their way to Africa (see Environment and Technology: Amerindian Foods in Africa).

The most tragic and dramatic transformation in the West Indies occurred in the human population. Chapter 16 detailed how the indigenous Arawak (Taino) peoples of the large islands were wiped out by disease and abuse within fifty years of Columbus's first voyage. As the plantation economy spread, the Carib surviving on the smaller islands were also pushed to the point of extinction. Far earlier and more completely than in any mainland colony, the West Indies were repeopled from across the Atlantic—first from Europe and then from Africa.

Amerindian Foods in Africa

The migration of European plants and animals across the Atlantic to the New World was one side of the Columbian Exchange (see Chapter 18). The Andean potato, for example, became a staple crop of the poor in Europe, and cassava (a Brazilian plant cultivated for its edible roots) and maize (corn) moved across the Atlantic to Africa.

Maize was a high-yielding grain that could produce much more food per acre than many grains indigenous to Africa. The varieties of maize that spread to Africa were not modern high-bred "sweet corn" but starchier types found in white and yellow corn meal. Cassava—not well known to modern North Americans except perhaps in the form of tapioca—became the most important New World food in Africa. Truly a marvel, cassava had the highest yield of calories per acre of any staple food and thrived even in poor soils and during droughts. Both the leaves and the root could be eaten. Ground into meal, the root could be made into a bread that would keep for up to six months, or it could be fermented into a beverage.

Cassava Plant   Both the leaves and the starchy root of the cassava plant could be eaten.   (Engraving from André Thevet, *Les Singularitez de la France Antarctique*. Paris: Maurice de la Porte, 1557. Courtesy of the James Bell Library, University of Minnesota)

Cassava and maize were probably accidentally introduced into Africa by Portuguese ships from Brazil that discarded leftover supplies after reaching Angola. It did not take long for local Africans to recognize the food value of these new crops, especially in drought-prone areas. As the principal farmers in Central Africa, women must have played an important role in learning how to cultivate, harvest, and prepare these foods. By the eighteenth century Lunda rulers hundreds of miles from the Angolan coast were actively promoting the cultivation of maize and cassava on their royal estates in order to provide a more secure food supply.

Some historians of Africa believe that in the inland areas these Amerindian food crops provided the nutritional base for a population increase that partially offset losses due to the Atlantic slave trade. By supplementing the range of food crops available and by enabling populations to increase in once lightly settled or famine-prone areas, cassava and maize, along with peanuts and other New World legumes, permanently altered Africans' environmental prospects.

Slaves' Lives

During the eighteenth century West Indian plantation colonies were the world's most polarized societies. On most islands 90 percent or more of the inhabitants were slaves. Power resided in the hands of a **plantocracy**, a small number of very rich men who owned most of the slaves and most of the land. Between the slaves and the masters might be found only a few others—some estate managers and government officials and, in the French islands, small farmers, both white and black. Thus it is only a slight simplification to describe eighteenth-century Caribbean society as being made up of a large, abject class of slaves and a small, powerful class of masters.

The profitability of a Caribbean plantation depended on extracting as much work as possible from the slaves. Their long workday might stretch to eighteen hours or more when the cane harvest and milling were in full swing. Sugar plantations achieved exceptional productivity through the threat and use of force. As Table 19.1 shows, on a typical Jamaican plantation about 80 percent of the slaves actively engaged in productive tasks; the only exceptions were infants, the seriously ill, and the very old. Everyone on the plantation, except those disabled by age or infirmity, had an assigned task.

Table 19.1 also illustrates how slave labor was organized by age, sex, and ability. As in other Caribbean colonies, only 2 or 3 percent of the slaves were house servants. About 70 percent of the able-bodied slaves worked in the fields, generally in one of three labor gangs. A "great gang," made up of the strongest slaves in the prime of life, did the heaviest work, such as breaking up the soil at the beginning of the planting season. A second gang of youths, elders, and less fit slaves did somewhat lighter work. A "grass gang," composed of children under the supervision of an elderly slave, was responsible for weeding and other simple work, such as collecting grass for the animals. Women often formed the majority of the field laborers, even in the great gang. Nursing mothers took their babies with them to the fields. Slaves too old for field labor tended the toddlers.

Because slave ships brought twice as many males as females from Africa, men outnumbered women on Caribbean plantations. As Table 19.1 shows, a little over half of the adult males were employed in nongang work. Some tended the livestock, including the mules and oxen that did the heavy carrying work; others were skilled craftsmen, such as blacksmiths and carpenters. The most important artisan slave was the head boiler, who oversaw the delicate process of reducing the cane sap to crystallized sugar and molasses.

Skilled slaves received rewards of food and clothing or time off for good work, but the most common reason for working hard was to escape punishment. A slave gang was headed by a privileged male slave, appropriately called the "**driver**," whose job was to ensure that the gang completed its work. Since production quotas were high, slaves toiled in the fields from sunup to sunset, except for meal breaks. Those who fell behind due to fatigue or illness soon felt the sting of the whip. Openly rebellious slaves who refused to work, disobeyed orders, or tried to escape were punished with flogging, confinement in irons, or mutilation. Sometimes slaves were punished with an "iron muzzle," which covered their faces and kept them from eating and drinking.

TABLE 19.1 Slave Occupations on a Jamaican Sugar Plantation, 1788

Occupations and Conditions	Men	Women	Boys and Girls	Total
Field laborers	62	78		140
Tradesmen	29			29
Field drivers	4			4
Field cooks		4		4
Mule-, cattle-, and stablemen	12			12
Watchmen	18			18
Nurse		1		1
Midwife		1		1
Domestics and gardeners		5	3	8
Grass-gang			20	20
Total employed	**125**	**89**	**23**	**237**
Infants			23	23
Invalids (18 with yaws)				32
Absent on roads				5
Superannuated [elderly]				7
Overall total				**304**

Source: Adapted from "Edward Long to William Pitt," in Michael Craton, James Walvin, and David Wright, eds., *Slavery, Abolition, and Emancipation* (London: Longman, 1976), 103. © Michael Craton, James Walvin, and David Wright, reprinted by permission of Pearson Education Limited.

Even though slaves did not work in the fields on Sunday, it was no day of rest, for they had to farm their own provisioning grounds to supplement meager rations, maintain their dwellings, and do other chores, such as washing and mending their rough clothes. Sunday markets, where slaves sold small amounts of produce or animals they had raised to get a little spending money, were common in the British West Indies.

Except for occasional holidays—including the Christmas-week revels in the British West Indies—there was little time for recreation and relaxation. Slaves might sing in the fields, but singing was simply a way to distract themselves from their fatigue and the monotony of the work. There was certainly no time for schooling, nor was there willingness to educate slaves beyond skills useful to the plantation.

Time for family life was also inadequate. Although the large proportion of young adults in plantation colonies ought to have had a high rate of natural increase, despite the sex imbalance that resulted from the slave trade, the opposite occurred. Poor nutrition and overwork

TABLE 19.2   Birth and Death on a Jamaican Sugar Plantation, 1779–1785

Year	Born Males	Born Females	Purchased	Died Males	Died Females	Proportion of Deaths
1779	5	2	6	7	5	1 in 26
1780	4	3	—	3	2	1 in 62
1781	2	3	—	4	2	1 in 52
1782	1	3	9	4	5	1 in 35
1783	3	3	—	8	10	1 in 17
1784	2	1	12	9	10	1 in 17
1785	2	3	—	0	3	1 in 99
Total	19	18	27	35	37	
	Born 37			Died 72		

Source: From "Edward Long to William Pitt," in Michael Craton, James Walvin, and David Wright, eds., *Slavery, Abolition, and Emancipation* (London: Longman, 1976), 105. © Michael Craton, James Walvin, and David Wright, reprinted by permission of Pearson Education Limited.

lowered fertility. The continuation of heavy fieldwork made it difficult for a woman who became pregnant to carry a child to term or, after a child's birth, to ensure the infant's survival. As a result of these conditions, along with disease and accidents from dangerous mill equipment, deaths heavily outnumbered births on West Indian plantations (see Table 19.2). Life expectancy for slaves in nineteenth-century Brazil was only 23 years of age for males and 25.5 years for females. The figures were probably similar for the eighteenth-century Caribbean. A callous opinion, common among slave owners in the Caribbean and in parts of Brazil, held that it was cheaper to import a youthful new slave from Africa than to raise one to the same age on a plantation.

The harsh conditions of plantation life played a major role in shortening slaves' lives, but the greatest killer was disease. The very young were carried off by dysentery caused by contaminated food and water. Slaves newly arrived from Africa went through the period of adjustment to a new environment known as **seasoning**, during which one-third, on average, died of unfamiliar diseases. Slaves also suffered from diseases brought with them, including malaria. On the plantation profiled in Table 19.1, for example, more than half of the slaves incapacitated by illness had yaws, a painful and debilitating skin disease common in Africa. As a consequence, only slave populations in the healthier temperate zones of North America experienced natural increase; those in tropical Brazil and the Caribbean had a negative rate of growth.

Such high mortality greatly added to the volume of the Atlantic slave trade, since plantations had to purchase new slaves every year or two just to replace those who died (see Table 19.2). The additional imports of

slaves to permit the expansion of the sugar plantations meant that the majority of slaves on most West Indian plantations were African-born. As a result, African religious beliefs, patterns of speech, styles of dress and adornment, and music were prominent parts of West Indian life.

Given the harsh conditions of their lives, it is not surprising that slaves in the West Indies often sought to

Punishment for Slaves   In addition to whipping and other cruel punishments, slave owners devised other ways to shame and intimidate slaves into obedience. This metal face mask prevented the wearer from eating or drinking. (By permission of the Syndics of Cambridge University Library)

regain the freedom into which most had been born. Individual slaves often ran away, hoping to elude the men and dogs that would track them. Sometimes large groups of plantation slaves rose in rebellion against their bondage and abuse. For example, a large rebellion in Jamaica in 1760 was led by a slave named Tacky, who had been a chief on the Gold Coast of Africa. One night his followers broke into a fort and armed themselves. Joined by slaves from nearby plantations, they stormed several plantations, setting them on fire and killing the planter families. Tacky died in the fighting that followed, and three other rebel leaders stoically endured cruel deaths by torture that were meant to deter others from rebellion.

Because they believed rebellions were usually led by slaves with the strongest African heritage, European planters tried to curtail African cultural traditions. They required slaves to learn the colonial language and discouraged the use of African languages by deliberately mixing slaves from different parts of Africa. In French and Portuguese colonies, slaves were encouraged to adopt Catholic religious practices, though African deities, beliefs, and practices survived, serving as the foundation for modern African-derived religions like candomblé. In the British West Indies, where only Quaker slave owners encouraged Christianity among their slaves before 1800, African herbal medicine remained strong, as did African beliefs concerning nature spirits and witchcraft.

Free Whites and Free Blacks

The lives of the small minority of free people were very different from the lives of slaves. In the French colony of Saint Domingue, which had nearly half of the slaves in the Caribbean in the eighteenth century, free people fell into three distinct groups. At the top of free society were the wealthy owners of large sugar plantations (the *grands blancs*°, or "great whites"), who dominated the economy and society of the island. Second came less-well-off Europeans (*petits blancs*°, or "little whites"). Most of them served as colonial officials and retail merchants or raised provisions for local consumption and crops such as coffee, indigo, and cotton for export. Most owned slaves. Third came the free blacks. Though nearly as numerous as the free whites and engaged in similar occupations, they ranked below whites socially. A surprising number of the more prosperous black artisans and small landowners also owned slaves.

grands blancs (grawn blawnk)   **petits blancs** (pay-TEE blawnk)

Online Study Center
Improve Your Grade
Primary Source: The Interesting Narrative of Olaudah Equt and Written by Himself

The dominance of the plantocracy was even greater in British colonies. Whereas sugar constituted about half of Saint Domingue's exports, in Jamaica the figure was over 80 percent. Such concentration on sugar cane left much less room for small cultivators, white or black, and confined most landholding to a few larger owners. At midcentury three-quarters of the farmland in Jamaica belonged to individuals who owned 1,000 acres (400 hectares) or more.

One source estimated that a planter had to invest nearly £20,000 ($100,000) to acquire even a medium-size Jamaican plantation of 600 acres (240 hectares) in 1774. A third of this money went for land on which to grow sugar and food crops, pasture animals, and cut timber and firewood. A quarter of the expense was for the sugar works and other equipment. The largest expense was to purchase 200 slaves at about £40 ($200) each. In comparison, the wage of an English rural laborer at this time was about £10 ($50) a year (one-fourth the price of a slave), and the annual incomes in 1760 of the ten wealthiest noble families in Britain averaged only £20,000 each.

Reputedly the richest Englishmen of this time, West Indian planters often translated their wealth into political power and social prestige. The richest planters put their plantations under the direction of managers and lived in Britain, often on rural estates that once had been the preserve of country gentlemen. Between 1730 and 1775 seventy of these absentee planters secured election to the British Parliament, where they formed an influential voting bloc. Those who resided in the West Indies had political power as well, for the British plantocracy controlled the colonial assemblies.

In most European plantation colonies it was possible to grant freedom to an individual slave or group of slaves. **Manumission** (the legal grant of freedom by an owner) was more common in Brazil and the Spanish and French colonies than in English colonies. Among English colonies, manumissions were more common in the Caribbean than in North America. Many plantation owners in the Caribbean were single males, and many of them took advantage of slave women for sexual favors or took slave mistresses. It was not uncommon for a slave owner who fathered a child by a female slave to give both mother and child their freedom. But across the Americas the largest group of freed slaves had purchased their freedom, especially in the colonies of

Cudjoe, Leader of the Jamaican Maroons, Negotiates a Peace Treaty In 1738 after decades of successful resistance to the British, Cudjoe negotiated a peace treaty that recognized the freedom of his runaway followers. Unable to defeat the maroons the British also granted land and effective self-government to the maroons in exchange for an end to raids on plantations and the promise to return slave runaways for a reward. (Courtesy of National Library, Institute of Jamaica)

and Hispaniola as well as in the interior of the Guianas°. Jamaican maroons, after withstanding several attacks by the colony's militia, signed a treaty in 1738 that recognized their independence in return for their cooperation in stopping new runaways and suppressing slave revolts. Similar treaties with the large maroon population in the Dutch colony of Surinam (Dutch Guiana) recognized their possession of large inland regions.

CREATING THE ATLANTIC ECONOMY

At once archaic in their cruel system of slavery and oddly modern in their specialization in a single product for export, the West Indian plantation colonies were the bittersweet fruits of a new Atlantic trading system. Changes in the type and number of ships crossing the Atlantic illustrate the rise of this new system. The Atlantic trade of the sixteenth century calls to mind the treasure fleet, an annual convoy of twenty to sixty ships laden with silver and gold bullion from Spanish America. Two different types of merchant vessels typify the far more numerous Atlantic voyages of the late seventeenth and eighteenth centuries. One was the sugar ship, returning to Europe from the West Indies or Brazil crammed with barrels of brown sugar destined for further refinement. At the end of the seventeenth century an average of 266 sugar ships sailed every year just from the small island of Barbados. The second type of vessel was the slave ship. At the trade's peak between 1760 and 1800, some 300 ships, crammed with an average of 250 African captives each, crossed the Atlantic to the Americas each year.

Many separate pieces went into the creation of the new Atlantic economy. Besides the plantation system itself, three other elements merit further investigation: new economic institutions, new partnerships between private investors and governments in Europe, and new working relationships between European and African merchants. The new trading system is a prime example of how European capitalist relationships were reshaping the world.

France, Spain, and Portugal, where self-purchase was a right protected by the courts.

In many colonies manumission led to the development of a significant free black population. Since legal condition followed that of the mother, slave families often struggled to free women in childbearing years first so that subsequent children would be born free. By the late eighteenth century free blacks were more numerous than slaves in most of the Spanish colonies. They made up almost 30 percent of the black population of Brazil and a smaller, but still significant, percentage in the French colonies.

As in Brazil (see Chapter 18) and Spanish mainland colonies, escaped slaves constituted another part of the free black population. In the Caribbean runaways were known as **maroons**. Maroon communities were especially numerous in the mountainous interiors of Jamaica

| Capitalism and Mercantilism | The Spanish and Portuguese voyages of exploration in the fifteenth and sixteenth centuries were often government |

ventures, and both countries tried to restrict the overseas

Guianas (guy-AHN-uhs)

trade of their colonies using royal monopolies (see Chapters 16 and 18). Monopoly control, however, proved both expensive and inefficient. The success of the Atlantic economy in the seventeenth and eighteenth centuries owed much to private enterprise, which made trading venues more efficient and profitable. European private investors were attracted by the profits they could make from an established and growing trading and colonial system, but their successful participation in the Atlantic economy depended on new institutions and a significant measure of government protection that reduced the likelihood of catastrophic loss.

Two European innovations enabled private investors to fund the rapid growth of the Atlantic economy. One was the ability to manage large financial resources through mechanisms that modern historians have labeled **capitalism**. The essence of early modern capitalism was the expansion of credit and the development of large financial institutions—banks, stock exchanges, and chartered trading companies—that enabled merchants and investors to conduct business at great distances from their homes while reducing risks and increasing profits. Originally developed for business dealings within Europe, the capitalist system expanded overseas in the seventeenth century, when slow economic growth in Europe led many investors to seek greater profits in the production and export of colonial products like sugar and tobacco and in satisfying the colonial demand for European products.

Banks were a central capitalist institution. By the early seventeenth century Dutch banks had developed such a reputation for security that individuals and governments from all over western Europe entrusted them with large sums of money. To make a profit, the banks invested these funds in real estate, local industries, loans to governments, and overseas trade.

Individuals seeking returns higher than the low rate of interest paid by banks could purchase shares in a joint-stock company, a sixteenth-century forerunner of the modern corporation. Shares were bought and sold in specialized financial markets called stock exchanges. The Amsterdam Exchange, founded in 1530, became the greatest stock market in the seventeenth and eighteenth centuries. To reduce risks in overseas trading, merchants and trading companies bought insurance on their ships and cargoes from specialized companies that agreed to cover losses. Both banks and stock markets appeared much later in the Iberian world, slowing the rate of economic growth.

The capitalism of these centuries was buttressed by **mercantilism**, policies adopted by European states to promote their citizens' overseas trade and accumulate capital in the form of precious metals, especially gold and silver. Mercantilist policies strongly discouraged citizens from trading with foreign merchants and used armed force when necessary to secure exclusive relations.

Chartered companies were one of the first examples of mercantilist capitalism. A charter issued by the government of the Netherlands in 1602 gave the Dutch East India Company a legal monopoly over all Dutch trade in the Indian Ocean. This privilege encouraged private investors to buy shares in the company. They were amply rewarded when the Dutch East India Company captured control of long-distance trade routes in the Indian Ocean from the Portuguese (see Chapter 20). As we have seen, a sister firm, the Dutch West India Company, was chartered in 1621 to engage in the Atlantic trade and to seize sugar-producing areas in Brazil and African slaving ports from the Portuguese.

Such successes inspired other governments to set up their own chartered companies. In 1672 a royal charter placed all English trade with West Africa in the hands of a new **Royal African Company (RAC)**, which established its headquarters at Cape Coast Castle, just east of Elmina on the Gold Coast. The French government also played an active role in chartering companies and promoting overseas trade and colonization. Jean Baptiste Colbert°, King Louis XIV's minister of finance from 1661 to 1683, chartered French East India and French West India Companies to reduce French colonies' dependence on Dutch and English traders.

French and English governments also used military force in pursuit of commercial dominance, especially to break the trading advantage of the Dutch in the Americas. Restrictions on Dutch access to French and English colonies provoked a series of wars with the Netherlands between 1652 and 1678 (see Chapter 18), during which the larger English and French navies defeated the Dutch and drove the Dutch West India Company into bankruptcy. Military and diplomatic pressure also forced Spain after 1713 to grant England and later France monopoly rights to supply slaves (the *asiento*) to its colonies.

With Dutch competition in the Atlantic reduced, the French and English governments moved to revoke the monopoly privileges of their chartered companies. England opened trade in Africa to any English subject in 1698 on the grounds that ending monopolies would be "highly beneficial and advantageous to this kingdom." It was hoped that such competition would also cut the cost of slaves to West Indian planters, though the demand for slaves soon drove the prices up again.

Colbert (kohl-BEAR)

Such new mercantilist policies fostered competition among a nation's own citizens, while using high tariffs and restrictions to exclude foreigners. In the 1660s England had passed a series of Navigation Acts that confined trade with its colonies to English ships and cargoes. The French called their mercantilist legislation, first codified in 1698, the *Exclusif*°, highlighting its exclusionary intentions. Other mercantilist laws defended manufacturing and processing interests in Europe against competition from colonies, imposing prohibitively high taxes on any manufactured goods and refined sugar imported from the colonies.

As a result of such mercantilist measures, the Atlantic became Britain, France, and Portugal's most important overseas trading area in the eighteenth century. Britain's imports from its West Indian colonies in this period accounted for over one-fifth of the value of total British imports. The French West Indian colonies played an even larger role in France's overseas trade. Only the Dutch, closed out of much of the American trade, found Asian trade of greater importance (see Chapter 20). Profits from the Atlantic economy, in turn, promoted further economic expansion and increased the revenues of European governments.

The Atlantic Circuit

At the heart of this trading system was a clockwise network of sea routes known as the **Atlantic Circuit** (see Map 19.1). It began in Europe, ran south to Africa, turned west across the Atlantic Ocean to the Americas, and then swept back to Europe. Like Asian sailors in the Indian Ocean, Atlantic mariners depended on the prevailing winds and currents to propel their ships. What drove the ships as much as the winds and currents was the desire for the profits that each leg of the circuit was expected to produce.

The first leg, from Europe to Africa, carried European manufactures—notably metal bars, hardware, and guns—as well as great quantities of cotton textiles brought from India. Some of these goods were traded for West African gold, ivory, timber, and other products, which were taken back to Europe. More goods went to purchase slaves, who were transported across the Atlantic to the plantation colonies in the part of the Atlantic Circuit known as the **Middle Passage**. On the third leg, plantation goods from the colonies returned to Europe. Each leg carried goods from where they were abundant and relatively cheap to where they were

Exclusif (ek-skloo-SEEF)

scarce and therefore more valuable. Thus, in theory, each leg of the Atlantic Circuit could earn much more than its costs, and a ship that completed all three legs could return a handsome profit to its owners. In practice, shipwrecks, deaths, piracy, and other risks could turn profit into loss.

Online Study Center
Improve Your Grade
Interactive Map: The Atlantic
Economy, ca. 1750

The three-sided Atlantic Circuit is only one of many different commercial routes of Atlantic trade. Many other trading voyages supplemented the basic circuit with the addition of distant ports of call. Cargo ships made long voyages from Europe to the Indian Ocean, passed southward through the Atlantic with quantities of African gold and American silver, and returned with the cotton textiles necessary to the African trade. Other sea routes brought the West Indies manufactured goods from Europe or foodstuffs and lumber from New England. In addition, some Rhode Island and Massachusetts merchants participated in a "Triangular Trade" that carried rum to West Africa, slaves to the West Indies, and molasses and rum back to New England. There was also a considerable two-way trade between Brazil and Angola that exchanged Brazilian tobacco and liquor for slaves. Brazilian tobacco also found its way north as a staple of the Canadian fur trade. On another route, Brazil and Portugal exchanged sugar and gold from their colonies for European imports.

European interests dominated the Atlantic system. The manufacturers who supplied the trade goods and the investors who provided the capital were all based in Europe, but so too were the principal consumers of plantation products. Before the seventeenth century, sugar had been rare and fairly expensive in western Europe. By 1700 annual consumption of sugar in England had risen to about 4 pounds (nearly 2 kilograms) per person. Rising western European prosperity and declining sugar prices promoted additional consumption, starting with the upper classes and working its way down the social ladder. People spooned sugar into popular new beverages imported from overseas—tea, coffee, and chocolate—to overcome the beverages' natural bitterness. By 1750 annual sugar consumption in Britain had doubled, and it doubled again to about 18 pounds (8 kilograms) per person by the early nineteenth century (well below the American average of about 100 pounds [45 kilograms] a year in 1960).

The flow of sugar to Europe depended on another key component of the Atlantic trading system: the flow

Map 19.1   The Atlantic Economy   By 1700 the volume of maritime exchanges among the Atlantic continents had begun to rival the trade of the Indian Ocean Basin. Notice the trade in consumer products, slave labor, precious metals, and other goods. Silver trade to East Asia laid the basis for a Pacific Ocean economy.

Map 19.2   The African Slave Trade, 1500–1800   After 1500 a vast new trade in slaves from sub-Saharan Africa to the Americas joined the ongoing slave trade to the Islamic states of North Africa, the Middle East, and India. The West Indies were the major destination of the Atlantic slave trade, followed by Brazil.

Online Study Center
Interactive Map:
The African Slave Trade, 1500–1800

of slaves from Africa (see Map 19.2). The rising volume of the Middle Passage also measures the Atlantic system's expansion. During the first 150 years after the European discovery of the Americas, some 800,000 Africans had begun the journey across the Atlantic. During the boom in sugar production between 1650 and 1800, the slave trade amounted to nearly 7.5 million. Of the survivors, over half landed in the West Indies and nearly a third in Brazil. Plantations in North America imported another 5 percent, and the rest went to other parts of Spanish America (see Figure 19.1).

In these peak decades, the transportation of slaves from Africa was a highly specialized trade, although it regularly attracted some amateur traders hoping to make a quick profit. Most slaves were carried in ships that had been specially built or modified for the slave trade by the construction between the ships' decks of additional platforms on which the human cargo was packed as tightly as possible.

Seventeenth-century mercantilist policies placed much of the Atlantic slave trade in the hands of chartered companies. During their existence the Dutch West India Company and the English Royal African Company each carried about 100,000 slaves across the Atlantic. In the eighteenth century private English traders from Liverpool and Bristol controlled about 40 percent of the slave trade. The French, operating out of Nantes and Bordeaux, handled about half as much, and the Dutch hung on to only 6 percent. The Portuguese supplying Brazil and other places had nearly 30 percent of the Atlantic slave trade, in contrast to the 3 percent carried in North American ships.

To make a profit, European slave traders had to buy slaves in Africa for less than the cost of the goods they

Slave Ship
This model of the English vessel
Brookes shows the specially built section of the hold where enslaved Africans were packed together
during the Middle Passage. Girls, boys, and women were confined separately.   (Wilberforce House
Museum, Hull, Humberside, UK/The Bridgeman Art Library)

traded in return. Then they had to deliver as many healthy slaves as possible across the Atlantic for resale in the plantation colonies. The treacherous voyage to the Americas lasted from six to ten weeks. Some ships completed it with all of their slaves alive, but large, even catastrophic, losses of life were common (see Figure 19.1). On average, however, slave transporters succeeded in lowering mortality during the Middle Passage from about 23 percent on voyages before 1700 to half that in the last half of the eighteenth century.

Some deaths resulted from the efforts of the captives to escape. As on the voyage of the *Hannibal* recounted at the beginning of the chapter, male slaves were shackled together to prevent them from trying to escape while they were still in sight of land. Because some still managed to jump overboard in pairs, slave ships were outfitted with special netting around the outside. Some slaves developed deep psychological depression, known to contemporaries as "fixed melancholy." Crews force-fed slaves who refused to eat, but some successfully willed themselves to death.

When opportunities presented themselves (nearness to land, illness among the crew), some enslaved Africans tried to overpower their captors. To inhibit such mutinies, African men were confined below deck during most of the voyage, except at mealtimes, when they were brought up in small groups under close supervision. In any event, "mutinies" were rarely successful and were put down with brutality that occasioned further losses of life.

Other deaths during the Middle Passage were due to ill treatment. Although it was in the interests of the captain and crew to deliver their slave cargo in good condition, whippings, beatings, and even executions were used to maintain order or force captives to take nourishment. Moreover, the dangers and brutalities of the slave trade were so notorious that many ordinary seamen shunned such work. As a consequence, cruel and brutal officers and crews abounded on slave ships.

Although examples of unspeakable cruelties are common in the records, most deaths in the Middle Passage were the result of disease rather than abuse. Dysentery spread by contaminated food and water caused many deaths. Other slaves died of contagious diseases such as smallpox carried by persons whose infections were not detected during medical examinations prior to boarding. Such maladies spread quickly in the crowded and unsanitary confines of the ships, claiming the lives of many slaves already physically weakened and mentally traumatized by their ordeals.

Crew members in close contact with the slaves were exposed to the same epidemics and also died in great numbers. Moreover, sailors often fell victim to tropical diseases, such as malaria, to which Africans had acquired resistance. It is a measure of the callousness of the age, as well as the cheapness of European labor, that over the course of a round-trip voyage from Europe the proportion of crew deaths could be as high as the slave deaths.

Africa, the Atlantic, and Islam

The Atlantic system took a terrible toll in African lives both during the Middle Passage and under the harsh conditions of plantation slavery. Many other Africans died while being marched to African coastal ports for sale overseas. The overall effects on Africa of these losses and of other aspects of the slave trade have been the subject of considerable historical debate. It is clear that the trade's impact depended on the intensity and terms of different African regions' involvement.

Online Study Center
Improve Your Grade
Primary Source: A Voyage to the
New Calabar River in the Year 1699

Any assessment of the Atlantic system's effects in Africa must also take into consideration the fact that some Africans profited from the trade by capturing and selling slaves. They chained the slaves together or bound them to forked sticks for the march to the coast, then bartered them to the European slavers for trade goods. The effects on the enslaver were different from the effects on the enslaved. Finally, a broader understanding of the Atlantic system's effects in sub-Saharan Africa comes from comparisons with the effects of Islamic contacts.

The Gold Coast and the Slave Coast

As Chapter 16 showed, early European visitors to Africa's Atlantic coast were interested more in trading than in colonizing or controlling the continent. As the Africa trade mushroomed after 1650, this pattern continued. African kings and merchants sold slaves and goods at many new coastal sites, but the growing slave trade did not lead to substantial European colonization.

The transition to slave trading was not sudden. Even as slaves were becoming Atlantic Africa's most valuable export, goods such as gold, ivory, and timber remained a significant part of the total trade. For example, during its eight decades of operation from 1672 to 1752, the Royal African Company made 40 percent of its profits from dealings in gold, ivory, and forest products. In some parts of West Africa, such nonslave exports remained predominant even at the peak of the trade.

African merchants were very discriminating about what merchandise they received in return for slaves or goods. A European ship that arrived with goods of low quality or not suited to local tastes found it hard to purchase a cargo at a profitable price. European guidebooks to the African trade carefully noted the color and shape of beads, the pattern of textiles, the type of guns, and the sort of metals that were in demand on each section of the coast. In the early eighteenth century the people of Sierra Leone had a strong preference for large iron kettles; brass pans were preferred on the Gold Coast; and iron and copper bars were in demand in the Niger Delta, where smiths turned them into useful objects (see Map 19.3).

Although preferences for merchandise varied, Africans' greatest demands were for textiles, hardware, and guns. Of the goods the Royal African Company traded in West Africa in the 1680s, over 60 percent were Indian and European textiles and 30 percent were hardware and weaponry. Beads and other jewelry made up 3 percent. The rest consisted of cowrie shells that were used as money. In the eighteenth century, tobacco and rum from the Americas became welcome imports.

Both Europeans and Africans attempted to drive the best bargain for themselves and sometimes engaged in deceitful practices. The strength of the African bargaining position, however, may be inferred from the fact that as the demand for slaves rose, so too did their price in Africa. In the course of the eighteenth century the goods needed to purchase a slave on the Gold Coast doubled and in some places tripled or quadrupled.

West Africans' trading strengths were reinforced by African governments on the Gold and Slave Coasts that made Europeans observe African trading customs and prevented them from taking control of African territory. Rivalry among European nations, each of which established its own trading "castles" along the Gold Coast, also reduced Europeans' bargaining strength. In 1700 the head of the Dutch East India Company in West Africa, Willem Bosman°, bemoaned the fact that, to stay competitive against the other European traders, his company had to include large quantities of muskets and gunpowder in the goods it exchanged, thereby adding to Africans' military power.

Bosman also related that before being allowed to buy slaves at Whydah on the Slave Coast, his agents first had to pay the king a substantial customs duty and then pay a premium price for whatever slaves the king had to sell. By African standards, Whydah was a rather small kingdom controlling only that port and its immediate hinterland. In 1727 it was annexed by the larger kingdom of Dahomey°, which maintained a strong trading position with

---

Willem Bosman (VIL-uhm boos-MAHN)
Dahomey (dah-HOH-mee)

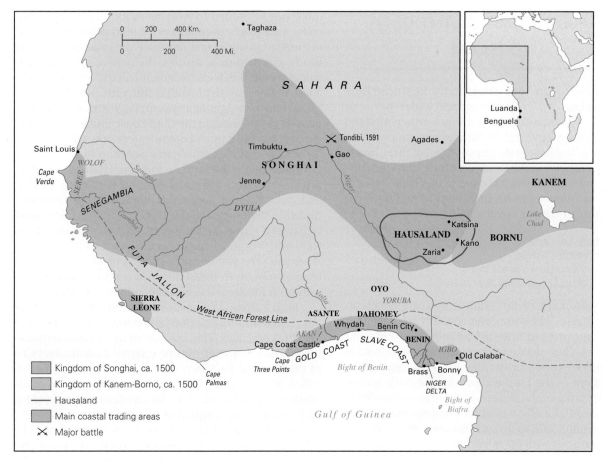

Map 19.3 West African States and Trade, 1500–1800   The Atlantic and the trans-Saharan trade brought West Africans new goods and promoted the rise of powerful states and trading communities. The Moroccan invasion of Songhai and Portuguese colonization of the Angolan ports of Luanda and Benguela showed the political dangers of such relations.

Europeans at the coast. Dahomey's rise in the 1720s depended heavily on the firearms that the slave trade supplied for its well-trained armies of men and women.

In the cases of two of Dahomey's neighbors, the connections between state growth and the Atlantic trade were more complex. One was the inland Oyo° kingdom to the northeast. Oyo cavalry overran Dahomey in 1730 and forced it to pay an annual tribute to keep its independence. The other was the newer kingdom of Asante°, west of Dahomey along the Gold Coast, which expanded rapidly after 1680. Both Oyo and Asante participated in the Atlantic trade, but neither kingdom was as dependent on it as Dahomey. Overseas trade formed a relatively modest part of the economies of these large and

populous states and was balanced by their extensive overland trade with their northern neighbors and with states across the Sahara. Like the great medieval empires of the western Sudan, Oyo and Asante were stimulated by external trade but not controlled by it.

How did African kings and merchants obtain slaves for sale? Bosman dismissed misconceptions prevailing in Europe in his day. "Not a few in our country," he wrote to a friend in 1700, "fondly imagine that parents here sell their children, men their wives, and one brother the other. But those who think so, do deceive themselves; for this never happens on any other account but that of necessity, or some great crime; but most of the slaves that are offered to us are prisoners of war, which are sold by the victors as their booty."[2] Other accounts agree that prisoners taken in war were the greatest source of slaves for the Atlantic trade, but it is difficult to say how often

---

Oyo (aw-YOH)   **Asante** (uh-SHAN-tee)

capturing slaves for export was the main cause of warfare. "Here and there," conclude two respected historians of Africa, "there are indications that captives taken in the later and more peripheral stages of these wars were exported overseas, but it would seem that the main impetus of conquest was only incidentally concerned with the slave-trade in any external direction."[3]

An early-nineteenth-century king of Asante had a similar view: "I cannot make war to catch slaves in the bush, like a thief. My ancestors never did so. But if I fight a king, and kill him when he is insolent, then certainly I must have his gold, and his slaves, and his people are mine too. Do not the white kings act like this?"[4] English rulers had indeed sentenced seventeenth-century Scottish and Irish prisoners to forced labor in the West Indies. One may imagine that the African and the European prisoners did not share their kings' view that such actions were legitimate.

The Bight of Biafra and Angola

In the eighteenth century the slave trade expanded eastward to the Bight° of Biafra. In contrast to the Gold and Slave Coasts, where strong kingdoms predominated, the densely populated interior of the Bight of Biafra contained no large states. Even so, the powerful merchant princes of the coastal ports made European traders give them rich presents. Because of the absence of sizable states, there were no large-scale wars and consequently few prisoners of war. Instead, kidnapping was the major source of slaves.

Through a network of markets and inland routes, some inland African merchants supplied European slave traders at the coast with debtors, victims of kidnapping, and convicted criminals. The largest inland traders of the Bight of Biafra were the Aro of Arochukwu, who used their control of a famous religious oracle to enhance their prestige. The Aro cemented their business links with powerful inland families and the coastal merchants through gifts and marriage alliances.

As the volume of the Atlantic trade along the Bight of Biafra expanded in the late eighteenth century, some inland markets evolved into giant fairs with different sections specializing in slaves and imported goods. In the 1780s an English ship's doctor reported that slaves were "bought by the black traders at fairs, which are held for that purpose, at a distance of upwards of two hundred miles from the sea coast." He reported seeing between twelve hundred and fifteen hundred enslaved men and women arriving at the coast from a single fair.[5]

The local context of the Atlantic trade was different south of the Congo estuary at Angola, the greatest source of slaves for the Atlantic trade (see Map 19.2). This was also the one place along the Atlantic coast where a single European nation, Portugal, controlled a significant amount of territory. Except when overrun by the Dutch for a time in the seventeenth century, Portuguese residents of the main coastal ports of Luanda and Benguela° served as middlemen between the caravans that arrived from the far interior and the ships that crossed from Brazil. From the coastal cities Afro-Portuguese traders guided large caravans of trade goods inland to exchange for slaves at special markets. Some markets met in the shadow of Portuguese frontier forts; powerful African kings controlled others.

Many of the slaves sold at these markets were prisoners of war captured by expanding African states. By the late eighteenth century slaves sold from Angolan ports were prisoners of wars fought as far as 600 to 800 miles (1,000 to 1,300 kilometers) inland. Many were victims of wars of expansion fought by the giant federation of Lunda kingdoms. As elsewhere in Africa, such prisoners usually seem to have been a byproduct of African wars rather than the purpose for which the wars were fought.

Research has linked other enslavement with environmental crises in the hinterland of Angola.[6] During the eighteenth century these southern grasslands periodically suffered severe droughts, which drove famished refugees to better-watered areas. Powerful African leaders gained control of these refugees in return for supplying them with food and water. These leaders built up their followings by assimilating refugee children, along with adult women, who were valued as food producers and for reproduction. However, they often sold adult male refugees, who were more likely than women and children to escape or challenge the ruler's authority, into the Atlantic trade. Rising Angolan leaders parceled out the Indian textiles, weapons, and alcohol they received in return for such slaves as gifts to attract new followers and to cement the loyalty of their established allies.

The most successful of these inland Angolan leaders became heads of powerful new states that stabilized areas devastated by war and drought and repopulated them with the refugees and prisoners they retained. The slave frontier then moved farther inland. This cruel system worked to the benefit of a few African rulers and merchants at the expense of the many thousands of

---

Bight (bite)

Benguela (ben-GWAY-luh)

Luanda, Angola Luanda was founded by the Portuguese in 1575 and became the center of the slave trade to Brazil. In this eighteenth-century print the city's warehouses and commercial buildings line the city streets. In the foreground captives are dragged to the port for shipment to the Western Hemisphere. (New York Public Library/Art Resource, NY)

Africans who were sent to death or perpetual bondage in the Americas.

Although the organization of the Atlantic trade in Africa varied, it was based on a partnership between European and African elites. To obtain foreign textiles, metals, and weapons, African rulers and merchants sold slaves and many products. Most of the exported slaves were prisoners taken in wars associated with African state growth. But strong African states also helped offset the Europeans' economic advantage and hindered them from taking control of African territory. Even in the absence of strong states, powerful African merchant communities everywhere dominated the movement of goods and people. The Africans who gained from these exchanges were the rich and powerful few. Many more Africans were losers in the exchanges.

Africa's European and Islamic Contacts

The ways in which sub-Saharan Africans were establishing new contacts with Europe paralleled their much older pattern of relations with the Islamic world. There were striking similarities and differences in Africans' political, commercial, and cultural interactions with these two external influences between 1500 and 1800.

During the three and a half centuries of contact up to 1800, Africans ceded very little territory to Europeans. Local African rulers kept close tabs on the European trading posts they permitted along the Gold and Slave Coasts and collected lucrative rents and fees from the traders who came there. Aside from some uninhabited islands off the Atlantic coast, Europeans established colonial beachheads in only two places. One was the Portuguese colony of Angola; the other was the Dutch East India Company's Cape Colony at the southern tip of the continent, which was tied to the Indian Ocean trade, not to the Atlantic trade. Unlike Angola, the Cape Colony did not export slaves; rather, most of the 25,750 slaves in its population in 1793 were imported from Madagascar, South Asia, and the East Indies.

North Africa had become a permanent part of the Islamic world in the first century of Islamic expansion. Sub-Saharan Africans had learned of Muslim beliefs and practices more gradually from the traders who crossed the Sahara from North Africa or who sailed from the Middle East to the Swahili trading cities of East Africa. However, the geography, trading skills, and military prowess of sub-Saharan Africans had kept them from being conquered by expansive Middle Eastern empires. During the sixteenth century all of North Africa except Morocco was annexed to the new Islamic Ottoman Empire, and Ethiopia lost

Traders Approaching Timbuktu   As they had done for centuries, traders brought their wares to this ancient desert-edge city. Timbuktu's mosques tower above the ordinary dwellings of the fabled city.   (The Art Archive)

extensive territory to other Muslim conquerors, but until 1590 the Sahara was an effective buttress against invasion.

The great **Songhai**° Empire of West Africa was pushing its dominion into the Sahara from the south. Like its predecessor Mali, Songhai drew its wealth from the trans-Saharan trade and was ruled by an indigenous Muslim dynasty (see Map 19.3). However, Songhai's rulers faced a challenge from the northwestern kingdom of Morocco, whose Muslim rulers sent a military expedition of four thousand men and ten thousand camels across the desert. Half the men perished on their way across the desert. Songhai's army of forty thousand cavalry and foot soldiers faced the survivors in 1591 but could not withstand the Moroccans, who had the advantage of firearms. Although Morocco was never able to annex the western Sudan, for the next two centuries the occupying troops extracted a massive tribute of slaves and goods from the local population and collected tolls from passing merchants.

Morocco's destruction of Songhai weakened the trans-Saharan trade in the western Sudan. The **Hausa** trading cities in the central Sudan soon attracted most of the caravans bringing textiles, hardware, and weapons

Songhai (song-GAH-ee)

across the Sahara. The goods the Hausa imported and distributed through their trading networks were similar to those coastal African traders commanded from the Atlantic trade, except for the absence of alcohol (which was prohibited to Muslims). The goods they sent back in return also resembled the major African exports into the Atlantic: gold and slaves. One unique export to the north was the caffeine-rich kola nut, a stimulant that was much in demand among Muslims in North Africa. The Hausa also exported cotton textiles and leather goods.

Few statistics of the slave trade to the Islamic north exist, but the size of the trade seems to have been substantial, if smaller than the transatlantic trade at its peak. Between 1600 and 1800, by one estimate, about 850,000 slaves trudged across the desert's various routes (see Map 19.2). A nearly equal number of slaves from sub-Saharan Africa entered the Islamic Middle East and India by way of the Red Sea and the Indian Ocean.

In contrast to the plantation slavery of the Americas, most African slaves in the Islamic world were soldiers and servants. In the late seventeenth and eighteenth centuries Morocco's rulers employed an army of 150,000 African slaves obtained from the south, whose loyalty they trusted more than the loyalty of recruits from their own lands. Other slaves worked for Moroccans on sugar plantations, as servants, and as artisans. Unlike the case in the Americas, the majority of African slaves in the Islamic world were women who served wealthy households as concubines, servants, and entertainers. The trans-Saharan slave trade also included a much higher proportion of children than did the Atlantic trade, including eunuchs meant for eventual service as harem guards. It is estimated that only one in ten of these boys survived the surgical removal of their genitals.

The central Sudanese kingdom of **Bornu** illustrates several aspects of trans-Saharan contacts. Ruled by the same dynasty since the ninth century, this Muslim state had grown and expanded in the sixteenth century as the result of guns imported from the Ottoman Empire. Bornu retained many captives from its wars or sold them as slaves to the north in return for the firearms and horses that underpinned the kingdom's military power. One Bornu king, Mai Ali, conspicuously displayed his kingdom's new power and wealth while on four pilgrimages to Mecca between 1642 and 1667. On the last, an enormous entourage of slaves—said to number fifteen thousand—accompanied him.

Like Christians of this period, Muslims saw no moral impediment to owning or trading in slaves. Indeed, Islam considered enslaving "pagans" to be a meritorious act because it brought them into the faith. Although Islam forbade the enslavement of Muslims, Muslim rulers in Bornu, Hausaland, and elsewhere were not strict observers of that rule (see Diversity and Dominance: Slavery in West Africa and the Americas).

Sub-Saharan Africans had much longer exposure to Islamic cultural influences than to European cultural influences. Scholars and merchants learned to use the Arabic language to communicate with visiting North Africans and to read the Quran. Islamic beliefs and practices as well as Islamic legal and administrative systems were influential in African trading cities on the southern edge of the Sahara and on the Swahili coast. In some places Islam had extended its influence among rural people, but in 1750 it was still very much an urban religion.

European cultural influence in Africa was even more limited. Some coastal Africans had shown an interest in Western Christianity during the first century of contact with the Portuguese, but in the 1700s only Angola had a significant number of Christians. Coastal African traders found it useful to learn one or more European languages, but African languages dominated inland trade routes. A few African merchants sent their sons to Europe to learn European ways. One of these young men, Philip Quaque°, who was educated in England, was ordained as a priest in the Church of England and became the official chaplain of

Quaque (KWAH-kay)

the Cape Coast Castle from 1766 until his death in 1816. A few other Africans learned to write in a European language, such as the Old Calabar trader Antera Duke, who kept a diary in English in the late eighteenth century.

Overall, how different and similar were the material effects of Islam and Europe in sub-Saharan Africa by 1800? The evidence is incomplete, but some assessment is possible with regard to population and possessions.

Although both foreign Muslims and Europeans obtained slaves from sub-Saharan Africa, there was a significant difference in the numbers they obtained. Between 1550 and 1800 some 8 million Africans were exported into the Atlantic trade, compared to perhaps 2 million in the Islamic trade to North Africa and the Middle East. What effect did these losses have on Africa's population? Scholars who have looked deeply into the question generally agree on three points: (1) even at the peak of the trade in the 1700s sub-Saharan Africa's overall population remained very large; (2) localities that contributed heavily to the slave trade, such as the lands behind the Slave Coast, suffered acute losses; (3) the ability of a population to recover from losses was related to the proportion of fertile women who were shipped away. The fact that Africans sold fewer women than men into the larger Atlantic trade somewhat reduced its long-term effects.

Many other factors played a role. Angola, for example, supplied more slaves over a longer period than any other part of Africa, but the trade drew upon different parts of a vast and densely populated hinterland. Moreover, the periodic population losses due to famine in this region may have been reduced by the increasing cultivation of high-yielding food plants from the Americas (see Environment and Technology: Amerindian Foods in Africa).

The impact of the goods received in sub-Saharan Africa from these trades is another topic of research. Africans were very particular about what they received, and their experience made them very adept at assessing the quality of different goods. Economic historians have questioned the older idea that the imports of textiles and metals undermined African weavers and metalworkers. First, they point out that on a per capita basis the volume of these imports was too small to have idled many African artisans. Second, the imports are more likely to have supplemented rather than replaced local production. The goods received in sub-Saharan Africa were intended for consumption and thus did not serve to develop the economy. Likewise, the sugar, tea, and chocolate Europeans consumed did little to promote economic development in Europe. However, both African and European merchants profited from trading these consumer goods. Because they directed the whole Atlantic system, Europeans gained far more wealth than Africans.

Slavery in West Africa and the Americas

*S*ocial diversity was common in Africa, and the domination of masters over slaves was a feature of many societies. Ahmad Baba (1556–1627) was an outstanding Islamic scholar in the city of Timbuktu. He came from an old Muslim family of the city. In about 1615 he replied to some questions that had been sent to him. His answers reveal a great deal about the official and unofficial condition of slavery in the Sudan of West Africa, especially in the Hausa states of Kano and Katsina (see Map 19.3).

You asked: What have you to say concerning the slaves imported from the lands of the Sudan whose people are acknowledged to be Muslims, such as Bornu, . . . Kano, Goa, Songhay, Katsina and others among whom Islam is widespread? Is it permissible to possess them [as slaves] or not?

Know—may God grant us and you success—that these lands, as you have stated are Muslim. . . . But close to each of them are lands in which are unbelievers whom the Muslim inhabitants of these lands raid. Some of these unbelievers are under the Muslims' protection and pay them [taxes]. . . . Sometimes there is war between the Muslim sultans of some of these lands and one attacks the other, taking as many prisoners as he can and selling the captive though he is a free-born Muslim. . . . This is a common practice among them in Hausaland; Katsina raids Kano, as do others, though their language is one and their situations parallel; the only difference they recognize among themselves is that so-and-so is a born Muslim and so-and-so is a born unbeliever. . . .

Whoever is taken prisoner in a state of unbelief may become someone's property, whoever he is, as opposed to those who have become Muslims of their own free will . . . and may not be possessed at all.

A little over a century later another African provided information about enslavement practices in the Western Sudan. Ayuba Suleiman Diallo (ah-YOO-bah SOO-lay-mahn JAH-loh) (1701–?) of the state of Bondu some 200 miles from the Gambia River was enslaved and transported to Maryland, where he was a slave from 1731 to 1733. When an Englishman learned of Ayuba's literacy in Arabic, he recorded his life story, anglicizing his name to Job Solomon. According to the account, slaves in Bondu did much of the hard work, while men of Ayuba's class were free to devote themselves to the study of Islamic texts.

In February, 1730, Job's father hearing of an English ship at Gambia River, sent him, with two servants to attend him, to sell two Negroes, and to buy paper, and some other necessaries; but desired him not to venture over the river, because the country of the Mandingoes, who are enemies to the people of Futa, lies on the other side. Job not agreeing with Captain Pike (who commanded the ship, lying then at Gambia, in the service of Captain Henry Hunt, brother to Mr. William Hunt, merchant, in Little Tower-street, London) sent back the two servants to acquaint his father with it, and to let him know that he intended to go no farther. Accordingly . . . he crossed the River Gambia, and disposed of his Negroes for some cows. As he was returning home, he stopped for some refreshment at the house of an old acquaintance; and the weather being hot, he hung up his arms in the house, while he refreshed himself. . . . It happened that a company of the Mandingoes, . . . passing by at that time, and observing him unarmed, rushed in, to the number of seven or eight at once, at a back door, and pinioned Job, before he could get his arms, together with his interpreter, who is a slave in Maryland still. They then shaved their heads and beards, which Job and his man resented as the highest indignity; tho' the Mandingoes meant no more by it, than to make them appear like slaves taken in war. On the 27th of February, 1730, they carried them to Captain Pike at Gambia, who purchased them; and on the first of March they were put on board. Soon after Job found means to acquaint Captain Pike that he was the same person that came to trade with him a few days before, and after what manner he had been taken. Upon this Captain Pike gave him free leave to redeem himself and his man; and Job sent to an acquaintance of his father's, near Gambia, who promised to send to Job's father, to inform him of what had happened, that he might take some course to have him set at liberty. But it being a fortnight's [two weeks'] journey between that friend's house and his father's, and the ship sailing in about a week after, Job was brought with the rest of the slaves to Annapolis in Maryland, and delivered to Mr. Vachell Denton. . . .

Mr. Vachell Denton sold Job to one Mr. Tolsey in Kent Island in Maryland, who put him to work in making tobacco; but he was soon convinced that Job had never been used to such labour. He every day showed more and more uneasiness under this exercise, and at last grew sick, being no way able to bear it; so his master was obliged to find easier work for him, and therefore put him to tend the cattle. Job would often leave the cattle, and withdraw into the woods to pray; but a white boy frequently watched him, and whilst he was at his devotion would mock him and throw dirt in his face. This very much disturbed Job, and added considerably to his other misfortunes; all which were increased by his ignorance of the English language, which prevented his complaining, or telling his case to any person about him. Grown in some measure desperate, by reason of his present hardships, he resolved to travel at a venture; thinking he might possibly be taken up by some master, who would use him better, or otherwise meet with some lucky accident, to divert or abate his grief. Accordingly, he travelled thro' the woods, till he came to the County of Kent, upon Delaware Bay. . . . There is a law in force, throughout the [mid-Atlantic] colonies . . . as far as Boston in New England, viz. that any Negroe, or white servant who is not known in the county, or has no pass, may be secured by any person, and kept in the common [jail], till the master of such servant shall fetch him. Therefore Job being able to give no account of himself, was put in prison there.

This happened about the beginning of June 1731, when I, who was attending the courts there, and heard of Job, went with several gentlemen to the [jailer's] house, being a tavern, and desired to see him. He was brought into the tavern to us, but could not speak one word of English. Upon our talking and making signs to him, he wrote a line to two before us, and when he read it, pronounced the words Allah and Mahommed; by which, and his refusing a glass of wine we offered him, we perceived he was a Mahometan [Muslim], but could not imagine of what country he was, or how he got thither; for by his affable carriage, and the easy composure of his countenance, we could perceive he was no common slave.

When Job had been some time confined, an old Negroe man, who lived in that neighborhood, and could speak the Jalloff [Wolof] language, which Job also understood, went to him, and conversed with him. By this Negroe the keeper was informed to whom Job belonged, and what was the cause of his leaving his master. The keeper thereupon wrote to his master, who soon after fetched him home, and was much kinder to him than before; allowing him place to pray in, and in some other conveniences, in order to make his slavery as easy as possible. Yet slavery and confinement was by no means agreeable to Job, who had never been used to it; he therefore wrote a letter in Arabick to his father, acquainting him with his misfortunes, hoping he might yet find means to redeem him. . . . It happened that this letter was seen by James Oglethorpe, Esq. [founder of the colony of Georgia and director of the Royal African Company]; who, according to his usual goodness and generosity, took compassion on Job, and [bought him from his master]; his master being very willing to part with him, as finding him no ways fit for his business.

In spring 1733 Job's benefactors took him to England, teaching him passable English during the voyage, and introduced him to the English gentry. Job attracted such attention that local men took up a collection to buy his freedom and pay his debts, and they also introduced him at the royal court. In 1735 Job returned to Gambia in a Royal African Company ship, richly clothed and accompanied by many gifts.

QUESTIONS FOR ANALYSIS

1. Since Ahmad Baba points out that Islamic law permitted a Muslim to raid and enslave non-Muslims, do you think that the non-Muslim Mandinka (Mandingos) would have considered it justifiable to enslave Ayuba, since he was a Muslim?

2. Which aspects of Ayuba Suleiman's experiences of enslavement were normal, and which unusual?

3. How different might Ayuba's experiences of slavery have been had he been sold in Jamaica rather than Maryland?

4. How strictly was the ban against enslaving Muslims observed in Hausaland?

Source: Thomas Hodgkin, ed., *Nigerian Perspectives: An Historical Anthology,* 2nd ed. (London: Oxford University Press, 1975), 154–156; Thomas Bluett, *Some Memoirs of the Life of Job, the Son of Solomon the High Priest of Boonda in Africa* (London: Richard Ford, 1734), 16–24.

Historians disagree in their assessment of how deeply European capitalism dominated Africa before 1800, but Europeans clearly had much less political and economic impact in Africa than in the West Indies or on the mainland of the Americas. Still, it is significant that Western capitalism was expanding rapidly in the seventeenth century, while the Ottoman Empire, the dominant state of the Middle East, was entering a period of economic and political decline (see Chapter 20). The tide of influence in Africa was thus running in the Europeans' direction.

COMPARATIVE PERSPECTIVES

The new Atlantic trading system had great importance in and momentous implications for world history. In the first phase of their expansion Europeans had conquered and colonized the Americas and captured major Indian Ocean trade routes. The development of the Atlantic system showed their ability to move beyond the conquest and capture of existing systems to create a major new trading system that could transform a region almost beyond recognition.

From the seventeenth century European powers expanded and created new colonies in the Caribbean. While these colonies remained fragile for decades, settlers found ways to profitably produce goods sought by European consumers. Tobacco dominated early but was supplanted by sugar. The West Indies felt the transforming power of capitalism more profoundly than did any other place outside Europe in this period. The establishment of sugar plantation societies was not just a matter of replacing native vegetation with alien plants and native peoples with Europeans and Africans. More fundamentally, it made these once-isolated islands part of a dynamic trading system controlled from Europe. To be sure, the West Indies was not the only place affected. Northeastern Brazil was the first region to profitably produce sugar and remained a major exporter of sugar into the nineteenth century. Other parts of the American tropics followed similar paths, producing cacao, cotton, coffee, and indigo and using slave labor.

Despite the central importance of their shared dependence on export markets and African slaves, there were important differences among the European colonies in the Caribbean region. Only the English experimented in significant ways with indentured labor, but once the English plantations began to use African slave labor the transition was accomplished very quickly because of the maritime and financial assets of this capitalist dynamo. Joint-stock companies and individual investors dominated this trade. The French entered the process late, but the French state and the monopoly companies sanctioned by the state quickly produced a massive flow of slaves while securing a profitable home market for the sugar of Saint Domingue, Guadeloupe, and France's smaller island possessions. The Dutch failed to capture and hold Portugal's sugar-producing colony of Brazil and slave-exporting colony of Angola. After this they became influential in the transfer of sugar technology to the Caribbean and also facilitated the expansion of the slave trade.

In the end they were marginalized in a series of wars with the English. While Spain had introduced sugar to the Caribbean and imported African slaves from the early sixteenth century, its most important Caribbean colony, Cuba, joined the sugar revolution late. Nevertheless, Cuba quickly became the major destination for the slave trade and the major producer of sugar by 1820.

Africa played an essential role in the Atlantic system, importing trade goods and exporting slaves to the Americas. Africa, however, was less dominated by the Atlantic system than were Europe's American colonies. Africans remained in control of their continent and interacted culturally and politically with the Islamic world more than with the Atlantic.

Historians have seen the Atlantic system as a model of the kind of highly interactive economy that became global in later centuries. For that reason the Atlantic system was a milestone in a much larger historical process, but not a monument to be admired. Its transformations were destructive as well as creative, producing victims as well as victors. Yet one cannot ignore that the system's awesome power came from its ability to create wealth.

SUMMARY

○ How important was sugar production to the European colonies of the West Indies and to the expansion of the African slave trade?

○ What effect did sugar plantations have on the natural environment and on living conditions?

○ What was the relationship between private investors and European governments in the development of the Atlantic economy?

○ How did sub-Saharan Africa's expanding contacts in the Atlantic compare with its contacts with the Islamic world?

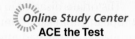

The islands of the West Indies were divided among a number of European powers. The devastating epidemics in the fifteenth and sixteenth centuries eliminated the indigenous populations of many of the islands. As a result, early settlers relied on slavery and indentured labor to produce a range of export crops. Tobacco was the most profitable of these early exports. Sugar and African slaves had been crucial to the development of Brazil, and the Caribbean imitated this model after 1650. When settlers and European investors realized sugar's profitability, they were willing to finance the forced transfer of hundreds of thousands of Africans to work the Caribbean plantations. Since Africans and their American-born descendants outnumbered Europeans across the area, African culture took root and served as an important basis for these new American societies.

Sugar plantations included the land where the sugar was harvested and the factory where sugar cane was crushed and processed. The intensive cultivation of this crop removed nutrients from the soil and led to soil exhaustion. Deforestation was also a problem, as land was rapidly cleared to keep productivity high. Finally, while new plants and animals introduced by Europeans were useful additions to the islands, they also crowded out indigenous species. All of these environmental impacts did not compare with the toll that the plantations took on human life, however. Over 90 percent of the island inhabitants were slaves forced to work in brutal conditions, while power resided in the hands of a very few rich men.

European merchants and investors played a central role in the creation of the Atlantic system. European merchants had expanded trade in the century before Columbus, trading over longer distances and using new credit mechanisms to facilitate transactions. They had engaged the markets of Asia through Muslim middlemen and initiated the first tentative contacts with African markets. By the seventeenth century a more confident and adventurous European investor class was ready to promote colonial production and long-distance trade in a much more aggressive way. The development of banks, stock exchanges, and chartered companies supported new ambitions. Chartered companies like the Royal African Company and the Dutch West India Company were not mere merchant enterprises; these companies owned fleets of armed merchant ships and maintained military forces to gain entry into new markets and to protect commercial outposts.

Sub-Saharan Africa had long-established trade connections with the Islamic world. Among the goods transported along these trade routes were slaves, and the slave trade to the Islamic north persisted long after the Atlantic trade began to decline. Islamic trade was accompanied by the spread of the religion south of the Sahara and the creation of Islamic states like Mali and Songhai (see Chapter 16). But the volume of the Atlantic trade was much larger than the Islamic trade, especially as the Caribbean islands began intensively producing sugar at the end of the seventeenth century. Between 1550 and 1800 four slaves crossed the Atlantic to European colonies for every slave carried across the Sahara. The Islamic trade took more women and children, and these slaves were seldom subjected to the brutal labor found on West Indian plantations.

KEY TERMS

Atlantic system *p. 550*
chartered companies *p. 550*
Dutch West India Company *p. 551*
plantocracy *p. 555*
driver *p. 556*
seasoning *p. 557*

manumission *p. 558*
maroon *p. 559*
capitalism *p. 560*
mercantilism *p. 560*
Royal African Company *p. 560*

Atlantic Circuit *p. 561*
Middle Passage *p. 561*
Songhai *p. 569*
Hausa *p. 569*
Bornu *p. 570*

SUGGESTED READING

The global context of early modern capitalism is examined by Immanuel Wallerstein, *The Modern World-System*, 3 vols. (1974–1989); by Fernand Braudel, *Civilization and Capitalism, 15th–18th Century*, 3 vols. (1982–1984); and in two volumes of scholarly papers edited by James D. Tracy, *The Rise of Merchant Empires* (1990) and *The Political Economy of Merchant Empires* (1991). Especially relevant are the chapters in *The Rise of Merchant Empires* by Herbert S. Klein, summarizing scholarship on the Middle Passage, and by Ralph A. Austen, on the trans-Saharan caravan trade between 1500 and 1800.

The best general introductions to the Atlantic system are Philip D. Curtin, *The Rise and Fall of the Plantation Complex* (1990); David Ellis, *The Rise of African Slavery in the Americas* (2000); and Robin Blackburn, *The Making of New World Slavery* (1997). Recent scholarly articles on subjects considered in this chapter are available in *The Atlantic Slave Trade: Effects on Economies, Societies, and Peoples in Africa, the Americas and Europe*, ed. Joseph E. Inikori and Stanley L. Engerman (1992); in *Slavery and the Rise of the Atlantic System*, ed. Barbara L. Solow (1991); and in *Africans in Bondage: Studies in Slavery and the Slave Trade*, ed. Paul Lovejoy (1986). Pieter Emmer has edited a valuable collection of articles on *The Dutch in the Atlantic Economy, 1580–1880: Trade, Slavery, and Emancipation* (1998).

Herbert S. Klein's *The Atlantic Slave Trade* (1999) provides a brief overview of research on that subject. A useful collection of debates is David Northrup, ed., *The Atlantic Slave Trade*, 2nd ed. (2002). Hugh Thomas's *The Slave Trade: The Story of the Atlantic Slave Trade, 1440–1870* (1999) and Basil Davidson's *The Atlantic Slave Trade*, rev. ed. (1980), are other useful historical narratives. More global in its conception is Patrick Manning, *Slave Trades, 1500–1800: Globalization of Forced Labor* (1996).

The connections of African communities to the Atlantic are explored by David Northrup, *Africa's Discovery of Europe, 1450–1850* (2002); John Thornton, *Africa and Africans in the Making of the Atlantic World, 1400–1800*, 2nd ed. (1998); and the authors of *Captive Passage: The Transatlantic Slave Trade and the Making of the Americas* (2002). Still valuable are Margaret E. Crahan and Franklin W. Knight, eds., *Africa and the Caribbean: The Legacies of a Link* (1979), and Richard Price, ed., *Maroon Societies: Rebel Slave Communities in the Americas*, 2nd ed. (1979). An important new contribution is Jane G. Landers and Barry M. Robinson, eds., *Slaves, Subjects, and Subversives: Blacks in Colonial Latin America* (2006). María Elena Díaz, *The Virgin, the King and the Slaves of El Cobre* (2000), offers a good introduction to the complexities of the Spanish slave system in Cuba before the sugar revolution.

Herbert S. Klein's *African Slavery in Latin America and the Caribbean* (1986) is an exceptionally fine synthesis of recent research on New World slavery. The larger context of Caribbean history is skillfully surveyed by Eric Williams, *From Columbus to Castro: The History of the Caribbean* (1984), and more simply surveyed by William Claypole and John Robottom, *Caribbean Story*, vol. 1, *Foundations*, 2nd ed. (1990). A useful collection of sources and readings is Stanley Engerman, Seymour Drescher, and Robert Paquette, eds., *Slavery* (2001).

Roland Oliver and Anthony Atmore, *The African Middle Ages, 1400–1800*, 2nd ed. (2003), summarize African history in this period. Students can pursue specific topics in more detail in Richard Gray, ed., *The Cambridge History of Africa*, vol. 4 (1975), and B. A. Ogot, ed., *UNESCO General History of Africa*, vol. 5 (1992). For recent research on slavery and the African, Atlantic, and Muslim slave trades with Africa, see Paul Lovejoy, *Transformations in Slavery: A History of Slavery in Africa*, 2nd ed. (2000); Claire C. Robertson and Martin A. Klein, eds., *Women and Slavery in Africa* (1983); and Patrick Manning, *Slavery and African Life: Occidental, Oriental, and African Slave Trades* (1990). See also Philip D. Curtin, ed., *Africa Remembered: Narratives by West Africans from the Era of the Slave Trade* (1968, 1997).

Those interested in Islam's cultural and commercial contacts with sub-Saharan Africa will find useful information in James L. A. Webb, Jr., *Desert Frontier: Ecological and Economic Change Along the Western Sahel, 1600–1850* (1995); Elizabeth Savage, ed., *The Human Commodity: Perspectives on the Trans-Saharan Slave Trade* (1992); and J. Spencer Trimingham, *The Influence of Islam upon Africa* (1968).

NOTES

1. Eric Williams, *Capitalism and Slavery* (Chapel Hill University of North Carolina Press, 1944), 7.
2. Willem Bosman, *A New and Accurate Description of Guinea, etc.* (London, 1705), quoted in David Northrup, ed., *The Atlantic Slave Trade* (Lexington, MA: D. C. Heath, 1994), 72.
3. Roland Oliver and Anthony Atmore, *The African Middle Ages, 1400–1800* (Cambridge, England: Cambridge University Press, 1981), 100.
4. King Osei Bonsu, quoted in Northrup, ed., *The Atlantic Slave Trade*, 93.
5. Alexander Falconbridge, *Account of the Slave Trade on the Coast of Africa* (London: J. Phillips, 1788), 12.
6. Joseph C. Miller, "The Significance of Drought, Disease, and Famine in the Agriculturally Marginal Zones of West-Central Africa," *Journal of African History* 23 (1982): 17–61.

Funeral Procession of Suleiman the Magnificent Each Ottoman sultan wore a distinctive turban, hence the visible turban representing the body in the hearse.
(© The Trustees of The Chester Beatty Library, T. 413, f. 13b and f. 14a)

○—How did the Ottoman Empire rise to power, and what factors contributed to its transformation?

○—How did the Safavid Empire both resemble and differ from its neighbors?

○—How did the Mughal Empire combine Muslim and Hindu elements into an effective state?

○—What role does maritime history play in the political and economic life of this period?

576

20 SOUTHWEST ASIA AND THE INDIAN OCEAN, 1500–1750

CHAPTER OUTLINE

The Ottoman Empire, to 1750

The Safavid Empire, 1502–1722

The Mughal Empire, 1526–1761

The Maritime Worlds of Islam, 1500–1750

DIVERSITY AND DOMINANCE: Islamic Law and Ottoman Rule

ENVIRONMENT AND TECHNOLOGY: Tobacco and Waterpipes

In 1541 a woman named Sabah appeared before an Ottoman judge in the town of Aintab in southern Turkey to answer several charges: that she had brought men and women together illegally and that she had fostered heresy. In her court testimony, she stated the following:

> I gather girls and brides and women in my home. I negotiated with Ibrahim b. Nazih and the two youths who are his apprentices, and in exchange for paying them a month's fee, I had them come every day to the girls and brides in my house and I had them preach and give instruction. There are no males at those sessions besides the said Ibrahim and his apprentices; there are only women and girls and young brides. This kind of thing is what I have always done for a living.[1]

Two male neighbors testified differently:

> She holds gatherings of girls and brides and women in her home. . . . While she says that she has [Ibrahim] preach, she actually has him

Online Study Center

This icon will direct you to interactive activities and study materials on the website: *college.hmco.com/pic/bulliet4e.*

speak evil things. She has him conduct spiritual conversations with these girls and brides. . . . [I]n the ceremonies, the girls and brides and women spin around waving their hands, and they bring themselves into a trancelike state by swaying and dancing. They perform the ceremonies according to Kizilbash teachings. We too have wives and families, and we are opposed to illegal activities like this.[2]

The judge made no finding on the charge of heresy, but he ordered Sabah to be publicly humiliated and banished from town for unlawfully mixing the sexes. Ibrahim was also banished.

This uncommon story taken from Ottoman religious court records sheds light on several aspects of daily life in a provincial town. It provides an example of a woman making her living by arranging religious instruction for other women. It also demonstrates the willingness of neighbors, in this case males, to complain in court about activities they considered immoral. And its suggestion that Sabah was promoting the qizilbash heresy, which at that time was considered a state threat because it was the ideology of the enemy Safavid Empire next door, shows that townspeople thought it plausible that women could act to promote religious doctrines.

Studies of everyday life through court records and other state and nonstate documents are a recent development in Ottoman and Safavid history. They produce an image of these societies that differs greatly from the pomp and formality conveyed by European travelers and official histories, such as one that contains the depiction of a sultan's funeral shown at the start of this chapter. As a consequence, accounts of capricious and despotic actions taken by shahs and sultans are increasingly being balanced by stories of common people, who were much more concerned with the maintenance of a sound legal and moral order than were some of the denizens of the imperial palaces. The doings of rulers remain an important historical focus, of course, but stories about ordinary folk perhaps give a better picture of the habits and mores of the majority of the population.

THE OTTOMAN EMPIRE, TO 1750

The most long-lived of the post-Mongol Muslim empires, the **Ottoman Empire** grew from a tiny nucleus in 1300 to encompass most of southeastern Europe by the late fifteenth century. Mamluk Syria and Egypt, along with the holy cities of Mecca and Medina, succumbed in the early sixteenth century, leaving the Ottomans with the largest Muslim empire since the original Islamic caliphate in the seventh century. However, the empire resembled the new centralized monarchies of France and Spain (see Chapter 17) more than any medieval model.

Enduring more than five centuries until 1922, the Ottoman Empire survived several periods of wrenching change, some caused by internal problems, others by the growing power of European adversaries. These periods of change reveal the problems faced by huge, land-based empires around the world.

Expansion and Frontiers

At first a tiny state in northwestern Anatolia built by Turkish nomad horsemen, zealous Muslim warriors, and a few Christian converts to Islam (see Map 20.1), the empire grew because of three factors: (1) the shrewdness of its founder Osman (from which the name *Ottoman* comes) and his descendants, (2) control of a strategic link between Europe and Asia at Gallipoli° on the Dardanelles strait, and (3) the creation of an army that took advantage of the traditional skills of the Turkish cavalryman and new military possibilities presented by gunpowder and Christian prisoners of war.

At first, Ottoman armies concentrated on Christian enemies in Greece and the Balkans, conquering a strong Serbian kingdom at the Battle of Kosovo° (in present-day Serbia) in 1389. Much of southeastern Europe and Anatolia was under the control of the sultans by 1402, when Bayazid° I, "the Thunderbolt," confronted Timur's challenge from Central Asia. After Timur defeated and captured Bayazid at the Battle of Ankara (1402), a generation of civil war followed, until Mehmed° I reunified the sultanate.

During a century and a half of fighting for territory both east and west of Constantinople, the sultans repeatedly eyed the heavily fortified capital of the slowly

---

Gallipoli (gah-LIP-po-lee)   **Kosovo** (KO-so-vo)
Bayazid (BAY-yah-zeed)   **Mehmed** (MEH-met)

C H R O N O L O G Y

	Ottoman Empire	Safavid Empire	Mughal Empire	Europeans in the Indian Ocean States
1500		**1502–1524** Shah Ismail establishes Safavid rule in Iran		**1511** Portuguese seize Malacca from local Malay ruler
	1514 Selim I defeats Safavid shah at Chaldiran; conquers Egypt and Syria (1516–1517)	**1514** Defeat by Ottomans at Chaldiran limits Safavid growth		
	1520–1566 Reign of Suleiman the Magnificent; peak of Ottoman Empire		**1526** Babur defeats last sultan of Delhi at Panipat	
	1529 First Ottoman siege of Vienna		**1539** Death of Nanak, founder of Sikh religion	
			1556–1605 Akbar rules in Agra; peak of Mughal Empire	
	1571 Ottoman naval defeat at Lepanto	**1587–1629** Reign of Shah Abbas the Great; peak of Safavid Empire		**1565** Spanish establish their first fort in the Philippines
1600				**1600** English East India company founded
				1602 Dutch East India Company founded
	1610 End of Anatolian revolts			**1606** Dutch reach Australia
		1622 Iranians oust Portuguese from Hormuz after 108 years		**1641** Dutch seize Malacca from Portuguese
			1658–1707 Aurangzeb imposes conservative Islamic regime	**1650** Omani Arabs capture Musqat from Portuguese
				1698 Omani Arabs seize Mombasa from Portuguese
1700	**1718–1730** Tulip Period; military decline apparent to Austria and Russia	**1722** Afghan invaders topple last Safavid shah		
		1736–1747 Nadir Shah temporarily reunites Iran; invades India (1739)	**1739** Iranians under Nadir Shah sack Delhi	**1741** Expansion of French Power in India

Map 20.1   Muslim Empires in the Sixteenth and Seventeenth Centuries   Iran, a Shi'ite state flanked by Sunni Ottomans on the west and Sunni Mughals on the east, had the least exposure to European influences. Ottoman expansion across the southern Mediterranean Sea intensified European fears of Islam. The areas of strongest Mughal control dictated that Islam's spread into Southeast Asia would be heavily influenced by merchants and religious figures from Gujarat instead of from eastern India.

Online Study Center
Improve Your Grade
Interactive Map: Muslim Empires in the Sixteenth and Seventeenth Century

Ottoman Empire, 1520
Ottoman Empire, 1566
Safavid Empire, ca. 1600
Mughal Empire, 1530
Mughal Empire, 1656
Major battles

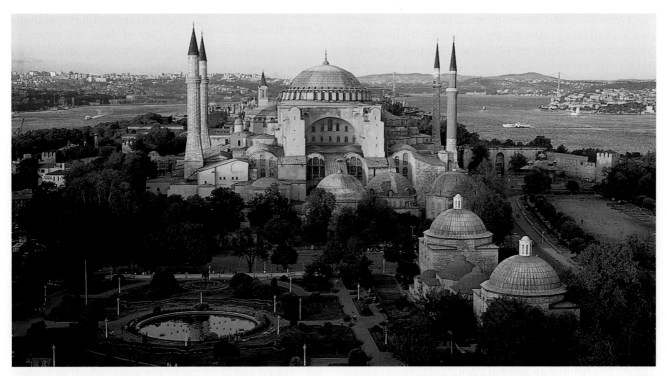

Aya Sofya Mosque in Istanbul   Originally a Byzantine cathedral, Aya Sofya (in Greek, Hagia Sophia) was transformed into a mosque after 1453, and four minarets were added. It then became a model for subsequent Ottoman mosques. To the right behind it is the Bosporus strait dividing Europe and Asia, to the left the Golden Horn inlet separating the old city of Istanbul from the newer parts. The gate to the Ottoman sultan's palace is to the right of the mosque. The pointed tower to the left of the dome is part of the palace.   (Robert Frerck/Woodfin Camp & Associates)

dying Byzantine Empire. In 1453 Sultan Mehmed II, "the Conqueror," laid siege to Constantinople, using enormous cannon to bash in the city's walls, dragging warships over a high hill from the Bosporus strait to the city's inner harbor to avoid its sea defenses, and finally penetrating the city's land walls through a series of infantry assaults. The fall of Constantinople—popularly known even before this event as Istanbul—brought over eleven hundred years of Byzantine rule to an end and made the Ottomans seem invincible.

In 1514, at the Battle of Chaldiran (in Armenia), Selim° I, "the Grim," ended a potential threat on his eastern frontier from the new and expansive realm of the Safavid shah in Iran (see below). Although warfare between the two recurred, the general border between the Ottomans and their eastern neighbor dates to this battle. Iraq became a contested and repeatedly ravaged frontier zone.

When Selim conquered the Mamluk Sultanate of Egypt and Syria in 1516 and 1517, the Red Sea became the Ottomans' southern frontier. In the west, the rulers of the major port cities of Algeria and Tunisia, some of them Greek or Italian converts to Islam, voluntarily joined the empire in the early sixteenth century, thereby strengthening its Mediterranean fleets.

The son of Selim I, **Suleiman° the Magnificent** (r. 1520–1566), known to his subjects as Suleiman Kanuni, "the Lawgiver," commanded the greatest Ottoman assault against European enemies. Suleiman seemed unstoppable as he conquered Belgrade in 1521, expelled the Knights of the Hospital of St. John from the island of Rhodes the following year, and laid siege to Vienna in 1529. Only the lateness of the season and the need to retreat before the onset of winter saved Vienna's valiant but overmatched garrison. In later centuries, Ottoman historians looked back on Suleiman's reign as a golden age when the imperial system worked to perfection. But they did this more to critique their current governments than to prove that the empire had once been perfectly ruled.

Selim (seh-LEEM)

Suleiman (SOO-lay-man)

While Ottoman armies pressed deeper and deeper into eastern Europe, the sultans also sought to control the Mediterranean. Between 1453 and 1502 the Ottomans fought the opening rounds of a two-century war with Venice, the most powerful of Italy's commercial city-states. From the Fourth Crusade of 1204 onward, Venice had assembled a profitable maritime empire that included major islands such as Crete and Cyprus along with strategic coastal strongpoints in Greece. Venice thereby became more than just a trading nation. Its island sugar plantations, exploiting cheap slave labor, competed favorably with Egypt in the international trade of the fifteenth century. With their rivals the Genoese, who traded through the strategic island of Chios, the Venetians stifled Ottoman maritime activities in the Aegean Sea.

The initial fighting left Venice with reduced military power and subject to an annual tribute payment, but it controlled its lucrative islands for another century. The Ottomans, like the Chinese, were willing to let other nations carry trade to and from their ports; they preferred trade of this sort as long as the other nations acknowledged Ottoman authority. They did not neglect their maritime frontiers in the Mediterranean Sea, Red Sea, and Indian Ocean, but fielding an army of a hundred thousand men to expand or defend their frontiers consumed more state resources.

In the south Muslims of the Red Sea and Indian Ocean region customarily traded by way of Egypt and Syria. In the early sixteenth century merchants from southern India and Sumatra sent emissaries to Istanbul requesting naval support against the Portuguese. The Ottomans responded vigorously to Portuguese threats close to their territories, such as at Aden at the southern entrance to the Red Sea, but their efforts farther afield fell short of eliminating Portuguese competition.

Nevertheless, eastern luxury products still flowed to Ottoman markets by sea as well as by land. The Portuguese demand that merchant vessels buy a certificate of protection, a practice not without precedent in the southern seas, did not enable them to monopolize trade. Portuguese power was territorially limited to fortified coastal points, such as Hormuz at the entrance to the Persian Gulf, Goa in western India, and Malacca in Malaya (see Chapter 16). The Ottomans did take the Portuguese threat seriously and at one point sent a small naval force to Indonesia, but they seem never to have followed a consistent Indian Ocean strategy.

Online Study Center
Improve Your Grade
Interactive Map: The Ottoman Empire at Its Height, 1566

Central Institutions

Heirs of the military traditions of Central Asia, the Ottoman army originally consisted of lightly armored mounted warriors skilled at shooting short bows made of compressed layers of bone, wood, and leather. The conquest of Balkan territories in the late fourteenth century, however, gave the Ottomans access to a new military resource: Christian prisoners of war induced to serve as military slaves.

Slave soldiery had a long history in Islamic lands. The Mamluk Sultanate of Egypt and Syria was built on that practice. The Mamluks, however, acquired their new blood from slave markets in Central Asia and the Caucasus. Enslaving Christian prisoners, an action of questionable legality in Islamic law, was an Ottoman innovation. Converted to Islam, these "new troops," called *yeni cheri* in Turkish and "**Janissaries°**" in English, gave the Ottomans great military flexibility.

When the sultans attacked rival Muslim states in western Asia, it is likely that they counted on these troops, brought up as Christians, to be more willing to do battle. Moreover, not coming from a culture of horse nomads, the Janissaries readily accepted the idea of fighting on foot and learning to use guns, which were then still too heavy and awkward for a horseman to load and fire. The Janissaries lived in barracks and trained all year round. Until the mid-sixteenth century, they were barred from holding jobs or marrying.

Selection for Janissary training changed early in the fifteenth century. The new system, called the **devshirme°** (literally "selection"), imposed a regular levy of male children on Christian villages in the Balkans and occasionally elsewhere, such as Greece and Hungary. Devshirme children were placed with Turkish families to learn their language before commencing military training. The most promising of them received their education at the sultan's palace in Istanbul, where they studied Islam and what we might call the liberal arts in addition to military matters. This regime, sophisticated for its time, produced not only the Janissary soldiers but also, from among the few who received special training in the inner service of the palace, senior military commanders and heads of government departments up to the rank of grand vizier, the administrative head of government.

The Ottoman Empire became cosmopolitan in character. The sophisticated court language, Osmanli° (Turkish for the word "Ottoman"), shared basic grammar and vocabulary with the Turkish spoken by Anatolia's

---

Janissary (JAN-nih-say-ree)   **devshirme** (dev-sheer-MEH)
Osmanli (os-MAHN-lee)

Ottoman Glassmakers on Parade Celebrations of the circumcisions of the sultan's sons featured parades organized by the craft guilds of Istanbul. This float features glassmaking, a common craft in Islamic realms. The most elaborate glasswork included oil lamps for mosques and colored glass for the small stained-glass windows below mosque domes. (Topkapi Palace Museum)

from the central treasury and trained in the most advanced weaponry. Greek, Turkish, Algerian, and Tunisian sailors manned the galley-equipped navy, usually under the command of an admiral from one of the North African ports.

The balance of the Ottoman land forces brought success to Ottoman arms in recurrent wars with the Safavids, who were much slower to adopt firearms, and in the inexorable advance into southeastern Europe. In naval matters, a major expedition against Malta that would have given the Ottomans a foothold in the western Mediterranean failed in 1565. The combined forces of Venice and the Holy Roman Empire also achieved a massive naval victory at the Battle of Lepanto, off Greece, in 1571. In a year's time, however, the sultan had replaced all of the galleys sunk in that battle, and in 1580 the Ottomans finally captured Cyprus from Venice.

Under the land-grant system, resident cavalrymen administered most rural areas in Anatolia and the Balkans. They maintained order, collected taxes, and reported for each summer's campaign with their horses, retainers, and supplies, all paid for from the taxes they collected. When not campaigning, they stayed at home. Some historians maintain that these cavalrymen, who did not own their land, had little interest in encouraging production or introducing new technologies; but since a militarily able son usually succeeded his father, the grant holders did have some interest in productivity.

The Ottoman conception of the world saw the sultan providing justice for his reaya and the military protecting them. In return, the reaya paid the taxes that supported both the sultan and the military. In reality, the central government, like most large territorial governments in premodern times, seldom intersected with the lives of most subjects. Arab, Turkish, and Balkan townsfolk sought justice in religious law courts and depended on local notables and religious leaders to represent them before Ottoman provincial officials. Balkan regions such as Albania and Bosnia had large numbers of converts, and Islam gradually became the majority religion. Thus the law of Islam (the Shari'a°), as interpreted by local ulama° (religious scholars), conditioned urban institutions and social life (see Diversity and Dominance: Islamic Law and Ottoman Rule). Local customs prevailed

nomads and villagers, but Arabic and Persian elements made it as distinct from that language as the Latin of educated Europeans was from the various Latin-derived Romance languages. People who served in the military or the bureaucracy and conversed in Osmanli belonged to the *askeri°*, or "military," class, which made them exempt from taxes and dependent on the sultan for their well-being. The mass of the population, whether Muslims, Christians, or Jews—Jews flooded into Ottoman territory after their expulsion from Spain in 1492 (see Chapter 17)—constituted the *reaya°*, literally "flock of sheep."

By the beginning of the reign of Sultan Suleiman, the Ottoman Empire was the most powerful and best-organized state in Europe and the Islamic world. Its military balanced mounted archers, primarily Turks supported by grants of land in return for military service, with Janissaries, mostly Turkified Albanians, Serbs, and Macedonians paid

---

askeri (AS-keh-ree)   **reaya** (RAH-yah)

Shari'a (sha-REE-ah)   **ulama** (oo-leh-MAH)

DIVERSITY + DOMINANCE

후세인 은신처 망
들과 함께 사망 가능
삼진지 구축… 이틀째 시가戰
령이 대중 앞에 나타나거나 애국심
을 고취하는 노래만을 내보내던 방
송마저 중단됐다.
라크 전후 대책을
의에서는 전후 노
영국 주도로 해

Islamic Law and Ottoman Rule

E bu's-Su'ud was the Mufti of Istanbul from 1545 to 1574, serving under the sultans Suleiman the Magnificent (1520–1566) and his son Selim II (1566–1574). Originally one of many city-based religious scholars giving opinions on matters of law, the mufti of Istanbul by Ebu's-Su'ud's time had become the top religious official in the empire and the personal adviser to the sultan on religious and legal matters. The position would later acquire the title Shaikh al-Islam.

Historians debate the degree of independence these muftis had. Since the ruler, as a Muslim, was subject to the Shari'a, the mufti could theoretically veto his policies. On important matters, however, the mufti more often seemed to come up with the answer that best suited the sultan who appointed him. This bias is not apparent in more mundane areas of the law.

The collection of Ebu's-Su'ud's fatwas, or legal opinions, from which the examples below are drawn shows the range of matters that came to his attention. They are also an excellent source for understanding the problems of his time, the relationship between Islamic law and imperial governance, and the means by which the state asserted its dominance over the common people. Some opinions respond directly to questions posed by the sultan. Others are hypothetical, using the names Zeyd, 'Amr, and Hind the way police today use John Doe and Jane Doe. While qadis, or Islamic judges, made findings of fact in specific cases on trial, muftis issued only opinions on matters of law. A qadi as well as a plaintiff or defendant might ask a question of a mufti. Later jurists consulted collections of fatwas for precedents, but the fatwas had no permanent binding power.

On the plan of Selim II to attack the Venetians in Crete in 1570 A land was previously in the realm of Islam. After a while, the abject infidels overran it, destroyed the colleges and mosques, and left them vacant. They filled the pulpits and the galleries with the tokens of infidelity and error, intending to insult the religion of Islam with all kinds of vile deeds, and by spreading their ugly acts to all corners of the earth.

His Excellency the Sultan, the Refuge of Religion, has, as zeal for Islam requires, determined to take the aforementioned land from the possession of the shameful infidels and to annex it to the realm of Islam.

When peace was previously concluded with the other lands in the possession of the said infidels, the aforenamed land was included. An explanation is sought as to whether, in accordance with the pure shari'a, this is an impediment to the Sultan's determining to break the treaty.

Answer: There is no possibility that it could ever be an impediment. For the Sultan of the People of Islam (may God glorify his victories) to make peace with the infidels is legal only when there is a benefit to all Muslims. When there is no benefit, peace is never legal. When a benefit has been seen, and it is then observed to be more beneficial to break it, then to break it becomes absolutely obligatory and binding.

His Excellency [Muhammad] the Apostle of God (may God bless him and give him peace) made a ten-year truce with the Meccan infidels in the sixth year of the Hegira. His Excellency 'Ali (may God ennoble his face) wrote a document that was corroborated and confirmed. Then, in the following year, it was considered more beneficial to break it and, in the eighth year of the Hegira, [the Prophet] attacked [the Meccans], and conquered Mecca the Mighty.

On war against the Shi'ite Muslim Safavids of Iran Is it licit according to the shari'a to fight the followers of the Safavids? Is the person who kills them a holy warrior, and the person who dies at their hands a martyr?

Answer: Yes, it is a great holy war and a glorious martyrdom.

Assuming that it is licit to fight them, is this simply because of their rebellion and enmity against the [Ottoman] Sultan of the People of Islam, because they drew the sword against the troops of Islam, or what?

Answer: They are both rebels and, from many points of view, infidels.

Can the children of Safavid subjects captured in the Nakhichevan campaign be enslaved?

Answer: No.

The followers of the Safavids are killed by order of the Sultan. If it turns out that some of the prisoners, young and old, are [Christian] Armenian[s], are they set free?

Answer: Yes. So long as the Armenians have not joined the Safavid troops in attacking and fighting against the troops of Islam, it is illegal to take them prisoner.

On the Holy Land   Are all the Arab realms Holy Land, or does it have specific boundaries, and what is the difference between the Holy Land and other lands?

Answer: Syria is certainly called the Holy Land. Jerusalem, Aleppo and its surroundings, and Damascus belong to it.

On land-grants   What lands are private property, and what lands are held by feudal tenure [i.e., assignment in exchange for military service]?

Answer: Plots of land within towns are private property. Their owners may sell them, donate them or convert them to trust. When [the owner] dies, [the land] passes to all the heirs. Lands held by feudal tenure are cultivated lands around villages, whose occupants bear the burden of their services and pay a portion of their [produce in tax]. They cannot sell the land, donate it or convert it to trust. When they die, if they have sons, these have the use [of the land]. Otherwise, the cavalryman gives [it to someone else] by *tapu* [title deed].

On the consumption of coffee   Zeyd drinks coffee to aid concentration or digestion. Is this licit?

Answer: How can anyone consume this reprehensible [substance], which dissolute men drink when engaged in games and debauchery?

The Sultan, the Refuge of Religion, has on many occasions banned coffee-houses. However, a group of ruffians take no notice, but keep coffee-houses for a living. In order to draw the crowds, they take on unbearded apprentices, and have ready instruments of entertainment and play, such as chess and backgammon. The city's rakes, rogues and vagabond boys gather there to consume opium and hashish. On top of this, they drink coffee and, when they are high, engage in games and false sciences, and neglect the prescribed prayers. In law, what should happen to a judge who is able to prevent the said coffee-sellers and drinkers, but does not do so?

Answer: Those who perpetrate these ugly deeds should be prevented and deterred by severe chastisement and long imprisonment. Judges who neglect to deter them should be dismissed.

On matters of theft   How are thieves to be "carefully examined"?

Answer: His Excellency 'Ali (may God ennoble his face) appointed Imam Shuraih as judge. It so happened that, at that time, several people took a Muslim's son to another district. The boy disappeared and, when the people came back, the missing boy's father brought them before Judge Shuraih. [When he brought] a claim [against them on account of the loss of his son], they denied it, saying: "No harm came to him from us." Judge Shuraih thought deeply and was perplexed.

When the man told his tale to His Excellency 'Ali, [the latter] summoned Judge Shuraih and questioned him. When Shuraih said; "Nothing came to light by the shari'a," ['Ali] summoned all the people who had taken the man's son, separated them from one another, and questioned them separately. For each of their stopping places, he asked: "What was the boy wearing in that place? What did you eat? And where did he disappear?" In short, he made each of them give a detailed account, and when their words contradicted each other, each of their statements was written down separately. Then he brought them all together, and when the contradictions became apparent, they were no longer able to deny [their guilt] and confessed to what had happened.

This kind of ingenuity is a requirement of the case. [This fatwa appears to justify investigation of crimes by the state instead of by the qadi. Judging from court records, which contain very few criminal cases, it seems likely that in practice, many criminal cases were dealt with outside the jurisdiction of the qadi's court.]

Zeyd takes 'Amr's donkey without his knowledge and sells it. Is he a thief?

Answer: His hand is not cut off.

Zeyd mounts 'Amr's horse as a courier and loses it. Is compensation necessary?

Answer: Yes.

In which case: What if Zeyd has a Sultanic decree [authorising him] to take horses for courier service?

Answer: Compensation is required in any case. He was not commanded to lose [the horse]. Even if he were commanded, it is the person who loses it who is liable.

On homicides   Zeyd enters Hind's house and tries to have intercourse forcibly. Since Hind can repel him by no other means, she strikes and wounds him with an axe. If Zeyd dies of the wound, is Hind liable for anything?

Answer: She has performed an act of Holy War.

QUESTIONS FOR ANALYSIS

1. What do these fatwas indicate with regard to the balance between practical legal reasoning and religious dictates?
2. How much was the Ottoman government constrained by the Shari'a?
3. What can be learned about day-to-day life from materials of this sort?

Source: Colin Imber, *Ebu's-Su'ud: The Islamic Legal Tradition* (Palo Alto, CA: Stanford University Press, 1997), 84–88, 93–94, 223–226, 250, 257. Copyright 1997 Colin Imber, originating publisher Stanford University Press. Used with permission of Stanford University Press: www.sup.org.

among non-Muslims and in many rural areas. Non-Muslims also looked to their own religious leaders for guidance in family and spiritual matters.

Crisis of the Military State, 1585–1650

As military technology evolved, cannon and lighter-weight firearms played an ever-larger role on the battlefield. Accordingly, the size of the Janissary corps—and its cost to the government—grew steadily, and the role of the Turkish cavalry, which continued to disdain firearms, diminished. In the mid-sixteenth century, to fill state coffers and pay the Janissaries, the sultan started reducing the number of landholding cavalrymen. Revenues previously spent on their living expenses and military equipment went directly into the imperial treasury. Some of the displaced cavalrymen, armed and unhappy, became a restive element in rural Anatolia.

In the late sixteenth century, inflation caused by a flood of cheap silver from the New World affected many of the remaining landholders, who collected taxes according to legally fixed rates. European traders with access to New World silver could buy more goods with the same quantity of precious metal than an Ottoman subject could. Prices rose as a result. Some landholders saw their purchasing power decline so much that they could not report for military service. This delinquency played into the hands of the government, which wanted to reduce the cavalry and increase the Janissary corps. As the central government recovered control of the land, more and more cavalrymen joined the ranks of dispossessed troopers. Students and professors in madrasas (religious colleges) similarly found it impossible to live on fixed stipends from madrasa endowments.

Constrained by religious law from fundamentally reforming the tax system, the government levied emergency surtaxes to obtain enough funds to pay the Janissaries and bureaucrats. For additional military strength, both on the Iranian front and in continuing forays in Europe, the government reinforced the Janissaries with partially trained, salaried soldiers hired for the duration of a campaign. Once the summer campaign season ended, these soldiers found themselves out of work and short on cash.

This complicated situation resulted in revolts that devastated Anatolia between 1590 and 1610. Former landholding cavalrymen, short-term soldiers released at the end of a campaign, peasants overburdened by emergency taxes, and even impoverished students of religion formed bands of marauders. Anatolia experienced the worst of the rebellions and suffered greatly from emigration

and loss of agricultural production. Banditry, made worse by the government's inability to stem the spread of muskets among the general public, beset other parts of the empire as well.

In the meantime, the Janissaries took advantage of their growing influence to gain relief from prohibitions on marrying and engaging in business. Janissaries who involved themselves in commerce lessened the burden on the state budget. Married Janissaries who enrolled sons or relatives in the corps made it possible in the seventeenth century for the government to save state funds by abolishing the devshirme system with its traveling selection officers. However, the increase in the total number of Janissaries and their steady deterioration as a military force more than offset these savings.

Economic Change and Growing Weakness, 1650–1750

A very different Ottoman Empire emerged from this period of crisis. The sultan once had led armies. Now he mostly resided in his palace and had little experience of the real world. This manner of living resulted from a gradually developed policy of keeping the sultan's male relatives confined to the palace to prevent them from plotting coups or meddling in politics. The sultan's mother and the chief eunuch overseeing the private quarters of the palace thus became important arbiters of royal favor, and even of succession to the sultanate, while the chief administrators—the grand viziers—oversaw the affairs of government. (Ottoman historians draw special attention to the negative influence of women in the palace after the time of Suleiman, but to some degree they reflect stereotypical male, and Muslim, fears about women in politics.)

The devshirme had been discontinued, and the Janissaries had taken advantage of their increased power and privileges to make membership in their corps hereditary. Together with several other newly prominent infantry regiments, they involved themselves in crafts and trading, both in Istanbul and in provincial capitals such as Cairo, Aleppo, and Baghdad. This activity took a toll on their military skills, but they continued to be a powerful faction in urban politics that the sultans could neither ignore nor reform.

Land grants in return for military service also disappeared. Tax farming arose in their place. Tax farmers paid specific taxes, such as customs duties, in advance in return for the privilege of collecting greater amounts from the actual taxpayers. In one instance, two tax farmers

advanced the government 18 million akches° (small silver coins) for the customs duties of the Aegean port of Izmir° and collected a total of 19,169,203 akches, for a profit of 6.5 percent.

Rural administration, already disrupted by the rebellions, suffered from the transition to tax farms. The military landholders had kept order on their lands to maintain their incomes. Tax farmers seldom lived on the land, and their tax collection rights could vary from year to year. The imperial government, therefore, faced greater administrative burdens and came to rely heavily on powerful provincial governors or on wealthy men who purchased lifelong tax collection rights that prompted them to behave more or less as private landowners.

Rural disorder and decline in administrative control sometimes opened the way for new economic opportunities. The port of Izmir, known to Europeans by the ancient name "Smyrna," had a population in 1580 of around two thousand, many of them Greek-speaking Christians. By 1650 the population had increased to between thirty thousand and forty thousand. Along with refugees from the Anatolian uprisings and from European pirate attacks along the coast came European merchants and large colonies of Armenians and Jews. A French traveler in 1621 wrote: "At present, Izmir has a great traffic in wool, beeswax, cotton, and silk, which the Armenians bring there instead of going to Aleppo . . . because they do not pay as many dues."[3]

Izmir transformed itself between 1580 and 1650 from a small town into a multiethnic, multireligious, multilinguistic entrepôt because of the Ottoman government's inability to control trade and the slowly growing dominance of European traders in the Indian Ocean. Spices from the East, though still traded in Aleppo and other long-established Ottoman centers, were not to be found in Izmir. Aside from Iranian silk brought in by caravan, European traders at Izmir purchased local agricultural products—dried fruits, sesame seeds, nuts, and olive oil. As a consequence, local farmers who previously had grown grain for subsistence shifted their plantings more and more to cotton and other cash crops, including, after its introduction in the 1590s, tobacco, which quickly became popular in the Ottoman Empire despite government prohibitions (see Environment and Technology: Tobacco and Waterpipes). In this way, the agricultural economy of western Anatolia, the Balkans, and the Mediterranean coast—the Ottoman lands most accessible to Europe (see Map 20.1)—became enmeshed in a growing European commercial network.

At the same time, military power slowly ebbed. The ill-trained Janissaries sometimes resorted to hiring substitutes to go on campaign, and the sultans relied on partially trained seasonal recruits and on armies raised by the governors of frontier provinces. A second mighty siege on Vienna failed in 1683, and by the middle of the eighteenth century it was obvious to the Austrians and Russians that the Ottoman Empire was weakening. On the eastern front, however, Ottoman exhaustion after many wars was matched by the demise in 1722 of their perennial adversary, the Safavid state of Iran.

The Ottoman Empire lacked both the wealth and the inclination to match European economic advances. Overland trade from the east dwindled as political disorder in Safavid Iran cut deeply into Iranian silk production (see below). Coffee from the highlands of Yemen, a product that rose from obscurity in the fifteenth century to become the rage first in the Ottoman Empire and then in Europe, traditionally reached the market by way of Egypt. By 1770, however, Muslim merchants trading in the Yemeni port of Mocha° (literally "the coffee place") paid 15 percent in duties and fees. But European traders, benefiting from long-standing trade agreements with the sultans, paid little more than 3 percent.

Such trade agreements, called capitulations, were first granted as favors by powerful sultans, but they eventually led to European domination of Ottoman seaborne trade. Nevertheless, the Europeans did not control strategic ports in the Mediterranean comparable to Malacca in the Indian Ocean and Hormuz on the Persian Gulf, so their economic power stopped short of colonial settlement or direct control in Ottoman territories.

A few astute Ottoman statesmen observed the growing disarray of the empire and advised the sultans to reestablish the land-grant and devshirme systems of Suleiman's reign. Most people, however, could not perceive the downward course of imperial power, much less the reasons behind it. Ottoman historians named the period between 1718 and 1730 the "**Tulip Period**" because of the craze for high-priced tulip bulbs that swept Ottoman ruling circles. The craze echoed a Dutch tulip mania that had begun in the mid-sixteenth century, when the flower was introduced into Holland from Istanbul, and had peaked in 1636 with particularly rare bulbs going for 2,500 florins apiece—the value of twenty-two

---

akche (AHK-cheh)   **Izmir** (IZ-meer)

Mocha (MOH-kuh)

ENVIRONMENT + TECHNOLOGY

Tobacco and Waterpipes

Tobacco, a plant native to the Western Hemisphere, may have been introduced into Ottoman Syria as early as 1570 and was certainly known in Istanbul by 1600. In Iran, one historian noted that when an Uzbek ruler entered the northeast province of Khurasan in 1612 and called for tobacco, it was quickly provided for him, while a Spanish diplomat remarked just a few years later that Shah Abbas, who had banned smoking as a sinful practice, nevertheless permitted an envoy from the Mughal sultan to indulge. European traders initially brought tobacco by sea, but it quickly became a cultivated crop in Mughal India, whence it was exported to Iran. By the middle of the seventeenth century, however, it had also become a significant crop in Ottoman and Safavid territories.

The waterpipe became a distinctive means of smoking in the Islamic world, but when the device came into use is disputed. Iranian historians assert that it was invented in Iran, where one reference in poetry goes back to before 1550. This early date suggests that waterpipes may have been used for smoking some other substance before tobacco became known. Straight pipes of clay or wood were also used, especially in Turkish areas and among poorer people.

The Persian word for a waterpipe, *qalyan*, comes from an Arabic verb meaning "to boil, or bubble." Arabic has two common words: *nargila*, which derives ultimately from the Sanskrit word for "coconut," and *shisha*, which means "glass" in Persian. In India, where coconuts were often used to contain the water, the usual term was *hookah*, meaning "jar." The absence of a clear linguistic indication of the country of origin enhances the possibility that waterpipes evolved and spread before the introduction of tobacco.

All levels of society took to smoking, with women enjoying it as much as men. The leisurely ceremony of preparing and lighting the waterpipe made it an ideal pastime in coffeehouses, which became popular in both the Ottoman and Safavid Empires. In other settings, the size and fragility of the waterpipe could cause inconvenience. When traveling, wealthy Iranian men sometimes had a pipe carrier in their entourage who carried the *qalyan* in his hand and had a small pot containing hot coals dangling from his saddle in case his master should wish to light up on the road.

Iranian Waterpipe   Moistened tobacco is placed in cup A, and a glowing coal is put on top of it to make it smolder. When the smoker draws on the stem sticking out to the side, the smoke bubbles up from beneath the water, which cools and filters it. The sophisticated manufacture shown in this drawing, which was rendered in 1622, supports the theory that the waterpipe went through a lengthy period of development before the seventeenth century.   (From Rudi Matthee, *The Pursuit of Pleasure: Drugs and Stimulants in Iranian History, 1500–1900* [Princeton: Princeton University Press] p. 125)

oxen. Far from seeing Europe as the enemy that would eventually dismantle the empire, the Istanbul elite experimented with European clothing and furniture styles and purchased printed books from the empire's first (and short-lived) press.

In 1730, however, gala soirees at which guests watched turtles with candles on their backs wander in the dark through massive tulip beds gave way to a conservative Janissary revolt with strong religious overtones. Sultan Ahmed III abdicated, and the leader of the revolt, Patrona Halil°, an Albanian former seaman and stoker of the public baths, swaggered around the capital for several months dictating government policies before he was seized and executed.

The Patrona Halil rebellion confirmed the perceptions of a few that the Ottoman Empire was facing severe difficulties. Yet decay at the center spelled benefit elsewhere. In the provinces, ambitious and competent governors, wealthy landholders, urban notables, and nomad chieftains took advantage of the central government's weakness. By the middle of the eighteenth century groups of Mamluks had regained a dominant position in Egypt. Though Selim I had defeated the Mamluk sultanate in the early sixteenth century, the practice of buying slaves in the Caucasus and training them as soldiers reappeared by the end of the century in several Arab cities. In Baghdad, Janissary commanders and Georgian mamluks competed for power, with the latter emerging triumphant by the mid-eighteenth century. In Aleppo and Damascus, however, the Janissaries came out on top. Meanwhile, in central Arabia, a puritanical Sunni movement inspired by Muhammad ibn Abd al-Wahhab began a remarkable rise beyond the reach of Ottoman power. Although no region declared full independence, the sultan's power was slipping away to the advantage of a broad array of lower officials and upstart chieftains in all parts of the empire while the Ottoman economy was reorienting itself toward Europe.

THE SAFAVID EMPIRE, 1502–1722

The **Safavid Empire** of Iran (see Map 20.1) resembled its longtime Ottoman foe in many ways: it initially used land grants to support its all-important cavalry; its population spoke several languages; it focused on land rather than sea power; and urban notables, nomadic chieftains, and religious scholars served as intermediaries between the people and the government. Certain other qualities, such as a royal tradition rooted in pre-Islamic legends and adoption of Shi'ism, continue to the present day to set Iran off from its neighbors.

The Rise of the Safavids

Timur had been a great conqueror, but his children and grandchildren contented themselves with modest realms in Afghanistan and Central Asia, while a number of would-be rulers vied for control elsewhere. In Iran itself, the ultimate victor in a complicated struggle for power among Turkish chieftains was a boy of Kurdish, Iranian, and Greek ancestry named Ismail°, the hereditary leader of a militant Sufi brotherhood called the "Safaviya" for his ancestor Safi al-Din. In 1502, at age sixteen, Ismail proclaimed himself shah of Iran. At around the same time, he declared that henceforward his realm would practice **Shi'ite Islam** and revere the family of Muhammad's son in-law Ali. He called on his subjects to abandon their Sunni beliefs.

Most of the members of the Safaviya spoke Turkish and belonged to nomadic groups known as *qizilbash*°, or "redheads," because of their distinctive turbans. Being at the extreme end of a wide spectrum of Sufi beliefs, many considered Ismail god incarnate and fought ferociously on his behalf. If Ismail wished his state to be Shi'ite, his word was law to the qizilbash. The Iranian subject population, however, resisted. Neighboring lands gave asylum to Sunni refugees whose preaching and intriguing helped stoke the fires that kept Ismail (d. 1524) and his son Tahmasp° (d. 1576) engaged in war after war. It took a century and a series of brutal persecutions to make Iran an overwhelmingly Shi'ite land. The transformation also involved the importation of Arab Shi'ite scholars from Lebanon and Bahrain to institute Shi'ite religious education at a high level.

Society and Religion

Although Ismail's reasons for compelling Iran's conversion are unknown, the effect was to create a deep chasm between Iran and its neighbors, all of which were Sunni. Iran's distinctiveness had been long in the making, however.

Patrona Halil (pa-TROH-nuh ha-LEEL)

Ismail (IS-ma-eel)   **qizilbash** (KIH-zil-bahsh)
Tahmasp (tah-MAHSP)

Safavid Shah with Attendants and Musicians   This painting by Ali-Quli Jubbadar, a European convert to Islam working for the Safavid armory, reflects Western influences. Notice the use of light and shadow to model faces and the costume of the attendant to the shah's right. The shah's waterpipe indicates the spread of tobacco, a New World crop, to the Middle East.   (Courtesy of Oriental Institute, Academy of Sciences, Leningrad. Reproduced from Album of Persian and Indian Miniatures [Moscow, 1962], ill. no. 98)

Persian, written in the Arabic script from the tenth century onward, had emerged as the second language of Islam. By 1500 an immense library of legal and theological writings; epic, lyric, and mystic poetry; histories; and drama and fiction had come into being. Iranian scholars and writers normally read Arabic as well as Persian and sprinkled their writings with Arabic phrases, but their Arab counterparts were much less inclined to learn Persian. Even handwriting styles differed, Iranians preferring more elaborate and difficult-to-read forms of the Arabic script.

This divergence between the two language areas had intensified after 1258 when the Mongols destroyed Baghdad, the capital of the Islamic caliphate, and thereby diminished the importance of Arabic-speaking Iraq. Syria and Egypt, under Mamluk rule, had become the heartland of the Arab world. However, the significant cultural achievements the Mamluk sultans encouraged in areas like architecture and metalwork remained little known in Iran, which developed largely on its own. Instead, Iran built fruitful contacts with India, whose

Muslim rulers made Persian the official language of government.

Where cultural styles had radiated in all directions from Baghdad during the heyday of the Islamic caliphate in the seventh through ninth centuries, now Iraq separated an Arab zone from a Persian zone. The post-Mongol period saw an immense burst of artistic creativity and innovation in Iran, Afghanistan, and Central Asia. Painted and molded tiles and tile mosaics, often in vivid turquoise blue, became the standard exterior decoration of mosques in Iran. Architects in Syria and Egypt followed different styles, as did those in the Ottoman Empire. The Persian poets Hafez (1319–1389?) and Sa'di (1215–1291) raised morally instructive and mystical-allegorical verse to a peak of perfection. Arabic poetry languished by comparison.

The Turks, who steadily came to dominate the political scene from Bengal to Istanbul, generally preferred Persian as a vehicle for literary and religious expression. The Mamluks in Egypt and Syria, however, showed greatest respect for Arabic. The Turkish language, which had a vigorous tradition of folk poetry, developed only slowly, primarily in the Ottoman Empire, as a language of literature and administration. Ironically, Ismail Safavi was a noted religious poet in the Turkish language of his qizilbash followers, while his mortal adversary, the Ottoman Selim I (r. 1512–1520), composed elegant poetry in Persian.

To be sure, Islam itself provided a tradition that crossed ethnic and linguistic borders. Mosque architecture differed, but Iranians, Arabs, and Turks, as well as Muslims in India, all had mosques. They also had madrasas that trained the ulama to sustain and interpret the Shari'a as the all-encompassing law of Islam. Yet local understandings of the common tradition differed substantially.

Each Sufi brotherhood had distinctive rituals and concepts of mystical union with God, but Iran stood out as the land where Sufism most often fused with militant political objectives. The Safaviya was not the first brotherhood to deploy armies and use the point of a sword to promote mystic union with God. The later Safavid shahs, however, banned (somewhat ineffectively) all Sufi orders from their domain.

Even prior to Shah Ismail's imposition of Shi'ism therefore, Iran had become a distinctive society. Nevertheless, the impact of Shi'ism was significant. Shi'ite doctrine says that all temporal rulers, regardless of title, are temporary stand-ins for the "**Hidden Imam**," the twelfth descendant of Ali, who was the prophet Muhammad's cousin and son-in-law. Shi'ites believe that leadership of the Muslim community rests solely with divinely appointed Imams from Ali's family, that the twelfth descendant (the Hidden Imam) disappeared as a child in the ninth century, and that the Shi'ite community will lack a proper religious authority until he returns. Some Shi'ite scholars concluded that the faithful should calmly accept the world as it was and wait quietly for the Hidden Imam's return. Others maintained that they themselves should play a stronger role in political affairs because they were best qualified to know the Hidden Imam's wishes. These two positions, which still play a role in Iranian Shi'ism, tended to enhance the self-image of the ulama as independent of imperial authority and slowed the trend of religious scholars' becoming subordinate government functionaries, as happened with many Ottoman ulama.

Shi'ism also affected the psychological life of the people. Commemoration of the martyrdom of Imam Husayn (d. 680), Ali's son and the third Imam, during the first two weeks of every Muslim lunar year regularized an emotional outpouring with no parallel in Sunni lands. Day after day for two weeks (as they do today) preachers recited the woeful tale to crowds of weeping believers, and chanting and self-flagellating men paraded past crowds of reverent onlookers in elaborate street processions, often organized by craft guilds. Passion plays in which Husayn and his family are mercilessly killed by the Sunni caliph's general became a unique form of Iranian public theater.

Of course, Shi'ites elsewhere observed some of the same rites of mourning for Imam Husayn, particularly in the Shi'ite pilgrimage cities of Karbala and Najaf° in Ottoman Iraq. But Iran, with over 90 percent of its population professing Shi'ism, felt the impact of these rites most strongly. Over time, the subjects of the Safavid shahs came to feel more than ever a people apart, even though many of them had been Shi'ite for only two or three generations.

A Tale of Two Cities: Isfahan and Istanbul

Isfahan° became Iran's capital in 1598 by decree of **Shah Abbas I** (r. 1587–1629). Outwardly, Istanbul and Isfahan looked quite different. Built on seven hills on the south side of the narrow Golden Horn inlet, Istanbul boasted a skyline punctuated by the gray lead domes and thin, pointed minarets of the great imperial mosques. Their design derived from Hagia Sophia, the Byzantine cathedral converted to a mosque and renamed Aya Sofya° after 1453 (see page 581). By contrast, the mosques surrounding the royal plaza in Isfahan featured brick domes covered with bright tiles and rising to gentle peaks and unobtrusive minarets. High walls surrounded the sultan's palace in Istanbul. Shah Abbas focused Isfahan on the giant royal plaza, which was large enough for his army to play polo, and he used an airy palace overlooking the plaza to receive dignitaries and review his troops. This public image contributed to Shah Abbas's being called "the Great."

The harbor of Istanbul, the primary Ottoman seaport, teemed with sailing ships and smaller craft, many of them belonging to a colony of European merchants perched on a hilltop on the north side of the Golden Horn. Isfahan, far from the sea, only occasionally received European visitors. Along with Jews and Hindus, a colony of Armenian Christians brought in by Shah Abbas who settled them in a suburb of the city handled most of its trade.

Beneath these superficial differences, the two capitals had much in common. Wheeled vehicles were scarce in hilly Istanbul and nonexistent in Isfahan, which was within the broad zone where camels supplanted wheeled transport after the rise of the Arab caravan cities in the pre-Islamic centuries. In size and layout both cities favored walking and, aside from the royal plaza in Isfahan,

---

Najaf (NAH-jaf) **Isfahan** (is-fah-HAHN)
Aya Sofya (AH-yah SOAF-yah)

Royal Square in Isfahan   Built by the order of Shah Abbas over a period of twenty years starting in 1598, the open space is as long as five football fields (555 by 172 yards). At the upper left end of the square in this drawing is the entrance to the covered bazaar, at the bottom the immense Royal Mosque. The left-hand side adjoins the shah's palace and state administrative office. A multistory pavilion for reviewing troops and receiving guests overlooks the square across from the smaller domed personal mosque of the shah.   (Reproduced with permission from Klaus Herdeg, *Formal Structure in Islamic Architecture of Iran and Turkestan* [New York: Rizzoli, 1990])

lacked the open spaces common in contemporary European cities. Away from the major mosque complexes, streets were narrow and irregular. Houses crowded against each other in dead-end lanes. Residents enjoyed the privacy of interior courtyards. Artisans and merchants organized themselves into guilds that had strong social and religious as well as economic bonds. The shops of the guilds adjoined each other in the markets.

Women seldom appeared in public, even in Istanbul's mazelike covered market or in Isfahan's long, serpentine bazaar. At home, the women's quarters—called anderun°, or "interior," in Iran and harem, or "forbidden area," in Istanbul—were separate from the public rooms where the men of the family received visitors. Low cushions, charcoal braziers for warmth, carpets, and small tables constituted most of the furnishings. In Iran and the Arab provinces, shelves and niches for books could be cut into thick, mud-brick walls. Residences in Istanbul were usually built of wood. Glazed tile in geometric or floral patterns covered the walls of wealthy men's reception areas.

The private side of family life has left few traces, but it is apparent that women's society—consisting of wives, children, female servants, and sometimes one or more eunuchs (castrated male servants)—had some connections with the outside world. Ottoman court records reveal that women using male agents bought and sold urban real estate, often dealing with inherited shares of their fathers' estates. Some even established religious endowments for pious purposes. The fact that Islamic law, unlike most European codes, permitted a wife to retain her property after marriage gave some women a stake in the general economy and a degree of independence from their spouses. Women also appeared in other types of court cases, where they often testified for themselves, for Islamic courts did not recognize the role of attorney. Although comparable Safavid court records do not survive, historians assume that a parallel situation prevailed in Iran.

---

anderun (an-deh-ROON)

Istanbul Family on the Way to a Bath House   Public baths, an important feature of Islamic cities, set different hours for men and women. Young boys, such as the lad in the turban shown here, went with their mothers and sisters. Notice that the children wear the same styles as the adults.   (Osterreichische Nationalbibliothek)

European travelers commented on the veiling of women outside the home, but miniature paintings indicate that ordinary female garb consisted of a long, ample dress with a scarf or long shawl pulled tight over the forehead to conceal the hair. Lightweight trousers, either close-fitting or baggy, were worn under the dress. This mode of dress differed little from that of men. Poor men wore light trousers, a long shirt, a jacket, and a brimless cap or turban. Wealthier men wore ankle-length caftans, often closely fitted around the chest, over their trousers. The norm for both sexes was complete coverage of arms, legs, and hair.

Men monopolized public life. Poetry and art, both somewhat more elegantly developed in Isfahan than in Istanbul, centered as much on the charms of beardless boys as of pretty maidens. Despite religious disapproval of homosexuality, attachments to adolescent boys were neither unusual nor hidden. Women on city streets included non-Muslims, the aged, the very poor, and slaves. Miniature paintings frequently depict female dancers, musicians, and even acrobats in attitudes and costumes that range from decorous to decidedly erotic.

Despite social similarities, the overall flavors of Isfahan and Istanbul were not the same. Isfahan had a prosperous Armenian quarter across the river from the city's center, but it was not a truly cosmopolitan capital. Like other rulers of extensive land empires, Shah Abbas located his capital toward the center of his domain, within comparatively easy reach of any threatened frontier and on a major trade route from the Persian Gulf to the Black Sea. Istanbul, in contrast, was a great seaport and crossroads located on the straits separating the sultan's European and Asian possessions, both of which were home to large non-Muslim communities. People of all sorts lived or spent time in Istanbul—Venetians, Genoese, Arabs, Turks, Greeks, Armenians, Albanians, Serbs, Jews, Bulgarians, and more. In this respect, Istanbul conveyed the cosmopolitan character of major seaports from London to Canton (Guangzhou) and belied the fact that its prosperity rested on the vast reach of the sultan's territories rather than on the voyages of its merchants.

Economic Crisis and Political Collapse

The silk fabrics of northern Iran, monopolized by the shahs, provided the mainstay of the Safavid Empire's foreign trade. However, the manufacture that eventually became most powerfully associated with Iran was the deep-pile carpet made by knotting colored yarns around stretched warp threads. Different cities produced distinctive carpet designs. Women and girls did much of the actual knotting work.

Carpets with geometrical or arabesque designs appear in Timurid miniature paintings, but no knotted "Persian rug" survives from the pre-Safavid era. One of the earliest dated carpets was produced in 1522 to adorn the tomb of Shaikh Safi al-Din, the fourteenth-century founder of the Safaviya. This use indicates the high value accorded these products within Iran. One German visitor to Isfahan remarked: "The most striking adornment of the banqueting hall was to my mind the carpets laid out over all three rostra [platforms to sit on for eating] in a most extravagant fashion, mostly woolen rugs from Kirman with animal patterns and woven of the finest wool."[4]

Overall, Iran's manufacturing sector was neither large nor notably productive. Most of the shah's subjects, whether Iranians, Turks, Kurds, or Arabs, lived by subsistence farming or herding. Neither area of activity recorded significant technological advances during the Safavid period. The shahs granted large sections of the country to the qizilbash nomads in return for mounted warriors for the army. Nomad groups held these lands in common, however, and did not subdivide them into individual landholdings as in the Ottoman Empire. Thus, many people in rural areas lived according to the will of a nomad chieftain who had little interest in building the agricultural economy.

The Safavids, like the Ottomans, had difficulty finding the money to pay troops armed with firearms. This crisis occurred somewhat later in Iran because of its greater distance from Europe. By the end of the sixteenth century, it was evident that a more systematic adoption of cannon and firearms in the Safavid Empire would be needed to hold off the Ottomans and the Uzbeks° (Turkish rulers who had succeeded the Timurids on Iran's Central Asian frontier; see Map 20.1). Like the Ottoman cavalry a century earlier, however, the nomad warriors refused to trade in their bows for firearms. Shah Abbas responded by establishing a slave corps of year-round soldiers and arming them with guns.

The Christian converts to Islam who initially provided the manpower for the new corps came mostly from captives taken in raids on Georgia in the Caucasus°. Some became powerful members of the court. They formed a counterweight to the nomad chiefs just as the Janissaries had earlier challenged the landholding Turkish cavalry in the Ottoman Empire. The strong hand of Shah Abbas kept the inevitable rivalries and intrigues between the factions under control. His successors showed less skill.

In the late sixteenth century the inflation caused by cheap silver spread into Iran; then overland trade through Safavid territory declined because of mismanagement of the silk monopoly after Shah Abbas's death in 1629. As a result, the country faced the unsolvable problem of finding money to pay the army and bureaucracy. Trying to remove the nomads from their lands to regain control of taxes proved more difficult and more disruptive militarily than the piecemeal dismantling of the land-grant system in the Ottoman Empire. Demands from the central government caused the nomads, who were still a potent military force, to withdraw to their mountain pastures until the pressure subsided. By 1722 the government had become so weak and commanded so little support from the nomadic groups that an army of marauding Afghans was able to capture Isfahan and effectively end Safavid rule.

Despite Iran's long coastline, the Safavids never possessed a navy. The Portuguese seized the strategic Persian Gulf island of Hormuz in 1517 and were expelled only in 1622, when the English ferried Iranian soldiers to the attack. Entirely land-oriented, the shahs relied on the English and Dutch for naval support and never considered confronting them at sea. Nadir Shah, a general who emerged from the confusion of the Safavid fall to reunify Iran briefly between 1736 and 1747, purchased some

naval vessels from the English and used them in the Persian Gulf. But his navy decayed after his death, and Iran did not have a navy again until the twentieth century.

THE MUGHAL EMPIRE, 1526–1761

As a land of Hindus ruled by a Muslim minority, the realm of the Mughal° sultans of India differed substantially from the empires of the Ottomans and Safavids. To be sure, the Ottoman provinces in the Balkans, except for Albania and Bosnia, remained mostly Christian, and there were large Greek and Armenian populations in Anatolia; but as a whole, the Ottoman Empire was overwhelmingly Muslim. The Ottoman sultans made much of their control of Mecca and Medina and resulting supervision of the annual pilgrimage caravans. All Muslims were expected to make the pilgrimage to Mecca at least once during their lifetime. As Shi'ite rulers, the Safavid shahs promoted pilgrimage to the shrine of the eighth Imam in Mashhad in northeastern Iran, as well as to even more sacred Shi'ite shrines in Iraq.

India, in contrast, lay far from the Islamic heartlands (see Map 20.1). Muslim dominion in northern India began with repeated military campaigns in the early eleventh century, and the Mughals had to contend with the Hindus' long-standing resentment of the destruction of their culture. Unlike the Balkan peoples who had struggled to maintain their separate identities in relation to the Byzantines, the crusaders, and one another before arrival of the Turks, the peoples of the Indian subcontinent had used centuries of relative freedom from foreign intrusion to forge a distinctive, if not politically unified, Hindu civilization that could not easily accommodate the world-view of Islam. Thus, the Mughals faced the challenge not just of conquering and organizing a large territorial state but also of finding a formula for Hindu-Muslim coexistence.

Political Foundations

Babur° (1483–1530), the founder of the **Mughal Empire**, descended from Timur. Though *Mughal* means "Mongol" in Persian, the Timurids were of Turkic rather than Mongol origin. Timur's marriage to a descendant of Genghis

---

Uzbeks (UHZ-bex)   Caucasus (CAW-kuh-suhs)

Mughal (MOH-guhl)   Babur (BAH-bur)

Elephants Breaking Bridge of Boats　This illustration of an incident in the life of Akbar illustrates the ability of Mughal miniature painters to depict unconventional action scenes. Because the flow of rivers in India and the Middle East varied greatly from dry season to wet season, boat bridges were much more common than permanent constructions.　(Victoria and Albert Museum, London/The Bridgeman Art Library)

of Genghis Khan—as a governor rather than an independent sovereign.

India proved to be the primary theater of Mughal accomplishment, however. Babur's grandson **Akbar** (r. 1556–1605), a brilliant but mercurial man whose illiteracy betrayed his upbringing in the wilds of Afghanistan, established the central administration of the expanding state. Under him and his three successors—the last of whom died in 1707—all but the southern tip of India fell under Mughal rule, administered first from Agra and then from Delhi°.

Akbar granted land revenues called *mansabs°*, to military officers and government officials in return for their service. As in the other Islamic empires, the central government kept careful track of these nonhereditary grants.

With a population of 100 million, a thriving trading economy based on cotton cloth, and a generally efficient administration, India under Akbar enjoyed great prosperity in the sixteenth century. Akbar and his successors faced few external threats and experienced mostly peaceful conditions in their northern Indian heartland. Nevertheless, they were capable of squandering immense amounts of blood and treasure fighting Hindu kings and rebels in the Deccan region or Afghans on their western frontier (see Map 20.1).

Foreign trade boomed at the port of Surat in the northwest, which also served as an embarkation point for pilgrims headed for Mecca. Like the Safavids, the Mughals had no navy, and Indian merchant ships were privately owned. The government saw the Europeans—now primarily Dutch and English, the Portuguese having lost most of their Indian ports—less as enemies than as

Khan had earned him the Mongol designation "son-in-law," but like the Ottomans, his family did not enjoy the political legitimacy that came with Genghisid decent experienced by lesser rulers in Central Asia and in the Crimea north of the Black Sea.

Invading from Central Asia, Babur defeated the last Muslim sultan of Delhi at the Battle of Panipat in 1526. Even though this victory marked the birth of a brilliant and powerful state in India, Babur's descendants continued to think of Central Asia as their true home, from time to time expressing intentions of recapturing Samarkand and referring to its Uzbek ruler—a genuine descendant

Delhi (DEL-ee)　**mansabs** (MAN-sabz)

shipmasters whose military support could be procured as needed in return for trading privileges. It never questioned the wisdom of selling Indian cottons for European coin—no one understood how cheap silver had become in Europe—and shipping them off to European customers in English and Dutch vessels.

Hindus and Muslims

India had not been dominated by a single ruler since the time of Harsha Vardhana (r. 606–647). Muslim destruction of Hindu cultural monuments, the expansion of Muslim territory, and the practice, until Akbar's time, of enslaving prisoners of war and compelling them to convert to Islam horrified the Hindus. But the politically divided Hindus did not put up a combined resistance. The Mughal state, in contrast, inherited traditions of unified imperial rule from both the Islamic caliphate and the more recent examples of Genghis Khan and Timur.

Those Mongol-based traditions did not necessarily mean religious intolerance. Seventy percent of the *mansabdars°* (officials holding land grants) appointed under Akbar were Muslim soldiers born outside India, but 15 percent were Hindus, mostly warriors from the north called **Rajputs°**. One of them rose to be a powerful revenue minister. Their status as mansabdars confirmed the policy of religious accommodation adopted by Akbar and his successors.

Akbar, the most illustrious Mughal ruler, differed from his Ottoman and Safavid counterparts—Suleiman the Magnificent and Shah Abbas the Great—in his striving for social harmony and not just for more territory and revenue. He succeeded to the throne at age thirteen, and his actions were dominated at first by a regent and then by his strong-minded childhood nurse. On reaching twenty, Akbar took command of the government. He married a Hindu Rajput princess, whose name is not recorded, and welcomed her father and brother to the court in Agra.

Other rulers might have used such a marriage as a means of humiliating a subject group, but Akbar signaled his desire for Muslim-Hindu reconciliation. A year later he rescinded the head tax that Muslim rulers traditionally levied on tolerated non-Muslims. This measure was more symbolic than real because the tax had not been regularly collected, but the gesture helped cement the allegiance of the Rajputs.

Akbar longed for an heir. Much to his relief, his Rajput wife gave birth to a son in 1569, ensuring that future rulers would have both Muslim and Hindu ancestry.

Akbar ruled that in legal disputes between two Hindus, decisions would be made according to village custom or Hindu law as interpreted by local Hindu scholars. Muslims followed Shari'a law. Akbar made himself the legal court of last resort in a 1579 declaration that he was God's infallible earthly representative. Thus, appeals could be made to Akbar personally, a possibility not usually present in Islamic jurisprudence.

He also made himself the center of a new "Divine Faith" incorporating Muslim, Hindu, Zoroastrian, Sikh°, and Christian beliefs. Sufi ideas attracted him and permeated the religious rituals he instituted at his court. To promote serious consideration of his religious principles, he monitored, from a high catwalk, debates among scholars of all religions assembled in his private octagonal audience chamber. When courtiers uttered the Muslim exclamation "Allahu Akbar"—"God is great"—its second grammatical meaning, "God is Akbar," was not lost on them. Akbar's religious views did not survive him, but the court culture he fostered, reflecting a mixture of Muslim and Hindu traditions, flourished until his zealous great-grandson Aurangzeb° (r. 1658–1707) reinstituted many restrictions on Hindus.

Mughal and Rajput miniature portraits of political figures and depictions of scantily clad women brought frowns to the faces of pious Muslims, who deplored the representation of human beings in art. Most of the leading painters were Hindus. In literature, in addition to the florid style of Persian verse favored at court, a new taste developed for poetry and prose in the popular language of the Delhi region. The modern descendant of this language is called Urdu in Pakistan, from the Turkish word *ordu*, meaning "army" (in India it is called Hindi).

Akbar's policy of toleration does not explain the pattern of conversion in Mughal India, most of which was to Sunni Islam. Some scholars maintain that most converts came from the lowest Hindu social groups, or castes, who hoped to improve their lot in life, but little evidence confirms this theory. Others argue that Sufi brotherhoods, which developed strongly in India, led the way in converting people to Islam, but this proposition has not been proved. The most heavily Muslim regions developed in the valley of the Indus River and in Bengal. The Indus center dates from the isolated establishment of Muslim rule there as early as the eighth century.

A careful study of local records and traditions from east Bengal indicates that the eastward movement of the delta of the Ganges River, caused by silting, and the spread of rice cultivation into forest clearings played the primary role in conversions to Islam there. Mansabdars (mostly Muslims) with land grants in east Bengal contracted with

---

mansabdars (man-sab-DAHRZ)   **Rajputs** (RAHJ-putz)

Sikh (sick)   **Aurangzeb** (ow-rang-ZEB)

local entrepreneurs to collect a labor force, cut down the forest, and establish rice paddies. Though some entrepreneurs were Hindu, most were non-Sufi Muslim religious figures. The latter centered their farming communities on mosques and shrines, using religion as a social cement. Most natives of the region were accustomed to worshiping local forest deities rather than the main Hindu gods. So the shift to Islam represented a move to a more sophisticated, literate culture appropriate to their new status as farmers producing for the commercial rice market. Gradual religious change of this kind often produced Muslim communities whose social customs differed little from those in neighboring non-Muslim communities. In east Bengal, common Muslim institutions, such as madrasas, the ulama, and law courts, were little in evidence.

The emergence of **Sikhism** in the Punjab region of northwest India constituted another change in Indian religious life in the Mughal period. Nanak (1469–1539), the religion's first guru (spiritual teacher), stressed meditation as a means of seeking enlightenment and drew upon both Muslim and Hindu imagery in his teachings. His followers formed a single community without differences of caste. However, after Aurangzeb ordered the ninth guru beheaded in 1675 for refusing to convert to Islam, the tenth guru dedicated himself to avenging his father's death and reorganized his followers into "the army of the pure," a religious order dedicated to defending Sikh beliefs. These devotees signaled their faith by leaving their hair uncut beneath a turban; carrying a comb, a steel bracelet, and a sword or dagger; and wearing military-style breeches. By the eighteenth century, the Mughals were encountering fierce opposition from the Sikhs as well as from Hindu guerrilla forces in the rugged and ravine-scarred province of Maharashtra on India's west coast.

| Central Decay and Regional Challenges, 1707–1761 | Mughal power did not long survive Aurangzeb's death in 1707. Some historians consider the land-grant system a central element in the rapid |

decline of imperial authority, but other factors played a role as well. Aurangzeb failed to effectively integrate new Mughal territories in southern India into the imperial structure, and a number of strong regional powers challenged Mughal military supremacy. The Marathas proved a formidable enemy as they carved out a swath of territory across India's middle, and Sikhs, Hindu Rajputs, and Muslim Afghans exerted intense pressure from the northwest. A climax came in 1739 when Nadir Shah, the general who had seized power in Iran after the fall of the Safavids, invaded the subcontinent and sacked Delhi,

which Akbar's grandson had rebuilt and beautified as the Mughal capital some decades before. He carried off to Iran, as part of the booty, the priceless, jewel-encrusted "peacock throne," symbol of Mughal grandeur. The later Mughals found another throne to sit on; but their empire, which survived in name to 1857, was finished.

In 1723 Nizam al-Mulk°, the powerful vizier of the Mughal sultan, gave up on the central government and established his own nearly independent state at Hyderabad in the eastern Deccan. Other officials bearing the title *nawab*° (from Arabic *na'ib* meaning "deputy" and Anglicized as "nabob") became similarly independent in Bengal and Oudh° in the northeast, as did the Marathas farther west. In the northwest, simultaneous Iranian and Mughal weakness allowed the Afghans to establish an independent kingdom.

Some of these regional powers and smaller princely states flourished with the removal of the sultan's heavy hand. Linguistic and religious communities, freed from the religious intolerance instituted during the reign of Aurangzeb, similarly enjoyed greater opportunity for political expression. However, this disintegration of central power favored the intrusion of European adventurers.

Joseph François Dupleix° took over the presidency of the east coast French stronghold of Pondicherry° in 1741 and began a new phase of European involvement in India. He captured the English trading center of Madras and used his small contingent of European and European-trained Indian troops to become a power broker in southern India. Though offered the title *nawab*, Dupleix preferred to operate behind the scenes, using Indian princes as puppets. His career ended in 1754 when he was called home. Deeply involved in European wars, the French government declined to pursue further adventures in India. Dupleix's departure cleared the way for the British, whose ventures in India are described in Chapter 26.

THE MARITIME WORLDS OF ISLAM, 1500–1750

As land powers, the Mughal, Safavid, and Ottoman Empires faced similar problems in the seventeenth and eighteenth centuries. Complex changes in military technology and in the world economy, along with the increasing difficulty of basing an extensive land empire on military forces paid through land grants, affected them

---

Nizam al-Mulk (nee-ZAHM al-MULK)   **nawab** (NAH-wab)
Oudh (OW-ad)   **Dupleix** (doo-PLAY)
Pondicherry (pon-dir-CHEH-ree)

all adversely. These difficulties contributed to the often dynamic development of power centers away from the imperial capital.

The new pressures faced by land powers were less important to seafaring countries intent on turning trade networks into maritime empires. Improvements in ship design, navigation accuracy, and the use of cannon gave an ever-increasing edge to European powers competing with local seafaring peoples. Moreover, the development of joint-stock companies, in which many merchants pooled their capital, provided a flexible and efficient financial instrument for exploiting new possibilities. The English East India Company was founded in 1600, the Dutch East India Company in 1602.

Although the Ottomans, Safavids, and Mughals did not effectively contest the growth of Portuguese and then Dutch, English, and French maritime power, the majority of non-European shipbuilders, captains, sailors, and traders were Muslim. Groups of Armenian, Jewish, and Hindu traders were also active, but they remained almost as aloof from the Europeans as the Muslims did. The presence in every port of Muslims following the same legal traditions and practicing their faith in similar ways cemented the Muslims' trading network. Islam, from its very outset in the life and preaching of Muhammad (570–632), had favored trade and traders. Unlike Hinduism, it was a proselytizing religion, a factor that encouraged the growth of coastal Muslim communities as local non-Muslims associated with Muslim commercial activities converted and intermarried with Muslims from abroad.

Although European missionaries, particularly the Jesuits, tried to extend Christianity into Asia and Africa (see Chapters 16 and 21), most Europeans, the Portuguese excepted, did not treat local converts or the offspring of mixed marriages as full members of their communities. Islam was generally more welcoming. As a consequence, Islam spread extensively into East Africa and Southeast Asia during precisely the time of rapid European commercial expansion. Even without the support of the Muslim land empires, Islam became a source of resistance to growing European domination.

Muslims in Southeast Asia

Historians disagree about the chronology and manner of Islam's spread in Southeast Asia. Arab traders appeared in southern China as early as the eighth century, so Muslims probably reached the East Indies (the island portions of Southeast Asia) at a similarly early date. Nevertheless, the dominance of Indian cultural influences in the area for several centuries thereafter indicates that early Muslim visitors had little impact on local beliefs. Clearer indications of conversion and the formation of Muslim communities date from roughly the fourteenth century, with the strongest overseas linkage being to the port of Cambay in India (see Map 20.2) rather than to the Arab world. Islam first took root in port cities and in some royal courts and spread inland only slowly, possibly transmitted by itinerant Sufis.

Although appeals to the Ottoman sultan for support against the Europeans ultimately proved futile, Islam strengthened resistance to Portuguese, Spanish, and Dutch intruders. When the Spaniards conquered the Philippines during the decades following the establishment of their first fort in 1565, they encountered Muslims on the southern island of Mindanao° and the nearby Sulu archipelago. They called them "Moros," the Spanish term for their old enemies, the Muslims of North Africa. In the ensuing Moro wars, the Spaniards portrayed the Moros as greedy pirates who raided non-Muslim territories for slaves. In fact, they were political, religious, and commercial competitors whose perseverance enabled them to establish the Sulu Empire based in the southern Philippines, one of the strongest states in Southeast Asia from 1768 to 1848.

Other local kingdoms that looked on Islam as a force to counter the aggressive Christianity of the Europeans included the actively proselytizing Brunei° Sultanate in northern Borneo and the **Acheh° Sultanate** in northern Sumatra. At its peak in the early seventeenth century, Acheh succeeded Malacca as the main center of Islamic expansion in Southeast Asia. It prospered by trading pepper for cotton cloth from Gujarat in India. Acheh declined after the Dutch seized Malacca from Portugal in 1641.

How well Islam was understood in these Muslim kingdoms is open to question. In Acheh, for example, a series of women ruled between 1641 and 1699. This practice ended when local Muslim scholars obtained a ruling from scholars in Mecca and Medina that Islam did not approve of female rulers. After this ruling scholarly understandings of Islam gained greater prominence in the East Indies.

Historians have looked at merchants, Sufi preachers, or both as the first propagators of Islam in Southeast Asia. The scholarly vision of Islam, however, took root in the sixteenth century by way of pilgrims returning from years of study in Mecca and Medina. Islam promoted the dissemination of writing in the region. Some of the returning pilgrims wrote in Arabic, others in Malay or Javanese. As Islam continued to spread, adat ("custom"), a form of Islam rooted in pre-Muslim religious and social practices, retained its preeminence in rural areas over practices centered on the Shari'a, the religious law. But

---

Mindanao (min-duh-NOW)   **Brunei** (BROO-nie)
Acheh (AH-cheh)

Map 20.2 European Colonization in the Indian Ocean, to 1750 Since Portuguese explorers were the first Europeans to reach India by rounding Africa, Portugal gained a strong foothold in both areas. Rival Spain was barred from colonizing the region by the Treaty of Tordesillas in 1494, which limited Spanish efforts to lands west of a line drawn through the mid-Atlantic Ocean. The line carried around the globe provided justification of Spanish colonization in the Philippines. French, British, and Dutch colonies date from after 1600, when joint-stock companies provided a new stimulus for overseas commerce.

Online Study Center
Improve Your Grade
Interactive Map: European Colonization in the Indian Ocean, to 1750

Colonial possessions

- British
- Portuguese
- French
- Dutch
- Spanish

the royal courts in the port cities began to heed the views of the pilgrim teachers. Though different in many ways, both varieties of Islam provided believers with a firm basis of identification in the face of the growing European presence. Christian missionaries gained most of their converts in regions that had not yet converted to Islam, such as the northern Philippines.

Muslims in Coastal Africa

Muslim rulers also governed the East African ports that the Portuguese began to visit in the fifteenth century, though they were not allied politically (see Map 20.2). People living in the millet and rice lands of the Swahili Coast—from the Arabic *sawahil°* meaning "coasts"—had little contact with those in the dry hinterlands. Throughout this period, the East African lakes region and the highlands of Kenya witnessed unprecedented migration and relocation of peoples because of drought conditions that persisted from the late sixteenth through most of the seventeenth century.

Cooperation among the trading ports of Kilwa, Mombasa, and Malindi was hindered by the thick bush country that separated the cultivated tracts of coastal land and by the fact that the ports competed with one another in the export of ivory; ambergris° (a whale byproduct used in perfumes); and forest products such as beeswax, copal tree resin, and wood. Kilwa also exported gold. In the eighteenth century slave trading, primarily to Arabian ports but also to India, increased in importance. Because Europeans—the only peoples who kept consistent records of slave-trading activities—played a minor role in this slave trade, few records have survived to indicate its extent. Perhaps the best estimate is that 2.1 million slaves were exported between 1500 and 1890, a little over 12.5 percent of the total traffic in African slaves during that period (see Chapter 19).

The Portuguese conquered all the coastal ports from Mozambique northward except Malindi, with whose ruler Portugal cooperated. A Portuguese description of the ruler names some of the cloth and metal goods that Malindi imported, as well as some local manufactures:

> The King wore a robe of damask trimmed with green satin and a rich [cap]. He was seated on two cushioned chairs of bronze, beneath a rough sunshade of crimson satin attached to a pole. An old man, who attended him as a page, carried a short sword in a silver sheath. There

were many players on [horns], and two trumpets of ivory richly carved and of the size of a man, which were blown through a hole in the side, and made sweet harmony with the [horns].[5]

Initially, the Portuguese favored the port of Malindi, which caused the decline of Kilwa and Mombasa. Repeatedly plagued by local rebellion, Portuguese power suffered severe blows when the Arabs of **Oman** in southeastern Arabia captured their south Arabian stronghold at Musqat (1650) and then went on to seize Mombasa (1698), which had become the Portuguese capital in East Africa. The Portuguese briefly retook Mombasa but lost control permanently in 1729. From then on, the Portuguese had to content themselves with Mozambique in East Africa and a few remaining ports in India (Goa) and farther east (Macao and Timor).

The Omanis created a maritime empire of their own, one that worked in greater cooperation with the African populations. The Bantu language of the coast, broadened by the absorption of Arabic, Persian, and Portuguese loanwords, developed into **Swahili°**, which was spoken throughout the region. Arabs and other Muslims who settled in the region intermarried with local families, giving rise to a mixed population that played an important role in developing a distinctive Swahili culture.

Islam also spread in the southern Sudan in this period, particularly in the dry areas away from the Nile River. This growth coincided with a waning of Ethiopian power as a result of Portugal's stifling of trade in the Red Sea. Yet no significant contact developed between the emerging Muslim Swahili culture and that of the Muslims in the Sudan to the north.

In northwest Africa the seizure by Portugal and Spain of coastal strongholds in Morocco provoked a militant response. The Sa'adi family, which claimed descent from the Prophet Muhammad, led a resistance to Portuguese aggression that climaxed in victory at the battle of al-Qasr al-Kabir (Ksar el Kebir) in 1578. The triumphant Moroccan sultan, Ahmad al-Mansur, restored his country's strength and independence. By the early seventeenth century naval expeditions from the port of Salé, referred to in British records as "the Sally Rovers," raided European shipping as far as Britain itself.

Corsairs, or sea raiders, working out of Algerian, Tunisian, and Libyan ports brought the same sort of warfare to the Mediterranean. European governments called these Muslim raiders pirates and slave-takers, and they leveled the same charges against other Muslim mariners

---

sawahil (suh-WAH-hil)   **ambergris** (AM-ber-grees)

Swahili (swah-HEE-lee)

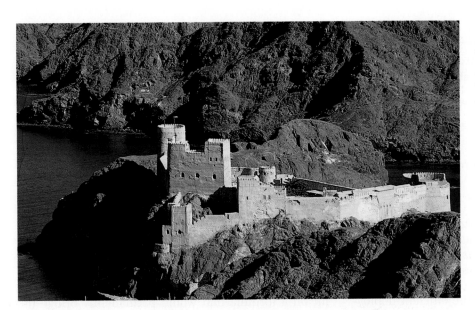

Portuguese Fort Guarding Musqat Harbor Musqat in Oman and Aden in Yemen, the best harbors in southern Arabia, were targets for imperial navies trying to establish dominance in the Indian Ocean. Musqat's harbor is small and circular, with one narrow entrance overlooked by this fortress. The palace of the sultan of Oman is still located at the opposite end of the harbor. (Robert Harding World Imagery)

in the Persian Gulf and the Sulu Sea. But there was little distinction between the actions of the Muslims and of their European adversaries.

European Powers in Southern Seas

The Dutch played a major role in driving the Portuguese from their possessions in the East Indies. They were better organized than the Portuguese through the Dutch East India Company. Just as the Portuguese had tried to dominate the trade in spices, so the Dutch concentrated at first on the spice-producing islands of Southeast Asia. The Portuguese had seized Malacca, a strategic town on the narrow strait at the end of the Malay Peninsula, from a local Malay ruler in 1511 (see Chapter 16). The Dutch took it away from them in 1641, leaving Portugal little foothold in the East Indies except the islands of Ambon° and Timor (see Map 20.2).

Although the United Netherlands was one of the least autocratic countries of Europe, the governors-general appointed by the Dutch East India Company deployed almost unlimited powers in their efforts to maintain their trade monopoly. They could even order the execution of their own employees for "smuggling"— that is, trading on their own. Under strong governors-general, the Dutch fought a series of wars against Acheh and other local kingdoms on Sumatra and Java. In 1628

and 1629 their new capital at **Batavia**, now the city of Jakarta on Java, was besieged by a fleet of fifty ships belonging to the sultan of Mataram°, a Javanese kingdom. The Dutch held out with difficulty and eventually prevailed when the sultan was unable to get effective help from the English.

Suppressing local rulers, however, was not enough to control the spice trade once other European countries adopted Dutch methods, learned more about where goods might be acquired, and started to send more ships to Southeast Asia. In the course of the eighteenth century, therefore, the Dutch gradually turned from being middlemen between Southeast Asian producers and European buyers to producing crops in areas they controlled, notably in Java. Javanese teak forests yielded high-quality lumber, and coffee, transplanted from Yemen, grew well in the western hilly regions. In this new phase of colonial export production, Batavia developed from being the headquarters town of a far-flung enterprise to being the administrative capital of a conquered land.

Beyond the East Indies, the Dutch utilized their discovery of a band of powerful eastward-blowing winds (called the "Roaring Forties" because they blow throughout the year between 40 and 50 degrees south latitude) to reach Australia in 1606. In 1642 and 1643 Abel Tasman became the first European to set foot on Tasmania and New Zealand and to sail around Australia, signaling European involvement in that region (see Chapter 26).

Ambon (am-BOHN)

Mataram (MAH-tah-ram)

SUMMARY

How did the Ottoman Empire rise to power, and what factors contributed to its transformation?

How did the Safavid Empire both resemble and differ from its neighbors?

How did the Mughal Empire combine Muslim and Hindu elements into an effective state?

What role does maritime history play in the political and economic life of this period?

Online Study Center
ACE the Test

Strategic location and a centralized army well balanced between mounted bowmen and an infantry armed with gunpowder weapons were keys to Ottoman success during the empire's first two centuries. With territorial growth, however, the borders became too distant from the capital for the efficient deployment of a centralized army, and economic pressures, notably those associated with a flood of cheap silver from the New World, forced modifications in the ruling system. Military, and increasingly political, power devolved to commanders and governors in provincial capitals and border districts, while new fiscal arrangements captured more tax revenue for the central government and the Istanbul elite.

The Safavid Empire embodied some of the same Turkish tribal traditions and Islamic governing institutions that were found among the Ottomans, but the formal adoption of Shi'ism as the state religion at the beginning of the sixteenth century created such a gulf between them that these similarities were seldom recognized. In some respects, such as their practice of using Christian prisoners of war as infantry, the Safavids followed the Ottoman lead. By contrast, the Mughals drew military forces from Central Asia and Afghanistan and adopted Persian as the language of government but never enjoyed the religious and cultural homogeneity that was a hallmark of Safavid Iran.

Dealing with the Hindu majority in their domain was a continuing problem for the Mughal rulers. Akbar took the path of accommodation by appointing Hindu officials and trying to harmonize religious differences. Aurangzeb, his great-grandson, took the opposite path of persecuting Hindus and exalting Islam. Both rulers enjoyed military success against various Indian adversaries, but neither hit on a formula that would permanently bridge the gap between the Muslim ruling minority and the non-Muslim majority. Nevertheless, by comparison with most earlier Indian states, and measured by the problems and successes of the contemporary Ottoman and Safavid realms, Mughal rule must be deemed effective.

Muslim rulers who saw greater opportunities and dangers along imperial land frontiers than at sea saw nothing threatening in the vigorous commercial activity of the non-Muslim merchants in their realms—Jews, Christians, and Hindus—or even the European trading companies. To be sure, the Ottoman navy was a formidable military force in the Mediterranean, and Muslim rulers in Morocco, Oman, and Southeast Asia sometimes reacted effectively to European maritime pressure. But the greatest battles were fought on land, and acquisition or loss of territory was taken by Muslims and non-Muslims alike as a more important sign of an empire's strength than its command of maritime trade routes. Over time, the economic gains made by the European trading companies changed the balance of power in the region, but local merchants never disappeared from the commercial scene, either as maritime traders or as manufacturers producing goods like Indian cotton cloth for export.

KEY TERMS

Ottoman Empire *p. 578*
Suleiman the Magnificent *p. 581*
Janissaries *p. 582*
devshirme *p. 582*
Tulip Period *p. 587*
Safavid Empire *p. 589*

Shi'ite Islam *p. 589*
Hidden Imam *p. 591*
Shah Abbas I *p. 591*
Mughal Empire *p. 594*
Akbar *p. 595*
mansabs *p. 595*

Rajputs *p. 596*
Sikhism *p. 597*
Acheh Sultanate *p. 598*
Oman *p. 600*
Swahili *p. 600*
Batavia *p. 601*

Online Study Center
Improve Your Grade
Flashcards

SUGGESTED READING

The best comprehensive and comparative account of the post-Mongol Islamic land empires, with an emphasis on social history, is Ira Lapidus, *A History of Islamic Societies* (1988). For a work of similar scope concentrating on intellectual history see Marshall G. S. Hodgson, *The Venture of Islam*, vol. 3, *The Gunpowder Empires and Modern Times* (1974).

On the Ottoman Empire in its prime see Colin Imber, *The Ottoman Empire, 1300–1650: The Structure of Power* (2002). Daniel Goffman, *The Ottoman Empire and Early Modern Europe* (2002), compares the Ottomans with contemporary European kingdoms. Jason Goodwin, *Lords of the Horizons: A History of the Ottoman Empire* (1999), offers a brief journalistic account. Ottoman origins are well covered in Cemal Kafadar, *Between Two Worlds* (1995). For a collection of articles on nonpolitical matters see Halil Inalcik and Donald Quataert, eds., *An Economic and Social History of the Ottoman Empire, 1300–1914* (1994). For a sociological analysis of change in the seventeenth century see Karen Barkey, *Bandits and Bureaucrats* (1994).

Some specialized studies of cities and regions give a sense of the major changes in Ottoman society and economy after the sixteenth century: Daniel Goffman, *Izmir and the Levantine World, 1550–1650* (1990); Abraham Marcus, *The Middle East on the Eve of Modernity: Aleppo in the Eighteenth Century* (1989); Bruce Mc-Gowan, *Economic Life in the Ottoman Empire: Taxation, Trade, and the Struggle for Land, 1600–1800* (1981); and Dina Rizk Khoury, *State and Provincial Society in the Ottoman Empire: Mosul, 1540–1834* (1997).

Articles in Benjamin Braude and Bernard Lewis, eds., *Christians and Jews in the Ottoman Empire: The Functioning of a Plural Society* (1982), deal with questions relating to religious minorities. Leslie Peirce skillfully treats the role of women in the governance of the empire in *The Imperial Harem: Women and Sovereignty in the Ottoman Empire* (1993), as well as problems in the day-to-day lives of women in *Morality Tales: Law and Gender in the Ottoman Court of Aintab* (2003). Ralph S. Hattox, *Coffee and Coffeehouses: The Origins of a Social Beverage in the Medieval Near East* (1988), is an excellent contribution to Ottoman social history.

The most comprehensive treatment of the history of Safavid Iran is in the articles in Peter Jackson and Laurence Lockhart, eds., *The Cambridge History of Iran*, vol. 6, *The Timurid and Safavid Periods* (1986). The articles by Hans Roemer in this volume provide solid political narratives of the pre-Safavid and Safavid periods. For a short and stimulating reinterpretation of Safavid rule see Andrew Newman, *Safavid Iran: Rebirth of a Persian Empire* (2006). Willem Floor and Edmend Herzig, eds., *Iran and the World in the Safavid Age* (2006), places Safavid Iran in a broader setting.

For the artistic side of Safavid history, abundantly illustrated, see Anthony Welch, *Shah Abbas and the Arts of Isfahan* (1973). Said Amir Arjomand, *The Shadow of God and the Hidden Imam: Religion, Political Order, and Societal Change in Shiite Iran from the Beginning to 1890* (1984), contains the best analysis of the complicated relationship between Shi'ism and monarchy. For Safavid economic history see Willem Floor, *A Fiscal History of Iran in the Safavid and Qajar Periods, 1500–1925* (1998); and Rudoph P. Matthee, *The Politics of Trade in Safavid Iran: Silk for Silver, 1600–1730* (1999). Rudi Matthee (same as Rudolph P.) also writes about both court life and popular culture in *The Pursuit of Pleasure: Drugs and Stimulants in Iranian History, 1500–1900* (2005).

A highly readable work that situates the Mughal Empire within the overall history of the subcontinent is Stanley Wolpert, *A New History of India*, 6th ed. (1999). For a broad treatment of the entire development of Islamic society in India with emphasis on the Mughal period, see S. M. Ikram, *History of Muslim Civilization in India and Pakistan* (1989). For an illuminating portrayal of more southerly parts of India during the same period see Richard M. Eaton, *A Social History of the Deccan, 1300–1761: Eight Indian Lives* (2005). Wheeler Thackston has made a lively translation of Babur's autobiography in *The Baburnama: Memoirs of Babur, Prince and Emperor* (1996). For a comprehensive history of the Mughals see John F. Richards, *The Mughal Empire* (1993). See also Richard Foltz, *Mughal India and Central Asia* (1999). Irfan Habib has edited an extensive collection of articles on the Mughal Empire in its prime entitled *Akbar and His India* (1997). For the history of the Sikhs see W. H. McLeod, *The Sikhs: History, Religion, and Society* (1989). Two specialized works on the economic and trading history of India are Ashin Das Gupta and M. N. Pearson, eds., *India and the Indian Ocean, 1500–1800* (1987), and Stephen Frederic Dale, *Indian Merchants and Eurasian Trade, 1600–1750* (1994).

The history of East Africa in this period is not well documented, but B. A. Ogot, ed., *UNESCO General History of Africa*, vol. 5, *Africa from the Sixteenth to the Eighteenth Century* (1992), provides a useful collection of articles. See also Tom Spear, *The Swahili* (1984), and James de Vere Allen, *Swahili Origins* (1993).

For a brief, general introduction to the relations between the Muslim land empires and the development of Indian Ocean trade, see Patricia Risso, *Merchants and Faith: Muslim Commerce and Culture in the Indian Ocean* (1995). Esmond Bradley Martin and Chryssee Perry Martin have written a popular and well-illustrated work on the western Indian Ocean entitled *Cargoes of the East: The Ports, Trade and Culture of the Arabian Seas and Western Indian Ocean* (1978). C. R. Boxer, *The Dutch Seaborne Empire, 1600–1800* (1973), is a classic account of all aspects of Dutch maritime expansion.

NOTES

1. Leslie Peirce, *Morality Tales: Law and Gender in the Ottoman Court of Aintab* (Berkeley: University of California Press, 2003), 258.
2. Ibid., 262.
3. Daniel Goffman, *Izmir and the Levantine World, 1550–1650* (Seattle: University of Washington Press, 1990), 52.
4. Quoted in Peter Jackson and Laurence Lockhart, eds., *The Cambridge History of Iran*, vol. 6, *The Timurid and Safavid Periods* (New York: Cambridge University Press, 1986), 703.
5. Edmund Bradley Martin and Chryssee Perry Martin, *Cargoes of the East: The Ports, Trade and Culture of the Arabian Seas and Western Indian Ocean* (1978), 17.

Russian Ambassadors to Holland Display Their Furs, 1576 Representatives from Muscovy impressed the court of King Maximilian II of Bohemia with their sable coats and caps. (Novositi)

- How did Japan respond to domestic social changes and the challenges posed by contact with foreign cultures?

- How did China deal with military and political challenges both inside and outside its borders?

- To what extent was Russia's expanding empire influenced by relations with western Europe in this period?

21

NORTHERN EURASIA, 1500–1800

CHAPTER OUTLINE

Japanese Reunification

The Later Ming and Early Qing Empires

The Russian Empire

Comparative Perspectives

ENVIRONMENT AND TECHNOLOGY: East Asian Porcelain

DIVERSITY AND DOMINANCE: Gendered Violence: The Yangzhou Massacre

The three centuries between 1500 and 1800 saw the rise of the Tokugawa Shogunate in Japan, the Qing Empire in China, and the Russian Empire. Each of these states experienced turbulence as they consolidated power domestically, faced challenges from their neighbors, and made new contacts with commercially and militarily powerful European governments.

In 1603, after a period of civil war and a devastating, if short-lived, conquest of Korea, Japanese rulers united under Tokugawa Ieyasu and established a centralized government. The Tokugawa Shogunate welcomed trade with European merchants for a time, but religious controversy arose when Catholic missionaries began to convert large numbers of Japanese. By the early seventeenth century there were

Online Study Center

This icon will direct you to interactive activities and study materials on the website: *college.hmco.com/pic/bulliet4e.*

605

some 300,000 Japanese Christians; the government responded with massive persecutions and in 1639 it cut off all trade with Europe.

An intriguing look at the rise of the Qing Empire is provided by the story of Li Zicheng°, an apprentice ironworker who lost his job, along with many other government employees, when the emperor needed money to fund more troops to defend Beijing° against attacks by **Manchu** armies. By 1630 Li had found work as a soldier, but he and his comrades mutinied when the government failed to provide them with needed supplies. A natural leader, Li headed a group of several thousand Chinese rebels. They captured towns, conscripted young men into their army, and won popular support with promises to end imperial abuses. In April 1644 they took Beijing without a fight, and the last Ming emperor hanged himself in the palace garden. Their success was short-lived: educated, violent men like Li and the Ming general Wu Sangui joined forces with the Manchu, and they retook Beijing in June.[1]

Shortly before his death in 1576, presiding over a Holy Roman Empire on the brink of collapse, Maximilian II met with Russian ambassadors to Holland who had come to show off their sable coats and caps. Within a century the Netherlands became the world's greatest commercial power, while the princes of Muscovy, led by Ivan IV, engaged in wars of conquest that laid the foundations of the Russian Empire. Under Tsar Peter the Great and his successors, Russia expanded its territory westward to Poland and eastward to Alaska.

JAPANESE
REUNIFICATION

Like China and Russia in the centuries between 1500 and 1800, Japan experienced three major changes: internal and external military conflicts, political growth and strengthening, and expanded commercial and cultural contacts. Along with its culturally homogenous population and natural boundaries, Japan's smaller size made the process of political unification shorter than in the great empires of China and Russia. Japan also differed in its responses to new contacts with western Europeans.

Civil War and the Invasion of Korea, 1500–1603

In the twelfth century Japan's imperial unity had disintegrated, and the country fell under the rule of numerous warlords known as *daimyo*°. Each of the daimyo had his own castle town, a small bureaucracy, and an army of warriors, the *samurai*°. Daimyo pledged a loose allegiance to the hereditary commander of the armies, the shogun, as well as to the Japanese emperor residing in the capital city of Kyoto°. The emperor and shogun were symbols of national unity but lacked political power.

Warfare among the different daimyo was common. In the late 1500s Japan experienced a prolonged civil war that brought the separate Japanese islands under powerful warlords. The most successful of these warlords was Hideyoshi°. In 1592, buoyed with his success in Japan, the supremely confident Hideyoshi launched an invasion of the Asian mainland with 160,000 men. His apparent intention was not just to conquer the Korean peninsula but to make himself emperor of China as well.

The Korean and Japanese languages are closely related, but the dominant influence on Korean culture had long been China. Korea generally accepted a subordinate relationship with its giant neighbor and paid tribute to the Chinese dynasty in power. In many ways the Yi dynasty that ruled Korea from 1392 to 1910 was a model Confucian state. Although Korea had developed its own system of writing in 1443 and made extensive use of printing with movable type from the fifteenth century on, most printing continued to use Chinese characters.

Against Hideyoshi's invaders the Koreans employed all the technological and military skill for which the Yi period was renowned. Ingenious covered warships, or "turtle boats," intercepted a portion of the Japanese fleet. The mentally unstable Hideyoshi countered with brutal punitive measures. The Koreans and their Chinese allies could not stop the Japanese conquest of the peninsula and their invasion of the Chinese province of Manchuria. However, after Hideyoshi's death in 1598, the other Japanese military leaders withdrew their forces, and the Japanese government made peace in 1606.

Li Zicheng (lee ZUH-cheng)   Beijing (bay-JING)

daimyo (DIE-mee-oh)   samurai (SAH-moo-rye)
Kyoto (KYOH-toh)   Hideyoshi (HEE-duh-YOH-shee)

C H R O N O L O G Y		
Korea and Japan	**China and Central Asia**	**Russia**

	Korea and Japan	China and Central Asia	Russia
1500		**1517** Portuguese embassy to China	
	1543 First Portuguese contacts		**1533-1584** Rule of Prince Ivan IV
			1582 Russians conquer Khanate of Sibir
	1592 Japanese invasion of Korea		
1600	**1603** Tokugawa Shogunate formed	**1601** Matteo Ricci allowed to reside in Beijing	**1613–1645** Rule of Mikhail, the first Romanov tsar
	1633–1639 Edicts close down trade with Europe	**1644** Qing conquest of Beijing	
		1662–1722 Rule of Emperor Kangxi	**1649** Subordination of serfs complete
		1689 Treaty of Nerchinsk with Russia	**1689–1725** Rule of Peter the Great
		1691 Qing control of Inner Mongolia	
1700	**1702** Trial of the Forty-Seven Ronin		**1712** St. Petersburg becomes Russia's capital
		1736–1795 Rule of Emperor Qianlong	
			1762–1796 Rule of Catherine the Great
	1792 Russian ships first spotted off the coast of Japan		**1799** Alaska becomes a Russian colony

Korea was severely devastated by the invasion. In the confusion after the Japanese withdrawal, the Korean *yangban* (nobility) and lesser royals were able to lay claim to so much tax-paying land that royal revenues may have fallen by two-thirds. But the most dramatic consequences of the Japanese invasion were in China. The battles in Manchuria weakened Chinese garrisons there, permitting Manchu opposition to consolidate. Manchu forces invaded Korea in the 1620s and eventually compelled the Yi to become a tributary state. As already related, the Manchu would be in possession of Beijing, China's capital, by 1644.

The Tokugawa Shogunate, to 1800	After Hideyoshi's demise, Japanese leaders brought the civil wars to an end, and in 1603 they established a more centralized

government. A new shogun, Tokugawa Ieyasu° (1543–1616),

Tokugawa Ieyasu (TOH-koo-GAH-wah ee-ay-YAH-soo)

had gained the upper hand in the conflict and established a new military government known as the **Tokugawa Shogunate**. The shoguns created a new administrative capital at Edo° (now Tokyo). Trade along the well-maintained road between Edo and the imperial capital of Kyoto promoted the development of the Japanese economy and the formation of other trading centers (see Map 25.3).

Although the Tokugawa Shogunate gave Japan more political unity than the islands had seen in centuries, the regional lords, the daimyo, still had a great deal of power and autonomy. Ieyasu and his successor shoguns had to work hard to keep this decentralized political system from disintegrating.

In some ways, economic integration was more a feature of Tokugawa Japan than was political centralization. Because Tokugawa shoguns required the daimyo to visit Edo frequently, good roads and maritime transport linked the city to the castle towns on three of the four main islands of Japan. Commercial

Edo (ED-oh)

Korean Turtle Boats This painting shows a fleet of Korean warships under the command of Admiral Yi Sun-shin who repelled numerous attacks by the Japanese in the last decade of the sixteenth century. Yi Sun-Shin is celebrated for his invention of the "turtle boat" – the world's first ironclad warship. (National Museum of Seoul/photo: Dr. Yushin Yoo)

traffic also developed along these routes. The shogun paid the lords in rice, and the lords paid their followers in rice. To meet their personal expenses, recipients of rice had to convert much of it into cash. This transaction stimulated the development of rice exchanges at Edo and at Osaka°, where merchants speculated in rice prices. By the late seventeenth century Edo was one of the largest cities in the world, with nearly a million inhabitants.

The domestic peace of the Tokugawa era forced the warrior class to adapt itself to the growing bureaucratic needs of the state. As the samurai became better educated, more attuned to the tastes of the civil elite, and more interested in conspicuous consumption, they became important customers for merchants dealing in silks, *sake*° (rice wine), fans, porcelain, lacquer ware, books, and moneylending. The state attempted—unsuccessfully—to curb the independence of the merchants when the economic well-being of the samurai was threatened, particularly when rice prices went too low or interest rates on loans were too high.

The 1600s and 1700s were centuries of high achievement in artisanship, and Japanese skills in steel making, pottery, and lacquer ware were joined by excellence in the production and decoration of porcelain (see Environment and Technology: East Asian Porcelain), thanks in no small part to Korean experts brought back to Japan after the invasion of 1592. In the early 1600s manufacturers and merchants amassed enormous family fortunes. Several of the most important industrial and financial companies—for instance, the Mitsui° companies—had their origins in sake breweries of the early Tokugawa period, then branched out into manufacturing, finance, and transport.

Wealthy merchant families usually cultivated close alliances with their regional daimyo and, if possible, with the shogun himself. In this way they could weaken the strict control of merchant activity that was an official part of Tokugawa policy. By the end of the 1700s the merchant families of Tokugawa Japan held the key to future modernization and the development of heavy industry, particularly in the prosperous provinces.

Online Study Center
Improve Your Grade
Primary Source: Some
Observation on Merchants

Osaka (OH-sah-kah)　**sake** (SAH-kay)

Mitsui (MIT-soo-ee)

East Asian Porcelain

By the 1400s artisans in China, Korea, and Japan were all producing high-quality pottery with lustrous surface glazes. The best quality, intended for the homes of the wealthy and powerful, was made of pure white clay and covered with a hard translucent glaze. Artisans often added intricate decorations in cobalt blue and other colors. Cheaper pottery found a huge market in East Asia.

Such pottery was also exported to Southeast Asia, the Indian Ocean, and the Middle East. Little found its way to Europe before 1600, but imports soared once the Dutch established trading bases in East Asia. Europeans called the high-quality ware "porcelain." Blue and white designs were especially popular.

One of the great centers of Chinese production was at the large artisan factory at Jingdezhen (JING-deh-JUHN). No sooner had the Dutch tapped into this source than the civil wars and Manchu conquests disrupted production in the middle 1600s. Desperate for a substitute source, the Dutch turned to porcelain from Japanese producers at Arita and Imari, near Nagasaki. Despite Japan's restriction of European trade, the Dutch East India Company transported some 190,000 pieces of Japanese ceramic ware to the Netherlands between 1653 and 1682.

In addition to a wide range of Asian designs, Chinese and Japanese artisans made all sorts of porcelain for the European market. These included purely decorative pottery birds, vases, and pots as well as utilitarian vessels and dishes intended for table use. The serving dish illustrated here came from dinnerware sets the Japanese made especially for the Dutch East India Company. The VOC logo at the center represents the first letters of the company's name in Dutch. It is surrounded by Asian design motifs.

After the return of peace in China, the VOC imported tens of thousands of Chinese porcelain pieces a year. The Chinese artisans sometimes produced imitations of Japanese designs that had become popular in Europe. Meanwhile, the Dutch were experimenting with making their own imitations of East Asian porcelain, right down to the Asian motifs and colors that had become so fashionable in Europe.

Japanese Export Porcelain Part of a larger set made for the Dutch East India Company. (Photograph courtesy Peabody Essex Museum, #83830)

Comprehensive Map of the Myriad Nations Thanks to the "Dutch studies" scholars and to overseas contacts, many Japanese were well informed about the cultures, technologies, and political systems of various parts of the world. This combination map and ethnographic text of 1671 enthusiastically explores the differences among the many peoples living or traveling in Asia. The map of the Pacific hemisphere has the north pole on the left and the south pole on the extreme right of the drawing. (The Fotomas Index/The Bridgeman Art Library)

Japan and the Europeans

Direct contacts with Europeans beginning in the mid-sixteenth century presented Japan with new opportunities and problems. The first major impact was on Japanese military technology. Within thirty years of the arrival of the first Portuguese in 1543, the daimyo were fighting with Western-style firearms, copied and improved upon by Japanese armorers. Japan's civil conflicts of the late sixteenth century launched the first East Asian "gunpowder revolution."

The Japanese also welcomed new trade with merchants from distant Portugal, Spain, the Netherlands, and England, but the government closely regulated their activities. Aside from the brief boom in porcelain exports in the seventeenth century, few Japanese goods went to Europe, and not much from Europe found a market in Japan. The Japanese sold the Dutch copper and silver, which the Dutch exchanged in China for silks that they then resold in Japan. The Japanese, of course, had their own trade with China.

Portuguese and Spanish merchant ships also brought Catholic missionaries. One of the first, Francis Xavier, went to India in the mid-sixteenth century looking for converts and later traveled throughout Southeast and East Asia. He spent two years in Japan and died in 1552, hoping to gain entry to China.

Japanese responses were decidedly mixed to Xavier and other Jesuits (members of the Catholic religious order the Society of Jesus). Large numbers of ordinary Japanese found the new faith deeply meaningful, but members of the Japanese elite were inclined to oppose it as disruptive and foreign. Nevertheless, by 1580 more than 100,000 Japanese had become Christians, and one daimyo gave Jesuit missionaries the port city of Nagasaki°. In 1613 Date Masamune°, the fierce and independent daimyo of northern Honshu°, sent his own embassy to the Vatican by way of the Philippines (where there were significant communities of Japanese merchants and pirates) and Mexico

Nagasaki (NAH-guh-SAHK-kee) **Date Masamune** (DAH-tay mah-suh-MOO-nay) **Honshu** (HOHN-shoo)

City. Some daimyo converts ordered their subjects to become Christians as well. Other Japanese were won over by the Jesuit, Dominican, and Franciscan missionaries.

By the early seventeenth century there were some 300,000 Japanese Christians and a few newly ordained Japanese priests. But these extraordinary events could not stand apart from the fractious politics of the day and suspicions about the larger intentions of the Europeans and their well-armed ships. The new shogunate in Edo became the center of hostility to Christianity. In 1614 a decree charging the Christians with seeking to overthrow true doctrine, change the government, and seize the land ordered the movement eliminated. Some missionaries left Japan, but others took their movement underground. The government began its persecutions in earnest in 1617, and the beheadings, crucifixions, and forced recantations over the next several decades destroyed almost the entire Christian community.

A series of decrees issued between 1633 and 1639 went much farther, ordering an end to European trade as the price to be paid for eliminating Christian influences. Europeans who entered illegally faced the death penalty. A new government office made sure Christianity did not reemerge; people were required to produce certificates from Buddhist temples attesting to their religious orthodoxy and thus their loyalty to the regime.

The closing of Japan to European influence was not total. A few Dutch were permitted to reside on a small artificial island in Nagasaki's harbor, and a few Japanese were licensed to supply their needs. The information these intermediaries acquired about European weapons technology, shipbuilding, mathematics and astronomy, anatomy and medicine, and geography was known as "Dutch studies."

The Tokugawa government also placed restrictions on the number of Chinese ships that could trade in Japan, but these were harder to enforce. Regional lords in northern and southern Japan not only pursued overseas trade and piracy but also claimed dominion over islands between Japan and Korea to the east and between Japan and Taiwan to the south, including present-day Okinawa. Despite such evasions, the larger lesson is the substantial success of the new shogunate in exercising its authority.

Elite Decline and Social Crisis

During the 1700s population growth put a great strain on the well-developed lands of central Japan. In more remote provinces, where the lords promoted new settlements and agricultural expansion, the rate of economic growth far outstripped the growth rate in central Japan.

Also destabilizing the Tokugawa government in the 1700s was the shogunate's inability to stabilize rice prices and halt the economic decline of the samurai. To finance their living, the samurai had to convert their rice to cash in the market. The Tokugawa government realized that the rice brokers might easily enrich themselves at the expense of the samurai if the price of rice and the rate of interest were not strictly controlled. Laws designed to regulate both had been passed early in the Tokugawa period, and laws requiring moneylenders to forgive samurai debts were added later. But these laws were not always enforced, sometimes because neither the lords nor the samurai wished them to be. By the early 1700s members of both groups were dependent on the willingness of merchants to provide credit.

The Tokugawa shoguns sought to protect the samurai from decline while curbing the growing power of the merchant class. Their legitimacy rested on their ability to reward and protect the interests of the lords and samurai who had supported the Tokugawa conquest. But the Tokugawa government, like the governments of China, Korea, and Vietnam, accepted the Confucian idea that agriculture should be the basis of state wealth and that merchants should occupy lowly positions in society because of their reputed lack of moral character.

Governments throughout East Asia used Confucian philosophy to attempt to limit the influence and power of merchants. The Tokugawa government, however, was at a special disadvantage. Its decentralized system limited its ability to regulate merchant activities and actually stimulated the growth of commercial activities. From the founding of the Tokugawa Shogunate in 1603 until 1800, the economy grew faster than the population. Household amenities and cultural resources that in China were found only in the cities were common in the Japanese countryside. Despite official disapproval, merchants and others involved in the growing economy enjoyed relative freedom and influence in eighteenth-century Japan. They produced a vivid culture of their own, fostering the development of *kabuki* theater, colorful woodblock prints and silk-screened fabrics, and restaurants.

The ideological and social crisis of Tokugawa Japan's transformation from a military to a civil society is captured in the "Forty-Seven Ronin°" incident of 1701–1703. A senior minister provoked a young daimyo into drawing his sword at the shogun's court. For this offense the young lord was sentenced to commit *seppuku°*,

---

ronin (ROH-neen) **seppuku** (SEP-poo-koo)

Woodblock Print of the "Forty-Seven Ronin" Story The saga of the forty-seven ronin and the avenging of their fallen leader has fascinated the Japanese public since the event occurred in 1702. This watercolor from the Tokugawa period shows the leaders of the group pausing on the snowy banks of the Sumida River in Edo (Tokyo) before storming their enemy's residence. (Private Collection)

the ritual suicide of the samurai. His own followers then became *ronin,* "masterless samurai," obliged by the traditional code of the warrior to avenge their deceased master. They broke into the house of the senior minister who had provoked their own lord, and they killed him and others in his household. Then they withdrew to a temple in Edo and notified the shogun of what they had done out of loyalty to their lord and to avenge his death.

A legal debate began in the shogun's government. To deny the righteousness of the ronin would be to deny samurai values. But to approve their actions would create social chaos, undermine laws against murder, and deny the shogunal government the right to try cases of samurai violence. The shogun ruled that the ronin had to die but would be permitted to die honorably by committing *seppuku.* Traditional samurai values had to surrender to

the supremacy of law. The purity of purpose of the ronin is still celebrated in Japan, but since then Japanese writers, historians, and teachers have recognized that the self-sacrifice of the ronin for the sake of upholding civil law was necessary.

The Tokugawa Shogunate put into place a political and economic system that fostered innovation, but the government itself could not exploit it. Thus, during the Tokugawa period the government remained quite traditional while other segments of society developed new methods of productivity and management.

THE LATER MING AND EARLY QING EMPIRES

Like Japan, China after 1500 experienced civil and foreign wars, an important change in government, and new trading and cultural relations with Europe and its neighbors. The internal and external forces at work in China were different in detail and operated on a much larger scale, but they led in similar directions. By 1800 China had a greatly enhanced empire, an expanding economy, and growing doubts about the importance of European trade and Christianity.

The Ming Empire, 1500–1644

The brilliant economic and cultural achievements of the early **Ming Empire** continued during the 1500s. Ming manufacturers had transformed the global economy with their techniques for the assembly-line production of porcelain. An international market eager for Ming porcelain, as well as for silk and lacquered furniture, stimulated the commercial development of East Asia, the Indian Ocean, and Europe. But this golden age was followed by many decades of political weakness, warfare, and rural woes until a new dynasty, the Qing° from Manchuria, guided China back to peace and prosperity.

The Europeans whose ships began to seek out new contacts with China in the early sixteenth century left many accounts of their impressions. Like others before them, they were astonished at Ming China's imperial power, exquisite manufactures, and vast population. European merchants bought such large quantities of the high-grade blue-on-white porcelain commonly

Qing (ching)

used by China's upper classes that in English all fine dishes became known simply as "china."

The growing integration of China into the world economy stimulated rapid growth in the silk, cotton, and porcelain industries. Agricultural regions that supplied raw materials to these industries and food for the expanding urban populations also prospered. In exchange for Chinese porcelain and textiles, tens of thousands of tons of silver from Japan and Latin America flooded into China in the century before 1640. The influx of silver led many Chinese to substitute payments in silver for various land taxes, labor obligations, and other kinds of dues.

Ming cities had long been culturally and commercially vibrant. Many large landowners and absentee landlords lived in the cities, as did officials, artists, and rich merchants who had purchased ranks or prepared their sons for the examinations. The elite classes had created a brilliant culture in which novels, operas, poetry, porcelain, and painting were all closely interwoven. Owners of small businesses catering to the urban elites could make money through printing, tailoring, running restaurants, or selling paper, ink, ink-stones, and writing brushes. The imperial government operated factories for the production of ceramics and silks. Enormous government complexes at Jingdezhen and elsewhere invented assembly-line techniques and produced large quantities of high-quality ceramics for sale in China and abroad.

Despite these achievements, serious problems were developing that left the Ming Empire economically exhausted, politically deteriorating, and technologically lagging behind both its East Asian neighbors and some European countries. Some of these problems were the result of natural disasters associated with climate change and disease. There is evidence that the climate changes known as the Little Ice Age in seventeenth-century Europe affected the climate in China as well (see Issues in World History: The Little Ice Age on page 632). Annual temperatures dropped, reached a low point about 1645, and remained low until the early 1700s. The resulting agricultural distress and famine fueled large uprisings that speeded the end of the Ming Empire. The devastation caused by these uprisings and the spread of epidemic disease resulted in steep declines in local populations.

Along with many benefits, the rapid growth in the trading economy also led to such problems as rapid urban growth and business speculation. Some provinces suffered from price inflation caused by the flood of silver. In contrast to the growing involvement of European governments in promoting economic growth, the Ming government showed little interest in developing the economy and pursued some policies that were inimical to it. Despite the fact that paper currency had failed to find general acceptance as far back as the 1350s, Ming governments persisted in issuing new paper money and promoting copper coins, even after abundant supplies of silver had won the approval of the markets. Corruption was also a serious government problem. By the end of the Ming period the factories were plagued by disorder and inefficiency. The situation became so bad during the late sixteenth and seventeenth centuries that workers held strikes with increasing frequency. During a labor protest at Jingdezhen in 1601, workers threw themselves into the kilns to protest working conditions.

Yet the urban and industrial sectors of later Ming society fared much better than the rural, agricultural sector. Following a period of economic growth and recovery from the population decline of the thirteenth century, the rural Ming economy did not maintain strong growth. After the beginning of the sixteenth century, China had knowledge, gained from European traders, of new crops from Africa and America. But they were introduced very slowly, and neither rice-growing regions in southern China nor wheat-growing regions in northern China experienced a meaningful increase in productivity under the later Ming. After 1500 economic depression in the countryside, combined with recurring epidemics in central and southern China, kept rural population growth in check.

Ming Collapse and the Rise of the Qing

Rising environmental, economic, and administrative problems weakened the Ming Empire but did not cause its fall. That was the result of growing rebellion within and the rising power of the Manchu outside China's borders.

Insecure boundaries were an indication of the later Ming Empire's difficulties. The Ming had long been under pressure from the powerful Mongol federations of the north and west. In the late 1500s large numbers of Mongols were unified by their devotion to the Dalai Lama°, or universal teacher, of Tibetan Buddhism, whom they regarded as their spiritual leader. Building on this spiritual unity, a brilliant leader named Galdan restored Mongolia as a regional military power around 1600. The Manchu, an agriculturally based people who controlled the region north of Korea, grew stronger in the northeast.

Dalai Lama (DAH-lie LAH-mah)

In the southwest, repeated uprisings occurred among native peoples crowded by the immigration of Chinese farmers. Pirates based in Okinawa and Taiwan, many of them Japanese, frequently looted the southeastern coastal towns. Ming military resources, concentrated against the Mongols and the Manchu in the north, could not be deployed to defend the coasts. As a result, many southern Chinese migrated to Southeast Asia to profit from the sea-trading networks of the Indian Ocean.

As the previous section related, the Japanese invasion of 1592 to 1598 set the Ming collapse in motion. To stop the Japanese the Ming brought Manchu troops into an international force and eventually paid a high price for that invitation. Weakened by the strain of repelling the Japanese, Chinese defenses in the northeast could not stop the advance of Manchu troops, who had already brought Korea under their sway.

Taking advantage of this situation, as the opening of this chapter related, the Chinese rebel leader Li Zicheng advanced and captured Beijing. With the emperor dead by his own hand and the imperial family in flight, a Ming general invited Manchu leaders to help his forces take Beijing from the rebels. The Manchu did so in the summer of 1644. Rather than restoring the Ming, they claimed China for their own and began a forty-year conquest of the rest of the Ming territories (see Diversity and Dominance: Gendered Violence: The Yangzhou Massacre). By the end of the century, the Manchu had gained control of south China and incorporated the island of Taiwan into imperial China for the first time (see Map 21.1). They also conquered parts of Mongolia and Central Asia.

Online Study Center
Improve Your Grade
Interactive Map: The Qing Empire, 1644–1783

Map 21.1 The Qing Empire, 1644–1783 The Qing Empire began in Manchuria and captured north China in 1644. Between 1644 and 1783 the Qing conquered all the former Ming territories and added Taiwan, the lower Amur River basin, Inner Mongolia, eastern Turkestan, and Tibet. The resulting state was more than twice the size of the Ming Empire.

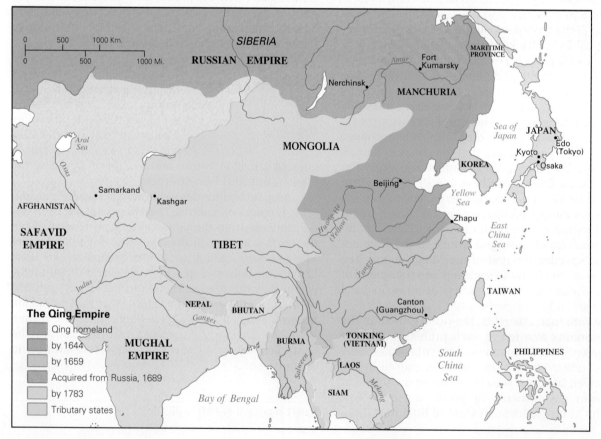

A Manchu family headed the new **Qing Empire**, and Manchu generals commanded the military forces. But the Manchu were a very small portion of the population, and one of several minorities. The overwhelming majority of Qing officials, soldiers, merchants, and farmers were ethnic Chinese. Like other successful invaders of China, the Qing soon adopted Chinese institutions and policies.

Trading Companies and Missionaries

For the European mariners who braved the long voyages to Asia, the China trade was second in importance only to the spice trade of southern Asia. China's vast population and manufacturing skills drew a steady supply of ships from western Europe, but enthusiasm for the trade developed more slowly, especially at the imperial court.

A Portuguese ship reached China at the end of 1513, but it was not permitted to trade. A formal Portuguese embassy in 1517 got bogged down in Chinese protocol and procrastination, and China expelled the Portuguese in 1522. Finally, in 1557 the Portuguese gained the right to trade from a base in Macao°. Spain's Asian trade was conducted from Manila in the Philippines, which served as the terminus of trans-Pacific trade routes from South America. For a time, the Spanish and the Dutch both maintained outposts for trade with China and Japan on the island of Taiwan, but in 1662 they were forced to concede control over the island to the Qing, who incorporated Taiwan for the first time as a part of China.

By then, the Dutch East India Company (VOC) had displaced the Portuguese as the major European trader in the Indian Ocean and, despite the setback on Taiwan, was establishing itself as the main European trader in East Asia. VOC representatives courted official favor in China by acknowledging the moral superiority of the emperor. They performed the ritual kowtow, in which the visitor knocked his head on the floor while crawling toward the throne.

Catholic missionaries accompanied the Portuguese and Spanish merchants to China, just as they did to Japan. While the Franciscans and Dominicans sought to replicate the conversion efforts at the bottom of society that had worked so well in Japan, the Jesuits concentrated their efforts among China's intellectual and political elite. In this they were far more successful than they had been in Japan—at least until the eighteenth century.

The outstanding Jesuit of late Ming China, Matteo Ricci° (1552–1610), became expert in the Chinese language and an accomplished scholar of the Confucian classics. Under Ricci's leadership, the Jesuits sought to adapt Catholic Christianity to Chinese cultural traditions while enhancing their status by introducing the Chinese to the latest science and technology from Europe. From 1601 Ricci was allowed to reside in Beijing on an imperial stipend as a Western scholar. Later Jesuits headed the office of astronomy that issued the official calendar.

Online Study Center
Improve Your Grade
Primary Source: Journals

Emperor Kangxi (r. 1662–1722)

The seventeenth and eighteenth centuries—particularly the reigns of the **Kangxi°** (r. 1662–1722) and Qianlong° (r. 1736–1796) emperors—were a period of great economic, military, and cultural achievement in China. The early Qing emperors wished to foster economic and demographic recovery in China. They repaired the roads and waterworks, lowered transit taxes, mandated comparatively low rents and interest rates, and established economic incentives for resettlement of the areas devastated during the peasant rebellions of the late Ming period. Foreign trade was encouraged. Vietnam, Burma, and Nepal sent regular embassies to the Qing tribute court and carried the latest Chinese fashions back home. Overland routes of communication from Korea to Central Asia were revived, and through its conquests the Qing Empire gained access to the superior horses of Afghanistan.

The early Qing conquest of Beijing and north China was carried out under the leadership of a group of Manchu aristocrats who dominated the first Qing emperor° based in China and were regents for his young son, who was declared emperor in 1662. This child-emperor, Kangxi, spent several years doing political battle with his regents, and in 1669 he gained real as well as formal control of the government by executing his chief regent. Kangxi was then sixteen. He was an intellectual prodigy who mastered classical Chinese, Manchu, and Mongolian at an early age and memorized the Chinese classics. His reign, lasting until his death in 1722, was marked not only by great expansion of the empire but by great stability as well.

Macao (muh-KOW)

Matteo Ricci (mah-TAY-oh REE-chee) **Kangxi** (KAHNG-shee)
Qianlong (chee-YEN-loong)

Gendered Violence:
The Yangzhou Massacre

*A*fter the fall of Beijing to the Manchu, the rest of China felt the dominance of the conquerors. The Qing were not eager for reminders of their brutal takeover to circulate. This rare eyewitness account, which survived because it was smuggled out of China, reveals not just the violence of the conquest but also the diversity of its impact on men and women.

The account begins in 1645 as rumors of approaching Manchu soldiers spread through Yangzhou, an important city near the juncture of the Yangzi River and the Grand Canal, and the soldiers charged with its defense begin to flee.

Crowds of barefoot and disheveled refugees were flocking into the city. When questioned, they were too distraught to reply. At that point dozens of mounted soldiers in confused waves came surging south looking as though they had given up all hope. Along them appeared a man who turned out to be the commandant himself. It seems he had intended to leave by the east gate but could not because the enemy soldiers outside the wall were drawing too near; he was therefore forced to cut across this part of town to reach the south gate. This is how we first learned for sure that the enemy troops would enter the city . . . .

My house backed against the city wall, and peeping through the chinks in my window, I saw the soldiers on the wall marching south then west, solemn and in step. Although the rain was beating down, it did not seem to disturb them. This reassured me because I gathered that they were well disciplined units.

. . . For a long time no one came. I retreated again to the back window and found that the regiment on the wall had broken ranks; some soldiers were walking about, others standing still.

All of a sudden I saw some soldiers escorting a group of women dressed in Yangzhou fashion. This was my first real shock. Back in the house, I said to my wife, "Should things go badly when the soldiers enter the city, you may need to end your life."

"Yes," she replied, "Whatever silver we have you should keep. I think we women can stop thinking about life in this world." She gave me all the silver, unable to control her crying. . . .

Soon my younger brother arrived, then my two older brothers. We discussed the situation and I said, "The people who live in our neighborhood are all rich merchants. It will be disastrous if they think we are rich too." I then urged my brothers to brave the rain and quickly take the women by the back route to my older brother's house. His home was situated behind Mr. He's graveyard and was surrounded by the huts of poor families. . . .

Finally, my eldest brother reappeared and said, "People are being killed in the streets! What are we waiting for here? It doesn't matter so much whether we live or die, as long as we brothers stay together." Immediately I gathered together our ancestral tablets and went with him to our second brother's house. . . .

The cunning soldiers, suspecting that many people were still hidden, tried to entice them out by posting a placard promising clemency. About fifty to sixty people, half of them women, emerged. My elder brother said, "We four by ourselves will never survive if we run into these vicious soldiers, so we had better join the crowd. Since there are so many of them, escape will be easier. Even if things do not turn out well, as long as we are together, we will have no cause for regret." In our bewilderment we could think of no other way to save our lives. Thus agreed, we went to join the group.

The leaders were three Manchu soldiers. They searched my brothers and found all the silver they were carrying, but left me untouched. At that point some women appeared, two of whom called out to me. I recognized them as the concubines of my friend Mr. Zhu Shu and stopped them anxiously. They were disheveled and partly naked, their feet bare and covered with mud up to the ankles. One was holding a girl whom the soldiers hit with a whip and threw into the mud. Then we were immediately driven on. One soldier, sword in hand, took the lead; another drove us from behind with a long spear; and a third walked along on our right and left flanks alternately, making sure no one escaped. In groups of twenty or thirty we were herded along like sheep and cattle. If we faltered we were struck, and some people were even killed on the spot. The women were tied together with long chains around their necks, like a clumsy string of pearls. Stumbling at every step, they were soon covered with mud. Here and there on the ground lay babies, trampled by people or horses. Blood and gore soaked the fields, which were filled with the sound of sobbing. We passed gutters and ponds piled high with corpses; the blood had turned the water to a deep greenish-red color and filled the ponds to the brim.

... We then entered the house of [a] merchant, ... which had been taken over by the three soldiers. Another soldier was already there. He had seized several attractive women and was rifling their trunks for fancy silks, which he piled in a heap. Seeing the three soldiers arrive, he laughed and pushed several dozen of us into the back hall. The women he led into a side chamber. ...

The three soldiers stripped the women of their wet clothing all the way to their underwear, then ordered the seamstress to measure them and give them new garments. The women, thus coerced, had to expose themselves and stand naked. What shame they endured! Once they had changed, the soldiers grabbed them and forced them to join them in eating and drinking, then did whatever they pleased with them, without any regard for decency.

[The narrator escapes and hides atop a wooden canopy over a bed.] Later on a soldier brought a woman in and wanted her to sleep with him in the bed below me. Despite her refusal he forced her to yield. "This is too near the street. It is not a good place to stay," the woman said. I was almost discovered, but after a time the soldier departed with the woman. ... [The narrator flees again and is reunited with his wife and relatives.]

At length, however, there came a soldier of the "Wolf Men" tribe, a vicious-looking man with a head like a mouse and eyes like a hawk. He attempted to abduct my wife. She was obliged to creep forward on all fours, pleading as she had with the others, but to no avail. When he insisted that she stand up, she rolled on the ground and refused. He then beat her so savagely with the flat of his sword that the blood flowed out in streams, totally soaking her clothes. Because my wife had once admonished me, "If I am unlucky I will die no matter what; do not plead for me as a husband or you will get caught too," I acted as if I did not know she was being beaten and hid far away in the grass, convinced she was about to die. Yet the depraved soldier did not stop there; he grabbed her by the hair, cursed her, struck her cruelly, and then dragged her away by the leg. ... Just then they ran into a body of mounted soldiers. One of them said a few words to the soldier in Manchu. At this he dropped my wife and departed with them. Barely able to crawl back, she let out a loud sob, every part of her body injured. ...

Unexpectedly there appeared a handsome looking man of less than thirty, a double-edged sword hung by his side, dressed in Manchu-style hat, red coat, and a pair of black boots. His follower, in a yellow jacket, was also very gallant in appearance. Immediately behind them were several residents of Yangzhou. The young man in red, inspecting me closely, said, "I would judge from your appearance that you are not one of these people. Tell me honestly, what class of person are you?"

I remembered that some people had obtained pardons and others had lost their lives the moment they said that they were poor scholars. So I did not dare come out at once with the truth and instead concocted a story. He pointed to my wife and son and asked who they were, and I told him the truth. "Tomorrow the prince will order that all swords be sheathed and all of you will be spared," he said and then commanded his followers to give us some clothes and an ingot of silver. He also asked me, "How many days have you been without food?"

"Five days," I replied.

"Then come with me," he commanded. Although we only half trusted him, we were afraid to disobey. He led us to a well-stocked house, full of rice, fish, and other provisions. "Treat these four people well," he said to a woman in the house and then left. ...

The next day was [April 30]. Killing and pillaging continued, although not on the previous scale. Still the mansions of the rich were thoroughly looted, and almost all the teenage girls were abducted. ... every grain of rice, every inch of silk now entered these tigers' mouths. The resulting devastation is beyond description.

[May 2]. Civil administration was established in all the prefectures and counties; proclamations were issued aimed at calming the people, and monks from each temple were ordered to burn corpses. The temples themselves were clogged with women who had taken refuge, many of whom had died of fright or starvation. The "List of Corpses Burned" records more than eight hundred thousand, and this list does not include those who jumped into wells, threw themselves into the river, hanged themselves, were burned to death inside houses, or were carried away by the soldiers. ...

When this calamity began there had been eight of us: my two elder brothers, my younger brother, my elder brother's wife, their son, my wife, my son, and myself. Now only three of us survived for sure, though the fate of my wife's brother and sister-in-law was not yet known. ...

From the 25th of the fourth month to the 5th of the fifth month was a period of ten days. I have described here only what I actually experienced or saw with my own eyes; I have not recorded anything I picked up from rumor or hearsay.

QUESTIONS FOR ANALYSIS

1. **What accounts for the soldiers' brutal treatment of the women?**

2. **What did different women do to protect themselves?**

3. **Having conquered, what did the Manchu do to restore order?**

Source: Reprinted with permission of the Free Press, a division of Simon and Schuster Adult Publishing Group from *Chinese Civilization: A Sourcebook,* Second Edition, edited by Patricia Buckley Ebrey, pp. 272–279. Copyright © 1993 by Patricia Buckley Ebrey.

Emperor Kangxi In a portrait from about 1690, the young Manchu ruler is portrayed as a refined scholar in the Confucian tradition. He was a scholar and had great intellectual curiosity, but this portrait would not suggest that he was also capable of leading troops in battle. (The Palace Museum, Beijing)

The Qing rulers were as anxious as the Ming to consolidate their northern frontiers, especially as they feared an alliance between Galdan's Mongol state and the expanding Russian presence along the **Amur° River**. In the 1680s Kangxi sent forces to attack the wooden forts on the northern bank of the Amur that hardy Russian scouts had built. Neither empire sent large forces into the Amur territories, and the contest was partly a struggle for the goodwill of the local Evenk and Dagur peoples. The Qing emperor emphasized the importance of treading lightly in the struggle and well understood the principles of espionage:

> Upon reaching the lands of the Evenks and the Dagurs you will send to announce that you have come to hunt deer. Meanwhile, keep a careful record of the distance and go, while hunting, along the northern bank of the Amur until you come by the shortest route to the town of Russian settlement at Albazin. Thoroughly reconnoiter its location and situation. I don't think the Russians will take a

Amur (AH-moor)

chance on attacking you. If they offer you food, accept it and show your gratitude. If they do attack you, don't fight back. In that case, lead your people and withdraw into our own territories. For I have a plan of my own.[2]

That delicacy gives a false impression of the intensity of the struggle between these two great empires. Qing forces twice attacked Albazin. The Qing were worried about Russian alliances with other frontier peoples, while Russia wished to protect its access to the furs, timber, and metals concentrated in Siberia, Manchuria, and Yakutsk. The Qing and Russians were also rivals for control of northern Asia's Pacific coast. Continued conflict would benefit neither side. In 1689 the Qing and Russian Empires negotiated the Treaty of Nerchinsk, using Jesuit missionaries as interpreters. The treaty fixed the border along the Amur River and regulated trade across it. Although this was a thinly settled area, the treaty proved important since the frontier it demarcated has long endured.

The next step was to settle the Mongolian frontier. Kangxi personally led troops in the great campaigns that defeated Galdan and brought Inner Mongolia under Qing control by 1691.

Kangxi was distinguished by his openness to new ideas and technologies from different regions. Unlike the rulers of Japan, who drove Christian missionaries out, he welcomed Jesuit advisers and put them in important offices. Jesuits helped create maps in the European style as practical guides to newly conquered regions and as symbols of Qing dominance. Kangxi considered introducing the European calendar, but protests from the Confucian elite were so strong that the plan was dropped. The emperor frequently discussed scientific and philosophical issues with the Jesuits. When he fell ill with malaria in the 1690s, Jesuit medical expertise (in this case, the use of quinine) aided his recovery. Kangxi also ordered the creation of illustrated books in Manchu detailing European anatomical and pharmaceutical knowledge.

To gain converts among the Chinese elite, the Jesuits made important compromises in their religious teaching. The most important was their toleration of Confucian ancestor worship. The matter caused great controversy between the Jesuits and their Catholic rivals in China, the Franciscans and Dominicans, and also between the Jesuits and the pope. In 1690 the disagreement reached a high pitch. Kangxi wrote to Rome supporting the Jesuit position. Further disagreement with a papal legate to China led Kangxi to order the expulsion of all missionaries who refused to

sign a certificate accepting his position. Most of the Jesuits signed, but relations with the imperial court were irreparably harmed. Jesuit presence in China declined in the eighteenth century, and later Qing emperors persecuted Christians rather than naming them to high offices.

Chinese Influences on Europe

The exchange of information between the Qing and the Europeans that Kangxi had fostered was never one-way. When the Jesuits informed the Qing court on matters of anatomy, for instance, the Qing were able to demonstrate an early form of inoculation, called "variolation," that had been used to stem the spread of smallpox after the Qing conquest of Beijing. The technique helped inspire the development of other vaccines later in Europe.

Similarly, Jesuit writings about the intellectual and cultural achievements of China excited admiration in Europe. The wealthy and the aspiring middle classes of Europe demanded Chinese things—or things that looked to Europeans as if they could be Chinese. Not only silk, porcelain, and tea were avidly sought, but also cloisonné jewelry, tableware and decorative items, lacquered and jeweled room dividers, painted fans, and carved jade and ivory (which originated in Africa and was finished in China). One of the most striking Chinese influences on European interior life in this period was wallpaper—an adaptation of the Chinese practice of covering walls with enormous loose-hanging watercolors or calligraphy scrolls. By the mid-1700s special workshops throughout China were producing wallpaper and other consumer items according to the specifications of European merchants. The items were shipped to Canton for export to Europe.

In political philosophy, too, the Europeans felt they had something to learn from the early Qing emperors. In the late 1770s poems supposedly written by Emperor Qianlong were translated into French and disseminated through the intellectual circles of western Europe. These works depicted the Qing emperors as benevolent despots who campaigned against superstition and ignorance, curbed the excesses of the aristocracy, and patronized science and the arts. European intellectuals who were questioning their own political systems found the image of a practical, secular, compassionate ruler intriguing. The French thinker Voltaire proclaimed the Qing emperors model philosopher-kings and advocated such rulership as a protection against the growth of aristocratic privilege.

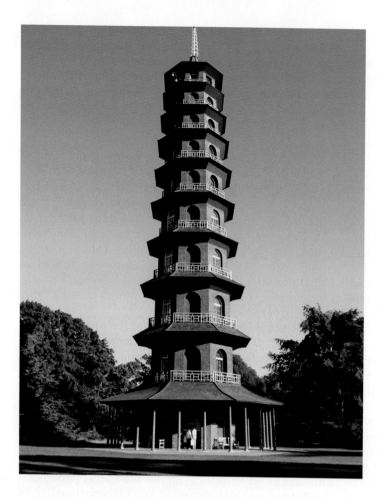

Great Pagoda at Kew Gardens A testament to Europeans' fascination with Chinese culture is the towering Pagoda at the Royal Botanic Gardens in London. Completed in 1762, it was designed by Sir William Chambers as the principal ornament in the pleasure grounds of the White House at Kew, residence of Augusta, the mother of King George III. (Martyn Vickery/Alamy)

Tea and Diplomacy

The Qing were eager to expand China's economic influence but were determined to control the trade very strictly. To make trade easier to tax and to limit piracy and smuggling, the Qing permitted only one market point for each foreign sector. Thus Europeans were permitted to trade only at Canton.

This system worked well enough for European traders until the late 1700s, when Britain became worried about its massive trade deficit with China. From bases in India and Singapore, British traders moved eastward to China and eventually displaced the Dutch as China's leading European trading partner. The directors of the East India Company (EIC) believed that China's technological achievements and gigantic potential markets made it the key to limitless profit. China had tea, rhubarb, porcelain, and silk to offer. By the early 1700s the EIC dominated European trading in Canton.

Tea from China had spread overland on Eurasian routes in medieval and early modern times to become a prized import in Russia, Central Asia, and the Middle East, all of which know it by its northern Chinese name, *cha*—as do the Portuguese. Other western Europeans acquired tea from the sea routes and thus know it by its name in the Fujian province of coastal China and Taiwan: *te.* In much of Europe, tea competed with chocolate and coffee as a fashionable drink by the mid-1600s.

Great fortunes were being made in the tea trade, but the English had not found a product to sell to China. They believed that China was a vast unexploited market, with hundreds of millions of potential consumers of lamp oil made from whale blubber, cotton grown in India or the American South, or guns manufactured in London or Connecticut. Particularly after the loss of the thirteen American colonies, Britain feared that its markets would diminish, and the EIC and other British merchants believed that only the Qing trade system—the

"Canton system," as the British called it—stood in the way of opening new paths for commerce.

The British government also worried about Britain's massive trade deficit with China. Because the Qing Empire rarely bought anything from Britain, British silver poured into China to pay for imported tea and other products. The Qing government, whose revenues were declining in the later 1700s while its expenses rose, needed the silver. But in Britain the imbalance of payments stirred anxiety and anger over the restrictions that the Qing placed on imported foreign goods. To make matters worse, the East India Company had managed its worldwide holdings badly, and as it teetered on bankruptcy, its attempts to manipulate Parliament became increasingly intrusive. In 1792 the British government dispatched Lord George Macartney, a well-connected peer with practical experience in Russia and India, to China. Including scientists, artists, and translators as well as guards and diplomats, the **Macartney mission** showed Britain's great interest in the Qing Empire as well as the EIC's desire to revise the trade system.

China was not familiar with the European system of ambassadors, and Macartney struggled to portray himself in Chinese terms as a "tribute emissary" come to salute the Qianlong emperor's eightieth birthday. He steadfastly refused to perform the kowtow to the emperor, but he did agree to bow on one knee as he would to his own monarch, King George III. The Qianlong emperor received Macartney courteously in September 1793, but he refused to alter the Canton trading system, open new ports of trade, or allow the British to establish a permanent mission in Beijing, The Qing had no interest in changing a system that provided revenue to the imperial family and lessened serious piracy problems. Qianlong sent a letter to King George explaining that China had no need to increase its foreign trade, had no use for Britain's ingenious devices and manufacturers, and set no value on closer diplomatic ties.

Online Study Center
Improve Your Grade
Primary Source: Edict on
Trade with Great Britain

Dutch, French, and Russian embassies soon attempted to achieve what Macartney had failed to do. When they also failed, European frustration with the Qing mounted. The great European admiration for China faded, and China was considered despotic, self-satisfied, and unrealistic. Political solutions seemed impossible because the Qing court would not communicate with foreign envoys or observe the simplest rules of the diplomatic system familiar to Europeans. In Macartney's view, China was like a venerable old warship, well maintained and splendid to look at, but obsolete and no longer up to the task.

Population and Social Stress

The Chinese who escorted Macartney and his entourage in 1792–1793 took them through China's prosperous cities and productive farmland. The visitors did not see evidence of the economic and environmental decline that had begun to affect China in the last decades of the 1700s. The population explosion had intensified demand for rice and wheat, for land to be opened for the planting of crops imported from Africa and the Americas, and for more thorough exploitation of land already in use.

In the peaceful decades of Qing rule, China's population had grown to three times its size in 1500. If one accepts an estimate of some 350 million in the late 1700s, China had twice the population of all of Europe. Despite the efficiency of Chinese agriculture and the gradual adoption of New World crops such as corn and sweet potatoes, population growth led to social and environmental problems. More people meant less land per person for farming. Increased demand for building materials and firewood sharply reduced China's remaining woodlands. Deforestation, in turn, accelerated wind and water erosion and increased the danger of flooding. Dams and dikes were not maintained, and silted-up river channels were not dredged. By the end of the eighteenth century parts of the thousand-year-old Grand Canal linking the rivers of north and south China were nearly unusable, and the towns that bordered it were starved for commerce.

The result was misery in many parts of interior China. Some districts responded by increasing production of cash crops such as tea, cotton, and silk that were tied to the export market. Some peasants sought seasonal jobs in better-off agricultural areas or worked in low-status jobs such as barge puller, charcoal burner, or night soil carrier. Many drifted to the cities to make their way by begging, prostitution, or theft. In central and southwestern China, where serious floods had impoverished many farmers, rebellions became endemic. Often joining in revolt were various indigenous peoples, who were largely concentrated in the less fertile lands in the south and in the northern and western borderlands of the empire (see Map 21.2).

The Qing government was not up to controlling its vast empire. Though twice the size of the Ming geographically, the Qing Empire employed about the same

Map 21.2   Climate and Diversity in the Qing Empire   The Qing Empire encompassed different environmental zones, and the climate differences corresponded to population density and cultural divisions. Wetter regions to the east of the 15-inch rainfall line also contained the most densely populated 20 percent of Qing land. The drier, less densely populated 80 percent of the empire was home to the greatest portion of peoples who spoke languages other than Chinese. Many were nomads, fishermen, hunters, and farmers who raised crops other than rice.

number of officials. The government's dependence on working alliances with local elites had led to widespread corruption and shrinking government revenues. As was the case with other empires, the Qing's spectacular rise had ended, and decline had set in.

THE RUSSIAN EMPIRE

From modest beginnings in 1500, Russia expanded rapidly during the next three centuries to create an empire that stretched from eastern Europe across northern Asia and into North America. Russia also became one of the major powers of Europe by 1750, with armies capable of mounting challenges to its Asian and European neighbors.

The Drive Across Northern Asia

The Russians were a branch of the Slavic peoples of eastern Europe, and most were Orthodox Christians like the Greeks. During the centuries just before 1500, their history had been dominated by Asian rule. The Mongol Khanate of the Golden Horde had ruled the Russians and their neighbors from the 1240s until 1480.

Under the Golden Horde Moscow became the most important Russian city and the center of political power. Moscow lay in the forest that stretched across northern

Eurasia, in contrast to the treeless steppe (plains) favored by Mongol horsemen for pasture. The princes of **Muscovy°**, the territory surrounding the city of Moscow, led the movement against the Golden Horde and ruthlessly annexed the great territories of the neighboring Russian state of Novgorod in 1478.

Once free from Mongol domination, the princes of Moscovy set out on conquests that in time made them masters of the old dominions of the Golden Horde and then of a far greater empire. Prince Ivan IV (r. 1533–1584) pushed the conquests south and east, expanding Russia's borders far to the east through the conquest of the Khanates of Kazan and Astrakhan and the northern Caucasus region (see Map 21.3).

At the end of the sixteenth century, Russians ruled the largest state in Europe and large territories on the Asian side of the **Ural Mountains** as well. Since 1547 the Russian ruler used the title **tsar°** (from the Roman imperial title "caesar"), the term Russians had used for the rulers of the Mongol Empire. The Russian church promoted the idea of Moscow as the "third Rome," successor to the Roman Empire's second capital, Constantinople, which had fallen to the Ottoman Turks in 1453. But such foreign titles were a thin veneer over a very Russian pattern of expansion.

Online Study Center
Improve Your Grade
Interactive Map: Expansion of Russia, to 1725

These claims to greatness were also exaggerated: in 1600 the Russian Empire was poor, backward, and landlocked. Only the northern city of Arkangelsk was connected by water to the rest of the world—when its harbor was not frozen. The independent Crimean peoples to the south were powerful enough to sack Moscow in 1571. Beyond them, the still vigorous Ottoman Empire controlled the shores of the Black Sea, while the Safavid rulers of Iran dominated the trade routes of southern Central Asia. The powerful kingdoms of Sweden and Poland-Lithuania to the west turned back Russian forces trying to gain access to the warmer waters of the Baltic Sea and pummeled them badly.

A path of less resistance lay to the east across **Siberia**, and it had much to recommend it. Many Russians felt more at home in the forested northern part of Siberia than on the open steppes, and the thinly inhabited region teemed with valuable resources. Most prominent of these resources was the soft, dense fur that forest animals grew to survive the long winter cold. Like their counterparts in Canada (see Chapter 18), hardy Russian pioneers in Siberia made a living from animal pelts. The

Muscovy (MUSS-koe-vee)   **tsar** (zahr)

merchants from western Europe and other lands who came to buy these furs in Moscow provided the tsars with revenues and access to European technology.

Early Russian exploration of Siberia was not the work of the state but of the Strogonovs, a wealthy Russian trading family. The small bands of hunting and fishing peoples who inhabited this cold and desolate region had no way of resisting the armed adventurers hired by the Strogonovs. Their troops attacked the only political power in the region, the Khanate of Sibir, and they used their rifles to destroy the khanate in 1582. Taking advantage of rivers to move through the almost impenetrable forests, Russian fur trappers reached the Pacific during the seventeenth century and soon crossed over into Alaska. Russian political control followed at a much slower pace. In the seventeenth century Siberia was a frontier zone with widely scattered forts, not a province under full control. Native Siberian peoples continued to resist Russian control fiercely, and the Russians had to placate local leaders with gifts and acknowledge their rights and authority. From the early seventeenth century the tsar also used Siberia as a penal colony for criminals and political prisoners.

The trade in furs and forest products helped ease Russian isolation and fund further conquests. The eastward expansion of the Russian state took second place during the seventeenth century to the tsars' efforts to build political and military power and establish control over the more numerous peoples of Siberia and the steppe.

In the 1640s Russian settlers had begun to move into the valley of the Amur River east of Mongolia in order to grow grain. The government's wooden forts aroused the concerns of the Ming about yet another threat on their northern frontier. As seen already, by the time the Qing were in a position to deal with the Russian presence, the worrisome threat of Galdan's Mongol military power had arisen. Equally concerned about the Mongols, the Russians were pleased to work out a frontier agreement with China. The 1689 Treaty of Nerchinsk recognized Russian claims west of Mongolia but required the Russians to withdraw their settlements east. Moreover, the negotiations showed China's recognition of Russia as an important and powerful neighbor.

Russian Society and Politics to 1725

Russian expansion produced far-reaching demographic changes and more gradual changes in the relations of the tsar with the elite classes. A third transformation was in the freedom and mobility of the Russian peasantry.

As the empire expanded, it incorporated people with different languages, religious beliefs, and ethnic identities. The emerging Russian Empire included peoples who

Map 21.3 The Expansion of Russia, 1500–1800 Sweden and Poland initially blocked Russian expansion in Europe, while the Ottoman Empire blocked the southwest. In the sixteenth century, Russia began to expand east, toward Siberia and the Pacific Ocean. By the end of the rule of Catherine the Great in 1796, Russia encompassed all of northern and northeastern Eurasia.

spoke Asian languages and who were not Christians. Language differences were not hard to overcome, but religious and other cultural differences often caused tensions, especially when differences were manipulated for political purposes. Orthodox missionaries made great efforts to turn people in Siberia into Christians, in much the same way that Catholic missionaries did in Canada. But among the more populous steppe peoples, Islam eventually replaced Christianity as the dominant religion. More fundamental than language, ethnicity, or religion were the differences in how people made their living. Russians tended to live as farmers, hunters, builders, scribes, or merchants, while those newly incorporated into the empire were mostly herders, caravan workers, and soldiers.

As people mixed, individual and group identities could become quite complex. Even among Russian speakers who were members of the Russian Orthodox Church there was wide diversity of identity. The **Cossacks** are a revealing example. The name probably came from a Turkic word for a warrior or mercenary soldier and referred to bands of people living on the steppes between Moscovy and the Caspian and Black Seas. In practice, Cossacks became highly diverse in their origins and beliefs. What mattered was that they belonged to close-knit bands, were superb riders and fighters, and were feared by both the villagers and the legal authorities. Cossacks made temporary allegiances with many rulers but were most loyal to their bands and to whoever was currently paying for their military services.

Many Cossacks were important allies in the expansion of the Russian Empire. They formed the majority of the soldiers and early settlers employed by the Strogonovs in the penetration of Siberia. Most historians believe that Cossacks founded all the major towns of Russian Siberia. They also manned the Russian camps on the Amur River. The Cossacks west of the Urals performed distinctive service for Russia in defending against Swedish and Ottoman incursions, but they also resisted any efforts to undermine their own political autonomy. Those in the rich and populous lands of the Ukraine, for example, rebelled when the tsar agreed to a division of their lands with Poland-Lithuania in 1667.

In the early seventeenth century Swedish and Polish forces briefly occupied Moscow on separate occasions. In the midst of this "Time of Troubles" the old line of Muscovite rulers was finally deposed, and the Russian aristocracy—the boyars°—allowed one of their own, Mikhail Romanov, to become tsar (r. 1613–1645). The early Romanov° rulers saw a close connection between the consolidation of their own authority and successful competition with neighboring powers. They tended to represent conflicts between Slavic Russians and Turkic peoples of Central Asia as being between Christians and "infidels" or between the civilized and the "barbaric." Despite this rhetoric, it is important to understand that these cultural groups were defined less by blood ties than by the way in which they lived.

The political and economic transformations of the Russian Empire had serious repercussions for the peasants who tilled the land in European Russia. As centralized power rose, the freedom of the peasants fell. The process was longer and more complex than the rise of slavery in the Americas. The Muscovite rulers and early tsars rewarded their loyal nobles with grants of land that included obligations of the local peasants to work for these lords. Law and custom permitted peasants to change masters during a two-week period each year, which encouraged lords to treat their peasants well, but the rising commercialization of agriculture also raised the value of these labor obligations.

The long periods of civil and foreign warfare in the late sixteenth and early seventeenth centuries caused such disruption and economic decline that many peasants fled to the Cossacks or across the Urals to escape. Some who couldn't flee sold themselves into slavery to ensure a steady supply of food. When peace returned, landlords sought to recover these runaway peasants and bind them more firmly to their land. A law change in 1649 completed the transformation of peasants into **serfs** by eliminating the period when they could change masters and removing limitations on the length of the period during which runaways could be forced to return to their masters.

Like slavery, serfdom was a hereditary status, but in theory the serf was tied to a piece of land, not owned by a master. In practice, the difference between serfdom and slavery grew finer as the laws regulating selfdom became stricter. By 1723 all Russian slaves were transformed into serfs. In the Russian census of 1795, serfs made up over half the population of Russia. The serfs were under the control of landowners who made up only 2 percent of Russia's population, similar to the size of the slave-owning class in the Caribbean.

Peter the Great

The greatest of the Romanovs was Tsar **Peter the Great** (r. 1689–1725), who made major changes to reduce Russia's isolation and increase the empire's size and power. Tsar Peter is remembered for his efforts to turn Russia away from its Asian cultural connections and toward what he deemed the civilization of the West. In fact, he accelerated trends under way for some time. By the time he ascended the throne, there

---

boyar (BOY-ar)   **Romanov** (ROH-man-off or roh-MAN-off)

Peter the Great This portrait from his time as a student in Holland in 1697 shows Peter as ruggedly masculine and practical, quite unlike most royal portraits of the day that posed rulers in foppish elegance and haughty majesty. Peter was a popular military leader as well as an autocratic ruler. (Collection, Countess Bobrinskoy/ Michael Holford)

were hundreds of foreign merchants in Moscow; western European soldiers had trained a major part of the army in new weapons and techniques; and Italian architects had made an impression on the city's churches and palaces. It was on this substantial base that Peter erected a more rapid transformation of Russia.

Peter matured quickly both physically and mentally. In his youth the government was in the hands of his half-sister Sophia, who was regent on behalf of him and her sickly brother Ivan. Living on an estate near the foreigners' quarter outside Moscow, Peter learned what he could of life outside Russia and busied himself with gaining practical skills in blacksmithing, carpentry, shipbuilding, and the arts of war. He organized his own military drill unit among other young men. When Princess Sophia tried to take complete control of the government in 1689, Peter rallied enough support to send her to a monastery, secure the abdication of Ivan, and take charge of Russia. He was still in his teens.

Peter concerned himself with Russia's expansion and modernization. To secure a warm-water port on the Black Sea, he constructed a small but formidable navy that could blockade Ottoman ports. Describing his wars with the Ottoman Empire as a new crusade to liberate Constantinople from the Muslim sultans, Peter also saw himself as the legal protector of Orthodox Christians living under Ottoman rule. Peter's forces had seized the port of Azov in 1696, but the fortress was lost again in 1713, and Russian expansion southward was blocked for the rest of Peter's reign.

In the winter of 1697–1698, after his Black Sea campaign, Peter traveled in disguise across Europe to discover how western European societies were becoming so powerful and wealthy. The young tsar paid special attention to ships and weapons, even working for a time as a ship's carpenter in the Netherlands. With great insight, he perceived that western European success owed as much to trade and toleration as to technology. Trade generated the money to spend on weapons, while toleration attracted talented persons fleeing persecution. Upon his return to Russia, Peter resolved to expand and reform his vast and backward empire.

In the long and costly Great Northern War (1700–1721), his modernized armies broke Swedish control of the Baltic Sea, establishing more direct contacts between Russia and Europe. Peter's victory forced the European powers to recognize Russia as a major power for the first time.

On land captured from Sweden at the eastern end of the Baltic, Peter built St. Petersburg, a new city that was to be his window on the West. In 1712 the city became Russia's capital. To demonstrate Russia's new sophistication, Peter ordered architects to build St. Petersburg's houses and public buildings in the baroque style then fashionable in France.

Peter also pushed the Russian elite to imitate western European fashions. He personally shaved off his noblemen's long beards to conform to Western styles and ordered them to wear Western clothing. To end the traditional seclusion of upper-class Russian women, Peter required officials, officers, and merchants to bring their wives to the social gatherings he organized in the capital. He also directed the nobles to educate their children.

Online Study Center
Improve Your Grade
Primary Source:
Edicts and Decrees

Another of Peter's strategies was to reorganize Russian government along the lines of the powerful German state of Prussia. To break the power of the boyars he sharply reduced their traditional roles in government

The Fontanka Canal in St. Petersburg in 1753   The Russian capital continued to grow as a commercial and administrative center. As in Amsterdam, canals were the city's major arteries. On the right is a new summer palace built by Peter's successor.   (Engraving, after M. I. Makhaiev, from the official series of 1753. Courtesy of the Trustees of the British Museum)

and the army. The old boyar council of Moscow was replaced by a group of advisers in St. Petersburg whom the tsar appointed. Members of the traditional nobility continued to serve as generals and admirals, but officers in Peter's modern, professional army and navy were promoted according to merit, not birth.

The goal of Peter's westernization strategy was to strengthen the Russian state and increase the power of the tsar. A decree of 1716 proclaimed that the tsar "is not obliged to answer to anyone in the world for his doings, but possesses power and authority over his kingdom and land, to rule them at his will and pleasure as a Christian ruler." Under this expansive definition of his role, Peter brought the Russian Orthodox Church more firmly under state control, built factories and iron and copper foundries to provide munitions and supplies for the military, and increased the burdens of taxes and forced labor on the serfs. Peter was an absolutist ruler of the sort then popular in western Europe, and he had no more intention of improving the conditions of the serfs, on whose labors the production of basic foodstuffs depended, than did the European slave owners of the Americas.

Consolidation of the Empire

Russia's eastward expansion also continued under Peter the Great and his successors. The frontier settlement with China and Qianlong's quashing of Inner Mongolia in 1689 freed Russians to concentrate on the northern Pacific. The Pacific northeast was colonized, and in 1741 an expedition led by Captain Vitus Bering crossed the strait (later named for him) into North America. In 1799 a Russian company of merchants received a monopoly over the Alaskan fur trade, and its agents were soon active along the entire northwestern coast of North America.

Far more important than these immense territories in the cold and thinly populated north were the populous agricultural lands to the west acquired during the reign of Catherine the Great (r. 1762–1796). A successful war with the Ottoman Empire gave Russia control of the rich north shore of the Black Sea by 1783. As a result of three successive partitions of the once powerful kingdom of Poland between 1772 and 1795, Russia's frontiers advanced 600 miles (nearly 1,000 kilometers) to the west (see Map 21.3). When Catherine died, the Russian Empire extended from Poland in the west to Alaska in the east, from the Barents Sea in the north to the Black Sea in the south.

Catherine also made important additions to Peter's policies of promoting industry and building a canal system to improve trade. Besides furs, the Russians had also become major exporters of gold, iron, and timber. Catherine implemented administrative reforms and showed a special talent for diplomacy. Through her promotion of the ideas of the Enlightenment, she expanded Peter's policies of westernizing the Russian elite.

COMPARATIVE PERSPECTIVES

China and Russia are examples of the phenomenal flourishing of empires in Eurasia between 1500 and 1800. Already a vast empire under the Ming, China doubled in size under the Qing, mostly through westward expansion into less densely populated areas. In expanding from a modestly sized principality into the world's largest land empire, Russia added rich and well-populated lands to the west and south and far larger but less populous lands to the east. Russia and China were land based, just like the Ottoman and Mughal Empires, with the strengths and problems of administrative control and tax collection that size entailed.

Japan was different. Though nominally headed by an emperor, Japan's size and ethnic homogeneity do not support calling it an empire in the same breath with China and Russia. Tokugawa Japan was similar in size and population to France, the most powerful state of western Europe, but its political system was much more decentralized. Japan's efforts to add colonies on the East Asian mainland had failed.

China had once led the world in military innovation (including the first uses of gunpowder), but the modern "gunpowder revolution" of the fifteenth and sixteenth centuries was centered in the Ottoman Empire and western European states. Although the centuries after 1500 were full of successful military operations, Chinese armies continued to depend on superior numbers and tactics for their success, rather than on new technology. As in the past, infantrymen armed with guns served alongside others armed with bows and arrows, swords, and spears.

The military forces of Japan and Russia underwent more innovative changes than those of China, in part through Western contacts. In the course of its sixteenth-century wars of unification, Japan produced its own gunpowder revolution but thereafter lacked the motivation and the means to stay abreast of the world's most advanced military technology. By the eighteenth century Russia had made greater progress in catching up with its European neighbors, but its armies still relied more on their size than on the sophistication of their weapons.

Naval power provides the greatest military contrast among the three. Eighteenth-century Russia constructed modern fleets of warships in the Baltic and Black Seas, but neither China nor Japan developed navies commensurate with their size and coastlines. China's defenses against pirates and other sea invaders were left to its maritime provinces, whose small war junks were armed with only a half-dozen cannon. Japan's naval capacity was similarly decentralized. In 1792, when Russian ships exploring the North Pacific turned toward the Japanese coast, the local daimyo used his own forces to chase them away. All Japanese daimyo understood that they would be on their own if foreign incursions increased.

The expansion of China and Russia incorporated not just new lands but also diverse new peoples. Chinese society had long been diverse, and its geographical, occupational, linguistic, and religious differences grew as the Qing expanded (see Map 21.2). China had also long used Confucian models, imperial customs, and a common system of writing to transcend such differences and to assimilate elites. Russia likewise approached its new peoples with a mixture of pragmatic tolerance and a propensity for seeing Russian ways and beliefs as superior. The Russian language was strongly promoted. Religion was a particular sore point, as Russian Orthodox missionaries, with the support of the tsars, encouraged conversion of Siberian peoples. Russia absorbed new ideas and styles from western Europe, although even among the elite these influences often overlay Russian traditions in a very superficial way. In contrast, Japan remained more culturally homogeneous, and the government reacted with great intolerance to the growing influence of converts to western Christianity.

Forced labor remained common in the Russian and Chinese Empires. Serfdom grew more brutal and widespread in Russia in the seventeenth and eighteenth centuries, although the expansion of the frontier eastward across Siberia also opened an escape route for many peasants and serfs. Some Chinese peasants also improved their lot by moving to new territories, but population growth increased overall misery in the eighteenth century. China was also notable for the size of its popular insurrections, especially the one that toppled the Ming.

SUMMARY

How did Japan respond to domestic social changes and the challenges posed by contact with foreign cultures?

How did China deal with military and political challenges both inside and outside its borders?

To what extent was Russia's expanding empire influenced by relations with western Europe in this period?

Online Study Center
ACE the Test

The formation of the Tokugawa Shogunate in Japan is a clear example of a society changing from within. Hideyoshi failed in his attempt to conquer Korea and China, and the Shogunate arose from the resolution of civil wars between rival daimyo. A decentralized government led to the rise of a powerful merchant class, but the Shogunate's inability to stabilize rice prices contributed to the economic decline of the samurai, who became dependent on merchants to extend them credit. The decisions of government to suppress the Christianity that some Japanese had adopted from European missionaries and to severely curtail commercial and intellectual contacts with distant Europe illustrate how readily Japan could control its dealings with outsiders.

China's history illustrates a more complex interplay of internal and external forces. In the world's most populous state, the already faltering Ming dynasty was greatly weakened by Hideyoshi's Japanese invasion through Korea, overthrown by Li Zicheng's rebels from within, and replaced by the conquering armies of the Manchu from across the northern frontier. The Qing's settlement of the Amur frontier with Russia illustrates how diplomacy and compromise could serve mutual interests. Finally, the Chinese added new European customers to already extensive internal and external markets and developed both positive and problematic cultural relations with the Jesuits and some other Europeans. From a Chinese perspective, European contacts could be useful but were neither essential nor of great importance.

The internal and external factors in Russia's history are the hardest to sort out. Especially problematic is assessing the rising importance of the West in light of Russia's growing trade in that direction, Russia's emergence as a European Great Power, and the stated policies of both Peter the Great and Catherine the Great to Westernize their people. Clearly, Western influences were important, but their importance can easily be exaggerated. The impetus for Muscovy's expansion came out of its own history and domination by the Mongols. Trade with western Europe was not the center of the Russian economy. Tsar Peter was interested in imitating Western technology, not the full range of Western culture. The Russian church was quite hostile to Catholics and Protestants, whom it regarded as heretics. Peter banned the Jesuits from Russia, considering them a subversive and backward influence.

KEY TERMS

Manchu *p. 606*

daimyo *p. 606*

samurai *p. 606*

Tokugawa Shogunate *p. 607*

Ming Empire *p. 612*

Qing Empire *p. 615*

Kangxi *p. 615*

Amur River *p. 618*

Macartney mission *p. 621*

Muscovy *p. 623*

Ural Mountains *p. 623*

tsar *p. 623*

Siberia *p. 623*

Cossacks *p. 625*

serfs *p. 625*

Peter the Great *p. 625*

Online Study Center
Improve Your Grade
Flashcards

SUGGESTED READING

A fascinating place to begin is with John E. Wills, Jr., *1688: A Global History* (2001), Part III, "Three Worlds Apart: Russia, China, and Japan."

On Japan in this period see Andrew Gordon, *A Modern History of Japan: From Tokugawa Times to the Present* (2003); *The Cambridge History of Japan*, vol. 4: *Early Modern Japan*, ed. John Whitney Hall (1991); Chie Nakane and Shinzaburo Oishi, *Tokugawa Japan: The Social and Economic Antecedents of Modern Japan*, trans. Conrad Totman (1990); and Tessa Morris-Suzuki, *The Technological Transformation of Japan from the Seventeenth to the Twenty-First Century* (1994). Mary Elizabeth Berry, *Hideyoshi* (1982), is an account of the reunification of Japan at the end of the sixteenth century and the invasion of Korea. See also Michael Cooper, ed., *They Came to Japan: An Anthology of European Reports on Japan, 1543–1640* (1995).

For China during the transition from the Ming to Qing periods, see Jonathan D. Spence, *The Search for Modern China* (1990); James W. Tong, *Disorder Under Heaven: Collective Violence in the Ming Dynasty* (1991); Frederic Wakeman, *The Great Enterprise: The Manchu Reconstruction of Imperial Order in Seventeenth-Century China* (1985); and Lynn A. Struve, *Voices from the Ming-Qing Cataclysm: China in Tiger's Jaws* (1993). The latest work on the late Ming is summarized in *The Cambridge History of China*, vol. 8, *The Ming Dynasty, 1368–1644, Part 2* (1998). On the history of the Manchu and of the Qing Empire, see Evelyn Sakakida Rawski, *The Last Emperors: A Social History of Qing Imperial Institutions* (1998), and Pamela Kyle Crossley, *The Manchus* (2002).

On Chinese society generally in this period, see two classic (though slightly dated) works by Ping-ti Ho, *The Ladder of Success in Imperial China: Aspects of Social Mobility, 1368–1911* (1962), and *Studies on the Population of China 1368–1953* (1959); and see the general study by Susan Naquin and Evelyn S. Rawski, *Chinese Society in the Eighteenth Century* (1987). On the two greatest of the Qing emperors and their times, see Jonathan D. Spence, *Emperor of China; Self Portrait of K'ang Hsi, 1654–1722* (1974). For a more scholarly treatment see Lawrence D. Kessler, *K'ang-hsi and the Consolidation of Ch'ing Rule, 1661–1684* (1976); Jonathan D. Spence, *Ts'ao Yin and the K'ang-hsi Emperor: Bondservant and Master* (1966); and Harold L.

Kahn, *Monarchy in the Emperor's Eyes: Image and Reality in the Ch'ien-lung Reign* (1971).

On the Qing trade systems see John E. Wills, *Embassies and Illusions: Dutch and Portuguese Envoys to K'ang-hsi, 1666–1687* (1984), and Craig Clunas, *Chinese Export Art and Design* (1987). There is a great deal published on the Macartney mission, much of it originating in the diaries and memoirs of the participants. See the exhaustively detailed Alain Peyrefitte, *The Immobile Empire*, trans. Jon Rothschild (1992). For a more theoretical discussion see James L. Hevia, *Cherishing Men from Afar: Qing Guest Ritual and the Macartney Embassy of 1793* (1995).

On early modern Russian history, see Robert O. Crummey, *Aristocrats and Servitors: The Boyar Elite in Russia, 1613–1689* (1983), and Andreas Kappeler, *The Russian Empire: A Multiethnic History* (2001). Western perceptions of Russia are examined in Marshall T. Poe, *A People Born to Slavery: Russia in Early Modern European Ethnography, 1476–1748* (2000), and Lloyd E. Berry and Robert O. Crummey, eds., *Rude and Barbarous Kingdom: Russia in the Accounts of Sixteenth-Century English Voyagers* (1968). Among the best-known recent books on Tsar Peter are Matthew Smith Anderson, *Peter the Great*, 2nd ed. (1995); Robert K. Massie, *Peter the Great: His Life and World* (1980); and Lindsey Hughes, *Russia in the Age of Peter the Great* (1998). For Russian naval development and Russian influence in the Pacific and in America, see Glynn Barratt, *Russia in Pacific Waters, 1715–1825: A Survey of the Origins of Russia's Naval Presence in the North and South Pacific* (1981), and Howard I. Kushner, *Conflict on the Northwest Coast: American-Russian Rivalry in the Pacific Northwest, 1790–1867* (1975).

For Jesuits in East Asia in the sixteenth and seventeenth centuries, see Michael Cooper, S.J., *Rodrigues the Interpreter: An Early Jesuit in Japan and China* (1974); David E. Mungello, *Curious Land: Jesuit Accommodation and the Origins of Sinology* (1989); and Jonathan D. Spence, *The Memory Palace of Matteo Ricci* (1984). Still useful are C. R. Boxer, *The Christian Century in Japan, 1549–1650* (1951), and Cornelius Wessels, *Early Jesuit Travellers in Central Asia, 1603–1721* (1924). On European images of and interactions with China connected to the Jesuits, see the relevant portions of Jonathan D. Spence, *The Chan's*

Great Continent: China in Western Minds (1998); Joanna Waley-Cohen, *The Sextants of Beijing: Global Currents in Chinese History* (1999); and David E. Mungello, *The Great Encounter of China and the West, 1500–1800,* 2nd ed. (2005).

On the East India companies see John E. Wills, *Pepper, Guns, and Parleys: The Dutch East India Company and China, 1662–1681* (2005); Dianne Lewis, *Jan Compagnie in the Straits of Malacca, 1641–1795* (1995); and John Keay, *The Honourable Company: A History of the English East India Company* (1994). On the development of global commerce in tea, coffee, and cocoa, see the relevant chapters in Roy Porter and Mikulás Teich, *Drugs and Narcotics in History* (1995).

NOTES

1. Adapted from Jonathan D. Spence, *The Search for Modern China* (New York: W. W. Norton, 1990), 21–25.

2. Adapted from G. V. Melikhov, "Manzhou Penetration into the Basin of the Upper Amur in the 1680s," in S. L. Tikhvinshii, ed., *Manzhou Rule in China* (Moscow: Progress Publishers, 1983).

The Little Ice Age

A giant volcanic eruption in the Peruvian Andes in 1600 affected the weather in many parts of the world for several years. When volcanic ash from the eruption of Mount Huanyaputina (hoo-AHN-yah-poo-TEE-nuh) shot into the upper atmosphere and spread around the world, it screened out sunlight. As a result, the summer of 1601 was the coldest in two hundred years in the northern hemisphere.

Archaeologist Brian Fagan has pointed out that Mount Huanyaputina's chilling effects were a spectacular event in a much longer pattern of climate change that has been called the Little Ice Age.[1] Although global climate had been cooling since the late 1200s, in the northern temperate regions the 1590s had been exceptionally cold. Temperatures remained cooler than normal throughout the seventeenth century.

The most detailed information on the Little Ice Age comes from Europe. Glaciers in the Alps grew much larger. Trade became difficult when rivers and canals that had once been navigable in winter froze solid from bank to bank. In the coldest years, the growing season in some places was as much as two months shorter than normal. Unexpectedly late frosts withered the tender shoots of newly planted crops in spring. Wheat and barley ripened more slowly during cooler summers and were often damaged by early fall frosts.

People could survive a smaller-than-average harvest in one year by drawing on food reserves, but when cold weather damaged crops in two or more successive years, the consequences were devastating. Deaths due to malnutrition and cold increased sharply when summer temperatures in northern Europe registered 2.7°F (1.5°C) lower than average in 1674 and 1675 and again in 1694 and 1695. The cold spell of 1694 and 1695 caused a famine in Finland that carried off a quarter to a third of the population.

At the time people had no idea what was causing the unusual cold of the Little Ice Age. Advances in climate history make it clear that the cause was not a single terrestrial event such as the eruption of Mount Huanyaputina. Nor was the Little Ice Age the product of human actions, unlike some climate changes such as today's global warming.

Ultimately, the earth's weather is governed by the sun. In the seventeenth century astronomers in Europe reported seeing fewer sunspots, dark spots on the sun's surface that are indicative of solar activity and thus the sun's warming power. Diminished activity in the sun was primarily responsible for the Little Ice Age.

If the sun was the root cause, the effects of global cooling should not have been confined to northern Europe. Although contemporary accounts are much scarcer in other parts of the world, there is evidence of climate changes around the world in this period. Observations of sunspots in China, Korea, and Japan drop to zero between 1639 and 1700. China experienced unusually cool weather in the seventeenth century, although the warfare and disruption accompanying the fall of the Ming and the rise of the Qing probably were much more to blame for the famines and rural distress of that period.

By itself, a relatively slight decrease in average annual temperature would not have a significant effect on human life outside the northern temperate areas. However, evidence suggests that there was also a significant rise in humidity in this period in other parts of the world. Ice cores drilled into ancient glaciers in the Arctic and Antarctic show increased snowfall. Information compiled by historian James L. A. Webb, Jr., shows that lands south of the Sahara received more rainfall between 1550 and 1750 than they had during the previous era.[2] Increased rainfall would have been favorable for pastoral people, whose herds found new pasture in what had once been desert, and for the farmers farther south, whose crops got more rain.

In the eighteenth century the sun's activity began to return to normal. Rising temperatures led to milder winters and better harvests in northern Eurasia. Falling rainfall allowed the Sahara to advance southward, forcing the agricultural frontier to retreat.

NOTES

1. Brian Fagan, *The Littlest Ice Age: How Climate Made History, 1300-1850* (New York: Basic Books, 2000).

2. James L. A. Webb, Jr., *Desert Frontier: Ecological Change Along the Western Sahel, 1600-1850* (Madison: University of Wisconsin Press, 1995).

PART SIX

REVOLUTIONS RESHAPE THE WORLD, 1750–1870

CHAPTER 22
Revolutionary Changes in the Atlantic World, 1750–1850

CHAPTER 23
The Early Industrial Revolution, 1760–1851

CHAPTER 24
Nation Building and Economic Transformation in the Americas, 1800–1890

CHAPTER 25
Land Empires in the Age of Imperialism, 1800–1870

CHAPTER 26
Africa, India, and the New British Empire, 1750–1870

Between 1750 and 1870, nearly every part of the world experienced dramatic political, economic, and social change. The beginnings of industrialization, the American, French, and Haitian revolutions, as well as the revolutions for independence in Latin America transformed political and economic life. European nations expanded into Africa, Asia, and the Middle East while Russia and the United States acquired vast new territories.

The Industrial Revolution introduced new technologies and patterns of work that made these societies wealthier and militarily more powerful. Western intellectual life became more secular. The Atlantic slave trade and later slavery itself were abolished, and the first efforts to improve the status of women were initiated.

The Industrial Revolution led to a new wave of imperialism. France conquered Algeria, and Great Britain expanded its colonial rule in India and established colonies in Australia and New Zealand. European political and economic influence also expanded in Africa and Asia. The Ottoman Empire

South America 1820s This map of South America from the 1820s records the comprehensive success of the independence movements. With the exception of the Guyanas, no colonial governments remain. As we examine this map, we are also reminded of the failure of two political experiments designed to hold together geographically and ethnically diverse regions in a single national government. In the northwest is Colombia (also called Gran Colombia) created by the era's greatest revolutionary leader, Simón Bolívar. It quickly broke apart to form the modern nations of Venezuela, Colombia, and Ecuador. The United Provinces of Río de la Plata, located in the southeast, also soon collapsed, giving birth to the nations of Argentina, Paraguay, and Uruguay. (Library of Congress)

and the Qing Empire met this challenge by implementing reform programs that preserved traditional structures while adopting elements of Western technology and organization. Though lagging behind western Europe in transforming its economy and political institutions, Russia attempted modernization efforts, including the abolition of serfdom.

The economic, political, and social revolutions that began in the mid-eighteenth century shook the foundations of European culture and led to the expansion of Western power around the globe. Some of the nations of Asia, Africa, and Latin America reformed and strengthened their own institutions and economies, while others pushed for more radical change. After 1870 Western imperialism became more aggressive, and few parts of the world were able to resist it.

Burning of Cap Français, Saint Domingue, in 1793 In 1791, the slaves of Saint Domingue, France's richest colony, began a rebellion that, after years of struggle, ended slavery and created the Western Hemisphere's second independent nation, Haiti. (Jean-Loup Charmet/The Bridgeman Art Library)

How did the costs of imperial wars and the Enlightenment challenge the established authority of monarchs and religion in Europe and the American colonies?

What were the direct causes of the American Revolution?

What were the origins and accomplishments of the French Revolution?

How did revolution in one country help incite revolution elsewhere?

22

REVOLUTIONARY CHANGES IN THE ATLANTIC WORLD, 1750–1850

CHAPTER OUTLINE

Prelude to Revolution: The Eighteenth-Century Crisis

The American Revolution, 1775–1800

The French Revolution, 1789–1815

Revolution Spreads, Conservatives Respond, 1789–1850

Comparative Perspectives

ENVIRONMENT AND TECHNOLOGY: The Guillotine

DIVERSITY AND DOMINANCE: Robespierre and Wollstonecraft Defend and Explain the Terror

O n the evening of August 14, 1791, more than two hundred slaves and black freedmen met in secret in the plantation district of northern Saint Domingue° (present-day Haiti) to set the date for an armed uprising against local slave owners. Although the delegates agreed to delay the attack for a week, violence began almost immediately. During the following decade and a half, slavery was abolished; military forces from Britain and France were defeated; and Haiti achieved independence.

The meeting was provoked by news and rumors about revolutionary events in France that had spread through the island's slave community. Events in France had also divided the island's white

Saint Domingue (san doe-MANG)

Online Study Center

This icon will direct you to interactive activities and study materials on the website: *college.hmco.com/pic/bulliet4e.*

population into competing camps of royalists (supporters of France's King Louis XVI) and republicans (who sought an end to monarchy). The free mixed-race population initially gained some political rights from the French Assembly but was then forced to rebel when the local slave-owning elite reacted violently.

A black freedman named François Dominique Toussaint eventually became leader of the insurrection. He proved to be one of the most remarkable representatives of the revolutionary era, later taking the name Toussaint L'Ouverture°. He organized the rebels into a potent military force, negotiated with the island's royalist and republican factions and with representatives of Great Britain and France, and wrote his nation's first constitution. Commonly portrayed as a fiend by slave owners throughout the Western Hemisphere, to the slaves Toussaint became a towering symbol of resistance to oppression.

The Haitian slave rebellion was an important episode in the long and painful political and cultural transformation of the modern Western world. Economic expansion and the growth of trade were creating unprecedented wealth. The first stage of the Industrial Revolution (see Chapter 23) increased manufacturing productivity and led to greater global interdependence, new patterns of consumerism, and altered social structures. At the same time, intellectuals were questioning the traditional place of monarchy and religion in society. An increasingly powerful class of merchants, professionals, and manufacturers created by the emerging economy provided an audience for these new intellectual currents and began to press for a larger political role.

This revolutionary era turned the Western world "upside down." The *ancien régime*°, the French term for Europe's old order, rested on medieval principles: politics dominated by powerful monarchs, intellectual and cultural life dominated by religion, and economics dominated by a hereditary agricultural elite. In the West's new order, politics was opened to vastly greater participation; science and secular inquiry took the place of religion in intellectual life; and economies were increasingly opened to competition.

This radical transformation did not take place without false starts and temporary setbacks. Imperial powers resisted the loss of colonies; monarchs and nobles struggled to retain their ancient privileges; and the church fought against the claims of science. Revolutionary steps forward were often matched by reactionary steps backward. The liberal and nationalist ideals of the eighteenth-century revolutionary movements were only imperfectly realized in Europe and the Americas in the nineteenth century. Despite setbacks, belief in national self-determination and universal suffrage and a passion for social justice continued to animate reformers into the twentieth century.

PRELUDE TO REVOLUTION: THE EIGHTEENTH-CENTURY CRISIS

In large measure, the cost of wars fought among Europe's major powers over colonies and trade precipitated the revolutionary era that began in 1775 with the American Revolution. Britain, France, and Spain were the central actors in these global struggles, but other imperial powers were affected as well. Unpopular and costly wars had been fought earlier and paid for with new taxes. But changes in the Western intellectual and political environments led to a much more critical response. Any effort to extend the power of a monarch or impose new taxes now raised questions about the rights of individuals and the authority of political institutions.

Colonial Wars and Fiscal Crises

The rivalry among European powers intensified in the early 1600s when the newly independent Netherlands began an assault on the American and Asian colonies of Spain and Portugal. The Dutch attacked Spanish treasure fleets in the Caribbean and Pacific and seized parts of Portugal's colonial empire in Brazil and Angola. Europe's other emerging sea power, Great Britain, also attacked

---

Toussaint L'Ouverture (too-SAN loo-ver-CHORE) **ancien régime** (ahn-see-EN ray-ZHEEM)

CHRONOLOGY

	The Americas	Europe
1750		
	1754–1763 French and Indian War	**1756–1763** Seven Years War
	1770 Boston Massacre	
1775	**1776** American Declaration of Independence	
	1778 United States alliance with France	**1778** Death of Voltaire and Rousseau
	1781 British surrender at Yorktown	
	1783 Treaty of Paris ends American Revolution	**1789** Storming of Bastille begins French Revolution; Declaration of Rights of Man and Citizen in France
	1791 Slaves revolt in Saint Domingue (Haiti)	**1793–1794** Reign of Terror in France
	1798 Toussaint L'Ouverture defeats British in Haiti	**1795–1799** The Directory rules France
1800		**1799** Napoleon overthrows the Directory
	1804 Haitians defeat French invasion and declare independence	**1804** Napoleon crowns himself emperor
		1814 Napoleon abdicates; Congress of Vienna opens
		1815 Napoleon defeated at Waterloo
		1830 Greece gains independence; revolution in France overthrows Charles X
		1848 Revolutions in France, Austria, Germany, Hungary, and Italy

Spanish fleets and seaports in the Americas. By the end of the seventeenth century expanding British sea power had checked Dutch commercial and colonial ambitions and ended the Dutch monopoly of the African slave trade.

As Dutch power ebbed, Britain and France began a long struggle for political preeminence in western Europe and for territory and trade outlets in the Americas and Asia. Both the geographic scale and the expense of this conflict expanded during the eighteenth century. Nearly all of Europe's great powers were engaged in the War of the Spanish Succession (1701–1714). In 1739 a war between Britain and Spain over smuggling in the Americas quickly broadened into a generalized European conflict, the War of the Austrian Succession (1740–1748). Conflict between French and English settlers in North America then helped ignite a long war that altered the colonial balance of power. War began along the American frontier between French and British forces and their Amerindian allies. Known as the French and Indian War,

this conflict helped lead to a wider struggle, the Seven Years War (1756–1763). British victory led to undisputed control of North America east of the Mississippi River while also forcing France to surrender most of its holdings in India.

The enormous costs of these conflicts distinguished them from earlier wars. Traditional taxes collected in traditional ways no longer covered the obligations of governments. For example, at the end of the Seven Years War in 1763, Britain's war debt reached £137 million. Britain's total budget before the war had averaged only £8 million. With the legacy of war debt, Britain's interest payments alone came to exceed £5 million. Even as European economies expanded because of increased trade and the early stages of the Industrial Revolution, fiscal crises overtook one European government after another. In an intellectual environment transformed by the Enlightenment, the need for new revenues provoked debate and confrontation within a vastly expanded and more critical public.

The Enlightenment and the Old Order

The complex and diverse intellectual movement called the **Enlightenment** applied the methods and questions of the Scientific Revolution of the seventeenth century to the study of human society. Dazzled by Copernicus's ability to explain the structure of the solar system and Newton's representation of the law of gravity, European intellectuals began to apply the logical tools of scientific inquiry to other questions. Some labored to systematize knowledge or organize reference materials. For example, Carolus Linnaeus° (a Swedish botanist known by the Latin form of his name) sought to categorize all living organisms, and Samuel Johnson published a comprehensive English dictionary with over forty thousand definitions. In France Denis Diderot° worked with other Enlightenment thinkers to create a compendium of human knowledge, the thirty-five-volume *Encyclopédie*.

Other thinkers pursued lines of inquiry that challenged long-established religious and political institutions. Some argued that if scientists could understand the laws of nature, then surely similar forms of disciplined investigation might reveal laws of human nature. Others wondered whether society and government might be better regulated and more productive if guided by science rather than by hereditary rulers and the church. These new perspectives and the intellectual optimism that fed them were to help guide the revolutionary movements of the late eighteenth century.

The English political philosopher John Locke (1632–1704) argued in 1690 that governments were created to protect life, liberty, and property and that the people had a right to rebel when a monarch violated these natural rights. Locke's closely reasoned theory began with the assumption that individual rights were the foundation of civil government. In *The Social Contract*, published in 1762, the French-Swiss intellectual Jean-Jacques Rousseau° (1712–1778) asserted that the will of the people was sacred and that the legitimacy of the monarch depended on the consent of the people. Although both men believed that government rested on the will of the people rather than on divine will, Locke emphasized the importance of individual rights secured institutionally, and Rousseau, much more distrustful of society and government, envisioned the people acting collectively because of their shared historical experience.

Online Study Center
Improve Your Grade
Primary Source: Rousseau Espouses
Popular Sovereignty and the General Will

All Enlightenment thinkers were not radicals like Rousseau. There was never a uniform program for political and social reform, and the era's intellectuals often disagreed about principles and objectives. The Enlightenment is commonly associated with hostility toward religion and monarchy, but few European intellectuals openly expressed republican or atheist sentiments. The church was most commonly attacked when it attempted to censor ideas or ban books. Critics of monarchial authority were as likely to point out violations of ancient custom as to suggest democratic alternatives. Even Voltaire, one of the Enlightenment's most critical intellects and great celebrities, believed that Europe's monarchs were likely agents of political and economic reform and even wrote favorably of China's Qing° emperors.

Indeed, sympathetic members of the nobility and reforming European monarchs such as Charles III of Spain (r. 1759–1788), Catherine the Great of Russia (r. 1762–1796), Joseph II of Austria (r. 1780–1790), and Frederick the Great of Prussia (r. 1740–1786) actively sponsored and promoted the dissemination of new ideas, providing patronage for many intellectuals. They recognized that elements of the Enlightenment critique of the ancien régime buttressed their own efforts to expand royal authority at the expense of religious institutions, the nobility, and regional autonomy. Goals such as the development of national bureaucracies staffed by civil servants selected on merit, the creation of national legal systems, and the modernization of tax systems united many of Europe's monarchs and intellectuals. Monarchs also understood that the era's passion for science and technology held the potential of fattening national treasuries and improving economic performance. Periodicals disseminating new technologies often gained the patronage of these reforming monarchs.

Though willing to embrace reform proposals when they served royal interests, Europe's monarchs moved quickly to suppress or ban radical ideas that promoted republicanism or directly attacked religion. However, too many channels of communication were open to permit a thoroughgoing suppression of ideas. In fact, censorship tended to enhance intellectual reputations, and persecuted intellectuals generally found patronage in the courts of foreign rivals.

Many of the major intellectuals of the Enlightenment maintained extensive correspondence with each other as well as with political leaders. This communication led to numerous firsthand contacts among the intellectuals of different nations and helped create a more

---

Carolus Linnaeus (kar-ROLL-uhs lin-NEE-uhs)
Denis Diderot (duh-nee DEE-duh-roe)
Jean-Jacques Rousseau (zhan-zhock roo-SOE)

Qing (ching)

coherent assault on what was typically called ignorance—beliefs and values associated with the ancien régime. Rousseau met the Scottish philosopher David Hume in Paris. Later, when Rousseau feared arrest, Hume helped him seek refuge in Britain. Similarly, Voltaire sought patronage and protection in England and later in Prussia.

Women were instrumental in the dissemination of the new ideas. In England educated middle-class women purchased and discussed the books and pamphlets of the era. Some were important contributors to intellectual life as writers and commentators, raising by example and in argument the issue of the rights of women. In Paris wealthy women made their homes centers of debate, intellectual speculation, and free inquiry. Their salons brought together philosophers, social critics, artists, and members of the aristocracy and commercial elite. Unlike their contemporaries in England, the women of the Parisian salons used their social standing more to direct the conversations of men than to give vent to their own opinions.

The intellectual ferment of the era deeply influenced the expanding middle class in Europe and the Western Hemisphere. Members of this class were eager consumers of books and the inexpensive newspapers and journals that were widely available. This broadening of the intellectual audience overwhelmed traditional institutions of censorship. Scientific discoveries, new technologies, and controversial work on human nature and politics also were discussed in the thousands of coffeehouses and teashops opening in major cities and market towns.

Many European intellectuals were interested in the Americas. Some Europeans continued to dismiss the New World as barbaric and inferior, but others used idealized accounts of the New World to support their critiques of European society. These thinkers looked to Britain's North American colonies for confirmation of their belief that human nature unconstrained by the corrupted practices of Europe's old order would quickly produce material abundance and social justice. More than any other American, the writer and inventor **Benjamin Franklin** came to symbolize both the natural genius and the vast potential of America.

Born in 1706 in Boston, the young Franklin was apprenticed to his older brother, a printer. At seventeen he ran away to Philadelphia, where he succeeded as a printer and publisher and was best known for his *Poor Richard's Almanac*. By age forty-two he was a wealthy man. He retired from active business to pursue writing, science, and public affairs. In Philadelphia Franklin was instrumental in the creation of the organizations that later became the Philadelphia Free Library, the American Philosophical Society, and the University of Pennsylvania.

Franklin's contributions were both practical and theoretical. He was the inventor of bifocal glasses, the lightning rod, and an efficient wood-burning stove. In 1751 he published a scientific work, *Experiments and Observations on Electricity*, that established his intellectual reputation in Europe. Intellectuals heralded the book as proof that the simple and unsophisticated world of America was a particularly hospitable environment for genius.

Franklin was also an important political figure. He served Pennsylvania as a delegate to the Albany (New York) Congress in 1754, which sought to coordinate colonial defense against attacks by the French and their Amerindian allies. Later he was a Pennsylvania delegate to the Continental Congress that issued the Declaration of Independence in 1776. His service in England as colonial lobbyist and later as the Continental Congress's ambassador to Paris allowed him to cultivate his European reputation. Franklin's wide achievement, witty conversation, and careful self-promotion make him a symbol of the era. In him the Enlightenment's most radical project, the freeing of human potential from the inhibitions of inherited privilege, found its most agreeable confirmation.

As Franklin's career demonstrates, the Western Hemisphere shared in the debates of Europe. New ideas penetrated the curricula of colonial universities and appeared in periodicals and books published in the New World. As scientific method was applied to economic and political questions, colonial writers, scholars, and artists were drawn into a debate that eventually was to lead to the rejection of colonialism itself. This radicalization of the colonial intellectual community was provoked by the European monarchies' efforts to reform colonial policies. As European authorities swept away colonial institutions and long-established political practices without consultation, colonial residents increasingly recognized their subordination to European rulers. Among people compelled to recognize this structural dependence and inferiority, the idea that government authority ultimately rested on the consent of the governed was potentially explosive.

In Europe and the colonies, many intellectuals resisted the Enlightenment, seeing it as a dangerous assault on the authority of the church and monarchy. This Counter Enlightenment was most influential in France and other Catholic nations. Its adherents argued the importance of faith to human happiness and social well-being. They also emphasized duty and obligation to the community of believers in opposition to the concern for individual rights and individual fulfillment common

***Beer Street* (1751)** This engraving by William Hogarth shows an idealized London street scene where beer drinking is associated with manly strength, good humor, and prosperity. The self-satisfied corpulent figure in the left foreground has been reading a copy of the king's speech to Parliament. We can imagine him offering a running commentary to his drinking companions as he reads. (The Art Archive)

in the works of the Enlightenment. Most importantly for the politics of the era, they rejected their enemies' enthusiasm for change and utopianism, reminding their readers of human fallibility and the importance of history. While the central ideas of the Enlightenment gained strength across the nineteenth century, the Counter Enlightenment provided the ideological roots of both conservatism and popular antidemocratic movements.

Folk Cultures and Popular Protest

While intellectuals and the reforming royal courts of Europe debated the rational and secular enthusiasms of the Enlightenment, most people in Western society remained loyal to competing cultural values grounded in the preindustrial past. These regionally distinct folk cultures were framed by the memory of shared local historical experience and nourished by religious practices that encouraged emotional release. They emphasized the obligations that people had to each other and local, rather than national, loyalties. Though never formally articulated, these cultural traditions composed a coherent expression of the mutual rights and obligations connecting the people and their rulers. Rulers who violated the con-

straints of these understandings were likely to face violent opposition.

In the eighteenth century, European monarchs sought to increase their authority and to centralize power by reforming tax collection, judicial practice, and public administration. Although monarchs viewed these changes as reforms, the common people often saw them as violations of sacred customs and sometimes expressed their outrage in bread riots, tax protests, and attacks on royal officials. These violent actions were not efforts to overturn traditional authority but were instead efforts to preserve custom and precedent. In Spain and the Spanish colonies, for example, protesting mobs commonly asserted the apparently contradictory slogan "Long live the King. Death to bad government." They expressed loyalty to and love for their monarch while at the same time assaulting his officials and preventing the implementation of changes to long-established customs.

Folk cultures were threatened by other kinds of reform as well. Rationalist reformers of the Enlightenment sought to bring order and discipline to the citizenry by banning or by altering the numerous popular cultural traditions—such as harvest festivals, religious holidays, and country fairs—that enlivened the drudgery of everyday life. These events were popular celebrations of sexuality and individuality as well as opportunities for masked and costumed celebrants to mock the greed, pretension, and foolishness of government officials, the wealthy, and the clergy. Hard drinking, gambling, and blood sports like cockfighting and bearbaiting were popular in this preindustrial mass culture. Because these customs were viewed as corrupt and decadent by reformers influenced by the Enlightenment, governments undertook efforts to substitute civic rituals, patriotic anniversaries, and institutions of self-improvement. These challenges to custom—like the efforts at political reform—often provoked protests, rebellions, and riots.

The efforts of ordinary men and women to resist the growth of government power and the imposition of new cultural forms provide an important political undercurrent to much of the revolutionary agitation and conflict between 1750 and 1850. Spontaneous popular uprisings and protests punctuated nearly every effort at reform in the eighteenth century. But these popular actions gained revolutionary potential only when they coincided with ideological divisions and conflicts within the governing class itself. In America and France the old order was swept away when the protests and rebellions of the rural and urban poor coincided with the appearance of revolutionary leaders who followed Enlightenment ideals in efforts to create secular republican states. Likewise, the slave rebellion in Saint Domingue (Haiti) achieved revolutionary potential when it attracted the support of black freedmen and disaffected poor whites radicalized by news of the French Revolution.

THE AMERICAN REVOLUTION, 1775–1800

In British North America, clumsy efforts to increase colonial taxes to cover rising defense expenditures and to diminish the power of elected colonial legislatures outraged a populace accustomed to effective local autonomy. Once begun, the American Revolution ushered in a century-long process of political and cultural transformation in Europe and the Americas. By the end of this revolutionary century the authority of monarchs had been swept away or limited by constitutions, and religion had lost its dominating place in Western intellectual life. Moreover, the medieval idea of a social order determined by birth had been replaced by a capitalist vision that emphasized competition and social mobility.

Frontiers and Taxes

After defeating the French in 1763, the British government faced two related problems in its North American colonies. As settlers pushed west into Amerindian lands, the government saw the likelihood of renewed conflict and rising military expenses. Already burdened with heavy debts from the French and Indian War, Britain tried to limit settler pressure on Amerindian lands and get colonists to shoulder more of the costs of imperial defense and colonial administration.

In the Great Lakes region the British tried to contain costs by reducing the prices paid for furs and by refusing to continue the French practice of giving gifts and paying rent for frontier forts to Amerindian peoples, who were now dependent on European trade goods, especially firearms, gunpowder, textiles, and alcohol. With the trade value of furs reduced, native peoples hunted more aggressively, putting new pressures on the environment and endangering some species. The situation got worse as settlers and white trappers pushed across the Appalachians to compete with indigenous hunters. The predictable result was renewed violence along the frontier led by Pontiac, an Ottawa chief. His broad alliance of native peoples drove the British military from some western outposts but was defeated within a year.

The British government's panicked reaction was the Proclamation of 1763, which sought to establish an effective western limit for settlement, throwing into question the claims of thousands of established farmers without effectively protecting Amerindian land. No one was satisfied. The 1774 decision of the British government to annex disputed western territory to the province of Quebec in the hope of slowing the movement of settlers onto Amerindian lands provoked bitter resentment in the eastern colonies.

Frontier issues increased hostility and suspicion between the British government and many of the colonists but did not directly lead to a breach. However, British efforts to transfer the cost of imperial wars to the colonists with a campaign of fiscal reforms and new taxes sparked a political confrontation that would lead to rebellion. The imposition of new commercial regulations that increased the cost of foreign molasses endangered New England's profitable trade with Spanish and French Caribbean sugar colonies. The outlawing of the colonial practice of issuing paper money, a custom made necessary by the colonies' chronic balance-of-payments deficits, led colonial legislatures to formally protest these measures and led angry colonists to organize boycotts of British goods.

The Stamp Act of 1765, which imposed a tax, to be paid in scarce coin, on all legal documents, newspapers, pamphlets, and nearly all printed material, proved particularly incendiary. Propertied colonists, including holders of high office and members of the colonial elite, now assumed leading roles in protests, using fiery political language that identified Britain's rulers as "parricides" and "tyrants." Women from many of the most prominent colonial families organized boycotts of British goods. The production of homespun textiles by colonial women was now viewed as a patriotic enterprise. A young girl in Boston proclaimed that she was a "daughter of liberty" because she had learned to spin.[1] Organizations such as the Sons of Liberty were more confrontational, holding public meetings, intimidating royal officials, and organizing committees to enforce the boycotts. The combination of violent protest and trade boycott forced the repeal of the Stamp Act, but new taxes and duties were soon imposed. More importantly, Parliament sent British troops to quell colonial riots. One indignant woman later sent her poignant perception of this injustice to a British officer:

> [T]he most ignorant peasant knows . . . that no man has the right to take their money without their consent. The supposition is ridiculous and absurd, as none but highwaymen and robbers attempt it. Can you, my friend, reconcile it with your own good sense, that a body of men in Great Britain, who have little intercourse with America . . . shall invest themselves with a power to command our lives and properties [?][2]

British authorities reacted to these boycotts and attacks on royal officials by threatening traditional liberties. The colonial legislature of Massachusetts was dissolved and two regiments of soldiers were dispatched to reestablish control of Boston's streets. Support for a complete break with Britain grew after March 5, 1770, when a British force fired on an angry Boston crowd, killing five civilians. This "Boston Massacre," which seemed to expose the naked force on which colonial rule rested, radicalized public opinion throughout the colonies.

Parliament attempted to calm opinion in the colonies by repealing some taxes and duties, but it then stumbled into another crisis by granting a monopoly for importing tea to the colonies to the British East India Company, raising anew the constitutional issue of Parliament's right to tax the colonies. The crisis came to a head when protesters dumped tea worth £10,000 into Boston harbor. Britain responded by appointing a military man, Thomas Gage, as governor of Massachusetts and by closing the port of

The Tarring and Feathering of a British Official, 1774   This illustration from a British periodical shows the unfortunate John Malcomb, commissioner of customs at Boston. By the mid-1770s British periodicals were focusing public opinion on mob violence and the breakdown of public order in the colonies. British critics of colonial political protests viewed the demand for liberty as little more than an excuse for mob violence.   (The Granger Collection, New York)

Boston. Public order in Boston now depended on British troops, and public administration was in the hands of a general. This militarization of colonial government in Boston undermined Britain's constitutional authority and made a military test of strength inevitable.

The Course of Revolution, 1775–1783

As the crisis mounted, patriot leaders created new governing bodies that made laws, appointed justices, and even took control of colonial militias, thus effectively deposing many British governors, judges, and customs officers. Simultaneously, radical leaders organized crowds to intimidate loyalists—people who were pro-British—and organized women to enforce boycotts of British goods.

When representatives elected to the Continental Congress met in Philadelphia in 1775, patriot militia had already met British troops at Lexington and Concord, Massachusetts (see Map 22.1), and blood had been shed. Events were propelling the colonies toward revolution. Congress assumed the powers of government, creating a currency and organizing an army led by **George Washington** (1732–1799), a Virginia planter who had served in the French and Indian War.

Popular support for independence was given a hard edge by the angry rhetoric of thousands of street-corner speakers and the inflammatory pamphlet *Common Sense*, written by Thomas Paine, a recent immigrant from England. Paine's pamphlet sold 120,000 copies. On July 4, 1776, Congress approved the Declaration of Independence, the document that proved to be the most enduring statement of the revolutionary era's ideology:

> We hold these truths to be self evident: That all men are created equal; that they are endowed by their creator with certain unalienable rights; that among these are life, liberty and the pursuit of happiness; that, to secure these rights, governments are instituted among men, deriving their just powers from the consent of the governed.

The Declaration's affirmation of popular sovereignty and individual rights would influence the language of revolution and popular protest around the world.

Online Study Center
Improve Your Grade
Primary Source: The United States
Declaration of Independence

Hoping to shore up British authority, Great Britain sent additional military forces to pacify the colonies. By 1778 British land forces numbered 50,000 and were supported by 30,000 German mercenaries. This military commitment proved futile. Despite the existence of a large loyalist community, the British army found it difficult to control the countryside. Although British forces won most of the battles, Washington slowly built a competent Continental army as well as the civilian support networks that provided supplies and financial resources.

The real problem for the British government was its inability to discover a compromise solution that would satisfy colonial grievances. Half-hearted efforts to resolve the bitter conflict over taxes failed, and an offer to roll back the clock and reestablish the administrative arrangements of 1763 made little headway. Overconfidence and poor leadership prevented the British from finding a political solution before revolutionary institutions were in place and the armies engaged. By allowing confrontation to occur, the British government lost the opportunity to mobilize and give direction to the large numbers of loyalists and pacifists in the colonies.

Along the Canadian border, both sides solicited Amerindians as allies and feared them as potential enemies. For over a hundred years, members of the powerful Iroquois Confederacy—Mohawk, Oneida, Onondaga, Cayuga, Seneca, and (after 1722) Tuscarora—had protected their traditional lands with a combination of diplomacy and warfare, playing a role in all the colonial wars of the eighteenth century. Just as the American Revolution forced settler families to join the rebels or remain loyal, it divided the Iroquois, who fought on both sides.

The Mohawk proved to be the most valuable British allies among the Iroquois. Their loyalist leader **Joseph Brant** (Thayendanegea°) organized Britain's most potent fighting force along the Canadian border. His raids along the northern frontier earned him the title "Monster" Brant, but he was actually a man who moved easily between European and Amerindian cultures. Educated by missionaries, he was fluent in English and helped translate Protestant religious tracts into Mohawk. He was tied to many of the wealthiest loyalist families through his sister, formerly the mistress of Sir William Johnson, Britain's superintendent of Indian affairs for North America. Brant had traveled to London and had an audience with George III (r. 1760–1820). He became a celebrity and was taken up by London's aristocratic society.

The defeat in late 1777 of Britain's general John Burgoyne by General Horatio Gates at Saratoga, New York, put the future of the Mohawk at risk. This victory, which gave heart to patriot forces that had recently suffered a string of defeats, led to destructive attacks on Iroquois villages. Brant's supporters fought on to the end of the war, but patriot victories along the frontier curtailed their political and military power. Brant eventually joined the loyalist exodus to Canada. For these Americans the success of the revolution certainly did not mean the protection of life and property.

The British defeat at Saratoga also convinced France to enter the war as an ally of the United States in 1778. French military help proved crucial, supplying American forces and forcing the British to defend their colonies in the Caribbean. The French contribution was most clear in the final decisive battle, fought at Yorktown, Virginia, in 1781 (see Map 22.1). With the American army supported by French soldiers and a French fleet, General Charles

---

Thayendanegea (ta-YEHN-dah-NEY-geh-ah)

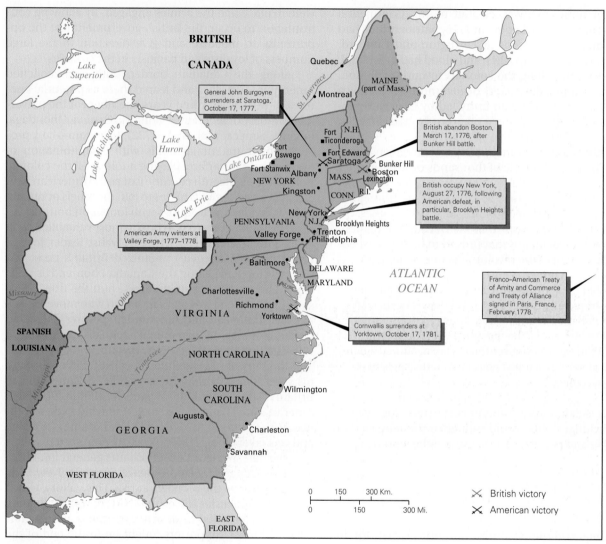

Map 22.1 The American Revolutionary War The British army won most of the major battles, and British troops held most of the major cities. Even so, the American revolutionaries eventually won a comprehensive military and political victory.

Online Study Center
Improve Your Grade
Interactive Map: The American Revolutionary War

Cornwallis surrendered to Washington as the British military band played "The World Turned Upside-Down."

This victory effectively ended the war. The Continental Congress sent representatives to the peace conference that followed with instructions to work in tandem with the French. Believing that France was more concerned with containing British power than with guaranteeing a strong United States, America's peace delegation chose to negotiate directly with Britain and gained a generous settlement. The Treaty of Paris (1783) granted unconditional independence and established generous boundaries for the former colonies. In return the United States promised to repay prewar debts due to British merchants and to allow loyalists to recover property confiscated by patriot forces. In the end, loyalists were poorly treated, and thousands of them decided to leave for Canada.

The Construction of Republican Institutions, to 1800

Even before the Declaration of Independence, many colonies had created new governments independent of British colonial authorities. After independence leaders in each of the new states (as the former colonies were called) summoned constitutional conventions to draft formal charters and submitted the results to voters for ratification. Europeans were fascinated by the drafting of written constitutions and by the formal ratification of these constitutions by a vote of the people. Many of these documents were quickly translated and published in Europe. Remembering conflicts between royal governors and colonial legislatures, the authors of state constitutions placed severe limits on executive authority but granted legislatures greater powers than in colonial times. Many state constitutions also included bills of rights to provide further protection against government tyranny.

An effective constitution for the new national government was developed with difficulty. The Second Continental Congress sent the Articles of Confederation—the first constitution of the United States—to the states for approval in 1777, but it was not accepted by all the states until 1781. It created a one-house legislature in which each state was granted a single vote. A simple majority of the thirteen states was sufficient to pass minor legislation, but nine votes were necessary for declaring war, imposing taxes, and coining or borrowing money. Executive power was exercised by committees, not by a president. Given the intended weakness of this government, it is remarkable that it successfully organized the human and material resources to defeat Great Britain.

With the coming of peace, many of the most powerful political figures in the United States recognized that the Confederation was unable to enforce unpopular requirements of the peace treaty such as the recognition of loyalist property claims, the payment of prewar debts, and even the payment of military salaries and pensions to veterans. In September 1786 Virginia invited the other states to discuss the government's failure to deal with trade issues. This led to a call for a new convention to meet in Philadelphia nine months later. A rebellion led by Revolutionary War veterans in western Massachusetts gave the assembling delegates a sense of urgency.

The **Constitutional Convention**, which began meeting in May 1787, achieved a nonviolent second American Revolution. The delegates pushed aside the announced purpose of the convention—"to render the constitution of the federal government adequate to the exigencies of the union"—and secretly undertook the creation of a new constitution. George Washington was elected presiding officer. His reputation and popularity provided a solid foundation on which the delegates could contemplate an alternative political model.

Debate focused on representation, electoral procedures, executive powers, and the relationship between the federal government and the states. Compromise solutions included distribution of political power among the executive, legislative, and judicial branches and the division of authority between the federal government and the states. The final compromise provided for a two-house legislature: the lower house (the House of Representatives) to be elected directly by voters and the upper house (the Senate) to be elected by state legislatures. The chief executive—the president—was to be elected indirectly by "electors" selected by ballot in the states.

Although the U.S. Constitution created the most democratic government of the era, only a minority of the adult population was given full rights. In some northern states where large numbers of free blacks had fought with patriot forces, there was some hostility to the continuation of slavery, but southern leaders were able to protect the institution. Although slaves were denied participation in the political process, slave states were permitted to count three-fifths of the slave population in the calculations that determined the number of congressional representatives, thus multiplying the political power of the slave-owning class. Southern delegates also gained a twenty-year continuation of the slave trade to 1808 and a fugitive slave clause that required all states to return runaway slaves to their masters.

Women were powerfully affected by their participation in revolutionary politics and by changes in the economy brought on by the break with Britain. They had led prewar boycotts and had organized relief and charitable organizations during the war. Some had served in the military as nurses, and a smaller number had joined the ranks disguised as men. Nevertheless, they were denied political rights in the new republic. Only New Jersey granted the right to vote to all free residents who met modest property requirements. As a result, women and African Americans who met property requirements were able to vote in New Jersey until 1807, when lawmakers eliminated this right.

THE FRENCH REVOLUTION, 1789–1815

The French Revolution undermined traditional monarchy as well as the power of the Catholic Church and the hereditary aristocracy but, unlike the American Revolution, did not create an enduring form of representative democracy. The colonial revolution in North America, however, did not confront so directly the entrenched privileges of an established church, monarchy, and aristocracy, and the American Revolution produced no symbolic drama comparable to the public beheading of the French king Louis XVI in early 1793. Among its achievements, the French Revolution expanded mass participation in political life and radicalized the democratic tradition inherited from the English and American experiences. But in the end, the passions unleashed by revolutionary events in France could not be sustained, and popular demagogues and the dictatorship of Napoleon stalled democratic reform.

French Society and Fiscal Crisis

French society was divided into three groups. The clergy, called the First Estate, numbered about 130,000 in a nation of 28 million. The Catholic Church owned about 10 percent of the nation's land and extracted substantial amounts of wealth from the economy in the form of tithes and ecclesiastical fees. Despite its substantial wealth, the church was exempted from nearly all taxes. The clergy was organized hierarchically, and members of the hereditary nobility held almost all the upper positions in the church.

The 300,000 members of the nobility, the Second Estate, controlled about 30 percent of the land and retained ancient rights on much of the rest. Nobles held the vast majority of high administrative, judicial, military, and church positions. Though traditionally barred from some types of commercial activity, nobles were important participants in wholesale trade, banking, manufacturing, and mining. Like the clergy, this estate was hierarchical: important differences in wealth, power, and outlook separated the higher from the lower nobility. The nobility was also a highly permeable class; in the eighteenth century it received an enormous infusion of wealthy commoners who purchased administrative and judicial offices that conferred noble status.

The Third Estate included everyone else, from wealthy financiers to homeless beggars. The bourgeoisie°, or middle class, grew rapidly in the eighteenth century. There were three times as many members of this class in 1774, when Louis XVI took the throne, as there had been in 1715, at the end of Louis XIV's reign. Commerce, finance, and manufacturing accounted for much of the wealth of the Third Estate. Wealthy commoners also owned nearly a third of the nation's land. This literate and socially ambitious class supported an expanding publishing industry, subsidized the fine arts, and purchased many of the extravagant new homes being built in Paris and other cities.

Peasants accounted for 80 percent of the French population. Artisans and other skilled workers, small shopkeepers and peddlers, and small landowners held a

bourgeoisie (boor-zwah-ZEE)

Parisian Stocking Mender   The poor lived very difficult lives. This woman uses a discarded wine barrel as a shop where she mends socks.   (Private Collection)

more privileged position in society. They owned some property and lived decently when crops were good and prices stable. By 1780 poor harvests had increased their cost of living and led to a decline in consumer demand for their products. They were rich enough to fear the loss of their property and status, well educated enough to be aware of the growing criticism of the king, but too poor and marginalized to influence policy.

The nation's poor were a large, growing, and troublesome sector. The poverty and vulnerability of peasant families forced younger children to seek seasonal work away from home and led many to crime and beggary. Raids by roving vagabonds on isolated farms were one measure of this social dislocation. In Paris and other French cities the vile living conditions and unhealthy diet of the working poor were startling to visitors from other European nations. Urban streets swarmed with beggars and prostitutes. Paris alone had 25,000 prostitutes in 1760. The wretchedness of the French poor is perhaps best indicated by the growing problem of child abandonment. On the eve of the French Revolution at least 40,000 children a year were given up by their parents. The convenient fiction was that these children would be adopted; in reality the majority died of neglect.

Unable to afford decent housing, obtain steady employment, or protect their children, the poor periodically erupted in violent protest and rage. In the countryside violence was often the reaction when the nobility or clergy increased dues and fees. In towns and cities an increase in the price of bread often provided the spark, for bread prices largely determined the quality of life of the poor. These explosive episodes, however, were not revolutionary in character. The remedies sought were conventional and immediate rather than structural and long-term. That was to change when the Crown tried to solve its fiscal crisis.

The expenses of the War of the Austrian Succession began the crisis. Louis XV (r. 1715–1774) first tried to impose new taxes on the nobility and on other groups that in the past had enjoyed exemptions. This effort failed in the face of widespread protest and the refusal of the Parlement of Paris, a court that heard appeals from local courts throughout France, to register the new tax. The crisis deepened when debts from the Seven Years War compelled the king to impose emergency fiscal measures. Again, the king met resistance from the Parlement of Paris. In 1768 frustrated authorities exiled the members of that Parlement and pushed through a series of unpopular fiscal measures. When the twenty-two-year-old Louis XVI assumed the throne in 1774, he attempted to gain popular support by recalling the exiled members of the Parlement of Paris, but he soon learned that provincial parlements had also come to see themselves as having a constitutional power to check any growth in monarchial authority.

In 1774 Louis's chief financial adviser warned that the government could barely afford to operate; as he put it, "the first gunshot [act of war] will drive the state to bankruptcy." Despite this warning, the French took on the heavy burden of supporting the American Revolution, delaying collapse by borrowing enormous sums and disguising the growing debt in misleading fiscal accounts. By the end of the war with Britain, more than half of France's national budget was required to pay the interest on the resulting debt. It soon became clear that fiscal reforms and new taxes, not new loans, were unavoidable.

In 1787 the desperate king called an Assembly of Notables to approve a radical and comprehensive reform of the economy and fiscal policy. Despite the fact that the members of this assembly were selected by the king's advisers from the high nobility, the judiciary, and the clergy, this privileged group proved unwilling to act as a rubber stamp for the proposed reforms or new taxes. Instead, these representatives of France's most privileged classes sought to protect their interests by questioning the competence of the king and his ministers to supervise the nation's affairs.

Protest Turns to Revolution, 1789–1792

In frustration, the king dismissed the Notables and attempted to implement some reforms on his own, but his effort was met by an increasingly hostile judiciary and by popular demonstrations. Because the king was unable to extract needed tax concessions from the French elite, he was forced to call the **Estates General**, the French national legislature, which had not met since 1614. The narrow self-interest and greed of the rich—who would not tolerate an increase in their own taxes—rather than the grinding poverty of the common people had created the conditions for political revolution.

In late 1788 and early 1789 members of the three estates came together throughout the nation to discuss grievances and elect representatives who would meet at Versailles°. The Third Estate's representatives were mostly men of substantial property, but even some of them were angry at the king's ministers and inclined to move France toward constitutional monarchy with an elected legislature. Many nobles and members of the clergy sympathized with the reform agenda of the Third Estate, but deep internal divisions over procedural and policy issues limited the power of the First and the Second Estates.

Traditionally, the three estates met separately, and a positive vote by two of the three was required for action. Tradition, however, was quickly overturned when the Third Estate refused to conduct business until the king ordered the other two estates to sit with it in a single body. During a six-week period of stalemate, many parish priests from the First Estate began to meet with the commoners. When this expanded Third Estate declared itself the **National Assembly**, the king and his advisers recognized that the reformers intended to force them to accept a constitutional monarchy.

After being locked out of their meeting place, the Third Estate appropriated an indoor tennis court and pledged to write a constitution. The Oath of the Tennis Court ended Louis's vain hope that he could limit the agenda to fiscal reform. The king's effort to solve the

---

Versailles (vuhr-SIGH)

Parisians Storm the Bastille This depiction of the storming of the Bastille on July 14, 1789, was painted by an artist who witnessed the epochal event still celebrated by the French as a national holiday. (Photos12.com-ARJ)

nation's fiscal crisis had become connected in unpredictable ways to the central ideas of the era: the people were sovereign, and the legitimacy of political institutions and individual rulers ultimately depended on their carrying out the people's will. Louis prepared for a confrontation with the National Assembly by moving military forces to Versailles. Before he could act, the people of Paris intervened.

A succession of bad harvests beginning in 1785 had propelled bread prices upward throughout France and provoked an economic depression as demand for nonessential goods collapsed. By the time the Estates General met, nearly a third of the Parisian work force was unemployed. Hunger and anger marched hand in hand through working-class neighborhoods.

When the people of Paris heard that the king was massing troops in Versailles to arrest the representatives, crowds of common people began to seize arms and mo-

bilize. On July 14, 1789, a crowd searching for military supplies attacked the Bastille°, a medieval fortress used as a prison. The futile defense of the Bastille cost ninety-eight lives before its garrison surrendered. Enraged, the attackers hacked the commander to death and then paraded through the city with his head and that of Paris's chief magistrate stuck on pikes.

These events coincided with uprisings by peasants in the country. Peasants sacked manor houses and destroyed documents that recorded their traditional obligations. They refused to pay taxes and dues to landowners and seized common lands. Forced to recognize the fury raging through rural areas, the National Assembly voted to end traditional obligations and to reform the tax system. Having forced acceptance of their narrow agenda, the peasants ceased their revolt.

Bastille (bass-TEEL)

These popular uprisings strengthened the hand of the National Assembly in its dealings with the king. One manifestation of this altered relationship was passage of the **Declaration of the Rights of Man**. There were clear similarities between the language of this declaration and the U.S. Declaration of Independence. Indeed, Thomas Jefferson, who had written the American document, was U.S. ambassador to Paris and offered his opinion to those drafting the French statement. The French declaration, however, was more sweeping in its language than the American. Among the enumerated natural rights were "liberty, property, security, and resistance to oppression." The Declaration of the Rights of Man also guaranteed free expression of ideas, equality before the law, and representative government.

Online Study Center
Improve Your Grade
Primary Source: The Declaration
of the Rights of Man and Citizen

While delegates debated political issues in Versailles, the economic crisis worsened in Paris. Women employed in the garment industry and in small-scale retail businesses were particularly hard hit. Because the working women of Paris faced high food prices every day as they struggled to feed their families, their anger had a hard edge. Public markets became political arenas where the urban poor met daily in angry assembly. Here the revolutionary link between the material deprivation of the French poor and the political aspirations of the French bourgeoisie was forged.

On October 5, market women organized a crowd of thousands to march the 12 miles (19 kilometers) to Versailles. Once there, they forced their way into the National Assembly to demand action from the frightened representatives: "the point is that we want bread." The crowd then entered the royal apartments, killed some of the king's guards, and searched for Queen Marie Antoinette°, whom they loathed as a symbol of extravagance. Eventually, the crowd demanded that the royal family return to Paris. Preceded by the heads of two aristocrats carried on pikes and hauling away the palace's supply of flour, the triumphant crowd escorted the royal family to Paris.

With the king's ability to resist democratic change overcome by the Paris crowd, the National Assembly achieved a radically restructured French society in the next two years. It passed a new constitution that dramatically limited monarchial power and abolished the nobility

---

Antoinette (ann-twah-NET)

---

as a hereditary class. Economic reforms swept away monopolies and trade barriers within France. The Legislative Assembly (the new constitution's name for the National Assembly) seized church lands to use as collateral for a new paper currency, and priests—who were to be elected—were put on the state payroll. When the government tried to force priests to take a loyalty oath, however, many Catholics joined a growing counterrevolutionary movement.

At first, many European monarchs had welcomed the weakening of the French king, but by 1791 Austria and Prussia threatened to intervene in support of the monarchy. The Legislative Assembly responded by declaring war. Although the war went badly at first for French forces, people across France responded patriotically to foreign invasions, forming huge new volunteer armies and mobilizing national resources to meet the challenge. By the end of 1792 French armies had gained a stalemate with the foreign forces.

The Terror, 1793–1794

In this period of national crisis and foreign threat, the French Revolution entered its most radical phase. A failed effort by the king and queen to escape from Paris and find foreign allies cost the king any remaining popular support. As foreign armies crossed into France, his behavior was increasingly viewed as treasonous. On August 10, 1792, a crowd similar to the one that had marched on Versailles invaded his palace in Paris and forced the king to seek protection in the Legislative Assembly. The Assembly suspended the king, ordered his imprisonment, and called for the formation of a new National Convention to be elected by the vote of all men.

Rumors of counterrevolutionary plots kept working-class neighborhoods in an uproar. In September mobs surged through the city's prisons, killing nearly half the prisoners. Swept along by popular passion, the newly elected National Convention convicted Louis XVI of treason, sentencing him to death and proclaiming France a republic. The guillotine ended the king's life in January 1793. Invented in the spirit of the era as a more humane way to execute the condemned, this machine was to become the bloody symbol of the revolution (see Environment and Technology: The Guillotine). By February 1793 these events helped to precipitate a wider war with France now confronting nearly all of Europe's major powers.

The National Convention—the new legislature of the new First Republic of France—convened in September. Almost all of its members were from the middle class,

The Guillotine

No machine more powerfully symbolizes the revolutionary era than the guillotine. The machine immortalizes Joseph Ignace Guillotin (1738–1814), a physician and member of the French Constituent Assembly. In 1789 Guillotin recommended that executions be made more modern and more humane by the use of a beheading device. He sought to replace hangings, used for commoners, and beheadings by axe, used for the nobility. Both forms of execution were often administered with little skill, leading to gruesome and painful deaths. Guillotin believed that a properly designed machine would produce predictable, nearly painless deaths. The universal application of this penalty would also remove the social distinction between commoners and nobles, now embarrassing in a more egalitarian age. As Guillotin said, the "privilege of decapitation will no longer be confined to nobles."

From 1791 execution by beheading became the common sentence for all capital crimes. The actual machine was invented by another physician, Antoine Louis, secretary of the College of Surgeons. Once directed to produce a suitable device, Louis, in many ways a typical technician of his time, systematically examined devices used elsewhere and experimented until satisfied with his results. At first called Louisette after its inventor, the guillotine was first used on a highwayman in 1792. Praised by contemporaries because it seemed to remove human agency, and therefore revenge, from the execution of the death penalty, the guillotine became the physical symbol of the Terror.

The Guillotine The guillotine, introduced as a more humane and democratic alternative to traditional executions, came to symbolize the arbitrary violence of the French Revolution. In this contemporary cartoon Robespierre, the architect of the Terror, is shown as an executioner surrounded by these terrifying machines. (The Art Archive)

and nearly all were **Jacobins**°—the most uncompromising democrats. Deep political differences, however, separated moderate Jacobins—called "Girondists°," after a region in southern France—and radicals known as "the Mountain." Members of the Mountain—so named because their seats were on the highest level in the assembly hall—were more sympathetic than the Girondists to the demands of the Parisian working class and more impatient with parliamentary procedure and constitutional constraints on government action. The Mountain came to be dominated by **Maximilien Robespierre**°, a young, little-known lawyer from the provinces who had been influenced by Rousseau's ideas.

With the French economy still in crisis and Paris suffering from inflation, high unemployment, and scarcity, Robespierre used the popular press and political clubs to

Jacobin (JAK-uh-bin)   **Girondist** (juh-RON-dist)

Robespierre (ROBES-pee-air)

Playing Cards from the French Revolution Even playing cards could be used to attack the aristocracy and Catholic Church. In this pack of cards, "Equality" and "Liberty" replaced kings and queens. (Jean-Loup Charmet/The Bridgeman Art Library)

forge an alliance with the volatile Parisian working class. His growing strength in the streets allowed him to purge and execute many of his enemies in the National Convention and to restructure the government. Executive power was placed in the hands of the newly formed Committee of Public Safety, which created special courts to seek out and punish domestic enemies.

Among the groups that lost ground were the active feminists of the Parisian middle class and the working-class women who had sought the right to bear arms in defense of the Revolution. These women had provided decisive leadership at crucial times, helping propel the Revolution toward widened suffrage and a more democratic structure. Armed women had actively participated in every confrontation with conservative forces. It is ironic that the National Convention—the revolutionary era's most radical legislative body, elected by universal male suffrage—chose to repress the militant feminist forces that had prepared the ground for its creation.

Faced with rebellion in the provinces and foreign invasion, Robespierre and his allies unleashed a period of repression called the Reign of Terror (1793–1794) (see Diversity and Dominance: Robespierre and Wollstonecraft Defend and Explain the Terror). During the Terror, approximately 40,000 people were executed or died in prison, and another 300,000 were imprisoned. New actions against the clergy were also approved, including the provocative measure of forcing priests to marry. Even time was subject to revolutionary change. A new republican calendar created twelve thirty-day months divided into ten-day weeks. Sunday, with its Christian meanings, disappeared from the calendar.

By spring 1794 the Revolution was secure from foreign and domestic enemies, but repression, now institutionalized, continued. Among the victims were some who had been Robespierre's closest political collaborators during the early stage of the Terror. The execution of these former allies prepared the way for Robespierre's own fall by undermining the sense of invulnerability that had secured the loyalty of his remaining partisans in the National Convention. After French victories eliminated the immediate foreign threat, conservatives in the Convention felt secure enough to vote for the arrest of Robespierre on July 27, 1794. Over the next two days, Robespierre and nearly a hundred of his remaining allies were executed by guillotine.

Reaction and the Rise of Napoleon, 1795–1815

Purged of Robespierre's collaborators, the Convention began to undo the radical reforms. It removed many of the emergency economic controls that had been holding down prices and protecting the working class. Gone also was toleration for violent popular demonstrations. When the Paris working class rose in protest in 1795, the Convention approved the use of overwhelming military force. Another retreat from radical objectives was signaled when the Catholic Church was permitted to regain much of its former influence. The church's confiscated wealth, however, was not returned. A more conservative constitution was also ratified. It protected property, established a voting process that reduced the power of the masses, and created a new executive authority, the Directory. Once installed in power, however, the Directory proved unable to end the foreign wars or solve domestic economic problems.

After losing the election of 1797 the Directory suspended the results. The republican phase of the Revolution was clearly dead. Legitimacy was now based on coercive power rather than on elections. Two years later, **Napoleon Bonaparte** (1769–1821), a brilliant young general in the

DIVERSITY + DOMINANCE

후세인 은신처 망

들과 함께 사망 가
령이 대중 앞에 나타나거나 애국심
을 고취하는 노래만을 내보내던 방
송마저 중단됐다.

라크 전후 대책을
의에서는 전후
영국 주도로 해

심견지 구축… 이틀째 시가戰

Robespierre and Wollstonecraft Defend and Explain the Terror

*M*any Europeans who had initially been sympathetic to the French Revolution were repelled by the Terror. In 1793 and 1794, while France was at war with Austria, Prussia, Great Britain, Holland, and Spain, about 2,600 people were executed in Paris, including the king and queen, members of the nobility, and Catholic clergy. The public nature of the judicial procedures and executions outraged many. Critics of the Revolution asked if these excesses were not worse than those committed by the French monarchy. Others defended the violence as necessary, arguing that the Terror had been provoked by enemies of the Revolution or was the consequence of earlier injustices.

The following two opinions date from 1794. Maximilien Robespierre was the head of the Committee of Public Safety, the effective head of the revolutionary government. Robespierre was a provincial lawyer who rose to power in Paris as the Revolution was radicalized. In the statement that follows he is unrepentant, arguing that violence was necessary in the defense of liberty. He made this statement on the eve of his political demise; in 1794 he was driven from power and executed by the revolutionary movement he had helped create.

Mary Wollstonecraft, an English intellectual and advocate for women's rights who was living in Paris at the time of the execution of Louis XVI, was troubled by the violence, and her discussion of these events is more an apology than a defense. She had published her famous A Vindication of the Rights of Woman in 1792, after which she left for Paris. Wollstonecraft left Paris after war broke out between France and Britain. She remained an important force in European intellectual life until her death from complications of childbirth in 1797.

Maximilien Robespierre, "On the Moral and Political Principles of Domestic Policy"

[L]et us deduce a great truth: the characteristic of popular government is confidence in the people and severity towards itself.

The whole development of our theory would end here if you had only to pilot the vessel of the Republic through calm waters; but the tempest roars, and the revolution imposes on you another task.

This great purity of the French revolution's basis, the very sublimity of its objective, is precisely what causes both our strength and our weakness. Our strength, because it gives to us truth's ascendancy over imposture, and the rights of the public interest over private interests; our weakness, because it rallies all vicious men against us, all those who in their hearts contemplated despoiling the people and all those who intend to let it be despoiled with impunity, both those who have rejected freedom as a personal calamity and those who have embraced the revolution as a career and the Republic as prey. Hence the defection of so many ambitious or greedy men who since the point of departure have abandoned us along the way because they did not begin the journey with the same destination in view. The two opposing spirits that have been represented in a struggle to rule nature might be said to be fighting in this great period of human history to fix irrevocably the world's destinies, and France is the scene of this fearful combat. Without, all the tyrants encircle you; within, all tyranny's friends conspire; they will conspire until hope is wrested from crime. We must smother the internal and external enemies of the Republic or perish with it; now in this situation, the first maxim of your policy ought to be to lead the people by reason and the people's enemies by terror.

If the spring of popular government in time of peace is virtue, the springs of popular government in revolution are at once virtue and terror: virtue, without which terror is fatal; terror, without which virtue is powerless. Terror is nothing other than justice, prompt, severe, inflexible; it is therefore an emanation of virtue; it is not so much a special principle as it is a consequence of the general principle of democracy applied to our country's most urgent needs.

It has been said that terror is the principle of despotic government. Does your government therefore resemble despotism? Yes, as the sword that gleams in the hands of the heroes of liberty resembles that with which the henchmen of tyranny are armed. Let the despot govern by terror his brutalized subjects; he is right, as a despot. Subdue by terror the enemies of liberty, and you will be right, as founders of the Republic. The government of the revolution is liberty's despotism against tyranny. Is force made only to protect crime? And is the thunderbolt not destined to strike the heads of the proud?

. . . Society owes protection only to peaceable citizens; the only citizens in the Republic are the republicans. For it, the royalists, the conspirators are only strangers or, rather, enemies. This terrible war waged by liberty against tyranny is it not indivisible? Are the enemies within not the allies of the enemies without? The assassins who tear our country apart, the intriguers who buy the consciences that hold the people's mandate; the traitors who sell them; the mercenary pamphleteers hired to dishonor the people's cause, to kill public virtue, to stir up the fire of civil discord, and to prepare political counterrevolution by moral counterrevolution—are all those men less guilty or less dangerous than the tyrants whom they serve?

Mary Wollstonecraft, "An Historical and Moral View of the Origin and Progress of the French Revolution"

Weeping scarcely conscious that I weep, O France! Over the vestiges of thy former oppression, which, separating man from man with a fence of iron, sophisticated [complicated] all, and made many completely wretched; I tremble, lest I should meet some unfortunate being, fleeing from the despotism of licentious freedom, hearing the snap of the guillotine at his heels, merely because he was once noble, or has afforded an asylum to those whose only crime is their name—and, if my pen almost bound with eagerness to record the day that leveled the Bastille [an abbey used as a prison before the Revolution] with the dust, making the towers of despair tremble to their base, the recollection that still the abbey is appropriated to hold the victims of revenge and suspicion [she means that the Bastille remained a prison for those awaiting revolutionary justice]. . . .

Excuse for the Ferocity of the Parisians   The deprivation of natural, equal, civil, and political rights reduced the most cunning of the lower orders to practice fraud, and the rest to habits of stealing, audacious robberies, and murders. And why? Because the rich and poor were separated into bands of tyrants and slaves, and the retaliation of slaves is always terrible. In short, every sacred feeling, moral and divine, has been obliterated, and the dignity of man sullied, by a system of policy and jurisprudence as repugnant to reason as at variance with humanity.

The only excuse that can be made for the ferocity of the Parisians is then simply to observe that they had not any confidence in the laws, which they had always found to be merely cobwebs to catch small flies [the poor]. Accustomed to be punished themselves for every trifle, and often for only being in the way of the rich, or their parasites, when, in fact,

had the Parisians seen the execution of a noble, or priest, though convicted of crimes beyond the daring of vulgar minds? When justice, or the law, is so partial, the day of retribution will come with the red sky of vengeance, to confound the innocent with the guilty. The mob were barbarous beyond the tiger's cruelty. . . .

Let us cast our eyes over the history of man, and we shall scarcely find a page that is not tarnished by some foul deed or bloody transaction. Let us examine the catalogue of the vices of men in a savage state, and contrast them with those of men civilized; we shall find that a barbarian, considered as a moral being, is an angel, compared with the refined villain of artificial life. Let us investigate the causes which have produced this degeneracy, and we shall discover that they are those unjust plans of government which have been formed by peculiar circumstances in every part of the globe.

Then let us coolly and impartially contemplate the improvements which are gaining ground in the formation of principles of policy; and I flatter myself it will be allowed by every humane and considerate being that a political system more simple than has hitherto existed would effectually check those aspiring follies, which, by imitation, leading to vice, have banished from governments the very shadow of justice and magnanimity.

Thus had France grown up and sickened on the corruption of a state diseased. . . . it is only the philosophical eye, which looks into the nature and weighs the consequences of human actions, that will be able to discern the cause, which has produced so many dreadful effects.

QUESTIONS FOR ANALYSIS

1. Why does Robespierre believe that revolution cannot tolerate diversity of opinion? Are his reasons convincing?

2. How does Robespierre distinguish the terror of despots from the terror of liberty?

3. How does Wollstonecraft explain the "ferocity" of the Parisians?

4. What does Wollstonecraft believe will come from this period of violence?

Sources: Maximilien Robespierre, "On the Moral and Political Principles of Domestic Policy," February 5, 1794, Modern History Sourcebook: Robespierre: Terror and Virtue, 1794, http://www.fordham.edu/halsall/mod/robespierre-terror.html; Mary Wollstonecraft, "An Historical and Moral View of the Origin and Progress of the French Revolution," A Mary Wollstonecraft Reader, ed. Barbara H. Solomon and Paula S. Berggren (New York: New American Library, 1983), 374–375, 382–383.

French army, seized power. Just as the American and French Revolutions had been the start of the modern democratic tradition, the military intervention that brought Napoleon to power in 1799 marked the advent of another modern form of government: popular authoritarianism.

The American and French Revolutions had resulted in part from conflicts over representation. If the people were sovereign, what institutions best expressed popular will? In the United States the answer was to expand the electorate and institute representative government. The French Revolution had taken a different direction with the Reign of Terror. Interventions on the floor of the National Convention by market women and soldiers, the presence of common people at revolutionary tribunals and at public executions, and expanded military service were all forms of political communication that temporarily satisfied the French people's desire to influence their government. Napoleon tamed these forms of political expression to organize Europe's first popular dictatorship. He succeeded because his military reputation promised order to a society exhausted by a decade of crisis, turmoil, and bloodshed.

In contrast to the National Convention, Napoleon proved capable of realizing France's dream of dominating Europe and providing effective protection for persons and property at home. Negotiations with the Catholic Church led to the Concordat of 1801. This agreement gave French Catholics the right to freely practice their religion, but it also recognized the French government's authority to nominate bishops and retain priests on the state payroll. In his comprehensive rewriting of French law, the Civil Code of 1804, Napoleon won the support of the peasantry and of the middle class by asserting two basic principles inherited from the moderate first stage of the French Revolution: equality in law and protection of property. Even some members of the nobility became supporters after Napoleon declared himself emperor and France an empire in 1804. However, the discrimination against women that had begun during the Terror was extended by the Napoleonic Civil Code. Women were denied basic political rights and were able to participate in the economy only with the guidance and supervision of their fathers and husbands.

While providing personal security, the Napoleonic system denied or restricted many individual rights. Free speech and free expression were limited. Criticism of the government, viewed as subversive, was proscribed, and most opposition newspapers disappeared. Spies and informers directed by the minister of police enforced these limits to political freedom. Thousands of the regime's enemies and critics were questioned or detained in the name of domestic tranquility.

Ultimately, the Napoleonic system depended on the success of French arms and French diplomacy (see

Map 22.2). From Napoleon's assumption of power until his fall, no single European state could defeat the French military. Even powerful alliances like that of Austria and Prussia were brushed aside with humiliating defeats and forced to become allies of France. Only Britain, protected by its powerful navy, remained able to thwart Napoleon's plans to dominate Europe. His effort to mobilize forces for an invasion of Britain failed in late 1805 when the British navy defeated the French and allied Spanish fleets off the coast of Spain at the Battle of Trafalgar.

Desiring to again extend French power to the Americas, Napoleon invaded Portugal in 1807 and Spain in 1808. French armies soon became tied down in a costly conflict with Spanish and Portuguese patriots who had forged an alliance with the only available European power, Great Britain. Frustrated by events on the Iberian Peninsula and faced with a faltering economy, Napoleon made the fateful decision to invade Russia. In June 1812 he began his campaign with the largest army ever assembled in Europe, approximately 600,000 men. After fighting an inconclusive battle at Borodino, Napoleon pressed on to Moscow. Five weeks after occupying Moscow, he was forced to retreat by Russian patriots who set the city on fire and by approaching armies. During the retreat, the brutal Russian winter and attacks by Russian forces destroyed his army. A broken and battered fragment of 30,000 men returned to France.

After the debacle in Russia, Austria and Prussia deserted Napoleon and entered an alliance with England and Russia. Unable to defend Paris, Napoleon was forced to abdicate the French throne in April 1814. The allies exiled Napoleon to the island of Elba off the coast of Italy and restored the French monarchy. The next year Napoleon escaped from Elba and returned to France. But his moment had passed. He was defeated in 1815 by an allied army at Waterloo, in Belgium, after only one hundred days in power. His final exile was on the distant island of St. Helena in the South Atlantic, where he died in 1821.

REVOLUTION SPREADS, CONSERVATIVES RESPOND, 1789–1850

Even as the dictatorship of Napoleon eliminated the democratic legacy of the French Revolution, revolutionary ideology was spreading and taking hold in Europe and the Americas. In Europe the French Revolution promoted nationalism and republicanism. In the Americas the legacies of the American and French

Map 22.2   Napoleon's Europe, 1810   By 1810 Great Britain was the only remaining European power at war with Napoleon. Because of the loss of the French fleet at the Battle of Trafalgar in 1805, Napoleon was unable to threaten Britain with invasion, and Britain was able to actively assist the resistance movements in Spain and Portugal, thereby helping weaken French power.

Haiti's Former Slaves Defend Their Freedom   In this representation, a veteran army sent by Napoleon to reassert French control in Haiti battles with Haitian forces in a tropical forest. The combination of Haitian resistance and yellow fever defeated the French invasion.   (Bettmann/Corbis)

Revolutions led to a new round of struggles for independence. News of revolutionary events in France destabilized the colonial regime in Saint Domingue (present-day Haiti), a small French colony on the western half of the island of Hispaniola, and resulted in the first successful slave rebellion. In Europe, however, the spread of revolutionary fervor was checked by reaction as monarchs formed an alliance to protect themselves from further revolutionary outbreaks.

The Haitian Revolution, 1789–1804

In 1789 the French colony of Saint Domingue was among the richest European colonies in the Americas. Its plantations produced sugar, cotton, indigo, and coffee. The colony accounted for two-thirds of France's tropical imports and generated nearly one-third of all French foreign trade. This impressive wealth depended on a brutal slave regime. Saint Domingue's harsh punishments and poor living conditions were notorious throughout the Caribbean. The colony's high mortality and low fertility rates created an insatiable demand for African slaves. As a result, in 1790 the majority of the colony's 500,000 slaves were African-born.

In 1789, when news of the calling of France's Estates General arrived on the island, wealthy white planters sent a delegation to Paris charged with seeking more home rule and greater economic freedom for Saint Domingue. The free mixed-race population, the *gens de couleur*°, also sent representatives. These nonwhite delegates were mostly drawn from the large class of slave-owning small planters and urban merchants. They focused on ending race discrimination and achieving political equality with whites. They did not seek freedom for slaves; the most prosperous gens de couleur were slave owners themselves. As the French Revolution became more radical, the gens de couleur forged an alliance with sympathetic French radicals, who came to identify the colony's wealthy planters as royalists and aristocrats.

The political turmoil in France weakened the ability of colonial administrators to maintain order. The authority

gens de couleur (zhahn deh koo-LUHR)

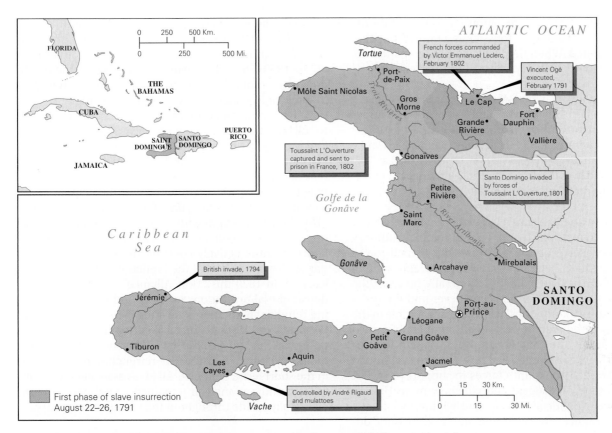

Map 22.3   The Haitian Revolution   On their way to achieving an end to slavery and gaining national independence, the Haitian revolutionaries were forced to defeat British and French military interventions as well as the local authority of the slave masters.

of colonial officials was no longer clear, and the very legitimacy of slavery was being challenged in France. In the vacuum that resulted, rich planters, poor whites, and the gens de couleur pursued their narrow interests, engendering an increasingly bitter and confrontational struggle. Given the slaves' hatred of the brutal regime that oppressed them and the accumulated grievances of the free people of color, there was no way to limit the violence once the control of the slave owners slipped. When Vincent Ogé°, leader of the gens de couleur mission to France, returned to Saint Domingue in 1790 to organize a military force, the planters captured, tortured, and executed him. This cruelty was soon repaid in kind.

By 1791 whites, led by the planter elite, and the gens de couleur were engaged in open warfare. This breach between the two groups of slave owners gave the slaves

an opening. A slave rebellion began on the plantations of the north and spread throughout the colony (see Map 22.3). Plantations were destroyed, masters and overseers killed, and crops burned. An emerging rebel leadership that combined elements of African political culture with revolutionary ideology from France mobilized and directed the rebelling slaves.

The rebellious slaves eventually gained the upper hand under the leadership of **François Dominique Toussaint L'Ouverture**, a former domestic slave, who created a disciplined military force. Toussaint was politically strengthened in 1794 when the radical National Convention in Paris abolished slavery in all French possessions. He overcame his rivals in Saint Domingue, defeated a British expeditionary force in 1798, and then led an invasion of the neighboring Spanish colony of Santo Domingo, freeing the slaves there. Toussaint continued to assert his loyalty to France but gave the French government no effective role in local affairs.

Ogé (oh-ZHAY)

As reaction overtook revolution in France, both the abolition of slavery and Toussaint's political position were threatened. When the Directory contemplated the reestablishment of slavery, Toussaint protested:

> Do they think that men who have been able to enjoy the blessing of liberty will calmly see it snatched away? They supported their chains only so long as they did not know any condition of life more happy than slavery. But today when they have left it, if they had a thousand lives they would sacrifice them all rather than be forced into slavery again.[3]

In 1802 Napoleon sent a large military force to Saint Domingue to reestablish both French colonial authority and slavery (see Map 22.3). At first the French forces were successful. Toussaint was captured and sent to France, where he died in prison. Eventually, however, the loss of thousands of lives to yellow fever and the resistance of the revolutionaries turned the tide. Visible in the resistance to the French were small numbers of armed women. During the early stages of the Haitian Revolution, very few slave women had taken up arms, although many had aided Toussaint's forces in support roles. But after a decade of struggle and violence, more Haitian women were politically aware and willing to join the armed resistance. In 1804 Toussaint's successors declared independence, and the free republic of Haiti joined the United States as the second independent nation in the Western Hemisphere. But independence and emancipation were achieved at a terrible price. Tens of thousands had died; the economy was destroyed; and public administration was corrupted by more than a decade of violence. Political violence and economic stagnation were to trouble Haiti throughout the nineteenth century.

The Congress of Vienna and Conservative Retrenchment, 1815–1820

In 1814–1815 representatives of Britain, Russia, Austria, and Prussia, along with representatives of other nations, met as the **Congress of Vienna** to reestablish political order in Europe. While they were meeting, Napoleon escaped from Elba and then was defeated at Waterloo. The French Revolution and Napoleon's imperial ambitions had threatened the very survival of Europe's old order. Ancient monarchies had been overturned and dynasties replaced with interlopers. Long-established political institutions had been tossed aside, and long-recognized international borders had been ignored. The very existence of the nobility and church had been put at risk. Under the leadership of the Austrian foreign minister, Prince Klemens von Metternich° (1773–1859), the allies worked together in Vienna to create a comprehensive peace settlement that they hoped would safeguard the conservative order.

The central objective of the Congress of Vienna was to roll back the clock in France. Because the participants believed that a strong and stable France was the best guarantee of future peace, the French monarchy was reestablished, and France's 1792 borders were recognized. Most of the continental European powers received some territorial gains, for Metternich sought to offset French strength with a balance of power. In addition, Austria, Russia, and Prussia formed a separate alliance to more actively confront the revolutionary and nationalist energies that the French Revolution had unleashed. In 1820 this "Holy Alliance" acted militarily to defeat liberal revolutions in Spain and Italy. By repressing republican and nationalist ideas in universities and the press, the Holy Alliance also attempted to meet the potential challenge posed by subversive ideas. Metternich's program of conservative retrenchment succeeded in the short term, but powerful ideas associated with liberalism and nationalism remained a vital part of European political life throughout the nineteenth century.

Nationalism, Reform, and Revolution, 1821–1850

Despite the power of the conservative monarchs, popular support for national self-determination and democratic reform grew throughout Europe. Greece had been under Ottoman control since the fifteenth century. In 1821 Greek patriots launched an independence movement. Metternich and other conservatives opposed Greek independence, but European artists and writers enamored with the cultural legacy of ancient Greece rallied political support for intervention. After years of struggle, Russia, France, and Great Britain forced the Ottoman Empire to recognize Greek independence in 1830.

Louis XVIII, brother of the executed Louis XVI, had been placed on the throne of France by the victorious allies in 1814. He ruled as a constitutional monarch until his death in 1824 and was followed to the throne by his brother Charles X. Charles attempted to rule in the prerevolutionary style of his ancestors, repudiating the constitution in 1830. Unwilling to accept this reactionary challenge, the people of Paris rose up and forced Charles

---

Metternich (MET-uhr-nik)

The Revolution of 1830 in Belgium After the 1830 uprising that overturned the restored monarchy in France, Belgians rose up to declare their independence from Holland. In Poland and Italy, similar uprisings combining nationalism and a desire for self-governance failed. This painting by Baron Gustaf Wappers romantically illustrates the popular nature of the Belgian uprising by bringing to the barricades men, women, and children drawn from both the middle and the working classes. (Musées Royaux des Beaux-Arts de Belgique, Brussels)

to abdicate. His successor was his cousin Louis Philippe° (r. 1830–1848), who accepted the reestablished constitution and extended voting privileges.

At the same time democratic reform movements appeared in both the United States and Great Britain. In the United States after 1790 the original thirteen states were joined by new states with constitutions granting voting rights to most free males. After the War of 1812 the right to vote was expanded in the older states as well. This broadening of the franchise led to the election of the populist president Andrew Jackson in 1828 (see Chapter 24).

However, revolutionary violence in France made the British aristocracy and the conservative Tory Party fearful

of expanded democracy and mass movements of any kind. In 1815 the British government passed the Corn Laws, which limited the importation of foreign grains. The laws favored the profits of wealthy landowners who produced grain at the expense of the poor, who were forced to pay more for their bread. When poor consumers organized to overturn these laws, the government outlawed most public meetings, using troops to crush protest in Manchester. Reacting against these policies, reformers gained the passage of laws that increased the power of the House of Commons, redistributed votes from agricultural to industrial districts, and increased the number of voters by nearly 50 percent. Although the most radical demands of these reformers, called Chartists, were defeated, new labor and economic reforms addressing the grievances of workers were passed (see Chapter 23).

Louis Philippe (loo-EE fee-LEEP)

Despite the achievement of Greek independence and limited political reform in France and Great Britain, conservatives continued to hold the upper hand in Europe. Finally, in 1848 the desire for democratic reform and national self-determination and the frustrations of urban workers led to upheavals across Europe. The **Revolutions of 1848** began in Paris, where members of the middle class and workers united to overthrow the regime of Louis Philippe and create the Second French Republic. Adult men were given voting rights; slavery was abolished in French colonies; the death penalty was ended; and a ten-hour workday was legislated for Paris. But Parisian workers' demands for programs to reduce unemployment and prices provoked conflicts with the middle class, which wanted to protect property rights. When workers rose up against the government, French troops were called out to crush them. Desiring the reestablishment of order, the French elected Louis Napoleon, nephew of the former emperor, president in December 1848. Three years later, he overturned the constitution as a result of popular plebiscite and, after ruling briefly as dictator, became Emperor Napoleon III. He remained in power until 1871.

Reformers in Hungary, Italy, Bohemia, and elsewhere pressed for greater national self-determination in 1848. When the Austrian monarchy did not meet their demands, students and workers in Vienna took to the streets to force political reforms similar to those sought in Paris. With revolution spreading throughout the Austrian Empire, Metternich, the symbol of reaction, fled Vienna in disguise. Little lasting change occurred, however, because the new Austrian emperor, Franz Joseph (r. 1848–1916) was able to use Russian military assistance and loyal Austrian troops to reestablish central authority.

Middle-class reformers and workers in Berlin joined forces in an attempt to compel the Prussian king to accept a liberal constitution and seek unification of the German states. But the Constituent Assembly called to write a constitution and arrange for national integration became entangled in diplomatic conflicts with Austria and Denmark. As a result, Frederick William IV (r. 1840–1861) was able to reassert his authority, thwarting both constitutional reform and unification.

Despite their heroism on the barricades of Paris, Vienna, Rome, and Berlin, the revolutionaries of 1848 failed to gain either their nationalist or their republican objectives. Monarchs retained the support not only of aristocrats but also of professional militaries, largely recruited from among peasants who had little sympathy for urban workers. Revolutionary coalitions, in contrast, were fragile and lacked clear objectives. Workers' demands for higher wages, lower prices, and labor reform often drove their middle-class allies into the arms of the reactionaries.

COMPARATIVE PERSPECTIVES

The last decades of the eighteenth century began a long period of revolutionary upheaval in the Atlantic world. Costly wars in Europe and along Europe's colonial frontiers in the Americas and Asia helped to provoke change, forcing European monarchs to impose new and unpopular taxes. The American Revolution initiated these transformations. Having defeated Britain, the citizens of this new American republic created the most democratic government of the time. While full rights were limited and slavery persisted, many Europeans saw this experiment as demonstrating the efficacy of the Enlightenment's most revolutionary political ideas. In the end, however, the compromises over slavery that had made the Constitution possible in 1787 failed, and, as discussed in Chapter 24, the new nation nearly disintegrated after 1860.

The French Revolution led temporarily to a more radical formulation of representative democracy, but it also led to the Terror, which cost thousands of lives, and the militarization of western Europe and a destructive cycle of wars. Yet, despite these terrible costs, the French Revolution propelled the idea of democracy and the ideal of equality far beyond the boundaries established earlier by the American Revolution. The Haitian Revolution, set in motion by events in France, not only created the second independent nation of the Western Hemisphere but also delivered a powerful blow to the institution of slavery. In Europe the excesses of the French Revolution and the wars that followed in its wake promoted the political ascent of Napoleon Bonaparte and democracy's modern nemesis, popular authoritarianism.

Each revolution had its own character. The revolutions in France and Haiti proved to be more violent and destructive than the American Revolution. First, there was no slave rebellion in North America. Although slavery was crucial to the most profitable exports, such as tobacco, cotton, and rice, slaves in British North America remained a minority except along the South Carolina coast. In addition, revolutionaries in France and Haiti faced more strongly entrenched and more powerful oppositions as well as greater social inequalities than did the revolutionaries in North America. The resistance of entrenched and privileged elites led inexorably to greater violence. Both French and Haitian revolutionaries also faced powerful foreign interventions that intensified the bloodshed and destructiveness of these revolutions.

The conservative retrenchment that followed the defeat of Napoleon succeeded in the short term. Monarchy, multinational empires, and the established church retained their hold on the loyalty of millions of Europeans and could count on the support of many of Europe's wealthiest and most powerful individuals. But liberalism and nationalism continued to stir revolutionary sentiment. The contest between adherents of the old order and partisans of change was to

continue well into the nineteenth century. In the end, the nation-state, the Enlightenment legacy of rational inquiry, broadened political participation, and secular intellectual culture prevailed. This outcome was determined in large measure by the old order's inability to satisfy the new social classes that appeared with the emerging industrial economy. The material transformation produced by industrial capitalism could not be contained in the narrow confines of a hereditary social system, nor could the rapid expansion of scientific learning be contained within the doctrines of traditional religion.

The revolutions of the late eighteenth century began the transformation of Western society, but they did not complete it. Only a minority gained full political rights. Women did not achieve full political rights until the twentieth century. Democratic institutions, as in revolutionary France, often failed. Moreover, as Chapter 24 discusses, slavery endured in the Americas past the mid-1800s, despite the revolutionary era's enthusiasm for individual liberty.

SUMMARY

○— How did the costs of imperial wars and the Enlightenment challenge the established authority of monarchs and religion in Europe and the American colonies?

○— What were the direct causes of the American Revolution?

○— What were the origins and accomplishments of the French Revolution?

○— How did revolution in one country help incite revolution elsewhere?

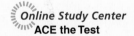

Online Study Center
ACE the Test

This era of revolution was, in large measure, the product of a long period of costly warfare among the imperial nations of Europe. Britain and France in particular faced fiscal crises as a result of colonial wars. Using taxes and institutions inherited from the past, they found it increasingly difficult to fund distant wars in the Americas or in Asia. In the British case, the costs of the French and Indian War led the government to attempt to impose unpopular taxes on its colonies. France faced an even more dire fiscal emergency as a result this war and later aid to the American revolutionaries. The refusal of powerful French interests to accept

new taxes would force the king to call the Estates General and lead ultimately to the French Revolution.

Meanwhile, the spread of literacy and the greater availability of books helped create an Enlightenment culture more open to reform and to the revolutionary change of existing institutions in Europe and in the Americas. But there were many distinct, even contradictory, currents in the Enlightenment. If the ideas of Locke and Rousseau guided critics of monarchy toward a new political culture of elections and representative institutions, these ideas were difficult to reconcile. Nevertheless, the intellectual ferment of the era gave educated men and women tools to criticize existing political institutions and the confidence to design new ones. The language of liberty and equality, even if poorly realized in the actions of revolutionary governments, proved a powerful solvent when applied to hierarchy and privilege.

The American Revolution grew from British colonial policy after the French and Indian War. To avoid new military costs, Britain tried unsuccessfully through the Quebec Act to restrict western settlement and thus reduce conflict with the Amerindians. To pay its war debt, Britain imposed new taxes, duties, and commercial regulations on the colonies, including the Stamp Act. These acts led to violent unrest that culminated with the "Boston Massacre." Parliament repealed some of these acts but then gave the British East India Company a tea monopoly, thus provoking more violence. Colonial patriots met in the Continental Congress, assumed government powers, raised an army, and issued the Declaration of Independence.

The French Revolution erupted from the crises provoked by France's archaic social and tax system, financial collapse, urban unrest, and division between the monarchy and aristocracy. The immediate cause was the crisis within the Estates General, during which the Third Estate broke away and declared itself the National Assembly. Uprisings in Paris and the countryside strengthened the Assembly's position, enabling it to press reforms embodied in the Declaration of the Rights of Man. Further reforms restructured France's society and economy. However, foreign intervention pushed the Legislative Assembly to radical extremes that culminated with the execution of Louis XVI and the Reign of Terror. Reaction against the Terror resulted in the conservative Directory and the even more repressive dictatorship of Napoleon Bonaparte. Napoleon's military adventures ultimately led to his fall, and the Congress of Vienna sought to establish a conservative balance of power. Despite this retrenchment, revolutionary struggles continued, especially in France, where the 1830 uprising replaced Charles X with Louis-Philippe. In 1848 nationalist and republican revolutions flared throughout Europe. These won few lasting gains, however, and in France they resulted in the imperial rule of Napoleon III.

Each new revolutionary development served as example and provocation for dissatisfied women and men elsewhere. French officers who took part in the American Revolution helped ignite the French Revolution. The constitutions of new American states and the new national constitution were published across Europe and read by thousands. Free black militiamen from Saint Domingue served along French units in support of the American Revolution. With the first stage of the French Revolution black freemen from Haiti traveled to France to seek their rights and returned to spread revolutionary passions. With the success of the Haitian Revolution, slaves throughout the Western Hemisphere took heart, and some rose in rebellion.

KEY TERMS

Enlightenment   *p. 640*

Benjamin Franklin   *p. 641*

George Washington   *p. 645*

Joseph Brant   *p. 647*

Constitutional Convention   *p. 649*

Estates General   *p. 649*

National Assembly   *p. 649*

Declaration of the Rights of Man   *p. 651*

Jacobins   *p. 652*

Maximilien Robespierre   *p. 652*

Napoleon Bonaparte   *p. 653*

gens de couleur   *p. 658*

François Dominique Toussaint L'Ouverture   *p. 659*

Congress of Vienna   *p. 660*

Revolutions of 1848   *p. 662*

Online Study Center
Improve Your Grade
Flashcards

SUGGESTED READING

The American Revolution has received a great amount of attention from scholars. Colin Bonwick, *The American Revolution* (1991), and Edward Countryman, *The American Revolution* (1985), provide excellent introductions. Garry Wills, *Inventing America, Jefferson's Declaration of Independence* (1978), and Edmund S. Morgan, *The Challenge of the American Revolution* (1976), are major works of interpretation. Gordon S. Wood, *The Radicalism of the American Revolution* (1992), is a brilliant examination of the ideological and cultural meanings of the Revolution. A contrarian view is offered by Francis Jennings, *The Creation of America Through Revolution to Empire* (2003). See also William Howard Adams, *The Paris Years of Thomas Jefferson* (1997). Lance Banning, *The Sacred Fire of Liberty: James Madison and the Founding of the Federal Republic* (1995), is a convincing revision of the story of Madison and his era. Gary Wills, *The Unknown American Revolution* (2005), is a very useful supplement. For the role of women in the American Revolution, see Linda K. Kerber, *Women of the Republic: Intellect and Ideology in Revolutionary America* (1980), and Mary Beth Norton, *Liberty's Daughters: The Revolutionary Experience of American Women, 1750–1800* (1980). Also recommended is Norton's *Founding Mothers and Fathers: Gendered Power and the Forming of American Society* (1996). Among the many works that deal with African Americans and Amerindians during the era, see Sylvia Frey, *Water from Rock: Black Resistance in a Revolutionary Age* (1991); Barbara Graymont, *The Iroquois in the American Revolution* (1972); and William N. Fenton, *The Great Law and the Longhouse: A Political History of the Iroquois Confederacy* (1998). For Benjamin Franklin's place in the intellectual life of the period, see Philip Dray, *Stealing God's Thunder* (2005).

For intellectual life in the era of the French Revolution, see Anne Goldgar, *Impolite Learning: Conduct and Community in the Republic of Letters, 1680–1750* (1995); Benedetta Craveri, *The Age of Conversation* (2005); and Dena Goodman, *The Republic of Letters: A Cultural History of the Enlightenment* (1994). James Swenson, *On Jean-Jacques Rousseau Considered as One of the First Authors of the Revolution* (2002), and Leo Damrosch, *Jean-Jacques Rousseau* (2005), situate this influential intellectual well in the ferment of the era. *Rousseau's Dog* (2005) by John Eidinow makes clear the contentiousness of the intellectual community. For the Counter Enlightenment see Darrin M. McMahon, *Enemies of the Enlightenment, The French Counter-Enlightenment and the Making of Modernity* (2001). For the "underside" of this era, see the discussion of "folk culture" in *Shaping History: Ordinary People in European Politics, 1500–1700* (1998), by Wayne Te Brake. François Furet, *Interpreting the French Revolution* (1981), breaks with interpretations that emphasize class and ideology. Georges Lefebvre, *The Coming of the French Revolution*, trans. R. R. Palmer (1947), presents the classic class-based analysis. George Rudé, *The Crowd in History: Popular Disturbances in France and England* (1981), remains the best introduction to the role of mass protest in the period. Lynn Hunt, *The Family Romance of the French Revolution* (1992), examines the gender content of revolutionary politics. For the role of women see Joan Landes, *Women and the Public Sphere in the Age of the French Revolution* (1988), and *The Women of Paris and Their French Revolution* (1998) by Dominique Godineau. Felix Markham, *Napoleon* (1963), and Robert B. Holtman, *The Napoleonic Revolution* (1967), provide reliable summaries of the period.

The Haitian Revolution has received less extensive coverage than the revolutions in the United States and France. C. L. R. James, *The Black Jacobins*, 2nd ed. (1963), is the classic study. Anna J. Cooper, *Slavery and the French Revolutionists, 1788–1805* (1988), also provides an overview of this important topic. Carolyn E. Fick, *The Making of Haiti: The Saint Domingue Revolution from Below* (1990), is the best recent synthesis. David P. Geggus, *Slavery, War, and Revolution* (1982), examines the British role in the revolutionary period. See also David Barry Gaspar and David Patrick Geggus, eds., *A Turbulent Time: The French Revolution and the Greater Caribbean* (1997).

For the revolutions of 1830 and 1848 see Arthur J. May's brief survey in *The Age of Metternich, 1814–48*, rev. ed. (1963). Henry Kissinger's *A World Restored* (1957) remains among the most interesting discussions of the Congress of Vienna. Eric Hobsbawm's *The Age of Revolution* (1962) provides a clear analysis of the class issues that appeared during this era. Paul Robertson's *Revolutions of 1848: A Social History* (1960) remains a valuable introduction. See also Peter Stearns and Herrick Chapman, *European Society in Upheaval* (1991). For the development of European social reform movements, see Albert Lindemann, *History of European Socialism* (1983).

For national events in Hungary see István Deák's examination of Hungary, *The Lawful Revolution: Louis Kossuth and the Hungarians, 1848–49* (1979). On Germany see Theodore S. Hamerow, *Restoration, Revolution, and Reaction, 1815–1871* (1966). For French events see Roger Price, *A Social History of Nineteenth-Century France* (1987). Barbara Taylor, *Eve and the New Jerusalem: Socialism and Feminism in the Nineteenth Century* (1983), analyzes connections between workers' and women's rights issues in England.

NOTES

1. Quoted in Ray Raphael, *A People's History of the American Revolution* (New York: Perennial, 2001), 142.
2. Ibid., 141.
3. Quoted in C. L. R. James, *The Black Jacobins,* 2nd ed. (New York: Vintage Books, 1963), 196.

Manchester, the First Industrial City
The first cotton mills, built on the banks of the River Irwell in northern England, transformed Manchester from a country town into a booming industrial city. The use of chemicals to bleach and dye the cloth and the introduction of steam engines in the early nineteenth century to power the spinning and weaving machines made Manchester, for a time, the most polluted city on earth. (The Royal Collection ©2006 Her Majesty Queen Elizabeth II)

- What caused the Industrial Revolution?

- What were the key innovations that increased productivity and drove industrialization?

- What was the impact of these changes on the society and environment of the industrializing countries?

- How did the Industrial Revolution influence the rise of new economic and political ideas?

- How did the Industrial Revolution affect the relations between the industrialized and the nonindustrialized parts of the world?

23

THE EARLY INDUSTRIAL REVOLUTION, 1760–1851

CHAPTER OUTLINE

Causes of the Industrial Revolution

The Technological Revolution

The Impact of the Early Industrial Revolution

New Economic and Political Ideas

The Limits of Industrialization Outside the West

DIVERSITY AND DOMINANCE: Adam Smith and the Division of Labor

ENVIRONMENT AND TECHNOLOGY: Gas Lighting

Manchester was just a small town in northern England in the early eighteenth century. A hundred years later, it had turned into the fastest-growing city in history. To contemporaries who visited the city, it was both a marvel and a horror. In the inner city, cotton mills and other factories were interspersed with workers' housing, built as cheaply as possible. Here is how the economist Nassau Senior described these workers' quarters:

> But when I went through their habitations . . . my only wonder was that tolerable health could be maintained by the inmates of such houses. These towns . . . have been erected by small speculators with an utter disregard to everything except immediate profit. . . . In one place we saw a whole street following the course of a ditch, in order to have deeper cellars (cellars for people, not for lumber) without the expense of excavation. Not a house in this street escaped cholera. And, generally speaking, . . . the streets are unpaved, with a dunghill or a pond in

Online Study Center

This icon will direct you to interactive activities and study materials on the website: *college.hmco.com/pic/bulliet4e.*

the middle; the houses built back to back, without ventilation or drainage, and whole families occupy each a corner of a cellar or of a garret.[1]

Not everyone deplored the living conditions in the new industrial city. Friedrich Engels, one of the foremost critics of industrial capitalism, recounts a meeting with a well-to-do citizen:

> One day I walked with one of these middle-class gentlemen into Manchester. I spoke to him about the disgraceful unhealthy slums and drew his attention to the disgusting condition of that part of the town in which the factory workers lived. I declared that I had never seen so badly built a town in my life. He listened patiently and at the corner of the street at which we parted company, he remarked: "And yet there is a great deal of money made here. Good morning, Sir!"[2]

Manchester's rise as a large, industrial city was a result of what historians call the **Industrial Revolution**, the most profound and wrenching transformation in human life since the development of agriculture 10,000 years earlier. The Industrial Revolution made it possible for increasing numbers of people (including those in Manchester) to lead longer, healthier, richer, and more productive lives than could have been possible before.

This revolution involved dramatic innovations in manufacturing, mining, transportation, and communications and equally rapid changes in society and commerce. New relationships between social groups created an environment that was conducive to technical innovation and economic growth. New technologies and new social and economic arrangements allowed the industrializing countries—first Britain, then western Europe and the United States—to unleash massive increases in production and productivity, exploit the world's natural resources as never before, and transform the environment and human life in unprecedented ways.

The distribution of power and wealth generated by the Industrial Revolution was very uneven, for industrialization widened the gap between rich and poor. The people who owned and controlled the innovations amassed wealth and power over nature and over other people. While some of them lived lives of spectacular luxury, workers, including children, worked long hours in dangerous factories and lived crowded together in unsanitary tenements.

The effect of the Industrial Revolution around the world was also very uneven. The first countries to industrialize grew rich and powerful. In Egypt and India, the economic and military power of the European countries stifled the tentative beginnings of industrialization. Regions that had little or no industry were easily taken advantage of. The disparity between the industrial and the developing countries that exists today has its origins in the early nineteenth century.

CAUSES OF THE INDUSTRIAL REVOLUTION

What caused the Industrial Revolution, and why did it begin in England in the late eighteenth century? These are two of the great questions of history. The basic preconditions of this momentous event seem to have been economic development propelled by population growth, an agricultural revolution, the expansion of trade, and an openness to innovation.

Population Growth The population of Europe rose in the eighteenth century—slowly at first, faster after 1780, then even faster in the early nineteenth century. The fastest growth took place in England and Wales. Population there rose from 5.5 million in 1688 to 9 million in 1801 and 18 million by 1851—increases never before experienced in European history.

The growth of population resulted from more widespread resistance to disease and more reliable food supplies, thanks to the new crops that originated in the Americas (see Chapter 18). More dependable food supplies and better job opportunities led people to marry at earlier ages and have more children. A high birthrate meant a large percentage of children in the general population. In the early nineteenth century some 40 percent of the population of Britain was under fifteen years of age. This high proportion of youths explains both the vitality of the British people in that period and the widespread use of child labor. People also migrated at an unprecedented rate—from the countryside to the cities, from Ireland to England, and, more

CHRONOLOGY

	Technology	Economy, Society, and Politics
1750	**1702–1712** Thomas Newcomen builds first steam engine	
	1759 Josiah Wedgwood opens pottery factory	
	1764 Spinning jenny	
	1769 Richard Arkwright's water frame; James Watt patents steam engine	**1776** Adam Smith's *Wealth of Nations* **1776–1783** American Revolution
	1779 First iron bridge	
	1785 Boulton and Watt sell steam engines; Samuel Crompton's mule	**1789–1799** French Revolution **1792** Mary Wollstonecraft's *A Vindication of the Rights of Woman*
	1793 Eli Whitney's cotton gin	
1800	**1800** Alessandro Volta's battery	**1804–1815** Napoleonic Wars
	1807 Robert Fulton's *North River*	
	1820s Construction of Erie Canal	**1820s** U.S. cotton industry begins
	1829 *Rocket,* first prize-winning locomotive	**1833** Factory Act in Britain **1834** German Zollverein; Robert Owen's Grand National Consolidated Trade Union
	1837 Wheatstone and Cooke's telegraph	
	1838 First ships steam across the Atlantic	
	1840 *Nemesis* sails to China	
	1843 Samuel Morse's Baltimore-to-Washington telegraph	**1846** Repeal of British Corn Laws **1847–1848** Irish famine **1848** Collapse of Chartist movement; revolutions in Europe
1850	**1851** Crystal Palace opens in London	**1854** First cotton mill in India

generally, from Europe to the Americas. Thanks to immigration, the population of the United States rose from 4 million in 1791 to 9.6 million in 1820 and 31.5 million in 1860—faster growth than in any other part of the world at the time.

The Agricultural Revolution

Innovations in manufacturing could only have taken place alongside a simultaneous revolution in farming that provided food for city dwellers and forced poorer peasants off the land. This **agricultural revolution** had begun long before the eighteenth century. One important aspect was the acceptance of the potato, introduced from South America in the sixteenth century. In the cool and humid regions of Europe from Ireland to Russia, potatoes yielded two or three times more food per acre than did the wheat, rye, and oats

they replaced. Maize (American corn) was grown across Europe from northern Iberia to the Balkans. Turnips, legumes, and clover did not deplete the soil and could be fed to cattle, which were sources of milk and meat. Manure from cattle in turn fertilized the soil for other crops.

The security of small-scale tenant farmers and sharecroppers depended on traditional methods and rural customs such as collecting plants left over in the fields after the harvest, pasturing their animals on common village lands, and gathering firewood in common woods. Only prosperous landowners with secure titles to their land could afford to bear the risk of trying new methods and new crops. Rich landowners therefore "enclosed" the land—that is, consolidated their holdings—and got Parliament to give them title to the commons that in the past had been open to all. Once in control of the land, they could drain and improve the soil, breed better livestock, and introduce crop rotation. This "enclosure movement" turned tenants and sharecroppers into landless farm laborers. Many moved to the cities to seek work; others became homeless migrants and vagrants; and still others emigrated to Canada, Australia, and the United States.

In eastern Europe, as in Britain, large estates predominated, and aristocratic landowners used such improvements to increase their wealth and political influence. In western Europe enclosure was hampered by the fact that the law gave secure property rights to numerous small farmers.

Trade and Inventiveness

In most of Europe the increasing demand that accompanied the growth of population was met by increasing production in traditional ways. Roads were improved so stagecoaches could travel faster. Royal manufacturers trained additional craftsmen to produce fine china, silks, and carpets by hand. In rural areas much production was carried out through cottage industries. Merchants delivered fibers, leather, and other raw materials to craftspeople (often farmers in the off-season) and picked up the finished products. The growth of the population and food supply was accompanied by the growth of trade. Most of it was local trade in traditional goods and services, but a growing share came from far away.

In the course of the eighteenth century, Europeans developed a craving for sweet foods. Sugar from Caribbean slave plantations became the most profitable item in international trade. Even people of modest means began drinking tea, coffee, and cocoa at home and eating pastries and candies. These habits in turn stimulated the demand for porcelain cups and other dinnerware. More and more people also wore clothes of silk or cotton imported from Asia.

Stimulated by the demands of an emerging consumer society, scientific discoveries, commercial enterprise, and technical skills became closely connected. Technology and innovation fascinated educated people throughout Europe and eastern North America. The French *Encyclopédie* contained thousands of articles and illustrations of crafts and manufacturing (see Diversity and Dominance: Adam Smith and the Division of Labor). The French and British governments sent expeditions around the world to collect plants that could profitably be grown in their colonies. They also offered prizes to anyone who could find a method of determining the longitude of a ship at sea to avoid the shipwrecks that had cost the lives of thousands of sailors. The American Benjamin Franklin, like many others, experimented with electricity. In France, the Montgolfier brothers invented a hot-air balloon. Claude Chappe° created the first semaphore telegraph. French artillery officers proposed making guns with interchangeable parts. The American Eli Whitney and his associate John Hall invented machine tools, that is, machines capable of making other machines. These machines greatly increased the productivity of manufacturing.

Britain and Continental Europe

Economic growth was evident throughout the North Atlantic area, yet industrialization did not take place everywhere at once. To understand why, we must look at the peculiar role of Great Britain. Britain enjoyed a rising standard of living during the eighteenth century, thanks to good harvests, a growing population, and a booming overseas trade. Britain was the world's leading exporter of tools, guns, hardware, clocks, and other craft goods (see Map 23.1). Its mining and metal industries employed engineers willing to experiment with new ideas. It had the largest merchant marine and produced more ships, naval supplies, and navigation instruments than other countries.

Until the mid-eighteenth century the British were better known for their cheap imitations than for their innovations or quality products. But they put inventions into practice more quickly than other people, as the engineer John Farey told a parliamentary committee in 1829: "The prevailing talent of English and Scotch people is to apply new ideas to use and to bring such applications to perfection, but they do not imagine as much as foreigners."

Before 1790 Britain also had a more fluid society than did the rest of Europe. The English royal court was less ostentatious, its aristocracy was less powerful, and the lines separating the social classes were not as sharply drawn as in Europe. Political power was not as centralized as on the European continent, and the government employed fewer bureaucrats and officials. Members of the gentry, and even some aristocrats, married into merchant families. Intermarriage among the families of petty merchants, yeoman farmers, and town craftsmen was common. Guilds, which resisted innovation, were relatively weak. Ancestry remained important, but wealth also commanded respect. A businessman with enough money could buy a landed estate, a seat in Parliament, and the social status that accompanied them.

At a time when transportation by land was very costly, Great Britain had good water transportation thanks to its

Chappe (SHAPP)

Map 23.1   The Industrial Revolution in Britain, ca. 1850
The first industries arose in northern and western England. These regions had abundant coal and iron-ore deposits for the iron industry, as well as moist climate and fast-flowing rivers, factors important for the cotton textile industry.

indented coastline, navigable rivers, and growing network of canals. It had a unified internal market with none of the duties and tolls that goods had to pay every few miles in France. This encouraged regional specialization, such as tin mining in Cornwall and cotton manufacturing in Lancashire, and a growing trade between regions.

Britain was also highly commercial; more people were involved in production for export and in trade and finance than in any other major country. It was especially active in overseas trade with the Americas, West Africa, the Middle East, and India. It had financial and insurance institutions able to support growing business enterprises and a patent system that offered inventors the hope of rich rewards. The example of men who became wealthy and respected for their inventions—such as Richard Arkwright, the cotton magnate, and James Watt, the steam engine designer—stimulated others.

In the eighteenth century, the economies of continental Europe also underwent a dynamic expansion, thanks to the efforts of individual entrepreneurs and investors. Yet growth was still hampered by high transportation costs, misguided government regulations, and rigid social structures. The Low Countries were laced with canals, but the terrain elsewhere in Europe made canal building costly and difficult. The ruling monarchies made some attempts to import British techniques and organize factory production, but they all foundered for lack of markets or management skills. From 1789 to 1815 Europe was scarred by revolutions and wars. Although war created opportunities for suppliers of weapons, uniforms, and horses produced by traditional methods, the interruption of trade between Britain and continental Europe slowed the diffusion of new techniques, and the insecurity of countries at war discouraged businessmen from investing in factories and machinery.

The political revolutions swept away the restrictions of the old regimes. After 1815 the economies of western Europe were ready to begin industrializing. Industrialization took hold in Belgium and northern France, as businessmen visited Britain to observe the changes and spy out industrial secrets. In spite of British laws forbidding the emigration of skilled workers and the export of textile machinery, many workers slipped through. By the 1820s several thousand Britons were at work on the continent of Europe setting up machines, training workers in the new methods, and even starting their own businesses.

Acutely aware of Britain's head start and the need to stimulate their own industries, European governments took action. They created technical schools. They eliminated internal tariff barriers, tolls, and other hindrances to trade. They encouraged the formation of joint-stock companies and banks to channel private savings into industrial investments. On the European continent, as in Britain, cotton cloth was the first industry. The mills of France, Belgium, and the German states served local markets but could not compete abroad with the more advanced British industry. By 1830 the political climate in western Europe was as favorable to business as Britain's had been a half-century earlier.

Abundant coal and iron-ore deposits determined the concentration of industries in a swath of territories running from northern France through Belgium and the Ruhr district of western Germany to Silesia in Prussia (now part of Poland). By the 1850s France, Belgium, and the German states were in the midst of an industrial boom like that of Britain, based on iron, cotton, steam engines, and railroads.

Adam Smith and the Division of Labor

*A*dam Smith (1723–1790), a Scottish social philosopher, is famous for one book, An Inquiry into the Nature and Causes of the Wealth of Nations, *which was first published in 1776 and has been reprinted many times and translated into many languages. It was the first work to explain the economy of a nation as a system. In it, Smith criticized the notion, common in the eighteenth century, that a nation's wealth was synonymous with the amount of gold and silver in the government's coffers. Instead, he defined wealth as the amount of goods and services produced by a nation's people. By this definition, labor and its products are an essential element in a nation's prosperity.*

In the passage that follows, Smith discusses the increase in productivity (to use a modern term) that results from dividing a craft into separate tasks, each of which is performed over and over by one worker. He contrasts two methods of making pins. In one a team of workers divided up the job of making pins and produced a great many every day; in the other pin workers "wrought separately and independently" and produced very few pins per day. It is clear that the division of labor produces more pins per worker per day. But who benefits? Left unsaid is that a pin factory had to be owned and operated by a manufacturer who hired workers and assigned a task to each one. Thus did industrialization reduce the diversity of self-employed craftsmen by replacing them with a system of dominance.

The illustration shows a pin-maker's workshop in late-eighteenth-century France. Each worker is performing a specific task on a few pins at once, and all the energy comes from human muscles. These are the characteristics of a proto-industrial workshop.

To take an example, therefore, from a very trifling manufacture—but one in which the division of labour has been very often taken notice of—the trade of the pin-maker: a workman not educated to this business (which the division of labour has rendered a distinct trade), nor acquainted with the use of machinery employed in it (to the invention of which the same division of labour has probably given occasion), could scarce, perhaps, with his utmost industry, make one pin in a day, and certainly could not make twenty. But in the way in which this business is now carried on, not only the whole work is a peculiar trade, but it is divided into a number of branches, of which the greater part are likewise peculiar trades. One man draws out the wire, another straights it, a third cuts it, a fourth points it, a fifth grinds it at the top for receiving the head; to make the head requires two or three distinct operations, to put it on, is a peculiar business, to whiten the pins is another; it is even a trade by itself to put them into the paper; and the important business of making a pin is, in this manner, divided into about eighteen distinct operations, which, in some manufactories, are all performed by distinct hands, though in others the same man will sometimes perform two or three of them. I have seen a small manufactory of this kind where ten men only were employed, and where some of them, consequently, performed two or three distinct operations. But though they were very poor, and therefore but indifferently accommodated with the necessary machinery, they could, when they exerted themselves, make among them about twelve pounds of pins in a day.

A Pin-Maker's Workshop The man in the middle (Fig. 2) is pulling wire off a spindle (G) and through a series of posts. This ensures that the wire will be perfectly straight. The worker seated on the lower right (Fig. 3) takes the long pieces of straightened wire and cuts them into shorter lengths. The man in the lower left-hand corner (Fig. 5) sharpens twelve to fifteen wires at a time by holding them against a grindstone turned by the worker in Fig. 6. The men in Figs. 4 and 7 put the finishing touches on the points. Other operations—such as forming the wire to the proper thickness, cleaning and coating it with tin, and attaching the heads—are depicted in other engravings in the same encyclopedia. (Division of Rare and Manuscript Collections, Cornell University Library)

There are in a pound upwards of four thousand pins of a middling size. Those ten persons, therefore, could make among them upwards of forty-eight thousand pins in a day. Each person, therefore, making a tenth part of forty-eight thousand pins, might be considered as making four thousand eight hundred pins a day. But if they had all wrought separately and independently, and without any of them having been educated to this peculiar business, they certainly could not each of them have made twenty, perhaps not one pin in a day; that is, certainly, not the two hundred and fortieth, perhaps not the four thousand eight hundredth part of what they are at present capable of performing, in consequence of a proper division and combination of their different operations.

QUESTIONS FOR ANALYSIS

1. Why does dividing the job of pin-making into ten or more operations result in the production of more pins per worker? How much more productive are these workers than if each one made complete pins from start to finish?

2. How closely does the picture of a pin-maker's workshop illustrate Smith's verbal description?

3. What disadvantage would there be to working in a pin factory where the job was divided as in Smith's example, compared to making entire pins from start to finish?

4. What other examples can you think of, from Adam Smith's day or from more recent times, of the advantages of the division of labor?

Source: *Adam Smith, An Inquiry into the Nature and Causes of the Wealth of Nations,* ed. Edward Gibbon Wakefield (London: Charles Knight and Co., 1843), 7–9.

THE TECHNOLOGICAL REVOLUTION

Five innovations spurred industrialization: (1) mass production through the division of labor, (2) new machines and mechanization, (3) a great increase in the manufacture of iron, (4) the steam engine and the changes it made possible in industry and transportation, and (5) the electric telegraph. China had achieved the first three of these during the Song dynasty (960–1279), but it had not developed the steam engine or electricity. The continued success of Western industrialization depended heavily on these new forms of energy.

Mass Production: Pottery

The pottery industry offers a good example of **mass production**, the making of many identical items by breaking the process into simple repetitive tasks. East Asian potters had long known how to make fine glazed porcelain, or "china," but the high cost of transporting it to Europe before the mid-eighteenth century meant that only the wealthy could afford fine Chinese porcelain. Middle-class people used pewter tableware, and the poor ate from wooden or earthenware bowls. Several royal manufactures—Meissen° in Saxony, Delft in Holland, and Sèvres° in France—produced exquisite handmade products for the courts and aristocracy, but their products were much too expensive for mass consumption. Meanwhile, more and more Europeans acquired a taste for Chinese tea as well as for cocoa and coffee, and they wanted porcelain that would not spoil the flavor of hot beverages. This demand created opportunities for inventive entrepreneurs.

Like other countries, Britain had many small pottery workshops where craftsmen made a few plates and cups at a time. Much of this activity took place in a part of the Midlands that possessed good clay, coal for firing, and lead for glazing. There **Josiah Wedgwood**, the son of a potter, started his own pottery business in 1759. He had a scientific bent and invented the pyrometer, a device to measure the extremely high temperatures that are found in kilns during the firing of pottery, for which he was elected a member of the Royal Society. Today the name Wedgwood is associated with expensive, highly decorated china. But Wedgwood's most important contribution lay in producing

Meissen (MY-sen) Sèvres (SEV-ruh)

ordinary porcelain cheaply by means of the **division of labor** (see Diversity and Dominance: Adam Smith and the Division of Labor).

Wedgwood subdivided the work into highly specialized and repetitive tasks, such as unloading the clay, mixing it, pressing flat pieces, dipping the pieces in glaze, putting handles on cups, packing kilns, and carrying things from one part of his plant to another. To prevent interruptions in production, he instituted strict discipline among his workers. He substituted the use of molds for the potter's wheel wherever possible, a change that not only saved labor but also created identical plates and bowls that could be stacked. He invested in toll roads and canals so that special pottery clay found in southwestern England could be economically shipped to his factories in the Midlands.

Wedgwood's Potteries In Staffordshire, England, Josiah Wedgwood established a factory to mass-produce beautiful and inexpensive china. The bottle-shaped buildings are kilns in which thousands of pieces of china could be fired at one time. Kilns, factories, and housing were all mixed together in pottery towns, and smoke from burning coal filled the air. (Mary Evans Picture Library)

Wedgwood's interest in applying technology to manufacturing was sparked by his membership in the Lunar Society, a group of businessmen, scientists, and craftsmen that met each month when the moon was full to discuss the practical application of knowledge. In 1782 the naturalist Erasmus Darwin encouraged him to purchase a steam engine from Boulton and Watt, the firm founded by two other members of the society. The engine that Wedgwood bought to mix clay and grind flint was one of the first to be installed in a factory.

These were radical departures from the age-old methods of craftsmanship. But the division of labor and new machinery allowed Wedgwood to lower the cost of his products while improving their quality, and to offer his wares for sale at lower prices. His factory grew far larger than his competitors' factories and employed several hundred workers. His salesmen traveled throughout England touting his goods, and his products were sold on the European continent as well.

| Mechanization: The Cotton Industry | The cotton industry, the larg-est industry in this period, illustrates the role of **mechanization**, the use of machines |

to do work previously done by hand. Cotton cloth had long been the most common fabric in China, India, and the Middle East, where it was spun and woven by hand. The cotton plant did not grow in Europe, but the cloth was so much cooler, softer, and cleaner than wool that wealthy Europeans developed a liking for the costly import. When the powerful English woolen industry persuaded Parliament to forbid the import of cotton cloth into England, that prohibition stimulated attempts to import cotton fiber and make the cloth locally. Here was an opportunity for enterprising inventors to reduce costs with laborsaving machinery.

To turn inventions into successful businesses, inventors had to link up with entrepreneurs or become businessmen themselves. Making a working prototype often took years, even decades, and many inventions led to dead ends. History remembers those who were successful, but even they struggled against great odds.

Beginning in the 1760s a series of inventions revolutionized the spinning of cotton thread. The first was the spinning jenny, invented in 1764, which mechanically drew out the cotton fibers and twisted them into thread. The jenny was simple, cheap to build, and easy for one person to operate. Early models spun six or seven threads at once, later ones up to eighty. The thread, however, was soft and irregular and could be used only in combination with linen, a strong yarn derived from the flax plant.

In 1769 **Richard Arkwright** invented another spinning machine, the water frame, which produced thread strong enough to be used without linen. Arkwright was both a gifted inventor and a successful businessman. His machine was larger and more complex than the jenny and required a source of power such as a water wheel, hence the name "water frame." To obtain the necessary energy he installed dozens of machines in a building next to a fast-flowing river. The resemblance to a flour mill gave such enterprises the name cotton mill.

In 1785 Samuel Crompton patented a machine that combined the best features of the jenny and the water frame. This device, called a mule, produced a strong thread that was thin enough to be used to make a better type of cotton cloth called muslin. The mule could make a finer, more even thread than could any human being, and at a lower cost. At last British industry could undersell high-quality handmade cotton cloth from India, and British cotton output increased tenfold between 1770 and 1790.

The boom in thread production and the soaring demand for cloth created bottlenecks in weaving, stimulating inventors to mechanize the rest of textile manufacturing. The first power loom was introduced in 1784 but was not perfected until after 1815. Other inventions of the period included carding machines, chlorine bleach, and cylindrical presses to print designs on fabric. By the 1830s large English textile mills powered by steam engines were performing all the steps necessary to turn raw cotton into printed cloth. This was a far cry from the cottage industries of the previous century.

Mechanization offered two advantages: (1) increased productivity for the manufacturer and (2) lower prices for the consumer. Whereas in India it took five hundred hours to spin a pound of cotton, the mule of 1790 could do so in three person-hours, and the self-acting mule—an improved version introduced in 1830—required only eighty minutes. Cotton mills needed very few skilled workers, and managers often hired children to tend the spinning machines. The same was true of power looms, which gradually replaced handloom weaving: the number of power looms rose from 2,400 in 1813 to 500,000 by 1850. Meanwhile, the price of cloth fell by 90 percent between 1782 and 1812 and kept on dropping.

The industrialization of Britain made cotton America's most valuable crop. In the 1790s most of Britain's cotton came from India, as the United States produced a mere 750 tons (729 metric tons), mostly from South Carolina. In 1793 the American Eli Whitney patented his cotton gin, a simple device that separated the bolls or seedpods from the fiber and made cotton growing economical. This invention permitted the spread of cotton farming into Georgia, then into Alabama, Mississippi, and Louisiana, and finally as far west as Texas. By the late 1850s the southern states were producing a million tons of cotton a year, five-sixths of the world's total.

With the help of British craftsmen who introduced jennies, mules, and power looms, Americans developed their own cotton industry in the 1820s. By 1840 the United States had twelve hundred cotton mills, two-thirds of them in New England, that served the booming domestic market.

The Iron Industry

Iron making also was transformed during the Industrial Revolution. Throughout Eurasia and Africa, iron had been in use for thousands of years for tools, swords and other weapons, and household items such as knives, pots, hinges, and locks. In the eleventh century, during the Song period, Chinese forges had produced cast iron in large quantities. Production declined after the Song, but iron continued to be common and inexpensive in China. Wherever iron was produced, however, deforestation eventually drove up the cost of charcoal (used for smelting) and restricted output. Furthermore, iron had to be repeatedly heated and hammered to drive out impurities, a difficult and costly process. Because of limited wood supplies and the high cost of skilled labor, iron was a rare and valuable metal outside China before the eighteenth century.

A first breakthrough occurred in 1709 when Abraham Darby discovered that coke (coal from which the impurities have been cooked out) could be used in place of charcoal. The resulting metal was of lower quality than charcoal-smelted iron but much cheaper to produce, for coal was plentiful. Just as importantly, in 1784 Henry Cort found a way to remove some of the impurities in coke-iron by puddling—stirring the molten iron with long rods. Cort's process made it possible to turn high-sulfur English coal into coke to produce wrought iron (a soft and malleable form of iron) very cheaply. By 1790 four-fifths of Britain's iron was made with coke, while other countries still used charcoal. Coke-iron was cheaper and less destructive of forests, and it allowed a great expansion in the size of individual blast furnaces, substantially reducing the cost of iron. There seemed almost no limit to the quantity of iron that could be produced with coke. Britain's iron production began rising fast, from 17,000 tons in 1740 to 3 million tons in 1844, as much as in the rest of the world put together.

In turn, there seemed no limit to the amount of iron that an industrializing society would purchase or to the novel applications for this cheap and useful material. In 1779 the iron manufacturer Abraham Darby III (grandson of the first Abraham Darby) built a bridge of iron across the Severn River. In 1851 Londoners marveled at the **Crystal Palace,** a huge greenhouse made entirely of iron and glass and large enough to enclose the tallest trees.

The availability of cheap iron made the mass production of objects such as guns, hardware, and tools appealing. However, fitting together the parts of these products required a great deal of labor. To reduce labor costs, manufacturers turned to the idea of interchangeable parts. This idea originated in the eighteenth century when French army officers attempted, without success, to persuade gun makers to produce precisely identical parts. Craftsmen continued to use traditional methods to make gun parts that had to be fitted together by hand. By the mid-nineteenth century, however,

Pit Head of a Coal Mine   This is a small coal mine. In the center of this picture stands a Newcomen engine used to pump water. The work of hauling coal out of the mine was still done by horses and mules. The smoke coming out of the smokestack is a trademark of the early industrial era. (The Board of Trustees of the National Museums and Galleries on Merseyside, Walker Art Gallery [WAG 659])

Transatlantic Steamship Race   In 1838, two ships equipped with steam engines, the *Sirius* and the *Great Western*, steamed from England to New York. Although the *Sirius* left a few days earlier, the *Great Western*—shown here arriving in New York harbor—almost caught up with it, arriving just four hours after the *Sirius*. This race inaugurated regular transatlantic steamship service.   (Courtesy of the Mariners' Museum, Newport News, VA)

interchangeable-parts manufacturing had been adopted in the manufacture of firearms, farm equipment, and sewing machines. At the Crystal Palace exhibition of 1851, Europeans called it the "American system of manufactures." In the next hundred years the use of machinery to mass-produce consumer items was to become the hallmark of American industry.

The Steam Engine

In the history of the world, there had been a number of periods of great technological inventiveness and economic growth. But in all previous cases, the dynamism eventually faltered for various reasons, such as the Mongol invasions that overthrew the Song dynasty in China and the Abassid Caliphate (750–1258) in the Middle East.

The Industrial Revolution that began in the eighteenth century, in contrast, has never slowed down but has instead only accelerated. One reason has been increased interactions between scientists, technicians, and businesspeople. Another has been access to an inexhaustible source of cheap energy, namely fossil fuels.

The first machine to transform fossil fuel into mechanical energy was the **steam engine**, a substitute for human and animal power as well as for wind and water power. Although the mechanization of manufacturing was very important, the steam engine was what set the Industrial Revolution apart from all previous periods of growth and innovation.

Before the eighteenth century, many activities had been limited by the lack of energy. For example, deep mines filled with water faster than horses could pump it out. Scientists understood the concept of atmospheric pressure and had created experimental devices to turn heat into motion, but they had not found a way to put those devices to practical use. Then, between 1702 and 1712 Thomas Newcomen developed the first practical steam engine, a crude but effective device. One engine could pump water out of mines as fast as four horses, and it could run day and night without getting tired.

The Newcomen engine's voracious appetite for fuel mattered little in coal mines, where fuel was cheap, but it made the engine too costly for other uses. In 1764 **James Watt**, a maker of scientific instruments at Glasgow University in Scotland, was asked to repair the university's model Newcomen engine. Watt realized that the engine wasted fuel because the cylinder had to be alternately heated and cooled. He developed a separate condenser—a vessel into which the steam was allowed to escape after it had done its work, leaving the cylinder always hot and the condenser always cold. Watt patented his idea in 1769. He enlisted the help of the iron manufacturer Matthew Boulton to turn his invention into a commercial product. Their first engines were sold to pump water out of copper and tin mines, where fuel was too costly for Newcomen engines. In 1781 Watt invented the sun-and-planet gear, which turned the back-and-forth action of the piston into rotary motion. This allowed steam engines to power machinery in flour and cotton mills, pottery manufactures, and other industries. Watt's steam engine was the most celebrated invention of the eighteenth century. Because there seemed almost no limit to the amount of coal in the ground, steam-generated energy appeared to be an inexhaustible source of power, and steam engines could be used where animal, wind, and water power were lacking.

Inspired by the success of Watt's engine, inventors in France in 1783, in the United States in 1787, and in England in 1788 put steam engines on boats. The need to travel great distances in the United States explains why the first commercially successful steamboat was Robert Fulton's *North River*, which steamed up and down the Hudson River between New York City and Albany, New York, in 1807.

Soon steamboats were launched on other American rivers, especially the Ohio and the Mississippi, gateways to the Midwest. In the 1820s the Erie Canal linked the Atlantic seaboard with the Great Lakes and opened Ohio, Indiana, and Illinois to European settlement. Steamboats proliferated west of the Appalachian Mountains; by 1830 some three hundred plied the Mississippi and its tributaries. To counter the competition from New York State, Pennsylvania built a thousand miles of canals by 1840. The United States was fast becoming a nation that moved by water.

Oceangoing steam-powered ships were much more difficult to build than river boats, for the first steam engines used so much coal that no ship could carry more than a few days' supply. The *Savannah*, which crossed the Atlantic in 1819, was a sailing ship with an auxiliary steam engine that was used for only ninety hours of its twenty-nine-day trip. Engineers soon developed more efficient engines, and in 1838 two steamers, the *Great Western* and the *Sirius*, crossed the Atlantic on steam power alone. Elsewhere, sailing ships held their own until late in the century. World trade was growing so fast that there was enough business for ships of every kind.

Railroads

On land as on water, the problem was not imagining uses for steam-powered vehicles but building ones that worked, for steam engines were too heavy and weak to pull any weight. After Watt's patent expired in 1800, inventors experimented with lighter, more powerful high-pressure engines—an idea Watt had

The *De Witt Clinton* Locomotive, 1835–1840   The *De Witt Clinton* was the first steam locomotive built in the United States. The high smokestack let the hot cinders cool so they would not set fire to nearby trees, an important consideration at a time when eastern North America was still covered with forest. The three passenger cars are clearly horse carriages fitted with railroad wheels.   (Bettmann/Corbis)

rejected as too dangerous. In 1804 the engineer Richard Trevithick built an engine that consumed twelve times less coal than Newcomen's and three times less than Watt's. With it, he built several steam-powered vehicles able to travel on roads or rails.

By the 1820s England had many railways on which horses pulled heavy wagons. On one of them, the Stockton and Darlington Railway, chief engineer George Stephenson began using steam locomotives in 1825. Four years later the owners of the Liverpool and Manchester Railway organized a contest between steam-powered locomotives and horse-drawn wagons. Stephenson and his son Robert easily won the contest with their locomotive *Rocket*, which pulled a 20-ton train at up to 30 miles (48 kilometers) per hour. After that triumph, a railroad-building mania that lasted for twenty years swept Britain. The first lines linked towns and mines with the nearest harbor or waterway. In the late 1830s passenger traffic soared, and entrepreneurs built lines between the major cities and then to small towns as well. Railroads were far cheaper, faster, and more comfortable than stagecoaches, and millions of people got in the habit of traveling.

In the United States entrepreneurs built railroads as quickly and cheaply as possible with an eye to fast profits, not long-term durability. By the 1840s, 6,000 miles

Map 23.2   Industrialization in Europe, ca. 1850   In 1850 industrialization was in its early stages on the European continent. The first industrial regions were comparatively close to England and possessed rich coal deposits: Belgium and the Ruhr district of Germany. Politics determined the location of railroads. Notice the star-shaped French network of rail lines emanating from Paris and the lines linking the different parts of the German Confederation.

(10,000 kilometers) of track connected and radiated westward from Boston, New York, Philadelphia, and Baltimore. The boom of the 1840s was dwarfed by the mania of the 1850s, when 21,000 miles (34,000 kilometers) of new track were laid, much of it westward across the Appalachians to Memphis, St. Louis, and Chicago. After 1856 the trip from New York to Chicago, which had once taken three weeks by boat and on horseback, could be made in forty-eight hours. More than anything else, it was the railroads that opened up the Midwest, turning the vast prairie into wheat fields and pasture for cattle to feed the industrial cities of the eastern United States.

Railways also triggered the industrialization of Europe (see Map 23.2). Belgium, independent since 1830, quickly copied the British railways. Because France and Prussia planned and supervised their railroad construction from the start, construction was delayed in those countries until the mid-1840s. When it began, however, it had an even greater impact than in Britain, for it not only satisfied the long-standing need for transportation but also stimulated the iron, machinery, and construction industries.

Communication over Wires

After the Italian scientist Alessandro Volta invented the battery in 1800, making it possible to produce an electric current, many inventors tried to apply electricity to communication. The first practical **electric telegraph** systems were developed almost simultaneously in England and America. In 1837 in England Charles Wheatstone and William Cooke introduced a five-wire telegraph that remained in use until the early twentieth century. That same year, the American Samuel Morse introduced a code of dots and dashes that could be transmitted with a single wire; in 1843 he erected a telegraph line between Washington and Baltimore.

The railroad companies were among the first users of the new electric telegraph. They allowed telegraph companies to string wires along the tracks in exchange for the right to send telegrams from station to station announcing the departure and arrival of trains. Such messages made railroads much safer as well as more efficient.

By the late 1840s telegraph wires were being strung throughout the eastern United States and western Europe. In 1851 the first submarine telegraph cable was laid across the English Channel from England to France; it was the beginning of a network that eventually connected the entire globe. The world was rapidly shrinking, to the applause of Europeans and Americans for whom speed was a clear measure of progress. No longer were communications limited to the speed of a sailing ship, a galloping horse, or a fast-moving train.

The Impact of the Early Industrial Revolution

The Industrial Revolution led to profound changes in society, politics, and the economy. At first, the changes were local. While some people became wealthy and built beautiful mansions, others lived in slum neighborhoods with polluted water and smoke-filled air. By the mid-nineteenth century, the worst local effects were being alleviated and cities became cleaner and healthier. Replacing them were more complex problems on a national scale: business cycles, labor conflicts, and the transformation of entire regions into industrial landscapes. At the international and global level, industrialization empowered the nations of western Europe and North America at the expense of the rest of the world.

The New Industrial Cities

The most dramatic environmental changes brought about by industrialization occurred in the towns. Never before had towns grown so fast. London, one of the largest cities in Europe in 1700 with 500,000 inhabitants, grew to 959,000 by 1800 and to 2,363,000 by 1850; it was then the largest city the world had ever known. Smaller towns grew even faster. Manchester, a small town of 20,000 in 1758, reached 400,000 a century later, a twentyfold increase. Liverpool grew sixfold in sixty years, from 82,000 in 1801 to 472,000 in 1861. New York City, already 100,000 strong in 1815, reached 600,000 (including Brooklyn) in 1850. European cities also grew, but more slowly; their fastest growth occurred after 1850 with increasing industrialization. In some areas, towns merged and formed megalopolises, such as Greater London, the English Midlands, central Belgium, and the Ruhr district of western Germany.

Industrialization made some people very prosperous. A great deal of this new wealth went into the building of fine homes, churches, museums, and theaters in wealthy neighborhoods in London, Berlin, and New York. Much of the beauty of London dates from the time of the Industrial Revolution. Yet, by all accounts, the industrial cities grew much too fast, and much of the growth occurred in the poorest neighborhoods. As poor migrants streamed in from the countryside, developers built cheap, shoddy row houses for them to rent. These tenements were dangerously overcrowded. Often, several families had to live in one small room.

Sudden population growth, overcrowding, and inadequate municipal services conspired to make urban problems more serious than in earlier times. Town dwellers recently arrived from the country brought country ways with them. People threw their sewage and trash out the windows to be washed down the gutters in the streets. The poor kept pigs and chickens; the rich kept horses; and pedestrians stepped into the street at their own risk. Factories and workers' housing were mixed together. Air pollution from burning coal, a problem since the sixteenth century, got steadily worse. Londoners in particular breathed dense and noxious coal smoke. People drank water drawn from wells and rivers contaminated by sewage and industrial runoff. The River Irwell, which ran through Manchester, was, in the words of one visitor, "considerably less a river than a flood of liquid manure."[3]

"Every day that I live," wrote an American visitor to Manchester, "I thank Heaven that I am not a poor man with a family in England."[4] In his poem "Milton," William Blake (1757–1827) expressed the revulsion of sensitive people at the spoliation of England's "mountains green" and "pleasant pastures":

> And did the Countenance Divine
> Shine forth upon our clouded hills?
> And was Jerusalem builded here
> Among these dark Satanic Mills?

Railroads invaded the towns, bringing noise and smoke into densely populated neighborhoods. Railroad

Paris Apartment at Night   This cutaway drawing in a French magazine shows the vertical segregation by social class that prevailed in the 1840s. The lower level is occupied by the concierge and her family. The first floor belongs to a wealthy family throwing a party for high-society friends. Middle-class people living on the next floor seem annoyed by the noise coming from below. Above them, a thief has entered an artist's studio. A poor seamstress and her child live in the garret under the roof. When elevators were introduced in the late nineteenth century, people of different income levels became segregated by neighborhoods instead of by floors.   (Bibliothèque nationale de France)

companies built their stations as close to the heart of cities as they could. On the outskirts of cities, railroad yards, sidings, and repair shops covered acres of land, surrounded by miles of warehouses and workers' housing. Farther out, far from the dangerous and polluted cities where their factories were located, newly rich industrialists created an environment halfway between country homes and townhouses: the first suburbs.

Under these conditions, diseases proliferated. To the long list of preindustrial urban diseases such as smallpox, dysentery, and tuberculosis, industrialization added new ailments. Rickets, a bone disease caused by lack of sunshine, became endemic in dark and smoky in-

dustrial cities. Steamships brought cholera from India, causing great epidemics that struck poor neighborhoods especially hard. In the 1850s, when the average life expectancy in England was forty years, it was only twenty-four years in Manchester, and around seventeen years in Manchester's poorest neighborhoods, because of high rates of infant mortality. Observers of nineteenth-century industrial cities documented the horrors of slum life in vivid detail. Their shocking reports led to municipal reforms, such as garbage removal, water and sewage systems, and parks and schools. These measures began to alleviate the ills of urban life after the mid-nineteenth century.

Rural Environments

Long before the Industrial Revolution began, practically no wilderness areas were left in Britain and very few in western Europe. Almost every piece of land was covered with fields, forests, or pastures shaped by human activity, or by towns; yet humans continued to alter the environment. The most serious problem was deforestation. As they had been doing for centuries, people cut timber to build ships and houses, to heat homes, and to manufacture bricks, iron, glass, beer, bread, and many other items.

Americans transformed their environment even faster than Europeans. In North America, the Canadian and American governments seized land from the Indians and made it available at low cost to white farmers and logging companies. After shipbuilding and construction had depleted the British forests in the early nineteenth century, Britain relied heavily on imports of Canadian lumber. East of the Appalachian Mountains, settlers viewed forests not as a valuable resource but as a hindrance to development. In their haste to "open up the wilderness," pioneers felled trees and burned them, built houses and abandoned them, and moved on. The cultivation of cotton in the southern United States was especially harmful. Planters cut down forests, grew cotton for a few years until it depleted the soil, then moved west, abandoning the land to scrub pines. This was slash-and-burn agriculture on an industrial scale.

Online Study Center
Improve Your Grade
Interactive Map: Territorial
Growth of the United States

At that time, America seemed immune to human depredations. Americans thought of nature as an obstacle to be overcome and dominated. This mindset persisted long after the entire continent was occupied and the environment truly endangered.

An Industrial Canal   In the late eighteenth and early nineteenth centuries, before railroads were introduced, many canals were constructed in England so that barges could transport heavy materials cheaply, such as coal for industrial works and steam engines, stone and bricks for buildings, and clay for pottery works. Canals such as this one, which ran alongside Josiah Wedgwood's famous Etruria china factory, contributed greatly to Britain's industrial development.   (The Art Archive)

Paradoxically, in some ways industrialization relieved pressures on the environment in Europe. Raw materials once grown on the land—such as wood, hay, and wool—were replaced by materials found underground, like iron ore and coal, or obtained overseas, like cotton. While Russia, Sweden, the United States, and other forested countries continued to smelt iron with charcoal, the British and western Europeans substituted coke made from coal. As the population increased and land grew scarcer, the cost of growing feed for horses rose, creating incentives to find new, less land-hungry means of transportation. Likewise, as iron became cheaper and wood more expensive, ships and many other objects formerly made of wood began to be made of iron.

To contemporaries, the most obvious changes in rural life were brought about by the new transportation systems. In the eighteenth century France had a national network of quality roads, which Napoleon extended into Italy and Germany. In Britain local governments' neglect of the roads that served long-distance traffic led to the formation of private enterprises—"Turnpike Trusts"—that built numerous toll roads. For heavy goods, horse-drawn wagons were costly even on good roads because of the need to feed the horses. The growing volume of heavy freight triggered canal-building booms in Britain, France, and the Low Countries in the late eighteenth century. Some canals, like the duke of Bridgewater's canal in England, connected coal mines to towns or navigable rivers. Others linked navigable rivers and created national transportation networks.

Canals were marvels of construction, with deep cuts, tunnels, and even aqueducts that carried barges over rivers. They also were a sort of school where engineers learned skills they were able to apply to the next great transportation system: the railroads. They laid track across rolling country by cutting deeply into hillsides and erecting daringly long bridges of stone and iron across valleys. Lesser lines snaked their way to small towns hidden in remote valleys. Soon, clanking trains pulled by puffing, smoke-belching locomotives were invading long-isolated districts.

Thus, in the century after industrialization began, the landscape of industrializing countries was transformed more rapidly than ever before. But the ecological changes, like the technological and economic changes that caused them, were only beginning.

Working Conditions

Industrialization offered new opportunities to the enterprising. Carpenters, metalworkers, and machinists were in great demand. Since industrial machines were fairly simple, some workers became engineers or went into business for themselves. The boldest in England moved to the European continent, the Americas, or India, using their skills to establish new industries.

The successful, however, were a minority. Most industrial jobs were unskilled, repetitive, and boring. Factory work did not vary with the seasons or the time of day but began and ended by the clock. Factories used the invention of gas lighting to expand the working day past sunset (see Environment and Technology: Gas Lighting). Workdays were long; there were few breaks; and foremen

ENVIRONMENT + TECHNOLOGY

Gas Lighting

Before the nineteenth century, the night was a dangerous time to be out. Oil lanterns and candles made of tallow or beeswax were too expensive for everyday use. Some hardy souls—like the engine designer James Watt, the pottery manufacturer Josiah Wedgwood, the chemist Joseph Priestley, the iron manufacturer Matthew Boulton, and the naturalist Erasmus Darwin—called themselves the Lunar Society because they only met on nights when there was a full moon so they could find their way home in the dark. Almost everyone else went to bed at sundown and got up at dawn.

There was a big demand for better lighting. For the managers of cotton mills and other industrial establishments, daylight hours were too short, especially in the winter months; they knew that they could keep running after sunset if they had light, but lanterns and candles were costly and dangerous. Wealthy people wanted to light up their homes. Businesses and government offices also needed light. The demand inspired inventors to look for new ways to produce light.

In France, the engineer Philippe Lebon knew that heating wood to make charcoal let off a flammable gas. In the 1790s he was able to channel this gas through pipes to illuminate a home and garden. In Britain, William Murdock, an engineer who worked for the steam engine manufacturers Boulton and Watt, extracted gas released in the process of heating coal to make coke and used it to light up a house. Moving from these experiments to commercial applications was a long and complicated process, however. Coal gas was smelly and explosive and full of impurities that gave off toxic fumes and smoke when it burned. Engineers had to learn ways to extract the gas efficiently, make strong pipes that did not leak, and market the product. In 1806 a German immigrant to England, Frederick Albert Winsor, founded the National Light and Heat Company to produce and distribute gas in London. By 1816, London had 26 miles of gas mains bringing gas to several neighborhoods. That same year, Baltimore became the first American city to install gas mains and streetlamps. In the following decades, engineers developed ways of removing the impurities from the gas to make it safer and cleaner. They also invented meters to measure the amount of gas consumed and burners that produced a brighter light. As a result of these improvements, the cost of gas dropped to less than a third

Gas Lighting For city dwellers, one of the most dramatic improvements brought by industrialization was the introduction of gas lighting in the early nineteenth century. The gas used was a by-product of heating coal to make coke for the iron industry, and the gas was distributed in iron pipes throughout the wealthier neighborhoods of big cities. Every evening at dusk, lamplighters went around lighting the street lamps. (Mary Evans Picture Library/ The Image Works)

that of oil lamps of equivalent lighting power. From the 1840s until the early twentieth century, gaslights were installed in homes, businesses, and factories and even along streets in the major cities of Europe and America.

The results were astonishing and delighted city dwellers. Mills and factories could operate on two eight- to ten-hour shifts instead of one long dawn-to-dusk shift. Businesses stayed open late. Theaters gave evening performances. And people could now walk the streets safely. Evening illumination also contributed to the tremendous increase in adult education, as working people attended classes after work. Sales of books soared, in part because the increasing number of people with gaslights in their homes could stay up late reading. The brightly lit cities attracted migrants from the still-dark countryside. Long before electricity, gas lighting had banished the terrors of the night.

watched constantly. Workers who performed one simple task over and over had little sense of achievement or connection to the final product. Industrial accidents were common and could ruin a family. Unlike even the poorest preindustrial farmer or artisan, factory workers had no control over their tools, jobs, or working hours.

Industrial work had a major impact on women and family life. Working-class women—that is, those who could not afford servants—had always worked, but mostly within the family: spinning and weaving, sewing hats and clothes, preparing food, washing, and doing a myriad other household chores. In rural areas, women also did farmwork, especially caring for gardens and small animals, as well as helping during the planting and harvesting seasons. With industrialization, however, their work was removed from the home. Women workers were concentrated in textile mills, partly because of ancient traditions, partly because textile work required less strength than metalworking, construction, or hauling. On average, women earned one-third to one-half as much as men. The economist Andrew Ure wrote in 1835: "It is in fact the constant aim and tendency of every improvement in machinery to supersede human labour altogether or to diminish its cost, by substituting the industry of women and children for that of men."[5] Young unmarried women worked to support themselves or to save for marriage. Married women took factory jobs when their husbands were unable to support the family. Mothers of infants faced a hard choice: whether to leave their babies with wet nurses at great expense and danger or bring them to the factory and keep them drugged. Rather than working together as family units, husbands and wives increasingly worked in different places.

In the early years of industrialization, even where factory work was available, it was never the main occupation of working women. Most young women who sought paid employment became domestic servants in spite of the low pay, drudgery, and risk of sexual abuse by male employers. Women with small children tried hard to find work they could do at home, such as laundry, sewing, embroidery, millinery, or taking in lodgers.

Even with both parents working, poor families found it hard to make ends meet. As in preindustrial societies, parents thought children should contribute to their upkeep as soon as they were able to. The first generation of

"Love Conquers Fear"   This is a sentimental Victorian drawing of children in a textile mill. Child labor was common in the first half of the nineteenth century, and workers were exposed to dangerous machines and moving belts, as well as to dust and dirt.   (British Library)

workers brought children as young as five or six with them to the factories and mines; they had little choice, since there were no public schools or day-care centers. Employers encouraged the practice and even hired orphans. They preferred children because they were cheaper and more docile than adults and were better able to tie broken threads or crawl under machines to sweep the dust.

In Arkwright's cotton mills two-thirds of the workers were children. In another mill 17 percent were under ten years of age, and 53 percent were between ten and seventeen; they worked fourteen to sixteen hours a day and were beaten if they made mistakes or fell asleep. Mine operators used children to pull coal carts along the low passageways from the coal face to the mine shaft. In the mid-nineteenth century, when the British government began restricting child labor, mill owners increasingly recruited adult immigrants from Ireland.

American industry began on a somewhat different note than the British. In the early nineteenth century Americans still remembered their revolutionary ideals. When Francis Cabot Lowell built a cotton mill in Massachusetts, he hired the unmarried daughters of New England farmers, promising them decent wages and housing in dormitories under careful moral supervision. Other manufacturers eager to combine profits with morality followed his example. Soon the profit motive won out, and manufacturers imposed longer hours, harsher working conditions, and lower wages. The young women protested: "As our fathers resisted with blood the lordly avarice of the British ministry, so we, their daughters, never will wear the yoke which has been prepared for us."[6] When they went on strike, the mill owners replaced them with Irish immigrant women willing to accept lower pay and worse conditions.

While the cotton boom enriched planters, merchants, and manufacturers, African-Americans paid for it with their freedom. In the 1790s, 700,000 slaves of African descent lived in the United States. The rising demand for cotton and the British and American prohibition of the African slave trade in 1808 caused an increase in the price of slaves. As the "Cotton Kingdom" expanded, the number of slaves rose through natural increase and the reluctance of slave owners to free their slaves. By 1850 there were 3.2 million slaves in the United States, 60 percent of whom grew cotton. Similarly, Europe's and North America's surging demand for tea and coffee prolonged slavery in the sugar plantations of the West Indies and caused it to spread to the coffee-growing regions of southern Brazil. In the British West Indies slavery was abolished in 1833, but elsewhere in the Americas it persisted for another thirty to fifty years.

Slavery was not, as white American southerners maintained, a "peculiar institution"—a consequence of biological differences, biblical injunctions, or African traditions. Slavery was just as much part and parcel of the Industrial Revolution as child labor in Britain, the clothes that people wore, and the beverages they drank.

Changes in Society

Industrialization accentuated the polarization of society and income disparities. In his novel *Sybil; or, The Two Nations*, the British politician Benjamin Disraeli° (1804–1881) spoke of "two nations between

Disraeli (diz-RAY-lee)

whom there is no intercourse and no sympathy, who are as ignorant of each other's habits, thoughts, and feelings as if they were dwellers in different zones, or inhabitants of different planets . . . the rich and the poor." [7]

In Britain the worst-off were those who clung to an obsolete skill or craft. The cotton-spinning boom of the 1790s briefly brought prosperity to weavers. Their high wages and low productivity, however, induced inventors to develop power looms. As a result, by 1811 the wages of handloom weavers had fallen by a third; by 1832, by two-thirds. Even by working longer hours, they could not escape destitution.

In the industrial regions of Britain and continental Europe, the wages and standard of living of factory workers did not decline steadily like those of handloom weavers; they fluctuated wildly. During the war years of 1792 to 1815, the price of food, on which the poor spent most of their income, rose faster than wages. The result was widespread hardship. Then, in the 1820s real wages and public health began to improve. Industrial production grew at over 3 percent a year, pulling the rest of the economy along. Prices fell and wages rose. Even the poor could afford comfortable, washable cotton clothes and underwear.

Improvement, however, was not steady. One reason was the effect of **business cycles**—recurrent swings from economic hard times to recovery and growth, then back to hard times. When demand fell, businesses contracted or closed, and workers found themselves unemployed. Most had few or no savings, and no government at the time provided unemployment insurance. Hard times returned in the "hungry forties." In 1847–1848 the potato crop failed in Ireland. One-quarter of the Irish population died in the resulting famine, and another quarter emigrated to England and North America. On the European continent the negative effects of economic downturns were tempered by the existence of small family farms to which urban workers could return when they were laid off.

Only in the 1850s did the benefits of industrialization—cheaper food, clothing, and utensils—begin to improve workers' standard of living. The real beneficiary of the early Industrial Revolution was the middle class. In Britain landowning gentry and merchants had long shared wealth and influence. In the late eighteenth century a new group arose: entrepreneurs whose money came from manufacturing. Most, like Arkwright and Wedgwood, were the sons of middling shopkeepers, craftsmen, or farmers. Their enterprises were usually self-financed, for little capital was needed to start a cotton-spinning or machine-building business. Many tried and some succeeded, largely by plowing their profits back into the business. A generation later, in the nineteenth century, some newly rich industrialists bought their way into high society. The same happened in western Europe after 1815.

Before the Industrial Revolution, wives of merchants had often participated in the family business; widows occasionally managed sizable businesses on their own. With industrialization came a "cult of domesticity" to justify removing middle-class women from contact with the business world. Instead, they became responsible for the home, the servants, the education of children, and the family's social life (see Chapter 27). Not all women accepted the change; Mary Wollstonecraft (1759–1797) wrote the first feminist manifesto, *Vindication of the Rights of Woman,* in 1792.

Middle-class people who attributed their success, often correctly, to their own efforts and virtues believed in individual responsibility: if some people could succeed through hard work, thrift, and temperance, then those who did not succeed had no one but themselves to blame. Many workers, however, were newly arrived from rural districts and earned too little to save for the long stretches of unemployment they experienced. The squalor and misery of life in factory towns led to a noticeable increase in drunkenness on paydays. While the life of the poor remained hard, the well-to-do attributed their own success to sobriety, industriousness, thrift, and responsibility. The moral position of the middle class mingled condemnation with concern, coupled with feelings of helplessness in the face of terrible social problems, such as drunkenness, prostitution, and child abandonment.

NEW ECONOMIC AND POLITICAL IDEAS

Changes as profound as the Industrial Revolution triggered political ferment and ideological conflict. So many other momentous events took place during those years—the American Revolution (1776–1783), the French Revolution (1789–1799), the Napoleonic Wars (1804–1815), the reactions and revolts that periodically swept over Europe after 1815—that we cannot neatly separate out the consequences of industrialization from the rest. But it is clear that by undermining social traditions and causing a growing gap between rich and poor, the Industrial Revolution strengthened the ideas of laissez faire° and socialism and sparked workers' protests.

---

laissez faire (LAY-say fair)

Laissez Faire and Its Critics

The most celebrated exponent of **laissez faire** ("let them do") was Adam Smith (1723–1790), a Scottish economist. In *The Wealth of Nations* (1776) Smith argued that if individuals were allowed to seek personal gain, the effect, as though guided by an "invisible hand," would be to increase the general welfare. The government should refrain from interfering in business, except to protect private property; it should even allow duty-free trade with foreign countries. By advocating free-market capitalism, Smith was challenging the prevailing economic doctrine of earlier centuries, **mercantilism**, which argued that governments should regulate trade in order to maximize their hoard of precious metals (Chapter 19).

Persuaded by Adam Smith's arguments, governments dismantled many of their regulations in the decades after 1815. Britain even lowered its import duties, though other countries kept theirs. Nonetheless, it was obvious that industrialization was not improving the general welfare but was instead causing widespread misery. Two other thinkers, Thomas Malthus (1766–1834) and David Ricardo (1772–1832), attempted to explain the poverty they saw without challenging the basic premises of laissez faire. The cause of the workers' plight, Malthus and Ricardo said, was the population boom, which outstripped the food supply and led to falling wages. The workers' poverty, they claimed, was as much a result of "natural law" as the wealth of successful businessmen, and the only way the working class could avoid mass famine was to delay marriage and practice self-restraint and sexual abstinence.

Laissez faire provided an ideological justification for a special kind of capitalism: banks, stock markets, and chartered companies allowed investors to obtain profits with reasonable risks but with much less government control and interference than in the past. In particular, removing guild and other restrictions allowed businesses to employ women and children and keep wages low.

Businesspeople in Britain eagerly adopted laissez-faire ideas that justified their activities and kept the government at bay. But not everyone accepted the grim conclusions of the "dismal science," as economics was then known. The British philosopher Jeremy Bentham (1748–1832) believed that it was possible to maximize "the greatest happiness of the greatest number," if only a Parliament of enlightened reformers would study the social problems of the day and pass appropriate legislation.

The German economist Friedrich List (1789–1846) rejected laissez faire and free trade as a British trick "to make the rest of the world, like the Hindus, its serfs in all industrial and commercial relations." To protect their "infant industries" from British competition, he argued, the German states had to eliminate tariff barriers between them but erect high barriers against imports from Britain. On the European continent, List's ideas were as influential as those of Smith and Ricardo and led in 1834 to the formation of the Zollverein°, a customs union of most of the German states.

Positivists and Utopian Socialists

Bentham optimistically advocated gradual improvements. In contrast, three French social thinkers, moved by sincere concern for the poor, offered a radically new vision of a just civilization. Espousing a philosophy called **positivism**, the count of Saint-Simon (1760–1825) and his disciple Auguste Comte° (1798–1857) argued that the scientific method could solve social as well as technical problems. They recommended that the poor, guided by scientists and artists, form workers' communities under the protection of benevolent business leaders. These ideas found no following among workers, but they attracted the enthusiastic support of bankers and entrepreneurs, for whom positivism provided a rationale for investing in railroads, canals, and other symbols of modernity. The third French thinker, Charles Fourier° (1768–1837), loathed capitalists and imagined an ideal society in which groups of sixteen hundred workers would live in dormitories and work together on the land and in workshops where music, wine, and pastries would soften the hardships of labor. Critics called his ideas **utopian° socialism**, from the Greek word *utopia* meaning "nowhere." Fourier's ideas are now considered a curiosity, but positivism resonates to this day among liberal thinkers, especially in Latin America.

The person who came closest to creating a utopian community was the Englishman Robert Owen (1771–1858), a successful cotton manufacturer who believed that industry could provide prosperity for all. Conscience-stricken by the plight of British workers, Owen took over the management of New Lanark, a mill town south of Glasgow. He improved the housing and added schools, a church, and other amenities. He also testified in Parliament against child labor and for government inspection of working conditions. Although he angered his fellow industrialists, he helped bring about long-overdue reforms.

Protests and Reforms

Workers benefited little from the ideas of these middle-class philosophers. Instead, they resisted the harsh working conditions in their own ways. They changed jobs frequently. They were often absent, especially on Mondays. When they were not closely watched, the quality of their work was likely to be poor.

Periodically, workers rioted or went on strike, especially when food prices were high and when downturns in the business cycle left many unemployed. In some places, craftsmen broke into factories and destroyed the machines that threatened their livelihoods. Such acts of resistance did nothing to change the nature of industrial work. Not until workers learned to act together could they hope to have much influence.

Gradually, workers formed benevolent societies and organizations to demand universal male suffrage and shorter workdays. In 1834 Robert Owen organized the Grand National Consolidated Trade Union to lobby for an eight-hour workday; it quickly gained half a million members but collapsed a few months later in the face of government prosecution of trade-union activities. A new movement called Chartism arose soon thereafter. It was led by the London cabinetmaker William Lovett and the Irish landlord Fergus O'Connor and appealed to miners and industrial workers. It demanded universal male suffrage, equal electoral districts, the secret ballot, salaries for members of Parliament, and annual elections. It gathered 1.3 million signatures on a petition, but Parliament rejected it. Chartism collapsed in 1848, but it left a legacy of labor organizing.

Eventually, mass movements persuaded political leaders to look into the abuses of industrial life, despite the prevailing laissez-faire philosophy. In the 1820s and 1830s the British Parliament began investigating conditions in factories and mines. The Factory Act of 1833 prohibited the employment of children younger than nine in textile mills. It also limited the working hours of children between the ages of nine and thirteen to eight hours a day and of fourteen- to eighteen-year-olds to twelve hours. The Mines Act of 1842 prohibited the employment of women and boys under age ten underground. Several decades passed before the government appointed enough inspectors to enforce the new laws.

Most important was the struggle over the Corn Laws—tariffs on imported grain. Their repeal in 1846, in the name of "free trade," was designed to lower the cost of food for workers and thereby allow employers to pay lower wages. A victory for laissez faire, the repeal also represented a victory for the rising class of

---

Zollverein (TSOLL-feh-rine) **Comte** (COMB-tuh)
Fourier (FOOR-yeh) **utopian** (you-TOE-pee-uhn)

manufacturers and other employers over the conservative landowners who had long dominated politics and whose harvests faced competition from cheaper imported food.

The British learned to seek reform through accommodation. On the European continent, in contrast, the revolutions of 1848 revealed widespread discontent with repressive governments but failed to soften the hardships of industrialization (see Chapter 27).

THE LIMITS OF INDUSTRIALIZATION OUTSIDE THE WEST

The spread of the Industrial Revolution in the early nineteenth century transformed the relations of western Europe and North America with the rest of the world. In Egypt and India cheap industrial imports, backed by the power of Great Britain, delayed industrialization for a century or more. China was defeated and humiliated by the products of industrial manufacture. In these three cases, we can discern the outlines of the Western domination that has characterized the history of the world since the late nineteenth century.

Egypt, strongly influenced by European ideas since the French invasion of 1798, began to industrialize in the early nineteenth century. The driving force was its ruler, Muhammad Ali (1769–1849), a man who was to play a major role not only in the history of Egypt but in the Middle East and East Africa as well (see Chapters 25 and 26). He wanted to build up the Egyptian economy and military in order to become less dependent on the Ottoman sultan, his nominal overlord. To do so, he imported advisers and technicians from Europe and built cotton mills, foundries, shipyards, weapons factories, and other industrial enterprises. To pay for all this, he made the peasants grow wheat and cotton, which the government bought at a low price and exported at a profit. He also imposed high tariffs on imported goods in order to force the pace of industrialization.

Muhammad Ali's efforts fell afoul of the British, who did not want a powerful country threatening to interrupt the flow of travelers and mail across Egypt, the shortest route between Europe and India. When Egypt went to war against the Ottoman Empire in 1839, Britain intervened and forced Muhammad Ali to eliminate all import duties in the name of free trade. Unprotected, Egypt's

A Railroad Bridge Across the Nile In the second half of the nineteenth century, eastern nations, especially Great Britain sent engineers and equipment to build railroads in less-industrialized parts of the world, such as India, South Africa, Latin America, and the Middle East. One such railway connected Cairo and Alexandria in Egypt. Here a railroad bridge crosses the Nile at Benha near the Pyramids. (Corbis)

fledgling industries could not compete with the flood of cheap British products. Thereafter, Egypt exported raw cotton, imported manufactured goods, and became, in effect, an economic dependency of Britain.

Until the late eighteenth century, India had been the world's largest producer and exporter of cotton textiles, handmade by skilled spinners and weavers. The British East India Company took over large parts of India just as the Industrial Revolution was beginning in Britain (see Chapter 26 and Map 26.2). It allowed cheap British factory-made yarn and cloth to flood the Indian market duty-free, putting spinners and later handloom weavers out of work. Unlike Britain, India had no factories to which displaced handicraft workers could turn for work. Most of them became landless peasants, eking out a precarious living.

Like other tropical regions, India became an exporter of raw materials and an importer of British industrial goods. To hasten the process, British entrepreneurs and colonial officials introduced railroads into the subcontinent. The construction of India's railroad network began in the mid-1850s, along with coal mining to fuel the locomotives and the installation of telegraph lines to connect the major cities.

Some Indian entrepreneurs saw opportunities in the atmosphere of change that the British created. In 1854 the Bombay merchant Cowasjee Nanabhoy Davar imported an engineer, four skilled workers, and several textile machines from Britain and started India's first textile mill. This was the beginning of India's mechanized cotton industry. Despite many gifted entrepreneurs, India's industrialization proceeded at a snail's pace, for the government was in British hands and the British did nothing to encourage Indian industry.

China's stagnation in the late eighteenth and early nineteenth centuries, at the very time when first Britain and then western Europe and North America were becoming industrialized, has long puzzled historians. China had the resources, both human and natural, to advance technologically and economically, but a conservative elite and a growing population of poor peasants stood in the way of change (see Chapter 21). As a result, when faced with Western industrial technology, China became weaker rather than stronger.

In January 1840 a shipyard in Britain launched a radically new ship. The *Nemesis* had an iron hull, a flat bottom that allowed it to navigate in shallow waters, and a steam engine to power it upriver and against the wind. In November it arrived off the coast of China, heavily armed. Though ships from Europe had been sailing to China for three hundred years, the *Nemesis* was the first steam-powered iron gunboat seen in Asian waters. A Chinese observer noted: "Iron is employed to make it strong. The hull is painted black, weaver's shuttle fashion. On each side is a wheel, which by the use of coal fire is made to revolve as fast as a running horse. . . . At the vessel's head is a Marine God, and at the head, stern, and sides are cannon, which give it a terrific appearance. Steam vessels are a wonderful invention of foreigners, and are calculated to offer delight to many."[8]

Instead of offering delight, the *Nemesis* and other steam-powered warships that soon joined it steamed up the Chinese rivers, bombarded forts and cities, and transported troops and supplies from place to place along the coast and up rivers far more quickly than Chinese soldiers could move on foot. With this new weapon, Britain, a small island nation half a world away, was able to defeat the largest and most populated country in the world (see Chapter 25).

The cases of Egypt, India, and China show how the demands of Western nations and the military advantage that industrialization gave them led them to interfere in the internal affairs of nonindustrial societies. As we shall see in Chapter 28, this was the start of a new age of Western dominance.

SUMMARY

—○— What caused the Industrial Revolution?

—○— What were the key innovations that increased productivity and drove industrialization?

—○— What was the impact of these changes on the society and environment of the industrializing countries?

—○— How did the Industrial Revolution influence the rise of new economic and political ideas?

—○— How did the Industrial Revolution affect the relations between the industrialized and the nonindustrialized parts of the world?

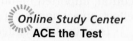
Online Study Center
ACE the Test

The Industrial Revolution arose from a combination of factors in European society in the eighteenth and early nineteenth centuries. The population grew, but so did the food supply, thanks to improvements in agriculture. Among upper- and middle-class Europeans, practical subjects like business, science, and technology became fashionable. Great Britain had a particularly fluid society open to talents and enterprise. On the European continent, the revolutions of 1789–1815 swept away the restrictions of the old aristocratic regimes.

A series of technological and organizational innovations transformed the manufacture of many products, reducing their costs and increasing their productivity. New machines, assembled in mills, mass-produced cotton yarn and cloth. Work formerly done by skilled craftsmen was divided into many simple tasks assigned to workers in factories. New techniques made iron cheap and abundant. Steam engines provided power to factories, ships, and railroads. And electricity found its first practical application in telegraphy.

The Industrial Revolution changed people's lives and the environments in which they lived. Cities grew huge and, for, most of their inhabitants, unsightly and unhealthy. While middle-class women were consigned to caring for the home and children, working-class women and children as well as men were obliged to earn their living in mines and factories. In the industrial cities, social problems such as unemployment, alcoholism, and the abandonment of children became acute. Rural environments were also transformed as roads, canals, and railroads crisscrossed open land.

Some thinkers defended the growing disparities between rich and poor in the name of laissez faire. Governments and businesspeople eagerly adopted many of the free-market capitalist views of Adam Smith. Others, such as positivists and utopian socialists, criticized the injustices caused by industrialization and offered a new vision of just communities. Workers created labor unions, leading political leaders to reexamine the working conditions of factories and mines, especially as they concerned women and children. However, not until the mid-nineteenth century did industrialization begin to raise living standards in the industrialized countries.

The Industrial Revolution changed life not only in the industrializing nations but also around the world because it gave the newly industrial nations of the West new powers to coerce non-Western societies. In particular, Britain snuffed out the incipient industrialization of Egypt and India and turned those countries into producers of raw materials, and British steam-powered gunboats forced China to open its doors to unequal trade.

KEY TERMS

Industrial Revolution *p. 668*
agricultural revolution *p. 669*
mass production *p. 674*
Josiah Wedgwood *p. 674*
division of labor *p. 674*

mechanization *p. 675*
Richard Arkwright *p. 675*
Crystal Palace *p. 676*
steam engine *p. 677*
James Watt *p. 677*
electric telegraph *p. 680*

business cycles *p. 685*
laissez faire *p. 686*
mercantilism *p. 686*
positivism *p. 687*
utopian socialism *p. 687*

Online Study Center
Improve Your Grade
Flashcards

SUGGESTED READING

General works on the history of technology give pride of place to industrialization. For an optimistic overview see Joel Mokyr, *The Lever of Riches: Technological Creativity and Economic Progress* (1990). Other important recent works include James McClellan III and Harold Dorn, *Science and Technology in World History* (1999); David Landes, *The Wealth and Poverty of Nations* (1998); and Ian Inkster, *Technology and Industrialization: Historical Case Studies and International Perspectives* (1998).

There is a rich literature on the British industrial revolution, beginning with T. S. Ashton's classic *The Industrial Revolution, 1760–1830*, published in 1948 and often reprinted. The interactions between scientists, technologists, and businessmen are described in Jenny Uglow, *The Lunar Men: Five Friends Whose Curiosity Changed the World* (2002), but see also Joel Mokyr, *The Gifts of Athena: Historical Origins of the Knowledge Economy* (2002). The importance of the steam engine is the theme of Jack Goldstone, "Efflorescences and Economic Growth in World History: Rethinking the 'Rise of the West' and the Industrial Revolution," in *Journal of World History* (Fall 2002).

The impact of industrialization on workers is the theme of E. P. Thompson's classic work *The Making of the English Working Class* (1963), but see also E. R. Pike, *"Hard Times": Human Documents of the Industrial Revolution* (1966). The role of women is most ably revealed in Lynn Y. Weiner, *From Working Girl to Working Mother: The Female Labor Force in the United States, 1820–1980* (1985), and in Louise Tilly and Joan Scott, *Women, Work, and Family* (1978).

European industrialization is the subject of J. Goodman and K. Honeyman, *Gainful Pursuits: The Making of Industrial Europe: 1600–1914* (1988); John Harris, *Industrial Espionage and Technology Transfer: Britain and France in the Eighteenth Century* (1998); and David Landes, *The Unbound Prometheus: Technological Change and Industrial Development in Western Europe from 1750 to the Present* (1972). On the beginnings of American industrialization see David Jeremy, *Artisans, Entrepreneurs and Machines: Essays on the Early Anglo-American Textile Industry, 1770–1840* (1998).

On the environmental impact of industrialization, see Richard Wilkinson, *Poverty and Progress: An Ecological Perspective on Economic Development* (1973), and Richard Tucker and John Richards, *Global Deforestation in the Nineteenth-Century World Economy* (1983).

The first book to treat industrialization as a global phenomenon is Peter Stearns, *The Industrial Revolution in World History* (1993); see also Louise Tilly's important article "Connections" in *American Historical Review* (February 1994). An important work comparing China and Europe in the eighteenth century is Kenneth Pomeranz, *The Great Divergence: Europe, China, and the Making of the Modern World Economy* (2000).

NOTES

1. Nassau W. Senior, *Letters on the Factory Act, as it affects the cotton manufacture, addressed to the Right Honourable, the President of the Board of Trade*, 2nd ed. (London: Fellows, 1844), 20.
2. Friedrich Engels, *Condition of the Working Class in England*, trans. and ed. by W. O. Henderson and W. H. Chaloner (Oxford: Blackwell, 1958), 312.
3. Quoted in Lewis Mumford, *The City in History* (New York: Harcourt Brace, 1961), 460.
4. Quoted in F. Roy Willis, *Western Civilization: An Urban Perspective*, vol. II (Lexington, MA: D.C. Heath, 1973), 675.
5. Quoted in Joan W. Scott, "The Mechanization of Women's Work," *Scientific American* 247, no. 3 (September 1982): 171.
6. Alice Kessler-Harris, *Women Have Always Worked: A Historical Overview* (Old Westbury, NY: The Feminist Press, 1981), 59.
7. J. P. T. Bury, *The New Cambridge Modern History*, vol. X (Cambridge: Cambridge University Press, 1967), 10.
8. *Nautical Magazine* 12 (1843): 346.

The Train Station in Orizaba, Mexico, 1877 In the last decades of the nineteenth century Mexico's political leaders actively promoted economic development. The railroad became the symbol of this ideal. (*Estación de Orizaba, 1877*. From Casimiro Castro, *Album del Ferro-Carril Mexicano: Coleccion de Vista Pintadas* [Victor Debray and Company, 1877] Typ 887.77.4162 PF, Department of Printing and Graphic Arts, Houghton Library, Harvard College Library)

- What were the causes of the revolutions for independence in Latin America?

- What major political challenges did Western Hemisphere nations face in the nineteenth century?

- How did economic modernization and the effects of abolition, immigration, and women's rights change the nations of the Western Hemisphere?

692

24

NATION BUILDING AND ECONOMIC TRANSFORMATION IN THE AMERICAS, 1800–1890

CHAPTER OUTLINE

Independence in Latin America, 1800–1830

The Problem of Order, 1825–1890

The Challenge of Social and Economic Change

Comparative Perspectives

DIVERSITY AND DOMINANCE: The Afro-Brazilian Experience, 1828

ENVIRONMENT AND TECHNOLOGY: Constructing the Port of Buenos Aires, Argentina

D uring the nineteenth century the newly independent nations of the Western Hemisphere sought to emulate the rapid economic progress of Europe under the influence of the Industrial Revolution. No technology seemed to represent that progress more perfectly than railroads. As a result, everywhere from Argentina to Canada governments sponsored railroad development. The great success story was the United States, where by 1850 there were 9,000 miles of track, as much as was found in the rest of the world. While Latin American nations committed to this technology more than three decades after the United States, railroads proved important to the growth of exports, to the development of new industries, and to the political and cultural integration of regions distant from national capitals.

Online Study Center

This icon will direct you to interactive activities and study materials on the website: *college.hmco.com/pic/bulliet4e.*

In Mexico the first concession for railroad construction was granted in 1837, but it was not until 1873 that the first significant rail line was inaugurated. No new project was proposed until 1880. It was during the long presidency of Porfirio Díaz (1876–1880 and 1884–1911) that railroad construction began in earnest. By 1910 Mexico had 12,000 miles of railroad track. Two characteristics of this development suggest the complex ways that economic development could affect national histories. First, vast areas of the Mexican interior that had remained in the hands of Amerindian peoples were made potentially profitable for the first time by railroads. As a result, powerful landed families used their political influence to strip this land from indigenous subsistence farmers and transform it to the production of export crops. Mexico certainly gained from this transformation, with as much as 50 percent of the growth in the economy in this period resulting from the greater efficiency and lower costs provided by railroads. But the Amerindian villagers lost ground and rural uprisings increased. Second, this rapid expansion of railroads after 1880 was made possible by foreign investment. By 1900 railroads accounted for more than half the total investment of Great Britain and the United States in Latin America. This dependence on foreign capital led to political protests and the rise of economic nationalism.

The Western Hemisphere witnessed radical political and social changes in addition to technological innovations and economic expansion. Most of the region's nations achieved independence by 1825, breaking free from European colonial powers. As was true in the earlier American and French Revolutions (see Chapter 22) rising nationalism and the ideal of political freedom helped organize and direct these changes. Despite the achievement of independence, Mexico and other nations in the hemisphere faced foreign interventions and other threats to sovereignty, including regionalism and civil war.

Throughout the nineteenth century the new nations in the Western Hemisphere wrestled with the difficult questions that independence raised. If colonies could reject submission to imperial powers, could not regions with distinct cultures, social structures, and economies refuse to accept the political authority of the newly formed nation-states? How could nations born in revolution accept the political strictures of written constitutions—even those they wrote themselves? How could the ideals of liberty and freedom expressed in those constitutions be reconciled with the denial of rights to Amerindians, slaves, recent immigrants, and women?

While trying to resolve these political questions, the new nations also attempted to promote economic growth. They introduced new technologies like railroads, opened new areas to settlement, and promoted immigration. But the legacy of colonial economic development, with its emphasis on agricultural and mining exports, inhibited efforts to promote diversification and industrialization, just as the legacy of class and racial division thwarted the realization of political ideals.

INDEPENDENCE IN LATIN AMERICA, 1800–1830

As the eighteenth century drew to a close, Spain and Portugal held vast colonial possessions in the Western Hemisphere, although their power had declined relative to that of their British and French rivals. Both Iberian empires had reformed their colonial administration and strengthened their military forces in the eighteenth century (see Chapter 18). Despite these efforts, the same economic and political forces that had undermined British rule in the colonies that became the United States were present in Spanish America and Brazil.

Roots of Revolution, to 1810

The great works of the Enlightenment as well as revolutionary documents like the American Declaration of Independence and the French Declaration of the Rights of Man circulated widely in Latin America by 1800, but very few colonial residents desired to follow the examples of the American and French Revolutions (see Chapter 22). Local-born members of Latin America's elites and middle classes were frustrated by the political and economic power of colonial officials and angered by high

C H R O N O L O G Y

	United States and Canada	Mexico and Central America	South America
1800	**1789** U.S. Constitution ratified **1803** Louisiana Purchase		**1808** Portuguese royal family arrives in Brazil **1808–1809** Revolutions for independence begin in Spanish South America
	1812–1815 War of 1812	**1810–1821** Mexican movement for independence	**1822** Brazil gains independence
1825			**1831** Brazil signs treaty with Great Britain to end slave trade. Illegal trade continues.
	1836 Texas gains independence from Mexico **1845** Texas admitted as a state	**1846–1848** War between Mexico and the United States **1847–1870** Caste War	
1850	**1848** Women's Rights Convention in Seneca Falls, New York **1861–1865** Civil War	**1857** Mexico's new constitution limits power of Catholic Church and military **1862–1867** French invade Mexico	**1850** Brazilian illegal slave trade suppressed **1865–1870** Argentina, Uruguay, and Brazil wage war against Paraguay
1875	**1867** Creation of Dominion of Canada **1876** Sioux and allies defeat U.S. Army in Battle of Little Bighorn	**1867** Emperor Maximilian executed	**1870s** Governments of Argentina and Chile begin final campaigns against indigenous peoples **1879–1881** Chile wages war against Peru and Bolivia; telegraph, refrigeration, and barbed wire introduced in Argentina **1888** Abolition of slavery in Brazil
	1890 "Jim Crow" laws enforce segregation in South **1890s** United States becomes world's leading steel producer		

taxes and imperial monopolies. But it was events in Europe that first pushed the colonies toward independence. Napoleon's decision to invade Portugal (1807) and Spain (1808), not revolutionary ideas, created the crisis of legitimacy that undermined the authority of colonial officials and ignited Latin America's struggle for independence.

In 1808 as a French army neared Lisbon, the royal family of Portugal fled to Brazil. King John VI maintained his court there for over a decade. In Spain, in contrast, Napoleon forced King Ferdinand VII to abdicate and placed his own brother, Joseph Bonaparte, on the throne. Spanish patriots fighting against the French created a

new political body, the Junta° Central, to administer the areas they controlled. Most Spaniards viewed the Junta as a temporary patriotic institution created to govern Spain while the king remained a French prisoner. The Junta, however, claimed the right to exercise the king's powers over Spain's colonies, and this claim provoked a crisis.

Large numbers of colonial residents in Spanish America, perhaps a majority, favored obedience to the Junta Central. A vocal minority, which included many wealthy

---

Junta (HUN-tah)

and powerful individuals, objected. The dissenters argued that they were subjects of the king, not dependents of the Spanish nation. They wanted to create local juntas and govern their own affairs until Ferdinand regained the throne. Spanish loyalists in the colonies resisted this tentative assertion of local autonomy and thus provoked armed uprisings. In late 1808 and 1809 popular movements overthrew Spanish colonial officials in Venezuela, Mexico, and Alto Peru (modern Bolivia) and created local juntas. In each case, Spanish officials quickly reasserted control and punished the leaders. This harsh repression, however, further polarized public opinion in the colonies and gave rise to a greater sense of a separate American nationality. By 1810 Spanish colonial authorities were facing a new round of revolutions more clearly focused on the achievement of independence.

| Spanish South America, 1810–1825 | In Caracas (the capital city of modern Venezuela) a revolutionary Junta led by creoles |

(colonial-born whites) declared independence in 1811. Although this group espoused popular sovereignty and representative democracy, its leaders were large landowners who defended slavery and opposed full citizenship for the black and mixed-race majority. Their aim was to expand their own privileges by eliminating Spaniards from the upper levels of Venezuela's government and from the church. The junta's narrow agenda spurred loyalists in the colonial administration and church hierarchy to rally thousands of free blacks and slaves to defend the Spanish Empire. Faced with this determined resistance, the revolutionary movement placed overwhelming political authority in the hands of its military leader **Simón Bolívar°** (1783–1830), who later became the preeminent leader of the independence movement in Spanish South America.

Online Study Center
Improve Your Grade
Primary Source:
The Jamaica Letter

The son of wealthy Venezuelan planters, Bolívar had studied both the classics and the works of the Enlightenment. He used the force of his personality to mobilize political support and to hold the loyalty of his troops. Defeated on many occasions, Bolívar successfully adapted his objectives and policies to attract new allies and build coalitions. Although initially opposed

---

Simón Bolívar (see-MOAN bow-LEE-varh)

to the abolition of slavery, for example, he agreed to support emancipation in order to draw slaves and freemen to his cause and to gain supplies from Haiti. Bolívar was also capable of using harsh methods to ensure victory. Attempting to force resident Spaniards to join the rebellion in 1813 he proclaimed: "Any Spaniard who does not . . . work against tyranny in behalf of this just cause will be considered an enemy and punished; as a traitor to the nation, he will inevitably be shot by a firing squad."[1]

Between 1813 and 1817 military advantage shifted back and forth between the patriots and loyalists. Bolívar's ultimate success was aided by his decision to enlist demobilized English veterans of the Napoleonic Wars and by a military revolt in Spain in 1820. The English veterans, hardened by combat, helped improve the battlefield performance of Bolívar's army. The revolt in Spain forced Ferdinand VII—restored to the throne in 1814 after the defeat of Napoleon—to accept a constitution that limited the powers of both the monarch and the church. Colonial loyalists who for a decade had fought to maintain the authority of monarch and church viewed these reforms as unacceptably liberal.

With the king's supporters divided, momentum swung to the patriots. After liberating present-day Venezuela, Colombia, and Ecuador, Bolívar's army occupied the area that is now Peru and Bolivia (named for Bolívar). Finally defeating the last Spanish armies in 1824, Bolívar and his closest supporters attempted to draw the former Spanish colonies into a formal confederation. The first step was to forge Venezuela, Colombia, and Ecuador into the single nation of Gran Colombia (see Map 24.1). With Bolívar's encouragement, Peru and Bolivia also experimented with unification. Despite his prestige, however, all of these initiatives had failed by 1830.

Buenos Aires (the capital city of modern Argentina) was the second important center of revolutionary activity in Spanish South America. In Buenos Aires news of Ferdinand VII's abdication led to the creation of a junta organized by militia commanders, merchants, and ranchers, which overthrew the viceroy in 1810. To deflect

Map 24.1 Latin America by 1830 By 1830 patriot ➤ forces had overturned the Spanish and Portuguese Empires of the Western Hemisphere. Regional conflicts, local wars, and foreign interventions challenged the survival of many of these new nations following independence.

Online Study Center
Improve Your Grade
Interactive Map:
Latin America by 1830

ATLANTIC
OCEAN

PACIFIC
OCEAN

OREGON
COUNTRY
(Joint U.S.-British
occupation)

BRITISH NORTH AMERICA
(Gr. Br.)

UNITED STATES

Colorado

Rio Grande

Mississippi

MEXICO
1821

San
Antonio

Gulf of Mexico

BAHAMA IS.
(Gr. Br.)

Havana

CUBA
(Spain)

HAITI 1804

PUERTO RICO (Spain)

Mexico City

Veracruz

BRITISH
HONDURAS (Gr. Br.)

JAMAICA (Gr. Br.)

GUATEMALA
Guatemala City

*Caribbean
Sea*

UNITED PROVINCES OF
CENTRAL AMERICA
1823—1839

Panama

Caracas

TRINIDAD (Gr. Br.)

VENEZUELA

BR. GUIANA (Gr. Br.)

DUTCH GUIANA (Neth.)

FRENCH GUIANA (France)

Magdalena

Socorro

Bogotá

GRAN COLOMBIA
1819—1830

*Galápagos
Islands*

Quito

ECUADOR

Amazon

EMPIRE OF BRAZIL
1822

PERU
1824

Lima

Salvador

BOLIVIA
1825

La Paz

Sucre

Paraná

PARAGUAY
1811

São Paulo

Rio de Janeiro

CHILE
1817

UNITED
PROVINCES OF
THE RÍO DE
LA PLATA
1816

Valparaíso

Santiago

URUGUAY
1828

ARGENTINA

Buenos Aires

Bahía
Blanca

Montevideo

1811   Year independence gained

Colony

0   500   1000 Km.

0   500   1000 Mi.

PATAGONIA
(Disputed between
Argentina and Chile)

Islas Malvinas
(Falkland Islands)

the opposition of loyalists and Spanish colonial officials, the junta claimed loyalty to the imprisoned king. After Ferdinand regained the Spanish throne, however, junta leaders dropped this pretense. In 1816 they declared independence as the United Provinces of the Río de la Plata.

Patriot leaders in Buenos Aires at first sought to retain control over the territory of the Viceroyalty of Río de la Plata, which had been created in 1776 and included modern Argentina, Uruguay, Paraguay, and Bolivia. But Spanish loyalists in Uruguay and Bolivia and a separatist movement in Paraguay defeated these ambitions. Even within the territory of Argentina, the government in Buenos Aires was unable to control regional rivalries and political differences. As a result, the region rapidly descended into political chaos.

A weak succession of juntas, collective presidencies, and dictators soon lost control over much of the interior of Argentina. However, in 1817 the government in Buenos Aires did manage to support a mixed force of Chileans and Argentines led by José de San Martín° (1778–1850), who crossed the Andes Mountains to attack Spanish military forces in Chile and Peru. During this campaign San Martín's most effective troops were former slaves, who had gained their freedom by enlisting in the army, and gauchos, the cowboys of the Argentine pampas (prairies). After gaining victory in Chile San Martín pushed on to Peru in 1820, but he failed to gain a clear victory there. The violent and destructive uprising of Tupac Amaru II in 1780 had traumatized the Andean region and made colonists fearful that support for independence might unleash another Amerindian uprising (see Chapter 18). Unable to make progress, San Martín surrendered command of patriot forces in Peru to Simón Bolívar, who overcame final Spanish resistance in 1824.

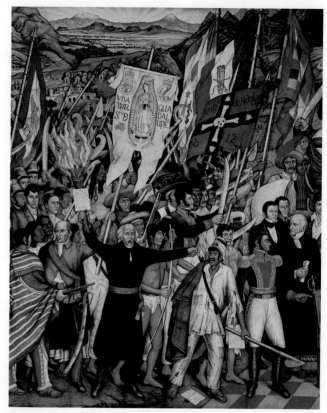

Padre Hidalgo   The first stage of Mexico's revolution for independence was led by Padre Miguel Hidalgo y Costilla, who rallied the rural masses of central Mexico to his cause. His defeat, trial, and execution made him one of Mexico's most important political martyrs.   (Schaalkwijk/Art Resource, NY)

Mexico, 1810–1823

In 1810 Mexico was Spain's wealthiest and most populous colony. Its silver mines were the richest in the world, and the colony's capital, Mexico City, was larger than any city in Spain. Mexico also had the largest population of Spanish immigrants among the colonies. Spaniards dominated the government, church, and economy. When news of Napoleon's invasion of Spain reached Mexico, conservative Spaniards in Mexico City overthrew the local viceroy because he was too sympathetic to the creoles. This action by Spanish loyalists underlined the new reality: with the king of Spain removed

from his throne by the French, colonial authority now rested on brute force.

The first stage of the revolution against Spain occurred in central Mexico. In this region wealthy ranchers and farmers had aggressively forced many Amerindian communities from their traditional agricultural lands. Crop failures and epidemics further afflicted the region's rural poor. At the same time, miners and the urban poor faced higher food prices and rising unemployment. With the power of colonial authorities weakened by events in Spain, anger and fear spread through towns and villages in central Mexico.

On September 16, 1810, **Miguel Hidalgo y Costilla°**, parish priest of the small town of Dolores, rang the church bells, attracting thousands. In a fiery speech he

---

José de San Martín (hoe-SAY deh san mar-TEEN)

Miguel Hidalgo y Costilla (mee-GEHL ee-DAHL-go ee cos-TEA-ah)

urged the crowd to rise up against the oppression of Spanish officials. Tens of thousands of the rural and urban poor joined his movement. They lacked military discipline and adequate weapons but knew who their oppressors were, spontaneously attacking the ranches and mines that had been exploiting them. Many Spaniards and colonial-born whites were murdered or assaulted. At first wealthy Mexicans were sympathetic to Hidalgo's objectives, but they eventually supported Spanish authorities when they recognized the threat posed to them by the angry masses following Hidalgo. The military tide quickly turned against Hidalgo and he was captured, tried, and executed in 1811.

The revolution continued under the leadership of another priest, **José María Morelos°**, a former student of Hidalgo's. A more adept military and political leader than his mentor, Morelos created a formidable fighting force and, in 1813, convened a congress that declared independence and drafted a constitution. Despite these achievements, loyalist forces also proved too strong for Morelos. He was defeated and executed in 1815. Although small numbers of insurgents continued to wage war against Spanish forces, colonial rule seemed secure in 1820. However, news of the military revolt in Spain unsettled the conservative groups and church officials who had defended Spanish rule against Hidalgo and Morelos. In 1821 Colonel Agustín de Iturbide° and other loyalist commanders forged an alliance with remaining insurgents and declared Mexico's independence. The conservative origins of Mexico's transition to independence were highlighted by the decision to create a monarchial form of government and crown Iturbide as emperor. In early 1823, however, the army overthrew Iturbide and Mexico became a republic. When Iturbide returned to Mexico from exile in 1824, he was captured and, like Hidalgo and Morelos, was executed by a firing squad.

Brazil, to 1831

The arrival of the Portuguese royal family in Brazil in 1808 helped maintain the loyalty of the colonial elite and stimulate the local economy. After the defeat of Napoleon in Europe, the Portuguese government called for King John VI to return to Portugal. He at first resisted this pressure. Then in 1820 the military uprising in Spain provoked a sympathetic liberal revolt in Portugal, and the Portuguese military garrison in Rio de Janeiro forced the king to permit the creation of juntas.

José María Morelos (hoe-SAY mah-REE-ah moh-RAY-los)
Agustín de Iturbide (ah-goos-TEEN deh ee-tur-BEE-deh)

John recognized that he needed to take dramatic action to protect his throne. In 1821 he returned to Portugal. Hoping to protect his claims to Brazil, he left his son Pedro in Brazil as regent.

By 1820 the Spanish colonies along Brazil's borders had experienced ten years of revolution and civil war, and some, like Argentina and Paraguay, had gained independence. Unable to ignore these struggles, some Brazilians began to reevaluate Brazil's relationship with Portugal. Many Brazilians resented their homeland's economic subordination to Portugal. The arrogance of Portuguese soldiers and bureaucrats led others to talk openly of independence. Rumors circulated that Portuguese troops were being sent to discipline Brazil and force the regent Pedro to join his father in Lisbon.

Unwilling to return to Portugal and committed to maintaining his family's hold on Brazil, Pedro aligned himself with the rising tide of independence sentiment. In 1822 he declared Brazilian independence. Pedro's decision launched Brazil into a unique political trajectory. Unlike its neighbors, which became constitutional republics, Brazil gained independence as a constitutional monarchy with Pedro I, heir to the throne of Portugal, as emperor.

Pedro I was committed to both monarchy and many liberal principles. He directed the writing of the constitution of 1824, which provided for an elected assembly and granted numerous protections for political opposition. But he made powerful enemies by attempting to protect the Portuguese who remained in Brazil from arbitrary arrest and seizure of their property. More dangerously still, he opposed slavery in a nation dominated by a slave-owning class. In 1823 Pedro I anonymously published an article that characterized slavery as a "cancer eating away at Brazil" (see Diversity and Dominance: The Afro-Brazilian Experience, 1828). Despite opposition, in 1831 he ratified a treaty with Great Britain to end Brazilian participation in the slave trade, but the political elite of Brazil's slave-owning regions opposed the treaty and for nearly two decades worked effectively to prevent enforcement until 1850. Pedro also continued his father's costly commitment of military forces to control neighboring Uruguay. As military losses and costs rose, the Brazilian public grew impatient. A small but vocal minority that opposed the monarchy and sought the creation of a democracy used these issues to rally public opinion against the emperor.

Confronted by street demonstrations, Pedro I abdicated the throne in 1831 in favor of his five-year-old son Pedro II. After a nine-year regency, Pedro II assumed full powers as emperor of Brazil. He reigned until he was overthrown by republicans in 1889.

The Afro-Brazilian Experience, 1828

Brazil was the most important destination for the Atlantic slave trade. From the sixteenth century to the 1850s more than 2 million African slaves were imported by Brazil, roughly twice the number of free European immigrants who arrived in the same period. Beginning in the 1820s Great Britain, Brazil's main trading partner, began to press for an end to the slave trade. British visitors to Brazil became an important source of critical information for those who sought to end the trade.

The following opinions were provided by a British clergyman, Robert Walsh, who traveled widely in Brazil in 1828 and 1829. Walsh's account reflects the racial attitudes of his time, but his testimony is valuable because of his ability to recognize the complex and sometimes unexpected ways that slaves and black freedmen were integrated into Brazilian society.

[At the Alfandega, or custom house,] . . . for the first time I saw the Negro population under circumstances so striking to a stranger. The whole labour of bearing and moving burdens is performed by these people, and the state in which they appear is revolting to humanity. Here were a number of beings entirely naked, with the exception of a covering of dirty rags tied about their waists. Their skins, from constant exposure to the weather, had become hard, crusty, and seamed, resembling the coarse black covering of some beast, or like that of an elephant, a wrinkled hide scattered with scanty hairs. On contemplating their persons, you saw them with a physical organization resembling beings of a grade below the rank of man. . . . Some of these beings were yoked to drays, on which they dragged heavy burdens. Some were chained by the necks and legs, and moved with loads thus encumbered. Some followed each other in ranks, with heavy weights on their heads, chattering the most inarticulate and dismal cadence as they moved along. Some were munching young sugar-canes, like beasts of burden eating green provender [animal feed], and some were seen near water, lying on the bare ground among filth and offal, coiled up like dogs, and seeming to expect or require no more comfort or accommodation, exhibiting a state and conformation so unhuman, that they not only seemed, but actually were, far below the inferior animals around them. Horses and mules were not employed in this way; they were used only for pleasure, and not for labour. They were seen in the same streets, pampered, spirited, and richly caparisoned, enjoying a state far superior to the negroes, and appearing to look down on the fettered and burdened wretches they were passing, as on beings of an inferior rank in the creation to themselves. . . .

The first impression of all this on my mind, was to shake the conviction I had always felt, of the wrong and hardship inflicted on our black fellow creatures, and that they were only in that state which God and nature had assigned them; that they were the lowest grade of human existence, and the link that connected it with the brute, and that the gradation was so insensible, and their natures so intermingled, that it was impossible to tell where one had terminated and the other commenced; and that it was not surprising that people who contemplated them every day, so formed, so employed, and so degraded, should forget their claims to that rank in the scale of beings in which modern philanthropists are so anxious to place them. I did not at the moment myself recollect, that the white man, made a slave on the coast of Africa, suffers not only a similar mental but physical deterioration from hardships and emaciation, and becomes in time the dull and deformed beast I now saw yoked to a burden.

A few hours only were necessary to correct my first impressions of the negro population, by seeing them under a different aspect. We were attracted by the sound of military music, and found it proceeded from a regiment drawn up in one of the streets. Their colonel had just died, and they attended to form a procession to celebrate his obsequies. They were all of different shades of black, but the majority were negroes. Their equipment was excellent; they wore dark jackets, white pantaloons, and black leather caps and belts, all which, with their arms, were in high order. Their band produced sweet and agreeable music, of the leader's own composition, and the men went through some evolutions with regularity and dexterity. They were only a militia regiment, yet were as well appointed and disciplined as one of our regiments of the line. Here then was the first step in that gradation by which the black population of this country ascend in the scale of humanity; he advances from the state below that of a beast of burden into a military rank, and he shows himself as capable of discipline and improvement as a human being of any other colour.

Our attention was next attracted by negro men and women bearing about a variety of articles for sale; some in baskets, some on boards and cases carried on their heads. They belonged to a class of small shopkeepers, many of whom vend their wares at home, but the greater number send them about in this way, as in itinerant shops. A few of these people were still in a state of bondage, and brought a certain sum every evening to their owners, as the produce of their daily labour. But a large proportion, I was informed, were free, and exercised this little calling on their own account. They were all very neat and clean in their persons, and had a decorum and sense of respectability about them, superior to whites of the same class and calling. All their articles were good in their kind, and neatly kept, and they sold them with simplicity and confidence, neither wishing to take advantage of others, nor suspecting that it would be taken of themselves. I bought some confectionary from one of the females, and I was struck with the modesty and propriety of her manner; she was a young mother, and had with her a neatly dressed child, of which she seemed very fond. I gave it a little comfit [candy covered nut], and it turned up its dusky countenance to her and then to me, taking my sweetmeat, and at the same time kissing my hand. As yet unacquainted with the coin of the country, I had none that was current about me, and was leaving the articles; but the poor young woman pressed them on me with a ready confidence, repeating in broken Portuguese, out of tempo, I am sorry to say, the "other time" never came, for I could not recognize her person afterwards to discharge her little debt, though I went to the same place for the purpose.

It soon began to grow dark, and I was attracted by a number of persons bearing large lighted wax tapers, like torches, gathering before a house. As I passed by, one was put into my hand by a man who seemed in some authority, and I was requested to fall into a procession that was forming. It was the preparation for a funeral, and on such occasions, I learned that they always request the attendance of a passing stranger, and feel hurt if they are refused. I joined the party, and proceeded with them to a neighbouring church. When we entered we arranged ourselves on each side of a platform which stood near the choir, on which was laid an open coffin, covered with pink silk and gold borders. The funeral service was chanted by a choir of priests, one of whom was a negro, a large comely man, whose jet black visage formed a strong and striking contrast to his white

vestments. He seemed to perform his part with a decorum and sense of solemnity, which I did not observe in his brethren. After scattering flowers on the coffin, and fumigating it with incense, they retired, the procession dispersed, and we returned on board. I had been but a few hours on shore, for the first time, and I saw an African negro under four aspects of society; and it appeared to me, that in every one his character depended on the state in which he was placed, and the estimation in which he was held. As a despised slave, he was far lower than other animals of burthen that surrounded him; more miserable in his look, more revolting in his nakedness, more distorted in his person, and apparently more deficient in intellect than the horses and mules that passed him by. Advanced to the grade of a soldier, he was clean and neat in his person, amenable to discipline, expert at his exercises, and showed the port [sic.] and being of a white man similarly placed. As a citizen, he was remarkable for the respectability of his appearance, and the decorum of his manners in the rank assigned him; and as a priest, standing in the house of God, appointed to instruct society on their most important interests, and in a grade in which moral and intellectual fitness is required, and a certain degree of superiority is expected, he seemed even more devout in his impressions, and more correct in his manners, than his white associates. I came, therefore, to the irresistible conclusion in my mind, that colour was an accident affecting the surface of a man, and having no more to do with his qualities than his clothes—that God had equally created an African in the image of his person, and equally given him an immortal soul; and that an European had no pretext but his own cupidity, for impiously thrusting his fellow man from that rank in the creation which the Almighty had assigned him, and degrading him below the lot of the brute beasts that perish.

QUESTIONS FOR ANALYSIS

1. What is the author's first impression of the Brazilian slave population?

2. What does the author later observe that changes this opinion?

3. How did slavery dehumanize slaves?

4. What circumstances or opportunities permitted Brazil's free blacks to improve their lives?

Source: Robert Edgar Conrad, *Children of God's Fire: A Documentary History of Black Slavery in Brazil* (Princeton, N.J.: Princeton University Press, 1983), 216–220. Reprinted by permission of the author.

THE PROBLEM OF ORDER, 1825–1890

All the newly independent nations of the Western Hemisphere had difficulties establishing stable political institutions. The idea of popular sovereignty found broad support across the hemisphere. As a result, written constitutions and elected assemblies were put in place, often before the actual achievement of independence. Even in the hemisphere's two monarchies, Mexico and Brazil, the emperors sought to legitimize their rule by accepting constitutional limits on their authority and by the creation of representative assemblies. Nevertheless, widespread support for constitutional order and for representative government failed to prevent bitter factional conflict, regionalism, and the appearance of charismatic political leaders and military uprisings.

Constitutional Experiments

In reaction to the arbitrary and tyrannical authority of colonial rulers, revolutionary leaders in both the United States and Latin America espoused constitutionalism. They believed that the careful description of political powers in written constitutions offered the best protection for individual rights and liberties. In practice, however, many new constitutions proved unworkable. In the United States George Washington, James Madison, and other leaders became dissatisfied with the nation's first constitution, the Articles of Confederation. They led the effort to write a new constitution, which was put into effect in 1789. In Latin America few constitutions survived the rough-and-tumble of national politics. Between 1811 and 1833 Venezuela and Chile ratified and then rejected a combined total of nine constitutions.

Important differences in colonial political experience influenced later political developments in the Americas. The ratification of a new constitution in the United States was the culmination of a long historical process that had begun with the development of English constitutional law and continued under colonial charters. Many more residents of the British North American colonies had had the experience of voting and holding political office than did people in Portuguese and Spanish colonies. The British colonies provided opportunities for holding elective offices in town governments and colonial legislatures, and, by the time of independence, citizens had grown accustomed to elections, political parties, and factions. In contrast, constitutional government and elections were only briefly experienced in Spanish America between 1812 and 1814—while Ferdinand VII was a prisoner of Napoleon—and this short period was disrupted by the early stages of the revolutions for independence. Brazil had almost no experience with popular politics before independence. Despite these differences in experience and constitutional forms, every new republic in the Americas initially limited the right to vote to free men of property.

Democratic passions and the desire for effective self-rule led to significant political reform in the Americas, even in some of the region's remaining colonies. British Canada was divided into separate colonies and territories, each with a separate and distinct government. Political life in each colony was dominated by a provincial governor and appointed advisory councils drawn from the local elite. Elected assemblies existed within each province, but they exercised limited power. Agitation to end oligarchic rule and make government responsive to the will of the assemblies led to armed rebellion in 1837. In the 1840s Britain responded by establishing limited self-rule in each of the Canadian provinces. By the 1860s regional political leaders interested in promoting economic development realized that railroads and other internal improvements required a government with a "national" character. Both the U.S. Civil War and raids from U.S. territory into Canada by Irish nationalists attempting to force an end to British control of Ireland gave the reform movement a sense of urgency and focused attention on the need to protect the border. Negotiations led to the **Confederation of 1867**, which included the provinces of Ontario, Quebec, New Brunswick, and Nova Scotia. The Confederation that created the new Dominion of Canada with a central government in Ottawa (see Map 24.2) was hailed by one observer as the "birthday of a new nationality."[2] The path to effective constitutional government was rockier to the south. Because neither Spain nor Portugal had permitted anything like the elected legislatures and municipal governments of colonial North America, the drafters of Latin American constitutions were less constrained by practical political experience. As a result, many of the new Latin American nations experimented with untested political institutions. For example, Simón Bolívar, who wrote the first constitutions of five South American republics, included in Bolivia's constitution a fourth branch of government that had "jurisdiction over the youth, the hearts of men, public spirit, good customs, and republican ethics."

Most Latin American nations found it difficult to define the political role of the Catholic Church after independence. In the colonial period the Catholic Church was

Map 24.2 Dominion of Canada, 1873   Although independence was not yet achieved and settlement remained concentrated along the U.S. border, Canada had established effective political and economic control over its western territories by 1873.

a religious monopoly that controlled all levels of education and dominated intellectual life. Many early constitutions aimed to reduce this power by making education secular and by permitting the practice of other religions. The church reacted by organizing its allies and financing conservative political movements. In Mexico, Colombia, Chile, and Argentina, conflicts between liberals who sought the separation of church and state and supporters of the church's traditional powers dominated political life until late in the nineteenth century.

Limiting the power of the military proved to be another significant stumbling block to the creation of constitutional governments in Latin America. The wars for independence elevated the prestige of military leaders. When the wars were over, Bolívar and other military commanders seldom proved willing to subordinate themselves to civilian authorities. At the same time, frustrated by the often-chaotic workings of constitutional democracy, few citizens were willing to support civilian politicians in any contest with the military. As a result, many Latin American militaries successfully resisted civilian control. Brazil, ruled by Emperor Pedro I, was the principal exception to this pattern.

Personalist Leaders   Successful patriot leaders in both the United States and Latin America gained mass followings during the wars for independence. They recruited and mobilized popular support by using patriotic symbols and by carefully associating their actions with national objectives. After independence, many patriot military leaders were able to use their personal followings to gain national political leadership. George Washington's ability to dominate the political scene in the early republican United States anticipated the later political ascendancy of revolutionary heroes such as Iturbide in Mexico and Bolívar in Gran Colombia. In each case, military reputation provided the foundation for personal political power. Washington was distinguished from most other early leaders by his willingness to surrender power. More commonly, **personalist leaders** relied on their ability to mobilize and direct the masses of these new nations rather than on the authority of constitutions and laws. Their model was Napoleon, who rose from the French army to become emperor, not James Madison, the primary author of the U.S. Constitution. In Latin America, a personalist leader who gained and held political power without constitutional sanction was called a *caudillo°*.

Latin America's slow development of stable political institutions made personalist politics more influential than they were in the United States. Nevertheless, charismatic politicians in the United States such as Andrew Jackson did sometimes challenge constitutional limits to their authority, as did the caudillos of Latin America.

Throughout the Western Hemisphere charismatic military men played key roles in attracting mass support for independence movements that were commonly dominated by colonial elites. Although this popular support was often decisive in the struggle for independence, the first constitutions of nearly all the American republics excluded large numbers of poor citizens from full political participation. But nearly everywhere in the Americas marginalized groups found populist leaders to articulate their concerns and challenge limits on their participation. Using informal means, these leaders sought to influence the selection of officeholders and to place their concerns in the public arena. Despite their success in overturning the deference-based politics of the colonial past, this populist political style at times threatened constitutional order and led to dictatorship.

Powerful personal followings allowed **Andrew Jackson** of the United States and **José Antonio Páez°** of Venezuela to challenge constitutional limits to their authority. During the independence wars in Venezuela and Colombia, Páez (1790–1873) organized and led Bolívar's most successful cavalry force. Like most of his followers, Páez was uneducated and poor, but his physical strength, courage, and guile made him a natural guerrilla leader and helped him build a powerful political base in Venezuela. Páez described his authority in the following manner: "[The soldiers] resolved to confer on me the supreme command and blindly to obey my will, confident . . . that I was the only one who could save them."[3] Able to count on the personal loyalty of his followers, Páez was seldom willing to accept the constitutional authority of a distant president.

After defeating the Spanish armies, Bolívar pursued his dream of forging a permanent union of former Spanish colonies modeled on the federal system of the United States. But he underestimated the strength of nationalist sentiment unleashed during the independence wars. Páez and other Venezuelan leaders resisted the surrender of their hard-won power to Bolívar's Gran Colombian government in distant Bogotá (the capital city of modern Colombia). When Bolívar's authority was challenged by political opponents in 1829, Páez declared Venezuela's independence. Merciless to his enemies and indulgent with his followers, Páez ruled the country as president or dictator for the next eighteen years. Despite implementing an economic program favorable to the elite, Páez remained popular with the masses by skillfully manipulating popular political symbols. Even as his personal wealth grew through land acquisitions and commerce, Páez took care to present himself as a common man.

Andrew Jackson (1767–1845) was the first U.S. president born in humble circumstances. A self-made man who eventually acquired substantial property and owned over a hundred slaves, Jackson was extremely popular among frontier residents, urban workers, and small farmers. Although he was notorious for his untidy personal life as well as for dueling, his courage, individualism, and willingness to challenge authority helped him attain political success as judge, general, congressman, senator, and president.

During his military career, Jackson proved to be impatient with civilian authorities. Widely known because of his victories over the Creek and Seminole peoples, he was elevated to the pinnacle of American politics by his celebrated defeat of the British at the Battle of New Orleans in 1815 and by his seizure of Florida from the Spanish in 1818. In 1824 he received a plurality of the popular votes cast for the presidency, but he failed to win a majority of the electoral votes and was denied the presidency when the House of Representatives chose John Quincy Adams.

Jackson's followers viewed his landslide election victory in 1828 and reelection in 1832 as the triumph of democracy over the entrenched aristocracy. In office Jackson challenged constitutional limits on his authority, substantially increasing presidential power at the expense of Congress and the Supreme Court. Like Páez, Jackson was able to dominate national politics by blending a populist political style that celebrated the virtues and cultural enthusiasms of common people with support for policies that promoted the economic interests of some of the nation's most powerful propertied groups.

Personalist leaders were common in both Latin America and the United States, but Latin America's weaker constitutional tradition, more limited protection of property rights, lower literacy levels, and less-developed

---

caudillo (kouh-DEE-yoh)
José Antonio Páez (hoe-SAY an-TOE-nee-oh PAH-ays)

communications systems provided fewer checks on the ambitions of popular politicians. The Constitution of the United States was never suspended, and no national election result in the United States was ever successfully overturned by violence. Latin America's personalist leaders, however, often ignored constitutional restraints on their authority, and election results seldom determined access to presidential power. As a result, by 1900 every Latin American nation had experienced periods of dictatorship.

The Threat of Regionalism

After independence, new national governments were generally weaker than the colonial governments they replaced. In debates over tariffs, tax and monetary policies, and, in many nations, slavery and the slave trade, regional elites were often willing to lead secessionist movements or to provoke civil war rather than accept laws that threatened their interests. Some of the hemisphere's newly independent nations did not survive these struggles; others lost territories to aggressive neighbors.

In Spanish America all of the postindependence efforts to forge large multistate federations failed. Central America and Mexico had been united in the Viceroyalty of New Spain and briefly maintained their colonial-era administrative ties following independence in 1821. After the overthrow of Iturbide's imperial rule in Mexico in 1823, however, regional politicians split with Mexico and created the independent Republic of Central America. Regional rivalries and civil wars during the 1820s and 1830s forced the breakup of that entity as well and led to the creation of five separate nations. Bolívar attempted to maintain the colonial unity of Venezuela, Colombia, and Ecuador by creating the nation of Gran Colombia with a capital in Bogotá. But even before his death in 1830 Venezuela and Ecuador had become independent states.

During colonial times Argentina, Uruguay, Paraguay, and Bolivia had been united in a single viceroyalty with its capital in Buenos Aires. With the defeat of Spain, political leaders in Paraguay, Uruguay, and Bolivia declared their independence from Buenos Aires. Argentina, the area that remained after this breakup, was itself nearly overwhelmed by these powerful centrifugal forces. After independence, Argentina's liberals took power in Buenos Aires. They sought a strong central government to promote secular education, free trade, and immigration from Europe. Conservatives dominated the interior provinces. They supported the Catholic Church's traditional control of education as well as the protection of local textile and winemaking

industries from European imports. In 1819, when political leaders in Buenos Aires imposed a national constitution that ignored these concerns, the conservatives of the interior rose in rebellion.

After a decade of civil war and rebellions a powerful local *caudillo*, Juan Manuel de Rosas°, came to power. For more than two decades he dominated Argentina, running the nation as if it were his private domain. The economy expanded under Rosas, but his use of intimidation, mob violence, and assassination created many enemies. In 1852 an alliance of foreign and domestic enemies overthrew him, but a new cycle of provincial rivalry and civil war prevented the creation of a strong central government until 1861.

Regionalism threatened the United States as well. The defense of state and regional interests played an important role in the framing of the U.S. Constitution. Many important constitutional provisions represented compromises forged among competing state and regional leaders. The creation of a Senate with equal representation from each state, for example, was an attempt to calm small states, which feared they might be dominated by larger states. The formula for representation in the House of Representatives was also an effort to compromise the divisions between slave and free states. Yet, despite these constitutional compromises, the nation was still threatened by regional rivalries.

Slavery increasingly divided the nation into two separate and competitive societies. A rising tide of immigration to the northern states in the 1830s and 1840s began to move the center of political power in the House of Representatives away from the south. Many southern leaders sought to protect slavery by expanding it to new territories. They supported the Louisiana Purchase in 1803 (see Map 24.3), an agreement with France that transferred to the United States a vast territory extending from the Gulf of Mexico to Canada. Southern leaders also supported statehood for Texas and war with Mexico (discussed later in the chapter).

The territorial acquisitions proved a mixed blessing to the defenders of slavery because they forced a national debate about slavery itself. Should slavery be allowed to expand into new territories? Could slavery be protected if new territories eligible for statehood were overwhelmingly free?

In 1860 Abraham Lincoln (1809–1865), who was committed to checking the spread of slavery, was elected president of the United States. In response, the planter elite in the southern states chose the dangerous course of secession from the federal Union. The seceding states formed a new government, the Confederate States of

---

Juan Manuel de Rosas (huan man-WELL deh ROH-sas)

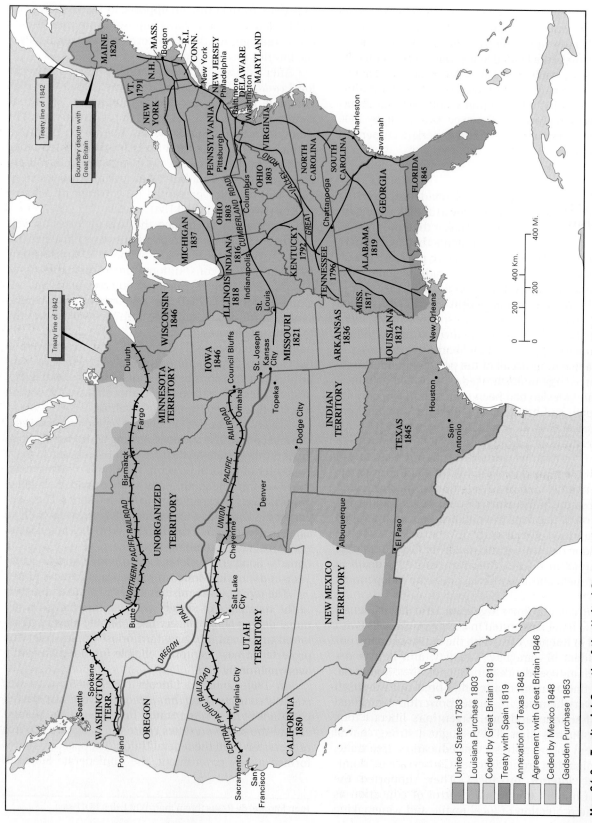

Map 24.3 Territorial Growth of the United States, 1783–1853 The rapid western expansion of the United States resulted from aggressive diplomacy and warfare against Mexico and Amerindian peoples. Railroad development helped integrate the trans-Mississippi west and promote economic expansion.

America, known as the Confederacy. Lincoln was able to preserve the Union, but his victory was purchased at an enormous cost. The U.S. Civil War (1861–1865), waged by southern Confederate forces and northern Union (U.S.) forces, was the most destructive conflict in the history of the Western Hemisphere. More than 600,000 lives were lost before the Confederacy surrendered in 1865. The Union victory led to the abolition of slavery. It also transferred national political power to a northern elite committed to industrial expansion and federal support for the construction of railroads and other internal improvements.

The Confederate States of America was better prepared politically and economically for independence than were the successful secessionist movements that broke up Gran Colombia and other Spanish American federations. Nevertheless, the Confederacy failed, in part because of poor timing. The new nations of the Western Hemisphere were most vulnerable during the early years of their existence; indeed, all the successful secessions occurred within the first decades following independence. In the case of the United States, southern secession was defeated by an experienced national government legitimated and strengthened by more than seven decades of relative stability reinforced by dramatic economic and population growth.

Foreign Interventions and Regional Wars

In the nineteenth century wars often determined national borders, access to natural resources, and control of markets in the Western Hemisphere. Even after the achievement of independence, some Western Hemisphere nations, like Mexico, had to defend themselves against Europe's great powers. Contested national borders and regional rivalries also led to wars between Western Hemisphere nations. By the end of the nineteenth century the United States, Brazil, Argentina, and Chile had all successfully waged wars against their neighbors and established themselves as regional powers.

Within thirty years of independence the United States fought a second war with England—the War of 1812 (1812–1815). The weakness of the new republic was symbolized by the burning of the White House and Capitol by British troops in 1814. This humiliation was soon overcome, however, and by the end of the nineteenth century the United States was the hemisphere's greatest military power. Its war against Spain in 1898–1899 created an American empire that reached from the Philippines in the Pacific Ocean to Puerto Rico in the Caribbean Sea (see Chapter 28).

Europe also challenged the sovereignty of Latin American nations. During the first decades after independence Argentina faced British and French naval blockades, and British naval forces systematically violated Brazil's territorial waters to stop the importation of slaves. Mexico faced more serious threats to its sovereignty, defeating a weak Spanish invasion in 1829 and a French assault on the city of Veracruz in 1838.

Mexico also faced a grave threat from the United States. In the 1820s Mexico had encouraged Americans to immigrate to its northern province of Texas. By the early 1830s Americans outnumbered Mexican nationals in Texas by four to one and were aggressively challenging Mexican laws such as the prohibition of slavery. In 1835 political turmoil in Mexico led to a rebellion in Texas by an alliance of Mexican liberals and American settlers. Mexico was defeated in a brief war, and in 1836 Texas gained its independence. In 1845 the United States made Texas a state, provoking war with Mexico a year later. The surrender of Mexico City to American forces compelled Mexico to accept a harsh treaty in 1848. Compounding the loss of Texas in 1836, the treaty of 1848 forced Mexico to cede vast territories to the United States, including present-day New Mexico, Arizona, and California. In return Mexico received $15 million. When gold was discovered in California in 1848, the magnitude of Mexico's loss became clear.

With the very survival of the nation at stake, Mexico's liberals took power and imposed sweeping reforms, including a new constitution in 1857 that limited the power of the Catholic Church and military. The reforms provoked a civil war with the conservatives (1858–1861). **Benito Juárez°** assumed the presidency and defeated the conservatives, who then turned to Napoleon III of France for assistance. In 1862, the French invaded Mexico, using unpaid government debts as an excuse, and Benito Juárez was forced to flee Mexico City. The French suspended the constitution and installed the Austrian Habsburg Maximilian as emperor of Mexico. Juárez organized an effective military resistance and after years of warfare drove the French army out of Mexico in 1867, aided by some U.S. diplomatic pressure. After capturing Maximilian, Juárez ordered his execution.

The victory over a powerful foreign enemy redeemed a nation that had earlier been humiliated by the United States. But the creation of democracy proved more elusive than the protection of Mexican sovereignty. Despite the Mexican constitution's prohibition of presidential reelection, Juárez would serve as president until his death in 1872.

Benito Juárez (beh-NEE-toh WAH-rez)

Execution of Emperor Maximilian of Mexico This painting by Edouard Manet shows the 1867 execution by firing squad of Maximilian and two of his Mexican generals. The defeat of the French intervention was a great triumph for Mexican patriots led by Benito Juárez. (Erich Lessing/Art Resource, NY)

As was clear in the Mexican-American War, wars between Western Hemisphere nations could lead to dramatic territorial changes. In two wars with neighbors Chile established itself as the leading military and economic power on the west coast of South America. Between 1836 and 1839 Chile defeated the Confederation of Peru and Bolivia. In 1879 Chilean and British investors in nitrate mines located in the Atacama Desert, a disputed border region, provoked a new war with Peru and Bolivia (War of the Pacific). The Chilean army and navy won a crushing victory in 1881, forcing Bolivia to cede its only outlet to the sea and Peru to yield the rich mining districts.

Argentina and Brazil fought over control of Uruguay in the 1820s, but a military stalemate eventually forced them to recognize Uruguayan independence. In 1865 Argentina and Uruguay joined Brazil to wage war against Paraguay (War of the Triple Alliance, or Paraguayan War). After five years of warfare the Paraguayan dictator Francisco Solano López° and more than 20 percent of the population of Paraguay had died. Paraguay suffered military occupation, lost territory to the victors, and was forced to open its markets to foreign trade.

Francisco Solano López (fran-CEES-co so-LAN-oh LOH-pehz)

Native Peoples and the Nation-State

Both diplomacy and military action shaped relations between the Western Hemisphere's new nation-states and the indigenous peoples living within them. During late colonial times, to avoid armed conflict and to limit the costs of frontier defense, Spanish, Portuguese, and British imperial governments attempted to restrict the expansion of settlements into territories already occupied by Amerindians. With independence, the colonial powers' role as mediator for and protector of native peoples ended.

Still-independent Amerindian peoples posed a significant military challenge to many Western Hemisphere republics. Weakened by civil wars and constitutional crises, many of the new nations were less able to maintain frontier peace than had the colonial governments. After independence Amerindian peoples in Argentina, the United States, Chile, and Mexico succeeded in pushing back some frontier settlements. But despite these early victories, by the end of the 1880s native military resistance was finally overcome in both North and South America.

After the American Revolution, the rapid expansion of agricultural settlements threatened native peoples in North America. Between 1790 and 1810 tens of

Navajo Leaders Gathered in Washington to Negotiate   As settlers, ranchers, and miners pushed west in the nineteenth century, leaders of Amerindian peoples were forced to negotiate territorial concessions with representatives of the U.S. government. In order to impress Amerindian peoples with the wealth and power of the United States, many of their leaders were invited to Washington, D.C. This photo shows Navajo leaders and their Anglo translators in Washington, D.C., in 1874.   (Frank McNitt Photograph Collection, Image #5851. Courtesy of the New Mexico State Records Center)

thousands of settlers entered territories guaranteed to Amerindians in treaties with the United States. More than 200,000 white settlers were present in Ohio alone by 1810. Indigenous leaders responded by seeking the support of British officials in Canada and by forging broad indigenous alliances. American forces decisively defeated one such Amerindian alliance in 1794 in Ohio. After 1800 two Shawnee leaders, the brothers **Tecumseh°** and Prophet (Tenskwatawa), created a larger and better organized alliance among Amerindian peoples in the Ohio River Valley and gained some support from Great Britain. In 1811 American military forces attacked and destroyed the ritual center of the alliance, Prophet Town. The final blow came during the War of 1812 when

Tecumseh, fighting alongside his British allies, was killed in battle.

In the 1820s white settlers forced native peoples living in Ohio, southern Indiana and Illinois, southwestern Michigan, most of Missouri, central Alabama, and southern Mississippi to cede their land. The 1828 presidential election of Andrew Jackson, a veteran of wars against native peoples, brought matters to a head. In 1830 Congress passed the Indian Removal Act, forcing the resettlement of the Cherokee, Creek, Choctaw, and other eastern peoples to land west of the Mississippi River. The removal was carried out in the 1830s, and nearly half of the forced migrants died on this journey, known as the Trail of Tears.

Amerindians living on the Great Plains offered formidable resistance to the expansion of white settlement. By the time substantial numbers of white buffalo hunters,

---

Tecumseh (teh-CUM-sah)

cattlemen, and settlers reached the American west, indigenous peoples were skilled users of horses and firearms. These technologies had transformed the cultures of the Sioux, Comanche, Pawnee, Kiowa, and other plains peoples. The improved efficiency of the buffalo hunt reduced their dependence on agriculture and expanded their territories. As a result, women, whose primary responsibility had been raising crops, lost prestige and social power to male hunters. Living arrangements also changed as the single-family tepees of migratory buffalo hunters replaced the multigenerational lodges of the traditional farming economy.

During the U.S. Civil War, native peoples experienced a disruption of their trade with Eastern merchants and the suspension of payments pledged by previous treaties. Then after the war a new wave of settlers pushed onto the plains. Buffalo herds were hunted to near extinction for their hides, and land was lost to farmers and ranchers. During nearly four decades of armed conflict with the United States Army, Amerindian peoples were gradually forced to give up their land and their traditional ways. The Comanche, who had dominated the southern plains during the period of Spanish and Mexican rule, were forced by the U.S. government to cede most of their land in Texas in 1865. The Sioux and their allies resisted. In 1876 they overwhelmed General George Armstrong Custer and the Seventh Cavalry in the Battle of Little Bighorn (in the southern part of the present-day state of Montana). But finally the Sioux were also forced to accept reservation life. Military campaigns in the 1870s and 1880s then broke the resistance of the Apache.

The indigenous peoples of Argentina and Chile experienced a similar trajectory of adaptation, resistance, and defeat. Herds of wild cattle provided indigenous peoples with a limitless food supply, and horses and metal weapons increased their military capacities. Thus, for a while, the native peoples of Argentina and Chile effectively checked the southern expansion of agriculture and ranching. Amerindian raiders operated within 100 miles (160 kilometers) of Buenos Aires into the 1860s. Unable to defeat these resourceful enemies, the governments of Argentina and Chile relied on an elaborate system of gift giving and prisoner exchanges to maintain peace on the frontier. By the 1860s, however, population increase, political stability, and military modernization allowed Argentina and Chile to take the offensive.

In the 1870s the government of Argentina used overwhelming military force to crush native resistance. Thousands of Amerindians were killed, and survivors were driven onto marginal land. In Chile the story was the same. When civil war and an economic depression weakened the Chilean government at the end of the 1850s, the Mapuches° (called "Araucanians" by the Spanish) attempted to push back frontier settlements. Despite early successes the Mapuches were defeated in the 1870s by modern weaponry. In Chile, as in Argentina and the United States, government authorities justified military campaigns against native peoples by demonizing them. Newspaper editorials and the speeches of politicians portrayed Amerindians as brutal and cruel, and as obstacles to progress. In April 1859 a Chilean newspaper commented:

> The necessity, not only to punish the Araucanian race, but also to make it impotent to harm us, is well recognized . . . as the only way to rid the country of a million evils. It is well understood that they are odious and prejudicial guests in Chile . . . conciliatory measures have accomplished nothing with this stupid race—the infamy and disgrace of the Chilean nation.[4]

Political divisions and civil wars within the new nations could also provide an opportunity for long-pacified native peoples to rebel. In the Yucatán region of Mexico, the owners of henequen (the agave plant that produces fiber used for twine) and sugar plantations had forced many Maya° communities off their traditional agricultural lands, reducing thousands to peonage. This same regional elite declared itself independent of the government in Mexico City that was convulsed by civil war in the late 1830s. The Mexican government was unable to reestablish control because it faced the greater threat of invasion by the United States. Seeing their oppressors divided, the Maya rebelled in 1847. This well-organized and popular uprising, known as the **Caste War**, nearly returned the Yucatán to Maya rule. Grievances accumulated over more than three hundred years led to great violence and property destruction. The Maya were not defeated until the war with the United States ended. Even then Maya rebels retreated to unoccupied territories and created an independent state, which they called the "Empire of the Cross." Organized around a mix of traditional beliefs and Christian symbols, this indigenous state resisted Mexican forces until 1870. A few defiant Maya strongholds survived until 1901.

Mapuches (mah-POO-chez)
Maya (MY-ah)

The Challenge of Social and Economic Change

During the nineteenth century the newly independent nations of the Western Hemisphere struggled to realize the Enlightenment ideals of freedom and individual liberty that had helped ignite the revolutions for independence. The achievement of these objectives was slowed by the persistence of slavery and other oppressive colonial-era institutions. Cultural and racial diversity also presented obstacles to reform. Nevertheless, by century's end reform movements in many of the hemisphere's nations had succeeded in ending the slave trade, abolishing slavery, expanding voting rights, and assimilating immigrants from Asia and Europe.

Increased industrialization and greater involvement in the evolving world economy challenged the region's political stability and social arrangements. A small number of nations embraced industrialization, but most Western Hemisphere economies became increasingly dependent on the export of agricultural goods and minerals during the nineteenth century. While the industrializing nations of the hemisphere became richer than the nations that remained exporters of raw materials, all the region's economies became more vulnerable and volatile as a result of greater participation in international markets. Like contemporary movements for social reform, efforts to assert national economic control produced powerful new political forces.

The Abolition of Slavery

In both the United States and Latin America strong antislavery sentiments were expressed during the struggles for independence. Revolutionary leaders of nearly all the new nations of the Western Hemisphere asserted ideals of universal freedom and citizenship that contrasted sharply with the reality of slavery. Men and women who wanted to outlaw slavery were called **abolitionists**. Despite their efforts, slavery survived in much of the hemisphere until the 1850s. In regions where the export of plantation products was most important—such as the United States, Brazil, and Cuba—the abolition of slavery was achieved with great difficulty.

In the United States slavery was weakened by abolition in some northern states and by the termination of the African slave trade in 1808. But this progress was stalled by the profitable expansion of cotton agriculture after the War of 1812. In Spanish America tens of thousands of slaves gained freedom by joining revolutionary armies during the wars for independence. After independence, most Spanish American republics prohibited the slave trade. Counteracting that trend was the growing international demand for sugar and coffee, products traditionally produced on plantations by slaves. As prices rose for plantation products in the first half of the nineteenth century, Brazil and Cuba (the island remained a Spanish colony until 1899) increased their imports of slaves.

During the long struggle to end slavery in the United States, American abolitionists argued that slavery offended both morality and the universal rights asserted in the Declaration of Independence. Abolitionist Theodore Weld articulated the religious objection to slavery in 1834:

> No condition of birth, no shade of color, no mere misfortune of circumstance, can annul the birth-right charter, which God has bequeathed to every being upon whom he has stamped his own image, by making him a free *moral agent* [emphasis in original], and that he who robs his fellow man of this tramples upon right, subverts justice, outrages humanity . . . and sacrilegiously assumes the prerogative of God.[5]

Two groups denied full rights of citizenship under the Constitution, women and free African Americans, played important roles in the abolition of slavery. Women served on the executive committee of the American Anti-Slavery Society and produced some of the most effective propaganda against slavery. Eventually, thousands of women joined the abolitionist cause, where they provided leadership and were effective speakers and propagandists. When social conservatives attacked this highly visible public role, many women abolitionists responded by becoming public advocates of female suffrage as well.

Frederick Douglass, a former slave, became one of the most effective abolitionist speakers and writers. More radical black leaders pushed the abolitionist movement to accept the inevitability of violence. They saw civil war or slave insurrection as necessary for ending slavery. In 1843 Henry Highland Garnet stirred the National Colored Convention when he demanded, "Brethren, arise, arise, arise! . . . Let every slave in the land do this and the days of slavery are numbered."[6] In the 1850s the growing electoral strength of the newly formed Republican Party forced a confrontation between slave and free states. After the election of Abraham Lincoln in 1860, the first of the eleven southern states that formed the Confederacy seceded from the Union. During the Civil War pressure for emancipation rose as tens of thousands of black freemen and escaped slaves joined the Union army. Hundreds of thousands of other slaves fled their masters' plantations and farms for the protection of advancing northern armies. In 1863, in the midst of the Civil War and two years after the abolition of serfdom in Russia (see Chapter 26), President Lincoln began the abolition of slavery by issuing the Emancipation Proclamation, which ended slavery in rebel states not occupied by the Union army. Final abolition was accomplished after the war, in 1865, by the Thirteenth Amendment to the Constitution. Most African Americans continued to live in harsh conditions as sharecroppers long after the end of slavery. By the end of the century nearly all southern states had instituted "Jim Crow" laws that segregated blacks in public transportation, jobs, and schools. This coincided with increased racial violence that saw an average of fifty blacks lynched each year.

In Brazil slavery survived for more than two decades after it was abolished in the United States. Progress toward abolition was not only slower but also depended on foreign pressure. In 1830 Brazil signed a treaty with the British ending the slave trade. Despite this agreement, Brazil illegally imported over a half-million more African slaves before the British navy finally forced compliance in the 1850s. In the 1850s and 1860s the Brazilian emperor, Pedro II, and many liberals worked to abolish slavery, but their desire to find a form of gradual emancipation acceptable to slave owners slowed progress.

During the war with Paraguay (1865–1870) large numbers of slaves joined the Brazilian army in exchange for freedom. Their loyalty and heroism undermined the military's support for slavery. Educated Brazilians increasingly viewed slavery as an obstacle to economic development and an impediment to democratic reform. In the 1870s, as abolitionist sentiment grew, reformers forced the passage of laws providing for the gradual emancipation of slaves. When political support for slavery weakened in the 1880s, growing numbers of slaves forced the issue by fleeing from bondage. By then army leaders were resisting demands to capture and return runaway slaves. Legislation abolishing slavery finally was passed by the Brazilian parliament and accepted by the emperor in 1888.

The plantations of the Caribbean region received almost 40 percent of all African slaves shipped to the New World. Throughout the region tiny white minorities lived surrounded by slave and free colored majorities. At the end of the eighteenth century the slave rebellion in Saint Domingue (see Chapter 22) spread terror among slave owners across the Caribbean. Because of fear that any effort to overthrow colonial rule might unleash new

A Former Brazilian Slave Returns from Military Service
The heroic participation of black freemen and slaves in the Paraguayan War (1865–1870) led many Brazilians to advocate the abolition of slavery. The original caption for this drawing reads: "On his return from the war in Paraguay: Full of glory, covered with laurels, after having spilled his blood in defense of the fatherland and to free a people from slavery, the volunteer sees his own mother bound and whipped! Awful reality!" (Courtesy, Fundacao Biblioteca Nacional, Brazil)

slave rebellions, there was little enthusiasm among free settlers in Caribbean colonies for independence. Nor did local support for abolition appear among white settlers or free colored populations. Thus abolition in most Caribbean colonies commonly resulted from political decisions made in Europe by colonial powers.

Nevertheless, like slaves in Brazil, the United States, and Spanish America, slaves in the Caribbean helped propel the movement toward abolition by rebelling, running away, and resisting in more subtle ways. Although initially unsuccessful, the rebellions that threatened other French Caribbean colonies after the Haitian Revolution (1791–1804) weakened France's support for slavery. Jamaica and other British colonies also experienced rebellions and saw the spread of communities of runaways. In Spanish Cuba as well, slave resistance forced increases in expenditures for police forces in the nineteenth century.

After 1800 the profitability of sugar plantations in the British West Indian colonies declined with increased competition from Cuba, and a coalition of labor groups, Protestant dissenters, and free traders in Britain pushed for the abolition of slavery. Britain, the major participant in the eighteenth-century expansion of slavery in the Americas, ended its participation in the slave trade in 1807. It then negotiated a series of treaties with Spain, Brazil, and other importers of slaves to eliminate the slave trade to the Americas. Once these treaties were in place, British naval forces acted to force compliance.

Slavery in British colonies was abolished in 1834. However, the law compelled "freed" slaves to remain with former masters as "apprentices." Abuses by planters and resistance to apprenticeship by former slaves led to complete abolition, the ending of forced apprenticeships, in 1838. A decade later slavery in the French Caribbean was abolished after upheavals in France led to the overthrow of the government of Louis Philippe (see Chapter 22). The abolition of slavery in the Dutch Empire in 1863 freed 33,000 slaves in Surinam and 12,000 in the Antilles. Slave owners were compensated for their loss, and the freedmen of Surinam were required to provide ten years of compensated labor to their former owners.

In the Caribbean, slavery lasted longest in Cuba and Puerto Rico, Spain's remaining colonies. Britain's use of diplomatic pressure and naval force to limit the arrival of African slaves weakened slavery after 1820. More important, however, was the growth of support for abolition in these colonies. Both Cuba and Puerto Rico had larger white and free colored populations than did the Caribbean colonies of Britain and France. As a result, there was less fear in Cuba and Puerto Rico that abolition would lead to the political ascendancy of former slaves (as had occurred in Haiti). In Puerto Rico, where slaves numbered approximately thirty thousand, local reformers secured the abolition of slavery in 1873. In the midst of a decade-long war to defeat forces seeking the independence of Cuba, the Spanish government gradually moved toward abolition. Initially, slave children born after September 18, 1868, were freed but obligated to work for their former masters for eighteen years. In 1880 all other slaves were freed on the condition that they serve their masters for eight additional years. Finally, in 1886 these conditions were eliminated; slavery was abolished; and Cuban patriots forged the multiracial alliance that was to initiate a war for Cuban independence in 1895 (see Chapter 28).

Immigration

During the colonial period free Europeans were a minority among immigrants to the Western Hemisphere. Between 1500 and 1760 African slaves entering the Western Hemisphere outnumbered European immigrants by nearly two to one. Another 4 million or so African slaves were imported before the effective end of the slave trade at the end of the 1850s. As the African slave trade came to an end, the arrival of millions of immigrants from Europe and Asia contributed to the further transformation of the Western Hemisphere. This nineteenth-century wave of immigration fostered rapid economic growth and the occupation of frontier regions in the United States, Canada, Argentina, Chile, and Brazil. It also promoted urbanization. By century's end nearly all of the hemisphere's fastest-growing cities (Buenos Aires, Chicago, New York, and São Paulo, for example) had large immigrant populations.

Europe provided the majority of immigrants to the Western Hemisphere during the nineteenth century. For much of the century they came primarily from western Europe, but after 1870 most came from southern and eastern Europe. The scale of immigration increased dramatically in the second half of the century. The United States received approximately 600,000 European immigrants in the 1830s, 1.5 million in the 1840s, and then 2.5 million per decade until 1880. In the 1890s an astonishing total of 5.2 million immigrants arrived. This helped push the national population from 39 million in 1871 to 63 million in 1891, an increase of 62 percent. Most of the immigrants ended up in cities. Chicago, for example, grew from 444,000 in 1870 to 1.7 million in 1900.

European immigration to Latin America also increased dramatically after 1880. Combined immigration to Argentina and Brazil rose from just under 130,000 in the 1860s to 1.7 million in the 1890s. By 1910, 30 percent of the Argentine population was foreign-born, more than twice the proportion in the U.S. population. Argentina was an extremely attractive destination for European immigrants, receiving more than twice as many immigrants as Canada between 1870 and 1930. Even so, immigration to Canada increased tenfold during this period.

Asian immigration to the Western Hemisphere increased after 1850. Between 1849 and 1875 approximately 100,000 Chinese immigrants arrived in Peru and another 120,000 entered Cuba. Canada attracted about 50,000 Chinese in the second half of the century. The United States, however, was the primary North American destination for Chinese immigrants, receiving 300,000 between 1854 and 1882. India also contributed to the social transformation of the Western Hemisphere, sending more than a half-million immigrants to the Caribbean region.

Chinese Funeral in Vancouver, Canada   In the 1890s Vancouver was an important Western Hemisphere destination for Chinese immigrants. This photo shows how an important element of traditional Chinese culture thrived among the storefronts and streetcar lines of the late-Victorian Canadian city.   (Vancouver Public Library, Special Collections, VPL #17064)

British Guiana alone received 238,000 immigrants, mostly indentured laborers, from the Asian subcontinent.

Despite the obvious economic benefits that accompanied this inflow of people, hostility to immigration mounted in many nations. Nativist political movements argued that large numbers of foreigners could not be successfully integrated into national political cultures. By the end of the century fear and prejudice led many governments in the Western Hemisphere to limit immigration or to distinguish between "desirable" and "undesirable" immigrants, commonly favoring Europeans over Asians.

Asians faced more obstacles to immigration than did Europeans and were more often victims of violence and extreme forms of discrimination in the New World. In the 1870s and 1880s anti-Chinese riots erupted in many western cities in the United States. Congress responded to this wave of racism by passing the Chinese Exclusion Act in 1882, which eliminated most Chinese immigration. In 1886 fears that Canada was being threatened by "inferior races" led to the imposition of a head tax that made immigration to Canada more difficult for Chinese families. During this same period strong anti-Chinese prejudice surfaced in Peru, Mexico, and Cuba. Japanese immigrants in Brazil and East Indians in the English-speaking Caribbean faced similar prejudice.

Immigrants from Europe also faced prejudice and discrimination. In the United States, Italians were commonly portrayed as criminals or anarchists. In Argentina, social scientists attempted to prove that Italian immigrants were more violent and less honest than the native-born population. Immigrants from Spain were widely stereotyped in Argentina as miserly and dishonest. Eastern European Jews seeking to escape pogroms and discrimination at home found themselves barred from many educational institutions and professional careers in both the United States and Latin America. Negative stereotypes were invented for Irish, German, Swedish, Polish, and Middle Eastern immigrants as well. The perceived grievances used to justify these common prejudices were remarkably similar from Canada to Argentina. Immigrants, it was argued, threatened the well-being of native-born workers by accepting low wages, and they threatened national culture by resisting assimilation.

Many intellectuals and political leaders wondered if the evolving mix of culturally diverse populations could sustain a common citizenship. As a result, efforts were directed toward compelling immigrants to assimilate. Schools became cultural battlegrounds where language, cultural values, and patriotic feelings were transmitted to the children of immigrants. Across the hemisphere, school curricula were revised to promote national culture. Ignoring Canada's large French-speaking population, an English-speaking Canadian reformer commented on recent immigration: "If Canada is to become in a real sense a nation, if our people are to become one people, we must have one language."[7] Fear and prejudice were among the emotions promoting the singing of patriotic songs, the veneration of national flags and other symbols, and the writing of national histories that emphasized patriotism and civic virtue.

American Cultures

Despite discrimination, immigrants continued to stream into the Western Hemisphere, introducing new languages, living arrangements, technologies, and work customs. Immigrants altered the politics of many of the hemisphere's nations as they sought to influence government policies. Where immigrants arrived in the greatest numbers, they put enormous pressure on housing, schools, and social welfare services. To compensate for their isolation from home, language, and culture, immigrants often created ethnically based mutual aid societies, sports and leisure clubs, and neighborhoods. Ethnic organizations and districts provided valuable social and economic support for recent arrivals while sometimes worsening the fears of the native-born that immigration posed a threat to national culture.

Immigrants were changed by their experiences in their adopted nations and by programs that forced them to accept new cultural values through education or, in some cases, service in the military. Similar efforts to forge national cultures were put in place in Europe by modernizing governments at the same time. The modification of the language, customs, values, and behaviors of a group as a result of contact with people from another culture is called **acculturation**.

Immigrants and their children, in turn, made their mark on the cultures of their adopted nations in the Americas. They learned the language spoken in their adopted countries as fast as possible in order to improve their earning capacity. At the same time, words and phrases from their languages entered the vocabularies of the host nations. Languages as diverse as Yiddish and Italian strongly influenced American English, Argentine Spanish, and Brazilian Portuguese. Dietary practices introduced from Europe and Asia altered the cuisine of nearly every American nation. In turn, immigrants commonly added native foods to their diets, especially the hemisphere's abundant and relatively cheap meats.

Throughout the hemisphere culture and popular music changed as well. For example, the Argentine tango, based on African-Argentine rhythms, was transformed by new instrumentation and orchestral arrangements brought by Italian immigrants. Mexican ballads blended with English folk music in the U.S. southwest, and Italian operas played to packed houses in Buenos Aires. Sports, games of chance, and fashion also experienced this process of borrowing and exchange.

Union movements and electoral politics in the hemisphere also felt the influence of new arrivals who aggressively sought to influence government and improve working conditions. The labor movements of Mexico, Argentina, and the United States, in particular, were influenced by the anarchist and socialist beliefs of European immigrants. Mutual benevolent societies and less-formal ethnic associations pooled resources to help immigrants

Arrest of Labor Activist in Buenos Aires   The labor movement in Buenos Aires grew in numbers and became more radical with the arrival of tens of thousands of Italian and Spanish immigrants. Fearful of socialist and anarchist unions, the government of Argentina used an expanded police force to break strikes by arresting labor leaders.   (Archivo General de la Nación, Buenos Aires)

open businesses, aid the immigration of relatives, or bury family members. They also established links with political movements, sometimes exchanging votes for favors.

Women's Rights and the Struggle for Social Justice

The abolition of slavery in the Western Hemisphere did not end racial discrimination or provide full political rights for every citizen. Not only blacks but also women, new immigrants, and native peoples in nearly every Western Hemisphere nation suffered the effects of political and economic discrimination. During the second half of the nineteenth century reformers struggled to remove these limits on citizenship while also addressing the welfare needs of workers and the poor.

In 1848 a group of women angered by their exclusion from an international antislavery meeting issued a call for a meeting to discuss women's rights. The **Women's Rights Convention** at Seneca Falls, New York, issued a statement that said, in part, "We hold these truths to be self-evident: that all men and women are equal." While moderates focused on the issues of greater economic independence and full legal rights, increasing numbers of women demanded the right to vote. Others lobbied to provide better conditions for women working outside the home, especially in textile factories. Sarah Grimké responded to criticism of women's activism:

> This has been the language of man since he laid aside the whip as a means to keep woman in subjection. He spares her body, but the war he has waged against her mind, her heart, and her soul, has been no less destructive to her as a moral being. How monstrous is the doctrine that woman is to be dependent on man![8]

Progress toward equality between men and women was equally slow in Canada and Latin America. Canada's first women doctors received their training in the United States because no woman was able to receive a medical degree in Canada until 1895. Full enfranchisement occurred in Canada in the twentieth century, but Canadian women did gain the right to vote in some provincial and municipal elections before 1900. Like women in the United States, Canadian women provided leadership in temperance, child welfare, and labor reform movements. Argentina and Uruguay were among the first Latin American nations to provide public education for women. Both nations introduced coeducation in the 1870s. Chilean women gained access to some careers in

medicine and law in the 1870s. In Argentina the first woman doctor graduated from medical school in 1899. In Brazil, where many women were active in the abolitionist movement, four women graduated in medicine by 1882. Throughout the hemisphere more rapid progress was achieved in lower-status careers that threatened male economic power less directly, and by the end of the century women dominated elementary school teaching throughout the Western Hemisphere.

From Canada to Argentina and Chile, the majority of working-class women had no direct involvement in these reform movements, but they succeeded in transforming gender relations in their daily lives. By the end of the nineteenth century, large numbers of poor women worked outside the home on farms, in markets, and, increasingly, in factories. Many bore full responsibility for providing for their children. Whether men thought women should remain in the home or not, by the end of the century women were unambiguously present in the economy (see also Chapter 27).

Throughout the hemisphere there was little progress toward eliminating racial discrimination. Blacks were denied the vote throughout the southern United States. They also were subjected to the indignity of segregation—consigned to separate schools, hotels, restaurants, seats in public transportation, and even water fountains. Racial discrimination against men and women of African descent was also common in Latin America, though seldom spelled out in legal codes. Unlike the southern states of the United States, Latin American nations did not insist on formal racial segregation or permit lynching. Nor did they enforce a strict color line. Many men and women of mixed background were able to enter the skilled working class or middle class. Latin Americans tended to view racial identity across a continuum of physical characteristics rather than in the narrow terms of black and white that defined race relations in the United States.

The abolition of slavery in Latin America did not lead to an end to racial discrimination. Some of the participants in the abolition struggles later organized to promote racial integration. They demanded access to education, the right to vote, and greater economic opportunity, pointing out the economic and political costs of denying full rights to all citizens. Their success depended on effective political organization and on forging alliances with sympathetic white politicians. Black intellectuals also struggled to overturn racist stereotypes. In Brazil, Argentina, and Cuba, as in the United States, political and literary magazines celebrating black cultural achievement became powerful weapons in the struggle against racial discrimination. Although men

New Technologies Change the Mining Industry   Powerful hydraulic technologies were introduced in western mining sites in the United States. This early photo shows how high-power water jets could transform the natural environment.   (Colorado Historical Society)

and women of African descent continued to experience prejudice and discrimination everywhere in the Americas, successful men and women of mixed descent in Latin America confronted fewer obstacles to their advancement than did similar groups in the United States.

Development and Underdevelopment

The Atlantic economy experienced three periods of economic contraction during the nineteenth century, but nearly all the nations of the Western Hemisphere were richer in 1900 than in 1800. The Industrial Revolution, worldwide population growth, and an increasingly integrated world market stimulated economic expansion (see Environment and Technology: Constructing the Port of Buenos Aires, Argentina). Wheat, corn, wool, meats, and nonprecious minerals joined the region's earlier exports of silver, sugar, dyes, coffee, and cotton. During the nineteenth century the United States was the only Western Hemisphere nation to industrialize, but nearly every government promoted new economic activities. Governments

and private enterprises invested in roads, railroads, canals, and telegraphs to better serve distant markets. Most governments adopted tariff and monetary policies to foster economic diversification and growth. Despite these efforts, by 1900 only three Western Hemisphere nations—the United States, Canada, and Argentina—achieved individual income levels similar to those of western Europe. All three nations had open land, temperate climates, diverse resources, and large inflows of immigrants.

New demands for copper, zinc, lead, coal, and tin unleashed by the Industrial Revolution led to mining booms in the western United States, Mexico, and Chile. Unlike the small-scale and often short-term gold- and silver-mining operations of the colonial era, the mining companies of the late nineteenth century were heavily capitalized international corporations that could bully governments and buy political favors. During this period, European and North American corporations owned most new mining enterprises in Latin America. Petroleum development, which occurred at the end of the century in Mexico and elsewhere, would follow this

ENVIRONMENT + TECHNOLOGY

Constructing the Port of Buenos Aires, Argentina

Located on the banks of the Río de la Plata, Buenos Aires had been a major commercial center and port since the late eighteenth century. But Buenos Aires was not a natural harbor. Because of the shallowness of the river, the largest oceangoing ships were forced to anchor hundreds of yards offshore while goods and passengers were unloaded by small boats or by specially built ox carts with huge wheels. Smaller vessels docked at a river port to the city's south.

By the 1880s the Argentine economy was being transformed by the growing demands of European consumers for meat and grain. As exports surged and land values exploded, the wages of Argentines rose, and the nation became a favored destination for European immigrants. Argentina was becoming the wealthiest nation in Latin America.

Excavation of Port of Buenos Aires, Argentina   Relying on foreign capital and engineering, the government of Argentina improved the port to facilitate the nation's rapidly expanding export economy. (Courtesy, Hack Hoffenburg, South American Resources)

The nation's political and economic elites decided that future growth required the modernization and expansion of port facilities. Two competing plans were debated. The first emphasized the incremental expansion and dredging of the river port. This was supported by local engineers and political groups suspicious of foreign economic interests. The second, and ultimately successful, plan involved dredging a port and deep-water channel from the low mud flats near the city center. This plan was more expensive, relying on British engineering firms, British banks, and British technology. It was supported by Argentine economic interests most closely tied to the European export trade and by national political leaders who believed progress and prosperity required the imitation of European models. Already the British were the nation's primary creditors as well as leaders in the development of the nation's railroads, streetcar lines, and gas works in Buenos Aires.

The photograph shows the construction of Puerto Madero, the new port of Buenos Aires, in the 1890s. The work force was almost entirely recruited from recent immigrants. The engineering staff was dominated by British experts. Most of the profits were culled by the local elite through real estate deals and commissions associated with construction. Puerto Madero, named after its local promoter, was opened in stages beginning in 1890. Cost overruns and corruption stretched out completion to 1898. By 1910 arrivals and departures reached thirty thousand ships and 18 million tons. But the project was poorly designed, and "improvements" were still being made in the 1920s.

Why had the government of Argentina chosen the costliest and most difficult design? Argentine politicians were seduced by the idea of modernity; they chose the most complex and technologically sophisticated solution to the port problem. And they believed that British engineering and British capital were guarantees of modernity. The new port facilities did facilitate a boom in exports and imports, and the huge public works budget did provide incomes for thousands of laborers. However, debts, design flaws, and the increased influence of foreign capital in Argentina left a legacy of problems that Argentina would be forced to deal with in the future. (See the discussion of Juan Perón in Chapter 31.)

pattern as well (see the discussion of the Mexican economy during the Díaz dictatorship in Chapter 31).

New technology accelerated economic integration, but the high cost of this technology often increased dependence on foreign capital. Many governments promoted railroads by granting tax benefits, free land, and monopoly rights to both domestic and foreign investors. By 1890 vast areas of the Great Plains in the United States, the Canadian prairie, the Argentine pampas, and parts of northern Mexico were producing grain and livestock for foreign markets opened by the development of railroads. Steamships also lowered the cost of transportation to distant markets, and the telegraph stimulated expansion by speeding information about the demand for and availability of products.

The simultaneous acquisition of several new technologies multiplied the effects of individual technologies. In Argentina the railroad, the telegraph, barbed wire, and refrigeration all appeared in the 1870s and 1880s. Although Argentina had had abundant livestock herds since the colonial period, the distance from Europe's markets prevented Argentine cattle raisers from exporting fresh meat or live animals. Technology overcame these obstacles. The combination of railroads and the telegraph lowered freight costs and improved information about markets. Steamships shortened trans-Atlantic crossings, and refrigerated ships made it possible to sell meat in the markets of Europe. As land values rose and livestock breeding improved, new investments were protected by barbed wire, the first inexpensive fencing available on the nearly treeless plains.

Growing interdependence and increased competition produced deep structural differences among Western Hemisphere economies by 1900. Two distinct economic tracks became clearly visible. One led to industrialization and prosperity, what is now called **development**. The other continued colonial dependence on exporting raw materials and on low-wage industries, now commonly called **underdevelopment**. By 1900 material prosperity was greater and economic development more diversified in English-speaking North America than in the nations of Latin America. With a temperate climate, vast fertile prairies, and an influx of European immigrants, Argentina was the only Latin American nation to approach the prosperity of the United States and Canada.

Changes in the performance of international markets helped determine the trajectory of Western Hemisphere economies as new nations promoted economic development. When the United States gained independence, the world capitalist economy was in a period of rapid growth. With a large merchant fleet, a diversified economy that included some manufacturing, and adequate banking and insurance services, the United States benefited from the expansion of the world economy. Rapid population growth due in large measure to immigration, high levels of individual wealth, widespread landownership, and relatively high literacy rates also fostered rapid economic development in the United States. The rapid expansion of railroad mileage suggests this success. In 1865 the United States had the longest network in the world. By 1915 it had multiplied eleven-fold (see Map 24.4). Steel production grew rapidly as well, with the United States overtaking Britain and Germany in the 1890s. One cost of the nation's industrialization was the vastly expanded power of monopolies, like Standard Oil, over political life.

Canada's struggle for greater political autonomy led to the Confederation of 1867, which coincided with a second period of global economic expansion. Canada also benefited from a special trading relationship with Britain, the world's preeminent industrial nation, and from a rising tide of immigrants after 1850. Nevertheless, some regions within each of these prosperous North American nations—Canada's Maritime Provinces and the southern part of the United States, for example—demonstrated the same patterns of underdevelopment found in Latin America.

Latin American nations gained independence in the 1820s, when the global economy was contracting due to the end of the Napoleonic Wars and market saturation provoked by the early stages of European industrialization. In the colonial period Spain and Portugal had promoted the production of agricultural and mining exports. After independence those raw-material exports faced increased competition. Although these sectors experienced periods of great prosperity in the nineteenth century, they also faced stiff competition and falling prices as new regions began production or new products captured markets. Sugar, coffee, nitrates, and copper all followed this pattern.

The history of the specialized Latin American economies, subject to periodic problems of oversupply and low prices, was one of boom and bust. Many Latin American governments sought to promote exports in the face of increased competition and falling prices by resisting union activity and demands for higher wages and by opening domestic markets to foreign manufactures. Resulting low wages and an abundance of foreign manufactured goods, in turn, undermined efforts to promote industrialization in Latin America.

Weak governments, political instability, and, in some cases, civil war also slowed Latin American economic

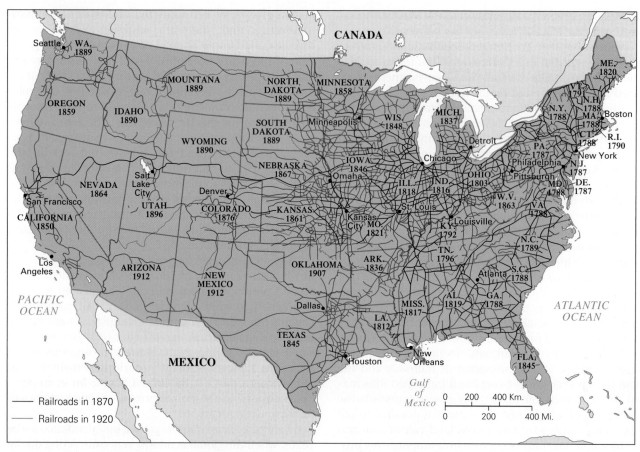

Map 24.4 The Expansion of the United States, 1850–1920 The settlement of western territories and their admission as states depended on migration, the exploitation of natural resources, and important new technologies like railroads and telegraphs that facilitated economic and political integration.

development. A comparative examination of Western Hemisphere economic history makes clear that stable and reliable public administration is a necessary part of the development process. Because Latin America was dependent on capital and technology from abroad, Great Britain and, by the end of the century, the United States were often able to impose unfavorable trade conditions or even intervene militarily to protect investments. The combined impact of these domestic and international impediments to development became clear when Mexico, Chile, and Argentina failed to achieve high levels of domestic investment in manufacturing late in the nineteenth century, despite a rapid accumulation of wealth derived from traditional exports.

Altered Environments

Population growth, economic expansion, new technologies, and the introduction of plants and animals to new regions dramatically altered the environment of the Western Hemisphere. Cuba's planters cut down many of the island's forests in the early nineteenth century to expand sugar production. Growing demand for meat led ranchers to expand livestock-raising into fragile environments in Argentina, Uruguay, southern Brazil, and the southwestern United States. Other forms of commercial agriculture also threatened the environment. Farmers in South Carolina and Georgia gained a short-term increase in cotton production by abandoning crop rotation after 1870, but this practice quickly led to soil exhaustion and erosion. Similarly, coffee planters in Brazil exhausted soil fertility with a destructive cycle of overplanting followed by expansion onto forest reserves cleared by cutting and burning. The landscapes of Argentina, Brazil, and the United States were transformed by massive transfers of land from public to private ownership in order to promote livestock-raising and agriculture. Not only was land worked more intensively, but new technologies had environmental effects as well. The use of steel plows on North American prairies and Argentine pampas eliminated many native grasses and increased the threat of soil erosion. While larger populations and new technologies led to dynamic economic expansion, fragile environments were put under extreme pressure.

Rapid urbanization also put heavy pressure on the environment. New York, Chicago, Rio de Janeiro, Buenos Aires, and Mexico City were among the world's fastest-growing cities in the nineteenth century. Governments strained to provide adequate sewers, clean water, and garbage disposal. Timber companies clear-cut large areas of Michigan, Wisconsin, and the Appalachian Mountains to provide lumber for railroad ties and frame houses, pulp for paper, and fuel for locomotives and foundries. Under the Timber and Stone Act of 1878, the U.S. government sold more than 3.5 million additional acres (1.4 million hectares) of public land to individual and corporations at low cost by 1900. At the same time, the forest industries of British Honduras (now Belize), Nicaragua, and Guatemala grew rapidly in response to demand in Europe and North America for tropical hardwoods like mahogany. As forest throughout the hemisphere was cleared, animal habitats and native plant species disappeared.

The scale of mining operation grew in Nevada, Montana, and California, accelerating erosion and pollution.

Similar results occurred in other mining areas. The expansion of nitrate mining and, later, open-pit copper mining in Chile scarred and polluted the environment. The state of Minas Gerais° in Brazil experienced a series of mining booms that began with gold in the late seventeenth century and continued with iron ore in the nineteenth. By the end of the nineteenth century its red soil was ripped open, its forests were depleted, and erosion was uncontrolled. Similar devastation afflicted parts of Bolivia and Mexico.

Efforts to meet increasing domestic demand for food and housing and to satisfy foreign demands for exports led to environmental degradation but also contributed significantly to the growth of the world economy and to regional prosperity. By the end of the nineteenth century small-scale conservation efforts were under way in many nations, and the first national parks and nature reserves had been created. In the United States large areas remained undeveloped. A few particularly beautiful areas were preserved in a national park system. In 1872 Yellowstone in Wyoming became the first national park. President Theodore Roosevelt (1901–1909) and the naturalist John Muir played major roles in preserving large areas of the western states. In Canada the first national park was created at Banff in 1885 and was expanded from 10 to 260 square miles (26 to 673 square kilometers) two years later. However, when confronted by a choice between economic growth and environmental protection, all the hemisphere's nations embraced growth.

Minas Gerais (ME-nas JER-aize)

COMPARATIVE PERSPECTIVES

While the new nations of the Western Hemisphere faced similar challenges in the nineteenth century, they had developed from different colonial traditions. The effort to establish stable constitutional systems proved difficult nearly everywhere. While the constitution of the United States endured, conflict over slavery led to a civil war that threatened the nation's survival. Elsewhere most constitutions had failed within a generation. In Argentina, for example, fifty years passed before a stable national government was in place. Personalist political leaders with large followings, like José Antonio Páez and Andrew Jackson, were often confined or thwarted by constitutions. Nations were divided by regions and by ideologies, which could promote civil war or lead to the overthrow of constitutional government.

New nations also faced foreign interventions and local wars with regional powers. By 1850 Mexico had lost 50 percent of its territory to the United States and then faced a French invasion in 1862. Bolivia and Peru lost territory to an expansive Chile, and Paraguay was crushed by an alliance of Argentina, Brazil, and Uruguay. In this process of strengthening the institutions of national government and settling territorial boundaries, the nations of the Americas also crushed the last vestiges of autonomous Amerindian culture in the Western Hemisphere by the 1880s. It is not an accident that the most successful of these expansive powers experienced the most rapid economic growth.

The nations of the hemisphere also witnessed a series of dramatic social and economic changes. Slavery left a terrible legacy (see Chapter 19). After a century of protest and political mobilization, Brazil's slaves were emancipated in 1888, but the institution had created societies characterized by racism and discrimination. These societies also had low levels of investment in education and internal improvements. By 1890 many of the hemisphere's poorest nations or poorest regions within nations were those that had depended on slavery. The American south and the northeast of Brazil, for example, became the poorest regions in these expanding nations.

Amerindian populations experienced centuries of exploitation, forced integration in market economies, and compulsory removal to marginal lands. They were also among the poorest peoples in the hemisphere by 1890. The indigenous peoples of nations like Guatemala and Bolivia, for example, were still subject to forced labor long after independence. Across the region, the most oppressive labor systems of the colonial era (see Chapter 18) created obstacles to both political stability and economic development.

Immigration transformed many Western Hemisphere nations. As a general rule, the millions of European immigrants that entered the Western Hemisphere in the nineteenth century avoided nations or regions within nations where slavery had been important or where large indigenous populations remained. Argentina, Brazil, Canada, and the United States were the most popular destinations, and immigrants to Brazil and the United States avoided the former plantation zones. Few immigrants went to indigenous regions of the Andes or Central America or to the Caribbean. Instead, hundreds of thousands of Chinese and East Indians, migrating as indentured laborers, were directed to plantation regions, where they faced mounting racism and discrimination.

By 1890 nearly all the nations of the Western Hemisphere were richer and more politically stable. Economic growth and political progress were clearly related, and both were linked historically to the character of colonial development. A small number of nations located in the temperate regions—Canada, the United States, Argentina, and Chile—had become prosperous regional powers relative to their neighbors. While most of the region's growth continued to depend on the export of agricultural goods and raw materials—sugar, cotton, grains, minerals, and livestock products—the United States had become a major industrial nation by 1890.

SUMMARY

○— What were the causes of the revolutions for independence in Latin America?

○— What major political challenges did Western Hemisphere nations face in the nineteenth century?

○— How did economic modernization and the effects of abolitionism, immigration, and women's rights change the nations of the Western Hemisphere?

Online Study Center
ACE the Test

The nineteenth century witnessed enormous political changes in the Western Hemisphere. Except in Canada, many Caribbean islands, and a handful of mainland colonies like Surinam, the Guyanas, and Belize, colonial regimes were overturned by the 1830s. The powerful new political ideas of the Enlightenment and an increased sense of national identity contributed to the desire for independence and self-rule. The success of the American and Haitian Revolutions began the assault on the colonial order, transforming the hemisphere's politics. Napoleon's invasion of Portugal and Spain proved crucial in provoking the movement toward independence in Latin America.

Once colonial rule was overturned, the creation of stable and effective governments proved difficult. Powerful personalist leaders resisted the constraints imposed by constitutions. National governments often confronted divisive regional political movements. From Argentina in the south to the United States in the north, regional political rivalries provoked civil wars that challenged the very survival of the new nations. Foreign military interventions and wars with native peoples also consumed resources and determined national boundaries. The effort to fulfill the promise of universal citizenship led to struggles to end slavery, extend civil and political rights to women and minorities, and absorb new immigrants. These objectives were only partially achieved.

Industrialization had a transforming effect on the hemisphere as well. Wealth, political power, and population were increasingly concentrated in urban areas. In most countries, bankers and manufacturers, rather than farmers and plantation owners, directed national destinies. The United States, the most industrialized nation in the Americas, played an aggressive economic role in the region's affairs and used its growing military power as

well. Industrialization altered the natural environment in dramatic ways. Modern factories consumed huge amounts of raw materials and energy. Copper mines in Chile and Mexico, Cuban sugar plantations, Brazilian coffee plantations, and Canadian lumber companies all left their mark on the natural environment, and all had ties to markets in the United States. The concentration of people in cities in the United States and Latin America put pressure on water supplies, sewage treatment, and food supplies.

By 1900, however, the hemisphere's national governments were much stronger than they had been at independence and were better able to meet the threats of foreign intervention and regionalism. Slavery had been abolished, and political rights had been extended to some formerly excluded citizens. Immigration of Europeans and Asians altered some societies culturally, Argentina, Uruguay, Canada and the United States in particular, while invigorating these economies. But broader political participation and more diverse populations also led to mass political movements, demands for wealth redistribution and social justice, and, in some places, greater political violence. Other serious challenges remained as well. Amerindian peoples and women were still excluded from national political life and had limited opportunities for advancement. The benefits of economic growth were not equitably distributed among the nations of the Western Hemisphere or within individual nations. In 1900 nearly every American nation was wealthier, better educated, more democratic, and more populous than at independence. But these nations were also more vulnerable to distant economic forces, more profoundly split between haves and have-nots, and more clearly divided into a rich north and a poorer south.

KEY TERMS

Simón Bolívar   *p. 696*

Miguel Hidalgo y Costilla
   p. 698

José María Morelos   *p. 699*

Confederation of 1867   *p. 702*

personalist leaders   *p. 704*

Andrew Jackson   *p. 704*

José Antonio Páez   *p. 704*

Benito Juárez   *p. 707*

Tecumseh   *p. 709*

Caste War   *p. 710*

abolitionists   *p. 711*

acculturation   *p. 715*

Women's Rights Convention
   p. 716

development   *p. 719*

underdevelopment   *p. 719*

Online Study Center
Improve Your Grade
Flashcards

SUGGESTED READING

For the independence era in Latin America see John Lynch, *The Spanish American Revolutions, 1808–1826*, 2nd ed. (1986); Jay Kinsbruner, *Independence in Spanish America*, 2nd ed. (2000); Jaime Rodriguez O., *The Origins of Mexican National Politics* (1997); and A. J. R. Russell-Wood, ed., *From Colony to Nation: Essays on the Independence of Brazil* (1976).

The postindependence political and economic struggles in Latin America can be traced in David Bushnell and Neil Macaulay, *The Emergence of Latin America in the Nineteenth Century* (1988). Tulio Halperin-Donghi, *The Contemporary History of Latin America* (1993), and E. Bradford Burns, *The Poverty of Progress: Latin America in the Nineteenth Century* (1980), argue in different ways that Latin America's economic and social problems originated in unfavorable trade relationships with more developed nations. See also an excellent collection of essays, Leslie Bethell, ed., *The Cambridge History of Latin America*, vol. 3, *From Independence to c. 1870* (1985).

There is an enormous literature on politics and nation building in the United States and Canada. Among the many worthy studies of the United States are John Lauritz Larson, *Internal Improvement: National Public Works and the Promise of Popular Government in the Early United States* (2001); William J. Cooper, *The South and the Politics of Slavery, 1828–1856* (1978); Kenneth M. Stampp, *America in 1857* (1991); and Lawrence Frederick Kohl, *The Politics of Individualism: Parties and the American Character in the Jacksonian Era* (1989). See also H. W. Brands, *Andrew Jackson, His Life and Times* (2005). For Canada see J. M. S. Careless, *The Union of the Canadas: The Growth of Canadian Institutions, 1841–1857* (1967); Ged Martin, ed., *The Causes of Canadian Confederation* (1990); and Arthur I. Silver, *The French-Canadian Idea of Confederation, 1864–1900* (1982).

The social and cultural issues raised in this chapter are also the subject of a vast literature. For an excellent history of the immigration era see Walter Nugent, *Crossing: The Great Transatlantic Migrations, 1870–1914* (1992). See also Gunther Barth, *Bitter Strength: A History of Chinese in the United States, 1850–1870* (1964); and Nicolás Sánchez-Albornoz, *The Population of Latin America: A History* (1974). For economic history, see Victor Bulmer Thomas, *The Economic History of Latin America Since Independence* (2003). On the creation of Latin American cultures in the age of immigration, see Leslie Bethell, *A Cultural History of Latin America* (1998).

On the issue of slavery see David Brion Davis, *Inhuman Bondage: The Rise and Fall of Slavery in the New World* (2006); and George M. Frederickson, *The Black Image in the White Mind: The Debate on Afro-American Character and Destiny, 1817–1914* (1971). Among the many fine studies of abolition see Benjamin Quarles, *Black Abolitionists* (1969), and John Stauffer, *The Black Hearts of Men* (2001). For the women's rights movement see Ellen C. Du Bois, *Feminism and Suffrage: The Emergence of an Independent Woman's Movement in the Nineteenth Century* (1984), and Lori D. Ginzberg, *Women and the Work of Benevolence: Morality, Politics, and Class in the Nineteenth-Century United States* (1990). Among numerous excellent studies of Indian policies see Robert M. Utley, *The Indian Frontier of the American West, 1846–1890* (1984), and the recent *Andrew Jackson and His Indian Wars* (2001) by Robert V. Remini. On those topics for Canada see J. R. Miller, *Skyscrapers Hide the Heavens: A History of Indian White Relations in Canada* (1989); Olive Patricia Dickason, *Canada's First Nations* (1993); and Alison Prentice, *Canadian Women: A History* (1988).

For abolition in Latin America and the Caribbean see Rebecca Scott, *Slave Emancipation in Cuba: The Transition to Free Labor, 1860–1899* (1985); Robert Conrad, *The Destruction of Brazilian Slavery, 1850–1888* (1973); and William A. Green, *British Slave Emancipation: The Sugar Colonies and the Great Experiment, 1830–1865* (1973). See George Reid Andrews, *Afro-Latin America, 1800–2000* (2004), for a synthesis of the Latin American experience. An introduction to the place of women in Latin American society is found in Francesca Miller, *Latin American Women and the Search for Social Justice* (1991), and Jane Jaquette, ed., *The Women's Movement in Latin America* (1989). See also David Barry Gaspar and Darlene Clark Hine, eds., *More Than Chattel: Black Women and Slavery in the Americas* (1996).

An introduction to the environmental consequences of North American development is provided by William Cronon, *Nature's Metropolis: Chicago and the Great West* (1991); Joseph M. Petulla, *American Environmental History* (1973); and Donald Worster, *Rivers of Empire: Water, Aridity, and the Growth of the American West* (1985). Shepard Krech III, *The Ecological Indian* (1999), is an important contribution. For Brazil see Warren Dean, *With Broadax and Firebrand: The Destruction of the Brazilian Atlantic Forest* (1995); and for Argentina, Uruguay, and Chile, see Alfred Crosby, *Ecological Imperialism: The Biological Expansion of Europe, 900–1900* (1986).

NOTES

1. Quoted in Lyman L. Johnson, "Spanish American Independence and Its Consequences," in *Problems in Modern Latin American History: A Reader,* ed. John Charles Chasteen and Joseph S. Tulchin (Wilmington, DE: Scholarly Resources, 1994), 21.

2. Quoted in Margaret Conrad, Alvin Finkel, and Cornelius Jaenen, *History of the Canadian Peoples,* vol. 1 (Toronto: Copp Clark Pittman Ltd., 1993), 606–607.

3. José Antonio Páez, *Autobiografía del General José Antonio Páez,* vol. 1 (New York: Hallety Breen, 1869), 83.

4. Quoted in Brian Loveman, *Chile: The Legacy of Hispanic Capitalism* (New York: Oxford University Press, 1979), 170.

5. Quoted in Bernard Bailyn, David Brion Davis, David Herbert Donald, John L. Thomas, Robert H. Wiebe, and Gordon S. Wood, *The Great Republic: A History of the American People* (Lexington, MA: D. C. Heath, 1981), 398.

6. Quoted in Mary Beth Norton et al., *A People and a Nation: A History of the United States,* 6th ed. (Boston: Houghton Mifflin, 2001), 284.

7. J. S. Woodsworth in 1909, quoted in R. Douglas Francis, Richard Jones, and Donald B. Smith, *Destinies: Canadian History Since Confederation,* 2nd ed. (Toronto: Holt, Rinehart and Winston, 1992), 141.

8. Sarah Grimké, "Reply to the Massachusetts Clergy," in *Early American Women: A Documentary History, 1600–1900,* ed. Nancy Woloch (Belmont, CA: Wadsworth, 1992), 343.

Trade Warehouse in Guangzhou European merchant enters in background while Chinese workers pack tea and porcelain. (Peabody Essex Museum, Salem, Massachusetts/The Bridgeman Art Library)

- What were the benefits and the drawbacks to the Ottoman Empire of the reforms adopted during the Tanzimat period?

- How did the Russian Empire maintain its status as both a European power and a great Asian land empire?

- How did the impact of European imperialism on China differ from its impact on Russia and the Ottoman Empire?

25

LAND EMPIRES IN THE AGE OF IMPERIALISM, 1800–1870

CHAPTER OUTLINE

The Ottoman Empire

The Russian Empire

The Qing Empire

Comparative Perspectives

ENVIRONMENT AND TECHNOLOGY: The Web of War

DIVERSITY AND DOMINANCE: Chinese Responses to Imperialism

When the emperor of the Qing° (the last empire to rule China) died in 1799, the imperial court received a shock. For decades officials had known that the emperor was indulging his handsome young favorite, Heshen°, allowing him extraordinary privileges and power. Senior bureaucrats hated Heshen, suspecting him of overseeing a widespread network of corruption. They believed he had been scheming to prolong the inconclusive wars against the native Miao° peoples of southwest China in the late 1700s. Glowing reports of successes against the rebels had poured into the capital, and enormous sums of government money had flowed to the battlefields. But there was no adequate accounting for the funds, and the war persisted.

After the emperor's death, Heshen's enemies ordered his arrest. When they searched his mansion, they discovered a magnificent

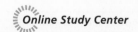
Online Study Center

This icon will direct you to interactive activities and study materials on the website: *college.hmco.com/pic/bulliet4e.*

Qing (ching)   **Heshen** (huh-shun)   **Miao** (mee-ow)

hoard of silk, furs, porcelain, furniture, and gold and silver. His personal cash alone exceeded what remained in the imperial treasury. The new emperor ordered Heshen to commit suicide with a rope of gold silk. The government seized Heshen's fortune, but the financial damage could not be undone. The declining agricultural base could not replenish the state coffers, and much of the income that did flow in was squandered by an increasingly corrupt bureaucracy. In the 1800s the Qing Empire faced increasing challenges from Europe and the United States with an empty treasury, a stagnant economy, and a troubled society.

The Qing Empire's problems were not unique. They were common to all the land-based empires of Eurasia, where old and inefficient ways of governing put states at risk. The international climate was increasingly dominated by industrializing European economies drawing on the wealth of their overseas colonies. The picture that opens this chapter depicts a European commercial establishment in China. During the early 1800s rapid population growth and slow agricultural growth affected much of Eurasia. Earlier military expansion had stretched the resources of imperial treasuries (see Chapter 21), leaving the land-based empires vulnerable to European military pressure. Responses to this pressure varied, with reform and adaptation gaining headway in some lands and tradition being reasserted in others. In the long run, attempts to meet western Europe's economic and political demands produced financial indebtedness to France, Britain, and other Western powers.

This chapter contrasts the experiences of the Qing Empire with the Russian and Ottoman Empires, with a particular look at the Ottomans' semi-independent province of Egypt. While the Qing opted for resistance, the others made varying attempts to adapt and reform. Russia eventually became part of Europe and shared in many aspects of European culture, while the Ottomans and the Qing became subject to ever-greater imperialist pressure. These different responses raise the question of the role of culture in shaping western Europe's relations with the rest of the world in the nineteenth century.

THE OTTOMAN EMPIRE

During the eighteenth century the central government of the Ottoman Empire lost much of its power to provincial governors, military commanders, ethnic leaders, and bandit chiefs. In several parts of the empire local officials and large landholders tried to increase their autonomy and divert imperial funds into their own coffers.

An army led by the central Arabian clan of Ibn Saud, which had adopted the puritanical and fundamentalist religious views of an eighteenth-century leader named Muhammad ibn Abd al-Wahhab°, took control of the holy cities of Mecca and Medina and deprived the sultan of the important honor of organizing the annual pilgrimage. In Egypt the Mamluk slave-soldiers purchased as boys in Georgia and nearby parts of the Caucasus and educated for war reasserted their influence. Such soldiers had ruled Egypt between 1260 and 1517, when they were defeated by the Ottomans. Now Ottoman weakness allowed Mamluk factions based on a revival of the slave-soldier tradition to reemerge as local military forces.

For the sultans, hopes of escaping still further decline were few. The inefficient Janissary corps wielded great political power in Istanbul. It used this power to force Sultan Selim III to abandon efforts to train a modern, European-style army at the end of the eighteenth century. This situation unexpectedly changed when France invaded Egypt.

Egypt and the Napoleonic Example, 1798–1840

Napoleon Bonaparte and an invasion force of 36,000 men and four hundred ships invaded Egypt in May 1798. The French quickly defeated the Mamluk forces that for several decades had dominated the country under the loose jurisdiction of the Ottoman sultan in Istanbul. Fifteen months later, after being stopped by Ottoman land and British naval forces in an attempted invasion of Syria, Napoleon secretly left Cairo and returned to France. Three months later he seized power and made himself emperor.

Back in Egypt, his generals tried to administer a country that they only poorly understood. Cut off from France by British ships in the Mediterranean, they had little hope of remaining in power and agreed to withdraw in 1801. For the second time in three years, a collapse of military power produced a power vacuum in Egypt. The winner of the

---

Muhammad ibn Abd al-Wahhab (moo-HAH-muhd ib-uhn abd ahl–wa-HAHB)

C H R O N O L O G Y

	Ottoman Empire	Russian Empire	Qing Empire
1800	**1805–1849** Muhammad Ali governs Egypt	**1801–1825** Reign of Alexander I	**1794–1804** White Lotus Rebellion
	1808–1839 Rule of Mahmud II	**1812** Napoleon's retreat from Moscow	
	1826 Janissary corps dissolved	**1825** Decembrist revolt	
	1829 Greek independence	**1825–1855** Reign of Nicholas I	
	1839 Abdul Mejid begins Tanzimat reforms		**1839–1842** Opium War
1850			**1850–1864** Taiping Rebellion
	1853–1856 Crimean War	**1853–1856** Crimean War	**1856–1860** Arrow War
		1855–1881 Reign of Alexander II	**1860** Sack of Beijing
		1861 Emancipation of the serfs	**1861–1873** Empress Dowager Cixi wields power during her son's minority
	1876 First constitution by an Islamic government		**1875–1908** After her son's death, Empress Dowager Cixi resumes power on behalf of minor successors

ensuing contest was **Muhammad Ali°**, the commander of a contingent of Albanian soldiers sent by the sultan to restore imperial control. By 1805 he had taken the place of the official Ottoman governor, and by 1811 he had dispossessed the Mamluks of their lands and privileges.

Muhammad Ali's rise to power coincided with the meteoric career of Emperor Napoleon I. It is not surprising, therefore, that he adopted many French practices in rebuilding the Egyptian state. Militarily, he dutifully followed the sultan's urging and sent an army to Arabia to expel the Saudi clan from Mecca and Medina. Losses during this successful war greatly reduced his contingent of Albanians, leaving him free to construct a new army. Instead of relying on picked groups of warriors like the Mamluks, Muhammad Ali instituted the French practice of conscription. For the first time since the days of the pharaohs, Egyptian peasants were compelled to become soldiers.

He also established special schools for training artillery and cavalry officers, army surgeons, military bandmasters, and other specialists. The curricula of these schools featured European skills and sciences, and

---

Muhammad Ali (moo-HAM-muhd AH-lee)

Muhammad Ali began to send promising young Turks and Circassians (an ethnic group from the Caucasus), the only people permitted to serve as military officers, to France for education. In 1824 he started a gazette devoted to official affairs, the first newspaper in the Islamic world.

To outfit his new army Muhammad Ali built all sorts of factories. These did not prove efficient enough to survive, but they showed a determination to achieve independence and parity with the European powers.

Money for these enterprises came from confiscation of lands belonging to Muslim religious institutions, under the pretext that the French occupation had canceled religious trusts established in earlier centuries, and from forcing farmers to sell their crops to the government at fixed prices. Muhammad Ali resold some of the produce abroad, making great profits as long as the Napoleonic wars kept European prices for wheat at a high level.

In the 1830s Muhammad Ali's son Ibrahim invaded Syria and instituted some of the changes already under way in Egypt. The improved quality of the new Egyptian army had been proven during the Greek war of independence, which lasted from 1821 to 1831, when Ibrahim had commanded an expeditionary force to help the sultan. In response, the sultan embarked on building his own new army in 1826. The two armies met in 1839 when Ibrahim attacked northward into Anatolia. The Egyptian army was victorious, and Istanbul would surely have fallen if not for European intervention.

In 1841 European pressure, highlighted by British naval bombardment of coastal cities in Egyptian-controlled Syria, forced Muhammad Ali to withdraw to the present-day border between Egypt and Israel. The great powers imposed severe limitations on his army and navy and forced him to dissolve his economic monopolies and allow Europeans to undertake business ventures in Egypt.

Muhammad Ali remained Egypt's ruler, under the suzerainty of the sultan, until his death in 1849; and his family continued to rule the country until 1952. But his dream of making Egypt a mighty country capable of standing up to Europe faded. What survived was the example he had set for the sultans in Istanbul.

| Ottoman Reform and the European Model, 1807–1853 | At the end of the eighteenth century Sultan Selim° III (r. 1789–1807), an intelligent and forward-looking ruler who stayed well informed about |

events in Europe, introduced reforms to create European-style military units, bring provincial governors under the control of the central government, and standardize taxation and land tenure. The rise in government expenditures to implement the reforms was supposed to be offset by taxes on selected items, primarily tobacco and coffee.

These reforms failed for political, more than economic, reasons. The most violent and persistent opposition came from the **Janissaries°**. Originally Christian boys taken from their homes in the Balkans, converted to Islam, and required to serve for life in the Ottoman army, in the eighteenth century the Janissaries became a significant political force in Istanbul and in provincial capitals like Damascus and Aleppo. Their interest in preserving special economic privileges made them resist the creation of new military units.

At times, the disapproval of the Janissaries produced military uprisings. An early example occurred in the Balkans, in the Ottoman territory of **Serbia,** where Janissaries acted as provincial governors. Their control in Serbia was intensely resented by the local residents, particularly Orthodox Christians who claimed that the Janissaries abused them. In response to the charges, Selim threatened to reassign the Janissaries to the Ottoman capital at Istanbul. Suspecting that the sultan's threat signaled the beginning of the end of their political power, in 1805 the

Janissaries revolted against Selim and massacred Christians in Serbia. Selim was unable to reestablish central Ottoman rule over Serbia. Instead, the Ottoman court had to rely on the ruler of Bosnia, a neighboring Balkan province, who joined his troops with the peasants of Serbia to suppress the Janissary uprising. The threat of Russian intervention prevented the Ottomans from disarming the victorious Serbians, so Serbia became effectively independent.

Other opponents of reform included ulama, or Muslim religious scholars, who distrusted the secularization of law and taxation that Selim proposed. In the face of widespread rejection of his reforms, Selim suspended his program in 1806. Nevertheless, a massive military uprising occurred at Istanbul, and the sultan was deposed and imprisoned. Reform forces rallied and recaptured the capital, but not before Selim had been executed. Selim's cousin Sultan Mahmud° II (r. 1808–1839) cautiously revived the reform movement. The fate of Selim III had taught the Ottoman court that reform needed to be more systematic and imposed more forcefully, but it took the concrete evidence of the effectiveness of radical reform in Muhammad Ali's Egypt to drive this lesson home. Mahmud II was able to use an insurrection in Greece, and the superior performance of Egyptian forces in the unsuccessful effort to suppress it, as a sign of the weakness of the empire and the pressing need for reform.

Greek independence in 1829 was a complex event that had dramatic international significance. A combination of Greek nationalist organizations and interlopers from Albania formed the independence movement. By the early nineteenth century interest in the classical age of Greece and Rome had intensified European desires to encourage and if possible aid the struggle for independence. Europeans considered the war for Greek independence a campaign to recapture the classical roots of their civilization from Muslim despots, and many—including the "mad, bad and dangerous to know" English poet Lord Byron, who lost his life in the war—went to Greece to fight as volunteers. The Ottomans called on Ibrahim Pasha° of Egypt, the son of Muhammad Ali, to help preserve their rule in Greece; but when the combined squadrons of the British, French, and Russian fleets, under orders to observe but not intervene in the war, made an unauthorized attack that sank the Ottoman fleet at the Battle of Navarino, not even Ibrahim's help could prevent defeat (see Map 25.1).

Europeans trumpeted the victory of the Greeks as a triumph of European civilization over the Ottoman Empire, and Mahmud II agreed that the loss of Greece

---

Selim (seh-LEEM)   **Janissaries** (JAN-nih-say-rees)

Mahmud (MAH-mood)
Ibrahim Pasha (ib-rah-HEEM PAH-shah)

Map 25.1 **The Ottoman and Russian Empires, 1829–1914** At its height the Ottoman Empire controlled most of the perimeter of the Mediterranean Sea. But in the 1800s Ottoman territory shrank as many countries gained their independence. The Black Sea, where the Turkish coast was vulnerable to assault, became a weak spot as Russian naval power grew. Russian challenges to the Ottomans at the eastern end of the Black Sea and to the Persians east and west of the Caspian aroused fears in Europe that Russia was trying to reach the Indian Ocean.

indicated a profound weakness—he considered it backwardness—in Ottoman military and financial organization. With popular outrage over the military setbacks in Greece strong, the sultan made his move in 1826. First he announced the creation of a new artillery unit, which he had secretly been training. When the Janissaries rose in revolt, he ordered the new unit to bombard the Janissary barracks. The Janissary corps was officially dissolved.

Like Muhammad Ali, Mahmud felt he could not implement major changes without reducing the political power of the religious elite. He visualized restructuring the bureaucracy and the educational and legal systems, where ulama power was strongest. Before such strong

measures could be undertaken, however, Ibrahim attacked from Syria in 1839. Battlefield defeat, the decision of the rebuilt Ottoman navy to switch sides and support Egypt, and the death of Mahmud, all in the same year, left the empire completely dependent on the European powers for survival.

Mahmud's reforming ideas received their widest expression in the **Tanzimat**° ("reorganization"), a series of reforms announced by his sixteen-year-old son and successor, Abdul Mejid°, in 1839 and strongly endorsed by the European ambassadors. One proclamation called for public trials and equal protection under the law for all,

---

Tanzimat (TAHNZ-ee-MAT)   **Abdul Mejid** (ab-dul meh-JEED)

whether Muslim, Christian, or Jew. It also guaranteed some rights of privacy, equalized the eligibility of men for conscription into the army (a practice copied from Egypt), and provided for a new, formalized method of tax collection that legally ended tax farming in the Ottoman Empire. It took many years and strenuous efforts by reforming bureaucrats, known as the "men of the Tanzimat," to give substance to these reforms. At a theoretical level, however, they opened a new chapter in the history of the Islamic world. European observers praised them for their noble principles and rejection of religious influences in government. Ottoman citizens were more divided; the Christians and Jews, for whom the Europeans showed the greatest concern, were generally more enthusiastic than the Muslims. Many historians see the Tanzimat as the dawn of modern thought and enlightened government in the Middle East. Others point out that removing the religious elite from influence in government also removed the one remaining check on authoritarian rule.

Online Study Center
Improve Your Grade
Primary Source:
Imperial Rescript

With the passage of time, one legal code after another—commercial, criminal, civil procedure—was introduced to take the place of the corresponding areas of religious legal jurisdiction. All the codes were modeled closely on those of Europe. The Shari'a, or Islamic law, gradually became restricted to matters of family law such as marriage and inheritance. As the Shari'a was displaced, job opportunities for the ulama shrank, as did the value of a purely religious education.

Like Muhammad Ali, Sultan Mahmud sent military cadets to France and the German states for training. Military uniforms were modeled on those of France. In the 1830s an Ottoman imperial school of military sciences, later to become Istanbul University, was established at Istanbul. Instructors imported from western Europe taught chemistry, engineering, mathematics, and physics in addition to military history. Reforms in military education became the model for more general educational reforms. In 1838 the first medical school was established to train army doctors and surgeons. Later, a national system of preparatory schools was created to feed graduates into the military schools. The subjects that were taught and many of the teachers were foreign, so the issue of whether Turkish would be a language of instruction in the new schools was a serious one. Because it was easier to import and use foreign textbooks than to write new ones in Turkish, French became the preferred language in all advanced professional and scientific training. In

numerical terms, however, the great majority of students still learned to read and write in Quran schools down to the twentieth century.

In the capital city of Istanbul, the reforms stimulated the growth of a small but cosmopolitan milieu embracing European language and culture. The first Turkish newspaper, a government gazette modeled on that of Muhammad Ali, appeared in 1831. Other newspapers followed, many written in French. Travel to Europe—particularly to England and France—became more common among wealthy Turks. Interest in importing European military, industrial, and communications technology remained strong through the 1800s.

The Ottoman rulers quickly learned that limited improvements in military technology had unforeseen cultural and social effects. Accepting the European notion that modern weapons and drill required a change in traditional military dress, beards were deemed unhygienic and, in artillery units, a fire hazard. They were restricted, along with the wearing of loose trousers and turbans. Military headgear also became controversial. European military caps, which had leather bills on the front to protect against the glare of the sun, were not acceptable because they interfered with Muslim soldiers' touching their foreheads to the ground during daily prayers. The compromise was the brimless cap now called the *fez*, which was adopted by the military and then by Ottoman civil officials in the early years of Mahmud II's reign.

The changes in military dress—so soon after the suppression of the Janissaries—were recognized as an indication of the empire's new orientation. Government ministries that traditionally drew young men from traditional bureaucratic families and trained them for ministerial service were gradually transformed into formal civil services hiring men educated in the new schools. Among self-consciously progressive men, particularly those in government service, European dress became the fashion in the Ottoman cities of the later 1800s. Traditional dress became a symbol of the religious, the rural, and the parochial.

Secularization of the legal code had special implications for the non-Muslim subjects of the Ottomans. Islamic law had required non-Muslims to pay a special head tax that was sometimes explained as a substitute for military service. Under the Tanzimat, the tax was abolished and non-Muslims became liable for military service—unless they bought their way out by paying a new military exemption tax. Under the new law codes, all male subjects had equal access to the courts, while the sphere of operation of the Islamic law courts shrank. Perhaps the biggest enhancement of the status of non-Muslims, however, was the strong and direct concern for

Modernized Ottoman Troops   This photograph of a contingent of Imperial Guards in the late nineteenth century shows them equipped and uniformed much like any other European army of the time. The only distinctive feature is the fez, a brimless hat adopted earlier in the century as a symbol of reform. Comparison with the soldiers in the funeral procession of Suleiman the Magnificent (page 576) shows the degree of change from the traditional military uniforms that were still being worn in the eighteenth century.   (From one of the original photographic albums of Sultan Abdul Hamid II, 1842–1918/Library of Congress)

their welfare consistently expressed by the European powers. The Ottoman Empire became a rich field of operation for Christian missionaries and European supporters of Jewish community life in the Muslim world.

The public rights and political participation granted during the Tanzimat applied specifically to men. Private life, including everything connected to marriage and divorce, remained within the sphere of religious law, and at no time was there a question of political participation or reformed education for women. Indeed, the reforms may have decreased the influence of women. The political changes ran parallel to economic changes that also narrowed women's opportunities.

The influx of silver from the Americas that had begun in the 1600s increased the monetarization of some sectors of the Ottoman economy, particularly in the cities. Workers were increasingly paid in cash rather than in goods, and businesses associated with banking, finance, and law developed. Competition drove women from the work force. Early industrial labor and the pro-

fessions were not open to women, and traditional "woman's work" such as weaving was increasingly mechanized and done by men.

Nevertheless, women retained considerable power in the management and disposal of their own property, gained mostly through fixed shares of inheritance, well into the 1800s. After marriage a woman was often pressured to convert her landholdings to cash in order to transfer her personal wealth to her husband's family, with whom she and her husband would reside; but this was not a requirement, since men were legally obligated to support their families single-handedly. Until the 1820s many women retained their say in the distribution of property through the creation of charitable trusts for their sons. Because these trusts were set up in the religious courts, they could be designed to conform to the wishes of family members, and they gave women of wealthy families an opportunity to exercise significant indirect control over property. Then, in the 1820s and 1830s the centralizing reforms of Mahmud II, which did not always produce happy results, transferred jurisdiction over the charitable trusts from religious courts to the state and ended women's control over this form of property. In addition, reforms in the military, higher education, the professions, and commerce all bypassed women.

The Crimean War and Its Aftermath, 1853–1877

Since the reign of Peter the Great (r. 1689–1725) the Russian Empire had been attempting to expand southward at the Ottomans' expense (see "Russia and Asia," below). By 1815 Russia had pried the Georgian region of the Caucasus away from the Ottomans, and the threat of Russian intervention had prevented the Ottomans from crushing Serbian independence. Russia seemed poised to exploit Ottoman weakness and acquire the long-sought goal of free access to the Mediterranean Sea. In the eighteenth century Russia had claimed to be the protector of Ottoman subjects of Orthodox Christian faith in Greece and the Balkans. When Muhammad Ali's Egyptian army invaded Syria in 1833, Russia signed a treaty in support of the Ottomans. In return, the sultan recognized an extension of this claim to cover all of the empire's Orthodox subjects. This set the stage for an obscure dispute that resulted in war.

In 1852 the sultan bowed to British and French pressure and named France Protector of the Holy Sepulchre in Jerusalem, a position with certain ecclesiastical privileges. Russia protested, but the sultan held firm. So Russia invaded Ottoman territories in what is today Romania, and Britain and France went to war as allies of the sultan. The real causes of the war went beyond church quarrels in Jerusalem. Diplomatic maneuvering among European powers over whether the Ottoman Empire should continue to exist and, if not, who should take over its territory lasted until the empire finally disappeared after World War I. The Eastern Question was the simple name given to this complex issue. Though the powers had agreed to save the empire from Ibrahim's invasion in 1839, Britain subsequently became very suspicious of Russian ambitions. A number of prominent British politicians were strongly anti-Russian. They feared that Russia would threaten the British hold on India either overland through Central Asia or by placing its navy in the Mediterranean Sea.

Between 1853 and 1856 the **Crimean° War** raged in Romania, on the Black Sea, and on the Crimean peninsula. Britain, France, and the Italian kingdom of Sardinia-Piedmont sided with the Ottomans, allowing Austria to mediate the final outcome. Britain and France trapped the Russian fleet in the Black Sea, where its commanders decided to sink the ships to protect the approaches to Sevastopol, their main base in Crimea. An army largely made up of British and French troops landed and laid siege to the city. A lack of railways and official corruption hampered Russian attempts to supply both its land and its sea forces. On the Romanian front, the Ottomans resisted effectively. At Sevastopol, the Russians were outmatched militarily and suffered badly from disease. As defeat became imminent, Tsar Nicholas died, leaving his successor, Alexander II (r. 1855–1881), to sue for peace when Sevastopol finally fell three months later.

A formal alliance among Britain, France, and the Ottoman Empire blocked further Russian expansion into eastern Europe and the Middle East. The terms of peace also gave Britain and France a means of checking each other's colonial ambitions in the Middle East; neither, according to the agreement that ended the war, was entitled to take Ottoman territory for its exclusive use.

The Crimean War brought significant changes to all the combatants. The tsar and his government, already beset by demands for the reform of serfdom, education, and the military (discussed later), were further discredited. In Britain and France, the conflict was accompanied by massive propaganda campaigns. For the first time newspapers were an important force in mobilizing public support for a war. Press accounts of British participation in the war were often so glamorized that the false impression has lingered ever since that Ottoman troops played a negligible role in the conflict. At the time, however, British and French military commanders noted the massive losses among Turkish troops in particular. The French press, dominant in Istanbul, promoted a sense of unity between Turkish and French society that continued to influence many aspects of Turkish urban culture.

The larger significance of the Crimean War was that it marked the transition from traditional to modern warfare (see Environment and Technology: The Web of War). A high casualty count resulted in part from the clash of mechanized and unmechanized means of killing. All the combatant nations had previously prided themselves on the effective use of highly trained cavalry to smash through the front lines of infantry. Cavalry coexisted with firearms until the early 1800s, primarily because early rifles were awkward to load, vulnerable to explosion, and not very accurate. Swift and expert cavalry could storm infantry lines during the intervals between volleys and even penetrate artillery barrages. In the 1830s and 1840s percussion caps that did away with pouring gunpowder into the barrel of a musket were widely adopted in Europe. In Crimean War battles many

Crimean (cry-ME-uhn)

The Web of War

The lethal military technologies of the mid-nineteenth century that were used on battlefields in the United States, Russia, India, and China were rapidly transmitted from one conflict to the next. This dissemination was due not only to the rapid development of communications but also to the existence of a new international network of soldiers who moved from one trouble spot to another, bringing expertise in the use of new techniques.

General Charles Gordon (1833–1885), for instance, was commissioned in the British army in 1852, then served in the Crimean War after Britain entered on the side of the Ottomans. In 1860 he was dispatched to China. He served with British forces during the Arrow War and took part in the sack of Beijing. Afterward, he stayed in China and was seconded to the Qing imperial government until the suppression of the Taipings in 1864, earning himself the nickname "Chinese" Gordon. Gordon later served the Ottoman rulers of Egypt as governor of territory along the Nile. He was killed in Egypt in 1885 while leading his Egyptian troops in defense of the city of Khartoum against an uprising by the Sudanese religious leader, the Mahdi.

Journalism played an important part in the developing web of telegraph communications that sped orders to and from the battlefields. Readers in London could learn details of the drama occurring in the Crimea or in China within a week—or in some cases days—after they occurred. Print and, later, photographic journalism created new "stars" from these war experiences. Charles Gordon was one. Florence Nightingale was another.

In the great wars of the 1800s, the vast majority of deaths resulted from infection or excessive bleeding, not from the wounds themselves. Florence Nightingale (1820–1910), while still a young woman, became interested in hospital management and nursing. She went to Prussia and France to study advanced techniques. Before the outbreak of the Crimean War she was credited with bringing about marked improvement in British health care. When the public reacted to news reports of the suffering in the Crimea, the British government sent Nightingale to the region. Within a year of her arrival the death rate in the military hospitals there dropped from 45 percent to under 5 percent. Her techniques for preventing septicemia and dysentery, essentially sanitary measures like washing bed linens after a death and emptying toilet buckets outside, were quickly adopted by those working for and with her. On her return to London, Nightingale established institutes for nursing that soon were recognized as leaders around the world. She herself was lionized by the British public and received the Order of Merit in 1907, three years before her death.

The importance of Nightingale's innovations in public hygiene is underscored by the life of her contemporary, Mary Seacole (1805–1881). A Jamaican woman who volunteered to nurse British troops in the Crimean War, Seacole was repeatedly excluded from nursing service by British authorities. She eventually went to Crimea and used her own funds to run a hospital there, bankrupting herself in the process. The drama of the Crimean War moved the British public to support Seacole after her sacrifices were publicized. She was awarded medals by the British, French, and Turkish governments and today is recognized with her contemporary Florence Nightingale as an innovative field nurse and a champion of public hygiene in peacetime.

Florence Nightingale During Crimean War This 1856 lithograph shows Florence Nightingale supervising nursing care in a hospital in Scutari (Uskudar) across the Bosphorus strait from Istanbul. Though the artist may have exaggerated the neatness and cleanliness of the ward, sanitary measures proved the key to Nightingale's raising of the survival rate of sick and wounded soldiers. (Private Collection/The Bridgeman Art Library)

Street Scene in Cairo This engraving from Edward William Lane's influential travel book, *Account of the Manners and Customs of the Modern Egyptians Written in Egypt During the Years 1833–1835* conveys the image of narrow lanes and small stores that became stock features of European thinking about Middle Eastern cities. (From Edward William Lane, *The Manners and Customs of the Modern Egyptians* [London: J. M. D & Co. 1860])

cavalry units were destroyed by the rapid and relatively accurate fire of rifles that loaded at the breech rather than down the barrel. That was the fate of the British Light Brigade, which was sent to relieve an Ottoman unit surrounded by Russian troops. Ironically, in the charge of the Light Brigade, the heroic but obsolete horsemen were on the side with the most advanced weaponry. In the long run, despite the pathos of Alfred Lord Tennyson's famous poem, the new military technologies pioneered

in the Crimean War, not its heroic events, made the conflict a turning point in the history of war.

After the Crimean War, declining state revenues and increasing integration with European commercial networks created hazardous economic conditions in the Ottoman Empire. The men of the Tanzimat dominated government affairs under Abdul Mejid's successors and continued to secularize Ottoman financial and commercial institutions, modeling them closely on European counterparts. The Ottoman imperial bank was founded in 1840, and a few years later currency reform pegged the value of Ottoman gold coins to the British pound. Sweeping changes in the 1850s expedited the creation of banks, insurance companies, and legal firms throughout the empire. These and other reforms facilitating trade contributed to a strong demographic shift in the Ottoman Empire between about 1850 and 1880, as many rural people headed to the cities. Within this period many of the major cities of the empire—Istanbul, Damascus, Beirut, Alexandria, Cairo—expanded. A small but influential urban professional class emerged, as did a considerable class of wage laborers. This shift was magnified by an influx into the northern Ottoman territories of refugees from Poland and Hungary, where rivalry between the European powers and the Russian Empire caused political tension and sporadic warfare, and from Georgia and other parts of the Caucasus, where Russian expansion forced many Muslims to emigrate (discussed later).

The Ottoman reforms stimulated commerce and urbanization, but no reform could repair the chronic insolvency of the imperial government. Declining revenues from agricultural yields and widespread corruption damaged Ottoman finances. Some of the corruption was exposed in the early 1840s. From the conclusion of the Crimean War in 1856 on, the Ottoman government became heavily dependent on foreign loans. In return the Ottoman government lowered tariffs to favor European imports, and European banks opened in Ottoman cities. Currency changes allowed more systematic conversion to European currencies. Europeans were allowed to live in their own enclaves in Istanbul and other commercial centers, subject to their own laws and exempt from Ottoman jurisdiction. This status was known as **extraterritoriality**.

As the cities prospered, they became attractive to laborers, and still more people moved from the countryside. But opportunities for wage workers reached a plateau in the bloated cities. Foreign trade brought in large numbers of imports, but—apart from tobacco and the Turkish opium that American traders took to China to compete against the Indian opium of the British—few exports were sent abroad from Anatolia. Together with the growing national debt, these factors aggravated inflationary trends that left urban populations in a precar-

Interior of the Ottoman Financial Bureau   This engraving from the eighteenth century depicts the governing style of the Ottoman Empire before the era of westernizing reforms. By the end of the Tanzimat period in 1876, government offices and the costumes of officials looked much more like those in contemporary European capitals.   (From Ignatius Mouradgea d'Ohsson, *Tableau General de l'Empire Ottoman,* large folio edition, Paris, 1787–1820, pl. 178, following p. 340)

ious position in the mid-1800s. By contrast, Egyptian cotton exports soared during the American Civil War, when American cotton exports plummeted, but the profits benefited Muhammad Ali's descendants, who had become the hereditary governors of Egypt, rather than the Ottoman government. The Suez Canal, which was partly financed by cotton profits, opened in 1869, and Cairo was redesigned and beautified. Eventually overexpenditure on such projects plunged Egypt into the same debt crisis that plagued the empire as a whole.

In the 1860s and 1870s reform groups demanded a constitution and entertained the possibility of a law permitting all men to vote. Spokesmen for the Muslim majority expressed dismay at the possibility that the Ottoman Empire would no longer be a Muslim society. Muslims were also suspicious of the motives of Christian elites, many of whom enjoyed close relations with European powers. Memories of attempts by Russia and France to interfere in Ottoman affairs for the benefit of Christians seemed to some to warrant hostility toward Christians in Ottoman territories.

The decline of Ottoman power and prosperity had a strong impact on a group of well-educated young urban men who aspired to wealth and influence. They believed that the empire's rulers and the Tanzimat officials who worked for them would be forced to—or would be willing to—allow the continued domination of the empire's political, economic, and cultural life by Europeans. Though lacking a sophisticated organization, these **Young Ottomans** (who are sometimes called Young Turks, though that term properly applies to a later movement) promoted a mixture of liberal ideas derived from Europe, national pride in Ottoman independence, and modernist views of Islam. Prominent Young Ottomans helped draft a constitution that was promulgated in 1876 by a new and as yet untried sultan, Abdul Hamid II. This apparent triumph of liberal reform was short-lived. With war against Russia again threatening in the Balkans in 1877, Abdul Hamid suspended the constitution and the parliament that had been elected that year. He ruthlessly opposed further political reforms, but the Tanzimat programs of extending modern schooling, utilizing European military practices and advisers, and making the government bureaucracy more orderly continued during his reign.

The Russian Empire

Awareness of western Europe among Russia's elite began with the reign of Peter the Great (r. 1689–1725), but knowledge of the French language, considered by Russians to be the language of European culture, spread only slowly among the aristocracy in the second half of the eighteenth century. In 1812, when Napoleon's march on Moscow ended in a disastrous retreat brought on more by what a later tsar called "Generals January and February" than by Russian military action, the European image of Russia changed. Just as Napoleon's withdrawal from Egypt paved the way for the brief emergence of Muhammad Ali's Egypt as a major power, so his withdrawal from Russia conferred status on another autocrat. Conservative Europeans still saw Russia as an alien, backward, and oppressive land, but they acknowledged its immensity and potential power and included Tsar Alexander I (r. 1801–1825) as a major partner in efforts to restore order and suppress revolutionary tendencies throughout Europe. Like Muhammad Ali, Alexander attempted reforms in the hope of strengthening his regime. Unlike Muhammad Ali, acceptance by the other European monarchs saved a rising Russia from being strangled in its cradle.

In several important respects Russia resembled the Ottoman Empire more than the conservative kingdoms of Europe whose autocratic practices it so staunchly supported. Socially dominated by nobles whose country estates were worked by unfree serfs, Russia had almost no middle class. Industry was still at the threshold of development by the standards of the rapidly industrializing European powers, though it was somewhat more dynamic than Ottoman industry. And the absolute power of the tsar was unchallenged. Like Egypt and the Ottoman Empire, Russia engaged in reforms from the top down under Alexander I, but when his conservative brother Nicholas I (r. 1825–1855) succeeded to the throne, iron discipline and suspicion of modern ideas took priority over reform.

Russia and Europe   In 1700 only 3 percent of the Russian people lived in cities, two-thirds of them in Moscow alone. By the middle of the nineteenth century the town population had grown tenfold, though it still accounted for only 6 percent of the population because the territo-

ries of the tsars had grown greatly through wars and colonization (see Chapter 21). Since mining and small-scale industry can be carried out in small communities, urbanization is only a general indicator of modern economic developments. These figures do demonstrate, however, that, like the Ottoman Empire, Russia was an overwhelmingly agricultural land. Moreover, Russian transportation was even worse than that of the Ottomans, since many of the latter's major cities were seaports. Both empires encompassed peoples speaking many different languages.

Well-engineered roads did not begin to appear until 1817, and steam navigation commenced on the Volga in 1843. Tsar Nicholas I built the first railroad in Russia from St. Petersburg, the capital, to his summer palace in 1837. A few years later his commitment to strict discipline led him to insist that the trunk line from St. Petersburg to Moscow run in a perfectly straight line. American engineers, among them the father of the painter James McNeill Whistler, who learned to paint in St. Petersburg, oversaw the laying of track and built locomotive workshops. This slow start in modern transportation compares better with that of Egypt, where work on the first railroad began in 1851, than with France, which saw railroad building soar during the 1840s. Industrialization projects depended heavily on foreign expertise. British engineers set up the textile mills that gave wool and cotton a prominent place among Russia's industries.

Until the late nineteenth century the Russian government's interest in industry was limited and hesitant. To be successful, an industrial revolution required large numbers of educated and independent-minded artisans and entrepreneurs. Suspicious of Western ideas, especially anything smacking of liberalism, socialism, or revolution, Nicholas feared the spread of literacy and modern education beyond the minimum needed to train the officer corps and the bureaucracy. Rather than run the risk of allowing the development of a middle class and a working class that might challenge his control, Nicholas I kept the peasants in serfdom and preferred to import most industrial goods and pay for them with exports of grain and timber.

Like Egypt and the Ottoman Empire, Russia aspired to Western-style economic development. But fear of political change caused the country to fall farther behind western Europe, economically and technologically, than it had been a half-century before. When France and Britain entered the Crimean War, they faced a Russian army equipped with obsolete weapons and bogged down by lack of transportation. At a time when European engineers were making major breakthroughs in fast loading of cannon through an opening at the breech end, muzzle-loading artillery remained the Russian standard.

Raising of the Alexander Monument in St. Petersburg The death of Alexander I in 1825 brought to power his conservative brother Nicholas I. Yet Alexander remained a heroic figure for his resistance to Napoleon. This monument in Winter Palace Square was erected in 1829. (Visual Connection Archive)

Despite these deficiencies in technology and its institutional supports, in some ways Russia bore a closer resemblance to other European countries than the Ottoman Empire did. From the point of view of the French and the British, the Cyrillic alphabet and the Russian Orthodox form of Christianity seemed foreign, but they were not nearly as foreign as the Arabic alphabet and the Muslim faith of the Turks, Arabs, Persians, and Muslim Indians. Britain and France feared Russia as a rival for power in eastern Europe and the eastern Mediterranean lands, but they increasingly accepted Tsar Nicholas's view of the Ottoman Empire as "the sick man of Europe," capable of surviving only so long as the European powers found it a useful buffer state.

From the Russian point of view, kinship with western Europe was of questionable value. Westernizers, like the men of the Tanzimat and later the Young Ottomans, put their trust in technical advances and governmental reform. Opposing them were intellectuals known as **Slavophiles**, who considered the Orthodox faith, the solidity of peasant life, and the tsar's absolute rule to be the proper bases of Russian civilization. After Russia's humiliating defeat in the Crimea, the Slavophile tendency gave rise to **Pan-Slavism**, a militant political doctrine advocating unity of all the Slavic peoples, including those living under Austrian and Ottoman rule.

On the diplomatic front, the tsar's inclusion among the great powers of Europe contrasted sharply with the sultan's exclusion. However, this did not prevent the development of a powerful sense of Russophobia in the west. Britain in particular saw Russia as a geostrategic threat and despised the continuing subjection of the serfs, who were granted their freedom by Tsar Alexander II only in 1861, twenty-eight years after the British had abolished slavery. The passions generated by the Crimean War and its outcome affected the relations of Russia, Europe, and the Ottoman Empire for the remainder of the nineteenth century.

Russia and Asia

The Russian drive to the east in the eighteenth century brought the tsar's empire to the Pacific Ocean and the frontiers of China (see Map 21.1) by century's end. In the nineteenth century Russian expansionism continued with a drive to the south. The growing inferiority of the Russian military in comparison with the European powers did not affect these Asian battlefronts, since the peoples they faced were even less industrialized and technologically advanced than the Russians. In 1860 Russia established a military outpost on the Pacific coast that would eventually grow into the great naval port of Vladivostok, today Russia's most southerly city. In Central Asia the steppe lands of the Kazakh nomads came under Russian control early in the century, setting the stage for a confrontation with three Uzbek states farther south. They succumbed to Russian pressure and military action one by one, beginning in 1865, giving rise to the new province of Turkestan, with its capital at Tashkent in present-day Uzbekistan. In the region of the Caucasus Mountains, the third area of southward expansion, Russia first took over Christian Georgia (1786), Muslim Azerbaijan° (1801), and Christian Armenia (1813) before embarking on the conquest of the many small principalities, each with its own language or languages, in the heart of the mountains. Between 1829 and 1864 Dagestan, Chechnya°, Abkhazia°, and other regions that were to gain political prominence only after the breakup of the Soviet Union at the end of the twentieth century became parts of the Russian Empire.

The drive to the south intensified political friction with Russia's new neighbors: Qing China and Japan in the east, Iran on the Central Asian and Caucasus frontiers, and the Ottoman Empire at the eastern end of the Black Sea. In the latter two instances, a flow of Muslim refugees from the territories newly absorbed by Russia increased anti-Russian feelings, but in some cases also brought talented people into Iran and the Ottoman lands. Armenian, Azerbaijani, and Bukharan exiles who had been exposed to Russian administration and education brought new ideas to Iran in the later decades of the century, and a massive migration of Crimean Turks and Circassians from Russia's Caucasian territories affected the demography of the Ottoman Empire, which resettled some of the immigrants as far away as Syria and Jordan and others as buffer populations on the Russian frontiers.

In a broader political perspective, the Russian drive to the south added a new element to the Eastern Question. Many British statesmen and strategists reckoned that a warlike Russia would press on until it had conquered all the lands separating it from British India, a prospect that made them shudder, given India's enormous contribution to Britain's prosperity. The competition that ensued over which power would control southern Central Asia resulted in a standoff in Afghanistan, which became a buffer zone under the control of neither, and direct competition in Iran, where both powers sought to gain an economic

and political advantage while preserving the independence of the Qajar dynasty of shahs.

Cultural Trends

Unlike Egypt and the Ottoman Empire, which began to send students to Europe for training only in the nineteenth century, Russia had been in cultural contact with western Europe since the time of Peter the Great (r. 1689–1725). Members of the Russian court knew Western languages, and the tsars employed officials and advisers from Western countries. Peter had also enlisted the well-educated Ukrainian clerics who headed the Russian Orthodox Church to help spread a Western spirit of education. As a result, Alexander I's reforms met a more positive reception than those of Muhammad Ali and Mahmud II.

While Muhammad Ali put his efforts into building a modern army and an economic system to support it, the reforms of Sultan Mahmud II and Alexander promised more on paper than they brought about in practice. Both monarchs hoped to create better organized and more efficient government bureaus, but it took many years to develop a sufficient pool of trained bureaucrats to make the reforms effective. Alexander's Council of State worked better than the new ministerial system he devised. The council coordinated ministry affairs and deliberated over new legislation. As for the ministries, Alexander learned a lesson from Napoleon's military organization. He made each minister theoretically responsible for a strict hierarchy of officers below him and ordered the ministers to report directly to him as commander-in-chief. But this system remained largely ineffective, as did the provincial advisory councils that were designed to extend the new governing ideas into outlying areas.

Ironically, much of the opposition to these reforms came from well-established families that were not at all unfriendly to Western ideas. Their fear was that the new government bureaucrats, who often came from humbler social origins, would act as agents of imperial despotism. This fear was realized during the conservative reign of Nicholas I in the same way that the Tanzimat-inspired bureaucracy of the Ottoman Empire served the despotic purposes of Sultan Abdul al-Hamid II after 1877. In both cases, historians have noted that administrative reforms made by earlier rulers began to take hold under conservative despots, though more because of accumulating momentum and training than because of those rulers' policies.

Individuals favoring more liberal reforms, including military officers who had served in western Europe, intellectuals who read Western political tracts, and members of Masonic lodges who exchanged views with

---

Azerbaijan (ah-zer-by-JAHN) **Chechnya** (CHECH-nee-yah)
Abkhazia (ab-KAH-zee-yah)

Freemasons in the west, formed secret societies of opposition. Some placed their highest priority on freeing the serfs; others advocated a constitution and a republican form of government. When Alexander I died in December 1825, confusion over who was to succeed him encouraged a group of reform-minded army officers to try to take over the government and provoke an uprising. The so-called **Decembrist revolt** failed, and many of the participants were severely punished. These events ensured that the new tsar, Nicholas I, would pay little heed to calls for reform over the next thirty years.

Though the great powers meeting in Paris to settle the Crimean War in 1856 compelled the Ottoman sultan to issue new reform decrees improving the status of non-Muslim subjects, Russia faced a heavier penalty, being forced to return land to the Ottomans in both Europe and Asia. This humiliation contributed to the determination of Nicholas's son and successor, Alexander II, to institute major new reforms to reinvigorate the country. The greatest of his reforms was the emancipation of the serfs in 1861 and the conferral on them of property rights to prevent them from simply becoming hired laborers of big landowners (see Chapter 27). He also authorized new joint-stock companies, projected a railroad network to tie the country together, and modernized the legal and administrative arms of government.

Intellectual and cultural trends that had germinated under Alexander I, and that grew slowly under Nicholas, flourished under Alexander II. More and more people became involved in intellectual, artistic, and professional life. Under Alexander I education had expanded both at the preparatory and university levels, though Alexander imposed curbs on liberal thought in his later years. Most prominent intellectuals received some amount of instruction at Moscow University, and some attended German universities. Universities also appeared in provincial cities like Kharkov in Ukraine and Kazan on the Volga River. Student clubs, along with Masonic lodges, became places for discussing new ideas.

Nicholas continued his brother's crackdown on liberal education in the universities, but he encouraged professional and scientific training. By the end of his reign Russian scholars and scientists were achieving recognition for their contributions to European thought. Scholarly careers attracted many young men from clerical families, and this helped stimulate reforms in religious education. Perhaps because political activism was prohibited, clubs, salons, and organizations promoting scientific and scholarly activities became more and more numerous. The ideas of Alexander Herzen (1812–1870), a Russian intellectual working abroad who praised traditional peasant assemblies as the heart of Russia, encour-

aged socialist and Slavophile thinking and gave rise, under Alexander II, to the *narodniki*, a political movement dedicated to making Russia a land of peasant communes. Feodor Dostoyevsky° (1821–1881) and Count Leo Tolstoy (1828–1910), both of whom began to publish their major novels during the reign of Alexander II, aired these and other reforming ideas in the debates of the characters they created.

The initially ineffective bureaucratic reforms of Alexander I, which set in motion cultural currents that would make Russia a dynamic center of intellectual, artistic, and political life under his nephew Alexander II, resemble in some ways the Tanzimat reforms of the Ottoman Empire that preceded the emergence of the Young Ottomans as a new and assertive political and intellectual force in the second half of the nineteenth century. There was more overlap between the two groups of reformers and intellectuals in the Ottoman case than in the Russian, but the resemblance indicates parallel attitudes toward change on the part of the rulers.

Unlike the Ottoman Empire, however, Russia belonged to two different spheres of development. It entered the nineteenth century as a recognized political force in European politics, but in other ways it fit the Ottoman model of change. Rulers in both empires instituted reforms, overcame opposition, and increased the power of their governments. These activities also stimulated intellectual and political trends that would ultimately work against the absolute rule of tsar and sultan. Yet Russia would eventually develop much closer relations with western Europe and become an arena for every sort of European intellectual, artistic, and political tendency, while the Ottoman Empire would ultimately succumb to European imperialism.

THE QING EMPIRE

In 1800 the Qing Empire faced many of the crises the Ottomans had encountered, but no early reform movement of the kind initiated by Sultan Selim III emerged in China. The reasons are not difficult to understand. The Qing Empire, created by the Manchus, had skillfully countered Russian strategic and diplomatic moves in the 1600s. Instead of a Napoleon threatening them with invasion, the Qing rulers enjoyed the admiration of Jesuit priests who likened them to enlightened philosopher-kings. In 1793, however, a British attempt to establish

---

Feodor Dostoyevsky (FE-oh-dor doh-stoh-YEHV-skee)

diplomatic and trade relations—the Macartney mission—turned European opinion against China (see Chapter 21).

For their part, the Qing rulers and bureaucrats faced serious crises of a depressingly familiar sort: rebellions by displaced indigenous peoples and the poor, protests against the injustice of the local magistrates, and official corruption of the sort discussed at the start of this chapter. They dealt with these problems in the usual way, by suppressing rebels and dismissing incompetent or untrustworthy officials, and paid little attention to contacts with far-off Europeans. Complaints from European merchants at Canton, who chafed against the restrictions of the "Canton system" by which the Qing limited and controlled foreign trade, were brushed off.

Economic and Social Disorder, 1800–1839

Early Qing successes and territorial expansion sowed the seeds of the domestic and political chaos of the later period. The Qing conquest in the 1600s brought stability to central China after decades of rebellion and agricultural shortages. The new emperors encouraged the recovery of farmland, the opening of previously uncultivated areas, and the restoration and expansion of the road and canal systems. The result was a great expansion of the agricultural base together with a doubling of the population between about 1650 and 1800. Enormous numbers of farmers, merchants, and day laborers migrated in search of less crowded conditions, and a permanent floating population of the unemployed and homeless emerged. By 1800 population strain on the land had caused serious environmental damage in some parts of central and western China.

While farmers tried to cope with agricultural deterioration, other groups vented grievances against the government: minority peoples in central and southwestern China complained about being driven off their lands during the boom of the 1700s; Mongols resented appropriation of their grazing lands and the displacement of their traditional elites. In some regions, village vigilante organizations took over policing and governing functions from Qing officials who had lost control. Growing numbers of people mistrusted the government, suspecting that all officials were corrupt. The growing presence of foreign merchants and missionaries in Canton and in the Portuguese colony of Macao aggravated discontent in neighboring districts.

In some parts of China the Qing were hated as foreign conquerors and were suspected of sympathy with the Europeans. Indeed, the White Lotus Rebellion (1794–1804)—partly inspired by a messianic ideology that predicted the restoration of the Chinese Ming dynasty and the coming of the Buddha—raged across central China for a decade. It initiated a series of internal conflicts that continued through the 1800s. Ignited by deepening social instabilities, these movements were sometimes intensified by local ethnic conflicts and by unapproved religions. The ability of some village militias to defend themselves and attack others intensified the conflicts, though the same techniques proved useful to southern coastal populations attempting to fend off British invasion.

The Opium War and Its Aftermath, 1839–1850

Unlike the Ottomans, the Qing believed that the Europeans were remote and only casually interested in trade. They knew little of the enormous fortunes being made in the early 1800s by European and American merchants smuggling opium into China. They did not know that silver gained in this illegal trade was helping finance the industrial transformation of England and the United States. But Qing officials slowly became aware of British colonies in India that grew and exported opium, and of the major naval base at Singapore through which British opium reached East Asia.

For more than a century, British officials had been frustrated by the trade deficit caused by the British demand for tea and the Qing refusal to facilitate the importation of any British product. In the early 1700s a few European merchants and their Chinese partners were importing small quantities of opium. In 1729 the first Qing law banning opium imports was promulgated. By 1800, however, opium smuggling had swelled the annual import level to as many as four thousand chests. British merchants had pioneered this extremely profitable trade; Chinese merchants likewise profited from distributing the drugs. A price war in the early 1820s stemming from competition between British and American importers raised demand so sharply that as many as thirty thousand chests were being imported by the 1830s. Addiction spread to people at all levels of Qing society, including very high-ranking officials. The Qing emperor and his officials debated whether to legalize and tax opium or to enforce the existing ban more strictly. Having decided to root out the use and importation of opium, in 1839 they sent a high official to Canton to deal with the matter.

Britain considered the ban on opium importation an intolerable limitation on trade, a direct threat to Britain's economic health, and a cause for war. British naval and marine forces arrived at the south China coast in late 1839. The power of modern naval forces dawned on the Qing slowly. Indeed, Qing strategists did not learn to distinguish a naval invasion from piracy until the Opium War was nearly ended.

The **Opium War** (1839–1842) broke out when negotiations between the Qing official and British representatives reached a stalemate. The war exposed the fact that the traditional, hereditary soldiers of the Qing Empire—the **Bannermen**—were, like the Janissaries of the Ottoman Empire, hopelessly obsolete. As in the Crimean War, the British excelled at sea, where they deployed superior technology. British ships landed marines who pillaged coastal cities and then sailed to new destinations (see Map 25.2). The Qing had no imperial navy, and until they were able to engage the British in prolonged fighting on land, they were unable to defend themselves against British attacks. Even in the land engagements, Qing resources proved woefully inadequate. The British could quickly transport their forces by sea along the coast; Qing troops moved primarily on foot. Moving Qing reinforcements from central to eastern China took more than three months, and when the defense forces arrived, they were exhausted and basically without weapons.

The Bannermen used the few muskets the Qing had imported during the 1700s. The weapons were matchlocks, which required the soldiers to ignite the load of gunpowder in them by hand. Firing the weapons was dangerous, and the canisters of gunpowder that each musketeer carried on his belt were likely to explode if a fire broke out nearby—a frequent occurrence in encounters with British artillery. Most of the Bannermen, however, had no guns and fought with swords, knives, spears, and clubs. Soldiers under British command—many of them were Indians—carried percussion-cap rifles, which were far quicker, safer, and more accurate than the matchlocks. In addition, the long-range British artillery could be moved from place to place and proved deadly in the cities and villages of eastern China.

Qing commanders thought that British gunboats rode so low in the water that they could not sail up the Chinese rivers. Hence, evacuating the coasts, they believed, would protect the country from the British threat. But the British deployed new gunboats for shallow waters and moved without difficulty up the Yangzi River.

When the invaders approached Nanjing, the former Ming capital, the Qing decided to negotiate. In 1842 the terms of the **Treaty of Nanking** (the British name for Nanjing) dismantled the old Canton system. The number of **treaty ports**—cities opened to foreign residents—increased from one (Canton) to five (Canton, Xiamen, Fuzhou, Ningbo, and Shanghai°), and the island of Hong Kong became a long-term British colony. British residents in China gained extraterritorial rights. The Qing government agreed to set a low tariff of 5 percent on imports and to pay Britain an indemnity of 21 million ounces of silver as a penalty for having started the war. A supplementary treaty the following year guaranteed **most-favored-nation status** to Britain. This meant that any privileges that China granted to another country would be automatically extended to Britain as well. This provision effectively prevented the colonization of China, because giving land to one country would have necessitated giving it to all.

With each round of treaties came a new round of privileges for foreigners. In 1860 a new treaty legalized their right to import opium. Later, French treaties established the rights of foreign missionaries to travel extensively in the Chinese countryside and preach their religion. The number of treaty ports grew, too; by 1900 they numbered more than ninety.

The treaty system and the principle of extraterritoriality resulted in the colonization of small pockets of Qing territory, where foreign merchants lived at ease. Greater territorial losses resulted when outlying regions gained independence or were ceded to neighboring countries. Districts north and south of the Amur River in the northeast fell to Russia by treaty in 1858 and 1860; parts of modern Kazakhstan and Kyrgyzstan in the northwest met the same fate in 1864. From 1865 onward the British gradually gained control of territories on China's Indian frontier. In the late 1800s France forced the court of Vietnam to end its vassalage to the Qing, while Britain encouraged Tibetan independence.

In Canton, Shanghai, and other coastal cities, Europeans and Americans maintained offices and factories that employed local Chinese as menial laborers. The foreigners built comfortable housing in zones where Chinese were not permitted to live, and they entertained themselves in exclusive restaurants and bars. Around the foreign establishments, gambling and prostitution offered employment to part of the local urban population.

Whether in town or in the countryside, Christian missionaries whose congregations sponsored hospitals, shelters, and soup kitchens or gave stipends to Chinese who attended church enjoyed a good reputation. But just as often the missionaries themselves were regarded as another evil. They seemed to subvert Confucian beliefs

---

Shanghai (shahng-hie)

Areas of Taiping rebellion
- 1853–1857
- 1857–1863
- Areas of Nian rebellion, 1853–1868
- Areas of Muslim revolts, 1855–1873

← British attacks during the Opium War, 1839–1842
← British and French attacks during the Arrow War, 1858–1860
★ Conflicts with Romanovs, 1850s
■ Treaty ports

Map 25.2 Conflicts in the Qing Empire, 1839–1870 In both the Opium War of 1839–1842 and the Arrow War of 1856–1860, the seacoasts saw most of the action. Since the Qing had no imperial navy, the well-armed British ships encountered little resistance as they shelled the southern coasts. In inland conflicts, such as the Taiping Rebellion, the opposing armies were massive and slow moving. Battles on land were often prolonged attempts by one side to starve out the other side before making a major assault.

Online Study Center
Improve Your Grade
Interactive Map: Conflicts in the Qing Empire, 1839–1870

by condemning ancestor worship, pressuring poor families to put their children into orphanages, or fulminating against footbinding, a centuries-old practice that crippled the feet of young girls to satisfy a male obsession with tiny feet as a standard of beauty. The growing numbers of foreigners, and their growing privileges, became targets of resentment for a deeply dissatisfied, daily more impoverished, and increasingly militarized society.

The Taiping Rebellion, 1851–1864

The inflammatory mixture of social unhappiness and foreign intrusion exploded in the great civil war usually called the **Taiping° Rebellion.** In Guangxi, where the Taiping movement originated, entrenched social problems had been generating disorders for half a century. Agriculture in the region was unstable, and many people made their living from arduous and despised trades such as disposing of human waste, making charcoal, and mining. Ethnic divi-

Taiping (tie-PING)

Nanjing Encircled For a decade the Taipings held the city of Nanjing as their capital. For years Qing and international troops attempted to break the Taiping hold. By the summer of 1864, Qing forces had built tunnels leading to the foundations of Nanjing's city walls and had planted explosives. The detonation of the explosives signaled the final Qing assault on the rebel capital. As shown here, the common people of the city, along with their starving livestock, were caught in the crossfire. Many of the Taiping leaders escaped the debacle at Nanjing, but nearly all were hunted down and executed. (Roger-Viollet/Getty Images)

sions complicated economic distress. The lowliest trades frequently involved a minority group, the Hakkas, and tensions between them and the majority were rising. Problems may have been intensified by the sharp fluctuations in the trade of opium, which flooded the coastal and riverine portions of China after 1842, then collapsed as domestically grown opium began to dominate the market. Also, the area was close enough to Canton to feel the cultural and economic impact of the growing number of Europeans and Americans.

Hong Xiuquan°, the founder of the Taiping movement, experienced all of these influences. Hong came

Hong Xiuquan (hoong shee-OH-chew-an)

from a humble Hakka background. After years of study, he competed in the provincial Confucian examinations, hoping for a post in government. He failed the examinations repeatedly, and it appears that he suffered a nervous breakdown in his late thirties. Afterward he spent some time in Canton, where he met both Chinese and American Protestant missionaries, who inspired him with their teachings. Hong had his own interpretation of the Christian message. He saw himself as the younger brother of Jesus, commissioned by God to found a new kingdom on earth and drive the Manchu conquerors, the Qing, out of China. The result would be universal peace. Hong called his new religious movement the "Heavenly Kingdom of Great Peace."

Hong quickly attracted a community of believers, primarily Hakkas like himself. They believed in the prophecy of dreams and claimed they could walk on air. Hong and his rivals for leadership in the movement went in and out of ecstatic trances. They denounced the Manchus as creatures of Satan. News of the sect reached the government, and Qing troops arrived to arrest the Taiping leaders. But the Taipings soundly repelled the imperial troops. Local loyalty to the Taipings spread quickly; their numbers multiplied; and they began to enlarge their domain.

The Taipings relied at first on Hakka sympathy and the charismatic appeal of their religious doctrine to attract followers. But as their numbers and power grew, they altered their methods of preaching and governing. They replaced the anti-Chinese appeals used to enlist Hakkas with anti-Manchu rhetoric designed to enlist Chinese. They forced captured villages to join their movement. Once people were absorbed, the Taipings strictly monitored their activities. They segregated men and women and organized them into work and military teams. Women were forbidden to bind their feet (the Hakkas had never practiced footbinding) and participated fully in farming and labor. Brigades of women soldiers took to the field against Qing forces.

As the movement grew, it began to move toward eastern and northern China (see Map 25.2). Panic preceded the Taipings. Villagers feared being forced into Taiping units, and Confucian elites recoiled in horror from the bizarre ideology of foreign gods, totalitarian rule, and walking, working, warring women. But the huge numbers the Taipings were able to muster overwhelmed attempts at local defense. The tremendous growth in the number of Taiping followers required the movement to establish a permanent base. When the rebel army conquered Nanjing in 1853, the Taiping leaders decided to settle there and make it the capital of the new "Heavenly Kingdom of Great Peace."

Qing forces attempting to defend north China became more successful as problems of organization and growing numbers slowed Taiping momentum. Increasing Qing military success resulted mainly from the flexibility of the imperial military commanders in the face of an unprecedented challenge. In addition, the military commanders received strong backing from a group of civilian provincial governors who had studied the techniques developed by local militia forces for self-defense. Certain provincial governors combined their knowledge of civilian self-defense and local terrain with more efficient organization and the use of modern weaponry. The result was the formation of new military units, in which many of the Bannermen voluntarily served under civilian governors. The Qing court agreed to special taxes to fund the new armies and acknowledged the new combined leadership of the civilian and professional force.

When the Taipings settled into Nanjing, the new Qing armies surrounded the city, hoping to starve out the rebels. The Taipings, however, had provisioned and fortified themselves well. They also had the services of several brilliant young military commanders, who mobilized enormous campaigns in nearby parts of eastern

Street Scene in Guangzhou This photograph taken in the 1860s by an Englishman shows a comparatively wide market street with signs advertising drugs, cushions, seals, ink, etc. The engraving of a Cairo street scene (page 736) shows a much more exotic stereotype of the orient, complete with young girl displaying her body while covering her face. (Photo by John Thomson/George Eastman House/Getty Images)

China, scavenging supplies and attempting to break the encirclement of Nanjing. For more than a decade the Taiping leadership remained ensconced at Nanjing, and the "Heavenly Kingdom" endured.

In 1856 Britain and France, freed from their preoccupation with the Crimean War, turned their attention to China. European and American missionaries had visited Nanjing, curious to see what their fellow Christians were up to. Their reports were discouraging. Hong Xiuquan and the other leaders appeared to lead lives of indulgence and abandon, and more than one missionary accused them of homosexual practices. Relieved of the possible accusation of quashing a pious Christian movement, the British and French surveyed the situation. Though the Taipings were not going to topple the Qing, rebellious Nian ("Bands") in northern China added a new threat in the 1850s. A series of simultaneous large insurrections might indeed destroy the empire. Moreover, since the Qing had not observed all the provisions of the treaties signed after the Opium War, Britain and France were now considering renewing war on the Qing themselves.

In 1856 the British and French launched a series of swift, brutal coastal attacks—a second opium war, called the Arrow War (1856–1860)—that culminated in a British and French invasion of Beijing and the sacking of the Summer Palace in 1860. A new round of treaties punished the Qing for not enacting all the provisions of the Treaty of Nanking. Having secured their principal objective, the British and French forces joined the Qing campaign against the Taipings. Attempts to coordinate the international forces were sometimes riotous and sometimes tragic, but the injection of European weaponry and money helped quell both the Taiping and the Nian rebellions during the 1860s.

The Taiping Rebellion ranks as the world's bloodiest civil war and the greatest armed conflict before the twentieth century. Estimates of deaths range from 20 million to 30 million. The loss of life came primarily from starvation and disease, for most engagements consisted of surrounding fortified cities and waiting until the enemy forces died, surrendered, or were so weakened that they could be easily defeated. Many sieges continued for months, and after starving for a year under the occupation of the rebels, people within some cities had to starve for another year under the occupation of the imperial forces. Reports of people eating grass, leather, hemp, and human flesh were widespread. The dead were rarely buried properly, and epidemic disease was common.

The area of early Taiping fighting was close to the regions of southwest China in which bubonic plague had been lingering for centuries. When the rebellion was suppressed, many Taiping followers sought safety in the highlands of Laos and Vietnam, which soon showed infestation by plague. Within a few years the disease reached Hong Kong. From there it spread to Singapore, San Francisco, Calcutta, and London. In the late 1800s there was intense apprehension over the possibility of a worldwide outbreak, and Chinese immigrants were regarded as likely carriers. This fear became a contributing factor in the passage of discriminatory immigration bans on Chinese in the United States in 1882.

The Taiping Rebellion devastated the agricultural centers of China. Many of the most intensely cultivated regions of central and eastern China were depopulated and laid barren. Some were still uninhabited decades later, and major portions of the country did not recover until the twentieth century.

Cities, too, were hard hit. Shanghai, a treaty port of modest size before the rebellion, saw its population multiplied many times by the arrival of refugees from war-blasted neighboring provinces. The city then endured months of siege by the Taipings. Major cultural centers in eastern China lost masterpieces of art and architecture; imperial libraries were burned or their collections exposed to the weather; and the printing blocks used to make books were destroyed. While the empire faced the mountainous challenge of dealing with the material and cultural destruction of the war, it also was burdened by a major ecological disaster in the north. The Yellow River changed course in 1855, destroying the southern part of impoverished Shandong province with flooding and initiating decades of drought along the former riverbed in northern Shandong.

Decentralization at the End of the Qing Empire, 1864–1875

The Qing government emerged from the 1850s with no hope of achieving solvency. The corruption of the 1700s, attempts in the very early 1800s to restore waterworks and roads, and declining yields from land taxes had bankrupted the treasury. By 1850, before the Taiping Rebellion, Qing government expenditures were ten times revenues. The indemnities demanded by Europeans after the Opium and Arrow Wars foreclosed any hope that the Qing would get out of debt. Vast stretches of formerly productive rice land were devastated, and the population was dispersed. Refugees pleaded for relief, and the imperial, volunteer, foreign, and mercenary troops that had suppressed the Taipings demanded unpaid wages.

Britain and France became active participants in the period of recovery that followed the rebellion. To ensure repayment of the debt to Britain, Robert Hart was installed as

Cixi's Allies   In the 1860s and 1870s, Cixi was a supporter of reform (see page 751). In later years she was widely regarded as corrupt and self-centered and as an obstacle to reform. Her greatest allies were the court eunuchs. Introduced to palace life in early China as managers of the imperial harems, eunuchs became powerful political parties at court. The first Qing emperors refused to allow the eunuchs any political influence, but by Cixi's time the eunuchs once again were a political factor.   (Freer Gallery of Art and Arthur M. Sackler Gallery Archives, Smithsonian Institution, Washington, D.C., Purchase, 1963–1964. Neg #SC-GR 261)

inspector-general of a newly created Imperial Maritime Customs Service. Britain and the Qing split the revenues he collected. Britons and Americans worked for the Qing government as advisers and ambassadors, attempting to smooth communications between the Qing, Europe, and the United States.

The real work of the recovery, however, was managed by provincial governors who had come to the forefront in the struggle against the Taipings. To prosecute the war, they had won the right to levy their own taxes, raise their own troops, and run their own bureaucracies. These special powers were not entirely canceled when the war ended. Chief among these governors was Zeng Guofan°, who oversaw programs to restore agriculture,

communications, education, and publishing, as well as efforts to reform the military and industrialize armaments manufacture.

Like many provincial governors, Zeng preferred to look to the United States rather than to Britain for models and aid. He hired American advisers to run his weapons factories, shipyards, and military academies. He sponsored a daring program in which promising Chinese boys were sent to Hartford, Connecticut, a center of missionary activity, to learn English, science, mathematics, engineering, and history. They returned to China to assume some of the positions previously held by foreign advisers. Though Zeng was never an advocate of participation in public life by women, his Confucian convictions taught him that educated mothers were more than ever a necessity. He not only encouraged but also partly oversaw the advanced classical

---

Zeng Guofan (zung gwoh-FAN)

Chinese Responses
to Imperialism

The Opium War, followed by the Taiping Rebellion, revealed China's weakness for all to see, but there was no agreement on what should be done to restore its strength. A few provincial officials were able to take effective action, but the competing ideas that were heard at the imperial court tended to cancel each other out.

Feng Guifen, an official and a scholar, came into contact with Westerners defending Shanghai when he took refuge there from the Taipings. The following is from a book of essays he published in 1861.

According to a general geography compiled by an Englishman, the territory of China is eight times that of Russia, ten times that of the United States, one hundred times that of France, and two hundred times that of Great Britain. . . . Yet we are shamefully humiliated by the four nations, not because our climate, soil, or resources are inferior to theirs, but because our people are inferior. . . . Now, our inferiority is not due to our allotment from Heaven [i.e., our inherent nature], but is rather due to ourselves. . . .

Why are the Western nations small and yet strong? Why are we large and yet weak? We must search for the means to become their equal, and that depends solely upon human effort. . . .

We have only one thing to learn from the barbarians, and that is strong ships and effective guns. . . . Funds should be allotted to establish a shipyard and arsenal in each trading port. A few barbarians should be employed, and Chinese who are good in using their minds should be selected to receive instruction so that in turn they may teach many craftsmen. When a piece of work is finished and is as good as that made by the barbarians, the makers should be rewarded with an official *juren* degree and be permitted to participate in the metropolitan examinations on the same basis as other scholars. Those whose products are of superior quality should be rewarded with the *jinshi* degree [ordinarily conferred in the metropolitan examinations] and be permitted to participate

in the palace examinations like others. The workers should be paid double so that they will not quit their jobs.

Our nation's emphasis on civil service examinations has sunk deep into people's minds for a long time. Intelligent and brilliant scholars have exhausted their time and energy in such useless things as the stereotyped examination essays, examination papers, and formal calligraphy. . . . We should now order one-half of them to apply themselves to the manufacturing of instruments and weapons and to the promotion of physical studies. . . . The intelligence and ingenuity of the Chinese are certainly superior to those of the various barbarians; it is only that hitherto we have not made use of them. When the government above takes delight in something, the people below will pursue it further: their response will be like an echo carried by the wind. There ought to be some people of extraordinary intelligence who can have new ideas and improve on Western methods. At first they may take the foreigners as their teachers and models; then they may come to the same level and be their equals; finally they may move ahead and surpass them. Herein lies the way to self-strengthening.

In 1867 the debate over how to resist foreign military pressure surged through the imperial court. Woren, a Mongol who held the rank of grand secretary, spoke for the conservatives.

Mathematics, one of the six arts, should indeed be learned by scholars as indicated in the imperial decree, and it should not be considered an unworthy subject. But according to the viewpoint of your servant, astronomy and mathematics are of very little use. If these subjects are going to be taught by Westerners as regular studies, the damage will be great. . . . Your servant has learned that the way to establish a nation is to lay emphasis on rites and rightness, not on power and plotting. The fundamental effort lies in the minds of people, not in techniques. Now, if we seek trifling arts and respect barbarians as teachers . . . all that can be accomplished is the

749

training of mathematicians. From ancient down to modern times, your servant has never heard of anyone who could use mathematics to raise the nation from a state of decline or to strengthen it in time of weakness. . . .

Since the conclusion of the peace, Christianity has been prevalent, and half of our ignorant people have been fooled by it. The only thing we can rely on is that our scholars should clearly explain to the people the Confucian tenets, which may be able to sustain the minds of the ignorant populace. Now if these brilliant and talented scholars, who have been trained by the nation and reserved for great future usefulness, have to change from their regular course of study to follow the barbarians, then the correct spirit will not be developed, and accordingly the evil spirit will become stronger. After several years it will end in nothing less than driving the multitudes of the Chinese people into allegiance to the barbarians.

The opposing group of ministers who backed the idea of "self-strengthening" responded.

Your ministers have examined the memorial of Woren: the principles he presents are very lofty and the opinion he maintains is very orthodox. Your ministers' point of view was also like that before they began to manage foreign affairs; and yet today they do not presume to insist on such ideas, because of actual difficulties that they cannot help. . . .

From the beginning of foreign relations to the present there have been twenty or thirty years. At first the officials inside and outside the capital did not grasp the crux of the matter, and whether they negotiated peace or discussed war, generally these were empty words without effect. . . . Therefore your ministers have pondered a long-term policy and discussed the situation thoroughly with all the provincial officials. Proposals to learn the written and spoken languages of foreign countries, the various methods of making machines, the training of troops with foreign guns, the dispatching of officials to travel in all countries, the investigation of their local customs and social conditions . . . all these painstaking and special decisions represent nothing other than a struggle for self-strengthening. . . .

We too are afraid that the people who are learning these things will have no power of discrimination and are likely to be led astray by foreigners, as Woren fears. Therefore we have deliberated and decided that those who participate in these examinations must be persons from regular scholastic channels. It is indeed those students who have read widely and who understand right principles and have their minds set upon upright and grand purposes—and the present situation is just what causes the scholars and officials to feel pain in heart and head—who would certainly be able to lie on faggots and taste gall [i.e., nurse vengeance] in order to encourage each other vigorously to seek the actual achievement of self-strengthening. They are different from those who have vague, easygoing, or indifferent ideas.

QUESTIONS FOR ANALYSIS

1. How do the views of the writers reflect their own backgrounds as officials who achieved their offices through the traditional examination system?
2. In what ways do these passages indicate a deep or a shallow understanding of the West?
3. How do the ideas expressed here compare with the attitudes toward reform in the Ottoman and Russian Empires as discussed elsewhere in this chapter?

Source: Wm. Theodore de Bary and Richard Lafrano, *Sources of Chinese Tradition*, vol. 2, 2nd ed. (New York: Columbia University Press, 2000), 235–236, 238–239.

education of his own daughters. Zeng's death in 1872 deprived the empire of a major force for reform.

The period of recovery marked a fundamental structural change in the Qing Empire. Although the emperors after 1850 were ineffective rulers, a coalition of aristocrats supported the reform and recovery programs (see Diversity and Dominance: Chinese Responses to Imperialism). Without their legitimization of the new powers of provincial governors like Zeng Guofan, the empire might have evaporated within a generation. A crucial member of this alliance was Cixi°, who was known as the "Empress Dowager" after the 1880s. Later observers, both Chinese and foreign, reviled her as a monster of corruption and arrogance. But in the 1860s and 1870s Cixi supported the provincial governors, some of whom became so powerful that they were managing Qing foreign policy as well as domestic affairs.

No longer a conquest regime dominated by a Manchu military caste and its Chinese civilian appointees, the empire came under the control of a group of reformist aristocrats and military men, independently powerful civilian governors, and a small number of foreign advisers. The Qing lacked strong, central, unified leadership and could not recover their powers of taxation, legislation, and military command once they had been granted to the provincial governors. From the 1860s forward, the Qing Empire disintegrated into a number of large power zones in which provincial governors handed over leadership to their protégés in a pattern that the Qing court eventually could only ritually legitimate.

Cixi (tsuh-shee)

COMPARATIVE PERSPECTIVES

Most of the subjects of the Ottoman, Russian, and Qing rulers did not think of European pressure or competition as determining factors in their lives during the first half of the nineteenth century. They continued to live according to the social and economic institutions they inherited from previous generations. By the 1870s, however, the challenge of Europe had become widely realized. The Crimean War, where European allies achieved a hollow victory for the Ottomans and then pressured the sultan for more reforms, confirmed both Ottoman and Russian military weakness. The Opium War did the same for China. But China, unlike the other empires, was also stricken by rampaging civil war and regional uprisings.

Though all three empires faced similar problems of reform, military rebuilding, and financial disarray, China was geographically remote from Europe and thus removed from the geostrategic tug-of-war between Britain and Russia. Yet despite British fears about Russian threats to India, the tsars enjoyed the advantage of being included in high-level deliberations among European powers. The Ottoman Empire, which had once dominated eastern Europe, was largely excluded from these deliberations. To many European diplomats and overseas investors, its final demise seemed only a matter of time, leaving up in the air the question of who would reap the benefits.

In analyzing the crises of the three empires, historians today stress European economic pressures and observe that all three empires ultimately became insolvent and saw the overthrow of their ruling dynasties. However, at the time what most impressed the Ottomans, Russians, and Chinese was European military superiority, as demonstrated in the Greek war of independence, the Crimean War, and the Opium War. Thus for all three empires, dealing with military emergency took priority over deeper reforms throughout most of the time period of this chapter.

SUMMARY

What were the benefits and the drawbacks to the Ottoman Empire of the reforms adopted during the Tanzimat period?

How did the Russian Empire maintain its status as both a European power and a great Asian land empire?

How did the impact of European imperialism on China differ from its impact on Russia and the Ottoman Empire?

Online Study Center
ACE the Test

Although the Tanzimat period began with the sultan declaring in 1839 a measure of equality for all Ottoman citizens, improving military performance was at the center of the reforming effort. This reform enhanced the role of the military while other administrative changes reduced the social role and governmental influence of the religious elite. The result was an unbalanced reform effort that eventually led to a military takeover of the country.

For Russians, defeat in the Crimean War and the revelation that Russian arms were no match for modern European weaponry were counterbalanced by the comparative weakness of the peoples to the east and south into whose territories they aggressively expanded. Thus Russia shared in the imperialist expansion that the other European states were engaged in even while lagging far behind in industrialization and efficient government.

The course of Russian expansion into Asia made it a neighbor of Qing China, but other European powers were seen as greater threats. Britain, France, and the United States used every means available to gain the freedom to exploit China economically. With respect to the empires nearer to home, however, European imperialists—the United States had minimal involvement—considered financial investment to be somewhat less important than limiting Russian expansion or weakening the Ottoman state and improving the lives of its Christian and Jewish populations.

KEY TERMS

Muhammad Ali   *p. 729*
Janissaries   *p. 730*
Serbia   *p. 730*
Tanzimat   *p. 731*
Crimean War   *p. 734*
extraterritoriality   *p. 736*

Young Ottomans   *p. 737*
Slavophile   *p. 739*
Pan-Slavism   *p. 739*
Decembrist revolt   *p. 741*
Opium War   *p. 743*
Bannermen   *p. 743*

Treaty of Nanking   *p. 743*
treaty ports   *p. 743*
most-favored-nation status   *p. 743*
Taiping Rebellion   *p. 744*

Online Study Center
Improve Your Grade
Flashcards

SUGGESTED READING

For general histories of the Ottoman Empire see Stanford Shaw, *History of the Ottoman Empire and Modern Turkey* (1976–1977); Bernard Lewis, *The Emergence of Modern Turkey*, 3rd ed. (2001); and Donald Quataert, *The Ottoman Empire, 1700–1922*, 2nd ed. (2005).

On the economy and society of the nineteenth-century Ottoman Empire see Huri Islamoglu-Inan, ed., *The Ottoman Empire and the World-Economy* (1987); Resat Kasaba, *The Ottoman Empire and the World Economy: The Nineteenth Century* (1988); Sevket Pamuk, *The Ottoman Empire and European Capitalism, 1820–1913: Trade, Investment, and Production* (1987); Kemal H. Karpat, *Ottoman Population, 1830–1914: Demographic and Social Characteristics* (1985); and Carter V. Findley, *Bureaucratic Reform in the Ottoman Empire: The Sublime Porte, 1789–1922* (1980). On the reform program and the emergence of national concepts see also Serif Mardin, *The Genesis of Young Ottoman Thought: A Study in the Modernization of Turkish Political Ideas* (reprint, 2000), and Selim Deringil, *The Well-Protected Domains: Ideology and the Legitimation of Power in the Ottoman Empire, 1876–1909* (1998).

Marc Raeff, *Understanding Imperial Russia* (1984), sets nineteenth-century Russian developments in a broad context and challenges many standard ideas. Andreas Kappeler, *The Russian Multi-Ethnic Empire* (2001), and Mark Bassin, *Imperial Visions: Nationalist Imagination and Geographical Expansion in the Russian Far East, 1840–1865* (1999), address Russian expansion and the problems inherent in diversity of population. On economic matters see W. L. Blackwell, *The Beginnings of Russian Industrialization, 1800–1860* (1968). Daniel Field, *The End of Serfdom: Nobility and Bureaucracy in Russia, 1855–1861* (1976), addresses the primary problem besetting Russian society during this period. On the intellectual debates see M. Malia, *Alexander Herzen and the Birth of Russian Socialism* (1961), and Andrzej Walicki, *The Slavophile Controversy* (1975). For a readable popular biography see Edvard Radzinsky, *Alexander II: The Last Great Tsar* (2005).

On the Qing Empire of the nineteenth century see Pamela Kyle Crossley, *Orphan Warriors: Three Manchu Generations and the End of the Qing World* (1990), and for a more detailed political history see Mary C. Wright, *The Last Stand of Chinese Conservatism: The T'ung-chih Restoration, 1862–1874* (1971). On indigenous economic development see Madeleine Zelin, *The Merchants of Zigong: Industrial Entrepreneurship in Early Modern China* (2005). There is a very large literature on both the Opium War and the Taiping Rebellion, including reprinted editions of contemporary observers. For general histories of the Opium War see Peter Ward Fay, *The Opium War, 1840–1842: Barbarians in the Celestial Empire in the Early Part of the Nineteenth Century and the War by Which They Forced Her Gates Ajar* (1975); Christopher Hibbert, *The Dragon Wakes: China and the West, 1793–1911* (1970); and the classic study by Chang Hsin-pao, *Commissioner Lin and the Opium War* (1964). For a recent, more monographic study on Qing political thought in the period of the Opium War see James M. Polachek, *The Inner Opium War* (1992). On the Taiping Rebellion, enduring sources are S. Y. Têng, *The Taiping Rebellion and the Western Powers: A Comprehensive Survey* (1971), and C. A. Curwen, *Taiping Rebel: The Deposition of Li Hsiuch'eng* (1976); see also Caleb Carr, *The Devil Soldier: The Story of Frederick Townsend Ward* (1992). The most recent study is Jonathan D. Spence, *God's Chinese Son: The Taiping Heavenly Kingdom of Hong Xiuquan* (1996).

Indian Railroad Station, 1866   British India built the largest network of railroads in Asia. People of every social class traveled by train.   (Private Collection)

○─ How did different African leaders and peoples interact with each other, and how did European nations' relationship to African peoples change during this period?

○─ How did Britain secure its hold on India, and what colonial policies led to the beginnings of Indian nationalism?

○─ What role did the abolition of slavery and the continued growth of British overseas trade play in the immigration to the Caribbean and elsewhere of peoples from Africa, India, and Asia?

26

AFRICA, INDIA, AND THE NEW BRITISH EMPIRE, 1750–1870

CHAPTER OUTLINE

Changes and Exchanges in Africa

India Under British Rule

Britain's Eastern Empire

Comparative Perspectives

DIVERSITY AND DOMINANCE: Ceremonials of Imperial Domination

ENVIRONMENT AND TECHNOLOGY: Whaling

After suppressing a rebellion instigated by a coalition of Hindus and Muslims in 1857, imperial Britain soon established near complete authority over the Indian subcontinent. The governance of such a vast amount of territory coincided with the Industrial Revolution (described in Chapter 23), and by 1870 India had the greatest rail network in all of Asia, transporting millions of passengers a year. By the middle of the next century these and other developments would empower Indians to reassert, and ultimately realize, their right to self-determination. This chapter will outline, among other topics, the history that made such an outcome possible.

In 1782 Tipu Sultan inherited the throne of the state of Mysore°, which his father had made the most powerful state in south India. The ambitious and talented new ruler also inherited a healthy

---

Mysore (my-SORE)

Online Study Center

This icon will direct you to interactive activities and study materials on the website: *college.hmco.com/pic/bulliet4e.*

distrust of the territorial ambitions of Great Britain's East India Company. In 1785, before the company could invade Mysore, Tipu Sultan launched his own attack. He then sent an embassy to France in 1788, seeking an alliance against Britain. Neither of these ventures was immediately successful.

Not until a decade later did the French agree to a loose alliance with Tipu Sultan as part of their plan to challenge Britain's colonial and commercial supremacy in the Indian Ocean. General Napoleon Bonaparte invaded Egypt in 1798 to threaten British trade routes to India and hoped to use the alliance with Tipu Sultan to drive the British out of India. The French invasion of Egypt went well enough at first, but a British naval blockade and the ravages of disease crippled the French force. As described in Chapter 25, Muhammad Ali took advantage of the situation to revitalize Egypt and expand its rule.

Meanwhile, Tipu's struggle with the East India Company was going badly. A military defeat in 1792 forced him to surrender most of his coastal lands. Despite the loose alliance with France, he was unable to stop further British advances. Tipu lost his life in 1799 while defending his capital against a British assault. Mysore was divided between the British and their Indian allies.

As these events illustrate, talented local leaders and European powers were all vying to expand their influence in South Asia and Africa between 1750 and 1870. Midway through that period, it was by no means clear who would gain the upper hand. Britain and France were as likely to fight each other as they were to fight an Asian or African state. In 1800 the two nations were engaged in their third major war for overseas supremacy since 1750. By 1870, however, Britain had gained a decisive advantage over France.

The new British Empire in the East included the subcontinent of India, settler colonies in Australia and New Zealand, and a growing network of trading outposts. By 1870 Britain had completed the campaign to replace the overseas slave trade from Africa with "legitimate" trade and had spearheaded new Asian and South Pacific labor migrations into a rejuvenated string of tropical colonies.

CHANGES AND EXCHANGES IN AFRICA

In the century before 1870 Africa underwent dynamic political changes and a great expansion of foreign trade. Indigenous African leaders as well as Middle Eastern and European imperialists built powerful new states and expanded old ones. As the continent's external slave trades to the Americas and to Islamic lands died slowly under British pressure, trade in goods such as palm oil, ivory, timber, and gold grew sharply. In return Africans imported large quantities of machine-made textiles and firearms. These complex changes are best understood by looking at African regions separately.

New African States   Internal forces produced clusters of new states in two parts of sub-Saharan Africa between 1750 and 1870. In southern Africa changes in warfare gave rise to a powerful Zulu kingdom and other new states. In inland West Africa Islamic reformers created the gigantic Sokoto° Caliphate and companion states (see Map 26.1).

For many centuries the Nguni° peoples had pursued a life based on cattle and agriculture in the fertile coastlands of southeastern Africa (in modern South Africa). Small independent chiefdoms suited their political needs until a serious drought hit the region at the beginning of the nineteenth century. Out of the conflict for grazing and farming lands, an upstart military genius named Shaka (r. 1818–1828) created the **Zulu** kingdom in 1818. Strict military drill and close-combat warfare featuring ox-hide shields and lethal stabbing spears made the Zulu the most powerful and most feared fighters in southern Africa.

Shaka expanded his kingdom by raiding his African neighbors, seizing their cattle, and capturing their women and children. Breakaway military bands spread this system of warfare and state building inland to the high plateau country, across the Limpopo River (in modern Zimbabwe°), and as far north as Lake Victoria. As the power and population of these new kingdoms increased, so too did the number of displaced and demoralized refugees around them.

To protect themselves from the Zulu, some neighboring Africans created their own states. The Swazi kingdom consolidated north of the Zulu, and the kingdom of

Sokoto (SOH-kuh-toh)   **Nguni** (ng-GOO-nee)
Zimbabwe (zim-BAH-bway)

C H R O N O L O G Y

	Empire	Africa	India
1750			**1756** Black Hole of Calcutta
	1763 End of Seven Years War		**1765** East India Company (EIC) rule of Bengal begins
	1769–1778 Captain James Cook explores New Zealand and eastern Australia		
	1795 End of Dutch East India Company	**1795** Britain takes Cape Colony	**1798** Britain annexes Ceylon
1800		**1798** Napoleon invades Egypt	**1799** EIC defeats Mysore
	1807 Britain outlaws slave trade	**1805** Muhammad Ali seizes Egypt	
		1808 Britain takes over Sierra Leone	
		1809 Sokoto Caliphate founded	
		1818 Shaka founds Zulu kingdom	**1818** EIC creates Bombay Presidency
		1821 Foundation of Republic of Liberia; Egypt takes control of Sudan	**1826** EIC annexes Assam and northern Burma
			1828 Brahmo Samaj founded
	1834 Britain frees slaves in its colonies	**1831–1847** Algerians resist French takeover	**1834** Indentured labor migrations begin
		1836–1839 Afrikaners' Great Trek	
		1840 Omani sultan moves capital to Zanzibar	
1850		**1869** Jaja founds Opobo	**1857–1858** Sepoy Rebellion leads to end of EIC rule and Mughal rule
	1867 End of Atlantic slave trade		
	1877 Queen Victoria becomes Empress of India		**1885** First Indian National Congress
		1889 Menelik unites modern Ethiopia	

Lesotho° grew by attracting refugees to strongholds in southern Africa's highest mountains. Both Lesotho and Swaziland survive as independent states to this day.

Although Shaka ruled for little more than a decade, he succeeded in creating a new national identity as well as a new kingdom. He grouped all the young people in his domains by age into regiments. Regiment members lived together and immersed themselves in learning Zulu lore and customs, including fighting methods for the males. A British trader named Henry Francis Fynn expressed his "astonishment at the order and discipline" he found everywhere in the Zulu kingdom. He witnessed public festivals of loyalty to Shaka at which regiments of young men and women numbering in the tens of thousands

danced around the king for hours. Parades showed off the king's enormous herds of cattle, a Zulu measure of wealth.

Meanwhile, Islamic reform movements were creating another cluster of powerful states in the savannas of West Africa. Islam had been a force in the politics and cities of this region for centuries, but it had made only slow progress among most rural people. As a consequence, most Muslim rulers had found it prudent to tolerate the older religious practices of their rural subjects. In the 1770s local Muslim scholars began preaching the need for a vigorous reform of Islamic practices. They condemned the accommodations Muslim rulers had made with older traditions and called for a forcible conquest of rural "pagans." The reformers followed a classic Muslim pattern: a *jihad* (holy war) added new lands, where governments enforced Islamic laws and promoted the religion's spread among conquered people.

Lesotho (luh-SOO-too)

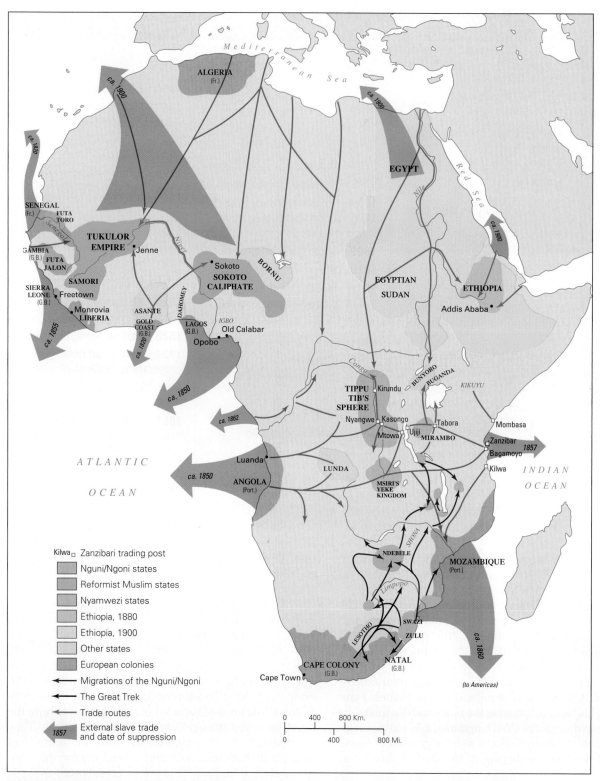

Map 26.1 Africa in the Nineteenth Century Expanding internal and overseas trade drew much of Africa into global networks, but foreign colonies in 1870 were largely confined to Algeria and southern Africa. Growing trade, Islamic reform movements, and other internal forces created important new states throughout the continent.

Zulu in Battle Dress, 1838 Elaborate costumes helped impress opponents with the Zulu's strength. Shown here are long-handled spears and thick leather shields. The stabbing spear is not shown. (Killie Campbell Africana Library. Photo: Jane Taylor/Sonia Halliday Photographs)

The largest of the new Muslim reform movements occurred in the Hausa° states (in what is now northern Nigeria) under the leadership of Usuman dan Fodio° (1745–1817), a Muslim cleric of the Fulani° people. He charged that the Hausa kings, despite their official profession of Islam, were "undoubtedly unbelievers . . . because they practice polytheistic rituals and turn people away from the path of God." Distressed by the lapses of a former pupil, the king of Gobir, Usuman issued a call in 1804 for a jihad to overthrow him. Muslims unhappy with their social or religious position spread the movement to other Hausa states. The successful armies united the conquered Hausa states and neighboring areas under a caliph (sultan) who ruled from the city of

Hausa (HOW-suh)   **Usuman dan Fodio** (OO-soo-mahn dahn FOH-dee-oh)   **Fulani** (foo-LAH-nee)

Sokoto. The **Sokoto Caliphate** (1809–1906) was the largest state in West Africa since the fall of Songhai in the sixteenth century.

As in earlier centuries, these new Muslim states became centers of Islamic learning and reform. Schools for training boys in Quranic subjects spread rapidly, and the great library at Sokoto attracted many scholars. Although officials permitted non-Muslims within the empire to follow their religions in exchange for paying a special tax, they suppressed public performances of dances and ceremonies associated with traditional religions. During the jihads, many who resisted the expansion of Muslim rule were killed, enslaved, or forced to convert.

Sokoto's leaders sold some captives into the Atlantic slave trade and many more into the trans-Saharan slave trade, which carried ten thousand slaves a year, mostly women and children, across the desert to North Africa and the Middle East. Slavery also increased greatly within the Sokoto Caliphate and other new Muslim states. It is estimated that by 1865 there were more slaves in the Sokoto Caliphate than in any remaining slave-holding state in the Americas.[1] Most of the enslaved persons raised food, making possible the seclusion of free women in their homes in accordance with reformed Muslim practice.

Modernization in Egypt and Ethiopia

While new states were arising elsewhere, in northeastern Africa the ancient states of Egypt and Ethiopia were undergoing growth and **modernization**. Napoleon's invading army had withdrawn from Egypt by 1801, but the shock of this display of European strength and Egyptian weakness was long-lasting. The successor to Napoleon's rule was **Muhammad Ali** (see Chapter 25), who ruled Egypt from 1805 to 1848. He began the political, social, and economic reforms that created modern Egypt. In the 1830s Muhammad Ali headed the strongest state in the Islamic world and the first to employ Western methods and technology for modernization. The process was far from blind imitation of the West. Rather, the technical expertise of the West was combined with Islamic religious and cultural traditions. For example, the Egyptian printing industry, begun to provide Arabic translations of technical manuals, turned out critical editions of Islamic classics and promoted a revival of Arabic writing and literature later in the century.

By the end of Muhammad Ali's reign in 1848, the modernization of Egypt was well under way. The population had nearly doubled; trade with Europe had expanded by almost 600 percent; and a new class of

Téwodros's Mighty Cannon Like other modernizers in the nineteenth century, Emperor Téwodros of Ethiopia sought to reform his military forces. In 1861 he forced resident European missionaries and craftsmen to build guns and cannon, including this 7-ton behemoth nicknamed "Sebastapol" after the Black Sea port that had been the center of the Crimean War. It took five hundred men to haul the cannon across Ethiopia's hilly terrain. (From Hormuzd Rassam, *Narrative of the British Mission to Theodore, King of Abyssinia, II,* London 1869, John Murray)

educated Egyptians had begun to replace the old ruling aristocracy. Egyptians were replacing many of the foreign experts, and the fledgling program of industrialization was providing the country with its own textiles, paper, weapons, and military uniforms. The demands on peasant families for labor and military service, however, were acutely disruptive.

Ali's grandson Ismail° (r. 1863–1879) placed even more emphasis on westernizing Egypt. "My country is no longer in Africa," Ismail declared, "it is in Europe."[2] His efforts increased the number of European advisers in Egypt—and Egypt's debts to French and British banks. In the first decade of his reign, revenues increased thirty-fold and exports doubled (largely because of a huge increase in cotton exports during the American Civil War).

By 1870 Egypt had a network of new irrigation canals, 800 miles (1,300 kilometers) of railroads, a modern postal service, and the dazzling new capital city of Cairo. When the market for Egyptian cotton collapsed after the American Civil War, however, Egypt's debts to British and French investors led to the country's partial occupation.

From the middle of the century, state building and reform also were under way in the ancient kingdom of Ethiopia, whose rulers had been Christian for fifteen hundred years. Weakened by internal divisions and the pressures of its Muslim neighbors, Ethiopia was a shadow of what it had been in the sixteenth century, but under Emperor Téwodros° II (r. 1833–1868) and his successor Yohannes° IV (r. 1872–1889) most highland regions were brought back under imperial rule. The only

Ismail (is-MAH-eel)

Téwodros (tay-WOH-druhs)   **Yohannes** (yoh-HAHN-nehs)

large part of ancient Ethiopia that remained outside Emperor Yohannes's rule was the Shoa kingdom, ruled by King Menelik° from 1865. When Menelik succeeded Yohannes as emperor in 1889, the merger of their separate realms created the modern boundaries of Ethiopia.

Beginning in the 1840s Ethiopian rulers purchased modern weapons from European sources and created strong armies loyal to the ruler. Emperor Téwodros also encouraged the manufacture of weapons locally. With the aid of Protestant missionaries his craftsmen even constructed a giant cannon capable of firing a half-ton shell. However, his efforts to coerce more technical aid by holding some British officials captive backfired when the British invaded instead. As the British forces advanced, Téwodros committed suicide to avoid being taken prisoner. Satisfied that their honor was avenged, the British withdrew. Later Ethiopian emperors kept up the program of reform and modernization.

European Penetration

More lasting than Britain's punitive invasion of Ethiopia was France's conquest of Algeria, a move that anticipated the general European "scramble" for Africa after 1870. Equally pregnant with future meaning was the Europeans' exploration of the inland parts of Africa in the middle decades of the century.

Long an exporter of grain and olive oil to France, the North African state of Algeria had even supplied Napoleon with grain for his 1798 invasion of Egypt. The failure of French governments to repay this debt led to many disputes between Algeria and France and eventually to a severing of diplomatic relations in 1827 after the ruler of Algeria, annoyed with the French ambassador, allegedly struck him with a fly whisk. Three years later an unpopular French government, hoping to stir French nationalism with an easy overseas victory, attacked Algeria on the pretext of avenging this insult.

The invasion of 1830 proved a costly mistake. The French government was soon overthrown, but the war in Algeria dragged on for eighteen years. The attack by an alien Christian power united the Algerians behind 'Abd al-Qadir°, a gifted and resourceful Muslim holy man. To achieve victory, the French built up an army of over 100,000 that broke Algerian resistance by destroying farm animals and crops and massacring villagers by the tens of thousands. After 'Abd al-Qadir was captured and exiled in 1847, the resistance movement fragmented, but the French occupiers faced resistance in the mountains

for another thirty years. Poor European settlers, who rushed in to take possession of Algeria's rich coastlands, numbered 130,000 by 1871.

Meanwhile, a more peaceful European intrusion was penetrating Africa's geographical secrets. Small expeditions of adventurous explorers, using their own funds or financed by private geographical societies, were seeking to uncover the mysteries of inner Africa that had eluded Europeans for four centuries. Besides discovering more about the course of Africa's mighty rivers, these explorers wished to assess the continent's mineral wealth or convert the African millions to Christianity.

Many of the explorers were concerned with tracing the course of Africa's great rivers. Explorers learned in 1795 that the Niger River in West Africa flowed from west to east (not the other way, as had often been supposed) and in 1830 that the great morass of small streams entering the Gulf of Guinea was in fact the Niger Delta.

The north-flowing Nile, whose annual floods made Egypt bloom, similarly attracted explorers bent on finding the headwaters of the world's longest river. In 1770 Lake Tana in Ethiopia was established as a major source, and in 1861–1862 Lake Victoria (named for the British sovereign) was found to be the other main source.

In contrast to the heavily financed expeditions with hundreds of African porters that searched the Nile, the Scottish missionary David Livingstone (1813–1873) organized modest treks through southern and Central Africa. The missionary doctor's primary goal was to scout out locations for Christian missions, but he was also highly influential in tracing the course of the Zambezi River between 1853 and 1856. He named its greatest waterfall for the British monarch Queen Victoria. Livingstone also traced the course of the upper Congo River, where in 1871 he was met by the Welsh-American journalist Henry Morton Stanley (1841–1904) on a publicity-motivated search for the "lost" missionary doctor. On an expedition from 1874 to 1877, Stanley descended the Congo River to its mouth.

One of the most remarkable features of the explorers' experiences in Africa was their ability to move unmolested from place to place. The strangers were seldom harmed without provocation. Stanley preferred large expeditions that fought their way across the continent, but Livingstone's modest expeditions, which posed no threat to anyone, regularly received warm hospitality.

Abolition and Legitimate Trade

No sooner was the mouth of the Niger River discovered than eager entrepreneurs began to send expeditions up the river to scout out its potential for trade. Along much of coastal

West Africa, commercial relations with Europeans remained dominant between 1750 and 1870. The value of trade between Africa and the other Atlantic continents more than doubled between the 1730s and the 1780s, then doubled again by 1870.[3] Before about 1825 the slave trade accounted for most of that increase, but thereafter African exports of vegetable oils, gold, ivory, and other goods drove overseas trade to new heights.

Europeans played a critical role in these changes in Africa's overseas trade. The Atlantic trade had arisen to serve the needs of the first European empires, and its transformation was linked to the ideas and industrial needs of Britain's new economy and empire.

One step in the Atlantic slave trade's extinction was the successful slave revolt in Saint Domingue in the 1790s (see Chapter 22). It ended slavery in the largest plantation colony in the West Indies, and elsewhere in the Americas it inspired slave revolts that were brutally repressed. As news of the slave revolts and their repression spread, humanitarians and religious reformers called for an end to the trade. Since it was widely believed that African-born slaves were more likely to rebel than were persons born into slavery, support for abolition of the slave trade was found even among Americans wanting to preserve slavery. In 1807 both Great Britain and the United States made carrying and importing slaves from Africa illegal for their citizens. Most other Western countries followed suit by 1850, but few enforced abolition with the vigor of the British.

Once the world's greatest slave traders, the British became the most aggressive abolitionists. Britain sent a naval patrol to enforce the ban along the African coast and negotiated treaties allowing the patrol to search other nations' vessels suspected of carrying slaves. During the half-century after 1815, Britain spent some $60 million (£12 million) to end the slave trade, a sum equal to the profits British slave traders had made in the fifty years before 1808. Although British patrols captured 1,635 slave ships and liberated over 160,000 enslaved Africans, the trade proved difficult to stop. Cuba and Brazil continued to import huge numbers of slaves, which drove prices up and persuaded some African rulers and merchants to continue to sell slaves and to help foreign slavers evade the British patrols. After British patrols quashed the slave trade along the Gold Coast, the powerful king of Asante° even tried to persuade a British official in 1820 that reopening the trade would be to their mutual profit. Because the slave trade moved to other parts of Africa, the trans-Atlantic slave trade did not end until 1867.

The demand for slaves in the Americas claimed the lives and endangered the safety of untold numbers of Africans, but the trade also satisfied other Africans' desires for the cloth, metals, and other goods that European traders brought in return. To continue their access to those imports, Africans expanded their "**legitimate**" **trade** (exports other than slaves). They revived old exports or developed new ones as the Atlantic slave trade was shut down. On the Gold Coast, for example, annual exports of gold climbed to nearly 25,000 ounces (750 kilograms) in the 1840s and 1850s, compared to 10,000 ounces (300 kilograms) in the 1790s.

The most successful of the new exports from West Africa was palm oil, a vegetable oil used by British manufacturers for soap, candles, and lubricants. Though still a major source of slaves until the mid-1830s, the trading states of the Niger Delta simultaneously emerged as the premier exporters of palm oil. In inland forests men climbed tall oil palms and cut down large palm-nut clusters, which women pounded to extract the thick oil. Coastal African traders bought the palm oil at inland markets and delivered it to European ships at the coast.

The dramatic increase in palm-oil exports—from a few hundred tons at the beginning of the century to tens of thousands of tons by midcentury—did not require any new technology, but it did alter the social structure of the coastal trading communities. Coastal traders grew rich and used their wealth to buy large numbers of male slaves to paddle the giant dugout canoes that transported palm oil from inland markets along the narrow delta creeks to the trading ports. Niger Delta slavery could be as harsh and brutal as slavery on New World plantations, but it offered some male and female slaves a chance to gain wealth and power. Some female slaves who married big traders exercised great authority over junior members of trading households. Male slaves who supervised canoe fleets were well compensated, and a few even became wealthy enough to take over the leadership of the coastal "canoe houses" (companies). The most famous, known as "Jaja" (ca. 1821–1891), rose from canoe slave to become the head of a major canoe house. In 1869, to escape discrimination by free-born Africans, he founded the new port of Opobo, which he ruled as king. In the 1870s Jaja of Opobo was the greatest palm-oil trader in the Niger Delta.

Another effect of the suppression of the slave trade was the spread of Western cultural influences in West Africa. To serve as a base for their anti-slave-trade naval squadron, the British had taken over the small colony of Sierra Leone° in 1808. Over the next several years, 130,000 men, women, and children taken from "captured" vessels

---

Asante (uh-SHAHN-tee)

Sierra Leone (see-ER-uh lee-OWN)

King Jaja of Opobo This talented man rose from slavery in the Niger Delta port of Bonny to head one of the town's major palm-oil trading firms, the Anna Pepple House, in 1863. Six years later, Jaja founded and ruled his own trading port of Opobo. (Reproduced from *West Africa: An Introduction to Its History*, by Michael Crowder, by courtesy of the publishers, Addison Wesley Longman)

Africanus Horton (1835–1882), the son of slaves liberated in Sierra Leone, became a doctor and the author of many studies of West Africa.

Other Western cultural influences came from people of African birth or descent returning to their ancestral homeland. In 1821, to the south of Sierra Leone, free black Americans began a settlement that grew into the Republic of Liberia, a place of liberty at a time when slavery was legal and flourishing in the United States. After their emancipation in 1865 other African Americans moved to Liberia. Emma White, a literate black woman from Kentucky, moved from Liberia to Opobo in 1875, where King Jaja employed her to write his commercial correspondence and run a school for his children. Edward Wilmot Blyden (1832–1912), born in the Danish West Indies and proud of his West African parentage, emigrated to Liberia in 1851 and became a professor of Greek and Latin (and later Arabic) at the fledgling Liberia College. Free blacks from Brazil and Cuba chartered ships to return to their West African homelands, bringing Roman Catholicism, architectural motifs, and clothing fashions from the New World. Although the number of Africans exposed to Western culture in 1870 was still small, this influence grew rapidly.

Secondary Empires in Eastern Africa

When British patrols hampered the slave trade in West Africa, slavers moved southward and then around the tip of southern Africa to eastern Africa. There the Atlantic slave trade joined an existing trade in slaves to the Islamic world that also was expanding. Two-thirds of the 1.2 million slaves exported from eastern Africa in the nineteenth century went to markets in North Africa and the Middle East; the other third went to plantations in the Americas and to European-controlled Indian Ocean islands.

Slavery also became more prominent within eastern Africa itself. Between 1800 and 1873 Arab and Swahili° owners of clove plantations along the coast purchased some 700,000 slaves from inland eastern Africa to do the labor-intensive work of harvesting this spice. The plantations were on Zanzibar Island and in neighboring territories belonging to the Sultanate of Oman, an Arabian kingdom on the Persian Gulf that had been expanding its control over the East African coast since 1698. The sultan had even moved his court to Zanzibar in 1840 to take better advantage of the burgeoning trade in cloves. Zanzibar also was an important center of slaves and ivory. Most of the ivory was shipped to India, where much of it was carved into decorative objects for European markets.

were liberated in Sierra Leone. Christian missionaries helped settle these impoverished and dispirited **recaptives** in and around Freetown, the capital. In time the mission churches and schools made many willing converts among such men and women.

Sierra Leone's schools also produced a number of distinguished graduates. For example, Samuel Adjai Crowther (1808–1891), freed as a youth from a slave ship by the British squadron in 1821, became the first Anglican bishop in West Africa in 1864, administering a pioneering diocese along the lower Niger River. James

Swahili (swah-HEE-lee)

Ivory caravans came to the coast from hundreds of miles inland under the direction of African and Arab merchants. Some of these merchants brought large personal empires under their control by using capital they had borrowed from Indian bankers and modern firearms they had bought from Europeans and Americans. Some trading empires were created by inland Nyamwezi° traders, who worked closely with the indigenous Swahili and Arabs in Zanzibar to develop the long-distance caravan routes.

The largest of these personal empires, along the upper Congo River, was created by Tippu Tip (ca. 1830–1905), a trader from Zanzibar, who was Swahili and Nyamwezi on his father's side and Omani Arab on his mother's. Livingstone, Stanley, and other explorers who received Tippu Tip's gracious hospitality in the remote center of the continent praised their host's intelligence and refinement. On an 1876 visit, for example, Stanley recorded in his journal that Tippu Tip was "a remarkable man," a "picture of energy and strength" with "a fine intelligent face: almost courtier-like in his manner."

Tippu Tip also composed a detailed memoir of his adventures in the heart of Africa, written in the Swahili language of the coast. In it he mocked innocent African villagers for believing that his gunshots were thunder. As the memoir and other sources make clear, modern rifles not only felled countless elephants for their ivory tusks but also inflicted widespread devastation and misery on the people of this isolated area.

One can blame Tippu Tip and other Zanzibari traders, along with their master, the sultan of Oman, for the pillage and havoc in the once-peaceful center of Africa. However, the circle of responsibility was broader. Europeans supplied the weapons and were major consumers of ivory and cloves. For this reason histories have referred to the states carved out of eastern Africa by the sultans of Oman, Tippu Tip, and others as "secondary empires," in contrast to the empire that Britain was establishing directly. At the same time, British officials pressured the sultan of Oman into halting the Indian Ocean slave trade from Zanzibar in 1857 and ending the import of slaves into Zanzibar in 1873.

Egypt's expansion southward during the nineteenth century can also be considered a secondary empire. Muhammad Ali had pioneered the conquest of the upper Nile, in 1821 establishing a major base at Khartoum° that became the capital of Egyptian Sudan. A major reason for his invasion of Sudan was to secure slaves for his army so that more Egyptian peasants could be left free to grow cotton for export. From the 1840s unscrupulous traders of many origins, leading forces armed with European weapons, pushed south to the modern frontiers of Uganda and Zaire in search of cattle, ivory, and slaves. They set one African community against another and reaped profit from the devastation they sowed.

INDIA UNDER BRITISH RULE

The people of South Asia felt the impact of European commercial, cultural, and colonial expansion more immediately and profoundly than did the people of Africa. While Europeans were laying claim to only small parts of Africa between 1750 and 1870, nearly all of India (with three times the population of all of Africa) came under Britain's direct or indirect rule. During the 250 years after the founding of the East India Company in 1600, British interests commandeered the colonies and trade of the Dutch, fought off French and Indian challenges, and picked up the pieces of the decaying Mughal° Empire. By 1763 the French were stymied; in 1795 the Dutch East India Company was dissolved; and in 1858 the last Mughal emperor was dethroned, leaving the vast subcontinent in British hands.

Company Men

As Mughal power weakened in the eighteenth century, Europeans were not the first outsiders to make a move. In 1739 Iranian armies defeated the Mughal forces, sacked Delhi, and returned home with vast amounts of booty. Indian states also took advantage of Mughal weakness to assert their independence. By midcentury, the Maratha° Confederation, a coalition of states in central India, controlled more land than the Mughals did (see Map 26.2). Also ruling their own powerful states were the **nawabs**° (a term used for Muslim princes who were deputies of the Mughal emperor, though in name only): the nawab of Bengal in the northeast; the nawab of Arcot in the southeast, Haidar Ali (1722–1782)—the father of Tipu Sultan and ruler of the southwestern state of Mysore; and many others.

Nyamwezi (nn-nyahm-WAY-zee)   **Khartoum** (khar-TOOM)

Mughal (MOO-guhl)   **Maratha** (muh-RAH-tuh)
nawab (NAH-wab)

Legend:
- Northern limit of Mughal Empire in 1707
- Muslim land in 1765
- Muslim land in 1805
- Area controlled by Hindus in 1805
- Land under British East India Company rule in 1805
- ✕ Site of important battle

Map 26.2 India, 1707–1805 As Mughal power weakened during the eighteenth century, other Indian states and the East India Company expanded their territories.

Online Study Center
Improve Your Grade
Interactive Map: India, 1707–1805

British, Dutch, and French companies were also eager to expand their profitable trade into India in the eighteenth century. Such far-flung European trading companies were speculative and risky ventures in 1750. Their success depended on hard-drinking and ambitious young "company men," who used hard bargaining, and hard fighting when necessary, to persuade Indian rulers to allow them to establish trading posts at strategic points along the coast. To protect their fortified warehouses from attack by other Europeans or by native states, the companies hired and trained Indian troops known as **sepoys**°. In divided India these private armies came to hold the balance of power.

---

sepoy (SEE-poy)

In 1691 Great Britain's East India Company (EIC) had convinced the nawab of the large state of Bengal in northeast India to let the company establish a fortified outpost at the fishing port of Calcutta. A new nawab, pressing claims for additional tribute from the prospering port, overran the fort in 1756 and imprisoned a group of EIC men in a cell so small that many died of suffocation. To avenge their deaths in this "Black Hole of Calcutta," a large EIC force from Madras, led by the young Robert Clive, overthrew the nawab. The weak Mughal emperor was persuaded to acknowledge the East India Company's right to rule Bengal in 1765. Fed by the tax revenues of Bengal as well as by profits from trade, the EIC was on its way. Calcutta grew into a city of 250,000 by 1788.

In southern India, Clive had used EIC forces from Madras to secure victory for the British Indian candidate for nawab of Arcot during the Seven Years War (1756–1763), thereby gaining an advantage over French traders who had supported the loser. The defeat of Tipu Sultan of Mysore at the end of the century (described at the start of the chapter) secured south India for the company and prevented a French resurgence.

Along with Calcutta and Madras, the third major center of British power in India was Bombay, on the western coast. There, after a long series of contests with Maratha Confederation rulers, the East India Company gained a decisive advantage in 1818, annexing large territories to form the core of what was called the "Bombay Presidency." Some states were taken over completely, as Bengal had been, but very many others remained in the hands of local princes who accepted the political control of the company.

Raj and Rebellion, 1818–1857

In 1818 the East India Company controlled an empire with more people than in all of western Europe and fifty times the population of the colonies the British had lost in North America. One thrust of **British raj** (reign) was to remake India on a British model through administrative and social reform, economic development, and the introduction of new technology. But at the same time the company men—like the Mughals before them—had to temper their interference with Indian social and religious customs lest they provoke rebellion or lose the support of their Indian princely allies. For this reason and because of the complexity of the task of ruling such a vast empire, there were many inconsistencies in Britain's policies toward India.

The main policy was to create a powerful and efficient system of government. British rule before 1850 relied heavily on military power—170 sepoy regiments and 16 European regiments. Another policy very much in the interests of India's new rulers was to disarm approximately 2 million warriors who had served India's many states and turn them to civilian tasks, mostly cultivation. A third policy was to give freer rein to Christian missionaries eager to convert and uplift India's masses. Few converts were made, but the missionaries kept up steady pressure for social reforms.

Another key British policy was to substitute ownership of private property for India's complex and overlapping patterns of landholding. In Bengal this reform worked to the advantage of large landowners, but in Mysore the peasantry gained. Private ownership made it easier for the state to collect the taxes that were needed to pay for administration, the army, and economic reform.

Such policies of "westernization, Anglicization, and modernization," as they have been called, were only one side of British rule. The other side was the bolstering of "traditions"—both real and newly invented. In the name of tradition the Indian princes who ruled nearly half of British India were frequently endowed by their British overlords with greater power and splendor and longer tenure than their predecessors had ever had. Hindu and Muslim holy men were able to expand their "traditional" power over property and people far beyond what had been the case in earlier times. Princes, holy men, and other Indians frequently used claims of tradition to resist British rule as well as to turn it to their advantage. The British rulers themselves invented many "traditions"—including elaborate parades and displays—half borrowed from European royal pomp, half freely improvised from Mughal ceremonies.

The British and Indian elites danced sometimes in close partnership, sometimes in apparent opposition. But the ordinary people of India suffered. Women of every status, members of subordinate Hindu castes, the "untouchables" and "tribals" outside the caste system, and the poor generally experienced less benefit from the British reforms and much new oppression from the taxes and "traditions" that exalted their superiors' status.

The transformation of British India's economy was also doubled-edged. On the one hand, British raj created many new jobs as a result of the growth of internal and external trade and the expansion of agricultural production, such as in opium in Bengal—largely for export to China (see Chapter 25)—coffee in Ceylon (an island off the tip of India), and tea in Assam (a state in northeastern India). On the other hand, competition from cheap cotton goods produced in Britain's industrial mills drove many Indians out of the handicraft textile industry. In the eighteenth century India had been the world's greatest exporter of cotton textiles; in the nineteenth century India increasingly shipped raw cotton fiber to Britain.

Even the beneficial economic changes introduced under Britain rule were disruptive, and there were no safety nets for the needy. Displaced ruling elites, disgruntled religious traditionalists, and the economically dispossessed fomented almost constant local rebellions during the first half of the nineteenth century. British rulers readily handled these isolated uprisings, but they were more concerned about the continuing loyalty of Indian sepoys in the East India Company's army. The EIC employed 200,000 sepoys in 1857, along with 38,000 British officers. Armed with the latest rifles and disciplined in fighting methods, the sepoys had a potential for successful rebellion that other groups lacked.

In fact, discontent was growing among Indian soldiers. In the early decades of EIC rule, most sepoys came from Bengal, one of the first states the company had annexed. The Bengali sepoys resented the active recruitment of other ethnic groups into the army after 1848, such as Sikhs° from Punjab and Gurkhas from Nepal. Many high-caste Hindus objected to a new law in 1856 requiring new recruits to be available for service overseas in the growing Indian Ocean empire, for their religion prohibited ocean travel. The replacement of the standard military musket by the far more accurate Enfield rifle in 1857 also caused problems. Soldiers were ordered to use their teeth to tear open the ammunition cartridges, which were greased with animal fat. Hindus were offended by this order if the fat came from cattle, which they considered sacred. Muslims were offended if the fat came from pigs, which they considered unclean.

Although the cartridge-opening procedure was quickly changed, the initial discontent grew into rebellion by Hindu sepoys in May 1857. British troubles mushroomed when Muslim sepoys, peasants, and discontented elites joined in. The rebels asserted old traditions to challenge British authority: sepoy officers in Delhi proclaimed their loyalty to the Mughal emperor; others rallied behind the Maratha leader Nana Sahib. The rebellion was put down by March 1858, but it shook this piecemeal empire to its core.

Historians have attached different names and meanings to the events of 1857 and 1858. Concentrating on the technical fact that the uprising was an unlawful action by soldiers, nineteenth-century British historians labeled it the "**Sepoy Rebellion**" or the "Mutiny," and these names are still commonly used. Seeing in these events the beginnings of the later movement for independence, some

Sikh (seek)

modern Indian historians have termed it the "Revolution of 1857." In reality, it was much more than a simple mutiny, because it involved more than soldiers, but it was not yet a nationalist revolution, for the rebels' sense of a common Indian national identity was weak.

Political Reform and Industrial Impact

Whatever it is called, the rebellion of 1857–1858 was a turning point in the history of modern India. Some say it marks the beginning of modern India. In its wake Indians gained a new centralized government, entered a period of rapid economic growth, and began to develop a new national consciousness.

The changes in government were immediate. In 1858 Britain eliminated the last traces of Mughal and Company rule. In their place, a new secretary of state for India in London oversaw Indian policy, and a new government-general in Delhi acted as the British monarch's viceroy on the spot. A proclamation by Queen Victoria in November 1858 guaranteed all Indians equal protection of the law and the freedom to practice their religions and social customs; it also assured Indian princes that so long as they were loyal to the queen British India would respect their control of territories and "their rights, dignity and honour."[4]

British rule continued to emphasize both tradition and reform after 1857. At the top, the British viceroys lived in enormous palaces amid hundreds of servants and gaudy displays of luxury meant to convince Indians that the British viceroys were legitimate successors to the Mughal emperors. They treated the quasi-independent Indian princes with elaborate ceremonial courtesy and maintained them in splendor. When Queen Victoria was proclaimed "Empress of India" in 1877 and periodically thereafter, the viceroys put on great pageants known as **durbars** (see page 770). The most elaborate was the durbar at Delhi in 1902–1903 to celebrate the coronation of King Edward VII, at which Viceroy Lord Curzon honored himself with a 101-gun salute and a parade of 34,000 troops in front of 50 princes and 173,000 visitors (see Diversity and Dominance: Ceremonials of Imperial Domination).

Behind the pomp and glitter, a powerful and efficient bureaucracy controlled the Indian masses. Members of the elite **Indian Civil Service** (ICS), mostly graduates of Oxford and Cambridge Universities, held the senior administrative and judicial posts. Numbering only a thousand at the end of the nineteenth century, these men visited the villages in their districts, heard lawsuits and complaints, and passed judgments. Beneath them were a far greater number of Indian officials

DIVERSITY + DOMINANCE

후세인 은신처 망

들과 함께 사망 가

형이 대중 앞에 나타나거나 애국심   라크 전후 대책
을 고취하는 노래만을 내보내던 방   의에서는 전후
송마저 중단했다.   영국 주도로 해

Ceremonials of Imperial Domination

*T*his letter to Queen Victoria from Edward Robert Bulwer-Lytton, the Earl of Lytton and the viceroy of India, describes the elaborate durbar that the government of India staged in 1876 in anticipation of her being named "Empress of India." It highlights the effects these ceremonies had on the Indian princes who governed many parts of India as agents ("feudatories") of the British or as independent rulers.

British India's power rested on the threat of military force, but the letter points up how much it also depended on cultivating the allegiance of powerful Indian rulers. For their part, as the letter suggests, such rulers were impressed with such displays of majesty and organization and found much to be gained from granting the British their support.

The day before yesterday (December 23), I arrived, with Lady Lytton and all my staff at Delhi. . . . I was received at the [railroad] station by all the native chiefs and princes, and, . . . after shaking hands . . . , I immediately mounted my elephant, accompanied by Lady Lytton, our two little girls following us on another elephant. The procession through Delhi to the camp . . . lasted upwards of three hours. . . . The streets were lined for many miles with troops; those of the native princes being brigaded with those of your Majesty. The crowd along the way, behind the troops, was dense, and apparently enthusiastic; the windows, walls, and housetops being thronged with natives, who salaamed, and Europeans, who cheered as we passed along. . . .

My reception by the native princes at the station was most cordial. The Maharaja of Jeypore informed Sir John Strachey that India had never seen such a gathering as this, in which not only all the great native princes (many of whom have never met before), but also chiefs and envoys from Khelat, Burmah, Siam, and the remotest parts of the East, are assembled to do homage to your Majesty. . . .

On Tuesday (December 26) from 10 A.M. till past 7 P.M., I was, without a moment's intermission, occupied in receiving visits from native chiefs, and bestowing on those entitled to them the banners, medals, and other honours given by your Majesty. The durbar, which lasted all day and long after dark, was most successful. . . . Your Majesty's portrait, which was placed over the Viceregal throne in the great durbar tent, was thought by all to be an excellent likeness of your Majesty. The native chiefs examined it with special interest.

On Wednesday, the 27th, I received visits from native chiefs, as before, from 10 A.M. til 1 P.M., and from 1:30 P.M. to 7:30 P.M., was passed in returning visits. I forgot to mention that on Tuesday and Wednesday evenings I gave great State dinners to the Governors of Bombay and Madras. Every subsequent evening of my stay at Delhi was similarly occupied by state banquets and receptions [for officials, foreign dignitaries, and] many distinguished natives. After dinner on Thursday, I held a levee [reception], which lasted till one o'clock at night, and is said to have been attended by 2,500 persons—the largest, I believe, ever held by any Viceroy or Governor-General in India. . . .

The satisfactory and cordial assurances received from [the ruler of] Kashmir are, perhaps, less important, because his loyalty was previously assumed. But your Majesty will, perhaps, allow me to mention, in connection with the name of this prince, one little circumstance which appears to me very illustrative of the effect which the assemblage has had on him and others. In the first interviews which took place months ago between myself and Kashmir, which resulted in my securing his assent to the appointment of a British officer at Gilgit, I noticed that, though perfectly courteous, he was extremely mistrustful of the British Government and myself. He seemed to think that every word I had said to him must have a hidden meaning against which he was bound to be on his guard. During our negotiations he carefully kept all his councillors round him, and he referred to them before answering any question I put to him, and, although he finally agreed to my proposals, he did so with obvious reluctance and suspicion, after taking a night to think them over. On the day following the Imperial assemblage, I had another private interview with Kashmir for the settlement of some further details. His whole manner and language on this last occasion were strikingly different. [He said:] "I am now convinced that you mean nothing that is not for the good of me and mine. Our interests are identical with those of the empire. Give me your orders and they shall be obeyed."

I have already mentioned to your Majesty that one of the sons of Kashmir acted as my page at the assemblage. I can truly affirm that all the native princes, great and small, with whom I was previously acquainted vied with each other in doing honor to the occasion, and I sincerely believe that this great gathering has also enabled me to establish the most cordial and confidential personal relations with a great many others whom I then met for the first time.

. . . If the vast number of persons collected together at Delhi, and all almost entirely under canvas, be fairly taken into consideration—a number alluding the highest executive officers of your Majesty's administration from every part of India, each with his own personal staff; all the members of my own Council, with their wives and families, who were entertained as the Viceroy's personal guests; all the representatives of the Press, native and European; upwards of 15,000 British troops, besides about 450 native princes and nobles, each with a following of from 2 to 500 attendants; the foreign ambassadors with their suites; the foreign consuls; a large number of the rudest and most unmanageable transfrontier chieftains with their horses and camels, &c.; and then an incalculably large concourse of private persons attracted by curiosity from every corner of the country—I say if all this be fairly remembered, no candid person will, I think, deny that to bring together, lodge, and feed so vast a crowd without a single case of sickness, or a single accident due to defective arrangements, without a moment's confusion or an hour's failure in the provision of supplies, and then to have sent them all away satisfied and loud in their expressions of gratitude for the munificent hospitality with which they had been entertained (at an expenditure of public money scrupulously moderate), was an achievement highly creditable to all concerned in carrying it out. Sir Dinkur Rao (Sindiah's great Minister) said to one of my colleagues: "If any man would understand why it is that the English are, and must necessarily remain, the masters of India, he need only go up to the Flagstaff Tower, and look down upon this marvellous camp. Let him notice the method, the order, the cleanliness, the discipline, the perfection of its whole organisation, and he will recognise in it at once the epitome of every title to command and govern which one race can possess over others." This anecdote reminds me of another which may perhaps please your Majesty. [The ruler of] Holkar said to me when I took leave of him: "India has been till now a vast heap of stones, some of them big, some of them small. Now the house is built, and from roof to basement each stone of it is in the right place."

The Khan of Khelat and his wild Sirdars were, I think, the chief objects of curiosity and interest to our Europeans. . . . On the Khan himself and all his Sirdars, the assemblage seems to have made an impression more profound even than I had anticipated. Less than a year ago they were all at war with each other, but they have left Delhi with mutual embraces, and a very salutary conviction that the Power they witnessed there is resolved that they shall henceforth keep the peace and not disturb its frontiers with their squabbles. The Khan asked to have a banner given to him. It was explained to His Highness that banners were only given to your Majesty's feudatories, and that he, being an independent prince, could not receive one without compromising his independence. He replied: "But I am a feudatory of the Empress, a feudatory quite as loyal and obedient as any other. I don't want to be an independent prince, and I do want to have my banner like all the rest. Pray let me have it."

I anticipate an excellent effect by and by from the impressions which the yet wilder envoys and Sirdars of Chitral and Yassin will carry with them from Delhi, and propagate throughout that important part of our frontier where the very existence of the British Government has hitherto been almost unrealised, except as that of a very weak power, popularly supposed in Kafristan to be exceedingly afraid of Russia. Two Burmese noblemen, from the remotest part of Burmah, said to me: "The King of Burmah fancies he is the greatest prince upon earth. When we go back, we shall tell all his people that he is nobody. Never since the world began has there been in it such a power as we have witnessed here." These Burmese are writing a journal or memoir of their impressions and experiences at Delhi, of which they have promised me a copy. I have no doubt it will be very curious and amusing. Kashmir and some other native princes have expressed a wish to present your Majesty with an imperial crown of great value; but as each insists upon it that the crown shall be exclusively his own gift, I have discouraged an idea which, if carried out, would embarrass your Majesty with the gift of half a dozen different crowns, and probably provoke bitter heart-burnings amongst the donors. The Rajpootana Chiefs talk of erecting a marble statue of the Empress on the spot where the assemblage was held; native noblemen have already intimated and several to me their intention of building bridges, or other public works, and founding charities, to be called after your Majesty in commemoration of the event.

QUESTIONS FOR ANALYSIS

1. What is significant about the fact that Lord Lytton and his family arrived in Delhi by train and then chose to move through the city on elephants?

2. What impression did the viceroy intend to create in the minds of the Indian dignitaries by assembling so many of them together and bestowing banners, medals, and honors on them?

3. What might account for some Indians' remarkable changes of attitude toward the viceroy and the empire? How differently might a member of the Indian middle class or an unemployed weaver have reacted?

Source: Lady Betty Balfour, *The History of Lord Lytton's Indian Administration, 1876 to 1880* (London: Longmans, Green, and Co., 1899), 116–125.

Delhi Durbar, January 1, 1903 The parade of Indian princes on ornately decorated elephants and accompanied by retainers fostered their sense of belonging to the vast empire of India that British rule had created. The durbar was meant to evoke the glories of India's earlier empires, but many of the details and ceremonies were nineteenth-century creations. (British Empire and Commonwealth Museum, Bristol, UK/The Bridgeman Art Library)

and employees. Recruitment into the ICS was by open examinations. In theory any British subject could take these exams. But they were given in England, so in practice the system worked to exclude Indians. In 1870 only one Indian was a member of the ICS. Subsequent reforms by Viceroy Lord Lytton led to fifty-seven Indian appointments by 1887, but there the process stalled.

The key reason qualified Indians were denied entry into the upper administration of their country was the racist contempt most British officials felt for the people they ruled. When he became commander-in-chief of the Indian army in 1892, Lord Kitchener declared:

> It is this consciousness of the inherent superiority of the European which had won for us India. However well educated and clever a native may be, and however brave he may have proved himself, I believe that no rank we can bestow on him would cause him to be considered an equal of the British officer.

A second transformation of India after 1857 resulted from involvement with industrial Britain. The government invested millions of pounds sterling in harbors, cities, irrigation canals, and other public works. British interests felled forests to make way for tea plantations, persuaded Indian farmers to grow cotton and jute for export, and created great irrigation systems to alleviate the famines that periodically decimated whole provinces. As a result, India's trade expanded rapidly.

Most of the exports were agricultural commodities for processing elsewhere: cotton fiber, opium, tea, silk, and sugar. In return India imported manufactured goods from Britain, including the flood of machine-made cotton textiles that severely undercut Indian hand-loom weavers. The effects on individual Indians varied enormously. Some women found new jobs, though at very low pay, on plantations or in the growing cities, where prostitution flourished. Others struggled to hold families together or ran away from abusive husbands. Everywhere in India poverty remained the norm.

The Indian government also promoted the introduction of new technologies into India not long after their appearance in Britain. Earlier in the century there were steamboats on the rivers and a massive program of canal building for irrigation. Beginning in the 1840s a railroad boom (paid for out of government revenues) gave India its first national transportation network, followed shortly by telegraph lines. Indeed, in 1870 India had the greatest rail network in Asia and the fifth largest in the world. Originally designed to serve British commerce, the railroads were owned by British companies, constructed with British rails and equipment, and paid dividends to British investors. Ninety-nine percent of the railroad employees were Indians, but Europeans occupied all the top positions—"like a thin film of oil on top of a glass of water, resting upon but hardly mixing with [those] below," as one official report put it.

Although some Indians opposed the railroads at first because the trains mixed people of different castes, faiths, and sexes, the Indian people took to rail travel with great enthusiasm. Indians rode trains on business, on pilgrimage, and in search of work. In 1870 over 18 million passengers traveled along the network's 4,775 miles (7,685 kilometers) of track, and more than a half-million messages were sent up and down the 14,000 miles (22,500 kilometers) of telegraph wire. By 1900 India's trains were carrying 188 million passengers a year.

But the freer movement of Indian pilgrims and the flood of poor Indians into the cities also promoted the spread of cholera°, a disease transmitted through water contaminated by human feces. Cholera deaths rose rapidly during the nineteenth century, and eventually the disease spread to Europe. In many Indian minds *kala mari* ("the black death") was a divine punishment for failing to prevent the British takeover. This chastisement also fell heavily on British residents, who died in large numbers. In 1867 officials demonstrated the close connection between cholera and pilgrims who bathed in and drank from sacred pools and rivers. The installation of a new sewerage system (1865) and a filtered water supply (1869) in Calcutta dramatically reduced cholera deaths there. Similar measures in Bombay and Madras also led to great reductions, but most Indians lived in small villages where famine and lack of sanitation kept cholera deaths high. In 1900 an extraordinary four out of every thousand residents of British India died of cholera. Sanitary improvements lowered the rate later in the twentieth century.

cholera (KAHL-uhr-uh)

Rising Indian Nationalism

Ironically, both the successes and the failures of British India stimulated the development of Indian nationalism. Stung by the inability of the rebellion of 1857 to overthrow British rule, some thoughtful Indians began to argue that the only way for Indians to regain control of their destiny was to reduce their country's social and ethnic divisions and promote Pan-Indian nationalism.

Individuals such as Rammohun Roy (1772–1833) had promoted development along these lines a generation

Rammohun Roy   This romantic portrait of the Indian reformer emphasizes his scholarly accomplishments and India's traditional architecture and natural beauty.   (Bristol City Museum and Art Gallery, UK/The Bridgeman Art Library)

earlier. A Western-educated Bengali from a Brahmin family, Roy was a successful administrator for the East India Company and a thoughtful student of comparative religion. His Brahmo Samaj° (Divine Society), founded in 1828, attracted Indians who sought to reconcile the values they found in the West with the ancient religious traditions of India. They supported efforts to reform some Hindu customs, including the restrictions on widows and the practice of child marriage. They advocated reforming the caste system, encouraged a monotheistic form of Hinduism, and urged a return to the founding principles of the Upanishads, ancient sacred writings of Hinduism.

Roy and his supporters had backed earlier British efforts to reform or ban some practices they found repugnant. Widow burning (*sati*°) was outlawed in 1829 and slavery in 1843. Reformers sought to correct other abuses of women: prohibitions against widows remarrying were revoked in 1856, and female infanticide was made a crime in 1870.

Although Brahmo Samaj remained an influential movement after the rebellion of 1857, many Indian intellectuals turned to Western secular values and nationalism as the way to reclaim India for its people. In this process the spread of Western education played an important role. Roy had studied both Indian and Western subjects, mastering ten languages in the process, and helped found the Hindu College in Calcutta in 1816. Other Western-curriculum schools quickly followed, including Bethune College in Calcutta, the first secular school for Indian women, in 1849. European and American missionaries played a prominent role in the spread of Western education. In 1870 there were 790,000 Indians in over 24,000 elementary and secondary schools, and India's three universities (established in 1857) awarded 345 degrees. Graduates of these schools articulated a new Pan-Indian nationalism that transcended regional and religious differences.

Many of the new nationalists came from the Indian middle class, which had prospered from the increase of trade and manufacturing. Such educated and ambitious people were angered by the obstacles that British rules and prejudices put in the way of their advancement. Hoping to increase their influence and improve their employment opportunities in the Indian government, they convened the first **Indian National Congress** in 1885. The members sought a larger role for Indians in the Civil Service. They also called for reductions in military expenditures, which consumed 40 percent of the government's budget, so that more could be spent on alleviating the poverty of the Indian masses. The Indian National Congress promoted unity among the country's many religions and social groups, but most early members were upper-caste Western-educated Hindus and Parsis (members of a Zoroastrian religious sect descended from Persians). The Congress effectively voiced the opinions of elite Indians, but until it attracted the support of the masses, it could not hope to challenge British rule.

BRITAIN'S EASTERN EMPIRE

In 1750 Britain's empire was centered on slave-based plantation and settler colonies in the Americas. A century later its main focus was on commercial networks and colonies in the East. In 1750 the French and Dutch were also serious contenders for global dominion. A century later they had been eclipsed by the British colossus that was straddling the world.

Several distinct changes facilitated the expansion and transformation of Britain's overseas empire. A string of military victories pushed aside other rivals for overseas trade and colonies; new policies favored free trade over mercantilism; and changes in shipbuilding techniques increased the speed and volume of maritime commerce. Linked to these changes were new European settlements in southern Africa, Australia, and New Zealand and the growth of a new long-distance trade in indentured labor.

Colonies and Commerce

As the story of Tipu Sultan told at the beginning of this chapter illustrates, France was still a serious rival for dominion in the Indian Ocean at the end of the eighteenth century. However, defeats in the wars of the French Revolution (see Chapter 22) ended Napoleon's dream of restoring French dominance overseas. The wars also dismantled much of the Netherlands' Indian Ocean empire. When French armies occupied the Netherlands, the Dutch ruler, who had fled to Britain in January 1795, authorized the British to take over Dutch possessions overseas in order to keep them out of French hands. During 1795 and 1796 British forces quickly occupied the Cape Colony at the tip of southern Africa, the strategic Dutch port of Malacca on the strait between the Indian Ocean and the South China Sea, and the island of Ceylon (see Map 26.3).

Bramo Samaj (BRAH-moh suh-MAHJ)   **sati** (suh-TEE)

Map 26.3   European Possessions in the Indian Ocean and South Pacific, 1870   After 1750 French and British competition for new territories generally expanded the European presence established earlier by the Portuguese, Spanish, and Dutch. By 1870 the British controlled much of India, were settling Australia and New Zealand, and possessed important trading enclaves throughout the region.

Then the British occupied Dutch Guiana° and Trinidad in the southern Caribbean. In 1811 they even seized the island of Java, the center of the Netherlands' East Indian empire. British forces had also attacked French possessions, gaining control of the islands of Mauritius° and Réunion in the southwestern Indian Ocean. At the end of the Napoleonic Wars in 1814, Britain returned Java to the Dutch and Réunion to the French but kept the Cape Colony, British Guiana (once part of Dutch Guiana), Trinidad, Ceylon, Malacca, and Mauritius.

The Cape Colony was valuable because of Cape Town's strategic importance as a supply station for ships making the long voyages between Britain and India. With the port city came some twenty thousand descendants of earlier Dutch and French settlers who occupied far-flung farms and ranches in its hinterland. Despite their European origins, these people thought of themselves as permanent residents of Africa and were beginning to refer to themselves as "Afrikaners°" ("Africans" in their dialect of Dutch). British governors prohibited any expansion of the white settler frontier because such expansion invariably led to wars with indigenous Africans. This decision, along with the imposition of laws protecting African rights within Cape Colony (including the emancipation of slaves in 1834), alienated many Afrikaners.

Between 1836 and 1839 parties of Afrikaners embarked on a "Great Trek," leaving British-ruled Cape Colony for the fertile high *veld* (plateau) to the north that two decades of Zulu wars had depopulated. The Great Trek led to the foundation of three new settler colonies in southern Africa by 1850: the Afrikaners' Orange Free State and Transvaal on the high veld and the British colony of Natal on the Indian Ocean coast. Although firearms enabled the settlers to win some important battles against the Zulu and other Africans, they were still a tiny minority surrounded by the populous and powerful independent African kingdoms that had grown up at the beginning of the century. A few thousand British settlers came to Natal and the Cape Colony by midcentury, but these colonies were important to Britain only as stopovers for shipping between Britain and British India.

Meanwhile, another strategic British outpost was being established in Southeast Asia. One prong of the advance was led by Thomas Stamford Raffles, who had governed Java during the period of British occupation from 1811 to 1814. After Java's return to the Dutch, Raffles helped the British East India Company establish a new free port at Singapore in 1824, on the site of a small Malay fishing

Great Trek Aided by African Servants   The ox-drawn wagons of the Afrikaners struggled over the Drakensberg Mountains to the high plains in an effort to escape British control.   (Hulton Archive/Getty Images)

village with a superb harbor. By attracting British merchants and Chinese businessmen and laborers, Singapore soon became the center of trade and shipping between the Indian Ocean and China. Along with Malacca and other possessions on the strait, Singapore formed the "Straits Settlements," which British India administered until 1867.

Further British expansion in Malaya (now Malaysia) did not occur until after 1874, but it came more quickly in neighboring Burma. Burma had emerged as a powerful kingdom by 1750, with plans for expansion. In 1785 Burma tried to annex neighboring territories of Siam (now Thailand) to the east, but a coalition of Thai leaders thwarted Burmese advances by 1802. Burma next attacked Assam to the west, but this action led to war with British India, which was concerned for the security of its own frontier with Assam. After a two-year war, India annexed Assam in 1826 and occupied two coastal provinces of northern Burma. As rice and timber trade from these provinces grew important, the occupation became permanent, and in 1852 British India annexed the port of Rangoon and the rest of coastal Burma.

Guiana (ghee-AH-nuh)   **Mauritius** (moh-RIHS-uhs)
Afrikaner (af-rih-KAHN-uhr)

Imperial Policies and Shipping

Through such piecemeal acquisitions, by 1870 Britain had added several dozen colonies to the twenty-six colonies it had in 1792, after the loss of the thirteen in North America (see Chapter 22). Nevertheless, historians usually portray Britain in this period as a reluctant empire builder, its leaders unwilling to acquire new outposts that could prove difficult and expensive to administer. This apparent contradiction is resolved by the recognition that the underlying goal of most British imperial expansion during these decades was trade rather than territory. Most of the new colonies were meant to serve as ports in the growing network of shipping that encircled the globe or as centers of production and distribution for those networks.

This new commercial expansion was closely tied to the needs of Britain's growing industrial economy and reflected a new philosophy of overseas trade. Rather than rebuilding the closed, mercantilist network of trade with its colonies, Britain sought to trade freely with all parts of the world. Free trade was also a wise policy in light of the independence of so many former colonies in the Americas (see Chapter 24).

Whether colonized or not, more and more African, Asian, and Pacific lands were being drawn into the commercial networks created by British expansion and industrialization. As was pointed out earlier, uncolonized parts of West Asia became major exporters to Britain of vegetable oils for industrial and domestic use and forest products for dyes and construction, while areas of eastern Africa free of European control exported ivory that ended up as piano keys and decorations in the elegant homes of the industrial middle class. From the far corners of the world came coffee, cocoa, and tea (along with sugar to sweeten them) for the tables of the new industrial classes in Britain and other parts of Europe, and indigo dyes and cotton fibers for their expanding textile factories.

In return, the factories of the industrialized nations supplied manufactured goods at very attractive prices. By the mid-nineteenth century a major part of their textile production was destined for overseas markets. Sales of cotton cloth to Africa increased 950 percent from the 1820s to the 1860s. British trade to India grew 350 percent between 1841 and 1870, while India's exports increased 400 percent. Trade with other regions also expanded rapidly. In most cases such trade benefited both sides, but there is no question that the industrial nations were the dominant partners.

A second impetus to global commercial expansion was the technological revolution in the construction of oceangoing ships under way in the nineteenth century.

The middle decades of the century were the golden age of the sailing ship. Using iron to fasten timbers together permitted shipbuilders to construct much larger vessels. Merchant ships in the eighteenth century rarely exceeded 300 tons, but after 1850 swift American-built **clipper ships** of 2,000 tons were commonplace in the British merchant fleet. Huge canvas sails hung from tall masts made the streamlined clippers faster than earlier vessels. Ships from the East Indies or India had taken six months to reach Europe in the seventeenth century; after 1850 the new ships could complete the voyage in half that time.

This increase in size and speed lowered shipping costs and further stimulated maritime trade. The growth in size and numbers of ships increased the tonnage of British merchant shipping by 400 percent between 1778 and 1860. To extend the life of such ships in tropical lands, clippers intended for Eastern service generally were built of teak and other tropical hardwoods from new British colonies in South and Southeast Asia. Although tropical forests began to be cleared for rice and sugar plantations as well as for timbers, the effects on the environment and people of Southeast Asia came primarily after 1870.

Colonization of Australia and New Zealand

The development of new ships and shipping contributed to a third form of British rule in the once-remote South Pacific. British settlers displaced indigenous populations in the new colonies of Australia and New Zealand, just as they had done in North America. This differs from India, where Britain ruled numerous indigenous populations, and Singapore and Cape Town, which were outposts of a commercial empire.

Portuguese mariners had sighted the continent of Australia in the early seventeenth century, but it was too remote to be of much interest to Europeans. However, after the English adventurer Captain James Cook systematically explored New Zealand and the fertile eastern coast of Australia between 1769 and 1778, expanding shipping networks brought in growing numbers of visitors and settlers.

At the time of Cook's visits Australia was the home of about 650,000 hunting-and-gathering people, whose Melanesian° ancestors had settled there some forty thousand years earlier. The two islands of New Zealand, lying 1,000 miles (1,600 kilometers) southeast of Australia, were inhabited by about 250,000 Maori°, who practiced hunting, fishing, and simple forms of agriculture, which

---

Melanesian (mel-uh-NEE-zhuhn)
Maori (MOW-ree [ow as in cow])

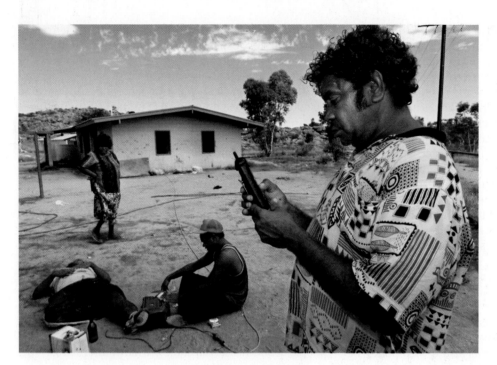

The Aborigines of Australia
Native peoples had been thriving in Australia for tens of thousands of years when the British established their first colonies there in the nineteenth century. Since then they have been the victims of racism and political oppression, and most live on reservations distant from urban areas populated by the descendents of Caucasian and Asian immigrants. (AFP/Getty Images)

their Polynesian ancestors had introduced around 1200 C.E. Because of their long isolation from the rest of humanity, the populations of Australia and New Zealand were as vulnerable as the Amerindians had been to unfamiliar diseases introduced by new overseas contacts. In the 1890s only 93,000 aboriginal Australians and 42,000 Maori survived. By then, British settler populations outnumbered and dominated the indigenous peoples.

The first permanent British settlers in Australia were 736 convicts, of whom 188 were women, sent into exile from British prisons in 1788. Over the next few decades, Australian penal colonies grew slowly and had only slight contact with the indigenous population, whom the British called "Aborigines." However, the discovery of gold in 1851 brought a flood of free European settlers (and some Chinese) and hastened the end of the penal colonies. When the gold rush subsided, government subsidies enabled tens of thousands of British settlers to settle "down under." Improved sailing ships made possible a voyage halfway around the world, although it still took more than three months to reach Australia from Britain. By 1860 Australia had a million immigrants, and the settler population doubled during the next fifteen years.

British settlers were drawn more slowly to New Zealand. Some of the first were temporary residents along the coast who slaughtered seals and exported seal pelts to Western countries to be made into men's felt hats. A single ship in 1806 took away sixty thousand sealskins.

By the early 1820s overhunting had nearly exterminated the seal population. Special ships also hunted sperm whales extensively near New Zealand for their oil, used for lubrication, soap, and lamps; ambergris°, an ingredient in perfume; and bone, used in women's corsets (see Environment and Technology: Whaling). Military action that overcame Maori resistance, a brief gold rush, and the availability of faster ships and subsidized passages attracted more British immigrants after 1860. The colony especially courted women immigrants to offset the preponderance of single men. By the early 1880s fertile agricultural lands of this most distant frontier of the British Empire had a settler population of 500,000.

Britain encouraged the settlers in Australia and New Zealand to become self-governing, following the 1867 model that had formed the giant Dominion of Canada out of the very diverse and thinly settled colonies of British North America. In 1901 a unified Australia emerged from the federation of six separate colonies. New Zealand became a self-governing dominion in 1907.

Britain's policies toward its settler colonies in Canada and the South Pacific reflected a desire to avoid the conflicts that had led to the American Revolution in the eighteenth century. By gradually turning over governing power to the colonies' inhabitants, Britain accomplished three

---

ambergris (AM-ber-grees)

ENVIRONMENT + TECHNOLOGY

Whaling

The rapid expansion of whaling aptly illustrates the growing power of technology over nature in this period. Many contemporaries, like many people today, were sickened by the killing of the planet's largest living mammals. American novelist Herman Melville captured the conflicting sentiments in his epic whaling story, *Moby Dick* (1851). One of his characters enthusiastically explains why the grisly and dangerous business existed:

> But, though the world scorns us as whale hunters, yet does it unwittingly pay us the profoundest homage; yea, an all abounding adoration! for almost all the tapers, lamps, and candles that burn around the globe, burn, as before so many shrines, to our glory!

Melville's character overstates the degree to which whale oil dominated illumination and does not mention its many other industrial uses. Neither does he describe the commercial importance of whalebone (baleen). For a time its use in corsets allowed fashionable women to achieve the hourglass shape that fashion dictated. Whalebone's use for umbrella stays, carriage springs, fishing rods, suitcase frames, combs, brushes, and many other items made it the plastic of its day.

New manufacturing technologies went hand in hand with new hunting technologies. The revolution in ship design enabled whalers from Europe and North America to extend the hunt into the southern oceans off New Zealand. By the nineteenth century whaling ships were armed with guns that shot a steel harpoon armed with vicious barbs deep into the whale. In the 1840s explosive charges on harpoon heads ensured the whale's immediate death. Yet, as this engraving of an expedition off New Zealand shows, flinging small harpoons from rowboats in the open sea continued to be part of the dangerous work.

Another century of extensive hunting devastated many whale species before international agreements finally limited the killing of these giant sea creatures.

South Pacific Whaling One boat was swamped, but the hunters killed the huge whale. (The Granger Collection, New York)

things. It satisfied the settlers' desire for greater control over their own territories; it muted demands for independence; and it made the colonial governments responsible for most of their own expenses. Indigenous peoples were outvoted by the settlers or even excluded from voting.

North American patterns also shaped the indigenous peoples' fate. An 1897 Australian law segregated the remaining Aborigines onto reservations, where they lacked the rights of Australian citizenship. The requirement that voters had to be able to read and write English kept Maori from voting in early New Zealand elections, but four seats in the lower house of the legislature were reserved for Maori from 1867 on.

In other ways the new settler colonies were more progressive. Australia developed very powerful trade unions, which improved the welfare of skilled and semi-skilled urban white male workers, promoted democratic values, and exercised considerable political clout. In New Zealand, where sheep raising was the main occupation, populist and progressive sentiments promoted the availability of land for the common person. Australia and New Zealand were also among the first states in the world to grant women the right to vote, beginning in 1894.

New Labor Migrations

Europeans were not the only people to transplant themselves overseas in the mid-nineteenth century. Between 1834 and 1870 many thousands of Indians, Chinese, and Africans responded to labor recruiters, especially to work overseas on sugar plantations. In the half-century after 1870 tens of thousands of Asians and Pacific islanders made similar voyages.

In part these migrations were linked to the end of slavery. After their emancipation in British colonies in 1834, the freed men and women were no longer willing to put in the long hours they had been forced to work as slaves. When given full freedom of movement in 1839, many left the plantations. To compete successfully with sugar plantations in Cuba, Brazil, and the French Caribbean that were still using slave labor, British colonies had to recruit new laborers.

India's impoverished people seemed one obvious alternative. After planters on Mauritius successfully introduced Indian laborers, the Indian labor trade moved to the British Caribbean in 1838. In 1841 the British government also allowed Caribbean planters to recruit Africans whom British patrols had rescued from slave ships and liberated in Sierra Leone and elsewhere. By 1870 nearly 40,000 Africans had settled in British colonies, along with over a half-million Indians and over 18,000 Chinese. After the French and Dutch abolished slavery in 1848, their colonies also recruited over 150,000 new laborers from Asia and Africa.

Slavery was not abolished in Cuba until 1886, but the rising cost of slaves led the burgeoning sugar plantations to recruit 138,000 new laborers from China between 1847 and 1873. Indentured labor recruits also became the mainstay of new sugar plantations in places that had never known slave labor. After 1850 American planters in Hawaii recruited labor from China and Japan; British planters in Natal recruited from India; and those in Queensland (in northeastern Australia) relied on laborers from neighboring South Pacific islands.

Larger, faster ships made transporting laborers halfway around the world affordable, though voyages from Asia to the Caribbean still took an average of three months. Despite close regulation and supervision of shipboard conditions, the crowded accommodations encouraged the spread of cholera and other contagious diseases that took many migrants' lives.

All of these laborers served under **contracts of indenture**, which bound them to work for a specified period (usually from five to seven years) in return for free passage to their overseas destination. They were paid a small salary and were provided with housing, clothing, and medical care. Indian indentured laborers also received the right to a free passage home if they worked a second five-year contract. British Caribbean colonies required forty women to be recruited for every hundred men as a way to promote family life. So many Indians chose to stay in Mauritius, Trinidad, British Guiana, and Fiji that they constituted a third or more of the total population of these colonies by the early twentieth century.

Although many early recruits from China and the Pacific Islands were kidnapped or otherwise coerced into leaving their homes, in most cases the new indentured migrants had much in common with contemporary emigrants from Europe (described in Chapter 23). Both groups chose to leave their homelands in hopes of improving their economic and social conditions. Both earned modest salaries. Many saved to bring money back when they returned home, or they used their earnings to buy land or to start a business in their new countries, where large numbers chose to remain. One major difference was that people recruited as indentured laborers were generally so much poorer than emigrants from Europe that they had to accept lower-paying jobs in less desirable areas because they could not pay their own way. However, it is also true that many European immigrants into distant places like Australia and New Zealand had their passages subsidized but did not have to sign a contract of indenture. This shows that racial and cultural preferences, not just economics, shaped the flow of labor into European colonies.

A person's decision to accept an indentured labor contract could also be shaped by political circumstances. In India disruption brought by British colonial policies and the suppression of the 1857 rebellion contributed significantly to people's desire to emigrate. Poverty, famine, and warfare had not been strangers in precolonial India.

Nor were these causes of emigration absent in China and Japan (see Chapter 25).

The indentured labor trade reflected the unequal commercial and industrial power of the West, but it was not an entirely one-sided creation. The men and women who signed indentured contracts were trying to improve their lives by emigrating, and many succeeded. Whether for good or ill, more and more of the world's peoples saw their lives being influenced by the existence of Western colonies, Western ships, and Western markets.

COMPARATIVE PERSPECTIVES

What is the global significance of these complex political and economic changes in southern Asia, Africa, and the South Pacific? One perspective stresses the continuing exploitation of the weak by the strong, of African, Asian, and Pacific peoples by aggressive Europeans. In this view, the emergence of Britain as a dominant power in the Indian Ocean Basin and South Pacific continues the European expansion that the Portuguese and the Spanish pioneered and the Dutch took over. Likewise, Britain's control over the densely populated lands of South and Southeast Asia and over the less populated lands of Australia and New Zealand can be seen as a continuation of the conquest and colonization of the Americas.

From another perspective what was most important about this period was not the political and military strength of the Europeans but their growing domination of the world's commerce, especially through long-distance ocean shipping. In this view, like other Europeans, the British were drawn to Africa and southern Asia by a desire to obtain new materials.

However, Britain's commercial expansion in the nineteenth century was also the product of Easterners' demand for industrial manufactures. The growing exchanges could be mutually beneficial. African and Asian consumers found industrially produced goods far cheaper and sometimes better than the handicrafts they replaced or supplemented. Industrialization created new markets for African and Asian goods, as in the case of the vegetable-oil trade in West Africa or cotton in Egypt and India. There

were also negative impacts, as in the case of the weavers of India and the damage to species of seals and whales.

Europeans' military and commercial strength did not reduce Africa, Asia, and the Pacific to mere appendages of Europe. While the balance of power shifted in the Europeans' favor between 1750 and 1870, other cultures were still vibrant and local initiatives often dominant. Islamic reform movements and the rise of the Zulu nation had greater significance for their respective regions of Africa than did Western forces. Despite some ominous concessions to European power, Southeast Asians were still largely in control of their own destinies. Even in India, most people's lives and beliefs showed more continuity with the past than with the change due to British rule.

Finally, it must not be imagined that Asians and Africans were powerless in dealing with European expansion. The Indian princes who extracted concessions from the British in return for their cooperation and the Indians who rebelled against the raj both forced the system to accommodate their needs. Moreover, some Asians and Africans were beginning to use European education, technology, and methods to transform their own societies. Leaders in Egypt, India, and other lands, like those in Russia, the Ottoman Empire, China, and Japan—the subject of Chapter 25—were learning to challenge the power of the West on its own terms. In 1870 no one could say how long and how difficult that learning process would be, but Africans and Asians would continue to shape their own futures.

SUMMARY

○— How did different African leaders and peoples interact with each other, and how did European nations' relationship to African peoples change during this period?

○— How did Britain secure its hold on India, and what colonial policies led to the beginnings of Indian nationalism?

○— What role did the abolition of slavery and the continued growth of British overseas trade play in the immigration to the Caribbean and elsewhere of peoples from Africa, India, and Asia?

Online Study Center
ACE the Test

New African states arose in this period, and ancient states underwent growth and modernization. Shaka established a powerful Zulu kingdom in the south, while the kingdoms of the Swazi and of Lesotho were able to maintain their independence. Usuman dan Fodio conquered the former Hausa states in the west and formed the Sokoto Caliphate. In Egypt Muhammad Ali combined Western expertise with Islamic traditions, and his grandson Ismail did much to develop the country's infrastructure, building irrigation canals, a railroad network, and a modern postal service. Under Emperor Téwodros and his successor, Christian Ethiopia grew stronger by purchasing European weapons and manufacturing them locally. When France invaded Algeria in 1830, Algerians united behind the Muslim cleric 'Abd al-Qadir, but the country was devastated. Commercial ties between Europe and Africa grew enormously, owing first to the slave trade and then to trade in vegetable oils, gold, and ivory. No country enforced the abolition of slavery more effectively than Britain. British antislavery naval operations freed more than one hundred thousand captives, settling them in Freetown, the capital of Sierra Leone. The slave trade then moved east to exploit an expanding market for slaves in North Africa and the Middle East.

While Europeans laid claim to only small parts of Africa, Britain gained nearly complete control of India. European companies established trading posts at strategic points along the coast and protected them by hiring private armies of sepoys. The British East India Company, using negotiation or force in dealing with local princes, was able to secure control of the cities of Calcutta, Madras, and Bombay. The British instituted a powerful colonial government and skillfully exploited native traditions and local rulers. The power given to Indians who governed on their behalf was greatly increased, even as the life of the masses deteriorated. In 1857–1858 the Sepoy Rebellion prompted a wave of reforms: Queen Victoria promised all Indians freedom of religion and equal protection under the law, and great sums of money were invested in harbors, canals, trains, and telegraph lines. However, the profits from such enterprises remained in colonial hands, and the loss of manufacturing jobs, epidemics of cholera, and an increasingly educated middle class led to the rise of Indian nationalism.

By 1850 the British Empire was no longer focused on slave-based colonies in the Americas but on commercial networks and colonies in the East. Faster and larger vessels, like the American-built clipper ships, facilitated the expansion of the British merchant fleet. With the demise of Napoleonic France and the backing of the Dutch, the British took control of the Cape Colony in southern Africa, the island of Ceylon, and the port of Malacca. In 1824 British founded a port at Singapore that soon became the center of trade between the Indian Ocean and China. After Britain, France, and the Netherlands had abolished slavery, thousands of Indians, Chinese, Africans, and Pacific islanders immigrated to British colonies, above all to the Caribbean, under contracts of indenture. By 1778, when James Cook had explored New Zealand and eastern Australia, expanding shipping networks brought growing numbers of settlers there, displacing the native Maori and Australian peoples. Europeans brought new and devastating diseases, as they had done to Amerindian peoples two centuries before (see Chapters 16 and 18): over 80 percent of native New Zealanders and Australians perished in just over a century.

KEY TERMS

Zulu *p. 756*	recaptives *p. 763*	durbar *p. 767*	*Online Study Center*
Sokoto Caliphate *p. 759*	nawab *p. 764*	Indian Civil Service *p. 767*	**Improve Your Grade**
modernization *p. 759*	sepoy *p. 765*	Indian National Congress *p. 772*	Flashcards
Muhammad Ali *p. 759*	British raj *p. 766*	clipper ship *p. 775*	
"legitimate" trade *p. 762*	Sepoy Rebellion *p. 767*	contract of indenture *p. 778*	

SUGGESTED READING

Volumes 2 and 3 of *The Oxford History of the British Empire*, ed. William Roger Louis (1998, 1999), are the most up-to-date global surveys of this period. Less Anglocentric in their interpretations are Immanuel Wallerstein's *The Second Era of Great Expansion of the Capitalist World-Economy, 1730–1840s* (1989) and William Woodruff's *Impact of Western Man: A Study of Europe's Role in the World Economy, 1750–1960* (1982). Atlantic relations are well handled by David Eltis, *Economic Growth and the Ending of the Transatlantic Slave Trade* (1987). For the Indian Ocean basin see Sugata Bose, *A Hundred Horizons: The Indian Ocean in the Age of Global Empire* (2006).

Roland Oliver and Anthony Atmore provide a brief introduction to Africa in *Africa Since 1800*, 5th ed. (2005). More advanced works are J. F. Ade Ajayi, ed., *UNESCO General History of Africa*, vol. 6, *Africa in the Nineteenth Century until the 1880s* (1989), and John E. Flint, ed., *The Cambridge History of Africa*, vol. 5, *From c. 1790 to c. 1870* (1976). Although specialized literature has refined some of their interpretations, the following are excellent introductions to their subjects: J. D. Omer-Cooper, *The Zulu Aftermath: A Nineteenth Century Revolution in Bantu Africa* (1978); Murray Last, *The Sokoto Caliphate* (1967); A. G. Hopkins, *An Economic History of West Africa* (1973); Robert W. July, *The Origins of Modern African Thought: Its Development in West Africa During the Nineteenth and Twentieth Centuries* (1968); and Robert I. Rotberg, ed., *Africa and Its Explorers: Motives, Methods, and Impact* (1970). For eastern and northeastern Africa see Norman R. Bennett, *Arab Versus European: Diplomacy and War in Nineteenth Century East Central Africa* (1986); P. J. Vatikiotis, *The History of Modern Egypt: From Muhammad Ali to Mubarak*, 4th ed. (1991); and, for the negative social impact of Egyptian modernization, Judith Tucker, "Decline of the Family Economy in Mid-Nineteenth-Century Egypt," *Arab Studies Quarterly* 1 (1979): 245–271.

Very readable introductions to India in this period are Sugata Bose and Ayeshia Jalal, *Modern South Asia: History, Culture, Political Economy*, 2nd ed. (2003); Burton Stein, *A History of India* (1998); and Stanley Wolpert, *A New History of India*, 7th ed.

(2004). More advanced treatments in the "New Cambridge History of India" series are P. J. Marshall, *Bengal: The British Bridgehead: Eastern India, 1740–1828* (1987); C. A. Bayly, *Indian Society and the Making of the British Empire* (1987); Sugata Bose, *Peasant Labour and Colonial Capital: Rural Bengal Since 1700* (1993); and Kenneth W. Jones, *Socio-Religious Reform Movements in British India* (1989). Environmental and technological perspectives on India are offered in the appropriate parts of Daniel Headrick, *The Tentacles of Progress: Technology Transfer in the Age of Imperialism, 1850–1940* (1988); and Madhav Gadgil and Ramachandra Guha, *This Fissured Land: An Ecological History of India* (1993). For Tipu Sultan see Kate Brittlebank, *Tipu Sultan's Search for Legitimacy: Islam and Kingship in a Hindu Domain* (1997).

A good introduction to the complexities of Southeast Asian history is D. R. SarDesai, *Southeast Asia: Past and Present*, 5th ed. (2004). More detail can be found in the appropriate chapters of Nicholas Tarling, ed., *The Cambridge History of South East Asia*, 2 vols. (1999). The second and third volumes of *The Oxford History of Australia*, ed. Geoffrey Bolton (1992, 1988), deal with the period covered by this chapter. A very readable multicultural and gendered perspective is provided by *Images of Australia: An Introductory Reader in Australian Studies,* ed. Gillian Whitlock and David Carter (1992). *The Oxford Illustrated History of New Zealand,* ed. Keith Sinclair (1996), provides a wide-ranging introduction to that nation.

For summaries of recent scholarship on the indentured labor trade see David Northrup, *Indentured Labor in the Age of Imperialism, 1834–1922* (1995), and Robin Cohen, ed., *The Cambridge Survey of World Migration*, part 3, "Asian Indentured and Colonial Migration" (1995).

An outstanding analysis of British whaling is Gordon Jackson's *The British Whaling Trade* (2005). Edouard A. Stackpole's *Whales & Destiny: The Rivalry Between America, France, and Britain for Control of the Southern Whale Fishery, 1785–1825* (1972) is more anecdotal.

NOTES

1. Paul E. Lovejoy and Jan S. Hogendorn, *Slow Death for Slavery: The Course of Abolition in Northern Nigeria, 1897–1936* (New York: Cambridge University Press, 1993).
2. Quoted in P. J. Vatikiotis, *The History of Modern Egypt: From Muhammad Ali to Mubarak*, 4th ed. (Baltimore: Johns Hopkins University Press, 1991), 74.
3. David Eltis, "Precolonial Western Africa and the Atlantic Economy," in *Slavery and the Rise of the Atlantic Economy,* ed. Barbara Solow (New York: Cambridge University Press, 1991), table 1.
4. Quoted by Bernard S. Cohn, "Representing Authority in Victorian India," in *The Invention of Tradition*, ed. Eric Hobsbawm and Terence Ranger (Cambridge, England: Cambridge University Press, 1983), 165.

State Power, the Census, and the Question of Identity

Between the American Revolution and the last decades of the nineteenth century, Europe and the Americas were transformed. The ancient power of kings and the authority of religion were eclipsed by muscular new ways of organizing political, economic, and intellectual life. The Western world was vastly different in 1870 than it had been a century earlier. One of the less heralded but enduringly significant changes was the huge expansion of government statistical services.

The rise of the nation-state was associated with the development of modern bureaucratic departments that depended on reliable statistics to measure the nation's achievements and discover its failures. The nation-state, whether democratic or not, mobilized resources on a previously unimaginable scale. Modern states were more powerful and wealthier, and they were also more ambitious and more intrusive. The growth of their power can be seen in the modernization of militaries, the commitment to internal improvements such as railroads, and the growth in state revenues. In recent years historians have begun to examine a less visible but equally important manifestation of growing state power: census taking.

Governments and religious authorities have counted people since early times. Our best estimates of the Amerindian population of the Western Hemisphere in 1500 rest almost entirely on what were little more than missionaries' guesses about the numbers of people they baptized. Spanish and Portuguese kings were eager to count native populations, since "indios" (adult male Amerindians) were subject to special labor obligations and tribute payments. So, from the mid-sixteenth century onward, imperial officials conducted regular censuses of Amerindians, adapting practices already in place in Europe.

The effort to measure and categorize populations was transformed in the last decades of the eighteenth century when the nature of European governments began to change. The Enlightenment belief that the scientific method could be applied to human society proved to be attractive both to political radicals, like the French Revolutionaries, and to reforming monarchs like Maria Theresa of Austria. Enlightenment philosophers had argued that a science of government could remove the inefficiencies and irrationalities that had long subverted the human potential for prosperity and happiness. The French intellectual Condorcet wrote in 1782:

> Those sciences, created almost in our own days, the object of which is man himself, the direct goal of which is the happiness of man, will enjoy a progress no less sure than that of the physical sciences. . . . In meditating on the nature of the moral sciences [what we now call the social sciences], one cannot help seeing that, as they are based like the physical sciences on the observation of fact, they must follow the method, acquire a language equally exact and precise, attaining the same degree of certainty.[1]

As confidence in this new "science" grew, the term previously used to describe the collection of numbers about society, *political arithmetic*, was abandoned by governments and practitioners in favor of *statistics*, a term that clearly suggests its close ties to the "state." In the nineteenth century the new objectives set out by Condorcet and others led to both the formal university training of statisticians and the creation of government statistical services.

The ambitions of governments in this new era were great. Nation-states self-consciously sought to transform society, sponsoring economic development, education, and improvements in health and welfare. They depended on statistics to measure the effectiveness of their policies and, as a result, were interested in nearly everything. They counted taverns, urban buildings, births and deaths, and arrests and convictions. They also counted their populations with a thoroughness never before seen. As statistical reporting became more uniform across Europe and the Americas, governments could measure not only their own progress but also that of their neighbors and rivals.

The revolutionary governments of France modernized the census practices of the overthrown monarchy. They spent much more money, hired many more census takers, and devoted much more energy to training the staff that designed censuses and analyzed results. Great Britain set up an official census in 1801, but it established a special administrative structure only in the 1830s. In the Western Hemisphere nearly every in-

---

[1]Quoted in James C. Scott, *Seeing like a State. How Certain Schemes to Improve the Human Condition Have Failed* (New Haven: Yale University Press, 1998), 91.

dependent nation provided for "scientific" censuses. In the United States the federal constitution required that a census be taken every ten years. Latin American nations, often torn by civil war in the nineteenth century, took censuses less regularly, but even the poorest nations took censuses when they could. It was as if the census itself confirmed the existence of the government, demonstrating its modernity and seriousness.

Until recently, historians who relied on these documents in their research on economic performance, issues of race and ethnicity, family life, and fertility and mortality asked few questions about the politics of census design. What could be more objective than rows of numbers? But the advocates of statistics who managed census taking were uninhibited in advertising the usefulness of reliable numbers to the governments that employed them. At the 1860 International Statistical Congress held in London one speaker said, "I think the true meaning to be attached to `statistics' is not every collection of figures, but figures collected with the sole purpose of applying the principles deduced from them to questions of importance to the state."[2] The desire to be useful meant that statistics could not be fully objective.

Subjectivity was an unavoidable problem with censuses. Censuses identified citizens and foreign residents by place of residence, sex, age, and family relationships within households as well as profession and literacy. These determinations were sometimes subjective. Modern scholars have demonstrated that census takers also often undercounted the poor and those living in rural areas.

Because census takers, as agents of nation-states, were determined to be useful, they were necessarily concerned with issues of nationality and, in the Americas, with race because these characteristics commonly determined political rights and citizenship. The assessment and recording of nationality and race would prove to be among the most politically problematic objectives of the new social sciences.

Nationality had not been a central question for traditional monarchies. For the emerging nation-state, however, nationality was central. A nation's strength was assumed to depend in large measure on the growth of its population, a standard that, once articulated, suggested that the growth of minority populations was

dangerous. Who was French? Who was Austrian or Hungarian? European statisticians relied on both *language of use* and *mother tongue* as proxies for *nationality*, the first term being flexible enough to recognize the assimilation of minorities, the second suggesting a more permanent identity based on a person's original language. Both terms forced bilingual populations to simplify their more complex identities. Ethnic minorities, once identified, were sometimes subject to discrimination such as exclusion from military careers or from universities. In parts of Spanish America language was used as a proxy for *race*. Those who spoke Spanish were citizens in the full sense, even if they were indistinguishable from Amerindians in appearance. Those who spoke indigenous languages were "indios" and therefore subject to special taxes and labor obligations and effectively denied the right to vote.

Beyond providing a justification for continuing discrimination, census categories compressed and distorted the complexity and variety of human society to fit the preconceptions of bureaucrats and politicians. Large percentages of the residents of Mexico, Peru, and Bolivia, among other parts of the Americas, were descended from both Europeans and Amerindians and, in the Caribbean region, from Europeans and Africans. Census categories never adequately captured the complexities of these biological and cultural mixtures. We now know that the poor were often identified as "indios" or "blacks" and the better-off were often called something else, "Americanos," "criollos" (creoles), or even whites. Since this process flattened and streamlined the complexities of identity, censuses on their own are not reliable guides to the distribution of ethnicity and race in a population.

In Europe the issue of nationality proved similarly perplexing for census takers and similarly dangerous to those identified as minorities. Linguistic and ethnic minorities had always lived among the politically dominant majorities: Jewish and Polish minorities in areas controlled by German speakers, German speakers among the French, and Serbo-Croatian speakers among Hungarians, for example. The frontiers between these minority populations and their neighbors were always porous. Sexual unions and marriages were common, and two or more generations of a family often lived together in the same household, with the elder members speaking one language and the younger members another. Who was what? In a very real sense, nationality, like race in the Americas, was ultimately fixed by the census process, where the nation-state forced a limited array of politically utilitarian categories onto the rich diversity of ethnicity and culture.

---

[2]This discussion relies heavily on Eliza Johnson (now Ablovatski), "Counting and Categorizing: The Hungarian Gypsy Census of 1893" (M.A. Thesis, Columbia University, 1996), especially Chapter III. She quotes from the *Proceedings of the Sixth International Statistical Congress Held in London, 1860,* 379.

PART SEVEN

GLOBAL DIVERSITY AND DOMINANCE, 1850–1945

CHAPTER 27
The New Power Balance, 1850–1900

CHAPTER 28
The New Imperialism, 1869–1914

CHAPTER 29
The Crisis of the Imperial Order, 1900–1929

CHAPTER 30
The Collapse of the Old Order, 1929–1949

CHAPTER 31
Striving for Independence: India, Africa, and Latin America, 1900–1949

In 1850, the world still embraced a huge diversity of societies, cultures, and states. During the century that followed, European nations, the United States, and Japan dominated much of the world in a wave of conquest we call the New Imperialism and tried to convert their new subjects to their own cultures and ways of life.

In Europe, mounting tensions and the awesome power of modern armaments led to the devastating Great War of 1914–1918. Russia and China erupted in revolution. Soon after, the heartland of the Ottoman Empire became modern Turkey, while its Arab provinces were taken over by France and Britain.

The political and economic system the European powers crafted after the war fell apart in the 1930s. While the capitalist nations fell into a deep

Highways of the Empire   In the late nineteenth century, Europeans believed the world revolved around their small subcontinent. World maps printed in Great Britain showed the British Empire in red, with informal dependencies and protectorates in pink. Most maps showed the world in a Mercator projection, centered on the intersection of the Greenwich meridian and the equator just off West Africa. This one, in contrast, is a polar projection with Britain in the exact center. It shows the lines of communication that bound Britain to her possessions worldwide: the major shipping routes and submarine telegraph cable lines that made London the center of global commerce and finance and insured the supremacy of the Royal Navy around the world.   (Victoria & Albert Museum, London/Art Resource, NY)

economic depression, the Soviet Union industrialized at breakneck speed. In Germany and Japan, extremists sought to solve their countries' grievances by military conquest.

In World War II, nationalism and industrial warfare led to the massacre of millions of people and the destruction of countless cities. The war also weakened Europe's control of its overseas empires. Nationalists in Asia, Latin America, and Africa were inspired by Western ideas and by the desire to acquire the benefits of industrialization. India gained its independence in 1947. Two years later, Mao Zedong led the Chinese communists to victory. Latin American leaders embraced nationalist economic and social policies. Of all the once great powers, only the United States and the Soviet Union remained to compete for global dominance.

Arrivals from the East   In 1853, Commodore Matthew Perry's fleet sailed into Edo (now Tokyo) Bay. The first steam-powered warships to appear in Japanese waters caused a sensation among the Japanese. In this print done after the Meiji Restoration, the traditionally dressed local samurai go out to confront the mysterious "black ships."   (Courtesy of the Trustees of the British Museum/The Art Archive)

○─ What new technologies and industries appeared between 1850 and 1900, and how did they affect the world economy?

○─ How did the societies of the industrial countries change during this period?

○─ How did industrialization contribute to the socialist and labor movements?

○─ How was nationalism transformed from a revolutionary to a conservative ideology?

○─ How did the forces of nationalism affect the major powers of Europe?

27

THE NEW POWER BALANCE, 1850–1900

CHAPTER OUTLINE

New Technologies and the World Economy

Social Changes

Socialism and Labor Movements

Nationalism and the Rise of Italy, Germany, and Japan

The Great Powers of Europe, 1871–1900

China, Japan, and the Western Powers

ENVIRONMENT AND TECHNOLOGY: Railroads and Immigration

MATERIAL CULTURE: Cotton Clothing

DIVERSITY AND DOMINANCE: Marx and Engels on Global Trade and the Bourgeoisie

On July 8, 1853, four American warships, two of them steam-powered, appeared in Edo Bay, close to the capital of Japan. The commander of the fleet, **Commodore Matthew Perry**, delivered a letter from the president of the United States, demanding that Japan open its ports to foreign trade. Although foreign ships had appeared from time to time in Japanese waters, Perry's "black ships," as the Japanese called them, were the first to break through the barriers that had kept Japan isolated from the rest of the world for two and a half centuries. It was not the foreign interlopers who created such a sensation among the Japanese, but the machines they came in.

Online Study Center

This icon will direct you to interactive activities and study materials on the website: *college.hmco.com/pic/bulliet4e.*

A year later, Perry returned with a fleet of seven ships to receive the answer from the Japanese government. The Americans also set up a track and a little steam locomotive, a short telegraph line, and other marvels of Western technology. For the next twenty years, Japanese society was torn between those who wanted to retreat into isolation and those who wished to embrace the foreign ways and acquire their machines and the industries that made them. For it soon became clear that industrialization gave power and that only by industrializing could Japan join the ranks of the powerful nations and escape the fate of weaker ones that were then being taken over by Europe and the United States.

In the late nineteenth century a very small number of states, known as "great powers," dominated the world. Great Britain, France, and Russia had been recognized as great powers long before the industrial age. Russia began industrializing in the late nineteenth century, as did Germany, the United States, and Japan. The rise of the United States was covered in Chapter 24; in this chapter we will turn to the other great powers of the age. In the next chapter, which deals with the era of the "New Imperialism" (1870–1914), we will see how these nations used their power to establish colonial empires in Asia and Africa and to control Latin America. Together, Chapters 27 and 28 describe an era in which a handful of wealthy industrialized nations imposed on the other peoples of the world a domination more powerful than any experienced before or since.

NEW TECHNOLOGIES AND THE WORLD ECONOMY

The Industrial Revolution marked the beginning of a massive transformation of the world. In the nineteenth century the technologies discussed in Chapter 23—textile mills, railroads, steamships, the telegraph, and others—spread from Britain to other parts of the world. By 1890 Germany and the United States had surpassed Great Britain as the world's leading industrial powers. Small companies, like those that flourished in Britain, were overshadowed by large corporations, some owned by wealthy capitalists, others (especially in Russia and Japan) by governments.

Industrialization did not consist only of familiar technologies spreading to new areas, but also of entirely new technologies that revolutionized everyday life and transformed the world economy. The motive force behind this second phase of industrialization consisted of deliberate combinations of business entrepreneurship, engineering, and science, especially physics and chemistry. The first Industrial Revolution that you read about in Chapter 23 also involved the interactions of science, crafts, and business through the friendships of people with different interests, as in the Lunar Society. By the mid-nineteenth century this potent combination was institutionalized in the creation of engineering schools and research laboratories, first in Germany and then in the United States. Electricity and the steel and chemical industries were the first results of this new force. Let us turn first to the diffusion of earlier technologies, and then to the newer industries of the late nineteenth century.

Railroads

By the mid-nineteenth century, steam engines had become the prime mover of industry and commerce. Nowhere was this more evident than in the spread of **railroads**. By 1850 the first railroads had proved so successful that every industrializing country, and many that aspired to become industrial, began to build lines. The next fifty years saw a tremendous expansion of the world's rail networks. After a rapid spurt of building new lines, British railroad mileage leveled off at around 20,000 miles (over 32,000 kilometers) in the 1870s. France and Germany built networks longer than Britain's, as did Canada and Russia. When Japan began building its railway network in the 1870s, it imported several hundred engineers from the United States and Britain, then replaced them with newly trained Japanese engineers in the 1880s. By the early twentieth century, rail lines reached every city and province in Japan (see Map 27.3 on page 807).

The largest rail network by far was in the United States. At the end of its Civil War in 1865 the United States already had 35,000 miles (over 56,000 kilometers) of track, three times as much as Britain. By 1915 the American network reached 390,000 miles (around 628,000 kilometers), more than the next seven longest networks combined.

Railroads were not confined to the industrialized nations; they could be constructed almost anywhere

CHRONOLOGY

	Political Events	Social, Cultural, and Technological Events
1850		**1851** Majority of British population living in cities
	1853–1854 Commodore Matthew Perry visits Japan	**1856** Bessemer converter; first synthetic dye
		1859 Charles Darwin, *On the Origin of Species*
1860	**1860–1870** Unification of Italy	**1861** Emancipation of serfs (Russia)
	1861–1865 American Civil War	**1866** Alfred Nobel develops dynamite
	1862–1908 Rule of Empress Dowager Cixi (China)	**1867** Karl Marx, *Das Kapital*
		1868–1894 Japan undergoes Western-style industrialization and societal changes
	1868 Meiji Restoration begins modernization drive in Japan	
1870	**1870–1871** Franco-Prussian War	
	1871 Unification of Germany	
	1875 Social Democratic Party founded in Germany	
1880		**1879** Thomas Edison develops incandescent lamp
1890	**1894–1906** Dreyfus affair (France)	
	1894 Sino-Japanese War	
1900	**1900** Boxer Uprising (China)	
	1904–1905 Russo-Japanese War	
	1905 Revolution of 1905 (Russia)	
	1910 Japan annexes Korea	

they would be of value to business or government. That included regions with abundant raw materials or agricultural products, like South Africa, Mexico, and Argentina, and densely populated countries like Egypt. The British built the fourth largest rail network in the world in India in order to reinforce their presence and develop trade with their largest colony. Until the opening of the Panama Canal in 1915, a railroad across the isthmus carried freight between the Atlantic and Pacific Oceans.

With one exception, European or American engineers built these railroads with equipment imported from the West. In 1855, barely a year after Commodore Perry's visit, the Japanese instrument maker Tanaka Hisashige built a model steam train that he demonstrated to an admiring audience. In the 1870s the Japanese government hired British engineers to build the first line from Tokyo to Yokohama, then sent them home again as soon as they had trained Japanese engineers. Within a few years, Japan began manufacturing its own equipment.

Railroads consumed huge amounts of land. Many old cities doubled in size to accommodate railroad stations, sidings, tracks, warehouses, and repair shops. In the countryside, railroads required bridges, tunnels, and embankments. Railroads also consumed vast quantities of timber for ties to hold the rails and for bridges, often using up whole forests for miles on either side of the tracks. Throughout the world, they opened new land to agriculture, mining, and other human exploitation of natural resources, whether for the benefit of the local inhabitants, as in Europe and North America, or for a distant power, as in the colonial empires.

Steamships and Telegraph Cables

Steam-powered ships dated back to the 1830s but were initially too costly for anything but first-class passenger traffic. Then, by midcentury, a series of developments radically transformed ocean shipping. First iron, then steel, replaced the wood that had been used for hulls since shipbuilding began. Propellers replaced paddle wheels. Engineers built more powerful and fuel-efficient engines. By the turn of the century a marine engine could convert the heat produced by burning a single sheet of paper into the power to move one ton over half a mile. The average size of freighters increased from 200 tons in 1850 to 7,500 tons in 1900. Coaling stations and ports able to handle large ships were built around the world. Most of all, the Suez Canal, constructed in 1869, shortened the distance between Europe and Asia and triggered a massive switch from sail power to steam (see Chapter 28).

The steamers of the turn of the century were so costly they had to be used as efficiently as possible. As the world's fleet of merchant ships grew from 9 million tons in 1850 to 35 million tons in 1910, new organizations developed to make the best use of them. One such organization was the shipping line, a company that offered fast, punctual, and reliable service on a fixed schedule. Passengers, mail, and perishable freight traveled on scheduled liners. Most ships, however, were tramp freighters that voyaged from one port to another under orders from their company headquarters in Europe or North America.

To control their ships around the globe, shipping companies used a new medium of communications: **submarine telegraph cables** laid on the ocean floor. Cables were laid across the Atlantic in 1866, to India in 1870, to China, Japan, and Australia in 1871 and 1872, to Latin America in 1872 and 1873, to East and South Africa in 1879, and to West Africa in 1886. By the turn of the century cables connected every country and almost every inhabited island. As cables became the indispensable tools of modern shipping and business, the public and the press extolled the "annihilation of time and space."

The Steel and Chemical Industries

Steel is a special form of iron, both hard and elastic. Until the nineteenth century it could be made only by skilled blacksmiths in very small quantities at a very high cost and was reserved for swords, knives, axes, and watch springs. Then came a series of inventions that made steel the cheapest and most versatile metal ever known. In the 1850s William Kelly, a Kentucky iron master, discovered that air forced through molten pig iron by powerful pumps turned the iron into steel without additional fuel. In 1856 the Englishman Henry Bessemer improved Kelly's method, producing steel at one-tenth the cost of earlier methods. Other new processes permitted steel to be made from scrap iron, an increasingly important raw material, and from the phosphoric iron ores common in western Europe. As a result, world steel production rose from a half-million tons in 1870 to 28 million in 1900, of which the United States produced 10 million, Germany 8 million, and Britain 4.9 million. Steel became cheap and abundant enough to make rails, bridges, ships, and even "tin" cans meant to be used once and thrown away.

The chemical industry followed a similar pattern. Until the late eighteenth century chemicals were produced by trial and error in small workshops. By the early nineteenth century soda, sulfuric acid, and chlorine bleach (used in the cotton industry) were manufactured on a large scale, especially in Britain. In 1856 the Englishman William Perkin created the first synthetic dye, aniline purple, from coal tar; the next few years were known in Europe as the "mauve decade" from the pale purple color of fashionable women's clothes. Industry began mass-producing other organic chemicals—compounds containing carbon atoms. Toward the end of the century German chemists synthesized red, violet, blue, brown, and black dyes as well. These bright, long-lasting colors were cheaper to manufacture and could be produced in much greater quantities than natural dyes. They delighted consumers but ruined the natural-dye producers in tropical countries, such as the indigo plantations of India. Chemistry also made important advances in the manufacture of explosives. The first of these, nitroglycerin, was so dangerous that it exploded when shaken. In 1866 the Swedish scientist Alfred Nobel found a way to turn nitroglycerin into a stable solid—dynamite. This and other new explosives were useful in mining and were critical in the construction of railroads and canals, including the all-important Suez Canal. They also enabled the armies and navies of the great powers to arm themselves with increasingly accurate and powerful rifles and cannon.

The growing complexity of industrial chemistry made it one of the first fields where science and technology interacted on a daily basis. This development gave a great advantage to Germany, which had the most advanced engineering schools and scientific institutes of the time. While the British government paid little attention to science and engineering, the German government funded research and encouraged cooperation between universities and industries. By the end of the nineteenth century, Germany was the world's leading producer of dyes, drugs, synthetic fertilizers, ammonia, and nitrates used in making explosives.

Industrialization affected entire regions such as the English Midlands, the German Ruhr, parts of Pennsylvania in the United States, and the regions around Tokyo

Paris Lit Up by Electricity, 1900 The electric light bulb was invented in the United States and Britain, but Paris made such extensive use of the new technology that it was nicknamed "City of Lights." To mark the Paris Exposition of 1900, the Eiffel Tower and all the surrounding buildings were illuminated with strings of light bulbs while powerful spotlights swept the sky. (Courtesy, Civiche Raccolte d'Art Applicata ed Incisioni [Raccolte Bertarelli] Photo: Foto Saporetti)

and Osaka in Japan. The new steel mills were hungry consumers of coal, iron ore, limestone, and other raw materials that were extracted from the ground. They took up as much space as whole towns, belched smoke and particulates, and left behind huge hills of slag and other waste products. Railroad locomotives and other steam engines polluted the air with coal smoke. The dyestuff and other chemical industries left behind toxic wastes that were usually dumped into nearby rivers. This phase of industrialization, unrestrained by environmental regulations, caused considerable damage to nature and to the health of nearby inhabitants.

Electricity

No innovation of the late nineteenth century changed people's lives as radically as **electricity**. At first, producing electric current was so costly that it was used only for electroplating and telegraphy. In 1831 the Englishman Michael Faraday showed that the motion of a copper wire through a magnetic field induced an electric current in the wire. Based on his discovery, inventors in the 1870s devised efficient generators that turned mechanical energy into electric current. As an energy source, electricity was more flexible and much easier to use than water power or the stationary steam engine, which had powered industrialization until then. This opened the way to a host of new applications.

Arc lamps lit up public squares, theaters, and stores. For a while, homes continued to rely on gas lamps, which produced a softer light. Then in 1879 in the United States **Thomas Edison** developed an incandescent lamp well suited to lighting small rooms. In 1882 Edison created the world's first electrical distribution network in New York City. By the turn of the century electric lighting was rapidly replacing dim and smelly gas lamps in the cities of Europe and North America.

Other uses of electricity quickly appeared. Electric streetcars and, later, subways helped reduce the traffic jams that clogged the large cities of Europe and North America. Electric motors replaced steam engines and power belts, increasing productivity and improving workers' safety. As demand for electricity grew, engineers learned to use waterpower to produce electricity, and hydroelectric plants were built. The plant at Niagara Falls, on the border between Ontario, Canada, and New York State, produced an incredible 11,000 horsepower when it opened in 1895. At the newly created Imperial College of Engineering in Japan, an Englishman, William Ayrton, became the first professor of electrical engineering anywhere in the world; his students later went on to found major corporations and government research institutes.

World Trade and Finance

World trade expanded tenfold between 1850 and 1913. Europe imported wheat from the United States and India, wool from Australia, and beef from Argentina, and it exported coal, railroad equipment, textiles, and machinery to Asia and the Americas. Because steamships were much more efficient than sailing ships, the cost of freight dropped between 50 and 95 percent, making it worthwhile to ship even cheap and heavy products over very long distances. The advantage that steamers had over sailing ships was especially pronounced close to industrial countries that produced coal, such as Britain and the United States. On seas and oceans to which coal had to be shipped halfway around the world, such as the Pacific Ocean, sailing ships retained a competitive advantage until the early twentieth century.

The growth of world trade transformed the economies of different parts of the world in different ways. The economies of western Europe and North America, the first to industrialize, grew more diversified and prosperous. Industries mass-produced consumer goods for a growing number of middle-class and even working-class customers: soap, canned and packaged foods, ready-made clothes, household items, and small luxuries like cosmetics and engravings.

Capitalist economies, however, were prey to sudden swings in the business cycle—booms followed by deep depressions in which workers lost their jobs and investors their fortunes. For example, because of the close connections among the industrial economies, the collapse of a bank in Austria in 1873 triggered a depression that spread to the United States, causing mass unemployment. Worldwide recessions occurred in the mid-1880s and mid-1890s as well.

In the late 1870s and early 1880s Germany, the United States, and other late-industrializing Western nations raised tariffs to protect their industries from British competition. Yet trade barriers could not insulate them from the business cycle, for money continued to flow almost unhindered around the world. One of the main causes of the growing interdependence of the global economy was the financial power of Great Britain. Long after German and American industries surpassed the British, Britain continued to dominate the flow of trade, finance, and information. In 1900 two-thirds of the world's submarine cables were British or passed through Britain. Over half of the world's shipping was British owned. Britain invested one-fourth of its national wealth overseas, much of it in the United States and Argentina. British money financed many of the railroads, harbors, mines, and other big projects outside Europe. While other currencies fluctuated, the pound sterling was as good as gold, and nine-tenths of international transactions used sterling.

Nonindustrial areas also were tied to the world economy as never before. They were more vulnerable to changes in price and demand than were the industrialized nations, for many of them produced raw materials that could be replaced by synthetic substitutes (like dyestuffs) or alternative sources of supply (like coffee from Brazil). Electricity created a huge demand for copper, tying Chile, Montana, and southern Africa to the world economy as never before. Even products in constant demand, like Cuban sugar or Bolivian tin, were subject to wild swings in price on the world market. Nevertheless, until World War I, the value of exports from the tropical countries generally kept up with the growth of their populations.

SOCIAL CHANGES

The technological and economic changes of the late nineteenth century sparked profound social changes in the industrial nations. A fast-growing population swelled cities to unprecedented size, and millions of Europeans emigrated to the Americas. Strained relations between industrial employers and workers spawned labor movements and new forms of radical politics. Women found their lives dramatically altered, both in the home and in the public sphere.

Population and Migrations

The population of Europe grew faster from 1850 to 1914 than ever before or since, almost doubling from 265 million to 468 million. In non-European countries with predominantly white populations—the United States, Canada, Australia, New Zealand, and Argentina—the increase was even greater because of the inflow of Europeans. There were many reasons for the mass migrations of this period: the Irish famine of 1847–1848; the persecution of Jews in Russia; poverty and population growth in Italy, Spain, Poland, and Scandinavia; and the cultural ties between Great Britain and English-speaking countries overseas. Equally important was the availability of cheap and rapid steamships and railroads serving travelers at both ends (see Environment and Technology: Railroads and Immigration). Between 1850 and 1900, on average,

ENVIRONMENT + TECHNOLOGY

Railroads and Immigration

Why did so many Europeans emigrate to North America in the late nineteenth and early twentieth centuries? The quick answer is that millions of people longed to escape the poverty or tyranny of their home countries and start new lives in a land of freedom and opportunity. Personal desire alone, however, does not account for the migrations. After all, poverty and tyranny existed long before the late nineteenth century. Two other factors helped determine when and where people migrated: whether they were allowed to migrate, and whether they were able to.

In the nineteenth century Asians were recruited to build railroads and work on farms. But from the 1890s on, the United States and Canada closed their doors to non-Europeans, so regardless of what they wanted, they could not move to North America. In contrast, emigrants from Europe were admitted until after the First World War.

The ability to travel was a result of improvements in transportation. Until the 1890s most immigrants came from Ireland, England, or Germany—countries with good rail transportation to their own harbors and low steamship fares to North America. As rail lines were extended into eastern and southern Europe, more and more immigrants came from Italy, Austria-Hungary, and Russia.

Similarly, until the 1870s most European immigrants to North America settled on the east coast. Then, as the railroads pushed west, more of them settled on farms in the central and western parts of the continent. The power of railroads moved people as much as their desires did.

Emigrant Waiting Room   The opening of the western region of the United States attracted settlers from the east coast and from Europe. These migrants are waiting for a train to take them to the Black Hills of Dakota during one of the gold rushes of the late nineteenth century.   (Library of Congress)

400,000 Europeans migrated overseas every year; between 1900 and 1914 the flood rose to over 1 million a year. From 1850 to 1910 the population of the United States and Canada rose from 25 million to 98 million, nearly a fourfold increase. The proportion of people of European ancestry in the world's population rose from one-fifth to one-third.

Why did the number of Europeans and their descendants overseas jump so dramatically? Much of the increase came from a drop in the death rate, as epidemics and starvation became less common. The Irish famine was the last peacetime famine in European history. As farmers plowed up the plains of North America and planted wheat, much of which was shipped to Europe, food supplies increased faster than the population. Fertilizers boosted crop yields, and canning and refrigeration made food abundant year-round. The diet of Europeans and North Americans improved as meat, fruit, vegetables, and oils became part of the daily fare of city dwellers in winter as well as in summer.

Asians also migrated in large numbers during this period, often as indentured laborers recruited to work on plantations, in mines, and on railroads. Indians went mainly to Africa, Southeast Asia, and other tropical colonies of Great Britain. Chinese and Indians emigrated to Southeast Asia, the East Indies, and the Caribbean to work in the sugar plantations after the emancipation of African slaves. Japanese migrated to Brazil and other parts of Latin America. Many Japanese, as well as Chinese and Filipinos, went to work in agriculture and menial trade in Hawaii and California, where they encountered growing hostility from European-Americans.

Urbanization and Urban Environments

In 1851 Britain became the first nation with a majority of its population living in towns and cities. By 1914, 80 percent of its population was urban, as were 60 percent of the German and 45 percent of the French populations. Cities grew to unprecedented size. London grew from 2.7 million in 1850 to 6.6 million in 1900. New York, a small town of 64,000 people in 1800, reached 3.4 million by 1900, a fiftyfold increase. Population growth and the building of railroads and industries allowed cities to invade the countryside, swallowing nearby towns and villages. In 1800 New York had covered only the southernmost quarter of Manhattan Island, some 3 square miles (nearly 8 square kilometers); by 1900 it covered 150 square miles (390 square kilometers). London in 1800 measured about 4 square miles (about 10 square kilometers); by 1900 it covered twenty times more area.

In the English Midlands, in the German Ruhr, and around Tokyo Bay, towns fused into one another, filling in the fields and woods that once had separated them.

As cities grew, they changed in character. Newly built railroads not only brought goods into the cities on a predictable schedule but also allowed people to live farther apart. At first, only the well-to-do could afford to commute by train; by the end of the century, electric streetcars and subways allowed working-class people to live miles from their workplaces.

In preindustrial and early industrial cities, the poor crowded together in tenements; sanitation was bad; water often was contaminated with sewage; and darkness made life dangerous. New urban technologies and the growing powers and responsibilities of governments transformed city life for all but the poorest residents. The most important change was the installation of pipes to bring in clean water and to carry away sewage. First gas lighting and then electric lighting made cities safer and more pleasant at night. By the turn of the twentieth century municipal governments provided police and fire protection, sanitation and garbage removal, building and health inspection, schools, parks, and other amenities unheard of a century earlier.

As sanitation improved, epidemics became rare. For the first time, urban death rates fell below birthrates. The decline in infant mortality was especially significant. Confident that their children would survive infancy, couples began to limit the number of children they had, and ancient scourges like infanticide and child abandonment became less frequent. By the beginning of the twentieth century middle-class and even working-class couples began using contraceptives.

To accommodate the growing population, builders created new neighborhoods, from crowded tenements for the poor to opulent mansions for the newly rich. In the United States planners laid out new cities, such as Chicago, on rectangular grids, and middle-class families moved to new developments on the edges of cities. In Paris older neighborhoods with narrow crooked streets and rickety tenements were torn down to make room for broad boulevards and modern apartment buildings. Brilliantly lit by gas and electricity, Paris became the "city of lights," a model for city planners from New Delhi to Buenos Aires. The rich continued to live in inner cities that contained the monuments, churches, and palaces of preindustrial times, while workers moved to the outskirts.

Lower population densities and better transportation divided cities into industrial, commercial, and residential zones occupied by different social classes. Improvements such as water and sewerage, electricity, and streetcars always benefited the wealthy first, then

Separate Spheres in Great Britain   In the Victorian Age, men and women of the middle and upper classes led largely separate lives. In *Aunt Emily's Visit* (1845), we see women and children at home, tended by a servant. *The Royal Exchange*, meanwhile, was a place for men to transact business.   (Mary Evans Picture Library)

the middle class, and finally the working class. In the complex of urban life, businesses of all kinds arose, and the professions—engineering, accounting, research, journalism, and the law, among others—took on increased importance. The new middle class exhibited its wealth in fine houses with servants and in elegant entertainment.

In fast-growing cities such as London, New York, or Chicago, newcomers arrived so quickly that housing construction and municipal services could not keep up. Immigrants who saved their money to reunite their families could not afford costly municipal services. As a result, the poorest neighborhoods remained as overcrowded, unhealthy, and dangerous as they had been since the early decades of industrialization.

While urban environments improved in many ways, air quality worsened. Coal, burned to power steam engines and heat buildings, polluted the air, creating unpleasant and sometimes dangerous "pea-soup" fog and coating everything with a film of grimy dust. The thousands of horses that pulled the carts and carriages covered the streets with their wastes, causing a terrible stench. The introduction of electricity helped alleviate some of these environmental problems. Electric motors and lamps did not pollute the air. Power plants were built at a distance from cities. As electric trains and streetcars began replacing horse-drawn trolleys and coal-burning locomotives, cities became cleaner and healthier. However, most of the environmental benefits of electricity were to come in the twentieth century.

Middle-Class Women's "Separate Sphere"

In English-speaking countries the period from about 1850 to 1901 is known as the "**Victorian Age**." The expression refers not only to the reign of Queen Victoria of England (r. 1837–1901) but also to rules of behavior and to an ideology surrounding the family and the relations between men and women. The Victorians contrasted the masculine ideals of strength and courage with the feminine virtues of beauty and kindness, and they idealized the home as a peaceful and loving refuge from the dog-eat-dog world of competitive capitalism.

Victorian morality claimed to be universal, yet it best fit upper- and middle-class European families. Men and women were thought to belong in "**separate spheres**." Successful businessmen spent their time at work or relaxing in men's clubs. They put their wives in charge of rearing the children, running the household, and spending the family money to enhance the family's social status.

Before electric appliances, maintaining a middle-class home involved enormous amounts of work. Not only were families larger, but middle-class couples entertained often and lavishly. Carrying out these tasks required servants. A family's status and the activities and lifestyle of the "mistress of the house" depended on the availability of servants to help with household tasks. Only families that employed at least one full-time servant were considered middle class.

Toward the turn of the century modern technology began to transform middle-class homes. Plumbing eliminated the pump and the outhouse. Central heating replaced fireplaces, stoves, trips to the basement for coal, and endless dusting. Gas and electricity lit houses and cooked food without soot, smoke, and ashes. In the early twentieth century wealthy families acquired the first vacuum cleaners and washing machines. These technological advances did not mean less housework for women. As families acquired new household technologies, they raised their standards of cleanliness, thus demanding just as much labor as before.

The most important duty of middle-class women was raising children. Unlike the rich of previous eras who handed their children over to wet nurses and tutors, Victorian mothers nursed their own babies and showered their children with love and attention. Even those who could afford nannies and governesses remained personally involved in their children's education. Girls received an education very different from that of boys. While boys were being prepared for the business world or the professions, girls were taught such skills as embroidery, drawing, and music, which offered no monetary reward or professional preparation but enhanced their social graces and marriage prospects.

Victorian morality frowned on careers for middle-class women. Young women could work until they got married, but only in genteel places like stores and offices, never in factories. When the typewriter and telephone were introduced into the business world in the 1880s, businessmen found that they could get better work at lower wages from educated young women than from men, and operating these machines was typecast as women's work.

Most professional careers were closed to women. Until late in the century few universities granted degrees to women. In the United States higher education was available to women only at elite colleges in the East and teachers' colleges in the Midwest. European women had fewer opportunities. Before 1914 very few women became doctors, lawyers, or professional musicians.

The first profession open to women was teaching, due to laws calling for universal compulsory education. By 1911, for instance, 73 percent of all teachers in England were women. They were considered well suited to teaching young children and girls—an extension of the duties of Victorian mothers. Teaching, however, was judged suitable only for single women. A married woman was expected to get pregnant right away and to stay home taking care of her own children rather than the children of other people.

A home life, no matter how busy, did not satisfy all middle-class women. Some became volunteer nurses or social workers, receiving little or no pay. Others organized to fight prostitution, alcohol, and child labor. By the turn of the century a few were challenging male domination of politics and the law. Women suffragists, led in Britain by Emmeline Pankhurst and in the United States by Elizabeth Cady Stanton and Susan B. Anthony, demanded the right to vote. By 1914 U.S. women had won the right to vote in twelve states. British women did not vote until 1918.

Emmeline Pankhurst Under Arrest   The leader of the British women's suffrage movement frequently called attention to her cause by breaking the law to protest discrimination against women. Here she is being arrested and carried off to jail by the police.   (Mary Evans Picture Library)

Working-Class Women

In the new industrial cities, men and women no longer worked together at home or in the fields. The separation of work and home affected women's lives even more than men's lives. Women formed a majority of the workers in the textile industries and in domestic service. Yet working-class women needed to keep homes and raise children as well as earn their living. As a result, they led lives of toil and pain, considerably harder than the lives of their menfolk. Parents expected girls as young as ten to contribute to the household. In Japan, as in Ireland and New England, tenant farmers, squeezed by rising taxes and rents, were forced to send their daughters to work in textile mills. Others became domestic servants, commonly working sixteen or more hours a day, six and a half days a week, for little more than room and board. Their living quarters, usually in attics or basements, contrasted with the luxurious quarters of their masters. Without appliances, much of their work was physically hard: hauling coal and water up stairs, washing laundry by hand.

Female servants were vulnerable to sexual abuse by their masters or their masters' sons. A well-known case is that of Helene Demuth, who worked for Karl and Jenny Marx all her life. At age thirty-one she bore a son by Karl Marx and put him with foster parents rather than leave the family. She was more fortunate than most; the majority of families fired servants who got pregnant, rather than embarrass the master of the house.

Young women often preferred factory work to domestic service. Here, too, Victorian society practiced a strict division of labor by gender. Men worked in construction, iron and steel, heavy machinery, or on railroads; women worked in textiles and the clothing trades, extensions of traditional women's household work (see Material Culture: Cotton Clothing). Appalled by the abuses of women and children in the early years of industrialization, most industrial countries passed protective legislation limiting the hours or forbidding the employment of women in the hardest and most dangerous occupations, such as mining and foundry work. Such legislation limited abuses but also reinforced gender divisions in industry, keeping women in low-paid, subordinate positions. Denied access to the better-paid jobs of foremen or machine repairmen, female factory workers earned between one-third and two-thirds of men's wages.

Married women with children were expected to stay home, even if their husbands did not make enough to support the family. Most working-class married women had double responsibilities within the home: not only the work of child rearing and housework but also that of contributing to the family's income. Families who had room to spare, even a bed or a corner in the kitchen, took in boarders. Many women did piecework such as sewing dresses, making hats or gloves, or weaving baskets. The hardest and worst-paid work was washing other people's clothes. Many women worked at home ten to twelve hours a day and enlisted the help of their small children, perpetuating practices long outlawed in factories. Since electric lighting and indoor plumbing cost more than most working-class families could afford, even ordinary household duties like cooking and washing remained heavy burdens.

SOCIALISM AND LABOR MOVEMENTS

Industrialization combined with the revolutionary ideas of the late eighteenth century to produce two kinds of movements calling for further changes: socialism and labor unions. **Socialism** was an ideology developed by radical thinkers who questioned the sanctity of private property and argued in support of industrial workers against their employers. **Labor unions** were organizations formed by industrial workers to defend their interests in negotiations with employers. The socialist and labor movements were never identical. Most of the time they were allies; occasionally they were rivals.

Marx and Socialism

Socialism began as an intellectual movement. By far the best-known socialist was **Karl Marx** (1818–1883), a German journalist and writer who spent most of his life in England and collaborated with another socialist, Friedrich Engels (1820–1895), author of *The Condition of the Working Class in England in 1844* (1845). Together, they combined German philosophy, French revolutionary ideas, and knowledge of British industrial conditions.

Marx expressed his ideas succinctly in the *Communist Manifesto* (1848) (see Diversity and Dominance: Marx and Engels on Global Trade and the Bourgeoisie on page 800) and in great detail in *Das Kapital*° (1867). He saw history as a long series of conflicts

---

Das Kapital (DUSS cop-ee-TAHL)

MATERIAL CULTURE

Cotton Clothing

Of all the things that bring us comfort, nothing compares to cotton. For clothes, sheets, and towels, it is the world's favorite textile. And no wonder: cotton is cool next to the skin, can be dyed in bright colors, absorbs moisture, and, unlike other fabrics such as wool, can be washed easily.

The use of cotton for clothing has a long history dating back to 3000 B.C.E., when it was grown in the Indus River Valley. Originally, the cotton plant was grown and the cloth woven only in India, Mexico, Peru, and a few other places in the tropics. The Mayans wove fine textiles from cotton and traded them with other parts of Mesoamerica. Indian cottons were particularly fine and exported as luxury items to China and Rome. Cotton replaced hemp clothing in China and was used extensively by the Mongols for turbans, pants, and other items of clothing. The Arabs spread cotton growing and weaving to the Middle East and Spain. By the tenth century, it was a major crop in Iran and elsewhere in the region. Many of our names for particular kinds of cotton fabric come from cities in India, like calico (from Calicut) or madras, or in the Middle East, like damask (from Damascus) or muslin (from Mosul in Iraq).

Around 800 C.E., Arab merchants brought cotton cloth to Europe, where it became as precious as silk. With the invention of machines like the spinning jenny and the water frame in the eighteenth century (see Chapter 23), cotton became less precious and more available. Cotton yarn and cloth were the first items to be mass-produced in the Industrial Revolution, with important consequences for India, the American South, and other countries.

Mass production means mass consumption. In the nineteenth century, for the first time, the poor could afford to wear bright, colorful clothes and—even more important—to wash them. These clothes were made almost exclusively by women. Wealthy European families hired seamstresses who came to the house, took measurements, and returned a few days later with finished clothes. Other women sewed clothes for themselves and their families.

Sewing by hand was very time-consuming and increasingly costly compared to the declining price of cloth. By the mid-nineteenth century, prosperity and a faster pace of life in Europe and America provided an incentive for inventors

The Sewing Machine
The Japanese imported many innovations from the West after the Meiji Restoration of 1868. Among the most popular were Western-style clothing and sewing machines. Sewing was a gendered activity in Japan as in the West, with the woman sewing and the man looking on.
(Private Collection)

to devise a machine that could sew. In 1850, Isaac Singer manufactured the first practical machine for commercial use. A few years later, he designed the "Singer Family Sewing Machine" with an iron stand and a foot-treadle for home use. By 1891 Singer alone had manufactured 10 million machines in the United States and Europe. Some were industrial machines sold to makers of ready-to-wear clothes in the new garment districts. Others were home models, some inexpensive enough for the working class. There were even portable models that seamstresses could take with them to their clients' homes.

The combination of cotton cloth and sewing machines revolutionized clothing. A shirt that took fourteen and a half hours to sew by hand could be made in an hour and a quarter on a machine; an apron could be made in nine minutes instead of an hour and a half. Now the poor could afford to own several shirts, skirts, or pants, even underwear. Better-off homemakers subscribed to fashion magazines, bought patterns, and made blouses and dresses, even complicated items like crinolines and hoopskirts, which would once have been too tedious to sew by hand.

Today, the world uses more cotton than any other fiber. China is the largest producer (and consumer) of cotton, followed by the United States, India, and Pakistan. Almost all of the cotton clothing sold is produced on powerful computerized machines in the developing countries of Asia and Latin America.

between social classes, the latest being between property owners (the bourgeoisie) and workers (the proletariat). He argued that the capitalist system allowed the bourgeoisie to extract the "surplus value" of workers' labor—that is, the difference between their wages and the value of the goods they manufactured. He saw business enterprises becoming larger and more monopolistic and workers growing more numerous and impoverished with every downturn in the business cycle. He concluded that this conflict would inevitably lead to a revolution and the overthrow of the bourgeoisie, after which the workers would establish a communist society without classes.

Online Study Center
Improve Your Grade
Primary Source: Working Men
of All Countries, Unite!

What Marx called "scientific socialism" provided an intellectual framework for the growing dissatisfaction with raw industrial capitalism. In the late nineteenth century business tycoons spent money lavishly on mansions, yachts, private railroad cars, and other displays of wealth that contrasted sharply with the poverty of the workers. Even though industrial workers were not becoming poorer as Marx believed, the class struggle between workers and employers was brutally real. What Marx did was to offer a persuasive explanation of the causes of this contrast and the antagonisms it bred.

Marx was not just a philosopher; he also had a direct impact on politics. In 1864 he helped found the International Working Man's Association (later known as the First International), a movement he hoped would bring about the overthrow of the bourgeoisie. However, it attracted more intellectuals than workers. Workers found other means of redressing their grievances, such as the vote and labor unions.

Labor Movements

Since the beginning of the nineteenth century, workers had united to create "friendly societies" for mutual assistance in times of illness, unemployment, or disability. Anticombination laws, however, forbade workers to strike. These laws were abolished in Britain in the 1850s and in the rest of Europe in subsequent decades. Labor unions sought not only better wages but also improved working conditions and insurance against illness, accidents, disability, and old age. They grew slowly because they required a permanent staff and a great deal of money to sustain their members during strikes. By the end of the century British labor unions counted 2 million members, and German and American unions had 1 million members each.

Just as labor unions strove to enable workers to share in the benefits of a capitalist economy, so did electoral politics persuade workers to become part of the existing political system instead of seeking to overthrow it. The nineteenth century saw a gradual extension of the right to vote throughout Europe and North America. Universal male suffrage became law in the United States in 1870, in France and Germany in 1871, in Britain in 1885, and in the rest of Europe soon thereafter. Because there were so many newly enfranchised workers, universal male suffrage meant that socialist politicians could expect to capture many seats in their nations' parliaments. Unlike Marx, who predicted that workers would seize power through revolution, the socialists expected workers to use their voting power to obtain concessions from government and eventually even to form a government.

The classic case of socialist electoral politics is the Social Democratic Party of Germany. Founded in 1875 with a revolutionary socialist program, within two years it won a half-million votes and several seats in the Reichstag° (the lower house of the German parliament). Through superb organizing efforts and important concessions wrung from the government, the party grew fast, garnering 4.2 million votes in 1912 and winning more seats in the Reichstag than any other party. In pursuit of electoral success, the Social Democrats became more reformist and less radical. By joining the electoral process, they abandoned the idea of violent revolution.

Working-class women, burdened with both job and family responsibilities, found little time for politics and were not welcome in the male-dominated trade unions or radical political parties. A few radical women, such as the German socialist Rosa Luxemburg and Emma Goldman in the United States, an **anarchist** who believed in the abolition of all governments, became famous but did not have a large following. It was never easy to reconcile the demands of workers and those of women. In 1889 the German socialist Clara Zetkin wrote: "Just as the male worker is subjected by the capitalist, so is the woman by the man, and she will always remain in subjugation until she is economically independent. Work is the indispensable condition for economic independence." Six years later, she recognized that the liberation

---

Reichstag (RIKES-tog)

Marx and Engels on Global Trade and the Bourgeoisie

In 1848 the German philosophers Karl Marx (1818–1883) and Friedrich Engels (1820–1895), who were living in England at the time, published a small book called Manifesto of the Communist Party. *In it, they tried to explain why owners of manufactures and business—the "bourgeoisie"—had become the wealthiest and most powerful class of people in industrializing countries like Britain, and why urban and industrial workers—the "proletariat"—lived in poverty. In their view, the dominance of the European commercial and industrial bourgeoisie was in the process of destroying the diversity of human cultures, reducing all classes in Europe and all cultures to the status of proletarians selling their labor.*

In the Manifesto, *Marx and Engels did not limit themselves to publicizing social inequities. They also called for a social revolution in which the workers would overthrow the bourgeoisie and establish a new society without private property or government. Their* Manifesto *was soon translated into many languages and became the best-known expression of radical communist ideology.*

Whatever one may think of their call to revolution, Marx and Engels's analysis of class relations has had a lasting impact on social historians. Their ideas are especially interesting from the perspective of global history because of the way in which they connect the rise of the bourgeoisie with world trade and industrial technology. The following paragraphs explain these connections.

The history of all hitherto existing society is the history of class struggles.

Freeman and slave, patrician and plebeian, lord and serf, guild-master and journeyman, in a word, oppressor and oppressed, stood in constant opposition to one another, carried on an uninterrupted, now hidden, now open fight, a fight that each time ended, either in a revolutionary re-constitution of society at large, or in the common ruin of the contending classes.

In the earlier epochs of history, we find almost everywhere a complicated arrangement of society into various orders, a manifold gradation of social rank. In ancient Rome we have patricians, knights, plebeians, slaves; in the middle ages, feudal lords, vassals, guild-masters, journeymen, apprentices,

serfs; in almost all of these classes, again, subordinate gradations.

The modern bourgeois society that has sprouted from the ruins of feudal society, has not done away with class antagonisms. It has but established new classes, new conditions of oppression, new forms of struggle in place of the old ones.

Our epoch, the epoch of the bourgeoisie, possesses, however, this distinctive feature; it has simplified the class antagonisms. Society as a whole is more and more splitting up into two great hostile camps, into two great classes directly facing each other: Bourgeoisie and Proletariat.

From the serfs of the Middle Ages sprang the chartered burghers of the earliest towns. From these burgesses the first elements of the bourgeoisie were developed.

The discovery of America, the rounding of the Cape, opened up fresh ground for the rising bourgeoisie. The East-Indian and Chinese markets, the colonization of America, trade with the colonies, the increase in the means of exchange and in commodities generally, gave to commerce, to navigation, to industry, an impulse never before known, and thereby, to the revolutionary element in the tottering feudal society, a rapid development.

The feudal system of industry, under which industrial production was monopolised by close guilds, now no longer sufficed for the growing wants of the new markets. The manufacturing system took its place. The guild-masters were pushed on one side by the manufacturing middle-class; division of labour between the different corporate guilds vanished in the face of division of labour in each single workshop.

Meantime the markets kept ever growing, the demand, ever rising. Even manufacture no longer sufficed. Thereupon, steam and machinery revolutionised industrial production. The place of manufacture was taken by the giant, Modern Industry, the place of the industrial middle-class, by industrial millionaires, the leaders of whole industrial armies, the modern bourgeois.

Modern industry has established the world-market, for which the discovery of America paved the way. This market has given an immense importance to commerce, to navigation, to communication by land. This development has, in its turn, reacted on the extension of industry; and in proportion as industry, commerce, navigation, railways extended, in the same proportion the bourgeoisie developed, increased its capital, and pushed into the background every class handed down from the Middle Ages.

We see, therefore, how the modern bourgeoisie is itself the product of a long course of development, of a series of revolutions in the modes of production and of exchange. . . .

[T]he bourgeoisie has at last, since the establishment of Modern Industry and of the world-market, conquered for itself, in the modern representative State, exclusive political sway. The executive of the modern State is but a committee for managing the common affairs of the whole bourgeoisie.

The bourgeoisie, historically, has played a most revolutionary part. . . .

It has been the first to show what man's activity can bring about. It has accomplished wonders far surpassing Egyptian pyramids, Roman aqueducts, and Gothic cathedrals; it has conducted expeditions that put in the shade all former Exoduses of nations and crusades.

The bourgeoisie cannot exist without constantly revolutionising the instruments of production, and thereby the relations of production, and with them the whole relations of society. Conservation of the old modes of production in unaltered form, was, on the contrary, the first condition of existence for all earlier industrial classes. Constant revolutionising of production, uninterrupted disturbance of all social conditions, everlasting uncertainty and agitation distinguish the bourgeois epoch from all earlier ones. All fixed, fast-frozen relations, with their train of ancient and venerable prejudices and opinions, are swept away, all new-formed ones become antiquated before they can ossify. All that is solid melts into air, all that is holy is profaned, and man is at last compelled to face with sober senses, his real conditions of life, and his relations with his kind.

The need of a constantly expanding market for its products chases the bourgeoisie over the whole surface of the globe. It must nestle everywhere, settle everywhere, establish connexions everywhere.

The bourgeoisie has through its exploitation of the world-market given a cosmopolitan character to production and consumption in every country. To the great chagrin of Reactionists, it has drawn from under the feet of industry the national ground on which it stood. All old-fashioned national industries have been destroyed or are daily being destroyed. They are dislodged by new industries, whose introduction becomes a life or death question for all civilised nations, by industries that no longer work up indigenous raw material, but raw material drawn from the remotest zones; industries whose products are consumed, not only at home, but in every quarter of the globe. In place of the old wants, satisfied by the productions of the country, we find new wants, requiring for their satisfaction the products of distant lands and climes. In place of the old local and national seclusion and self-sufficiency, we have intercourse in every direction, universal inter-dependence of nations. And as in material, so also in intellectual production. The intellectual creations of individual nations become common property. National

one-sidedness and narrow-mindedness become more and more impossible, and from the numerous national and local literatures there arises a world-literature.

The bourgeoisie, by the rapid improvement of all instruments of production, by the immensely facilitated means of communication, draws all, even the most barbarian, nations into civilisation. The cheap prices of its commodities are the heavy artillery with which it batters down all Chinese walls, with which it forces the barbarians' intensely obstinate hatred of foreigners to capitulate. It compels all nations, on pain of extinction, to adopt the bourgeois mode of production; it compels them to introduce what it calls civilisation into their midst, i.e., to become bourgeois themselves. In a word, it creates a world after its own image.

The bourgeoisie has subjected the country to the rule of the towns. It has created enormous cities, has greatly increased the urban population as compared with the rural, and has thus rescued a considerable part of the population from the idiocy of rural life. Just as it has made the country dependent on the towns, so it has made barbarian and semi-barbarian countries dependent on the civilised ones, nations of peasants on nations of bourgeois, the East on the West. . . .

The bourgeoisie, during its rule of scarce one hundred years, has created more massive and more colossal productive forces than have all preceding generations together. Subjection of Nature's forces to man, machinery, application of chemistry to industry and agriculture, steam-navigation, railways, electric telegraphs, clearing of whole continents for cultivation, canalization of rivers, whole populations conjured out of the ground—what earlier century had even a presentiment that such productive forces slumbered in the lap of social labour?

QUESTIONS FOR ANALYSIS

1. How did the growth of world trade since the European discovery of America affect relations between social classes in Europe?

2. Compare Marx and Engels's views on industrial production with those of Adam Smith that you read in Chapter 23. Do they contradict each other? Or does Smith's description of pin-making explain the rise of what Marx and Engels call "the giant, Modern Industry"?

3. What effect did the growth of trade and industry have on products, intellectual creations, and consumer tastes around the world?

4. Why do Marx and Engels think the bourgeoisie requires constant changes in technology and social relations? How well does that description fit the world you live in?

Source: Karl Marx and Frederick Engels, *Manifesto of the Communist Party,* Authorized English Translation: Edited and Annotated by Frederick Engels (Chicago: Charles H. Kerr & Company, 1906), pp. 12–20.

of women would have to await a change in the position of the working class as a whole: "The proletarian woman cannot attain her highest ideal through a movement for the equality of the female sex, she attains salvation only through the fight for the emancipation of labor."[1]

NATIONALISM AND
THE RISE OF ITALY, GERMANY,
AND JAPAN

The most influential idea of the nineteenth century was **nationalism**. The French revolutionaries had defined people, who had previously been considered the subjects of a sovereign, as the citizens of a *nation*—a concept identified with a territory, the state that ruled it, and the culture of its people. While Italians and Germans looked inward to create unified nations, the Japanese would eventually look outward, embracing Western ideas and institutions as a way to protect and strengthen their country.

Language and National Identity in Europe Before 1871

Language was usually the crucial element in creating a feeling of national unity. It was important both as a way to unite the people of a nation and as the means of persuasion by which political leaders could inspire their followers. Language was the tool of the new generation of political activists, most of them lawyers, teachers, students, and journalists. Yet language and citizenship seldom coincided.

The fit between France and the French language was closer than in most large countries, though some French-speakers lived outside of France and some French people spoke other languages. Italian- and German-speaking people, however, were divided among many small states. Living in the Austrian Empire were peoples who spoke German, Czech, Slovak, Hungarian, Polish, and other languages. Even where people spoke a common language, they could be divided by religion or institutions. The Irish, though English-speaking, were mostly Catholic, whereas the English were primarily Protestant; and in the United States, different economic systems and the issue of slavery divided the south from the north.

The idea of redrawing the boundaries of states to accommodate linguistic, religious, or cultural differences was revolutionary. In Italy and Germany it led to the forging of large new states out of many small ones in

1871. In central and eastern Europe, nationalism threatened to break up large states into smaller ones.

Until the 1860s nationalism was associated with **liberalism**, the revolutionary middle-class ideology that emerged from the French Revolution, asserted the sovereignty of the people, and demanded constitutional government, a national parliament, and freedom of expression. The most famous nationalist of the early nineteenth century was the Italian liberal Giuseppe Mazzini° (1805–1872), the leader of the failed revolution of 1848 in Italy. Mazzini not only sought to unify the Italian peninsula into one nation but also associated with like-minded revolutionaries elsewhere to bring nationhood and liberty to all peoples oppressed by tyrants and foreigners. Although the governments of Russia, Prussia, and Austria censored the new ideas, they could not be quashed. To staff bureaucracies and police forces to maintain law and order, even conservative regimes required educated personnel, and education meant universities, the seedbeds of new ideas transmitted by a national language.

Although the revolutions of 1848 failed except in France, the strength of the revolutionary movements convinced conservatives that governments could not forever keep their citizens out of politics, and that mass politics, if properly managed, could strengthen rather than weaken the state. A new generation of conservative political leaders learned how to preserve the social status quo through public education, universal military service, and colonial conquests, all of which built a sense of national unity.

The Unification of Italy, 1860–1870

The Austrian statesman Prince Metternich had famously described Italy as "a geographical expression." By midcentury, however, popular sentiment was building throughout Italy for unification. Opposing it were Pope Pius IX, who abhorred everything modern, and Austria, which controlled two Italian provinces, Lombardy and Venetia (see Map 27.1). The prime minister of the Kingdom of Piedmont-Sardinia, Count Camillo Benso di Cavour, saw the rivalry between France and Austria as an opportunity to unify Italy. He secretly formed an alliance with France, then instigated a war with Austria in 1858. The war was followed by uprisings throughout northern and central Italy in favor of joining Piedmont-Sardinia, a moderate constitutional monarchy under King Victor Emmanuel.

Giuseppe Mazzini (jew-SEP-pay mots-EE-nee)

Map 27.1   Unification of Italy, 1859–1870   The unification of Italy was achieved by the expansion of the kingdom of Piedmont-Sardinia, with the help of France.

If the conservative, top-down approach to unification prevailed in the north, a more radical approach was still possible in the south. In 1860 the fiery revolutionary **Giuseppe Garibaldi°** and a small band of followers landed in Sicily and then in southern Italy, overthrew the Kingdom of the Two Sicilies, and prepared to found a democratic republic. The royalist Cavour, however, took advantage of the unsettled situation to sideline Garibaldi and expand Piedmont-Sardinia into a new Kingdom of Italy. Unification was completed with the addition of Venetia in 1866 and the Papal States in 1870.

Giuseppe Garibaldi (jew-SEP-pay gary-BAHL-dee)

The process of unification illustrates the shift of nationalism from a radical democratic idea to a conservative method of building popular support for a strong centralized government, even an aristocratic and monarchical one.

The Unification of Germany, 1866–1871

Because the most widely spoken language in nineteenth-century Europe was German, the unification of most German-speaking people into a single state in 1871 had momentous consequences for the world. Until the 1860s the region of central Europe where people spoke German (the former Holy Roman Empire) consisted of Prussia, the western half of the Austrian Empire, and numerous smaller states (see Map 27.2). Some German nationalists wanted to unite all Germans under the Austrian throne. Others wanted to exclude Austria with its many non-Germanic peoples and unite all other German-speaking areas under Prussia. The divisions were also religious: Austria and southwestern Germany were Catholic; Prussia and the northeast were Lutheran. The Prussian state had two advantages: (1) the newly developed industries of the Rhineland, and (2) the first European army to make use of railroads, telegraphs, breechloading rifles, steel artillery, and other products of modern industry.

During the reign of King Wilhelm I (r. 1861–1888) Prussia was ruled by the brilliant and authoritarian aristocrat, Chancellor **Otto von Bismarck°** (1815–1898). Bismarck was determined to use Prussian industry and German nationalism to make his state the dominant power in Germany. In 1866 Prussia attacked and defeated Austria. To everyone's surprise, Prussia took no Austrian territory. Instead, Prussia and some smaller states formed the North German Confederation, the nucleus of a future Germany. Then in 1870, confident that Austria would not hinder him, Bismarck took advantage of French Emperor Napoleon III's hostility to the North German Confederation to start a war with France. Prussian armies, joined by troops from southern as well as northern Germany, used their superior firepower and tactics to achieve a quick victory. "Blood and iron" were the foundation of the new German Empire.

The spoils of victory included a large indemnity and two provinces of France bordering on Germany: Alsace and Lorraine. The French paid the indemnity easily enough but resented the loss of their provinces. To the Germans, this region was German because a majority of its inhabitants spoke German. To the French, it was French because it had been so when the nation of France was forged in the Revolution and because most of its inhabitants considered themselves French. These two conflicting definitions of nationalism kept enmity between France and Germany smoldering for decades. In this case, nationalism turned out to be a divisive rather than a unifying force.

The West Challenges Japan

In Japan a completely different political organization was in place. The emperor was revered but had no power. Instead, Japan was governed by the Tokugawa Shogunate—a secular government under a military leader, or *shogun*, that had come to power in 1600 (see Chapter 21). Local lords, called *daimyos*, were permitted to control their lands and populations with very little interference from the shogunate.

When threatened from outside, this system showed many weaknesses. It did not permit the coordination of resources necessary to resist a major invasion. Shoguns attempted to minimize exposure to foreign powers. In the early 1600s they prohibited foreigners from entering Japan and Japanese from going abroad. The penalties for breaking these laws was death, but many Japanese ignored them anyway. The most flagrant violators were powerful lords in southern Japan who ran large and very successful pirate or black-market operations. In their entrepreneurial activities these lords benefited from the decentralization of the shogunal political system. But when a genuine foreign threat was suggested—as when, in 1792, Russian and British ships were spotted off the Japanese coast—the local lords realized that Japan was too weak and decentralized to resist a foreign invasion. As a result, a few of the regional lords began to develop their own reformed armies, arsenals, and shipyards.

By the 1800s Satsuma° and Choshu°, two large domains in southern Japan, had become wealthy and ambitious. They enjoyed high rates of revenue and population growth. Their remoteness from the capital Edo (now Tokyo) and their economic vigor also fostered a strong sense of local self-reliance.

In 1853, as mentioned in the chapter opening, the American commodore Matthew C. Perry arrived off the coast of Japan and demanded that Japan open its

---

Otto von Bismarck (UTT-oh von BIS-mark)

Satsuma (SAT-soo-mah)   **Choshu** (CHOE-shoo)

Map 27.2   The Unification of Germany, 1866–1871   Germany was united after a series of short, successful wars by the kingdom of Prussia against Austria in 1866 and against France in 1871.

ports to trade and allow American ships to refuel and take on supplies during their voyages between China and California. He promised to return a year later to receive the Japanese answer. Perry's demands sparked a crisis in the shogunate. After consultation with the provincial daimyos, the shogun's advisers advocated capitulation to Perry. They pointed to China's humiliating

defeats in the Opium and Arrow Wars. In 1854, when Perry returned, representatives of the shogun indicated their willingness to sign the Treaty of Kanagawa°, modeled on the unequal treaties between China and the

---

Kanagawa (KAH-nah-GAH-wah)

Western powers. Angry and disappointed, some provincial governors began to encourage an underground movement calling for the destruction of the Tokugawa regime and the banning of foreigners from Japan.

Tensions between the shogunate and some provincial leaders, particularly in Choshu and Satsuma, increased in the early 1860s. When British and French ships shelled the southwestern coasts in 1864 to protest the treatment of foreigners, the action enraged the provincial samurai who rejected the Treaty of Kanagawa and resented the shogunate's inability to protect the country. Young, ambitious, educated men who faced mediocre prospects under the rigid Tokugawa class system emerged as provincial leaders. In 1867 the Choshu leaders Yamagata Aritomo and Ito Hirobumi finally realized that they should stop warring with their rival province, Satsuma, and join forces to lead a rebellion against the shogunate.

The Meiji Restoration and the Modernization of Japan, 1868–1894

The civil war was intense but brief. In 1868 provincial rebels overthrew the Tokugawa Shogunate and declared young emperor Mutsuhito° (r. 1868–1912) "restored." The new leaders called their regime the "**Meiji° Restoration**" after Mutsuhito's reign name (*Meiji* means "enlightened rule"). The "Meiji oligarchs," as the new rulers were known, were extraordinarily talented and far-sighted. Determined to

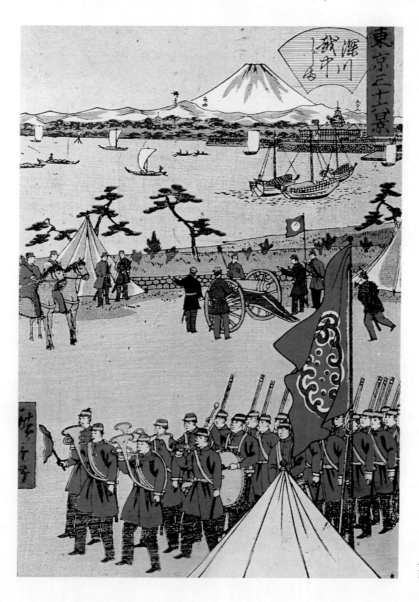

Japan's New Army   After the Meiji Restoration in 1868, the leaders of the new government set out to make Japan "a rich country with a strong army." They modeled the new army on the European armies of the time, with Western-style uniforms, rifles, cannon, and musical instruments. (Tsuneo Tamba Collection/Laurie Platt Winfrey, Inc.)

Mutsuhito (moo-tsoo-HE-toe)   **Meiji** (MAY-gee)

protect their country from Western imperialism, they encouraged its transformation into "a rich country with a strong army" with world-class industries. Though imposed from above, the Meiji Restoration marked as profound a change as the French Revolution (see Map 27.3).

Online Study Center
Improve Your Grade
Primary Source: Letter to
Mitsubishi Employees

The oligarchs were under no illusion that they could fend off the Westerners without changing their institutions and their society. In the Charter Oath issued in 1868, the young emperor included a prophetic phrase: "Knowledge shall be sought throughout the world and thus shall be strengthened the foundation of the imperial polity." It was to be the motto of a new Japan, which embraced all foreign ideas, institutions, and techniques that could strengthen the nation. The literacy

Map 27.3 Expansion and Modernization of Japan, 1868–1918 As Japan acquired modern industry, it followed the example of the European powers in seeking overseas colonies. Its colonial empire grew at the expense of its neighbors: Taiwan was taken from China in 1895; Karafutu (Sakhalin) from Russia in 1905; and all of Korea became a colony in 1910.

rate in Japan was the highest in Asia at the time, and the oligarchs shrewdly exploited it in their introduction of new educational systems, a conscript army, and new communications. The government was able to establish heavy industry through the use of judicious deficit financing without extensive foreign debt, thanks to decades of experimentation with industrial development and financing in the provinces in the earlier 1800s. With a conscript army and a revamped educational system, the oligarchs attempted to create a new citizenry that was literate and competent but also loyal and obedient.

The Meiji leaders copied the government structure of imperial Germany. They modeled the new Japanese navy on the British and the army on the Prussian. They introduced Western-style postal and telegraph services, railroads and harbors, banking, clocks, and calendars. To learn the secrets of Western strength, they sent hundreds of students to Britain, Germany, and the United States. Western-style clothing, including military and police uniforms, and hairstyles became popular. Even pastimes were affected, with garden parties and formal dances becoming common.

The government was especially interested in Western technology. It opened vocational, technical, and agricultural schools and founded four imperial universities. It brought in foreign experts to advise on medicine, science, and engineering. To encourage industrialization, the government set up state-owned enterprises to manufacture cloth and inexpensive consumer goods for sale abroad. The first Japanese industries, some of which had been founded in the early nineteenth century, exploited their workers ruthlessly, just as the first industries in Europe and America had done. In 1881, to pay off its debts, the government sold these enterprises to private investors, mainly large *zaibatsu°*, or conglomerates. It encouraged individual technological innovation. Thus the carpenter Toyoda Sakichi founded the Toyoda Loom Works (now Toyota Motor Company) in 1906; ten years later he patented the world's most advanced automatic loom.

Nationalism and Social Darwinism

The Franco-Prussian War of 1870–1871 changed the political climate of Europe. France became more liberal. The kingdom of Italy completed the unification of the peninsula. Germany, Austria-Hungary (as the Austrian Empire had renamed itself in 1867), and Russia remained conservative and used nationalism to maintain the status quo.

Nationalism and parliamentary elections made politicians of all parties appeal to public opinion. They were greatly aided by the press, especially cheap daily newspapers that sought to increase circulation by publishing sensational articles about overseas conquests and foreign threats. As governments increasingly came to recognize the advantages of an educated population in the competition between states, they opened public schools in every town and admitted women into public-service jobs for the first time. The spread of literacy allowed politicians and journalists to appeal to the emotions of the poor, diverting their anger from their employers to foreigners and their votes from socialist to nationalist parties.

In many countries the dominant group used nationalism to justify imposing its language, religion, or customs on minority populations. The Russian Empire attempted to "Russify" its diverse ethnic populations. The Spanish government made the Spanish language compulsory in the schools, newspapers, and courts of its Basque- and Catalan-speaking provinces. Immigrants to the United States were expected to learn English to safeguard national unity.

Nationalism soon spread. By the 1880s signs of national consciousness appeared in Egypt, Japan, India, and other non-Western countries, inspiring anti-Western and anticolonial movements.

Western culture in the late nineteenth century exalted the powerful over the weak, men over women, rich over poor, Europeans over other races, and humans over nature. Some people looked to science for support of political dominance. One of the most influential scientists of the century, and the one whose ideas were most widely cited and misinterpreted, was the English biologist Charles Darwin (1809–1882).

In his 1859 book *On the Origin of the Species by Means of Natural Selection*, Darwin argued that the earth was much older and the time frame for all biological life was far longer than most persons had previously believed. He proposed that over the course of hundreds of thousands of years living beings had either evolved in the struggle for survival or become extinct.

The philosopher Herbert Spencer (1820–1903) and others took up Darwin's ideas of "natural selection" and "survival of the fittest" and applied them to human society. Extreme Social Darwinists developed elaborate pseudo-scientific theories of racial differences, claiming that they were the result not of history but of biology. They viewed the poor and disenfranchised as people struggling with their social environment and did not want the state

---

zaibatsu (zye-BOT-soo)

to intervene in this natural process. Although not based on any research, these ideas became very popular at the turn of the century, for they gave a scientific-sounding justification for the power of the privileged.

THE GREAT POWERS OF EUROPE, 1871–1900

After the middle of the century, politicians and journalists discovered that minor incidents involving foreigners could be used to stir up popular indignation against neighboring countries. Military officers, impressed by the awesome power of the weapons that industry provided, began to think that the weapons were invincible. Rivalries over colonial territories, ideological differences between liberal and conservative governments, and even minor border incidents or trade disagreements contributed to a growing atmosphere of international tension.

Germany at the Center of Europe

International relations revolved around a united Germany because Germany was located in the center of Europe and had the most powerful army on the European continent. After creating a unified Germany in 1871, Bismarck declared that his country had no further territorial ambitions, and he put his effort into maintaining the peace in Europe. To isolate France, the only country with a grudge against Germany, he forged a loose coalition with Austria-Hungary and Russia, the other two conservative powers. Despite the competing ambitions of Austria and Russia in the Balkans, he was able to keep his coalition together for twenty years.

Bismarck proved equally adept at strengthening German national unity at home. To weaken the influence of middle-class liberals, he extended the vote to all adult men, thereby allowing Socialists to win seats in the *Reichstag* or parliament. By imposing high tariffs on manufactured goods and wheat, he gained the support of both the wealthy industrialists of the Rhineland and the great landowners of eastern Germany, traditional rivals for power. Though he repressed labor unions, he gained the acquiescence of industrial workers by introducing social legislation—medical, unemployment, and disability insurance and old-age pensions—long before other industrial countries. His government supported public and technical education. Under his leadership,

Online Study Center
Improve Your Grade
Primary Source: Extracts from History of Germany in the Nineteenth Century and Historical Political Writings

the German people developed a strong sense of national unity and pride in their industrial and military power.

In 1888 Wilhelm I was succeeded by his grandson Wilhelm II (r. 1888–1918), an insecure and arrogant man who tried to gain respect by using bullying tactics. Within two years he had dismissed Chancellor Bismarck and surrounded himself with yes men. Whereas Bismarck had shown little interest in acquiring colonies overseas, Wilhelm II talked about his "global policy" and demanded a colonial empire. Ruler of the nation with the mightiest army and the largest industrial economy in Europe, he felt that Germany deserved "a place in the sun." His intemperate speeches made him seem far more belligerent than he really was.

The Liberal Powers: France and Great Britain

France, once the dominant nation in Europe, had difficulty reconciling itself to being in second place. Though a prosperous country with flourishing agriculture and a large colonial empire, the French republic had some serious weaknesses. Its population was scarcely growing; in 1911 France had only 39 million people compared to Germany's 64 million. In an age when the power of nations was roughly proportional to the size of their armies, France could field an army only two-thirds the size of Germany's. Another weakness was the slow growth of French industry compared to Germany's, due in part to the loss of the iron and coal mines of Lorraine.

The French people were deeply divided over the very nature of the state: some were monarchists and Catholic; a growing number held republican and anticlerical views. These divisions came to a head at the turn of the century over the case of Captain Alfred Dreyfus, a Jewish officer falsely convicted of spying for the Germans in 1894. French society, even families, split between those who felt that reopening the case would only dishonor the army and those who believed that letting injustice go unchallenged dishonored the nation. The case reawakened the dormant anti-Semitism in French society. Not until 1906, after twelve painful years, was Dreyfus exonerated. Yet if French political life seemed fragile and frequently in crisis, a long tradition of popular participation in politics and a strong sense of nationhood, reinforced by a fine system of public education, gave the French people a deeper cohesion than appeared on the surface.

Great Britain had a long experience with parliamentary elections and competing parties. The British government alternated smoothly between the Liberal and Conservative Parties, and the income gap between rich and poor gradually narrowed. Nevertheless, Britain had problems that grew more apparent as time went on. One problem was Irish resentment of English rule. Nationalism had strengthened the allegiance of the English, Scots, and Welsh to the British crown and state. But the Irish, excluded because they were Catholic and predominantly poor, saw the British as a foreign occupying force.

Another problem was the British economy. Once the workshop of the world, Great Britain had fallen behind the United States and Germany in such important industries as iron and steel, chemicals, electricity, and textiles. Even in shipbuilding and shipping, Britain's traditional specialties, Germany was catching up.

Also, Britain was preoccupied with its enormous and fast-growing empire. A source of wealth for investors and the envy of other imperialist nations, the empire was also a constant drain on Britain's finances. The revolt of 1857 against British rule in India (see Chapter 25) was crushed with difficulty and kept British politicians worried thereafter. The empire required Britain to station several costly fleets of warships throughout the world.

For most of the nineteenth century Britain turned its back on Europe and pursued a policy of "splendid isolation." Only in 1854 did it intervene militarily in Europe, joining France in the Crimean War of 1854–1856 against Russia (see Chapter 25). Britain's preoccupation with India and the shipping routes through the Mediterranean led British statesmen to exaggerate the Russian threat to the Ottoman Empire and to the Central Asian approaches to India. Periodic "Russian scares" and Britain's age-old rivalry with France for overseas colonies diverted the attention of British politicians away from the rise of a large, powerful, united Germany.

The Conservative Powers: Russia and Austria-Hungary

The forces of nationalism weakened rather than strengthened Russia and Austria-Hungary. Their populations were far more divided, socially and ethnically, than were the German, French, or British peoples.

Nationalism was most divisive in south-central Europe, where many different language groups lived in close proximity. In 1867 the Austrian Empire renamed itself the Austro-Hungarian Empire to appease its Hungarian critics. Its attempts to promote the cultures of its Slavic-speaking minorities did little to gain their political allegiance. The Austro-Hungarian Empire still thought of itself as a great power, but instead of seeking conquests in Asia or Africa, it attempted to dominate the Balkans. This strategy irritated Russia, which thought of itself as the protector of Slavic peoples everywhere. The Austrian annexation of the former Turkish province of Bosnia-Herzegovina in 1908 worsened relations between the Austro-Hungarian and Russian Empires. As we will see in Chapter 29, festering quarrels over the Balkans—the "tinderbox of Europe"—eventually pushed Europe into war.

Ethnic diversity also contributed to the instability of imperial Russia. The Polish people, never reconciled to being annexed by Russia in the eighteenth century, rebelled in 1830 and 1863–1864. The tsarist empire also included Finland, Estonia, Latvia, Lithuania, and Ukraine, the very mixed peoples of the Caucasus, and the Muslim population of Central Asia conquered between 1865 and 1881. Furthermore, Russia had the largest Jewish population in Europe, despite the harshness of its anti-Semitic laws and periodic *pogroms* (massacres), which prompted many Jews to flee to America. All in all, only 45 percent of the peoples of the tsarist empire spoke Russian. This meant that Russian nationalism and the state's attempts to impose the Russian language on its subjects were divisive instead of unifying forces.

In 1861 the moderate conservative Tsar Alexander II (r. 1855–1881) emancipated the peasants from serfdom. He did so partly out of a genuine desire to strengthen the bonds between the monarchy and the Russian people, and partly to promote industrialization by enlarging the labor pool. That half-hearted measure, however, did not create a modern society on the western European model. It only turned serfs into communal farmers with few skills and little capital. Though technically "emancipated," the great majority of Russians had little education, few legal rights, and no say in the government. After Alexander's assassination in 1881, his successors Alexander III (r. 1881–1894) and Nicholas II (r. 1894–1917) reluctantly permitted half-hearted attempts at social change. Although the Russian government employed many bureaucrats and policemen, its commercial middle class was small and had little influence. Industrialization consisted largely of state-sponsored projects, such as railroads, iron foundries, and armament factories, and led to social unrest among urban workers. Wealthy landowning aristocrats continued to dominate the Russian court and administration and succeeded in blocking most reforms.

The Doss House   Late-nineteenth-century cities showed more physical than social improvements. This painting by Makovsky of a street in St. Petersburg contrasts the broad avenue and impressive new buildings with
the poverty of the crowd.   (Courtesy, The State Russian Museum/Smithsonian Institution Traveling Exhibit)

The weaknesses in Russia's society and government
became glaringly obvious during a war with Japan in
1904 and 1905. The fighting in the Russo-Japanese War
took place in Manchuria, a province in northern China
far from European Russia. The Russian army, which received all its supplies by means of the inefficient Trans-
Siberian Railway, was soon defeated by the better-trained
and better-equipped Japanese. The Russian navy, after a
long journey around Europe, Africa, and Asia, was met
and sunk by the Japanese fleet at the Battle of Tsushima
Strait in 1905.

The shock of defeat caused a popular uprising, the
Revolution of 1905, that forced Tsar Nicholas II to grant a
constitution and an elected Duma (parliament). But as
soon as he was able to rebuild the army and the police,
he reverted to the traditional despotism of his forefa-
thers. Small groups of radical intellectuals, angered by

the contrast between the wealth of the elite and the
poverty of the common people, began plotting the violent overthrow of the tsarist autocracy.

CHINA, JAPAN, AND THE WESTERN POWERS

After 1850 China and Japan—the two largest countries
in East Asia—felt the influence of the Western powers as never before, but their responses were completely
opposite. China resisted Western influence and became
weaker, while Japan transformed itself into a major industrial and military power. One reason for this difference was the Western powers' heavy involvement in
China and the distance to Japan, the nation most remote

from Europe by ship. More important was the difference between the Chinese and Japanese elites' attitudes toward foreign cultures.

China in Turmoil

China had been devastated by the Taiping° Rebellion that raged from 1850 to 1864 (see Chapter 25). The French and British took advantage of China's weakness to demand treaty ports where they could trade at will. The British took over China's customs and allowed the free import of opium until 1917. A Chinese "self-strengthening movement" tried in vain to bring about significant reforms by reducing government expenditures and eliminating corruption. The **Empress Dowager Cixi**° (r. 1862–1908), who had once encouraged the construction of shipyards, arsenals, and telegraph lines, opposed railways and other foreign technologies that could carry foreign influences to the interior. Government officials, who did not dare resist the Westerners outright, secretly encouraged crowds to attack and destroy the intrusive devices. They were able to slow the foreign intrusion, but in doing so, they denied themselves the best means of defense against foreign pressure.

Japan Confronts China

The late nineteenth century marked the high point of European power and arrogance, as the nations of Europe, in a frenzy known as the "New Imperialism," rushed to gobble up the last remaining unclaimed pieces of the world, as we will see in Chapter 28. Yet at that very moment two nations outside Europe were becoming great powers. One of them, the United States, was inhabited mainly by people of European origin. As we saw in Chapter 24, its rise to great-power status had been predicted early in the nineteenth century by astute observers like the French statesman Alexis de Tocqueville. The other one, Japan, seemed so distant and exotic in 1850 that no European

The Boxer Uprising   In 1900 a Chinese secret society, the Righteous Fists, rose up with the encouragement of the Empress Dowager Cixi and attacked foreigners and their establishments. In the Western press they were known as "Boxers" and shown in lurid poses, such as these men putting up a poster that read "Death to Foreigners!"   (Mary Evans Picture Library/The Image Works)

Taiping (tie-PING)   **Cixi** (TSUH-shee)

had guessed that it would join the ranks of the great powers.

The motive for the transformation of Japan was defensive—to protect the nation from the Western powers—but the methods that strengthened Japan against the imperial ambitions of others could also be used to carry out its own conquests. Japan's path to imperialism was laid out by **Yamagata Aritomo**, a leader of the Meiji oligarchs. He believed that to be independent Japan had to define a "sphere of influence" that included Korea, Manchuria, and part of China (see Map 27.3). If other countries controlled this sphere, Japan would be at risk. To protect this sphere of influence, Yamagata insisted, Japan must sustain a vigorous program of military industrialization, culminating in the building of battleships.

Meanwhile, as Japan grew stronger, China was growing weaker. In 1894 the two nations went to war over Japanese encroachments in Korea. The Sino-Japanese War lasted less than six months, and it forced China to evacuate Korea, cede Taiwan and the Liaodong° Peninsula,

---

Liaodong (li-AH-oh-dong)

and pay a heavy indemnity. France, Germany, Britain, Russia, and the United States, upset at seeing a newcomer join the ranks of the imperialists, made Japan give up Liaodong in the name of the "territorial integrity" of China. In exchange for their "protection," the Western powers then made China grant them territorial and trade concessions, including ninety treaty ports.

In 1900 Chinese officials around the Empress Dowager Cixi encouraged a series of antiforeign riots known as the Boxer Uprising. Military forces from the European powers, Japan, and the United States put down the riots and occupied Beijing. Emboldened by China's obvious weakness, Japan and Russia competed for possession of the mineral-rich Chinese province of Manchuria.

Japan's participation in the suppression of the Boxer Uprising demonstrated its military power in East Asia. In 1905 Japan surprised the world by defeating Russia in the Russo-Japanese War. By the Treaty of Portsmouth that ended the war, Japan established a protectorate over Korea. In spite of Western attempts to restrict it to the role of junior partner, Japan continued to increase its influence. It gained control of southern Manchuria, with its industries and railroads. In 1910 it finally annexed Korea, joining the ranks of the world's colonial powers.

SUMMARY

○── What new technologies and industries appeared between 1850 and 1900, and how did they affect the world economy?

○── How did the societies of the industrial countries change during this period?

○── How did industrialization contribute to the socialist and labor movements?

○── How was nationalism transformed from a revolutionary to a conservative ideology?

○── How did the forces of nationalism affect the major powers of Europe?

Online Study Center
ACE the Test

After World War I broke out in 1914, many people, especially in Europe, looked back on the period from 1850 to 1914 as a golden age. For some, and in certain ways, it was. Industrialization was a powerful torrent changing Europe, North America, and East Asia. While other technologies like shipping and railroads increased their global reach, new ones—electricity, the steel and chemical industries, and the global telegraph network—contributed to the enrichment and empowerment of the industrial nations. World trade increased tenfold

during this period, and many countries' economies were transformed.

With these new technologies, memories of the great scourges—famines, wars, and epidemics—faded. Clean water, electric lights, and railways began to improve the lives of city dwellers, even the poor. Municipal services made city life less dangerous and chaotic. Goods from distant lands, even travel to other continents, came within the reach of millions. While middle-class women continued to focus on domestic pursuits and lived in a "separate sphere" from men, many working-class women took jobs in the textile industry. Yet their work outside the home did not lessen their domestic and child-rearing responsibilities.

Industrialization created a large class of factory and railroad workers. Karl Marx predicted a class struggle between workers and employers, but socialism became more of an intellectual movement. Through labor unions, workers achieved some measure of recognition and security. By the turn of the century, liberal political reforms had taken hold in western Europe and seemed about to triumph in Russia as well. Universal male suffrage became law in the United States in 1870 and in various parts of Europe by the 1880s. Morality and legislation aimed at providing security for women and families, though equality between the sexes was still beyond reach.

The framework for all these changes was the nation-state. Until the 1860s nationalism was associated with liberalism, but later generations of conservatives used public education, military service, and colonial conquests to build a sense of national unity. By 1871 both Italy and Germany had become unified states. In Japan, the Meiji Restoration restored power to the emperor and ushered in a period of Western influences. By the 1880s nationalist views had taken hold in many non-Western countries such as Egypt, India, and Japan.

The world economy, international politics, and even cultural and social issues revolved around a handful of countries—the great powers—that believed they controlled the destiny of the world. These included the most powerful European nations of the previous century, as well as three newcomers—Germany, the United States, and Japan—that were to play important roles in the future. Under the leadership of Bismarck, the German people developed a strong sense of national pride. Religious differences proved to be a hindrance to nationalism in France, especially with the anti-Semitism of the Dreyfus affair. Great Britain's problems were due to Irish resentment of English rule and economic issues.

KEY TERMS

Commodore Matthew Perry   *p. 787*

railroads   *p. 788*

submarine telegraph cables   *p. 790*

steel   *p. 790*

electricity   *p. 791*

Thomas Edison   *p. 791*

Victorian Age   *p. 795*

"separate spheres"   *p. 795*

socialism   *p. 797*

labor unions   *p. 797*

Karl Marx   *p. 797*

anarchists   *p. 799*

nationalism   *p. 802*

liberalism   *p. 802*

Giuseppe Garibaldi   *p. 803*

Otto von Bismarck   *p. 804*

Meiji Restoration   *p. 806*

Empress Dowager Cixi   *p. 812*

Yamagata Aritomo   *p. 813*

Online Study Center
Improve Your Grade
Flashcards

SUGGESTED READING

More has been written on the great powers in the late nineteenth century than on any previous period in their histories. The following are some interesting recent works and a few classics.

Industrialization is the subject of Peter Stearns, *The Industrial Revolution in World History* (1993), and David Landes, *The Unbound Prometheus: Technological Change and Industrial Development in Western Europe from 1750 to the Present* (1969). On the "second industrial revolution," see Vaclav Smil, *Creating the Twentieth Century: Technical Innovations of 1867–1914 and Their Lasting Impact* (2005).

Two interesting works on nationalism are E. J. Hobsbawm, *Nation and Nationalism Since 1780* (1990), and Benedict Anderson, *Imagined Communities: Reflections on the Origin and Spread of Nationalism* (1991).

Barrington Moore, *The Social Origins of Dictatorship and Democracy* (1966), is a classic essay on European society. On European women see Renate Bridenthal, Susan Mosher Stuard, and Merry E. Wiesner, eds., *Becoming Visible: Women in European History,* 3rd ed. (1998); Patricia Branca, *Silent Sisterhood: Middle-Class Women in the Victorian Home* (1975); Louise Tilly and Joan Scott, *Women, Work, and Family* (1987); and Theresa McBride, *The Domestic Revolution: The Modernization of Household Service in England and France, 1820–1920* (1976). The history of family life is told in Beatrice Gottlieb, *The Family in the Western World from the Black Death to the Industrial Age*

(1993). Albert Lindemann, *A History of European Socialism* (1983), covers the labor movements as well.

There are many excellent histories of individual countries. On Germany in the nineteenth century see David Blackbourne, *The Long Nineteenth Century: A History of Germany, 1780–1918* (1998), and Gordon A. Craig, *Germany, 1866–1945* (1980). The standard works on Bismarck and the unification of Germany are Otto Pflanze, *Bismarck and the Development of Germany* (1990), and Lothar Gall, *Bismarck, the White Revolutionary* (1986). On Britain see Donald Read, *The Age of Urban Democracy: England, 1868–1914* (1994), and David Thomson, *England in the Nineteenth Century, 1815–1914* (1978). On France, Eugen Weber, *Peasants into Frenchmen* (1976), and Roger Price, *A Social History of Nineteenth-Century France* (1987), are especially recommended. For Austria see Alan Sked, *The Decline and Fall of the Habsburg Empire, 1815–1918* (1989). Two good introductions to Russian history are Hans Rogger, *Russia in the Age of Modernization and Revolution, 1881–1917* (1983), and Gregory L. Freeze, ed., *Russia: A History* (1997).

There are several interesting books on Japan, in particular Peter Duus, *The Rise of Modern Japan,* 2nd ed. (1998), and Tessa Morris-Suzuki, *The Technological Transformation of Japan* (1994). Two fine books that cover the history of modern China are John King Fairbank, *The Great Chinese Revolution, 1800–1985* (1987), and Jonathan D. Spence, *The Search for Modern China* (1990).

NOTES

1. Quoted in Bonnie S. Anderson and Judith P. Zinsser, *A History of Their Own: Women in Europe from Prehistory to the Present,* vol. 2 (New York: Harper & Row, 1988), 372, 387.

Opening the Suez Canal When the canal opened in 1869, thousands of dignitaries and ordinary people gathered to watch the ships go by. (Bildarchiv Preussischer Kulturbesitz/Art Resource, NY)

○—What motivated the industrial nations to conquer new territories, and what means did they use?

○—Why were imperialists drawn to the natural resources of Africa, and how did their presence on that continent change the environment?

○—What were the social and cultural effects of imperialism in Asia?

○—What were the economic motives behind imperialism in Latin America?

○—How did imperialism contribute to the growth and globalization of the world economy?

28

THE NEW IMPERIALISM, 1869–1914

CHAPTER OUTLINE

The New Imperialism: Motives and Methods

The Scramble for Africa

Imperialism in Asia and the Pacific

Imperialism in Latin America

The World Economy and the Global Environment

DIVERSITY AND DOMINANCE: Two Africans Recall the Arrival of the Europeans

ENVIRONMENT AND TECHNOLOGY: Imperialism and Tropical Ecology

In 1869 Ismail°, the khedive° (ruler) of Egypt, invited all the Christian princes of Europe and all the Muslim princes of Asia and Africa—except the Ottoman sultan, his nominal overlord—to celebrate the inauguration of the greatest construction project of the century: the **Suez Canal**. Among the sixteen hundred dignitaries from the Middle East and Europe who assembled at Port Said° were Emperor Francis Joseph of Austria-Hungary and Empress Eugénie of France. A French journalist wrote:

> This multitude, coming from all parts of the world, presented the most varied and singular spectacle. All races were represented. . . . We saw, coming to attend this festival of civilization, men of the Orient wearing clothes of dazzling colors, chiefs of African tribes

---

Ismail (is-mah-EEL)   **khedive** (kuh-DEEV)   **Port Said** (port sah-EED)

Online Study Center

This icon will direct you to interactive activities and study materials on the website: *college.hmco.com/pic/bulliet4e.*

wrapped in their great coats, Circassians in war costumes, officers of the British army of India with their shakos [hats] wrapped in muslin, Hungarian magnates wearing their national costumes.[1]

Ismail used the occasion to emphasize the harmony and cooperation between the peoples of Africa, Asia, and Europe and to show that Egypt was not only independent but was also an equal of the great powers. To bless the inauguration, Ismail had invited clergy of the Muslim, Orthodox, and Catholic faiths. A reporter noted: "The Khedive . . . wished to symbolize thereby the unity of men and their brotherhood before God, without distinction of religion; it was the first time that the Orient had seen such a meeting of faiths to celebrate and bless together a great event and a great work."[2]

The canal was a great success, but not in the way Ismail intended. Ships using it could travel between Europe and India in less than two weeks—much less time than the month or longer consumed by sailing around Africa and across the Indian Ocean. By lowering freight costs, the canal stimulated shipping and the construction of steamships, giving an advantage to nations that had heavy industry and a large maritime trade over land-based empires and countries with few merchant ships. Great Britain, which long opposed construction of the canal for fear that it might fall into enemy hands, benefited more than any other nation. France, which provided half the capital and most of the engineers, came in a distant second, for it had less trade with Asia than Britain did. Egypt, which contributed the other half of the money and most of the labor, was the loser. Instead of making Egypt powerful and independent, the Suez Canal provided the excuse for a British invasion and occupation of that country.

Far from inaugurating an era of harmony among the peoples of three continents and three faiths, the canal triggered a wave of European domination over Africa and Asia. Between 1869 and 1914 Germany, France, Britain, Russia, Japan, and the United States used industrial technology to impose their will on the nonindustrial parts of the world. Historians use the expression **New Imperialism** to describe this exercise of power.

THE NEW IMPERIALISM: MOTIVES AND METHODS

Europe had a long tradition of imperialism reaching back to the twelfth-century Crusades against the Arabs, and the United States greatly expanded its territory after achieving independence in 1783 (see Map 24.3). During the first two-thirds of the nineteenth century the European powers continued to increase their influence overseas (see Chapter 26). The New Imperialism was characterized by an explosion of territorial conquests even more rapid than the Spanish conquests of the sixteenth century. Between 1869 and 1914, in a land grab of unprecedented speed, Europeans seized territories in Africa and Central Asia, and both Europeans and Americans took territories in Southeast Asia and the Pacific. Approximately 10 million square miles (26 million square kilometers) and 150 million people fell under the rule of Europe and the United States in this period.

Online Study Center
Improve Your Grade
Interactive Map: European Colonization, Nineteenth and Twentieth Centuries

The New Imperialism was more than a land grab. The imperial powers used economic and technological means to reorganize dependent regions and bring them into the world economy as suppliers of foodstuffs and raw materials and as consumers of industrial products. In Africa and other parts of the world, this was done by conquest and colonial administration. In the Latin American republics the same result was achieved indirectly. Even though they remained politically independent, they became economic dependencies of the United States and Europe.

What inspired Europeans and Americans to venture overseas and impose their will on other societies? There is no simple answer to this question. Economic, cultural, and political motives were involved in all cases.

Political Motives

The great powers of the late nineteenth century, as well as less powerful countries like Italy, Portugal, and Belgium, were competitive and hypersensitive about their status. French leaders, humiliated by their

C H R O N O L O G Y

	Africa	Asia and the Pacific	Latin America
1870	**1869** Opening of the Suez Canal **1874** Warfare between the British and the Asante (Gold Coast) **1877–1879** Warfare between the British and the Xhosa and between the British and the Zulu (South Africa) **1882** British forces occupy Egypt **1884–1885** Berlin Conference; Leopold II obtains Congo Free State	**1862–1895** French conquer Indochina **1865–1876** Russian forces advance into Central Asia **1878** United States obtains Pago Pago Harbor (Samoa)	**1870–1910** Railroad building boom; British companies in Argentina and Brazil; U.S. companies in Mexico.
1890	**1896** Ethiopians defeat Italian army at Adowa; warfare between the British and the Asante **1898** Battle of Omdurman	**1885** Britain completes conquest of Burma **1887** United States obtains Pearl Harbor (Hawaii) **1894–1895** China defeated in Sino-Japanese War **1895** France completes conquest of Indochina	**1895–1898** Cubans revolt against Spanish rule
1900	**1899–1902** South African War between Afrikaners and the British **1902** First Aswan Dam completed (Egypt)	**1898** United States annexes Hawaii and Guam and purchases Philippines from Spain **1899–1902** U.S. forces conquer and occupy Philippines **1903** Russia completes Trans-Siberian Railway **1904–1905** Russia defeated in Russo-Japanese War	**1898** Spanish-American War; United States annexes Puerto Rico and Guam **1901** United States imposes Platt Amendment on Cuba **1903** United States backs secession of Panama from Colombia **1904–1907, 1916** U.S. troops occupy Dominican Republic **1904–1914** United States builds Panama Canal
1910	**1908** Belgium annexes Congo		**1912** U.S. troops occupy Nicaragua and Honduras

defeat by Prussia in 1871 (see Chapter 27), sought to reestablish their nation's prestige through territorial acquisitions overseas. Great Britain, already in possession of the world's largest and richest empire, felt the need to protect India, its "jewel in the crown," by acquiring colonies in East Africa and Southeast Asia. German Chancellor Otto von Bismarck had little interest in acquiring colonies, but many Germans believed that a country as important as theirs required an impressive empire overseas.

Political motives were not limited to statesmen in the capital cities. Colonial governors, even officers posted to the farthest colonial outposts, practiced their own diplomacy. They often decided on their own to claim a piece of land before some rival got it. Armies fighting frontier wars found it easier to defeat their neighbors than to make peace with them. In response to border skirmishes with neighboring states, colonial agents were likely to send in troops, take over their neighbors' territories, and then inform their home governments. Governments felt obligated to back up their men-on-the-spot in order not to lose face. The great powers of Europe acquired much of West Africa, Southeast Asia, and the Pacific islands in this manner.

Cultural Motives

The late nineteenth century saw a Christian revival in Europe and North America, as both Catholics and Protestants founded new missionary societies. Their purpose was not only religious—to convert nonbelievers, whom they regarded as "heathen"—but also cultural in a broader sense. They sought to export their own norms of "civilized" behavior: they were determined to abolish slavery in Africa and bring Western education, medicine, hygiene, and monogamous marriage to all the world's peoples.

Among those attracted by religious work overseas were many women who joined missionary societies to become teachers and nurses, positions of greater authority than they could hope to find at home. Although they did not challenge colonialism directly, their influence often helped soften the harshness of colonial rule—for example, by calling attention to issues of maternity and women's health. Mary Slessor, a British missionary who lived for forty years among the people of southeastern Nigeria, campaigned against slavery, human sacrifice, and the killing of twins and, generally, for women's rights. In India missionaries denounced the customs of child marriages and *sati* (the burning of widows on their husbands' funeral pyres). Such views often clashed with the customs of the people among whom they settled.

The sense of moral duty and cultural superiority was not limited to missionaries. Many Europeans and Americans equated technological innovations with "progress" and "change for the better." They believed that Western technology proved the superiority of Western ideas, customs, and culture. This attitude included the idea that non-Western peoples could achieve, through education, the same cultural level as Europeans and Americans. More harmful were racist ideas that relegated non-Europeans to a status of permanent inferiority. Racists assigned different stages of biological development to peoples of different races and cultures (see Chapter 27). They divided humankind into several races based on physical appearance and ranked these races in a hierarchy that ranged from "civilized" at the highest level down through "semi-barbarous," "barbarian," and finally, at the bottom, "savage." Caucasians—whites—were always at the top of this ranking. Such

ideas were often presented as an excuse for permanent rule over Africans and Asians.

Imperialism first interested small groups of explorers, clergy, and businessmen but soon attracted people from other walks of life. Young men, finding few opportunities for adventure and glory at home in an era of peace, sought them overseas as the Spanish conquistadors had done over three centuries earlier. At first, European people and parliaments were indifferent or hostile to overseas adventures, but a few easy victories in the 1880s helped to overcome their reluctance. The United States was fully preoccupied with its westward expansion until the 1880s, but in the 1890s popular attention shifted to lands outside U.S. borders. Newspapers, which achieved wide readership in the second half of the nineteenth century, discovered that they could boost circulation with reports of wars and conquests. By the 1890s imperialism was a popular cause; it was the overseas extension of the nationalism propelling the power politics of the time.

Economic Motives

The industrialization of Europe and North America stimulated the demand for minerals—copper for electrical wiring, tin for canning, chrome and manganese for the steel industry, coal for steam engines, and, most of all, gold and diamonds. The demand for such industrial crops as cotton and rubber and for stimulants such as sugar, coffee, tea, and tobacco also grew. These products were found in the tropics, but never in sufficient quantities.

An economic depression lasting from the mid-1870s to the mid-1890s caused European merchants, manufacturers, and shippers to seek protection against foreign competition (see below). They argued that their respective countries needed secure sources of tropical raw materials and protected markets for their industries. Declining business opportunities at home prompted entrepreneurs and investors to look for profits from mines, plantations, and railroads in Asia, Africa, and Latin America. Since investment in countries so different from their own was extremely risky, businessmen sought the backing of their governments, preferably with soldiers.

These reasons explain why Europeans and Americans wished to expand their influence over other societies in the late nineteenth and early twentieth centuries. Yet motives do not adequately explain the events of that time. It was possible to conquer a piece of Africa, convert the "heathen," and start a plantation because of the sudden increase in the power that industrial peoples could wield over nonindustrial peoples and over the forces of nature. Technological advances explain both the motives and the outcome of the New Imperialism.

The Tools of the Imperialists

To succeed, empire builders needed the means to achieve their objectives at a reasonable cost. These means were provided by the Industrial Revolution (see Chapter 23). In the early part of the nineteenth century technological innovations began to tip the balance of power in favor of Europe.

Europeans had dominated the oceans since about 1500, and their naval power increased still more with the introduction of steamships. The first steamer reached India in 1825 and was soon followed by regular mail service in the 1830s. The long voyage around Africa was at first too costly for cargo steamers, for coal had to be shipped from England. The building of the Suez Canal and the development of increasingly efficient engines solved this problem and led to a boom in shipping to the Indian Ocean and East Asia. Whenever fighting broke out, passenger liners were requisitioned as troopships, giving European forces greater mobility than Asians and Africans. Their advantage was enhanced even more by the development of a global network of submarine telegraph cables connecting Europe with North America in the 1860s, with Latin America and Asia in the 1870s, with Africa in the 1880s, and finally across the Pacific in 1904.

Until the middle of the nineteenth century, western Europeans were much weaker on land than at sea. Thereafter, Europeans used gunboats with considerable success in China, Burma, Indochina, and the Congo Basin. Although gunboats opened the major river basins to European penetration, the invaders often found themselves hampered by other natural obstacles. *Falciparum* malaria, found only in Africa, was so deadly to Europeans that few explorers survived before the 1850s. In 1854 a British doctor discovered that the drug quinine, taken regularly during one's stay in Africa, could prevent the disease. This and a few sanitary precautions reduced the annual death rate among whites in West Africa from between 250 and 750 per thousand in the early nineteenth century to between 50 and 100 per thousand after 1850. This reduction was sufficient to open the continent to merchants, officials, and missionaries.

Muzzle-loading smoothbore muskets had been used in Europe, Asia, and the Americas since the late seventeenth century, and by the early nineteenth century they were also common in much of Africa. The development of new and much deadlier firearms in the 1860s and 1870s shifted the balance of power on land between Westerners and other peoples. One of these was the breechloader, which could be fired accurately ten times as fast as, and five or six times farther than, a musket. By the 1870s all armies in Europe and the United States had switched to these new rifles. Two more innovations appeared in the 1880s: smokeless powder, which did not foul the gun or reveal the soldier's position, and repeating rifles, which could shoot fifteen rounds in fifteen seconds. In the 1890s European and American armies began using machine guns, which could fire eleven bullets per second.

In the course of the century Asians and Africans also acquired better firearms, mostly old weapons that European armies had discarded. As European firearms improved, the firepower gap widened, making colonial conquests easier than ever before. By the 1880s and 1890s European-led forces of a few hundred could defeat non-European armies of thousands. Against the latest weapons, African and Asian soldiers armed with muskets or, in some cases, with spears did not stand a chance, no matter how numerous and courageous they were.

A classic example is the **Battle of Omdurman** in Sudan. On September 2, 1898, forty thousand Sudanese attacked an Anglo-Egyptian expedition that had come up the Nile on six steamers and four other boats to avenge the defeat of General Charles Gordon in 1885 (see Chapter 25). General Horatio Kitchener's troops had twenty machine guns and four artillery pieces; the Sudanese were equipped with muskets and spears. Within a few hours eleven thousand Sudanese and forty-eight British lay dead. Winston Churchill, the future British prime minister, witnessed the battle and called it

the most signal triumph ever gained by the arms of science over barbarians. Within the space of five hours the strongest and best-armed savage army yet arrayed against a modern European Power had been destroyed and dispersed, with hardly any difficulty, comparatively small risk, and insignificant loss to the victors.[3]

Colonial Agents and Administration

Once colonial agents took over a territory, their home government expected them to cover their own costs and, if possible, return some profit to the home country. The system of administering and exploiting colonies for the benefit of the home country is known as **colonialism**. In some cases, such as along the West African coast or in Indochina, there was already a considerable trade that could be taxed. In other places profits could come only from investments and a thorough reorganization of the indigenous societies. In applying modern scientific and

The Battle of Omdurman   In the late nineteenth century, most battles between European (or European-led) troops and African forces were one-sided encounters because of the disparity in the opponents' firearms and tactics. The Battle of Omdurman in Sudan in 1898 is a dramatic example. The forces of the Mahdi, some on horseback, were armed with spears and single-shot muskets. The British troops and their Egyptian allies, lined up in the foreground, used repeating rifles and machine guns able to shoot much farther than the Sudanese weapons. As a result, there were many Sudanese casualties but very few British and Egyptian.   (The Art Archive)

industrial methods to their colonies, colonialists started the transformation of Asian and African societies and landscapes that has continued to our day.

Legal experts and academics emphasized the differences between various systems of colonial government and debated whether colonies eventually should be assimilated into the ruling nation, associated in a federation, or allowed to rule themselves. Colonies that were protectorates retained their traditional governments, even their monarchs, but had a European "resident" or "consul-general" to "advise" them. Other colonies were directly administered by a European governor. In fact, the impact of colonial rule depended much more on economic and social conditions than on narrow legal distinctions.

One important factor was the presence or absence of European settlers. In Canada, Australia, and New Zealand, whites were already in the majority by 1869, and their colonial "mother-country," Britain, encouraged them to elect parliaments and rule themselves. Where European settlers were numerous but still a minority of the population, as in Algeria and South Africa, settlers and the home country struggled for control over the indigenous population. In colonies with few white settlers, the European governors ruled autocratically.

In the early years of the New Imperialism, colonial administrations consisted of a governor and his staff, a few troops to keep order, and a small number of tax collectors and magistrates. Nowhere could colonialism operate without the cooperation of indigenous elites, because no colony was wealthy enough to pay the salaries of more than a handful of European officials. In most cases the colonial governors exercised power through

A Colonial Lady   In many tropical colonies in the nineteenth century, there were few good roads, but labor was abundant. European colonial officials and their wives often traveled in a tonjon, or sedan chair carried by porters. This image of a lady in India dates from 1828.   (Eileen Tweedy/The Art Archive)

traditional rulers willing to cooperate, as in the Princely States of India (see Chapter 26). In addition, colonial governments educated a few local youths for "modern" jobs as clerks, nurses, policemen, customs inspectors, and the like. Thus colonialism relied on two rival indigenous elites.

European and American women seldom took part in the early stages of colonial expansion. As conquest gave way to peaceful colonialism and as steamships and railroads made travel less difficult, colonial officials and settlers began bringing their wives to the colonies. By the 1880s the British Women's Emigration Association was recruiting single women to go out to the colonies to marry British settlers. As one of its founders, Ellen Joyce, explained, "The possibility of the settler marrying his own countrywoman is of imperial as well as family importance."

The arrival of white women in Asia and Africa led to increasing racial segregation. Sylvia Leith-Ross, wife of a colonial officer in Nigeria, explained: "When you are alone, among thousands of unknown, unpredictable people, dazed by unaccustomed sights and sounds, bemused by strange ways of life and thought, you need to remember who you are, where you come from, what your standards are." Many colonial wives found themselves in command of numerous servants and expected to follow the complex etiquette of colonial entertainment in support of their husbands' official positions. Occasionally they found opportunities to exercise personal initiatives, usually charitable work involving indigenous women and children. However well meaning, their efforts were always subordinate to the work of men.

THE SCRAMBLE FOR AFRICA

Until the 1870s African history was largely shaped by internal forces and the spread of Islam (see Chapter 26). Outside Algeria and southern Africa, only a handful of Europeans had ever visited the interior of Africa, and European countries possessed only small enclaves on the coasts. As late as 1879 Africans ruled more than 90 percent of the continent. Then, within a decade, Africa was invaded and divided among the European powers in a movement often referred to as the **"scramble" for Africa** (see Map 28.1). This invasion affected all regions of the continent. Let us look at the most significant cases, beginning with Egypt, the wealthiest and most populated part of the continent.

Egypt

Ironically, European involvement in Egypt resulted from Egypt's attempt to free itself from Ottoman rule. Throughout the mid-nineteenth century the khedives of Egypt had tried to modernize their armed forces; build canals, harbors, railroads,

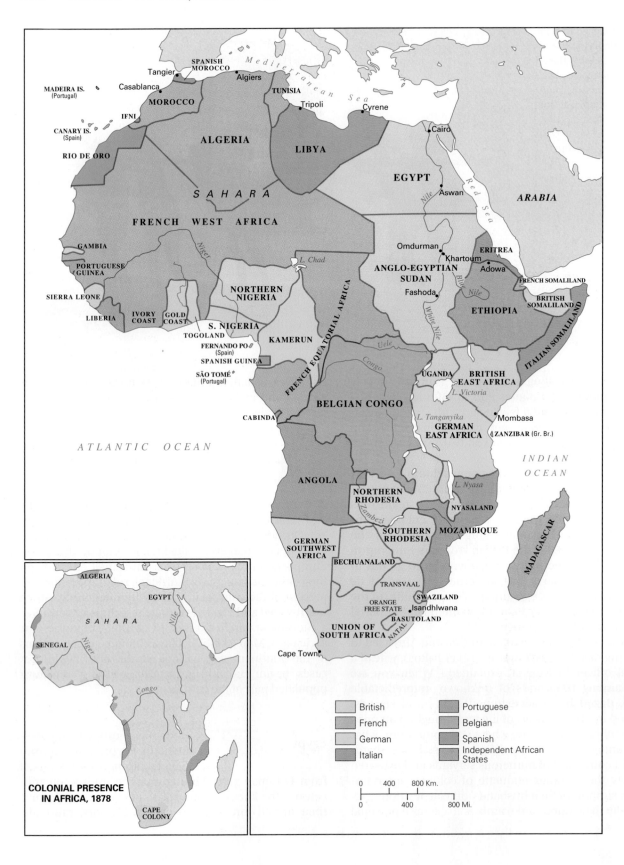

British

French

German

Italian

Portuguese

Belgian

Spanish

Independent African States

0   400   800 Km.

0   400   800 Mi.

COLONIAL PRESENCE IN AFRICA, 1878

◄ **Map 28.1 Africa in 1878 and 1914** In 1878 the European colonial presence was limited to a few coastal enclaves, plus portions of Algeria and South Africa. By 1914, Europeans had taken over all of Africa except Ethiopia and Liberia.

and other public works; and reorient agriculture toward export crops, especially cotton (see Chapters 23 and 26). Their interest in the Suez Canal was also part of this policy. Khedive Ismail even tried to make Egypt the center of an empire reaching south into Sudan and Ethiopia.

These ambitions cost vast sums of money, which the khedives borrowed from European creditors at high interest rates. By 1876 Egypt's foreign debt had risen to £100 million sterling, and the interest payments alone consumed one-third of its foreign export earnings. To avoid bankruptcy the Egyptian government sold its shares in the Suez Canal to Great Britain and accepted four foreign "commissioners of the debt" to oversee its finances. French and British bankers, still not satisfied, lobbied their governments to secure the loans by stronger measures. In 1878 the two governments obliged Ismail to appoint a Frenchman as minister of public works and a Briton as minister of finance. When high taxes caused hardship and popular discontent, the French and British persuaded the Ottoman sultan to depose Ismail. This foreign intervention provoked a military uprising under Egyptian army colonel Arabi Pasha, which threatened the Suez Canal.

Online Study Center
Improve Your Grade
Primary Source: Convention on Free Navigation of the Suez Canal Between the European Powers and the Ottoman Empire, October 29, 1888

Fearing for their investments, the British sent an army into Egypt in 1882. They intended to occupy Egypt for only a year or two. But theirs was a seaborne empire that depended on secure communications between Britain and India. So important was the Suez Canal to their maritime supremacy that they stayed for seventy years. During those years the British ruled Egypt "indirectly"—that is, they maintained the Egyptian government and the fiction of Egyptian sovereignty but retained real power in their own hands.

Eager to develop Egyptian agriculture, especially cotton production, the British brought in engineers and contractors to build the first dam across the Nile, at Aswan in upper Egypt. When completed in 1902, it was one of the largest dams in the world. It captured the annual Nile flood and released its waters throughout the year, allowing farmers to grow two, sometimes three, crops a year. This doubled the effective acreage compared with the basin system of irrigation practiced since the time of the pharaohs, in which the annual floodwaters of the Nile were retained by low dikes around the fields.

The economic development of Egypt by the British enriched a small elite of landowners and merchants, many of them foreigners. Egyptian peasants got little relief from the heavy taxes collected to pay for their country's crushing foreign debt and the expenses of the British army of occupation. Western ways that conflicted with the teachings of Islam—such as the drinking of alcohol and the relative freedom of women—offended Muslim religious leaders. Most Egyptians found British rule more onerous than that of the Ottomans. By the 1890s Egyptian politicians and intellectuals were demanding that the British leave, to no avail.

Western and Equatorial Africa

While the British were taking over Egypt, the French were planning to extend their empire into the interior of West Africa. Starting from the coast of Senegal, which had been in French hands for centuries, they hoped to build a railroad from the upper Senegal River to the upper Niger in order to open the interior to French merchants. This in turn led the French military to undertake the conquest of western Sudan.

Meanwhile, the actions of three individuals, rather than a government, brought about the occupation of the Congo Basin, an enormous forested region in the heart of equatorial Africa (see Map 28.1). In 1879 the American journalist **Henry Morton Stanley**, who had explored the area (see Chapter 26), persuaded **King Leopold II** of Belgium to invest his personal fortune in "opening up" equatorial Africa. With Leopold's money, Stanley returned to Africa from 1879 to 1884 to establish trading posts along the southern bank of the Congo River. At the same time, **Savorgnan de Brazza**, an Italian officer serving in the French army, obtained from an African ruler living on the opposite bank a treaty that placed the area under the "protection" of France.

These events sparked a flurry of diplomatic activity. German chancellor Bismarck called the **Berlin Conference** on Africa of 1884 and 1885. There the major powers agreed that henceforth "effective occupation" would replace the former trading relations between Africans and Europeans. This meant that every country with colonial ambitions had to send troops into Africa and participate in the division of the spoils. As a reward for triggering the "scramble" for Africa, Leopold II acquired a personal

A Steamboat for the Congo River   Soon after the Congo Basin was occupied by Europeans, the new colonial rulers realized they needed to improve transportation. Since access from the sea was blocked by rapids on the lower Congo River, steamboats had to be brought in sections, hauled from the coast by thousands of Congolese over very difficult terrain. This picture shows the pieces arriving at Stanley Pool, ready to be reassembled.   (From H. M. Stanley, *The Congo,* vol. 2, London, 1885)

domain under the name "Congo Free State," while France and Portugal took most of the rest of equatorial Africa. In this manner, the European powers and King Leopold managed to divide Africa among themselves, at least on paper.

"Effective occupation" required many years of effort. In the interior of West Africa, Muslim rulers resisted the French invasion for up to thirty years. The French advance encouraged the Germans to stake claims to parts of the region and the British to move north from their coastal enclaves, until the entire region was occupied by Britain, France, and Germany.

Because West Africa had long had a flourishing trade, the new rulers took advantage of existing trade networks, taxing merchants and farmers, investing the profits in railroads and harbors, and paying dividends to European stockholders. In the Gold Coast (now Ghana) British trading companies bought the cocoa grown by African farmers at low prices and resold it for large profits. The interior of French West Africa lagged behind. Although the region could produce cotton, peanuts,

and other crops, the difficulties of transportation limited its development before 1914.

Compared to West Africa, equatorial Africa had few inhabitants and little trade. Rather than try to govern these vast territories directly, authorities in the Congo Free State, the French Congo, and the Portuguese colonies of Angola and Mozambique farmed out huge pieces of land to private concession companies, offering them monopolies on the natural resources and trade of their territories and the right to employ soldiers and tax the inhabitants. The inhabitants, however, had no cash crops that they could sell to raise the money they needed to pay their taxes.

Freed from outside supervision, the companies forced the African inhabitants at gunpoint to produce cash crops and carry them, on their heads or backs, to the nearest railroad or navigable river. The worst abuses took place in the Congo Free State, where a rubber boom lasting from 1895 to 1905 made it profitable for private companies to coerce Africans to collect latex from vines that grew in the forests. One Congolese refugee told the

British consul Roger Casement who investigated the atrocities:

> We begged the white men to leave us alone, saying we could get no more rubber, but the white men and their soldiers said: "Go. You are only beasts yourselves, you are only *nyama* (meat)." We tried, always going further into the forest, and when we failed and our rubber was short, the soldiers came to our towns and killed us. Many were shot, some had their ears cut off; others were tied up with ropes around their necks and bodies and taken away.[4]

After 1906 the British press began publicizing the horrors. The public outcry that followed, coinciding with the end of the rubber boom, convinced the Belgian government to take over Leopold's private empire in 1908.

Southern Africa

The history of southern Africa between 1869 and 1914 differs from that of the rest of the continent in several important respects. One was that the land had long attracted settlers. African pastoralists and farmers had inhabited the region for centuries. **Afrikaners**, descendants of Dutch settlers on the Cape of Good Hope, moved inland throughout the nineteenth century; British prospectors and settlers arrived later in the century; and, finally, Indians were brought over by the British and stayed.

Southern Africa attracted European settlers because of its good pastures and farmland and its phenomenal deposits of diamonds, gold, and copper, as well as coal and iron ore. This was the new El Dorado that imperialists had dreamed of since the heyday of the Spanish Empire in Peru and Mexico in the sixteenth century.

The discovery of diamonds at Kimberley in 1868 lured thousands of European prospectors as well as Africans looking for work. It also attracted the interest of Great Britain, colonial ruler of the Cape Colony, which annexed the diamond area in 1871, thereby angering the Afrikaners. Once in the interior, the British defeated the Xhosa° people in 1877 and 1878. Then in 1879 they confronted the Zulu, militarily the most powerful of the African peoples in the region.

The Zulu, led by their king Cetshwayo°, resented their encirclement by Afrikaners and British. A growing sense of nationalism and their proud military tradition led them into a war with the British in 1879. At first they held their own, defeating the British at Isandhlwana°, but a few months later they were defeated. Cetshwayo was captured and sent into exile, and the Zulu lands were given to white ranchers. Yet throughout those bitter times, the Zulu's sense of nationhood remained strong.

Relations between the British and the Afrikaners, already tense as a result of British encroachment, took a turn for the worse when gold was discovered in the Afrikaner republic of Transvaal° in 1886. In the gold rush that ensued, the British soon outnumbered the Afrikaners.

Britain's invasion of southern Africa was driven in part by the ambition of **Cecil Rhodes** (1853–1902), who once declared that he would "annex the stars" if he could. Rhodes made his fortune in the Kimberley diamond fields, founding De Beers Consolidated, a company that has dominated the world's diamond trade ever since. He then turned to politics. He encouraged a concession company, the British South Africa Company, to push north into Central Africa, where he named two new colonies after himself: Southern Rhodesia (now Zimbabwe) and Northern Rhodesia (now Zambia). The Ndebele° and Shona peoples, who inhabited the region, resisted this invasion, but the machine guns of the British finally defeated them.

British attempts to annex the two Afrikaner republics, Transvaal and Orange Free State, and the inflow of English-speaking whites into the gold- and diamond-mining areas led to the South African War, which lasted from 1899 to 1902. At first the Afrikaners had the upper hand, for they were highly motivated, possessed modern rifles, and knew the land. In 1901, however, Great Britain brought in 450,000 troops and crushed the Afrikaner armies. Ironically, the Afrikaners' defeat in 1902 led to their ultimate victory. Wary of costly commitments overseas, the British government expected European settlers in Africa to manage their own affairs, as they were doing in Canada, Australia, and New Zealand. Thus, in 1910 the European settlers created the Union of South Africa, in which the Afrikaners eventually emerged as the ruling element.

Unlike Canada, Australia, and New Zealand, South Africa had a majority of indigenous inhabitants and substantial numbers of Indians and "Cape Coloureds" (people of mixed ancestry). Yet the Europeans were both numerous enough to demand self-rule and powerful enough to deny the vote and other civil rights to the majority. In 1913 the South African parliament passed the Natives Land Act, assigning Africans to reservations and forbidding them to own land elsewhere. This and other

---

Xhosa (KOH-sah)   **Cetshwayo** (set-SHWAH-yo)

Isandhlwana (ee-sawn-dull-WAH-nuh)   **Transvaal** (trans-VAHL)
Ndebele (en-duh-BELL-ay)

Victorious Ethiopians Among the states of Africa, Ethiopia alone was able to defend itself against European imperialism. In the 1880s, hemmed in by Italian advances to its east and north and by British advances to its south and west, Ethiopia purchased modern weapons and trained its army to use them. Thus prepared, the Ethiopians defeated an Italian invasion at Adowa in 1896. These Ethiopian army officers wore their most elaborate finery to pose for a photograph after their victory. (National Archives)

racial policies turned South Africa into a land of segregation, oppression, and bitter divisions.

Political and Social Consequences

At the time of the European invasion, Africa contained a wide variety of societies. Some parts of the continent had long-established kingdoms with aristocracies or commercial towns dominated by a merchant class. In other places agricultural peoples lived in villages without any outside government. Still elsewhere pastoral nomads were organized along military lines. In some remote areas people lived from hunting and gathering. Not surprisingly, these societies responded in very different ways to the European invasion.

Some peoples welcomed the invaders as allies against local enemies. Once colonial rule was established, they sought work in government service or in European firms and sent their children to mission schools. In exchange, they were often the first to receive benefits such as clinics and roads.

Others, especially peoples with a pastoral or a warrior tradition, fought tenaciously. Examples abound, from the Zulu and Ndebele of southern Africa to the pastoral Herero° people of Southwest Africa (now Namibia), who rose up against German invaders in 1904; in repressing their uprising, the Germans exterminated two-thirds of them. In the Sahel, a belt of grasslands south of the Sahara, charismatic leaders rose up in the name of a purified Islam, gathered a following of warriors, and led them on part-religious, part empire-building campaigns called *jihads*. These leaders included Samori Toure in western Sudan (now Mali), Rabih in the Chad basin, and the Mahdi° in eastern Sudan (see Chapter 26). All of them eventually came into conflict with European-led military expeditions and were defeated.

Some commercial states with long histories of contact with Europeans also fought back. The kingdom of **Asante°** in Gold Coast rose up in 1874, 1896, and 1900 before it was finally overwhelmed. In the Niger Delta, the ancient city of Benin, rich with artistic treasures, resisted colonial control until 1897, when a British "punitive expedition" set it on fire and carted its works of art off to Europe.

One resistance movement succeeded, to the astonishment of Europeans and Africans alike. When **Menelik** became emperor of Ethiopia in 1889 (see Chapter 26), his country was threatened by Sudanese Muslims to the west and by France and Italy, which controlled the coast of the Red Sea to the east. For many years, Ethiopia had been purchasing European and American weapons. By the Treaty of Wichelle (1889), Italy agreed to sell more weapons to Ethiopia. Six years later, when Italians attempted to establish a protectorate over Ethiopia, they found the Ethiopians armed with thousands of rifles and even a few machine guns and artillery pieces. Although Italy sent twenty thousand troops to attack Ethiopia, in 1896 they were defeated at Adowa° by a larger and better-trained Ethiopian army.

Herero (hair-AIR-oh) Mahdi (MAH-dee)
Asante (uh-SHAWN-tee) Adowa (AH-do-ah)

Most Africans neither joined nor fought the European invaders but tried to continue living as before. They found this increasingly difficult because colonial rule disrupted every traditional society. The presence of colonial officials meant that rights to land, commercial transactions, and legal disputes were handled very differently and that traditional rulers lost all authority, except where Europeans used them as local administrators.

Changes in landholding were especially disruptive, for most Africans were farmers or herders for whom access to land was a necessity. In areas with a high population density, such as Egypt and West Africa, colonial rulers left peasants in place, encouraged them to grow cash crops, and collected taxes on the harvest. Elsewhere, the new rulers declared any land that was not farmed to be "waste" or "vacant" and gave it to private concession companies or to European planters and ranchers. In Kenya, Northern Rhodesia, and South Africa, Europeans found the land and climate to their liking, in contrast to other parts of Africa, where soldiers, officials, missionaries, or traders stayed only a few years. White settlers forced Africans to become squatters, sharecroppers, or ranch hands on land they had farmed for generations. In South Africa they forced many Africans off their lands and onto "reserves," much like the nomadic peoples of North America, Russia, and Australia (see Chapter 24).

Although the colonial rulers harbored designs on the land, they were even more interested in African labor. They did not want to pay wages high enough to attract workers voluntarily. Instead, they imposed various taxes, such as the hut tax and the head tax, which Africans had to pay regardless of their income. To find the money, Africans had little choice but to accept whatever work the Europeans offered. In this way Africans were recruited to work on plantations, railroads, and other modern enterprises. In the South African mines Africans were paid, on average, one-tenth as much as Europeans.

Some Africans came to the cities and mining camps seeking a better life than they had on the land. Many migrated great distances and stayed away for years at a time. Most migrant workers were men who left their wives and children behind in villages and on reserves. In some cases the authorities did not allow them to bring their families and settle permanently in the towns. This caused great hardship for African women, who had to grow food for their families during the men's absences and care for sick and aged workers. Long separations between spouses also led to an increase in prostitution and to the spread of sexually transmitted diseases.

Some African women welcomed colonial rule, for it brought an end to fighting and slave raiding, but others were led into captivity (see Diversity and Dominance: Two Africans Recall the Arrival of the Europeans). A few succeeded in becoming wealthy traders or owners of livestock. On the whole, however, African women benefited less than men from the economic changes that colonialism introduced. In areas where the colonial rulers replaced communal property (traditional in most of Africa) with private property, property rights were assigned to the head of the household—that is, to the man. Almost all the jobs open to Africans, even those considered "women's work" in Europe, such as nursing and domestic service, were reserved for men.

Cultural Responses

Africans had more contact with missionaries than with any other Europeans. Missionaries, both men and women, opened schools to teach reading, writing, and arithmetic to village children. Boys were taught crafts such as carpentry and blacksmithing, while girls learned domestic skills such as cooking, laundry, and childcare.

Along with basic skills, the first generation of Africans educated in mission schools acquired Western ideas of justice and progress. Samuel Ajayi Crowther, a Yoruba rescued from slavery as a boy and educated in mission schools in Sierra Leone, went on to become an Anglican minister and, in 1864, the first African bishop. Crowther thought that Africa needed European assistance in achieving both spiritual and economic development:

> Africa has neither knowledge nor skill . . . to bring out her vast resources for her own improvement. . . . Therefore to claim Africa for the Africans alone, is to claim for her the right of a continued ignorance. . . . For it is certain, unless help [comes] from without, a nation can never rise above its present state.[5]

After the first generation, many of the teachers in mission schools were African, themselves the products of a mission education. They discovered that Christian ideals clashed with the reality of colonial exploitation. One convert wrote in 1911:

> There is too much failure among all Europeans in Nyasaland. The three combined bodies—Missionaries, Government and Companies or gainers of money— do form the same rule to look upon the native with mockery eyes. . . . If we had enough power to communicate ourselves to Europe, we would advise them not to call themselves Christendom, but Europeandom. Therefore the life of the three combined bodies is altogether too cheaty, too thefty, too mockery. Instead of "Give," they say "Take away from." There is too much breakage of God's pure law.[6]

Two Africans Recall the Arrival of the Europeans

We know a great deal about the arrival of the Europeans into the interior of Africa from the perspective of the conquerors, but very little about how the events were experienced by Africans. Here are two accounts by African women, one from northern Nigeria whose land was occupied by the British, the other from the Congo Free State, a colony of King Leopold II of Belgium. They show not only how Africans experienced European colonial dominance, but also the great diversity of experiences of Africans.

Baba of Karo, a Nigerian Woman, Remembers her Childhood

When I was a maiden the Europeans first arrived. Ever since we were quite small the *malams* had been saying that the Europeans would come with a thing called a train, they would come with a thing called a motor-car, in them you would go and come back in a trice. They would stop wars, they would repair the world, they would stop oppression and lawlessness, we should live at peace with them. We used to go and sit quietly and listen to the prophecies. They would come, fine handsome people, they would not kill anyone, they would not oppress anyone, they would bring all their strange things. . . .

I remember when a European came to Karo on a horse, and some of his foot soldiers went into the town. Everyone came out to look at them, but in Zerewa they didn't see the European. Everyone at Karo ran away—"There's a European, there's a European!" He came from Zaria with a few black men, two on horses and four on foot. We were inside the town. Later on we heard that they were there in Zaria in crowds, clearing spaces and building houses. One of my younger "sisters" was at Karo, she was pregnant, and when she saw the European she ran away and shut the door.

At that time Yusufu was the king of Kano. He did not like the Europeans, he did not wish them, he would not sign their treaty. Then he say that perforce he would have to agree, so he did. We Habe wanted them to come, it was the Fulani who did not like it. When the Europeans came the Habe saw that if you worked for them they paid you for it, they didn't say, like the Fulani, "Commoner, give me this! Commoner, bring me that!" Yes, the Habe wanted them; they saw no harm in them. From Zaria they came to Rogo, they were building their big road to Kano City. They called out the people and said they were to come and make the road, if there were trees in the way they cut them down. The Europeans paid them with goods, they collected the villagers together and each man brought his large hoe. Money was not much use to them, so the Europeans paid them with food and other things.

The Europeans said that there were to be no more slaves; if someone said "Slave!" you could complain to the *alkali* who would punish the master who said it, the judge said, "That is what the Europeans have decreed." The first order said that any slave, if he was younger than you, was your younger brother, if he was older than you was your elder brother—they were all brothers of their master's family. No one used the word "slave" any more. When slavery was stopped, nothing much happened at our *rinji* except that some slaves whom we had bought in the market ran away. Our own father went to his farm and worked, he and his son took up their large hoes; they loaned out their spare farms. Tsoho our father and Kadiri my brother with whom I live now and Babambo worked, they farmed guineacorn and millet and groundnuts and everything; before this they had supervised the slaves' work—now they did their own. When the midday food was ready, the women of the compound would give us children the food, one of us drew water, and off we went to the farm to take the men their food at the foot of a tree; I was about eight or nine at that time, I think. . . .

In the old days if the chief liked the look of your daughter he would take her and put her in his house; you could do nothing about it. Now they don't do that.

Ilanga, a Congolese Woman, Recounts her Capture by Agents of the Congo Free State

Our village is called Waniendo, after our chief Niendo. . . . It is a large village near a small stream, and surrounded by large fields of *mohago* (cassava) and *muhindu* (maize) and other foods, for we all worked hard at our plantations, and always had plenty to eat. The men always worked in the fields clearing the ground, or went hunting. . . . We never had war in our country, and the men had not many arms except knives; but our chief Niendo had a gun, which he had bought long ago from another chief for forty-three beads, but he had no powder or caps, and only carried it when he went on a journey.

. . . we were all busy in the fields hoeing our plantations, for it was the rainy season, and the weeds sprang quickly up, when a runner came to the village saying that a large band of men was coming, that they all wore red caps and blue cloth, and carried guns and long knives, and that many white men were with them, the chief of whom was *Kibalanga* (Michaux). Niendo at once called all the chief men to his house, while the drums were beaten to summon the people to the village. A long consultation was held, and finally we were all told to go quietly to the fields and bring in ground-nuts, plantains, and cassava for the warriors who were coming, and goats and fowl for the white men. The women all went with baskets and filled them, and put them in the road, which was blocked up, so many were there. Niendo then commanded everyone to go and sit quietly in the houses until he gave other orders. This we did, everyone remaining quietly seated while Niendo went up the road with the head men to meet the white chief. We did not know what to think, for most of us feared that so many armed men coming boded evil; but Niendo thought that, by giving presents of much food, he would induce the strangers to pass on without harming us. And so it proved, for the soldiers took the baskets, and were then ordered by the white men to move off through the village. Many of the soldiers looked into the houses and shouted at us words we did not understand. We were glad when they were all gone, for we were much in fear of the white men and the strange warriors, who are known to all the people as being great fighters, bringing war wherever they go. . . .

When the white men and their warriors had gone, we went again to our work, and were hoping that they would not return; but this they did in a very short time. As before, we brought in great heaps of food; but this time *Kibalanga* did not move away directly, but camped near our village, and his soldiers came and stole all our fowl and goats and tore up our cassava; but we did not mind as long as they did not harm us. The next morning it was reported that the white men were going away; but soon after the sun rose over the hill, a large band of soldiers came into the village, and we all went into the houses and sat down. We were not long seated when the soldiers came rushing in shouting, and threatening Niendo with their guns. They rushed into the houses and dragged the people out. Three or four came to our house and caught hold of me, also my husband Oleka and my sister Katinga. We were dragged into the road, and were tied together with cords about our necks, so that we could not escape. We were all crying, for now we knew that we were to be taken away to be slaves. The soldiers beat us with the iron sticks from their guns, and compelled us to march to the camp of *Kibalanga*, who ordered the women to be tied up separately, ten to each cord, and the men in the same way. When we were all collected—and there were many from other villages whom we now saw, and many from Waniendo—the soldiers brought baskets of food for us to carry, in some of which was smoked human flesh (*niama na nitu*).

We then set off marching very quickly. My sister Katinga had her baby in her arms, and was not compelled to carry a basket; but my husband Oleka was made to carry a goat. We marched until the afternoon, when we camped near a stream, where we were glad to drink, for we were much athirst. We had nothing to eat, for the soldiers would give us nothing, so we lay upon the ground, and at night went to sleep. The next day we continued the march, and when we camped at noon were given some maize and plantains, which were gathered near a village from which the people had run away. So it continued each day until the fifth day, when the soldiers took my sister's baby and threw it in the grass, leaving it to die, and made her carry some cooking pots which they found in the deserted village. On the sixth day we became very weak from lack of food and from constant marching and sleeping in the damp grass, and my husband, who marched behind us with the goat, could not stand up longer, and so he sat down beside the path and refused to walk more. The soldiers beat him, but still he refused to move. Then one of them struck him on the head with the end of his gun, and he fell upon the ground. One of the soldiers caught the goat, while two or three others stuck the long knives they put on the ends of their guns into my husband. I saw the blood spurt out, and then saw him no more, for we passed over the brow of a hill and he was out of sight. Many of the young men were killed the same way, and many babies thrown into the grass to die. A few escaped; but we were so well guarded that it was almost impossible.

After marching ten days we came to the great water (Lualaba) and were taken in canoes across to the white men's town at Nyangwe. Here we stayed for six or seven days, and were then put in canoes and sent down the river; . . . but on the way we could get nothing to eat, and were glad to rest here, where there are good houses and plenty of food; and we hope we will not be sent away.

QUESTIONS FOR ANALYSIS

1. How do Baba and Ilanga recall their existence before the Europeans came?

2. What did they expect when they first heard of the arrival of Europeans? Instead, what happened to them, their relatives, and their towns?

3. How do you explain the difference between these two accounts?

Source: From M. F. Smith, ed., *Baba of Karo: A Woman of the Muslim Hausa* (New York: Philosophical Library, 1955), 66–68. Edgar Canisius, *A Campaign Amongst Cannibals* (London: R. A. Everett & Co., 1903), 250–256. Used by permission of the Philosophical Library.

Christian missionaries from Europe and America were not the only ones to bring religious change to Africa. In southern and Central Africa indigenous preachers adapted Christianity to African values and customs and founded new denominations known as "Ethiopian" churches.

Christianity proved successful in converting followers of traditional religions but made no inroads among Muslims. Instead, Islam, long predominant in northern and eastern Africa, spread southward as Muslim teachers established Quranic schools in the villages and founded Muslim brotherhoods. European colonialism unwittingly helped the diffusion of Islam. By building cities and increasing trade, colonial rule permitted Muslims to settle in new areas. As Islam—a universal religion without the taint of colonialism—became increasingly relevant to Africans, the number of Muslims in sub-Saharan Africa probably doubled between 1869 and 1914.

IMPERIALISM IN ASIA AND THE PACIFIC

From 1869 to 1914 the pressure of the industrial powers was felt throughout Asia, the East Indies, and the Pacific islands. As trade with these regions grew in the late nineteenth century, so did their attractiveness to imperialists eager for economic benefits and national prestige.

Europeans had traded along the coasts of Asia and the East Indies since the early sixteenth century. By 1869 Britain already controlled most of India and Burma; Spain occupied the Philippines; and the Netherlands held large parts of the East Indies (now Indonesia). Between 1862 and 1895 France conquered Indochina (now Vietnam, Kampuchea, and Laos). The existence of these Asian colonial possessions had inspired the building of the Suez Canal.

We have seen the special cases of British imperialism in India (Chapter 26) and of Japanese imperialism in China and Korea (Chapter 27). Here let us look at the impact of the New Imperialism on Central and Southeast Asia, Indonesia, the Philippines, and Hawaii (see Map 28.2).

Central Asia

For over seven centuries Russians had been at the mercy of the nomads of the Eurasian steppe extending from the Black Sea to Manchuria. When the nomadic tribesmen were united, as they were under the Mongol ruler Genghis Khan (r. 1206–1227),

they could defeat the Russians; when they were not, the Russians moved into the steppe. This age-old ebb and flow ended when Russia acquired modern rifles and artillery.

Between 1865 and 1876 Russian forces advanced into Central Asia. Nomads like the Kazakhs, who lived east of the Caspian Sea, fought bravely but in vain. The fertile agricultural land of Kazakhstan attracted 200,000 Russian settlers. Although the governments of Tsar Alexander II (r. 1855–1881) and Tsar Alexander III (r. 1881–1894) claimed not to interfere in indigenous customs, they declared communally owned grazing lands "waste" or "vacant" and turned them over to farmers from Russia. By the end of the nineteenth century the nomads were fenced out and reduced to starvation. Echoing the beliefs of other European imperialists, an eminent Russian jurist declared: "International rights cannot be taken into account when dealing with semibarbarous peoples."

South of the Kazakh steppe land were deserts dotted with oases where the fabled cities of Tashkent, Bukhara, and Samarkand served the caravan trade between China and the Middle East. For centuries the peoples of the region had lived under the protection of the Mongols, Timur and his descendants, and later the Qing Empire. But by the 1860s and 1870s the Qing Empire was losing control over Central Asia, so it was fairly easy for Russian expeditions to conquer the indigenous peoples. Russia thereby acquired land suitable for cotton, along with a large and growing Muslim population.

Russian rule brought few benefits to the peoples of the Central Asian oases and few real changes. The Russians abolished slavery, built railroads to link the region with Europe, and planted hundreds of thousands of acres of cotton. Unlike the British in India, however, they did not attempt to change the customs, languages, or religious beliefs of their subjects.

Southeast Asia and Indonesia

The peoples of the Southeast Asian peninsula and the Indonesian archipelago had been in contact with outsiders—Chinese, Indians, Arabs, Europeans—for centuries. Java and the smaller islands—the fabled Spice Islands (the Moluccas)—had long been subject to Portuguese and later to Dutch domination. Until the mid-nineteenth century, however, most of the region was made up of independent kingdoms.

As in Africa, there is considerable variation in the history of different parts of the region, yet all came under intense imperialist pressure during the nineteenth century.

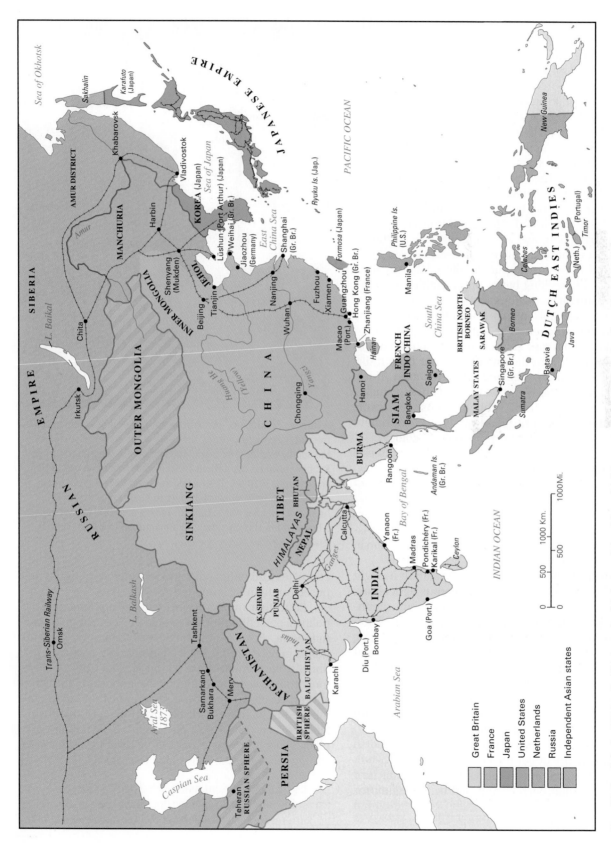

Map 28.2 Asia in 1914 By 1914, much of Asia was claimed by colonial powers. The southern rim, from the Pacific Gulf to the Pacific, was occupied by Great Britain, France, the Netherlands, and the United States. Central Asia had been incorporated into the Russian Empire. Japan, now industrialized, had joined the Western imperialist powers in expanding its territory and influence at the expense of China.

Burma (now Myanmar), nearest India, was gradually taken over by the British in the course of the century, until the last piece was annexed in 1885. Indochina fell under French control piece by piece until it was finally subdued in 1895. Similarly, Malaya (now Malaysia) came under British rule in stages during the 1870s and 1880s. By the early 1900s the Dutch had subdued northern Sumatra, the last part of the Dutch East Indies to be conquered. Only Siam (now Thailand) remained independent, although it lost several border provinces.

Despite their varied political histories, all these regions had features in common. They all had fertile soil, constant warmth, and heavy rains. Furthermore, the peoples of the region had a long tradition of intensive gardening, irrigation, and terracing. In parts of the region where the population was not very dense, Europeans found it easy to import landless laborers from China and India seeking better opportunities overseas. Another reason for the region's wealth was the transfer of commercially valuable plants from other parts of the world. Tobacco, cinchona° (an antimalarial drug), manioc (an edible root crop), maize (corn), and natural rubber were brought from the Americas; sugar from India; tea from China; and coffee and oil palms from Africa. By 1914 much of the world's supply of these valuable products—in the case of rubber, almost all—came from Southeast Asia and Indonesia (see Environment and Technology: Imperialism and Tropical Ecology).

Most of the wealth of Southeast Asia and Indonesia was exported to Europe and North America. In exchange, the inhabitants of the region received two benefits from colonial rule: peace and a reliable food supply. As a result, their numbers increased at an unprecedented rate. For instance, the population of Java (an island the size of Pennsylvania) doubled from 16 million in 1870 to over 30 million in 1914.

Colonialism and the growth of population brought many social changes. The more numerous agricultural and commercial peoples gradually moved into mountainous and forested areas, displacing the earlier inhabitants who practiced hunting and gathering or shifting agriculture. The migrations of the Javanese to Borneo and Sumatra are but one example. Immigrants from China and India (see Chapter 26) changed the ethnic composition and culture of every country in the region. Thus the population of the Malay Peninsula became one-third Malay, one-third Chinese, and one-third Indian.

As in Africa, European missionaries attempted to spread Christianity under the colonial umbrella. Islam, however, was much more successful in gaining new converts, for it had been established in the region for

cinchona (sin-CHO-nah)

A Rubber Plantation   As bicycles and automobiles proliferated in the early twentieth century, the demand for rubber outstripped the supply available from wild rubber trees in the Amazon forest. Rubber grown on plantations in Southeast Asia came on the market from 1910 on. The rubber trees had to be tapped very carefully and on a regular schedule to obtain the latex or sap from which rubber was extracted. In this picture a woman and a boy perform this operation on a plantation in British Malaya. (Mary Evans Picture Library/The Image Works)

centuries and people did not consider it a religion imposed on them by foreigners.

Education and European ideas had an impact on the political perceptions of the peoples of Southeast Asia and Indonesia. Just as important was their awareness of events in neighboring Asian countries: India, where a nationalist movement arose in the 1880s; China, where modernizers were undermining the authority of the Qing; and especially Japan, whose rapid industrialization culminated in its brilliant victory over Russia in the Russo-Japanese War (1904–1905; see Chapter 27). The spirit of a rising generation was expressed by a young Vietnamese writing soon after the Russo-Japanese War:

> I, . . . an obscure student, having had occasion to study new books and new doctrines, have discovered in a recent history of Japan how they have been able

ENVIRONMENT + TECHNOLOGY

Imperialism and Tropical Ecology

Like all conquerors before them, the European imperialists of the nineteenth century exacted taxes and rents from the peoples they conquered. But they also sent botanists and agricultural experts to their tropical colonies to increase the production of commercial crops, radically changing the landscapes.

The most dramatic effects were brought about by the deliberate introduction of new crops—an acceleration of the Columbian Exchange that had begun in the fifteenth century. In the early nineteenth century tea was transferred from China to India and Ceylon. In the 1850s British and Dutch botanists smuggled seeds of the cinchona tree from the Andes in South America to India and Java. They had to operate in secret because the South American republics, knowing the value of this crop, prohibited the export of seeds. With the seeds, the British and Dutch established cinchona plantations in Ceylon and Java, respectively, to produce quinine, which was essential as an antimalarial drug and a flavoring for tonic water. Similarly, in the 1870s British agents stole seeds of rubber trees from the Amazon rain forest and transferred them to Malaya and Sumatra.

Before these transfers, vast forests covered the highlands of India, Southeast Asia, and Indonesia, precisely the lands where the new plants grew best. So European planters had the forests cut down and replaced with thousands of acres of commercially profitable trees and bushes, all lined up in perfect rows and tended by thousands of indigenous laborers to satisfy the demands of customers in faraway lands. The crops that poured forth from the transformed environments brought great wealth to the European planters and the imperial powers. In 1909 the British botanist John Willis justified the transformation in these terms:

> Whether planting in the tropics will always continue to be under European management is another question, but the northern powers will not permit that the rich and as yet comparatively undeveloped countries of the tropics should be entirely wasted by being devoted merely to the supply of the food and clothing wants of their own people, when they can also supply the wants of the colder zones in so many indispensable products.

This quotation raises important questions about trade versus self-sufficiency. If a region's economy supplies the food and clothing wants of its own people, is its output "entirely wasted"? What is the advantage of trading the products of one region (such as the tropics) for those of another (such as the colder zones)? Is this trade an obligation? Should one part of the world (such as the "northern powers") let another refuse to develop and sell its "indispensable products"? Can you think of a case where a powerful country forced a weaker one to trade?

Branch of a Cinchona Tree   The bark of the cinchona tree was the source of quinine, the only antimalarial drug known before the 1940s. Quinine made it much safer for Europeans to live in the tropics.   (From Bentley & Trimen's Medicinal Plants. Hunt Institute for Botanical Documentation, Carnegie Mellon University)

Source: The quotation is from John Christopher Willis, *Agriculture in the Tropics: An Elementary Treatise* (Cambridge: Cambridge University Press, 1909), 38–39.

Emilio Aguinaldo In 1896, a revolt led by Emilio Aguinaldo attempted to expel Spaniards from the Philippines. When the United States purchased the Philippines from Spain two years later, the Filipino people were not consulted. Aguinaldo continued his campaign, this time against the American occupation forces, until his capture in 1901. In this picture, he appears on horseback, surrounded by some of his troops. (Corbis)

to conquer the impotent Europeans. This is the reason why we have formed an organization. . . . We have selected from young Annamites [Vietnamese] the most energetic, with great capacities for courage, and are sending them to Japan for study. . . . Several years have passed without the French being aware of the movement. . . . Our only aim is to prepare the population for the future.[7]

Hawaii and the Philippines, 1878–1902

By the 1890s the United States had a fast-growing population and industries that produced more manufactured goods than they could sell at home. Merchants and bankers began to look for export markets. The political mood was also expansionist, and many echoed the feelings of the naval strategist Alfred T. Mahan°: "Whether they will or no, Americans must now begin to look outward. The growing production of the country requires it."

Some Americans had been looking outward for quite some time, especially across the Pacific to China and Japan. In 1878 the United States obtained the harbor of Pago Pago in Samoa as a coaling and naval station, and in 1887 it secured the use of Pearl Harbor in Hawaii for the same purpose. Six years later American settlers in

Hawaii deposed Queen Liliuokalani (1838–1917) and offered the Hawaiian Islands to the United States. At the time President Grover Cleveland (1893–1897) was opposed to annexation, and the settlers had to content themselves with an informal protectorate. By 1898, however, the United States under President William McKinley (1897–1901) had become openly imperialistic, and it annexed Hawaii as a steppingstone to Asia. As the United States became ever more involved in Asian affairs, Hawaii's strategic location brought an inflow of U.S. military personnel, and its fertile land caused planters to import farm laborers from Japan, China, and the Philippines. These immigrants soon outnumbered the native Hawaiians.

While large parts of Asia were falling under colonial domination, the people of the Philippines were chafing under their Spanish rulers. The movement for independence began among young Filipinos studying in Europe. José Rizal, a young doctor working in Spain, was arrested and executed in 1896 for writing patriotic and anticlerical novels. Thereafter, the center of resistance shifted to the Philippines, where **Emilio Aguinaldo**, leader of a secret society, rose in revolt and proclaimed a republic in 1899. The revolutionaries had a good chance of winning independence, for Spain had its hands full with a revolution in Cuba (see below).

Unfortunately for Aguinaldo and his followers, the United States went to war against Spain in April 1898 and quickly overcame Spanish forces in the Philippines

Mahan (mah-HAHN)

and Cuba. President McKinley had not originally intended to acquire the Philippines, but after the Spanish defeat, he realized that a weakened Spain might lose the islands to another imperialist power. Japan, having recently defeated China in the Sino-Japanese War (1894–1895) and annexed Taiwan (see Chapter 27), was eager to expand its empire. So was Germany, which had taken over parts of New Guinea and Samoa and several Pacific archipelagoes during the 1880s. To forestall them, McKinley purchased the Philippines from Spain for $20 million.

The Filipinos were not eager to trade one master for another. For a while, Aguinaldo cooperated with the Americans in the hope of achieving full independence. When his plan was rejected, he rose up again in 1899 and proclaimed the independence of his country. In spite of protests by anti-imperialists in the United States, the U.S. government decided that its global interests outweighed the interests of the Filipino people. In rebel areas, a U.S. army of occupation tortured prisoners, burned villages and crops, and forced the inhabitants into "reconcentration camps." Many American soldiers tended to look on Filipinos with the same racial contempt with which Europeans viewed their colonial subjects. By the end of the insurrection in 1902, the war had cost the lives of 5,000 Americans and 200,000 Filipinos.

After the insurrection ended, the United States attempted to soften its rule with public works and economic development projects. New buildings went up in the city of Manila; roads, harbors, and railroads were built; and the Philippine economy was tied ever more closely to that of the United States. In 1907 Filipinos were allowed to elect representatives to a legislative assembly, but ultimate authority remained in the hands of a governor appointed by the president of the United States. In 1916 the Philippines were the first U.S. colony to be promised independence, a promise fulfilled thirty years later.

IMPERIALISM IN LATIN AMERICA

Nations in the Americas followed two divergent paths (see Chapter 24). In Canada and the United States manufacturing industries, powerful corporations, and wealthy financial institutions arose. Latin America and the Caribbean exported raw materials and foodstuffs and imported manufactured goods. The poverty of their people, the preferences of their elites, and the pressures of the world economy made them increasingly dependent on the industrialized countries. Their political systems saved them from outright annexation by the

colonial empires. But their natural resources made them attractive targets for manipulation by the industrial powers, including the United States, in a form of economic dependence called **free-trade imperialism**.

In the Western Hemisphere, therefore, the New Imperialism manifested itself not by a "scramble" for territories but in two other ways. In the larger republics of South America, the pressure was mostly financial and economic. In Central America and the Caribbean, it also included military intervention by the United States.

Railroads and the Imperialism of Free Trade

Latin America's economic potential was huge, for the region could produce many agricultural and mineral products in demand in the industrial countries. What was needed was a means of opening the interior to development. Railroads seemed the perfect answer.

Foreign merchants and bankers as well as Latin American landowners and politicians embraced the new technology. Starting in the 1870s almost every country in Latin America acquired railroads, usually connecting mines or agricultural regions with the nearest port rather than linking up the different parts of the interior. Since Latin America did not have any steel or mechanical industries, all the equipment and building material came from Britain or the United States. So did the money to build the networks, the engineers who designed and maintained them, and the managers who ran them.

Argentina, a land of rich soil that produced wheat, beef, and hides, gained the longest and best-developed rail network south of the United States. By 1914, 86 percent of the railroads in Argentina were owned by British firms; 40 percent of the employees were British; and the official language of the railroads was English, not Spanish. The same was true of mining and industrial enterprises and public utilities throughout Latin America.

In many ways, the situation resembled those of India and Ireland, which also obtained rail networks in exchange for raw materials and agricultural products. The Argentine nationalist Juan Justo saw the parallel:

> English capital has done what English armies could not do. Today our country is tributary to England . . . the gold that the English capitalists take out of Argentina or carry off in the form of products does us no more good than the Irish get from the revenues that the English lords take out of Ireland.[8]

The difference was that the Indians and Irish had little say in the matter because they were under British rule. But in Latin America the political elites encouraged foreign companies with generous concessions as the most rapid way to modernize their countries and enrich the property owners. In countries where the majority of the poor were Indians (as in Mexico and Peru) or of African origin (as in Brazil), they were neither consulted nor allowed to benefit from the railroad boom.

American Expansionism and the Spanish-American War, 1898

After 1865 Europeans used their financial power to penetrate Latin America. But they avoided territorial acquisitions for four reasons: (1) they were overextended in Africa and Asia; (2) there was no need, because the Latin American governments provided the political backing for the economic arrangements; (3) the Latin Americans had shown themselves capable of resisting invasions, most recently when Mexico fought off the French in the 1860s (see Chapter 24); and (4) the United States, itself a former colony, claimed to defend the entire Western Hemisphere against all outside intervention. This claim, made in the Monroe Doctrine (1823), did not prevent the United States itself from intervening in Latin American affairs.

The United States had long had interests in Cuba, the closest and richest of the Caribbean islands and a Spanish colony. American businesses had invested great sums of money in Cuba's sugar and tobacco industries, and tens of thousands of Cubans had migrated to the United States. In 1895 the Cuban nationalist José Martí started a revolution against Spanish rule. American newspapers thrilled readers with lurid stories of Spanish atrocities; businessmen worried about their investments; and politicians demanded that the U.S. government help liberate Cuba.

On February 15, 1898, the U.S. battleship *Maine* accidentally blew up in Havana harbor, killing 266 American sailors. The U.S. government immediately blamed Spain and issued an ultimatum that the Spanish evacuate Cuba. Spain agreed to the ultimatum, but the American press and Congress were eager for war, and President McKinley did not restrain them.

The Spanish-American War was over quickly. On May 1, 1898, U.S. warships destroyed the Spanish fleet at Manila in the Philippines. Two months later the United States Navy sank the Spanish Atlantic fleet off Santiago, Cuba. By mid-August Spain was suing for peace. U.S. Secretary of State John Hay called it "a splendid little war." The United States purchased the Philippines from Spain but took over Puerto Rico and Guam as war booty. The two islands remain American possessions to this day. Cuba became an independent republic, subject, however, to intense interference by the United States.

American Intervention in the Caribbean and Central America, 1901–1914

The nations of the Caribbean and Central America were small and poor, and their governments were corrupt, unstable, and often bankrupt. They seemed to offer an open invitation to foreign interference. A government would borrow money to pay for railroads, harbors, electric power, and other symbols of modernity. When it could not repay the loan, the lending banks in Europe or the United States would ask for assistance from their home governments, which sometimes threatened to intervene. To ward off European intervention, the United States sent in the marines on more than one occasion.

Presidents Theodore Roosevelt (1901–1909), William Taft (1909–1913), and Woodrow Wilson (1913–1921) felt impelled to intervene in the region, though they differed sharply on the proper policy the United States should follow toward the small nations to the south. Roosevelt encouraged regimes friendly to the United States, like Porfirian Mexico; Taft sought to influence them through loans from American banks; and the moralist Wilson tried to impose clean governments through military means.

Having "liberated" Cuba from Spain, the United States forced the Cuban government to accept the Platt Amendment in 1901. The amendment gave the United States the "right to intervene" to maintain order on the island. The United States used this excuse to occupy Cuba militarily from 1906 to 1909, in 1912, and again from 1917 to 1922. In all but name Cuba became an American protectorate. U.S. troops also occupied the Dominican Republic from 1904 to 1907 and again in 1916, Nicaragua and Honduras in 1912, and Haiti in 1915. They brought sanitation and material progress but no political improvements.

The United States was especially forceful in Panama, which was a province of Colombia. Here the issue was not corruption or debts but a more vital interest: the construction of a canal across the isthmus of Panama to speed shipping between the east and west coasts of the United States. In 1878 the Frenchman Ferdinand de Lesseps, builder of the Suez Canal, had obtained a concession from Colombia to construct a canal across the isthmus, which lay in Colombian territory. Financial scandals and yellow fever, however, doomed his project.

When the United States acquired Hawaii and the Philippines, it recognized the strategic value of a canal that would allow warships to move quickly between the Atlantic and Pacific Oceans. The main obstacle was Colombia, whose senate refused to give the United States a piece of its territory. In 1903 the U.S. government supported a Panamanian rebellion against Colombia and quickly recognized the independence of Panama. In exchange, it obtained the right to build a canal and to occupy a zone 5 miles

(8 kilometers) wide on either side of it. Work began in 1904, and the **Panama Canal** opened on August 15, 1914.

THE WORLD ECONOMY AND THE GLOBAL ENVIRONMENT

The New Imperialists were not traditional conquerors or empire builders like the Spanish conquistadors. Although their conquests were much larger (see Map 28.3), their aim was not only to extend their power over new territories and peoples but also to control both the natural world and indigenous societies and put them to work more efficiently than had ever been done before. Both their goals and their methods were industrial. A railroad, for example, was an act of faith as well as a means of transportation. They expressed their belief in progress and their good intentions in the clichés of the time: "the conquest of nature," "the annihilation of time and space," "the taming of the wilderness," and "our civilizing mission."

Expansion of the World Economy

For centuries Europe had been a ready market for spices, sugar, silk, and other exotic or tropical products. The Industrial Revolution vastly expanded this demand. Imports of foods and stimulants such as tea, coffee, and cocoa increased substantially during the nineteenth century. The trade in industrial raw materials grew even faster. Some were the products of agriculture, such as cotton, jute for bags, and palm oil for soap and lubricants. Others were minerals such as diamonds, gold, and copper. There also were wild forest products that only later came to be cultivated: timber for buildings and railroad ties, cinchona bark, rubber for rainwear and tires, and gutta-percha° (the sap of a Southeast Asian tree) to insulate electric cables.

The growing needs of the industrial world could not be met by the traditional methods of production and transportation of the nonindustrial world. When the U.S. Civil War interrupted the export of cotton to England in the 1860s, the British turned to India and Egypt. But they found that Indian cotton was ruined by exposure to rain and dust during the long trip on open carts from the interior of the country to the harbors. To prevent the expansion of their industry from being stifled by the technological backwardness of their newly conquered territories, the imperialists made every effort to bring those territories into the mainstream of the world market.

One great change was in transportation. The Suez and Panama Canals cut travel time and lowered freight costs dramatically. Steamships became more numerous, and as their size increased, new, deeper harbors were needed. The Europeans also built railroads throughout the world; India alone had 37,000 miles (nearly 60,000 kilometers) of track by 1915, almost as much as Germany or Russia. Railroads reached into the interior of Latin America, Canada, China, and Australia. In 1903 the Russians completed the Trans-Siberian Railway from Moscow to Vladivostok on the Pacific. Visionaries even made plans for railroads from Europe to India and from Egypt to South Africa.

Transformation of the Global Environment

The economic changes brought by Europeans and Americans also altered environments around the world. The British, whose craving for tea could not be satisfied with the limited exports available from China, introduced tea into the warm, rainy hill country of Ceylon and northeastern India. In those areas and in Java thousands of square miles of tropical rain forests were felled to make way for tea plantations.

Economic botany and agricultural science were applied to every promising plant species. European botanists had long collected and classified exotic plants from around the world. In the nineteenth century they founded botanical gardens in Java, India, Mauritius°, Ceylon, Jamaica, and other tropical colonies. These gardens not only collected local plants but also exchanged plants with other gardens. They were especially active in systematically transferring commercially valuable plant species from one tropical region to another. Cinchona, tobacco, sugar, and other crops were introduced, improved, and vastly expanded in the colonies of Southeast Asia and Indonesia (see Environment and Technology: Imperialism and Tropical Ecology). Cocoa and coffee growing spread over large areas of Brazil and Africa; oil-palm plantations were established in Nigeria and the Congo Basin. Rubber, used to make waterproof garments and bicycle tires, originally came from the latex of *Hevea* trees growing wild in the Brazilian rain forest. Then, in the 1870s, British agents smuggled seedlings from Brazil to the Royal Botanic Gardens at Kew near London, and from there to the Botanic Garden of Singapore. These plants formed the nucleus of the enormous rubber economy of Southeast Asia.

Throughout the tropics land once covered with forests or devoted to shifting slash-and-burn agriculture was transformed into permanent farms and plantations.

---

gutta-percha (gut-tah-PER-cha)

Mauritius (maw-REE-shuss)

Map 28.3 The Great Powers and Their Colonial Possessions in 1913 By 1913, a small handful of countries claimed sovereignty over more than half the land area of the earth. Global power was closely connected with industries and a merchant marine, rather than with a large territory. This explains why Great Britain, the smallest of the great powers, possessed the largest empire.

The colonial powers and their possessions

- Germany
- France
- Great Britain
- Russia
- United States
- Japan

- Belgium
- Netherlands
- Portugal
- Italy
- Spain
- Major shipping routes

Even in areas not developed to export crops, growing populations put pressure on the land. In Java and India farmers felled trees to obtain arable land and firewood. They terraced hillsides, drained swamps, and dug wells.

Irrigation and water control transformed the dry parts of the tropics as well. In the 1830s British engineers in India had restored ancient canals that had fallen into disrepair. Their success led them to build new irrigation canals, turning thousands of previously barren acres into well-watered, densely populated farmland. The migration of European experts spread the newest techniques of irrigation engineering around the world. By the turn of the century irrigation projects were under way wherever rivers flowed through dry lands. In Egypt and Central Asia irrigation brought more acres under cultivation in one forty-year span than in all previous history.

Railroads had voracious appetites for land and resources. They cut into mountains, spanned rivers and canyons with trestles, and covered as much land with their freight yards as whole cities had needed in previous centuries. They also consumed vast quantities of iron, timber for ties, and coal or wood for fuel. Most important of all, railroads brought people and their cities, farms, and industries to areas previously occupied by small, scattered populations.

Prospectors looking for valuable minerals opened the earth to reveal its riches: gold in South Africa, Australia, and Canada; tin in Nigeria, Malaya, and Bolivia; copper in Chile and Central Africa; iron ore in northern India; and much else. Where mines were dug deep inside

South African Diamond Mine   When diamonds were found in Kimberley, South Africa, in 1868, the discovery precipitated a rush of prospectors from Europe and America. As soon as surface deposits were exhausted, their claims were bought by large companies that could afford the heavy equipment needed to mine deep underground. By the early twentieth century, diamonds came from major industrial mines like the Premier Mine shown here.   (Corbis)

the earth, the dirt and rocks brought up with the ores formed huge mounds near mine entrances. Open mines dug to obtain ores lying close to the surface created a landscape of lunar craters, and runoff from the minerals poisoned the water for miles around. Refineries that processed the ores fouled the environment with slag heaps and more toxic runoff.

The transformation of the land by human beings, a constant throughout history, accelerated sharply. Only the changes occurring since 1914 can compare with the transformation of the global environment that took place between 1869 and 1914.

SUMMARY

○— What motivated the industrial nations to conquer new territories, and what means did they use?

○— Why were imperialists drawn to the natural resources of Africa, and how did their presence on that continent change the environment?

○— What were the social and cultural effects of imperialism in Asia?

○— What were the economic motives behind imperialism in Latin America?

○— How did imperialism contribute to the growth and globalization of the world economy?

Online Study Center
ACE the Test

European and American imperial powers were driven by economic, cultural, and political motives. Many governments used overseas colonies as a way to help reestablish their nations' prestige and power. Catholic and Protestant missionaries sought not only to convert the native peoples to their religious beliefs but also to "civilize" their behavior. This sense of moral and cultural superiority was common among the colonizing nations. Finally, colonizing nations were led by the demand for minerals and natural resources. The imperialists used tools provided by the Industrial Revolution, such as steamships, gunboats, and improved firearms, to build their empires.

Africans ruled over 90 percent of the continent until the European "scramble" for Africa began after the 1870s. Europeans took control of African resources to further their own military and economic power. After the Egyptians secured the Suez Canal, they constructed a dam across the Nile to help develop agriculture. In other parts of the continent, European companies took over profits from local trade in rubber, diamonds, and other resources. Local reaction to colonial rule varied greatly, traditional land use patterns were disrupted, and all Africans were affected by changes in social and cultural customs.

The effects of colonialism varied throughout Asia, although in all regions the economic profits benefited the Europeans rather than the indigenous workers. Southeast Asia's fertile soil and heavy rains made farming of various crops, most importantly rubber, quite profitable. As laborers were brought in from overseas, they gradually displaced the earlier inhabitants. A similar situation occurred in Hawaii, where U.S. military personnel and foreign farm laborers eventually outnumbered the native Hawaiians. Europeans differed in their approach to indigenous cultures and religions. In Central Asia, the Russians did not attempt to impose their customs, language, or religious beliefs on their subjects. Christian missionaries in Southeast Asia, meanwhile, worked to spread their beliefs. Their efforts gained only limited success in a land in which Islam had been dominant for centuries.

Latin America had great economic potential because of its wealth of agricultural and mineral products. The construction of railroads, using equipment, labor, and funding from Britain and the United States, helped to connect the interior regions with the coastal ports. Americans also saw economic potential in Cuba and invested heavily in the sugar and tobacco industries there. After the Spanish-American War, they issued the Platt Amendment to maintain their influence in the region. The United States also became involved in another war of independence in 1903, this time supporting a Panamanian rebellion against Colombia. Again, there was an economic motivation behind the American involvement: the Panama Canal.

Imperialism, both formal and informal, opened up the world to increased trade and communication. Shipping, canals, and railroads were the most visible means of globalization. Other activities—farming, mining, labor migrations, and urbanization—were profoundly affected as well. In the process, natural environments were transformed as never before. Forests were replaced by plantations. Irrigation schemes opened dry lands to agriculture. And railroads and mines cut into the landscape, leaving scars and pollution.

KEY TERMS

Suez Canal   *p. 817*
New Imperialism   *p. 818*
Battle of Omdurman   *p. 821*
colonialism   *p. 821*
"scramble" for Africa   *p. 823*
Henry Morton Stanley   *p. 825*

King Leopold II   *p. 825*
Savorgnan de Brazza   *p. 825*
Berlin Conference   *p. 825*
Afrikaners   *p. 827*
Cecil Rhodes   *p. 827*
Asante   *p. 828*

Menelik   *p. 828*
Emilio Aguinaldo   *p. 836*
free-trade imperialism   *p. 837*
Panama Canal   *p. 839*

Online Study Center
Improve Your Grade
Flashcards

SUGGESTED READING

Two good introductions to imperialism are D. K. Fieldhouse, *Colonialism, 1870–1945* (1981), and Scott B. Cook, *Colonial Encounters in the Age of High Imperialism* (1996). The debate on the theories of imperialism is presented in Roger Owen and Robert Sutcliffe, *Studies in the Theory of Imperialism* (1972), and in Winfried Baumgart, *Imperialism* (1982). The British Empire is the subject of Bernard Porter, *The Lion's Share: A Short History of British Imperialism, 1850–1970* (1976).

On Africa in this period see Roland Oliver and Anthony Atmore, *Africa Since 1800*, new ed. (1994); Roland Oliver and G. N. Sanderson, eds., *From 1870 to 1905* (1985), and A. D. Roberts, ed., *From 1905 to 1940* (1986), in *The Cambridge History of Africa*; and A. Adu Boahen, ed., *Africa Under Colonial Domination, 1880–1935* (1985), in *UNESCO General History of Africa*. The European conquest of Africa is recounted in Thomas Pakenham, *The Scramble for Africa* (1991); Bruce Vandervort, *Wars of Imperial Conquest in Africa, 1830–1914* (1998); and Ronald Robinson and John Gallagher, *Africa and the Victorians: The Climax of Imperialism* (1961). Adam Hochschild's *King Leopold's Ghost: A Story of Greed, Terror, and Heroism in Colonial Africa* (1998) is a very readable account of imperialism in the Belgian Congo. The classic novel about the impact of colonial rule on African society is Chinua Achebe's *Things Fall Apart* (1958).

Imperial rivalries in Asia are the subject of Akira Iriye, *Across the Pacific: An Inner History of American-East Asian Relations*, rev. ed. (1992); David Gillard, *The Struggle for Asia, 1828–1914: A Study in British and Russian Imperialism* (1977); and Peter Hopkirk, *The Great Game: The Struggle for Empire in Central Asia* (1994). On other aspects of imperialism in Asia see Clifford Geertz, *Agricultural Involution: The Process of Ecological Change in Indonesia* (1963), especially chapters 4 and 5; and Stanley Karnow, *In Our Image: America's Empire in the Philippines* (1989).

On Latin America in this period see David Bushnell and Neill Macauley, *The Emergence of Latin America in the Nineteenth Century* (1994). Free-trade imperialism is the subject of D. C. M. Platt, *Latin America and British Trade, 1806–1914* (1973). On American expansionism see David Healy, *Drive to Hegemony:*

The United States in the Caribbean, 1898–1917 (1989), and Walter LaFeber, *The Panama Canal*, rev. ed. (1990).

On race relations in the colonial world see Noel Mostert, *Frontiers: The Epic of South Africa's Creation and the Tragedy of the Xhosa People* (1992), and Robert Huttenback, *Racism and Empire: White Settlers and Colored Immigrants in the British Self-Governing Colonies, 1830–1910* (1976). Gender relations are the subject of Caroline Oliver, *Western Women in Colonial Africa* (1982), and Cheryl Walker, ed., *Women and Gender in Southern Africa to 1945* (1990). Franz Fanon, *The Wretched of the Earth* (1966), and Albert Memmi, *The Colonizer and the Colonized* (1967), examine colonialism from the point of view of the colonized.

The impact of technology on the New Imperialism is the subject of Daniel R. Headrick, *The Tools of Empire: Technology and European Imperialism in the Nineteenth Century* (1981) and *The Tentacles of Progress: Technology Transfer in the Age of Imperialism, 1850–1940* (1988); and Clarence B. Davis and Kenneth E. Wilburn, Jr., eds., *Railway Imperialism* (1991).

On the economic and demographic transformation of Africa and Asia see Eric Wolf, *Europe and the People Without History* (1982), especially chapters 11 and 12. David Northrup's *Indentured Labor in the Age of Imperialism, 1834–1922* (1995) discusses migrations and labor.

The impact of imperialism on the environment is the subject of R. P. Tucker and J. F. Richards, *Deforestation and the Nineteenth-Century World Economy* (1983); Donal McCracken, *Gardens of Empire: Botanical Institutions of the Victorian British Empire* (1997); Lucile H. Brockway, *Science and Colonial Expansion: The Role of the British Royal Botanic Gardens* (1979); Richard Drayton, *Nature's Government: Science, Imperial Britain, and the 'Improvement' of the World* (2000); John MacKenzie, *Imperialism and the Natural World* (1990); and David Arnold and Ramchandra Guha, eds., *Nature, Culture, Imperialism: Essays on the Environmental History of South Asia* (1995). In *Late Victorian Holocausts: El Niño Famines and the Making of the Third World* (2001), Mike Davis argues that imperialism exacerbated the social and demographic effects of famines.

NOTES

1. *Journal Officiel* (November 29, 1869), quoted in Georges Douin, *Histoire du Règne du Khédive Ismaïl* (Rome: Reale Societá di Geografia d'Egitto, 1933), 453.
2. E. Desplaces in *Journal de l'Union des Deux Mers* (December 15, 1869), quoted ibid., 453.
3. Winston Churchill, *The River War: An Account of the Reconquest of the Soudan* (New York: Charles Scribner's Sons, 1933), 300.
4. "Correspondence and Report from His Majesty's Consul at Boma respecting the Administration of the Independent State of the Congo," *British Parliamentary Papers, Accounts and Papers, 1904* (Cd. 1933), lxii, 357.
5. Robert W. July, *A History of the African People*, 3d ed. (New York: Charles Scribner's Sons, 1980), 323.
6. George Shepperson and Thomas Price, *Independent African* (Edinburgh: University Press, 1958), 163–164, quoted in Roland Oliver and Anthony Atmore, *Africa Since 1800*, 4th ed. (Cambridge: Cambridge University Press, 1994), 150.
7. Thomas Edson Ennis, *French Policy and Development in Indochina* (Chicago: University of Chicago Press, 1936), 178, quoted in K. M. Panikkar, *Asia and Western Dominance* (New York: Collier, 1969), 167.
8. Quoted in Stanley J. Stein and Barbara H. Stein, *The Colonial Heritage of Latin America* (New York: Oxford University Press, 1970), 151.

The Western Front in World War I In a landscape ravaged by artillery fire, two soldiers dash for cover amid shell holes and the charred remains of a forest. (Imperial War Museum/The Art Archive)

- What led to the outbreak of the First World War?

- How did the war lead to revolution in Russia?

- What role did the war play in eroding European dominance in the world?

- Why did China and Japan follow such divergent paths in this period?

- How did the Middle East change as a result of the war?

- How did European and North American society and technology change in the aftermath of the war?

29

The Crisis of the Imperial Order, 1900–1929

CHAPTER OUTLINE

Origins of the Crisis in Europe and the Middle East

The "Great War" and the Russian Revolutions, 1914–1918

Peace and Dislocation in Europe, 1919–1929

China and Japan: Contrasting Destinies

The New Middle East

Society, Culture, and Technology in the Industrialized World

Comparative Perspectives

DIVERSITY AND DOMINANCE: The Middle East After World War I

ENVIRONMENT AND TECHNOLOGY: The Birth of Civil Aviation

Online Study Center

This icon will direct you to interactive activities and study materials on the website: *college.hmco.com/pic/bulliet4e.*

O n June 28, 1914, Archduke Franz Ferdinand, heir to the throne of Austria-Hungary, was riding in an open carriage through Sarajevo, capital of Bosnia-Herzegovina, a province Austria had annexed six years earlier. When the carriage stopped momentarily, Gavrilo Princip, member of a pro-Serbian conspiracy, fired his pistol twice, killing the archduke and his wife.

Those shots ignited a global conflict. All previous wars had caused death and destruction, but they were also marked by heroism and glory. In this new war, on the crucial battlefield in Belgium and northern France, four years of bitter fighting produced no victories, no gains, and no glory, only death for millions of soldiers. The war became global as the Ottoman Empire fought against Britain in the Middle East and Japan attacked German positions in China. France and Britain involved their empires in the war and brought Africans, Indians, Australians, and Canadians to Europe to fight and labor on the front lines. Finally, in 1917, the United States entered the fray.

The next three chapters tell a story of violence and hope. In this chapter, we will look at the causes of war between the great powers, the consequences of that conflict in Europe, the Middle East, and Russia, and the upheavals in China and Japan. At the same time, we will review the accelerating rate of technological change, which made the first half of the twentieth century so violent and so hopeful. Industrialization continued apace. Entirely new technologies, and the organizations that produced and applied them, made war more dangerous, yet also allowed far more people to live healthier, more comfortable, and more interesting lives than ever before.

ORIGINS OF THE CRISIS IN EUROPE AND THE MIDDLE EAST

When the twentieth century opened, the world seemed firmly under the control of the great powers that you read about in Chapter 27. The first decade of the twentieth century was a period of relative peace and economic growth in most of the world. Trade boomed. Several new technologies—airplanes, automobiles, radio, and cinema—aroused much excitement. The great powers consolidated their colonial conquests of the previous decades. Their alliances were so evenly matched that they seemed, to observers at the time, likely to maintain peace. The only international war of the period, the Russo-Japanese War (1904–1905), ended quickly with a decisive Japanese victory.

However, two major changes were undermining the apparent stability of the world. In Europe, tensions mounted as Germany, with its growing industrial and military might, challenged Britain at sea and France in Morocco. The Ottoman Empire grew weaker, leaving a dangerous power vacuum. The resulting chaos in the Balkans, the unstable borderlands between a predominantly Christian Europe and a predominantly Muslim Middle East, gradually drew the European powers into a web of hostilities.

The Ottoman Empire and Balkans

From the fifteenth to the nineteenth centuries the Ottoman Empire was one of the world's richest and most powerful states. By the late nineteenth century, however, it had fallen behind economically, technologically, and militarily, and Europeans referred to it as the "sick man of Europe."

As the Ottoman Empire weakened, it began losing outlying provinces situated closest to Europe. Macedonia rebelled in 1902–1903. In 1908 Austria-Hungary annexed Bosnia. Crete, occupied by European "peacekeepers" since 1898, merged with Greece in 1909. A year later Albania became independent. In 1912 Italy conquered Libya, the Ottomans' last foothold in Africa. In 1912–1913 in rapid succession came two Balkan Wars in which Serbia, Bulgaria, Romania, and Greece chased the Turks out of Europe, except for a small enclave around Constantinople.

The European powers meddled in the internal affairs of the Ottoman Empire, sometimes cooperatively but often as rivals. Russia saw itself as the protector of the Slavic peoples of the Balkans. France and Britain, posing as protectors of Christian minorities, controlled Ottoman finances, taxes, railroads, mines, and public utilities. Austria-Hungary coveted Ottoman lands inhabited by Slavs, thereby angering the Russians.

In reaction, the Turks began to assert themselves against rebellious minorities and meddling foreigners. Many officers in the army, the most Europeanized segment of Turkish society, blamed Sultan Abdul Hamid II (r. 1876–1909) for the decline of the empire. The group known as "Young Turks" began conspiring to force a constitution on the sultan. They alienated other anti-Ottoman groups by advocating centralized rule and the Turkification of ethnic minorities.

In 1909 the parliament, dominated by Young Turks, overthrew Abdul Hamid and replaced him with his brother. The new regime began to reform the police, the bureaucracy, and the educational system. At the same time, it cracked down on Greek and Armenian minorities. Galvanized by their defeat in the Balkan Wars, the Turks turned to Germany, the European country that had meddled least in Ottoman affairs, and hired a German general to modernize their armed forces.

Nationalism, Alliances, and Military Strategy

The assassination of Franz Ferdinand triggered a chain of events over which military and political leaders lost control. The escalation from assassination to global war had causes that went back many

CHRONOLOGY

	Europe and North America	Middle East	East Asia
1900			1900 Boxer uprising in China
			1904–1905 Russo-Japanese War
	1904 British-French Entente		
	1907 British-Russian Entente		
1910		1909 Young Turks overthrow Sultan Abdul Hamid	1911 Chinese revolutionaries led by Sun Yat-sen overthrow Qing dynasty
	1912–1913 Balkan Wars	1912 Italy conquers Libya, last Ottoman territory in Africa	
	1914 Assassination of Archduke Franz Ferdinand sparks World War I	1915 British defeat at Gallipoli	1915 Japan presents Twenty-One Demands to China
	1916 Battles of Verdun and the Somme	1916 Arab Revolt in Arabia	
	1917 Russian Revolutions; United States enters the war	1917 Balfour Declaration	
	1918 Armistice ends World War I		
	1918–1921 Civil war in Russia		
	1919 Treaty of Versailles	1919–1922 War between Turkey and Greece	1919 May Fourth Movement in China
1920	1920 First commercial radio broadcast (United States)		
	1921 New Economic Policy in Russia	1922 Egypt nominally independent	
		1923 Mustafa Kemal proclaims Turkey a republic	
	1927 Charles Lindbergh flies alone across the Atlantic		1927 Guomindang forces occupy Shanghai and expel Communists

years. One was nationalism, which bound citizens to their ethnic group and led them, when called upon, to kill people they viewed as enemies. Another was the system of alliances and military plans that the great powers had devised to protect themselves from their rivals. A third was Germany's yearning to dominate Europe.

Nationalism was deeply rooted in European culture. As we saw in Chapter 27, it united the citizens of France, Britain, and Germany behind their respective governments and gave them tremendous cohesion and strength of purpose. Only the most powerful feelings could inspire millions of men to march obediently into battle and could sustain civilian populations through years of hardship.

Nationalism could also be a dividing force. The large but fragile multinational Russian, Austro-Hungarian, and Ottoman Empires contained numerous ethnic and religious minorities. The dominant ethnic groups—Russians, Austrians, Hungarians, and Turks—were themselves becoming more nationalistic. Having repressed the other minorities for centuries, the governments could never count on their full support. The very existence of an independent Serbia threatened Austria-Hungary by stirring up the hopes and resentments of its Slavic populations.

Because of the spread of nationalism, most people viewed war as a crusade for liberty or as long-overdue revenge for past injustices. In the course of the nineteenth century, as memories of the misery and carnage caused by the Napoleonic Wars faded, revulsion against war gradually weakened. The few wars fought in Europe after 1815, such as the Crimean War of 1853–1856 and the Franco-Prussian War of 1871, had been short and caused few casualties or long-term consequences. And in the wars of the New Imperialism (see Chapter 28), Europeans almost always had been victorious at a small cost in money and manpower. The well-to-do began to believe that only war could heal the class divisions in their societies and make workers unite behind their "natural" leaders.

What turned an incident in a small town in the Balkans into a conflict involving all the great powers was the system of alliances that had grown up over the previous decades. At the center of Europe stood Germany, the most heavily industrialized country in Europe. Its army was the best trained and equipped. It challenged Great Britain's naval supremacy by building "dreadnoughts"—heavily armed battleships. It joined Austria-Hungary and Italy in the Triple Alliance in 1882, while France allied itself with Russia. In 1904 Britain joined France in an Entente° ("understanding"), and in 1907 Britain and Russia buried their differences and formed an Entente. Europe was thus divided into two blocs of roughly equal power (see Map 29.1).

The alliance system was cursed by inflexible military planning. In 1914 western and central Europe had highly developed railroad networks but very few motor vehicles. European armies had grown to include millions of soldiers and more millions of reservists. To mobilize these forces and transport them to battle would be an enormous project requiring thousands of trains running on precise schedules. As a result, once under way, a country's mobilization could not be canceled or postponed without causing chaos.

In the years before World War I, military planners in France and Germany had worked out elaborate railroad timetables to mobilize their respective armies in a few days. Other countries were less prepared. Russia, a large country with an underdeveloped rail system, needed several weeks to mobilize its forces. Britain, with a tiny volunteer army, had no mobilization plans, and German planners believed that the British would stay out of a war on the European continent. So that Germany could avoid having to fight France and Russia at the same time, German war plans called for German generals to defeat France in a matter of days, then transport the entire army across Germany to the Russian border by train before Russia could fully mobilize.

On July 28, emboldened by the backing of Germany, Austria-Hungary declared war on Serbia. Diplomats, statesmen, and monarchs sent one another frantic telegrams, but they had lost control of events, for the declaration of war triggered the general mobilization plans of Russia, France, and Germany. On July 29 the Russian government ordered general mobilization to force Austria to back down. On August 1 France honored its treaty obligation to Russia and ordered general mobilization. Minutes later Germany did likewise. Because of the rigid railroad timetables, war was now automatic.

Entente (on-TONT)

The German plan was to wheel around through neutral Belgium and into northwestern France. The German General Staff expected France to capitulate before the British could get involved. But on August 3, when German troops entered Belgium, Britain demanded their withdrawal. When Germany refused, Britain declared war on Germany.

THE "GREAT WAR" AND THE RUSSIAN REVOLUTIONS, 1914–1918

Throughout Europe, people greeted the outbreak of war with parades and flags, expecting a quick victory. German troops marched off to the front shouting "To Paris!" Spectators in France encouraged marching French troops with shouts of "Send me the Kaiser's moustache!" The British poet Rupert Brooke began a poem with the line "Now God be thanked Who has matched us with His hour." The German sociologist Max Weber wrote: "This war, with all its ghastliness, is nevertheless grand and wonderful. It is worth experiencing." When the war began, very few imagined that their side might not win, and no one foresaw that everyone would lose.

In Russia the effect of the war was especially devastating, for it destroyed the old society, opened the door to revolution and civil war, and introduced a radical new political system. By clearing away the old, the upheaval of war prepared Russia to industrialize under the leadership of professional revolutionaries.

Stalemate, 1914–1917

The war that erupted in 1914 was known as the "Great War" until the 1940s, when a far greater one overshadowed it. Its form came as a surprise to all belligerents, from the generals on down. In the classic battles—from Alexander's to Napoleon's—that every officer studied, the advantage always went to the fastest-moving army led by the boldest general. In 1914 the generals' carefully drawn plans went awry from the start. Believing that a spirited attack would always prevail, French generals hurled their troops, dressed in bright blue-and-red uniforms, against the well-defended German border and suffered a crushing defeat. In battle after battle the much larger German armies defeated the French and the British. By early September the Germans held Belgium and northern France and were fast approaching Paris.

Map 29.1   Europe in 1913   On the eve of World War I, Europe was divided between two great alliance systems—the Central Powers (Germany, Austria-Hungary, and Italy) and the Entente (France, Great Britain, and Russia)—and their respective colonial empires. These alliances were not stable. When war broke out, the Central Powers lost Italy but gained the Ottoman Empire.

German victory seemed assured. But German troops, who had marched and fought for a month, were exhausted, and their generals wavered. When Russia attacked eastern Germany, troops needed for the final push into France were shifted to the Russian front. A gap opened between two German armies along the Marne River, into which General Joseph Joffre moved France's last reserves. At the Battle of the Marne (September 5–12, 1914), the Germans were thrown back several miles.

During the next month, both sides spread out until they formed an unbroken line extending over 300 miles (some 500 kilometers) from the North Sea to the border of Switzerland. All along this **Western Front**, the opposing troops prepared their defenses. Their most potent weapons were machine guns, which provided an almost impenetrable defense against advancing infantry but were useless for the offensive because they were too heavy for one man to carry and took too much time to set up.

To escape the deadly streams of bullets, soldiers dug holes in the ground, connected the holes to form shallow trenches, then dug communications trenches to the rear. Within weeks, the battlefields were scarred by lines of trenches several feet deep, their tops protected by sandbags and their floors covered with planks. Despite all the work they put into the trenches, the soldiers spent much of the year soaked and covered with mud. Trenches were nothing new. What was extraordinary was that the trenches along the entire Western Front were connected, leaving no gaps through which armies could advance (see Map 29.2). How, then, could either side ever hope to win?

For four years, generals on each side again and again ordered their troops to attack. They knew the casualties would be enormous, but they expected the enemy to run out of young men before their own side did. In battle after battle, thousands of young men on one side climbed out of their trenches, raced across the open fields, and were mowed down by enemy machine-gun fire. Hoping to destroy the machine guns, the attacking force would saturate the entrenched enemy lines with artillery barrages. But this tactic alerted the defenders to an impending attack and allowed them to rush in reinforcements and set up new machine guns.

The year 1916 saw the bloodiest and most futile battles of the war. The Germans attacked French forts at Verdun, losing 281,000 men and causing 315,000 French casualties. In retaliation, the British attacked the Germans at the Somme River and suffered 420,000 casualties—60,000 on the first day alone—while the Germans lost 450,000 and the French 200,000.

Warfare had never been waged this way before. It was mass slaughter in a moonscape of mud, steel, and flesh. Both sides attacked and defended, but neither side could win, for the armies were stalemated by trenches

Map 29.2 The First World War in Europe   Most of the fighting in World War I took place on two fronts. After an initial surge through Belgium into northern France, the German offensive bogged down for four years along the Western Front. To the East, the German armies conquered a large part of Russia during 1917 and early 1918. Despite spectacular victories in the east, Germany lost the war because its armies collapsed along the strategically important Western Front.

and machine guns. During four years of the bloodiest fighting the world had ever seen, the Western Front moved no more than a few miles one way or another.

At sea, the war was just as inconclusive. As soon as war broke out, the British cut the German overseas telegraph cables, blockaded the coasts of Germany and Austria-Hungary, and set out to capture or sink all enemy ships still at sea. The German High Seas Fleet, built at enormous cost, seldom left port. Only once, in May 1916, did it confront the British Grand Fleet. At the Battle of Jutland, off the coast of Denmark, the two fleets lost roughly equal numbers of ships, and the Germans escaped back to their harbors.

Britain ruled the waves but not the ocean below the surface. In early 1915, in retaliation for the British naval blockade, Germany announced a blockade of Britain by submarines. Unlike surface ships, submarines could not rescue the passengers of a sinking ship or distinguish between neutral and enemy ships. German submarines attacked every vessel they could. One of their victims was the British ocean liner *Lusitania*. The death toll from that attack was 1,198 people, 139 of them Americans. When the United States protested, Germany ceased its submarine campaign, hoping to keep America neutral.

Other than machine guns and submarines, military innovations had only minor effects. Airplanes were used for reconnaissance and engaged in spectacular but inconsequential dogfights above the trenches. Poison gas, introduced on the Western Front in 1915, killed and wounded attacking soldiers as well as their intended victims, adding to the horror of battle. Primitive tanks aided, but did not cause, the collapse of the German army in the last weeks of the war. Although these weapons were of limited effectiveness in World War I, they offered an insight into the future of warfare.

The Home Front and the War Economy

Trench-bound armies demanded ever more weapons, ammunition, and food, so civilians had to work harder, eat less, and pay higher taxes. Textiles, coal, meat, fats, and imported products such as tea and

ALSACE

Cologne

Rhine

Strasbourg

Moselle

Saar

LUXEMBOURG

LORRAINE

NETHERLANDS

Liège

Nancy

BELGIUM

Meuse

Sedan

Antwerp

Argonne Forest

Verdun

Brussels

FLANDERS

Passchendaele

Somme

Aisne

Reims

Marne

Ypres

Somme

Marne

Ostend

Calais

Dover

Amiens

Paris

FRANCE

English Channel

Seine

Germany, 1914

German offensive, 1914

Farthest German advance,
Sept. 1914

Front at beginning of 1915

German offensive, Summer 1918

Armistice line, November 1918

Major battles

Caspian Sea

RUSSIA

Moscow

OTTOMAN EMPIRE

Treaty of Brest-Litovsk, March 1918

St. Petersburg

Black Sea

Constantinople

Dardanelles

Kiev

Bucharest

ROMANIA

FINLAND

Helsinki

Riga

Brest-Litovsk

Warsaw

POLAND

Gallipoli
1915

BULGARIA

SERBIA

GREECE

Sarajevo

AUSTRIA-HUNGARY

MONTENEGRO

ALBANIA

Vienna

SWEDEN

Baltic
Sea

Berlin

GERMANY

ITALY

Rome

NORWAY

DENMARK

Danube

Jutland 1916

British
blockade line

Rhine

SWITZ.

LUX.

North Sea

NETH.

BELG.

ICELAND

GREAT
BRITAIN

London

Paris

FRANCE

Mediterranean Sea

IRELAND

ATLANTIC
OCEAN

SPAIN

PORTUGAL

Entente Powers and Allies

Central Powers

Neutral nations

Farthest German-Austrian advance

Major battles

400 Mi.

400 Km.

200

200

0

0

Women in World War I Women played a more important role in World War I than in previous wars. As the armies drafted millions of men, employers hired women for essential war work. This poster extolling the importance of women workers in supplying munitions was probably designed to recruit women for factory jobs. (Imperial War Museum/The Art Archive)

sugar were strictly rationed. Governments gradually imposed stringent controls over all aspects of their economies. Socialists and labor unions participated actively in the war effort, for they found government regulation more to their liking than unfettered free enterprise.

The war economy transformed civilian life. In France and Britain food rations were allocated according to need, improving nutrition among the poor. Unemployment vanished. Thousands of Africans, Indians, and Chinese were recruited for heavy labor in Europe. Employers hired women to fill jobs in steel mills, mines, and munitions plants vacated by men off to war. Some women became streetcar drivers, mail carriers, and police officers. Others found work in the burgeoning government bureaucracies. Many joined auxiliary military services as doctors, nurses, mechanics, and ambulance drivers; after 1917, as the war took its toll of young men, the British government established women's auxiliary units for the army, navy, and air force. Though clearly intended "for the duration only," these positions gave thousands of women a sense of participation in the war effort and a taste of personal and financial independence.

German civilians paid an especially high price for the war, for the British naval blockade severed their overseas trade. The German chemical industry developed synthetic explosives and fuel, but synthetic food was not an option. Wheat flour disappeared, replaced first by rye, then by potatoes and turnips, then by acorns and chestnuts, and finally by sawdust. After the failure of the potato crop in 1916 came the "turnip winter," when people had to survive on 1,000 calories per day, half the normal amount that an active adult needed. Women, children, and the elderly were especially hard hit. Soldiers at the front went hungry and raided enemy lines to scavenge food.

When the war began, the British and French overran German Togo on the West African coast. The much larger German colonies of Southwest Africa and German Cameroon were conquered in 1915. In German East Africa, the Germans remained undefeated until the end of the war.

The war also brought hardships to Europe's African colonies. The Europeans requisitioned foodstuffs, imposed heavy taxes, and forced Africans to grow export crops and sell them at low prices. Many Europeans stationed in Africa joined the war, leaving large areas with little or no European presence. In Nigeria, Libya, Nyasaland (now Malawi), and other colonies, the combination of increased demands on Africans and fewer European officials led to uprisings that lasted for several years.

Over a million Africans served in the various armies, and perhaps three times that number were drafted as porters to carry army equipment. Faced with a shortage of young Frenchmen, France drafted Africans into its army, where many fought side by side with Europeans. The Senegalese Blaise Diagne°, the first African elected to France's Chamber of Deputies in 1914, campaigned for African support of the war effort. Put in charge of recruiting African soldiers, he insisted on equal rights for

---

Blaise Diagne (blez dee-AHN-yuh)

African and European soldiers and an extension of the franchise to educated Africans. These demands were only partially met.

One country grew rich during the war: the United States. For two and a half years the United States stayed technically neutral—that is, it did not fight but did a roaring business supplying France and Britain. When the United States entered the war in 1917, businesses engaging in war production made spectacular profits. Civilians were exhorted to help the war effort by investing their savings in war bonds and growing food in backyard "victory gardens." Facing labor shortages, employers hired women and African Americans. Employment opportunities created by the war played a major role in the migration of black Americans from the rural south to the cities of the north.

The Ottoman Empire at War

On August 2, 1914, the Turks signed a secret alliance with Germany. In November they joined the fighting, hoping to gain land at Russia's expense. But the campaign in the Caucasus proved disastrous for both armies and for the civilian populations as well. The Turks deported the Armenians, whom they suspected of being pro-Russian, from their homelands in eastern Anatolia to Syria and other parts of the Ottoman Empire. During the forced march across the mountains in the winter, hundreds of thousands of Armenians died of hunger and exposure. This massacre was a precedent for even ghastlier tragedies still to come.

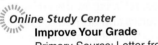

Online Study Center
Improve Your Grade
Primary Source: Letter from
Turkey, Summer 1915

The Turks also closed the Dardanelles, the strait between the Mediterranean and Black Seas (see Map 29.2). Seeing little hope of victory on the Western Front, British officials tried to open the Dardanelles by landing troops on the nearby Gallipoli Peninsula in 1915. Turkish troops pushed the invaders back into the sea.

Having failed at the Dardanelles, the British tried to subvert the Ottoman Empire from within by promising the emir (prince) of Mecca, Hussein ibn Ali, a kingdom of his own if he would lead an Arab revolt against the Turks. In 1916 Hussein rose up and was proclaimed king of Hejaz° (western Arabia). His son **Faisal**° led an Arab army in support of the British advance from

Online Study Center
Improve Your Grade
Interactive Map: The Disintegration
of the Ottoman Empire, 1829–1914

Egypt into Palestine and Syria. The Arab Revolt of 1916 did not affect the struggle in Europe, but it did contribute to the defeat of the Ottoman Empire.

The British made promises to Jews as well as Arabs. For centuries, Jewish minorities had lived in eastern and central Europe, where they developed a thriving culture despite frequent persecutions. By the early twentieth century a nationalist movement called Zionism, led by **Theodore Herzl**, arose among those who wanted to return to their ancestral homeland in Palestine. The concept of a Jewish homeland appealed to many Europeans, Jews and gentiles alike, as a humanitarian solution to the problem of anti-Semitism.

By 1917 Chaim Weizmann°, leader of the British Zionists, had persuaded several British politicians that a Jewish homeland in Palestine should be carved out of the Ottoman Empire and placed under British protection, thereby strengthening the Allied cause (as the Entente was now called). In November, as British armies were advancing on Jerusalem, Foreign Secretary Sir Arthur Balfour wrote:

> His Majesty's Government view with favor the establishment in Palestine of a national home for the Jewish people and will use their best endeavours to facilitate the achievement of that object, it being clearly understood that nothing shall be done which may prejudice the civil and religious rights of existing non-Jewish communities in Palestine.

The British did not foresee that this statement, known as the **Balfour Declaration**, would lead to conflicts between Palestinians and Jewish settlers.

Britain also sent troops to southern Mesopotamia (now Iraq) to secure the oil pipeline from Iran. Then they moved north, taking Baghdad in early 1917. The officers for the Mesopotamian campaign were British, but most of the troops and equipment came from India. Most Indians, like other colonial subjects of Britain, supported the war effort despite the hardships it caused. Their involvement in the war bolstered the movement for Indian independence (see Chapter 31).

Hejaz (hee-JAHZ)   **Faisal** (FIE-sahl)

Chaim Weizmann (hi-um VITES-mun)

Double Revolution in Russia

At the beginning of the war Russia had the largest army in the world, but its generals were incompetent, supplies were lacking, and soldiers were poorly trained and equipped. In August 1914 two Russian armies invaded eastern Germany but were thrown back. The Russians defeated the Austro-Hungarian army several times, only to be defeated in turn by the Germans.

In 1916, after a string of defeats, the Russian army ran out of ammunition and other essential supplies. Soldiers were ordered into battle unarmed and told to pick up the rifles of fallen comrades. With so many men in the army, railroads broke down for lack of fuel and parts, and crops rotted in the fields. Civilians faced shortages and widespread hunger. In the cities food and fuel became scarce. During the bitterly cold winter of 1916–1917 factory workers and housewives had to line up in front of grocery stores before dawn to get food. The court of Tsar Nicholas II, however, remained as extravagant and corrupt as ever.

In early March 1917 (February by the old Russian calendar) food ran out in Petrograd (St. Petersburg), the capital. Housewives and women factory workers staged mass demonstrations. Soldiers mutinied and joined striking workers to form soviets (councils) to take over factories and barracks. A few days later the tsar abdicated, and leaders of the parliamentary parties, led by Alexander Kerensky, formed a Provisional Government. Thus began what Russians called the "February Revolution."

Revolutionary groups formerly hunted by the tsar's police came out of hiding. Most numerous were the Social Revolutionaries, who advocated the redistribution of land to the peasants. The Social Democrats, a Marxist party, were divided into two factions: Mensheviks and Bolsheviks. The Mensheviks advocated electoral politics and reform in the tradition of European socialists and had a large following among intellectuals and factory workers. The **Bolsheviks**, their rivals, were a small but tightly disciplined group of radicals obedient to the will of their leader, **Vladimir Lenin** (1870–1924).

Lenin, the son of a government official, became a revolutionary in his teens when his older brother was executed for plotting to kill the tsar. He spent years in exile, first in Siberia and later in Switzerland, where he devoted his full attention to organizing his followers. He professed Marx's ideas about class conflict (see Chapter 27), but he never visited a factory or a farm. His goal was to create a party that would lead the revolution rather than wait for it. He explained: "Classes are led by parties and parties are led by individuals. . . . The will of a class is sometimes fulfilled by a dictator."

In early April 1917 the German government, hoping to destabilize Russia, allowed Lenin to travel from Switzerland to Russia in a sealed railway car. As soon as he arrived in Petrograd, he announced his program: immediate peace, all power to the soviets, and transfers of land to the peasants and factories to the workers. This plan proved immensely popular among soldiers and workers exhausted by the war.

The next few months witnessed a tug-of-war between the Provisional Government and the various revolutionary factions in Petrograd. When Kerensky ordered another offensive against the Germans, Russian soldiers began to desert by the hundreds of thousands, throwing away their rifles and walking back to their villages. As the Germans advanced, Russian resistance melted, and the government lost the little support it had.

Meanwhile, the Bolsheviks were gaining support among the workers of Petrograd and the soldiers and sailors stationed there. On November 6, 1917 (October 24 in the Russian calendar), they rose up and took over the city, calling their action the "October Revolution." Their sudden move surprised rival revolutionary groups that believed that a "socialist" revolution could happen only after many years of "bourgeois" rule. Lenin, however, was more interested in power than in the fine points of Marxist doctrine. He overthrew the Provisional Government and arrested Mensheviks, Social Revolutionaries, and other rivals.

Seizing Petrograd was only the first step, for the rest of Russia was in chaos. The Bolsheviks nationalized all private land and ordered the peasants to hand over their crops without compensation. The peasants, having seized their landlords' estates, resisted. In the cities the Bolsheviks took over the factories and drafted the workers into compulsory labor brigades. To enforce his rule Lenin created the Cheka, a secret police force with powers to arrest and execute opponents.

The Bolsheviks also sued for peace with Germany and Austria-Hungary. By the Treaty of Brest-Litovsk, signed on March 3, 1918, Russia lost territories containing a third of its population and wealth. Poland, Finland, and the Baltic states (Estonia, Latvia, and Lithuania) became independent republics. Russian colonies in Central Asia and the Caucasus broke away temporarily.

The End of the War in Western Europe, 1917–1918

Like many other Americans, President **Woodrow Wilson** wanted to stay out of the European conflict. For nearly three years he kept the United States neutral and tried to persuade the belligerents to compromise. But in late 1916 German leaders decided to starve the British into submission by using submarines to sink merchant ships carrying food supplies to Great Britain. The Germans knew that unrestricted submarine warfare was likely to bring the United States into the war, but they were willing to gamble that Britain and France would collapse before the United States could send enough troops to help them.

The submarine campaign resumed on February 1, 1917, and the German gamble failed. The British organized their merchant ships into convoys protected by destroyers, and on April 6 President Wilson asked the United States Congress to declare war on Germany.

On the Western Front, the two sides were so evenly matched in 1917 that the war seemed unlikely to end until one side or the other ran out of young men. Losing hope of winning, soldiers began to mutiny. In May 1917, before the arrival of U.S. forces, fifty-four of one hundred French divisions along the Western Front refused to attack. During the summer Italian troops also mutinied, panicked, or deserted.

In January 1918, President Wilson presented his **Fourteen Points**, a peace plan that called for the German evacuation of occupied lands, the settling of territorial disputes by the decisions of the local populations, and the formation of an association of nations to guarantee the independence and territorial integrity of all states. Germany rejected this plan. Instead, General Erich von Ludendorff launched a series of surprise attacks that broke through the front at several places and pushed to within 40 miles (64 kilometers) of Paris. But victory eluded him. Meanwhile, every month was bringing another 250,000 American troops to the front. In August the Allies counterattacked, and the Germans began a retreat that could not be halted, for German soldiers, many of them sick with the flu, had lost the will to fight.

In late October Ludendorff resigned, and sailors in the German fleet mutinied. Two weeks later Kaiser Wilhelm fled to Holland as a new German government signed an armistice. On November 11 at 11 A.M. the guns on the Western Front went silent.

PEACE AND DISLOCATION IN EUROPE, 1919–1929

The Great War lasted four years. It took almost twice as long for Europe to recover. Millions of people had died or been disabled; political tensions and resentments lingered; and national economies remained depressed until the mid-1920s. In the late 1920s peace and prosperity finally seemed assured, but this hope proved to be illusory.

The Impact of the War

The war left more dead and wounded and more physical destruction than any previous conflict. It is estimated that between 8 million and 10 million people died, almost all of them young men. Perhaps twice that many returned home wounded, gassed, or shell-shocked, many of them injured for life. Among the dead were about 2 million Germans, 1.7 million Russians, and 1.7 million Frenchmen. Austria-Hungary lost 1.5 million, the British Empire a million, Italy 460,000, and the United States 115,000.

Besides ending over 8 million lives, the war dislocated whole populations, creating millions of refugees. War and revolution forced almost 2 million Russians, 750,000 Germans, and 400,000 Hungarians to flee their homes. War led to the expulsion of hundreds of thousands of Greeks from Anatolia and Turks from Greece.

Many refugees found shelter in France, which welcomed 1.5 million people to bolster its declining population. The preferred destination, however, was the United States, the most prosperous country in the world. About 800,000 immigrants succeeded in reaching the United States before immigration laws passed in 1921 and 1924 closed the door to eastern and southern Europeans. Canada, Australia, and New Zealand adopted similar restrictions on immigration. The Latin American republics welcomed European refugees, but their economies were hard hit by the drop in the prices of their main exports, and their poverty discouraged potential immigrants.

One unexpected byproduct of the war was the great influenza epidemic of 1918–1919, which started among soldiers heading for the Western Front. This was no ordinary flu but a virulent strain that infected almost everyone on earth and killed one person in every forty. It caused the largest number of deaths in so short a time in the history of the world. Half a million Americans perished in the epidemic—five times as many as died in the war. Worldwide, some 20 million people died.

The war also caused serious damage to the environment. No place was ever so completely devastated as the scar across France and Belgium known as the Western Front. The fighting ravaged forests and demolished towns. The earth was gouged by trenches, pitted with craters, and littered with ammunition, broken weapons, chunks of concrete, and the bones of countless soldiers. After the war, it took a decade to clear away the debris, rebuild the towns, and create dozens of military cemeteries with neat rows of crosses stretching for miles. To this day, farmers plow up fragments of old weapons and ammunition, and every so often a long-buried shell explodes. The war also hastened the buildup of industry, with mines, factories, and railroad tracks.

The Peace Treaties

In early 1919 delegates of the victorious powers met in Paris. The defeated powers were kept out until the treaties were ready for signing. Russia, in the throes of civil war, was not invited.

From the start, three men dominated the Paris Peace Conference: U.S. president Wilson, British prime minister David Lloyd George, and French premier Georges Clemenceau°. They ignored the Italians, who had joined the Allies in 1915. They paid even less attention to the delegates of smaller European nations and none at all to non-European nationalities. They rejected the Japanese proposal that all races be treated equally. They ignored the Pan-African Congress organized by the African American W. E. B. Du Bois to call attention to the concerns of African peoples around the world. They also ignored the ten thousand other delegates of various nationalities that did not represent sovereign states—the Arab leader Faisal, the Zionist Chaim Weizmann, and several Armenian delegations—who came to Paris to lobby for their causes. They were, in the words of Britain's Foreign Secretary Balfour, "three all-powerful, all-ignorant men, sitting there and carving up continents" (see Map 29.3).

Each had his own agenda. Wilson, a high-minded idealist, wanted to apply the principle of self-determination to European affairs, by which he meant creating nations that reflected ethnic or linguistic divisions. He proposed a **League of Nations**, a world organization to safeguard the peace and foster international cooperation. His idealism clashed with the more hardheaded and self-serving nationalism of the Europeans. To satisfy his constituents, Lloyd George insisted that Germany pay a heavy indemnity. Clemenceau wanted Germany to give Alsace and Lorraine (a part of France before 1871) and the industrial Saar region to France and demanded that the Rhineland be detached from Germany to form a buffer state.

The result was a series of compromises that satisfied no one. The European powers formed a League of Nations, but the United States Congress, reflecting the isolationist feelings of the American people, refused to let the United States join. France recovered Alsace and Lorraine but was unable to detach the Rhineland and had to content itself with vague promises of British and American protection if

Germany ever rebuilt its army. Britain acquired new territories in Africa and the Middle East but was greatly weakened by human losses and the disruption of its trade.

On June 28, 1919, the German delegates reluctantly signed the **Treaty of Versailles°**. Germany was forbidden to have an air force and was permitted only a token army and navy. It gave up large parts of its eastern territory to a newly reconstituted Poland. The Allies made Germany promise to pay reparations to compensate the victors for their losses, but they did not set a figure or a period of time for payment. A "guilt clause," which was to rankle for years to come, obliged the Germans to accept "responsibility for causing all the loss and damage" of the war. The Treaty of Versailles left Germany humiliated but largely intact and potentially the most powerful nation in Europe. Establishing a peace neither of punishment nor of reconciliation, the treaty was one of the great failures in history.

Online Study Center
Improve Your Grade
Primary Source: Comments of the German Delegation to the Peace Conference on the Conditions of Peace, October 1919

Online Study Center
Improve Your Grade
Primary Source: An Economist Analyzes the Versailles Treaty and Finds It Lacking

Meanwhile, the Austro-Hungarian Empire had fallen apart. In the Treaty of Saint-Germain° (1920) Austria and Hungary each lost three-quarters of its territory. New countries appeared in the lands lost by Russia, Germany, and Austria-Hungary: Poland, resurrected after over a century; Czechoslovakia, created from the northern third of Austria-Hungary; and Yugoslavia, combining Serbia and the former south Slav provinces of Austria-Hungary. The new boundaries coincided with the major linguistic groups of eastern Europe, but they all contained disaffected minorities. These small nations were safe only as long as Germany and Russia lay defeated and prostrate.

Russian Civil War and the New Economic Policy

The end of the Great War did not bring peace to all of Europe. Fighting continued in Russia for another three years. The Bolshevik Revolution had provoked Allied intervention. French troops occupied Odessa in the south; the British and Americans landed in Archangel and

---

Georges Clemenceau (zhorzh cluh-mon-SO)

Versailles (vuhr-SIGH) **Saint-Germain** (san–zhair-MEN)

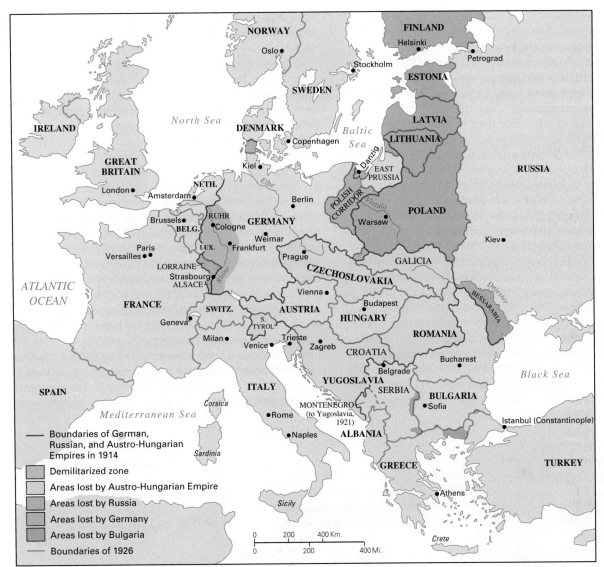

Map 29.3 Territorial Changes in Europe After World War I Although the heaviest fighting took place in western Europe, the territorial changes there were relatively minor; the two provinces taken by Germany in 1871, Alsace and Lorraine, were returned to France. In eastern Europe, in contrast, the changes were enormous. The disintegration of the Austria-Hungary Empire and the defeat of Russia allowed a belt of new countries to arise, stretching from Finland in the north to Yugoslavia in the south.

Online Study Center
Improve Your Grade
Interactive Map: Territorial Changes in Europe After World War I

Murmansk in the north; and the Japanese occupied Vladivostok in the far east. Liberated Czech prisoners of war briefly seized the Trans-Siberian Railway.

Also, in December 1918, civil war broke out in Russia. The Communists—as the Bolsheviks called themselves after March 1918—held central Russia, but all the surrounding provinces rose up against them. Counterrevolutionary armies led by former tsarist officers obtained weapons and supplies from the Allies. For three years the two sides fought each other. They burned farms and confiscated crops, causing a famine that claimed 3 million victims, more than had died in Russia in seven years of fighting. By 1921 the Communists had defeated most of their enemies, for the anti-Bolshevik forces were never united, and the peasants feared that a tsarist victory would mean the return of their landlords.

The Communists' victory was also due to the superior discipline of their Red Army and the military genius of their army commander, Leon Trotsky.

Finland, the Baltic states, and Poland remained independent, but the Red Army reconquered other parts of the tsar's empire one by one. In December 1920 Ukrainian Communists declared the independence of a Soviet Republic of Ukraine, which merged with Russia in 1922 to create the Union of Soviet Socialist Republics (USSR), or Soviet Union. The provinces of the Russian Empire in the Caucasus and Central Asia had also declared their independence in 1918. Although the Bolsheviks staunchly supported anticolonialist movements in Africa and Asia, they opposed what they called "feudalism" in the former Russian colonies. They were also eager to control the oil fields in both regions. In 1920–1921 the Red Army reconquered the Caucasus and replaced the indigenous leaders with Russians. In 1922 the new Soviet republics of Georgia, Armenia, and Azerbaijan joined the USSR. In this way the Bolsheviks rid Russia of the taint of tsarist colonialism but retained control over lands and peoples that had been part of the tsar's empire.

Years of warfare, revolution, and mismanagement ruined the Russian economy. By 1921 it had declined to one-sixth of its prewar level. Factories and railroads had shut down for lack of fuel, raw materials, and parts. Farmland had been devastated and livestock killed, causing hunger in the cities. Finding himself master of a country in ruin, Lenin decided to release the economy from party and government control. In March 1921 he announced The **New Economic Policy** (N.E.P.). It allowed peasants to own land and sell their crops, private merchants to trade, and private workshops to produce goods and sell them on the free market. Only the biggest businesses, such as banks, railroads, and factories, remained under government ownership.

The relaxation of controls had an immediate effect. Production began to climb, and food and other goods became available. In the cities food remained scarce because farmers used their crops to feed their livestock rather than sell them. But the N.E.P. reflected no change in the ultimate goals of the Communist Party. It merely provided breathing space, what Lenin called "two steps back to advance one step forward." The Communists had every intention of creating a modern industrial economy without private property, under party guidance. This meant investing in heavy industry and electrification and moving farmers to the cities to work in the new industries. It also meant providing food for the urban workers without spending scarce resources to purchase it from the peasants. In other words, it meant making the peasants, the great majority of the Soviet

Lenin the Orator The leader of the Bolshevik revolutionaries was a spellbinding orator. Here Lenin is addressing Red Army soldiers in Sverdlov Square, Moscow, in 1920. (Trotsky, who originally appeared in this picture, was airbrushed out.) At the time, the Bolsheviks were mopping up the last of the anti-Bolshevik forces and were fully engaged in a war with Poland. The fate of the Revolution depended on the fighting spirit of the Red Army soldiers and on their loyalty to Lenin. (David King Collection)

people, pay for the industrialization of Russia. This turned them into bitter enemies of the Communists.

When Lenin died in January 1924, his associates jockeyed for power. The leading contenders were Leon Trotsky, commander of the Red Army, and Joseph Stalin, general secretary of the Communist Party. Trotsky had the support of many "Old Bolsheviks" who had joined the party before the revolution. Having spent years in exile, he saw the revolution as a spark that would ignite a world revolution of the working class. Stalin, the only leading Communist who had never lived abroad, insisted that socialism could survive "in one country."

Stalin filled the party bureaucracy with individuals loyal to himself. In 1926–1927 he had Trotsky expelled for "deviation from the party line." In January 1929 he forced Trotsky to flee the country. Then, as absolute master of the party, he prepared to industrialize the Soviet Union at breakneck speed.

| An Ephemeral Peace | The 1920s were a decade of apparent progress hiding irreconcilable tensions. After the |

enormous sacrifices made during the war, the survivors developed hugely unrealistic expectations and were soon disillusioned. Conservatives in Britain and France longed for a return to the stability of the prewar era—the hierarchy of social classes, prosperous world trade, and European dominance over the rest of the world. All over the rest of the world, people's hopes had been raised by the rhetoric of the war, then dashed by its outcome. In Europe, Germans felt cheated out of a victory that had seemed within their grasp, and Italians were disappointed that their sacrifices had not been rewarded at Versailles with large territorial gains. In the Middle East and Asia, Arabs and Indians longed for independence; the Chinese looked for social justice and a lessening of foreign intrusion; and the Japanese hoped to expand their influence in China. In Russia, the Communists were eager to consolidate their power and export their revolution to the rest of the world.

The decade after the end of the war can be divided into two distinct periods: five years of painful recovery and readjustment (1919–1923), followed by six years of growing peace and prosperity (1924–1929). In 1923 Germany suspended reparations payments. In retaliation for the French occupation of the Ruhr, the German government began printing money recklessly, causing the most severe inflation the world had ever seen. Soon German money was worth so little that it took a wheelbarrow full of it to buy a loaf of bread. As Germany teetered on the brink of civil war, radical nationalists

called for revenge and tried to overthrow the government. Finally, the German government issued a new currency and promised to resume reparations payments, and the French agreed to withdraw their troops from the Ruhr.

Beginning in 1924 the world enjoyed a few years of calm and prosperity. After the end of the German crisis of 1923, the western European nations became less confrontational, and Germany joined the League of Nations. The vexed issue of reparations also seemed to vanish, as Germany borrowed money from New York banks to make its payments to France and Britain, which used the money to repay their wartime loans from the United States. This triangular flow of money, based on credit, stimulated the rapid recovery of the European economies. France began rebuilding its war-torn northern zone; Germany recovered from its hyperinflation; and a boom began in the United States that was to last for five years.

While their economies flourished, governments grew more cautious and businesslike. Even the Communists, after Lenin's death, seemed to give up their attempts to spread revolution abroad. Yet neither Germany nor the Soviet Union accepted its borders with the small nations that had arisen between them. In 1922 they signed a secret pact allowing the German army to conduct maneuvers in Russia (in violation of the Versailles treaty) in exchange for German help in building up Russian industry and military potential.

The League of Nations proved adept at resolving numerous technical issues pertaining to health, labor relations, and postal and telegraph communications. But the League could carry out its main function, preserving the peace, only when the great powers (Britain, France, and Italy) were in agreement. Without U.S. participation, sanctions against states that violated League rules carried little weight.

CHINA AND JAPAN: CONTRASTING DESTINIES

China and Japan share a common civilization, and both were subject to Western pressures, but their modern histories have been completely opposite. China clung much longer than Japan to a traditional social structure and economy, then collapsed into chaos and revolution. Japan experienced reform from above (see Chapter 27), acquiring industry and a powerful military, which it used to take advantage of China's weakness. Their different reactions to the pressures of the West put these two great nations on a collision course.

Social and Economic Change

China's population—about 400 million in 1900—was the largest of any country in the world and growing fast. But China had little new land to put into cultivation. In 1900 peasant plots averaged between 1 and 4 acres (less than 2 hectares) apiece, half as large as they had been two generations earlier. Farming methods had not changed in centuries. Landlords and tax collectors took more than half of the harvest. Most Chinese worked incessantly, survived on a diet of grain and vegetables, and spent their lives in fear of floods, bandits, and tax collectors.

Constant labor was needed to prevent the Yellow River from bursting its dikes and flooding the low-lying fields and villages on either side. In times of war and civil disorder, when flood-control precautions were neglected, disasters ensued. Between 1913 and 1938 the river burst its dikes seventeen times, each time killing thousands of people and making millions homeless.

Japan had few natural resources and very little arable land on which to grow food for its rising population. It did not suffer from devastating floods like China, but it was subject to other natural calamities. Typhoons regularly hit its southern regions. Earthquakes periodically shook the country, which lies on the great ring of tectonic fault lines that surround the Pacific Ocean. The Kanto earthquake of 1923 destroyed all of Yokohama and half of Tokyo and killed as many as 200,000 people.

Above the peasantry, Chinese society was divided into many groups and strata. Landowners lived off the rents of their tenants. Officials, chosen through an elaborate examination system, enriched themselves from taxes and the government's monopolies on salt, iron, and other products. Wealthy merchants handled China's growing import-export trade in collaboration with foreign companies. Shanghai, China's financial and commercial center, was famous for its wealthy foreigners and its opium addicts, prostitutes, and gangsters.

Although foreign trade represented only a small part of China's economy, contact with the outside world had a tremendous impact on Chinese politics. Young men living in the treaty ports saw no chance for advancement in the old system of examinations and official positions. Some learned foreign ideas in Christian mission schools or abroad. The contrast between the squalor in which most urban residents lived and the luxury of the foreigners' enclaves in the treaty ports sharpened the resentment of educated Chinese.

Japan's population reached 60 million in 1925 and was increasing by a million a year. The crash program of industrialization begun in 1868 by the Meiji oligarchs (see Chapter 27) accelerated during the First World War, when Japan exported textiles, consumer goods, and munitions. In the war years, its economy grew four times as fast as western Europe's, eight times faster than China's.

In the 1880s electrification was still in its infancy, so Japan became competitive very early on. Blessed with a rainy climate and many fast-flowing rivers, Japan quickly expanded its hydroelectric capacity. By the mid-1930s, 89 percent of Japanese households had electric lights, compared with 68 percent of U.S. and 44 percent of British households.

Economic growth aggravated social tensions. The *narikin* ("new rich") affected Western ways and lifestyles that clashed with the austerity of earlier times. In the big cities *mobos* (modern boys) and *mogas* (modern girls)

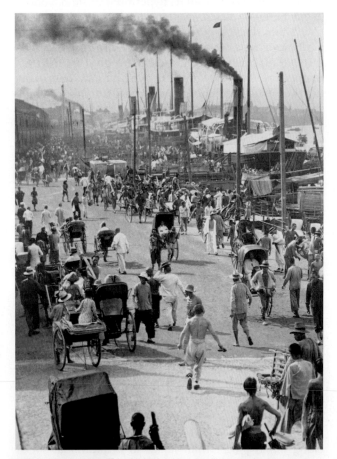

The Bund, Shanghai   Shanghai was the most important port and industrial city in China. This picture shows the Bund, or waterfront, where ocean-going ships docked and where Chinese and foreign merchants did business. Many of the people you see in the picture were stevedores, who loaded and unloaded ships, and drivers of rickshaws or man-powered taxis.   (Corbis)

shocked traditionalists with their foreign ways: dancing together, wearing short skirts and tight pants, and behaving like Americans. Students who flirted with dangerous thoughts were called "Marx boys."

The main beneficiaries of prosperity were the *zaibatsu*°, or conglomerates, four of which—Mitsubishi, Sumitomo, Yasuda, and Mitsui—controlled most of Japan's industry and commerce. Farmers, who constituted half of the population, remained poor; in desperation some sold their daughters to textile mills or into domestic service, where young women formed the bulk of the labor force. Labor unions were weak and repressed by the police.

Japanese prosperity depended on foreign trade and imperialism in Asia. The country exported silk and light manufactures and imported almost all its fuel, raw materials, and machine tools, and even some of its food. Though less at the mercy of the weather than China, Japan was much more vulnerable to swings in the world economy.

Revolution and War, 1900–1918

In 1900 China's Empress Dowager Cixi°, who had seized power in a palace coup two years earlier, encouraged a secret society, the Righteous Fists, or Boxers, to rise up and expel all the foreigners from China. When the Boxers threatened the foreign legation in Beijing, an international force from the Western powers and Japan captured the city and forced China to pay a huge indemnity. Shocked by these events, many Chinese students became convinced that China needed a revolution to get rid of the Qing dynasty and modernize their country. In Shanghai dissidents published works that would have been forbidden elsewhere in China.

Online Study Center
Improve Your Grade
Primary Source: Two Proclamations
of the Boxer Rebellion

When Cixi died in 1908, the Revolutionary Alliance led by **Sun Yat-sen**° (Sun Zhongshan, 1867–1925) prepared to take over. Sun had spent much of his life in Japan, England, and the United States, plotting the overthrow of the Qing dynasty. His ideas were a mixture of nationalism, socialism, and Confucian philosophy. His patriotism, his powerful ambition, and his tenacious spirit attracted a large following.

Online Study Center
Improve Your Grade
Primary Source: The Three People's Principles
and the Future of the Chinese People

The military thwarted Sun's plans. After China's defeat in the war with Japan in 1895, the government had agreed to equip the army with modern rifles and machine guns. The combination of traditional regional autonomy with modern tactics and equipment led to the creation of local armies beholden to local generals known as warlords, rather than to the central government. When a regional army mutinied in October 1911, **Yuan Shikai**°, the most powerful of the regional generals, refused to defend the Qing. A revolutionary assembly at Nanjing elected Sun president of China in December 1911, and the last Qing ruler, the boy-emperor Puyi, abdicated the throne. But Sun had no military forces at his command. To avoid a clash with the army, he resigned after a few weeks, and a new national assembly elected Yuan president of the new Chinese republic.

Yuan was an able military leader, but he had no political program. When Sun reorganized his followers into a political party called **Guomindang**° (National People's Party), Yuan quashed every attempt at creating a Western-style government and harassed Sun's followers. Victory in the first round of the struggle to create a new China went to the military.

The Japanese were quick to join the Allied side in World War I. They saw the war as an opportunity to advance their interests while the Europeans were occupied elsewhere. The war created an economic boom, as the Japanese suddenly found their products in greater demand. But it also created hardships for workers, who rioted when the cost of rice rose faster than their wages.

The Japanese soon conquered the German colonies in the northern Pacific and on the coast of China, then turned their attention to the rest of China. In 1915 Japan presented China with Twenty-One Demands, which would have turned it into a virtual protectorate. Britain and the United States persuaded Japan to soften the demands but could not prevent it from keeping the German coastal enclaves and extracting railroad and mining concessions at China's expense. In protest, anti-Japanese riots and boycotts broke out throughout China. Thus began a bitter struggle between the two countries that was to last for thirty years.

---

zaibatsu (zie-BOT-soo) **Cixi** (TSUH-shee)
Sun Yat-sen (soon yot-SEN)

Yuan Shikai (you-AHN she-KIE) **Guomindang** (gwo-min-dong)

Chinese Warlords and the Guomindang, 1919–1929

At the Paris Peace Conference, the great powers accepted Japan's seizure of the German enclaves in China. To many educated Chinese, this decision was a cruel insult. On May 4, 1919, students demonstrated in front of the Forbidden City of Beijing. Despite a government ban, the May Fourth Movement spread to other parts of China. A new generation was growing up to challenge the old officials, the regional generals, and the foreigners.

China's regional generals—the warlords—still supported their armies through plunder and arbitrary taxation. They frightened off trade and investment in railroads, industry, and agricultural improvement. While neglecting the dikes and canals on which the livelihood of Chinese farmers depended, they fought one another and protected the gangsters who ran the opium trade. During the warlord era only the treaty ports prospered, while the rest of China grew poorer and weaker.

Sun Yat-sen tried to make a comeback in Canton (Guangzhou) in the early 1920s. Though not a Communist, he was impressed with the efficiency of Lenin's revolutionary tactics and let a Soviet adviser reorganize the Guomindang along Leninist lines. He also welcomed members of the newly created Chinese Communist Party into the Guomindang.

When Sun died in 1925, the leadership of his party passed to Jiang Jieshi, known in the West as **Chiang Kai-shek°** (1887–1975).

An officer and director of the military academy, Chiang trained several hundred young officers who remained loyal to him thereafter. In 1927 he determined to crush the regional warlords. As his army moved north from its base in Canton, he briefly formed an alliance with the Communists. Once his troops had occupied Shanghai, however, he allied himself with local gangsters to crush the labor unions and decimate the Communists, whom he considered a threat. He then defeated or co-opted most of the other warlords and established a dictatorship.

Chiang's government issued ambitious plans to build railroads, develop agriculture and industry, and modernize China from the top down. However, his followers were neither competent administrators like the Japanese officials of the Meiji Restoration nor ruthless modernizers like the Russian Bolsheviks. Instead, the government attracted thousands of opportunists whose goals were to "become officials and get rich" by taxing and plundering businesses. In the countryside tax collectors and landowners squeezed the peasants ever harder, even in times of natural disasters. What little money reached the government's coffers went to the military. For twenty years after the fall of the Qing, China remained mired in poverty, subject to corrupt officials and the whims of nature.

THE NEW MIDDLE EAST

Having contributed to the Allied victory, the Arab peoples expected to have a say in the outcome of the Great War. But the victorious French and British planned to treat the Middle East like a territory open to colonial rule. The result was a legacy of instability that has persisted to this day.

The Mandate System

At the Paris Peace Conference France, Britain, Italy, and Japan proposed to divide the former German colonies and the territories of the Ottoman Empire among themselves, but their ambitions clashed with President Wilson's ideal of national self-determination. Eventually, the victors arrived at a compromise solution called the **mandate system**: colonial rulers would administer the territories but would be accountable to the League of Nations for "the material and moral well-being and the social progress of the inhabitants."

Class C Mandates—those with the smallest populations—were treated as colonies by their conquerors. South Africa replaced Germany in Southwest Africa (now Namibia). Britain, Australia, New Zealand, and Japan took over the German islands in the Pacific. Class B Mandates, larger than Class C but still underdeveloped, were to be ruled for the benefit of their inhabitants under League of Nations supervision. They were to receive autonomy at some unspecified time in the future. Most of Germany's African colonies fell into this category.

The Arab-speaking territories of the old Ottoman Empire were Class A Mandates. The League of Nations declared that they had "reached a state of development where their existence as independent nations can be provisionally recognized subject to the rendering of administrative advice and assistance by a Mandatory, until such time as they are able to stand alone." Arabs interpreted this ambiguous wording as a promise of independence. Britain and France sent troops into the region "for the benefit of its inhabitants." Palestine (now Israel), Transjordan (now Jordan), and Iraq (formerly Mesopotamia) became British mandates; France claimed

---

Chiang Kai-shek (chang kie-shek)

Syria and Lebanon (see Map 29.4). (See Diversity and Dominance: The Middle East After World War I.)

Mustafa Kemal Atatürk   After World War I, Mustafa Kemal was determined to modernize Turkey on the Western model. Here he is shown wearing a European-style suit and teaching the Latin alphabet.   (Stock Montage)

The Rise of Modern Turkey

At the end of the war, as the Ottoman Empire teetered on the brink of collapse, France, Britain, and Italy saw an opportunity to expand their empires, and Greece eyed those parts of Anatolia inhabited by Greeks. In 1919 French, British, Italian, and Greek forces occupied Constantinople and parts of Anatolia. By the Treaty of Sèvres (1920) the Allies made the sultan give up most of his lands.

In 1919 Mustafa Kemal, a hero of the Gallipoli campaign, had formed a nationalist government in central Anatolia with the backing of fellow army officers. In 1922, after a short but fierce war against invading Greeks, his armies reconquered Anatolia and the area around Constantinople. The victorious Turks forced hundreds of thousands of Greeks from their ancestral homes in Anatolia. In response the Greek government expelled all Muslims from Greece. The ethnic diversity that had prevailed in the region for centuries ended.

As a war hero and proclaimed savior of his country, Kemal was able to impose wrenching changes on his people faster than any other reformer would have dared. An outspoken modernizer, he was eager to bring Turkey closer to Europe as quickly as possible. He abolished the sultanate, declared Turkey a secular republic, and introduced European laws. In a radical break with Islamic tradition, he suppressed Muslim courts, schools, and religious orders and replaced the Arabic alphabet with the Latin alphabet.

Kemal attempted to westernize the traditional Turkish family. Women received civil equality, including the right to vote and to be elected to the national assembly. Kemal forbade polygamy and instituted civil marriage and divorce. He even changed people's clothing, strongly discouraging women from veiling their faces, and replaced the fez, until then the traditional Turkish men's hat, with the European brimmed hat. He ordered everyone to take a family name, choosing the name **Atatürk** ("father of the Turks") for himself. His reforms spread quickly in the cities; but in rural areas, where Islamic traditions remained strong, people resisted them for a long time.

Arab lands and the Question of Palestine

Among the Arab people, the thinly disguised colonialism of the mandate system set off protests and rebellions not only in the mandated territories, but even as far away as Morocco. Arabs viewed the European presence not as "liberation" from Ottoman "oppression," but as foreign occupation.

After World War I Middle Eastern society underwent dramatic changes. Nomads disappeared from the deserts as trucks replaced camel caravans. The rural population grew fast, and many landless peasants migrated to the swelling cities. The population of the region is estimated to have increased by 50 percent between 1914 and 1939, while that of large cities such as Constantinople, Baghdad, and Cairo doubled.

The urban and mercantile middle class, encouraged by the transformation of Turkey, adopted Western ideas, customs, and styles of housing and clothing. Some families sent their sons to European secular or mission schools, then to Western colleges in Cairo and Beirut or universities abroad, to prepare for jobs in government and business. Among the educated elite were a few women who became schoolteachers or nurses. There were great variations, ranging from Lebanon, with its strong French influence, to Arabia and Iran, which retained their cultural traditions.

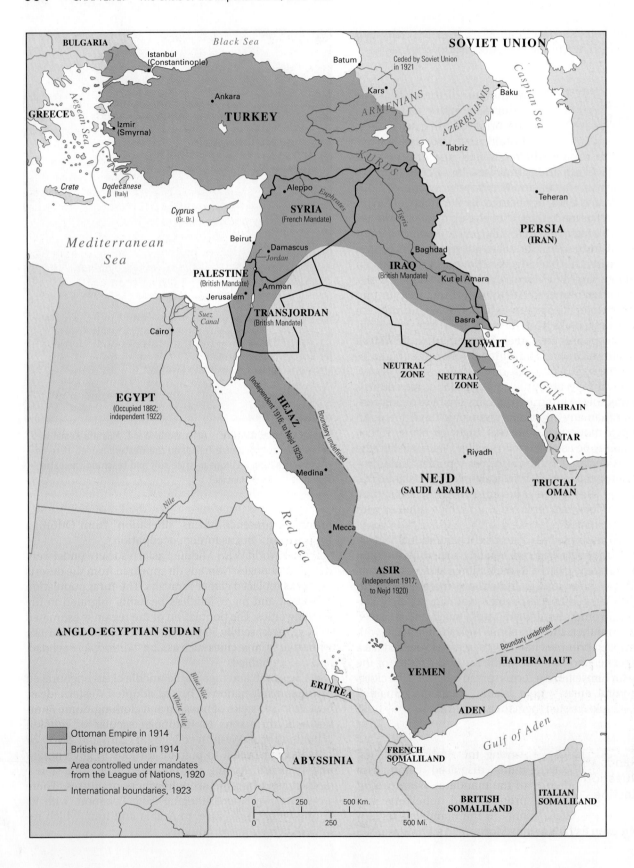

BULGARIA

Black Sea

Istanbul
(Constantinople)

Batum

Ceded by Soviet Union
in 1921

SOVIET UNION

Caspian Sea

Ankara

Kars

Baku

GREECE

Aegean Sea

Izmir
(Smyrna)

TURKEY

ARMENIANS

AZERBAIJANIS

Tabriz

Crete

Dodecanese
(Italy)

Aleppo

Euphrates

KURDS

Teheran

Cyprus
(Gr. Br.)

SYRIA
(French Mandate)

Tigris

PERSIA
(IRAN)

*Mediterranean
Sea*

Beirut

Damascus

Jordan

Baghdad

PALESTINE
(British Mandate)

Amman

IRAQ
(British Mandate)

Kut el Amara

Jerusalem

*Suez
Canal*

Cairo

TRANSJORDAN
(British Mandate)

Basra

KUWAIT

**NEUTRAL
ZONE**

**NEUTRAL
ZONE**

Persian Gulf

EGYPT
(Occupied 1882;
independent 1922)

HEJAZ
(Independent 1916; to Nejd 1925)

Boundary undefined

BAHRAIN

QATAR

Riyadh

Medina

NEJD
(SAUDI ARABIA)

**TRUCIAL
OMAN**

Nile

Red Sea

Mecca

ASIR
(Independent 1917;
to Nejd 1920)

Boundary undefined

ANGLO-EGYPTIAN SUDAN

HADHRAMAUT

Blue Nile

White Nile

YEMEN

ERITREA

ADEN

Gulf of Aden

Ottoman Empire in 1914

British protectorate in 1914

Area controlled under mandates
from the League of Nations, 1920

International boundaries, 1923

ABYSSINIA

**FRENCH
SOMALILAND**

**BRITISH
SOMALILAND**

**ITALIAN
SOMALILAND**

0   250   500 Km.

0   250   500 Mi.

◀ **Map 29.4   Territorial Changes in the Middle East After World War I**   The defeat and dismemberment of the Ottoman Empire at the end of World War I resulted in an entirely new political map of the region. The Turkish Republic inherited Anatolia and a small piece of the Balkans, while the Ottoman Empire's Arab provinces were divided between France and Great Britain as "Class A Mandates." The French acquired Syria and Lebanon, and the British got Palestine (now Israel), Transjordan (now Jordan), and Iraq. Only Iran and Egypt remained as they had been.

The region in closest contact with Europe was the Maghrib—Algeria, Tunisia, and Morocco—which the French army considered its private domain. Alongside the old native quarters, the French built modern neighborhoods inhabited mainly by Europeans. France had occupied Algeria since 1830 and had encouraged European immigration. The settlers owned the best lands and monopolized government jobs and businesses, while Arabs and Berbers remained poor and suffered intense discrimination. Nationalism was only beginning to appear before World War II, and the settlers quickly blocked attempts at reform.

The British attempted to control the Middle East with a mixture of bribery and intimidation. They helped Faisal, leader of the Arab Revolt, become king of Syria. When the French ousted him, the British made him king of Iraq. They used bombers to quell rural insurrections in Iraq. In 1931 they reached an agreement with King Faisal's government: official independence for Iraq in exchange for the right to keep two air bases, a military alliance, and an assured flow of petroleum. France, meanwhile, sent thousands of troops to Syria and Lebanon to crush nationalist uprisings.

In Egypt, as in Iraq, the British substituted a phony independence for official colonialism. They declared Egypt independent in 1922 but reserved the right to station troops along the Suez Canal to secure their link with India in the event of war. Most galling to the Wafd (Nationalist) Party was the British attempt to remove Egyptian troops from Sudan, a land many

Egyptians considered a colony of Egypt. Britain was successful in keeping Egypt in limbo—neither independent nor a colony—thanks to an alliance with King Fouad and conservative Egyptian politicians who feared both secular and religious radicalism.

Before the war, a Jewish minority lived in Palestine, as in other Arab countries. Small numbers of Jews had been immigrating to Palestine since the nineteenth century, but as soon as Palestine became a British mandate in 1920, many more came from Europe, encouraged by the Balfour Declaration of 1917. Most settled in the cities, but some established *kibbutzim*, or communal farms, on land purchased by the World Zionist Organization. Their goals were to become self-sufficient and to reestablish their ties to the land of their ancestors. The purchases of land by Jewish agencies angered the indigenous Palestinians, especially tenant farmers who had been evicted to make room for settlers. In 1920–1921 riots erupted between Jews and Arabs. When far more Jewish immigrants arrived than they had anticipated, the British tried to limit immigration, thereby alienating the Jews without mollifying the Arabs. Increasingly, Jews arrived without papers, smuggled in by militant Zionist organizations. In the 1930s the country was torn by strikes

The Jewish Settlement of Palestine   The Jewish population of Israel originated with the immigration to Palestine of thousands of Jews fleeing persecution and discrimination in Europe. Many settled on the land and founded kibbutzim, or collective farms. In this picture taken in 1912, an 84-year-old immigrant from Russia learns to plow the land.   (Hulton Archive/Getty Images)

The Middle East After World War I

*D*uring the First World War, Entente forces invaded the Arab provinces of the Ottoman Empire and occupied Palestine, Mesopotamia, and Syria. This raised the question of what to do with these territories after the war. Would they be returned to the Ottoman Empire? Would they simply be added to the colonial empires of Britain and France? Or would they become independent Arab states?

The following documents illustrate the diversity of opinions among various groups planning the postwar settlement: Great Britain concerned with defeating Germany and maintaining its empire; the United States, basing its policies on lofty principles; and Arab delegates from the Middle East, seeking self-determination.

In the early twentieth century, in response to the rise of anti-Semitism in Europe, a movement called Zionism had arisen among European Jews. Zionists, led by Theodore Herzl, hoped for a return to Israel, the ancestral homeland of the Jewish people. For two thousand years this land had been a province of various empires—the Roman, Byzantine, Arab, and Ottoman—and was inhabited by Arabic-speaking people, most of whom practiced the Islamic religion.

During the war the British government eagerly sought the support of the American Jewish community to balance the hostility of Irish-Americans and German-Americans toward the British war effort. It was therefore receptive to the idea of establishing a Jewish homeland in Palestine. As a result, the British government found itself torn between two contradictory impulses: it was motivated by the short-term need to win the war, but not without thought of the more distant future. The result was a policy statement, sent by Foreign Secretary Arthur James Balfour to Baron Rothschild, a prominent supporter of the Zionist movement in England. This statement, called the "Balfour Declaration," has haunted the Middle East ever since.

The Balfour Declaration of 1917

Foreign Office
November 2nd, 1917

Dear Lord Rothschild:

I have much pleasure in conveying to you, on behalf of His Majesty's Government, the following declaration of sympathy with Jewish Zionist aspirations which have been submitted to, and approved by, the Cabinet:

> His Majesty's Government view with favor the establishment in Palestine of a national home for the Jewish people, and will use their best endeavors to facilitate the achievement of this object, it being clearly understood that nothing shall be done which may prejudice the civil and religious rights of existing non-Jewish communities in Palestine, or the rights and political status enjoyed by Jews in any other country.

I should be grateful if you would bring this declaration to the knowledge of the Zionist Federation.

Yours,
Arthur James Balfour

*O*n January 8, 1918, the American president Woodrow Wilson issued his famous Fourteen Points proposal to end the war. Much of his speech was devoted to European affairs or to international relations in general, but two of his fourteen points were understood as referring to the Arab world.

Woodrow Wilson's Fourteen Points

We entered this war because violations of right had occurred which touches us to the quick and made the life of our own people impossible unless they were corrected and the world secured once for all against their recurrence. What we demand in this war, therefore, is nothing peculiar to ourselves. It is that the world be made fit and safe to live in; and particularly that it be made safe for every peace-loving nation which, like our own, wishes to live its own life, determine its own institutions, be assured of justice and fair dealing by the other peoples of the world as against force and selfish aggression. All the peoples of the world are in effect partners in this interest, and for our own part we see very clearly that unless justice be done to others it will not be done to us. The programme of the world's peace, therefore, is our programme; and that programme, the only possible programme, as we see it, is this:

V. A free, open-minded, and absolutely impartial adjustment of all colonial claims, based upon a strict observance of the principle that in determining all such questions of sovereignty the interests of the populations concerned must have equal weight with the equitable claims of the government whose title is to be determined.

XII. The Turkish portions of the present Ottoman Empire should be assured a secure sovereignty, but the other nationalities which are now under Turkish rule should be assured an undoubted security of life and an absolutely unmolested opportunity of autonomous development. . . .

When the war ended, the victorious Allies assembled in Paris to determine, among other things, the fate of the former Arab provinces of the Ottoman Empire. This was a matter of grave concern to both Zionists and leaders of the Arab populations. Arab leaders, in particular, had reason to doubt the intentions of the great powers, especially Britain and France. When the Allies decided to create mandates in the Arab territories on the grounds that the Arab peoples were not ready for independence, Arab leaders expressed their misgivings, as the following statement shows:

Memorandum of the General Syrian Congress, July 2, 1919

We the undersigned members of the General Syrian Congress, meeting in Damascus on Wednesday, July 2nd, 1919, made up of representatives from the three Zones, viz., The Southern, Eastern, and Western, provided with credentials and authorizations by the inhabitants of our various districts, Moslems, Christians, and Jews, have agreed upon the following statement of the desires of the people of the country who have elected us. . . .

1. We ask absolutely complete political independence for Syria. . . .

2. We ask that the government of this Syrian country should be a democratic civil constitutional Monarchy on broad decentralization principles, safeguarding the rights of minorities, and that the King be the Emir Feisal, who carried on a glorious struggle in the cause of our liberation and merited our full confidence and entire reliance.

3. Considering the fact that the Arabs inhabiting the Syrian area are not naturally less gifted than other more advanced races and that they are by no means less developed than the Bulgarians, Serbians, Greeks, and Roumanians at the beginning of their independence, we protest against Article 22 of the Covenant of the League of Nations, placing us among the nations in their middle stage of development which stand in need of a mandatory power.

4. In the event of the rejection of the Peace Conference of this just protest for certain considerations that we may not understand, we, relying on the declarations of President Wilson that his object in waging war was to put an end to the ambition of conquest and colonization, we can only regard the mandate mentioned in the Covenant of the League of Nations as equivalent to the rendering of economical and technical assistance that does not prejudice our complete independence. And desiring that our country should not fall a prey to colonization and believing that the American Nation is furthest from any thought of colonization and has no political ambition in our country, we will seek the technical and economic assistance from the United States of America, provided that such assistance does not exceed 20 years.

5. In the event of America not finding herself in a position to accept our desire for assistance, we will seek this assistance from Great Britain, also provided that such does not prejudice our complete independence and unity of our country and that the duration of such assistance does not exceed that mentioned in the previous article.

6. We do not acknowledge any right claimed by the French Government in any part whatever of our Syrian country and refuse that she should assist us or have a hand in our country under any circumstances and in any place.

7. We opposed the pretensions of the Zionists to create a Jewish commonwealth in the southern part of Syria, known as Palestine, and oppose Zionist migration to any part of our country; for we do not acknowledge their title but consider them a grave peril to our people from the national, economical, and political points of view. Our Jewish compatriots shall enjoy our common rights and assume our common responsibilities.

QUESTIONS FOR ANALYSIS

1. Was there a contradiction between Balfour's proposal to establish "a national home for the Jewish people" and the promise "that nothing shall be done which may prejudice the civil and religious rights of existing non-Jewish communities in Palestine"? If so, why did he make two contradictory promises?

2. How would Woodrow Wilson's statements about "the interests of the populations concerned" and "an absolutely unmolested opportunity of autonomous development" apply to Palestine?

3. Why did the delegates to the Syrian General Congress object to the plan to create mandates in the former Ottoman provinces? What alternatives did they offer?

4. Why did the delegates object to the creation of a Jewish commonwealth?

Source: The Balfour Declaration, *The Times* (London), November 9, 1917. Memorandum of the General Syrian Congress, *Foreign Relations of the United States: Paris Peace Conference*, vol. 12 (Washington, DC: Government Printing Office, 1919), 780–781.

Online Study Center
Improve Your Grade
Primary Source:
The Balfour Declaration

and guerrilla warfare that the British could not control. In the process, Britain earned the hatred of both sides and of many other people in the Arab world.

SOCIETY, CULTURE, AND TECHNOLOGY IN THE INDUSTRIALIZED WORLD

With the signing of the peace treaties, the countries that had fought for four years turned their efforts toward building a new future. The war had left a deep imprint on European society and culture. Advances in science offered astonishing new insights into the mysteries of nature and the universe. New technologies, many of them pioneered in the United States, promised to change the daily lives of millions of people.

Class and Gender

After the war, class distinctions began to fade. Many European aristocrats had died on the battlefields, and with them went their class's long domination of the army, the diplomatic corps, and other elite sectors of society. The United States and Canada had never had as rigidly defined a class structure as European societies or as elaborate a set of traditions and manners. During the war, displays of wealth and privilege seemed unpatriotic. On both sides of the Atlantic, engineers, businessmen, lawyers, and other professionals rose to prominence, increasing the relative importance of the middle class.

The activities of governments had expanded during the war and continued to grow. Governments provided housing, highways, schools, public health facilities, broadcasting, and other services. This growth of government influence created a need for thousands more bureaucrats. Department stores, banks, insurance companies, and other businesses also increased the white-collar work force.

In contrast with the middle class, the working class did not expand. The introduction of new machines and new ways of organizing work, such as the automobile assembly line that Henry Ford devised, increased workers' productivity so that greater outputs could be achieved without a larger labor force.

Women's lives changed more rapidly in the 1920s than in any previous decade. Although the end of the war marked a retreat from wartime job opportunities, some women remained in the work force as wage earners and as salaried professionals. The young and wealthy enjoyed more personal freedoms than their mothers had before the war; they drove cars, played sports, traveled alone, and smoked in public. For others the upheavals of war brought more suffering than liberation. Millions of women had lost their fathers, brothers, sons, husbands, and fiancés in the war or in the great influenza epidemic. After the war the shortage of young men caused many single women to lead lives of loneliness and destitution.

In Europe and North America advocates of women's rights had been demanding the vote for women since the 1890s. New Zealand was the only nation to grant women the vote before the twentieth century. Women in Norway were the first to obtain it in Europe, in 1915. Russian women followed in 1917, and Canadians and Germans in 1918. Britain gave women over age thirty the vote in 1918 and later extended it to younger women. The Nineteenth Amendment to the U.S. Constitution granted suffrage to American women in 1920. Women in Turkey began voting in 1934. Most other countries did not allow women to vote until after 1945.

In dictatorships voting rights for women made no difference, and in democratic countries women tended to vote like their male relatives. In the British elections of 1918—the first to include women—they overwhelmingly voted for the Conservative Party. Everywhere, their influence on politics was less radical than feminists had hoped and conservatives had feared. Even when it did not alter politics and government, however, the right to vote was a potent symbol.

Women were active in many other areas besides the suffrage movement. On both sides of the Atlantic women participated in social reform movements to prevent mistreatment of women and children and of industrial workers. In the United States such reforms were championed by Progressives such as Jane Addams (1860–1935), who founded a settlement house in a poor neighborhood and received the Nobel Peace Prize in 1931. In Europe reformers were generally aligned with Socialist or Labour Parties.

Since 1874 the Women's Christian Temperance Union had campaigned against alcohol and taverns. In the early twentieth century the American Carrie Nation (1846–1911) became famous for destroying saloons and for lectures in the United States and Europe against the evils of liquor. As a result of this campaign the Eighteenth Amendment imposed prohibition in the United States from 1919 until it was revoked by the Twenty-First Amendment fourteen years later.

Among the most controversial, and eventually most effective of the reformers, were those who advocated contraception, such as the American **Margaret Sanger** (1883–1966). Her campaign brought her into conflict with the authorities, who equated birth control with pornography. Finally, in 1923 she was able to found a birth control clinic in New York. In France, however, the government prohibited contraception and abortion in 1920 in an effort to increase the birthrate and make up for the loss of so many young men in the war. Only the Russian communists allowed abortion, for ideological reasons (see Diversity and Dominance: Women, Family Values, and the Russian Revolution in Chapter 30).

Revolution in the Sciences

For two hundred years scientists following in Isaac Newton's footsteps had applied the same laws and equations to astronomical observations and to laboratory experiments. At the end of the nineteenth century, however, a revolution in physics undermined all the old certainties about nature. Physicists discovered that atoms, the building blocks of matter, are not indivisible, but consist of far smaller subatomic particles. In 1900 the German physicist **Max Planck** (1858–1947) found that atoms emit or absorb energy only in discrete amounts, called *quanta,* instead of continuously, as assumed in Newtonian physics. These findings seemed strange enough, but what really undermined Newtonian physics was the general theory of relativity developed by **Albert Einstein** (1879–1955), another German physicist. In 1916 Einstein announced that not only is matter made of insubstantial particles, but that time, space, and mass are not fixed but are relative to one another. Other physicists said that light is made up of either waves or particles, depending on the observer, and that an experiment could determine either the speed or the position of a particle of light, but never both.

To nonscientists it seemed as though theories expressed in arcane mathematical formulas were replacing truth and common sense. Far from being mere speculation, however, the new physics promised to unlock the secrets of matter and provide humans with plentiful—and potentially dangerous—sources of energy.

The new social sciences were even more unsettling than the new physics, for they challenged Victorian morality, middle-class values, and notions of Western superiority. **Sigmund Freud** (1856–1939), a Viennese physician, developed the technique of psychoanalysis to probe the minds of his patients. He found not only rationality but also hidden layers of emotion and desire repressed by social restraints. "The primitive, savage and evil impulses have not vanished from any individual, but continue their existence, although in a repressed state," he warned. Meanwhile, sociologists and anthropologists had begun the empirical study of societies, both Western and non-Western. Before the war the French sociologist Emile Durkheim (1858–1917) had come to the then-shocking conclusion that "there are no religions that are false. All are true in their own fashion."

If the words *primitive* and *savage* applied to Europeans as well as to other peoples, and if religions were all equally "true," then what remained of the superiority of Western civilization? Cultural relativism, as the new approach to human societies was called, was as unnerving as relativity in physics.

Although these ideas had been expressed before 1914, wartime experiences called into question the West's faith in reason and progress. Some people accepted the new ideas with enthusiasm. Others condemned and rejected them, clinging to the sense of order and faith in progress that had energized European and American culture before the war. Yet others were overcome with feelings of uncertainty and despair in a world in which human existence seemed to have lost its meaning and purpose.

The New Technologies of Modernity

Some Europeans and Americans viewed the sciences with mixed feelings, but the new technologies aroused almost universal excitement. In North America even working-class people could afford some of the new products of scientific research, inventors' ingenuity, and industrial production. Mass consumption lagged in Europe, but science and technology were just as advanced, and public fascination with the latest inventions—the cult of the modern—was just as strong.

Of all the innovations of the time, none attracted public interest as much as airplanes. In 1903 two young American mechanics, **Wilbur and Orville Wright**, built the first aircraft that was heavier than air and could be maneuvered in flight. From that moment on, wherever they appeared, airplanes fascinated people. During the war the exploits of air aces relieved the tedium of news from the front. In the 1920s aviation became a sport and a form of entertainment, and flying daredevils achieved extraordinary fame by pushing their planes to the very limit—and often beyond. Among the most celebrated pilots were three Americans. Amelia Earhart was the first woman to fly across the Atlantic Ocean, and her example encouraged other women to fly. Richard Byrd flew over

The Archetypal Automobile City   As Los Angeles grew from a modest town into a sprawling metropolis, broad avenues, parking lots, and garages were built to accommodate automobiles. By 1929, most families owned a car and streetcar lines had closed for lack of passengers. This photograph shows a street in the downtown business district.   (Ralph Morris Archives/Los Angeles Public Library)

the North Pole in 1926. The most admired of all was Charles Lindbergh, the first person to fly alone across the Atlantic in 1927. The heroic age of flight lasted until the late 1930s, when aviation became a means of transportation, a business, and a male preserve (see Environment and Technology: The Birth of Civil Aviation).

Electricity, produced in industrial quantities since the 1890s (see Chapter 27), began to transform home life. The first home use of electricity was for lighting, thanks to the economical and long-lasting tungsten bulb. Then, having persuaded people to wire their homes, electrical utilities joined manufacturers in advertising electric irons, fans, washing machines, hot plates, and other appliances.

Radio—or wireless telegraphy, as it was called—had served ships and the military during the war as a means of point-to-point telecommunication. After the war, amateurs used surplus radio equipment to talk to one another. The first commercial station began broadcasting in Pittsburgh in 1920. By the end of 1923 six hundred stations were broadcasting news, sports, soap operas, and advertising to homes throughout North America. By

1930, 12 million families owned radio receivers. In Europe radio spread more slowly because governments reserved the airwaves for cultural and official programs and taxed radio owners to pay for the service.

Another medium that spread explosively in the 1920s was film. Motion pictures had begun in France in 1895 and flourished there and elsewhere in Europe, where the dominant concern was to reproduce stage plays. In the United States filmmaking started at almost the same time, but American filmmakers considered it their business to entertain audiences rather than preserve outstanding theatrical performances. In competing for audiences they looked to cinematic innovation, broad humor, and exciting spectacles, in the process developing styles of filmmaking that became immensely popular.

Diversity was a hallmark of the early film industry. After World War I filmmaking took root and flourished in Japan, India, Turkey, Egypt, and a suburb of Los Angeles, California, called Hollywood. American and European movie studios were successful in exporting films, since silent movies presented no language problems. In 1929,

The Birth of Civil Aviation

Antoine de Saint-Exupéry, best known for his children's book *The Little Prince*, was a pilot for Aéropostale, a French airline that served South America. In his book *Vol de Nuit* (Night Flight), he tells a harrowing tale of a pilot blown out to sea in a storm over Argentina:

> One of the radio operators at the Comodoro Rivadavia station in Patagonia made a sudden gesture and all those who were keeping a helpless vigil there crowded around him. . . .
>
> "Storm?"
>
> He nodded yes; static prevented him from hearing the message. Then he scrawled some illegible signs, then words. Then the text came out:
>
> "Cut off at 12,000 feet above the storm. Proceeding due west toward interior; we were carried out to sea. No visibility below. Do not know if still flying over sea. Report if storm extends interior." . . .

> Buenos Aires transmitted a reply.
>
> "Storm covers all interior. How much gasoline left?"
>
> "Half an hour."
>
> These words sped from post to post back to Buenos Aires. The plane was doomed to plunge in less than half an hour into a hurricane that would smash it to earth. . . .

Today, airplanes are safer than cars and we are shocked when we hear of a crash. But in the 1920s, when regular airline service began, air travel was dangerous. Airplanes, many of them converted World War I bombers, were made of wood and cloth, with open cockpits for the pilot and navigator and wicker chairs for passengers. They had a compass, an altimeter, and a radio. Pilots located their position by looking for towns and railroad tracks. At night and in cloudy weather, they often got lost. And yet, with these machines they conquered the skies.

Source: Antoine de Saint-Exupéry, *Vol de nuit* (Paris: Gallimard, 1939), 147–149.

An Early Passenger Plane After World War I, aviators and aircraft manufacturers turned their attention to civil aviation, such as air-mail service, crop dusting, and carrying passengers. This British-made De Havilland-34 bi-plane, photographed before 1924, was designed to carry up to ten passengers. (Mary Evans Picture Library/The Image Works)

out of an estimated 2,100 films produced worldwide, 510 were made in the United States and 750 in Japan. But by then the United States had introduced the first "talking" motion picture, *The Jazz Singer* (1927), which changed all the rules.

The number of Americans who went to see their favorite stars in thrilling adventures and heart-breaking romances rose from 40 million in 1922 to 100 million in 1930, at a time when the population of the country was about 120 million. Europeans had the technology and the art but neither the wealth nor the huge market of the United States. Hollywood studios began the diffusion of American culture that has continued to this day.

Health and hygiene were also part of the cult of modernity. Advances in medicine—some learned in the war—saved many lives. Wounds were regularly disinfected, and x-ray machines helped diagnose fractures. Since the late nineteenth century scientists had known that disease-causing bacteria could be transmitted through contaminated water, spoiled food, or fecal matter. After the war cities built costly water supply and sewage treatment systems. By the 1920s indoor plumbing and flush toilets were becoming common even in working-class neighborhoods.

Interest in cleanliness altered private life. Doctors and home economists bombarded women with warnings and advice on how to banish germs. Soap and appliance manufacturers filled women's magazines with advertisements for products to help housewives keep their family's homes and clothing spotless and their meals fresh and wholesome. The decline in infant mortality and improvements in general health and life expectancy in this period owe as much to the cult of cleanliness as to advances in medicine.

Technology and the Environment

Two new technologies—the skyscraper and the automobile—transformed the urban environment even more radically than the railroad had done in the nineteenth century. At the end of the nineteenth century architects had begun to design ever-higher buildings using load-bearing steel frames and passenger elevators. Major corporations in Chicago and New York competed to build the most daring buildings in the world, such as New York's fifty-five-story Woolworth Building (1912) and Chicago's thirty-four-story Tribune Tower (1923). A building boom in the late 1920s produced dozens of skyscrapers, culminating with the eighty-six-story, 1,239-foot (377-meter) Empire State Building in New York, completed in 1932.

European cities restricted the height of buildings to protect their architectural heritage; Paris forbade buildings over 56 feet (17 meters) high. In innovative designs, however, European architects led the way. In the 1920s the Swiss architect Charles Edouard Jeanneret (1887–1965), known as Le Corbusier°, outlined a new approach to architecture that featured simplicity of form, absence of surface ornamentation, easy manufacture, and inexpensive materials. Other architects—including the Finn Eero Saarinen, the Germans Ludwig Mies van der Rohe° and Walter Gropius, and the American Frank Lloyd Wright—also contributed their own designs to create what became known as the International Style.

While central business districts were reaching for the sky, outlying areas were spreading far into the countryside, thanks to the automobile. The assembly line pioneered by Henry Ford mass-produced vehicles in ever-greater volume and at falling prices. By 1929 the United States had one car for every five people, five-sixths of the world's automobiles. Far from being blamed for their exhaust emissions, automobiles were praised as the solution to urban pollution. As cars replaced carts and carriages, horses disappeared from city streets, as did tons of manure.

The most important environmental effect of automobiles was suburban sprawl. Middle-class families could now live in single-family homes too spread apart to be served by public transportation. By the late 1920s paved roads rivaled rail networks both in length and in the surface they occupied. As middle- and working-class families bought cars, cities acquired rings of automobile suburbs. Los Angeles, the first true automobile city, consisted of suburbs spread over hundreds of square miles and linked together by broad avenues. In sections of the city where streetcar lines went out of business, the automobile, at first a plaything for the wealthy, became a necessity for commuters. Many Americans saw Los Angeles as the portent of a glorious future in which everyone would have a car; only a few foresaw the congestion and pollution that would ensue.

Technological advances also transformed rural environments. Automobile owners quickly developed an interest in "motoring"—driving their vehicles out into the country on weekends or on holiday trips. Farmers began buying cars and light trucks, using them to transport produce as well as passengers. Governments obliged by building new roads and paving old ones to make automobile travel smoother and safer.

Le Corbusier (luh cor-booz-YEH)
Ludwig Mies van der Rohe (LOOD-vig MEES fon der ROW-uh)

Until the 1920s horses remained the predominant source of energy for pulling plows and reapers and powering threshing machines on American farms. Only the wealthiest farmers could afford the slow and costly steam tractors. In 1915 Ford introduced a gasoline-powered tractor, and by the mid-1920s these versatile machines began replacing horses. Larger farms profited most from this innovation, while small farmers sold their land and moved to the cities. Tractors and other expensive equipment hastened the transforma-tion of agriculture from family enterprises to the large agribusinesses of today.

In India, Australia, and the western United States, where there was little virgin rain-watered land left to culti-vate, engineers built dams and canals to irrigate dry lands. Dams offered the added advantage of producing electric-ity, for which there was a booming demand. The immedi-ate benefits of irrigation—land, food, and electricity—far outweighed such distant consequences as salt deposits on irrigated lands and harm to wildlife.

COMPARATIVE PERSPECTIVES

In the late 1920s it seemed as though the victors in the Great War might reestablish the prewar prosperity and European dominance of the globe. But the spirit of the 1920s was not real peace; instead it was the eye of a hurricane.

The Great War caused a major realignment among the nations of the world. France and Britain, the two leading colonial powers, emerged economically weakened despite their victory. The war brought defeat and humiliation to Germany but did not reduce its military or industrial poten-tial. It destroyed the old regime and the aristoc-racy of Russia, leading to civil war and revolution from which the victorious powers sought to iso-late themselves. Two other old empires—the Aus-tro-Hungarian and the Ottoman—were divided into many smaller and weaker nations.

Only two countries benefited from the war. Japan took advantage of the European conflict to develop its industries and press its demands on a China weakened by domestic turmoil and social unrest. The United States emerged as the most prosperous and potentially most powerful nation, restrained only by the isolationist senti-ments of many Americans.

In the Middle East, the fall of the Ottoman Empire awakened aspirations of nationhood among the Turkish and Arab inhabitants and Jewish immigrants. These aspirations were thwarted when France and Great Britain tried to impose their rule upon the former Ottoman lands, causing conflicts and bitter enmities.

SUMMARY

○— What led to the outbreak of the First World War?

○— How did the war lead to revolution in Russia?

○— What role did the war play in eroding European dominance in the world?

○— Why did China and Japan follow such divergent paths in this period?

○— How did the Middle East change as a result of the war?

○— How did European and North American society and technology change in the aftermath of the war?

Online Study Center
ACE the Test

In 1914 the great powers of Europe had not had a major conflict in decades and believed a war would be quick and victorious. Each of the two alliances they formed—the Central Powers and the Entente—was locked into a rigid timetable of mobilizations and railroad schedules. When competing nationalisms in the Balkans triggered a conflict between Serbia and Austria-Hungary, the alliances quickly drew Russia, Germany, France, and Britain into the conflict.

Of all the European powers, Russia was the least prepared for war. Chaotic mobilization and a string of defeats disrupted the economy, causing shortages of food and other essential goods. As the war progressed, soldiers began to desert, farmers rose up against their landlords, city women demanded bread, and the government lost control of the army and the population. The moderate government that replaced the tsar in March 1917 could neither satisfy the people nor pursue the war. Its failure allowed the Bolsheviks to overthrow it in a second revolution in November.

The war caused the defeat of Germany and the collapse of the once-powerful Russian, Austro-Hungarian, and Ottoman Empires. France, Great Britain, and Italy expected to reap the benefits of victory and expand their empires at the expense of the defeated. However, the victorious Allies, with the exception of the United States, which withdrew to the Western Hemisphere, were exhausted and impoverished by the war and had lost the will to fight in colonial wars. Meanwhile, the idea of self-determination had spread to the Middle East and Asia, where nationalist politicians and their followers were determined to resist European dominance.

Though united by a common civilization, China and Japan reacted to the West in opposite ways. After 1868, Japan established a strong government and built up an industrial economy comparable to that of Europe. Meanwhile China, long ruled by the Qing dynasty, erupted after 1911 in civil wars in which warlords and political factions vied for power. The Japanese military and major industries seized the opportunity of Europe's involvement in the Great War to build up Japan's economy at China's expense.

After the war, France and Britain expected to divide up the Arab lands of the former Ottoman Empire between them. In Anatolia, the heartland of the Ottoman Empire, a movement for national unity led by Kemal Atatürk created a Turkish republic that fought foreign encroachment and expelled the Greek Christian population. In the predominantly Arab regions of western Asia the population resisted the Europeans. An influx of Jews into Palestine provoked a violent reaction from the Muslim Palestinians, which their British overlords found hard to control.

The war challenged social traditions in many ways. Many women who had participated in the war effort remained in the work force and demanded voting and other rights. Governments took on new responsibilities for education, public health, and social welfare. Automobiles, movies, and radio broadcasts were eagerly adopted by western Europeans and North Americans, and aviation aroused tremendous enthusiasm. Advances in the sciences, especially in physics and psychology, undermined the old cultural certainties, while birth control and family planning provoked considerable opposition from traditionalists.

KEY TERMS

Western Front   p. 850
Faisal   p. 853
Theodore Herzl   p. 853
Balfour Declaration   p. 853
Bolsheviks   p. 854
Vladimir Lenin   p. 854
Woodrow Wilson   p. 854
Fourteen Points   p. 855

League of Nations   p. 856
Treaty of Versailles   p. 856
New Economic Policy   p. 858
Sun Yat-sen   p. 861
Yuan Shikai   p. 861
Guomindang   p. 861
Chiang Kai-shek   p. 862
mandate system   p. 862

Atatürk   p. 863
Margaret Sanger   p. 869
Max Planck   p. 869
Albert Einstein   p. 869
Sigmund Freud   p. 869
Wilbur and Orville Wright   p. 869

Online Study Center
Improve Your Grade
Flashcards

SUGGESTED READING

Bernadotte Schmitt and Harold C. Bedeler, *The World in the Crucible, 1914–1918* (1984), and John Keegan, *The First World War* (1999), are two engaging overviews of World War I. Imanuel Geiss, *July 1914: The Outbreak of the First World War* (1967), argues that Germany caused the conflict. Barbara Tuchman's *The Guns of August* (1962) and Alexander Solzhenitsyn's *August 1914* (1972) recount the first month of the war in detail. Keegan's *The Face of Battle* (1976) vividly describes the Battle of the Somme from the soldiers' perspective. On the technology of warfare see William H. McNeill, *The Pursuit of Power: Technology, Armed Force, and Society* (1982), and John Ellis, *The Social History of the Machine Gun* (1975). The role of women and the home front is the subject of essays in Margaret Higonnet et al., eds., *Behind the Lines: Gender and the Two World Wars* (1987), and sections of Lynn Weiner, *From Working Girl to Working Mother* (1985). The definitive work on the flu epidemic is Alfred W. Crosby, *America's Forgotten Pandemic: The Influenza of 1918* (1989). Two famous novels about the war are Erich Maria Remarque's *All Quiet on the Western Front* (1928) and Robert Graves's *Goodbye to All That* (1929). Ernest Jünger, *Storm of Steel* (1920), describes the war more favorably. The war in English literature is the subject of Paul Fussell, *The Great War and Modern Memory* (1975).

For the background to the Russian Revolution read Theodore von Laue's *Why Lenin? Why Stalin?* 2nd ed. (1971); but see also Richard Pipes, *The Russian Revolution* (1990), and Orlando Figes, *A People's Tragedy: The Russian Revolution, 1891–1924* (1996). The classic eyewitness account of the Revolution is John Reed's *Ten Days That Shook the World* (1919). On gender issues see Wendy Goldman, *Women, the State, and Revolution: Soviet Family Policy and Social Life, 1917–1936* (1993). The best-known novel about the Revolution and civil war is Boris Pasternak's *Doctor Zhivago* (1958).

John Maynard Keynes's *The Economic Consequences of the Peace* (1920) is a classic critique of the Paris Peace Conference. Arno Mayer's *Political Origins of the New Diplomacy, 1917–1918* (1959) analyzes the tensions and failures of great-power politics.

The 1920s are discussed in Raymond Sontag's *A Broken World, 1919–1939* (1971).

The best recent book on Japan in the twentieth century is Daikichi Irokawa's *The Age of Hirohito: In Search of Modern Japan* (1995). See also Richard Storry, *A History of Modern Japan* (1982), and Tessa Morris-Suzuki, *The Technological Transformation of Japan* (1994). In the large and fast-growing literature on twentieth-century China, two general introductions are especially useful: John K. Fairbank, *The Great Chinese Revolution, 1800–1985* (1986), and Jonathan Spence, *The Search for Modern China* (1990). On the warlord and Guomindang periods see Lucien Bianco, *Origins of the Chinese Revolution, 1915–1949* (1971).

On the war and its aftermath in the Middle East see David Fromkin, *A Peace to End All Peace* (1989), and M. E. Yapp, *The Near East Since the First World War* (1991). Bernard Lewis, *The Emergence of Modern Turkey* (1968), is a good introduction. On Africa in this period see A. Adu Boahen, ed., *Africa Under Colonial Domination, 1880–1935*, vol. 7 of the *UNESCO General History of Africa* (1985), and A. D. Roberts, ed., *Cambridge History of Africa*, vol. 7, *1905–1940* (1986).

The cultural transformation of Europe is captured in H. Stuart Hughes, *Consciousness and Society: The Reorientation of European Social Thought, 1890–1930* (1958). The towering intellectuals of that era are the subject of Peter Gay, *Freud: A Life for Our Time* (1988), and Abraham Pais, *Subtle Is the Lord: The Science and Life of Albert Einstein* (1982). Three books capture the enthusiastic popular response to technological innovations: David E. Nye, *Electrifying America: Social Meanings of a New Technology* (1990); Peter Fritzsche, *A Nation of Fliers: German Aviation and the Popular Imagination* (1992); and the sweeping overview by Thomas Hughes, *American Genesis: A Century of Invention and Technological Enthusiasm, 1870–1970* (1989). On the role of women is this period, see Ellen DuBois, *Woman Suffrage and Women's Rights* (1998); Sheila Rowbotham, *A Century of Women: The History of Women in Britain and the United States* (1997); and Renate Bridenthal, Claudia Koonz, and Susan Stuard, eds., *Becoming Visible: Women in European History* (1987).

German Dive-Bomber over Eastern Europe
A German Messerschmidt Bf-110 fighter plane attacks a Soviet troop convoy on the Eastern Front.   (akg-images)

- How did the Soviet Union change under Stalin, and at what cost?

- What caused the Depression, and what effects did it have on the world?

- How did fascism in Italy and Germany lead to the Second World War?

- What were the economic reasons behind Japan's invasion of Manchuria?

- How was the war fought, and why did Japan and Germany lose?

- How did science and technology change the nature of warfare?

30

THE COLLAPSE OF THE OLD ORDER, 1929–1949

CHAPTER OUTLINE

The Stalin Revolution

The Depression

The Rise of Fascism

East Asia, 1931–1945

The Second World War

The Character of Warfare

DIVERSITY AND DOMINANCE: Women, Family Values, and the Russian Revolution

ENVIRONMENT AND TECHNOLOGY: The Enigma Machine

B efore the First World War the Italian futurist poet Filippo Marinetti exalted violence as noble and manly: "We want to glorify war, the world's only hygiene—militarism, deed, destroyer of anarchisms, the beautiful ideas that are death-bringing, and the subordination of women." His friend Gabriele d'Annunzio added: "If it is a crime to incite citizens to violence, I shall boast of this crime." Poets are sometimes more prescient than they imagine.

In the nineteenth century the great powers had created a world order with three dimensions. Their constitutional governments were manipulated by politicians—some liberal, some conservative— through appeals to popular nationalism. Internationally, the world

Online Study Center

This icon will direct you to interactive activities and study materials on the website: *college.hmco.com/pic/bulliet4e.*

order relied on the maintenance of empires, formal or informal, by military or economic means. And the global economy was based on free-market capitalism in which the industrial countries exchanged manufactured goods for the agricultural and mineral products of the nonindustrial world.

After the trauma of World War I the world seemed to return to what U.S. president Warren Harding called "normalcy": prosperity in Europe and America, European colonialism in Asia and Africa, American domination of Latin America, and peace almost everywhere. But in1929 the normalcy of the twenties fell apart. As the Great Depression spread around the world, governments turned against one another in a desperate attempt to protect their people's livelihood. Even wholly agricultural nations and colonies suffered as markets for their exports shriveled.

Most survivors of the war had learned to abhor violence. For a few, however, war and domination became a creed, a goal, and a solution to their problems. The Japanese military tried to save their country from the Depression by conquering China, which erupted in revolution. In Germany the Depression reawakened resentments against the victors of the Great War; people who blamed their troubles on Communists and Jews turned to the Nazis, who promised to save German society by crushing others. In the Soviet Union Stalin used energetic and murderous means to force his country into a Communist version of the Industrial Revolution.

As the old order collapsed, the world was engulfed by a second Great War, one far more global and destructive than the first. Unlike World War I, this was a war of movement in which entire countries could be conquered in a matter of days or weeks. It was also a war of machines: fighter planes and bombers that targeted civilians, tanks, aircraft carriers, and, finally, atomic bombs that obliterated entire cities.

At the end of World War II much of Europe and East Asia lay in ruins, and millions of destitute refugees sought safety in other lands. The colonial powers were either defeated or so weakened that they could no longer hold on to their empires when Asian and African peoples asserted their desire for independence.

THE STALIN REVOLUTION

During the 1920s other countries ostracized the Soviet Union as it recovered from the Revolutions of 1917 and the civil war that followed (see Chapter 29). After Stalin achieved total mastery over this huge nation in early 1929, he led it through another revolution—an economic and social transformation that turned it into a great industrial and military power and intensified both admiration for and fear of communism throughout the world.

Five-Year Plans

Joseph Stalin (1879–1953) was born Joseph Vissarionovich Dzhugashvili into the family of a poor shoemaker. Before becoming a revolutionary, he studied for the priesthood. Under the name "Stalin" (Russian for "man of steel") he played a small part in the Revolutions of 1917. He was a hard-working and skillful administrator who rose within the party bureaucracy and filled its upper ranks with men loyal to himself. By 1927 he had ousted Leon Trotsky, the best-known revolutionary after Lenin, from the party. He then proceeded to squeeze all other rivals out of positions of power, make himself absolute dictator, and transform Soviet society.

Stalin's ambition was to turn the Union of Soviet Socialist Republics (USSR) into an industrial nation. Industrialization was to serve a different purpose in the USSR than in other countries, however. It was not expected to produce consumer goods for a mass market, as in Britain and the United States, or to enrich individuals. Instead, its aim was to increase the power of the Communist Party domestically and the power of the Soviet Union in relation to other countries.

By building up Russia's industry, Stalin was determined to prevent a repetition of the humiliating defeat Russia had suffered at the hands of Germany in 1917. His goal was to quintuple the output of electricity and double that of heavy industry—iron, steel, coal, and machinery—in five years. To do so, he devised the first of a series of **Five-Year Plans**, a system of centralized control copied from the German experience of World War I.

Beginning in October 1928 the Communist Party and government created whole industries and cities from scratch, then trained millions of peasants to work in the new factories, mines, and offices. In every way except actual fighting, Stalin's Russia resembled a nation at war.

Rapid industrialization hastened environmental changes. Hydroelectric dams turned rivers into strings of reservoirs. Roads, canals, and railroad tracks cut the landscape. Forests and grassland were turned into farmland.

C H R O N O L O G Y

	United States, Europe, and North Africa	Asia and the Pacific
1920s	**1928** Stalin introduces Five Year Plans and the collectivization of agriculture	
1930	**1929** Great Depression begins in U.S.	**1931** Japanese forces occupy Manchuria
	1931 Great Depression reaches Europe	
	1933 Hitler comes to power in Germany	**1934–1935** Mao leads Communists on Long March
1935		
	1936 Hitler invades the Rhineland	**1937** Japanese troops invade China, conquer coastal provinces; Chiang Kai-shek flees to Sichuan
	1939 (Sept. 1) German forces invade Poland	**1937–1938** Japanese troops take Nanjing
1940	**1940 (March–April)** German forces conquer Denmark, Norway, the Netherlands, and Belgium	
	1940 (May–June) German forces conquer France	
	1940 (June–Sept.) Battle of Britain	
	1941 (June 21) German forces invade USSR	**1941 (Dec. 7)** Japanese aircraft bomb Pearl Harbor
	1942–1943 Allies and Germany battle for control of North Africa	**1942 (Jan.–March)** Japanese conquer Thailand, Philippines, Malaya
		1942 (June) United States Navy defeats Japan at Battle of Midway
	1943 Soviet victory in Battle of Stalingrad	
	1943–1944 Red Army slowly pushes Wehrmacht back to Germany	
	1944 (June 6) D-day: U.S., British, and Canadian troops land in Normandy	
1945	**1945 (May 7)** Germany surrenders	**1945 (Aug. 6)** United States drops atomic bomb on Hiroshima
		1945 (Aug. 14) Japan surrenders
		1945–1949 Civil war in China
		1949 (Oct. 1) Communist defeat Guomindang; Mao proclaims People's Republic

From an environmental perspective, the outcome of the Five-Year Plans resembled the transformation that had occurred in the United States and Canada a few decades earlier.

Collectivization of Agriculture

Since the Soviet Union was still a predominantly agrarian country, the only way to pay for these massive investments, provide the labor, and feed the millions of new industrial workers was to squeeze the peasantry. Stalin therefore proceeded with the most radical social experiment conceived up to that time: the collectivization of agriculture.

Collectivization meant consolidating small private farms into vast collectives and making the farmers work together in commonly owned fields. Each collective was expected to supply the government with a fixed amount of food and distribute what was left among its members. Machine Tractor Stations leased agricultural machinery to several farms in exchange for the government's share of the crop. Collectives were to become outdoor factories where food was manufactured through the techniques of mass production and the application of machinery.

The Collectivization of Soviet Agriculture   One of the goals of collectivization was to introduce modern farm machinery. This poster shows delighted farmers operating new tractors and threshers.   (David King Collection)

Collectivization was an attempt to replace what Lenin called the peasants' "petty bourgeois" attitudes with an industrial way of life, the only one Communists respected. Collectivization was expected to bring the peasants under government control so they never again could withhold food supplies, as they had done during the Russian civil war of 1918–1921.

When collectivization was announced, the government mounted a massive propaganda campaign and sent party members into the countryside to enlist the farmers' support. At first all seemed to go well, but soon *kulaks*° ("fists"), the better-off peasants, began to resist giving up all their property. When soldiers came to force them into collectives at gunpoint, the kulaks burned their own crops, smashed their own equipment, and slaughtered their own

kulaks (COO-lox)

livestock. Within a few months they slaughtered half of the Soviet Union's horses and cattle and two-thirds of the sheep and goats. In retaliation, Stalin ruthlessly ordered the "liquidation of kulaks as a class" and incited the poor peasants to attack their wealthier neighbors. Over 8 million kulaks were arrested. Many were executed. The rest were sent to slave labor camps, where most starved to death.

The peasants who were left had been the least successful before collectivization and proved to be the least competent after. Many were sent to work in factories. The rest were forbidden to leave their farms. With half of their draft animals gone, they could not plant or harvest enough to meet the swelling demands of the cities. Yet government agents took whatever they could find, leaving little or nothing for the farmers themselves. After bad harvests in 1933 and 1934, a famine swept through the countryside, killing some 5 million people, about one in every twenty farmers.

Stalin's second Five-Year Plan, designed to run from 1933 to 1937, was originally intended to increase the output of consumer goods. But when the Nazis took over Germany in 1933 (see below), Stalin changed the plan to emphasize heavy industries that could produce armaments. Between 1927 and 1937 the Soviet output of metals and machines increased fourteen-fold while consumer goods became scarce and food was rationed. After a decade of Stalinism, the Soviet people were more poorly clothed, fed, and housed than they had been during the years of the New Economic Policy.

Terror and Opportunities

The 1930s brought both terror and new opportunities to the Soviet people. The forced pace of industrialization, the collectivization of agriculture, and the uprooting of millions of people could be accomplished only under duress. To prevent any possible resistance or rebellion, the NKVD, Stalin's secret police force, created a climate of suspicion and fear. The terror that pervaded the country was a reflection of Stalin's own paranoia, for he distrusted everyone and feared for his life.

As early as 1930 Stalin had hundreds of engineers and technicians arrested on trumped-up charges of counterrevolutionary ideas and sabotage. Three years later, he expelled a million members of the Communist Party—one-third of the membership—on similar charges. He then turned on his most trusted associates.

In December 1934 Sergei Kirov, the party boss of Leningrad (formerly called Petrograd), was assassinated, perhaps on Stalin's orders. Stalin made a public display of mourning Kirov while blaming others for the crime. He then ordered a series of spectacular purge trials in which he accused most of Lenin's associates of "antiparty activities," the worst form of treason. In 1937 he had his eight top generals and many lesser officers charged with treason and executed, leaving the Red Army dangerously weakened. He even executed the head of the dreaded NKVD, which was enforcing the terror. Under torture or psychological pressure, almost all the accused confessed to the "crimes" they were charged with.

While "Old Bolsheviks" and high officials were being put on trial, terror spread steadily downward. The government regularly made demands that people could not meet, so everyone was guilty of breaking some regulation or other. People from all walks of life were arrested, sometimes on mere suspicion or because of a false accusation by a jealous coworker or neighbor, sometimes for expressing a doubt or working too hard or not hard enough, sometimes for being related to someone previously arrested, sometimes for no reason at all. Millions of people were sentenced without trials. At the height of the terror, some 8 million were sent to *gulags°* (labor camps), where perhaps a million died each year of exposure or malnutrition. To its victims the terror seemed capricious and random. Yet it turned a sullen and resentful people into docile hard-working subjects of the party.

In spite of the fear and hardships, many Soviet citizens supported Stalin's regime. Suddenly, with so many people gone and new industries and cities being built everywhere, there were opportunities for those who remained, especially the poor and the young. Women entered careers and jobs previously closed to them, becoming steelworkers, physicians, and office managers; but they retained their household and child-rearing duties, receiving little help from men (see Diversity and Dominance: Women, Family Values, and the Russian Revolution). People who moved to the cities, worked enthusiastically, and asked no questions could hope to rise into the upper ranks of the Communist Party, the military, the government, or the professions—where the privileges and rewards were many.

Stalin's brutal methods helped the Soviet Union industrialize faster than any country had ever done. By the late 1930s the USSR was the world's third largest industrial power, after the United States and Germany. To foreign observers it seemed to be booming with construction projects, production increases, and labor shortages. Even anti-Communist observers admitted that only a planned economy subject to strict government control could avoid the Depression. To millions of Soviet citizens who took pride in the new strength of their country, and to many foreigners who contrasted conditions in the Soviet Union with the unemployment and despair in the West, Stalin's achievement seemed worth any price.

---

gulag (GOO-log)

THE DEPRESSION

On October 24, 1929—"Black Thursday"—the New York stock market went into a dive. Within days stocks had lost half their value. The fall continued for three years. Millions of investors lost money, as did the banks and brokers from whom they had borrowed the money. People with savings accounts rushed to make withdrawals, causing thousands of banks to collapse.

Economic Crisis What began as a stock-market crash soon turned into the deepest and most widespread depression in history. As consumers reduced their purchases, businesses cut production. Companies laid off thousands of workers, throwing them onto public charity. Business and government agencies laid off their female employees, arguing that men had to support families while women worked only for "pin money." Jobless men deserted their families. As farm prices fell, small farmers went bankrupt and lost their land. By mid-1932 the American economy had shrunk by half, and unemployment had risen to an unprecedented 25 percent of the work force. Many observers thought that free-enterprise capitalism was doomed.

In 1930 the U.S. government, hoping to protect American industries from foreign competition, imposed the Smoot-Hawley tariff, the highest import duty in American history. In retaliation, other countries raised their tariffs in a wave of "beggar thy neighbor" protectionism. The result was crippled export industries and shrinking world trade. While global industrial production declined by 36 percent between 1929 and 1932, world trade dropped by a breathtaking 62 percent.

Depression in Industrial Nations Frightened by the stock-market collapse, the New York banks called in their loans to Germany and Austria. Without American money, Germany and Austria stopped paying reparations to France and Britain, which then could not repay their war loans to America. By 1931 the Depression had spread to Europe. Governments canceled reparations payments and war loans, but it was too late to save the world economy.

Though their economies stagnated, France and Britain weathered the Depression by making their colonial empires purchase their products rather than the products of other countries. Nations that relied on exports to pay for imported food and fuel, in particular Japan and

Women, Family Values, and the Russian Revolution

The Bolsheviks were of two minds on the subject of women. Following in the footsteps of Marx, Engels, and other revolutionaries, they were opposed to bourgeois morality and to the oppression of women, especially working-class women, under capitalism, with its attendant evils of prostitution, sexual abuse, and the division of labor. But what to put in its place?

Alexandra Kollontai was the most outspoken of the Bolsheviks on the subject of women's rights and the equality of the sexes. Before and during the Russian Revolution, she advocated the liberation of women, the replacement of housework by communal kitchens and laundries, and divorce on demand. Under socialism, love, sex, and marriage would be entirely equal, reciprocal, and free of economic obligations. Childbearing would be encouraged, but children would be raised communally, rather than individually by their fathers and mothers: "The worker mother . . . must remember that there are henceforth only our children, those of the communist state, the common possession of all workers."

In a lecture she gave at Sverdlov University in 1921, Kollontai declared:

. . . it is important to preserve not only the interests of the woman but also the life of the child, and this is to be done by giving the woman the opportunity to combine labour and maternity. Soviet power tries to create a situation where a woman does not have to cling to a man she has learned to loathe only because she has nowhere else to go with her children, and where a woman alone does not have to fear for her life and the life of her child. In the labour republic it is not the philanthropists with their humiliating charity but the workers and peasants, fellow-creators of the new society, who hasten to help the working woman and strive to lighten the burden of motherhood. The woman who bears the trials and tribulations of reconstructing the economy on an equal footing with the man, and who participated in the civil war, has a right to demand that in this most important hour of her life, at the moment when she presents society with a new

member, the labour republic, the collective, should take upon itself the job of caring for the future of the new citizen. . . . I would like to say a few words about a question which is closely connected with the problem of maternity—the question of abortion, and Soviet Russia's attitude toward it. On 20 November 1920 the labour republic issued a law abolishing the penalties that had been attached to abortion. What is the reason behind this new attitude? Russia after all suffers not from an overproduction of living labour but rather from a lack of it. Russia is thinly, not densely populated. Every unit of labour power is precious. Why then have we declared abortion to be no longer a criminal offence? Hypocrisy and bigotry are alien to proletarian politics. Abortion is a problem connected with the problem of maternity, and likewise derives from the insecure position of women (we are not speaking here of the bourgeois class, where abortion has other reasons—the reluctance to "divide" an inheritance, to suffer the slightest discomfort, to spoil one's figure or miss a few months of the season, etc.).

Abortion exists and flourishes everywhere, and no laws or punitive measures have succeeded in rooting it out. A way round the law is always found. But "secret help" only cripples women; they become a burden on the labour government, and the size of the labour force is reduced. Abortion, when carried out under proper medical conditions, is less harmful and dangerous, and the woman can get back to work quicker. Soviet power realizes that the need for abortion will only disappear on the one hand when Russia has a broad and developed network of institutions protecting motherhood and providing social education, and on the other hand when women understand that *childbirth is a social obligation*; Soviet power has therefore allowed abortion to be performed openly and in clinical conditions.

Besides the large-scale development of motherhood protection, the task of labour Russia is to strengthen in women the healthy instinct of motherhood, to make motherhood and labour for the collective compatible and thus do away with the need for abortion. This is the approach of the labour republic to the question of abortion, which still faces women in the bourgeois countries in all its magnitude. In these countries women are exhausted by the dual burden of hired labour for capital and motherhood. In Soviet Russia the working woman and peasant woman are helping the Communist Party to build a new society and to undermine the old way of life that has enslaved women. As soon as woman is viewed as being essentially a labour unit, the key to the solution of the complex question of maternity can be found. In bourgeois society, where housework complements the system of capitalist economy and private property creates a stable basis for the isolated form of the family, there is no way out for the working woman. The emancipation of women can only be completed when a fundamental transformation of living is effected; and life-styles will change only with the fundamental transformation of all production and the establishment of a communist economy. The revolution in everyday life is unfolding before our very eyes, and in this process the liberation of women is being introduced in practice.

Fifteen years later Joseph Stalin reversed the Soviet policy on abortion.

The published draft of the law prohibiting abortion and providing material assistance to mothers has provoked a lively reaction throughout the country. It is being heatedly discussed by tens of millions of people and there is no doubt that it will serve as a further strengthening of the Soviet family. Parents' responsibility for the education of their children will be increased and a blow will be dealt at the lighthearted, negligent attitude toward marriage.

When we speak of strengthening the Soviet family, we are speaking precisely of the struggle against the survivals of a bourgeois attitude towards marriage, women, and children. So-called "free love" and all disorderly sex life are bourgeois through and through, and have nothing to do with either socialist principles or the ethics and standards of conduct of the Soviet citizens. Socialist doctrine shows this, and it is proved by life itself.

The elite of our country, the best of the Soviet youth, are as a rule also excellent family men who dearly love their children. And vice versa: the man who does not take marriage seriously, and abandons his children to the whims of fate, is usually also a bad worker and a poor member of society.

Fatherhood and motherhood have long been virtues in this country. This can be seen at first glance, without searching enquiry. Go through the parks and streets of Moscow or of any other town in the Soviet Union on a holiday, and you will see not a few young men walking with pink-cheeked, well-fed babies in their arms. . . .

It is impossible even to compare the present state of the family with that which obtained before the Soviet regime—so great has been the improvement towards greater stability and, above all, greater humanity and goodness. The single fact that millions of women have become economically independent and are no longer at the mercy of men's whims, speaks volumes.

Compare, for instance, the modern woman collective farmer who sometimes earns more than her husband, with the pre-revolutionary peasant woman who completely depended on her husband and was a slave in the household. Has not this fundamentally changed family relations, has it not rationalized and strengthened the family? The very motives for setting up a family, for getting married, have changed for the better, have been cleansed of atavistic and barbaric elements. Marriage has ceased to be a matter of sell-and-buy. Nowadays a girl from a collective farm is not given away (or should we say "sold away"?) by her father, for now she is her own mistress, and no one can give her away. She will marry the man she loves. . . .

We alone have all the conditions under which a working woman can fulfill her duties as a citizen and as a mother responsible for the birth and early upbringing of her children.

A woman without children merits our pity, for she does not know the full joy of life. Our Soviet women, full-blooded citizens of the freest country in the world, have been given the bliss of motherhood. We must safeguard the family and raise and rear healthy Soviet heroes!

QUESTIONS FOR ANALYSIS

1. How does Kollontai expect women to be both workers and mothers without depending on a man? How would Soviet society make this possible?

2. Why does Alexandra Kollontai advocate the legalization of abortion in Soviet Russia? Does she view abortion as a permanent right or as a temporary necessity?

3. Why does Stalin characterize a "lighthearted, negligent attitude toward marriage" and "all disorderly sex life" as "bourgeois through and through"?

4. How does Stalin's image of the Soviet family differ from Kollontai's? Are his views a variation of her views, or the opposite?

5. Do the views of Kollontai and Stalin on the role of women represent a diversity of opinions within the Communist Party, or the dominance of one view over others?

Source: First selection from Alexandra Kollontai, "The Labour of Women in the Revolution of the Economy," in *Selected Writings of Alexandra Kollontai,* translated by Alix Holt (Lawrence Hill Books, 1977), 148–149. Reprinted with permission. Second selection from Joseph Stalin, *Law on the Abolition of Legal Abortion* (1936).

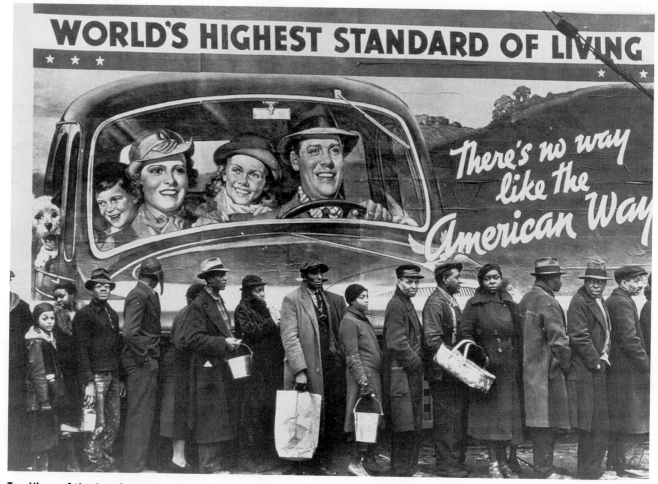

Two Views of the American Way   In this classic photograph, *Life* magazine photographer Margaret Bourke-White captured the contrast between advertisers' view of the ideal American family and the reality of bread lines for the poor in a land of plenty.   (Time Life Pictures/Getty Images)

Germany, suffered much more. In Germany unemployment reached 6 million by 1932, twice as high as in Britain. Half the German population lived in poverty. Thousands of teachers and engineers were laid off, and those who kept their jobs saw their salaries cut and their living standards fall. In Japan the burden of the Depression fell hardest on the farmers and fishermen, who saw their incomes drop sharply.

This massive economic upheaval had profound political repercussions. Nationalists everywhere called for autarchy, or independence from the world economy. Many people in capitalist countries began calling for government intervention in the economy. In the United States Franklin D. Roosevelt was elected president in 1932 on a "New Deal" platform of government programs to stimulate and revitalize the economy. Although

the American, British, and French governments intervened in their economies, they remained democratic. In Germany and Japan, as economic grievances worsened long-festering political resentments, radical leaders came to power and turned their nations into military machines, hoping to acquire, by war if necessary, empires large enough to support self-sufficient economies.

Depression in Non-industrial Regions   The Depression also spread to Asia, Africa, and Latin America, but very unevenly. In 1930 India erected a wall of import duties to protect its infant industries from foreign competition; its living standards stagnated but did not drop.

Except for its coastal regions, China was little affected by trade with other countries; as we shall see, its problems were more political than economic.

Countries that depended on exports—sugar from the Caribbean, coffee from Brazil and Colombia, wheat and beef from Argentina, tea from Ceylon and Java, tin from Bolivia, and many other products—were hard hit by the Depression. Malaya, Indochina, and the Dutch East Indies produced most of the world's natural rubber; when automobile production dropped by half in the United States and Europe, so did imports of rubber, devastating their economies. Egypt's economy, dependent on cotton exports, was also affected, and in the resulting political strife, the government became autocratic and unpopular.

Throughout Latin America unemployment and homelessness increased markedly. The industrialization of Argentina and Brazil was set back a decade or more. During the 1920s Cuba had been a playground for Americans who basked in the sun and quaffed liquor forbidden at home by Prohibition; when the Depression hit, the tourists vanished, and with them went Cuba's prosperity. Disenchanted with liberal politics, military officers seized power in several Latin American countries. Consciously imitating dictatorships emerging in Europe, they imposed authoritarian control over their economies, hoping to stimulate local industries and curb imports.

Other than the USSR, only southern Africa boomed during the 1930s. As other prices dropped, gold became relatively more valuable. Copper deposits, found in Northern Rhodesia (now Zambia) and the Belgian Congo, proved to be cheaper to mine than Chilean copper. But this mining boom benefited only a small number of European and white South African mine owners. For Africans it was a mixed blessing; mining provided jobs and cash wages to men while women stayed behind in the villages, farming, herding, and raising children without their husbands' help.

THE RISE OF FASCISM

The Russian Revolution and its Stalinist aftermath frightened property owners in Europe and North America. In the democracies of western Europe and North America, where there was little fear of Communist uprisings or electoral victories, middle- and upper-income voters took refuge in conservative politics. Political institutions in southern and central Europe, in contrast, were frail and lacked popular legitimacy. The war had turned people's hopes of victory to bitter disappointment. Many were bewildered by modernity—with its cities, factories, and department stores—which they blamed on ethnic minorities, especially Jews. In their yearning for a mythical past of family farms and small shops, increasing numbers rejected representative government and sought more dramatic solutions.

Radical politicians quickly learned to apply wartime propaganda techniques to appeal to a confused citizenry, especially young and unemployed men. They promised to use any means necessary to bring back full employment, stop the spread of communism, and achieve the territorial conquests that World War I had denied them. While defending private property from communism, they borrowed the communist model of politics: a single party and a totalitarian state with a powerful secret police that ruled by terror and intimidation.

Mussolini's Italy

The first country to seek radical answers was Italy. World War I, which had never been popular, left thousands of veterans who found neither pride in their victory nor jobs in the postwar economy. Unemployed veterans and violent youths banded together into *fasci di combattimento* (fighting units) to demand action and intimidate politicians. When workers threatened to strike, factory and property owners hired gangs of these *fascisti* to defend them.

Benito Mussolini (1883–1945) had been expelled by the Socialist Party for supporting Italy's entry into the war. A spellbinding orator, he quickly became the leader of the **Fascist Party**, which glorified warfare and the Italian nation. By 1921 the party had 300,000 members, many of whom used violent methods to repress strikes, intimidate voters, and seize municipal governments. A year later Mussolini threatened to march on Rome if he was not appointed prime minister. The government, composed of timid parliamentarians, gave in.

Mussolini proceeded to install Fascist Party members in all government jobs, crush all opposition parties, and jail anyone who criticized him. The party took over the press, public education, and youth activities and gave employers control over their workers. The Fascists lowered living standards but reduced unemployment and provided social security and public services. On the whole, they proved to be neither ruthless radicals nor competent administrators.

What Mussolini and the Fascist movement really excelled at was publicity: bombastic speeches, spectacular parades, and signs everywhere proclaiming "Il Duce° [the Leader] is always right!" Mussolini's genius was to apply the techniques of modern mass communications

---

Il Duce (eel DOO-chay)

and advertisement to political life. Movie footage and radio news bulletins galvanized the masses in ways never before done in peacetime. His techniques of whipping up public enthusiasm were not lost on other radicals. By the 1930s fascist movements had appeared in most European countries, as well as in Latin America, China, and Japan. Fascism appealed to many people who were frightened by rapid changes and the insecurity of life and placed their hopes in mass movement dominated by charismatic leaders. Of all of Mussolini's imitators, none was as sinister as Adolf Hitler.

Hitler's Germany

Germany had lost the First World War after coming very close to winning. The hyperinflation of 1923 wiped out the savings of middle-class families. Less than ten years later the Depression caused more unemployment and misery than in any other country. Millions of Germans blamed Socialists, Jews, and foreigners for their troubles. Few foresaw that they were about to get a dictatorship dedicated to war and mass murder.

Adolf Hitler (1889–1945) joined the German army in 1914 and was wounded at the front. He later looked back fondly on the clear lines of authority and the camaraderie he had experienced in battle. After the war he used his gifts as an orator to lead a political splinter group called the National Socialist German Workers' Party—**Nazis** for short. While serving a brief jail sentence he wrote *Mein Kampf*° (*My Struggle*), in which he outlined his goals and beliefs.

When it was published in 1925 *Mein Kampf* attracted little notice. Its ideas seemed so insane that almost no one took it, or its author, seriously. Hitler's ideas went far beyond ordinary nationalism. He believed that Germany should incorporate all German-speaking areas, even those in neighboring countries. He distinguished among a "master race" of Aryans (he meant Germans, Scandinavians, and Britons), a degenerate "Alpine" race of French and Italians, and an inferior race of Russian and eastern European Slavs, fit only to be slaves of the master race. He reserved his most intense hatred for Jews, on whom he blamed every disaster that had befallen Germany, especially the defeat of 1918. He glorified violence and looked forward to a future war in which the "master race" would defeat and subjugate all others.

Hitler's first goal was to repeal the humiliation and military restrictions of the Treaty of Versailles. Then he planned to annex all German-speaking territories to a greater Germany, then conquer *Lebensraum*° (room to live) at the expense of Poland and the USSR. Finally, he planned to eliminate all Jews from Europe.

From 1924 to 1930 Hitler's followers remained a tiny minority, for most Germans found his ideas too extreme. But when the Depression hit, the Nazis gained supporters among the unemployed, who believed their promises of jobs for all, and among property owners frightened by the growing popularity of Communists. In March 1933 President Hindenburg called on Hitler to become chancellor of Germany.

Once in office Hitler quickly assumed dictatorial power. He put Nazis in charge of all government agencies, educational institutions, and professional organizations. He banned all other political parties and threw their leaders into concentration camps. The Nazis deprived Jews of their citizenship and civil rights, prohibited them from marrying "Aryans," ousted them from the professions, and confiscated their property. In August 1934 Hitler proclaimed himself *Führer*° ("leader") and called Germany the "Third Reich," the third German empire after the Holy Roman Empire of medieval times and the German Empire of 1871 to 1918.

The Nazis' economic and social policies were spectacularly effective. The government undertook massive public works projects. Businesses got contracts to manufacture weapons for the armed forces. Women, who had entered the work force during and after World War I, were urged to return to "Kinder, Kirche, Küche" (children, church, kitchen), releasing jobs for men. By 1936 business was booming; unemployment was at its lowest level since the 1920s; and living standards were rising. Hitler's popularity soared because most Germans believed that their economic well-being outweighed the loss of liberty.

Online Study Center
Improve Your Grade
Interactive Map: The Growth of Nazi Germany

The Road to War, 1933–1939

Hitler's goal was not prosperity or popularity, but conquest. As soon as he came to office, he began to build up the armed forces. Meanwhile, he tested the reactions of the other powers through a series of surprise moves followed by protestations of peace.

Mein Kampf (mine compf)

Lebensraum (LAY-bens-rowm)   *Führer* (FEW-rer)

A Nazi Rally   In the years leading up to World War II, Hitler organized mass rallies at Nuremberg to whip up popular support for his regime and to indoctrinate young Germans with a martial spirit. Thousands of men in uniform marched in torch-lit parades before Hitler and his top officials.   (AP/Wide World Photos)

In 1933 Hitler withdrew Germany from the League of Nations. Two years later he announced that Germany was going to introduce conscription, build up its army, and create an air force—in violation of the Versailles treaty. Instead of protesting, Britain signed a naval agreement with Germany. The message was clear: neither Britain nor France was willing to risk war by standing up to Germany. The United States, absorbed in its domestic economic problems, turned its back on Europe but stayed actively involved in Latin America and East Asia.

In 1935, emboldened by the weakness of the democracies, Italy invaded Ethiopia, the last independent state in Africa and a member of the League of Nations. The League and the democracies protested but refused to close the Suez Canal to Italian ships or impose an oil embargo. The following year, when Hitler sent troops into the Rhineland on the borders of France and Belgium, the other powers merely protested.

By 1938 Hitler decided that his rearmament plans were far enough advanced that he could afford to escalate his demands. In March Germany invaded Austria. Most Austrians were German-speakers and accepted the annexation of their country without protest. Then came Czechoslovakia, where a German-speaking minority lived along the German border. Hitler first demanded their autonomy from Czech rule, then their annexation to Germany. Throughout the summer he threatened to go to war. At the Munich Conference of September 1938 he met with the leaders of France, Britain, and Italy, who gave him everything he wanted without consulting Czechoslovakia. Once again, Hitler learned that aggression paid off and that the democracies would always give in.

The weakness of the democracies—now called "appeasement"—ran counter to the traditional European balance of power. It had three causes. The first was the deep-seated fear of war among people who had lived through World War I. Unlike the dictators, politicians in the democracies could not ignore their constituents' yearnings for peace. Politicians and most other people believed that the threat of war might go away if they wished for peace fervently enough.

The second cause of appeasement was fear of communism among conservative politicians who were more afraid of Stalin than of Hitler, because Hitler claimed to respect Christianity and private property. Distrust of the Soviet Union prevented them from re-creating the only viable counterweight to Germany: the prewar alliance of Britain, France, and Russia.

The third cause was the very novelty of fascist tactics. Britain's prime minister Neville Chamberlain assumed that political leaders (other than the Bolsheviks) were honorable men and that an agreement was as valid as a business contract. Thus, when Hitler promised to incorporate only German-speaking people into Germany and said he had "no further territorial demands," Chamberlain believed him.

After Munich it was too late to stop Hitler, short of war. Germany and Italy signed an alliance called the Axis. In March 1939 Germany invaded what was left of Czechoslovakia. Belatedly realizing that Hitler could not be trusted, France and Britain sought Soviet help. Stalin, however, distrusted the "capitalists" as much as they distrusted him. When Hitler offered to divide Poland between Germany and the Soviet Union, Stalin accepted. The Nazi-Soviet Pact of August 23, 1939, freed Hitler from the fear of a two-front war and gave Stalin time to build up his armies. One week later, on September 1, German forces swept into Poland, and the war was on.

EAST ASIA, 1931–1945

When the Depression hit, China and the United States erected barriers against Japanese imports. The collapse of demand for silk and rice ruined thousands of Japanese farmers; to survive, many sold their daughters into prostitution while their sons flocked to the military. Ultra-nationalists, including young army officers, resented their country's dependence on foreign trade. If only Japan had a colonial empire, they thought, it would not be beholden to the rest of the world. But Europeans and Americans had already taken most potential colonies in Asia. Japan had only Korea, Taiwan, and a railroad in Manchuria. China, however, had not yet been conquered. Japanese nationalists saw the conquest of China, with its vast population and resources, as the solution to their country's problems.

| The Manchurian Incident of 1931 | Meanwhile, in China the Guomindang° was becoming stronger and preparing to challenge the Japanese presence in |

Manchuria, a province rich in coal and iron ore. Junior

officers in the Japanese army guarding the South Manchurian Railway, frustrated by the caution of their superiors, wanted to take action. In September 1931 an explosion on a railroad track, probably staged, gave them an excuse to conquer the entire province. In Tokyo weak civilian ministers were intimidated by the military. Informed after the fact, they acquiesced to the attack to avoid losing face, but privately one said: "From beginning to end the government has been utterly fooled by the army."

When Chinese students, workers, and housewives boycotted Japanese goods, Japanese troops briefly took over Shanghai, China's major industrial city, and the area around Beijing. Japan thereupon recognized the "independence" of Manchuria under the name "Manchukuo°."

The U.S. government condemned the Japanese conquest. The League of Nations refused to recognize Manchukuo and urged the Japanese to remove their troops from China. Persuaded that the Western powers would not fight, Japan simply resigned from the League.

During the next few years the Japanese built railways and heavy industries in Manchuria and northeastern China and sped up their rearmament. At home, production was diverted to the military, especially to building warships. The government grew more authoritarian, jailing thousands of dissidents. On several occasions, superpatriotic junior officers mutinied or assassinated leading political figures. The mutineers received mild punishments, and generals and admirals sympathetic to their views replaced more moderate civilian politicians.

| The Chinese and the Long March | Until the Japanese seized Manchuria, the Chinese government seemed to be consolidating its power and creating |

conditions for a national recovery. The main challenge to the government of **Chiang Kai-shek°** came from the Communists. The Chinese Communist Party was founded in 1921 by a handful of intellectuals. For several years it lived in the shadow of the Guomindang, kept there by orders of Joseph Stalin, who expected it to subvert the government from within. All its efforts to manipulate the Guomindang and to recruit members among industrial workers came to naught in 1927, when Chiang Kai-shek arrested and executed Communists and labor leaders alike. The few Communists who escaped the mass arrests fled to the remote mountains of Jiangxi°, in southeastern China.

Guomindang (gwo-min-dong)

Manchukuo (man-CHEW-coo-oh)
Chiang Kai-shek (chang kie-shek)   **Jiangxi** (jang-she)

Among them was **Mao Zedong**° (1893–1976), a farmer's son who had left home to study philosophy. He was not a contemplative thinker, but rather a man of action whose first impulse was to call for violent effort: "To be able to leap on horseback and to shoot at the same time; to go from battle to battle; to shake the mountains by one's cries, and the colors of the sky by one's roars of anger." In the early 1920s Mao discovered the works of Karl Marx, joined the Communist Party, and soon became one of its leaders.

In Jiangxi Mao began studying conditions among the peasants, in whom Communists had previously shown no interest. He planned to redistribute land from the wealthier to the poorer peasants, thereby gaining adherents for the coming struggle with the Guomindang army. In this, he was following the example of innumerable leaders of peasant rebellions over the centuries. His goal, however, was not just a nationalist revolution against the traditional government and foreign intervention, but a complete social revolution from the bottom up. Mao's reliance on the peasantry was a radical departure from Marxist-Leninist ideology, which stressed the backwardness of the peasants and pinned its hopes on industrial workers. Mao therefore had to be careful to cloak his pragmatic tactics in Communist rhetoric in order to allay the suspicions of Stalin and his agents.

Mao was also an advocate of women's equality. Radical ideas such as those of Margaret Sanger, the American leader of the birth-control movement, and the feminist play *A Doll's House* by the Norwegian playwright Henrik Ibsen inspired veterans of the May Fourth Movement (see Chapter 29) and young women attending universities and medical or nursing schools. Before 1927 the Communists had organized the women who worked in Shanghai's textile mills, the most exploited of all Chinese workers. Later, in their mountain stronghold in Jiangxi, they organized women farmers, allowed divorce, and banned arranged marriages and footbinding. But they did not admit women to leadership positions, for the party was still run by men whose primary task was warfare.

The Guomindang army pursued the Communists into the mountains, building small forts throughout the countryside. Rather than risk direct confrontations, Mao responded with guerrilla warfare. He harassed the army at its weak points with hit-and-run tactics, relying on the terrain and the support of the peasantry. Government troops often mistreated civilians,

but Mao insisted that his soldiers help the peasants, pay a fair price for food and supplies, and treat women with respect.

In spite of their good relations with the peasants of Jiangxi, the Communists gradually found themselves encircled by government forces. In 1934 Mao and his followers decided to break out of the southern mountains and trek to Shaanxi°, an even more remote province in northwestern China. The so-called **Long March** took them 6,000 miles (nearly 9,700 kilometers) in one year, 17 miles (27 kilometers) a day over desolate mountains and through swamps and deserts, pursued by the army and bombed by Chiang's aircraft. Of the 100,000 Communists who left Jiangxi in October 1934, only 4,000 reached Shaanxi a year later (see Map 30.1). Chiang's government thought it was finally rid of the Communists.

The Sino-Japanese War, 1937–1945

In Japan politicians, senior officers, and business leaders disagreed on how to solve their country's economic problems. Some proposed a quick conquest of China; others advocated war with the Soviet Union. While their superiors hesitated, junior officers decided to take matters into their own hands.

On July 7, 1937, Japanese troops attacked Chinese forces near Beijing. As in 1931, the junior officers who ordered the attack quickly obtained the support of their commanders and then, reluctantly, of the government. Within weeks Japanese troops seized Beijing, Tianjin, Shanghai, and other coastal cities, and the Japanese navy blockaded the entire coast of China.

Once again, the United States and the League of Nations denounced the Japanese aggression. Yet the Western powers were too preoccupied with events in Europe and with their own economic problems to risk a military confrontation in Asia. When the Japanese sank a U.S. gunboat and shelled a British ship on the Yangzi River, the U.S. and British governments responded only with righteous indignation and pious resolutions.

The Chinese armies were large and fought bravely, but they were poorly led and armed and lost every battle. Japanese planes bombed Hangzhou, Nanjing, and Guangzhou, while soldiers on the ground broke dikes and burned villages, killing thousands of civilians. Within a year Japan controlled the coastal provinces of China and

---

Mao Zedong (ma-oh zay-dong)

Shaanxi (SHAWN-she)

0 250 500 Km.	
0 250 500 Mi.	

SOVIET UNION

OUTER MONGOLIA
(Independent 1924)

MANCHURIA

Qiqihar   Jiamusi

Harbin

Amur

Ussuri

Baotou

Zhangjiakou
(Kalgan)

Beijing

Jinzhou   Shenyang
(Mukden)

Tianjin

Lüshun
(Port Arthur)

KOREA
(Japanese 1910–1945)

Taiyuan

Yan'an

Lanzhou

SHAANXI

Xi'an

Huang He

(Yellow)

Luoyang   Zhengzhou

SHANDONG

Jinan

Qingdao

Yellow Sea

Xuzhou

CHINA

Chengdu

SICHUAN

Chongqing

Chang Jiang
(Yangtze)

Wuhan

Nanjing

Hangzhou

Shanghai

Zunyi

Changsha

Nanchang

Jiangxi Soviet under
Mao Zedong, 1929–1934

Guiyang

HUNAN

Kunming

Ji'an

Shantou

Xiamen
(Amoy)

TAIWAN
(Japanese
1895–1945)

*PACIFIC
OCEAN*

BURMA

Guangzhou
(Canton)

Hong Kong
(British)

**FRENCH
INDO-CHINA**

Areas under Communist control before Nov. 1934

Areas under Communist control, 1929–1938

Areas occupied by Japan by end of 1938

→ Route of the Long March, Oct. 1934–Oct. 1935: Main forces from Ji'an

→ Other forces

the lower Yangzi and Yellow River Valleys, China's richest and most populated regions (see Map 30.1).

In spite of Japanese organizational and fighting skills, the attack on China did not bring the victory Japan had hoped for. The Chinese people continued to resist, either in the army or, increasingly, with the Communist guerrilla forces. Japan's periodic attempts to turn the tide by conquering one more piece of China only pushed Japan deeper into the quagmire. For the Japanese people, life became harsher and more repressive as taxes rose, food and fuel became scarce, and more and more young men were drafted. Japanese leaders belatedly realized that the war with China was a drain on the Japanese economy and manpower and that their war machine was becoming increasingly dependent on the United States for steel and machine tools and for nine-tenths of its oil.

Warfare between the Chinese and Japanese was incredibly violent. In the winter of 1937–1938 Japanese troops took Nanjing, raped 20,000 women, killed 200,000 prisoners and civilians, and looted and burned the city. To slow them down, Chiang ordered the Yellow River dikes blasted open, causing a flood that destroyed four thousand villages, killed 890,000 people, and made 12.5 million homeless. Two years later, when the Communists ordered a massive offensive, the Japanese retaliated with a "kill all, burn all, loot all" campaign, destroying hundreds of villages down to the last person, building, and farm animal.

The Chinese government, led by Chiang Kai-shek, escaped to the mountains of Sichuan in the center of the country. There Chiang built up a huge army, not to fight Japan but to prepare for a future confrontation with the Communists. The army drafted over 3 million men, even though it had only a million rifles and could not provide food or clothing for all its soldiers. The Guomindang raised farmers' taxes, even when famine forced farmers to eat the bark of trees. Such taxes were not enough to support both a large army and the thousands of government officials and hangers-on who had fled to Sichuan. To avoid taxing its wealthy supporters the government printed money, causing inflation, hoarding, and corruption.

From his capital of Yan'an in Shaanxi province, Mao also built up his army and formed a government.

Until early 1941 he received a little aid from the Soviet Union; then, after Stalin signed a Soviet-Japanese Neutrality Pact, none at all. Unlike the Guomindang, the Communists listened to the grievances of the peasants, especially the poor, to whom they distributed land confiscated from wealthy landowners. They imposed rigid discipline on their officials and soldiers and tolerated no dissent or criticism from intellectuals. Though they had few weapons, the Communists obtained support and intelligence from farmers in Japanese-occupied territory. They turned military reversals into propaganda victories, presenting themselves as the only group in China that was serious about fighting the Japanese.

THE SECOND WORLD WAR

Many people feared that the Second World War would be a repetition of the First. Instead, it was much bigger in every way. It was fought around the world, from Norway to New Guinea and from Hawaii to Egypt, and on every ocean. It killed far more people than World War I. It was a total war, involving all productive forces and all civilians, and it showed how effectively industry, science, and nationalism could be channeled into mass destruction.

The War of Movement

Defensive maneuvers had dominated in World War I. In World War II motorized weapons gave back the advantage to the offensive. Opposing forces moved fast, their victories hinging as much on the aggressive spirit of their commanders and the military intelligence they obtained as on numbers of troops and firepower.

The Wehrmacht°, or German armed forces, was the first to learn this lesson. It not only had tanks, trucks, and fighter planes but perfected their combined use in a tactic called *Blitzkrieg°* (lightning war): fighter planes scattered enemy troops and disrupted communications, and tanks punctured the enemy's defenses and then, with the help of the infantry, encircled and captured enemy troops. At sea, the navies of both Japan and the United States had developed aircraft carriers that could launch planes against targets hundreds of miles away.

Yet the very size and mobility of the opposing forces made the fighting far different from any the world had

Wehrmacht (VAIR-mokt) **Blitzkrieg** (BLITS-creeg)

ever seen. Instead of engaging in localized battles, armies ranged over vast theaters of operation. Countries were conquered in days or weeks. The belligerents mobilized the economies of entire continents, squeezing them for every possible resource. They tried not only to defeat their enemies' armed forces but—by means of blockades, submarine attacks on shipping, and bombing raids on industrial areas—to damage the economies that supported those armed forces. They thought of civilians not as innocent bystanders but as legitimate targets and, later, as vermin to be exterminated.

Soviet Tanks at Stalingrad In the winter of 1942/1943, the Red Army encircled a German army at Stalingrad, a strategic city on the Volga River in southern Russia, that marked the furthest eastward advance of the Wehrmacht. The Soviets deployed their new T-34s, the best tanks in the world at the time. Unlike the Germans, Soviet soldiers were equipped with warm winter uniforms with a white outer layer for camouflage in the snow. (TASS-Sovfoto)

War in Europe and North Africa

It took less than a month for the Wehrmacht to conquer Poland (see Map 30.2). Britain and France declared war on Germany but took no military action. Meanwhile, the Soviet Union invaded eastern Poland and the Baltic republics of Lithuania, Latvia, and Estonia. Although the Poles fought bravely, the Polish infantry and cavalry were no match for German and Russian tanks. During the winter of 1939–1940 Germany and the Western democracies faced each other in what soldiers called a "phony war" and watched as the Soviet Union attacked Finland, which resisted for many months.

In March 1940 Hitler went on the offensive again, conquering Denmark, Norway, the Netherlands, and Belgium in less than two months. In May he attacked France. Although the French army had as many soldiers, tanks, and aircraft as the Wehrmacht, its morale was low and it quickly collapsed. By the end of June Hitler was master of all of Europe between Russia and Spain.

Germany still had to face one enemy: Britain. The British had no army to speak of, but they had other assets: the English Channel, the Royal Navy and Air Force, and a tough new prime minister, Winston Churchill. The Germans knew they could invade Britain only by gaining control of the airspace over the Channel, so they launched a massive air attack—the Battle of Britain—lasting from June through September. The attack failed, however, because the Royal Air Force had better fighters and used radar and code-breaking to detect approaching German planes.

Frustrated in the west, Hitler turned his attention eastward, even though it meant fighting a two-front war. So far he had gotten the utmost cooperation from Stalin, who supplied Germany with grain, oil, and strategic raw materials. Yet he had always wanted to conquer Lebensraum in the east and enslave the Slavic peoples who lived there, and he feared that if he waited, Stalin would build a dangerously strong army. In June 1941 Hitler launched the largest attack in history, with 3 million soldiers and thousands of planes and tanks. Within five months the Wehrmacht conquered the Baltic states, Ukraine, and half of European Russia; captured a million prisoners of war; and stood at the very gates of Moscow and Leningrad. The USSR seemed on the verge of collapse when the weather turned cold, machines froze, and the fighting came to a halt. Like Napoleon, Hitler had ignored the environment of Russia to his peril.

The next spring the Wehrmacht renewed its offensive. It surrounded Leningrad in a siege that was to cost a million lives. Leaving Moscow aside, it turned toward the Caucasus and its oil wells. In August the Germans attacked **Stalingrad** (now Volgagrad), the key to the Volga River and the supply of oil. For months German and Soviet soldiers fought over every street and every house. When winter came the Red Army counterattacked and encircled the city. In February 1943 the remnants of the German army in Stalingrad surrendered.

Map 30.2 World War II in Europe and North Africa In a series of quick and decisive campaigns from September 1939 to December 1941, German forces overran much of Europe and North Africa. There followed three years of bitter fighting as the Allies slowly pushed the Germans back. This map shows the maximum extent of Germany's conquests and alliances, as well as the key battles and the front lines at various times.

Online Study Center
Improve Your Grade
Interactive Map:
World War II in Europe

Hitler had lost an army of 200,000 men and his last chance of defeating the Soviet Union and of winning the war (see Map 30.2).

From Europe the war spread to Africa. When France fell in 1940 Mussolini began imagining himself a latter-day Roman emperor and decided that the time had come to realize his imperial ambitions. Italian forces quickly overran British Somaliland, then invaded Egypt. Their victories were ephemeral, however, for when the British counterattacked, Italian resistance crumbled. During 1941 British forces conquered Italian East Africa and invaded Libya as well. The Italian rout in North Africa brought the Germans to their rescue. During 1942 the German army and the forces of the British Empire (now known as the Commonwealth) seesawed back and forth across the deserts of Libya and Egypt. At **El Alamein** in northern Egypt the British prevailed because they had more weapons and supplies. Thanks to their success at breaking German codes, they also were better informed about their enemies' plans. The Germans were finally expelled from Africa in May 1943.

War in Asia and the Pacific

The fall of France and the involvement of Britain and the USSR against Germany presented Japan with the opportunity it had been looking for. Suddenly the European colonies in Southeast Asia, with their abundant oil, rubber, and other strategic materials, seemed ripe for the taking. In July 1941 the French government allowed Japanese forces to occupy Indochina. In retaliation, the United States and Britain stopped shipments of steel, scrap iron, oil, and other products that Japan desperately needed. This left Japan with three alternatives: accept the shame and humiliation of giving up its conquests, as the Americans insisted; face economic ruin; or widen the war. Japan chose war.

Admiral Isoroku Yamamoto, commander of the Japanese fleet, told Prime Minister Fumimaro Konoye: "If I am told to fight regardless of the consequences, I shall run wild for the first six months or a year, but I have utterly no confidence for the second or third year. . . . I hope that you will endeavor to avoid a Japanese-American war." Ignoring his advice, the war cabinet made plans for a surprise attack on the United States Navy, followed by an invasion of Southeast Asia.

They knew they could not hope to defeat the United States, but they calculated that the shock of the attack would be so great that isolationist Americans would accept the Japanese conquest of Southeast Asia as readily as they had acquiesced to Hitler's conquests in Europe.

On December 7, 1941, Japanese planes bombed the U.S. naval base at **Pearl Harbor**, Hawaii, sinking or damaging scores of warships, but missing the aircraft carriers, which were at sea. Then, between January and March 1942, the Japanese bombed Hong Kong and Singapore and invaded Thailand, the Philippines, and Malaya. Within a few months they occupied all of Southeast Asia and the Dutch East Indies. The Japanese claimed to be liberating the inhabitants of these lands from European colonialism. But they soon began to confiscate food and raw materials and demand heavy labor from the inhabitants, whom they treated with contempt. Those who protested were brutally punished.

Online Study Center
Improve Your Grade
Interactive Map:
World War II in the Pacific

Japan's dream of an East Asian empire seemed within reach, for its victories surpassed even Hitler's in Europe. Yamamoto's fears were justified, however, because the United States, far from being cowed into submission, joined Britain and the Soviet Union in an alliance called the United Nations (or the Allies) and began preparing for war. In April 1942 American planes bombed Tokyo. In May the United States Navy defeated a Japanese fleet in the Coral Sea, ending Japanese plans to conquer Australia. A month later, at the **Battle of Midway**, Japan lost four of its six largest aircraft carriers. Japan did not have enough industry to replace them, for its war production was only one-tenth that of the United States. In the vastness of the Pacific Ocean aircraft carriers held the key to victory, and without them, Japan faced a long and hopeless war (see Map 30.3).

The End of War

After the Battle of Stalingrad the advantage on the Eastern Front shifted to the Soviet Union. By 1943 the Red Army was receiving a growing stream of supplies from factories in Russia and the United States. Slowly at first and then with increasing vigor, it pushed the Wehrmacht back toward Germany.

The Western powers, meanwhile, staged two invasions of Europe. Beginning in July 1943 they captured Sicily and invaded Italy. Italy signed an armistice, but German

Map 30.3 World War II in Asia and the Pacific   After having conquered much of China between 1937 and 1941, Japanese forces launched a sudden attack on Southeast Asia, Indonesia, and the Pacific in late 1941 and early 1942. American forces slowly reconquered the Pacific islands and the Philippines until August 1945, when the atomic bombing of Hiroshima and Nagasaki forced Japan's surrender.

troops held off the Allied advance for two years. In November, at a meeting with Stalin in Teheran, Roosevelt and Churchill promised to open another front in France as soon as possible. On June 6, 1944—forever after known as D-day—156,000 British, American, and Canadian troops landed on the coast of Normandy in western France—the largest shipborne assault ever staged. Within a week the Allies had more troops in France than Germany did, and by September Germany faced an Allied army of over 2 million men with half a million vehicles of all sorts.

Although the Red Army was on the eastern border of Germany, ready for the final push, Hitler transferred part of the Wehrmacht westward. Despite overwhelming odds, Germany held out for almost a year, a result of the fighting qualities of its soldiers and the terror inspired by the Nazi regime, which commanded obedience to the end. In February 1945 the three Allied leaders met again in Yalta on the Black Sea to plan the future of Europe after the war. On May 7, 1945, a week after Hitler committed suicide, German military leaders surrendered.

Japan fought on a while longer, in large part because the United States had aimed most of its war effort at Germany. In the Pacific U.S. forces "leap-frogged" some heavily fortified Japanese island bases in order to capture others closer to Japan itself. Other islands, such as Saipan, Iwo Jima, and Okinawa, had to be captured by amphibious landings, with high casualty rates on both sides. By June 1944 U.S. bombers were able to attack Japan. Meanwhile, U.S. submarines sank ever larger numbers of Japanese merchant ships, gradually cutting Japan off from its sources of oil and other raw materials. In 1944 a terrible earthquake devastated the city of Nagoya, compounding the misery of war and bombing raids. After May 1945, with the Japanese air force grounded for lack of fuel, U.S. planes began destroying Japanese shipping, industries, and cities at will.

Even as their homeland was being pounded, the Japanese still held strong positions in Asia. At first, Asian nationalists such as the Indonesian Achmed Sukarno were glad to get rid of the white colonialists and welcomed the Japanese. Yet despite its name, "Greater East Asian Co-Prosperity Sphere," the Japanese occupation was harsh and brutal. By 1945 Asians were eager to see the Japanese leave, but not to welcome back the Europeans. Instead, they looked forward to independence (see Chapters 31 and 32).

On August 6, 1945, the United States dropped an atomic bomb on **Hiroshima**, killing some 80,000 people

Hiroshima After the Atomic Bomb   On August 6, 1945, an atomic bomb destroyed the city, killing some eighty thousand people. This photo shows the devastation of the city center, where only a few concrete buildings remained standing.   (Wide World Photos)

in a flash and leaving about 120,000 more to die in agony from burns and radiation. Three days later another atomic bomb destroyed Nagasaki. On August 14 Japan offered to surrender, and Emperor Hirohito himself gave the order to lay down arms. Two weeks later Japanese leaders signed the terms of surrender. The war was officially over.

Online Study Center
Improve Your Grade
Primary Source: The Decision
to Use the Bomb

Were these atomic weapons necessary? At the time, Americans believed that the conquest of the Japanese homeland would take more than a year and cost the lives of hundreds of thousands of American soldiers. Henry Stimson, secretary of war, later explained the official position of the United States government:

> As we understood it in July, there was a very strong possibility that the Japanese government might determine upon resistance to the end, in all areas of the Far East under its control. In such an event the Allies would be faced with the enormous task of destroying an armed force of five million men and five thousand suicide aircraft, belonging to a race which had already amply demonstrated its ability to fight literally to the death. . . .
>
> The total U.S. military and naval force involved in this grand design was of the order of 5,000,000 men; if all those indirectly concerned are included, it was larger still. . . . I was informed that such operations might be expected to cost over a million casualties to American forces alone. . . .
>
> A question then comes: Is there any alternative to such a forceful occupation of Japan which will secure for us the equivalent of an unconditional surrender of her forces and a permanent destruction of her power again to strike an aggressive blow. . . ? For such a purpose the atomic bomb was an eminently suitable weapon.[1]

Although some believed the Japanese were determined to fight to the bitter end, others thought they would surrender if they could retain their emperor. Military leaders such as Generals Eisenhower and Marshall objected to the use of the bomb, and Winston Churchill wrote: "It would be a mistake to suppose that the fate of Japan was settled by the atomic bomb. Her defeat was certain before the first bomb fell. . . ."[2]

Chinese Civil War and Communist Victory

The formal Japanese surrender in September 1945 came as a surprise to the Guomindang. American transport planes flew Guomindang officials and troops to all the cities of China. The United States gave millions of dollars of aid and weapons to the Guomindang, all the while urging "national unity" and a "coalition government" with the Communists. But Chiang used American aid and all other means available to prepare for a civil war. By late 1945 he had an army of 2.7 million, more than twice the size of the Communist forces.

From 1945 to 1949 the contest between the Guomindang and the Communists intensified. Guomindang forces started with more troops and weapons, U.S. support, and control of China's cities. But their behavior eroded whatever popular support they had. As they moved into formerly Japanese-held territory, they acted like an occupation force. They taxed the people they "liberated" more heavily than the Japanese had, looted businesses, confiscated supplies, and enriched themselves at the expense of the population. To pay its bills Chiang's government printed money so fast that it soon lost all its value, ruining merchants and causing hoarding and shortages. In the countryside the Guomindang's brutality alienated the peasants.

Meanwhile, the Communists obtained Japanese equipment seized by the Soviets in the last weeks of the war and American weapons brought over by deserting Guomindang soldiers. In Manchuria, where they were strongest, they pushed through a radical land reform program, distributing the properties of wealthy landowners among the poorest peasants. In battles against government forces, the higher morale and popular support they enjoyed outweighed the heavy equipment of the Guomindang, whose soldiers began deserting by the thousands.

In April 1947, as Chinese Communist forces surrounded Nanjing, the British frigate *Amethyst* sailed up the Yangzi River to evacuate British civilians. Dozens of times since the Opium War of 1839–1842, foreign powers had dispatched warships up the rivers of China to rescue their citizens, enforce their treaty rights, or intimidate the Chinese. Foreign warships deep in the heart of China were the very symbols of its weakness. This time, however, Chinese Communist artillery damaged the *Amethyst* and beat back other British warships sent to its rescue.

By 1949 the Guomindang armies were collapsing everywhere, defeated more by their own greed and ineptness than by the Communists. As the Communists advanced, high-ranking members of the Guomindang fled to Taiwan, protected from the mainland by the

Sale of Gold in the Last Days of the Guomindang   This picture was taken by famed French photojournalist Henri Cartier-Bresson in Shanghai just before the arrival of the Communist-led People's Liberation Army in 1949. It shows people desperate to buy gold before their Guomindang currency becomes worthless. (Henri Cartier-Bresson/Magnum Photos)

United States Navy. On October 1, 1949, Mao Zedong announced the founding of the People's Republic of China.

THE CHARACTER OF WARFARE

The war left an enormous death toll. Recent estimates place the figure at close to 60 million deaths, six to eight times more than in World War I. Over half of the dead were civilian victims of massacres, famines, and bombs. The Soviet Union lost between 20 million and 25 million people, more than any other country. China suffered 15 million deaths; Poland lost some 6 million, of whom half were Jewish; the Jewish people lost another 3 million outside Poland. Over 4 million Germans and over 2 million Japanese died. Great Britain lost 400,000 people, and the United States 300,000. In much of the world, almost every family mourned one or more of its members.

Many parts of the world were flooded with refugees. Some 90 million Chinese fled the Japanese advance. In Europe millions fled from the Nazis or the Red Army or were herded back and forth on government orders. Many refugees never returned to their homes, creating new ethnic mixtures more reminiscent of the New World than of the Old.

One reason for the terrible toll in human lives and suffering was a change in moral values, as belligerents identified not just soldiers but entire peoples as enemies. Some belligerents even labeled their own ethnic miniorities as "enemies." Another reason for the devastation was the appearance of new technologies that carried destruction deep into enemy territory, far beyond the traditional battlefields. Let us consider the new technologies of warfare, the changes in morality, and their lethal combination.

The Science and Technology of War

As fighting spread around the world, the features that had characterized the early years of the war—the mobilization of manpower and economies and the mobility of the armed forces—grew increasingly powerful. Meanwhile, new aspects of war took on a growing importance. One of these was the impact of science on the technology of warfare. Chemists found ways to make synthetic rubber from coal or oil. Physicists perfected radar, which warned of approaching enemy aircraft and submarines. Cryptanalysts broke enemy codes and were able to penetrate secret military communications (see Environment and Technology: The Enigma Machine). Pharmacologists developed antibiotics that saved the lives of countless wounded soldiers, who in any earlier war would have died of infections.

Aircraft development was especially striking. As war approached, German, British, and Japanese aircraft manufacturers developed fast, maneuverable fighter planes. U.S. industry produced aircraft of every sort but was especially noted for heavy bombers designed to fly in huge formations and drop tons of bombs on enemy cities. The Japanese developed the Mitsubishi "Zero" fighter plane—light, fast, and agile, but dangerous to fly. Unable to produce heavy planes in large numbers, Germany responded with radically new designs, including the first jet fighters, low-flying buzz bombs, and, finally, V-2 missiles, against which there was no warning or defense.

Military planners no longer dismissed the creations of civilian inventors, as they had done before World War I. Now they expected scientists to furnish secret weapons that could doom the enemy. In October 1939 President Roosevelt received a letter from physicist Albert Einstein, a Jewish refugee from Nazism, warning of the dangers of nuclear power: "There is no doubt that sub-atomic energy is available all around us, and that one day man will release and control its almost infinite power. We cannot prevent him from doing so and can only hope that he will not use it exclusively in blowing up his next door neighbor." Fearing that Germany might develop a nuclear bomb first, Roosevelt placed the vast resources of the U.S. government at the disposal of physicists and engineers, both Americans and refugees from Europe. By 1945 they had built two atomic bombs, each one powerful enough to annihilate an entire city.

Bombing Raids

German bombers damaged Warsaw in 1939 and Rotterdam and London in 1940. Yet Germany lacked a strategic bomber force capable of destroying whole cities. In this area, the British and Americans excelled. Since it was very hard to pinpoint individual buildings, especially at night, the British Air Staff under British air chief marshal Arthur "Bomber" Harris decided that "operations should now be focused on the morale of the enemy civilian population and in particular the industrial workers."

In May 1942, 1,000 British planes dropped incendiary bombs on Cologne, setting fire to most of the old city. Between July 24 and August 2, 1943, 3,330 British and American bombers set fire to Hamburg, killing 50,000 people, mostly women and children. Later raids destroyed Berlin, Dresden, and other German cities. All in all, the bombing raids against Germany killed 600,000 people—more than half of them women and children—and injured 800,000. If the air strategists had hoped thereby to break the morale of the German people, they failed. German armament production continued to increase until late 1944, and the population remained obedient and hard working. The only effective bombing raids were those directed against oil depots and synthetic fuel plants; by early 1945 they had almost brought the German war effort to a standstill.

Japanese cities were also the targets of American bombing raids. As early as April 1942 sixteen planes launched from an aircraft carrier bombed Tokyo. Later, as American forces captured islands close to Japan, the raids intensified. Their effect was even more devastating than the fire-bombing of German cities, for Japanese cities were made of wood. In March 1945 bombs set Tokyo ablaze, killing 80,000 people and leaving a million homeless. It was a portent of worse destruction to come.

The Holocaust

In World War II, for the first time, more civilians than soldiers were deliberately put to death. The champions in the art of killing defenseless civilians were the Nazis. Their murders were not the accidental byproducts of some military goal but a calculated policy of exterminating whole races of people.

Their first targets were Jews. Soon after Hitler came to power, he deprived German Jews of their citizenship

The Enigma Machine

Since ancient times, governments and armies have used various methods of encrypting messages, that is, making them unreadable to people who do not possess the proper code (words replaced by other words using a codebook) or cipher (letters replaced by numbers). The introduction of radio, which could be easily monitored by agents of foreign powers, turned cryptography (secret writing) into a necessity of diplomacy and war. Yet encrypting and decrypting messages required expert code clerks and took time. Furthermore, since each nation used several codes and ciphers and changed them periodically, a breakthrough in one code or cipher did not necessarily make other messages easier to decrypt.

After World War I, inventors in several countries set out to create machines that could encrypt and decrypt messages automatically while also making them harder to crack than manual codes and ciphers. The invention that was most successful was the Enigma, first produced by a German company in 1923. It consisted of a typewriter keyboard, a set of rotors containing electrical wires and contacts, and a series of lights marked with letters. When the operator entered a letter on the keyboard, an electrical current went through the rotors and lit up a letter different from the one entered. With each keystroke, the rotors also turned, so that the next time the same key was pushed, a different light went on. At the receiving end, if the operator had set his rotors in the same pattern as the sender, entering the encrypted letters on the keyboard lit up the letters of the original plaintext. Anyone who had an Enigma but was not privy to the rotor settings and attempted to read an encrypted message would have to try an almost infinite number of settings. This might take months or years, by which time the information would no longer have any value.

As war approached, the German armed forces purchased thousands of Enigma machines, each the size of a portable typewriter. They accompanied ships at sea, frontline troops, and squadrons of airplanes. The Germans considered their cipher unbreakable and their secrets safe from enemy eyes. They were wrong. Before the war began, Polish cryptanalysts had figured out how the Enigma worked and built some replicas. They also devised an electromechanical device they called "bomba" that went through rotor settings at blazing speed until it encountered an expression, such as "Heil Hitler," that often appeared in German messages. When the war broke out, they fled to France.

From there, the secret of the bomba passed to British cryptanalysts at a secret installation at Bletchley Park, north of London.

With this breakthrough, the British were able to read many Luftwaffe signals during the Battle of Britain in 1940. Cracking the German navy and army Enigmas proved to be much more difficult, for the other services used more rotors, changed the settings more frequently, and, most importantly, learned to avoid stock phrases. Nonetheless, by the spring of 1942, Bletchley Park had a staff of 1,500 handling some 40,000 German military messages a month. Their ability to read German messages was instrumental in the Allied victories against General Rommel in North Africa in 1942 and against the German U-boats in the Battle of the Atlantic in 1943.

The Enigma Machine During World War II, German armed forces used Enigma machines like the one seen here in the vehicle of a German tank commander. With Enigmas, they could encrypt and decrypt radio messages, keeping them secret (they believed) from enemy code-breakers. (Courtesy, Brian Johnson)

and legal rights. When eastern Europe fell under Nazi rule, the Nazis herded its large Jewish population into ghettos in the major cities, where many died of starvation and disease. Then, in early 1942, the Nazis decided to carry out Hitler's "final solution to the Jewish problem" by applying modern industrial methods to the slaughter of human beings. German companies built huge extermination camps in eastern Europe, while thousands of ordinary German citizens supported and aided the genocide. Every day trainloads of cattle cars arrived at the camps and disgorged thousands of captives and the corpses of those who had died of starvation or asphyxiation along the way. The strongest survivors were put to work and fed almost nothing until they died. Women, children, the elderly, and the sick were shoved into gas chambers and asphyxiated with poison gas. **Auschwitz**, the biggest camp, was a giant industrial complex designed to kill up to twelve thousand people a day. Most horrifying of all were the tortures inflicted on prisoners selected by Nazi doctors for "medical experiments." This mass extermination, now called the **Holocaust** ("burning"), claimed some 6 million Jewish lives.

Online Study Center
Improve Your Grade
Primary Source:
Memoirs

Besides the Jews, the Nazis also killed 3 million Polish Catholics—especially professionals, army officers, and the educated—in an effort to reduce the Polish people to slavery. They also exterminated homosexuals, Jehovah's Witnesses, Gypsies, the disabled, and the mentally ill—all in the interests of "racial purity." Whenever a German was killed in an occupied country, the Nazis retaliated by burning a village and all its inhabitants. After the invasion of Russia the Wehrmacht was given orders to execute all captured communists, government employees, and officers. They also worked millions of prisoners of war to death or let them die of starvation.

U.S. Army Medics and Holocaust Victims   At the end of World War II, Allied troops entered the Nazi concentration camps, where they found the bodies of thousands of victims of the Holocaust. In this picture, taken at Dachau in southern Germany, two U.S. Army medics are overseeing a truckload of corpses to be taken to a burial site.   (Hulton Deutsch Collection/Corbis)

The Home Front in Europe and Asia

In the First World War there had been a clear distinction between the "front" and the "home front." Not so in World War II, where rapid military movements and air power carried the war into people's homes. For the civilian populations of China, Japan, Southeast Asia, and Europe, the war was far more terrifying than their worst nightmares. Armies swept through the land, confiscating food, fuel, and anything else of value. Bombers and heavy artillery pounded cities into rubble, leaving only the skeletons of buildings, while survivors cowered in cellars and scurried like rats. Even when a city was not targeted, air-raid sirens awakened people throughout the night. In countries occupied by the Germans the police arrested civilians, deporting many to die in concentration camps or to work as slave laborers in armaments factories. Millions fled their homes in terror, losing their families and friends. Even in Britain, which was never invaded, children and the elderly were taken from their families for their own safety and sent to live in the countryside.

The war demanded an enormous and sustained effort from all civilians, but more so in some countries than in others. In 1941, even as the Wehrmacht was routing the Red Army, the Soviets dismantled over fifteen hundred factories and rebuilt them in the Ural Mountains and Siberia, where they soon turned out more tanks and artillery than the Axis.

Half of the ships afloat in 1939 were sunk during the war, but the Allied losses were more than made up for by American shipyards, while Axis shipping was reduced to nothing by 1945. The production of aircraft, trucks, tanks, and other materiel showed a similar imbalance. Although the Axis powers made strenuous efforts to increase their production, they could not compete with the vast outpouring of Soviet tanks and American materiel.

The Red Army eventually mobilized 22 million men; Soviet women took over half of all industrial and three-quarters of all agricultural jobs. In the other Allied countries, women also played major roles in the war effort, replacing men in fields, factories, and offices. The Nazis, in contrast, believed that German women should stay home and bear children, and they imported 7 million "guest workers"—a euphemism for war prisoners and captured foreigners.

The Home Front in the United States

The United States flourished during the war. Safe behind their oceans, Americans felt no bombs, saw no enemy soldiers, had almost no civilian casualties, and suffered fewer military casualties than other belligerents. The economy, still depressed in 1939, went into a prolonged boom after 1940. By 1944 the United States was producing twice as much as all the Axis powers combined. Thanks to huge military orders, jobs were plentiful and opportunities beckoned. Bread lines disappeared, and nutrition and health improved. Consumer goods ranging from automobiles to nylon stockings were in short supply, and most Americans saved part of their paychecks, laying the basis for a phenomenal postwar consumer boom. Many Americans later looked back on the conflict as the "good war."

War always exalts such supposedly masculine qualities as physical courage, violence, and domination. These were the official virtues of the Axis powers, but they were highly valued in the United States as well. Yet World War II also did much to weaken the hold of traditional ideas, as employers recruited women and members of racial minorities to work in jobs once reserved for white men. For example, 6 million women entered the labor force during the war, 2.5 million of them in manufacturing jobs previously considered "men's work." In a book entitled *Shipyard Diary of a Woman*

Welder (1944), Augusta Clawson recalled her experiences in a shipyard in Oregon:

> The job confirmed my strong conviction—I have stated it before—what exhausts the woman welder is not the work, not the heat, nor the demands upon physical strength. It is the apprehension that arises from inadequate skill and consequent lack of confidence; and this *can* be overcome by the right kind of training. . . . I know I can do it if my machine is correctly set, and I have learned enough of the vagaries of machines to be able to set them. And so, in spite of the discomforts of climbing, heavy equipment, and heat, I enjoyed the work today because *I could do it.*

At the beginning, many men resisted the idea that women, especially mothers of young children, should take jobs that would take them away from their families. As the labor shortage got worse, however, employers and politicians grudgingly admitted that the government ought to help provide day care for the children of working mothers. The entry of women into the labor force proved to be one of the most significant consequences of the war. As one woman put it: "War jobs have uncovered unsuspected abilities in American women. Why lose all these abilities because of a belief that 'a woman's place is in the home'? For some it is, for others not."

The war loosened racial bonds as well, bringing hardships for some and benefits for others. Seeking work in war industries, 1.2 million African Americans migrated to the north and west. In the southwest Mexican immigrants took jobs in agriculture and war industries. But no new housing was built to accommodate the influx of migrants to the industrial cities, and as a result many suffered from overcrowding and discrimination. Much worse was the fate of 112,000 Japanese-Americans living on the west coast of the United States; they were rounded up and herded into internment camps in the desert until the war was over, ostensibly for fear of spying and sabotage, but actually because of their race.

War and the Environment

During the Depression, construction and industry had slowed to a crawl, reducing environmental stress. The war reversed this trend, sharply accelerating pressures on the environment.

One reason for the change was the fighting itself. Battles scarred the landscape, leaving behind spent ammunition and damaged equipment. Retreating armies flooded large areas of China and the Netherlands. The bombing of cities left ruins that remained visible for a generation or more. Much of the damage eventually was repaired, although the rusted hulls of ships still darken the lagoons of once-pristine coral islands in the Pacific.

The main cause of environmental stress, however, was not the fighting but the economic development that sustained it. The war's half-million aircraft required thousands of air bases, many of them in the Pacific, China, Africa, and other parts of the world that had seldom seen an airplane before. Barracks, shipyards, docks, warehouses, and other military construction sprouted on every continent.

As war industries boomed—the United States increased its industrial production fourfold during the war—so did the demand for raw materials. Mining companies opened new mines and towns in Central Africa to supply strategic minerals. Brazil, Argentina, and other Latin American countries deprived of manufactured imports began building their own steel mills, factories, and shipyards. In India, China, and Europe, timber felling accelerated far beyond the reproduction rate of trees, replacing forests with denuded land. In a few instances the war was good for the environment. For example, submarine warfare made fishing and whaling so dangerous that fish and whale populations had a few years in which to increase.

We must keep the environmental effects of the war in perspective. Except for the destruction of cities, much of the war's impact was simply the result of industrial development only temporarily slowed by the Depression. During the war the damage that military demand caused was tempered by restraints on civilian consumption. From the vantage point of the present, the environmental impact of the war seems quite modest in comparison with the damage inflicted on the earth by the long consumer boom that began in the post–World War II years.

SUMMARY

○— How did the Soviet Union change under Stalin, and at what cost?

○— What caused the Depression, and what effects did it have on the world?

○— How did fascism in Italy and Germany lead to the Second World War?

○— What were the economic reasons behind Japan's invasion of Manchuria?

○— How was the war fought, and why did Japan and Germany lose?

○— How did science and technology change the nature of warfare?

Online Study Center
ACE the Test

After the Great War ended, the world seemed to return to its prewar state, but it was an illusion. In the Soviet Union, Joseph Stalin was determined to turn his country into a modern industrial state at breakneck speed, regardless of the human cost. Several million people—most of them peasants—died and millions more were enslaved during the Five Year Plans and the collectivization of agriculture, and by 1941 Soviet industry was much better prepared for a war with Germany than it had been in 1914–1917.

In 1929, after a few years of prosperity, excessive speculation based on shaky loans caused the New York stock market to collapse; within a few months, the world economy fell into the Great Depression, which threw millions out of work, not only in the industrial nations but also throughout the world. Countries such as France and Britain survived the Depression by making their colonial empires purchase their products. Countries that were dependent on exports, such as Germany and Japan, suffered more. Only the USSR and southern Africa, where gold became more valuable, boomed during the 1930s.

In Italy, the government that was already fascist became more tyrannical. Mussolini installed Fascist Party members in all government jobs and jailed anyone who criticized him. In Germany, economic collapse led people to entrust their government to Adolf Hitler and his Nazi followers, who quickly set to work establishing a totalitarian government. Nazi Germany's rebuilding of its military and its invasion of Austria and Czechoslovakia were greeted with a policy of appeasement by Western democracies, until finally they could no longer overlook Germany's intentions. The Depression hit Japan hard because the worldwide demand for silk and rice collapsed. Japan saw China as a potential new colony with a vast population and resources to help solve its economic problems. In 1931, Japan conquered Manchuria and proceeded to build railways and heavy industries there. The United States and the League of Nations protested but did little else. The Sino-Japanese War, which began with the Japanese invasion of Beijing in 1937, was a long and brutal war that became a drain on the Japanese economy and resources. Meanwhile, the Communists, led by Mao Zedong, were slowly gaining support in the Chinese countryside.

Italy conquered Ethiopia in 1935, and Japan attacked China in 1937, while the Western democracies disapproved but took no action. The war spread to Europe in 1939 when Germany conquered Poland, then Denmark, Norway, the Low Countries, and, in 1940, France. The war turned global when Germany invaded the Soviet Union and Japan attacked the United States in 1941. The Allies won because of Russia's hard fighting and its victory at Stalingrad; the Allies' overwhelming materiel resources, especially those of the United States; the invasion of D-Day, which put enough men on the European continent to finally drive back Germany; and U.S. naval victories in the Pacific and its use of atomic weapons against Japan.

The Second World War was by far the deadliest and most horrific in history. Modern mechanized forces swept across entire nations and oceans. Their targets were not only each other's armed forces, but their civilian populations as well. Though Germany had considerable scientific and technical talent, the war favored the nations with the most heavy industries, namely, the United States and the Soviet Union. The Allies destroyed German and Japanese cities with fire-bombs, and the United States dropped atomic bombs on Hiroshima and Nagasaki. Of the roughly 60 million people who died in the war, most of them were civilians.

KEY TERMS

Joseph Stalin   *p. 878*

Five-Year Plans   *p. 878*

Benito Mussolini   *p. 885*

Fascist Party   *p. 885*

Adolf Hitler   *p. 886*

Nazi Party   *p. 886*

Chiang Kai-shek   *p. 888*

Mao Zedong   *p. 889*

Long March   *p. 889*

Stalingrad   *p. 892*

El Alamein   *p. 894*

Pearl Harbor   *p. 894*

Battle of Midway   *p. 894*

Hiroshima   *p. 896*

Auschwitz   *p. 901*

Holocaust   *p. 901*

Online Study Center
Improve Your Grade
Flashcards

SUGGESTED READING

The literature on the period from 1929 to 1945 is enormous and growing fast. The following list is but a very brief introduction.

Charles Kindelberger's *The World in Depression, 1929–39* (1973) and Robert McElvaine's *The Great Depression: America, 1929–1941* (1984) provide sophisticated economic analyses of the Depression. A. J. H. Latham's *The Depression and the Developing World, 1914–1939* (1981) gives a global perspective.

The best recent book on Japan in the twentieth century is Daikichi Irokawa's *The Age of Hirohito: In Search of Modern Japan* (1995). On Japanese expansion see W. G. Beasley, *Japanese Imperialism, 1894–1945* (1987). The race to war is covered in Akira Iriye, *The Origins of the Second World War in Asia and the Pacific* (1987); Michael Barnhart, *Japan Prepares for Total War* (1987), is short and well written. The Japanese invasion of China is the subject of James Hsiung and Steven Levine, eds., *China's Bitter Victory: The War with Japan, 1937–1945* (1992). See also Iris Chang, *The Rape of Nanking: The Forgotten Holocaust of World War II* (1997), and Masahiro Yamamoto, *Nanking: Anatomy of an Atrocity* (2000). Haruko Taya Cook and Theodore Cook, eds., *Japan at War: An Oral History* (1992), recounts the experiences of ordinary Japanese in their own words. John Dower, *War Without Mercy: Race and Power in the Pacific War* (1987), is a seminal work.

In the large and fast-growing literature on twentieth-century China, two general introductions are especially useful: John K. Fairbank, *The Great Chinese Revolution, 1800–1985* (1986), and Jonathan Spence, *The Search for Modern China* (1990). On the warlord and Guomindang periods see Lucien Bianco, *Origins of the Chinese Revolution, 1915–1949* (1971). Jung Chang, *Wild Swans: Three Daughters of China* (1991), is a fascinating account of women's experiences during the Revolution and the Mao era by the daughter of two Communist officials.

Among recent biographies of Stalin, see Dmitrii Volkogonov's *Stalin: Triumph and Tragedy* (1991) and Robert Tucker's *Stalin as Revolutionary, 1879–1929* (1973) and *Stalin in Power: The Revolution from Above, 1928–1941* (1990). On the transformation of the USSR, see Roy Medvedev's *Let History Judge: The Origins and Consequences of Stalinism* (1989) and Stephen Kotkin's *Magnetic Mountain: Stalinism as Civilization* (1995). Stalin's collectivization of agriculture is vividly portrayed in Robert Conquest's *Harvest of Sorrow* (1986); see also Sheila Fitzpatrick's *Stalin's Peasants: Resistance and Survival in the Russian Village After Collectivization* (1994). Conquest's *The Great Terror: A Reassessment* (1990) describes the purges of the 1930s. Alexander Solzhenitsyn, a veteran of Stalin's prisons, explores them in a detailed history, *The Gulag Archipelago, 1918–1956* (3 vols., 1974–1978), and in a short but brilliant novel *One Day in the Life of Ivan Denisovich* (1978).

Alexander De Grand provides an excellent interpretation of fascism in *Italian Fascism: Its Origins and Development*, 2nd ed. (1989). William Shirer's *The Rise and Fall of the Third Reich* (1960) is a long but very dramatic eyewitness description of Nazi Germany by a journalist. The dictators are the subject of two fine biographies: Denis Mack Smith's *Mussolini* (1982) and Ian Kershaw's *Hitler* (2001). See also A. J. P. Taylor's controversial classic *The Origins of the Second World War* (1966) and Michael Burleigh's *Third Reich: A New History* (2000).

Two very detailed books on World War II are John Keegan, *The Second World War* (1990), and Gerhard Weinberg, *A World at Arms: A Global History of World War II* (1994). Particular aspects of the war in Europe are covered in David Glanz and Jonathan House, *When Titans Clashed: How the Red Army Stopped Hitler* (1998) and Conrad Crane, *Bombs, Cities, and Civilians* (1993). One of the most readable accounts of the war in Asia and the Pacific is Ronald Spector's *Eagle Against the Sun* (1988). Also see Akira Iriye, *Power and Culture: The Japanese-American War, 1941–1945* (1981), and Peter Schrijvers, *The GI War Against Japan: American Soldiers in Asia and the Pacific During World War II* (2002).

The terror of life under Nazi rule is the subject of two powerful memoirs: Anne Frank's *The Diary of a Young Girl* and Eli Wiesel's *Night* (1960). On the Holocaust see Lucy Dawidowicz, *The War Against the Jews, 1933–1945,* 2nd ed. (1986); Leni Yahil, *The Holocaust: The Fate of European Jewry* (1990); and Christopher Browning's *Ordinary Men: Reserve Police Battalion 101 and the Final Solution in Poland* (1992).

Among the many books that capture the scientific side of warfare, two are especially recommended: Richard Rhodes's long but fascinating *The Making of the Atomic Bomb* (1986), and F. H. Hinsley and Alan Stripp, eds., *Code Breakers* (1993).

Among the many books on the home front in the United States, the most vivid is Studs Terkel, *"The Good War": An Oral History of World War Two* (1984). Margaret Higonnet et al., eds., *Behind the Lines: Gender and the Two World Wars* (1987), discusses the role of women in the war. On women in Germany, see Jill Stephenson, *Women in Nazi Germany* (2001).

NOTES

1. Henry L. Stimson, "The Decision to Use the Atomic Bomb," *Harper's Magazine* (February 1947): 97–107.

2. Gar Alperowitz, *Atomic Diplomacy: Hiroshima and Potsdam* (New York: Simon & Schuster, 1965), 176–181 and 236–242.

Rush Hour in Brazil   In Latin American countries, modern conveniences, when first introduced, were often insufficient to meet the demand from eager customers. Here the Sao Januario streetcar in Rio de Janeiro carries twice as many passengers as it was designed for.   (Genevieve Naylor, photographer/ Reznikoff Artistic Partnership, NY)

Why did the educated elites of India want independence? What were ordinary Indians hoping for?

What changes did foreign rule bring to Africa, and how did Africans respond?

What could Latin Americans do to achieve social justice and economic development? Were these two goals compatible?

31

STRIVING FOR INDEPENDENCE: INDIA, AFRICA, AND LATIN AMERICA, 1900–1949

CHAPTER OUTLINE

The Indian Independence Movement, 1905–1947

Sub-Saharan Africa, 1900–1945

Mexico, Argentina, and Brazil, 1900–1949

Comparative Perspectives

ENVIRONMENT AND TECHNOLOGY: Gandhi and Technology

DIVERSITY AND DOMINANCE: A Vietnamese Nationalist Denounces French Colonialism

Modern technologies, such as the mass transit system of Brazil shown here, first appeared in the wealthier countries of Europe and North America. When they were transferred to Asia, Africa, and Latin America, they reinforced the dependence of these less developed parts of the world on the industrialized countries and widened the gap between their social classes. The tensions of modernization contributed to popular movements for independence and social justice.

The previous two chapters focused on a world convulsed by war and revolution. The world wars involved Europe, East Asia, the Middle East, and the United States, and they sparked violent revolutions in Russia and China. They accelerated the development of aviation, electronics, nuclear power, and other technologies. Although these momentous events dominate the history of the first half of the twentieth century, parts of the world that were little touched by war also underwent profound changes in this period, partly for internal reasons and partly because of the warfare and revolution in other parts of the world.

In this chapter we examine the changes that took place in India, in sub-Saharan Africa, and in three major countries of Latin America—Mexico, Brazil, and Argentina. These three regions represent three very distinct cultures, yet they had much in common. India and Africa were colonies of Europe, both politically and economically. Though politically independent, the Latin American republics were dependent on Europe and the United States for the sale of raw materials and commodities and for imports of manufactured goods, technology, and capital. In all three regions independence movements tried to wrest control from distant foreigners and improve the livelihood of their peoples. Their success was partial at best.

THE INDIAN INDEPENDENCE MOVEMENT, 1905–1947

India was a colony of Great Britain from the late eighteenth to the mid-twentieth centuries. Under British rule the subcontinent acquired many of the trappings of Western-style economic development, such as railroads, harbors, modern cities, and cotton and steel mills, as well as an active and worldly middle class. The economic transformation of the region awakened in this educated middle class a sense of national dignity that demanded political fulfillment. In response, the British gradually granted India a limited amount of political autonomy while maintaining overall control. Religious and communal tensions among the Indian peoples were carefully papered over under British rule. Violent conflicts tore India apart after the withdrawal of the British in 1947 (see Map 31.1).

The Land and the People

Much of India is fertile land, but it is vulnerable to the vagaries of nature, especially droughts caused by the periodic failure of the monsoons. When the rains failed from 1896 to 1900, 2 million people died of starvation.

Despite periodic famines the Indian population grew from 250 million in 1900 to 319 million in 1921 and 389 million in 1941. This growth created pressures in many areas. Landless young men converged on the cities, exceeding the number of jobs available in the slowly expanding industries. To produce timber for construction and railroad ties, and to clear land for tea and rubber plantations, government foresters cut down most of the tropical hardwood forests that had covered the subcontinent in the nineteenth century. In spite of deforestation and extensive irrigation, the amount of land available to peasant families shrank with each successive generation. Economic development—what the British called the "moral and material progress of India"—hardly benefited the average Indian.

Indians were divided into many classes. Peasants, always the great majority, paid rents to the landowner, interest to the village moneylender, and taxes to the government and had little left to improve their land or raise their standard of living. The government protected property owners, from village moneylenders all the way up to the maharajahs°, or ruling princes, who owned huge tracts of land. The cities were crowded with craftsmen, traders, and workers of all sorts, most very poor. Although the British had banned the burning of widows on their husbands' funeral pyres, in other respects women's lives changed little under British rule.

The peoples of India spoke many different languages: Hindi in the north, Tamil in the south, Bengali in the east, Gujerati around Bombay, Urdu in the northwest, and dozens of others. As a result of British rule and increasing trade and travel, English became, like Latin in medieval Europe, the common medium of communication of the Western-educated middle class. This new class of English-speaking government bureaucrats, professionals, and merchants was to play a leading role in the independence movement.

The majority of Indians practiced Hinduism and were subdivided into hundreds of castes, each affiliated with a particular occupation. Hinduism discouraged intermarriage and other social interactions among the castes and with people who were not Hindus. Muslims constituted one-quarter of the people of India but formed a majority in the northwest and in eastern Bengal. Muslim rulers had dominated northern and central India until they were displaced by the British in the eighteenth century. More reluctant than Hindus to learn English, Muslims felt discriminated against by both British and Hindus.

---

maharajah (mah-huh-RAH-juh)

CHRONOLOGY

	India	Africa	Latin America
			1876–1910 Porfirio Díaz, dictator of Mexico
1900	**1905** Viceroy Curzon splits Bengal; mass demonstrations	**1900s** Railroads connect ports to the interior	
	1906 Muslims found All-India Muslim League	**1909** African National Congress founded	
	1911 British transfer capital from Calcutta to Delhi		**1911–1919** Mexican Revolution; Emiliano Zapata and Pancho Villa against Constitutionalists
			1917 New constitution proclaimed in Mexico
1920	**1919** Amritsar Massacre	**1920s** J. E. Casely Hayford organizes political movement in British West Africa	**1928** Plutarco Elías Calles founds Mexico's National Revolutionary Party
	1929 Gandhi leads March to the Sea		**1930–1945** Getulio Vargas, dictator of Brazil
1930	**1930s** Gandhi calls for independence; he is repeatedly arrested		**1934–1940** Lázaro Cárdenas, president of Mexico
			1938 Cárdenas nationalizes Mexican oil industry; Vargas proclaims Estado Novo in Brazil
	1939 British bring India into World War II	**1939–1945** A million Africans serve in World War II	
1940	**1940** Muhammad Ali Jinnah demands a separate nation for Muslims		**1943** Juan Perón leads military coup in Argentina
	1947 Partition and independence of India and Pakistan		**1946** Perón elected president of Argentina

British Rule and Indian Nationalism

Colonial India was ruled by a viceroy appointed by the British government and administered by a few thousand members of the Indian Civil Service. These men, imbued with a sense of duty toward their subjects, formed one of the more honest (if not efficient) bureaucracies of all time. Drawn mostly from the English gentry, they liked to think of India as a land of lords and peasants. They believed it was their duty to protect the Indian people from the dangers of industrialization, while defending their own positions from Indian nationalists.

As Europeans they admired modern technology but tried to control its introduction into India so as to maximize the benefits to Britain and to themselves. For example, they encouraged railroads, harbors, telegraphs, and other communications technologies, as well as irrigation and plantations, because they increased India's foreign trade and strengthened British control. At the same time, they discouraged the cotton and steel industries and limited the training of Indian engineers, ostensibly to spare India the social upheavals that had accompanied the Industrial Revolution in Europe, while protecting British industry from Indian competition.

At the turn of the century the majority of Indians—especially the peasants, landowners, and princes—accepted British rule. But the Europeans' racist attitude toward dark-skinned people increasingly offended Indians who had learned English and absorbed English ideas of freedom and representative government, only to discover that thinly disguised racial quotas excluded them from the Indian Civil Service, the officer corps, and prestigious country clubs.

In 1885 a small group of English-speaking Hindu professionals founded a political organization called the **Indian National Congress**. For twenty years its members

Map 31.1   The Partition of India, 1947   Before the British, India was divided among many states, ethnic groups, and religions. When the British left in 1947, the subcontinent split along religious lines. The predominantly Muslim regions of Sind and Punjab in the northwest and East Bengal in the east formed the new nation of Pakistan. The predominantly Hindu center became the Republic of India. Jammu and Kashmir remained disputed territories and poisoned relations between the two new countries.

Online Study Center
Improve Your Grade
Interactive Map: The
Partition of India, 1947

respectfully petitioned the government for access to the higher administrative positions and for a voice in official decisions, but they had little influence outside intellectual circles. Then, in 1905, Viceroy Lord Curzon divided the province of **Bengal** in two to improve the efficiency of its administration. This decision, made without consulting anyone, angered not only educated Indians, who saw it as a way to lessen their influence, but also millions of uneducated Hindu Bengalis, who suddenly found themselves outnumbered by Muslims in East Bengal. Soon Bengal was the scene of demonstrations, boycotts of British goods, and even incidents of violence against the British.

Online Study Center
Improve Your Grade
Primary Source: An Indian Nationalist
Condemns the British Empire

Construction Site in Colonial India British civil engineers were active throughout India building roads, railroads, and canals. Here, a British official supervises Indian workers building a bridge. (The Billie Love Collection)

In 1906, while the Hindus of Bengal were protesting the partition of their province, Muslims, fearful of Hindu dominance elsewhere in India, founded the **All-India Muslim League**. Caught in an awkward situation, the government responded by granting Indians a limited franchise based on wealth. Muslims, however, were on average poorer than Hindus, for many poor and low-caste Hindus had converted to Islam to escape caste discrimination. Taking advantage of these religious divisions, the British instituted separate representation and different voting qualifications for Hindus and Muslims. Then, in 1911, the British transferred the capital of India from Calcutta to Delhi°, the former capital of the Mughal° emperors. These changes disturbed Indians of all classes and religions and raised their political consciousness. Politics, once primarily the concern of westernized intellectuals, turned into two mass movements: one by Hindus and one by Muslims.

To maintain their commercial position and prevent social upheavals, the British resisted the idea that India

could, or should, industrialize. Their geologists looked for minerals, such as coal or manganese, that British industry required. However, when the only Indian member of the Indian Geological Service, Pramatha Nath Bose, wanted to prospect for iron ore, he had to resign because the government wanted no part of an Indian steel industry that could compete with that of Britain. Bose joined forces with Jamsetji Tata, a Bombay textile magnate who decided to produce steel in spite of British opposition. With the help of German and American engineers and equipment, Tata's son Dorabji opened the first steel mill in India in 1911, in a town called Jamshedpur in honor of his father. Although it produced only a fraction of the steel that India required, Jamshedpur became a powerful symbol of Indian national pride. It prompted Indian nationalists to ask why a country that could produce its own steel needed foreigners to run its government.

During World War I Indians supported Britain enthusiastically; 1.2 million men volunteered for the army, and millions more voluntarily contributed money to the government. Many expected the British to reward their loyalty

Delhi (DEL-ee) **Mughal** (MOO-guhl)

with political concessions. Others organized to demand concessions and a voice in the government. In 1917, in response to the agitation, the British government announced "the gradual development of self-governing institutions with a view to the progressive realization of responsible government in India as an integral part of the British Empire." This sounded like a promise of self-government, but the timetable was so vague that nationalists denounced it as a devious maneuver to postpone India's independence.

In late 1918 and early 1919 a violent influenza epidemic broke out among soldiers in the war zone of northern France. Within a few months it spread to every country on earth and killed over 20 million people. India was especially hard hit; of the millions who died, two out of three were Indian. This dreadful toll increased the mounting political tensions. Leaders of the Indian National Congress declared that the British reform proposals were too little, too late.

On April 13, 1919, in the city of Amritsar in Punjab, General Reginald Dyer ordered his troops to fire into a peaceful crowd of some 10,000 demonstrators, killing at least 379 and wounding 1,200. Waves of angry demonstrations swept over India, but the government waited six months to appoint a committee to investigate the massacre. After General Dyer retired, the British House of Lords voted to approve his actions, and a fund was raised in appreciation of his services. Indians interpreted these gestures as showing British contempt for their colonial subjects. In the charged atmosphere of the time, the period of gradual accommodation between the British and the Indians came to a close.

Mahatma Gandhi and Militant Nonviolence

For the next twenty years India teetered on the edge of violent uprisings and harsh repression, possibly even war. That it did not succumb was due to **Mohandas K. Gandhi°** (1869–1948), a man known to his followers as "Mahatma," the "great soul."

Gandhi began life with every advantage. His family was wealthy enough to send him to England for his education. After his studies he lived in South Africa and practiced law for the small Indian community there. During World War I he returned to India and was one of many Western-educated Hindu intellectuals who joined the Indian National Congress.

Gandhi had some unusual political ideas. Unlike many radical political thinkers of his time, he denounced the popular ideals of power, struggle, and combat. Instead,

inspired by both Hindu and Christian concepts, he preached the saintly virtues of *ahimsa°* (nonviolence) and *satyagraha°* (the search for truth). He refused to countenance violence among his followers, and he called off several demonstrations when they turned violent.

Gandhi had an affinity for the poor that was unusual even among socialist politicians. In 1921 he gave up the Western-style suits worn by lawyers and the fine raiment of wealthy Indians and henceforth wore simple peasant garb: a length of homespun cloth below his waist and a shawl to cover his torso (see Environment and Technology: Gandhi and Technology). He spoke for the farmers and the outcasts, whom he called *harijan°*, "children of God." He attracted ever-larger numbers of followers among the poor and the illiterate, who soon began to revere him; and he transformed the cause of Indian independence from an elite movement of the educated into a mass movement with a quasi-religious aura.

Gandhi was a brilliant political tactician and a master of public relations gestures. In 1929, for instance, he led a few followers on an 80-mile (129-kilometer) walk, camped on a beach, and gathered salt from the sea in a blatant and well-publicized act of civil disregard for the government's monopoly on salt. But he discovered that unleashing the power of popular participation was one thing and controlling its direction was quite another. Within days of his "Walk to the Sea," demonstrations of support broke out all over India, in which the police killed a hundred demonstrators and arrested over sixty thousand.

Many times during the 1930s Gandhi threatened to fast "unto death," and several times he did come close to death, to protest the violence of both the police and his followers and to demand independence. He was repeatedly arrested and spent a total of six years in jail. But every arrest made him more popular. He became a cult figure not only in his own country but also in the Western media. He never won a battle or an election; instead, in the words of historian Percival Spear, he made the British "uncomfortable in their cherished field of moral rectitude," and he gave Indians the feeling that theirs was the ethically superior cause.

India Moves Toward Independence

In the 1920s, slowly and reluctantly, the British began to give in to the pressure of the Indian National Congress and the Muslim League. They handed over control of "national" areas such as education, the economy, and public works. They

Gandhi (GAHN-dee)

ahimsa (uh-HIM-sah)   **satyagraha** (suh-TYAH-gruh-huh)
harijan (HAH-ree-jahn)

Gandhi and Technology

In the twentieth century all political leaders but one embraced modern industrial technology. That one exception is Gandhi.

After deciding to wear only handmade cloth, Gandhi made a bonfire of imported factory-made cloth and began spending half an hour every day spinning yarn on a simple spinning wheel, a task he called a "sacrament." The spinning wheel became the symbol of his movement and was later incorporated into the Indian flag. Any Indian who wished to come before him had to dress in handwoven cloth.

Gandhi had several reasons for reviving this ancient craft. One was his revulsion against "the incessant search for material comforts," an evil to which he thought Europeans were "becoming slaves." Not only had materialism corrupted the people of the West, it had also caused massive unemployment in India. In particular, he blamed the impoverishment of the Indian people on the cotton industries of England and Japan, which had ruined the traditional cotton manufacturing by which India had once supplied all her own needs.

Gandhi looked back to a time before India became a colony of Britain, when "our women spun fine yarns in their own cottages, and supplemented the earnings of their husbands." The spinning wheel, he believed, was "presented to the nation for giving occupation to the millions who had, at least four months of the year, nothing to do." Not only would a return to the spinning wheel provide employment to millions of Indians, but it would also become a symbol of "national consciousness and a contribution by every individual to a definite constructive national work."

Nevertheless, Gandhi was a shrewd politician who understood the usefulness of modern devices for mobilizing the masses and organizing his followers. He wore a watch and used the telephone and the printing press to keep in touch with his followers. When he traveled by train, he rode third class—but in a third-class railroad car of his own. His goal was the independence of his country, and he pursued it with every nonviolent means he could find.

Gandhi's ideas challenge us to rethink the purpose of technology. Was he opposed on principle to all modern devices? Was he an opportunist who used those devices that served his political ends and rejected those that did not? Or did he have a higher principle that accounts for his willingness to use the telephone and the railroad but not factory-made cloth?

Gandhi at the Spinning Wheel   Mahatma Gandhi chose the spinning wheel as his symbol because it represented the traditional activity of millions of rural Indians whose livelihoods were threatened by industrialization.   (Margaret Bourke-White, Time Life Pictures/Getty Images *LIFE Magazine* © Time Warner Inc.)

also gradually admitted more Indians into the Civil Service and the officer corps.

India took its first tentative steps toward industrialization in the years before the First and then the Second World Wars. Indian politicians obtained the right to erect high tariff barriers against imports in order to protect India's infant industries from foreign, even British, competition. Behind these barriers, Indian entrepreneurs built plants to manufacture iron and steel, cement, paper, cotton and jute textiles, sugar, and other products. This early industrialization provided jobs, though not enough to improve the lives of the Indian peasants or urban poor. These manufactures, however, helped create a class of wealthy Indian businessmen. Far from being satisfied by the government's policies, they supported the Indian National Congress and its demands for independence. Though paying homage to Gandhi, they preferred his designated successor as leader of the Indian National Congress, **Jawaharlal Nehru°** (1889–1964). A highly educated nationalist and subtle thinker, Nehru, unlike Gandhi, looked forward to creating a modern industrial India.

Congress politicians won regional elections but continued to be excluded from the viceroy's cabinet, the true center of power. When World War II began in September 1939, Viceroy Lord Linlithgow declared war without consulting a single Indian. The Congress-dominated provincial governments resigned in protest and found that boycotting government office increased their popular support. When the British offered to give India its independence once the war ended, Gandhi called the offer a "postdated cheque on a failing bank" and demanded full independence immediately. His "Quit India" campaign aroused popular demonstrations against the British and provoked a wave of arrests, including his own. Nehru explained: "I would fight Japan sword in hand, but I can only do so as a free man." The Second World War divided the Indian people. Most Indian soldiers felt they were fighting to defend their country rather than to support the British Empire. As in World War I, Indians contributed heavily to the Allied war effort, supplying 2 million soldiers and enormous amounts of resources, especially the timber needed for emergency construction. A small number of Indians, however, were so anti-British that they joined the Japanese side.

India's subordination to British interests was vividly demonstrated in the famine of 1943 in Bengal. Unlike previous famines, this one was caused not by drought but by the Japanese conquest of Burma, which cut off supplies of Burmese rice that normally went to Bengal. Although food was available elsewhere in India, the British army had requisitioned the railroads to transport troops and equipment in preparation for a Japanese invasion. As a result, supplies ran short in Bengal and surrounding areas, while speculators hoarded whatever they could find. Some 2 million people starved to death before the army was ordered to supply food.

Partition and Independence

When the war ended, Britain's new Labour Party government prepared for Indian independence, but deep suspicions between Hindus and Muslims complicated the process. The break between the two communities had started in 1937, when the Indian National Congress won provincial elections and refused to share power with the Muslim League. In 1940 the leader of the League, **Muhammad Ali Jinnah°** (1876–1948), demanded what many Muslims had been dreaming of for years: a country of their own, to be called Pakistan (from "Punjab-Afghans-Kashmir-Sind" plus the Persian suffix *-stan* meaning "kingdom").

As independence approached, talks between Jinnah and Nehru broke down and battle lines were drawn. Violent rioting between Hindus and Muslims broke out in Bengal and Bihar. Gandhi's appeals for tolerance and cooperation fell on deaf ears. In despair, he retreated to his home near Ahmedabad. The British made frantic proposals to keep India united, but their authority was waning fast.

By early 1947 the Indian National Congress had accepted the idea of a partition of India into two states, one secular but dominated by Hindus, the other Muslim. In June Lord Mountbatten, the last viceroy, decided that independence must come immediately. On August 15 British India gave way to a new India and Pakistan. The Indian National Congress, led by Nehru, formed the first government of India; Jinnah and the Muslim League established a government for the provinces that made up Pakistan.

The rejoicing over independence was marred by violent outbreaks between Muslims and Hindus. In protest against the mounting chaos, Gandhi refused to attend the independence day celebration. Throughout the land, Muslim and Hindu neighbors turned on one another, and armed members of one faith hunted down people of the other faith. For centuries Hindus and Muslims had intermingled throughout most of India. Now, leaving most of their possessions behind, Hindus

---

Nehru (NAY-roo)

Jinnah (JEE-nah)

The Partition of India   When India became independent, Muslims fled from Hindu regions, and Hindus fled from Muslims. Margaret Bourke-White photographed a long line of refugees, with their cows, carts, and belongings, trudging down a country road toward safety.   (Margaret Bourke-White, Time Life Pictures/Getty Images)

fled from predominantly Muslim areas, and Muslims fled from Hindu areas. Trainloads of desperate refugees of one faith were attacked and massacred by members of the other or were left stranded in the middle of deserts. Within a few months some 12 million people had abandoned their ancestral homes and a half-million lay dead. In January 1948 Gandhi died too, gunned down by an angry Hindu refugee.

After the sectarian massacres and flights of refugees, few Hindus remained in Pakistan, and Muslims were a minority in all but one state of India. That state was Kashmir, a strategically important region in the foothills of the Himalayas. India annexed Kashmir because the local maharajah was Hindu and because the state held the headwaters of the rivers that irrigated millions of acres of farmland in the northwestern part of the subcontinent. The majority of the inhabitants of Kashmir were Muslims, however, and would probably have joined Pakistan if they had been allowed to vote on the matter. The consequence of the partition and of Kashmir in particular was to turn India and Pakistan into bitter enemies that have fought several wars in the past half-century.

SUB-SAHARAN AFRICA, 1900–1945

Of all the continents, Africa was the last to come under European rule (see Chapter 28). The first half of the twentieth century, the time when nationalist movements threatened European rule in Asia (see Diversity and Dominance: A Vietnamese Nationalist Denounces French Colonialism), was Africa's period of classic colonialism. After World War I Britain, France, Belgium, and South Africa divided Germany's African colonies among themselves. In the 1930s Italy invaded Ethiopia. The colonial empires reached their peak shortly before World War II.

Colonial Africa: Economic and Social Changes

Outside of Algeria, Kenya, and South Africa, few Europeans lived in Africa. In 1930 Nigeria, with a population of 20 million, was ruled by 386 British officials and by 8,000 policemen and military, of whom

A Vietnamese Nationalist Denounces French Colonialism

The regions described in this chapter were not the only ones whose inhabitants chafed at the dominance of the great powers and sought more control over their own national destinies. Movements for independence were a worldwide phenomenon. The tactics that different peoples used to achieve their goals differed widely. Among countries that were formal colonies, the case of India is unique in that its nationalist movement was led by Mahatma Gandhi, a man who subordinated the goal of national independence to his commitment to nonviolent passive resistance. In Mexico, as in China, Russia, and other parts of the world, revolutionary movements were often associated with violent uprisings. French Indochina is a case in point.

Indochina, comprising the countries we now call Vietnam, Kampuchea, and Laos, was conquered piecemeal by the French from 1862 to 1895, but only after overcoming fierce resistance. Thereafter, France modernized the cities and irrigation systems and transformed the country into a leading producer of tea, rice, and natural rubber. This meant transferring large numbers of landless peasants to new plantations and destroying the traditional social structure. To govern Indochina, the French brought in more soldiers and civil administrators than the British had in all of India, a far larger colony. Even though they succeeded in crushing the resistance of the peasants and the old Confucian elites, the French were educating a new elite in the French language. These newly educated youths, inspired by French ideas of liberty and nationhood and by the examples of the Guomindang and the Communist Party in neighboring China, formed the core of two new revolutionary movements.

One movement was the Vietnamese Revolutionary Youth League founded by Ho Chi Minh (1890–1969) in 1925, which later became the Indochinese Communist Party. The other was the Viet Nam Quoc Dan Dang, or Vietnamese Nationalist Party, modeled after Sun Yat-sen's Guomindang, founded in 1927 by a schoolteacher named Nguyen Thai Hoc (1904–1930). This party attracted low-level government employees, soldiers, and small businessmen. At first Nguyen

Thai Hoc lobbied the colonial government for reforms, but in vain. Two years later he turned to revolutionary action. In February 1930 he led an uprising at Yen Bay that the French quickly crushed. He and many of his followers were executed four months later, leaving Ho Chi Minh's Communists as the standard-bearers of nationalist revolution in Vietnam.

While awaiting his execution, Nguyen Thai Hoc wrote the following letter to the French Chamber of Deputies to justify his actions.

Gentlemen:

I, the undersigned, Nguyen Thai Hoc, a Vietnamese citizen, twenty-six years old, chairman and founder of the Vietnamese Nationalist Party, at present arrested and imprisoned at the jail of Yen Bay, Tongking, Indochina, have the great honor to inform you of the following facts:

According to the tenets of justice, everyone has the right to defend his own country when it is invaded by foreigners, and according to the principles of humanity, everyone has the duty to save his compatriots when they are in difficulty or in danger. As for myself, I have assessed the fact that my country has been annexed by you French for more than sixty years. I realize that under your dictatorial yoke, my compatriots have experienced a very hard life, and my people will without doubt be completely annihilated, by the naked principle of natural selection. Therefore, my right and my duty have compelled me to seek every way to defend my country which has been invaded and occupied, and to save my people who are in great danger.

At the beginning, I had thought to cooperate with the French in Indochina in order to serve my compatriots, my country and my people, particularly in the areas of cultural and economic development. As regards economic development, in 1925 I sent a memorandum to Governor General Varenne, describing to him all our aspirations concerning the protection of local industry and commerce in Indochina. I urged strongly in the same letter the creation of a Superior School of Industrial Development in Tongking. In 1926 I again addressed another letter to the then Governor General of Indochina in which I included some explicit suggestions to relieve the hardships of our poor people. In 1927, for a third time, I sent a letter to the Résident Supérieur [provincial administrator] in Tongking, requesting permission to publish a weekly magazine with the aim of safeguarding and encouraging local industry and commerce. With regard to the cultural domain, I sent a letter to the Governor General in 1927, requesting (1) the privilege of opening tuition-free schools for the children of the lower classes, particularly children of workers and peasants; (2) freedom to open popular publishing houses and libraries in industrial centers.

It is absolutely ridiculous that every suggestion has been rejected. My letters were without answer; my plans have not been considered; my requests have been ignored; even the articles that I sent to newspapers have been censored and rejected. From the experience of these rejections, I have come to the conclusion that the French have no sincere intention of helping my country or my people. I also concluded that we have to expel France. For this reason, in 1927, I began to organize a revolutionary party, which I named the Vietnamese Nationalist Party, with the aim of overthrowing the dictatorial and oppressive administration of our country. We aspire to create a Republic of Vietnam, composed of persons sincerely concerned with the happiness of the people. My party is a clandestine organization, and in February 1929, it was uncovered by the security police. Among the members of my party, a great number have been arrested. Fifty-two persons have been condemned to forced labor ranging from two to twenty years. Although many have been detained and many others unjustly condemned, my party has not ceased its activity. Under my guidance, the Party continues to operate and progress towards its aim.

During the Yen Bay uprising someone succeeded in killing some French officers. The authorities accused my party of having organized and perpetrated this revolt. They have accused me of having given the orders for the massacre. In truth, I have never given such orders, and I have presented before the Penal Court of Yen Bay all the evidence showing the inanity of this accusation. Even so, some of the members of my party completely ignorant of that event have been accused of participating in it. The French Indochinese government burned and destroyed their houses. They sent French troops to occupy their villages and stole their rice to divide it among the soldiers. Not just members of my party have been suffering from this injustice—we should rather call this cruelty rather than injustice—but also many simple peasants, interested only in their daily work in the rice fields, living miserable lives like buffaloes and horses, have been compromised in this reprisal. At the present time, in various areas there are tens of thousands of men, women, and children, persons of all ages, who have been massacred. They died either of hunger or exposure because the French Indochinese government burned their homes. I therefore beseech you in tears to redress this injustice which otherwise will annihilate my people, which will stain French honor, and which will belittle all human values.

I have the honor to inform you that I am responsible for all events happening in my country under the leadership of my party from 1927 until the present. You only need to execute me. I beg your indulgence for all the others who at the present time are imprisoned in various jails. I am the only culprit, all the others are innocent. They are innocent because most of them are indeed members of my party, and have joined it only because I have succeeded in convincing them of their duties as citizens of this country, and of the humiliations of a slave with a lost country. Some of them are not even party members. They have been wrongly accused by their enemy or by the security police; or they simply are wrongly accused by their friends who have not been able to bear the tortures inflicted by the security police. I have the honor to repeat once again that you need execute only me. If you are not satisfied with killing one man, I advise you to kill also the members of my family, but I strongly beg your indulgence towards those who are innocent.

Finally, I would like to declare in conclusion: if France wants to stay in peace in Indochina, if France does not want to have increasing troubles with revolutionary movements, she should immediately modify the cruel and inhuman policy now practiced in Indochina. The French should behave like friends to the Vietnamese, instead of being cruel and oppressive masters. They should be attentive to the intellectual and material sufferings of the Vietnamese people, instead of being harsh and tough. Please, Gentlemen, receive my gratitude.

QUESTIONS FOR ANALYSIS

1. When he first became involved in politics, what were Nguyen Thai Hoc's views of French colonialism?

2. What were his first initiatives, and what response did he get from the French colonial administration?

3. What motivated Nguyen Thai Hoc to organize an uprising, and what was the response of the French?

4. Compare Nguyen Thai Hoc's views and methods and the French response with the situation in India.

Source: Harry Benda and John Larkin, *The World of Southeast Asia* (New York: Harper & Row, 1967), 182–185. Reprinted by permission of the author.

African Farmers in the Gold Coast African farmers in the Gold Coast (now Ghana) sold their cocoa beans to government agents. The government kept the prices artificially low in order to profit on the transactions. (Popperfoto/Robertstock.com)

150 were European. Yet even such a small presence stimulated deep social and economic changes.

Since the turn of the century the colonial powers had built railroads from coastal cities to mines and plantations in the interior, in order to provide raw materials to the industrial world. The economic boom of the interwar years benefited few Africans. Colonial governments took lands that Africans owned communally and sold or leased them to European companies or, in eastern and southern Africa, to white settlers. Large European companies dominated wholesale commerce, while immigrants from various countries—Indians in East Africa, Greeks and Syrians in West Africa—handled much of the retail trade. Airplanes and automobiles were even more alien to the experience of Africans than railroads had been to an earlier generation.

Where land was divided into small farms, some Africans benefited from the boom. Farmers in the Gold Coast (now Ghana°) profited from the high price of cocoa, as did palm-oil producers in Nigeria and coffee growers in East Africa. In most of Africa women played a major role in the retail trades, selling pots and pans, cloth, food, and other items in the markets. Many maintained their economic independence and kept their household finances separate from those of their husbands, following a custom that predated the colonial period.

For many Africans economic development meant working in European-owned mines and plantations, often under compulsion. Colonial governments were eager to develop the resources of the territories under their control but could not afford to pay high enough wages to attract workers. Instead, they used their police powers to force Africans to work under harsh conditions for little or no pay. In the 1920s, when the government of French Equatorial Africa decided to build a railroad from Brazzaville to the Atlantic coast, a distance of 312 miles (502 kilometers), it drafted 127,000 men to carve a roadbed across mountains and through rain forests. For lack of food, clothing, and medical care, 20,000 of them died, an average of 64 deaths per mile of track.

Europeans prided themselves on bringing modern health care to Africa; yet before the 1930s there was too little of it to help the majority of Africans, and other aspects of colonialism actually worsened public health. Migrants to cities, mines, and plantations and soldiers moving from post to post spread syphilis, gonorrhea, tuberculosis, and malaria. Sleeping sickness and smallpox epidemics raged throughout Central Africa. In recruiting men to work, colonial governments depleted rural areas of farmers needed to plant and harvest crops. Forced requisitions of food to feed the workers left the remaining populations undernourished and vulnerable to diseases. Not until the 1930s did colonial governments realize the negative consequences of their labor policies and begin to invest in agricultural development and health care for Africans.

In 1900 Ibadan° in Nigeria was the only city in sub-Saharan Africa with more than 100,000 inhabitants; fifty years later, dozens of cities had reached that size, including Nairobi° in Kenya, Johannesburg in South Africa, Lagos in Nigeria, Accra in Gold Coast, and Dakar in Senegal. Africans migrated to cities because they offered hope of jobs and excitement and, for a few, the chance to become wealthy.

Ghana (GAH-nuh)

Ibadan (ee-BAH-dahn)　**Nairobi** (nie-ROE-bee)

A Quranic School In Muslim countries, religious education is centered on learning to read, write, and recite the Quran, the sacred book of the Islamic religion, in the original Arabic. This picture shows boys in a Libyan madrassa (Quranic school) studying writing and religion. (Olivier Martel/Corbis)

However, migrations damaged the family life of those involved, for almost all the migrants were men leaving women in the countryside to farm and raise children. Cities built during the colonial period reflected the colonialists' attitudes with racially segregated housing, clubs, restaurants, hospitals, and other institutions. Patterns of racial discrimination were most rigid in the white-settler colonies of eastern and southern Africa.

Religious and Political Changes

Traditional religious belief could not explain the dislocations that foreign rule, migrations, and sudden economic changes brought to the lives of Africans. Many therefore turned to one of the two universal religions, Christianity and Islam, for guidance.

Christianity was introduced into Africa by Western missionaries, except in Ethiopia, where it was indigenous. It was most successful in the coastal regions of West and South Africa, where the European influence was strongest. A major attraction of the Christian denominations was their mission schools, which taught both craft skills and basic literacy, providing access to employment as minor functionaries, teachers, and shopkeepers. These schools educated a new elite, many of whom learned not only skills and literacy but Western political ideas as well. Many Africans accepted Christianity enthusiastically, reading the suffering of their own peoples into the biblical stories of Moses and the parables of Jesus. The churches trained some of the brighter pupils to become catechists, teachers, and clergymen. A few rose to high positions, such as James Johnson, a Yoruba who became the Anglican bishop of the Niger Delta Pastorate. Independent Christian churches—known as "Ethiopian" churches—associated Christian beliefs with radical ideas of racial equality and participation in politics.

Islam spread inland from the East African coast and southward from the Sahel° toward the West African coast, through the influence and example of Arab and African merchants. Islam also emphasized literacy—in Arabic through Quranic schools rather than in a European language—and was less disruptive of traditional African customs such as polygamy.

In a few places, such as Dakar in Senegal and Cape Town in South Africa, small numbers of Africans could obtain secondary education. Even smaller numbers went on to college in Europe or America. Though few in number, they became the leaders of political movements. The contrast between the liberal ideas imparted by Western education and the realities of racial discrimination under colonial rule contributed to the rise of nationalism among educated Africans. In Senegal **Blaise Diagne**° agitated for African participation in politics and fair treatment in the French army during World War I. In

---

Sahel (SAH-hel)   **Diagne** (dee-AHN-yuh)

the 1920s J. E. Casely Hayford began organizing a movement for greater autonomy in British West Africa. These nationalist movements were inspired by the ideas of Pan-Africanists from America such as W. E. B. Du Bois and Marcus Garvey, who advocated the unity of African peoples around the world, as well as by European ideas of liberty and nationhood. To defend the interests of Africans, Western-educated lawyers and journalists in South Africa founded the **African National Congress** in 1912 in emulation of the Indian National Congress. Before World War II, however, these nationalist movements were small and had little influence.

The Second World War (1939–1945) had a profound effect on the peoples of Africa, even those far removed from the theaters of war. The war brought hardships, such as increased forced labor, inflation, and requisitions of raw materials. Yet it also brought hope. During the campaign to oust the Italians from Ethiopia, Emperor **Haile Selassie°** (r. 1930–1974) led his own troops into Addis Ababa, his capital, and reclaimed his title. A million Africans served as soldiers and carriers in Burma, North Africa, and Europe, where many became aware of Africa's role in helping the Allied war effort. They listened to Allied propaganda in favor of European liberation movements and against Nazi racism, and they returned to their countries with new and radical ideas.

The early twentieth century was a relatively peaceful period for sub-Saharan Africa. But this peace—enforced by the European occupiers—masked profound changes that were to transform African life after the Second World War. The building of cities, railroads, and other enterprises brought Africa into the global economy, often at great human cost. Colonialism also brought changes to African culture and religion, hastening the spread of Christianity and Islam. And the foreign occupation awakened political ideas that inspired the next generation of Africans to demand independence (see Chapter 32).

MEXICO, ARGENTINA, AND BRAZIL, 1900–1949

In the nineteenth century Latin America achieved independence from Spain and Portugal but did not industrialize. Throughout much of the century most Latin American republics suffered from ideological divisions, unstable governments, and violent upheavals. By trading their raw materials and agricultural products for foreign

manufactured goods and capital investments, they became economically dependent on the wealthier countries to the north, especially on the United States and Great Britain. Their societies, far from fulfilling the promises of their independence, remained deeply split between wealthy landowners and desperately poor peasants.

Mexico, Brazil, and Argentina contained well over half of Latin America's land, population, and wealth, and their relations with other countries and their economies were quite similar. Mexico, however, underwent a traumatic social revolution, while Argentina and Brazil evolved more peaceably.

Background to Revolution: Mexico in 1910

Mexico was the Latin American country most influenced by the Spanish during three centuries of colonial rule. After achieving independence in 1821, it suffered from a half-century of political turmoil. At the beginning of the twentieth century Mexican society was divided into rich and poor and into persons of Spanish, Indian, and mixed ancestry. A few very wealthy families of Spanish origin, less than 1 percent of the population, owned 85 percent of Mexico's land, mostly in huge *haciendas* (estates). Closely tied to this elite were the handful of American and British companies that controlled most of Mexico's railroads, silver mines, plantations, and other productive enterprises. At the other end of the social scale were Indians, many of whom did not speak Spanish. *Mestizos°*, people of mixed Indian and European ancestry, were only slightly better off; most of them were peasants who worked on the haciendas or farmed small communal plots near their ancestral villages.

During the colonial period, the Spanish government had made halfhearted efforts to defend Indians and mestizos from the land-grabbing tactics of the haciendas. After independence in 1821 wealthy Mexican families and American companies used bribery and force to acquire millions of acres of good agricultural land from villages in southern Mexico. Peasants lost not only their fields but also their access to firewood and pasture for their animals. Sugar, cotton, and other commercial crops replaced corn and beans, and peasants had little choice but to work on haciendas. To survive, they had to buy food and other necessities on credit from the landowner's store; eventually, they fell permanently into debt. Sometimes whole communities were forced to relocate.

Haile Selassie (HI-lee seh-LASS-ee)

mestizo (mess-TEE-so)

Despite many upheavals in Mexico in the nineteenth century, in 1910 the government seemed in control. For thirty-four years General Porfirio Díaz° (1830–1915) had ruled Mexico under the motto "Liberty, Order, Progress." To Díaz "liberty" meant freedom for rich hacienda owners and foreign investors to acquire more land. The government imposed "order" through rigged elections and a policy of *pan o palo* (bread or the stick)—that is, bribes for Díaz's supporters and summary justice for those who opposed him. "Progress" meant mainly the importing of foreign capital, machinery, and technicians to take advantage of Mexico's labor, soil, and natural resources.

During the Díaz years (1876–1910) Mexico City—with paved streets, streetcar lines, electric street lighting, and public parks—became a showplace, and new telegraph and railroad lines connected cities and towns throughout Mexico. But this material progress benefited only a handful of well-connected businessmen. The boom in railroads, agriculture, and mining at the turn of the century actually caused a decline in the average Mexican's standard of living.

Though a mestizo himself, Díaz discriminated against the nonwhite majority of Mexicans. He and his supporters tried to eradicate what they saw as Mexico's embarrassingly rustic traditions. On many middle- and upper-class tables French cuisine replaced traditional Mexican dishes. The wealthy replaced sombreros and ponchos with European garments. Though bullfighting and cockfighting remained popular, the well-to-do preferred horse racing and soccer. To the educated middle class—the only group with a strong sense of Mexican nationhood—this devaluation of Mexican culture became a symbol of the Díaz regime's failure to defend national interests against foreign influences.

Revolution and Civil War in Mexico

Many Mexicans feared or anticipated a popular uprising after Díaz. Unlike the independence movement in India, the Mexican Revolution was a social revolution and was not the work of one party with a well-defined ideology. Instead, it developed haphazardly, led by a series of ambitious but limited leaders, each representing a different segment of Mexican society.

The first was Francisco I. Madero (1873–1913), the son of a wealthy landowning and mining family, educated in the United States. When minor uprisings broke

Emiliano Zapata   Zapata, the leader of a peasant rebellion in southern Mexico during the Mexican Revolution, stands in full revolutionary regalia: sword, rifles, bandoleers, boots, and sombrero.   (Brown Brothers)

out in 1911, the government collapsed and Díaz fled into exile. The Madero presidency was welcomed by some, but it aroused opposition from peasant leaders like **Emiliano Zapata**° (1879–1919). In 1913, after two years as president, Madero was overthrown and murdered by one of his former supporters, General Victoriano Huerta. Woodrow Wilson (1856–1924), president of the United States, showed his displeasure by sending the United States Marines to occupy Veracruz.

Díaz (DEE-as)

Zapata (sah-PAH-tah)

Map 31.2   The Mexican Revolution   The Mexican Revolution began in two distinct regions of the country. One was the mountainous and densely populated area south of Mexico City, particularly Morelos, homeland of Emiliano Zapata. The other was the dry and thinly populated ranch country of the north, such as Chihuahua, home of Pancho Villa. The fighting that ensued crisscrossed the country along the main railroad lines, shown on the map.

The inequities of Mexican society and foreign intervention in Mexico's affairs angered Mexico's middle class and industrial workers. They found leaders in Venustiano Carranza, a landowner, and in Alvaro Obregón°, a schoolteacher. Calling themselves Constitutionalists, Carranza and Obregón organized private armies and succeeded in overthrowing Huerta in 1914. By then, the revolution had spread to the countryside.

As early as 1911 Zapata, an Indian farmer, had led a revolt against the haciendas in the mountains of Morelos, south of Mexico City (see Map 31.2). His soldiers were peasants, some of them women, mounted on horseback and armed with pistols and rifles. For several years they periodically came down from the mountains, burned hacienda buildings, and returned land to the Indian villages to which it had once belonged.

Obregón (oh-bray-GAWN)

Another leader appeared in Chihuahua, a northern state where seventeen individuals owned two-fifths of the land and 95 percent of the people had no land at all. Starting in 1913 **Francisco "Pancho" Villa** (1877–1923), a former ranch hand, mule driver, and bandit, organized an army of three thousand men, most of them cowboys. They too seized land from the large haciendas, not to rebuild traditional communities as in southern Mexico but to create family ranches.

Zapata and Villa were part agrarian rebels, part social revolutionaries. They enjoyed tremendous popular support but could never rise above their regional and peasant origins and lead a national revolution. The Constitutionalists had fewer soldiers than Zapata and Villa; but they held the major cities, controlled the country's exports of oil, and used the proceeds of oil sales to buy modern weapons. Fighting continued for years, and gradually the Constitutionalists took over most of Mexico. In 1919 they defeated and killed Zapata; Villa was

***The Agitator*, a Mural by Diego Rivera**   Diego Rivera (1886–1957) was politically committed to the Mexican Revolution and widely admired as an artist. This mural, painted at the National Agricultural School at Chapingo near Mexico City, shows a political agitator addressing peasants and workers. With one hand, the speaker points to miners laboring in a silver mine; with the other, to a hammer and sickle.   (© Banco de Mexico, Diego Rivera & Frida Kahlo Museums Trust.)

assassinated four years later. An estimated 2 million people lost their lives in the civil war, and much of Mexico lay in ruins.

During their struggle to win support against Zapata and Villa, the Constitutionalists adopted many of their rivals' agrarian reforms, such as restoring communal lands to the Indians of Morelos. The Constitutionalists also proposed social programs designed to appeal to workers and the middle class. The Constitution of 1917 promised universal suffrage and a one-term presidency; state-run education to free the poor from the hold of the Catholic Church; the end of debt peonage; restrictions on foreign ownership of property; and laws specifying minimum wages and maximum hours to protect laborers. Although these reforms were too costly to implement right away, they had important symbolic significance, for they enshrined the dignity of Mexicans and the equality of Indians, mestizos, and whites, as well as of peasants and city people. In the early 1920s, after a decade of violence that exhausted all classes, the Mexican Revolution lost momentum. Only in Morelos did peasants receive land, and President Obregón and his closest associates made all the important decisions. In 1928 Obregón was assassinated. His successor, Plutarco Elías Calles°, founded the National Revolutionary Party, or PNR (the abbreviation of its

name in Spanish). The PNR was a forum where all the pressure groups and vested interests—labor, peasants, businessmen, landowners, the military, and others—worked out compromises. The establishment of the PNR gave the Mexican Revolution a second wind.

Lázaro Cárdenas°, chosen by Calles to be president in 1934, brought peasants' and workers' organizations into the party, renamed it the Mexican Revolutionary Party (PRM), and removed the generals from government positions. Then he set to work implementing the reforms promised in the Constitution of 1917. Cárdenas redistributed 44 million acres (17.6 million hectares) to peasant communes, replaced church-run schools with government schools, and nationalized the railroads and numerous other businesses.

Cárdenas's most dramatic move was the expropriation of foreign-owned oil companies. In the early 1920s Mexico was the world's leading producer of oil, but a handful of American and British companies exported almost all of it. In 1938 Cárdenas seized the foreign-owned oil industry, more as a matter of national pride than of economics. The oil companies expected the governments of the United States and Great Britain to come to their rescue, perhaps with military force. But Mexico and the United States chose to resolve the issue

---

Calles (KAH-yace)

Lázaro Cárdenas (LAH-sah-roe KAHR-dih-nahs)

through negotiation, and Mexico retained control of its oil industry.

When Cárdenas's term ended in 1940, Mexico, like India, was still a land of poor farmers with a small industrial base. The Revolution had brought great changes, however. The political system was free of both chaos and dictatorships. A small group of wealthy people no longer monopolized land and other resources. The military was tamed; the Catholic Church no longer controlled education; and the nationalization of oil had demonstrated Mexico's independence from foreign corporations and military intervention.

In the arts the Mexican Revolution sparked a surge of creativity. The political murals of José Clemente Orozco and Diego Rivera and the paintings of Frida Kahlo focused on social themes, showing peasants, workers, and soldiers in scenes from the Revolution. These works of art gave Mexicans a sense of national unity and pride in the achievements of the Revolution that lasted long after the revolutionary fervor had dissipated.

What did the Mexican Revolution accomplish? It did not fulfill the democratic promise of Madero's campaign, for it brought to power a party that monopolized the government for eighty years. However, it allowed far more sectors of the population to participate in politics and made sure no president stayed in office more than six years. The Revolution also promised far-reaching social reforms, such as free education, higher wages and more security for workers, and the redistribution of land to the peasants. These long-delayed reforms began to be implemented during the Cárdenas administration. They fell short of the ideals expressed by the revolutionaries, but they laid the foundation for the later industrialization of Mexico.

The Transformation of Argentina

Most of Argentina consists of *pampas*°, flat, fertile land that is easy to till, much like the prairies of the midwestern United States and Canada. Throughout the nineteenth century Argentina's economy was based on two exports: the hides of longhorn creole cattle and the wool of merino sheep, which roamed the pampas in huge herds. Centuries earlier, Europeans had haphazardly introduced the animals and the grasses they ate. Natural selection had made the animals tough and hardy.

At the end of the nineteenth century railroads and refrigerator ships, which allowed the safe transportation of meat, changed not only the composition of Argentina's

exports but also the way they were produced—in other words, the land itself. European consumers preferred the soft flesh of Lincoln sheep and Hereford cattle to the tough, sinewy meat of creole cattle and merino sheep. But the valuable Lincolns and Herefords could not be allowed to roam and graze on the pampas. They were carefully bred and received a diet of alfalfa and oats. To safeguard them, the pampas had to be divided, plowed, cultivated, and fenced with barbed wire to keep out predators and other unwelcome animals. Once fenced, the land could be used to produce wheat as well as beef and mutton. Within a few years grasslands that had stretched to the horizon were transformed into farmland. Like the North American Midwest, the pampas became one of the world's great producers of wheat and meat.

Argentina's government represented the interests of the *oligarquía*°, a very small group of wealthy landowners. Members of this elite controlled enormous haciendas where they raised cattle and sheep and grew wheat for export. They also owned fine homes in Buenos Aires°, a city that was built to look like Paris. They traveled frequently to Europe and spent so lavishly that the French coined the superlative "rich as an Argentine." They showed little interest in any business other than farming, however, and were content to let foreign companies, mainly British, build Argentina's railroads, processing plants, and public utilities. In exchange for its agricultural exports Argentina imported almost all its manufactured goods from Europe and the United States. So important were British interests in the Argentinean economy that English, not Spanish, was used on the railroads, and the biggest department store in Buenos Aires was a branch of Harrods of London.

Brazil and Argentina, to 1929

Before the First World War Brazil produced most of the world's coffee and cacao, grown on vast estates, and natural rubber, gathered by Indians from rubber trees growing wild in the Amazon rain forest. Brazil's elite was made up of coffee and cacao planters and rubber exporters. Like their Argentinean counterparts, they spent their money lavishly, building palaces in Rio de Janeiro° and one of the world's most beautiful opera houses in Manaus°, deep in the Amazon. They had little interest in other forms of development; let British companies build railroads, harbors, and other infrastructure; and imported most manufactured goods. At the time this seemed to

---

pampas (POM-pus)

oligarquía (oh-lee-gar-KEE-ah) **Buenos Aires** (BWAY-nihs AIR-eze) **Rio de Janeiro** (REE-oh day zhuh-NAIR-oh) **Manaus** (meh-NOWSE) allow each country to do what it did best. If the British did not grow coffee, why should Brazil build locomotives?

Both Argentina and Brazil had small but outspoken middle classes that demanded a share in government and looked to Europe as a model. Beneath each middle class were the poor. In Argentina these were mainly Spanish and Italian immigrants who had ended up as landless farm laborers or workers in urban packing plants. In Brazil there was a large class of sharecroppers and plantation workers, many of them descendants of slaves.

Rubber exports collapsed after 1912, replaced by cheaper plantation rubber from Southeast Asia. The outbreak of war in 1914 put an end to imports from Europe as Britain and France focused all their industries on war production and Germany was cut off entirely. The disruption of the old trade patterns weakened the landowning class. In Argentina the urban middle class obtained the secret ballot and universal male suffrage in 1916 and elected a liberal politician, **Hipólito Irigoyen**°, as president. To a certain extent, the United States replaced the European countries as suppliers of machinery and consumers of coffee. European immigrants built factories to manufacture textiles and household goods. Desperate for money to pay for the war, Great Britain sold many of its railroad, streetcar, and other companies to the governments of Argentina and Brazil.

In contrast to Mexico, the postwar years were a period of prosperity in South America. Trade with Europe resumed; prices for agricultural exports remained high; and both Argentina and Brazil used profits accumulated during the war to industrialize and improve their transportation systems and public utilities. Yet it was also a time of social turmoil, as workers and middle-class professionals demanded social reforms and a larger voice in politics. In Argentina students' and workers' demonstrations were brutally crushed. In Brazil junior officers rose up several times against the government, calling for universal suffrage, social reforms, and freedom for labor unions. Though they accomplished little, they laid the groundwork for later reformist movements. In neither country did the urban middle class take power away from the wealthy landowners. Instead, the two classes shared power at the expense of both the landless peasants and the urban workers.

Yet as Argentina and Brazil were moving forward, new technologies again left them dependent on the advanced industrial countries. Brazilians are justly proud that the first person to fly an airplane outside the United States was Alberto Santos-Dumont, a Brazilian. He did so in 1906 in France, where he lived most of his life and

had access to engine manufacturers and technical assistance. Aviation reached Latin America after World War I, when European and American companies such as Aéropostale and Pan American Airways introduced airmail service between cities and linked Latin America with the United States and Europe.

Before and during World War I radio, then called "wireless telegraphy," was used not for broadcasting but for point-to-point communications. Transmitters powerful enough to send messages across oceans or continents were extraordinarily complex and expensive: their antennas covered many acres; they used as much electricity as a small town; and they cost tens of thousands of pounds sterling (millions of dollars in today's money).

Right after the war, the major powers scrambled to build powerful transmitters on every continent to compete with the telegraph cable companies and to take advantage of the boom in international business and news reporting. At the time, no Latin American country possessed the knowledge or funds to build its own transmitters. In 1919, therefore, President Irigoyen of Argentina granted a radio concession to a German firm. France and Britain protested this decision, and eventually four powerful radio companies—one British, one French, one German, and one American—formed a cartel to control all radio communications in Latin America. This cartel set up a national radio company in each Latin American republic, installing a prominent local politician as its president, but the cartel held all the stock and therefore received all the profits. Thus, even as Brazil and Argentina were taking over their railroads and older industries, the major industrial countries controlled the diffusion of the newer aviation and radio technologies.

The Depression and the Vargas Regime in Brazil

The Depression hit Latin America as hard as it hit Europe and the United States; in many ways, it marks a more important turning point for the region than either of the world wars. As long-term customers cut back their orders, the value of agricultural and mineral exports fell by two-thirds between 1929 and 1932. Argentina and Brazil could no longer afford to import manufactured goods. An imploding economy also undermined their shaky political systems. Like European countries, Argentina and Brazil veered toward authoritarian regimes that promised to solve their economic problems.

In 1930 **Getulio Vargas**° (1883–1954), a state governor, staged a coup and proclaimed himself president of

---

Hipólito Irigoyen (ee-POH-lee-toe ee-ree-GO-yen)

Getulio Vargas (jay-TOO-lee-oh VAR-gus)

Brazil. He proved to be a masterful politician. He wrote a new constitution that broadened the franchise and limited the president to one term. He raised import duties and promoted national firms and state-owned enterprises, culminating in the construction of the Volta Redonda steel mill in the 1930s. By 1936 industrial production had doubled, especially in textiles and small manufactures. Under his guidance, Brazil was on its way to becoming an industrial country. Vargas's policy, called **import-substitution industrialization**, became a model for other Latin American countries as they attempted to break away from neocolonial dependency.

The industrialization of Brazil brought all the familiar environmental consequences. Powerful new machines allowed the reopening of old mines and the digging of new ones. Cities grew as poor peasants looking for work arrived from the countryside. Around the older neighborhoods of Rio de Janeiro and São Paulo°, the poor turned steep hillsides and vacant lands into immense *favelas*° (slums) of makeshift shacks.

The countryside also was transformed. Scrubland was turned into pasture, and new acreage was planted in wheat, corn, and sugar cane. Even the Amazon rain forest—half of the land area of Brazil—was affected. In 1930 American industrialist Henry Ford invested $8 million to clear land along the Tapajós River and prepare it to become the site of the world's largest rubber plantation. Ford encountered opposition from Brazilian workers and politicians; the rubber trees proved vulnerable to diseases; and he had to abandon the project—but not before leaving 3 million acres (1.2 million hectares) denuded of trees. The ecological changes of the Vargas era, however, were but a tiny forerunner of the degradation of the Brazilian environment that was to take place later in the century.

Vargas instituted many reforms favorable to urban workers, such as labor unions, pension plans, and disability insurance, but he refused to take any measures that might help the millions of landless peasants or harm the interests of the great landowners. Although the Brazilian economy recovered from the Depression, the benefits of recovery were so unequally distributed that communist and fascist movements demanded even more radical changes.

In 1938, prohibited by his own constitution from being reelected, Vargas staged another coup, abolished the constitution, and instituted the Estado Novo°, or "New State," with himself as supreme leader. He abolished political parties, jailed opposition leaders, and turned Brazil into a fascist state. When the Second World War broke

Juan and Eva Perón Juan Perón's presidency of Argentina (1946-1955) relied on his, and especially on his wife Eva's, popularity with the working class. They often organized parades and demonstrations, in imitation of the fascist dictators of Europe, in order to sustain their popularity. This picture shows them riding in a procession in Buenos Aires in 1952. (Bettmann/Corbis)

out, however, Vargas aligned Brazil with the United States and contributed troops and ships to the Allied war effort.

Despite his economic achievements, Vargas harmed Brazil. By running roughshod over laws, constitutions, and rights, he infected not only Brazil but also all of South America with the temptations of political violence. It is ironic, but not surprising, that Vargas was overthrown in 1945 by a military coup.

Argentina After 1930

Economically, the Depression hurt Argentina almost as badly as it hurt Brazil. Politically, however, the consequences were delayed for many years. In 1930 General José Uriburu° overthrew the popularly elected President Irigoyen. The Uriburu government represented the large landowners and big business interests. For thirteen years the generals and the oligarchy ruled, doing nothing to lessen the poverty of the workers or the frustrations of the middle

São Paulo (sow PAL-oh)   **favelas** (feh-VEL-luhs)
Estado Novo (esh-TAH-doe NO-vo)

José Uriburu (hoe-SAY oo-ree-BOO-roo)

class. When World War II broke out, Argentina sympathized with the Axis but remained officially neutral.

In 1943 another military revolt flared, this one among junior officers angry at conservative politicians. It was led by Colonel **Juan Perón**° (1895–1974). The intentions of the rebels were clear:

> Civilians will never understand the greatness of our ideal; we shall therefore have to eliminate them from the government and give them the only mission which corresponds to them: work and obedience.[1]

Once in power the officers took over the highest positions in government and business and began to lavish money on military equipment and their own salaries. Their goal, inspired by Nazi victories, was nothing less than the conquest of South America.

As the war turned against the Nazis, the officers saw their popularity collapse. Perón, however, had other plans.

Inspired by his charismatic wife **Eva Duarte Perón**° (1919–1952), he appealed to the urban workers. Eva Perón became the champion of the *descamisados*°, or "shirtless ones," and campaigned tirelessly for social benefits and for the cause of women and children. With his wife's help, Perón won the presidency in 1946 and created a populist dictatorship in imitation of the Vargas regime in Brazil.

Like Brazil, Argentina industrialized rapidly under state sponsorship. Perón spent lavishly on social welfare projects as well as on the military, depleting the capital that Argentina had earned during the war. Though a skillful demagogue who played off the army against the navy and both against the labor unions, Perón could not create a stable government out of the chaos of coups and conspiracies. He had to back down from a plan to make Eva his vice president. When she died in 1952, he lost his political skills (or perhaps they were hers), and soon thereafter he was overthrown in yet another military coup.

Juan Perón (hoo-AHN pair-OWN)

Eva Duarte Perón (AY-vuy doo-AR-tay pair-OWN)
descamisados (des-cah-mee-SAH-dohs)

COMPARATIVE PERSPECTIVES

The wars and revolutions that engulfed the Northern Hemisphere between 1900 and 1949 affected India, sub-Saharan Africa, and Latin America by placing heavy demands on their peoples and raising their hopes for a better life. Sub-Saharan Africa and India were still under colonial rule, and their political life revolved around the desire of their elites for political independence while ordinary people yearned for social justice. Mexico, Argentina, and Brazil were politically independent, but their economies, like those of Africa and India, were closely tied to the economies of the industrial nations with which they traded. When the Depression hit, all three turned to state intervention and import-substitution industrialization. Like all industrializing countries, they did so by mining, farming, ranching, cutting down forests, and irrigating land, all at the expense of the natural environment. Their deeply polarized societies and the stresses caused by their dependence on the industrial countries clashed with the expectations of ever larger numbers of their peoples.

In Mexico these stresses brought about a long and violent social revolution, out of which Mexicans forged a lasting sense of national identity. Argentina and Brazil moved toward greater economic independence, but the price was social unrest, militarism, and dictatorship.

They languished under conservative regimes devoted to the interests of wealthy landowners, sporadically interrupted by military coups and populist demagogues. In India the conflict between growing expectations and the reality of colonial rule produced both a movement for independence and an ethnic split that tore the nation apart. In sub-Saharan Africa demands for national self-determination and economic development were only beginning to be voiced by 1949 and did not come to fruition until the second half of the century.

Nationalism and the yearning for social justice were the two most powerful forces for change in the early twentieth century. These ideas originated in the industrialized countries but resonated in the independent countries of Latin America as well as in colonial regions such as the Indian subcontinent and sub-Saharan Africa. However, they did not always unite people against their colonial rulers or foreign oppressors; instead, they often divided them along social, ethnic, or religious lines. Western-educated elites looked to industrialization as a means of modernizing their country and ensuring their position in it, while peasants and urban workers supported nationalist and revolutionary movements in the hope of improving their lives. Often these goals were not compatible.

SUMMARY

— Why did the educated elites of India want independence? What were ordinary Indians hoping for?

— What changes did foreign rule bring to Africa, and how did Africans respond?

— What could Latin Americans do to achieve social justice and economic development? Were these two goals compatible?

Online Study Center
ACE the Test

In the late nineteenth century, educated Indians began to resent the racist condescension with which they were treated by their colonial masters. They believed that they could govern India and develop its economy better than the British could. Poorer Indians were persuaded by Mahatma Gandhi, the Indian National Congress, and the Muslim League that national independence would alleviate their poverty.

Sub-Saharan Africa was radically transformed by its colonial rulers, who built cities, railroads, harbors, mines, and plantations. Africans were forced to provide the labor for these projects and received few benefits from them. Many turned to Christianity or Islam for spiritual guidance during these upheavals.

Latin Americans sought both economic development and social justice, but they found these two goals hard to reconcile. Decades of modernization had left most Mexicans poorer than before. The Revolution that broke out in 1911 promised to repair the injustices of the past, but it fell short of the ideals for which it was fought. Brazil and Argentina avoided a revolution but remained dependent on Britain and the United States. In both countries, as in Mexico, economic growth was difficult to achieve, democracy was fragile and often repressed by dictators, and social justice proved just as elusive as in earlier centuries.

KEY TERMS

Indian National Congress   *p. 909*
Bengal   *p. 910*
All-India Muslim League   *p. 911*
Mohandas K. Gandhi   *p. 912*
Jawaharlal Nehru   *p. 914*
Muhammad Ali Jinnah   *p. 914*
Blaise Diagne   *p. 919*
African National Congress   *p. 920*
Haile Selassie   *p. 920*

Emiliano Zapata   *p. 921*
Francisco "Pancho" Villa   *p. 922*
Lázaro Cárdenas   *p. 923*
Hipólito Irigoyen   *p. 925*
Getulio Vargas   *p. 925*
import-substitution industrialization   *p. 926*
Juan Perón   *p. 927*
Eva Duarte Perón   *p. 927*

Online Study Center
Improve Your Grade
Flashcards

SUGGESTED READING

For a general introduction to Indian history, see Sumit Sarkar, *Modern India, 1885–1947* (1983), and Percival Spear, *India: A Modern History*, rev. ed. (1972). On the influenza epidemic of 1918–1919 see Alfred W. Crosby, *America's Forgotten Pandemic: The Influenza of 1918* (1989). The Indian independence movement has received a great deal of attention. Judith M. Brown's most recent book on Gandhi is *Gandhi: Prisoner of Hope* (1989). *Gandhi's Truth: On the Origin of Militant Nonviolence* (1969) by noted psychoanalyst Erik Erikson is also recommended. Two collections of memoirs of the last decades of British rule are worth looking at: Charles Allen, ed., *Plain Tales of the Raj: Image of British India in the Twentieth Century* (1975), and Zareer Masani, ed., *Indian Tales of the Raj* (1988). Both the novel *A Passage to India* by E. M. Forster and the film by the same name give an insightful picture of Anglo-Indian relations during the 1920s. The transition from colonialism to partition and independence is the subject of the very readable *Freedom at Midnight* (1975) by Larry Collins and Dominique Lapierre. The environment is discussed in M. Gadgil and R. Guha, *This Fissured Land: An Ecological History of India* (1993). The best film on the independence movement is *Gandhi*. Thomas Skidmore and Peter Smith, *Modern Latin America*, 3rd ed. (1992), offers the best brief introduction.

On Africa under colonial rule the classic overview is Melville Herskovits, *The Human Factor in Changing Africa* (1958). Two excellent general introductions are Roland Oliver and Anthony Atmore, *Africa Since 1800*, 4th ed. (1994), and A. E. Afigbo et al., *The Making of Modern Africa*, vol. 2, *The Twentieth Century* (1986). More detailed and challenging are *UNESCO General History of Africa*, vols. 7 and 8; *The Cambridge History of Africa*, vols. 7 and 8; and Adu Boahen, *African Perspectives on Colonialism* (1987). Outstanding novels about Africa in the colonial era include Chinua Achebe, *Arrow of God* (1964); Buchi Emecheta, *The Joys of Motherhood* (1980); and Peter Abraham, *Mine Boy* (1946).

Two fine general overviews of modern Mexican history are Enrique Krauze, *Mexico: Biography of Power: A History of Modern Mexico, 1810–1996* (1997); Colin MacLachlan and William Beezley, *El Gran Pueblo: A History of Greater Mexico* (1994), and Michael Meyer and William Beezley, *Oxford History of Mexico* (2000). On the Mexican Revolution, two recent books are essential: Alan Knight, *The Mexican Revolution*, 2 vols. (1986), and John M. Hart, *Revolutionary Mexico: The Coming and Process of the Mexican Revolution* (1987). But see also two classics by sympathetic Americans: Frank Tannenbaum, *Peace by Revolution: Mexico After 1910* (1933), and Robert E. Quirk, *The Mexican Revolution, 1914–1915* (1960). Mexico's most celebrated revolutionary is the subject of Manuel Machado, *Centaur of the North: Francisco Villa, the Mexican Revolution, and Northern Mexico* (1988). Mariano Azuela, *The Underdogs* (1988), is an interesting fictional account of this period.

The standard work on Brazil is E. Bradford Burns, *A History of Brazil*, 3rd ed. (1993). On the environmental history of Brazil, see Warren Dean, *Brazil and the Struggle for Rubber: A Study in Environmental History* (1987). The history of modern Argentina is ably treated in David Rock, *Argentina, 1517–1987: From Spanish Colonization to Alfonsín* (1987). Mark Jefferson, *Peopling the Argentine Pampas* (1971), and Jeremy Adelman, *Frontier Development: Land, Labour and Capital on the Wheatlands of Argentina and Canada, 1890–1914* (1994), describe the transformation of the Argentinean environment.

NOTES

1. George Blankstein, *Perón's Argentina* (Chicago: University of Chicago Press, 1953), 37.

Famines and Politics

Nature is never reliable, and all living things periodically suffer from a catastrophic drop in food supplies. Human history is filled with tales of famines—times when crops failed, food supplies ran out, and people starved.

Natural Famines India, dependent on the monsoon rains, has been particularly prone to such calamities, with famines striking two to four times a century, whenever the rains failed for several years in succession. Three times in the eighteenth century (1702–1704, 1769–1770, and 1790–1792) famines killed several million people in different parts of the subcontinent. The nineteenth century was worse, with famines in 1803–1804, 1837–1838, 1868–1870, and 1876–1878. The latter also afflicted northern China, causing between 9 and 13 million deaths from hunger and from the diseases of malnutrition. There were even incidents of cannibalism, as starving adults killed and ate starving children.

When a drought hit a region, it decimated not only the human population but also the animals they relied on to transport goods and plow the land. Likewise, droughts lowered the water levels in rivers and canals, so food could not be moved from one place to another, food supplies ran out, and people starved.

Commercial Famines That all changed in the nineteenth century. Railroads and steamships could transport foodstuffs across great distances in a matter of days or weeks, regardless of drought or heavy rains. Great Britain became dependent on imports of wheat from Russia and the American Midwest, and later of beef from Argentina. Yet famines were worse than ever, and the global death toll from starvation has been far higher since the mid-nineteenth century than it ever was in earlier times. Why?

Consider the Irish famine of 1845–1848. By the early nineteenth century the potato had become the main source of nutrition for the Irish people. Potatoes grew abundantly in the cool, moist climate of Ireland and produced more calories per acre than any other crop. Most of the Irish were poor tenant farmers, and potatoes had allowed their population to increase far more than wheat or rye could have.

In fall 1845 the blight turned the potatoes in the fields black, mushy, and inedible. The harvest was ruined the following year as well. It recovered slightly in 1847 but was bad again in 1848. Tens of thousands died of starvation, while hundreds of thousands died from the diseases that strike malnourished people, especially dysentery, typhus, and cholera. Travelers saw corpses rotting in their hovels or on the sides of roads. Altogether, a million or more people died, while another million managed to emigrate, reducing the population of Ireland by half.

Throughout those years, wheat grew in Ireland, but much of it was exported to England, where customers had money to pay for it. Like any other commodity, food cost money. The Irish farmers, poor even before the famines, were destitute and could not afford to buy the wheat. The British government, wedded to the ideology of laissez faire, was convinced that interfering with the free market would only make things worse. Relief efforts were half-hearted at best; the official responsible for Irish affairs preferred to leave the situation to "the operation of natural causes."

The same held true in India, like Ireland a colony of Great Britain. The drought of 1876–1878 killed over 5 million Indians in the Deccan region, while British officials were helpless or indifferent. Part of the problem was transportation. In the 1870s only a few railway lines connected major cities. Most goods were still transported in bullock carts, but the bullocks also starved during the drought. Another obstacle was political. The idea that a government should be responsible for feeding the population was unthinkable at the time. And so, while millions were starving in the Deccan, the Punjab region was exporting wheat to Britain.

Over the next twenty years so-called famine railways were built in the regions historically most affected by the failures of the monsoon. When drought struck again at the end of the century, the railways were ready to transport food to areas that had previously been accessible only by bullock carts. However, the inhabitants of the affected regions had no money with which to buy what little food there was, and the government was still reluctant to interfere with free enterprise. Grain merchants bought all the stocks, hoarded them until the price rose, then used the railways to transport them out of the famine regions to regions where the harvests were better and people had more money.

In the twentieth century commercial famines have become rare, as governments have come to realize that they have a responsibility for food supplies not only for their own people, but for people in other countries as well. Yet commercial famines have not entirely disappeared. In 1974, when a catastrophic flood covered half of Bangladesh, the government was too disorganized to distribute its stocks of rice, while merchants bought what they could and exported it to India. Thousands died, and thousands more survived only because of belated shipments of food from donor countries.

Political Famines To say that governments are responsible for food supplies does not mean that they exercise that responsibility for the good of the people. Some do, but in many instances food is used as a weapon. In the twentieth century global food supplies were always adequate for the population of the world, and transportation was seldom a problem. Yet the century witnessed the most murderous famines ever recorded.

War-induced famines were not new. In 1812, as the Russian army retreated, it practiced a "scorched-earth" policy of burning food stocks to prevent them from falling into the hands of Napoleon's army. In doing so, it also caused a famine among Russian peasants. Similar famines resulted from the destruction or requisitioning of crops in the Russian civil war of 1921–1922, the Japanese occupation of Indochina in 1942–1945, and the Biafran war in Nigeria in 1967–1969.

The Bengal famine of 1943 was also war-related. In 1942 the Japanese army had conquered Burma, a rich rice-producing colony. Food supplies in Bengal, which imported rice from Burma, dropped by 5 percent. As prices began to rise, merchants bought stocks of rice and held them in the hope that prices would continue to increase. Sharecroppers sold their stocks to pay off their debts to landlords and village moneylenders. Meanwhile, the railroads that in peacetime would have carried food from other parts of India were fully occupied with military traffic. In October 1943, when a new viceroy, Lord Wavell, arrived in India and ordered the army to transport food to Bengal, food prices dropped to a level that the poor could afford. By then, however, between 1.5 and 2 million Bengalis had starved to death.

Worst of all were the famines that happened in peacetime as a result of the deliberate decisions of governments. The most famous of these political famines was caused by Stalin's collectivization of agriculture in 1932–1934. The Communist Party tried to force the peasants to give up their land and livestock and join collectives, where they could be made to work harder and provide food for the growing cities and industries. When they resisted, their crops were seized. Millions were sent to prison camps, and millions of others died of starvation. Stalin chided the overly enthusiastic party members who had caused the famine for being "dizzy with success."

An even worse famine took place in China from 1958 to 1961 during the "Great Leap Forward" (see Chapter 32). Communist Party Chairman Mao Zedong decided to hasten the transformation of China into a communist state and industrial power by relying not on the expertise of economists and technocrats but on the enthusiasm of the masses. All farms were consolidated into huge communes. Peasants were mobilized to work on giant construction projects or to make steel out of household utensils and tools in backyard furnaces. The harvest of 1959 was poor, and later ones were even worse. The amount of grain per person declined from 452 pounds (205 kilograms) in 1957 to 340 pounds (154 kilograms) in 1961. Since the Central Statistical Bureau had been shut down, the central government was unaware of the shortages and demanded ever higher requisitions of food to feed the army and urban and industrial workers and to export to the Soviet Union to pay off China's debts. The amount of food left to the farmers was between one-fifth and one-half of their usual subsistence diet. From 1958 to 1961 between 20 and 30 million Chinese are estimated to have starved or died of the diseases of malnutrition in the most catastrophic famine in the history of the world. The leaders of the Communist Party either were unaware of its extent or, if they knew, did not dare mention it for fear of displeasing Mao, who denied its existence.

Nothing quite as horrible has happened since the Great Leap Forward. During the droughts in Africa in the 1970s and 1980s, most people in the affected regions received international food aid, but the governments of Ethiopia and Sudan either denied that their people were hungry or prevented food shipments from reaching drought victims in order to crush rebellions.

In the world today, natural disasters are as frequent as ever, and many countries are vulnerable to food shortages. No one now claims, as many did in the nineteenth century, that governments have no business providing free food to the starving. Though food is not equitably distributed, there is enough for all human beings now, and there will be enough for the foreseeable future. However, humanitarian feelings compete with other political agendas, and the specter of politically motivated famines still stalks the world.

PART EIGHT

PERILS AND PROMISES OF A GLOBAL COMMUNITY, 1945 TO THE PRESENT

CHAPTER 32
The Cold War and Decolonization, 1945–1975

CHAPTER 33
The End of the Cold War and the Challenge of Economic Development and Immigration, 1975–2000

CHAPTER 34
Globalization in the New Millennium

An increasingly interconnected world faced new hopes and fears after World War II. The United Nations promoted peace, international co-operation, and human rights. Colonized peoples gained independence, and global trade expanded.

However, Cold War rhetoric and nuclear stalemate dispelled dreams of world peace. Wars in Korea and Vietnam, as well as proxy conflicts from Nicaragua to Afghanistan, pitted the United States against communist regimes. Following the Cold War nuclear proliferation and terrorism became top concerns. The 9/11 attacks by Muslim zealots on the World Trade Center and the Pentagon triggered an American "global war on terrorism." The ensuing invasions of Afghanistan and Iraq made the Middle East a top danger spot.

The industrialized nations, including Germany and Japan, recovered well from World War II. Elsewhere economic development came slowly, except in a handful of countries: South Korea, Taiwan, Brazil, Argentina, and, after 2000, China and India. In Africa and other poor regions, population growth usually offset economic gains.

Satellite Photograph of the Globe Photography from space revolutionized mapping. Physical features became more important than political boundaries. Photography also displayed transient features, such as cloud coverage and storm patterns. In this photograph the distinctive whorl of a tropical storm is visible off the east coast of Japan. More specialized photographic techniques are used to appraise natural resources and environmental problems. (NASA/Getty Images)

Although the Green Revolution of the 1960s and genetic engineering thirty years later alleviated much world hunger, industrial growth and automobile use increased pollution and competition for petroleum supplies. Global warming became an international concern, along with overfishing, deforestation, and endangerment of wild species.

Globalization affected culture as well. Transnational corporations selling uniform products threatened localized economic enterprises, and Western popular culture aroused fears of cultural imperialism. The Internet and the emergence of English as the global language improved international communication but also stimulated fears that cultural diversity would be lost.

Fidel Castro Arrives in Havana   Castro and his supporters overthrew a brutal dictatorship and began the revolutionary transformation of Cuba. This led to a confrontation with the United States.
(Bettmann/Corbis)

— What were the major threats to world peace during the Cold War?

— How were the experiences of Asia, Africa, and Latin America similar in this period?

— How did the rivalry between the Cold War superpowers affect the rest of the world?

32

THE COLD WAR AND DECOLONIZATION, 1945–1975

CHAPTER OUTLINE

The Cold War

Decolonization and Nation Building

Beyond a Bipolar World

Comparative Perspectives

ENVIRONMENT AND TECHNOLOGY: The Green Revolution

DIVERSITY AND DOMINANCE: Race and the Struggle for Justice in South Africa

O n January 1, 1959, Fidel Castro entered Havana, Cuba, after having successfully defeated the dictatorship of Fulgencio Batista°. Castro had initiated his revolution in 1953 with an attack on a military barracks. When the attack failed, Castro and other survivors stood trial. Many had died in the attack or been captured, tortured, and executed. In his legal defense, later published as *History Will Absolve Me*, Castro set out the objectives of his revolution: the restoration of Cuban democracy and an ambitious program of social and economic reforms designed to ameliorate the effects of underdevelopment. There was no direct criticism at the time of the United States, Cuba's major trading partner and the source of most of the island's foreign investment.

Fulgencio Batista (ful-HEHN-see-oh bah-TEES-tah)

Online Study Center

This icon will direct you to interactive activities and study materials on the website: *college.hmco.com/pic/bulliet4e.*

On September 26, 1960, Castro addressed the United Nations General Assembly. In the interim, relations between the Castro government and the United States had deteriorated, and both nations had begun to move toward confrontation. In his speech, Castro offered a broad internationalist and anti-imperialist criticism of the world's developed nations and of the United Nations. In particular, he attacked the role of the United Nations in the Congo, suggesting that it had supported Colonel Mobutu Sese Seko, a client of imperialism, rather than Patrice Lumumba, identified by the United States as a dangerous radical. Castro also supported the independence struggle of the Algerians against the French and demanded that China be seated in the United Nations.

In this speech, Castro outlined an ambitious program of revolutionary reforms in Cuba that he knew would lead to further confrontation with the United States. He charged that the United States had supported the Batista dictatorship as a means of defending the exploitative actions of American investors. Cuba, Castro said, "had yesterday been a hopeless land, a land of misery and a land of illiterates [and] is gradually becoming one of the most enlightened and advanced and civilized peoples of the continent."

Cuba became a flash point in the Cold War, and the United States tried and failed to overthrow Castro in 1961. Castro solidified his alliance with the Soviet Union, and in 1962 the Soviet placement of nuclear weapons in Cuba led to the Cuban missile crisis, which took the world to the brink of war.

The intensity of the Cold War, with its accompanying threat of nuclear destruction, sometimes obscured a postwar phenomenon of more enduring importance. Western domination was greatly reduced in most of Asia, Africa, and Latin America, and the colonial empires of the New Imperialism were gradually dismantled. The new generation of national leaders heading the states in these regions sometimes skillfully used Cold War antagonism to their own advantage. Some, like Castro, became frontline participants in this struggle. Most focused their attention on nation building, an enterprise charged with almost insurmountable problems and conflicts.

Each region subjected to imperialism had its own history and conditions and followed its own route to independence. Thus the new nations had difficulty finding a collective voice in a world increasingly oriented toward two superpowers, the United States and the Soviet Union. Some sided openly with one or the other. Others banded together in a posture of neutrality and spoke with one voice about their need for economic and technical assistance and the obligation of the wealthy nations to satisfy those needs.

The Cold War military rivalry stimulated extraordinary advances in weaponry and associated technologies, but many new nations faced basic problems of educating their citizens, nurturing industry, and escaping the economic constraints imposed by their former imperialist masters. The environment suffered severe pressures from oil exploration and transport to support the growing economies of the wealthy nations and from deforestation in poor regions challenged by the need for cropland. Neither rich nor poor nations understood the costs associated with these environmental changes.

THE COLD WAR

The wartime alliance between the United States, Great Britain, and the Soviet Union had been uneasy. Fear of working-class revolution, which the Nazis had played on in their rise to power, was not confined to Germany. For more than a century political and economic leaders committed to free markets and untrammeled capital investment had loathed socialism in its several forms. After World War II the iron curtain in Europe and communist insurgencies in China and elsewhere seemed to confirm the threat of worldwide revolution.

Western leaders quickly came to perceive the Soviet Union as the nerve center of world revolution and as a military power capable of launching a war as destructive and terrible as the one that had recently ended. As early as 1946 Great Britain's wartime leader, Winston Churchill, said in a speech in Missouri, "From Stettin in the Baltic to Trieste in the Adriatic, an iron curtain has descended across the Continent. . . . I am convinced there is nothing

C H R O N O L O G Y	
Cold War	**Decolonization**

	Cold War	Decolonization
1945		
	1948–1949 Berlin airlift	**1947** Partition of India
	1949 NATO formed	**1949** Dutch withdraw from Indonesia
1950	**1950–1953** Korean War	
	1952 United States detonates first hydrogen bomb	
	1954 Jacobo Arbenz overthrown in Guatemala, supported by CIA	**1954** CIA intervention in Guatemala; defeat at Dienbienphu ends French hold on Vietnam
1955	**1955** Warsaw Pact created	**1955** Bandung Conference
	1956 Soviet Union suppresses Hungarian revolt	
	1957 Soviet Union launches first artificial satellite into earth orbit	**1957** Ghana becomes first British colony in Africa to gain independence
		1959 Triumph of Fidel Castro's revolution Cuba
1960		**1960** Shootings in Sharpeville intensify South African struggle against apartheid; Nigeria becomes independent
	1961 East Germany builds Berlin Wall	
	1961 Bay of Pigs (Cuba)	
	1962 Cuban missile crisis	**1962** Algeria wins independence
	1968 Nuclear Non-Proliferation Treaty	
1970		
		1971 Bangladesh secedes from Pakistan
	1975 Helsinki Accords; end of Vietnam War	

they [the communists] so much admire as strength, and there is nothing for which they have less respect than weakness, especially military weakness." The phrase "**iron curtain**" became a watchword of the **Cold War**, the state of political tension and military rivalry then beginning between the United States and its allies and the Soviet Union and its allies.

After the United States and the nations of western Europe established the **North Atlantic Treaty Organization (NATO)** military alliance in 1949, Soviet leaders felt surrounded by hostile forces just when they were trying to recover from the terrible losses sustained in the war against the Axis. The Soviet Union created its own military alliance, the **Warsaw Pact**, in 1955. The distrust and suspicion between the two sides played out on a worldwide stage. The United Nations provided the venue for face-to-face debate.

Online Study Center
Improve Your Grade
Interactive Map:
The Cold War

The United Nations

In 1944 representatives from the United States, Great Britain, the Soviet Union, and China drafted proposals that finally bore fruit in the treaty called the United Nations Charter, ratified on October 24, 1945. Like the earlier League of Nations, the **United Nations** had two main bodies: the General Assembly, with representatives from all member states; and the Security Council, with five permanent members—China, France, Great Britain, the United States, and the Soviet Union—and seven rotating members. A full-time bureaucracy headed by a Secretary General carried out the day-to-day business of both bodies. Various agencies focused on specialized international problems—for example, UNICEF (United Nations Children's Emergency Fund), FAO (Food and Agriculture Organization), and UNESCO (United Nations Educational, Scientific and Cultural Organization) (see Environment and Technology: The Green Revolution). Unlike the League of Nations, which required unanimous agreement in both deliberative bodies, the United Nations operated by majority vote, except that the five permanent members of the Security Council had veto power in that chamber.

ENVIRONMENT + TECHNOLOGY

The Green Revolution

Concern about world food supplies grew directly out of serious shortages caused by the devastation and trade disruptions of World War II. The Food and Agriculture Organization of the United Nations, the Rockefeller Foundation, and the Ford Foundation took leading roles in fostering crop research and educating farmers about agricultural techniques. In 1966 the International Rice Research Institute (established in 1960–1962) began distributing seeds for an improved rice variety known as IR-8. Crop yields from this and other new varieties, along with improved farming techniques, were initially so impressive that the term *Green Revolution* was coined to describe a new era in agriculture.

On the heels of the successful new rice strains, new varieties of corn and wheat were introduced. Building on twenty years of Rockefeller-funded research in Mexico, the Centro Internacional de Mejoramiento de Maiz y Trigo (International Center for the Improvement of Maize and Wheat) was established in

1966 under Norman Borlaug, who was awarded the Nobel Peace Prize four years later. This organization distributed short, stiff-strawed varieties of wheat that were resistant to disease and responsive to fertilizer.

By 1970 other centers for research on tropical agriculture had been established in Ibadan, Nigeria, and Cali, Colombia. But the success of the Green Revolution and the growing need for its products called for a more comprehensive effort. The Consultative Group on International Agricultural Research brought together World Bank expertise, private foundations, international organizations, and national foreign aid agencies to undertake worldwide support of efforts to increase food productivity and improve natural resource management. More recently, the optimism that followed these innovations has been muted by the realization that population growth, soil depletion, the costs of irrigation and fertilizer, and the growing concentration of land in the export sector combined to reduce the effects of improved crop technology in poor countries.

Miracle Rice New strains of so-called miracle rice made many nations in South and Southeast Asia self-sufficient in food production after decades of worry that population growth would outstrip agricultural productivity. (Victor Englebert)

All signatories to the United Nations Charter renounced war and territorial conquest. Nevertheless, peacekeeping, the sole preserve of the Security Council, became a vexing problem. The permanent members exercised their vetoes to protect their friends and interests. Throughout the Cold War the United Nations was seldom able to forestall or quell international conflicts, though from time to time it sent observers or peacekeeping forces to monitor truces or agreements otherwise arrived at.

The decolonization of Africa and Asia greatly swelled the size of the General Assembly but not of the Security Council. Many of the new nations looked to the United Nations for material assistance and access to a wider political world. While the vetoes of the Security Council's permanent members often stymied actions that even indirectly touched on Cold War concerns,

Cold War Confrontation in 1959   U.S. vice president Richard M. Nixon and Soviet premier Nikita Khrushchev had a heated exchange of views during Nixon's visit to a Moscow trade fair. Two years earlier, the Soviet Union had launched the world's first space satellite. (Seymour Raskin/Magnum Photos, Inc.)

the General Assembly became an arena for opinions on many issues involving decolonization, a movement that the Soviet Union strongly encouraged but the Western colonial powers resisted.

In the early years of the United Nations, General Assembly resolutions carried great weight. An example is a 1947 resolution that sought to divide Palestine into sovereign Jewish and Arab states. Gradually, though, the flood of new members produced a voting majority concerned more with poverty, racial discrimination, and the struggle against imperialism than with the Cold War. As a result, the Western powers increasingly disregarded the General Assembly, in effect allowing the new nations of the world to have their say, but not the means to act collectively.

Capitalism and Communism

In July 1944, with Allied victory a foregone conclusion, economic specialists representing over forty countries met at Bretton Woods, a New Hampshire resort, to devise a new international monetary system. The signatories eventually agreed to fix exchange rates and to create the International Monetary Fund (IMF) and World Bank (formally the International Bank for Reconstruction and Development). The IMF was to use currency reserves from member nations to finance temporary trade deficits, and the **World Bank** was to provide funds for reconstructing Europe and helping needy countries after the war.

The Soviet Union attended the Bretton Woods Conference and signed the agreements, which went into effect in 1946. But deepening suspicion and hostility between the Soviet Union and the United States and Britain undermined cooperation. While the United States held reserves of gold and the rest of the world held reserves of dollars in order to maintain the stability of the monetary system, the Soviet Union established a closed monetary system for itself and the new communist regimes in eastern Europe. Similar differences were found across the economies of the two alliances. In the Western countries, supply and demand determined prices; in the Soviet command economy, government agencies allocated goods and set prices according to governmental priorities, irrespective of market forces.

Many leaders of newly independent states, having won the struggle against imperialism, preferred the Soviet Union's socialist example to the capitalism of their former colonizers. Thus, the relative success of economies patterned on Eastern or Western models became part of

Cold War rivalry. Each side trumpeted economic successes measured by industrial output, changes in per capita income, and productivity gains.

During World War II the U.S. economy finally escaped the lingering effects of the Great Depression (see Chapter 30). Increased military spending and the draft brought full employment and high wages. The wartime conversion of factories from the production of consumer goods had created demand for those goods. With peace, the United States enjoyed prosperity and an international competitive advantage because of massive destruction in Europe.

The economy of western Europe was heavily damaged during World War II, and the early postwar years were bleak in many European countries. With prosperity, the United States was able to support the reconstruction of western Europe. The **Marshall Plan** provided $12.5 billion in aid to friendly European countries between 1948 and 1952. Most of the aid was in the form of food, raw materials, and other goods. By 1961 more than $20 billion in economic aid had been disbursed. European determination backed by American aid spurred recovery, and by 1963 the resurgent European economy had doubled its 1940 output.

Western European governments generally increased their role in economic management during this period. In Great Britain, for example, the Labour Party government of the early 1950s nationalized coal, steel, railroads, and health care. Similarly, the French government nationalized public utilities; the auto, banking, and insurance industries; and parts of the mining industry. These steps provided large infusions of capital for rebuilding and acquiring new technologies.

In 1948 European governments also launched a process of economic cooperation and integration with the creation of the Organization of European Economic Cooperation (OEEC). Cooperative policies were first focused on coal and steel. Often located in disputed border areas, these industries had previously been flash points that led to war. Successes in these crucial areas encouraged some OEEC countries to begin lowering tariffs to encourage the movement of goods and capital. In 1957 France, West Germany, Italy, the Netherlands, Belgium, and Luxembourg signed a treaty creating the European Economic Community, also known as the Common Market. By the 1970s the Common Market nations had nearly overtaken the United States in industrial production. The economic alliance expanded between 1973 and 1995, when Great Britain, Denmark, Greece, Ireland, Spain, Portugal, Finland, Sweden, and Austria joined. The enlarged alliance called itself the **European Community (EC)**.

Prosperity brought dramatic changes to the societies of western Europe. Average wages increased, unemployment fell, and social welfare benefits were expanded. Governments increased spending on health care, unemployment benefits, old-age pensions, public housing, and grants to poor families with children. The combination of economic growth and income redistribution raised living standards and fueled demand for consumer goods, leading to the development of a mass consumer society. Automobile ownership, for example, grew approximately ninefold between 1950 and 1970.

The Soviet experience was dramatically different. The rapid growth of a powerful Soviet state after 1917 had challenged traditional Western assumptions about economic development and social policy. From the 1920s the Soviet state relied on bureaucratic agencies and political processes to determine the production, distribution, and price of goods. Housing, medical services, retail shops, factories, the land—even musical compositions and literary works—were viewed as collective property and were therefore regulated and administered by the state.

The economies of the Soviet Union and its eastern European allies were just as devastated at the end of the Second World War as those of western Europe. However, the Soviet command economy had enormous natural resources, a large population, and abundant energy at its disposal. Moreover, Soviet planners had made large investments in technical and scientific education, and the Soviet state had developed heavy industry in the 1930s and during the war years. Finally, Soviet leadership was willing to use forced labor on an enormous scale. For example, Bulgaria's postwar free work force of 361,000 was supplemented by 100,000 slave laborers.[1]

As a result, recovery was rapid at first, creating the structural basis for modernization and growth. Then, as the postwar period progressed, bureaucratic control of the economy grew less responsive and efficient at the same time that industrial might came to be more commonly measured by the production of consumer goods such as television sets and automobiles, rather than by tons of coal and steel. In the 1970s the gap with the West widened. Soviet industry failed to meet domestic demand for clothing, housing, food, automobiles, and consumer electronics, while Soviet agricultural inefficiency compelled increased reliance on food imports.

The socialist nations of eastern Europe were compelled to follow the Soviet economic model, with some national differences. Poland and Hungary, for example, implemented agricultural collectivization more slowly than did Czechoslovakia. Nevertheless, economic planners throughout the region coordinated industrialization and production plans with the Soviet Union. Significant growth occurred in all the socialist economies, but the inefficiencies and failures that plagued the Soviet economy troubled them as well.

Outside Europe, the United States and the Soviet Union competed in providing loans and grants and supplying arms (at bargain prices) to countries willing to align with them. Thus the relative success or failure of capitalism and communism in Europe and the United States was not necessarily the strongest consideration in other parts of the world when the time came to construct new national economies.

West Versus East in Europe and Korea

For Germany, Austria, and Japan, peace brought foreign military occupation and new governments that were initially controlled by the occupiers. When relations with the Western powers cooled at the end of the war, the Soviet Union sought to prevent the reappearance of hostile regimes on its borders. Initially, the Soviet Union seemed willing to accept governments in neighboring states that included a mix of parties as long as they were not hostile to local communist groups or to the Soviets. The nations of central and eastern Europe were deeply split by the legacies of the war, and many were willing to embrace the communists as a hedge against those who had supported fascism or cooperated with the Germans. As relations between the Soviets and the West worsened in the late 1940s, local communists, their strength augmented by Soviet military occupation, gained victories across eastern Europe. Western leaders saw the rapid emergence of communist regimes in Poland, Czechoslovakia, Hungary, Bulgaria, Romania, Yugoslavia, and Albania as a threat.

It took two years for the United States to shift from viewing the Soviet Union as an ally against Germany to seeing it as a worldwide enemy. In the waning days of World War II the United States had seemed amenable to the Soviet desire for free access to the Bosporus and Dardanelles straits that, under Turkish control, restricted naval deployments from the Black Sea to the Mediterranean. But in July 1947 the **Truman Doctrine** offered military aid to help both Turkey and Greece resist Soviet military pressure and subversion, and in 1951 both were admitted to NATO. The Western powers' decision to allow West Germany to rearm within limits set by NATO (see Map 32.1) led in 1955 to the creation of the Soviet counterpart to NATO, the Warsaw Pact.

The much-feared and long-prepared-for third great war in Europe did not occur. The Soviet Union tested Western resolve in 1948–1949 by blockading the British, French, and American zones in Berlin (located in Soviet-controlled East Germany), but airlifts of food and fuel defeated the blockade. In 1961 the East German government accentuated Germany's political division by building the Berlin Wall, a structure designed primarily to prevent its citizens from fleeing to the noncommunist western part of the city. In turn, the West tested the East by encouraging a rift between the Soviet Union and Yugoslavia. Western aid and encouragement resulted in Yugoslavia's signing a defensive treaty with Greece and Turkey (but not with NATO) and deciding against joining the Warsaw Pact.

Soviet power set clear limits on how far any eastern European country might stray from Soviet domination. In 1956 Soviet troops crushed an armed anti-Soviet revolt in Hungary. Then in 1968 Soviet troops repressed a peaceful reform effort in Czechoslovakia. The West, by being a passive onlooker, effectively acknowledged the Soviet Union's ability to intervene in the domestic affairs of any Soviet-bloc nation whenever it wished.

A more explosive crisis erupted in Korea, where the Second World War had left Soviet troops in control north of the thirty-eighth parallel and American troops in control to the south. When no agreement could be reached on holding countrywide elections, communist North Korea and noncommunist South Korea became independent states in 1948. Two years later North Korea invaded South Korea. The United Nations Security Council, in the absence of the Soviet delegation, voted to condemn the invasion and called on members of the United Nations to come to the defense of South Korea. The ensuing **Korean War** lasted until 1953. The United States was the primary ally of South Korea. The People's Republic of China supported North Korea.

The conflict in Korea remained limited to the Korean peninsula because the United States feared that launching attacks into China might prompt China's ally, the Soviet Union, to retaliate, beginning the dreaded third world war. Americans and South Koreans advanced from a toehold in the south to the North Korean–Chinese border. China sent troops across the border, and the North Koreans and Chinese pushed the Americans and South Koreans back. The fighting then settled into a static war in the mountains along the thirty-eighth parallel. The two sides eventually agreed to a truce along that line; but the cease-fire lines remained fortified, and no peace treaty was concluded. The possibility of renewed warfare between the two Koreas continued well past the end of the Cold War and remains a disturbing possibility today.

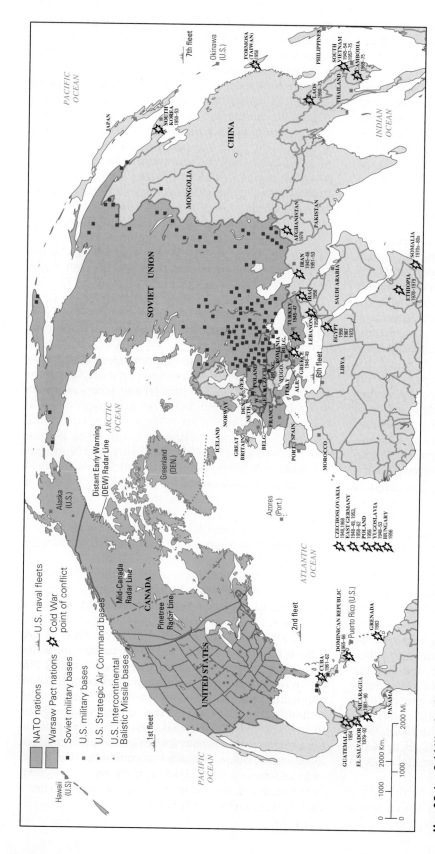

Map 32.1   Cold War Confrontation   A polar projection is shown on this map because Soviet and U.S. strategists planned to attack one another by missile in the polar region; hence the Canadian-American radar lines. Military installations along the southern border of the Soviet Union were directed primarily at China.

Japan benefited from the Korean War in an unexpected way. Massive purchases of supplies by the United States and spending by American servicemen on leave stimulated the Japanese economy similar to the way the Marshall Plan had stimulated Europe's economy.

United States Defeat in Vietnam

The most important postwar communist movement arose in the part of Southeast Asia known as French Indochina. Ho Chi Minh° (1890–1969), who had spent several years in France during World War I, played the pivotal role. Ho had helped form the Communist Party in France. In 1930, after training in Moscow, he returned to Vietnam to found the Indochina Communist Party. Forced to take refuge in China during World War II, Ho cooperated with the United States while Japan controlled Vietnam.

At war's end the new French government was determined to keep its prewar colonial possessions. Ho Chi Minh's nationalist coalition, then called the Viet Minh, fought the French with help from the People's Republic of China. After a brutal struggle, the French stronghold of Dienbienphu° fell in 1954, marking the end of France's colonial enterprise. Ho's Viet Minh government took over in the north, and a noncommunist nationalist government ruled in the south.

The United States had given some support to the French. President Dwight D. Eisenhower (1953–1961) and his foreign policy advisers debated long and hard about whether to aid France militarily during the battle for Dienbienphu. They decided not to prop up French colonial rule in Vietnam, perceiving that the European colonial empires were doomed. After winning independence, communist North Vietnam eventually supported a communist guerrilla movement—the Viet Cong—against the noncommunist government of South Vietnam. At issue was the ideological and economic orientation of an independent Vietnam.

President John F. Kennedy (served 1961–1963) and his advisers decided to support the South Vietnamese government of President Ngo Dinh Diem°. While they knew that the Diem government was corrupt and unpopular, they feared that a communist victory would encourage communist movements throughout Southeast Asia and alter the Cold War balance of power. Kennedy steadily increased the number of American military advisers from 685 to almost 16,000, while secretly encouraging the overthrow of Diem. The execution of Diem following his overthrow instigated a public debate as well as a critical reevaluation within the administration.

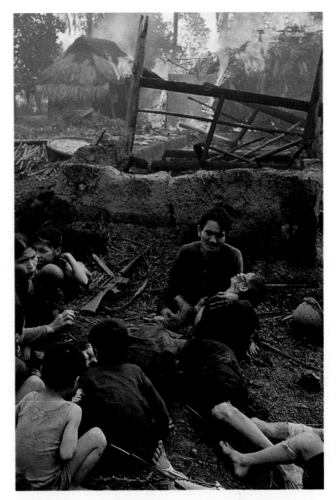

The Vietnamese People at War American and South Vietnamese troops burned many villages to deprive the enemy of civilian refuges. This policy undermined support for the South Vietnamese government in the countryside. (Dana Stone/stockphoto.com)

Lyndon Johnson, who became president (served 1963–1969) after Kennedy was assassinated, obtained support from Congress for unlimited expansion of U.S. military deployment after an alleged, but now disputed, North Vietnamese attack on two U.S. destroyers in the Gulf of Tonkin. But in South Vietnam there was little support for the nation's new rulers, who soon revealed themselves to be just as corrupt and unpopular as the earlier Diem government. Instead, many South Vietnamese were drawn to the heroic nationalist image of North Vietnam's leader Ho Chi Minh, who had led the struggles against the Japanese and French. By the end of 1966, 365,000 U.S. troops were engaged in the **Vietnam War**,

---

Ho Chi Minh (hoe chee min)
Dienbienphu (dee-yen-bee-yen-FOO)   **Diem** (dee-YEM)

but they were unable to achieve a comprehensive victory. While suffering significant losses, the Viet Cong guerrillas and their North Vietnamese allies gained significant military credibility in the massive 1968 Tet Offensive. With a battlefield victory becoming less likely, the antiwar movement in the United States grew in strength.

In 1973 a treaty between North Vietnam and the United States ended U.S. involvement in the war and promised future elections. Two years later, in violation of the treaty, Viet Cong and North Vietnamese troops overran the South Vietnamese army and captured the southern capital of Saigon, renaming it Ho Chi Minh City. The two parts of Vietnam were reunited in a single state ruled from the north. Over a million Vietnamese and 58,000 Americans had been killed in the war.

President Johnson had begun his administration committed to a broad program of social reforms and civil rights initiatives, called the Great Society. The civil rights campaign in the South led by Martin Luther King, Jr., and others led to a broad examination of issues of social justice and spawned numerous organizations that challenged the status quo. As the commitment of U.S. troops grew, a massive antiwar movement applied the tactics of the civil rights movement to government military policies. Many members of the military and their civilian supporters, on the other hand, were angered by limitations placed on the conduct of operations, despite fears that a wider war would lead to Chinese involvement and possible nuclear confrontation. The rising tide of antiwar rallies, now international in character, and growing economic problems undermined support for Johnson, who declined to seek reelection. By the mid-1970s both antiwar and prowar groups had drawn lessons from Vietnam, the former seeing any use of military force overseas as dangerous and unnecessarily destructive, and the latter believing that overwhelming force was required in warfare.

The Race for Nuclear Supremacy

Fear of nuclear warfare affected strategic decisions in the Korean and Vietnam Wars. It also affected all other aspects of Cold War confrontation. The devastation of Hiroshima and Nagasaki by atomic weapons (see Chapter 30) had ushered in a new era. Nuclear weapons fed into a logic of total war that was already reaching a peak in Nazi genocide and terror bombing and in massive Allied air raids on large cities. After the Soviet Union exploded its first nuclear device in 1949, fears of a worldwide holocaust grew. Fears increased when the United States exploded a far more powerful weapon, the hydrogen bomb, in 1952 and the Soviet Union followed suit less than a year later. The possibility of the theft of nuclear secrets by Soviet spies fostered paranoia in the United States, and the conviction that the nuclear superpowers were willing to use their terrible weapons if their vital interests were threatened spread despair around the world.

In 1954 President Eisenhower warned Soviet leaders against attacking western Europe. In response to such an attack, he said, the United States would reduce the Soviet Union to "a smoking, radiating ruin at the end of two hours." A few years later the Soviet leader Nikita Khrushchev° made an equally stark promise: "We will bury you." He was referring to economic competition, but Americans interpreted the statement to mean literal burial. Rhetoric aside, both men—and their successors—had the capacity to deliver on their threats, and everyone in the world knew that all-out war with nuclear weapons would produce the greatest global devastation in human history.

Everyone's worst fears seemed about to be realized in 1962 when the Soviet Union deployed nuclear missiles in Cuba. Khrushchev and Cuban president Fidel Castro were reacting to U.S. efforts to overthrow the government of Cuba. When the missiles were discovered, the United States prepared for an invasion of Cuba. Confronted by unyielding diplomatic pressure and military threats, Khrushchev pulled the missiles from Cuba. Subsequently, the United States removed its missiles from Turkey. As frightening as the **Cuban missile crisis** was, the fact that the superpower leaders accepted tactical defeat rather than launch an attack gave reason for hope that nuclear weapons might be contained.

The number, means of delivery, and destructive force of nuclear weapons increased enormously. The bomb dropped on Hiroshima, equal in strength to 12,500 tons of TNT, had destroyed an entire city. By the 1960s explosive yields were measured in megatons (millions of tons) of TNT, and a single missile could contain several weapons of this scale, each of which could be targeted to a different site. When the missiles were placed on submarines, a major component of U.S. nuclear forces, defending against them seemed impossible.

Arms limitation also progressed. In 1963 Great Britain, the United States, and the Soviet Union agreed to ban the testing of nuclear weapons in the atmosphere, in space, and under water, thus reducing the environmental danger of radioactive fallout. In 1968 the United States and the Soviet Union together proposed a

---

Khrushchev (KROOSH-chef)

world treaty against further proliferation of nuclear weapons. The Nuclear Non-Proliferation Treaty (NPT) was signed by 137 countries later that year. Not until 1972, however, did the two superpowers truly recognize the futility of squandering their wealth on ever-larger missile forces. They began the arduous and extremely slow process of negotiating weapons limits, a process made even slower by the vested interests of military officers and arms industries in each country—what President Eisenhower had called the "military-industrial complex."

In Europe, the Soviet-American arms race outran the economic ability of atomic powers France and Britain to keep pace. Instead, the European states sought to relax tensions. Between 1972 and 1975 the Conference on Security and Cooperation in Europe (CSCE) brought delegates from thirty-seven European states, the United States, and Canada to Helsinki. The goal of the Soviet Union was European acceptance of the political boundaries of the Warsaw Pact nations. The Helsinki Final Act—commonly known as the **Helsinki Accords**—affirmed that no boundaries should be changed by military force. It also contained formal (but nonbinding) declarations calling for economic, social, and governmental contacts across the iron curtain, and for cooperation in humanitarian fields, a provision that paved the way for dialogue about human rights.

Space exploration was another offshoot of the nuclear arms race. The contest to build larger and more accurate missiles prompted the superpowers to prove their skills in rocketry by launching space satellites. The Soviet Union placed a small *Sputnik* satellite into orbit around the earth in October 1957. The United States responded with its own satellite three months later. The space race was on, a contest in which accomplishments in space were understood to signify equivalent achievements in the military sphere. *Sputnik* administered a deep shock to American pride and confidence, but when in 1969 Neil A. Armstrong and Edwin E. ("Buzz") Aldrin became the first humans to walk on the moon, America demonstrated its technological superiority.

Despite rhetorical Cold War saber-rattling by Soviet and American leaders, the threat of nuclear war forced a measure of restraint on the superpower adversaries. Because fighting each other directly would have risked escalation to the level of nuclear exchange, they carefully avoided crises that might provoke such confrontations. Even when arming third parties to do their fighting by proxy, they set limits on how far such fighting could go. Some of these proxy combatants, however, understood the limitations of the superpowers well enough to manipulate them for their own purposes.

Decolonization and Nation Building

After World War I Germany, Austria-Hungary, and the Ottoman Empire lost their empires, and many foreign colonies and dependencies were transferred to the victors, especially to Great Britain and France. Following World War II the victors lost nearly all their imperial possessions. As a result of independence movements in Africa, Asia, and the Americas and growing anti-imperialist movements at home, most of the colonies of Great Britain, France, the Netherlands, Belgium, and the United States were transformed into independent states (see Map 32.2).

Circumstances differed profoundly from place to place. In some Asian countries, where colonial rule was of long standing, newly independent states found themselves in possession of viable industries, communications networks, and education systems. In other countries, notably in Africa, decolonized nations faced dire economic problems and internal disunity that resulted from internal language and ethnic differences.

Political independence had been achieved by most of Latin America in the nineteenth century (see Chapter 22). Following World War II mass political movements in this region focused on the related issue of economic sovereignty—freedom from growing American economic domination. Great Britain still retained colonies in the Caribbean after World War II. Barbados, Guyana, Jamaica, and Trinidad Tobago gained independence in the 1960s. The smaller British colonies followed in the 1970s and 1980s, as did Surinam, which was granted independence by the Netherlands.

Despite their differences, a sense of kinship arose among the new and old nations of Latin America, Africa, and Asia. All shared feelings of excitement and rebirth. As the North Americans, Europeans, and Chinese settled into the exhausting deadlock of the Cold War, visions of independence and national growth captivated the rest of the world.

New Nations in South and Southeast Asia

After partition in 1947 the independent states of India and Pakistan were strikingly dissimilar. Muslim Pakistan defined itself according to religion and quickly fell under the control of military leaders. India, a secular republic led by Prime Minister Jawaharlal Nehru, was much larger and inherited most of the considerable

Online Study Center
Improve Your Grade
Interactive Map:
Decolonization, 1947–1990

Map 32.2 Decolonization, 1947–1990 Notice that independence came a decade or so earlier in South and Southeast Asia than in Africa. Numerous countries that gained independence after World War II in the Caribbean, in South and Central America, and in the Pacific are not shown.

industrial and educational resources the British had developed, along with the larger share of trained civil servants and military officers. Ninety percent of its population was Hindu, most of the rest Muslim.

Adding to the tensions of independence (see Chapter 31) was the decision by the Hindu ruler of the northwestern state known as Jammu and Kashmir, without consulting his overwhelmingly Muslim subjects, to join India. War between India and Pakistan over Kashmir broke out in 1947 and ended with an uneasy truce negotiated at the end of 1948. War over Kashmir began again in 1965, this time involving large military forces and the use of air power by both sides. Kashmir has remained a flash point, with new clashes in 1999 and 2000.

Despite recurrent predictions that multilingual India might break up into a number of linguistically homogeneous states, most Indians recognized that unity benefited everyone; and the country pursued a generally democratic and socialist line of development. Pakistan, in contrast, did break up. In 1971 its Bengali-speaking eastern section seceded to become the independent country of Bangladesh. During the fighting Indian military forces again struck against Pakistan. Despite their shared political heritage, India, Pakistan, and Bangladesh have found cooperation difficult and have pursued markedly different economic, political, religious, and social paths.

As the Japanese had supported anti-British Indian nationalists, so they encouraged the dreams of some anticolonialists in the countries they had occupied in Southeast Asia. Other nationalists, particularly those belonging to communist groups, saw the Japanese as an imperialist enemy; and the harsh character of Japanese occupation eventually alienated most people in the occupied countries. Nevertheless, the defeats the Japanese inflicted on British, French, and Dutch colonial armies set an example of an Asian people standing up to European colonizers.

In the Dutch East Indies, Achmad Sukarno (1901–1970) cooperated with the Japanese in the hope that the Dutch, who had dominated the region economically since the seventeenth century, would never return. After military confrontation, Dutch withdrawal was finally negotiated in 1949, and Sukarno became the dictator of the resource-rich but underdeveloped island nation. He ruled until 1965, when a military coup ousted him and brutally eliminated Indonesia's powerful communist party.

Elsewhere in the region, nationalist movements won independence as well. Britain granted independence to Burma (now Myanmar°) in 1948 and established the

---

Myanmar (myahn-MAR)

Online Study Center
Improve Your Grade
Interactive Map: The New
States in Africa and Asia

Malay Federation the same year. Singapore, once a member of the federation, became an independent city-state in 1965. In 1946 the United States kept its promise of postwar independence for the Philippine Islands but retained close economic ties and leases on military bases.

The Struggle for Independence in Africa

The postwar French government was as determined to hold on to Algeria as it was to keep Vietnam. Since invading the country in 1830 France had followed policies very different from those of the British in India. French settlement had been strongly encouraged, and Algeria had been declared an actual part of France rather than a colony. By the mid-1950s, 10 percent of the Algerian population was of French or other European origin. The Algerian economy was strongly oriented toward France. Though Islam, the religion of 90 percent of the people, prohibited the drinking of alcohol, Algerian vineyards produced immense quantities of wine for French tables. Algerian oil and gas fields were the mainstay of the French petroleum industry.

The Algerian revolt in 1954 was pursued with great brutality by both sides. The Algerian revolutionary organization, the Front de Libération National (FLN), was supported by Egypt and other Arab countries acting on the principle that all Arab peoples should be able to choose their own governments. French colonists, however, considered the country rightfully theirs and swore to fight to the bitter end. When Algeria finally won independence in 1962, a flood of angry colonists returned to France. Their departure undermined the Algerian economy because very few Arabs had received technical training or acquired management experience. Despite bitter feelings left by the war, Algeria retained close and seemingly indissoluble economic ties to France, and Algerians increasingly fled unemployment at home by emigrating to France and taking low-level jobs.

Online Study Center
Improve Your Grade
Primary Source: Comments
on Algeria, April 11, 1961

In most of sub-Saharan Africa independence from European rule was achieved through negotiation. However, in colonies with significant white settler minorities, African peoples had to resort to armed struggle to gain independence, since settler populations strongly resisted majority rule. Throughout Africa, nationalists had to overcome many obstacles, but they were also able to take advantage of the consequential changes that colonial rule had brought.

In the 1950s and 1960s economic growth and growing support for liberation overcame worries about economic and environmental problems that would develop after independence. In the cities that hosted colonial authorities, educated African nationalists used the languages introduced by colonial governments to help build multiethnic coalitions within the artificial colonial boundaries. Missionary and colonial schools had produced few high school and college graduates, but graduates of these colonial school systems were often frustrated by obstacles to their advancement and joined the independence movements. Africans who had obtained advanced education in Europe and the United States also played an important role in the struggle for independence, as did African veterans of Allied armies during World War II.

The networks of roads and railroads built to facilitate colonial exports were used by African truckers and railroad workers to promote Africa's new political consciousness and to spread anticolonial ideas. Improvements in medical care and public health had led to rapid population growth. The region's young population enthusiastically embraced the goal of self-rule.

The young politicians who led the nationalist movements devoted their lives to ridding their homelands of foreign occupation. An example is Kwame Nkrumah° (1909–1972), who in 1957 became prime minister of Ghana (formerly the Gold Coast), the first British colony in West Africa to achieve independence. After graduating from a Catholic mission school and a government teacher-training college, Nkrumah spent a decade studying philosophy and theology in the United States, where he absorbed ideas about black pride and independence then being propounded by W. E. B. Du Bois and Marcus Garvey.

During a brief stay in Britain, Nkrumah joined Kenyan nationalist Jomo Kenyatta, a Ph.D. in anthropology, to found an organization devoted to African freedom. In 1947 Nkrumah returned to the Gold Coast to work for independence. The time was right. There was no longer strong public support in Britain for colonialism and, as a result, Britain's political leadership was not enthusiastic about investing resources to hold restive colonies. After Nkrumah's party won a decisive election

Jomo Kenyatta   Jomo Kenyatta, newly elected premier, is cheered by crowds in Nairobi in 1963. Kenyatta (waving ceremonial "wisk") had led the struggle to end British colonial rule in Kenya.   (Corbis)

victory in 1951, the Gold Coast governor released him from prison (where he had been held on "sedition" charges) and appointed him prime minister. Full independence came in 1957. Nkrumah turned out to be more effective as an international spokesman for colonized peoples than as an administrator, and in 1966 a group of army officers ousted him.

After Ghana won independence, Britain quickly granted independence to its other West African colonies, including large and populous Nigeria in 1960. However, white settler opposition in some British colonies in eastern and southern Africa delayed this process. In Kenya a small but influential group of wealthy coffee planters seized upon a protest movement among the Kikuyu° people as proof that Africans were unready for self-government. The settlers called the movement "Mau Mau," a made-up name meant to evoke primitive savagery. When violence between settlers and anticolonial fighters escalated after 1952, British troops hunted down the

---

Kwame Nkrumah (KWAH-mee nn-KROO-muh)

Kikuyu (kih-KOO-you)

movement's leaders and resettled the Kikuyu in fortified villages to prevent contact with rebel bands. The British also declared a state of emergency, banned all African political protest, and imprisoned Kenyatta and many other nationalists for eight years on charges of being Mau Mau leaders. Released in 1961, Kenyatta negotiated with the British to write a constitution for an independent Kenya. In 1964 he was elected the first president of the Republic of Kenya. He proved to be an effective, though autocratic, ruler. Kenya benefited from greater stability and prosperity than Ghana.

African leaders in the sub-Saharan French colonies were more reluctant than their counterparts in British colonies to call for full independence. They visualized political change in terms of promises made in 1944 by the Free French movement of General Charles de Gaulle at a conference in Brazzaville, in French Equatorial Africa. Acknowledging the value of his African territorial base, his many African troops, and the food supplied by African farmers, de Gaulle had promised more democratic government and broader suffrage, though not representation in the French National Assembly. He also had promised to abolish forced labor and imprisonment of Africans without charges; to expand French education down to the village level; to improve health services; and to open more administrative positions, though not the top ones, to Africans. The word *independence* was never mentioned at Brazzaville, but the politics of postwar colonial self-government led in that direction.

Most new African politicians who sought election in the colonies of French West Africa were civil servants. Because of the French policy of job rotation, they had typically served in a number of different colonies and thus had a broad outlook. They realized that some colonies—such as Ivory Coast, with coffee and cacao exports, fishing, and hardwood forests—had good economic prospects and others, such as landlocked, desert Niger, did not. Furthermore, they recognized the importance of French public investment in the region—a billion dollars between 1947 and 1956—and their own dependence on civil service salaries, which in places totaled 60 percent of government expenditures. The Malagasy politician Philibert Tsirinana° said at a press conference in 1958: "When I let my heart talk, I am a partisan of total and immediate independence [for Madagascar]; when I make my reason speak, I realize that it is impossible."

When Charles de Gaulle returned to power in France in 1958, at the height of the Algerian war, he warned that a rush to independence would have costs, saying: "One cannot conceive of both an independent territory and a France which continues to aid it." Ultimately, African patriotism prevailed in all of France's West African and Equatorial African colonies. Guinea, under the dynamic leadership of Sékou Touré°, gained full independence in 1958 and the rest in 1960.

Independence in the Belgian Congo was chaotic and violent. Contending political and ethnic groups found external allies; some were aided by Cuba and the Soviet Union, others by the West or by business groups tied to the rich mines. Civil war, the introduction of foreign mercenaries, and the rhetoric of Cold War confrontation roiled the waters and led to heavy loss of life as well as property destruction. In 1965 Mobuto Sese Seko seized the reins in a military coup that included the assassination of Patrice Lumumba, the first prime minister, and held on in one of the region's most corrupt governments until driven from power in 1997.

Decolonization in southern Africa was delayed by the opposition of European settlers, some with deep roots in Africa but many others who were new arrivals after 1945. While the settler minority tried to defend white supremacy, African-led liberation movements were committed to the creation of nonracial societies and majority rule. In the 1960s Africans began guerrilla movements against Portuguese rule in Angola and Mozambique, eventually prompting the Portuguese army to overthrow the undemocratic government of Portugal in 1974. The new Portuguese government granted independence to Angola and Mozambique the following year. In 1980, after a ten-year fight, European settlers in the British colony of Southern Rhodesia accepted African majority rule. The new government changed the country's name, which had honored the memory of the British imperialist Cecil Rhodes, to Zimbabwe, the name of a great stone city built by Africans long before the arrival of European settlers. This left only South Africa and neighboring Namibia in the hands of ruling European minorities.

A succession of South African governments had constructed a state and society based on a policy of racial separation, or *apartheid*°, after World War II. Fourteen percent of the population was descended from Dutch and English settlers. By law, whites controlled the most productive tracts of land, the industrial, mining, and commercial enterprises, and the government. Other laws imposed segregated housing, schools, and jobs on South Asians and people of mixed parentage classified as "nonwhite." The 74 percent of the population made up of indigenous Africans were subjected to far stricter

---

Tsirinana (tsee-REE-nah-nah)

Sékou Touré (SAY-koo too-RAY)   **apartheid** (uh-PAHRT-ate)

limitations on place of residence, right to travel, and access to jobs and public facilities. African "homelands," somewhat similar to Amerindian reservations in the United States, were created in parts of the country, often far from the more dynamic and prosperous urban and industrial areas. Overcrowded and lacking investment, these restricted "homelands" were very poor and squalid, with few services and fewer opportunities.

Online Study Center
Improve Your Grade
Primary Source: The Rivonia
Trial Speech to the Court

The African National Congress (ANC), formed in 1912, and other organizations led the opposition to apartheid (see Diversity and Dominance: Race and the Struggle for Justice in South Africa). After police fired on demonstrators in the African town of Sharpeville in 1960 and banned all peaceful political protest by Africans, an African lawyer named Nelson Mandela (b. 1918) organized guerrilla resistance by the ANC. Mandela was sentenced to life in prison in 1964. The ANC operated from outside the country. The armed struggle against apartheid continued until 1990, when Mandela was released from prison (see Chapter 34).

The Quest for Economic Freedom in Latin America

Latin American independence from European rule was achieved more than a hundred years earlier, but European and, by the end of the nineteenth century, American economic domination continued (see Chapters 28 and 31). Chile's copper, Cuba's sugar, Colombia's coffee, and Guatemala's bananas were largely controlled from abroad. The communications networks of several countries were in the hands of ITT (International Telephone and Telegraph Company), a U.S. corporation. From the 1930s, however, support for economic nationalism grew. During the 1930s and 1940s populist political leaders had experimented with programs that would constrain foreign investors or, alternatively, promote local efforts to industrialize (see discussion of Getulio Vargas and Juan Perón in Chapter 31).

In Mexico the revolutionary constitution of 1917 had begun an era of economic nationalism that culminated in the expropriation of foreign oil interests in 1938. Political stability had been achieved under the Institutional Revolutionary Party, or PRI (the abbreviation of its name in Spanish), which controlled the government until the 1990s. Stability allowed Mexico to experience significant economic expansion during the war years, but a yawning gulf between rich and poor, urban and rural, persisted. Although the government dominated important industries like petroleum and restricted foreign investment, rapid population growth, uncontrolled migration to Mexico City and other urban areas, and political corruption challenged efforts to lift the nation's poor. Economic power was concentrated at the top of society, with two thousand elite families benefiting disproportionally from the three hundred foreign and eight hundred Mexican companies that dominated the country. At the other end of the economic scale were the peasants, the 14 percent of the population classified as Indian, and the urban poor.

While Mexico's problems derived only partly from the effects of foreign influence, Guatemala's situation was more representative. Jacobo Arbenz Guzmán, elected in 1951, was typical of Latin American leaders, including Perón of Argentina and Vargas of Brazil (see Chapter 31), who tried to confront powerful foreign interests. An American corporation, the United Fruit Company, was Guatemala's largest landowner; it also controlled much of the nation's infrastructure, including port facilities and railroads. To suppress banana production and keep prices high, United Fruit kept much of its Guatemalan lands fallow. Arbenz attempted land reform, which would have transferred these fallow lands to the nation's rural poor. The threatened expropriation angered the United Fruit Company. Simultaneously, Arbenz tried to reduce U.S. political influence, raising fears in Washington that he sought closer ties to the Soviet Union. Reacting to the land reform efforts and to reports that Arbenz was becoming friendly to communism, the U.S. Central Intelligence Agency (CIA), in one of its first major overseas operations, sponsored a takeover by the Guatemalan military in 1954. CIA intervention removed Arbenz, but it also condemned Guatemala to decades of governmental instability and growing violence between leftist and rightist elements in society.

In Cuba economic domination by the United States prior to 1960 was overwhelming. U.S. companies effectively controlled sugar production, the nation's most important industry, as well as banking, transportation, tourism, and public utilities. The United States was the most important market for Cuba's exports and the most important source of Cuba's imports. The needs of the U.S. economy largely determined the ebb and flow of Cuban foreign trade. A 1934 treaty had granted preferential treatment (prices higher than world market prices) to Cuban sugar in the American market in return for access to the Cuban market by American manufacturers. Since U.S. companies dominated the sugar business, this was actually a kind of tax imposed on American consumers for the benefit of American corporations. By 1956 sugar accounted for 80 percent of Cuba's exports and 25 percent of Cuba's national income. But demand in the United States dictated keeping only 39 percent of the land owned by the sugar companies in production, while Cuba experienced chronic underemployment. Similarly, immense deposits of nickel in Cuba went untapped because the U.S. government, which owned them, considered them to be a reserve.

Profits went north to the United States or to a small class of wealthy Cubans, many of them, like the owners of the Bacardi rum company, of foreign origin. Between 1951 and 1958 Cuba's economy grew at 1.4 percent per year, less than the rate of population increase. Cuba's government was notoriously corrupt and subservient to the wishes of American interests. In 1953 Fulgencio Batista, a former military leader and president, illegally returned to power in a coup. Cuban aversion to corruption, repression, and foreign economic domination spread quickly.

A popular rebellion forced Batista to flee the country in 1959. The dictator had been opposed by student groups, labor unions, and supporters of Cuba's traditional parties. The revolution was led by Fidel Castro (b. 1927), a young lawyer who had been jailed and then exiled when a 1953 uprising failed. Castro established his revolutionary base in the countryside and utilized guerrilla tactics. When he and his youthful followers took power, they vowed not to suffer the fate of Arbenz and the Guatemalan reformers. Ernesto ("Che") Guevara°, Castro's chief lieutenant who became the main theorist of communist revolution in Latin America, had been in Guatemala at the time of the CIA coup. He and Castro took for granted that confrontation with the United States was inevitable. As a result, they quickly removed the existing military leadership, executing many Batista supporters and creating a new military.

They also moved rapidly to transform Cuban society. Castro gave a number of speeches in the United States in the wake of his victory and was cheered as a heroic enemy of dictatorship and American economic imperialism. Within a year his government redistributed land, lowered urban rents, and raised wages, effectively transferring 15 percent of the national income from the rich to the poor. Within twenty-two months the Castro government seized the property of almost all U.S. corporations in Cuba as well as the wealth of Cuba's elite.

To achieve his revolutionary transformation Castro sought economic support from the Soviet Union. The

Che Guevara (CHAY-guh-VAHR-uh)

Cuban Poster of Charismatic Leader Ernesto ("Che") Guevara
A leading theorist of communist revolution in Latin America, Argentine-born Guevara was in Guatemala at the time of the CIA-sponsored coup against Jacobo Arbenz in 1954. He later met Fidel Castro and became an important leader of the Cuban Revolution. He was killed in 1967 while leading an insurgency in Bolivia. (Christopher Morris/stockphoto.com)

United States responded by suspending the sugar agreement and seeking to destabilize the Cuban economy. These punitive measures, the nationalization of so much of the economy, and the punishment of Batista supporters caused tens of thousands of Cubans to leave. Initially, most emigrants were from wealthy families and the middle-class, but when the economic failures of the regime eventually became clear, many poor Cubans fled to the United States or to other Latin American nations.

Little evidence supports the view that Castro undertook his revolution to install a communist government, but he certainly sought to break the economic and political power of the United States in Cuba and to install dramatic social reforms based on an enhanced role for the state in the economy. With relations between Castro and Washington reaching crisis and Castro openly seeking the support of the Soviet Union, in April 1961 the United States attempted to apply the strategy that had removed Arbenz from power in Guatemala. Some fifteen hundred Cuban exiles trained and armed by the CIA were landed at the Bay of Pigs in an effort to overthrow Castro. The

Race and the Struggle for Justice in South Africa

One of South Africa's martyrs in the struggle against apartheid was Steve Biko (1946–1977), a thinker and activist especially concerned with building pride among Africans and asserting the importance of African cultures. Biko was one of the founders of the Black Consciousness Movement, focusing on the ways in which white settlers had stripped Africans of their freedom. As a result of his activism, he was restricted to his hometown in 1973. Between 1975 and 1977 he was arrested and interrogated four times by the police. After his arrest in August 1977 he was severely beaten while in custody. He died days later without having received medical care. His death caused worldwide outrage.

But these are not the people we are concerned with [those who support apartheid]. We are concerned with that curious bunch of nonconformists who explain their participation in negative terms: that bunch of do-gooders that goes under all sorts of names—liberals, leftists etc. These are the people who argue that they are not responsible for white racism and the country's "inhumanity to the black man." These are the people who claim that they too feel the oppression just as acutely as the blacks and therefore should be jointly involved in the black man's struggle for a place under the sun. In short, these are the people who say that they have black souls wrapped up in white skins.

The role of the white liberal in the black man's history in South Africa is a curious one. Very few black organisations were not under white direction. True to their image, the white liberals always knew what was good for the blacks and told them so. The wonder of it all is that the black people have believed in them for so long. It was only at the end of the 50s that the blacks started demanding to be their own guardians.

Nowhere is the arrogance of the liberal ideology demonstrated so well as in their insistence that the problems of the country can only be solved by a bilateral approach involving both black and white. This has, by and large, come to be taken in all seriousness as the modus operandi in South Africa by all those who claim they would like a change in the status quo. Hence the multiracial political organisations and parties and the "nonracial" student organisations, all of which insist on integration not only as an end goal but also as a means.

The integration they talk about is first of all artificial in that it is a response to conscious manoeuvre rather than to the dictates of the inner soul. In other words the people forming the integrated complex have been extracted from various segregated societies with their in built [sic] complexes of superiority and inferiority and these continue to manifest themselves even in the "nonracial" setup of the integrated complex. As a result the integration so achieved is a one-way course, with the whites doing all the talking and the blacks the listening. Let me hasten to say that I am not claiming that segregation is necessarily the natural order; however, given the facts of the situation where a group experiences privilege at the expense of others, then it becomes obvious that a hastily arranged integration cannot be the solution to the problem. It is rather like expecting the slave to work together with the slave-master's son to remove all the conditions leading to the former's enslavement.

Secondly, this type of integration as a means is almost always unproductive. The participants waste lots of time in an internal sort of mudslinging designed to prove that A is more of a liberal than B. In other words the lack of common ground for solid identification is all the time manifested in internal strifes [sic] inside the group.

It will not sound anachronistic to anybody genuinely interested in real integration to learn that blacks are asserting themselves in a society where they are being treated as perpetual under-16s. One does not need to plan for or actively encourage real integration. Once the various groups within a given community have asserted themselves to the point that mutual respect has to be shown then you have the ingredients for a true and meaningful integration. At the heart of true integration is the provision for each man, each group to rise and attain the envisioned self. Each group must be able to attain its style of existence without encroaching on or being thwarted by another. Out of this mutual respect for each other and complete freedom of self-determination there will obviously arise a genuine fusion of the life-styles of the various groups. This is true integration.

From this it becomes clear that as long as blacks are suffering from [an] inferiority complex—a result of 300 years of deliberate oppression, denigration and derision—they will be useless as co-architects of a normal society where man is nothing else but man for his own sake. Hence what is necessary as a prelude to anything else that may come is a very strong grassroots build-up of black consciousness such that blacks can learn to assert themselves and stake their rightful claim.

Thus in adopting the line of a nonracial approach, the liberals are playing their old game. They are claiming a "monopoly on intelligence and moral judgement" and setting the pattern and pace for the realisation of the black man's aspirations. They want to remain in good books with both the black and white worlds. They want to shy away from all forms of "extremisms," condemning "white supremacy" as being just as bad as "Black Power!" They vacillate between the two worlds, verbalising all the complaints of the blacks beautifully while skilfully extracting what suits them from the exclusive pool of white privileges. But ask them for a moment to give a concrete meaningful programme that they intend adopting, then you will see on whose side they really are. Their protests are directed at and appeal to white conscience, everything they do is directed at finally convincing the white electorate that the black man is also a man and that at some future date he should be given a place at the white man's table.

In the following selection Anglican bishop Desmond Tutu (b. 1931) expressed his personal anguish at the death of Steve Biko. He summarized Biko's contributions to the struggle for justice in South Africa. Tutu won the Noble Peace Prize in 1984 and was named archbishop in 1988. From 1995 to 1998 he chaired the Truth and Reconciliation Commission, which investigated atrocities in South Africa during the years of apartheid. He stated that his objective was to create "a democratic and just society without racial divisions."

When we heard the news "Steve Biko is dead" we were struck numb with disbelief. No, it can't be true! No, it must be a horrible nightmare, and we will awake and find that really it is different—that Steve is alive even if it be in detention. But no, dear friends, he is dead and we are still numb with grief, and groan with anguish "Oh God, where are you? Oh God, do you really care—how can you let this happen to us?"

It all seems such a senseless waste of a wonderfully gifted person, struck down in the bloom of youth, a youthful bloom that some wanted to see blighted. What can be the purpose of such wanton destruction? God, do you really love us? What must we do which we have not done, what must we say which we have not said a thousand times over, oh, for so many years—that all we want is what belongs to all God's children, what belongs as an inalienable right—a place in the sun in our own beloved mother country. Oh God, how long can we go on? How long can we go on appealing for a more just ordering of society where we all, black and white together, count not because of some accident of birth or a biological irrelevance—where all of us black and white count because we are human persons, human persons created in your own image.

God called Steve Biko to be his servant in South Africa—to speak up on behalf of God, declaring what the will of this God must be in a situation such as ours, a situation of evil, injustice, oppression and exploitation. God called him to be the founder father of the Black Consciousness Movement against which we have had tirades and fulminations. It is a movement by which God, through Steve, sought to awaken in the Black person a sense of his intrinsic value and worth as a child of God, not needing to apologise for his existential condition as a black person, calling on blacks to glorify and praise God that he had created them black. Steve, with his brilliant mind that always saw to the heart of things, realised that until blacks asserted their humanity and their personhood, there was not the remotest chance for reconciliation in South Africa. For true reconciliation is a deeply personal matter. It can happen only between persons who assert their own personhood, and who acknowledge and respect that of others. You don't get reconciled to your dog, do you? Steve knew and believed fervently that being pro-black was not the same thing as being anti-white. The Black Consciousness Movement is not a "hate white movement," despite all you may have heard to the contrary. He had a far too profound respect for persons as persons, to want to deal with them under readymade, shopsoiled [sic] categories.

All who met him had this tremendous sense of a warmhearted man, and as a notable acquaintance of his told me, a man who was utterly indestructible, of massive intellect and yet reticent; quite unshakeable in his commitment to principle and to radical change in South Africa by peaceful means; a man of real reconciliation, truly an instrument of God's peace, unshakeable in his commitment to the liberation of all South Africans, black and white, striving for a more just and more open South Africa.

QUESTIONS FOR ANALYSIS

1. What are Steve Biko's charges against white liberals in South Africa?
2. What was the proper role for whites in the antiapartheid movement according to Biko?
3. How does Bishop Tutu's eulogy differ from the political spirit and point of view expressed in Biko's 1970 essay?
4. According to Bishop Tutu, what were Biko's strongest characteristics? Were these characteristics demonstrated in Biko's essay?

Source: First selection from Steve Biko, *I Write What I Like,* ed. by Aelred Stubbs (Harper & Row, 1972). Reprinted with the permission of Bowerdean Publishing Co., Ltd.; second selection from *Crying in the Wilderness: The Struggle for Justice in South Africa,* ed. John Webster (William B. Eerdmans Publishing Co., 1982) pp. 61–63. Reprinted by permission of the Continuum International Publishing Group.

Cuban army defeated the attempted invasion in a matter of days, partly because the new U.S. president, John F. Kennedy, decided to provide less air support than had been planned by the Eisenhower administration. The failed overthrow of Castro helped precipitate the Cuban missile crisis. Fearful of a U.S. invasion, Castro and Khrushchev placed nuclear weapons as well as missiles and bombers in Cuba to forestall the anticipated attack.

The failure of the Bay of Pigs tarnished the reputation of the United States and the CIA and gave heart to revolutionaries all over Latin America. But the armed revolutionary movements that imitated the tactics, objectives, and even appearance of Cuba's bearded revolutionaries experienced little success. Among the thousands to lose their lives was Che Guevara, who was executed after capture in Bolivia in 1967. Nevertheless, Castro had demonstrated that American power could be successfully challenged and that a radical program of economic and social reform could be put in place in the Western Hemisphere.

Challenges of Nation Building

Decolonization occurred on a vast scale. Fifty-one nations signed the United Nations Charter in the closing months of 1945. During the United Nations' first decade twenty-five new members joined, a third of them upon gaining independence. During the next decade forty-six more new members were admitted, nearly all of them former colonial territories.

Each of these nations had to organize and institute some form of government. Comparatively few were able to do so without experiencing coups, rewritten constitutions, or regional rebellions. Leaders did not always agree on the form independence should take. In the absence of established constitutional traditions, leaders frequently tried to impose their own visions by force. Most of the new nations, while trying to establish political stability, also faced severe economic challenges, including foreign ownership and operation of key resources and the need to build infrastructure. Overdependence on world demand for raw materials and on imported manufactured goods persisted in many places long after independence.

Because the achievement of political and economic goals called for educated and skilled personnel, education was another common concern in newly emerging nations. Addressing that concern required more than building and staffing schools. In some countries, leaders had to decide which language to teach and how to inculcate a sense of national unity in students from different—and sometimes historically antagonistic—ethnic, religious, and linguistic groups. Another problem was how to provide satisfying jobs for new graduates, many of whom had high expectations because of their education.

Only rarely were the new nations able to surmount these hurdles. Even the most economically and educationally successful, such as South Korea, suffered from tendencies toward authoritarian rule. Similarly, Costa Rica, a country with a remarkably stable parliamentary regime from 1949 onward and a literacy rate of 90 percent, remained heavily dependent on world prices for agricultural commodities and on importation of manufactured goods.

BEYOND A BIPOLAR WORLD

Although no one doubted the dominating role of the East–West superpower rivalry in world affairs, the newly independent states had concerns that were primarily domestic and regional. Their challenge was to pursue their ends within the bipolar structure of the Cold War—and possibly to take advantage of the East–West rivalry. Where nationalist forces sought to assert political or economic independence, Cold War antagonists provided arms and political support even when the nationalist goals were quite different from those of the superpowers. For other nations, the ruinously expensive superpower arms race opened opportunities to expand industries and exports. In short, the superpowers dominated the world but did not control it. And as time progressed, they dominated it less and less.

The Third World

As one of the most successful leaders of the decolonization movement, Indonesia's President Sukarno was an appropriate figure to host a meeting in 1955 of twenty-nine African and Asian countries at Bandung, Indonesia. The conferees proclaimed solidarity among all peoples fighting against colonial rule. The Bandung Conference marked the beginning of an effort by the many new, poor, mostly non-European nations emerging from colonialism to gain more influence in world affairs by banding together. The terms **nonaligned nations** and **Third World**, which became commonplace in the following years, signaled these countries' collective stance toward the rival sides in the Cold War. If the West, led by the United States, and the East, led by the

Bandung Conference, 1955 India's Jawaharlal Nehru (in white hat) was a central figure at the conference held in Indonesia to promote solidarity among nonaligned developing nations. The nonalignment movement failed to achieve the influence that Nehru, Egypt's Nasir, and Indonesia's Sukarno sought. (Wide World Photos)

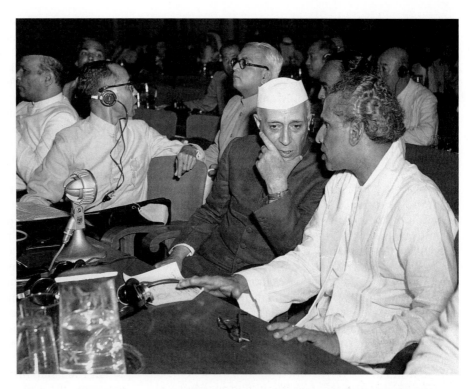

Soviet Union, represented two worlds locked in mortal struggle, the Third World consisted of everyone else.

Leaders of so-called Third World countries preferred the label *nonaligned,* which signified freedom from membership on either side. However, many leaders in the West noted that the Soviet Union supported national liberation movements and that the nonaligned movement included communist countries such as China and Yugoslavia. As a result, they decided not to take the term *nonaligned* seriously. In a polarized world, they saw Sukarno, Nehru, Nkrumah, and Egypt's Gamal Abd al-Nasir° as stalking horses for a communist takeover of the world. This may also have been the view of some Soviet leaders, since the Soviet Union was quick to offer some of these countries military and financial aid.

For the movement's leaders, however, nonalignment was primarily a way to extract money and support from one or both superpowers. By flirting with the Soviet Union or its ally, the People's Republic of China, a country could get cheap or free weapons, training, and barter agreements that offered an alternative to selling agricultural or mineral products on Western-dominated world markets. The same flirtation might also prompt the United States and its allies to proffer grants and loans, cheap or free surplus grain, and investment in industry and infrastructure.

When skillful, nonaligned countries could play the two sides against each other and profit from both. Egypt under Nasir, who had led a military coup against the Egyptian monarchy in 1952, and under Nasir's successor Anwar al-Sadat° after 1970 played the game well. The United States offered to build a dam at Aswan°, on the Nile River, to increase Egypt's electrical generating and irrigation capacity. When Egypt turned to the Soviet Union for arms, the United States reneged on the dam project in 1956. The Soviet Union then picked it up and completed the dam in the 1960s. In 1956 Israel, Great Britain, and France conspired to invade Egypt. Their objective was to overthrow Nasir, regain the Suez Canal (he had recently nationalized it), and secure Israel from any Egyptian threat. The invasion succeeded militarily, but the United States and the Soviet Union both pressured the invaders to withdraw, thus saving Nasir's government. In 1972 Sadat evicted his Soviet military advisers, but a year later he used his Soviet

---

Gamal Abd al-Nasir (gah-MAHL AHB-d al–NAH-suhr)

al-Sadat (al-seh-DAT)   **Aswan** (AS-wahn)

weapons to attack Israel. After he lost that war, he announced his faith in the power of the United States to solve Egypt's political and economic problems.

Numerous other countries adopted similar balancing strategies. In each case, local leaders were trying to develop their nation's economy and assert or preserve their nation's interests. Manipulating the superpowers was a means toward those ends and implied very little about true ideological orientation.

Japan and China

No countries took better advantage of the opportunities presented by the superpowers' preoccupation than did Japan and China. Japan signed a peace treaty with most of its former enemies in 1951 and regained independence from American occupation the following year. Renouncing militarism and its imperialist past (see Chapter 27), Japan remained on the sidelines throughout the Korean War. Its new constitution, written under American supervision in 1946, allowed only a limited self-defense force, banned the deployment of Japanese troops abroad, and gave the vote to women.

The Japanese turned their talents and energies to rebuilding their industries and engaging in world commerce. Peace treaties with countries in Southeast Asia specified reparations payable in the form of goods and services, thus reintroducing Japan to that region as a force for economic development rather than as a military occupier. Nevertheless, bitterness over wartime oppression remained strong, and Japan had to move slowly in developing new regional markets for its manufactured goods. The Cold War isolated Japan and excluded it from most world political issues. It thus provided an exceptionally favorable environment for Japan to develop its economic strength.

Three industries that took advantage of government aid and the newest technologies paved the way for Japan's emergence as an economic superpower after 1975. Electricity was in short supply in 1950; Tokyo itself suffered evening power outages. Projects producing 60 million kilowatts of electricity were completed between 1951 and 1970, almost a third through dams on Japan's many rivers. Between 1960 and 1970 steel production more than quadrupled, reaching 15.7 percent of the total capacity of countries outside the Soviet bloc. The shipbuilding industry produced six times as much tonnage in 1970 as in 1960, almost half the new tonnage produced worldwide outside the Soviet bloc.

While Japan benefited from being outside the Cold War, China was deeply involved in Cold War politics. When Mao Zedong° and the communists defeated the nationalists in 1949 and established the People's Republic of China (PRC), their main ally and source of arms was the Soviet Union. By 1956, however, the PRC and the Soviet Union were beginning to diverge politically, partly in reaction to the Soviet rejection of Stalinism and partly because of China's reluctance to be cast forever in the role of student. Mao had his own notions of communism, focusing strongly on the peasantry, whom the Soviets ignored in favor of the industrial working class.

Mao's Great Leap Forward in 1958 was supposed to vault China into the ranks of world industrial powers by maximizing the use of labor in small-scale, village-level industries and by mass collectivization in agriculture. These policies demonstrated Mao's willingness to carry out massive economic and social projects of his own devising in the face of criticism by the Soviets and by traditional economists. However, these revolutionary reforms failed comprehensively by 1962, leading to an estimated 30 million deaths.

In 1966 Mao instituted another radical nationwide program, the **Cultural Revolution**, and ordered the mass mobilization of Chinese youth into Red Guard units. His goal was to kindle revolutionary fervor in a new generation to ward off the stagnation and bureaucratization he saw in the Soviet Union. But this was also a strategy for increasing Mao's power within the Communist Party. Red Guard units criticized and purged teachers, party officials, and intellectuals for "bourgeois values." The young militants themselves suffered from factionalism, which caused more violence. Executions, beatings, and incarcerations were widespread, leading to a half-million deaths and three million purged by 1971. Finally, Mao admitted that attacks on individuals had gotten out of hand and intervened to reestablish order. The last years of the Cultural Revolution were dominated by radicals led by Mao's wife Jiang Qing°, who focused on restricting artistic and intellectual activity.

Online Study Center
Improve Your Grade
Primary Source: One Hundred Items for Destroying the Old and Establishing the New

---

Mao Zedong (maow dzuh-dong)   **Jiang Qing** (jyahn ching)

Chinese Red Guards   During the Cultural Revolution young Chinese militants joined the Red Guards, identifying enemies of the Communist Party and Chairman Mao. They also turned on their teachers and sometimes their parents and neighbors, labeling them enemies of the people or members of the bourgeoisie. Here a victim is paraded wearing a dunce cap on which his crimes are written.   (Wide World Photos)

In the meantime, the rift between the PRC and the Soviet Union had opened so wide that U.S. President Richard Nixon (served 1969–1974), by reputation a staunch anticommunist, put out secret diplomatic feelers to revive relations with China. In 1971 the United States agreed to allow the PRC to join the United Nations and occupy China's permanent seat on the Security Council. This decision necessitated the expulsion of the Chinese nationalist government based on the island of Taiwan, which had persistently claimed to be the only legal Chinese authority. The following year, Nixon visited Beijing, initiating a new era of enhanced cooperation between the People's Republic of China and the United States.

The Middle East

The superpowers could not control all dangerous international disputes. Independence had come gradually to the Arab countries of the Middle East. Britain granted Syria and Lebanon independence after World War II. Iraq, Egypt, and Jordan enjoyed nominal independence between the two world wars but remained under indirect British control until the 1950s. Military coups overthrew King Faruq° of Egypt in 1952 and King Faysal° II of Iraq in 1958. King Husayn° of Jordan dismissed his British military commander in 1956 in response to the Suez crisis, but his poor desert country remained dependent on British and later American financial aid.

Overshadowing all Arab politics, however, was the struggle with Israel. British policy on Palestine between the wars oscillated between sentiment favoring Zionist Jews—who emigrated to Palestine, encouraged by the Balfour Declaration—and sentiment for the indigenous Palestinian Arabs, who felt themselves being pushed aside and suspected that the Zionists were aiming at an independent state. As more and more Jews sought a safe haven from persecution by the Nazis, Arabs felt more and more threatened. The Arabs unleashed a guerrilla uprising against the British in 1936, and Jewish groups turned to militant tactics a few years later. Occasionally, Arabs and Jews confronted each other in riots or killings, making it clear that peaceful coexistence in Palestine would be difficult or impossible to achieve.

After the war, under intense pressure to resettle European Jewish refugees, Britain conceded that it saw no way of resolving the dilemma and turned the Palestine problem over to the United Nations. In November 1947 the General Assembly voted in favor of partitioning Palestine into two states, one Jewish and the other Arab. The Jewish community made plans to declare independence, while the Palestinians, who felt that the proposed land division was unfair, reacted with horror and took up arms. When Israel declared its independence in May 1948, neighboring Arab countries sent armies to help the Palestinians crush the newborn state.

Israel prevailed on all fronts. Some 700,000 Palestinians became refugees, finding shelter in United Nations refugee camps in Jordan, Syria, Lebanon, and the Gaza Strip (a bit of coastal land on the Egyptian-Israeli border). The right of these refugees to return home

---

Faruq (fuh-ROOK)   **Faysal** (FIE-suhl)   **Husayn** (hoo-SANE)

remains a focal point of Arab politics. In 1967 Israel responded to threatening military moves by Egypt's Nasir by preemptively attacking Egyptian and Syrian air bases. In six days Israel won a smashing victory. When Jordan entered the war, Israel won control of Jerusalem, which it had previously split with Jordan, and the West Bank. Acquiring all of Jerusalem satisfied Jews' deep longing to return to their holiest city, but Palestinians continued to regard Jerusalem as their destined capital, and Muslims in many countries protested Israeli control of the Dome of the Rock, a revered Islamic shrine located in the city. Israel also occupied the Gaza Strip, the strategic Golan Heights in southern Syria, and the entire Sinai Peninsula (see Map 32.3). These acquisitions resulted in a new wave of Palestinian refugees.

Shortage at the Pumps As prices rose in the late 1970s consumers tried to hoard supplies by filling gas cans at neighborhood stations. For the first time gas prices exceeded $1 a gallon. (James Pozarik/Getty Images)

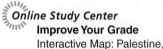
Online Study Center
Improve Your Grade
Interactive Map: Palestine,
Israel, and the Middle East

The rival claims to Palestine continued to plague Middle Eastern politics. The Palestine Liberation Organization (PLO), headed by Yasir Arafat°, waged guerrilla war against Israel, frequently engaging in acts of terrorism. The militarized Israelis were able to blunt or absorb these attacks and launch counterstrikes that likewise involved assassinations and bombings. Though the United States was a firm friend to Israel and the Soviet Union armed the Arab states, neither superpower saw the struggle between Zionism and Palestinian nationalism as a vital concern—until oil became a political issue.

Online Study Center
Improve Your Grade
Primary Source: The
Palestinian National Charter

The phenomenal concentration of oil wealth in the Middle East—Saudi Arabia, Iran, Iraq, Kuwait, Libya, Qatar, Bahrain, and the United Arab Emirates—was not fully realized until after World War II, when

demand for oil rose sharply as civilian economies recovered. In 1960, as a world oversupply diminished in the face of rising demand, oil-producing states formed the **Organization of Petroleum Exporting Countries (OPEC)** to promote their collective interest in higher revenues.

Oil politics and the Arab-Israeli conflict intersected in October 1973. A surprise Egyptian attack across the Suez Canal threw the Israelis into temporary disarray. Within days the war turned in Israel's favor, and an Egyptian army was trapped at the canal's southern end. The United States then arranged a ceasefire and the disengagement of forces. But before that could happen, the Arab oil-producing countries voted to embargo oil shipments to the United States and the Netherlands as punishment for their support of Israel.

The implications of using oil as an economic weapon profoundly disturbed the worldwide oil industry. Prices rose—along with feelings of insecurity. In 1974 OPEC responded to the turmoil in the oil market by quadrupling prices, setting the stage for massive transfers of wealth to the producing countries and provoking a feeling of crisis throughout the consuming countries.

Map 32.3 Middle East Oil and the Arab-Israeli Conflict, ➤
1947–1973 Oil resources were long controlled by private European and American companies. In the 1960s most countries, guided by OPEC, negotiated agreements for sharing control, eventually leading to national ownership. This set the stage for the use of oil as a weapon in the 1973 Arab-Israeli war and for subsequent price increases.

Arafat (AR-uh-fat)

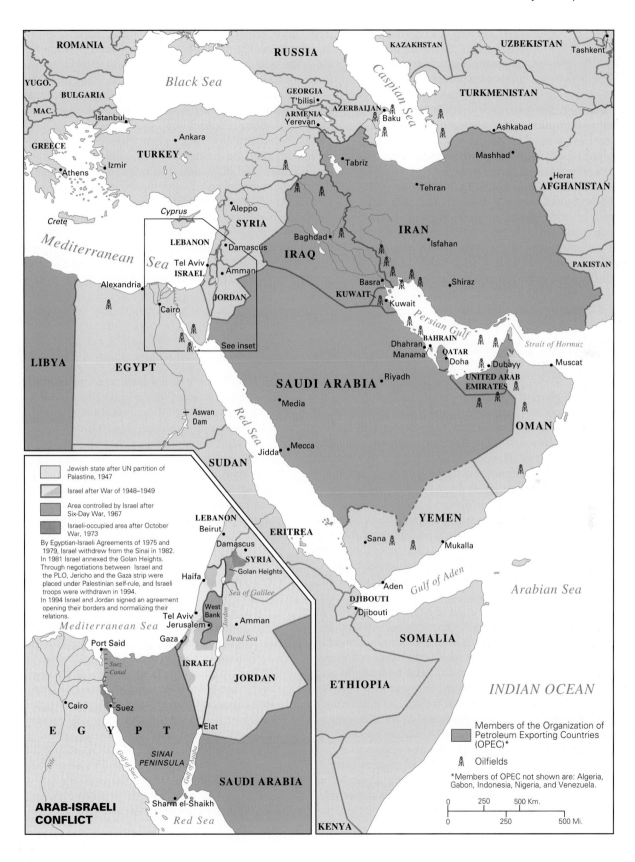

ROMANIA

RUSSIA

KAZAKHSTAN

UZBEKISTAN

Tashkent

YUGO.

Black Sea

BULGARIA

GEORGIA
T'bilisi

TURKMENISTAN

MAC.

ARMENIA
Yerevan

AZERBAIJAN
Baku

Ashkabad

Istanbul

GREECE

Ankara

TURKEY

Mashhad

Izmir

Tabriz

Tehran

Herat
AFGHANISTAN

Athens

Crete

Aleppo

SYRIA

IRAN

Isfahan

PAKISTAN

Cyprus

Mediterranean

LEBANON

Damascus

Baghdad

Sea

Tel Aviv
ISRAEL

Amman

IRAQ

Basra

Shiraz

Alexandria

JORDAN

KUWAIT

Cairo

See inset

Kuwait

Persian Gulf

LIBYA

EGYPT

Dhahran
Manama

BAHRAIN

QATAR
Doha

Dubayy

Strait of Hormuz

Muscat

SAUDI ARABIA

Riyadh

UNITED ARAB
EMIRATES

Aswan
Dam

Media

OMAN

Red Sea

Mecca

Jidda

SUDAN

Sana

YEMEN

Mukalla

Gulf of Aden

Aden

Arabian Sea

DJIBOUTI
Djibouti

SOMALIA

ETHIOPIA

INDIAN OCEAN

KENYA

Legend (inset)

	Jewish state after UN partition of Palastine, 1947
	Israel after War of 1948–1949
	Area controlled by Israel after Six-Day War, 1967
	Israeli-occupied area after October War, 1973

By Egyptian-Israeli Agreements of 1975 and 1979, Israel withdrew from the Sinai in 1982. In 1981 Israel annexed the Golan Heights. Through negotiations between Israel and the PLO, Jericho and the Gaza strip were placed under Palestinian self-rule, and Israeli troops were withdrawn in 1994.
In 1994 Israel and Jordan signed an agreement opening their borders and normalizing their relations.

ARAB-ISRAELI CONFLICT (inset)

LEBANON
Beirut

ERITREA

Damascus

SYRIA

Golan Heights

Haifa

Sea of Galilee

Mediterranean Sea

West
Bank

Amman

Tel Aviv
Jerusalem

Dead Sea

Gaza

Port Said

Suez Canal

ISRAEL

JORDAN

E G Y P T

Cairo

Suez

Nile

Elat

SINAI
PENINSULA

Gulf of Suez

Gulf of Aqaba

SAUDI ARABIA

Sharm el-Shaikh

Red Sea

Members of the Organization of Petroleum Exporting Countries (OPEC)*

Oilfields

*Members of OPEC not shown are: Algeria, Gabon, Indonesia, Nigeria, and Venezuela.

0   250   500 Km.

0   250   500 Mi.

The Emergence of Environmental Concerns

The Cold War and the massive investments made in postwar economic recovery had focused public and governmental attention on technological innovations and enormous projects such as hydroelectric dams and nuclear power stations. Only a few people warned that untested technologies and all-out drives for industrial productivity were rapidly degrading the environment. The superpowers were particularly negligent of the environmental impact of pesticide and herbicide use, automobile exhaust, industrial waste disposal, and radiation.

The wave of student unrest that swept many parts of the world in 1968 and the early 1970s created a new awareness of environmental issues and a new constituency for environmental action. As the current of youth activism grew, governments in the West began to pass new environmental regulations. Earth Day, a benchmark of the new awareness, was first celebrated in 1970, the year in which the United States established its Environmental Protection Agency.

The problem of finite natural resources became more broadly recognized when oil prices skyrocketed. Making gasoline engines and home heating systems more efficient and lowering highway speed limits to conserve fuel became matters of national debate in the United States, while poorer countries struggled to find the money to import oil. A widely read 1972 study called *The Limits of Growth* forecast a need to cut back on consumption of natural resources in the twenty-first century. As the most dangerous moments of the Cold War seemed to be passing, ecological and environmental problems of worldwide impact vied for public attention with superpower rivalry and Third World nation building.

COMPARATIVE PERSPECTIVES

The alliance between the Soviet Union and the Western democracies led by the United States did not survive into the post–World War II era. Shortly after the war both sides began to prepare for a new round of hostilities, establishing competing military alliances and attempting to influence the new governments of nations formerly occupied by the Axis. Each side portrayed this tension as a struggle between irreconcilably different social and economic systems, and each side emphasized the corruption, injustice, and unfairness of its opponent. When Winston Churchill spoke in 1946 of Soviet control in eastern Europe as an iron curtain, he suggested that the Soviet system was, in effect, a prison.

The boundary that separated the United States and its allies and the Soviet Union and its allies was soon defended by massive armies armed with increasingly sophisticated weapons, including nuclear weapons that were far more destructive than those dropped on Japan. This Cold War quickly became global in character as distant civil wars, regional conflicts, and nationalist revolutions were transformed by support provided by these contestants for global ascendancy.

Many of the flash points in this war were provided by the desire of colonized peoples to throw off imperial controls and establish independent nations. The Western nations had defined World War II as a war for freedom and self-determination. The Free French had promised greater autonomy to African colonies, the United States had used nationalist forces to fight against the Japanese in the Philippines and in Vietnam, and the British also had used forces recruited throughout its empire to fight the war. Once organized and set in motion, these nationalist energies could not be easily contained again in the confines of traditional colonial rule. The most powerful force in the postwar era was nationalism, the desire of peoples to control their own destinies. This reality, clear now, was obscured by the global contest of the Cold War.

In Africa, the Middle East, South Asia, and Latin America this desire to throw off foreign controls would lead to the creation of scores of new nations by the 1970s. Each nation's struggle had its own character. While in India these passions led to independence, similar sentiments led in China to the overthrow of a government seen as weak and subordinate to foreign powers and to the creation of a communist dictatorship. In much of Africa, the Middle East, and the Caribbean, nationalism was manifested as traditional anticolonial struggles, not unlike the conflict that gave birth to the United States. In the Middle East the desire for self-government was complicated by the creation of the state of Israel. In Latin America, where most nations had been independent for well over a century, the era's nationalist sentiment manifested itself as a desire for economic independence and an end to foreign interventions. For this reason Castro found it easy to connect his revolutionary ambitions to anticolonial movements elsewhere.

The end of Japanese control in Korea and Vietnam led to territorial partitions that separated Soviet-leaning and Western-allied polities. Civil war and foreign interventions soon followed. In both cases the Soviet Union and China supported communist forces. The United States committed large military forces to protect the anticommunist governments, gaining a stalemate in Korea and eventually losing in Vietnam. While the outcomes were mixed for the superpowers, the wars were contained and managed so as to prevent direct engagement and nuclear conflict.

SUMMARY

What were the major threats to world peace during the Cold War?

How were the experiences of Asia, Africa, and Latin America similar in this period?

How did the rivalry between the Cold War superpowers affect the rest of the world?

Online Study Center
ACE the Test

The arms race associated with the rivalry between the West and the Soviets produced the largest peacetime militaries in world history. The reliance of both sides on large inventories of nuclear weapons meant that any direct conflict had the potential of provoking massive retaliation. For more than fifty years massed armies faced each other across Europe. In the end this confrontation was projected into space, as each side sought to advertise its technological capacity through satellite launches and finally a moon landing. During the Cold War leaders of the opposing alliances viewed their struggle as a global conflict between irreconcilable systems. This meant that every popular movement, revolution, or civil war was strategically important and could involve the superpowers or their allies.

Africa, Asia, and Latin America were all powerfully affected by nationalism in the postwar period. In Africa and South Asia nationalist forces gathered strength and swept away colonial rule. In China nationalist frustration with the weak and corrupt government, viewed as incapable of defending national sovereignty, helped to propel communist revolutionaries led by Mao Zedong to power. Latin American nationalists aimed for economic independence and an end to foreign intervention, and Fidel Castro identified these goals with those of countries struggling for independence in Asia and Africa. Many newly installed nationalist governments experimented with forms of state-directed economic development, nationalizing important industries and seizing natural resources. Even while rejecting communism, these nationalist government adapted Soviet economic institutions and policies, such as five-year plans and central planning, to their own purposes. While some new governments supported the Soviets and others supported the United States, there was broad agreement on the importance of political and economic self-determination.

The Cold War rivalry never led to direct conflict between the major powers. Emerging nations were sometimes able to use this rivalry to gain foreign aid for development projects or infrastructure projects such as roads and schools. More typically, military aid flowed to political allies, leading to destructive and bloody conflicts. Both the West and the Soviets armed and trained contestants in civil wars, revolutions, and regional conflicts. The independence of the Congo turned into a protracted civil war financed in part by this rivalry, and a series of wars between Israel and its Arab neighbors were made possible by the transfer of massive amounts of military equipment. In the wake of the communist success in China, the United States went to war twice in Asia—in Korea and in Vietnam—to prevent further communist advances. The United States also supported the overthrow of the Guatemalan government in 1954 and attempted in 1961 to overthrow Castro as well. The Soviet Union crushed Hungarian nationalists in 1956 and Czechoslovakian patriots in 1968. No region of the world completely escaped the costs associated with the Cold War.

KEY TERMS

iron curtain *p. 937*

Cold War *p. 937*

North Atlantic Treaty Organization (NATO) *p. 937*

Warsaw Pact *p. 937*

United Nations *p. 937*

World Bank *p. 939*

Marshall Plan *p. 940*

European Community (EC) *p. 940*

Truman Doctrine *p. 941*

Korean War *p. 941*

Vietnam War *p. 943*

Cuban missile crisis *p. 944*

Helsinki Accords *p. 945*

nonaligned nations *p. 954*

Third World *p. 954*

Cultural Revolution (China) *p. 956*

Organization of Petroleum Exporting Countries (OPEC) *p. 958*

Online Study Center
Improve Your Grade
Flashcards

SUGGESTED READING

The period since 1945 has been particularly rich in memoirs by government leaders. Some that are particularly relevant to the Cold War and decolonization are Dean Acheson (U.S. secretary of state under Truman), *Present at the Creation* (1969); Nikita Khrushchev, *Khrushchev Remembers* (1970); and Anthony Eden (British prime minister), *Full Circle* (1960). Geoffrey Barraclough, *An Introduction to Contemporary History* (1964), is a remarkable early effort at understanding the broad sweep of history during this period. See also David Reynolds, *One World Divisible: A Global History Since 1945* (2000).

Scholarship on the origins of the Cold War is extensive and includes Akira Iriye, *The Cold War in Asia: A Historical Introduction* (1974); and Bruce Kuniholm, *The Origins of the Cold War in the Middle East* (1980). For Africa see Madelaine Kalb, *The Congo Cables: The Cold War in Africa—From Eisenhower to Kennedy* (1982); and Ludo De Witte, *The Assassination of Lumumba*, trans. Ann Wright (2003). For Latin America see Stephen G. Rabe, *The Most Dangerous Area in the World: John F. Kennedy Confronts Communist Revolution in Latin America* (1999); and Rabe's earlier *Eisenhower and Latin America: The Foreign Policy of Anticommunism* (1988).

Good general histories of the Cold War include Martin Walker, *The Cold War: A History* (1993), and Walter Lafeber, *America, Russia, and the Cold War, 1945–1992* (1993). The latter emphasizes how the Cold War eroded American democratic values. See also Michael J. Hogan, *A Cross of Iron: Harry S Truman and the Origins of the National Security State* (1998). For a recent reconsideration of earlier historical viewpoints see Melvyn P. Leffler and David S. Painter, eds., *Origins of the Cold War: An International History* (1994). For a look at the Cold War from the Soviet perspective see William Taubman, *Stalin's America Policy* (1981). An important study of Soviet objectives and strategy is Vladislav Zubok and Constantine Pleshakov, *Inside the Kremlin's Cold War: From Stalin to Khrushchev* (1997). For the American perspective see John Lewis Gaddis, *Strategies of Containment: A*

Critical Appraisal of Postwar American National Security Policy (1982). The Cuban missile crisis is well covered in Graham Allison, *Essence of Decision: Explaining the Cuban Missile Crisis* (1971), and Michael Beschloss, *The Crisis Years: Kennedy and Khrushchev, 1960–1963* (1991). Also see Aleksandr Fursenko and Timothy Naftali, *"One Hell of a Gamble": Khrushchev, Castro, and Kennedy, 1958–1964: The Secret History of the Cuban Missile Crisis* (1997); and the more recent John L. Gaddis, *We Now Know: Rethinking Cold War History* (1997); Mark Mazower, *Dark Continent* (1999); and William Hitchcock, *The Struggle for Europe: The Turbulent History of a Divided Continent 1945–2002* (2003).

The nuclear arms race and the associated Soviet–U.S. competition in space are well covered by McGeorge Bundy, *Danger and Survival: Choices About the Bomb in the First Fifty Years* (1988), and Walter MacDougall, *The Heavens and the Earth: A Political History of the Space Age* (1985). Among the many novels illustrating the alarming impact of the arms race on the general public are Philip Wylie, *Tomorrow!* (1954), and Nevil Shute, *On the Beach* (1970). At a technical and philosophical level, Herman Kahn's *On Thermonuclear War* (1961) had a similar effect.

The end of the European empires is broadly treated by D. K. Fieldhouse, *The Colonial Empires* (1982); a broad view is provided by D. A. Low, *The Egalitarian Moment: Asia and Africa, 1950–1980* (1996); for the British Empire in particular, see Brian Lapping, *End of Empire* (1985). M. Chamberlain, *Decolonization: The Fall of the European Empires*, 2nd ed. (1999), provides good coverage of the Caribbean. For a critical view of American policies toward the decolonized world see Gabriel Kolko, *Confronting the Third World: United States Foreign Policy, 1945–1980* (1988).

For books on some of the specific episodes of decolonization treated in this chapter see, on Algeria, Alistaire Horne, *A Savage War of Peace: Algeria, 1954–1962* (1987); on Africa, H. S. Wilson, *African Decolonization* (1994), and Frederick Cooper, *Decolonization and African Society: The Labor Question in French and*

British Africa (1996); on Cuba, Hugh Thomas, *Cuba: The Pursuit of Freedom* (1971); on the Suez crisis of 1956, Keith Kyle, *Suez 1956* (1991); on Britain's role in the Middle East over the period of the birth of Israel, William Roger Louis, *The British Empire in the Middle East, 1945–1951* (1984); on Vietnam, George Herring, *America's Longest War: The United States and Vietnam, 1950–1975* (1986), Stanley Karnow, *Vietnam: A History* (1991), and the recent Sandra C. Taylor, *Vietnamese Women at War: Fighting for Ho Chi Minh and the Revolution* (1999); and on Latin America, Thomas E. Skidmore and Peter H. Smith, *Modern Latin America*, 5th ed. (2001).

The special cases of Japan and China in this period are covered by Takafusa Nakamura, *A History of Showa Japan, 1926–1989* (1998); John Dower, *Embracing Defeat: Japan in the Wake of World War II* (1999); Marius B. Jansen, *Japan and China: From War to Peace, 1894–1972* (1975); and Maurice Meisner, *Mao's China and After: A History of the People's Republic* (1986). On the consequences of the Great Leap Forward see Jasper Becker, *Hungry Ghosts* (1998); and on the Cultural Revolution see Lynn T. White, *Policies of Chaos: The Organizational Causes of Violence in China's Cultural Revolution* (1989). John Merrill, *Korea: The Peninsular Origins of the War* (1989), presents the Korean War as a civil and revolutionary conflict as well as an episode of the Cold War. Among the hundreds of books on the Arab-Israeli conflict, Charles D. Smith, *Palestine and the Arab-Israel Conflict* (1992), and Trevor N. Dupuy, *Elusive Victory: The Arab-Israeli Wars, 1947–1974* (1978), stand out.

NOTES

1. From Mark Mazower, *Dark Continent: Europe's Twentieth Century* (New York: Alfred A. Knopf, 1999), 271.

Shanghai—Old Meets New The city of Shanghai is one of the great success stories in a rapidly growing Chinese economy. The prosperity of its modern industries has left many behind, however. In this photo a poor woman walks past Shanghai's modern skyline carrying goods to market in baskets and a neck yoke, a technology thousands of years old. (Dennis Cox/China Stock)

- How did the Cold War affect politics in Latin America and the Middle East in the 1970s and 1980s?

- What forces led to the collapse of the Soviet Union?

- What explains differences in the rate of population growth among the world's cultural regions?

- How does wealth inequality among nations impact international migration patterns?

- How has technological change affected the global environment in the recent past?

33

THE END OF THE COLD WAR AND THE CHALLENGE OF ECONOMIC DEVELOPMENT AND IMMIGRATION, 1975–2000

CHAPTER OUTLINE

Postcolonial Crises and Asian Economic Expansion

The End of the Bipolar World

The Challenge of Population Growth

Unequal Development and the Movement of Peoples

Technological and Environmental Change

Comparative Perspectives

DIVERSITY AND DOMINANCE: The Struggle for Women's Rights in an Era of Global Political and Economic Change

ENVIRONMENT AND TECHNOLOGY: The Personal Computer

MATERIAL CULTURE: Fast Food

China began an ambitious program of economic reforms at the end of the 1970s. Until then China, with the world's largest population, lagged far behind the mature industrialized nations of Europe and North America in economic performance, as well as behind neighboring nations like Japan and South Korea. Since the reforms China has experienced rapid economic growth and has become one of the few socialist nations to successfully make the transition from a socialist to a market economy. Despite this remarkable expansion, as many as 100 million Chinese still lived in poverty in 2000. As is indicated in the opening illustration, ancient technology and poverty can exist in close proximity with modernity and affluence in China.

Online Study Center

This icon will direct you to interactive activities and study materials on the website: *college.hmco.com/pic/bulliet4e.*

These same problems of poverty and inequality are found across the globe. In an era of astounding technological change and spreading prosperity, 1.2 billion of the world's population live on less than a dollar per day.

At the end of the twentieth century many of the nations of the developing world found that population growth continued to outstrip economic resources. In wealthy industrialized nations as well, politicians and social reformers still worry about the effects of unemployment, family breakdown, substance abuse, and homelessness. As had been true during the Industrial Revolution in the eighteenth century (see Chapter 23), dramatic economic expansion, increased global economic integration, and rapid technological progress in the last decades of the twentieth century coincided with problems of social dislocation and inequality. Among the most important events of the period were the emergence of new industrial powers in Asia and the precipitous demise of the Soviet Union and its socialist allies.

POSTCOLONIAL CRISES AND ASIAN ECONOMIC EXPANSION

Between 1975 and the end of the century, wars and revolutions provoked by a potent mix of ideology, nationalism, ethnic hatred, and religious fervor spread death and destruction through many of the world's least-developed regions. These conflicts often had ties to earlier colonialism and foreign intervention, but the character and objectives of each conflict reflected specific historical experiences. Throughout these decades of conflict the two superpowers sought to avoid direct military confrontation while working to gain strategic advantages. The United States and the Soviet Union each supplied arms and financial assistance to nations or insurgent forces hostile to its superpower rival. Once they became linked to this geopolitical rivalry, conflicts provoked by local and regional causes tended to become more deadly and long-lasting. Conflicts in which the rival superpowers financed and armed competing factions or parties were called **proxy wars**.

In Latin America the rivalry of the superpowers helped transform conflicts over political rights, social justice, and economic policies into a violent cycle of revolution, military dictatorship, and foreign meddling. In Iran and Afghanistan resentment against foreign intrusion and a growing religious hostility to secular culture led to revolutionary transformations. Here again superpower ambitions and regional political instability helped provoke war and economic decline. These experiences were not universal. During this period some Asian nations experienced rapid transformation. Japan became one of the world's leading industrial powers. A small number of other Asian economies entered the ranks of industrial and commercial powers, including socialist China, which initiated market-based economic reforms.

The collapse of the Soviet system in eastern Europe at the end of the 1980s ended the Cold War and undermined socialist economies elsewhere. As developing and former socialist nations opened their markets to foreign investment and competition, economic transformation was often accompanied by wrenching social change. The world's growing economic interconnectedness coincided with increased inequality. While the world's wealthiest industrial nations continued to prosper in the 1990s, some developing nations also reaped substantial benefits from rapid technological change and world economic integration.

This period also witnessed a great increase in world population and increased international immigration. Population growth and increased levels of industrialization had a dramatic impact on the global environment. Every continent felt the destructive effects of forest depletion, soil erosion, and pollution. Wealthy nations with slow population growth found it easier to respond to these environmental challenges than did poor nations experiencing rapid population growth.

Revolutions, Repression, and Democratic Reform in Latin America

In the 1970s Latin America entered a dark era of political violence. As revolutionary movements challenged the established order in many nations, democratic governments were overturned by military revolts. A region of weak democracy in 1960 became a region of military dictatorships fifteen years later. The new authoritarian leaders had little patience with civil liberties and human rights.

The ongoing confrontation between Fidel Castro and the government of the United States (see Chapter 32) helped propel the region toward crisis. The fact that the Cuban communist government survived efforts by the United States to overthrow it energized the revolutionary

CHRONOLOGY

	The Americas	Middle East/Africa	Asia	Eastern Europe
1970	**1970** Salvador Allende elected president of Chile			
	1973 Allende overthrown		**1975** Vietnam War ends	
	1976 Military takeover in Argentina			**1978** USSR sends troops to Afghanistan
	1979 Sandinistas overthrow Anastasio Somoza in Nicaragua	**1979** Shah of Iran overthrown in Islamic Revolution	**1979** China begins economic reforms	
1980		**1980–1988** Iran-Iraq War		
	1983–1990 Democracy returns in Argentina, Brazil, and Chile		**1986** Average Japanese income overtakes income in United States	**1985** Mikhail Gorbachev becomes Soviet head of state
	1989 United States invades Panama	**1989** USSR withdraws from Afghanistan	**1989** Tiananmen Square confrontation	**1989** Berlin Wall falls **1989–1991** Communism ends in eastern Europe
1990	**1990** Sandinistas defeated in elections in Nicaragua	**1990** Iraq invades Kuwait **1991** Persian Gulf War	**1990s** Japanese recession	**1990** Reunification of Germany **1992** Yugoslavia disintegrates; Croatia and Slovenia become independent nations **1992–1995** Bosnia crisis
	1998 Election of Hugo Chávez in Venezuela	**1994** Nelson Mandela elected president of South Africa; Tutsi massacred in Rwanda	**1997** Asian financial crisis begins	

left throughout Latin America. Fearful that revolution would spread across Latin America, the United States increased support for its political and military allies in that region. Many of the military leaders who would come to power in this period were trained by the United States.

Brazil was the first nation to experience the full effects of the conservative reaction to the Cuban Revolution. Claiming that Brazil's civilian political leaders could not protect the nation from communist subversion, the army overthrew the constitutional government of President João Goulart° in 1964. The military sus-

pended the constitution, outlawed all existing political parties, and exiled former presidents and opposition leaders. Death squads—illegal paramilitary organizations sanctioned by the government—detained, tortured, and executed thousands of citizens. The dictatorship also undertook an ambitious economic program that promoted industrialization through import substitution, using tax and tariff policies to compel foreign-owned companies to increase investment in manufacturing.

This combination of dictatorship, violent repression, and government promotion of industrialization came to be called the "Brazilian Solution" in Latin America. Elements of this "solution" were imposed across much of the

---

João Goulart (ju-wow go-LARHT)

The Nicaraguan Revolution Overturns Somoza A revolutionary coalition that included Marxists drove the dictator Anastasio Somoza from power in 1979. The Somoza family had ruled Nicaragua since the 1930s and maintained a close relationship with the United States. (Susan Meiselas/ Magnum Photos, Inc.)

region in the 1970s and early 1980s. In 1970 Chile's new president, **Salvador Allende°**, undertook an ambitious program of socialist reforms. He also nationalized most of Chile's heavy industry and mines, including the American-owned copper companies that dominated the Chilean economy. From the beginning of Allende's presidency the administration of President Richard Nixon (served 1969–1973) organized opposition to Allende's reforms. Afflicted by inflation, mass consumer protests, and declining foreign trade, Allende was overthrown in 1973 by a military uprising led by General Augusto Pinochet° and supported by the United States. President Allende and thousands of Chileans died in the uprising, and thousands more were illegally seized, tortured, and imprisoned without trial. Once in power Pinochet rolled back Allende's social reforms, dramatically reduced state participation in the economy, and encouraged foreign investment.

In 1976 Argentina followed Brazil and Chile into dictatorship. Isabel Martínez de Perón° became president after the death of her husband Juan Perón in 1974 (see Chapter 31). Argentina was wracked by high inflation, terrorism, and labor protests. Impatient with the policies of the president, the military seized power and suspended the constitution. During the next seven years the military fought what it called the **Dirty War** against terrorism. More than

nine thousand Argentines lost their lives, and thousands of others endured arrest, torture, and the loss of property.

Despite these reverses, revolutionary movements persisted. The high-water mark of the revolutionary movement came in 1979 in Nicaragua with the overthrow of the corrupt dictatorship of Anastasio Somoza. The broad alliance of revolutionaries and reformers that took power called themselves **Sandinistas°**. They took their name from Augusto César Sandino, who had led Nicaraguan opposition to U.S. military intervention between 1927 and 1932. Once in power, the Sandinistas sought to imitate the command economies of Cuba and the Soviet Union, nationalizing properties owned by members of the Nicaraguan elite and U.S. citizens.

During his four-year term U.S. president Jimmy Carter (served 1977–1980) championed human rights in the hemisphere and stopped the flow of U.S. arms to regimes with the worst records. Carter also agreed to the reestablishment of Panamanian sovereignty in the Canal Zone at the end of 1999, but his effort to find common ground with the Sandinistas failed.

In 1981 Ronald Reagan became president. He was committed to reversing the results of the Nicaraguan Revolution and defeating a revolutionary movement in neighboring El Salvador. His options, however, were limited by

Salvador Allende (sal-vah-DOR ah-YEHN-day)
Augusto Pinochet (ah-GOOS-toh pin-oh-CHET)
Isabel Martínez de Perón (EES-ah-bell mar-TEEN-ehz deh pair-OWN)

Sandinistas (sahn-din-EES-tahs)

the U.S. Congress, which resisted using U.S. combat forces in Nicaragua and El Salvador and put strict limits on military aid. The Reagan administration sought to roll back the Nicaraguan Revolution by the use of punitive economic measures and by the recruitment and arming of anti-Sandinista Nicaraguans, called Contras (counter-revolutionaries).

Confident that they were supported by the majority of Nicaraguans and assured that the U.S. Congress was close to cutting off aid to the Contras, the Sandinistas called for free elections in 1990. But they had miscalculated politically. Exhausted by more than a decade of violence, a majority of Nicaraguan voters rejected the Sandinistas and elected a middle-of-the-road coalition led by Violeta Chamorro°.

The revolutionaries of El Salvador hoped to imitate the initial success of the Sandinistas of Nicaragua. Taking their name from a martyred leftist leader of the 1930s, the FMLN (Farabundo Martí° National Liberation Front) organized an effective guerrilla force. The United States responded by providing hundreds of millions of dollars in military assistance and by training units of the El Salvadoran army.

The assassination of Archbishop Oscar Romero and other members of the Catholic clergy by death squads tied to the Salvadoran government as well as the murder of thousands of noncombatants by military units made it difficult for the Reagan administration to sustain its policy of military aid as opposition grew in the U.S. Congress. In the end, external events finally brought peace to El Salvador. With the electoral defeat of the Sandinistas in Nicaragua and the collapse of the Soviet Union (see below), popular support for armed struggle waned and the FMLN rebels negotiated an end to the war, transforming themselves into a civilian political party.

The military dictatorships established in Brazil, Chile, and Argentina all came to an end between 1983 and 1990. In each case reports of kidnappings, tortures, and corruption by military governments undermined public support. In Argentina the military junta's foolish decision in 1982 to seize the Falkland Islands—the Argentines called them the "Malvinas"—from Great Britain ended in an embarrassing military defeat and precipitated the return to civilian rule. In Chile and Brazil the military dictatorships ended without the drama of foreign war. Despite significant economic growth under Pinochet, Chileans resented the violence and corruption of the military. In 1988 Pinochet called a plebiscite to extend his authority, but the majority vote went against him. A year later Chile elected its first civilian president in eighteen years. Brazil's

military initiated a gradual transition to civilian rule in 1985 and four years later had its first popular presidential election. By 2000 nearly 95 percent of Latin America's population lived under civilian rule.

At the same time Latin America was more dominated by the United States than it had been in 1975. The United States had thwarted the left in Nicaragua and El Salvador by funding military proxies. It used its own military in the 1983 invasion of the tiny Caribbean nation of Grenada and again in 1989 to overthrow and arrest dictator General Manuel Noriega° of Panama. These actions were powerful reminders to Latin Americans of prior interventions (see Chapter 24), but they also served as reminders of American power at a time when socialism was discredited by the collapse of the Soviet bloc.

With its influence uncontested, the United States urged Latin American nations to reform their economies by reducing the economic role of the state. Called neoliberalism in Latin America and other developing regions, these free-market policies reduced protections afforded local industries, government social welfare policies, and public-sector employment. Governments sold public-sector industries, like national airlines, manufacturing facilities, and public utilities, to foreign corporations, but popular support eroded because of political scandals and a slowing economy. Between 2001 and 2002 Argentina, which had ambitiously pursued neoliberal reforms, experienced an economic and political meltdown. This contributed to the appearance of a reinvigorated nationalist left in Latin America that began to roll back neoliberal reforms (see Diversity and Dominance: The Struggle for Women's Rights in an Era of Global Political and Economic Change). Among the most vocal critic of neo-liberalism and American influence was Hugo Chávez°, elected president of Venezuela in 1998.

Islamic Revolutions in Iran and Afghanistan

Although the Arab-Israel conflict and the oil crisis (see Chapter 32) concerned both superpowers, the prospect of direct military involvement remained remote. When unexpected crises developed in Iran and Afghanistan, however, significant strategic issues came to the foreground. Both countries adjoined Soviet territory, making Soviet military intervention more likely. Exercising post–Vietnam War caution, the United States reacted with restraint. The Soviet Union chose a bolder and ultimately disastrous course.

Violeta Chamorro (vee-oh-LET-ah cha-MOR-roe)
Farabundo Martí (fah-rah-BOON-doh mar-TEE)

Manuel Noriega (MAN-wel no-ree-EGG-ah)
Hugo Chávez (HUGH-go SHAH-vez)

The Struggle for Women's Rights in an Era of Global Political and Economic Change

*The struggle for women's rights is one of the most important social movements of the twentieth century. Although fundamental similarities in objectives can be identified across cultural and political boundaries, women in less-developed nations are forced to recognize that their objectives and strategies must take into account international inequalities in power and wealth. In this section Gladys Acosta, a militant Peruvian feminist, discusses the appropriate agenda for this struggle in the era after the fall of the Soviet Union and the rise of **neo-liberalism**.*

Neo-liberalism is the term used in Latin America to identify the free-market economic policies advocated by the United States. Among its chief characteristics are an end to the protection of local industries, a reduction in government social welfare policies, a reduction in public-sector employment, a commitment to paying debts to international creditors, and the removal of impediments to foreign investment. Many Latin Americans believe neo-liberalism is a new form of imperialism.

No one can abstain from the debate about the great historical systems of our time. Not even those of us who are trying to change the complex web of human relationships from a feminist perspective. Everywhere people are talking about the end of ideologies. But before we can grasp the significance of current events and their consequences, we need to pinpoint our various doubts and blank spots. Capitalism is the main pivot of our lives because we were born under its influence. It [has] hegemony. . . .

Gender, the main distinction between all people, is ignored in most philosophical, political or economic discussions. The reason for this lies partly in the low level of women's participation, but not entirely, because women are not always aware of the system of submission and repression to which we are subjected against our will. We need to find something which unites women in a gender-specific manner.

That doesn't mean sweeping under the carpet all the differences between us, like social position, culture or age. . . .

Neo-Liberalism in Action

For those of us who live under the influence of the capitalist system, the situation is different. When I talk of neo-liberalism, I mean austerity measures, foreign debts, and increased liberties for all those who have the power of money at their disposal and the power of repression over those who make demands. We have now reached a new form of capitalist accumulation. The world's economic system is in a state of change and capital has become more concentrated and centralised. I would not go as far as to say countries don't exist anymore but national identities do certainly play a different role now. It is important to understand the dynamics because otherwise historical responsibilities are obscured and we no longer know whom we're fighting against. If we look at the bare face of neo-liberalism from a woman's point of view, we cannot fail to notice its murderous consequences. To create a more humane society we must continue to reject neo-liberalism here and now in the hope of being able to change the dead present into a living future. Under neo-liberalism there is a breathtaking circulation of commodities, but also an exchange of ideas, illusions and dreams. At the moment we're experiencing capitalism's greatest ideological offensive. It's all business: everything is bought and sold and everything has its price.

The Consequences of Neo-Liberal Politics

We women play an important role in this ever-more internationalized economy because we represent, as ever, a particularly exploitable workforce. A number of studies have revealed the existence of subcontractor chains who work for transnational companies "informally" and mainly employ women. Basically we are dealing with a kind of integration into the world market which often uses our own homes as its outlet. Obviously, this work is badly paid and completely un-protected and has to be done without any of those social rights which were formerly achieved by trade union strug-gles. The most important thing for us is to keep hold of just one thread of the enterprise so we can show how the com-modities make their way to their final destination. As it ad-vances worldwide, this capitalism also encourages the expansion of certain kinds of tourism. A visible increase in prostitution is part of this, whereby women from poor coun-tries are smuggled into large, internationally operated rings which exploit them. The reports of Filipina women traded on the West German market send shivers down our spines. . . . What kind of freedom are you talking about there?

How the Adoption of Austerity Measures Affects Women's Lives

It is obvious that foreign debt is one of the most inhuman forms of exploitation in our countries when one considers the ratio between work necessary for workers' needs and work producing profit for employers. The experts have already ex-plained how the prevailing exchange and investment struc-tures have created international finance systems which keep whole populations in inhuman conditions. Although many people might think it crazy, the development model of the global economy has a marked relation to gender. As long as prices were slapped on some luxury consumer items there weren't any serious problems; but now the snares have been set around basic commodities. Women in every household are suffering every day as a result of impoverished economies and those who are most exposed to the effects of foreign debt are women.

When it comes to shopping, caring for sick children or the impossibility of meeting their schooling costs, the illusion of "leaving poverty behind" evaporates. Yet the problem is not only of an economic nature because under such circum-stances the constant tension leads to grave, often lasting ex-haustion. The psychosocial damage is alarming. The situation is ready to explode, so to speak. . . . The adoption of austerity measures means a curtailment of the state's commitment to social services with a direct effect on women. Daily life be-comes hell for them. The lack of even minimal state welfare presents women (and obviously children too) with crushing working days. There is a constant expenditure of human en-ergy without any hope of rest! No relaxation, no breaks. . . . And if we consider what happens within the family, we no-tice that women keep the smallest portion of the meagre

family income. They give everything to their children or those adults who bring home a pay packet. As a result mal-nutrition among women is increasing at an alarming rate and their frequent pregnancies represent a superhuman physical achievement.

Women's valiant achievements in defending life and survival are not acknowledged by society. The efforts of women's organisations, whether it be communal kitchens, the glass-of-milk committees [milk distribution among the poor] or health services don't get the appropriate so-cial esteem. The social value of women cannot be calcu-lated. Perhaps in years to come the fate of millions of women who sacrifice everything to support the children and youth of Peru and other countries in Latin America will be acknowledged. We should not ignore the fact that violence of every form . . . goes hand-in-hand with the difficult situation I have described.[1] It's nothing new for women because the open wounds of sexual violence, abuse at home and the contempt of this *machista* culture, have always featured in our lives and our mothers' lives. The challenge is to prevent these from also affecting our future generations.

QUESTIONS FOR ANALYSIS

1. What is neo-liberalism?

2. According to Acosta, how does global economic inte-gration fostered by neo-liberalism affect the lives of women as workers?

3. Acosta claims that indebtedness to foreign lenders leads to austerity measures. How does this impact fam-ilies in poor countries?

Source: From Gladys Acosta, "The View of a Peruvian Militant," in *Com-pañeras. Voices from the Latin American Women's Movement*, edited by Gaby Küppers (London: Latin American Bureau, 1994), 167–172. Reprinted with permission of the publisher.

1. In the last report of the Comisaria de mujeres in Lima (the only one in the country at present) 4,800 rapes were filed for 1990, of which 4,200 went to trial. The police commissioner, in reading the document, personally ac-knowledged the alarming social problem which is posed by the violence of men who are connected to their victims in some way and. which, in-deed, persists throughout all levels of society.

Muhammad Reza Pahlavi° succeeded his father as shah of Iran in 1941. In 1953 covert intervention by the U.S. Central Intelligence Agency (CIA) helped the shah retain his throne in the face of a movement to overturn royal power. Even when he finally nationalized the foreign-owned oil industry, the shah continued to enjoy American support. As oil revenues increased following the price increases of the 1970s, the United States encouraged the shah to spend his nation's growing wealth on equipping the Iranian army with advanced American weaponry.

Resentment in Iran against the Pahlavi family's autocracy dated from the 1925 seizure of power by the shah's father. The shah's dependence on the United States stimulated further opposition. By the 1970s popular resentment against the ballooning wealth of the elite families that supported the shah and the brutality, inefficiency, malfeasance, and corruption of his government led to mass opposition.

Ayatollah Ruhollah Khomeini°, a Shi'ite° philosopher-cleric who had spent most of his eighty-plus years in religious and academic pursuits, became the voice and symbolic leader of the opposition. Massive street demonstrations and crippling strikes forced the shah to flee Iran and ended the monarchy in 1979. In the Islamic Republic of Iran, which replaced the monarchy, Ayatollah Khomeini was supreme arbiter of disputes and guarantor of religious legitimacy. He oversaw a parliamentary regime based on European models, but he imposed religious control over legislation and public behavior. Elections were held, but the electoral process was not open to all: monarchists, communists, and other groups opposed to the Islamic Republic were barred from running for office. Shi'ite clerics with little training for government service held many of the highest posts, and stringent measures were taken to combat Western styles and culture. Universities were temporarily closed, and their faculties were purged of secularists and monarchists. Women were compelled to wear modest Islamic garments outside the house, and semiofficial vigilante committees policed public morals and cast a pall over entertainment and social life.

Online Study Center
Improve Your Grade
Primary Source:
Islamic Government

The United States under President Carter had criticized the shah's repressive regime, but the overthrow of a long-standing ally and the creation of the Islamic Republic were blows to American prestige. The new Iranian

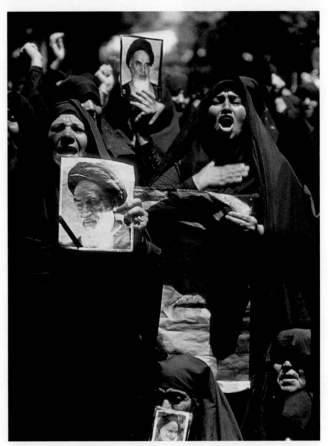

Muslim Women Mourning the Death of Ayatollah Khomeini in 1989 An Islamic revolution overthrew the shah of Iran in 1979. Ayatollah Khomeini sought to lead Iran away from the influences of Western culture and challenged the power of the United States in the Persian Gulf. (Alexandra Avakian/Woodfin Camp & Associates)

regime was religiously doctrinaire. It also was anti-Israeli and anti-American. Khomeini saw the United States as a "Great Satan" opposed to Islam, and he helped foster Islamic revolutionary movements elsewhere, which threatened the interests of both the United States and Israel. In November 1979 Iranian radicals seized the U.S. embassy in Tehran and held fifty-two diplomats hostage for 444 days. Americans felt humiliated by their inability to do anything, particularly after the failure of a military rescue attempt.

In the fall of 1980, shortly after negotiations for the release of the hostages began, **Saddam Husain°**, the

---

Reza Pahlavi (REH-zah PAH-lah-vee) **Ayatollah Ruhollah Khomeini** (A-yat-ol-LAH ROOH-ol-LAH ko-MAY-nee) **Shi'ite** (SHE-ite)

Saddam Husain (sah-DAHM hoo-SANE)

ruler of neighboring Iraq, invaded Iran to topple the Islamic Republic. His own dictatorial rule rested on a secular, Arab-nationalist philosophy and long-standing friendship with the Soviet Union, which had provided him with advanced weaponry. He feared that the fervor of Iran's revolutionary Shi'ite leaders would infect his own country's Shi'ite majority and threaten his power. The war pitted American weapons in the hands of the Iranians against Soviet weapons in the hands of the Iraqis, but the superpowers avoided overt involvement during eight years of bloodshed. Covertly, however, the United States used Israel to transfer arms to Iran, hoping to gain the release of other American hostages held by radical Islamic groups in Lebanon and to help finance the Contra war against the Sandinista government of Nicaragua. When this deal came to light in 1986, the resulting political scandal intensified American hostility to Iran. Openly tilting toward Iraq, President Reagan sent the United States Navy to the Persian Gulf, ostensibly to protect nonbelligerent shipping. The move helped force Iran to accept a cease-fire in 1988.

While the United States experienced anguish and frustration in Iran, the Soviet Union found itself facing even more serious problems in neighboring Afghanistan. In 1978 a Marxist party with a secular reform agenda seized power in Afghanistan. Offended by these efforts to reform education and grant rights to women, traditional ethnic and religious leaders led a successful rebellion. The Soviet Union responded by sending its army into Afghanistan to install a communist regime. With the United States, Saudi Arabia, and Pakistan paying, equipping, and training Afghan rebels, the Soviet Union found itself in an unwinnable war like the one the United States had stumbled into in Vietnam. Unable to justify the continuing drain on manpower, morale, and economic resources, and facing widespread domestic discontent over the war, Soviet leaders finally withdrew their troops in 1989. The Afghan communists held on for another three years. But once rebel groups took control of the entire country, they began to fight among themselves over who should rule.

Asian Transformation

Japan has few mineral resources and is dependent on oil imports, but the Japanese economy weathered the oil price shocks of the 1970s better than did the economies of Europe and the United States. In fact, Japan experienced a faster rate of economic growth in the 1970s and 1980s than did any other major developed economy, growing at about 10 percent a year. Average income also

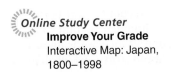

Online Study Center
Improve Your Grade
Interactive Map: Japan, 1800–1998

increased rapidly, overtaking that of the United States in 1986. While average income today lags behind that of the United States, Japan remains the world's second largest economy.

There are some major differences between the Japanese and U.S. industrial models. During the American occupation, Japanese industrial conglomerates known as *zaibatsu* (see Chapter 29) were broken up. Although ownership of major industries became less concentrated as a result, new industrial alliances appeared. During the period of dramatic growth there were six major **keiretsu°**, each of which included a major bank and firms in industry, commerce, and construction tied together in an interlocking ownership structure. There were also minor keiretsu dominated by a major corporation, like Toyota. Government assistance in the form of tariffs and import regulations inhibiting foreign competition were crucial in the early stages of development of Japan's automobile and semiconductor industries, among others.

Through the 1970s and 1980s Japanese success at exporting manufactured goods produced huge trade surpluses with other nations, prompting the United States and the European Community to engage in tough negotiations to try to force open the Japanese market. These efforts had only limited success. In 1990 Japan's trade surplus with the rest of the world was double its size in 1985. Many experts assumed that Japan's competitive advantages would propel it past the United States as the world's preeminent industrial economy, but problems began to appear in the 1980s and have proved difficult to solve. Japanese housing and stock markets had become highly overvalued, in part because the large and profitable trade surpluses led to real estate and stock market speculation. The close relationship of government, banks, and industries also contributed to speculation and corruption that undermined the nation's confidence. As the crisis deepened and prices collapsed, the close relationships between industry, government, and banks that had helped propel the postwar expansion proved to be a liability, propping up inefficient companies. By the end of the decade Japan's GDP (gross domestic product) had suffered a loss greater than that suffered by the United States in the Great Depression.

keiretsu (kay-REHT-soo)

The Japanese model of close cooperation between government and industry was imitated by other Asian states in the 1970s. The most important was the Republic of Korea, commonly called South Korea, which had a number of assets that helped promote economic development. The combination of inexpensive labor, strong technical education, and substantial domestic capital reserves allowed South Korea to overcome the devastation of the Korean War in little more than a decade. Despite large defense expenditures, South Korea developed heavy industries such as steel and shipbuilding as well as consumer industries such as automobiles and consumer electronics.

Taiwan, Hong Kong, and Singapore also developed modern industrial and commercial economies. As a result of their rapid economic growth, these three nations and South Korea were often referred to as the **Asian Tigers**. Taiwan suffered a number of political reverses, including the loss of its United Nations seat to the People's Republic of China in 1971 and the withdrawal of diplomatic recognition by the United States. Nevertheless, it achieved remarkable economic progress, based on smaller, more specialized companies and investment in the economy of the People's Republic of China.

Hong Kong and Singapore—both former British colonies with extremely limited resources—also enjoyed rapid economic development. Singapore's initial economic takeoff was based on its busy port and on banking and commercial services. After separating from Malaysia in 1965, this society of around 4 million people diversified by building textile and electronics industries. Hong Kong's economic prosperity, based on its port as well as its banking and commercial services, was increasingly tied to China's growing economy. Worried about Hong Kong's reintegration into the People's Republic of China in 1997, local capitalists moved significant amounts of capital to safe havens like the United States and Canada, but in recent years Hong Kong has regained its dynamism and is now even more closely tied to the rapidly expanding Chinese economy.

These **newly industrialized economies (NIEs)** shared many characteristics that helped explain their rapid industrialization. All had disciplined and hardworking labor forces, and all invested heavily in education. For example, as early as 1980 Korea had as many engineering graduates as Germany, Britain, and Sweden combined. All had very high rates of personal saving, about 35 percent of GDP, that allowed them to generously fund investment in new technology. All emphasized outward-looking export strategies. And, like Japan, all benefited from government sponsorship and protection. They were also beneficiaries of the extraordinary expansion in world trade and international communication that permitted technology to be disseminated more rapidly than at any time in the past.

Despite this momentum the region was shaken by a deep crisis that began in 1997. Like the recession that had already afflicted Japan, the Asian financial crisis was provoked by the burdens of bad loans, weak banks, and the international effects of currency speculation. The situation was stabilized by relief efforts of the United States, Japan, and international institutions like the International Monetary Fund.

China Rejoins the World Economy

In China after Mao Zedong's death in 1976 the communist leadership introduced comprehensive economic reforms that relaxed state control of the economy, allowing more initiative and permitting individuals to accumulate wealth. The results were remarkable. Under China's leader **Deng Xiaoping°** these reforms were expanded across the nation. China also began to permit foreign investment for the first time since the communists came to power in 1949. Between 1979 and 2005 foreign direct investment in China grew to $618 billion as McDonald's, General Motors, Coca-Cola, Airbus, and many other foreign companies began doing business there. As a result, China became a major industrial exporter and the world's sixth most important trading nation. But more than 100 million workers were still employed in state-owned enterprises, and most foreign-owned companies were segregated in special economic zones. The result was a dual industrial sector—one modern, efficient, and connected to international markets, the other directed by political decisions.

When Mao came to power in 1949, the meaning of the Chinese Revolution was made clear in the countryside, where collective ownership and organization were imposed. Deng Xiaoping did not privatize land, but he did abolish communes and permit the contracting of land to families, who were free to consume or sell whatever they produced. By 1984, 93 percent of China's agricultural land was in effect in private hands and producing for the market, tripling agricultural output.

Perhaps the best measure of the success of Deng's reforms is that between 1980 and 1993 China's per capita output more than doubled. Exports to the developed nations of the West, especially to Europe and the United States, were crucial to this expansion. Between 1979 and 2001 Chinese GDP grew from $177 billion to $1.16 trillion.

Deng Xiaoping (dung shee-yao-ping)

Best estimates of per capita wealth indicate that during this same period per capita GDP in China grew from $200 to $920. By comparison, South Korea had a per capita GDP twelve times larger and Singapore twenty times larger. Nevertheless, it is clear that economic reforms combined with massive investments and technology transfers from the United States, Europe, and Japan had propelled China into the twenty-first century as one of the world's major industrial powers.

Much of China's command economy remained in place, and the leadership of the Chinese Communist Party resisted serious political reform. Deng Xiaoping's strategy of balancing change and continuity avoided some of the social and political costs experienced by Russia and other socialist countries that abruptly embraced capitalism and democracy. However, the nation's leadership faced a major challenge in 1989. Responding to inflation and to worldwide mass movements in favor of democracy, Chinese students and intellectuals, many of whom had studied outside China, led a series of protests demanding more democracy and an end to corruption. This movement culminated in **Tiananmen° Square**, in the heart of Beijing. Hundreds of thousands of protesters gathered and refused to leave. After weeks of standoff, tanks pushed into the square, killing hundreds and arresting thousands.

China's continuing economic growth is sustained by direct foreign investment and by one of the world's highest savings rates. China's industries are modern and compete with more established industries in Japan and the West. But there are challenges. Increasing inequality, high levels of migration from the countryside to the cities, relatively weak infrastructure, poor protection of intellectual property rights, and corruption could retard future growth.

THE END OF THE BIPOLAR WORLD

After the end of World War II competition between the United States and the Soviet Union and their respective allies created a bipolar world. Every conflict, no matter how local its origins, had the potential of engaging the attention of one or both of the superpowers. The Korean War, decolonization in Africa, the Vietnam War, the Cuban Revolution, hostilities between Israel and its neighbors, and numerous other events increased tension between the superpowers, each armed with nuclear weapons. Given this succession of provocations, budgets within both blocs were dominated by defense expenditures, and political culture everywhere was dominated by arguments over the relative merits of the two competing economic and political systems.

Few in 1980 predicted the startling collapse of the Soviet Union and the socialist nations of the Warsaw Pact. Western observers tended to see communist nations as both more uniform in character and more subservient to the Soviet Union than was true. Long before the 1980s deep divisions had appeared among communist states. In general, the once-independent nations and ethnic groups that had been brought within the Soviet Union seemed securely transformed by the experiences and institutions of communism. By 1990, however, nationalism was resurgent, and communism was nearly finished.

Crisis in the Soviet Union

Under U.S. president Ronald Reagan and the Soviet Union's general secretary Leonid Brezhnev°, the rhetoric of the Cold War remained intense. Massive new U.S. investments in armaments placed heavy burdens on a Soviet economy unable to absorb the cost of developing similar weapons. Soviet economic problems were systemic; shortages had become a part of Soviet life. Obsolete industrial plants and centralized planning that stifled initiative led to a declining standard of living relative to the West, while the arbitrariness of the bureaucracy, the cynical manipulation of information, and deprivations created a generalized crisis in morale.

Despite the unpopularity of the war in Afghanistan and growing discontent, Brezhnev refused to modify his rigid and unsuccessful policies. But he was unable to contain an underground current of protest. In a series of powerful books, the writer Alexander Solzhenitzyn° castigated the Soviet system and particularly the Stalinist prison camps. He won a Nobel Prize in literature but was charged with treason and expelled from the country in 1974. Self-published underground writings (*samizdat°*) by critics of the regime circulated widely despite government efforts to suppress them.

By the time **Mikhail Gorbachev°** took up the reins of the Soviet government in 1985, weariness with war in Afghanistan, economic decay, and vocal protest had reached critical levels. Casting aside Brezhnev's hard

Tiananmen (tee-yehn-ahn-men)

Leonid Brezhnev (leh-oh-NEED BREZ-nef)
Solzhenitzen (sol-zhuh-NEET-sin)   samizdat (sah-meez-DAHT)
Gorbachev (GORE-beh-CHOF)

line, Gorbachev authorized major reforms in an attempt to stave off total collapse. His policy of political openness (*glasnost*) permitted criticism of the government and the Communist Party. His policy of **perestroika°** ("restructuring") was an attempt to address long-suppressed economic problems by moving away from central state planning and toward a more open economic system. In 1989 he ended the unpopular war in Afghanistan.

Online Study Center
Improve Your Grade
Primary Source: The Last Heir of Lenin Explains His Reform Plans: Perestroika and Glastnost

The Collapse of the Socialist Bloc

Events in eastern Europe were important in forcing change on the Soviet Union. In 1980 protests by Polish shipyard workers in the city of Gdansk led to the formation of **Solidarity**, a labor union that soon enrolled 9 million members. The Roman Catholic Church in Poland, strengthened by the elevation of a Pole, Karol Wojtyla°, to the papacy as John Paul II in 1978, gave strong moral support to the protest movement.

The Polish government imposed martial law in 1981 in response to the growing power of Solidarity and its allies, giving the army effective political control. Seeing Solidarity under tight controls and many of its leaders in prison, the Soviet Union decided not to intervene. But Solidarity remained a potent force with a strong institutional structure and nationally recognized leaders. As Gorbachev loosened political controls in the Soviet Union after 1985, communist leaders elsewhere lost confidence in Soviet resolve, and critics and reformers in Poland and throughout eastern Europe were emboldened.

Beleaguered Warsaw Pact governments vacillated between relaxation of control and suppression of dissent. Just as the Catholic clergy in Poland had supported Solidarity, Protestant and Orthodox religious leaders aided the rise of opposition groups elsewhere. This combination of nationalism and religion provided a powerful base for opponents of the communist regimes. Threatened by these forces, communist governments sought to quiet opposition by seeking solutions to their severe economic problems. They turned to the West for trade and financial assistance. They also opened their nations to

The Fall of the Berlin Wall The Berlin Wall was the most important symbol of the Cold War. Constructed to keep residents of East Germany from fleeing to the West and defended by armed guards and barbed wire, for many in the West it was the public face of communism. As the Soviet system fell apart, the residents of East and West Berlin broke down sections of the wall. Here young people straddle the wall, signaling the end of an era. (Bossu Regis/Corbis Sygma)

travelers, ideas, styles, and money from Western countries, all of which accelerated the demand for change.

By the end of 1989 communist governments across eastern Europe had fallen. The dismantling of the Berlin Wall, the symbol of a divided Europe and the bipolar world, vividly represented this transformation. Communist leaders in Poland, Hungary, Czechoslovakia, and Bulgaria decided that change was inevitable and initiated political reforms. In Romania the dictator Nicolae Ceausescu° refused to surrender power but was overthrown and executed. The comprehensiveness of these changes became clear in 1990, when Solidarity leader Lech Walesa° was elected president of Poland and dissident playwright Vaclav Havel° was elected president of Czechoslovakia.

---

perestroika (per-ih-STROY-kuh)
Karol Wojtyla (KAH-rol voy-TIL-ah)

Nicolae Ceausescu (nehk-oh-LIE chow-SHES-koo)
Lech Walesa (leck wah-LEN-sah)   Vaclav Havel (vah-SLAV hah-VEL)

Map 33.1 The End of the Soviet Union When communist hardliners failed to overthrow Gorbachev in 1991, popular anticommunist sentiment swept the Soviet Union. Following Boris Yeltsin's lead in Russia, the republics that constituted the Soviet Union declared their independence.

Online Study Center
Improve Your Grade
Interactive Map: The End of Soviet Domination in Eastern Europe

Following the fall of the Berlin Wall, a tidal wave of patriotic enthusiasm swept aside the once-formidable communist government of East Germany. In the chaotic months that followed, East Germans crossed to West Germany in large numbers, and government services in the eastern sector nearly disappeared. The collapse of the East German government led quickly in 1990 to reunification. Although numerous problems appeared, including high levels of unemployment and budget deficits, the nearly fifty years of confrontation and tension that had dominated Europe seemed to end overnight.

Soviet leaders looked on with dismay at the collapse of communism in the Warsaw Pact countries. They knew that similarly powerful nationalist sentiments existed within the Soviet Union as well. The year 1990 brought declarations of independence by Lithuania, Estonia, and Latvia, three small states on the Baltic Sea that the Soviet Union had annexed in 1939. Gorbachev tried to accommodate the rising pressures for change, but the tide was running too fast.

The end of the Soviet Union came suddenly in 1991 (see Map 33.1). After communist hardliners botched a poorly conceived coup against Gorbachev, disgust with communism boiled over. Boris Yeltsin, the president of the Russian Republic and longtime member of the Communist Party, led popular resistance to the coup in Moscow and emerged as the most powerful leader in the country. Russia, the largest republic in the Soviet Union, was effectively taking the place of the disintegrating USSR. With the central government scarcely functioning, nationalism, long repressed by Soviet authorities, reappeared throughout the Soviet Union. In September 1991 the Congress of People's Deputies—the central legislature of the USSR, long subservient to the Communist Party—voted to dissolve the union. In December a loose successor organization with little central control, the

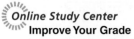

Online Study Center
Improve Your Grade
Interactive Map: Russia
and the Successor States

Commonwealth of Independent States (CIS), was created. The same month Mikhail Gorbachev resigned.

The ethnic and religious passions that fueled the breakup of the Soviet Union soon overwhelmed the Balkan state of Yugoslavia. In 1991 it dissolved into a morass of separatism and warring ethnic and religious groups. Slovenia and Croatia, the most westerly provinces, both heavily Roman Catholic, became independent states in 1992. Reflecting centuries of Muslim, Catholic, and Orthodox competition in the Balkans, the people of the province of Bosnia and Herzegovina were more mixed: 40 percent were Muslims, 30 percent Serbian Orthodox, and 18 percent Catholics. Following the declaration of Bosnian national independence in 1992, the Orthodox Serbs attempted to rid the state of Muslims, a violent campaign identified as **ethnic cleansing** in the international press. At first, no European power acted to stop this tragedy. Finally, after extensive television coverage of atrocities and wanton destruction seemed to force the issue, the United States intervened and eventually brokered a settlement in 1995.

In 1999 new fighting and a new round of ethnic cleansing occurred in the southernmost Yugoslavian province of Kosovo. Once the ancient homeland of the Serbs, Kosovo now had a predominantly Muslim and Albanian population. When NATO's warnings went unheeded, the United States, Britain, and France launched an aerial war against Serbia that forced the withdrawal of Serbian forces from Kosovo. While attention was focused on the Balkans, destructive ethnic and religious conflict also characterized the transitional period in Armenia, Georgia, and Chechnya.

Progress and Conflict in Africa

Since independence democracy has had mixed results in sub-Saharan Africa. Many elected leaders have used their offices to enrich themselves and limit or eliminate political opposition. Military coups and conflicts over resources such as diamonds have also been distressingly common. Southern Africa, however, has seen democratic progress and a steady decline in armed conflicts since 1991. A key change came in South Africa in 1994, when long-time political prisoner Nelson Mandela and his African National Congress (ANC) won the first national elections in which the African majority could participate equally. Since then, the lively politics of this ethnically diverse country have been a model of how democracy can resolve conflicts. Also hopeful has been the return to democracy of Nigeria, Africa's most populous state, after decades of military rulers. In 1999, after a succession of military governments, Nigerians elected President Olusegun Obasanjo° (a former coup leader), and a 2003 vote renewed his term, despite serious voting irregularities. Similarly, in 2002 Kenyans voted out the party that had held power for thirty-nine years.

Unfortunately, Africa was also the scene of ethnic cleansing. In 1994 the political leaders of the Central African nation of Rwanda incited Hutu people to massacre their Tutsi neighbors. The major powers avoided characterizing the slaughter as genocide because an international agreement mandated intervention to stop genocide. Without action by foreign powers, the carnage continued until some 750,000 people were dead and millions of refugees had fled into neighboring states. Finally, the United States and other powers intervened and the United Nations set up a tribunal to try those responsible for the genocide. In 1998 violence spread from Rwanda to neighboring Congo, where growing opposition and ill health had forced President Joseph Mobutu from office after over three decades of dictatorial misrule. Various peacemaking attempts failed to restore order. By mid-2003 more than 3 million Congolese had died from disease, malnutrition, and injuries related to the fighting.

The Persian Gulf War

The first significant conflict to occur after the breakup of the Soviet Union and the end of the Cold War was the Persian Gulf War. The immediate causes were local and bilateral. Iraq's ruler, Saddam Husain, had borrowed a great deal of money from neighboring Kuwait and sought unsuccessfully to get Kuwait's royal family to reduce the size of this debt. He was also eager to gain control of Kuwait's oil fields. Husain believed that the smaller and militarily weaker nation could be quickly defeated, and he suspected, as a result of a conversation with an American diplomat, that the United States would not react. The invasion came in August 1990.

The United States convinced the government of Saudi Arabia that it was a possible target of Iraq's aggression. Saudi Arabia, an important regional ally of the United States and a major oil producer, was the key to any military action by the United States. The United States and its allies concentrated an imposing military force of 500,000 in the region. With his intention to use

---

Olusegun Obasanjo (oh-LOO-she-gun oh-BAH-san-jo)

force endorsed by the United Nations and with many Islamic nations supporting military action, President George H. W. Bush ordered an attack in early 1991. Iraq proved incapable of countering the sophisticated weaponry of the coalition. The missiles and bombs of the United States destroyed not only military targets but also "relegated [Iraq] to a pre-industrial age," the United Nations reported after the war. Although Iraq's military defeat was comprehensive, Husain remained in power, and the country was not occupied. In fact Husain crushed an uprising in the months following this defeat. The United States and its key allies then imposed "no-fly" zones that denied Iraq's military aircraft access to the northern and southern regions of the country. As a result, military tensions and periodic armed confrontations continued.

In the United States the results were interpreted to mean that the U.S. military defeat in the Vietnam War could be forgotten and that U.S. military capability was unrivaled. Unable to deter military action by the U.S.-led coalition or to meaningfully influence the diplomacy that surrounded the war, Russia had been of little use to its former ally Iraq, and its impotence was clear.

THE CHALLENGE OF POPULATION GROWTH

For most of human history population growth was viewed as beneficial, and human beings were seen as a source of wealth. Since the late eighteenth century, however, population increases have been viewed with increasing alarm. At first it was feared that food supplies could not keep up with population growth. Then social critics expressed concern that growing population would lead to class and ethnic struggle as numbers overwhelmed resources. By the second half of the twentieth century population growth was increasingly seen as a threat to the environment. Are urban sprawl, pollution, and soil erosion inevitable results of population growth? The questions and debates continue today, but clearly population is both a cause and a result of increased global interdependency.

Demographic Transition

The population of Europe almost doubled between 1850 and 1914, putting enormous pressure on rural land and urban housing and overwhelming fragile public institutions that provided some crisis assistance (see Chapter 27). This dramatic growth forced a large wave of immigration across the Atlantic, helping to develop the Western Hemisphere and invigorating the Atlantic economy (see Chapter 24). Population growth also contributed to Europe's Industrial Revolution by lowering labor costs and increasing consumer demand.

Educated Europeans of the nineteenth century were ambivalent about the rapid increase in human population. Some saw it as a blessing that would promote economic well-being. Others warned that the seemingly relentless increase would bring disaster. The best-known pessimist was the English cleric **Thomas Malthus**, who in 1798 argued that unchecked population growth would outstrip food production. When Malthus looked at Europe's future, he used a prejudiced image of China to terrify his European readers. A visitor to China, he claimed, "will not be surprised that mothers destroy or expose many of their children; that parents sell their daughters for a trifle; . . . and that there should be such a number of robbers. The surprise is that nothing still more dreadful should happen."[1]

The generation that came of age in the years immediately following World War II inherited a world in which the views of Malthus were casually dismissed. Industrial and agricultural productivity had multiplied supplies of food and other necessities. Cultural changes associated with expanded female employment, older age at marriage, and more effective family planning had combined to slow the rate of population increase. And by the late 1960s Europe and other industrial societies had made what was called the **demographic transition** to lower fertility rates (average number of births per woman) and reduced mortality. The number of births in the developed nations was just adequate for the maintenance of current population levels.

By the late 1970s, however, the demographic transition had not occurred in the Third World, and the issue of population growth had become politicized. The leaders of some developing nations actively promoted large families, arguing that larger populations would increase national power. These arguments remained a persistent part of the debate between developed and developing nations. Industrialized, mostly white, nations raised concerns about rapid population growth in Asia, Africa, and Latin America. Populist political leaders in those regions asked whether these concerns were not fundamentally racist.

The question exposed the influence of racism in the population debate and temporarily disarmed Western advocates of birth control. However, once the economic shocks of the 1970s and 1980s revealed the vulnerability of developing economies, governments in the developing world jettisoned policies that promoted population growth. Mexico is a good example. In the

Chinese Family-Planning Campaign   Hoping to slow population growth, the Chinese government has sought to limit parents to a single child. Billboards and other forms of mass advertising have been an essential part of the campaign to gain compliance with national family-planning directives.   (Picard/Sipa Press)

1970s the government had encouraged high fertility, and population growth rose to 3 percent per year. In the 1980s Mexico rejected these policies and promoted birth control. As a result Mexico's annual population growth fell to 2.3 percent per year by the end of the decade and in the 1990s to 1.7 percent.

World population exploded in the twentieth century (see Table 33.1). Although the rate of growth has slowed since the 1980s, world population still increases by a number equal to the total population of the United States every three years. If fertility remains constant from today, with a world average of 2.5 children per woman, world population will reach nearly 30 billion in 2150, more than three times the 2050 projection found in Table 33.1.

This is not likely. Fertility is already declining in many developing nations, and many scholars see world population in 2150 in the 10 to 15 billion range. Mortality rates have also increased in some areas as immigration, commercial expansion, and improved transportation facilitate the transmission of disease. The rapid spread of HIV/AIDS is an example of this phenomenon. Less-developed regions with poorly funded public health institutions and with few resources to invest in prevention and treatment experience the highest rates of infection and the greatest

mortality. In Russia, for example, new HIV infections rose from under five thousand in 1997 to over ninety thousand in 2001. AIDS has spread at a similar pace in China. But the disease has developed most quickly and with the most devastating results in Africa, the home of 28 million of the world's 40 million infected people.

Unlike population growth in the eighteenth and nineteenth centuries, when much of the increase occurred in the wealthiest nations, population growth at the end of the twentieth century was overwhelmingly in the poorest nations. Although fertility rates dropped in most developing nations, they remained much higher than rates in the industrialized nations. At the same time, improvements in hygiene and medical treatment caused mortality rates to fall, despite recent catastrophes, such as HIV/AIDS. The result has been rapid population growth.

The Industrialized Nations

In the developed industrial nations of western Europe and in Japan at the beginning of the twenty-first century, fertility levels are so low that population will fall unless immigration

Table 33.1 **Population for World and Major Areas, 1750–2050**

Population Size (Millions)

Major Area	1750	1800	1850	1900	1950	1995	2050*
World	791	978	1,262	1,650	2,521	5,666	9,076
Africa	106	107	111	133	221	697	1,937
Asia	502	635	809	947	1,402	3,437	5,217
Europe	163	203	276	408	547	728	653
Latin America and the Caribbean	16	24	38	74	167	480	783
North America	2	7	26	82	172	297	438
Oceania	2	2	2	6	13	28	48

Percentage Distribution

Major Area	1750	1800	1850	1900	1950	1995	2050*
World	100	100	100	100	100	100	100
Africa	13.4	10.9	8.8	8.1	8.8	12	21.3
Asia	63.5	64.9	64.1	57.4	55.6	61	57.5
Europe	20.6	20.8	21.9	24.7	21.7	13	7.2
Latin America and the Caribbean	2.0	2.5	3.0	4.5	6.6	8	8.6
North America	0.3	0.7	2.1	5.0	6.8	5	4.8
Oceania	0.3	0.2	0.2	0.4	0.5	1	0.5

* Estimated

Source: J. D. Durand, "Historical Estimates of World Population: An Evaluation" (Philadelphia: University of Pennsylvania, Population Studies Center, 1974, mimeographed); United Nations, *The Determinants and Consequences of Population Trends,* vol. 1 (New York: United Nations, 1973); United Nations, *World Population Prospects as Assessed in 1963* (New York: United Nations, 1966); United Nations, *World Population Prospects: The 1998 Revision* (New York: United Nations, forthcoming); United Nations Population Division, Department of Economic and Social Affairs, http://www.un.org/esa/population/publications/WPP2004/2004Highlights-finalrevised.pdf. The medium fertility estimate is used for the 2050 population projection.

increases. Japanese women have an average of 1.39 children; in Italy the number is 1.2. Although Sweden tries to promote fertility with cash payments, tax incentives, and job leaves to families with children, the average number of births per woman has fallen to 1.4 in recent years. The low fertility found in mature industrial nations is tied to higher levels of female education and employment, the material values of consumer culture, and access to contraception and abortion. Educated women now defer marriage and child rearing until they are established in careers. An Italian woman in Bologna, the city with the lowest fertility in the world, put it this way: "I'm an only child and if I could, I'd have more than one child. But most couples I know wait until their 30's to have children. People want to have their own life, they want to have a successful career. When you see life in these terms, children are an impediment."[2]

In industrialized nations life expectancy has improved as fertility has declined. The combination of abundant food, improved hygiene, and more effective medicines and medical care has lengthened human lives. In 2000 about 20 percent of the population in the more-developed nations was sixty-five or over. By 2050 this proportion should rise to one-third. Italy soon will have more than twenty adults fifty years old or over for each five-year-old child. Because of higher fertility and greater levels of immigration, the United States is moving in this direction more slowly than western Europe; by 2050 the median age in Europe will be fifty-two, while it will be thirty-five in the United States.

The combination of falling fertility and rising life expectancy in the industrialized nations presents a challenge very different from the one foreseen by Malthus. These nations generally offer a broad array of social services, including retirement income, medical services, and housing supplements for the elderly. As the number of retirees increases relative to the number of people who are employed, the costs of these services may become unsustainable. Economists track this problem using the PSR (potential support ratio). This is the ratio of persons fifteen to sixty-four years old (likely workers) to persons sixty-five or older (likely retirees). Between 1950 and 2000 the world's PSR fell from twelve to nine. By 2050 it will fall to four. Clearly, nations with the oldest populations, especially Japan and the nations of western Europe, will have to reexamine programs that encourage early retirement as the ratio of workers to retirees drops.

In Russia and other former socialist nations, current birthrates are now actually lower than death rates—levels inadequate to sustain the current population size. Birthrates were already low before the collapse of the socialist system and have contracted further with recent economic problems. Since 1975 fertility rates have fallen between 20 and 40 percent across the former Soviet bloc. By the early 1980s abortions were as common as births in much of eastern Europe.

Life expectancy has also fallen. Life expectancy for Russian men is now only fifty-seven years, down almost ten years since 1980. In the Czech Republic, Hungary, and Poland, life expectancy is improving in response to improved economic conditions, but most of the rest of eastern Europe has experienced the Russian pattern of declining life expectancy. High unemployment, low incomes, food shortages, and the dismantling of the social welfare system of the communist era have all contributed to this decline.

The Developing Nations

Even if the industrialized nations decided to promote an increase in family size in the twenty-first century, they would continue to fall behind the developing nations as a percentage of world population. At current rates 95 percent of all future population growth will be in developing nations (see Map 33.2 and Table 33.1). A comparison between Europe and Africa illustrates these changes. In 1950 Europe had twice the population of Africa. By 1985 Africa's population had drawn even with Europe's. According to projections, Africa's population will be three times larger than Europe's by 2025.

As the 1990s ended other developing regions had rapid population growth as well. While all developing nations had an average birthrate of 33.6 per thousand inhabitants, Muslim countries had a rate of 42.1. This rate is more than 300 percent higher than the 13.1 births per thousand in the developed nations of the West. The populations of Latin America and Asia were also expanding, but at rates slower than sub-Saharan Africa and the Muslim nations. Latin America's population increased from 165 million in 1950 to 511 million in 1999 and is projected to reach 809 million in 2050, despite declining birthrates.

In Asia, the populations of India and China continued to grow despite government efforts to reduce family size. Today these two nations account for roughly one-third of the world's population. In China efforts to enforce a limit of one child per family led initially to female infanticide as rural families sought to produce male heirs. This is no longer the case. India's policies of forced sterilization created widespread outrage and led to the electoral defeat of the ruling Congress Party. Yet both countries achieved some successes. Between 1960 and 1982 India's birthrate fell from 48 to 34 per thousand, while China's rate declined even more sharply—from 39 to 19 per thousand. Still, by 2025 both China, which today has 1.13 billion people, and India, with 853 million, will likely reach 1.5 billion.

Old and Young Populations

Population pyramids generated by demographers clearly illustrate the profound transformation in human reproductive patterns and life expectancy in the years since World War II. Figure 33.1 shows the 2001 age distributions in Pakistan, South Korea, and Sweden—nations at three different stages of economic development. Sweden is a mature industrial nation. South Korea is rapidly industrializing and has surpassed many European nations in both industrial output and per capita wealth. Pakistan is a poor, traditional Muslim nation with rudimentary industrialization, low educational levels, and little effective family planning.

In 2001 nearly 50 percent of Pakistan's population was under age sixteen. The resulting pressures on the economy have been extraordinary. Every year approximately 150,000 men reach age sixty-five—and another 1.2 million turn sixteen. Pakistan, therefore, has to create more than a million new jobs a year or face steadily growing unemployment and steadily declining wages. Sweden confronts a different problem. Sweden's aging population, growing demand for social welfare benefits, and declining labor pool means that its industries may become less competitive and living standards may decline. In South Korea, a decline in fertility dramatically altered the ratio of children to adults, creating an age distribution similar to that of western Europe earlier in the twentieth century. South Korea does not face Pakistan's impossible task of creating new jobs or Sweden's growing demands for welfare benefits for the aged.

The demographic problem and potential technological adjustments are most clearly visible in Japan. Japan has the oldest population in the world, with a

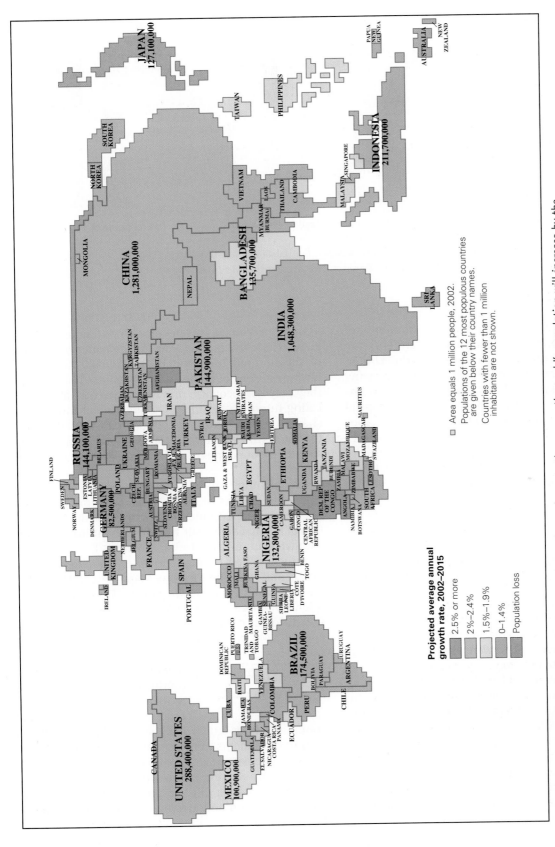

Map 33.2 **World Population Growth** At current rates of growth, every three years the world's population will increase by the equivalent of a nation the size of the United States. Most of this population increase will be in some of the world's poorest nations. By 2050, for example, Pakistan, a nation of only 40 million in 1950, will surpass the United States and become the country with the world's third largest population. *Source:* Data from www.worldbank.org.

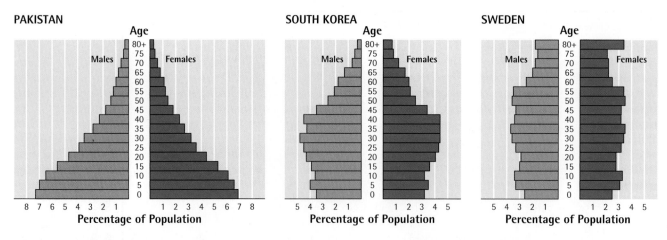

Figure 33.1   Age Structure Comparison: Islamic Nation (Pakistan), Non-Islamic Developing Nation (South Korea), and Developed Nation (Sweden), 2001   *Source:* U.S. Bureau of the Census, *International Database, 2001.*

current median age of forty-one. Large numbers of young immigrants from poorer nations are entering the work forces of Canada, Germany, the United States, and most other industrialized nations, slowing the aging of these populations. Japan has resisted immigration, instead investing heavily in technological solutions to the problems created by its aging labor force. As of 1994 Japan had 75 percent of the world's industrial robots. Although Japanese industries are able to produce more goods with fewer workers, Japan will still face long-term increases in social welfare payments.

UNEQUAL DEVELOPMENT AND THE MOVEMENT OF PEOPLES

Two characteristics of the postwar world should now be clear. First, despite decades of experimentation with state-directed economic development, most nations that were poor in 1960 were as poor or poorer in 2000. The only exceptions were a few rapidly developing Asian industrial nations and an equally small number of oil-exporting nations. Second, world population increased to startlingly high levels, and most of the increase was, and will continue to be, in the poorest nations.

The combination of intractable poverty and growing population generated a surge in international immigration. Few issues stirred more controversy. Even moderate voices sometimes framed the discussion of immigration

as a competition among peoples. One commentator analyzed the situation this way: "As the better-off families of the northern hemisphere individually decide that having only one or at the most two children is sufficient, they may not recognize that they are in a small way vacating future space (that is, jobs, parts of inner cities, shares of population, shares of market preferences) to faster-growing ethnic groups both inside and outside their boundaries. But that, in fact, is what they are doing."[3]

Large numbers of legal and illegal immigrants from poor nations with growing populations are entering the developed industrial nations, with the exception of Japan. Large-scale migrations within developing countries are a related phenomenon. The movement of impoverished rural residents to the cities of Asia, Africa, and Latin America (see Map 33.2 and Table 33.2) has increased steadily since the 1970s. This internal migration often serves as the first step toward migration abroad.

The Problem of Growing Inequality

Since 1945 global economic productivity has expanded more rapidly than at any other time in the past. Faster, cheaper communications and transportation have combined with improvements in industrial and agricultural technologies to create material abundance that would have amazed those who experienced the first Industrial Revolution (see Chapter 23). Despite this remarkable economic expansion and growing market integration, the

Table 33.2 The World's Largest Cities (Population of 10 Million or More)

City	1950	City	1975	City	2000	City	2015
1 New York	12.3	1 Tokyo	19.8	1 Tokyo	26.4	1 Tokyo	27.2
		2 New York	15.9	2 Mexico City	18.1	2 Dhaka	22.8
		3 Shanghai	11.4	3 Bombay	18.1	3 São Paulo	21.2
		4 Mexico City	11.2	4 São Paulo	17.8	4 Delhi	20.9
		5 São Paulo	10.0	5 New York	16.6	5 Mumbai	20.5
				6 Lagos	13.4	6 Mexico City	20.4
				7 Los Angeles	13.1	7 New York	17.9
				8 Calcutta	12.9	8 Jakarta	17.3
				9 Shanghai	12.9	9 Calcutta	16.8
				10 Buenos Aires	12.6	10 Karachi	16.2
				11 Dhaka	12.3	11 Lagos	16.0
				12 Karachi	11.8	12 Los Angeles	14.5
				13 Delhi	11.7	13 Shanghai	13.6
				14 Jakarta	11.0	14 Buenos Aires	13.2
				15 Osaka	11.0	15 Metro Manila	12.6
				16 Metro Manila	10.9	16 Beijing	11.7
				17 Beijing	10.8	17 Rio de Janeiro	11.5
				18 Rio de Janeiro	10.6	18 Cairo	11.5
				19 Cairo	10.6	19 Istanbul	11.4
						20 Osaka	11.0
						21 Tianjin	10.3
						22 Bangkok	10.0
						23 Seoul	10.0

Source: From the International Migration Report 2002, United Nations, Department of Economic and Social Affairs, Population Division, "World Urbanization Prospects: The 1999 Revision," p. 6. Reprinted by permission of United Nations. The 2015 projection is from United Nations Human Settlements Programme, *Global Report on Human Settlements 2003, The Challenge of Slums* (2003).

majority of the world's population remains in poverty. The industrialized nations of the Northern Hemisphere now enjoy a larger share of the world's wealth than they did a century ago. The United States, Japan, and the nations of the European Union accounted for a startling 74 percent of the world's economy in 1998.

The gap between rich and poor nations has grown much wider since 1945. But among both groups dramatic changes have resulted from changes in competitiveness, technology transfers, and market conditions. In 2001 Luxembourg and Switzerland had the highest per capita GNI (gross national income)—$39,840 and $35,630, respectively; the U.S. figure was $34,280; and Greece, the poorest nation in the European Union, had a per capita GNI of $11,430. The nations of the former Soviet Union and eastern Europe had per capita GNIs lower than some developing nations in the Third World. Russia's per capita GNI was $1,750 in 2001, less than Mexico's $5,530, Brazil's $3,070, and South Africa's

$2,820, but higher than Bolivia's $950 and the Philippines' $1,030. Among other developing economies, Algeria and Thailand had per capita GNIs of $1,650 and $1,940, respectively. Nigeria, India, and China had GNIs below $1,000. Even in the industrialized world, people were divided into haves and have-nots. Tax reforms in the 1980s in the United States increased wealth inequality dramatically. This trend continues to the present, driven by the stock market boom of the 1990s and another round of tax reforms under President George W. Bush (elected 2000). Wealth inequality is now as great as on the eve of the 1929 stock market crash. Scholars estimate that the wealthiest 1 percent of households in the United States now control more than 30 percent of the nation's total wealth, while the poorest households have average incomes of under $5,000. Even in Europe, where tax and inheritance laws redistributed wealth, unemployment, homelessness, and substandard housing have become increasingly common.

Garbage Dump in Manila, Philippines Garbage pickers are a common feature of Third World urban development. Thousands of poor families in nearly every Third World city sort and sell bottles, aluminum cans, plastic, and newspapers to provide household income. (Geoff Tompkinson/Aspect Picture Library Ltd.)

Internal Migration: The Growth of Cities

In developing nations migration from rural areas to urban centers increased threefold between 1925 and 1950, and the pace accelerated after that (see Table 33.2). Shantytowns around major cities in developing nations are commonly seen as signs of social breakdown and economic failure. Nevertheless, city life was generally better than life in the countryside. A World Bank study estimated that three out of four migrants to cities made economic gains. Residents of cities in sub-Saharan Africa, for example, were six times more likely than rural residents to have safe water. An unskilled migrant from the depressed northeast of Brazil could triple his or her income by moving to Rio de Janeiro.

However, as the scale of rural-to-urban migration grew, these benefits became more elusive. In the cities of the developing world basic services have been crumbling under the pressure of rapid population growth. In cities like Mexico City and Manila, which are among the world's largest cities, tens of thousands live in garbage dumps, scavenging for food and clothing. In Rio de Janeiro and other Latin American cities, large numbers of abandoned children live in the streets and parks, begging, selling drugs, stealing, and engaging in prostitution to survive. In Rio alone it is estimated that 350,000 abandoned children are on the streets. Worsening conditions

and the threat of crime and political instability have led many governments to try to return people to the countryside. Indonesia, for example, has relocated more than a half-million urban residents since 1969. Despite some successes with slowing the rate of internal migration, nearly every poor nation still faces the challenge of rapidly growing cities.

Global Migration

Each year hundreds of thousands of men and women leave the developing world to emigrate to industrialized nations. After 1960 this movement increased in scale, and ethnic and racial tensions in the host nations worsened. Political refugees and immigrants faced murderous violence in Germany; growing anti-immigrant sentiment led to a right-wing political movement in France and to a recent series of riots in cities with large immigrant populations; and the United States expanded its effort to more effectively seal the border with Mexico. Throughout the 1990s rising levels of immigration posed daunting social and cultural challenges for both host nations and immigrants.

Immigrants from the developing nations brought host nations many of the same benefits that the great migration of Europeans to the Americas provided a century earlier (see Chapter 24). Many European nations actively promoted guest worker programs and other inducements to immigration in the 1960s, when an expanding European economy first confronted labor shortages. However, attitudes toward immigrants changed as the size of the immigrant population grew and as European economies slowed in the 1980s. Facing higher levels of unemployment, native-born workers saw immigrants as competitors willing to work for lower wages and less likely to support labor unions. However, because cultural and ethnic characteristics have traditionally formed the basis of national identity in many European countries (see Chapter 27), worsening relations between immigrants and the native-born may have been inevitable. Put simply, many Germans are unable to think of the German-born son or daughter of Turkish immigrants as a German.

Because immigrants are generally young adults and commonly retain positive attitudes toward early marriage and large families dominant in their native cultures, immigrants in Europe and the United States have tended to have higher fertility rates than do host populations. In Germany in 1975, for example, immigrants made up only 7 percent of the population but accounted for nearly 15 percent of all births. Although immigrant fertility rates decline with prolonged residence in industrialized societies, the family size of second-generation immigrants is still larger than that of the host population. Therefore, even without additional immigration, immigrant groups grow faster than longer-established populations.

As the Muslim population in Europe and the Asian and Latin American populations in the United States expand in the twenty-first century, cultural conflicts will test definitions of citizenship and nationality. The United States will have some advantages in meeting these challenges because of long experience with immigration and relatively open access to citizenship. Yet at the end of the twentieth century the United States was moving slowly in the direction of asserting control over the border with Mexico and debating a culturally conservative definition of nationality focused in part on demanding the use of English in government.

TECHNOLOGICAL AND ENVIRONMENTAL CHANGE

Technological innovation powered the economic expansion that began after World War II. New technologies increased productivity and disseminated human creativity. They also altered the way people lived, worked, and played. Because most of the economic benefits were concentrated in the advanced industrialized nations, technology increased the power of those nations relative to the developing world. Even within developed nations, postwar technological innovations did not benefit all classes, industries, and regions equally. There were losers as well as winners.

Population growth and increased levels of migration and urbanization led to the global expansion of agricultural and industrial production. This multiplication of farms and factories intensified environmental threats. At the end of the twentieth century loss of rain forest, soil erosion, global warming, air and water pollution, and extinction of species threatened the quality of life and the survival of human societies. Here again, differences between nations were apparent. Environmental protection, like the acquisition of new technology, had progressed most in societies with the greatest economic resources.

New Technologies and the World Economy

Nuclear energy, jet engines, radar, and tape recording were among the many World War II developments that later had an impact on consumers' lives. When applied to industry, new technology increased productivity, reduced labor requirements, and improved the flow of information that made markets more efficient. Pent-up demand for consumer goods also spurred new research and the development of new technologies. As the Western economies recovered from the war and incomes rose, consumers wanted new products that reduced their workloads or provided entertainment. The consumer electronics industry rapidly developed new products, changes that can be summarized by the music industry's movement from vinyl records to 8-track tapes, CDs, and MP3 technologies.

Improvements in existing technologies accounted for much of the developed world's productivity increases during the 1950s and 1960s. Larger and faster trucks, trains, and airplanes cut transportation costs. Both capitalist and socialist governments built highway systems, improved railroad tracks, and constructed airports. Governments also bore much of the cost of developing and constructing nuclear power plants.

No technology has proved more influential in the last three decades than the computer, which transformed both work and leisure (see Environment and Technology: The Personal Computer). The first computers were expensive, large, and slow. Only large corporations, governments, and universities could afford them. But by the mid-1980s desktop computers had replaced typewriters in most of the developed world's offices, and

ENVIRONMENT + TECHNOLOGY

The Personal Computer

The period since World War II has witnessed wave after wave of technological innovations. Few of them have had a greater impact on the way people work, learn, and live than the computer. Until the 1970s most computing was done on large and expensive mainframe computers, access to computers was controlled by the government agencies, universities, and large corporations that owned them, and computers were used mainly for data storage and analysis. Today most computer use is devoted to communication and information searches.

Few anticipated the technological innovations of the last three decades that revolutionized the computer industry. In rapid succession transistors replaced vacuum tubes in mainframes and then silicon chips replaced hard-wired transistors. The race to miniaturize was on. The key development was the microprocessor, a computer processor (in effect the computer's brains) on a silicon chip. Computers became smaller and cheaper as memory chips and microprocessors were made smaller and more powerful. Today, laptop computers weigh only a few pounds and can be carried any-

where. As new companies entered the market, prices fell, and computers became a part of modern consumer culture.

Each new generation of computers has been more powerful, smaller, and less expensive. A modern 5-gigahertz Intel Pentium V chip is more than twenty times faster than the first desktop processor just forty years ago. By the mid-1990s desktop and laptop computers had replaced the mainframe for most uses. The Internet was developed to facilitate defense research in the 1960s. The establishment of the World Wide Web as a graphic interface in the 1990s allowed the smaller, faster computers to become research portals that accessed a vast international database of research, opinion, entertainment, and commerce. The computer revolution and the Web have had a revolutionary impact, allowing individuals and groups—without the support of governments, corporations, or other powerful institutions—to collect and disseminate information more freely than at any time in the past (see Chapter 34).

Among the revolutionary changes that impact modern women and men is the mounting tide of e-mails used to conduct business, arrange people's social lives, and pass on jokes and political opinions. E-mail traffic has exploded from 5.1 million messages in 2000 to 135.6 million messages in 2005. This important and intrusive part of modern life has been facilitated by wireless connections and hand-held devices like BlackBerries that allow us to remain connected in airport waiting rooms, restaurants, and sporting events.

From Mainframe to Laptops and PDAs During the last forty years the computer revolution has changed the way we work. (left: Dagmar Fabricius; right: AP/Wide World Photos)

the technology continued to advance. Each new generation of computers was smaller, faster, and more powerful than the one before.

Computers also altered manufacturing. Small dedicated computers were used to control and monitor machinery in most industries. In the developed world companies forced by competition to improve efficiency and product quality brought robots into factories. Europe quickly followed Japan's lead in robotics, especially in automobile production and mining. Although the United States introduced robots more slowly because it enjoyed lower labor costs, it has now fully embraced this technology.

The transnational corporation became the primary agent of these technological changes. Since the eighteenth century powerful commercial companies have conducted business across national borders. By the twentieth century the growing economic power of corporations in industrialized nations allowed them to invest directly in the mines, plantations, and public utilities of less-developed regions. In the post–World War II years many of these companies became truly transnational, having multinational ownership and management. International trade agreements and open markets furthered the process. Ford Motor Company not only produced and sold cars internationally, but its shareholders, workers, and managers also came from numerous nations. Symbolic of these changes, the Japanese automaker Honda manufactured cars in Ohio and imported them into Japan, while Germany's Volkswagen made cars in Mexico for sale in the United States.

The location of manufacturing plants overseas and the acquisition of corporate operations by foreign buyers rendered such global firms as transnational as the products they sold. In the 1970s and 1980s American brand names like Levi's, Coca-Cola, Marlboro, Gillette, McDonald's, and Kentucky Fried Chicken were global phenomena (see Material Culture: Fast Food). But in time Asian names—Hitachi, Sony, Sanyo, and Mitsubishi—were blazoned in neon and on giant video screens on the sides of skyscrapers, along with European brands such as Nestlé, Mercedes, Pirelli, and Benetton.

As transnational manufacturers, agricultural conglomerates, and financial giants became wealthier and more powerful, they increasingly escaped the controls imposed by national governments. If labor costs were too high in Japan, antipollution measures too intrusive in the United States, or taxes too high in Great Britain, transnational companies relocated—or threatened to do so. In 1945, for example, the U.S. textile industry was located in low-wage southern states, dominating the American market and exporting to the world. As wages in the South rose and global competition increased, producers began relocating plants to Puerto Rico in the 1980s and to Mexico after NAFTA went into effect in 1994 (see Chapter 34). Now China is the primary manufacturer of textiles. The relatively low Mexican wages that attracted investments in the early 1990s now appear high in comparison with wages in China. As industries moved around, searching for profits, the governments in the developing world were often hard-pressed to control their actions. As a result, the worst abuses of labor and of the environment usually occurred in poor nations.

Conserving and Sharing Resources

In the 1960s environmental activists and political leaders began warning about the devastating environmental consequences of population growth, industrialization, and the expansion of agriculture onto marginal lands. Assaults on rain forests and redwoods, the disappearance of species, and the poisoning of streams and rivers raised public consciousness. Environmental damage occurred both in the advanced industrial economies and in the poorest of the developing nations. Perhaps the worst environmental record was achieved in the former Soviet Union, where industrial and nuclear wastes were often dumped with little concern for environmental consequences. The accumulated effect of scientific studies and public debate led to national and international efforts to slow, if not undo, damage to the environment.

The expanding global population required increasing quantities of food, fresh water, housing, energy, and other resources as the twentieth century ended (see Map 33.3). In the developed world industrial activity increased much more rapidly than population grew, and the consumption of energy (coal, electricity, and petroleum) rose proportionally. Indeed, the consumer-driven economic expansion of the post–World War II years became an obstacle to addressing environmental problems. Modern economies depend on the profligate consumption of goods and resources. Stock markets closely follow measures of consumer confidence—the willingness of people to make new purchases. When consumption slows, industrial nations enter a recession. How could the United States, Germany, or Japan change consumption patterns to protect the environment without endangering corporate profits, wages, and employment levels?

Since 1945 population growth has been most dramatic in the developing countries, where environmental pressures have also been extreme. In Brazil, India, and China, for example, the need to expand food production led to rapid deforestation and the extension of farming and grazing onto marginal lands. The results were predictable: erosion and water pollution. Population growth

MATERIAL CULTURE

Fast Food

Since early times foods and beverages have been moved across national borders and cultural boundaries by empires and commercial enterprises. The list of examples is very long. Sugar, coffee, tea, chocolate, corn, manioc, potatoes, wheat, wine, beer, distilled alcohols, tomatoes, and bananas are a small number of the foods and beverages carried from their origins to new continents and new peoples. In each case, host cultures accepted these additions to the indigenous cuisine while at the same time changing their preparation and altering their cultural meanings. Chocolate, a bitter ritual beverage consumed by the Aztec elite, for example, was sweetened with sugar and became a beverage of mass consumption in Europe.

In modern industrialized nations fast food outlets have appeared everywhere to meet the needs of populations transformed by cultural changes. Women and men in these societies marry later or not at all, and families have fewer meals together because of the schedules of school and work. The traditional boundaries between work and family life have been blurred. Individuals work long hours, travel long distances, and eat on the run. In 2003 there were 1.9 billion fast food outlets worldwide, with annual sales of $282 billion.

With globalization, increased immigration and travel, and greater cultural connectivity promoted by films, television, and the Web, cuisine and associated ideas about preparation and delivery have been internationalized. McDonald's now operates more than 30,000 restaurants in 119 countries. When a new franchise opened in Kuwait City, the drive-through line was over 10 kilometers long. Generally meals cost the same in each cultural setting. In the United States, one of the richest countries in the world, McDonald's provides low-cost food to the masses, while in Pakistan, one of the poorest, the meals are luxuries. What is the attraction? For many in the developing world the fast food cuisines, restaurant designs, and styles of preparation represent the world of modernity and sophistication, not unlike the enthusiasm in the developed world for Mexican, Thai, or Ethiopian restaurants and cuisines.

Indeed, McDonald's is merely one of numerous examples of fast food globalization. The one-thousandth KFC outlet opened recently in China, surpassing McDonald's presence in this dynamic economy. Papa John's opened its fortieth outlet in Seoul and its twentieth outlet in Shanghai. Wendy's,

Pizza Hut in India
The booming, cosmopolitan city of Mumbai hosts India's most modern industries and many of the country's strictest vegetarians, as seen by the vegetarian menu advertised by this Pizza Hut restaurant. (Ajaz Rahi/AP/Wide World Photos)

Dominos, Cinnabon, and Subway have followed. Even Brazilian brands like Habib's and British brands like Dixy Chicken have expanded into the Middle East and India, respectively.

Many have condemned this process as Yankee imperialism or as the unwanted homogenization of global culture. Tens of thousands have demonstrated, and some have gone to jail as a result of attacks on these symbols of foreign cultural penetration. Yet, as in earlier examples of unequal cultural exchange, local cultures have found ways to impose their tastes and values on these powerful international businesses. In Singapore McDonald's serves its signature hamburger on rice cakes instead of buns, and in Israel McDonald's has established Kosher outlets. KFC, the most successful American chain in China, serves a Beijing Duck Wrap with spring onions and rice gruel for breakfast. In India, with its large vegetarian population, McDonald's, Pizza Hut, and other successful franchises devote as much as 75 percent of their menu to vegetarian foods. Not only have menus been altered, but local preferences for a more leisurely style of dining have also forced chains like Pizza Hut and KFC to modify restaurant design to provide more seating and table service.

Societies produce an enormous range of products that serve as class and culture markers and as forms of self-expression. In the modern world food helps mark consumers as "traditional" or "sophisticated" and as "rich" or "poor." Both the global success of fast food companies and the popular protests against them suggest the complexity of this form of cultural transmission.

Map 33.3 **Fresh Water Resources** This map links population density and the availability of water. Red areas are highly stressed environments where populations use at least 40 percent or more of available water. Less stressed environments are blue. The deeper the shade of red or blue the greater the environmental stress. *Source: National Geographic,* September, 2002. Reprinted by permission of The National Geographic Society. *Source:* From "Global Water Stress," *National Geographic,* September 2002, pp. 14–16. Reprinted by permission of the National Geographic Society.

Loss of Brazilian Rain Forest   The destruction of large portions of Brazil's virgin rain forest has come to symbolize the growing threat to the environment caused by population growth and economic development. In this photograph we see a tragic moonscape of tree stumps and fragile topsoil ripped open by settlers. The name given to this place is "Bom Futuro" ("Good Future" in English).   (Jacques Jangoux/Peter Arnold, Inc.)

in Indonesia forced the government to permit the cutting of nearly 20 percent of the total forest area. These and many other poor nations also attempted to force industrialization because they believed that providing for their rapidly growing populations depended on the completion of the transition from agriculture to manufacturing. The argument was compelling: Why should Indians or Brazilians remain poor while Americans, Europeans, and Japanese grew rich?

Responding to Environmental Threats

Despite the gravity of environmental threats, there were many successful efforts to preserve and protect the environment. The Clean Air Act, the Clean Water Act, and the Endangered Species Act were passed in the United States in the 1970s as part of an environmental effort that included the nations of the European Community and Japan. Grassroots political movements and the media encouraged environmental awareness, and most nations in the developed world enforced strict antipollution laws and sponsored massive recycling efforts. Many also encouraged resource conservation by rewarding energy-efficient factories and manufacturers of fuel-efficient cars and by promoting the use of alternative energy sources such as solar and wind power. These efforts were implemented most comprehensively in Europe, where both energy conservation and new technologies like wind turbines were embraced.

Environmental efforts produced significant results. In western Europe and the United States air quality improved dramatically. Smog levels in the United States fell nearly a third from 1970 to 2000, even though the number of automobiles increased more than 80 percent. Emissions of lead and sulfur dioxide were down as well. The Great Lakes, Long Island Sound, and Chesapeake Bay were all much cleaner at the end of the century than they had been in 1970. The rivers of North America and Europe also improved. Still, in the United States more than thirty thousand deaths each year are attributed to exposure to pesticides and other chemicals.

New technologies made much of the improvement possible. Pollution controls on automobiles, planes, and factory smokestacks reduced harmful emissions. Scientists identified the chemicals that threaten the ozone layer, and their use in new appliances and cars began to be phased out.

Clearly, the desire to preserve the natural environment was growing around the world. In the developed nations continued political organization and enhanced awareness of environmental issues seemed likely to lead to step-by-step improvements in environmental policy. In the developing world and most of the former Soviet bloc, however, population pressures and weak governments were major obstacles to effective environmental policies. Since the 1990s the rapid expansion of China's industrial sector has put additional pressure on the environment as is indicated by the fact that respiratory disease caused by industrial pollution is now the leading cause of death.

Thus it was likely that the industrialized nations would have to fund global improvements, and the cost was likely to be high. Nevertheless, growing evidence of environmental degradation continued to propel reform efforts. The media drew attention to the precipitous shrinkage of Peru's Andean glaciers, which have lost a quarter of their volume in the last three decades; to oil spills, loss of rain forest in Brazil, and deforestation in Indonesia; and to erosion in parts of Africa. A growing, vocal movement pushed reluctant politicians to act.

In Kyoto, Japan, in 1997 representatives from around the world negotiated a far-reaching treaty to reduce greenhouse gases that contribute to global warming. Although it was affirmed by nearly all other industrial nations, President Bush has opposed American participation. Without broad agreement among the rich nations, the economic and political power necessary for environmental protections on a global scale will be very difficult to institute.

COMPARATIVE PERSPECTIVES

The world was profoundly altered between 1975 and 2000. Both the United States and the Soviet Union feared that every conflict and every regime change represented a potential threat to their strategic interests, and every conflict threatened to provoke confrontation between them. As a result, the superpowers were drawn into a succession of civil wars and revolutions. The costs in lives and property were terrible, the gains small. As defense costs escalated, the Soviet system crumbled. By 1991 the Soviet Union and the socialist Warsaw Pact had disappeared, transforming the international stage.

The world was also altered by economic growth and integration, by population growth and movement, and by technological and environmental change. Led by the postwar recovery of the industrial powers and the remarkable economic expansion of Japan, the Asian Tigers, and more recently China, the world economy grew dramatically. The development and application of new technology contributed significantly

to this process. International markets were more open and integrated than at any other time. The new wealth and exciting technologies of the postwar era were not shared equally, however. The capitalist West and a handful of Asian nations grew richer and more powerful, while most of the world's nations remained poor.

Population growth in the developing world was one reason for this divided experience. Most of the world's population growth in recent decades is in developing nations with limited economic growth. Unable to find adequate employment or, in many cases, bare subsistence, people in developing nations have migrated across borders, hoping to improve their lives. These movements have often provided valuable labor in the factories and farms of the developed world, but they have also provoked cultural, racial, and ethnic tension. Problems of inequality, population growth, and international migration will continue to challenge the global community in the coming decades.

SUMMARY

— How did the Cold War affect politics in Latin America and the Middle East in the 1970s and 1980s?

Online Study Center
ACE the Test

— What forces led to the collapse of the Soviet Union?

— What explains differences in the rate of population growth among the world's cultural regions?

— How does wealth inequality among nations impact international migration patterns?

— How has technological change affected the global environment in the recent past?

During the Cold War the United States and the Soviet Union were engaged in a global contest for dominance. While the superpowers avoided direct conflict, they both were drawn into revolutions, civil wars, and regional conflicts when they found opportunities to undercut each other. Fear that the Cuban (1959) and later Nicaraguan (1979) revolutions would spread across Latin America led the United States to support the rise of military dictatorships across the region. In the Middle East, the United States and the Soviet Union both armed and trained the militaries of Israel and the Arab nations. Earlier U.S. support for the government of the shah of Iran helped to produce a religious and nationalist uprising that overthrew the shah and led to a long confrontation with the United States. The Soviet Union, pursuing the establishment of friendly regimes on its borders, sent an army into Afghanistan and set up a puppet government. However, with the United States, Saudi Arabia, and Pakistan supplying the insurgency, the Soviet Union was forced to withdraw.

The Soviet Union ultimately collapsed at the end of the 1980s. Although its economy had made great strides in the decades immediately after World War II, central planning proved uncompetitive with the West, especially in meeting demands for consumer products and technological innovation. The Soviets also found it increasingly difficult to control the nationalist passions that circulated below the surface of its constituent republics. Nationalism was more dangerous still in the satellite nations. Use of military force to crush uprisings in Hungary in 1956 and Czechoslovakia in 1968 were the clearest indications that the Soviet empire was based on force. As the cost of the Cold War grew in the 1980s, the Soviet system began to crumble. Between 1989 and 1991 the socialist bloc and then the Soviet Union itself dissolved.

In the mature industrial nations and Japan, fertility declined in the period after 1945. Populations in the developed world have grown slowly or not at all. This is largely because women are better educated and have entered the workforce in larger numbers. As a result, they marry later and have fewer children. The effects are mitigated by longer life expectations. A more extreme pattern is found in Russia and the other nations of the old Soviet Union. In these nations birthrates have crashed and life expectancy has declined as well, leading to falling population levels. In the developing world the educational levels and workforce participation rates of women are more traditional. Birthrates remain high while life expectancy has generally improved. As a result, population is growing rapidly. While in Korea, China, and other newly industrialized economies birthrates are now close to those in the developed world, birthrates remain high in sub-Saharan Africa and the Muslim world. As a result, more than 95 percent of the world's future population growth will occur in the poorest developing nations.

With population growing most rapidly in the world's poorest nations and the richest nations producing fewer children and growing older, people have begun to migrate from poorer nations to richer nations, especially to the United States and Canada, Australia and New Zealand, and western Europe. In addition, within developing nations migrants leave the poorest agricultural regions to seek opportunities in slightly-better-off urban centers. These patterns were growing in strength at the end of the twentieth century.

Growing population and the development process have forced marginal lands into production and stimulated the exploitation of new resources. The need to feed a rapidly growing world population has also pressured ocean resources. As the world's population has reached 6 billion and the largest cities have reached 20 million, the need to produce and deliver raw materials and finished goods has put tremendous stress on the environment. In the 1990s these pressures were compounded with the rapid development of the Chinese and Indian economies.

At the same time, new technologies and the wealth produced by economic expansion have allowed the world's richest nations to implement ambitious programs of environmental protection. As a result, pollution produced by automobiles and factories has actually declined in the richest nations. The question that remains is whether rapidly developing nations, such as China and India, will move more quickly than the mature industrial nations did to introduce these new technologies.

KEY TERMS

proxy wars   *p. 966*
Salvador Allende   *p. 968*
Dirty War   *p. 968*
Sandinistas   *p. 968*
neo-liberalism   *p. 970*
Ayatollah Ruhollah Khomeini
   p. 972

Saddam Husain   *p. 972*
keiretsu   *p. 973*
Asian Tigers   *p. 974*
newly industrialized economies
   (NIEs)   *p. 974*
Deng Xiaoping   *p. 974*
Tiananmen Square   *p. 975*

Mikhail Gorbachev   *p. 975*
perestroika   *p. 976*
Solidarity   *p. 976*
ethnic cleansing   *p. 978*
Thomas Malthus   *p. 979*
demographic transition
   p. 979

Online Study Center
Improve Your Grade
Flashcards

SUGGESTED READING

Among the works devoted to postwar economic performance are W. L. M. Adriaasen and J. G. Waardensburg, eds., *A Dual World Economy: Forty Years of Development Experience* (1989); P. Krugman, *The Age of Diminished Expectations: U.S. Economic Policy in the 1990s* (1990); B. J. McCormick, *The World Economy: Patterns of Growth and Change* (1988); and H. van der Wee, *Prosperity and Upheaval: The World Economy, 1945–1980* (1986).

For Latin America, Thomas E. Skidmore and Peter H. Smith, *Modern Latin America*, 4th ed. (1996), provides an excellent general introduction to the period 1975 to 1991. The literature on the era of repression is large. *Nunca Mas* (1986), the official report of the Argentine government, provides a moving introduction. Also see news stories in 1999 and 2000 about the arrest of Augusto Pinochet in London and the resulting legal proceedings. The movie *Official Story* (available with subtitles or dubbed) offers an effective look at the legacy of the Dirty War in Argentina. For Central America see Walter La Feber, *Inevitable Revolutions: The United States in Central America* (1983).

For Africa in the recent past see Martin Meredith, *The Fate of Africa: From the Hopes of Freedom to the Heart of Despair* (2005); and Leonard Thompson, *A History of South Africa,* 3rd ed. (2005). For the life of Nelson Mandela see his autobiography, *Long Walk to Freedom: The Autobiography of Nelson Mandela* (1995); and Anthony Sampson, *Mandela: The Authorized Biography* (2000). For events in Rwanda see John A. Berry and Carol Pott Berry, eds., *Genocide in Rwanda: A Collective Memory* (1999). For the Congo see Robert Edgerton, *The Troubled Heart of Africa: A History of the Congo* (2002).

For the Pacific Rim see Jonathan Spence, *The Search for Modern China* (1990); Edwin O. Reischauer, *The Japanese* (1988); and Staffan B. Linder, *Pacific Century: Economic and Political Consequences of Asian-Pacific Dynamism* (1986). For the recent experience of China see Oded Shenkar, *The Chinese Century: The Rising Chinese Economy and Its Impact on the Global Economy, the Balance of Power, and Your Job* (2004); and Nicholas R. Lardy, *China's Unfinished Economic Revolution* (1998). For India see Tim Dyson et al., eds., *Twenty-first Century India: Population, Economy, Human Development, and the Environment* (2005); and Kaushik Basu, ed., *India's Emerging Economy: Performance and Prospects in the 1990s and Beyond* (2004).

There are many fine studies of Europe and the Soviet system in the Cold War era. See, for example, John Lewis Gaddis, *The Cold War: A New History* (2005); and Odd Arne Westad, *The Global Cold War: Third World Interventions and the Making of Our Times* (2005). More focused examinations of the Soviet bloc are provided in Peter Kenez, *A History of the Soviet Union from the Beginning to the End* (2006); Richard Sakwa, *The Rise and Fall of the Soviet Union, 1917–1991* (1999); David Remnick, *Lenin's Tomb: The Last Days of the Soviet Empire* (1993); and Charles Maier, *Dissolution: The Crisis of Communism and the End of East Germany* (1997). See also Katherine Verdery, *What Was Socialism, and What Comes Next?* (1996).

The story of the Iranian Revolution and the early days of the Islamic Republic of Iran is told well by Shaul Bakhash, *The Reign of the Ayatollahs: Iran and the Iranian Revolution* (1990). Barnet Rubin, *The Fragmentation of Afghanistan* (1995), provides excellent coverage of the struggle between Soviet forces and the Muslim resistance in that country.

A number of studies examine the special problems faced by women in the postwar period. See, for example, Barbara Engel and Christine Worobec, eds., *Russia's Women: Accommodation, Resistance, Transformation* (1990); Elisabeth Croll, *Feminism and Socialism in China* (1978); J. Ginat, *Women in Muslim Rural Society: Status and Role in Family and Community* (1982); June Hahner, *Women in Latin America* (1976); P. Hudson, *Third World Women Speak Out* (1979); A. de Souza, *Women in Contemporary India and South Asia* (1980); and M. Wolf, *Revolution Postponed: Women in Contemporary China* (1985).

For general discussions of economic, demographic, and environmental problems facing the world see R. N. Gwynne, *New Horizons? Third World Industrialization in an International Framework* (1990); W. Alonso, ed., *Population in an Interacting World* (1987); P. R. Ehrlich and A. E. Ehrlich, *The Population Explosion* (1990); James Fallows, *More like Us: Making America Great Again* (1989); Paul M. Kennedy, *Preparing for the Twenty-first Century* (1993); W. W. Rostow, *The Great Population Spike and After: Reflections on the 21st Century* (1998); and J. L. Simon, *Population Matters: People, Resources, Environment and Immigration* (1990). Coverage of the recent past is found in Joseph E. Stiglitz, *Globalization and Its Discontents* (2003).

For issues associated with technological and environmental change see M. Feshbach and A. Friendly, *Ecocide in the U.S.S.R.* (1992); John Bellamy Foster, *Economic History of the Environment* (1994); S. Hecht and A. Cockburn, *The Fate of the Forest: Developers, Destroyers, and Defenders of the Amazon* (1989); K. Marton, *Multinationals, Technology, and Industrialization: Implications and Impact in Third World Countries* (1986); S. P. Huntington, *The Third Wave: Demoralization in the Late Twentieth Century* (1993); John R. McNeill, *Something New Under the Sun: An Environmental History of the Twentieth Century World* (2000); and B. L. Turner II et al., eds., *The Earth as Transformed by Human Action: Global and Regional Changes in the Biosphere over the Past 300 Years* (1990).

NOTES

1. Quoted in Antony Flew, "Introduction," in Thomas Robert Malthus, *An Essay on the Principle of Population and a Summary View of the Principle of Population* (New York: Penguin Books, 1970), 30.

2. "Population Implosion Worries a Graying Europe," *New York Times,* July 10, 1998.

3. Paul M. Kennedy, *Preparing for the Twenty-first Century* (New York: Random House, 1993), 45.

Lower Manhattan, 11 March 2002
Six months after the terrorist attacks, beams of light commemorated the destroyed twin towers of the World Trade Center and those who perished in them.   (AFP Photo/ Doug Kanter/Getty Images)

○—What are the main benefits and dangers of growing political, economic, and cultural integration?

○—What roles do religious beliefs and secular ideologies play in the contemporary world?

○—How has technology contributed to the process of global interaction?

34

GLOBALIZATION IN THE NEW MILLENNIUM

CHAPTER OUTLINE

Global Economic and Political Currents

Trends and Visions

Global Culture

ENVIRONMENT AND TECHNOLOGY: Global Warming

DIVERSITY AND DOMINANCE: World Literature in English

The workday began normally at the World Trade Center in lower Manhattan on the morning of September 11, 2001. The 50,000 people who work there were making their way to the two 110-story towers, as were some 140,000 others who visited on a typical day. Suddenly, at 8:46 A.M., an American Airlines Boeing 767 with 92 people on board, traveling at a speed of 470 miles per hour (756 kilometers per hour), crashed into floors 94 to 98 of the north tower, igniting the 10,000 gallons (38,000 liters) of fuel in its tanks. Just before 9:03 A.M. a United Airlines flight with 65 people on board and a similar fuel load hit floors 78 to 84 of the south tower.

As the burning jet fuel engulfed the collision areas, the buildings' surviving occupants struggled through smoke-filled corridors and down dozens of flights of stairs. Many of those trapped above the crash sites used cell phones to say good-bye to loved ones. Rather than endure the flames and fumes, a few jumped to their deaths.

Online Study Center

This icon will direct you to interactive activities and study materials on the website: *college.hmco.com/pic/bulliet4e.*

Just before 10 o'clock, temperatures that had risen to 2,300° Fahrenheit (1,260° Celsius) caused the steel girders in the impacted area of the south tower to give way. The collapsing upper floors crushed the floors underneath one by one, engulfing lower Manhattan in a dense cloud of dust. Twenty-eight minutes later the north tower pancaked in a similar manner. Miraculously, most of the buildings' occupants had escaped before the towers collapsed. Besides the people on the planes, nearly 2,600 lost their lives, including some 200 police officers and firefighters helping in the evacuation.

That same morning another American Airlines jet crashed into the Pentagon, killing all 64 people on board and 125 others inside the military complex near Washington, D.C. Passengers on a fourth plane managed to overpower their hijackers, and the plane crashed in rural Pennsylvania, killing all 45 on board.

The four planes had been hijacked by teams of Middle Eastern men who slit the throats of service and flight personnel and seized control. Of the nineteen hijackers, fifteen were from Saudi Arabia. All had links to an extremist Islamic organization, al-Qaeda° (the base or foundation), commanded by a rich Saudi named Usama bin Laden°, who was incensed with American political, military, and cultural influence in the Middle East. The men were educated and well traveled, had lived in the United States, and spoke English. Some had trained as pilots so that they could fly the hijacked aircraft.

The hijackers left few records of their personal motives, but the acts spoke for themselves. The Pentagon was the headquarters of the American military, the most technologically sophisticated and powerful fighting force the world had ever seen. The fourth plane was probably meant to hit the Capitol or the White House, the legislative and executive centers of the world's only superpower. The Twin Towers may have been targeted because they were the tallest buildings in New York, but they were not just American targets. The World Trade Center housed 430 companies involved in international commerce and finance.

Among the dead were people from more than half the countries in the world. New York was the site of the attack, but the World Trade Center was a powerful symbol of the international economy.

The events of September 11, which became commonly referred to as 9/11, can be understood on many levels. The hijackers and their supporters saw themselves as engaged in a holy struggle against economic, political, and military institutions they believed to be evil. They believed so deeply in their mission that they were willing to give their lives for it and to take as many other lives as they could. People directly affected and political leaders around the world tended to describe the attacks as evil acts against innocent victims.

To understand why the nineteen attackers were heroes to some and terrorists to others, one needs to explore the historical context of global changes at the turn of the millennium and the ideological tensions they have generated. While the advancing economic, political, and cultural integration of the world is welcomed by some, it seems threatening to others. The unique prominence of the United States in every major aspect of global integration, as well as its support for pro-American governments overseas, also elicits sharply divergent views.

Online Study Center
Improve Your Grade
Primary Source:
The Last Night

GLOBAL ECONOMIC AND POLITICAL CURRENTS

The turn of the millennium saw the intensification of **globalization** trends that had been building since the 1970s. Growing trade and travel and new technologies were bringing all parts of the world into closer economic, political, and cultural integration and interaction. The collapse of the Soviet Union had completed the dissolution of territorial empires that had been under way throughout the twentieth century. Autonomous national states (numbering about two hundred) became an almost universal norm, and a growing number of them had

---

al-Qaeda (ahl–KAW-eh-duh)
Usama bin Laden (oo-SAH-mah bin LAH-din)

C H R O N O L O G Y

	Politics	Economics and Society
2000	**2000** Al-Qaeda attacks American destroyer USS *Cole* in Yemen	
2001	**2001** Terrorists destroy the World Trade Center and damage the Pentagon on September 11	**2001–2003** Terrorist attacks trigger global recession **2001** Shanghai Cooperation Organization formed **2001** U.S. withdraws from Kyoto Protocol on global warming **2001** Al-Jazeera television in Qatar begins broadcasting statements by Usama bin Laden
2002	**2002** United Nations weapons inspectors return to Iraq	**2002** Euro currency adopted in twelve European countries
2003	**2003** United States and Britain invade and occupy Iraq	
2004	**2004** Terrorists bomb Spanish trains **2004** Hamid Karzai becomes first democratically elected president of Afghanistan	**2004** Ten new members admitted to European Union
2005	**2005** Terrorists bomb London transport system **2005** Iraqis adopt new constitution **2005** Anti-American president Mahmoud Ahmedinejad elected president of Iran	
2006	**2006** Iran announces ability to enrich uranium **2006** Iraqis elect new government **2006** Hamas movement defeats PLO in Palestinian election **2006** Israel attacks Hezbollah in Lebanon in response to its seizure of Israeli soldiers **2006** In midterm elections, American voters rejected Bush policies.	

embraced democratic institutions. The rapid integration of world trade and markets had convinced world leaders of the need to balance national autonomy with international agreements and associations.

An Interconnected Economy

The heated expansion of trade, global interconnections, and privatization of government enterprises that gained momentum with the dismantling of Soviet-style socialist economies in the 1990s cooled abruptly in the wake of 9/11. The rate of growth in world trade fell from 13 percent in 2000 to only 1 percent in 2001. The importance of the United States, and therefore of American economic and foreign policies, to the world economic system appears clearly in Map 34.1, which shows global disparities in national economies and per capita incomes in 2002. The gigantic U.S. economy, larger than the economies of the next five countries combined—Japan, Germany, Great Britain, China (including Hong Kong), and France—also consumed by far the largest portion of the world's natural resources, including over a quarter of annual global oil production.

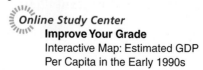

Online Study Center
Improve Your Grade
Interactive Map: Estimated GDP
Per Capita in the Early 1990s

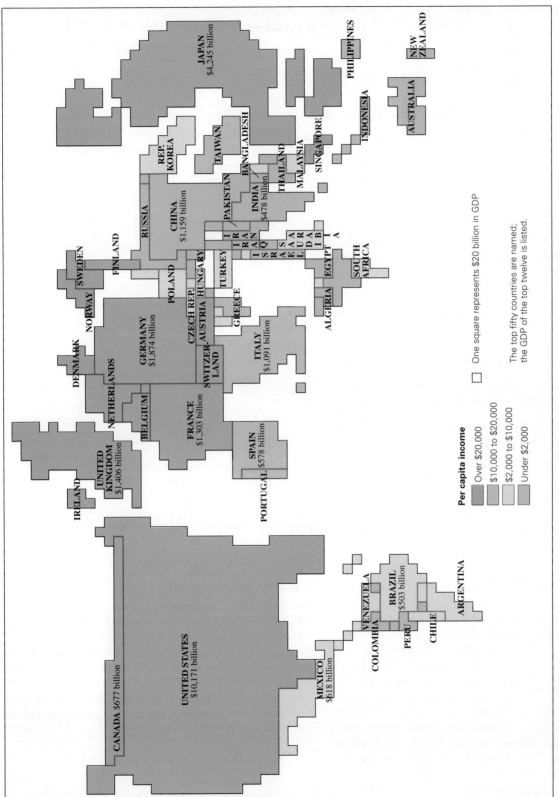

Map 34.1 Global Distribution of Wealth Industrialization and good government have given the citizens of Japan and Western countries access to tremendous wealth. Elsewhere, warfare and political mismanagement have slowed or reversed economic growth, while high population growth (see Map 33.2) has slowed increases in per capita wealth. In nearly all countries the distribution of wealth among individuals varies tremendously. Wealth is clearly concentrated in some parts of the world, but its geographical distribution is more complex than the often-cited divide between a rich north and a poor south.

Palm Island, Dubai The vast wealth that continues to pour into the oil-producing states of the Persian Gulf poses problems of how to invest the money sensibly. The Emirate of Dubai, one of the United Arab Emirates, is seeking to attract wealthy vacationers to this artificial island resort shaped like a palm tree. Its publicists say that "'Palm Island' will include 2,000 villas, up to 40 luxury hotels, shopping complexes, cinemas, and the Middle East's first marine park" and will be "visible from the moon." (Jorge Ferrari/epa/Corbis Sygma)

Economic growth in China and India resumed quickly after the shock of 2001, and the very large populations of these two countries marked them as future world economic powers. Their growth put particular pressure on world energy supplies. OPEC's manipulation of world oil prices, combined with political events like the Iranian Revolution of 1979 and Iraq's ensuing invasion of Iran, had caused crude oil prices to soar between 1973 and 1985. But aside from those years, the average price of oil remained consistently below $20 per barrel (adjusted for inflation) throughout the second half of the twentieth century. In the year 2000, however, oil prices began a new period of increase caused not by OPEC but by rising demand, especially in the United States and Asia, and by political turmoil in the Middle East (see below). By the middle of 2006, the price of a barrel of crude had crept past $70, with little prospect of a reversal of the trend. This increase not only boosted the national incomes of major producing countries such as Russia, Iran, and Saudi Arabia, but it also caused energy security to overtake the formation of international trade associations as a matter of global economic concern.

Among the regional trade associations that had come into being to promote growth, reduce the economic vulnerability of member states, and, less explicitly, balance American economic dominance, the European Union (EU) was the most successful (see Map 34.2). Twelve member states adopted a new common currency, the euro, in 2002, making the Euro-bloc a formidable competitor with the United States for investment and banking. Ten new members from eastern Europe and the Mediterranean were admitted to the EU in May 2004, and other countries, including Turkey, Bulgaria, and Romania, had aspirations to join.

Despite the EU's expansion, the North American Free Trade Agreement (NAFTA), which eliminated tariffs among the United States, Canada, and Mexico in 1994, governed the world's largest free-trade zone. However, a heated debate in the United States over illegal immigration across the Mexican border, as well as conservative fears that Spanish speakers might somehow dilute American culture and identity, limited popular enthusiasm for the agreement. The third largest free-trade zone, Mercosur, created by Argentina, Brazil, Paraguay, and Uruguay in 1991, decided in 2002 to allow the free movement of people within its area and gave equal employment rights to the citizens of all member states. Other free-trade associations operated in West Africa, southern Africa, Southeast Asia, Central America, the Pacific Basin, and the Caribbean.

The Shanghai Cooperation Organization (SCO), which formed in 2001 with China, Russia, and four former parts of the USSR—Kazakhstan°, Kyrgyzstan°, Tajikistan°,

---

Kazakhstan (KAH-zahk-stahn)   **Kyrgyzstan** (KER-gihz-stahn)
Tajikistan (tah-JEHK-ih-stahn)

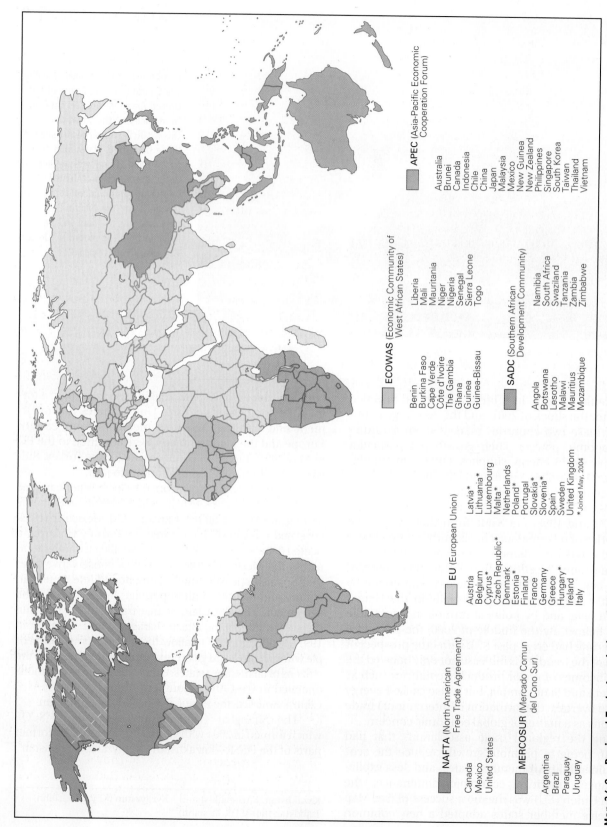

NAFTA (North American Free Trade Agreement)

Canada
Mexico
United States

MERCOSUR (Mercado Comun del Cono Sur)

Argentina
Brazil
Paraguay
Uruguay

EU (European Union)

Austria
Belgium
Cyprus*
Czech Republic*
Denmark
Estonia*
Finland
France
Germany
Greece
Hungary*
Ireland
Italy
Latvia*
Lithuania*
Luxembourg
Malta*
Netherlands
Poland*
Portugal
Slovakia*
Slovenia*
Spain
Sweden
United Kingdom
*Joined May, 2004

ECOWAS (Economic Community of West African States)

Benin
Burkina Faso
Cape Verde
Côte d'Ivoire
The Gambia
Ghana
Guinea
Guinea-Bissau
Liberia
Mali
Mauritania
Niger
Nigeria
Senegal
Sierra Leone
Togo

SADC (Southern African Development Community)

Angola
Botswana
Lesotho
Malawi
Mauritius
Mozambique
Namibia
South Africa
Swaziland
Tanzania
Zambia
Zimbabwe

APEC (Asia-Pacific Economic Cooperation Forum)

Australia
Brunei
Canada
Chile
China
Indonesia
Japan
Malaysia
Mexico
New Guinea
New Zealand
Philippines
Singapore
South Korea
Taiwan
Thailand
Vietnam

Map 34.2 Regional Trade Associations, 2004   International trade and development are major concerns of governments in developed and developing countries. NAFTA, Mercosur, and the EU are free-trade areas. The other associations promote trade and development.

and Uzbekistan°—as members, originally pursued common security interests, such as combating separatist movements and terrorism. But its announced twenty-year plan for reducing barriers to trade and population movements took a step forward in 2006 when Mahmoud Ahmedinejad, the president of Iran, a country with observer status, signaled Iran's desire to expand relations with the SCO. Bringing Iran's oil-rich economy into alignment with a rapidly developing China and a similarly oil-rich Russia, then recovering from the period of post-Soviet economic turmoil, promised to complicate the world economic and political picture.

Because of the inequalities and downturns that are intrinsic to free economic markets, the global bodies that tried to manage world trade and finance found it hard to convince poorer nations that they were not concerned only with the welfare of richer countries. In 1995 the world's major trading powers established the **World Trade Organization (WTO)**. The WTO encourages reduced trading barriers and enforces international trade agreements. Despite a membership of 149 nations by 2006, the WTO had many critics and regularly encountered street protests during its ministerial meetings. Some protesters feared that low-cost foreign manufacturers would shrink the job opportunities in richer states; others demanded continuing tariff protection for local farmers.

Countries in economic trouble had little choice but to turn to the international financial agencies for funds to keep things from getting worse. The International Monetary Fund (IMF) and World Bank (see Chapter 32) made their assistance conditional on internal economic reforms that were often politically unpopular, such as terminating government subsidies for basic foodstuffs, cutting social programs, and liberalizing investment. The bitter pill of economic reform sometimes paid off in long-term improvement, but it could also fuel popular criticism of the international economic system and of the governments that acceded to its demands.

The emphasis on free trade led to changes in government-to-government aid programs. During the Cold War countries had often gained funds for economic development by allying themselves with one of the superpowers. Not surprisingly, when the Cold War ended, foreign economic aid to poor nations fell by a third. On an African tour in 2000 President Bill Clinton told African countries that the days of large handouts were over and that they would have to rely on their own efforts to expand their economies.

In the face of rising criticism at home and protests at international meetings, however, world leaders rethought their positions and pledged to increase attention to the problem of economic despair, especially in Africa. At a Millennium Summit in September 2000 the states of the United Nations agreed to make sustainable development and the elimination of world poverty their highest priorities. A 2002 United Nations meeting in Monterrey, Mexico, called for special commitments to Africa. Late in 2002 President George W. Bush proposed a substantial increase in American foreign aid. In practice, however, special consideration of Africa's economic plight seldom resulted in major increases in support.

Globalization and Democracy

The last decades of the twentieth century saw rapid increases in democratic institutions and personal freedom. In 2003, 140 countries regularly held elections; people in 125 had access to free (or partly free) presses; and most people lived in fully democratic states.[1]

The great appeal of democracy in modern times has been that elections offer a peaceful way to settle the inevitable differences among a country's social classes, cultural groups, and regions. Although majority votes swing from one part of the political spectrum to another, democracies tend to encourage political moderation. Moreover, wars between fully democratic states are extremely rare.

Democratic gains were made especially in the nations of eastern Europe that had been under Soviet control, though some newly democratic states became subject to great mood swings among the electorate. In Ukraine, for example, the election in 1999 of Viktor Yushchenko, a reform-minded prime minister, came undone a year and a half later when a no-confidence vote supported by communist hardliners and big business interests removed him from office. Violent demonstrations followed in which protesters demanded the impeachment of the authoritarian president Leonid Kuchma. Kuchma yielded in 2004, and his hand-picked candidate seemingly outpolled Yushchenko in the election to succeed him. But when international monitors presented evidence of massive electoral fraud, pro-Yushchenko demonstrations, designated "the Orange Revolution," led to the Supreme Court invalidating the results. After a new election in 2005, Yushchenko finally became president. This experience, which had parallels in other former Soviet territories, demonstrated that working democracies can be hard to establish in countries with a history of authoritarianism.

Uzbekistan (ooz-BEHK-ih-stahn)

Sectarian Strife in India   Hours after these Hindu youths clambered atop the sixteenth-century Babri Mosque in December 1992, hundreds of angry Hindu nationalists completely demolished the structure. The Hindus claimed that the Muslim place of worship in the northern Indian province of Uttar Pradesh had been erected upon the site of a temple commemorating the birthplace of Lord Ram, the incarnation of the Hindu god Vishnu. Thousands died in the riots that followed the razing of the temple. An Indian government archaeological team uncovered the foundation of an earlier temple-like structure.   (Douglas E. Curran/Getty Images)

Asian democracies proved somewhat more stable. Beginning with free parliamentary elections in 1999, the populous state of Indonesia moved from years of authoritarian and corrupt rule toward more open political institutions. The following years witnessed many problems: a violent independence movement of the Acheh district of northern Sumatra, the secession in 2002 of East Timor after years of brutal Indonesian military occupation, terrorist bombings on the island of Bali in 2004, and a devastating earthquake and tsunami in 2004. But democratic elections were regularly held. The losing candidates left office peacefully, and the populace at large accepted the results.

In India a major political shift occurred in 1998 when the Bharatiya Janata Party (BJP) secured an electoral victory that ended four decades of Congress Party rule. The BJP success came through blatant appeals to Hindu nationalism, the condoning of violence against India's Muslims, and opposition to the social and economic progress of the Untouchables (those traditionally confined to the dirtiest jobs). In 2004, however, in a major upset, the BJP lost a national election to the Congress Party and peacefully handed over power.

In sub-Saharan Africa, democracy had mixed results. Nelson Mandela, the leader of the African National Congress (ANC) who had become the first postapartheid president of South Africa in 1994 (see Chapter 33), left

office in 1999 and was succeeded by the deputy president and ANC leader Thabo Mbeki. Mbeki was reelected in 2004. The lively politics of this ethnically diverse country have been a model of how democracy can resolve conflicts. Nigeria, Africa's most populous state, also tried democracy in 1999 when General Olusegun Obasanjo°, running on an anticorruption and reform platform, was elected president after decades of military rule. However, his reelection in 2003 was tainted by voting irregularities, and a campaign by his supporters to amend the constitution so he could run for a third term failed in 2006. In the meantime, Nigeria was wracked by periodic Muslim-Christian violence in the cities of the north and east, and a guerrilla movement in the Niger Delta aimed at sabotaging and threatening the oil industry in order to gain more of its benefits for local communities.

Regime Change in Iraq and Afghanistan

The most closely watched experiments in democratization took place in Iraq and Afghanistan, countries that the United States invaded in response to the terrorist attacks of 9/11. While the use of Afghanistan

Olusegun Obasanjo (oh-LOO-say-goon oh-bah-SAHN-joh)

Iranian President Mahmoud Ahmedinejad After two terms under the comparatively liberal, but ineffective, government of President Mohammad Khatami, voters in the Islamic Republic of Iran elected a relatively unknown conservative in 2006. President Ahmedinejad has taken confrontational positions on international affairs, notably his denial of Israel's legitimacy as a state and his assertion of Iran's right to develop nuclear technology. This has enhanced his domestic popularity, while convincing many analysts that with the American defeat of Saddam Husain, Iran had become a major power in the Middle East and the Islamic world. (IRNA/Reuters/Corbis)

as a safe haven for Usama bin Laden and his al-Qaeda organization was the unequivocal justification given for the overthrow in December 2001 of the militantly religious Taliban regime that protected him, the rationale for invading Iraq underwent a change. During the leadup to the war the American government contended that Iraq was a clear and present danger to the United States because it possessed **weapons of mass destruction** (WMDs), nuclear, chemical, and biological weapons that it might supply to terrorists like bin Laden. In November 2002 the Bush administration persuaded the United Nations Security Council to pass a resolution ordering the return of United Nations weapons inspectors to Iraq and requiring the Iraqi government to specify what WMDs it still possessed. When the new United Nations inspectors failed to find any evidence of banned weapons, a split widened between those nations wanting to continue inspections and those, led by the United States and Britain, wanting to intervene militarily. Abandoning efforts to gain explicit Security Council authorization, an American-led "coalition of the willing" began the invasion of Iraq with a massive aerial bombardment of Baghdad on March 20, 2003. Twenty-five days later the United States declared that "major fighting" had ended, little realizing that a guerrilla insurgency would continue for years.

Though Iraq then fell into a deep state of turmoil because the coalition army was too small or otherwise unprepared to prevent the looting and destruction of government facilities and other lawlessness, a thorough search was launched for prohibited weapons. This search failed to turn up any WMDs, just as intelligence analysis failed to uncover any evidence that Saddam Husain, Iraq's fallen dictator, had been in league with Usama bin Laden or had played a role in the 9/11 attacks.

However, American concern for WMDs was not eliminated. North Korea had an open program to build nuclear weapons, and Iran was suspected of having a covert plan based in part on technological aid secretly given by the head of Pakistan's successful nuclear arms program. Iran's outspokenly anti-American and anti-Israeli president, Mahmoud Ahmedinejad, elected in 2005, and North Korea's dictator Kim Jong-il presented the United States with difficult challenges, but the military invasion option chosen for Iraq was not talked of.

The failure to find Iraqi WMDs having become an embarrassment to the United States, President George W. Bush declared that the rationale for invading Iraq had actually been to liberate the Iraqi people and substitute democracy for oppression. Though an intense debate followed within the United States about whether the Bush administration had used deception in leading the nation into war, the question of whether the war would ultimately be termed a success or a failure came to hinge on the establishment of democratic institutions in both Afghanistan and Iraq.

Though Afghanistan had a far less developed economy and was suffering from the devastation caused by years of guerrilla war against the Soviet Union and from the harsh and stifling rule of the Taliban, the democratic process started well with an assembly of traditional tribal leaders selecting Hamid Karzai as interim president in 2002. Two years later Karzai was elected president in Afghanistan's first democratic elections.

Unfortunately, the power of the new Afghan government did not extend effectively over the entire country. Traditional warlords retained control in some areas, and in 2006 an effort by the Taliban to regain power gave rise to assassinations and guerrilla warfare in various parts of the country. Though the United States was able to enlist the participation of NATO forces in helping to police Afghanistan, the number of foreign troops and the amount of monetary aid made available to the Karzai government were insufficient to ensure either security or economic recovery. To the frustration of the countries trying to help Afghanistan with its many problems, opium produced for the world drug trade remained a mainstay of the country's farm income.

When the "major fighting" ended in Iraq, the United States and its allies established a Coalition Provisional Authority to govern the country while democratic institutions were being designed. After sixteen months of American direct rule, the authority appointed an Iraqi Governing Council composed mostly of Iraqi exiles who had opposed Saddam Husain's dictatorship. The council adopted a Transitional Administrative Law to serve as a temporary constitution and then passed authority on to an Iraqi Interim Government, which in turn gave way to an Iraqi Transitional Government elected in January 2006. This election, the first under a constitution adopted three months earlier, marked the culmination of the democratization process.

At every turning point along this twisting path to democratic rule, the United States declared that Iraq was finally emerging from chaos and anarchy, but in fact the growth of democracy was mirrored by the spread of a lethal resistance movement that attacked coalition forces and Iraqis who were helping them, especially newly recruited soldiers and police. When the elections produced a parliament in which Shi'ite political parties, representing the country's majority population and closely aligned with Iran, formed the largest bloc of votes, the insurgency increasingly targeted Shi'ite civilians and mosques. In response, Shi'ite militiamen, some of them incorporated within the government's security forces, attacked Sunni Arabs in Baghdad and elsewhere. The question was soon being asked whether Iraq was on the verge of, or already in the midst

of, a civil war. Though the Bush administration continued to claim that, despite the violence, democracy would eventually succeed in both Iraq and Afghanistan, public opinion polls showed that most Americans had doubts about this and worried about how and when American troops might be able to return home. In the 2006 midterm elections, opposition to the war led to Democrats capturing both the U.S. Senate and House of Representatives.

With the democratization process in Afghanistan and Iraq in question, other Middle Eastern countries hesitated to follow American urgings to liberalize their political systems. Though some small oil-producing countries in the Persian Gulf took cautious steps toward democratization and Kuwait for the first time allowed women to vote in 2006, large countries like Egypt and Syria talked about liberalization but continued to suppress most critics. These countries were fearful that free elections would lead to Islamic political parties gaining a share of power, or even forming a new government, as the religious Shi'ite parties had in Iraq. The capture of 23 out of 128 seats in the Lebanese parliament by the Lebanese Shi'ite movement Hezbollah in 2005 and the absolute majority of seats won by the militantly anti-Israeli Hamas movement in elections for the Palestine Governing Authority in 2006 seemed to confirm this fear, since both movements were strongly religious in their goals and policies. Attacks launched by Israel against both Hamas and Hezbollah in response to kidnappings of Israeli soldiers in 2006 suggested that fear of domination by Islamic movements might in the future become more important than democratization in the Middle East, regardless of American policies.

TRENDS AND VISIONS

As people around the world faced the opportunities and problems of globalization, they tried to make sense of these changes in terms of their own cultures and beliefs. With 6 billion people, the world was big enough to include many different approaches, whether religious or secular, local or international, traditional or visionary. In some cases, however, conflicting visions fed violence.

Faith and Politics

Religious beliefs increasingly inspired political actions during the second half of the twentieth century, and the trend intensified as the new century began (see Map 34.3). Though for Americans this change reversed two centuries of growing secularism, Western analysts did not agree on the cause of the religious revival.

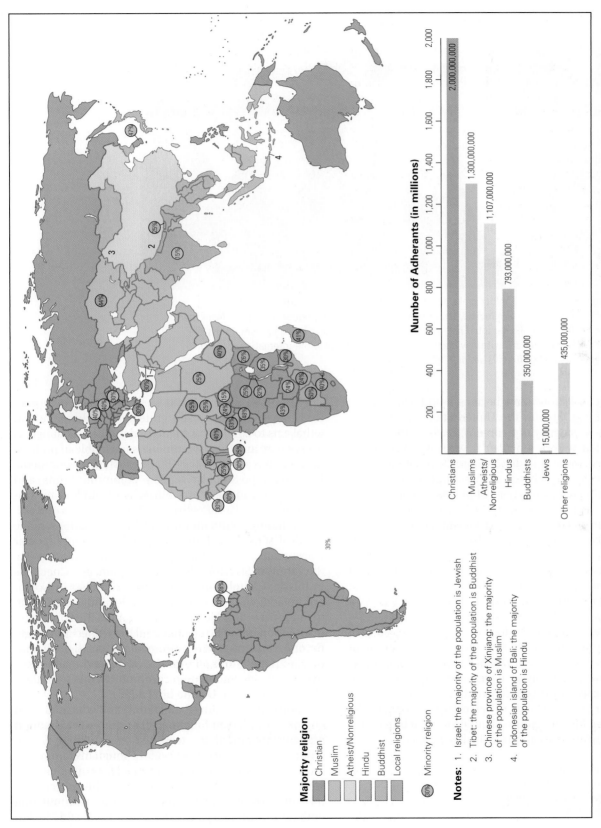

Majority religion
- Christian
- Muslim
- Atheist/Nonreligious
- Hindu
- Buddhist
- Local religions

⬤ Minority religion

Notes: 1. Israel: the majority of the population is Jewish

2. Tibet: the majority of the population is Buddhist

3. Chinese province of Xinjiang: the majority of the population is Muslim

4. Indonesian island of Bali: the majority of the population is Hindu

Number of Adherants (in millions)

Religion	Number
Christians	2,000,000,000
Muslims	1,300,000,000
Atheists/Nonreligious	1,107,000,000
Hindus	793,000,000
Buddhists	350,000,000
Jews	15,000,000
Other religions	435,000,000

Map 34.3 **World Religions** The distribution of Buddhism, Christianity, and Islam reflects centuries of missionary efforts. Hinduism and Judaism have expanded primarily through trade and migration. Chinese governments have actively curtailed religious practice. As religion revives as a source of social identity or a rationale for political assertion or mass mobilization, the possibility of religious activism across broad geographic regions becomes greater, as does the likelihood of domestic discord in multireligious states. (Data from *The New York Times 2003 Almanac*, ed. John W. Wright [New York: Penguin Books, 2002], 484–488. Copyright © The New York Times Company, 2002.)

Darfur Refugees In 2003 a conflict broke out in the Darfur region of western Sudan. Marauding bands, largely from nomadic backgrounds, struck farming villages, killing ten of thousands. More than 100,000 people crossed the border into Chad as refugees. With both sides being of more or less the same ethnicity and religion, and with few great power interests at stake, the international community proved unable to take effective action. (Patrick Robert/Corbis)

Evangelical Protestants became a powerful conservative political force in the United States, particularly during the presidency of George W. Bush. Catholic conservatives led by Pope John Paul II, who died in 2005, and his successor Pope Benedict XVI forcefully reiterated politically sensitive teachings, such as opposition to abortion, homosexuality, marriage of priests, and admission of women to the priesthood. In Israel, hyperorthodox Jews known as *haredim* played a leading role in settling the West Bank and Gaza, the Palestinian territories captured by Israel in 1967, and vehemently resisted both Israel's unilateral withdrawal from Gaza in 2005 and subsequent plans for withdrawal from parts of the West Bank. And in India, Hindu zealots made the BJP party a powerful political force (see above).

Yet Islam became the focus of most discussions of faith and politics. The birth of the Islamic Republic of Iran in the revolution of 1979 made the current of Muslim political assertiveness, which had been building in several Muslim countries for twenty years, visible to all. But by the year 2000 acts of **terrorism** perpetrated by non-Iranian Muslim groups claiming to be acting for religious reasons were capturing the headlines.

Terrorism as a political tactic by which comparatively weak militants used grotesquely inhumane and lethal acts to convince a frightened public that danger is everywhere and the government is incapable of protecting them has a long history. But the instantaneous media links made possible by satellite communications, and the tradition in the news business of publicizing violence, increased its effectiveness from the 1980s onward.

Bombings, kidnappings, and assassinations made political sense to all sorts of political groups: secular Palestinians confronting Israel; national separatists like the Tamils in Sri Lanka, Basques in Spain, and Chechens in Russia; Catholic and Protestant extremists in Northern Ireland; and racialist militias in Rwanda and Darfur, to name a few. But Muslim groups gained the lion's share of attention because they targeted the United States and Europe, concentrated on spectacular attacks, drew from Muslim populations all over the world, and made effective use of video and audio communications from their charismatic leader, **Usama bin Laden.**

Born into a wealthy Saudi family and educated as an engineer, bin Laden fought against the Soviet Union in Afghanistan and there recruited and trained a core group of fighters called al-Qaeda. Though his family disowned him and Saudi Arabia stripped him of his citizenship, his calls for a holy war (*jihad*) and his portrayal of the United States as an evil puppet-master manipulating both non-Muslim (e.g., Israel, India, Russia) and Muslim

Online Study Center

Improve Your Grade

Primary Source: Declaration of Jihad
Against Americans Occupying Land
of the Two Holy Mosques

(e.g., Egypt, Algeria, Saudi Arabia) governments to murder and oppress innocent Muslims made sense to millions of Muslims, even if only a very few committed themselves to follow him into battle.

Al-Qaeda blew up the American embassies in Kenya and Tanzania in 1998, crippled the U.S. Navy destroyer *Cole* while it was making a port call in Yemen in 2000, and then capped everything by crashing hijacked jetliners into the World Trade Center and the Pentagon in 2001. Though the "global war on terrorism" declared in response by President Bush successfully destroyed the Afghan government that had given bin Laden safe haven as well as the dictatorship of Saddam Husain that the United States claimed was a real or potential supporter of terrorism, bin Laden and his primary deputy, the Egyptian Ayman Zawahiri, could not be found. Further terrorist attacks—by Indonesians on tourists on the island of Bali in 2002, by North Africans on commuter trains servicing Madrid in 2004, and by English-born Muslims on the London transit system in 2005—made it clear that the current of violence unleashed by al-Qaeda had become decentralized and that recruits and cells might no longer be taking orders from bin Laden. In the meantime, the primary center of terrorist activity had shifted to Iraq, where suicide bombings became commonplace and a growing insurgency attacked coalition soldiers, the Iraqi citizens who worked for them, and Iraqis who belonged to opposing Muslim sects.

In trying to explain a current of violence that could strike anywhere in the world but seemed to be centered on Muslims, some analysts argued that the religion of Islam encouraged violence against non-Muslims. The counterargument pointed out that terrorists came from many backgrounds and that the vast majority of Muslims saw their religion as one of peace. Others maintained that rigidly conservative Muslims like Usama bin Laden were blindly opposed to freedom and modernity. The counterargument pointed out that al-Qaeda used modern military and propaganda techniques and that many of its operatives, like bin Laden himself, graduated from modern technical programs. A third school of thought felt that the United States instigated al-Qaeda's wrath through policies like supporting Israel and stationing troops in Saudi Arabia. The counterargument pointed out that the United States had also championed the Muslim cause in Bosnia and driven the secular dictator

Saddam Husain out of Kuwait, an act that most Arab governments supported.

Whether Islam and the West were destined to fight one another in a "clash of civilizations," as political scientist Samuel Huntington predicted, or whether their differences would eventually be resolved within a common "Islamo-Christian civilization," as Richard W. Bulliet maintained in response to Huntington, fear of terrorism became pervasive throughout the world, and many peaceful Muslims found themselves suspect because of their beliefs.

Universal Rights and Values

Alongside the growing influence of religion on politics, efforts to promote adherence to universal standards of human rights also expanded. Religious leaders had been the first to voice the notion that all people are equal, but the modern human rights movement grew out of the secular statements of the French Declaration of the Rights of Man (1789) and the U.S. Constitution (1788) and Bill of Rights (1791). Over the next century, the logic of universal rights moved Westerners to undertake international campaigns to end slave trading and slavery throughout the world and to secure equal legal rights (and eventually voting rights) for women.

International organizations in the twentieth century secured agreement on labor standards, the rules of war, and the rights of refugees. The pinnacle of these efforts was the **Universal Declaration of Human Rights,** passed by the United Nations General Assembly in 1948, which proclaimed itself "a common standard of achievement for all peoples and nations." Its thirty articles condemned slavery, torture, cruel and inhuman punishment, and arbitrary arrest, detention, and exile. The Declaration called for freedom of movement, assembly, and thought. It asserted rights to life, liberty, and security of person; to impartial public trials; and to education, employment, and leisure. The principle of equality was most fully articulated in Article 2:

> Everyone is entitled to all the rights and freedoms set forth in this Declaration, without distinction of any kind, such as race, color, sex, language, religion, or political or other opinion, national or social origin, property, birth or other status.[2]

This passage reflected an international consensus against racism and imperialism and a growing acceptance of the importance of social and economic equality. Most newly independent countries joining the United Nations willingly signed the Declaration because it implicitly condemned European colonial regimes.

The idea of universal human rights has not gone unchallenged. Some have asked whether a set of principles whose origins are so clearly Western can be called universal. Others have been uneasy with the idea of subordinating the traditional values of their culture or religion to a broader philosophical standard. Despite these objections, important gains have been made in implementing these standards.

Besides the official actions of the United Nations and various national governments, individual human rights activists, often working through international philanthropic bodies known as **nongovernmental organizations (NGOs)**, have been important forces for promoting human rights. Amnesty International, founded in 1961 and numbering 1.8 million members in 162 countries by the 1990s, concentrates on gaining the freedom of people who have been tortured or imprisoned without trial and campaigns against summary execution by government death squads or other gross violations of rights. Arguing that no right is more fundamental than the right to life, other NGOs have devoted themselves to famine relief, refugee assistance, and health care around the world. Médecins Sans Frontières (Doctors Without Borders), founded in 1971, was awarded the Nobel Peace Prize for 1999 for the medical assistance it offered in scores of crisis situations.

While NGOs often worked on individual situations in specific countries, other universal goals became enshrined in international agreements. Such agreements have made genocide a crime and have promoted environmental protection of the seas, of Antarctica, and of the atmosphere. The United States and a few other nations were greatly concerned that such treaties would unduly limit their sovereignty or threaten their national interests. For this reason the U.S. Congress delayed ratifying the 1949 convention on genocide until 1986. More recently the United States drew widespread international criticism for demanding exemption for Americans from the jurisdiction of the International Criminal Court, created in 2002 to try international criminals, and for declaring that "enemy combatants" taken prisoner during the "global war on terrorism" should not be treated in accordance with the Third Geneva Convention (1950) on humane treatment of prisoners of war. While these two actions grew out of America's acknowledged role as the one superpower capable of intervening in military crises anywhere in the world, the American withdrawal in 2001 from the 1997 Kyoto Protocol requiring industrial nations to sharply reduce emissions of pollutants that damage the atmosphere (see Environment and Technology: Global Warming) reflected a purely economic interest, namely, a fear that curbing emissions would impose great cost on power producers, vehicle makers, and manufacturers.

Women's Rights

The women's rights movement, which began on both sides of the North Atlantic in the nineteenth century, became an important human rights issue in the twentieth century. Rights for women became accepted in Western countries and were enshrined in the constitutions of many nations newly freed from colonial rule. In 1979 the United Nations General Assembly adopted the Convention on the Elimination of

Beijing Women's Conference in 1995 This gathering of women from every part of the world, under United Nations auspices, illustrated the challenges posed by women's search for equality. The Chinese government, consistent with its policies of suppressing dissent and closely regulating social life, tried to limit press access to the conference. As in many other instances, these efforts to silence or control women's voices on issues like abortion and family planning proved ineffective. (Boulat/Sipa Press)

Global Warming

Until the 1980s environmental alarms focused mainly on localized episodes of air and water pollution, exposure to toxic substances, waste management, and the disappearance of wilderness. The development of increasingly powerful computers and complex models of ecological interactions in the 1990s, however, made people aware of the global scope of certain environmental problems.

Many scientists and policymakers came to perceive global warming, the slow increase of the temperature of the earth's lower atmosphere, as an environmental threat requiring preventive action on an international scale. The warming is caused by a layer of atmospheric gases (carbon dioxide, methane, nitrous oxide, and ozone) that allow solar radiation to reach earth and warm it but that keep infrared energy (heat) from radiating from earth's surface into space. Called the *greenhouse effect*, this process normally keeps the earth's temperature at a level suitable for life. However, increases in greenhouse-gas emissions—particularly from the burning of fossil fuels in industry and transportation—have added to this insulating atmospheric layer.

Recent events have confirmed predictions of global temperature increases and melting glaciers and icecaps. Globally, the five warmest years on record were 1995, 1997, 1998, 2001, and 2002. Record heat hit northern Europe in the summer of 2003. Greenland glaciers and Arctic Ocean sea ice melted at record rates during 2002, and a huge section of the Antarctic ice shelf broke up and floated away. Andean glaciers are shrinking so fast they could disappear in a decade, imperiling water supplies for drinking, irrigation, and hydroelectric production. Drought has affected much of the United States in recent years, and in 2002 Australia experienced the "Big Dry," its worst drought in a century.

Despite this evidence, governments of the industrialized countries that produce the most greenhouse gasses have been slow to adopt measures stringent enough to reduce emissions because of the negative effects they believe this could have on their economies. There is also fear that it may be already too late to reverse global warming. The pledges that representatives from 178 countries made at the first Earth Summit in Rio de Janeiro in 1992 to limit their *increase* in greenhouse-gas production have so far been ineffective. Fearing limits on gas emissions could cripple their plans for industrial and economic expansion, many nations hesitated to sign the 1997 Kyoto Protocol, the first international agreement to impose penalties on countries that failed to cut greenhouse-gas emissions. It was a major environmental victory when Japan added its signature in March 2001, but to the consternation of many world leaders President George W. Bush rejected the agreement. Ostensibly, he acted because he was unconvinced by the scientific evidence for global warming and reluctant to impose burdens on American businesses, but global security concerns also made the environment a lower American priority. Until the destructive effects of global warming, such as the inundation of coastal regions and large cities by rising sea levels, match the destruction of terrorists, the political focus is unlikely to shift.

Flooding in Bangladesh   Typhoon-driven floods submerge the low-lying farmlands of Bangladesh with tragic regularity. Any significant rise in the sea level will make parts of the country nearly uninhabitable.   (D. Aubert/Sygma)

All Forms of Discrimination Against Women, and in 1985 the first international conference on the status of women, sponsored by the United Nations Division for the Advancement of Women, was held in Nairobi, Kenya. A second conference in Beijing ten years later added momentum to the women's rights movement. By 2006, 183 countries had endorsed the 1979 convention.

Besides highlighting the similarity of the problems women face around the world, international conferences have also revealed great variety in the views and concerns of women. Feminists from the West, who had been accustomed to dictating the agenda and who had pushed for the liberation of women in other parts of the world, sometimes found themselves accused of having narrow concerns and condescending attitudes. Some non-Western women complained about Western feminists' endorsement of sexual liberation and about the deterioration of family life in the West. They found Western feminists' concern with matters such as comfortable clothing misplaced and trivial compared to the issues of poverty and disease.

Other cultures came in for their share of criticism. Western women and many secular leaders in Muslim countries protested Islam's requirement that a woman cover her head and wear loose-fitting garments to conceal the shape of her body, practices enforced by law in countries such as Iran and Saudi Arabia. Nevertheless, many outspoken Muslim women voluntarily donned concealing garments as expressions of personal belief, statements of resistance to secular dictatorship, or defense against coarse male behavior. Much Western criticism focused on the African custom of circumcising girls, a form of genital mutilation that can cause chronic infections or permanently impair sexual enjoyment. While not denying the problems this practice can lead to, many African women saw deteriorating economic conditions, rape, and AIDS as more important issues (see Figure 34.1).

The conferences were more important for the attention they focused on women's issues than for the solutions they generated. The search for a universally accepted women's rights agenda proved elusive because of local concerns and strong disagreement on abortion and other issues. Nevertheless, increases in women's education, access to employment, political participation, and control of fertility augured well for the eventual achievement of gender equality.

Such efforts raised the prominence of human rights as a global concern and put pressure on governments to consider human rights when making foreign policy decisions. Skeptics observed, however, that a Western country could successfully prod a non-Western country to

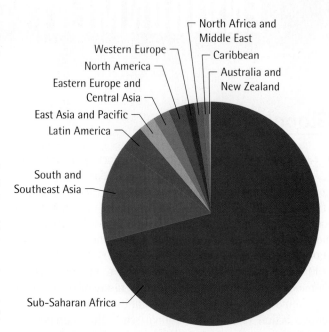

Figure 34.1 World Distribution of HIV/AIDS Cases (2001 estimates) *Source:* United Nations AIDS and World Health Organization, *Report on the Global HIV/AIDS Epidemic* (June 2000).

improve its human rights performance—for example, by granting women more equal access to education and careers—but that reverse criticism of a Western country often fell on deaf ears—for example, condemnation of the death penalty in the United States. For such critics the human rights movement was seen not as an effort to make the world more humane but as another form of Western cultural imperialism, a club with which to beat former colonial societies into submission. Still, support for universal rights has grown, especially because increasing globalization has made common standards of behavior more important.

GLOBAL CULTURE

Along with the human rights movement, other kinds of cultural globalization were also proceeding rapidly at the turn of the millennium. A global language, a global educational system, and global forms of artistic expression have all come into being. Trade, travel, and migration have made a common culture necessary. Electronic communications that were once confined to members of a jet-setting elite have enabled global cultural influences to move deeper into many societies, and a sort of global popular culture has also emerged. These changes have angered some and delighted others.

The Media and the Message

Although cultural influences from every continent travel around the world, the fact that the most pervasive elements of global culture have their origins in the West raises concerns in many quarters about **cultural imperialism**. Critics complain that entertainment conglomerates are flooding the world's movie theaters and television screens with Western tastes and styles and that manufacturers are flooding world markets with Western goods—both relying on sophisticated advertising techniques that promote consumption and cultural conformity. In this view, global marketing is an especially insidious effort not only to overwhelm the world with a single Western outlook shaped by capitalist ideology, but also to suppress or devalue traditional cultures and alternative ideologies. As the leader of the capitalist world, the United States is seen as the primary culprit.

But in truth, technology plays a more central role than ideology in spreading Western culture. Even though imperialist forces old and new shape choices, strongly democratic forces are also at work as people around the world make their selections in the cultural marketplace. Thus, a diversity of voices is more characteristic of cultural globalization than the cultural imperialism thesis maintains.

The pace of cultural globalization began to quicken during the economic recovery after World War II. The Hollywood films and American jazz recordings that had become popular in Europe and parts of Asia continued to spread. But the birth of electronic technology opened contacts with large numbers of people who could never have afforded to go to a movie or buy a record.

The first step was the development of cheap transistor radios that could run for months on a couple of small batteries. Perfected by American scientists at Bell Telephone Laboratories in 1948, solid-state electronic transistors replaced power-hungry and less reliable electron tubes in radios and a wide array of other devices. Just as tube radios had spread in Europe and America in the decades before the war, small portable transistor radios, most made in Japan and elsewhere in Asia, spread rapidly in parts of the world where homes lacked electricity.

Because the transistor radios sold in Asia and Africa were designed to receive shortwave broadcasts, they brought people in remote villages the news, views, and music that American, European, Soviet, and Chinese transmitters beamed to the world. For the first time in history, the whole world could learn of major political and cultural events simultaneously. Although such broadcasts came in local and regional languages, many were in English. Electronic audiotape and CD players added to the diversity of music available to individuals everywhere.

Television, made possible by the invention of an electron scanning gun in 1928, became widely available to consumers in Western countries in the 1950s. In poorer parts of the world TVs were not common until the 1980s and 1990s, after mass production and cheap transistors made sets more affordable and reliable. Outside the United States, television broadcasting was usually a government monopoly at first, following the pattern of telegraph and postal service and radio broadcasting. Governments expected news reports and other programming to disseminate a unified national viewpoint.

Government monopolies eroded as the high cost of television production opened up global markets for rebroadcasts of American soap operas, adventure series, and situation comedies. By the 1990s a global network of satellites brought privately owned television broadcasting to even remote areas of the world, and the VCR (videocassette recorder) brought an even greater variety of programs to people everywhere. In the following decade DVD players continued the trend. British programs found a secondary market in the United States, Canada, Australia, and other countries. As a result of wider circulation of programming, people often became familiar with different dialects of English and other languages. People in Portugal, for example, who in the 1960s had found it difficult to understand Brazilian Portuguese, have become avid fans of Brazilian soap operas. Immigrants from Albania and North Africa often arrive in Italy with a command of Italian learned from Italian stations whose signals they could pick up at home.

Further internationalization of culture resulted from satellite transmission of TV signals. Specializing in rock music videos aimed at a youth audience, MTV (Music Television) became an international enterprise offering special editions in different parts of the world. Music videos shown in Uzbekistan, for example, often featured Russian bands, and Chinese groups appeared in MTV programs shown in Singapore. CNN (Cable News Network) expanded its international market after becoming the most-viewed and informative news source during the 1991 Persian Gulf War, when it broadcast live from Baghdad. CNN's fundamentally American view of the news stimulated broadcasters in other countries to develop their own round-the-clock coverage. Al-Jazeera, based in the Persian Gulf emirate of Qatar, broadcast various statements by Usama bin Laden from 2001 onward and offered video footage and interpretation that differed greatly from American news coverage after the war in Iraq began in 2003.

The Internet, a linkage of academic, government, and business computer networks developed in the 1960s, began to transform world culture in the early years of the twenty-first century. Personal computers proliferated in the 1980s, and with the establishment of the easy-to-use graphic interface of the World Wide Web in 1994, the number of Internet users skyrocketed. Myriad new companies formed to exploit "e-commerce," the commercial dimension of the Internet, and college students were soon spending less time studying conventional books and scholarly resources than they were exploring the Web for information and entertainment. Blogs, or weblogs, offered a vehicle for anyone in the world to place his or her opinions, experiences, and creative efforts before anyone with access to a computer.

As had happened so often throughout history, technological developments had unanticipated consequences. Although the new telecommunications and entertainment technologies derived disproportionately from American invention, industry, and cultural creativity, Japan and other East Asian nations came to dominate the manufacture and refinement of computer devices. In the 1990s Japan introduced digital television broadcasting at about the time that disks containing digitized movies and computer programs with movielike action became increasingly available. High-definition television (HDTV), mostly in digital format, debuted in the first decade of the twenty-first century and seemed destined to become the global standard. At the miniaturized end of the visual scale, cell phones became increasingly used for taking and transmitting pictures and connecting to the Internet.

Japanese Adult Male Comic Book After World War II comic magazines emerged as a major form of publication and a distinctive product of culture in Japan. Different series are directed to different age and gender groups. Issued weekly and running to some three hundred pages in black and white, the most popular magazines sell as many copies as do major newsmagazines in the United States. (Private Collection)

The Spread of Pop Culture

New technologies changed perceptions of culture as well as its distribution around the world and among different social classes. For most of history, popular culture was folk culture, highly localized ways of dress, food, music, and expression. Only the educated and urban few had access to the riches of a broader "great tradition," such as Confucianism in East Asia or Western culture in Europe and the Americas. The schools of modern nation-states promoted national values and beliefs, as well as tastes in painting, literature, and art. Governments also promoted a common language or dialect and frequently suppressed local traditions and languages. In a more democratic way, the transistor helped break down barriers and create a global popular culture that transcended regional great traditions and national cultures.

Initially, the content of **global pop culture** was heavily American. Singer Michael Jackson was almost as well known to the youth of Dar-es-Salaam (Tanzania) and Bangkok (Thailand) as to American fans. Basketball star Michael Jordan became a worldwide celebrity, heavily promoted by Nike, McDonald's, and television. American television programs such as Wheel of Fortune and Friends acquired immense followings and inspired local imitations. American movies, which had long had great popular appeal, steadily increased their share of world markets.

Internet Search Engine
Students, journalists, researchers, and virtually everyone else who had access to the Internet became accustomed to using search engines like Google to get incredibly fast information on any subject imaginable. (Screenshot © Google Inc. Used with permission.)

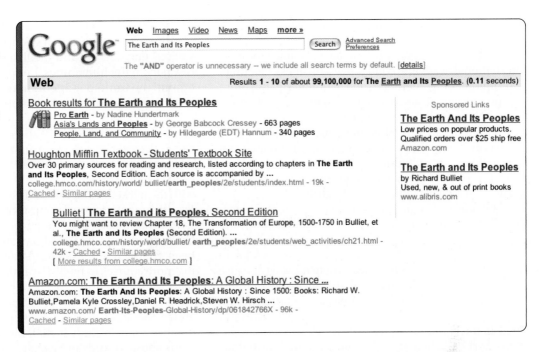

But the United States did not have a lock on global pop culture. Latin American soap operas, *telenovelas*, had a vast following in the Americas, eastern Europe, and elsewhere. Bombay, India, long the largest producer of films in the world, began to make more films for an international audience, rather than just for the home market. And the highly successful martial arts filmmakers of Hong Kong saw their style flourish in high-budget international spectaculars like director Ang Lee's Academy Award–winning *Crouching Tiger, Hidden Dragon* (2000), and the *Matrix* trilogy (1999–2003), which relied heavily on the skills of Hong Kong fight choreographers

Emerging Global Culture

While the globalization of popular culture has been criticized, cultural links across national and ethnic boundaries at a more elite level have generated little controversy. The end of the Cold War reopened intellectual and cultural contacts between former adversaries, making possible such things as Russian-American collaboration on space missions and extensive business contacts among former rivals. The English language, modern science, and higher education became the key elements of this **global elite culture**.

The emergence of English as the first global language depended on developments that had been building for centuries. The British Empire introduced the language to far-flung colonies. When the last parts of the empire gained independence after World War II, most former colonies chose to continue using English as an official language because it provided national unity and a link to the outside world that the dozens or hundreds of local languages could not. After independence, representatives of former British colonies formed the Commonwealth on the basis of their shared language and commercial ties. Newly independent countries that made a local language official for nationalist reasons often found the decision counterproductive. Indian nationalists had pushed for Hindi to be India's official language, but they found that students taught in Hindi were unable to compete internationally because of poor knowledge of English. Sri Lanka, which had made Sinhala its official language in 1956, reversed itself after local reporters revealed in 1989 that prominent officials were sending their children to English-medium private schools.

The use of English as a second language was greatly stimulated by the importance of the United States in postwar world affairs. Individuals recognized the importance of mastering English for successful business, diplomatic, and military careers. After the collapse of Soviet domination, students in eastern Europe flocked to study English instead of Russian. Ninety percent of students in Cambodia (a former French colony) chose to study English, even though a Canadian agency offered a sizable cash bonus if they would study French. In the 1990s China made the study of English as a second language nearly universal from junior high school onwards, but it also forced an English-medium school in Hong Kong to teach most subjects in Chinese.

English has become the language of choice for most international academic conferences, business meetings, and diplomatic gatherings. International organizations that provide equal status to many languages, such as the United Nations and the European Union, tend to conduct all informal committee meetings in English. English has even replaced Latin as the working language for international consultations in the Catholic Church. In cities throughout the world, signs and notices are now posted in the local language and English.

The utility of English as a global language is also evident in the emergence of an international literature in English (see Diversity and Dominance: World Literature in English). The trend has been evident for decades in former British colonies in Africa, where most writers use English to reach both a national audience and an international one. Wole Soyinka, the first sub-Saharan African to win the Nobel Prize in literature for 1986, wrote in English, the national language of Nigeria, rather than his native Yoruba. When Arundhati Roy won the prestigious Booker Prize in 1997 for *The God of Small Things,* a novel set in her native state of Kerala in southwest India, she was part of an English-language literary tradition that has been growing in India for a century. V. S. Naipaul of Trinidad, winner of the Nobel Prize in literature for 2001, is a good example of the way global migration has fostered the use of English. Naipaul's ancestors had emigrated from India in the nineteenth century.

World literature remains highly diverse in form and language, but science and technology have become standardized components of global culture. Though imperialism helped spread the Western disciplines of biology, chemistry, and physics around the world, their popularity continued to expand even after imperial systems ended because they worked so much better than other approaches to the natural world. Their truth was universal even if plants and animals continue to be classified in Latin and the less common elements are called by names originally derived from Latin and Greek. Global manufacturing could not function without a common system of applied science. Because of their scientific basis Western medicine and drugs are increasingly accepted as the best treatments, even though many cultures also use traditional remedies.

The third pillar of global elite culture is the university. The structure and curricula of modern universities are nearly indistinguishable around the world, permitting students today to cross national boundaries as freely as students in the Latin West or the Muslim world did in medieval times. Instruction in the pure sciences

varies little from place to place, and standardization is nearly as common in social science and applied sciences such as engineering and medicine. There may be more diversity in the humanities, but professors and students around the world pay attention to the latest literary theories and topics of historical interest.

While university subjects are taught in many languages, instruction in English is spreading rapidly. Because discoveries are often first published in English, advanced students in science, business, and international relations need to know that language to keep up with the latest developments. The global mobility of professors and students also promotes classroom instruction in the most global language. Many courses in the Netherlands and in Scandinavian countries have long been offered in English, and elsewhere in Europe offering more courses in English was the obvious way to facilitate the EU's efforts to encourage students to study outside their countries of origin. When South Africa ended the apartheid educational systems that had required people to study in their own languages, most students chose to study in English.

Because global elite culture is so deeply rooted in years of training, complex institutions, and practical utility, it is less subject to fads and commercial promotion than is global pop culture. Because such elite culture is confined to a distinct minority in most places, it poses little threat to national and folk cultures and, therefore, is much less controversial.

Enduring Cultural Diversity

Although protesters regularly denounce the "Americanization" of the world, a closer look suggests that cultural globalization is more complex and multifaceted. Just as English has largely spread as a second language, so global culture is primarily a second culture that dominates some contexts but does not displace other traditions. From this perspective, American music, fast food, and fashions are more likely to add to a society's options than to displace local culture.

Japan first demonstrated that a country with a non-Western culture could perform at a high industrial level. Individuality was less valued in Japan than the ability of each person to fit into a group, whether as an employee, a member of an athletic team, or a student in a class. Moreover, the Japanese considered it unmannerly to directly contradict, correct, or refuse the request of another person. From a Western point of view, these Japanese customs seemed to discourage individual initiative and personality development and to preserve traditional

World Literature
in English

The linguistic diversity of the world is part of its richness, but it is also an impediment to global communication. In this essay novelist and Indian diplomat Shashi Tharoor explains why he chooses to write in English. His decision to use English is not unusual among writers in India and many other lands where English is not the first language. Mr. Tharoor has worked for the United Nations since 1978. In 2002 he became Under-Secretary-General for Communications and Public Information.

For the record, the national languages of India are Hindi (spoken by 30 percent of the population) and English, which dominates communication among India's elite. Fourteen other languages are official at the provincial level, with English having official status in the provinces of East Bengal, Kerala, and Orissa.

As an Indian writer living in New York, I find myself constantly asked a question with which my American confreres never have to contend: "But whom do you write for?" In my case, the question is complicated by both geography and language. I live in the United States (because of my work at the United Nations) and I write about India; and I do so in English, a language mastered, if the last census is to be believed, by only 2 percent of the Indian population. There is an unspoken accusation implicit in the question: Am I not guilty of the terrible sin of inauthenticity, of writing about my country for foreigners? . . .

This is ironic, because few developments in world literature have been more remarkable than the emergence, over the last two decades, of a new generation of Indian writers in English.

Beginning with Salman Rushdie's *Midnight's Children* in 1981, they have expanded the boundaries of their craft and their nation's literary heritage, enriching English with the rhythms of ancient legends and the larger-then-life complexities of another civilization, while reinventing India in the confident cadences of English prose. Of the unintended consequences of empire, it is hard to imagine one of greater value to both colonizers and colonized.

The new Indian writers dip into a deep well of memory and experience far removed from those of their fellow novelists in the English language. But whereas Americans or Englishmen or Australians have also set their fictions in distant lands Indians write of India without exoticism, their insights undimmed by the dislocations of foreignness. And they do so in an English they have both learned and lived, an English of freshness and vigor, a language that is as natural to them as their quarrels at the school playground or the surreptitious notes they slipped each other in their classrooms.

Yet Indian critics still suggest that there is something artificial and un-Indian about an Indian writing in English. One critic disparagingly declared that the acid test ought to be, "Could this have been written only by an Indian?" I have never been much of a literary theoretician—I always felt that for a writer to study literature at university would be like learning about girls at medical school—but for most, though not all, of my own writing, I would answer that my works could not only have been written only by an Indian, but only by an Indian *in English.*

I write for anyone who will read me, but first of all for Indians like myself, Indians who have grown up speaking, writing, playing, wooing and quarreling in English, all over India. (No writer really chooses a language: the circumstances of his upbringing ensure that the language chooses him.)

Members of this class have entered the groves of academe and condemned themselves in terms of bitter self-reproach: one Indian scholar, Harish Trivedi, has asserted (in English) that Indian writers in that language are "cut off from the experiential mainstream and from that common cultural matrix . . . shared with writers of all other Indian languages." Dr. Trivedi metaphorically cites the fictional English-medium school in an R. K. Narayan story where the students must first rub off the sandalwood-paste caste marks from their foreheads before they enter its portals: "For this golden gate is only for the déraciné to pass through, for those who have erased their antecedents." [R. K. Narayan (1906–2001) pioneered writing in English in Madras in the 1930s, publishing three dozen novels and many short stories and essays.]

It's an evocative image, even though I thought the secular Indian state was supposed to encourage the erasure of casteism from the classroom. But the more important point is that writers like myself do share a "common cultural matrix," albeit one devoid of helpfully identifying caste marks. It is one that consists of an urban upbringing and a pannational outlook on the Indian reality. I do not think this is any less authentically "Indian" than the worldviews of writers in other Indian languages. Why should the rural peasant or the small-town schoolteacher with his sandalwood-smeared forehead be considered more quintessentially Indian than the punning collegian or the Bombay socialite, who are as much a part of the Indian reality?

India is a vast and complex country; in Whitman's phrase, it contains multitudes. I write of an India of multiple truths and multiple realities, an India that is greater than the sum of its parts. English expresses that diversity better than any Indian language precisely because it is not "rooted" in any one region of my vast country. At the same time, as an Indian, I remain conscious of, and connected to, my pre-urban and non-Anglophone antecedents: my novels reflect an intellectual heritage that embraces the ancient epic the Mahabharata, the Kerala folk dance called the ottamthullal (of which my father was a gifted practitioner) and the Hindi B-movies of Bollywood [the large movie-making industry of Bombay], as well as Shakespeare, Wodehouse and the Beatles.

As a first-generation urbanite myself, I keep returning to the Kerala villages of my parents, in my life as in my writing. Yet I have grown up in Bombay, Calcutta and Delhi, Indian cities a thousand miles apart from one another; the mother of my children is half-Kashmiri, half-Bengali; and my own mother now lives in the southern town of Coimbatore. This may be a wider cultural matrix than the good Dr. Trivedi imagined, but it draws from a rather broad range of Indian experience. And English is the language that brings those various threads of my India together, the language in which my wife could speak to her mother-in-law, the language that enables a Calcuttan to function in Coimbatore, the language that serves to express the complexity of that polyphonous Indian experience better than any other language I know.

As a novelist, I believe in distracting in order to instruct— my novels are, to some degree, didactic works masquerading as entertainments. Like Molière I believe that you have to entertain in order to edify. But the entertainment, and the edification, might strike different readers differently.

My first novel, The Great Indian Novel, as a satirical reinvention of the Mahabharata inevitably touches Indians in a way that most foreigners will not fully appreciate. But my publishers in the West enjoyed its stories and the risks it took with narrative form. My second, Show Business, did extremely well with American reviewers and readers, who enjoyed the way I tried to portray the lives and stories of Bollywood as a metaphor for Indian society. With India: From Midnight to the Millennium, an attempt to look back at the last 50 years of India's history, I found an additional audience of Indian-Americans seeking to rediscover their roots; their interest has helped the American edition outsell the Indian one.

In my new novel, Riot, for the first time I have major non-Indian characters, Americans as it happens, and that is bound to influence the way the book is perceived in the United States, and in India. Inevitably the English fundamentally affects the content of each book, but it does not determine the audience of the writer; as long as translations exist, language is a vehicle, not a destination.

Of course, there is no shame in acknowledging that English is the legacy of the colonial connection, but one no less useful and valid than the railway, the telegraphs or the law courts that were also left behind by the British. Historically, English helped us to find our Indian voice: that great Indian nationalist Jawaharlal Nehru wrote The Discovery of India in English. But the eclipse of that dreadful phrase "the Indo-Anglian novel" has occurred precisely because Indian writers have evolved well beyond the British connection to their native land.

The days when Indians wrote novels in English either to flatter or rail against their colonial masters are well behind us. Now we have Indians in India writing as naturally about themselves in English as Australians or South Africans do, and their tribe has been supplemented by India's rich diaspora in the United States, which has already produced a distinctive crop of impressive novelists, with Pulitzer Prizes and National Book Awards to their names.

Their addresses don't matter because writers really live inside their heads and on the page, and geography is merely a circumstance. They write secure of themselves in a heritage of diversity, and they write free of the anxiety of audience, for theirs are narratives that appeal as easily to Americans as to Indians—and indeed to readers irrespective of ethnicity.

Surely that's the whole point about literature—that for a body of fiction to constitute a literature it must rise above its origins, its setting, even its language, to render accessible to a reader anywhere some insight into the human condition. Read my books and those of other Indian writers not because we're Indian, not necessarily because you are interested in India; but because they are worth reading in and of themselves. And dear reader, whoever you are, if you pick up one of my books, ask not for whom I write: I write for you.

QUESTIONS FOR ANALYSIS

1. What does Shashi Tharoor mean when he states that his novels could only have been written in English?

2. What is the relationship between national literature and global literature?

3. What does the author mean when he says that for writers "geography is merely a circumstance"?

Source: Shashi Tharoor, "A Bedeviling Question in the Cadence of English," New York Times, July 30, 2001. Copyright © 2001 by Shashi Tharoor. Originally published in The New York Times. All rights reserved. Reprinted by arrangement with Mary Evans Inc.

hierarchies. Japanese women, for example, even though they often worked outside the home, responded only slowly to the American and European feminist advocacy of equality in economic and social relations. However, the Japanese approach to social relations was well suited to an industrial economy. The efficiency, pride in workmanship, and group solidarity of Japanese workers, supported by closely coordinated government and corporate policies, played a major role in transforming Japan from a defeated nation with a demolished industrial base in 1945 to an economic power by the 1980s.

Japan's success in the modern industrial world called into question the older assumption that successful industrialization required the adoption of Western culture. As awareness of the economic impact of Japanese culture and society began to spread, it became apparent that Taiwan and South Korea, along with Singapore and Hong Kong (a British colony before being reunited with China in 1997), were developing dynamic industrial economies of their own. The prospect of India and the People's Republic of China following the same path led many observers to surmise that by the end of the twenty-first century, the United States and Europe would no longer dominate the globe in industrial creativity and might. This does not mean that the world's culture diversity is secure. Every decade a number of minority languages cease to be spoken, usually as the result of the spread of national languages. Many religious practices are also disappearing in the face of the successful expansion of Islam, Christianity, and other religions, although secular values also play a role. Televised national ceremonies or performances for tourists may prevent folk customs and costumes from dying out, but they also tend to standardize rituals that once had many local variations. While it was possible to recognize the nationality of people from their clothing and grooming a century ago, today most urban men dress the same the world over, although women's clothing shows much greater variety. As much as one may regret the disappearance or commercialization of some folkways, most anthropologists would agree that change is characteristic of all healthy cultures. What doesn't change risks extinction.

CONCLUSION

Have we entered a golden age, or is the world descending into a fiery abyss? The future is unknowable, but the study of history suggests that neither extreme is likely. Golden ages and dark ages are rare, and our understanding of our own time is easily swayed by hopes, fears, and other emotions. If the exuberant optimism of the 1990s now seems excessive, the pessimism of the early 2000s may in time seem equally far off the mark.

What is undeniable is that the turn of the millennium has been a time of important global changes. The Iron Curtain that had divided Europe since the end of the Second World War fell, taking with it the tensions and risks of the Cold War. The great Soviet Empire broke up, while dozens of countries joined new economic coalitions. The bastions of communism embraced capitalism with varying degrees of enthusiasm. As trading barriers tumbled, world trade surged, creating new wealth and new inequalities in its distribution. Yet international terrorism and the proliferation of nuclear weapons cast shadows on the future, and the aggressive response of the United States to the attacks of 9/11 caused some people to worry about a new form of superpower imperialism.

History teaches that change is always uneven. The rate of change in global telecommunications and international economic institutions was notably faster than in international political institutions. The nation-state remained supreme. The structure of the United Nations was little different than at its founding six decades earlier. States resisted limits on their autonomy, and the more powerful ones took unilateral actions, whether supported or opposed by international public opinion. Rather than giving ground to globalization, many older ideas and values continued to be strong. The less powerful adapted slowly, dug in their heels to resist change, or raised voices and fists against it. Protests forced new attention on global poverty, disease, exploitation, and environmental damage that globalization caused or failed to relieve. Adjustments were made, but on the whole change on these fronts also came slowly. It is possible that historians surveying the broad sweep of history will one day conclude that the attacks of 9/11 constituted a watershed that significantly deflected the world's political evolution. But it is equally possible that the most potent development of the first decade of the twenty-first century will ultimately prove to be the Internet, with its unlimited potential for affecting the course of cultural change throughout the world.

KEY TERMS

globalization   *p. 998*
World Trade Organization (WTO)   *p. 1003*
weapons of mass destruction   *p. 1005*
terrorism   *p. 1008*
Usama bin Laden   *p. 1008*
Universal Declaration of Human Rights
   p. 1009

nongovernmental organizations (NGOs)
   p. 1010
cultural imperialism   *p. 1013*
global pop culture   *p. 1014*
global elite culture   *p. 1015*

Online Study Center
Improve Your Grade
Flashcards

SUGGESTED READING

Among those attempting to describe the world at the turn of the millennium are Benjamin R. Barber, *Jihad vs. McWorld: How Globalism and Tribalism Are Reshaping the World* (1995); Thomas L. Friedman, *The Lexus and the Olive Tree* (1999); Samuel P. Huntington, *The Clash of Civilizations and the Remaking of the World Order* (1996); Paul Kennedy, *Preparing for the Twenty-first Century* (1993); and Richard W. Bulliet, *The Case for Islamo-Christian Civilization* (2004).

Recent studies of American military policies and the widening split with Europe include Dana Priest, *The Mission: Waging War and Keeping Peace with America's Military* (2003); Robert Kaplan, *Of Paradise and Power: America and Europe in the New World Order* (2002); Charles A. Kulpchan, *The End of the American Era: U.S. Foreign Policy and the Geopolitics of the Twenty-first Century* (2002); and Joseph S. Nye, Jr., *The Paradox of American Power: Why the World's Only Superpower Can't Go It Alone* (2002).

Mike Moore, a former director-general of the WTO, provides an insider's view of the global economy in *A World Without Walls: Freedom, Development, Free Trade and Global Governance* (2003). Amy Chua, *World on Fire: How Exporting Free Market Democracy Breeds Ethnic Hatred and Global Instability* (2003), offers a quite different perspective.

Among the many books on the Middle East crisis are Mahmood Mamdani, *Good Muslim, Bad Muslim: America, the Cold War, and the Roots of Terror* (2004); Fawaz Gerges, *The Far Enemy: Why Jihad Went Global* (2005); and Rashid Khalidi, *Resurrecting Empire: Western Footprints and America's Perilous Path in the Middle East* (2004). Terrorism is well covered by Bruce Hoffman, *Inside Terrorism*, 2nd ed. (2006), and Mia Bloom, *Dying to Kill: The Allure of Suicide Terror* (2005).

Standard reviews of human rights include Thomas Buergenthal et al., *International Human Rights in a Nutshell*, 3rd ed. (2002); Carol Devine and Carol Rae Hansen, *Human Rights: The Essential Reference* (1999); and Jack Donnelly, *International Human Rights*, 2nd ed. (1998). Ronald Inglehart and Pippa Norris, *Rising Tide: Gender Equality and Cultural Change Around the World* (2003), surveys the condition of women.

The interrelationships between high culture and popular culture during the twentieth century are treated from different perspectives in Arjun Appadurai, *Modernity at Large: Cultural Dimensions of Globalization* (1996); Peter L. Berger and Samuel Huntington, eds., *Many Globalizations: Cultural Diversity in the Contemporary World* (2002); Tyler Cowen, *Creative Destruction: How Globalization Is Changing the World's Cultures* (2002); and Diana Crane, Nobuko Kawashima, and Kenichi Kawasaka, eds., *Global Culture: Media Arts, Policy* (2002). Two very readable books by James B. Twitchell detail the rise of popular culture in the United States and present various reactions to this phenomenon: *Carnival Culture: The Trashing of Taste in America* (1992) and *Adcult USA: The Triumph of Advertising in American Culture* (1996).

On global English see David Crystal, *English as a Global Language* (1997); Alistaire Pennycock, *The Cultural Politics of English as an International Language* (1994); and Robert Phillipson, *Linguistic Imperialism* (1992).

NOTES

1. "Liberty's Great Advance," *The Economist*, June 28–July 4, 2003, pp. 5–6.

2. "Universal Declaration of Human Rights," in *Twenty-five Human Rights Documents* (New York: Center for the Study of Human Rights, Columbia University, 1994), 6.

GLOSSARY

The glossary for *The Earth and Its Peoples,* 4/e is for the complete text, Chapters 1 through 34.

Abbasid Caliphate Descendants of the Prophet Muhammad's uncle, al-Abbas, the Abbasids overthrew the **Umayyad Caliphate** and ruled an Islamic empire from their capital in Baghdad (founded 762) from 750 to 1258. (*p. 258*)

abolitionists Men and women who agitated for a complete end to slavery. Abolitionist pressure ended the British transatlantic slave trade in 1808 and slavery in British colonies in 1834. In the United States the activities of abolitionists were one factor leading to the Civil War (1861–1865). (*p. 711*)

acculturation The adoption of the language, customs, values, and behaviors of host nations by immigrants. (*p. 715*)

Acheh Sultanate Muslim kingdom in northern Sumatra. Main center of Islamic expansion in Southeast Asia in the early seventeenth century, it declined after the Dutch seized **Malacca** from Portugal in 1641. (*p. 598*)

Aden Port city in the modern south Arabian country of Yemen. It has been a major trading center in the Indian Ocean since ancient times. (*p. 419*)

African National Congress An organization dedicated to obtaining equal voting and civil rights for black inhabitants of South Africa. Founded in 1912 as the South African Native National Congress, it changed its name in 1923. Though it was banned and its leaders were jailed for many years, it eventually helped bring majority rule to South Africa. (*p. 920*)

Afrikaners South Africans descended from Dutch and French settlers of the seventeenth century. Their Great Trek founded new settler colonies in the nineteenth century. Though a minority among South Africans, they held political power after 1910, imposing a system of racial segregation called apartheid after 1949. (*p. 827*)

Agricultural Revolutions (ancient) The change from food gathering to food production that occurred between ca. 8000 and 2000 B.C.E. Also known as the Neolithic Revolution. (*p. 18*)

agricultural revolution (eighteenth century) The transformation of farming that resulted in the eighteenth century from the spread of new crops, improvements in cultivation techniques and livestock breeding, and the consolidation of small holdings into large farms from which tenants and sharecroppers were forcibly expelled. (*p. 669*)

Aguinaldo, Emilio (1869–1964) Leader of the Filipino independence movement against Spain (1895–1898). He proclaimed the independence of the Philippines in 1899, but his movement was crushed and he was captured by the United States Army in 1901. (*p. 836*)

Akbar I (1542–1605) Most illustrious sultan of the Mughal Empire in India (r. 1556–1605). He expanded the empire and pursued a policy of conciliation with Hindus. (*p. 595*)

Akhenaten Egyptian pharaoh (r. 1353–1335 B.C.E.). He built a new capital at Amarna, fostered a new style of naturalistic art, and created a religious revolution by imposing worship of the sun-disk. The Amarna letters, largely from his reign, preserve official correspondence with subjects and neighbors. (*p. 93*)

Alexander (356–323 B.C.E.) King of Macedonia in northern Greece. Between 334 and 323 B.C.E. he conquered the Persian Empire, reached the Indus Valley, founded many Greek-style cities, and spread Greek culture across the Middle East. Later known as Alexander the Great. (*p. 150*)

Alexandria City on the Mediterranean coast of Egypt founded by Alexander. It became the capital of the Hellenistic kingdom of the **Ptolemies.** It contained the famous Library and the Museum—a center for leading scientific and literary figures. Its merchants engaged in trade with areas bordering the Mediterranean and the Indian Ocean. (*p. 152*)

Allende, Salvador (1908–1973) Socialist politician elected president of Chile in 1970 and overthrown by the military in 1973. He died during the military attack. (*p. 968*)

All-India Muslim League Political organization founded in India in 1906 to defend the interests of India's Muslim minority. Led by Muhammad Ali Jinnah, it attempted to negotiate with the **Indian National Congress.** In 1940, the League began demanding a separate state for Muslims, to be called Pakistan. (See also **Jinnah, Muhammad Ali.**) (*p. 911*)

altepetl An ethnic state in ancient Mesoamerica, the common political building block of that region. (*p. 348*)

amulet Small charm meant to protect the bearer from evil. Found frequently in archaeological excavations in Mesopotamia and Egypt, amulets reflect the religious practices of the common people. (*p. 41*)

Amur River This river valley was a contested frontier between northern China and eastern Russia until the settlement arranged in Treaty of Nerchinsk (1689). (*p. 618*)

anarchists Revolutionaries who wanted to abolish all private property and governments, usually by violence, and replace them with free associations of groups. (*p. 799*)

Anasazi Important culture of what is now the southwest United States (1000–1300 C.E.). Centered on Chaco Canyon in New Mexico and Mesa Verde in Colorado, the Anasazi culture built multistory residences and worshiped in subterranean buildings called kivas. (*p. 352*)

aqueduct A conduit, either elevated or underground, using gravity to carry water from a source to a location—usually a city—that needed it. The Romans built many aqueducts in a period of substantial urbanization. (*p. 175*)

Arawak Amerindian peoples who inhabited the Greater Antilles of the Caribbean at the time of Columbus. (*p. 465*)

Arkwright, Richard (1732–1792) English inventor and entrepreneur who became the wealthiest and most successful textile manufacturer of the early **Industrial Revolution.** He invented the water frame, a machine that, with minimal human supervision, could spin many strong cotton threads at once. (*p. 675*)

Armenia One of the earliest Christian kingdoms, situated in eastern Anatolia and the western Caucasus and occupied by speakers of the Armenian language. (*p. 244*)

Asante   African kingdom on the **Gold Coast** that expanded rapidly after 1680. Asante participated in the Atlantic economy, trading gold, slaves, and ivory. It resisted British imperial ambitions for a quarter century before being absorbed into Britain's Gold Coast colony in 1902. (*p. 828*)

Ashikaga Shogunate (1336–1573)   The second of Japan's military governments headed by a shogun (a military ruler). Sometimes called the Muromachi Shogunate. (*p. 396*)

Ashoka   Third ruler of the **Mauryan Empire** in India (r. 273–232 B.C.E.). He converted to Buddhism and broadcast his precepts on inscribed stones and pillars, the earliest surviving Indian writing. (*p. 204*)

Asian Tigers   Collective name for South Korea, Taiwan, Hong Kong, and Singapore—nations that became economic powers in the 1970s and 1980s. (*p. 974*)

Atahualpa (1502?–1533)   Last ruling Inca emperor of Peru. He was executed by the Spanish. (*p. 482*)

Atatürk, Kemal (1880–1938)   The founder of modern Turkey. An army officer, he distinguished himself in the defense of Gallipoli in World War I and expelled a Greek expeditionary army from Anatolia in 1921–1922. He abolished the sultanate and replaced the Ottoman Empire with the Turkish Republic in 1923. As president until his death in 1938, he pushed through a radical Westernization and reform of Turkish society. (*p. 863*)

Atlantic Circuit   The network of trade routes connecting Europe, Africa, and the Americas that underlay the Atlantic system. (*p. 561*)

Atlantic system   The network of trading links after 1500 that moved goods, wealth, people, and cultures around the Atlantic Ocean Basin. (*p. 550*)

Augustus (63 B.C.E.–14 C.E.)   Honorific name of Octavian, founder of the **Roman Principate,** the military dictatorship that replaced the failing rule of the **Roman Senate.** After defeating all rivals, between 31 B.C.E. and 14 C.E. he laid the groundwork for several centuries of stability and prosperity in the Roman Empire. (*p. 170*)

Auschwitz   Nazi extermination camp in Poland, the largest center of mass murder during the **Holocaust.** Close to a million Jews, Gypsies, Communists, and others were killed there. (*p. 901*)

australopithecines   The several extinct species of humanlike primates that existed during the Pleistocene era (genus *Australopithecus*). (*p. 7*)

ayllu   Andean lineage group or kin-based community. (*p. 355*)

Aztecs   Also known as Mexica, the Aztecs created a powerful empire in central Mexico (1325–1521 C.E.). They forced defeated peoples to provide goods and labor as a tax. (*p. 348*)

Babylon   The largest and most important city in Mesopotamia. It achieved particular eminence as the capital of the Amorite king **Hammurabi** in the eighteenth century B.C.E. and the Neo-Babylonian king Nebuchadnezzar in the sixth century B.C.E. (*p. 30*)

balance of power   The policy in international relations by which, beginning in the eighteenth century, the major European states acted together to prevent any one of them from becoming too powerful. (*p. 512*)

Balfour Declaration   Statement issued by Britain's Foreign Secretary Arthur Balfour in 1917 favoring the establishment of a Jewish national homeland in Palestine. (*p. 853*)

Bannermen   Hereditary military servants of the **Qing Empire,** in large part descendants of peoples of various origins who had fought for the founders of the empire. (*p. 743*)

Bantu   Collective name of a large group of sub-Saharan African languages and of the peoples speaking these languages. (*p. 242*)

Batavia   Fort established ca. 1619 as headquarters of Dutch East India Company operations in Indonesia; today the city of Jakarta. (*p. 601*)

Battle of Midway   U.S. naval victory over the Japanese fleet in June 1942, in which the Japanese lost four of their best aircraft carriers. It marked a turning point in World War II. (*p. 894*)

Battle of Omdurman   British victory over the Mahdi in the Sudan in 1898. General Kitchener led a mixed force of British and Egyptian troops armed with rapid-firing rifles and machine guns. (*p. 821*)

Beijing   China's northern capital, first used as an imperial capital in 906 and now the capital of the People's Republic of China. (*p. 386*)

Bengal   Region of northeastern India. It was the first part of India to be conquered by the British in the eighteenth century and remained the political and economic center of British India throughout the nineteenth century. The 1905 split of the province into predominantly Hindu West Bengal and predominantly Muslim East Bengal (now Bangladesh) sparked anti-British riots. (*p. 910*)

Berlin Conference (1884–1885)   Conference that German chancellor Otto von Bismarck called to set rules for the partition of Africa. It led to the creation of the Congo Free State under King **Leopold II** of Belgium. (See also **Bismarck, Otto von.**) (*p. 825*)

Bhagavad-Gita   The most important work of Indian sacred literature, a dialogue between the great warrior Arjuna and the god Krishna on duty and the fate of the spirit. (*p. 205*)

bin Laden, Usama   Saudi-born Muslim extremist who funded the al Qaeda organization that was responsible for several terrorist attacks, including those on the World Trade Center and the Pentagon in 2001. (*p. 1008*)

bipedalism   The ability to walk upright on two legs, characteristic of **hominids.** (*p. 8*)

Bismarck, Otto von (1815–1898)   Chancellor (prime minister) of Prussia from 1862 until 1871, when he became chancellor of Germany. A conservative nationalist, he led Prussia to victory against Austria (1866) and France (1870) and was responsible for the creation of the German Empire in 1871. (*p. 804*)

Black Death   An outbreak of **bubonic plague** that spread across Asia, North Africa, and Europe in the mid-fourteenth century, killing off a third of western Europeans. (*p. 433*)

Bolívar, Simón (1783–1830)   The most important military leader in the struggle for independence in South America. Born in Venezuela, he led military forces there and in Colombia, Ecuador, Peru, and Bolivia. (*p. 696*)

Bolsheviks   Radical Marxist political party founded by Vladimir Lenin in 1903. Under Lenin's leadership, the Bolsheviks seized power in November 1917 during the Russian Revolution. (See also **Lenin, Vladimir.**) (*p. 854*)

Bonaparte, Napoleon.   See **Napoleon I.**

Bornu   A powerful West African kingdom at the southern edge of the Sahara in the Central Sudan, which was important in trans-Saharan trade and in the spread of Islam. Also known as Kanem-Bornu, it endured from the ninth century to the end of the nineteenth. (*p. 570*)

Borobodur   A massive stone monument on the Indonesian island of Java, erected by the Sailendra kings around 800 C.E. The winding ascent through ten levels, decorated with rich relief carving, is a Buddhist allegory for the progressive stages of enlightenment. (*p. 215*)

bourgeoisie In early modern Europe, the class of well-off town dwellers whose wealth came from manufacturing, finance, commerce, and allied professions. (*p. 499*)

Brant, Joseph (1742–1807) Mohawk leader who supported the British during the American Revolution. (*p. 645*)

Brazza, Savorgnan de (1852–1905) Franco-Italian explorer sent by the French government to claim part of equatorial Africa for France. Founded Brazzaville, capital of the French Congo, in 1880. (*p. 825*)

British raj The rule over much of South Asia between 1765 and 1947 by the East India Company and then by a British government. (*p. 766*)

bronze An alloy of copper with a small amount of tin (or sometimes arsenic), it is harder and more durable than copper alone. The term *Bronze Age* is applied to the era—the dates of which vary in different parts of the world—when bronze was the primary metal for tools and weapons. The demand for bronze helped create long-distance networks of trade. (*p. 41*)

bubonic plague A bacterial disease of fleas that can be transmitted by flea bites to rodents and humans; humans in late stages of the illness can spread the bacteria by coughing. Because of its very high mortality rate and the difficulty of preventing its spread, major outbreaks have created crises in many parts of the world. (See also **Black Death.**) (*pp. 315, 379*)

Buddha (563–483 B.C.E.) An Indian prince named Siddhartha Gautama, who renounced his wealth and social position. After becoming "enlightened" (the meaning of *Buddha*) he enunciated the principles of Buddhism. This doctrine evolved and spread throughout India and to Southeast, East, and Central Asia. (See also **Mahayana Buddhism, Theravada Buddhism.**) (*p. 199*)

business cycles Recurrent swings from economic hard times to recovery and growth, then back to hard times and a repetition of the sequence. (*p. 685*)

Byzantine Empire Historians' name for the eastern portion of the Roman Empire from the fourth century onward, taken from "Byzantium," an early name for Constantinople, the Byzantine capital city. The empire fell to the Ottomans in 1453. (See also **Ottoman Empire.**) (*p. 276*)

caliphate Office established in succession to the Prophet Muhammad, to rule the Islamic empire; also the name of that empire. (See also **Abbasid Caliphate; Sokoto Caliphate; Umayyad Caliphate.**) (*p. 256*)

calpolli A group of up to a hundred families that served as a social building block of an **altepetl** in ancient Mesoamerica. (*p. 348*)

capitalism The economic system of large financial institutions—banks, stock exchanges, investment companies—that first developed in early modern Europe. *Commercial capitalism*, the trading system of the early modern economy, is often distinguished from *industrial capitalism*, the system based on machine production. (*p. 560*)

caravel A small, highly maneuverable three-masted ship used by the Portuguese and Spanish in the exploration of the Atlantic. (*p. 468*)

Cárdenas, Lázaro (1895–1970) President of Mexico (1934–1940). He brought major changes to Mexican life by distributing millions of acres of land to the peasants, bringing representatives of workers and farmers into the inner circles of politics, and nationalizing the oil industry. (*p. 923*)

Carthage City located in present-day Tunisia, founded by **Phoenicians** ca. 800 B.C.E. It became a major commercial center and naval power in the western Mediterranean until defeated by Rome in the third century B.C.E. (*p. 113*)

Caste War A rebellion of the Maya people against the government of Mexico in 1847. It nearly returned the Yucatán to Maya rule. Some Maya rebels retreated to unoccupied territories where they held out until 1901. (*p. 710*)

Catholic Reformation Religious reform movement within the Latin Christian Church, begun in response to the **Protestant Reformation.** It clarified Catholic theology and reformed clerical training and discipline. (*p. 494*)

Celts Peoples sharing a common language and culture that originated in central Europe in the first half of the first millennium B.C.E. After 500 B.C.E. they spread as far as Anatolia in the east, Spain and the British Isles in the west, and later were overtaken by Roman conquest and Germanic invasions. Their descendants survive on the western fringe of Europe (Brittany, Wales, Scotland, Ireland). (*p. 75*)

Champa rice Quick-maturing rice that can allow two harvests in one growing season. Originally introduced into Champa from India, it was later sent to China as a tribute gift by the Champa state. (See also **tributary system.**) (*p. 332*)

Chang'an City in the Wei Valley in eastern China. It became the capital of the Qin and early Han Empires. Its main features were imitated in the cities and towns that sprang up throughout the Han Empire. (*p. 184*)

Charlemagne (742–814) King of the Franks (r. 768–814); emperor (r. 800–814). Through a series of military conquests he established the Carolingian Empire, which encompassed all of Gaul and parts of Germany and Italy. Though illiterate himself, he sponsored a brief intellectual revival. (*p. 276*)

chartered companies Groups of private investors who paid an annual fee to France and England in exchange for a monopoly over trade to the West Indies colonies. (*p. 550*)

Chavín The first major urban civilization in South America (900–250 B.C.E.). Its capital, Chavín de Huántar, was located high in the Andes Mountains of Peru. Chavín became politically and economically dominant in a densely populated region that included two distinct ecological zones, the Peruvian coastal plain and the Andean foothills. (*p. 81*)

Chiang Kai-shek (1887–1975) Chinese military and political leader. Succeeded Sun Yat-sen as head of the **Guomindang** in 1925; headed the Chinese government from 1928 to 1948; fought against the Chinese Communists and Japanese invaders. After 1949 he headed the Chinese Nationalist government in Taiwan. (*pp. 862, 888*)

chiefdom Form of political organization with rule by a hereditary leader who held power over a collection of villages and towns. Less powerful than kingdoms and empires, chiefdoms were based on gift giving and commercial links. (*p. 353*)

Chimu Powerful Peruvian civilization based on conquest. Located in the region earlier dominated by **Moche.** Conquered by **Inca** in 1465. (*p. 357*)

chinampas Raised fields constructed along lake shores in Mesoamerica to increase agricultural yields. (*p. 343*)

city-state A small independent state consisting of an urban center and the surrounding agricultural territory. A characteristic political form in early Mesopotamia, Archaic and Classical Greece, Phoenicia, and early Italy. (See also **polis.**) (*p. 33*)

civilization An ambiguous term often used to denote more complex societies but sometimes used by anthropologists to describe any group of people sharing a set of cultural traits. (*p. 30*)

Cixi, Empress Dowager (1835–1908) Empress of China and mother of Emperor Guangxi. She put her son under house arrest, supported antiforeign movements, and resisted reforms of the Chinese government and armed forces. (*p. 812*)

clipper ship Large, fast, streamlined sailing vessel, often American built, of the mid-to-late nineteenth century rigged with vast canvas sails hung from tall masts. (*p. 775*)

Cold War (1945–1991) The ideological struggle between communism (Soviet Union) and capitalism (United States) for world influence. The Soviet Union and the United States came to the brink of actual war during the **Cuban missile crisis** but never attacked one another. The Cold War came to an end when the Soviet Union dissolved in 1991. (See also **North Atlantic Treaty Organization; Warsaw Pact.**) (*p. 937*)

colonialism Policy by which a nation administers a foreign territory and develops its resources for the benefit of the colonial power. (*p. 821*)

Columbian Exchange The exchange of plants, animals, diseases, and technologies between the Americas and the rest of the world following Columbus's voyages. (*p. 520*)

Columbus, Christopher (1451–1506) Genoese mariner who in the service of Spain led expeditions across the Atlantic, establishing contact between the peoples of the Americas and the Old World and opening the way to Spanish conquest and colonization. (*p. 470*)

Confederation of 1867 Negotiated union of the formerly separate colonial governments of Ontario, Quebec, New Brunswick, and Nova Scotia. This new Dominion of Canada with a central government in Ottawa is seen as the beginning of the Canadian nation. (*p. 702*)

Confucius Western name for the Chinese philosopher Kongzi (551–479 B.C.E.). His doctrine of duty and public service had a great influence on subsequent Chinese thought and served as a code of conduct for government officials. (*p. 66*)

Congress of Vienna (1814–1815) Meeting of representatives of European monarchs called to reestablish the old order after the defeat of **Napoleon I.** (*p. 660*)

conquistadors Early-sixteenth-century Spanish adventurers who conquered Mexico, Central America, and Peru. (See **Cortés, Hernán; Pizarro, Francisco.**) (*p. 479*)

Constantine (306–337 C.E.) Roman emperor (r. 312–337). After reuniting the Roman Empire, he moved the capital to Constantinople and made Christianity a favored religion. (*p. 176*)

Constitutional Convention Meeting in 1787 of the elected representatives of the thirteen original states to write the Constitution of the United States. (*p. 647*)

contract of indenture A voluntary agreement binding a person to work for a specified period of years in return for free passage to an overseas destination. Before 1800 most **indentured servants** were Europeans; after 1800 most indentured laborers were Asians. (*p. 778*)

Cortés, Hernán (1485–1547) Spanish explorer and conquistador who led the conquest of Aztec Mexico in 1519–1521 for Spain. (*p. 479*)

Cossacks Peoples of the Russian Empire who lived outside the farming villages, often as herders, mercenaries, or outlaws. Cossacks led the conquest of Siberia in the sixteenth and seventeenth centuries. (*p. 625*)

Council of the Indies The institution responsible for supervising Spain's colonies in the Americas from 1524 to the early eighteenth century, when it lost all but judicial responsibilities. (*p. 523*)

***coureurs des bois* (runners of the woods)** French fur traders, many of mixed Amerindian heritage, who lived among and often married with Amerindian peoples of North America. (*p. 539*)

creoles In colonial Spanish America, term used to describe someone of European descent born in the New World. Elsewhere in the Americas, the term is used to describe all non-native peoples. (*p. 529*)

Crimean War (1853–1856) Conflict between the Russian and Ottoman Empires fought primarily in the Crimean Peninsula. To prevent Russian expansion, Britain and France sent troops to support the Ottomans. (*p. 734*)

Crusades (1095–1204) Armed pilgrimages to the Holy Land by Christians determined to recover Jerusalem from Muslim rule. The Crusades brought an end to western Europe's centuries of intellectual and cultural isolation. (*p. 298*)

Crystal Palace Building erected in Hyde Park, London, for the Great Exhibition of 1851. Made of iron and glass, like a gigantic greenhouse, it was a symbol of the industrial age. (*p. 676*)

Cuban missile crisis (1962) Brink-of-war confrontation between the United States and the Soviet Union over the latter's placement of nuclear-armed missiles in Cuba. (*p. 944*)

cultural imperialism Domination of one culture over another by a deliberate policy or by economic or technological superiority. (*p. 1013*)

Cultural Revolution (China) (1966–1976) Campaign in China ordered by **Mao Zedong** to purge the Communist Party of his opponents and instill revolutionary values in the younger generation. (*p. 956*)

culture Socially transmitted patterns of action and expression. *Material culture* refers to physical objects, such as dwellings, clothing, tools, and crafts. Culture also includes arts, beliefs, knowledge, and technology. (*p. 12*)

cuneiform A system of writing in which wedge-shaped symbols represented words or syllables. It originated in Mesopotamia and was used initially for Sumerian and Akkadian but later was adapted to represent other languages of western Asia. Because so many symbols had to be learned, literacy was confined to a relatively small group of administrators and **scribes.** (*p. 41*)

Cyrus (600–530 B.C.E.) Founder of the Achaemenid Persian Empire. Between 550 and 530 B.C.E. he conquered Media, Lydia, and **Babylon.** Revered in the traditions of both Iran and the subject peoples, he employed Persians and Medes in his administration and respected the institutions and beliefs of subject peoples. (*p. 129*)

czar See **tsar.**

daimyo Literally, great name(s). Japanese warlords and great landowners, whose armed **samurai** gave them control of the Japanese islands from the eighth to the later nineteenth century. Under the **Tokugawa Shogunate** they were subordinated to the imperial government. (*p. 606*)

Daoism Chinese school of thought, originating in the Warring States Period with Laozi (604–531 B.C.E.). Daoism offered an alternative to the Confucian emphasis on hierarchy and duty. Daoists believe that the world is always changing and is devoid of absolute morality or meaning. They accept the world as they find it, avoid futile struggles, and deviate as little as possible from the *Dao*, or "path" of nature. (See also **Confucius.**) (*p. 67*)

Darius I (ca. 558–486 B.C.E.) Third ruler of the Persian Empire (r. 521–486 B.C.E.). He crushed the widespread initial resistance to his rule and gave all major government posts to Persians rather than to Medes. He established a system of provinces and tribute, began construction of Persepolis, and expanded Persian control in the east (Pakistan) and west (northern Greece). (*p. 130*)

Decembrist revolt Abortive attempt by army officers to take control of the Russian government upon the death of Tsar Alexander I in 1825. (*p. 741*)

Declaration of the Rights of Man (1789) Statement of fundamental political rights adopted by the French **National Assembly** at the beginning of the French Revolution. (*p. 651*)

deforestation The removal of trees faster than forests can replace themselves. (*p. 503*)

Delhi Sultanate (1206–1526) Centralized Indian empire of varying extent, created by Muslim invaders. (*p. 405*)

democracy A system of government in which all "citizens" (however defined) have equal political and legal rights, privileges, and protections, as in the Greek **city-state** of Athens in the fifth and fourth centuries B.C.E. (*p. 141*)

demographic transition A change in the rates of population growth. Before the transition, both birthrates and death rates are high, resulting in a slowly growing population; then the death rate drops but the birthrate remains high, causing a population explosion; finally the birthrate drops and the population growth slows down. This transition took place in Europe in the late nineteenth and early twentieth centuries, in North America and East Asia in the mid-twentieth, and, most recently, in Latin America and South Asia. (*p. 979*)

Deng Xiaoping (1904–1997) Communist Party leader who forced Chinese economic reforms after the death of **Mao Zedong.** (*p. 974*)

development In the nineteenth and twentieth centuries, the economic process that led to industrialization, urbanization, the rise of a large and prosperous middle class, and heavy investment in education. (*p. 719*)

devshirme "Selection" in Turkish. The system by which boys from Christian communities were taken by the Ottoman state to serve as **Janissaries.** (*p. 582*)

dhow Ship of small to moderate size used in the western Indian Ocean, traditionally with a triangular sail and a sewn timber hull. (*p. 415*)

Diagne, Blaise (1872–1934) Senegalese political leader. He was the first African elected to the French National Assembly. During World War I, in exchange for promises to give French citizenship to Senegalese, he helped recruit Africans to serve in the French army. After the war, he led a movement to abolish forced labor in Africa. (*p. 919*)

Dias, Bartolomeu (1450?–1500) Portuguese explorer who in 1488 led the first expedition to sail around the southern tip of Africa from the Atlantic and sight the Indian Ocean. (*p. 470*)

Diaspora A Greek word meaning "dispersal," used to describe the communities of a given ethnic group living outside their homeland. Jews, for example, spread from Israel to western Asia and Mediterranean lands in antiquity and today can be found throughout the world. (*p. 110*)

Dirty War War waged by the Argentine military (1976–1983) against leftist groups. Characterized by the use of illegal imprisonment, torture, and executions by the military. (*p. 968*)

divination Techniques for ascertaining the future or the will of the gods by interpreting natural phenomena such as, in early China, the cracks on oracle bones or, in ancient Greece, the flight of birds through sectors of the sky. (*p. 62*)

division of labor A manufacturing technique that breaks down a craft into many simple and repetitive tasks that can be performed by unskilled workers. Pioneered in the pottery works of Josiah Wedgwood and in other eighteenth-century factories, it greatly increased the productivity of labor and lowered the cost of manufactured goods. (See also **Wedgwood, Josiah.**) (*p. 674*)

driver A privileged male slave whose job was to ensure that a slave gang did its work on a plantation. (*p. 556*)

Druids The class of religious experts who conducted rituals and preserved sacred lore among some ancient Celtic peoples. They provided education, mediated disputes between kinship groups, and were suppressed by the Romans as a potential focus of opposition to Roman rule. (See also **Celts.**) (*p. 76*)

durbar An elaborate display of political power and wealth in British India in the nineteenth century, ostensibly in imitation of the pageantry of the **Mughal Empire.** (*p. 767*)

Dutch West India Company (1621–1794) Trading company chartered by the Dutch government to conduct its merchants' trade in the Americas and Africa. (*p. 551*)

Edison, Thomas (1847–1931) American inventor best known for inventing the electric light bulb, acoustic recording on wax cylinders, and motion pictures. (*p. 791*)

Einstein, Albert (1879–1955) German physicist who developed the theory of relativity, which states that time, space, and mass are relative to each other and not fixed. (*p. 869*)

El Alamein Town in Egypt, site of the victory by Britain's Field Marshal Bernard Montgomery over German forces led by General Erwin Rommel (the "Desert Fox") in 1942–1943. (*p. 894*)

electricity A form of energy used in telegraphy from the 1840s on and for lighting, industrial motors, and railroads beginning in the 1880s. (*p. 791*)

electric telegraph A device for rapid, long-distance transmission of information over an electric wire. It was introduced in England and North America in the 1830s and 1840s and replaced telegraph systems that utilized visual signals such as semaphores. (See also **submarine telegraph cables.**) (*p. 680*)

encomienda A grant of authority over a population of Amerindians in the Spanish colonies. It provided the grant holder with a supply of cheap labor and periodic payments of goods by the Amerindians. It obliged the grant holder to Christianize the Amerindians. (*p. 528*)

English Civil War (1642–1649) A conflict over royal versus Parliamentary rights, caused by King Charles I's arrest of his parliamentary critics and ending with his execution. Its outcome checked the growth of royal absolutism and, with the Glorious Revolution of 1688 and the English Bill of Rights of 1689, ensured that England would be a constitutional monarchy. (*p. 507*)

Enlightenment A philosophical movement in eighteenth-century Europe that fostered the belief that one could reform society by discovering rational laws that governed social behavior and that were just as scientific as the laws of physics. (*pp. 498, 640*)

equites In ancient Italy, prosperous landowners second in wealth and status to the senatorial aristocracy. The Roman emperors allied with this group to counterbalance the influence of the old aristocracy and used the *equites* to staff the imperial civil service. (*p. 170*)

Estates General France's traditional national assembly with representatives of the three estates, or classes, in French society: the clergy, nobility, and commoners. The calling of the Estates General in 1789 led to the French Revolution. (*p. 649*)

Ethiopia   East African highland nation lying east of the Nile River. (See also **Menelik II; Selassie, Haile.**) (*p. 244*)

ethnic cleansing   Effort to eradicate a people and its culture by means of mass killing and the destruction of historical buildings and cultural materials. Ethnic cleansing was used by both sides in the conflicts that accompanied the disintegration of Yugoslavia in the 1990s. (*p. 978*)

European Community (EC)   The European Economic Community, an organization promoting economic unity, became the European Community in 1967, consolidating earlier, more limited, agreements. Replaced by the European Union (EU) in 1993. (*p. 940*)

evolution   The biological theory that, over time, changes occurring in plants and animals, mainly as a result of natural selection and genetic mutation, result in new species. (*p. 6*)

extraterritoriality   The right of foreign residents in a country to live under the laws of their native country and disregard the laws of the host country. In the nineteenth and early twentieth centuries, European and American nationals living in certain areas of Chinese and Ottoman cities were granted this right. (*p. 736*)

Faisal (1885–1933)   Arab prince, leader of the Arab Revolt in World War I. The British made him king of Iraq in 1921, and he reigned under British protection until 1933. (*p. 853*)

Fascist Party   Italian political party created by Benito Mussolini during World War I. It emphasized aggressive nationalism and was Mussolini's instrument for the creation of a dictatorship in Italy from 1922 to 1943. (See also **Mussolini, Benito.**) (*p. 885*)

fief   In medieval Europe, land granted in return for a sworn oath to provide specified military service. (*p. 286*)

First Temple   A monumental sanctuary built in Jerusalem by King Solomon in the tenth century B.C.E. to be the religious center for the Israelite god Yahweh. The Temple priesthood conducted sacrifices, received a tithe or percentage of agricultural revenues, and became economically and politically powerful. The First Temple was destroyed by the Babylonians in 587 B.C.E., rebuilt on a modest scale in the late sixth century B.C.E., and replaced by King Herod's Second Temple in the late first century B.C.E. (destroyed by the Romans in 70 C.E.) (*p. 106*)

Five-Year Plans   Plans that Joseph Stalin introduced to industrialize the Soviet Union rapidly, beginning in 1928. They set goals for the output of steel, electricity, machinery, and most other products and were enforced by the police powers of the state. They succeeded in making the Soviet Union a major industrial power before World War II. (See also **Stalin, Joseph.**) (*p. 904*)

foragers   People who support themselves by hunting wild animals and gathering wild edible plants and insects. (*p. 15*)

Fourteen Points   A peace program presented to the U.S. Congress by President Woodrow Wilson in January 1918. It called for the evacuation of German-occupied lands, the drawing of borders and the settling of territorial disputes by the self-determination of the affected populations, and the founding of an association of nations to preserve the peace and guarantee their territorial integrity. It was rejected by Germany, but made Wilson the moral leader of the Allies in the last year of World War I. (*p. 855*)

Franklin, Benjamin (1706–1790)   American intellectual, inventor, and politician. He helped negotiate French support for the American Revolution. (*p. 641*)

free-trade imperialism   Economic dominance of a weaker country by a more powerful one, while maintaining the legal independence of the weaker state. In the late nineteenth century, free-trade imperialism characterized the relations between the Latin American republics, on the one hand, and Great Britain and the United States, on the other. (*p. 837*)

Freud, Sigmund (1856–1939)   Austrian psychiatrist, founder of psychoanalysis. He argued that psychological problems were caused by traumas, especially sexual experiences in early childhood, that were repressed in later life. His ideas caused considerable controversy among psychologists and in the general public. Although his views on repressed sexuality are no longer widely accepted, his psychoanalytic methods are still very influential. (*p. 869*)

Fujiwara   Aristocratic family that dominated the Japanese imperial court between the ninth and twelfth centuries. (*p. 330*)

Funan   An early complex society in Southeast Asia between the first and sixth centuries C.E. It was centered in the rich rice-growing region of southern Vietnam, and it controlled the passage of trade across the Malaysian isthmus. (*p. 214*)

Gama, Vasco da (1460–1524)   Portuguese explorer. In 1497–1498 he led the first naval expedition from Europe to sail to India, opening an important commercial sea route. (*p. 470*)

Gandhi, Mohandas K. (Mahatma) (1869–1948)   Leader of the Indian independence movement and advocate of nonviolent resistance. After being educated as a lawyer in England, he returned to India and became leader of the **Indian National Congress** in 1920. He appealed to the poor, led nonviolent demonstrations against British colonial rule, and was jailed many times. Soon after independence he was assassinated for attempting to stop Hindu-Muslim rioting. (*p. 912*)

Gaozu   The throne name of Liu Bang, one of the rebel leaders who brought down the Qin and founded the Han dynasty in 202 B.C.E. (*p. 181*)

Garibaldi, Giuseppe (1807–1882)   Italian nationalist and revolutionary who conquered Sicily and Naples and added them to a unified Italy in 1860. (*p. 803*)

Genghis Khan (ca. 1167–1227)   The title of Temüjin when he ruled the Mongols (1206–1227). It means the "oceanic" or "universal" leader. Genghis Khan was the founder of the Mongol Empire. (*p. 372*)

gens de couleur   Free men and women of color in Haiti. They sought greater political rights and later supported the Haitian Revolution. (See also **L'Ouverture, François Dominique Toussaint.**) (*p. 658*)

gentry   In China, the class of prosperous families, next in wealth below the rural aristocrats, from which the emperors drew their administrative personnel. Respected for their education and expertise, these officials became a privileged group and made the government more efficient and responsive than in the past. The term *gentry* also denotes the class of landholding families in England below the aristocracy. (*pp. 184, 502*)

Ghana   First known kingdom in sub-Saharan West Africa between the sixth and thirteenth centuries C.E. Also the modern West African country once known as the Gold Coast. (*p. 239*)

global elite culture   At the beginning of the twenty-first century, the attitudes and outlook of well-educated, prosperous, Western-oriented people around the world, largely expressed in European languages, especially English. (*p. 1015*)

global pop culture Popular cultural practices and institutions that have been adopted internationally, such as music, the Internet, television, food, and fashion. (*p. 1014*)

globalization The economic, political, and cultural integration and interaction of all parts of the world brought about by increasing trade, travel, and technology. (*p. 998*)

Gold Coast (Africa) Region of the Atlantic coast of West Africa occupied by modern Ghana; named for its gold exports to Europe from the 1470s onward. (*p. 470*)

Golden Horde Mongol khanate founded by Genghis Khan's grandson Batu. It was based in southern Russia and quickly adopted both the Turkic language and Islam. Also known as the Kipchak Horde. (*p. 379*)

Gorbachev, Mikhail (b. 1931) Head of the Soviet Union from 1985 to 1991. His liberalization effort improved relations with the West, but he lost power after his reforms led to the collapse of communist governments in eastern Europe. (*p. 975*)

Gothic cathedrals Large churches originating in twelfth-century France; built in an architectural style featuring pointed arches, tall vaults and spires, flying buttresses, and large stained-glass windows. (*p. 441*)

Grand Canal The 1,100-mile (1,771-kilometer) waterway linking the Yellow and the Yangzi Rivers. It was begun in the **Han** period and completed during the Sui Empire. (*p. 310*)

Great Ice Age Geological era that occurred between ca. 2 million and 11,000 years ago. As a result of climate shifts, large numbers of new species evolved during this period, also called the Pleistocene epoch. (See also **Holocene**.) (*p. 8*)

"great traditions" Historians' term for a literate, well-institutionalized complex of religious and social beliefs and practices adhered to by diverse societies over a broad geographical area. (See also **"small traditions."**) (*p. 240*)

Great Western Schism A division in the Latin (Western) Christian Church between 1378 and 1417, when rival claimants to the papacy existed in Rome and Avignon. (*p. 448*)

Great Zimbabwe City, now in ruins (in the modern African country of Zimbabwe), whose many stone structures were built between about 1250 and 1450, when it was a trading center and the capital of a large state. (*p. 418*)

guild In medieval Europe, an association of men (rarely women), such as merchants, artisans, or professors, who worked in a particular trade and banded together to promote their economic and political interests. Guilds were also important in other societies, such as the Ottoman and Safavid Empires. (*p. 438*)

Gujarat Region of western India famous for trade and manufacturing; the inhabitants are called Gujaratis. (*p. 413*)

gunpowder A mixture of saltpeter, sulfur, and charcoal, in various proportions. The formula, brought to China in the 400s or 500s, was first used to make fumigators to keep away insect pests and evil spirits. In later centuries it was used to make explosives and grenades and to propel cannonballs, shot, and bullets. (*p. 323*)

Guomindang Nationalist political party founded on democratic principles by **Sun Yat-sen** in 1912. After 1925, the party was headed by **Chiang Kai-shek**, who turned it into an increasingly authoritarian movement. (*p. 861*)

Gupta Empire (320–550 C.E.) A powerful Indian state based, like its Mauryan predecessor, on a capital at Pataliputra in the Ganges Valley. It controlled most of the Indian subcontinent through a combination of military force and its prestige as a center of sophisticated culture. (See also **theater-state**.) (*p. 206*)

Habsburg A powerful European family that provided many Holy Roman Emperors, founded the Austrian (later Austro-Hungarian) Empire, and ruled sixteenth- and seventeenth-century Spain. (*p. 505*)

hadith A tradition relating the words or deeds of the Prophet Muhammad; next to the **Quran**, the most important basis for Islamic law. (*p. 263*)

Hammurabi Amorite ruler of **Babylon** (r. 1792–1750 B.C.E.). He conquered many city-states in southern and northern Mesopotamia and is best known for a code of laws, inscribed on a black stone pillar, illustrating the principles to be used in legal cases. (*p. 37*)

Han A term used to designate (1) the ethnic Chinese people who originated in the Yellow River Valley and spread throughout regions of China suitable for agriculture and (2) the dynasty of emperors who ruled from 202 B.C.E. to 220 C.E. (*p. 178*)

Hanseatic League An economic and defensive alliance of the free towns in northern Germany, founded about 1241 and most powerful in the fourteenth century. (*p. 437*)

Harappa Site of one of the great cities of the Indus Valley civilization of the third millennium B.C.E. It was located on the northwest frontier of the zone of cultivation (in modern Pakistan), and may have been a center for the acquisition of raw materials, such as metals and precious stones, from Afghanistan and Iran. (*p. 50*)

Hatshepsut Queen of Egypt (r. 1473–1458 B.C.E.). She dispatched a naval expedition down the Red Sea to Punt (possibly northeast Sudan or Eretria), the faraway source of myrrh. There is evidence of opposition to a woman as ruler, and after her death her name and image were frequently defaced. (*p. 92*)

Hausa An agricultural and trading people of central Sudan in West Africa. Aside from their brief incorporation into the Songhai Empire, the Hausa city-states remained autonomous until the **Sokoto Caliphate** conquered them in the early nineteenth century. (*p. 569*)

Hebrew Bible A collection of sacred books containing diverse materials concerning the origins, experiences, beliefs, and practices of the Israelites. Most of the extant text was compiled by members of the priestly class in the fifth century B.C.E. and reflects the concerns and views of this group. (*p. 103*)

Hellenistic Age Historians' term for the era, usually dated 323–30 B.C.E., in which Greek culture spread across western Asia and northeastern Africa after the conquests of **Alexander** the Great. The period ended with the fall of the last major Hellenistic kingdom to Rome, but Greek cultural influence persisted until the spread of Islam in the seventh century C.E. (*p. 151*)

Helsinki Accords (1975) Political and human rights agreement signed in Helsinki, Finland, by the Soviet Union and western European countries. (*p. 945*)

Henry the Navigator (1394–1460) Portuguese prince who promoted the study of navigation and directed voyages of exploration down the western coast of Africa. (*p. 467*)

Herodotus (ca. 485–425 B.C.E.) Heir to the technique of *historia*—"investigation"—developed by Greeks in the late Archaic period. He came from a Greek community in Anatolia and traveled extensively, collecting information in western Asia and the Mediterranean lands. He traced the antecedents of and chronicled the **Persian Wars** between the Greek city-states and the Persian Empire, thus originating the Western tradition of historical writing. (*p. 142*)

Herzl, Theodore (1860–1904) Austrian journalist and founder of the Zionist movement urging the creation of a Jewish national homeland in Palestine. (*p. 853*)

Hidalgo y Costilla, Miguel (1753–1811) Mexican priest who led the first stage of the Mexican independence war in 1810. He was captured and executed in 1811. (*p. 698*)

Hidden Imam Last in a series of twelve descendants of Muhammad's son-in-law Ali, whom **Shi'ites** consider divinely appointed leaders of the Muslim community. In occlusion since ca. 873, he is expected to return as a messiah at the end of time. (*p. 591*)

hieroglyphics A system of writing in which pictorial symbols represented sounds, syllables, or concepts. It was used for official and monumental inscriptions in ancient Egypt. Because of the long period of study required to master this system, literacy in hieroglyphics was confined to a relatively small group of **scribes** and administrators. Cursive symbol-forms were developed for rapid composition on other media, such as **papyrus**. (*p. 45*)

Hinduism A general term for a wide variety of beliefs and ritual practices that have developed in the Indian subcontinent since antiquity. Hinduism has roots in ancient Vedic, Buddhist, and south Indian religious concepts and practices. It spread along the trade routes to Southeast Asia. (*p. 200*)

Hiroshima City in Japan, the first to be destroyed by an atomic bomb, on August 6, 1945. The bombing hastened the end of World War II. (*p. 896*)

history The study of past events and changes in the development, transmission, and transformation of cultural practices. (*p. 12*)

Hitler, Adolf (1889–1945) Born in Austria, Hitler became a radical German nationalist during World War I. He led the National Socialist German Workers' Party—the **Nazis**—in the 1920s and became dictator of Germany in 1933. He led Europe into World War II. (*p. 886*)

Hittites A people from central Anatolia who established an empire in Anatolia and Syria in the Late Bronze Age. With wealth from the trade in metals and military power based on chariot forces, the Hittites vied with New Kingdom Egypt for control of Syria-Palestine before falling to unidentified attackers ca. 1200 B.C.E. (See also **Ramesses II.**) (*p. 90*)

Holocaust Nazis' program during World War II to kill people they considered undesirable. Some 6 million Jews perished during the Holocaust, along with millions of Poles, Gypsies, Communists, Socialists, and others. (*p. 901*)

Holocene The geological era since the end of the **Great Ice Age** about 11,000 years ago. (*p. 21*)

Holy Roman Empire Loose federation of mostly German states and principalities, headed by an emperor elected by the princes. It lasted from 962 to 1806. (*pp. 21, 288, 505*)

hominid The biological family that includes humans and humanlike primates. (*p. 8*)

Homo erectus An extinct human species. It evolved in Africa about 2 million years ago. (*p. 9*)

Homo habilis The first human species (now extinct). It evolved in Africa about 2.5 million years ago. (*p. 9*)

Homo sapiens The current human species. It evolved in Africa about 200,000 years ago. It includes archaic forms such as Neanderthals (now extinct) and all modern humans. (*p. 9*)

hoplite A heavily armored Greek infantryman of the Archaic and Classical periods who fought in the close-packed phalanx formation. Hoplite armies—militias composed of middle- and upper-class citizens supplying their own equipment—were for centuries superior to all other military forces. (*p. 138*)

horse collar Harnessing method that increased the efficiency of horses by shifting the point of traction from the animal's neck to the shoulders; its adoption favors the spread of horse-drawn plows and vehicles. (*p. 297*)

House of Burgesses Elected assembly in colonial Virginia, created in 1618. (*p. 535*)

humanists (Renaissance) European scholars, writers, and teachers associated with the study of the humanities (grammar, rhetoric, poetry, history, languages, and moral philosophy), influential in the fifteenth century and later. (*p. 445*)

Hundred Years War (1337–1453) Series of campaigns over control of the throne of France, involving English and French royal families and French noble families. (*p. 450*)

Husain, Saddam (b. 1937) President of Iraq from 1979 until overthrown by an American-led invasion in 2003. Waged war on Iran from 1980 to 1988. His invasion of Kuwait in 1990 was repulsed in the Persian Gulf War in 1991. (*p. 972*)

Ibn Battuta (1304–1369) Moroccan Muslim scholar, the most widely traveled individual of his time. He wrote a detailed account of his visits to Islamic lands from China to Spain and the western Sudan. (*p. 401*)

Il-khan A "secondary" or "peripheral" khan based in Persia. The Il-khans' khanate was founded by Hülegü, a grandson of **Genghis Khan,** and was based at Tabriz in modern Azerbaijan. It controlled much of Iran and Iraq. (*p. 379*)

import-substitution industrialization An economic system aimed at building a country's industry by restricting foreign trade. It was especially popular in Latin American countries such as Mexico, Argentina, and Brazil in the mid-twentieth century. It proved successful for a time but could not keep up with technological advances in Europe and North America. (*p. 926*)

Inca Largest and most powerful Andean empire. Controlled the Pacific coast of South America from Ecuador to Chile from its capital of Cuzco. (*p. 360*)

indentured servant A migrant to British colonies in the Americas who paid for passage by agreeing to work for a set term ranging from four to seven years. (*p. 535*)

Indian Civil Service The elite professional class of officials who administered the government of British India. Originally composed exclusively of well-educated British men, it gradually added qualified Indians. (*p. 767*)

Indian National Congress A movement and political party founded in 1885 to demand greater Indian participation in government. Its membership was middle class, and its demands were modest until World War I. Led after 1920 by Mohandas K. Gandhi, it appealed increasingly to the poor, and it organized mass protests demanding self-government and independence. (See also **Gandhi, Mohandas K.**) (*pp. 772*)

Indian Ocean Maritime System In premodern times, a network of seaports, trade routes, and maritime culture linking countries on the rim of the Indian Ocean from Africa to Indonesia. (*p. 231*)

indulgence The forgiveness of the punishment due for past sins, granted by the Catholic Church authorities as a reward for a pious act. Martin Luther's protest against the sale of indulgences is often seen as touching off the **Protestant Reformation.** (*p. 492*)

Industrial Revolution The transformation of the economy, the environment, and living conditions, occurring first in England in the eighteenth century, that resulted from the use of steam engines, the mechanization of manufacturing in factories, and innovations in transportation and communication. (*p. 668*)

investiture controversy Dispute between the popes and the Holy Roman Emperors over who held ultimate authority over bishops in imperial lands. (*p. 289*)

Irigoyen, Hipólito (1850–1933) Argentine politician, president of Argentina from 1916 to 1922 and 1928 to 1930. The first president elected by universal male suffrage, he began his presidency as a reformer, but later became conservative. (*p. 925*)

Iron Age Historians' term for the period during which iron was the primary metal for tools and weapons. The advent of iron technology began at different times in different parts of the world. (*p. 88*)

iron curtain Winston Churchill's term for the Cold War division between the Soviet-dominated East and the U.S.-dominated West. (*p. 937*)

Iroquois Confederacy An alliance of five northeastern Amerindian peoples (six after 1722) that made decisions on military and diplomatic issues through a council of representatives. Allied first with the Dutch and later with the English, the Confederacy dominated the area from western New England to the Great Lakes. (*p. 537*)

Islam Religion expounded by the Prophet **Muhammad** (570–632 C.E.) on the basis of his reception of divine revelations, which were collected after his death into the **Quran.** In the tradition of Judaism and Christianity, and sharing much of their lore, Islam calls on all people to recognize one creator god—Allah—who rewards or punishes believers after death according to how they led their lives. (See also **hadith.**) (*p. 255*)

Israel In antiquity, the land between the eastern shore of the Mediterranean and the Jordan River, occupied by the Israelites from the early second millennium B.C.E. The modern state of Israel was founded in 1948. (*p. 103*)

Jackson, Andrew (1767–1845) First president of the United States to be born in humble circumstances. He was popular among frontier residents, urban workers, and small farmers. He had a successful political career as judge, general, congressman, senator, and president. After being denied the presidency in 1824 in a controversial election, he won in 1828 and was reelected in 1832. (*p. 704*)

Jacobins Radical republicans during the French Revolution. They were led by Maximilien Robespierre from 1793 to 1794. (See also **Robespierre, Maximilien.**) (*p. 652*)

Janissaries Infantry, originally of slave origin, armed with firearms and constituting the elite of the Ottoman army from the fifteenth century until the corps was abolished in 1826. (See also *devshirme.*) (*pp. 582, 730*)

jati. See **varna.**

Jesus (ca. 5 B.C.E.–34 C.E.) A Jew from Galilee in northern Israel who sought to reform Jewish beliefs and practices. He was executed as a revolutionary by the Romans. Hailed as the Messiah and son of God by his followers, he became the central figure in Christianity, a belief system that developed in the centuries after his death. (*p. 173*)

Jinnah, Muhammad Ali (1876–1948) Indian Muslim politician who founded the state of Pakistan. A lawyer by training, he joined the **All-India Muslim League** in 1913. As leader of the League from the 1920s on, he negotiated with the British and the **Indian National Congress** for Muslim participation in Indian politics. From 1940 on, he led the movement for the independence of India's Muslims in a separate state of Pakistan, founded in 1947. (*p. 914*)

joint-stock company A business, often backed by a government charter, that sold shares to individuals to raise money for its trading enterprises and to spread the risks (and profits) among many investors. (*p. 502*)

Juárez, Benito (1806–1872) President of Mexico (1858–1872). Born in poverty in Mexico, he was educated as a lawyer and rose to become chief justice of the Mexican supreme court and then president. He led Mexico's resistance to a French invasion in 1863 and the installation of Maximilian as emperor. (*p. 707*)

junk A very large flat-bottom sailing ship produced in the **Tang, Ming,** and **Song Empires,** specially designed for long-distance commercial travel. (*p. 323*)

Kamakura Shogunate The first of Japan's decentralized military governments (1185–1333). (*p. 331*)

kamikaze The "divine wind," which the Japanese credited with blowing Mongol invaders away from their shores in 1281. (*p. 395*)

Kangxi (1654–1722) Qing emperor (r. 1662–1722). He oversaw the greatest expansion of the **Qing Empire.** (*p. 615*)

karma In Indian tradition, the residue of deeds performed in past and present lives that adheres to a "spirit" and determines what form it will assume in its next life cycle. The doctrines of karma and reincarnation were used by the elite in ancient India to encourage people to accept their social position and do their duty. (*p. 198*)

keiretsu Alliances of corporations and banks that dominate the Japanese economy. (*p. 973*)

khipu System of knotted colored cords used by preliterate Andean peoples to transmit information. (*p. 355, 973*)

Khomeini, Ayatollah Ruhollah (1900?–1989) Shi'ite philosopher and cleric who led the overthrow of the shah of Iran in 1979 and created an Islamic republic. (*p. 972*)

Khubilai Khan (1215–1294) Last of the Mongol Great Khans (r. 1260–1294) and founder of the **Yuan Empire.** (*p. 386*)

Kievan Russia State established at Kiev in Ukraine ca. 882 by Scandinavian adventurers asserting authority over a mostly Slavic farming population. (*p. 276*)

Korean War (1950–1953) Conflict that began with North Korea's invasion of South Korea and came to involve the United Nations (primarily the United States) allying with South Korea and the People's Republic of China allying with North Korea. (*p. 941*)

Koryo Korean kingdom founded in 918 and destroyed by a Mongol invasion in 1259. (*p. 329*)

Kush An Egyptian name for Nubia, the region alongside the Nile River south of Egypt, where an indigenous kingdom with its own distinctive institutions and cultural traditions arose beginning in the early second millennium B.C.E. It was deeply influenced by Egyptian culture and at times under the control of Egypt, which coveted its rich deposits of gold and luxury products from sub-Saharan Africa carried up the Nile corridor. (*p. 72*)

labor union An organization of workers in a particular industry or trade, created to defend the interests of members through strikes or negotiations with employers. (*p. 797*)

laissez faire The idea that government should refrain from interfering in economic affairs. The classic exposition of laissez-faire principles is Adam Smith's *Wealth of Nations* (1776). (*p. 686*)

lama In Tibetan Buddhism, a teacher. (*p. 386*)

Las Casas, Bartolomé de (1474–1566)   First bishop of Chiapas, in southern Mexico. He devoted most of his life to protecting Amerindian peoples from exploitation. His major achievement was the New Laws of 1542, which limited the ability of Spanish settlers to compel Amerindians to labor for them. (See also **encomienda**.) (*p. 526*)

Latin West   Historians' name for the territories of Europe that adhered to the Latin rite of Christianity and used the Latin language for intellectual exchange in the period ca. 1000–1500. (*p. 430*)

League of Nations   International organization founded in 1919 to promote world peace and cooperation but greatly weakened by the refusal of the United States to join. It proved ineffectual in stopping aggression by Italy, Japan, and Germany in the 1930s, and it was superseded by the **United Nations** in 1945. (*p. 856*)

Legalism   In China, a political philosophy that emphasized the unruliness of human nature and justified state coercion and control. The **Qin** ruling class invoked it to validate the authoritarian nature of their regime and its profligate expenditure of subjects' lives and labor. It was superseded in the **Han** era by a more benevolent Confucian doctrine of governmental moderation. (*p. 70*)

"legitimate" trade   Exports from Africa in the nineteenth century that did not include the newly outlawed slave trade. (*p. 762*)

Lenin, Vladimir (1870–1924)   Leader of the Bolshevik (later Communist) Party. He lived in exile in Switzerland until 1917, then returned to Russia to lead the Bolsheviks to victory during the Russian Revolution and the civil war that followed. (*p. 854*)

Leopold II (1835–1909)   King of Belgium (r. 1865–1909). He was active in encouraging the exploration of Central Africa and became the ruler of the Congo Free State (to 1908). (*p. 825*)

liberalism   A political ideology that emphasizes the civil rights of citizens, representative government, and the protection of private property. This ideology, derived from the **Enlightenment,** was especially popular among the property-owning middle classes of Europe and North America. (*p. 802*)

Library of Ashurbanipal   A large collection of writings drawn from the ancient literary, religious, and scientific traditions of Mesopotamia. It was assembled by the seventh-century B.C.E. Assyrian ruler Ashurbanipal. The many tablets unearthed by archaeologists constitute one of the most important sources of present-day knowledge of the long literary tradition of Mesopotamia. (*p. 103*)

Linear B   A set of syllabic symbols, derived from the writing system of **Minoan** Crete, used in the Mycenaean palaces of the Late Bronze Age to write an early form of Greek. It was used primarily for palace records, and the surviving Linear B tablets provide substantial information about the economic organization of Mycenaean society and tantalizing clues about political, social, and religious institutions. (*p. 97*)

Li Shimin (599–649)   One of the founders of the **Tang Empire** and its second emperor (r. 626–649). He led the expansion of the empire into Central Asia. (*p. 310*)

Little Ice Age   A century-long period of cool climate that began in the 1590s. Its ill effects on agriculture in northern Europe were notable. (*p. 503*)

llama   A hoofed animal indigenous to the Andes Mountains in South America. It was the only domesticated beast of burden in the Americas before the arrival of Europeans. It provided meat and wool. The use of llamas to transport goods made possible specialized production and trade among people living in different ecological zones and fostered the integration of these zones by **Chavín** and later Andean states. (*p. 81*)

loess   A fine, light silt deposited by wind and water. It constitutes the fertile soil of the Yellow River Valley in northern China. Because loess soil is not compacted, it can be worked with a simple digging stick, but it leaves the region vulnerable to devastating earthquakes. (*p. 61*)

Long March (1934–1935)   The 6,000-mile (9,600-kilometer) flight of Chinese Communists from southeastern to northwestern China. The Communists, led by **Mao Zedong,** were pursued by the Chinese army under orders from **Chiang Kai-shek.** The four thousand survivors of the march formed the nucleus of a revived Communist movement that defeated the **Guomindang** after World War II. (*p. 889*)

L'Ouverture, François Dominique Toussaint (1743–1803)   Leader of the Haitian Revolution. He freed the slaves and gained effective independence for Haiti despite military interventions by the British and French. (*p. 659*)

ma'at   Egyptian term for the concept of divinely created and maintained order in the universe. Reflecting the ancient Egyptians' belief in an essentially beneficent world, the divine ruler was the earthly guarantor of this order. (See also **pyramid**.) (*p. 44*)

Macartney mission (1792–1793)   The unsuccessful attempt by the British Empire to establish diplomatic relations with the **Qing Empire.** (*p. 621*)

Magellan, Ferdinand (1480?–1521)   Portuguese navigator who led the Spanish expedition of 1519–1522 that was the first to sail around the world. (*p. 472*)

Mahabharata   A vast epic chronicling the events leading up to a cataclysmic battle between related kinship groups in early India. It includes the Bhagavad-Gita, the most important work of Indian sacred literature. (*p. 205*)

Mahayana Buddhism   "Great Vehicle" branch of Buddhism followed in China, Japan, and Central Asia. The focus is on reverence for **Buddha** and for bodhisattvas, enlightened persons who have postponed nirvana to help others attain enlightenment. (*p. 200*)

Malacca   Port city in the modern Southeast Asian country of Malaysia, founded about 1400 as a trading center on the Strait of Malacca. Also spelled Meleka. (*p. 420*)

Mali   Empire created by indigenous Muslims in western Sudan of West Africa from the thirteenth to fifteenth century. It was famous for its role in the trans-Saharan gold trade. (See also **Mansa Kankan Musa** and **Timbuktu**.) (*p. 406*)

Malthus, Thomas (1766–1834)   Eighteenth-century English intellectual who warned that population growth threatened future generations because, in his view, population growth would always outstrip increases in agricultural production. (*p. 979*)

Mamluks   Under the Islamic system of military slavery, Turkic military slaves who formed an important part of the armed forces of the **Abbasid Caliphate** of the ninth and tenth centuries. Mamluks eventually founded their own state, ruling Egypt and Syria (1250–1517). (*p. 258*)

Manchu   Federation of Northeast Asian peoples who founded the **Qing Empire.** (*p. 606*)

Mandate of Heaven   Chinese religious and political ideology developed by the **Zhou,** according to which it was the prerogative of Heaven, the chief deity, to grant power to the ruler of China and to take away that power if the ruler failed to conduct himself justly and in the best interests of his subjects. (*p. 65*)

mandate system Allocation of former German colonies and Ottoman possessions to the victorious powers after World War I, to be administered under League of Nations supervision. (*p. 862*)

manor In medieval Europe, a large, self-sufficient landholding consisting of the lord's residence (manor house), outbuildings, peasant village, and surrounding land. (*p. 285*)

mansabs In India, grants of land given in return for service by rulers of the **Mughal Empire.** (*p. 595*)

Mansa Kankan Musa Ruler of Mali (r. 1312–1337). His pilgrimage through Egypt to **Mecca** in 1324–1325 established the empire's reputation for wealth in the Mediterranean world. (*p. 407*)

manumission A grant of legal freedom to an individual slave. (*p. 558*)

Mao Zedong (1893–1976) Leader of the Chinese Communist Party (1927–1976). He led the Communists on the **Long March** (1934–1935) and rebuilt the Communist Party and Red Army during the Japanese occupation of China (1937–1945). After World War II, he led the Communists to victory over the **Guomindang.** He ordered the **Cultural Revolution** in 1966. (*p. 889*)

maroon A slave who ran away from his or her master. Often a member of a community of runaway slaves in the West Indies and South America. (*p. 559*)

Marshall Plan U.S. program to support the reconstruction of western Europe after World War II. By 1961 more than $20 billion in economic aid had been dispersed. (*p. 940*)

Marx, Karl (1818–1883) German journalist and philosopher, founder of the Marxist branch of **socialism.** He is known for two books: *The Communist Manifesto* (1848) and *Das Kapital* (Vols. I–III, 1867–1894). (*p. 797*)

mass deportation The forcible removal and relocation of large numbers of people or entire populations. The mass deportations practiced by the Assyrian and Persian Empires were meant as a terrifying warning of the consequences of rebellion. They also brought skilled and unskilled labor to the imperial center. (*p. 101*)

mass production The manufacture of many identical products by the division of labor into many small repetitive tasks. This method was introduced into the manufacture of pottery by Josiah Wedgwood and into the spinning of cotton thread by Richard Arkwright. (See also **Arkwright, Richard; Industrial Revolution; Wedgwood, Josiah.**) (*p. 674*)

Mauryan Empire The first state to unify most of the Indian subcontinent. It was founded by Chandragupta Maurya in 324 B.C.E. and survived until 184 B.C.E. From its capital at Pataliputra in the Ganges Valley it grew wealthy from taxes on agriculture, iron mining, and control of trade routes. (See also **Ashoka.**) (*p. 203*)

Maya Mesoamerican civilization concentrated in Mexico's Yucatán Peninsula and in Guatemala and Honduras but never unified into a single empire. Major contributions were in mathematics, astronomy, and development of the calendar. (*p. 344*)

Mecca City in western Arabia; birthplace of the Prophet **Muhammad,** and ritual center of the Islamic religion. (*p. 253*)

mechanization The application of machinery to manufacturing and other activities. Among the first processes to be mechanized were the spinning of cotton thread and the weaving of cloth in late-eighteenth- and early-nineteenth-century England. (*p. 675*)

medieval Literally "middle age," a term that historians of Europe use for the period ca. 500 to ca. 1500, signifying its intermediate point between Greco-Roman antiquity and the Renaissance. (*p. 276*)

Medina City in western Arabia to which the Prophet Muhammad and his followers emigrated in 622 to escape persecution in Mecca. (*p. 255*)

megaliths Structures and complexes of very large stones constructed for ceremonial and religious purposes in **Neolithic** times. (*p. 23*)

Meiji Restoration The political program that followed the destruction of the **Tokugawa Shogunate** in 1868, in which a collection of young leaders set Japan on the path of centralization, industrialization, and imperialism. (See also **Yamagata Aritomo.**) (*p. 806*)

Memphis The capital of Old Kingdom Egypt, near the head of the Nile Delta. Early rulers were interred in the nearby **pyramids.** (*p. 45*)

Menelik II (1844–1911) Emperor of Ethiopia (r. 1889–1911). He enlarged Ethiopia to its present dimensions and defeated an Italian invasion at Adowa (1896). (*p. 828*)

mercantilism European government policies of the sixteenth, seventeenth, and eighteenth centuries designed to promote overseas trade between a country and its colonies and accumulate precious metals by requiring colonies to trade only with their motherland country. The British system was defined by the Navigation Acts, the French system by laws known as the *Exclusif.* (*pp. 560, 686*)

Meroë Capital of a flourishing kingdom in southern Nubia from the fourth century B.C.E. to the fourth century C.E. In this period Nubian culture shows more independence from Egypt and the influence of sub-Saharan Africa. (*p. 72*)

mestizo The term used by Spanish authorities to describe someone of mixed Amerindian and European descent. (*p. 533*)

Middle Passage The part of the **Atlantic Circuit** involving the transportation of enslaved Africans across the Atlantic to the Americas. (*p. 511, 561*)

Ming Empire (1368–1644) Empire based in China that Zhu Yuanzhang established after the overthrow of the **Yuan Empire.** The Ming emperor **Yongle** sponsored the building of the Forbidden City and the voyages of **Zheng He.** The later years of the Ming saw a slowdown in technological development and economic decline. (*pp. 464, 612*)

Ming Empire (1368–1644) Empire based in China that Zhu Yuanzhang established after the overthrow of the **Yuan Empire.** The Ming emperor **Yongle** sponsored the building of the Forbidden City and the voyages of **Zheng He.** The later years of the Ming saw a slow down in technological development and economic decline. (*p. 396*)

Minoan Prosperous civilization on the Aegean island of Crete in the second millennium B.C.E. The Minoans engaged in far-flung commerce around the Mediterranean and exerted powerful cultural influences on the early Greeks. (*p. 95*)

mit'a Andean labor system based on shared obligations to help kinsmen and work on behalf of the ruler and religious organizations. (*p. 355*)

Moche Civilization of north coast of Peru (200–700 C.E.). An important Andean civilization that built extensive irrigation networks as well as impressive urban centers dominated by brick temples. (*p. 356*)

Moctezuma II (1466?–1520) Last Aztec emperor, overthrown by the Spanish conquistador Hernán Cortés. (*p. 480*)

modernization   The process of reforming political, military, economic, social, and cultural traditions in imitation of the early success of Western societies, often with regard for accommodating local traditions in non-Western societies. (*p. 759*)

Mohenjo-Daro   Largest of the cities of the Indus Valley civilization. It was centrally located in the extensive floodplain of the Indus River in contemporary Pakistan. Little is known about the political institutions of Indus Valley communities, but the large-scale of construction at Mohenjo-Daro, the orderly grid of streets, and the standardization of building materials are evidence of central planning. (*p. 50*)

moksha   The Hindu concept of the spirit's "liberation" from the endless cycle of rebirths. There are various avenues—such as physical discipline, meditation, and acts of devotion to the gods—by which the spirit can distance itself from desire for the things of this world and be merged with the divine force that animates the universe. (*p. 199*)

monasticism   Living in a religious community apart from secular society and adhering to a rule stipulating chastity, obedience, and poverty. It was a prominent element of medieval Christianity and Buddhism. Monasteries were the primary centers of learning and literacy in medieval Europe. (*p. 292*)

Mongols   A people of this name is mentioned as early as the records of the **Tang Empire,** living as nomads in northern Eurasia. After 1206 they established an enormous empire under **Genghis Khan,** linking western and eastern Eurasia. (*p. 372*)

monotheism   Belief in the existence of a single divine entity. Some scholars cite the devotion of the Egyptian pharaoh **Akhenaten** to Aten (sun-disk) and his suppression of traditional gods as the earliest instance. The Israelite worship of Yahweh developed into an exclusive belief in one god, and this concept passed into Christianity and Islam. (*p. 109*)

monsoon   Seasonal winds in the Indian Ocean caused by the differences in temperature between the rapidly heating and cooling landmasses of Africa and Asia and the slowly changing ocean waters. These strong and predictable winds have long been ridden across the open sea by sailors, and the large amounts of rainfall that they deposit on parts of India, Southeast Asia, and China allow for the cultivation of several crops a year. (*pp. 196, 402*)

Morelos, José María (1765–1815)   Mexican priest and former student of Miguel Hidalgo y Costilla, he led the forces fighting for Mexican independence until he was captured and executed in 1815. (See also **Hidalgo y Costilla, Miguel.**) (*p. 699*)

most-favored-nation status   A clause in a commercial treaty that awards to any later signatories all the privileges previously granted to the original signatories. (*p. 743*)

movable type   Type in which each individual character is cast on a separate piece of metal. It replaced woodblock printing, allowing for the arrangement of individual letters and other characters on a page, rather than requiring the carving of entire pages at a time. It may have been invented in Korea in the thirteenth century. (See also **printing press.**) (*p. 324*)

Mughal Empire   Muslim state (1526–1857) exercising dominion over most of India in the sixteenth and seventeenth centuries. (*p. 594*)

Muhammad (570–632 C.E.)   Arab prophet; founder of religion of Islam. (*p. 253*)

Muhammad Ali (1769–1849)   Leader of Egyptian modernization in the early nineteenth century. He ruled Egypt as an Ottoman governor, but had imperial ambitions. His descendants ruled Egypt until overthrown in 1952. (*pp. 729, 759*)

mulatto   The term used in Spanish and Portuguese colonies to describe someone of mixed African and European descent. (*p. 534*)

mummy   A body preserved by chemical processes or special natural circumstances, often in the belief that the deceased will need it again in the afterlife. In ancient Egypt the bodies of people who could afford mummification underwent a complex process of removing organs, filling body cavities, dehydrating the corpse with natron, and then wrapping the body with linen bandages and enclosing it in a wooden sarcophagus. (*p. 49*)

Muscovy   Russian principality that emerged gradually during the era of Mongol domination. The Muscovite dynasty ruled without interruption from 1276 to 1598. (*p. 623*)

Muslim   An adherent of the Islamic religion; a person who "submits" (in Arabic, *Islam* means "submission") to the will of God. (*p. 255*)

Mussolini, Benito (1883–1945)   Fascist dictator of Italy (1922–1943). He led Italy to conquer Ethiopia (1935), joined Germany in the Axis pact (1936), and allied Italy with Germany in World War II. He was overthrown in 1943 when the Allies invaded Italy. (*p. 885*)

Mycenae   Site of a fortified palace complex in southern Greece that controlled a Late Bronze Age kingdom. In Homer's epic poems Mycenae was the base of King Agamemnon, who commanded the Greeks besieging Troy. Contemporary archaeologists call the complex Greek society of the second millennium B.C.E. "Mycenaean." (*p. 96*)

Napoleon I (1769–1821)   Overthrew French Directory in 1799 and became emperor of the French in 1804. Failed to defeat Great Britain and abdicated in 1814. Returned to power briefly in 1815 but was defeated and died in exile. (*p. 653*)

Nasir al-Din Tusi (1201–1274)   Persian mathematician and cosmologist whose academy near Tabriz provided the model for the movement of the planets that helped to inspire the Copernican model of the solar system. (*p. 381*)

National Assembly   French Revolutionary assembly (1789–1791). Called first as the Estates General, the three estates came together and demanded radical change. It passed the **Declaration of the Rights of Man** in 1789. (*p. 649*)

nationalism   A political ideology that stresses people's membership in a nation—a community defined by a common culture and history as well as by territory. In the late eighteenth and early nineteenth centuries, nationalism was a force for unity in western Europe. In the late nineteenth century it hastened the disintegration of the Austro-Hungarian and Ottoman Empires. In the twentieth century it provided the ideological foundation for scores of independent countries emerging from **colonialism.** (*p. 802*)

nawab   A Muslim prince allied to British India; technically, a semi-autonomous deputy of the Mughal emperor. (*p. 764*)

Nazis   German political party joined by Adolf Hitler, emphasizing nationalism, racism, and war. When Hitler became chancellor of Germany in 1933, the Nazis became the only legal party and an instrument of Hitler's absolute rule. The party's formal name was National Socialist German Workers' Party. (See also **Hitler, Adolf.**) (*p. 886*)

Nehru, Jawaharlal (1889–1964) Indian statesman. He succeeded Mohandas K. Gandhi as leader of the **Indian National Congress.** He negotiated the end of British colonial rule in India and became India's first prime minister (1947–1964). (*p. 914*)

Neo-Assyrian Empire An empire extending from western Iran to Syria-Palestine, conquered by the Assyrians of northern Mesopotamia between the tenth and seventh centuries B.C.E. They used force and terror and exploited the wealth and labor of their subjects. They also preserved and continued the cultural and scientific developments of Mesopotamian civilization. (*p. 99*)

Neo-Babylonian kingdom Under the Chaldaeans (nomadic kinship groups that settled in southern Mesopotamia in the early first millennium B.C.E.), **Babylon** again became a major political and cultural center in the seventh and sixth centuries B.C.E. After participating in the destruction of Assyrian power, the monarchs Nabopolassar and Nebuchadnezzar took over the southern portion of the Assyrian domains. By destroying the **First Temple** in Jerusalem and deporting part of the population, they initiated the **Diaspora** of the Jews. (*p. 116*)

neo-Confucianism Term used to describe new approaches to understanding classic Confucian texts that became the basic ruling philosophy of China from the **Song** period to the twentieth century. (*p. 323*)

neo-liberalism The term used in Latin America and other developing regions to describe free-market policies that include reducing tariff protection for local industries; the sale of public-sector industries, like national airlines and public utilities, to private investors or foreign corporations; and the reduction of social welfare policies and public-sector employment. (*p. 970*)

Neolithic The period of the Stone Age associated with the ancient **Agricultural Revolution(s).** It follows the **Paleolithic** period. (*p. 13*)

Nevskii, Alexander (1220–1263) Prince of Novgorod (r. 1236–1263). He submitted to the invading Mongols in 1240 and received recognition as the leader of the Russian princes under the **Golden Horde.** (*p. 384*)

New Economic Policy Policy proclaimed by Vladimir Lenin in 1921 to encourage the revival of the Soviet economy by allowing small private enterprises. Joseph Stalin ended the N.E.P. in 1928 and replaced it with a series of **Five-Year Plans.** (See also **Lenin, Vladimir.**) (*pp. 788, 858*)

New France French colony in North America, with a capital in Quebec, founded 1608. New France fell to the British in 1760. (*p. 539*)

New Imperialism Historians' term for the late-nineteenth and early-twentieth-century wave of conquests by European powers, the United States, and Japan, which were followed by the development and exploitation of the newly conquered territories for the benefit of the colonial powers. (*p. 818*)

newly industrialized economies (NIEs) Rapidly growing, new industrial nations of the late twentieth century, including the **Asian Tigers.** (*p. 974*)

new monarchies Historians' term for the monarchies in France, England, and Spain from 1450 to 1600. The centralization of royal power was increasing within more or less fixed territorial limits. (*p. 451*)

nomadism A way of life, forced by a scarcity of resources, in which groups of people continually migrate to find pastures and water. (*p. 372*)

nonaligned nations Developing countries that announced their neutrality in the **Cold War.** (*p. 954*)

nongovernmental organizations (NGOs) Nonprofit international organizations devoted to investigating human rights abuses and providing humanitarian relief. Two NGOs won the Nobel Peace Prize in the 1990s: International Campaign to Ban Landmines (1997) and Doctors Without Borders (1999). (*p. 1010*)

North Atlantic Treaty Organization (NATO) Organization formed in 1949 as a military alliance of western European and North American states against the Soviet Union and its east European allies. (See also **Warsaw Pact.**) (*p. 937*)

Olmec The first Mesoamerican civilization. Between ca. 1200 and 400 B.C.E., the Olmec people of central Mexico created a vibrant civilization that included intensive agriculture, wide-ranging trade, ceremonial centers, and monumental construction. The Olmec had great cultural influence on later Mesoamerican societies, passing on artistic styles, religious imagery, sophisticated astronomical observation for the construction of calendars, and a ritual ball game. (*p. 78*)

Oman Arab state based in Musqat, the main port in the southwest region of the Arabian peninsula. Oman succeeded Portugal as a power in the western Indian Ocean in the eighteenth century. (*p. 600*)

Opium War (1839–1842) War between Britain and the **Qing Empire** that was, in the British view, occasioned by the Qing government's refusal to permit the importation of opium into its territories. The victorious British imposed the one-sided **Treaty of Nanking** on China. (*p. 743*)

Organization of Petroleum Exporting Countries (OPEC) Organization formed in 1960 by oil-producing states to promote their collective interest in generating revenue from oil. (*p. 958*)

Ottoman Empire Islamic state founded by Osman in northwestern Anatolia ca. 1300. After the fall of the **Byzantine Empire,** the Ottoman Empire was based at Istanbul (formerly Constantinople) from 1453 to 1922. It encompassed lands in the Middle East, North Africa, the Caucasus, and eastern Europe. (*pp. 385, 578*)

Páez, José Antonio (1790–1873) Venezuelan soldier who led Simón Bolívar's cavalry force. He became a successful general in the war and built a powerful political base. He was unwilling to accept the constitutional authority of Bolívar's government in distant Bogotá and declared Venezuela's independence from Gran Colombia in 1829. (*p. 704*)

Paleolithic The period of the Stone Age associated with the **evolution** of humans. It predates the **Neolithic** period. (*p. 13*)

Pan-Slavism Movement among Russian intellectuals in the second half of the nineteenth century to identify culturally and politically with the Slavic peoples of eastern Europe. (*p. 739*)

Panama Canal Ship canal cut across the isthmus of Panama by United States Army engineers; it opened in 1914. It greatly shortened the sea voyage between the east and west coasts of North America. The United States turned the canal over to Panama on January 1, 2000. (*p. 839*)

papacy The central administration of the Roman Catholic Church, of which the pope is the head. (*pp. 288, 492*)

papyrus A reed that grows along the banks of the Nile River in Egypt. From it was produced a coarse, paperlike writing medium used by the Egyptians and many other peoples in the ancient Mediterranean and Middle East. (*p. 46*)

Parthians Iranian ruling dynasty between ca. 250 B.C.E. and 226 C.E. (*p. 226*)

patron/client relationship In ancient Rome, a fundamental social relationship in which the patron—a wealthy and powerful individual—provided legal and economic protection and assistance to clients, men of lesser status and means, and in return the clients supported the political careers and economic interests of their patron. (*p. 165*)

Paul (ca. 5–65 C.E.) A Jew from the Greek city of Tarsus in Anatolia, he initially persecuted the followers of Jesus but, after receiving a revelation on the road to Syrian Damascus, became a Christian. Taking advantage of his Hellenized background and Roman citizenship, he traveled throughout Syria-Palestine, Anatolia, and Greece, preaching the new religion and establishing churches. Finding his greatest success among pagans ("gentiles"), he began the process by which Christianity separated from Judaism. (*p. 173*)

pax romana Literally, "Roman peace," it connoted the stability and prosperity that Roman rule brought to the lands of the Roman Empire in the first two centuries C.E. The movement of people and trade goods along Roman roads and safe seas allowed for the spread of cultural practices, technologies, and religious ideas. (*p. 171*)

Pearl Harbor Naval base in Hawaii attacked by Japanese aircraft on December 7, 1941. The sinking of much of the U.S. Pacific Fleet brought the United States into World War II. (*p. 894*)

Peloponnesian War A protracted (431–404 B.C.E.) and costly conflict between the Athenian and Spartan alliance systems that convulsed most of the Greek world. The war was largely a consequence of Athenian imperialism. Possession of a naval empire allowed Athens to fight a war of attrition. Ultimately, Sparta prevailed because of Athenian errors and Persian financial support. (*p. 148*)

perestroika Policy of "restructuring" was an attempt to address long-suppressed economic problems by moving away from central state planning toward a more open economic system. (See also **Gorbachev, Mikhail.**) (*p. 976*)

Pericles (ca. 495–429 B.C.E.) Aristocratic leader who guided the Athenian state through the transformation to full participatory democracy for all male citizens, supervised construction of the Acropolis, and pursued a policy of imperial expansion that led to the **Peloponnesian War.** He formulated a strategy of attrition but died from the plague early in the war. (*p. 143*)

Perón, Eva Duarte (1919–1952) Wife of **Juan Perón** and champion of the poor in Argentina. She was a gifted speaker and popular political leader who campaigned to improve the life of the urban poor by founding schools and hospitals and providing other social benefits. (*p. 927*)

Perón, Juan (1895–1974) President of Argentina (1946–1955, 1973–1974). As a military officer, he championed the rights of labor. Aided by his wife **Eva Duarte Perón,** he was elected president in 1946. He built up Argentinean industry, became very popular among the urban poor, but harmed the economy. (*p. 927*)

Perry, Commodore Matthew A navy commander who, on July 8, 1853, became the first foreigner to break through the barriers that had kept Japan isolated from the rest of the world for 250 years. (*p. 787*)

Persepolis A complex of palaces, reception halls, and treasury buildings erected by the Persian kings **Darius I** and Xerxes in the Persian homeland. It is believed that the New Year's festival was celebrated here, as well as the coronations, weddings, and funerals of the Persian kings, who were buried in cliff-tombs nearby. (*p. 131*)

Persian Wars Conflicts between Greek city-states and the Persian Empire, ranging from the Ionian Revolt (499–494 B.C.E.) through Darius's punitive expedition that failed at Marathon (490 B.C.E.) and the defeat of Xerxes' massive invasion of Greece by the Spartan-led Hellenic League (480–479 B.C.E.). This first major setback for Persian arms launched the Greeks into their period of greatest cultural productivity. **Herodotus** chronicled these events in the first "history" in the Western tradition. (*p. 144*)

personalist leaders Political leaders who rely on charisma and their ability to mobilize and direct the masses of citizens outside the authority of constitutions and laws. Nineteenth-century examples include José Antonio Páez of Venezuela and Andrew Jackson of the United States. Twentieth-century examples include Getulio Vargas of Brazil and Juan Perón of Argentina. (See also **Jackson, Andrew; Páez, José Antonio; Perón, Juan; Vargas, Getulio.**) (*p. 704*)

Peter the Great (1672–1725) Russian tsar (r. 1689–1725). He enthusiastically introduced Western languages and technologies to the Russian elite, moving the capital from Moscow to the new city of St. Petersburg. (*p. 625*)

pharaoh The central figure in the ancient Egyptian state. Believed to be an earthly manifestation of the gods, he used his absolute power to maintain the safety and prosperity of Egypt. (*p. 44*)

Phoenicians Semitic-speaking Canaanites living on the coast of modern Lebanon and Syria in the first millennium B.C.E. From major cities such as Tyre and Sidon, Phoenician merchants and sailors explored the Mediterranean, engaged in widespread commerce, and founded **Carthage** and other colonies in the western Mediterranean. (*p. 110*)

pilgrimage Journey to a sacred shrine by Christians seeking to show their piety, fulfill vows, or gain absolution for sins. Other religions also have pilgrimage traditions, such as the Muslim pilgrimage to **Mecca** and the pilgrimages made by early Chinese Buddhists to India in search of sacred Buddhist writings. (*p. 298*)

Pilgrims Group of English Protestant dissenters who established Plymouth Colony in Massachusetts in 1620 to seek religious freedom after having lived briefly in the Netherlands. (*p. 536*)

Pizarro, Francisco (ca. 1478–1541) Spanish explorer who led the conquest of the **Inca** Empire of Peru in 1531–1533. (*p. 481*)

Planck, Max (1858–1947) German physicist who developed quantum theory and was awarded the Nobel Prize for physics in 1918. (*p. 869*)

plantocracy In the West Indian colonies, the rich men who owned most of the slaves and most of the land, especially in the eighteenth century. (*p. 555*)

polis The Greek term for a **city-state,** an urban center and the agricultural territory under its control. It was the characteristic form of political organization in southern and central Greece in the Archaic and Classical periods. Of the hundreds of city-states in the Mediterranean and Black Sea regions settled by Greeks, some were oligarchic, others democratic, depending on the powers delegated to the Council and the Assembly. (*p. 138*)

positivism A philosophy developed by the French count of Saint-Simon. Positivists believed that social and economic problems could be solved by the application of the scientific method, leading to continuous progress. Their ideas became popular in France and Latin America in the nineteenth century. (*p. 687*)

Potosí Located in Bolivia, one of the richest silver mining centers and most populous cities in colonial Spanish America. (*p. 526*)

printing press A mechanical device for transferring text or graphics from a woodblock or type to paper using ink. Presses using movable type first appeared in Europe in about 1450. See also **movable type.** (*p. 446*)

Protestant Reformation Religious reform movement within the Latin Christian Church beginning in 1519. It resulted in the "protesters" forming several new Christian denominations, including the Lutheran and Reformed Churches and the Church of England. (*p. 493*)

proxy wars During the **Cold War,** local or regional wars in which the superpowers armed, trained, and financed the combatants. (*p. 966*)

Ptolemies The Macedonian dynasty, descended from one of Alexander the Great's officers, that ruled Egypt for three centuries (323–30 B.C.E.). From their magnificent capital at Alexandria on the Mediterranean coast, the Ptolemies largely took over the system created by Egyptian pharaohs to extract the wealth of the land, rewarding Greeks and Hellenized non-Greeks serving in the military and administration. (*p. 151*)

Puritans English Protestant dissenters who believed that God predestined souls to heaven or hell before birth. They founded Massachusetts Bay Colony in 1629. (*p. 536*)

pyramid A large, triangular stone monument, used in Egypt and Nubia as a burial place for the king. The largest pyramids, erected during the Old Kingdom near Memphis with stone tools and compulsory labor, reflect the Egyptian belief that the proper and spectacular burial of the divine ruler would guarantee the continued prosperity of the land. (See also **ma'at.**) (*p. 44*)

Qin A people and state in the Wei Valley of eastern China that conquered rival states and created the first Chinese empire (221–206 B.C.E.). The Qin ruler, **Shi Huangdi,** standardized many features of Chinese society and ruthlessly marshaled subjects for military and construction projects, engendering hostility that led to the fall of his dynasty shortly after his death. The Qin framework was largely taken over by the succeeding **Han** Empire. (*p. 178*)

Qing Empire Empire established in China by Manchus who overthrew the **Ming Empire** in 1644. At various times the Qing also controlled Manchuria, Mongolia, Turkestan, and Tibet. The last Qing emperor was overthrown in 1911. (*p. 615*)

Quran Book composed of divine revelations made to the Prophet **Muhammad** between ca. 610 and his death in 632; the sacred text of the religion of **Islam.** (*p. 256*)

railroads Networks of iron (later steel) rails on which steam (later electric or diesel) locomotives pulled long trains at high speeds. The first railroads were built in England in the 1830s. Their success caused a railroad-building boom throughout the world that lasted well into the twentieth century. (*p. 788*)

Rajputs Members of a mainly Hindu warrior caste from northwest India. The Mughal emperors drew most of their Hindu officials from this caste, and **Akbar I** married a Rajput princess. (*p. 596*)

Ramesses II A long-lived ruler of New Kingdom Egypt (r. 1290–1224 B.C.E.). He reached an accommodation with the **Hittites** of Anatolia after a standoff in battle at Kadesh in Syria. He built on a grand scale throughout Egypt. (*p. 93*)

Rashid al-Din (d. 1318) Adviser to the **Il-khan** ruler Ghazan, who converted to Islam on Rashid's advice. (*p. 381*)

recaptives Africans rescued by Britain's Royal Navy from the illegal slave trade of the nineteenth century and restored to free status. (*p. 763*)

reconquest of Iberia Beginning in the eleventh century, military campaigns by various Iberian Christian states to recapture territory taken by Muslims. In 1492 the last Muslim ruler was defeated, and Spain and Portugal emerged as united kingdoms. (*p. 452*)

Renaissance (European) A period of intense artistic and intellectual activity, said to be a "rebirth" of Greco-Roman culture. Usually divided into an Italian Renaissance, from roughly the mid-fourteenth to mid-fifteenth century, and a Northern (trans-Alpine) Renaissance, from roughly the early fifteenth to early seventeenth century. (*pp. 443, 491*)

Revolutions of 1848 Democratic and nationalist revolutions that swept across Europe. The monarchy in France was overthrown. In Germany, Austria, Italy, and Hungary the revolutions failed. (*p. 662*)

Rhodes, Cecil (1853–1902) British entrepreneur and politician involved in the expansion of the British Empire from South Africa into Central Africa. The colonies of Southern Rhodesia (now Zimbabwe) and Northern Rhodesia (now Zambia) were named after him. (*p. 827*)

Robespierre, Maximilien (1758–1794) Young provincial lawyer who led the most radical phases of the French Revolution. His execution ended the Reign of Terror. See **Jacobins.** (*p. 652*)

Romanization The process by which the Latin language and Roman culture became dominant in the western provinces of the Roman Empire. The Roman government did not actively seek to Romanize the subject peoples, but indigenous peoples in the provinces often chose to Romanize because of the political and economic advantages that it brought, as well as the allure of Roman success. (*p. 172*)

Roman Principate A term used to characterize Roman government in the first three centuries C.E., based on the ambiguous title *princeps* ("first citizen") adopted by Augustus to conceal his military dictatorship. (*p. 170*)

Roman Republic The period from 507 to 31 B.C.E., during which Rome was largely governed by the aristocratic **Roman Senate.** (*p 163*)

Roman Senate A council whose members were the heads of wealthy, landowning families. Originally an advisory body to the early kings, in the era of the **Roman Republic** the Senate effectively governed the Roman state and the growing empire. Under Senate leadership, Rome conquered an empire of unprecedented extent in the lands surrounding the Mediterranean Sea. In the first century B.C.E. quarrels among powerful and ambitious senators and failure to address social and economic problems led to civil wars and the emergence of the rule of the emperors. (*p. 163*)

Royal African Company (RAC) A trading company chartered by the English government in 1672 to conduct its merchants' trade on the Atlantic coast of Africa. (*p. 560*)

sacrifice A gift given to a deity, often with the aim of creating a relationship, gaining favor, and obligating the god to provide some benefit to the sacrificer, sometimes in order to sustain the deity and thereby guarantee the continuing vitality of the natural world. The object devoted to the deity could be as simple as a cup of wine poured on the ground, a live animal slain on the altar, or, in the most extreme case, the ritual killing of a human being. (*p. 141*)

Safavid Empire   Iranian kingdom (1502–1722) established by Ismail Safavi, who declared Iran a Shi'ite state. (*p. 589*)

Sahel   Belt south of the Sahara; literally "coastland" in Arabic. (*p. 237*)

samurai   Literally "those who serve," the hereditary military elite of the **Tokugawa Shogunate.** (*p. 606*)

Sandinistas   Members of a leftist coalition that overthrew the Nicaraguan dictatorship of Anastasia Somoza in 1979 and attempted to install a socialist economy. The United States financed armed opposition by the Contras. The Sandinistas lost national elections in 1990. (*p. 968*)

Sanger, Margaret (1883–1966)   American nurse and author; pioneer in the movement for family planning; organized conferences and established birth control clinics. (*p. 869*)

Sasanid Empire   Iranian empire, established ca. 224, with a capital in Ctesiphon, Mesopotamia. The Sasanid emperors established **Zoroastrianism** as the state religion. Islamic Arab armies overthrew the empire ca. 651. (*p. 250*)

satrap   The governor of a province in the Achaemenid Persian Empire, often a relative of the king. He was responsible for protection of the province and for forwarding tribute to the central administration. Satraps in outlying provinces enjoyed considerable autonomy. (*p. 130*)

savanna   Tropical or subtropical grassland, either treeless or with occasional clumps of trees. Most extensive in **sub-Saharan Africa** but also present in South America. (*p. 240*)

schism   A formal split within a religious community. See **Great Western Schism.** (*p. 278*)

scholasticism   A philosophical and theological system, associated with Thomas Aquinas, devised to reconcile Aristotelian philosophy and Roman Catholic theology in the thirteenth century. (*p. 444*)

Scientific Revolution   The intellectual movement in Europe, initially associated with planetary motion and other aspects of physics, that by the seventeenth century had laid the groundwork for modern science. (*p. 497*)

"scramble" for Africa   Sudden wave of conquests in Africa by European powers in the 1880s and 1890s. Britain obtained most of eastern Africa, France most of northwestern Africa. Other countries (Germany, Belgium, Portugal, Italy, and Spain) acquired lesser amounts. (*p. 823*)

scribe   In the governments of many ancient societies, a professional position reserved for men who had undergone the lengthy training required to be able to read and write using **cuneiforms, hieroglyphics,** or other early, cumbersome writing systems. (*p. 39*)

seasoning   An often difficult period of adjustment to new climates, disease environments, and work routines, such as that experienced by slaves newly arrived in the Americas. (*p. 557*)

Selassie, Haile (1892–1975)   Emperor of Ethiopia (r. 1930–1974) and symbol of African independence. He fought the Italian invasion of his country in 1935 and regained his throne during World War II, when British forces expelled the Italians. He ruled **Ethiopia** as a traditional autocracy until he was overthrown in 1974. (*p. 920*)

Semitic   Family of related languages long spoken across parts of western Asia and northern Africa. In antiquity these languages included Hebrew, Aramaic, and Phoenician. The most widespread modern member of the Semitic family is Arabic. (*p. 33*)

"separate spheres"   Nineteenth-century idea in Western societies that men and women, especially of the middle class, should have clearly differentiated roles in society: women as wives, mothers, and homemakers; men as breadwinners and participants in business and politics. (*p. 795*)

sepoy   A soldier in South Asia, especially in the service of the British. (*p. 765*)

Sepoy Rebellion   The revolt of Indian soldiers in 1857 against certain practices that violated religious customs; also known as the Sepoy Mutiny. (*p. 767*)

Serbia   The Ottoman province in the Balkans that rose up against **Janissary** control in the early 1800s. After World War II the central province of Yugoslavia. Serb leaders struggled to maintain dominance as the Yugoslav federation dissolved in the 1990s. (*p. 730*)

serf   In medieval Europe, an agricultural laborer legally bound to a lord's property and obligated to perform set services for the lord. In Russia some serfs worked as artisans and in factories; serfdom was not abolished there until 1861. (*pp. 285, 625*)

shaft graves   A term used for the burial sites of elite members of Mycenaean Greek society in the mid-second millennium B.C.E. At the bottom of deep shafts lined with stone slabs, the bodies were laid out along with gold and bronze jewelry, implements, weapons, and masks. (*p. 96*)

Shah Abbas I   The fifth and most renowned ruler of the **Safavid** dynasty in Iran (r. 1587–1629). Abbas moved the royal capital to Isfahan in 1598. (*p. 591*)

shamanism   The practice of identifying special individuals (shamans) who will interact with spirits for the benefit of the community. Characteristic of the Korean kingdoms of the early medieval period and of early societies of Central Asia. (*p. 327*)

Shang   The dominant people in the earliest Chinese dynasty for which we have written records (ca. 1750–1045 B.C.E.). Ancestor worship, divination by means of oracle bones, and the use of bronze vessels for ritual purposes were major elements of Shang culture. (*p. 61*)

Shi Huangdi   Founder of the short-lived **Qin** dynasty and creator of the Chinese Empire (r. 221–210 B.C.E.). He is remembered for his ruthless conquests of rival states, standardization of practices, and forcible organization of labor for military and engineering tasks. His tomb, with its army of life-size terracotta soldiers, has been partially excavated. (*p. 178*)

Shi'ites   Muslims belonging to the branch of Islam believing that God vests leadership of the community in a descendant of Muhammad's son-in-law Ali. Shi'ism is the state religion of Iran. (See also **Sunnis.**) (*pp. 256, 589*)

Siberia   The extreme northeastern sector of Asia, including the Kamchatka Peninsula and the present Russian coast of the Arctic Ocean, the Bering Strait, and the Sea of Okhotsk. (*p. 623*)

Sikhism   Indian religion founded by the guru Nanak (1469–1539) in the Punjab region of northwest India. After the Mughal emperor ordered the beheading of the ninth guru in 1675, Sikh warriors mounted armed resistance to Mughal rule. (*p. 597*)

Silk Road   Caravan routes connecting China and the Middle East across Central Asia and Iran. (*p. 226*)

Sima Qian   Chief astrologer for the Han dynasty emperor Wu. He composed a monumental history of China from its legendary origins to his own time and is regarded as the Chinese "father of history." (*p. 182*)

Slavophiles Russian intellectuals in the early nineteenth century who favored resisting western European influences and taking pride in the traditional peasant values and institutions of the Slavic people. (*p. 739*)

"small traditions" Historians' term for a localized, usually nonliterate, set of customs and beliefs adhered to by a single society, often in conjunction with a **"great tradition."** (*p. 240*)

socialism A political ideology that originated in Europe in the 1830s. Socialists advocated government protection of workers from exploitation by property owners and government ownership of industries. This ideology led to the founding of socialist or labor parties throughout Europe in the second half of the nineteenth century. (See also **Marx, Karl.**) (*p. 797*)

Socrates Athenian philosopher (ca. 470–399 B.C.E.) who shifted the emphasis of philosophical investigation from questions of natural science to ethics and human behavior. He attracted young disciples from elite families but made enemies by revealing the ignorance and pretensions of others, culminating in his trial and execution by the Athenian state. (*p. 146*)

Sokoto Caliphate A large Muslim state founded in 1809 in what is now northern Nigeria. (*p. 759*)

Solidarity Polish trade union created in 1980 to protest working conditions and political repression. It began the nationalist opposition to communist rule that led in 1989 to the fall of communism in eastern Europe. (*p. 976*)

Song Empire Empire in central and southern China (960–1126) while the Liao people controlled the north. Empire in southern China (1127–1279; the "Southern Song") while the Jin people controlled the north. Distinguished for its advances in technology, medicine, astronomy, and mathematics. (*p. 319*)

Songhai A people, language, kingdom, and empire in western Sudan in West Africa. At its height in the sixteenth century, the Muslim Songhai Empire stretched from the Atlantic to the land of the **Hausa** and was a major player in the trans-Saharan trade. (*p. 569*)

Srivijaya A state based on the Indonesian island of Sumatra, between the seventh and eleventh centuries C.E. It amassed wealth and power by a combination of selective adaptation of Indian technologies and concepts, control of the lucrative trade routes between India and China, and skillful showmanship and diplomacy in holding together a disparate realm of inland and coastal territories. (See also **theater-state.**) (*p. 214*)

Stalin, Joseph (1879–1953) Bolshevik revolutionary, head of the Soviet Communist Party after 1924, and dictator of the Soviet Union from 1928 to 1953. He led the Soviet Union with an iron fist, using **Five-Year Plans** to increase industrial production and terror to crush all opposition. (*p. 878*)

Stalingrad City in Russia, site of a Red Army victory over the German army in 1942–1943. The Battle of Stalingrad was the turning point in the war between Germany and the Soviet Union. Today Volgograd. (*p. 892*)

Stanley, Henry Morton (1841–1904) British-American explorer of Africa, famous for his expeditions in search of Dr. David Livingstone. Stanley helped King **Leopold II** establish the Congo Free State. (*p. 825*)

steam engine A machine that turns the energy released by burning fuel into motion. Thomas Newcomen built the first crude but workable steam engine in 1712. **James Watt** vastly improved his device in the 1760s and 1770s. Steam power was later applied to moving machinery in factories and to powering ships and locomotives. (*p. 677*)

steel A form of iron that is both durable and flexible. It was first mass-produced in the 1860s and quickly became the most widely used metal in construction, machinery, and railroad equipment. (*p. 790*)

steppes Treeless plains, especially the high, flat expanses of northern Eurasia, which usually have little rain and are covered with coarse grass. They are good lands for nomads and their herds. Living on the steppes promoted the breeding of horses and the development of military skills that were essential to the rise of the Mongol Empire. (*p. 240*)

stirrup Device for securing a horseman's feet, enabling him to wield weapons more effectively. First evidence of the use of stirrups was among the Kushan people of northern Afghanistan in approximately the first century C.E. (*p. 230*)

stock exchange A place where shares in a company or business enterprise are bought and sold. (*p. 502*)

Stone Age The historical period characterized by the production of tools from stone and other nonmetallic substances. It was followed in some places by the Bronze Age and more generally by the **Iron Age.** (*p. 13*)

submarine telegraph cables Insulated copper cables laid along the bottom of a sea or ocean for telegraphic communication. The first short cable was laid across the English Channel in 1851; the first successful transatlantic cable was laid in 1866. (See also **electric telegraph.**) (*p. 790*)

sub-Saharan Africa Portion of the African continent lying south of the Sahara. (*p. 240*)

Suez Canal Ship canal dug across the isthmus of Suez in Egypt, designed by Ferdinand de Lesseps. It opened to shipping in 1869 and shortened the sea voyage between Europe and Asia. Its strategic importance led to the British conquest of Egypt in 1882. (*p. 817*)

Suleiman the Magnificent (1494–1566) The most illustrious sultan of the **Ottoman Empire** (r. 1520–1566); also known as Suleiman Kanuni, "The Lawgiver." He significantly expanded the empire in the Balkans and eastern Mediterranean. (*p. 581*)

Sumerians The people who dominated southern Mesopotamia through the end of the third millennium B.C.E. They were responsible for the creation of many fundamental elements of Mesopotamian culture—such as irrigation technology, **cuneiform,** and religious conceptions—taken over by their **Semitic** successors. (*p. 31*)

Sunnis Muslims belonging to branch of Islam believing that the community should select its own leadership. The majority religion in most Islamic countries. (See also **Shi'ites.**) (*p. 256*)

Sun Yat-sen (1867–1925) Chinese nationalist revolutionary, founder and leader of the **Guomindang** until his death. He attempted to create a liberal democratic political movement in China but was thwarted by military leaders. (*p. 861*)

Swahili Bantu language with Arabic loanwords spoken in coastal regions of East Africa. (*p. 600*)

Swahili Coast East African shores of the Indian Ocean between the Horn of Africa and the Zambezi River; from the Arabic *sawahil,* meaning "shores." (*p. 417*)

Taiping Rebellion (1851–1864) The most destructive civil war before the twentieth century. A Christian-inspired rural rebellion that threatened to topple the **Qing Empire.** (*p. 744*)

Tamil kingdoms The kingdoms of southern India, inhabited primarily by speakers of Dravidian languages, which developed in partial isolation, and somewhat differently, from the Aryan north. They produced epics, poetry, and performance arts. Elements of Tamil religious beliefs were merged into the Hindu synthesis. (*p. 205*)

Tang Empire   Empire unifying China and part of Central Asia, founded 618 and ended 907. The Tang emperors presided over a magnificent court at their capital, Chang'an. (*p. 310*)

Tanzimat   "Restructuring" reforms by the nineteenth-century Ottoman rulers, intended to move civil law away from the control of religious elites and make the military and the bureaucracy more efficient. (*p. 731*)

Tecumseh (1768–1813)   Shawnee leader who attempted to organize an Amerindian confederacy to prevent the loss of additional territory to American settlers. He became an ally of the British in War of 1812 and died in battle. (*p. 709*)

Tenochtitlan   Capital of the Aztec Empire, located on an island in Lake Texcoco. Its population was about 125,000 on the eve of Spanish conquest. Mexico City was constructed on its ruins. (*p. 348*)

Teotihuacan   A powerful **city-state** in central Mexico (100 B.C.E.–750 C.E.). Its population was about 150,000 at its peak in 600. (*p. 342*)

terrorism   Political belief that extreme and seemingly random violence will destabilize a government and permit the terrorists to gain political advantage. Though an old technique, terrorism gained prominence in the late twentieth century with the growth of worldwide mass media that, through their news coverage, amplified public fears of terrorist acts. (*p. 1008*)

theater-state   Historians' term for a state that acquires prestige and power by developing attractive cultural forms and staging elaborate public ceremonies (as well as redistributing valuable resources) to attract and bind subjects to the center. Examples include the **Gupta Empire** in India and **Srivijaya** in Southeast Asia. (*p. 206*)

Thebes   Capital city of Egypt and home of the ruling dynasties during the Middle and New Kingdoms. Amon, patron deity of Thebes, became one of the chief gods of Egypt. Monarchs were buried across the river in the Valley of the Kings. (*p. 45*)

Theravada Buddhism   "Way of the Elders" branch of Buddhism followed in Sri Lanka and much of Southeast Asia. Therevada remains close to the original principles set forth by the **Buddha;** it downplays the importance of gods and emphasizes austerity and the individual's search for enlightenment. (*p. 200*)

Third-Century Crisis   Historians' term for the political, military, and economic turmoil that beset the Roman Empire during much of the third century C.E.: frequent changes of ruler, civil wars, barbarian invasions, decline of urban centers, and near-destruction of long-distance commerce and the monetary economy. After 284 C.E. Diocletian restored order by making fundamental changes. (*p. 176*)

Third World   Term applied to a group of developing countries who professed nonalignment during the **Cold War.** (*p. 954*)

three-field system   A rotational system for agriculture in which one field grows grain, one grows legumes, and one lies fallow. It gradually replaced two-field system in medieval Europe. (*p. 432*)

Tiananmen Square   Site in Beijing where Chinese students and workers gathered to demand greater political openness in 1989. The demonstration was crushed by Chinese military with great loss of life. (*p. 975*)

Tibet   Country centered on the high, mountain-bounded plateau north of India. Tibetan political power occasionally extended farther to the north and west between the seventh and thirteen centuries. (*p. 316*)

Timbuktu   City on the Niger River in the modern country of Mali. It was founded by the Tuareg as a seasonal camp sometime after 1000. As part of the **Mali** Empire, Timbuktu became a major terminus of the trans-Saharan trade and a center of Islamic learning. (*p. 421*)

Timur (1336–1405)   Member of a prominent family of the Mongols' Jagadai Khanate, Timur through conquest gained control over much of Central Asia and Iran. He consolidated the status of Sunni Islam as orthodox, and his descendants, the Timurids, maintained his empire for nearly a century and founded the **Mughal Empire** in India. (*p. 381*)

Tiwanaku   Name of capital city and empire centered on the region near Lake Titicaca in modern Bolivia (375–1000 C.E.). (*p. 357*)

Tokugawa Shogunate (1603–1868)   The last of the three shogunates of Japan. (*p. 607*)

Toltecs   Powerful postclassic empire in central Mexico (900–1168 C.E.). It influenced much of Mesoamerica. Aztecs claimed ties to this earlier civilization. (*p. 347*)

trans-Saharan caravan routes   Trading network linking North Africa with **sub-Saharan Africa** across the Sahara. (*p. 235*)

Treaty of Nanking (1842)   The treaty that concluded the **Opium War.** It awarded Britain a large indemnity from the **Qing Empire,** denied the Qing government tariff control over some of its own borders, opened additional ports of residence to Britons, and ceded the island of Hong Kong to Britain. (*p. 743*)

Treaty of Versailles (1919)   The treaty imposed on Germany by France, Great Britain, the United States, and other Allied Powers after World War I. It demanded that Germany dismantle its military and give up some lands to Poland. It was resented by many Germans. (*p. 856*)

treaty ports   Cities opened to foreign residents as a result of the forced treaties between the **Qing Empire** and foreign signatories. In the treaty ports, foreigners enjoyed **extraterritoriality.** (*p. 743*)

tributary system   A system in which, from the time of the **Han** Empire, countries in East and Southeast Asia not under the direct control of empires based in China nevertheless enrolled as tributary states, acknowledging the superiority of the emperors in China in exchange for trading rights or strategic alliances. (*p. 314*)

tribute system   A system in which defeated peoples were forced to pay a tax in the form of goods and labor. This forced transfer of food, cloth, and other goods subsidized the development of large cities. An important component of the Aztec and Inca economies. (*p. 349*)

trireme   Greek and Phoenician warship of the fifth and fourth centuries B.C.E. It was sleek and light, powered by 170 oars arranged in three vertical tiers. Manned by skilled sailors, it was capable of short bursts of speed and complex maneuvers. (*p. 145*)

tropical rain forest   High-precipitation forest zones of the Americas, Africa, and Asia lying between the Tropic of Cancer and the Tropic of Capricorn. (*p. 240*)

tropics   Equatorial region between the Tropic of Cancer and the Tropic of Capricorn. It is characterized by generally warm or hot temperatures year-round, though much variation exists due to altitude and other factors. Temperate zones north and south of the tropics generally have a winter season. (*p. 402*)

Truman Doctrine   Foreign policy initiated by U.S. president Harry Truman in 1947. It offered military aid to help Turkey and Greece resist Soviet military pressure and subversion. (*p. 941*)

tsar (czar)   From Latin *caesar,* this Russian title for a monarch was first used in reference to a Russian ruler by Ivan III (r. 1462–1505). (*pp. 385, 623*)

Tulip Period (1718–1730) Last years of the reign of Ottoman sultan Ahmed III, during which European styles and attitudes became briefly popular in Istanbul. (*p. 587*)

Tupac Amaru II Member of Inca aristocracy who led a rebellion against Spanish authorities in Peru in 1780–1781. He was captured and executed with his wife and other members of his family. (*p. 543*)

tyrant The term the Greeks used to describe someone who seized and held power in violation of the normal procedures and traditions of the community. Tyrants appeared in many Greek **city-states** in the seventh and sixth centuries B.C.E., often taking advantage of the disaffection of the emerging middle class and, by weakening the old elite, unwittingly contributing to the evolution of **democracy.** (*p. 140*)

Uighurs A group of Turkic-speakers who controlled their own centralized empire from 744 to 840 in Mongolia and Central Asia. (*p. 316*)

ulama Muslim religious scholars. From the ninth century onward, the primary interpreters of Islamic law and the social core of Muslim urban societies. (*p. 261*)

Umayyad Caliphate First hereditary dynasty of Muslim caliphs (661 to 750). From their capital at Damascus, the Umayyads ruled an empire that extended from Spain to India. Overthrown by the **Abbasid Caliphate.** (*p. 256*)

umma The community of all Muslims. A major innovation against the background of seventh-century Arabia, where traditionally kinship rather than faith had determined membership in a community. (*p. 255*)

underdevelopment The condition experienced by economies that depend on colonial forms of production such as the export of raw materials and plantation crops with low wages and low investment in education. (*p. 716*)

United Nations International organization founded in 1945 to promote world peace and cooperation. It replaced the **League of Nations.** (*p. 937*)

Universal Declaration of Human Rights A 1948 United Nations covenant binding signatory nations to the observance of specified rights. (*p. 1009*)

universities Degree-granting institutions of higher learning. Those that appeared in the **Latin West** from about 1200 onward became the model of all modern universities. (*p. 444*)

Ural Mountains This north-south range separates Siberia from the rest of Russia. It is commonly considered the boundary between the continents of Europe and Asia. (*p. 623*)

Urdu A Persian-influenced literary form of Hindi written in Arabic characters and used as a literary language since the 1300s. (*p. 421*)

utopian socialism A philosophy introduced by the Frenchman Charles Fourier in the early nineteenth century. Utopian socialists hoped to create humane alternatives to industrial capitalism by building self-sustaining communities whose inhabitants would work cooperatively. (See also **socialism.**) (*p. 687*)

Vargas, Getulio (1883–1954) Dictator of Brazil from 1930 to 1945 and from 1951 to 1954. Defeated in the presidential election of 1930, he overthrew the government and created Estado Novo ("New State"), a dictatorship that emphasized industrialization and helped the urban poor but did little to alleviate the problems of the peasants. (*p. 925*)

varna/jati Two categories of social identity of great importance in Indian history. *Varna* are the four major social divisions: the *Brahmin* priest class, the *Kshatriya* warrior/administrator class, the *Vaishya* merchant/farmer class, and the *Shudra* laborer class. Within the system of *varna* are many *jati,* regional groups of people who have a common occupational sphere, and who marry, eat, and generally interact with other members of their group. (*pp. 197, 198*)

vassal In medieval Europe, a sworn supporter of a king or lord committed to rendering specified military service to that king or lord. (*p. 286*)

Vedas Early Indian sacred "knowledge"—the literal meaning of the term—long preserved and communicated orally by Brahmin priests and eventually written down. These religious texts, including the thousand poetic hymns to various deities contained in the Rig Veda, are our main source of information about the Vedic period (ca. 1500–500 B.C.E.). (*p. 197*)

Versailles The huge palace built for French King Louis XIV south of Paris in the town of the same name. The palace symbolized the preeminence of French power and architecture in Europe and the triumph of royal authority over the French nobility. (*p. 510*)

Victorian Age The reign of Queen Victoria of Great Britain (r. 1837–1901). The term is also used to describe late-nineteenth-century society, with its rigid moral standards and sharply differentiated roles for men and women and for middle-class and working-class people. (See also **"separate spheres."**) (*p. 795*)

Vietnam War (1954–1975) Conflict pitting North Vietnam and South Vietnamese communist guerrillas against the South Vietnamese government, aided after 1961 by the United States. (*p. 943*)

Villa, Francisco "Pancho" (1877–1923) A popular leader during the Mexican Revolution. An outlaw in his youth, when the revolution started, he formed a cavalry army in the north of Mexico and fought for the rights of the landless in collaboration with **Emiliano Zapata.** He was assassinated in 1923. (*p. 922*)

Wari Andean civilization culturally linked to **Tiwanaku,** perhaps beginning as a colony of Tiwanaku. (*p. 357*)

Warsaw Pact The 1955 treaty binding the Soviet Union and countries of eastern Europe in an alliance against the **North Atlantic Treaty Organization.** (*p. 937*)

Washington, George (1732–1799) Military commander of the American Revolution. He was the first elected president of the United States (1789–1799). (*p. 645*)

water wheel A mechanism that harnesses the energy in flowing water to grind grain or to power machinery. It was used in many parts of the world but was especially common in Europe from 1200 to 1900. (*p. 434*)

Watt, James (1736–1819) Scot who invented the condenser and other improvements that made the **steam engine** a practical source of power for industry and transportation. The watt, an electrical measurement, is named after him. (*p. 677*)

weapons of mass destruction Nuclear, chemical, and biological devices that are capable of injuring and killing large numbers of people. (*p. 1005*)

Wedgwood, Josiah (1730–1795) English industrialist whose pottery works were the first to produce fine-quality pottery by industrial methods. (*p. 674*)

Western Front A line of trenches and fortifications in World War I that stretched without a break from Switzerland to the North Sea. Scene of most of the fighting between Germany, on the one hand, and France and Britain, on the other. (*p. 850*)

Wilson, Woodrow (1856–1924) President of the United States (1913–1921) and the leading figure at the Paris Peace Conference of 1919. He was unable to persuade the U.S. Congress to ratify the **Treaty of Versailles** or join the **League of Nations.** (*p. 854*)

witch-hunt The pursuit of people suspected of witchcraft, especially in northern Europe in the late sixteenth and seventeenth centuries. (*p. 496*)

Women's Rights Convention An 1848 gathering of women angered by their exclusion from an international antislavery meeting. They met at Seneca Falls, New York, to discuss women's rights. (*p. 716*)

World Bank A specialized agency of the United Nations that makes loans to countries for economic development, trade promotion, and debt consolidation. Its formal name is the International Bank for Reconstruction and Development. (*p. 939*)

World Trade Organization (WTO) An international body established in 1995 to foster and bring order to international trade. (*p. 1003*)

Wright, Wilbur (1867–1912), and Orville (1871–1948) American bicycle mechanics; the first to build and fly an airplane, at Kitty Hawk, North Carolina, December 7, 1903. (*p. 869*)

Xiongnu A confederation of nomadic peoples living beyond the northwest frontier of ancient China. Chinese rulers tried a variety of defenses and stratagems to ward off these "barbarians," as they called them, and finally succeeded in dispersing the Xiongnu in the first century C.E. (*p. 180*)

Yamagata Aritomo (1838–1922) One of the leaders of the **Meiji Restoration.** (*pp. 746, 813*)

Yi (1392–1910) The Yi dynasty ruled Korea from the fall of the **Koryo** kingdom to the colonization of Korea by Japan. (*p. 394*)

yin/yang In Chinese belief, complementary factors that help to maintain the equilibrium of the world. Yang is associated with masculine, light, and active qualities; yin with feminine, dark, and passive qualities. (*p. 70*)

Yongle Reign period of Zhu Di (1360–1424), the third emperor of the **Ming Empire** (r. 1403–1424). He sponsored the building of the Forbidden City, a huge encyclopedia project, the expeditions of **Zheng He,** and the reopening of China's borders to trade and travel. (*p. 390*)

Young Ottomans Movement of young intellectuals to institute liberal reforms and build a feeling of national identity in the Ottoman Empire in the second half of the nineteenth century. (*p. 737*)

Yuan Empire (1271–1368) Empire created in China and Siberia by **Khubilai Khan.** (*p. 377*)

Yuan Shikai (1859–1916) Chinese general and first president of the Chinese Republic (1912–1916). He stood in the way of the democratic movement led by **Sun Yat-sen.** (*p. 861*)

Zapata, Emiliano (1879–1919) Revolutionary and leader of peasants in the Mexican Revolution. He mobilized landless peasants in south-central Mexico in an attempt to seize and divide the lands of the wealthy landowners. Though successful for a time, he was ultimately defeated and assassinated. (*p. 921*)

Zen The Japanese word for a branch of **Mahayana Buddhism** based on highly disciplined meditation. It is known in Sanskrit as *dhyana*, in Chinese as *chan*, and in Korean as *son*. (*p. 324*)

Zheng He (1371–1435) An imperial eunuch and Muslim, entrusted by the Ming emperor **Yongle** with a series of state voyages that took his gigantic ships through the Indian Ocean, from Southeast Asia to Africa. (*pp. 390, 464*)

Zhou The people and dynasty that took over the dominant position in north China from the **Shang** and created the concept of the **Mandate of Heaven** to justify their rule. The Zhou era, particularly the vigorous early period (1045–771 B.C.E.), was remembered in Chinese tradition as a time of prosperity and benevolent rule. In the later Zhou period (771–221 B.C.E.), centralized control broke down, and warfare among many small states became frequent. (*p. 64*)

ziggurat A massive pyramidal stepped tower made of mud bricks. It is associated with religious complexes in ancient Mesopotamian cities, but its function is unknown. (*p. 40*)

Zoroastrianism A religion originating in ancient Iran with the prophet Zoroaster. It centered on a single benevolent deity—Ahuramazda—who engaged in a twelve-thousand-year struggle with demonic forces before prevailing and restoring a pristine world. Emphasizing truth-telling, purity, and reverence for nature, the religion demanded that humans choose sides in the struggle between good and evil. Those whose good conduct indicated their support for Ahuramazda would be rewarded in the afterlife. Others would be punished. The religion of the Achaemenid and Sasanid Persians, Zoroastrianism may have spread within their realms and influenced Judaism, Christianity, and other faiths. (*p. 132*)

Zulu A people of modern South Africa whom King Shaka united in 1818. (*p. 756*)

INDEX

Abbas I, Shah, 588, 591, 592*(illus.)*, 594

'Abd al-Qadir, 761

Abdul Hamid II, Sultan, 737, 740, 846

Abdul Mejid, Sultan, 731, 736

Abkhazia, 740

Abolition (abolitionist movement), 634. *See also* Slave trade, African, end of; Bolívar and, 696; in Cuba, 711, 712–713, 778; in Dutch colonies, 713, 778; in French colonies, 636*(illus.)*, 637, 660, 662, 712–713, 778; Great Britain and, 685, 699, 712, 762; legitimate trade with Africa and, 761–763; in Mexico, 707; in United States, 707, 711–712; in Western Hemisphere, 711–713

Aborigines, Australian, 775, 776 *and illus.*, 778

Abortion, 869, 981, 1012; in Soviet bloc, 869, 882, 883, 982. *See also* Birth control

Absolutism: *See also* Dictatorship; of French monarchs, 510; of Russiam tsars, 627, 739

Accra, Gold Coast, 918

Acheh, 1004

Acheh Sultanate, 598, 601

Acosta, Gladys, 970–971

Adal, 474

Adams, John Quincy, 704

Addams, Jane, 868

Addis Ababa, 920

Aden, 475, 478, 582

Administration: *See also* Bureaucracy; Civil Service; British North America, 537, 643, 645; Spanish colonial, 523, 524–525, 532, 541, 705; Ottoman, 582, 586, 740; Mughal India, 595; in Japan, 607; empire and, 628; European reform, 642; Haitian, 658–659, 660; Latin American development and, 720; in British India, 766, 767, 770, 910; New Imperialism and, 821–823

Adowa, Battle of, 828 *and illus.*

Advertising, 1013. *See also* Propaganda; family planning in China, 980*(illus.)*

Aegean Sea, 582

Aéropostale, 871, 925

Afghans (Afghanistan), 589, 590, 594; Mughal India and, 595; horses of, 615; Russia and, 740; Soviet war in, 969, 973, 975, 976, 1006; Islamic Revolution in, 966; regime change in, 1004, 1006; Taliban regime in, 1005

Afonso I (Kongo), 474, 476–477

Africa, trade with. *See* Gold (gold trade); Slave trade, African; Trans-Saharan trade

Africa (Africans). *See also* East Africa; North Africa; Southern Africa; Sub-Saharan Africa; in Madagascar, 463; Atlantic exploration, 465; in China, 464–465; Portuguese exploration of, 469*(map)*, 470, 482; chronology (1500–1730), 551;

Amerindian foods in, 554, 555 *and illus.*; Slave Coast in, 568, 565–567; Atlantic system and, 573; chronology (1795-1889), 757; in nineteenth century, 758*(map)*; new states in, 756–759; changes and exchanges in, 756–764; secondary empires in, 763–764; abolition and legitimate trade, 761–763; as laborers in British colonies, 778; British trade with, 775, 779; European penetration, 761, 821, 823–832; New Imperialism and, 818, 823, 824*(map)*, 825–832; chronology (1869-1908), 819; in 1878 and 1914, 824*(map)*; arrival of Europeans and, 830–831; Christianity in, 829, 832; in World War I armies, 852–853; chronology (1900s–1945), 909; World War II and, 903, 948; famine and drought in, 931; decolonization of, 946*(map)*, 947–950; HIV/AIDS in, 980; population growth in, 979, 981*(table)*, 982, 983*(map)*; development aid to, 1003; female circumcision in, 1012

African-Americans, 647. *See also* Slaves (slavery), African; abolitionist movement and, 711; after Civil War, 712; in Liberia, 763; World War I and, 853; World War II and, 902

African National Congress (ANC), 920, 950, 1004

African slaves. *See* Slaves (slavery), African

African slave trade. *See* Slave trade, African

Afrikaners, 774 *and illus.*, 827

Afro-Brazilians, 532–533, 542*(illus.)*, 700–701, 838; in West Africa, 763

Age distributions of populations, 982, 984*(figure)*

Agitator, The (Rivera), 923*(illus.)*

Agrarian reform: in China, 891, 897; in Mexico, 922, 923, 924; in Cuba, 951; in Guatemala, 950

Agriculture: *See also* Cotton; Farmers; Landowners; Peasants; Sugar plantations, *and specific crops*; American crops in Europe and, 503, 522; Amerindian women and, 528; Columbian exchange and, 522; in colonial Latin America, 526; in colonial North America, 537; soil erosion and, 553–554, 720–721; Ottoman, 587; Chinese, 613, 621, 742, 747; Japanese, 612; Industrial Revolution and, 669–670; North American Amerindians and, 708; Russian, 738; in Southeast Asia, 834; irrigation for, in British India, 770, 771, 841, 873; irrigation for, in Egypt, 760, 825, 841; shifting, 834; Soviet collectivization of, 879–880 *and illus.*, 931; tractors for, 873, 879, 880*(illus.)*; Green Revolution, 938 *and illus.*; South American exports, 925; collectivization of, in China, 931, 956;

collectivization of, in Eastern Europe, 940; privatization, in China, 974; global environment and, 987

Aguinaldo, Emilio, 836–837 *and illus.*

Ahmed III, Sultan, 589

Ahmedinejad, Mahmoud, 1003, 1005*(illus.)*

AIDS (Acquired Immune Deficiency Syndrome), 980, 1012*(figure)*

Aircraft (aviation): in Berlin blockade (1948–1949), 941; invention of, 869; World War I, 850; World War II, 876*(illus.)*, 891, 892, 896, 899, 903; in Latin America, 871 *and illus.*, 925; no-fly zones in Iraq, 979; September 11 (2001) attacks, 997–998, 1009

Aircraft carriers, 891, 894

Air pollution (air quality): Industrial Revolution and, 680; in late nineteenth century, 791, 795; in late twentieth century, 992

Akbar, Sultan, 478, 595

Alabama, 675; native peoples in, 709

Alaska, Russia and, 624*(map)*, 627

Albania (Albanians), 583, 729, 730, 846, 941; Kosovo crisis and (1999), 978

Albany (New York) Congress (1754), 641

Albazin, 619

Alcoholic beverages: wine, 503; Amerindians and, 535, 539; beer, 500, 503, 642*(illus.)*; rum, 553, 565, 951; Muslim prohibition on, 569, 825, 947; Prohibition (United States), 868

Aldrin, Edwin E. "Buzz," 945

Aleppo, 589, 730

Alexander I (Russia), 739*(illus.)*, 741; reforms of, 738, 740

Alexander II (Russia), 734, 741, 832; freeing of the serfs by, 738, 741, 810

Alexander III (Russia), 810, 832

Alexandria, 736; patriarch of, 475

Algeria, 581, 822, 915, 985; as French colony, 761, 865, 936; independence of, 947

Algerian War, 947, 949

Algonquin peoples, 539, 540

Ali (son-in-law of Muhammad), 589, 591

Al-Jazeera (Arab satellite TV), 1013–1014

Allende, Salvador, 968

Alliances: Muslim-Italian, 467; Portuguese-Ethiopian, 474–475; Amerindian-Spanish, 480, 481; in early modern Europe, 512; marriage and, 502, 523, 567; Mongol-Chinese, 613, 618; North American Amerindians, 643, 645, 709 (*See also* Iroquois Confederacy); against Napoleon, 656, 660; Anglo-Egyptian, 688–689, 821, 822*(illus.)*; World War I, 846–848, 849*(map)*, 853, 855, 856; Cuban-Soviet, 936; Cold War, 937, 942*(map)*

Allies (United Nations) World War II, 894, 895, 897

All-India Muslim League, 911, 912, 914
Alphabet, in Turkey, 863 *and illus.*
Al Qaeda, 998, 1005, 1008–1009
Al-Qasr al-Kabir, Battle of (1578), 600
Al-Mansur, Ahmad, 600
Alsace and Lorraine, 804, 805(*map*), 809, 856, 857(*map*)
Al-Umari, 465
Amazon rain forest, 835, 924, 926
Ambergris, 600, 776
Ambon, 601
American Anti-Slavery Society, 711
Americanization, 1016
American Revolution (1775–1783), 643–647, 646(*map*), 662–663; course of, 644–646; French and, 645–646, 649; frontiers and taxes, 643–644; republican institutions in, 646–647; women in, 644, 647
American system of manufactures, 677
Americas, colonial. *See* Brazil, colonial; British North America; French North America; Latin America, colonial
Americas, the (New World; Western Hemisphere). *See also* Andean region; Caribbean region; Central America; Latin America; North America; South America; *and specific countries;* Spanish conquest of, 479–482; small pox in, 479; African slaves in, 503, 762; chronology (1754–1804), 639; immigration to, 521, 536–537, 669, 713–715, 722; new foods from, 503, 554, 555 *and illus.*, 668; silver and gold from, 514, 586, 594; abolition of slavery in, 711–713; Enlightenment ideas in, 641; immigration to, 669, 670, 713–715, 979; social and economic change in, 711–722; altered environments, 720–722; constitutional experiments, 702–703; development and underdevelopment in, 717, 718–719; personalist leaders, 703–705, 722; foreign interventions and regional wars, 707–710, 722; independence movements in, 711; problem of order in, 702–710; raw materials from, 711, 719; regionalist threat in, 705, 707; women's rights and struggle for social justice, 716–717; racial discrimination in, 716–717, 722; Monroe Doctrine and, 838; chronology (1970-1998), 967
Amerindian alliances, 643, 645, 709. *See also* Iroquois Confederacy
Amerindians (native peoples). *See also specific peoples;* Pacific voyages of, 462; as noble savages, 499; disease and, 460, 473, 479, 481, 482, 488, 520–522; epidemics and, 526, 528, 532, 540; in Caribbean, 465, 466(*map*); Christianity and, 525–526, 540; fur trade and, 535, 539 *and illus.*, 643; in colonial Latin America, 523, 525–526, 528, 529, 532, 533(*illus.*), 534; in colonial North America, 518(*illus.*), 519–520, 535, 538(*illus.*), 539 *and illus.*, 541, 639; traveling in Europe, 504; French and Indian War and, 541, 639; horses and, 522, 523, 540, 710; labor of, 526, 528, 535, 722, 782; lands of, 532, 643, 694, 698, 710; rebellions by, 543, 698; as slaves,

479, 528, 535, 552; tobacco and, 550; American Revolution and, 643; in Mexico, 520, 708, 710, 838, 920, 923; in nineteenth century, 708–710, 722; women, 528, 539, 710; census of, 782, 783
Amethyst Incident (1947), 897
Amnesty International, 1010
Amritsar (India) massacre (1919), 912
Amsterdam, 500, 502 *and illus.*
Amsterdam Exchange, 502(*illus.*), 560
Amur River region, 618, 619, 625, 743
Anarchists, 799
Anatolia. *See also* Turkey; after World War I, 863, 864(*map*); Ottoman Empire and, 578
ANC. *See* African National Congress (ANC)
Ancestor worship, in China, 619
Ancien régime (old order), 638, 640–641, 663
Andean region: *See also* Bolivia; Peru; Spanish conquest, 481–482; Inca, 481–482, 520, 523, 528, 532; Amerindian uprising in, 543, 698; volcanic eruption in, 632; glacier shrinkage in, 993, 1011
Anglicanism (Church of England), 495(*map*), 507, 510, 536; in Africa, 763, 829, 919, 953
Anglo-Dutch Wars (1652-1678), 502, 560
Angola: Amerindian foods in, 555 *and illus.*; slave trade in, 551, 567; Christianity in, 570; trade with Brazil, 561; as Portuguese colony, 567, 568 *and illus.*, 573, 638, 826; independence in, 949
Ankara, Battle of (1402), 578
Anthony, Susan B., 796
Antibiotics, 899
Anticombination Laws (Britain), 799
Antigua, sugar plantation on, 554(*illus.*)
Anti-Semitism. *See also* Jews; French, 809; Russian, 810; Nazi German, 886
Antiwar movement, 944
Antwerp Painters Guild, 491
Apache peoples, 523, 710
Apartheid, in South Africa, 949–950, 952–953, 1016
Appalachian Mountains, 721
Appeasement of Nazi Germany, 887
Aqueducts, 527, 553
Arabia (Arabian Peninsula): *See also* Saudi Arabia; Wahhabism in, 589, 728
Arabic language, 570, 588, 590, 759, 919
Arab-Israeli conflict: (1947–1973), 957–958, 959(*map*); oil politics and, 958 *and illus.*
Arab Revolt (1916), 853, 865
Arabs: *See also* Islam; Middle East; Muslims; Omani, 600, 601(*illus.*); as traders, 598, 764, 798; after World War I, 862–868; Palestine question and, 863, 865–866, 939; independence, after World War II, 947
Arafat, Yasir, 958
Aragon, 467, 471, 505, 506(*map*)
Araucanians (Mapuches), 523, 710
Arawak (Taino), 465, 479, 550, 554
Arbenz Guzmán, Jacobo, 950
Architecture: *See also* Housing; in Safavid Iran, 590; in St. Petersburg, 626, 627(*illus.*); modern skyscrapers, 872, 964(*illus.*)
Arcot, 764, 766
Argentina: livestock industry in, 522, 719; independence of, 635(*map*), 696, 698,

699; Catholic Church in, 703, 705; Amerindians in, 708, 710; foreign naval blockades of, 707; income levels in, 717, 718; immigrants in, 713, 714, 715 *and illus.*, 722; labor movement in, 715 *and illus.*; racial discrimination in, 716; regional wars and, 705, 722; technology and development in, 718 *and illus.*, 720; education of women in, 716; government stability in, 722; pampas of, 523, 721, 924; railroads in, 719, 837, 924; European immigrants in, 718; British investment in, 792, 837; Depression of 1930s in, 885, 926; transformation of, 924; after 1930, 926–927 *and illus.*; and Brazil compared, 924–925; industry in, 903; military takeover and rule in (1976–1992), 968, 969; Falkland Islands (Malvinas) war and, 969; Mercosur and, 1001, 1002(*map*)
Aristocracy (nobility): *See also* Elite class; Landowners; European bourgeoisie and, 502; taxation and, 514; *hidalgos*, in Latin America, 529; Korean, 607; Qing China, 615; Russian, 625, 626–627, 738, 810; Enlightenment and, 640; pre-revolutionary France, 647, 648; British, 661
Aristotle, 497, 498
Aritomo, Yamagata, 806, 813
Arkangelsk, 623
Arkwright, Richard, 671, 675, 684, 685
Armed forces. *See also* Cavalry; Infantry; Military, the; Navy; Warrior elite, *and specific wars;* Portuguese, 475, 552; Inca, 482; Dutch, 514; early modern Europe, 511–512; Songhai, 569; Safavid Iran, 594; Ottoman, 582; Russian, 623, 811; Chinese, 606, 616–617, 628, 743, 746, 889; American Revolution, 645, 646(*map*); French, 651, 656, 658(*illus.*), 660, 695, 761; Latin American independence and, 696; black, in Americas, 711, 712 *and illus.*; Egyptian, 729–730, 823; Ottoman Empire modernization of, 732, 733(*illus.*); Crimean War, 734, 736; Indian (Sepoys), under British rule, 765, 766, 767; Japanese (Meiji), 806(*illus.*), 807; Prussian, 804, 808; New Imperialism and, 819–820, 821, 828 *and illus.*; United States, in Philippines, 837; before World War I, 848; women in, 852; World War I, 848, 850–851(*map*), 852, 853–854; Guomindang, 897; Japanese, 888, 889; Nazi Wehrmacht, 887, 891, 892, 894–896, 900 *and illus.* , 902; Soviet (Red Army), 876(*illus.*), 881, 892 *and illus.*, 894, 895, 941; Korean War, 941; Vietnam War, 943–944; Persian Gulf war, 978–979
Armenia (Armenians), 740, 856; merchants, 500, 587, 591, 593; in Ottoman Empire, 846, 853; Soviet Republic of, 858, 978
Arms control: nuclear weapons, 944–945; weapons of mass destruction, 1005
Armstrong, Neil A., 945
Aro of Arochukwu, 567
Arrow War (1856-1860), 744(*map*), 747
Art and artists. *See also* Paintings; *and specific artist;* Renaissance, 492; Flemish, 490(*illus.*), 491; Dutch, 500(*illus.*); colonial

religious, 525(illus.); Mexican Revolution and, 923(illus.), 924
Articles of Confederation (United States), 647, 702
Artillery, 731, 738, 743, 901, 902. See also Bombs and bombing; Cannon; New Imperialism and, 828, 832; Chinese Communist, 897
Artisans (craftspeople): apprenticeship in, 504; Dutch, 500; leatherworking, 569; slave, 556; Ottoman glassmakers, 583(illus.); Japanese, 608, 609; French Revolution and, 648; cottage industry and, 670; gunmaking and, 676
Aryans (Nazi master race), 886
Asante kingdom, 566, 567, 762, 828
Asia (Asians). See also Central Asia; East Asia; East Indies; Southeast Asia; maritime exploration from, 460; immigrants to Americas from, 713–714; indentured labor from, 714, 778–779; Russia and, 739–740; as railroad workers, 793; chronology (1862–1905), 819; New Imperialism in (1914), 832, 833(map), 834–836; chronology (1931–1949), 879; World War II in, 894, 895(map), 896; chronology (1975–1997), 967; economic transformation in (1960s–1990s), 966, 973–974; electronics industry in, 974, 1013, 1014; in United States, 987; population in (1750–2050), 981(table), 982; rising oil demand in, 1001; trade agreement in (APEC), 1001, 1002(map)
Asian Tigers, 974, 993
Askeri (Ottoman military), 583
Assam, 766, 774. See also Vietnam
Assembly-line manufacturing, 868, 872. See also Mass production; of porcelain, 609(illus.), 612, 613
Assembly of Notables (France), 649
Assinoboine people, 523
Astrakhan, 623
Astrolabe, 467
Astronomy, European revolution in, 497–498
Aswan dam (Egypt), 825, 955
Atacama Desert (Chile), 708
Atahualpa, 481(illus.), 482
Atlantic Ocean: chronology (770–1536), 461; exploration of, before 1500, 465, 467; Portuguese exploration of, 467–468; Spanish exploration of, 470, 472; steamships in, 677(illus.)
Atlantic trading system (Atlantic economy), 559–565, 562(map). See also Slave trade, African; triangular trade in, 561; capitalism and mercantilism, 559–561; Atlantic Circuit in, 561–564; chronology (1530–1713), 551; New England and, 537; sugar in, 561, 573; contraction of, 717
Atomic bombs: See also Nuclear weapons; bombing of Japan (1945), 895(map), 896–897 and illus., 944; development of, 899
Atomic theory, 869
Aurangzeb, Sultan, 596, 597
Auschwitz death camp, 901
Australia, 846, 862, 873; European immigrants in, 601, 670, 792, 822, 855;

Aborigines of, 775, 776 and illus., 778; as British colony, 756, 773(map), 779; penal colonies in, 776; drought in, 1011
Austria-Hungary (1867-1918): immigrants from, 793; Balkans and, 810; languages of, 802; nationalism in, 810; as conservative power, 808, 810; as great power, 809; Serbian independence and, 845, 847; expansion of, 846; World War I and, 848, 849(map), 850, 851(map), 854, 855; division of, after World War I, 856, 857(map), 873
Austria (to 1867 and 1918 to present), 512, 587, 792; Habsburg dynasty of, 505; Holy Alliance and, 660; French Revolution and, 651, 656; Revolution of 1848 in, 662; Crimean War and, 734; German unification and, 804; Italian unification and, 802; after World War I, 856, 857(map); Great Depression in, 881; German annexation of (1938), 887; in European Community, 940
Autarchy (self-sufficiency), 884
Authoritarianism, 888, 925, 954. See also Dictatorship; Fascism; of Napoleon, 656; in Iran, 972; end of, in Indonesia, 1004; end of, in Ukraine, 1003
Automobiles, 868, 870(illus.), 872, 940; air pollution and, 933, 992; Japanese, 973, 989
Aviation. See Aircraft
Axis powers, World War II, 888, 902. See also Germany; Italy; Japan, in World War II
Aya Sofya, in Istanbul, 581(illus.), 591
Ayrton, William, 791
Ayuba Suleiman Diallo, 571–572 and illus.
Azerbaijan, 740, 858
Azores, 465, 467, 470, 528
Aztecs (Aztec Empire), 479–481, 526, 532

Baba, Ahmad, 571
Baba of Karo, 830
Babur, 594, 595
Bach, Johann Sebastian, 491
Baghdad, 589, 590, 853, 863; invasion of (2003), 1005
Bahamas, 465, 479
Bahia, Brazil, 528
Bahrain, 958
Balance of power, 779. See also Great powers; in European alliances, 492, 510, 512; Congress of Vienna and, 660; in British India, 765; (1850–1900), 787–788; New Imperialism and, 821; before World War II, 887; Cold War, 943
Balboa, Vasco Núñez de, 472
Balfour, Sir Arthur, 853, 856, 866
Balfour Declaration (1917), 853, 865, 866, 957
Bali, 1004, 1009
Balkans: See also specific states; Orthodox Christians in, 730, 734, 978; Ottoman Empire and, 578, 582, 583, 730, 734, 737; Austria-Hungary and, 810; early twentieth century crisis in, 846; breakup of Yugoslavia, 977(map); ethnic cleansing in, 978

Baltic states, 626. See also Estonia; Latvia; Lithuania; independence of, 854, 858, 977; Soviet invasion of, 892
Bananas, 554, 950
Bandung Conference (1955), 954–955 and illus.
Bangladesh, 947; flooding in, 931, 1011
Banks and banking, 671; Dutch, 500, 514, 560; European, in Ottoman Empire, 736; Japanese industry and, 973; World Bank, 938, 939, 986, 1003
Bannermen (China), 743, 746
Bantu language, 600
Barbados, 536, 550, 945; sugar plantations in, 552, 553, 559
Barbed-wire fencing, 719, 924
Bastille, storming of (1789), 650 and illus., 655
Batavia (modern Jakarta), 601
Batista, Fulgencio, 935, 951
Bayazid I, Sultan, 578
Bay of Pigs invasion (1961), 951, 954
Beer, 500, 503, 642(illus.)
Beer Street (Hogarth), 642(illus.)
Beijing, 747, 957; Manchu capture of, 606, 614; Boxer Uprising in (1900), 813; student protests in, 862; Japanese seizure of (1937), 888, 889; Tiananmen massacre in (1989), 975
Beijing Women's Conference (1995), 1010(illus.), 1012
Belgian Congo, 824(map), 825–827, 830, 885; independence in, 949
Belgium, 818, 940; industrialization in, 671, 679(map); cities in, 680; coal in, 679(map); railroads in, 679 and map; Revolution of 1830 in, 661(illus.); colonies of, 824(map), 840(map); World War I and, 845, 848, 855; German invasion of, World War II, 892; decolonization of, 945
Belize (British Honduras), 721
Bell Telephone Laboratories, 1013
Benedict XVI, Pope, 1008
Bengal (Bengalis): Islam in, 596–597; East India Company and, 766, 767; opium in, 766; famine in (1943), 914, 931; independence movement in, 910–911
Benguela, 566(map), 567
Benin, 473–474 and illus., 828
Bentham, Jeremy, 686
Berbers, 865
Bering, Vitus, 627
Berlin, 662, 680; bombing of (1944), 899; blockade and airlift (1948–1949), 941
Berlin Conference (1884–1885), 825
Berlin Wall, 941; fall of (1989), 976 and illus., 977
Bessemer, Henry, 790
Bethune College, 772
Bharatiya Janata Party (BJP; India), 1004, 1008
Bible, the, 493; scientific revolution and, 497, 498; vernacular translations, 496, 498
Bight of Biafra, 567
Biko, Steven, 952–953
Bill of Rights (England, 1688), 507
Bill of Rights (United States, 1791), 1009
Bin Laden, Usama, 998, 1005, 1008, 1014
Bipolar world. See Cold War (Bipolar world)

Birth control (contraception), 794, 869, 979–980 *and illus.*, 982. *See also* Abortion

Birthrate. *See also* Fertility rate; in medieval Europe, 504; Industrial Revolution and, 668; urban sanitation and, 794; decline in, in industrial nations, 980–982; in developing world, 979–980, 982

Bishops: in England, 507; in France, 656; in Africa, 763, 829, 919, 953; El Salvadorean death squads and, 969

Bismarck, Otto von, 804, 825; German unification and, 809; imperialism and, 819

Black Consciousness Movement, 952–953

Blackfoot peoples, 523

"Black Hole of Calcutta," 766

Blacks: *See also* Africa (Africans); African-Americans; Afro-Brazilians; Free blacks; Slaves (slavery), African; racial discrimination and, 716–717

Black Sea region, 623, 731*(map)*; Russia and, 626, 627; Crimean War in, 734

"Black ships" of Perry, 786*(illus.)*, 787

Black Thursday (1929), 881

Blake, William, 680

Blitzkrieg warfare, 891

Blyden, Edward Wilmot, 763

Bohemia, 662

Bolívar, Simón, 698, 702, 703; Gran Colombia and, 635*(map)*, 696, 704

Bolivia, 702, 985; Amerindians of, 543, 722; silver mining in, 526–527 *and illus.*, 528; Bolivar and, 696; independence of, 696, 697*(map)*, 698; mining in, 721, 885; war with Chile, 708, 722; Guevara in, 954

Bolshevik Revolution (October Revolution; Russia), 854, 856

Bolsheviks, 857–859, 881, 882, 888. *See also* Communist Party (Soviet Union)

Bombay film industry (Bollywood), 1015, 1018

Bombay Presidency, 766

Bombs and bombing (explosives), 745*(illus.)*, 852. *See also* Nuclear weapons; Weapons and military technology; dynamite, 790; in World War II, 889, 894, 901; atomic bombing of Hiroshima and Nagasaki, 895*(map)*, 896–897 *and illus.*, 944; terrorist, in Bali (2004), 1004; in Iraq, 1005, 1009

Books: *See also* Literacy; Printing; Enlightenment, 499, 641; libraries, 590, 641, 759; scientific, 498; gas lighting and, 683; adult comics, in Japan, 1014*(illus.)*

Bordeaux, 504, 563

Borlaug, Norman, 938

Borneo, 598, 834

Borodino, Battle of (1812), 656

Bose, Pramatha Nath, 911

Bosman, Willem, 565, 566

Bosnia, 583, 730, 1009

Bosnia and Herzegovina, 810, 845, 977*(map)*; ethnic cleansing in, 978

Bosporus Strait, 581

Boston, colonial, 537, 644

Botany, global economy and, 835 *and illus.*, 839

Boulton, Matthew, 675, 677–678, 683

Bourbon dynasty, 510 *and table*, 512, 513*(map)*; colonial Latin America and, 541, 542–543

Bourgeoisie, 499–500, 502, 504. *See also* Middle class; French Revolution and, 648, 651; Marx on, 799, 800–801

Bourke-White, Margaret, 884*(photo)*, 914*(photo)*

Bows and arrows (archers): crossbows, 464; Ottoman, 582; Safavid Iran, 594; Chinese, 628

Boxer Uprising (1900, China), 812 *and illus.*, 813, 861

Boyars (Russian elite), 625, 626–627

Boycotts, 644, 647; in British India, 910, 914

Boyle, Robert, 498

Brahe, Tycho, 497 *and illus.*

Brahmins, in India, 772. *See also* Hindus

Brahmo Samaj (Divine Society), 772

Brant, Joseph (Thayendanegea), 645

Brazil. *See also* Brazil, colonial; independence in, 697*(map)*, 699; coffee production in, 543, 685, 720, 839, 885, 924, 925; constitutionalism in, 699, 702; Portuguese monarchy and, 699, 703; Afro-Brazilians, 700–701; end of slave trade in, 712; environmental degradation in, 720–721; immigrants in, 713, 714, 722, 778, 794; legacy of slavery in, 722; mining in (Minas Gerais), 721; nineteenth century wars, 707, 722; racial discrimination in, 716; women's rights in, 716; rush hour in Rio de Janeiro, 906*(illus.)*; Vargas regime in, 925–926; Argentina compared to, 924–925, 927; Depression of 1930s and, 885, 925–926; industry in, 903, 967; military rule in (1964–1985), 967–968, 969; deforestation in, 989, 992*(illus.)*, 993; wealth inequality in, 985; Mercosur (trade agreement) and, 1001, 1002*(map)*

Brazil, colonial, 479, 524*(map)*; Amerindians and disease in, 520; Cabral and, 470, 472; chronology (1530s–1777), 521; church and state in, 525; Afro-Brazilians, 532–533, 542*(illus.)*; Dutch and, 551, 552, 638; slaves and slave trade in, 528, 532, 533, 549, 557, 563 *and map*, 567, 762; livestock in, 522; manumission of slaves in, 558; market in, 542*(illus.)*; reform in, 543; sugar plantations in, 525, 526, 528, 529, 532, 533, 551, 573, 778; tobacco in, 561

"Brazilian Solution," 967–968

Brazza, Savorgnan de, 825

Brazzaville, 918

Brazzaville Conference (1944), 949

Brest-Litovsk, Treaty of (1918), 851*(map)*, 854

Bretton Woods Conference (1946), 939

Brezhnev, Leonid, 975

Bridges: in India, 595*(illus.)*; iron, in Britain, 676, 682; railroads and, 682, 688*(illus.)*; in British India, 911*(illus.)*

Britain, Battle of (1940–1941), 892, 893*(map)*, 900

British East India Company. *See* East India Company, English (EIC)

British Empire (British colonies). *See also* Great Britain; India, under British rule *and specific colonies;* in West Indies, 550–551 (*See also* Jamaica); trade and, 502, 529, 772, 774, 779; Australia and New Zealand, 756, 775–776, 778, 779; chronology (1763-1877), 757; in Indian Ocean and South Pacific, 773*(map)*; policies and shipping, 775; labor migrations to, 778–779; lines of communication in, 785*(map)*; as financial drain, 810; in Asia (1914), 833*(map)*; New Imperialism and, 819, 840*(map)*; World War I and, 846; Great Depression and, 881; English language and, 1015, 1016

British Guiana, 774; immigrants to, 714, 778

British investment: in Americas, 720, 792, 837, 920, 924, 925; in India, 770

British navy, 512 *and illus.*, 638–639, 656, 707, 713; Egypt and, 728, 730, 756; end of slave trade and, 762; Opium War and, 742–743, 744*(map)*; cost of, 810; in World War I, 848, 850, 852; in World War II, 892

British North America, 512, 534–538, 540*(map)*. *See also* Canada; chronology (1583–1763), 521; early experiments, 534; French and Indian War in, 541, 639; land ownership in, 553; Middle Atlantic, 537–538; New England, 536–537; population in, 537, 544; reform in, 543; slavery in, 535, 536, 563; South, 534–536; American Revolution, 643–647, 662–663; constitutionalism in, 646–647; Enlightenment in, 641

British Raj. *See* India, under British rule

British South Africa Company, 827

British West Indies (Caribbean colonies), 552. *See also* Jamaica; abolition of slavery in, 685, 712–713, 714, 778; labor migrations to, 714, 778

British Women's Emigration Association, 823

Brooke, Rupert, 848

Brookes (slave ship), 564*(illus.)*

Brueghel, Peter, 490*(illus.)*, 491

Brunei Sultanate, 598

Bubonic plague, in China, 747

Buddhism: in Japan, 611; Tibetan, 613; spread of, 1007*(map)*

Buenos Aires, 713, 721, 924; independence movement in, 696, 698, 705; labor movement in, 715*(illus.)*; port construction in, 718 *and illus.*

Buffalo (bison) hunters, Amerindian, 523, 710

Bukhara, 740, 832

Bulgaria, 846, 857*(map)*, 940, 976, 1001

Bulliet, Richard W., 1009

Bulwer-Lytton, Edward Robert, 768–769, 770

Bureaucracy (bureaucrats). *See also* Administration; Civil service; in Benin, 473; Safavid Iran, 594; Enlightenment ideas and, 640; Ottoman reform of, 730, 732, 737–738 *and illus.*; Chinese, 728; in British India, 767; Russian reforms, 740, 741; census and, 782; expansion of, after World War I, 868; Soviet, 859, 940, 956; United Nations, 937

Burgoyne, John, 645

Burma (Myanmar), 615; British in, 769, 774, 834; Japanese conquest of, 914, 931; independence of, 947

Bush, George H. W., 979

Bush, George W., 985, 993, 1003, 1009; Christian conservatism of, 1008; global warming denied by, 1011; war in Iraq and, 1005, 1006

Business (companies). *See also* Capitalism; Corporations; Entrepreneurs; Industries; Mercantilism; Monopoly; Trade; bourgeoisie and, 500, 504; chartered trading companies, 550, 560, 563, 686; in colonial Americas, 534, 536; British, 671; insurance, 502, 560, 736; invention and, 675; Japanese, 608; joint-stock, 500–501, 536, 560, 573, 598, 671, 741; laissez faire theory and, 686; industrialization and, 788; cycle of, 685, 687, 792, 799; New Imperialism and, 820

Byrd, Richard, 869–870

Byron, Lord (George Gordon Noel), 730

Byzantine Empire, 581

Cable News Network (CNN), 1013

Cabral, Pedro Alvares, 470, 472

Cacao. See Chocolate; Cocoa (cacao)

Cairo, 736 *and illus.*, 737, 760, 863

Cajamarca, 482

Cakchiquel of Guatemala, 521

Calcutta, 747, 771, 772, 911; East India Company in, 766; future growth of, 985*(table)*

Calendars: Gregorian, 498; Qing China and, 615, 619; French Revolution and, 653

Cali, Colombia, 938

Calicut, 464, 475, 478

California, 721; gold in, 707

Caliphate, Sokoto, 756, 758*(map)*, 759

Calles, Plutarco Elías, 923

Calvin, John, 493–494

Calvinism, 494, 495*(map). See also* Puritans

Cambodia (Kampuchea), 916, 1015

Canada, 868; colonial fur trade in, 537, 539 *and illus.*, 561; French in, 538–541, 715; Amerindians in, 539–540 *and illus.*, 541, 709; immigration to, 670, 713, 714 *and illus.*, 715, 717, 722, 792–794, 855; American Revolution and, 645, 646; forest products of, 681; British (Dominion of), 702, 703*(map)*, 719, 776; income levels in, 717; technology and development in, 719; women's rights in, 716; national park in, 721; railroads in, 719, 788; self-rule in, 702, 719, 822; in World War I, 846; in World War II, 895; North American Free Trade Agreement and, 1001, 1002*(map)*

Canal du Midi (France), 502

Canals: *See also* Suez Canal; Russian, 627*(illus.)*, 628; British, 671, 682*(illus.)*; Europe, 502, 682; Industrial Revolution and, 671, 678; United States, 678; irrigation, 760, 770, 771, 841; Panama, 838–839, 968

Canary Islands, 465, 470, 472, 554

Cannon, 511, 512, 515, 790; conquistadors, 481, 482; naval warfare, 464, 468, 628; Ottoman, 581; Safavid Iran, 594; Russian, 738; Ethiopian, 760*(illus.)*, 761

Canoes: African, 465, 762; Polynesian, 461–462, 463*(illus.)*; Canadian fur trader, 539*(illus.)*

Canton (Guangzhou), 619, 620–621, 862, 889; street scene in, 746*(illus.)*; trade warehouse in, 726*(illus.)*

Canton system, 742, 743

Cape Coast Castle, 560, 570

Cape Colony, 568, 772, 774, 827

Cape Town, 774, 775, 919

Cape Verde Islands, 528

Capitalism, 526, 559–560. *See also* Free trade; Mercantilism; European, in Africa, 573; laissez faire, 686–687; industrialization and, 663, 792; free market and, 686, 878, 969; Marx's view of, 799; Great Depression and, 881; Communism and, 939–941

Caracas, Venezuela, 696

Caramansa, 473

Caravan trade and routes, 764, 832. *See also* Trans-Saharan trade

Caravel (ship), 468, 471 *and illus.*, 472

Cárdenas, Lázaro, 923–924

Caribbean region (West Indies): native peoples of, 465, 466*(map)*, 479, 550, 554; Columbus in, 479; Atlantic trading system and, 559; disease in, 520, 521; sugar plantations in, 533, 548*(illus.)*, 549, 551–557, 558, 573, 643, 778, 885; chronology (1500–1760), 551; tobacco in, 550–551, 552, 554, 573; slave trade in, 533, 563*(map)*; abolition of slavery in, 712–713; Chinese and Indian immigrants in, 713, 714, 778, 794; U.S. intervention in (1901-1914), 838–839; decolonization in, 945; population in (1750–2050), 981*(table)*

Carib peoples, 465, 466*(map)*, 550, 554

Carolina, colonial, 535–536, 543

Carpet manufacture, 593

Carranza, Venustiano, 922

Carrío de la Vandera, Alonso, 530

Carter, James Earl "Jimmy," 968, 972

Cartier, Jacques, 538–539

Cartier-Bresson, Henri, 898*(photo)*

Cartography. *See* Mapmaking

Casement, Roger, 827

Cassava, 479, 555 *and illus.*

Castas (mixed-race), 533*(illus.)*, 534

Caste system (India), 464, 766, 772, 908, 912

Caste War (Mexico, 1847), 710

Castile, 467, 471, 505, 506*(map)*

Castro, Fidel, 934*(illus.)*, 935–936, 966; CIA plot to overthrow, 951, 954; Cuban missile crisis and, 936, 944

Catherine of Aragon, 507

Catherine the Great (Russia), 627–628, 640

Catholic Church. *See also* Papacy; Protestant Reformation and, 492–494, 495*(map)*; scientific revolution and, 498; European monarchies and, 505, 507, 514; in colonial Latin America, 525–526, 532, 534, 542; Enlightenment and, 641–642;

French Revolution and, 647, 648, 651, 656; in Latin America, 702–703, 705; in Africa, 763; in Argentina, 703, 705; in Mexico, 526, 703, 707, 923, 924; in Ireland, 802, 810; in Poland, 901, 976; in Balkans, 978; Conservatism in, 1008; English language in, 1016

Catholic missionaries, 605, 610, 615, 820. *See also* Dominicans; Franciscan order; Jesuits

Catholic Reformation, 494

Cattle (cattle raising): in Americas, 522 *and illus.*, 523, 554, 710, 719, 924; Zulu, in Africa, 756, 757

Caucasus region, 728, 858; Russia and, 623, 734, 736, 740, 810; World War I and, 854; World War II and, 892

Caudillo (personalist leader), 704, 705

Cavalry (horsemen): conquistador, 480; Ottoman Turk, 578, 582, 583, 586; Argentine gauchos, 698; Crimean War and, 734, 736; Ethiopian, 828*(illus.)*

Cavour, Camillo Benso di, 802, 803

Cayuga peoples, 537, 645

Ceausescu, Nicolae, 976

Censorship, 640, 641, 802

Census, state power and, 782–783

Central America, 542, 697*(map). See also specific country*; Amerindians of, 520; Republic of, 705; United States' intervention in, 838–839, 968–969

Central Asia, 858. *See also specific country and people*; chronology (1517–1795), 607; Turkic peoples of, 589, 590, 625; Timurids in, 589, 593, 594; Mughal India and, 594–595; Russia and, 623, 625, 740, 810, 832, 854; irrigation in, 841; New Imperialism in, 832; Qing China and, 832

Central Intelligence Agency (CIA): Bay of Pigs invasion (1961), 951, 954; coup in Guatemala (1954), 950, 951; Iran and, 972

Centralization: *See also* Communist Party; European Community; Fascism; Monarchy; in Japan, 607

Central Powers (Austria-Hungary, Germany, and Italy), 849*(map)*, 851*(map)*

Centro Internacional de Mejoramiento de Maíz y Trigo, 938

Cervantes, Miguel de, 491

Cetshwayo (Zulu), 827

Ceuta, Portuguese in, 467

Ceylon (Sri Lanka), 772, 774; coffee in, 766; tea in, 835, 839, 885; English in, 1015

Chaldiran, Battle of (1514), 581

Chamberlain, Neville, 888

Chambers, William, 620*(illus.)*

Chamorro, Violeta, 969

Champlain, Samuel de, 539

Chappe, Claude, 670

Charcoal, for iron industry, 503, 676

Charitable trusts, in Ottoman Empire, 733–734

Charles I (England), 507

Charles II (England), 537, 541, 543

Charles III (Spain), 640

Charleston, South Carolina, 536

Charles V (Holy Roman emperor), 505, 506*(map)*, 514

Charles X (France), 660

Chartered trading companies, 550, 560, 563, 686

Charter Oath (Japan), 807

Chartists (Great Britain), 661, 687

Chávez, Hugo, 969

Chechnya, 740, 978

Cheka (Russian secret police), 854

Chemistry and chemical industry, 498, 790, 852; poison gas in warfare, 850; pesticides, 992

Cherokee peoples, 709

Chesapeake Bay region, 535, 992

Cheyenne people, 540

Chiang Kaishek (Jiang Jieshi), 862, 888, 891; Chinese civil war (1945–1949) and, 897

Chicago, 721, 794, 872; immigrants in, 713, 795

Chiefdoms: Iranian, 593, 594; South African, 756

Child labor: on slave plantations, 556; in France, 648; in textile mills, 668, 675, 684 *and illus.*; restrictions on, 687

Children. *See also* Education; Family; Schools; Ottoman devshirme, 582, 586, 587; French Revolution and, 649; Victorian Age, 795, 796, 797; declining mortality of, 681, 794, 872; female infanticide, 772, 982; Russian Revolution and, 882–883; or career, for European women, 981; Rio de Janiero homeless, 986

Chile: colonial, 524(map), 542; independence of, 697(map), 698; Amerindians in, 708, 710; Catholic Church in, 703; constitution and political institutions in, 702, 703; underdevelopment in, 720; wars with Bolivia and Peru, 707, 708, 722; women's rights in, 716; mining in, 717, 721, 792; military rule in, 968, 969

China, imperial, 839. *See also* Chinese immigrants; Qing Empire; Ming Empire, 463–465 *and illus.*, 612–614; exploration by (Zheng He), 462(map), 464 *and illus.*, 465, 468, 471; Portuguese port in, 475, 615; world map in, 501; agriculture in, 613, 621, 742, 747; chronology (1517–1795), 607; climate change in, 632; Dutch trade with, 615; expansion of, 489, 614(map), 615, 628; Jesuit missionaries in, 499, 501, 615, 619; Korea and, 606–607; population in, 613, 621, 742, 860, 979; porcelain production in, 609; rebellions in, 606, 613–614, 621, 629; Russia and, 618–619; stagnation in, 688, 689; Yangzhou Massacre, 616–617; flooding in, 747, 861, 891, 903; France and, 744(map), 747, 812; Heavenly Kingdom of Great Peace, 745–746, 747; opium trade in, 736, 766, 812, 862; Taiping Rebellion (1850–1864), 744–747 *and map*; Zeng Guofan and, 748, 751; footbinding of women in, 744, 746, 889; Boxer Uprising (1900), 812 *and illus.*, 813, 861; cotton clothing in, 798; Western powers and, 811; flooding in, 747, 891, 903; treaty ports in, 743, 812, 860, 862; revolution and war in (1900–1918), 861;

social and economic change, 860; fascism in, 886; Guomindang in, 861, 888, 889, 891, 897–898, 916

China, Japan and, 613, 614, 805, 859–862, 873; Japanese invasion of Korea and, 606; social and economic changes, 860–861; war between (1894–1895), 812–813, 837, 861; Twenty-One Demands (1915), 861; Boxer Uprising (1900), 813, 861; Japanese seizure of Manchuria, 888; war between (1937–1945), 861, 889–891 *and map*

China, Nationalist (Guomindang), 888, 889, 891. *See also* Taiwan; war with Japan (1937–1945), 890(map); civil war and defeat of (1945–1949), 897–898; Sun Yat-sen and, 861, 862, 916

China, People's Republic of (PRC). *See also* Communist Party (China); Mao Zedong; civil war in (1945–1949), 897–898; cotton production in, 798; famine in (1958–1961), 931; Great Leap Forward in, 931, 956; Korean War and, 941, 961; Vietnam War and, 943, 944, 961; United Nations and, 936; Cultural Revolution in, 956, 957(illus.); United States' policy toward, 957; Taiwan and, 974; textile industry in, 989; Hong Kong and, 974; economic boom in, 965, 993, 1019; reforms of Deng Xiaoping, 974–975; foreign investment in, 974, 975; population growth in, 982; deforestation in, 989; family-planning campaign in, 980(illus.), 982; industrial pollution and disease, 992; English language in, 1015; in Shanghai Cooperative Organization, 1001, 1003; suppression of dissent in, 1010(illus.)

Chinese Exclusion Act (1882, United States), 714

Chinese immigrants: in Americas, 713; bubonic plague and, 747; in Canada, 714 *and illus.*; in Cuba, 713, 714, 778; in Southeast Asia, 614, 774, 794, 834; in United States, 714; in Hawaii, 836

Chocolate, 522, 561, 620, 990. *See also* Cocoa

Choctaw peoples, 518(illus.), 519–520, 541, 709

Cholera, 778, 930; in India, 681, 771

Choshu (Japan), 804, 806

Christianity (Christians): *See also* Bible, the; Christian Orthodoxy; Missionaries, Christian; *and specific cults, denominations and sects;* militancy of, 467, 470; Ethiopian, 474–475, 760, 832, 919; in colonial Americas, 472, 479; in Ottoman Empire, 587, 732; reformation and, 505, 507, 534; Caribbean slaves and, 558; in Angola, 570; Armenian, in Iran, 591; in Japan, 605–606, 610–611, 629; in Ottoman Empire, 737; in Balkans, 846; global spread of, 1007(map)

Christian Orthodoxy: in Balkans, 730, 734, 978; Russian, 623, 625, 626, 627, 628, 739, 740

Church buildings, Saint Peter's Basilica, 492

Churchill, Winston, 821; iron curtain speech of, 936–937, 960; in World War II, 892, 895, 897

Church of England. *See* Anglicanism

Church-state separation, 703

Cinchona tree, 834, 835 *and illus.*, 839

Circassians, 729, 740

Cities and towns (urban areas): *See also* City-states; Urbanization; *and specific cities;* Indian Ocean trade, 463, 475; Swahili Coast, 464–465, 475; European bourgeoisie and, 499–500; poverty in European, 503–504; colonial Americas, 526, 537, 538; Ottoman and Safavid compared, 591–592; Japanese, 608; Chinese, 613, 621; French Revolution and, 648–649; gas lighting in, 683 *and illus.*; industrialization, 666(illus.), 667–668; in Latin America, 698; Middle Eastern, 736 *and illus.*, 863; Chinese treaty ports, 743, 812, 860; late-nineteenth century, 794–795; bombing of, in World War II, 899, 901; automobile and suburban sprawl, 870 *and illus.*, 872; in colonial Africa, 918–919; migration from rural areas to, 926; global growth of, 985(table), 986

Citizenship: cultural diversity and, 714; denied to blacks and women, 711, 716; denied to native peoples, 778; denied to German Jews, 886, 899; nationality and, 987

City-states, in Europe, 505; northern Italy, 467. *See also* Florence; Genoa; Venice

Civil Code of 1804 (France), 656

Civil rights campaign (United States), 944

Civil service, 640. *See also* Administration; Bureaucracy; Chinese examinations for, 613, 749, 860; Indian (ICS), 767, 770, 772, 909, 947; in French West Africa, 949

Civil wars: Amerindian, 481, 482, 520; English (1642), 507; Japanese (late 1500s), 606, 607; Mexican (1858–1861), 707; Mexican (1830s), 710; United States (1861–1865), 702, 707, 710, 711–712, 737, 839; Chinese (1851–1864), 744–747, 744(map); Russian (1921–1922), 856–858, 931; Japanese (1867–1868), 806; Chinese (1945–1949), 897–898; Mexican (1910–1920), 921–923 *and map*; Congo, 949; Iraqi (2006), 1006

Cixi, Empress Dowager (China), 748(illus.), 751; Boxer Rebellion and, 812, 813, 861

Clash of Civilizations and the Remaking of the World Order (Huntington), 1009

Class struggle, Marx on, 799, 800. *See also* Social class

Clawson, Augusta, 902

Clemenceau, Georges, 856

Clergy (priests): *See also* Bishops; Papacy; Religion; in colonial Latin America, 525–526; Japanese, 611; French Revolution and, 648, 649, 651, 653, 656; Suez Canal and, 818; El Salvadorean death squads and, 969; collapse of Communism and, 976

Cleveland, Grover, 836

Climate and weather (climate change): *See also* Monsoons; Natural disasters; Rainfall; Little Ice Age, 503, 613, 632; and diversity, in China, 622; global warming, 933, 993, 1011

Clinton, William Jefferson "Bill," 1003

Clipper ships, 775

Clive, Robert, 766

Clothing (costume): *See also* Textiles; colonial Americas, 531; Safavid Iran, 593; Russian, 604*(illus.)*, 626; industrialization and, 685; Ottoman reforms, 732, 733*(illus.)*, 737*(illus.)*; Zulu warrior, 759*(illus.)*; cotton, 798; Ethiopian cavalry, 828*(illus.)*; Gandhi and, 912, 913*(illus.)*; Islamic women, 972 *and illus.*, 1012

CNN (Cable News Network), 1013

Coal, industrialization and, 682, 689; in Britain, 503, 671*(map)*; coal gas, 683; in Europe, 671, 679*(map)*; pollution from, 680, 795; steam engines and, 676*(illus.)*, 677–678, 792

Cochin, 478

Cocoa (cacao), 553, 670, 674, 775, 826, 839, 918. *See also* Chocolate

Code-breaking, World War II, 892, 894, 899; Enigma machine and, 900 *and illus.*

Coffee, 553, 561, 620, 658, 670, 674, 730, 775, 820; in Brazil, 543, 685, 720, 839, 885, 924, 925; in Ceylon, 766; in Java, 601, 834; slavery and, 711

Coffeehouses, 641; in Ottoman Empire, 585, 588

Coinage: copper, in China, 613; gold, 470, 736; Ottoman, 736

Coke-iron production, 503, 676, 682

Colbert, Jean Baptiste, 502, 503, 514, 560

Cold War (Bipolar world; 1946–1991). *See also* Superpowers, Cold War; aid to poor nations in, 938, 1003; capitalism and communism in, 939–941; China and, 956–957; chronology (1945–1975), 937; collapse of Soviet bloc and, *(map)*; Cuba in, 934*(illus.)*, 935–936; decolonization and (1947–1990), 949; eastern Europe and, 937, 940–941, 960, 976–978 *and map*; Japan and, 956, 961; Korean War and, 941, 943, 961; Middle East, 957–958, 959*(map)*; nuclear arms race and, 944–945; proxy wars in, 932, 945, 961, 966; Third World and, 954–955; United Nations and, 937, 939; Vietnam War and, 943–944 *and illus.*; environment and, 960; Latin America and, 966–969; Persian Gulf War and, 978–979; collapse of Soviet bloc, 976–978; Soviet Union crisis, 975–976; end of (1989–1991), 966, 975–979

Collectivization of agriculture: in China, 931, 956; in Soviet Union, 879–880 *and illus.*, 931

Colleges and universities: *See also* Education; in colonial Americas, 525, 526, 641; Islamic madrasas, 586, 591, 919 *and illus.*; in Istanbul, 732; in Russia, 741; British, 767; in India, 772; in Liberia, 763; industry and, 790; for women, 796; in Japan, 808; English language in, 1016

Cologne, bombing of (1942), 899

Colombia, 462, 703, 705, 885, 950; independence of, 635*(map)*, 696, 704; Panama and, 838

Colonies (colonialism), 641, 821, 865. *See also* British Empire; Decolonialization;

Expansion; French colonies; Imperialism; New Imperialism; Plantations; Latin America, colonial *and specific colonies and colonial powers;* Polynesian, 462; Enlightenment and, 641; European, in Indian Ocean and South Pacific, 773*(map)*; of great powers (1913), 840*(map)*

Columbian exchange, 520–523; animal and plant transfer in, 522–523 *and illus.*, 555; disease in, 520–522, 554

Columbus, Christopher, 469*(map)*, 470–472, 473, 479

Comanche people, 523, 540, 710

Comic book, in Japan, 1014*(illus.)*

Commerce. *See* Business; Merchants; Trade (commerce); Trade routes

Commercial famines, 930–931

Committee of Public Safety (France), 653, 654

Common Market (European Economic Community), 940

Common Sense (Paine), 645

Commonwealth of Independent States (CIS), 978

Communication: *See also* Telegraph; overland China, 615; Enlightenment, 640–641; Crimean War, 735; Ottoman reforms and, 732; British Empire, 785*(map)*; radio, 870, 871, 925, 1013; computers and, 987–989, 1014; mass media, 885–886, 1008, 1013–1014; television, 1013, 1014

Communism (communist countries): appeasement of Nazi Germany and, 887; fascist fears of, 885, 886; in Vietnam, 916, 943–944; rivalry with capitalism, 939–941; Cuban, 951; collapse of, 976–977 *and map*

Communist Manifesto (Marx and Engels), 797, 800–801

Communist Party (China), 957*(illus.)*. *See also* China, People's Republic of; Mao Zedong; civil war (1945–1949) and victory of, 785, 897; famine and, 891, 931; Guomindang and, 862, 888, 889; Long March (1934–1935) and, 889, 890*(map)*; peasants and, 889, 891, 897, 956; as victor in civil war, 897–898; Vietnam and, 916; Deng Xiaoping's reform of, 975

Communist Party (Soviet Union), 858–859, 878, 881. *See also* Soviet Union; Russian civil war and (1918), 857–858; famine and, 880, 931; Gorbachev's reforms and, 976; fall of (1990), 977

Companies. *See* Business (companies)

Company Men (India), 764–766. *See also* East India Company, English (EIC)

Compass, 467, 515

Computers, 987–989, 1014

Comte, Auguste, 687

Concentration camps, 886, 901 *and illus.*, 902

Concordat of 1804 (France), 656

Condition of the Working Class in England (Engels), 797

Condorcanqui, José Gabriel, 543

Condorcet, Marie-Jean-Antoine, 782

Confederate States of America (Confederacy), 705, 707

Confederation of 1867 (Canada), 702, 719

Conference on Security and Cooperation in Europe (CSCE), 945

Confucianism, 606, in Qing China, 612, 615, 618*(illus.)*, 743, 746, 750, 861

Congo, 936, 978. *See also* Kongo

Congo Free State (Belgian Congo), 825–827, 830

Congo River, 761, 764, 825, 826*(illus.)*, 839

Congress of People's Deputies (Soviet Union), 977

Congress of Vienna (1814-1815), 660

Congress Party (India), 982, 1004. *See also* Indian National Congress

Congress (United States), 709, 855, 856; Vietnam and, 943; Central America and, 969; genocide convention ratified by, 1010

Conquistadors, 479–482, 523, 529

Conscription (military draft), 732, 808; in China, 891; in Egypt, 729; in Nazi Germany, 887

Conservation, environmental, 721. *See also* Environment, the

Conservatism, 656, 663, 810; Congress of Vienna and, 660; Catholic Church and, 703; nationalism and, 802, 804; in Europe, post World War I, 859; fascism and, 885; Christian, in United States, 1008

Conservative Party (Great Britain), 868

Constantinople, 578, 581, 846, 863. *See also* Istanbul; Ottoman conquest of, 623, 626

Constitutional Convention (1787, United States), 647

Constitutionalists (Mexico), 922–923

Constitutional monarchy: in Brazil, 699; in France, 649, 660; in Russia, 811; in Spain, 696; in Syria, 867

Constitutions: French, 651, 653, 661, 662; Haitian, 638; Prussia, 662; in Latin America, 694, 702–703; Mexico (1813), 699; Ottoman Empire, 737, 846; Mexico (1917), 923, 950; Brazilian, 926; Kenya, 949; Japanese (1946), 956; Iraq (2005), 1006

Constitution (United States), 646–647, 702, 704, 705, 1009; abolition of slavery and, 711, 712, 722; Amendments to, 712, 868; France and, 661, 662

Construction and building techniques: *See also* Architecture *and specific buildings;* Mughal India, 595*(illus.)*; British India, 911*(illus.)*

Consultative Group on International Agricultural Research, 938

Consumers (consumer goods), 608, 792, 798, 989; electronics, 987

Continental Congress, 641, 645, 646, 647

Contraceptives. *See* Birth control

Contracts of indenture, 778–779

Contra War (Nicaragua), 969, 973

Cook, James, 775

Cooke, William, 680

Copernicus, Nicolas, 497–498, 640

Copper, 792, 827, 885; in Chile, 721, 950

Copper coinage, 613

Le Corbusier (Charles-Edouard Jeanneret), 872

Córdoba (Argentina), 531

Corn. *See* Maize (corn)

Corn Laws (Great Britain), 661, 687

Cornwallis, Charles, 645–646

Corporations, 788. *See also* Business; Japanese *zaibatsu,* 808, 861, 973; transnational, 717, 933, 989

Corruption: in China, 613, 727–728, 751; in Cuba, 951; in Africa, 949; in Japan, 973

Cort, Henry, 676

Cortés, Hernán, 479–481, 520

Cosmopolitanism, 475, 593; in Istanbul, 732

Cossacks (Russia), 625

Costa Rica, 954

Côte d'Ivoire (Ivory Coast), 949

Cotton (cotton industry), 522, 569, 658, 826. *See also* Spinning; Textiles; Brazilian, 543; Ottoman, 587; Chinese, 613; child labor in, 684 *and illus.*; British, 666*(illus.),* 671 *and map,* 675, 685, 766–767, 770, 775; women in, 684–685; Egyptian, 688, 689, 737, 764, 825, 839, 885; Indian, 561, 689, 766–767, 770, 798, 839, 913; in United States, 675–676, 681, 685, 711, 720; mechanization of, 675–676, 689; African slave trade and, 711; clothing, 798; Central Asian, 832

Cotton gin, 675

Council of the Indies (Spain), 523

Council of Trent (1545–1563), 494

Counter Enlightenment, 641–642

Coureurs de bois, in Canada, 539 *and illus.*

Crafts and craftspeople. *See* Artisans

Credit, 560, 611. *See also* Foreign debt; World War I reparations and, 859

Creek people, 704, 709

Creoles, in Latin America: colonial era, 529, 531, 532, 533, 542; independence and, 696, 698

Crete, 582; Greece and, 846

Crime: in early modern Europe, 503; in pre-revolutionary France, 648; in modern cities, 986

Crimea, Russia and, 623

Crimean War (1853-1856), 734–736, 738, 751, 810, 847; modernization of warfare in, 734, 736

Croatia, 977*(map),* 978

Crompton, Samuel, 675

Cromwell, Oliver, 507, 543

Crossbows, 464. *See also* Bows and arrows

Crouching Tiger, Hidden Dragon (film), 1015

Crowther, Samuel Adjai, 763, 829

Crusades, 582

Cruzado (gold coin), 470

Cryptography. *See* Codebreaking, World War II

Crystal Palace (London), 676, 677

Cuba, 479, 949. *See also* Castro, Fidel; colonial elite, 542; slave trade in, 552, 762; abolition of slavery in, 711, 712–713, 778; Chinese immigrants in, 713, 714, 778; deforestation in, 720; free blacks in, 763; racial discrimination in, 716; Spain and, 836–837, 838; sugar production in, 573, 720, 778, 792, 838, 950–951; Depression of 1930s and, 885; United

States and, 838, 966; revolution in (1959), 934*(illus.),* 935–936, 967

Cuban missile crisis (1962), 936, 944, 954

Cuban Revolution (1959), 934*(illus.),* 935–936, 967

Cudjoe (maroon), 559*(illus.)*

Cult of domesticity, 686

Cultural imperialism, 933, 1013

Cultural relativism, 869

Cultural Revolution (China), 956, 957*(illus.)*

Culture (cultural factors): *See also* Art and artists; Folk culture; Literature; Society (social conditions) Westernization; *and specific cultures;* Latin American, 526; Americas and immigration, 520, 715; Russian Empire, 740–741; New Imperialism and, 820, 829, 832; enduring diversity, 1016, 1019; global, 1012–1019; media and message, 1013–1014; Mexican, 921; popular, 870, 1014–1015; English language and, 1015–1018

Currency: *See also* Coinage; Monetary system; paper, 613, 643, 651; Ottoman reform, 736; speculation in, and Asia crisis, 974; launch of Euro, 1001

Curzon, Lord George, 767, 910

Custer, George Armstrong, 710

Cyprus, 582, 583

Cyrillic alphabet, 739

Czechoslovakia (Czechs), 940; independence of, 856, 857*(map);* Nazi Germany and, 887, 888; Soviet Union and, 940, 941; fall of Communism in, 976, 977*(map)*

Czech Republic, 977*(map),* 982

Dachau death camp, 901*(illus.)*

Da Gama, Christopher, 474

Da Gama, Vasco, 469*(map),* 470; ships of, 464*(illus.),* 471*(illus.),* 474

Dagestan, 740

Dagur peoples, 618

Dahomey, 565–566. *See also* Benin

Daimyo (Japanese warlord), 606, 607, 610, 612, 628, 804

Dakar, Senegal, 918, 919

Dalai Lama, 613

Dams, 825, 955; hydroelectric, 791, 860, 873, 878, 956, 960

D'Annunzio, Gabriele, 878

Darby, Abraham, 676

Darby, Abraham, III, 676

Dardanelles Strait, 578, 941; World War I and, 853

Darfur refugees, Sudan, 1008*(illus.)*

Darwin, Charles, 808

Darwin, Erasmus, 675, 683

Date Masamune, 610

Davar, Cowasjee Nanabhoy, 689

D-day (World War II; 1944), 895

Death squads, 1010; in Brazil, 967; in El Salvador, 969

De Beers Consolidated, 827, *(illus.)*

Debt peonage, in Mexico, 920, 923. *See also* Foreign debt (international loans); War debt

Deccan, 597, 930

Decembrist revolt (Russia), 741

Declaration of Independence (1776, United States), 641, 645, 651, 694, 1009

Declaration of the Rights of Man (1789, France), 651, 694, 1009

Decolonization (1947–1990), 936, 945–954, *(map). See also* Independence; of Africa, 946*(map),* 947–950; Bandung Conference (1955) and, 954–955 *and illus.;* chronology (1947–1971), 937; nation building and, 945, 954; of South and Southeast Asia, 945–946 *and map,* 947; United Nations and, 939

Deforestation: in colonial sugar plantations, 553–554, 775; and mining, in Latin America, 526, 527; in China, 621, 989; in Europe, 681; in Americas, 721; in Caribbean area, 720; in India, 835, 841, 908, 989; in Southeast Asia, 835; World War II and, 903; in Brazil, 989, 992*(illus.),* 993; in Indonesia, 835, 993

De Gaulle, Charles, 949

Delft, porcelain in, 674

Delhi, 764, 767, 985*(table);* durbars in, 767, 768–769, 770*(illus.);* as capital of India, 911

Delhi Sultanate, 595

Democracy (democratic reforms): House of Burgesses and, 535; Revolutions of 1848 and, 662; French Revolution and, 648; in Great Britain and United States, 647, 661, 662; in British Canada, 702; in Latin America, 699; personalist leaders and, 704; in Brazil, 712; in Sub-Saharan Africa, 978; in Eastern Europe, 1003; in India, 1004; in Iraq and Afghanistan, 1005–1006

Demographic changes: *See also* Migrations; Population; Urbanization; in Columbian exchange, 520–522, 554; 1960s-1990s, 979–980

Demonstrations. *See* Protests; Strikes

Demuth, Helene, 797

Deng Xiaoping, 974–975

Denmark, 662, 940; German invasion of, 892

Depression (economic), 792; Ming China, 613; French Revolution and, 650; (1870s–1880s), 820; Great (1930s), 878, 881, 884–885, 925–926, 927

Developed nations. *See* Industrial nations

Developing nations (Third World). *See also* Nonindustrial world; Cold War and, 954–955; environmental degradation in, 989, 992; global economy and, 985; immigrants from, 986–987; population growth in, 979, 980, 982, 992, 993; rural-to-urban migration in, 984

Development, underdevelopment and, 717, 719–720, 935. *See also* Economic factors; Economy; Industrialization

Devil, witch hunts and, 492, 496

Devshirme, 582, 586, 587

De Witt Clinton (locomotive), 678*(illus.)*

Dhows (ships), 463, 475

Diagne, Blaise, 852–853, 919

Diamond mining, in South Africa, 827, 841*(illus.),* 978

Dias, Bartolomeu, 469*(map),* 470

Díaz, Porfirio, 694, 838
Dictatorship: *See also* Authoritarianism; personalist leaders, 704; fascist, in Europe, 885–886; Guomindang China, 862; populist, 656, 927; in Cuba, 935, 936; in Latin America, 705, 927, 966; in Indonesia, 947
Diderot, Denis, 640, 670
Diem, Ngo Dinh, 943
Dienbienphu, Battle of (1954), 943
Diplomacy: *See also* Politics; and warfare, in early modern Europe, 511–512; McCartney mission to China, 621; Russian, 628; French, 656
Directory (France), 653, 660
Dirty War against terrorism (Argentina), 968
Disease. *See also* Epidemics; Health Care; Medicine; diptheria, 520; Amerindians and, 460, 473, 479, 481, 482, 488, 520, 528; in Columbian exchange, 520–522, 554; smallpox, 479, 481, 520, 522, 550, 564, 681, 918; African slaves and, 528, 550, 552, 557; dysentery, 550, 557, 564, 681, 735, 930; influenza, 520, 521, 855, 912; malaria, 521, 527, 564, 619, 821, 835 *and illus.*; yellow fever, 521–522, 658*(illus.)*, 660; in Australia and New Zealand, 776; industrialization and, 681; cholera, 681, 771, 778; bubonic plague, 747; rickets, 681; sexually-transmitted, 829, 918; in colonial Africa, 821, 829, 918; tuberculosis, 681, 918; typhus, 520, 930; famine and, 931; HIV/AIDS, 980, 1012*(figure)*
Disraeli, Benjamin, 685
Diu, 475, 478
Divine kingship, in Mughal India, 596
Divine Society (Brahmo Samaj), 772
Division of labor, 672–673 *and illus.*, 797
Doctors without Borders, 1010
A Doll's House (Ibsen), 889
Dome of the Rock (Jerusalem), 958
Domesticity, cult of, 686
Domestic servants, women as, 684, 795, 797, 861
Dominican order, 525 *and illus.*, 526, 615, 619
Dominican Republic, 838
The Doss House (Makovsky), 811*(illus.)*
Dostoyevsky, Feodor, 741
Douglass, Frederick, 711
Drake, Francis, 489*(map)*
Dresden, bombing of (1944), 899
Dreyfus, Alfred, 809
"Drivers" of slave gangs, 556
Drought: African slavery and, 567; in Africa, 600, 756, 931; in China, 747; famine in India and, 908, 930; global warming and, 1011
Dubai, Palm Island, 1001*(illus.)*
Du Bois, W. E. B., 856, 920, 948
Duke, Antara, 570
Duma (Russian Parliament), 811
Dupleix, Joseph François, 597
Durand, J. D., 981*(table)*
Durbars, in India, 767, 768–769, 770*(illus.)*

Durkheim, Emile, 869
Dutch (Afrikaners) in South Africa, 774 *and illus.*, 827
Dutch East India Company (VOC), 500, 502*(illus.)*, 598; African trade and, 565; in China, 615; Indian Ocean trade and, 568; porcelain and, 609 *and illus.*; spice trade and, 601; trade monopoly of, 502, 560
Dutch East Indies, 833*(map)*, 834, 885. *See also* Indonesia; nationalist movement in, 896; World War II and, 894, 947
Dutch Empire, 772, 840*(map)*. *See also* Dutch East Indies; Netherlands, the
Dutch Guiana (Surinam), 559, 713, 774, 945
Dutch studies, in Japan, 610*(illus.)*, 611
Dutch West India Company, 500, 502, 537, 551–552, 560
Dutch World Map (1641), 501 *and illus.*
Dyer, Reginald, 912
Dynamite, 790
Dysentery, 550, 557, 564, 681, 735, 930

Earhart, Amelia, 869
Earth Day (1970), 960
Earthquakes: Lisbon (1755), 496; Japan (1923), 860; Japan (1944), 896; and tsunami, in Sumatra (2004), 1004
East Asia. *See also* Southeast Asia *and specific countries*; porcelain in, 609 *and illus.*; Confucianism in, 612; Japanese military power in, 813; chronology (1900–1927), 847; events in (1931–1945), 888–891; Chinese Communists and Long March in, 888–889, 890*(map)*; trade with, 821; Sino-Japanese War (1937–1945), 889–891 *and map*; electronics industry in, 1014
Easter Island, 461, 462 *and map*
Eastern Africa, 918. *See also specific countries*; Portuguese and, 474–475; Swahili Coast, 464–465, 475, 568; Muslim traders in, 598; secondary empires in, 763–764; ivory trade and, 763–764, 775
Eastern Europe, 960. *See also specific countries*; slavery and serfdom in, 503; Ottoman threat to, 582; Slavs of, 623; immigrants to Americas from, 714; World War II in, 876*(illus.)*; Nazi Holocaust in, 901 *and illus.*; chronology in (1978–1995), 967; economies of, 940–941, 966; fall of communist governments in, 976–977 *and map*; Warsaw Pact and, 937, 941, 942*(map)*; birthrates and life expectancy in, 982; global economy and, 985; English language in, 1015
East Germany, 941, 976*(illus.)*. *See also* Germany; reunification and, 977 *and map*
East India Company, English (EIC), 598, 774. *See also* Dutch East India Company (VOC); China trade and, 620, 621; American revolution and, 644; British India and, 689, 756, 764–766, 765*(map)*, 767, 772
East India Company, French, 560
East Indies (maritime Southeast Asia), 568. *See also* Indian Ocean states; Southeast

Asia; Portuguese in, 459; Muslim traders in, 598; Dutch, 833*(map)*, 834, 885, 894, 896, 947 (*See also* Indonesia)
East Timor, independence of, 1004
Ebu's-Su'ud, 584
Economic crisis: *See also* Depression; Great Depression; French Revolution, 648–649, 650, 651; recession, 792
Economic growth: *See also* Global economy; Dutch, 514; in colonial Americas, 537, 541–542, 543; in Japan, 607, 611, 860, 861, 956; Qing China, 615; Revolutionary era, 638; in Mexico, 692*(illus.)*, 694; and immigration to Americas, 713; in United States, 719, 940; slavery as obstacle to, 712; and expansion, in Americas, 722; European industrialization and, 728; World War II and, 903; British India, 908; in Africa, 918; in Europe, after World War II, 940; in Asia, 966, 973–974; sustainable development, 1003
Economics (economic theories). *See also* Capitalism; Free trade; business cycles, 685; laissez faire, 686–687; of Malthus and Ricardo, 686; of Marx, 797, 799; of Lenin, 858; Cold War ideology and, 939–941; neo-liberalism, 969, 970–971; chronology (2001-2004), 999
Economy (economic factors). *See also* Business; Fiscal policies; Industrialization; Inflation; Taxation; Trade; Spanish decline and, 514, 543; sugar plantation, 551; Atlantic trade, 559–565; Ottoman Empire, 587, 733; Ming China depression, 613; government role in, 717; Americas (nineteenth century), 719–720; Qing Chinese, 742; British India, 766; British, 810; Latin American nationalism and, 694, 785; New Imperialism and, 820–821, 837–838; Philippines, 837; World War I, 850, 852; Japanese, and war with China, 889, 891; Soviet Union, 881; World War II, 892; Brazilian, 967–968; Cold War and, 939–941; Latin American, 818, 945, 961 (*See also specific countries*); Cuban, 950–951; Soviet reforms, 975–976; Chinese (1980s-1990s), 965; Hong Kong, 974; Singapore, 974, 975; South Korean, 974, 975; Taiwanese, 974; pollution controls and, 1010
Ecuador, 462, 705; independence of, 635*(map)*, 696
Edict of Nantes (1685), 507
Edison, Thomas, 791
Education (educational institutions): *See also* Colleges and universities; Literacy; Schools and scholars; European bourgeoisie, 504; Latin American church and, 703, 705; Ottoman Empire, 582, 732; military, in Egypt, 729; of women, 716, 748, 772, 796, 889, 981; Victorian Age, 796; British India, 772; conservatism and, 802; France and Germany, 809; Japan, 808; Middle East, 863; Southeast Asia, 834; colonial Africa, 919, 948; state-run, in Mexico, 923, 924; Korea, 974

Edward VI (Great Britain), 767

Egypt, 808, 829, 947, 1006; Ottoman Empire and, 474, 478, 582, 688, 728–730; Mamluks in, 578, 581, 582, 589, 590; Britain and, 688–689, 761, 818, 821, 822(illus.), 825, 865; industrialization in, 688, 760; irrigation in, 760, 825, 841; modernization in, 759–760, 823; under Muhammad Ali, 688, 729, 730, 731, 732, 734, 738, 740, 756, 759, 764; Napoleon's invasion of, 728–729, 738, 756, 759, 761; foreign debt of, 737, 760, 825; railroads in, 688(illus.), 738, 760; Suez Canal and, 737, 790, 816(illus.), 817–818, 825; cotton production in, 688, 689, 737, 764, 825, 839, 885; World War II and, 894; Aswan dam and, 825, 955; Israeli-Arab wars and, 955–956, 958

Eiffel Tower (Paris), 791(illus.)

Einstein, Albert, 869, 899

Eisenhower, Dwight D., 897, 943, 944, 954; on military-industrial complex, 945

El Alamein, in World War II, 894

Elba, Napoleon on, 656, 660

Elections: See also Voting rights; and civilian rule, in Latin America, 969; in Ukraine, 1003

Electricity, 670, 791–792. See also Hydroelectric dams; Franklin's experiments with, 641; home use of, 791, 796, 870; in Paris, 791(illus.), 794; telegraph and, 679–680; urban pollution and, 795; in Japan, 860, 956

Electronics industry, 1013–1014; in Asia, 974, 1013, 1014; computers, 987–989, 1014

Elephants, 595(illus.), 764. See also Ivory trade; in Indian ceremonials, 768, 770(illus.)

Elite class: See also Aristocracy (nobility); Warrior elite; colonial Latin American, 523, 524, 525, 532, 542; Caribbean planter, 535, 536, 553, 555, 558; Japanese oligarchs, 610; Chinese, 613, 619; Revolutionary era, 663; economic interests of, 704; British India, 766; indigenous colonial, 822–823; Latin American, 694, 699, 718, 837–838; Brazilian, 924; Mexican, 921; Iranian, 972; global culture and, 1015–1016

Elizabeth I (England), 489(map), 509

Elmina, 473, 474, 551–552

El Salvador, 969

Emancipation Proclamation (1863), 712

Embargo, oil (1973), 958

Empire of the Cross, 710

Empires. See Colonies; Expansion; Imperialism; New Imperialism, and specific empires and emperors

Empire State Building (New York City), 872

Enclosure movement (England), 669–670

Encomienda labor, 528, 529, 532

Encyclopédie (Diderot), 640, 670

Energy consumption, 989. See also Electricity; Oil (oil industry)

Enfranchisement. See Voting rights

Engels, Friedrich, 668, 797, 800–801

Engineering: See also Construction and building techniques; Technology;

Industrial Revolution, 670, 683; for port of Buenos Aires, 718 and illus.; foreign, in Russia, 738; colleges and schools for, 790, 791; foreign, in Japan, 788, 789, 791; in British India, 841, 909, 911(illus.)

England: See also British Empire; Great Britain; religion and state in, 507; Enlightenment science in, 498, 499; social inequality in, 499; Dutch rivalry with, 502; iron industry in, 503; royal dynasties in, 507, 510 and table; merchant fleet of, 502, 514; Atlantic trade and, 560; chartered companies and, 550, 560; slave trade and, 563; Mughal India and, 595–596; sugar consumption in, 561; McCartney mission to China, 621; war with France, 520, 541, 543, 639; population growth in, 668; Irish in, 685; emigration from, 793

English language: immigrants to United States and, 808, 987; in India, 908, 909, 1015, 1016, 1017–1018; as global second language, 933, 1015–1016; world literature in, 1017–1018

Enigma machine, 900 and illus.

Enlightenment, the, 662, 782; Catholic response to, 641–642; folk cultures and, 642–643; independence in Americas and, 696, 711; intellectuals of, 639–641, 663; reforms of, 498–499, 640, 641

Entente (France, Great Britain, and Russia), 848, 849(map), 851(map), 853, 866

Entrepreneurs: See also Business; Industrial Revolution and, 671, 674, 675, 678, 689; New Imperialism and, 820; in Tokugawa Japan, 804; in British India, 914

Environment, the (environmental stress). See also Climate and weather; Deforestation; Natural disasters; colonial sugar plantation, 553–554; sheep grazing and, 522; soil erosion and, 553–554, 720–721, 989, 992(illus.), 993; colonial Canada, 539; in Western Hemisphere, 720–721; mining and, 526, 527, 721, 841; industrialization and, 668, 681–682, 688, 791, 926, 927; in Qing China, 742; air pollution and, 795; urbanization and, 721, 794–795; tropical ecology, imperialism and, 835, 839; world economy and, 839, 841; World War I and, 844(illus.), 855–856; World War II and, 902–903; Cold War and, 989; emergence of concern over (1970s), 960; population growth and, 966, 979, 987, 989; sharing and conserving resources, 989, 991–992; world economy and, 987, 989; fast food and, 990; global fresh water resources, 991(illus.); in Brazil, 992(illus.); responding to threats, 992–993, 1010; global warming and, 993, 1011; technology and, 987–993

Environmental Protection Agency (United States), 960, 992

Epidemics, 681. See also Disease; Amerindians and, 526, 528, 532, 540; in China, 613, 747; in Columbian exchange, 522; influenza (1918–1919), 855, 912

Equality principle, 1009. See also Gender differences; Human rights; Inequality

Ericsson, Leif, 465

Erie Canal, 678

Erosion, soil, 553–554, 720–721, 989, 993; in Brazil, 992(illus.)

Estado Nuovo (New State; Brazil), 926

Estates General (France), 510, 649, 650, 658

Estonia, 810; independence of, 854, 857(map), 977; Soviet invasion of, 892

Ethiopia, 568–569, 758(map); Christianity in, 474–475, 760, 832, 919; famine and drought in, 600, 931; modernization in, 760–761 and illus.; defeat of Italian invasion by (1895), 828 and illus.; Italian invasion of (1935), 887, 920

Ethiopian Christianity, 474–475, 760, 832, 919

Ethnic cleansing, in Balkans, 978. See also Genocide

Ethnicity, and race in Latin America, 530–532

Ethnic minorities. See also Mixed race; census and, 783; nationalism and, 847; organizations for, 715–716; in Russia, 810, 847

Eugénie (France), 817

Eunuchs: in Chinese court, 748(illus.); as harem slaves, 570, 592

Euro (currency), launch of, 1001

Europe (1500–1750): bourgeoisie in, 499–500, 502, 504; chronology, 493; culture and ideas in, 492–499; Enlightenment ideas in, 498–499; great powers of (1740), 513(map); Holy Roman Empire in, 505, 506(map), 511; mapmaking in, 501 and illus.; monarchies in, 507, 510 and table; peasants and laborers in, 502–504; political craft in, 508–509; political innovations in, 505–514; religious policies, 507; religious reformation, 492–494, 495(map); Renaissance, 490(illus.), 491; scientific revolution in, 497–498; social and economic life, 499–505; taxation in, 512, 514; warfare and diplomacy in, 511–512; witch hunts in, 496; women and family in, 504–505

Europe, great powers of (1740), 513(map)

Europe, great powers of (1871–1900), 707, 809–811; conservative countries, 810–811; Germany, 809; liberal countries, 809–810; New Imperialism and, 818

Europe, great powers of (1900–1913), 840(map), 846, 847

European Economic Community (Common Market), 940, 973, 992

European immigrants (Europeans): to Americas, 488, 521, 536–537, 669, 713, 714, 722, 979; in Latin America, 523, 525, 526, 532, 855; as indentured servants, 550–551, 552–553; in Indian Ocean states, 579; in North America, 544, 792–794 and illus., 822; in Argentina, 718, 792; in Australia and New Zealand, 778, 792, 822, 855; labor movement and, 715 and illus.; in Algeria, 761, 865, 915; post-World War I, 855; in South Africa, 827, 829, 918

European maritime expansion (1400–1550), 465–472, 469(map); Americas and,

479–482; Eastern Africa, 474–475; Indian Ocean states, 475, 478–479; motives for, 466–467; Portuguese voyages, 467–470, 469(map); Spanish voyages, 458–460, 469(map), 470–472; Western Africa and, 473–474, 476–477

European Union (EU), 985, 1002(map); English language in, 1016

Europe (Europeans): See also Eastern Europe; Industrial nations; Western Europe; and specific regions, peoples, countries, and empires; sugar consumption in, 561; African trade and, 565–566; Asian porcelain in, 609; Atlantic economy and, 561; Chinese trade and, 619, 620 and illus.; chronology (1756–1848), 639; conservativism in, 660, 662; ancien régime in, 638; Enlightenment in, 640–642; as merchants, 500, 587, 598, 605, 612; Japan and, 605–606, 610–611; middle class in, 619; India and, 597; Indian Ocean trade and, 587; Napoleonic, 656, 657(map); industrialization in, 671, 679(map) (See also Industrial Revolution); Greek independence and, 730; Ottoman reforms and, 731, 732, 733; nationality and census in, 783; possessions in Indian Ocean and South Pacific, 773(map); Qing China and, 621, 751; Russia and, 626, 738–739, 751; trading companies of, 615, 765; universal male suffrage in, 799; nationalism, 802–804, 805(map), 877; population of, 792; chronology (1904-1927), 847; in 1913, 849(map); World War I in, 848–852, 851(map); peace and dislocation in (1919–1929), 855–859; territorial changes in, after World War I, 857(map); radio in, 872; film industry in, 872; chronology (1931–1945), 879; Great Depression in, 881; World War II, 892–896, 893(map), 899, 900–902; Bretton Woods Conference (1944), 939; Cold War and, 945; demographic transition in, 979; investment in China, 975; population of (1750–2050), 981(table); wealth inequality in, 985; guest workers in, 986–987; industrial robots in, 989; Muslim terrorism in, 1008

Evenk peoples, 618

Examination system: in China, 613, 749, 860; in India, 770. See also Civil service

Exclusif (France, 1698), 561

Expansion (expansionism): See also Colonies; European maritime expansion; Imperialism; Maritime expansion; New Imperialism; and specific empires and emperors; Polynesian, 460–462 and map; Inca, 481; global, 488; France, 512; West African, 473, 565–566; Mughal India, 595; Napoleonic France, 656, 657(map); Ottoman, 578, 580(map), 581–582; Russian Empire, 489, 606, 618, 622–623, 624(map), 626, 628, 629, 731(map), 734, 736, 739–740; imperial Chinese, 489, 614(map), 615, 628; United States, 705, 706(map), 720(map), 820, 836–837, 838;

Zulu, 756; British Empire, 772, 775; British India, 765(map), 766; Egyptian, 764; European, 779; world economy, 717, 719, 839; Japanese, 807(map), 888; Nazi German, 886–888

Experiments and Observations on Electricity (Franklin), 641

Exploration (expeditions): See also specific explorers; Chinese (Zheng He), 462(map), 464 and illus., 465, 468, 471; Drake, 489(map); Portuguese maritime, 459, 465, 467–470, 468(illus.), 469(map); Spanish maritime, 458(illus.), 459–460, 461, 469(map), 470–472; Europeans in Africa, 761; in outer space, 933(illus.), 945, 1015

Explosives, 745(illus.), 790, 852. See also Bombs and bombing

Extraterritoriality, 736, 743. See also Treaty ports, in China

Factories, 684. See also Manufacturing; tobacco, 529(illus.); gas lighting for, 682; women in, 716, 852 and illus.; industrial robots in, 989

Factory Act of 1833 (Great Britain), 687

Fagan, Brian, 632

Faisal (Syria), 853, 856, 867

Falkland Islands (Malvinas) war, 969

Family: See also Children; Marriage; Women; in Europe, 504–505; Latin American elite, 532; slave, on plantations, 533, 556–557; in Istanbul, 593(illus.); industrialization and, 684; Victorian Age, 795–796 and illus., 797; Russian Revolution and, 882–883; fast food and, 990

Family-Planning Campaign (China), 980(illus.), 982

Famine, 632; in Angola, 570; in Ireland (1847-1848), 685, 792, 794, 930; in World War I, 852; in China, 613, 891, 931; in Russia (1916–1917), 854, 857; in Bengal (1943), 914, 931; in India, 908; in Soviet Union, 880, 931; politics and, 930–931

Farabundo Martí National Liberation Front (FMLN), 969

Faraday, Michael, 791

Farey, John, 670

Farmers (farming): See also Agriculture; Peasants; African women, 555; Caribbean, 555; colonial America, 538, 643; sharecroppers and tenants, 669, 670, 797, 930; Mexican, 694, 698; Amerindian women, 710; in British India, 770; North American, 794; Chinese, 614, 742, 891; in colonial Africa, 829; Japanese, 861; Great Depression and, 881, 884; kibbutzim, in Palestine, 865 and illus.; twentieth century advances and, 872–873; Gandhi and, 912; in Ghana, 918 and illus.; tariff protections for, 1003

Faruq (Egypt), 957

Fascism (1930s), 885–888; appeasement of, 887; Hitler's Germany, 886–888; Mussolini's Italy, 885–886; Brazil, 926

Fascist Party (Italy), 885–886

Fatwas, 584–585

Faysal II (Iraq), 957

February Revolution (1917, Russia), 854

Feminism (feminists), 686, 970, 1012, 1019. See also Women's rights; French Revolution and, 653

Feng Guifen, 749

Ferdinand (Spain), 471

Ferdinand VII (Spain), 695, 696, 698, 702

Fertility rates: See also Birthrate; for slaves, 557 and table; (1970s-1990s), 979–981, 982; of immigrant groups, 987

Festivals: European traditions, 643; Zulu, 757; durbars in India, 767, 768–769, 770(illus.)

Feudalism, in Russian colonies, 858

Fez (headgear), 732, 733(illus.), 863

Fiji, 460, 462(map), 778

Film (motion pictures), 870, 872, 1013; Indian, 1015, 1018

Finance. See also Banks; Coinage; Currency; Economic factors; Economy; Fiscal crisis; Foreign debt; Inflation; Taxation: Ottoman bureau, 737(illus.); global trade and, 792; crisis in Asia (1997), 974

Financial markets (stock exchanges), 502, 560, 985, 989

Financial revolution, in Europe, 514

Finland (Finns), 810, 892, 940; famine in, 632; independence of, 854, 857(map), 858

Finney, Ben, 462

Firearms (guns), 515. See also Cannon; Gunpowder; Weapons and military technology; African trade in, 474, 565, 569, 570, 774; Amerindians and, 480, 519, 535, 539; muskets, 565, 734, 743, 767, 821, 822(illus.); Ottoman, 582, 583, 586; in Japan, 610; interchangeable parts for, 670, 676–677; rifles, 623, 746, 767, 821, 822(illus.), 828; machine guns, 821, 822(illus.), 828, 850, 861; Safavid Iran, 594

First Estate (France), 648, 649

First International, 799

First World War. See World War I

Fiscal crises: French Revolution and, 648–650, 651; in revolutionary era, 639

Fishing (fishermen), 537, 884, 903

Fishwife, The (Ostade), 500(illus.)

Five-year plans (Soviet Union), 878–879, 880

Flanders, art of, 490(illus.), 491. See also Belgium

Floods (flooding): in China, 747, 861, 891, 903; in Bangladesh, 931, 1011

Florence, 492, 500

Florida, colonial, 479, 704

Folk cultures (folk customs): witchcraft and, 496; African slaves and, 558; Shari'a and, 598; and popular protest, in Europe, 642–643; Mexican, 921; diversity and, 1019

Fontanka Canal, St. Petersburg, 627(illus.)

Food and Agriculture Organization (UN), 937, 938

Food crops: See also specific food crops; Amerindian in Africa, 554, 555 and illus.; Asian and African, in New World, 522, 554; from Americas, 488, 503, 520, 522, 668; American in China, 621; Green Revolution in, 938 and illus.

Food (diet; nutrition). *See also* Agriculture *and specific foods;* African slaves, 550; and immigration to Americas, 715, 794; fast food, 990
Food shortages. *See* Famine
Footbinding, in China, 744, 746, 889
Ford, Henry, 868, 872, 873, 926
Ford Foundation, 938
Ford Motor Company, 989
Foreign debt (international loans): war, 514; British war, 639, 643; American Revolution, 646, 647; French, 649; Egyptian, 737, 760, 825; Chinese, 747; Ottoman, 736; Central American, 838; Japanese, 808; war reparations and, 859; World War I, 881; neo-liberalism and, 971
Foreign investment: *See also* British investment; New Imperialism and, 820; American, in Cuba, 935, 936; in China, 974, 975; in Latin America, 694, 719, 720, 920, 968, 970
Foreign policy, human rights and, 1012
Forests and forest products: *See also* Deforestation; African, 565; Russian, 503, 623; Javanese, 601; North American, 681; Burmese, 774; for railroads, 789; tropical, 775, 835 *and illus.,* 839, 924, 926, 992 *and illus.;* global economy and, 839
Fortifications: cannon and, 511; Portuguese, in Musqat, 600, 601*(illus.);* in British India, 766
"Forty-Seven Ronin" incident, 611*(illus.),* 612
Fouad (Egypt), 865
Fourier, Charles, 687
Fourteen Points (Wilson), 855, 866–867
France. *See also* French colonies; French Revolution; women's salons in, 505; canals in, 502; deforestation in, 503; army of, 511; dynasties in, 510*(table);* taxation of nobles in, 502, 510, 514, 649; peasant revolts in, 504; religion and state in, 507, 510; war with British, 520, 541, 543, 639; bourgeoisie in, 499, 648, 651; trading companies of, 560, 573; Atlantic economy and, 562*(map);* Seven Years War (1756-1763), 541, 639, 766; Greece and, 660; American Revolution and, 645, 646 *and map,* 649; Counter Enlightenment in, 641; conservative retrenchment in, 660; monarchy in, 647, 649, 656, 660; Revolution of 1848 in, 662; roads in, 682; technology and innovation in, 670, 678, 683; industrialization in, 671; Louisiana sale and, 705; railroads in, 679 *and map,* 738, 788; invasion of Mexico by, 707; Ottoman Empire and, 732, 737; Russia and, 737, 739; India and, 766; Indian Ocean trade and, 756, 772; Napoleon's invasion of Egypt, 728–729, 738, 756, 759, 761; Algeria and, 761, 865, 936; Crimean War and, 734, 738, 810; Qing China and, 744*(map),* 747, 812; as great power, 788; census in, 782; male suffrage in, 799; as liberal power, 809–810; urbanization in, 794; Italian unification and, 802; language and nation in, 802;

Suez Canal and, 818, 955; African colonies of, 824*(map),* 826; in Indochina, 833*(map),* 834, 916–197; war with Prussia (1870-1871), 804, 808, 818–819, 847; alliances of, 848; World War I and, 845–846, 849–851 *and maps,* 852–853, 855; World War I peace and, 856, 859, 873; in Ruhr following World War I, 859; Middle East and, 862; appeasement of Germany by, 887; Depression of 1930s and, 881; filmmaking in, 870; World War II and, 892, 893*(map),* 894, 895; nationalization in, 940; United Nations and, 937; Vietnam and, 743, 916–917, 943; Cold War and, 945; Kosovo crisis and, 978; anti-immigrant sentiment in, 986
Franciscan order, 525–526, 615, 619
Francis I (France), 505
Franco-Prussian War (1870–1871), 804, 808, 818–819, 847
Franklin, Benjamin, 641, 670
Franz Ferdinand, assassination of, 845, 846
Franz Josef (Austria), 662, 817
Frederick the Great (Prussia), 640
Frederick William IV (Denmark), 662
Free blacks, 532, 533, 542*(illus.),* 558–559; in Haitian rebellion, 637–638, 659; in Latin America, 696, 712*(illus.);* in United States, 647
Free French movement, 949, 960
Freemasons, 740–741
Free trade (free market), 878, 969. *See also* Capitalism; as British policy, 686–687, 688–689, 772, 775; imperialism and, 837–838; women's rights and, 970–971; regional trade associations, 1001–1003 *and map*
French and Indian War (1756–1763), 541, 639, 649
French Assembly, 649–651
French colonies (French Empire), 772, 774, 840*(map). See also* French North America; in Indian Ocean, 597, 599*(map),* 773*(map);* in West Indies, 550, 551, 558, 559, 561, 643, 778 (*See also* St. Dominigue (Haiti)); abolition of slavery in, 636*(illus.),* 637, 660, 662, 712–713, 778; Vietnam as, 743, 916–917, 943; in Africa, 824*(map),* 826, 918, 949; independence of, 945, 949
French East India Company, 560
French Equatorial Africa, 918
French Indochina, 833*(map),* 834, 916–917
French language, 715, 732, 738; national identity and, 802; in Indochina, 916
French North America, 538–541, 540*(map);* Amerindians in, 518*(illus.),* 519–520, 539–540 *and illus.,* 541; chronology (1534-1760), 521; fur trade in, 522, 539 *and illus.,* 541; Louisiana, 518*(illus.),* 519–520, 541, 676, 705, 706*(map)*
French Revolution, 647–656; American Revolution compared to, 662–663; guillotine in, 651, 652; Haiti and, 637–638, 658, 659–660; National Assembly and, 649–651; playing cards from, 653*(illus.);* protest beginning, 649–651; radical

reforms of, 651, 653; reaction to, and rise of Napoleon, 653, 656; Reign of Terror (1793–1794), 651–653, 654–655, 656, 662; society and fiscal crisis, 648–649; war against Austria and Prussia, 656; women and, 651, 653, 656
French West Africa, 826, 949
French West India Company, 560
French West Indies, 550, 551, 558, 559, 561, 643. *See also* St. Domingue (Haiti); labor migration to, 778
Freud, Sigmund, 869
Front de Libération National (FLN), 947
Fugitive slave clause, 647
Fulani people, 759
Fulton, Robert, 678
Funerals: Afro-Brazilian, 701; Ottoman, 576*(illus.)*
Fur trade (furs): North American, 522, 535, 536, 539 *and illus.,* 541, 561, 643; Russian, 604*(illus.),* 606, 623, 627
Fynn, Henry Francis, 757

Gage, Thomas, 644
Galdan (Mongolia), 613, 618, 619, 623
Galilei, Maria Celeste, 505
Galileo Galilei, 498
Gallipoli Peninsula, 578, 853
Gambia, 571, 572
Gandhi, Mohandas K. (Mahatma), 912–915; militant nonviolence and, 912, 916; technology and, 913 *and illus.;* assassination of, 915
Ganges River Delta, 596
Garibaldi, Giuseppe, 803
Garnet, Henry Highland, 711
Garvey, Marcus, 920, 948
Gas lighting, 682, 683 *and illus.,* 794
Gates, Horatio, 645
Gaza Strip, 957, 958, 1008
Gender differences: *See also* Women; in slave society, 556; reform movements and, 716; in Victorian Age, 795–796 *and illus.;* division of labor and, 797; and class, in industrialized world, 868–869
General Assembly, United Nations, 936, 937; Israel and, 957; Universal Declaration of Human Rights and, 1009; women's rights and, 1010, 1012
Geneva Convention (1950), 1010
Genghis Khan, 594–595, 832
Genoa, 465, 467, 479, 500, 582
Genocide, 978, 1010; Nazi Holocaust, 899, 901 *and illus.*
Gens de couleur, in Haiti, 658–659
Gentry, British, 502, 670, 685, 909
George III (Great Britain), 621, 645
Georgia (Caucasus), 728, 734, 736, 740; Soviet Republic of, 858, 978
Georgia (United States), 675, 720
German language, 804
Germany (Germans), 868, 989. *See also* East Germany; Prussia; West Germany; nationalism in, 493, 505; Wars of Religion in, 505; in North America colonies, 538, 645; industrialization of, 671, 788, 790,

810; customs union in, 687; immigrants from, 714, 793; railroads in, 679(map); Ruhr district, 671, 679(map), 680, 790; as great power, 788; chemical industry in, 790, 852; socialist electoral politics in, 799; steel production in, 790; unification of, 662, 804, 805(map); urbanization in, 794; African colonies of, 824(map), 826, 828, 852, 862; colonies, 809, 819, 837, 840(map), 861, 862; Ottoman alliance with, 846, 853; before World War I, 846, 847–848; World War I and, 846, 848–851 and maps, 852, 853, 854–855; World War I peace and, 856, 857(map), 862, 873; economic crisis in (1923), 859, 886; reparations after World War I, 859, 881; Great Depression in, 878, 881, 884; in World War II, 887, 891, 892, 894–896 (See also Wehrmacht); Nazis in, 886–888, 896; Nazi-Soviet Pact (1939), 888; alliance with Italy, 888; bombing of, World War II, 899; casualties, in World War II, 888, 898, 899, 901 and illus.; fall of Berlin Wall and, 976(illus.); reunification of (1990), 977 and map; immigration to, 986, 987

Ghana, 948. See also Gold Coast

Gilbert, Humphrey, 534

Girondists (France), 652

Glaciers: in Little Ice Age, 632; melting of, in twenty-first century, 1011

Glasnost (Soviet reform), 976

Glassmakers, Ottoman, 583(illus.)

Global culture, 1012–1019; diversity in, 1016, 1019; English language and, 1015–1018; fast food and, 990; popular culture and, 1014–1015; technology and, 1012–1014, 1016

Global economy (world economy), 711. See also Globalization; American silver and, 528; European domination of, 728; expansion of, 717, 719; chemical industry, 790; steamships and, 789–790, 839; steel industry, 790, 791; technology and (1850–1900), 788–792; trade and finance, 792; Marx on, 800–801; before World War I, 846; environmental stress and, 839, 841; New Imperialism and, 818; Great Depression and, 881; free market and, 878; inequality and, 984–985; per capita GNIs, 985; colonial Africa in, 920; expansion of, 839, 993; World Trade center as symbol of, 998; return of China to, 974–975; current political currents and, 998–1006

Globalization, 998, 1019. See also Global economy (world economy); culture and (See Global culture); faith and politics, 1006–1009; global warming, 993, 1011; Islamic terrorism and, 1008–1009; population growth and, 979; spread of democracy and, 1003–1004; universal rights and values, 1009–1010; women's rights, 1010, 1012; world religions and, 1007(map)

Global warming, 933, 993, 1011

Glorious Revolution of 1688 (England), 507, 543

GNI (gross national income), trends in, 985

Goa, Portuguese in, 475, 582

The God of Small Things (Roy), 1016

Golan Heights (Syria), 958

Gold Coast, 560, 568. See also Ghana; Portuguese trade and, 467, 470, 473; Asante kingdom in, 566, 567, 762, 828; cocoa farmers in, 918; end of slave trade in, 762; slave trade and, 565; European imperialism in, 826

Gold coinage: cruzado, 470; Ottoman, 736

Golden Hind (ship), 489(map)

Golden Horde khanate, 622–623

"The Golden Speech of Queen Elizabeth," 509

Gold (gold trade), 939; in Caribbean, 479; African, 467, 470, 561, 565, 600; from colonial Americas, 482, 489, 514, 525, 526, 559; in Brazil, 529, 543; in California, 707; in Australia, 776; in Black Hills (Dakota), 793(illus.); in Gold Coast, 762; in South Africa, 827, 885; in Shanghai, 898(photo)

Goldman, Emma, 799

Gomes, Fernão, 470

Gorbachev, Mikhail, 975–976, 977–978

Gordon, Charles, 735, 821

Goulart, João, 967

Government: See also Administration; Bureaucracy; Constitutions; Monarchy; Political systems; Self-government; water transport and, 502; colonial Latin American, 523–524, 705; Dutch, 514; colonial North America, 535, 541, 543, 639, 644, 645; Ottoman, 581, 582, 583, 586, 589; Tokugawa Japan, 611, 612; Enlightenment view of, 640; French Revolution and, 653, 654; popular protest of, 642–643; Qing China, 615, 621–622, 748; United States, 646–647; industrialization and, 670, 671; laissez faire economics and, 686; Constitutionalism in Americas, 702–703; economic management by, 717, 884; immigrant cultures and, 715; Ottoman reforms, 732; power of, and census, 782–783; British colonial, 776, 778, 822; in British India, 766, 767, 771; in colonial Africa, 828, 918 and illus.; Japanese, 808, 888; New Imperialism and, 819–820, 822–823; Russian, 810; Soviet, 858, 878, 880; Guomindang, in China, 862; in fascist Italy, 885; in industrialized world, 868; nation building and, 954; neoliberalism, in Latin America and, 969; industry in Asia and, 973–974, 1019; European cooperation, 940; national language and, 1014; subsidies by, 1003; transitional, in Iraq, 1006

Granada, 467, 471

Gran Colombia, 697(map), 703, 705, 707; Bolívar and, 635(map), 696, 704

Grand Canal (China), 621

Grand National Consolidated Trade Union, 687

Great Britain: See also under British; England; India, British rule in; Atlantic economy and, 562(map); China trade and, 620–621; sea power of, 638–639; American Revolution and, 643–646, 647; Napoleon era France and, 656; democratic reforms in, 647, 661; enclosure movement in, 669–670; Greece and, 660; free trade in, 686–687, 688–689; war with United States (1812), 661, 707, 709; abolition of slavery and slave trade in, 685, 699, 712, 762; Canada and, 681, 719; railroads in, 671(map), 678, 679, 680; Latin America and, 694; Indian Ocean colonies of, (map); Argentina and, 718 and illus.; health care in, 735; Crimean War and, 734, 735–736, 738, 810; Qing China and, 741–743, 744(map), 747–748, 766, 812; Russia and, 739; Sierra Leone and, 762–763; United States and, 706(map), 792; census in, 782; Egypt and, 688–689, 761, 818, 821, 822(illus.), 825, 865; as great power, 788; steel production in, 790; universal male suffrage in, 799; financial power of, 792; Suez Canal and, 818, 825; urbanization in, 794; investment by, 720, 770; Ireland and, 507, 512, 534, 810, 837, 930; Japan and, 789; African colonies of, 824(map), 826, 948 (See also Cape Colony); Egypt and, 825, 865, 955; Middle East and, 862; Palestinian question and, 862, 865–866, 868, 957; Victorian "separate spheres," 795–796 and illus.; alliances of, 847, 848, 849(map); World War I and, 848, 850, 852, 853; World War I peace and, 856, 859, 873; Great Depression and, 881; women's rights in, 796 and illus., 868; Nazi Germany and, 887–888; World War II and, 892, 894, 895, 901; World War II casualties, 898; Mexican nationalization and, 923; South American infrastructure and, 925; United Nations and, 937; Cold War and, 944, 945; nationalization in, 940; Falklands War and, 969; Kosovo crisis and, 978

Great Britain, Industrial Revolution in (1760–1851), 670–671; canal-building in, 682 and illus.; changes in society, 685–686; child labor in, 668, 684 and illus.; cotton industry in, 666, 675, 684; disease and, 681; gas lighting in, 683; industrial cities, 666(illus.), 667–668, 680, 681; iron industry in, 676; laissez faire, 686–687; population growth and, 668; pottery industry, 674–675 and illus.; protests and reforms, 687–688; railroads in, 671(map), 678, 679, 680, 788; steam power in, 677–678; telegraph in, 680

Great Depression (1930s): economic crisis of, 881; in Germany, 878, 881, 884; in industrial nations, 881; in nonindustrial regions, 884–885; in Brazil and Argentina, 925–926, 927

Greater Antilles, 465, 479, 480. See also Caribbean region

Greater East Asia Co-Prosperity Sphere, 896

Great Lakes region (North America), 522, 539, 643, 992

Great Leap Forward (China), 931, 956

Great Northern War (1700–1721), 512, 626
Great Plains (United States), 709–710, 719, 794
Great powers: of Europe (1740), 513(map); of Europe (1871–1900), 707, 809–811, 877; Japan as (1868–1900), 788, 812–813; United States as (1865–1900), 788; of Europe (1900–1913), 846, 847; colonial possessions of (1913), 840(map)
Great Society reforms (United States), 944
Great Trek (southern Africa), 758(map), 774 and illus.
Great Western (steamship), 677(illus.), 678
Greco-Roman tradition, 492, 497, 730
Greece (Greeks), 582, 855, 940, 985; independence of, 660, 662, 729, 730; Orthodox Christians in, 734; in Ottoman Empire, 846; Crete and, 846; Turkey and, 863, 941; in West Africa, 918
Greenhouse effect: See also Global warming, 1011
Greenland, 465, 1011
Green Revolution, 933, 938 and illus.
Gregory XIII, Pope, 498
Grenada, invasion of, 969
Grimké, Sarah, 716
Gropius, Walter, 872
Gross national income (GNI), trends in, 985
Guadeloupe, 550, 552, 573
Guam, 838
Guaman Poma de Ayala, Felipe, 481(illus.)
Guangxi, 744
Guangzhou (Canton), 619, 620–621, 862, 889; street scene in, 746(illus.); trade warehouse in, 726(illus.)
Guatemala, 521, 722; CIA-sponsored military coup in (1954), 950, 951
Guerrilla warfare: Hindu, 597; in China, 889, 891; in Vietnam, 943–944; in Africa, 949, 950; in Cuba, 951; in El Salvador, 969; in Middle East, 868, 957, 958; in Afghanistan, 1006; in Iraq, 1005, 1006; in Niger, 1004
Guevara, Ernest "Che," 951 and illus., 954
Guianas, 559, 714, 774, 778
Guilds, 670, 686; merchant, 529; Ottoman, 583(illus.), 592
Guillotin, Joseph Ignaz, 652
Guillotine, 651, 652
Guinea, 949
Gujarat, 475, 478, 598
Gulags (Soviet labor camps), 880, 881
Gullah dialect, 536
Gunboats (warships), 689, 743, 821
Gunpowder, 565, 578, 734; in Japan, 610, 628; smokeless, 821
Guns. See Firearms
Guomindang (China), 861, 862, 891; civil war and defeat of, 897–898; Communists and, 862, 888, 889; Vietnam and, 916
Gurkhas (Nepal), 767

Habsburg dynasty, 505, 506(map), 510(table), 513(map), 541, 707
Haciendas (estates), 920–921, 922, 924
Hafez (poet), 590
Haidar Ali, 764

Haiti. See St. Domingue (Haiti)
Hakkas, in China, 745–746
Halil, Patrona, rebellion of, 589
Hall, John, 670
Hamas movement, 1006
Hamburg, 500; bombing of (1943), 899
Hannibal (slave ship), 550, 564
Hanoverian dynasty, 510(table)
Harding, Warren, 878
Harris, Arthur "Bomber," 899
Harsha Vardhana, 596
Hart, Robert, 747
Hausa states, 566(map), 569, 570, 571; Muslim reforms in, 759
Havana, Cuba, 553, 838, 934(illus.)
Havel, Vaclav, 976
Hawaii, 461, 462 and map, 778; Pearl Harbor in, 836, 894; United States and, 836, 838
Hay, John, 838
Hayford, J. E. Casely, 920
Headgear, Turkish fez, 732, 733(illus.), 863
Health care, 685, 872. See also Medicine (physicians); Crimean War and, 735; in colonial Africa, 918, 948
Heavenly Kingdom of Great Peace (China), 745–746, 747
Hebrew Bible, 496. See also Bible, the
Helena (Ethiopia), 474
Helsinki Accords (1975), 945
Henry of Navarre, 507
Henry the Navigator, 467–470, 469(map)
Henry VIII (England), 507, 512
Herero people, 828
Heresy, 526, 577–578
Herzegovina. See Bosnia and Herzegovina
Herzen, Alexander, 741
Herzl, Theodore, 853, 866
Heshen, 727–728
Heyerdahl, Thor, 462
Hezbollah (Lebanon), 1006
Hidalgo y Costilla, Miguel, 698–699 and illus.
Hidden Imam, 591
Hideyoshi, 606
Hindi language, 1015, 1017
Hindus (Hinduism), 464, 591, 947, 1008; in British India, 766, 767, 772; Deccan, 595; Indian independence and, 914; Muslim relations, 596–597, 908, 914, 1004 and illus.; social classes and; spread of, 1007(map)
Hirobumi, Ito, 806
Hirohito (Japan), 897
Hiroshima, atomic bombing of, 895(map), 896–897 and illus., 944
Hisashige, Tanaka, 789
Hispaniola, 479, 526, 553, 559. See also St. Domingue (Haiti)
History Will Absolve Me (Castro), 935
Hitler, Adolf, 886–888, 892, 894, 895; Holocaust and, 899, 901; suicide of, 896
HIV/AIDS, 980, 1012(figure)
Ho Chi Minh, 916, 943
Ho Chi Minh City (Saigon), 944
Hogarth, William, 642(illus.)
Hokulea (canoe), 462
Holland. See Netherlands (the Dutch)

Hollywood films, 870, 872, 1013
Holocaust, 899, 901 and illus.
Holy Alliance, 660
Holy Land, 585
Holy Roman Empire, 505, 506(map), 511, 513(map), 583, 606
Honda, 989
Hondius, Jodocus, 489(map)
Honduras, 838
Hong Kong, 743, 747, 894, 1015, 1019; China and, 974, 1016
Hong Xiuquan, 745–746, 747
Hookah (waterpipe), 588 and illus., 590(illus.)
Hormuz, 475, 582, 594
Horses, 615. See also Cavalry; Conquistador, 481; Amerindians and, 522, 523, 540, 710; urban pollution and, 795, 872
Horton, James Africanus, 763
Hospitallers, 581
House of Burgesses (Virginia), 535
House of Commons (Britain), 507, 537, 661
House of Lords (Britain), 507, 912
House of Representatives (United States), 647, 705. See also Congress (United States)
Housing (dwellings): See also Architecture; colonial Americas, 538(illus.); in Isfahan, 591–592; for industrial workers, 667–668, 680; Paris apartment, 681(illus.)
Huanyaputina, Mount, 632
Huascar, 481, 482
Huayna Capac, 481
Hudson River Valley, 537, 539, 678
Huerta, Victoriano, 921, 922
Huguenots, 495(map)
Human rights, 1009–1010. See also Rights; in Latin America, 968
Human sacrifice, Aztec, 480
Hume, David, 641
Hungary (Hungarians), 582, 662, 736, 847. See also Austria-Hungary (1867–1917); after World War I, 855, 856, 857(map); Soviet Union and, 940, 941; fall of Communism in, 976; life expectancy in, 982
Hunters in the Snow (Brueghel), 490(illus.), 491
Hunting: by Amerindians, 523, 535, 539, 540, 643, 710; of seals, off New Zealand, 776
Hunting-and-gathering peoples, 775, 828, 834
Huntington, Samuel P., 1009
Huron peoples, 539, 540
Husain, Saddam, 972–973, 1006; invasion of Kuwait by, 978–979, 1009; weapons of mass destruction and, 1005
Husain (Jordan), 957
Husayn (Shi'ite martyr), 591
Hussein ibn Ali, 853
Hutu-Tutsi rivalry (Rwanda), 978
Hydraulic technology, 717. See also under Water
Hydroelectric dams, 791, 873, 878, 960; in Japan, 860, 956
Hydrogen bomb, 944. See also Nuclear weapons
Hygiene, 872, 980, 981. See also Sanitation

Ibadan, Nigeria, 918, 938
Iberian expansion, 465–466. *See also* Portuguese exploration; Spanish exploration
Ibrahim Pasha (Egypt), 729–730, 731, 734
Ibsen, Henrik, 889
Ice Age, Little (1590s), 503, 613, 632
Iceland, Vikings in, 465
Ideology, popular protest and, 643. *See also* Political thought (ideology)
Ignatius of Loyola, 494
Ilanga (Congolese woman), 830–831
Illinois, 678; native peoples in, 709
IMF. *See* International Monetary Fund
Immigrants (immigration): *See also* European immigrants; Migration; acculturation and, 714–715; to Americas, 521, 536–537, 669, 670, 713–715, 722; to Australia and New Zealand, 601, 775, 776; Chinese, 614, 713, 714 *and illus.*, 747, 774, 778; to Hawaii, 836; Jews, in Palestine, 865–866 *and illus.*, 873; to United States, 669, 670, 705, 715, 719, 808, 986, 987, 1001; railroads and, 793; Russian Empire; World War I refugees, 855; and colonial African trade, 918; to industrialized nations, 984, 986–987
Imperialism: *See also* Colonies; Expansion; New Imperialism; *and specific empires and emperors;* Industrial Revolution and, 634; Qing China and, 749–750; Japanese, 861; in Latin America, 837–839; tropical ecology and, 835 *and illus.*; Castro's denouncement of, 936; United Nations and, 939; cultural, 933, 1013
Imperial Maritime Customs Service (Britain), 748
Import duties, 686, 881, 884. *See also* Tariffs
Import-substitution industrialization, 926; in Brazil, 967
Inca (Inca Empire), 523, 528; Spanish conquest of, 481–482, 532; population loss in, 520
Indentured labor, 550–551, 552–553, 573; of Asian immigrants, 714, 778–779, 794
Independence (independence movements). *See also* Decolonization (1947-1990); Latin American independence; Netherlands, 551; Haitian, 637, 660; American Revolution and, 645–646; Greek, 660, 662, 729, 730; Cuban, 713; Philippine, 837; Serbian, 734, 847; Young Ottomans and, 737; after World War I, 854, 856, 857*(map)*; League of Nations mandate and, 862; in India (1905-1945), 785, 908–915, 927; in sub-Saharan Africa, 947–950; in Indonesia, 1004
India, 985. *See also* India, under British rule; Mughal Empire (India); Chinese in, 464; Malabar Coast, 475, 478; Portuguese in, 478 *and illus.*; cotton textiles from, 561, 675, 798; African ivory trade and, 600, 763–764; British trade with; deforestation in, 835, 841, 908, 989; independence movement in, 908–915; Pakistan and, 945, 947; population growth in, 982;

deforestation in, 989; vegetarian fast food in, 990*(illus.)*; Hindu-Muslim strife in, 1004 *and illus.*; industrialization in, 1019; English language in, 1015, 1016, 1017–1018
India, independence movement in (1905-1945), 908–915, 927; Gandhi and, 912–914 *and illus.*, 916; Indian National Congress and, 909–910, 912, 914; land and people, 908; Muslim League and, 911, 912, 914; Nehru and, 914, 945; partition and (1947), 910*(map)*, 914–915; "Quit India" campaign, 914
India, under British rule, 764–772, 775, 819, 837, 947; (1707-1805), *(map)*; administration, 766, 767, 770; China and, 743; cholera in, 681, 771; chronology (1756-1885), 757; company men in, 764–766; cotton production and, 689, 770, 839; durbar ceremonials in, 767, 768–769; immigrant labor from, 713, 714, 794, 827, 834; industrialization in, 771, 914; tea production in, 766, 770, 835, 839; irrigation projects in, 770, 771, 841, 873; nationalism in (1828–1900), 767, 771–772, 808, 834, 1015; opium trade and, 766; political reform in, 767; traditions in, 766, 767; railroads in, 689, 754*(illus.)*, 755, 771, 789, 833*(map)*, 839, 930; raj and rebellion in (1818–1857), 766–767, 779, 810; trade in, 770, 775; Russia and, 740; independence movement in (1905–1945), 908–915, 927; population growth in (1900–1941), 908; World War I and, 853; civil engineering in, 841, 909, 911*(illus.)*; Depression of 1930s and, 884; famine in, 908, 930; influenza epidemic in (1918–1919), 912; women in, 772, 820, 908
Indiana, 678; native peoples in, 709
Indian Civil Service (ICS), 767, 770, 772, 909, 947
Indian National Congress, 772, 909–910, 912, 914, 920
Indian Ocean (Indian Ocean states), 821. *See also* East Indies; *and specific states;* chronology (1405–1539), 461; exploration of, before 1500, 462–465, 462*(map)*; Portuguese exploration of, 469*(map)*; chronology (1511–1741), 579; British domination of, 779; European colonies in, 773*(map)*
Indian Ocean trade (maritime system): Muslims and, 463; Portuguese and, 471, 472, 475, 478–479, 482, 489, 615; Dutch supremacy in, 500, 560, 568; Atlantic trading system and, 573; Europe and, 587; France and, 772
Indian Removal Act (U.S., 1830), 709
Indigo plantations, 536, 658, 775, 790
Individual rights: *See also* Human rights; Rights; Voting rights; Enlightenment view of, 640, 641; Declaration of Independence (US) and, 645; in Napoleonic France, 656; and constitutionalism, in Americas, 702

Indochina, 885. *See also* Burma; Cambodia; Laos; Southeast Asia; Thailand; Vietnam; Communist party in, 943; French in, 833*(map)*, 834, 916–917; Japanese occupation of, 894, 931
Indonesia (Indonesians), 954. *See also* Dutch East Indies; Java; New Imperialism in, 832, 834, 835; nationalism in, 896; relocation program in, 986; deforestation in, 992, 993; East Timor independence from, 1004; Muslim terrorism in, 1009
Indulgence selling, 492
Indus River Valley: cotton in, 798; Islam in, 596
Industrialization. *See also* Industrial nations; Industrial Revolution; capitalism and, 663; in Japan, 608; in Europe, 679*(map)*; in Egypt, 688, 760; laissez faire economics and, 686–687; nonindustrial world and, 688–689; environmental effects of, 681–682, 791; in Americas, 711, 717, 719; in Russia, 738, 788, 810; in Japan, 788, 808, 813, 834, 860; in Soviet Union, 785, 811, 858–859, 878, 880, 881, 940; technological change and, 846; in Brazil and Argentina, 925, 926, 927; in British India, 911, 913 *and illus.*, 914; in China, 926, 956, 974; in Latin America, 967; working women and, 881; World War II, 903; environmental effects of, 926, 987, 992; import-substitution, 926, 967; Asian governments and, 973–974; Western culture and, 1019
Industrial nations (developed world), 936. *See also* Industrialization; Industrial Revolution; overseas trade of, 792; social transformations in (1850–1900), 792–799; women's changing roles in, 795–797; technology in (1850-1900), 788–792; New Imperialism and, 820, 837; scientific revolution in, 869; class and gender in, 868–869; Depression (1930s) in, 881, 884; immigration to, 984, 986–987; Latin American dependence on, 927; population growth in, 980–981; growing wealth of, 985; modern technology and, 869–872, 907, 925; resource consumption in, 989; technology and, 987; environmental concerns in, 992, 993; Kyoto Protocol and, 1010, 1011
Industrial Revolution (1760–1851), 634, 667–690. *See also* Great Britain, Industrial Revolution in; United States, Industrial Revolution in; agriculture and, 669–670; causes of, 668–671; chronology, 669; cities and towns in, 666*(illus.)*, 667–668, 680–681; in continental Europe, 671, 679*(map)*; division of labor in, 672–673 *and illus.*; entrepreneurs in, 671, 674, 675, 678, 689; gas lighting, 683; impact of, 638, 680–686; iron industry, 676–677, 682; limits of, outside the West, 688–689; mass production in, 674–675; mechanization of cotton industry in, 675–676; new economic and political ideas, 686–688; population growth and, 668–669, 979; railroads and, 678–679 *and illus.*; rural areas and, 670,

Industrial Revolution *(Continued)*
681–682; steam engines, 676*(illus.)*,
677–678; telegraph and, 679–680; trade
and inventiveness in, 638, 670, 671;
women and, 684, 685; working conditions
in, 682, 684–685
Industries. *See also* Industrialization; Iron
industry; Manufacturing; Textile industry;
tobacco in colonial Mexico, 529*(illus.)*;
chemical, 790, 852; gender divisions in,
797; iron, 503, 512, 671, 676–677,
679*(map)*, 682; porcelain, 608, 609 *and
illus.*, 612–613, 674; silk, 587, 593, 594,
613; wool, 523, 675; World War II boom,
903; robots for, 989
Inequality: *See also* Social classes; in Mexico,
950; global poverty and, 966, 985; wealth,
984–985, 993, 1000*(map)*, 1001*(illus.)*
Infantry. *See also* Armed forces; Ottoman
Empire, 581; Chinese, 628; Crimean War
and, 734; in World War I, 850
Inflation: *See also* Prices (price inflation); in
Spain, 514; in Ottoman Empire, 586, 736;
in Safavid Iran, 594; in Ming China, 613; in
French Revolution, 652; German crisis
(1923), 859, 886; in Guomindang China,
891, 898*(illus.)*
Influenza, 520, 521; epidemic (1918–1919),
855, 912
Inheritance, women and, 592, 733
Inner Mongolia, 619, 627
Inquisition, 498
Institutes of the Christian Religion (Calvin), 494
Institutional Revolutionary Party (PRI), 950
Insurance companies, 502, 560, 736
Intellectual life (intellectuals): Enlightenment,
498–499, 639–641; in Ming China, 615;
European, 619; in Revolutionary era, 638,
663; Latin American independence
movements and, 703; socialism and, 797,
799; racial discrimination and, 716; Russian,
739, 741, 811, 854; Indian nationalism and,
772; British India, 912; in China, 891, 956
Interchangeable-parts manufacturing, 670,
676–677
Interest rates, 611. *See also* Credit; Foreign
debt
International Center for the Improvement of
Maize and Wheat, 938
International corporations: *See also*
Transnational corporations; mining and, 717
International Criminal Court, 1010
International Monetary Fund (IMF), 939,
974, 1003
International Rice Research Institute, 938
International Statistical Congress (1860), 783
International Style in architecture, 872
International Working Man's Association, 799
Internet, 933, 988, 1014, 1019
Inventions. *See* Technology *and specific
inventions*
Iran, 740, 853, 1005*(illus.)*, 1012. *See also*
Safavid Empire (Iran); cotton production
in, 798; Mughal India and, 764; after
World War II, 863, 864*(map)*; oil wealth of,
958, 959*(map)*, 972, 1001, 1003; Islamic

Revolution in, 966, 972–973, 1001, 1008;
Shi'ite Islam and, 971, 1006; war with Iraq,
972–973, 1001
Iraq, 957; oil wealth of, 958, 959*(map)*;
Shi'ite Islam in, 591, 1006; after World
War I, 862, 864*(map)*, 865; war with Iran,
972–973, 1001; Persian Gulf War
(1990–1991) and, 978–979; invasion and
regime change in, 1004–1006
Ireland (Irish), 940; in Canada, 702;
Catholicism in, 802, 810; Great Britain
and, 507, 512, 534, 810, 837, 930;
emigration from, 684–685, 714, 793, 930;
famine in (1847–1848), 685, 792, 794,
930; potatoes in, 503, 685
Irigoyen, Hipólito, 925, 926
Iron curtain, 936–937, 960, 1019. *See also*
Cold War; Warsaw Pact
Iron industry. *See also under* Steel; British,
503, 512; deforestation and, 676; in
Europe, 671, 679*(map)*; Industrial
Revolution and, 676–677, 682; mass
production and, 676–677
Iroquois Confederacy, 537, 538*(illus.)*, 539;
American Revolution and, 645
Irrigation: environmental impact of, 841; in
British India, 770, 771, 841, 873; in Egypt,
760, 825, 841
Isabella (Spain), 471
Isfahan, 591–592 and *illus.*, 593
Islamic Empires, 489. *See* Mughal Empire;
Ottoman Empire; Safavid Empire
Islamic law. *See* Shari'a (Islamic law)
Islamic Revolutions, 966, 969, 972–973
Islam (Islamic civilization). *See also* Muslims;
maritime worlds of (1500–1750), 597–601;
mosques, 581*(illus.)* 590, 591; African
trade and, 568–570; converts to, 583, 594,
596–597; pilgrims in, 465, 570, 598, 728;
Indian Ocean trade and, 463; in Russia,
625; prohibition on alcohol, 569, 825, 947;
spread of, in Africa, 600, 832; Sufism, 589,
591, 596, 598; women and, 759; reforms,
in West Africa, 757, 759, 779; Quranic
schools, 732, 759, 832, 919 *and illus.*;
jihad (holy war), 757, 759, 828, 1008;
Shi'ite, 584, 589, 591, 1006; in Southeast
Asia, 598, 600, 834; Sunni, 589, 596,
1006; Wahhabism, 589, 728; in Turkey, 863;
in Algeria, 947; terrorist militants in, 1008
Ismail, Shah, 589, 591
Ismail (Egypt), 760, 817–818, 825
Isolationism, in United States, 856, 873, 887
Israel, 865 *and illus.*, 961, 973; Arab conflict
with (1947–1973), 957–958, 959*(map)*;
attacks on Lebanon (2006), 1006;
hyperorthodox Jews in, 1008; Palestinian
guerilla war against, 957–958; Palestinian
terrorist groups and, 958; Suez Canal crisis
and (1956), 955; war with Egypt (1972),
955–956
Istanbul, 734. *See also* Constantinople; craft
guilds of, 583*(illus.)*; expansion of, 736; and
Isfahan compared, 591–592, 593; Janissary
power in, 728; mosque in, 581*(illus.)*, 591;
Ottoman reforms and, 730

Istanbul University, 732
Italy (Italian peninsula), 662, 818; city-states
of, 467, 500; Holy Alliance and, 660;
nationalism in, 661; immigrants from,
714, 715, 792, 793; unification of,
802–804 *and map*; alliances, in World War I,
848, 849*(map)*, 855; conquest of Libya by,
846; colonies of, 824*(map)*, 840*(map)*;
futurist poets in, 877; alliance with Nazi
Germany, 888; invasion of Ethiopia by, 828
and illus. 887, 920; Mussolini's fascism in,
885–886; World War II and, 888, 894;
declining fertility in, 981; in European
Union, 940
ITT (International Telephone and Telegraph
Company), 950
Iturbide, Agustín de, 699, 703, 705
Ivan IV (Ivan the Terrible; Russia), 606,
623, 626
Ivory Coast (Côte d'Ivoire), 949
Ivory trade, 565, 600, 763–764, 775
Iwo Jima, in World War II, 896
Izmir (Smyrna), 587

Jackson, Andrew, 661, 704, 709, 722
Jacobins (France), 652
Jaja of Opobo, 762, 763*(illus.)*
Jakarta, 601, 985*(table)*
Jamaica, 839, 945; free blacks in, 559 *and
illus.*; sugar plantations in, 553, 556*(table)*,
558; slave rebellions in, 558, 711
James I (England), 507, 550
James II (England), 507, 537, 543
Jamestown, 534–535
Jammu, 910*(map)*, 947
Jamshedpur, steel mill in, 911
Janissaries, 582, 587; Mahmud II's defeat of,
732; Selim III's reforms and, 728, 730;
uprisings by, 586, 589
Japan, China and, 613, 614, 805, 859–862,
873, 975; Japanese invasion of Korea and,
606; Boxer Uprising (1900), 813, 861; war
between (1894–1895), 812–813, 837;
Twenty-One Demands (1915), 861;
Japanese seizure of Manchuria, 888;
war between (1937–1945), 861, 889–891
and map
Japanese Americans, internment of, 902
Japan (Japanese). *See also* Japan, China and;
Tokugawa shogunate, 605, 607–612, 628;
Christianity in, 605–606, 610–611, 629;
civil war in, 606, 607, 806; chronology
(1543–1792), 607; elite decline and social
crisis in, 611–612; invasion of Korea by,
606–607, 608*(illus.)*; Europeans and,
605–606, 610–611; reunification of,
606–612; emigrants from, 714, 794, 836;
Meiji Restoration and modernization of,
806–808; Perry's opening of, 786*(illus.)*,
787–788, 804–805; birth of imperialism in
(1894–1905), 813; railroads in, 789; as
great power (1868–1900), 812–813; women
in textile industry of, 797; expansion of,
840*(map)*, 861; war with Russia
(1904–1905), 811, 813, 834, 846; fascism
in, 886; industrialization in, 788, 808,

813, 834; Korea and, 833*(map)*;
earthquakes in, 860, 896; in Vladivostok,
857; World War I and, 861; filmmaking
in, 872; Great Depression in, 888;
ultranationalism in, 888; economy and
trade of, 943, 966, 973–974, 985, 993;
militarization in, 878, 884; World War II
and, 894, 895*(map)*, 896–897 *and illus.*,
898, 899; World War II casualties, 896–897
and illus., 898, 899; Southeast Asian
nationalists and, 947; automobile
manufacture in, 973, 989; low fertility in,
980–981; aging population in, 982, 984;
environmental awareness in, 992;
electronics industry in, 1013, 1014;
wealth of, 1000*(illus.)*; adult male comic
book, 1014*(illus.)*; cultural traditions in,
1016, 1019
Java, 774, 835, 839, 841, 885; coffee on,
601, 834
The Jazz Singer (film), 872
Jefferson, Thomas, 651
Jerusalem, 734, 853, 958
Jesuits (Society of Jesus), 498, 542, 598; in
North America, 540; Reformation and,
494; in Japan, 610; in China, 499, 501,
615 619, 741
Jews, 591. *See also* Israel; mapmaking by,
467; expelled from Spain, 514; in Germany,
500; in Ottoman Empire, 583, 587, 732,
733; immigrants in Americas, 714;
anti-Semitism and, 809, 810, 885; in
Palestine, 853, 865–866 *and illus.*, 867,
939, 957; in Russia/Soviet Union, 792,
810; Nazi Germany and, 886; Holocaust of
World War II, 898, 899, 901 *and illus.*;
Zionist, 853, 856, 865–866, 867, 957,
958; *haredim*, in Israel, 1008
Jiang Jieshi. *See* Chiang Kaishek
Jiang Qing, 956
Jiangxi region (China), 888–889
Jihad (holy war), 757, 759, 828, 1008
Jim Crow laws (United States), 712
Jingdezhen, 609, 613
Jinnah, Muhammad Ali, 914
João Teixera, 476
Job Solomon, 571–572
Joffre, Joseph, 850
Johannesburg, South Africa, 918
John Paul II, Pope, 976, 1008
Johnson, James, 919
Johnson, Lyndon, 943
Johnson, Samuel, 640
Johnson, William, 645; home of, 538*(illus.)*
John VI (Portugal), 695, 699
Joint-stock companies, 500–501, 536, 598,
671, 741; Atlantic trade and, 560, 573
Jordan (Transjordan), 862, 864*(map)*, 958
Joseph Bonaparte (Spain), 695
Joseph II (Austria), 640
Joyce, Ellen, 823
Juan, Jorge, 530
Juárez, Benito, 707, 708*(illus.)*
Jubbadar, Ali-Quli, 590*(illus.)*
Junk (ship), 463–464 *and illus.*, 468
Junta Central (Spain), 695

Juntas, in Latin America, 696, 698
Justo, Juan, 837
Jutland, Battle of (1916), 850

Kahlo, Frida, 924
Kampuchea (Cambodia), 916
Kanagawa, Treaty of (1854), 805, 806
Kangxi (China), 615, 618–619 *and illus.*
Kanto earthquake (Japan, 1923), 860
Das Kapital (Marx), 797
Karzai, Hamid, 1006
Kashmir, 768; Pakistan-India dispute over,
910*(map)*, 914, 947
Kazakhstan (Kazakhs), 740, 743, 832, 1001
Kelly, William, 790
Kemal Atatürk, Mustafa, 863 *and illus.*
Kennedy, John F., 943, 954
Kenya, 600, 829, 915, 918, 978, 1009;
independence of, 949; Kikuyu protest in,
948–949
Kenyatta, Jomo, 948 *and illus.*, 949
Kepler, Johannes, 497
Kerensky, Alexander, 854
Kew Royal Botanic Gardens, 620*(illus.)*, 839
Khartoum, 764
Khelat, khan of, 769
Khomeini, Ayatollah Ruhollah, 972 *and illus.*
Khrushchev, Nikita, 939*(illus.)*, 944, 954
Kikuyu people, 948–949
Kilwa, 600
Kimberley diamond fields (South Africa), 827,
841*(illus.)*
Kim Jong-il (North Korea), 1005
King, Martin Luther, Jr., 944
Kiowa people, 710
Kitchener, Lord Horatio, 770, 821
Kizilbash heresy, 578
Knights of the Hospital of St. John, 581
Knights Templar, 470
Kollantai, Alexandra, 882–883
Kongo, 474, 476–477, 482. *See also* Congo
Konoye, Fumimaro, 894
Kon Tiki (raft), 462
Korea (Koreans): *See also* North Korea; South
Korea; China and, 606; Japan and, 606–607,
608*(illus.)*, 807*(map)*, 813, 888;
industrialization in, 974; education in, 974
Korean War (1950-1958), 941, 943, 956, 961
Kosovo, Battle of (1389), 578
Kosovo crisis (1999), 978
Kowtow (ritual bow), 615, 620
Kremer, Gerhard (Mercator), 501 *and illus.*
Ksar el Kebir, Battle of (1578), 600
Kuchma, Leonid, 1003
Kulaks (Soviet peasants), 880
Kuwait, 1006; invasion of, by Iraq (1990–1991),
978, 1009; oil wealth of, 958, 959*(map)*
Kyoto, 606, 607
Kyoto Protocol (1997), 993, 1010, 1011
Kyrgyzstan, 743, 1001

Labor camps: *See also* Concentration camps;
Soviet *gulags*, 880, 881
Labor (labor force): *See also* Labor
movements; Labor unions; Slaves; Workers;
Amerindian, 526, 528, 535, 722, 782,

783; Andean mit'a, 528, 543; indentured,
535, 552–553, 714, 778–779; division of,
672–673 *and illus.*; Asian immigrant,
778–779; gender division of, 797; African
colonial, 829; World War II shortages, 902;
Mexican reforms and, 923; Soviet bloc,
940; aging of, in industrialized world,
981–982, 987
Labor movement: in Argentina, 715 *and
illus.*; immigrants and, 715; women and,
799, 802
Labor unions (trade unions), 778, 852,
861, 862; in late nineteenth century, 687,
797, 799
Labour Party (Great Britain), 868, 914, 940
Lagos, Nigeria, 918, 985*(table)*
Laissez faire economics, 686–687. *See also*
Free trade; famine and, 930
Lake Victoria, 756, 761
Land grants: in colonial North America, 537;
for free blacks, 559 *and illus.*; mansabhars,
in India, 595, 596, 597; Ottoman, 583,
585, 586, 587; for railroads, 789; in
Safavid Iran, 589, 593; in Russia, 625
Landowners (landownership): European
nobility and, 502, 514; colonial Latin
America, 532, 542, 696; Amerindian, 532,
643, 694, 698, 710; French Revolution
and, 648, 650; Ottoman, 587; Russian serfs
and, 625; enclosure movement, 669–670;
British, 661, 688; British India, 766, 908;
United States, 719; New Zealand, 778;
Egyptian, 825; Argentine *oligarquía*, 924,
926; Brazilian, 926; Chinese, 860, 862;
colonial Africa, 827, 829, 918; Cuban,
951; Mexican *haciendas*, 920–921, 922
Land reform: in China, 891, 897; in Mexico,
922, 923, 924; in Cuba, 951; in
Guatemala, 950
Lane, Edward William, 736*(illus.)*
Languages: *See also* English language;
Malayo-Polynesian, 462 *and map*; Arabic,
570, 588, 590, 759; of African slaves, 536,
558; Osmanli, 582–583; in India, 596, 908,
947, 1015, 1016, 1017–1018; in Safavid
Iran, 588, 590–591; Latin, and Romance,
583; Urdu, 596; Turkish, 590–591, 732;
Bantu, 600; Russian, 625, 628; Swahili,
600, 764; and immigrants to Americas,
715; census and, 782; French, 715, 732,
738; nationalism and, 802, 987, 1014;
African independence and, 948
Laos, 747, 916
Las Casas, Bartolomé de, 526
Lateen sails, 468, 471 *and illus.*, 472
Latin alphabet, in Turkey, 863 *and illus.*
Latin America. *See also* Americas; the South
America; *and specific countries;* foreign
investment in, 694, 719; regionalist threat
in, 705; positivism in, 687; railroads in,
693, 837–838; abolition in, 711;
constitutional experiments in, 702–703; in
1830, 696*(map)*; personalist leaders in,
703, 704–705; racial discrimination in,
716–717; underdevelopment in, 719–720;
census in, 782; foreign investment in, 694,

Latin America *(Continued)*
719, 720; immigrants in, 713, 794, 855; women's rights in, 716; chronology (1870–1912), 819; Depression of 1930s in, 885; fascism in, 886; imperialism in, 837–839; industry in, 903; chronology (1876–1946), 909; economic freedom of, 818, 945, 950–951, 961; revolutionary movements in (1970s–1980s), 966–967, 968–969 *and illus.*; superpower rivalry and, 950, 966; United States and, 950–951, 954, 966–969, 987; neoliberalism in, 969, 970–971; abandoned children in cities of, 986; military coups and dictatorships in (1960s–1970s), 885, 927, 966, 967–968; population growth in, 979, 981*(table)*, 982; population in (1750–2050), 981*(table)*; soap operas (telenovelas), 1013, 1015

Latin America, colonial, 523–534, 524*(map)*. *See also* Brazil; *and specific colony;* Amerindians in, 523, 525–526, 528, 529, 532, 533*(illus.)*, 534, 543; chronology (1518–1780s), 521; culture of, 526; economy in, 526, 528–529, 541–542; elite in, 523, 524, 525, 532, 542; forced labor in, 526, 528, 535; gold and silver from, 526–528 *and illus.*, 542, 559, 613; imperial reforms and, 541–543; Mexico, 520, 522, 542, 920; Peru, 523, 524*(map)*, 528, 542; race and ethnicity in, 530–531; rebellion in, 543; society in, 529, 532–534; state and church in, 523, 525–526, 542

Latin American independence, 694, 697*(map)*, 702; Brazil, 695; chronology (1808–1888), 695; freedom for slaves in, 711; Mexico (1810–1823), 698–699, 920; roots of revolution (to 1810), 694–695; Spanish South America, 635*(map)*, 696, 698

Latin language, 583, 1016

Latvia, 810; independence of, 854, 57*(map)*, 977; Soviet invasion of, 892

Laws (legal codes): *See also* Shari'a (Islamic law); Enlightenment reforms and, 499, 640; legal training, 504; mercantilist, 561; Ottoman, 583; Japanese, 612; in France, under Napoleon, 656; British factory, 687; natural, 499, 686; working women and, 797; Jim Crow (United States), 712; Ottoman reforms, 731–732; anticombination (Europe), 799; social, in Germany, 809; environmental protection, 992

League of Nations, 856, 859; German withdrawal from, 887; Italian invasion of Ethiopia and, 887; Japanese withdrawal from, 888, 889; mandate system and, 862–863, 864*(map)*; United Nations and, 937

Lebanon, 863, 864*(map)*, 973; Hezbollah in, 1006; independence of, 957

Lebensraum (room to live), 886, 892

Lebon, Philippe, 683

Lee, Ang, 1015

Legislative Assembly (France), 651

Legislature: *See also* Congress; Laws; Parliament; *specific legislative body;* colonial America, 643–644, 646, 702

Leith-Ross, Sylvia, 823

Lenin, Vladimir I., 854, 858*(illus.)*, 862, 880, 889; death of, 859; economic policy of, 858

Leningrad, Seige of (1942), 892

Leopold II (Belgium), 825–827, 830

Leo X, Pope, 492–493

Lepanto, Battle of (1571), 583

Le Roy, Loys, 515

Lesseps, Ferdinand de, 838

Liaodong Peninsula (China), 813

Liberalism, 660, 809–810. *See also* Neo-liberalism; nationalism and, 638, 663, 802

Liberia, 763

Libraries: in Safavid Iran, 590; Franklin and, 641; Sokoto (Africa), 759

Libya, 852, 894, 958; Italian conquest of, 846; Quranic school in, 919*(illus.)*

Life expectancy: for slaves, 557; in nineteenth century Europe, 681; cult of cleanliness and, 872; for industrialized nations, 981–982; in Russia and former Soviet bloc, 982

Lighting: gas, 682, 683 *and illus.*, 794; electric, 791 *and illus.*, 794

Liliuokalani (Hawaii), 836

Lima, Peru, 523

The Limits of Growth, 960

Lincoln, Abraham, 705, 707, 711–712

Lindbergh, Charles, 870

Linlithgow, Lord, 914

Linnaeus, Carolus, 640

Lisbon earthquake (1755), 496

List, Frederich, 686–687

Literacy: *See also* Education; Schools; of European women, 505; in United States, 719; nationalism and, 808; Islam and, in Africa, 919 *and illus.*; in Costa Rica, 954

Literature. *See also* Books; Poets and poetry; in early modern Europe, 491; Safavid (Iran) poetry, 590–591; of Mughal India, 596; Soviet underground, 975; international, in English, 1016, 1017–1018

Lithuania, 810. *See also* Poland-Lithuania; Soviet invasion of, 892; independence of, 854, 857*(map)*, 977

Little Bighorn, Battle of (1876), 710

Little Ice Age (1590s), 503, 613, 632

Liverpool, 563, 678, 680

Livestock. *See also* Cattle; in colonial Americas, 522 *and illus.*, 526; on sugar plantations, 556; in Argentina, 522, 719, 720; in colonial Africa, 829

Living standards: industrialization and, 670, 685; Great Depression and, 884 *and illus.*; population growth, and decline in, 982; Soviet decline in, 975; in Western Europe, 940

Livingstone, David, 761, 764

Li Zicheng, 606, 614

Lloyd George, David, 856

Loans. *See* Foreign debt (international loans)

Locke, John, 510, 640

London, 747, 1009; Royal Society, 498; growth of, 499, 680; growth of (1850–1914), 794, 795; Crystal Palace, 676, 677; street

scene (1751), 642*(illus.)*; bombing of, in World War II, 899

Long March (China), 889, 890*(map)*

Looms, power, 675, 676

Lorraine. *See* Alsace and Lorraine

Los Angeles, 985*(table)*; automobiles in, 870 *(illus.)*, 872

Louis, Antoine, 652

Louisiana, 676; Choctaw of, 518*(illus.)*, 519–520, 541

Louisiana Purchase, 705, 706*(map)*

Louis Napoleon (Napoleon III), 662, 707, 804

Louis Philippe (France), 661, 662, 713

Louis XIII (France), 507

Louis XIV (France), 502, 507, 510, 512

Louis XV (France), 649

Louis XVI (France), 638, 649–650; beheading of, 647, 651

Louis XVIII (France), 660

Lovett, William, 687

Lowell, Francis Cabot, 685

Luanda, 551, 566*(map)*, 567, 568*(illus.)*

Ludendorff, Erich von, 855

Lumumba, Patrice, 936, 949

Lunar Society, 675, 683, 788

Lunda kingdoms, 555, 567

Lusitania (ocean liner), 850

Luther, Martin, 492–493, 494 *and illus.*, 498, 505

Lutheranism, 493, 494, 495*(map)*, 505, 804

Luxembourg, 940, 985

Luxemburg, Rosa, 799

Lytton, Lord (Bulwer-Lytton, Edward Robert), 768–769, 770

Macao, 475, 615, 742

Macartney, George (Macartney mission), 621, 741–742

Macchiavelli, Niccoló, 508–509

McDonald's restaurants, 990, 1014

Macedonia, 846, 977*(map)*

Machine guns, 821, 822*(illus.)*, 828, 850, 861

Machine tools, 670. *See also* Mechanization

McKinley, William, 836–837, 838

Madagascar, 462–463 *and map*, 568, 949

Madeira, 465, 467, 528

Madero, Francisco I., 921, 924

Madison, James, 702, 704

Madras, India, 597, 766

Madrasas (Islamic colleges), 586, 591, 919 *and illus.. See also* Quran schools

Magellan, Ferdinand, 458*(illus.)*, 459–460, 461, 469*(map)*, 472

Mahabharata, 1018

Mahan, Alfred T., 836

Maharashtra, 597

Mahdi, 822*(illus.)*, 828

Mahmud II, Sultan, 730–731, 732, 733, 740

Mai Ali (Bornu), 570

Maine (battleship), 838

Maize (corn), 479, 522, 834; in Africa, 555; in China, 621; in Europe, 503, 669; Green Revolution and, 938

Makovsky, 811*(illus.)*

Malabar Coast, 475, 478

Malacca, 475, 582, 598, 601; British in, 772, 774

Malaria: slaves and, 521, 557, 564; quinine and, 619, 821, 835 *and illus.; falciparium,* 821

Malawi (Nyasaland), 829, 852

Malaya (Malay Peninsula), 885. *See also* Malaysia; as British colony, 774, 834; rubber plantations in, 834 *and illus.,* 835

Malay Federation, 947

Malayo-Polynesian languages, 462 *and map*

Malay peoples, 460, 462 *and map*

Malaysia, 974. *See also* Malaya

Malcomb, John, 644*(illus.)*

Malindi, 464–465, 474, 600

Malintzin (Malinche), 480

Malta, 583

Malthus, Thomas, 686, 979, 981

Malvinas (Falkland Islands) war, 969

Mamluks, in Syria, 578, 582, 590

Mamluk sultanate (Egypt), 578, 590; Muhammad Ali and, 729; Ottoman Empire and, 581, 582, 589, 728

Manchester, England, 666*(illus.),* 667–668, 680, 681; protest in, 661

Manchukuo, 888. *See also* Manchuria

Manchuria, 607, 619; Russo-Japanese War (1904-1905), 811; Japan and, 606, 813; Japanese seizure of (1931), 888; Chinese Communists in, 897

Manchurian Incident (1931), 888

Manchus, 606, 613–615, 741. *See also* Qing Empire (China)

Manco Inca, 482

Mandate system, 862–863, 864*(map),* 867

Mandela, Nelson, 950, 978, 1004

Manila, Philippines, 615, 985*(table);* Spanish-American War and, 837, 838; garbage pickers in, 986 *and illus.*

Manioc, 522, 834

Mansabhars, 595, 596, 597

Mansa Kankan Musa, 465

Mansa Muhammad, 465

Manuel (Portugal), 475

Manufactured goods (manufacturing). *See also* Industrialization; Industrial Revolution (1760-1851); *and specific manufactures;* Dutch, 500; English, 543 in Safavid Iran, 593; promotion of, in Europe, 514, 561; assembly-line, 609*(illus.),* 612, 613; Japanese, 608; Ming porcelain, 612, 613; cottage industry, 670; Industrial Revolution and, 670; interchangeable parts for, 670, 676–677; British, in India, 770, 775, 914; division of labor in, 672–673 *and illus.;* mass production of, 674–675 *and illus.;* imported, in Latin America, 719, 720, 837, 924, 954; whalebone in, 777; consumer goods, 608, 792, 798, 987; Japanese, 956; computers and, 989; English language and, 1016

Manumission (freedom), 533, 558. *See also* Abolition

Maori people, 775–776, 778

Mao Zedong, 785, 898; Great Leap Forward and, 931, 956; Long March and, 889; death of, 974

Mapmaking: Jewish, 467; Portuguese, 468*(illus.);* world map (1595), 489*(map);* Dutch, 501 *and illus.;* Japanese, 610*(illus.);* Chinese, 619; British Empire and, 785*(illus.);* satellite photos, 933*(illus.)*

Mapuches (Araucanians), 523, 710

Maratha Confederation, 764, 765*(map),* 766, 767

Marathas, 597

Maria Theresa (Austria), 782

Marie Antoinette (France), 651

Marinetti, Filippo, 878

Maritime expansion: *See also* European maritime expansion; before 1450, 460–465; Atlantic Ocean, 465; Indian Ocean, 462–465, 462*(map);* Pacific Ocean, 460–462 *and map*

Markets, 582, 918. *See also* Trade; African slave trade, 567; in Latin America, 528, 542*(illus.);* sugar plantation, 556; global culture and, 1013

Marne, Battle of the (1914), 850, 851*(map)*

Maroons, in Jamaica, 559 *and illus.*

Marquesas Islands, 460–461, 462*(map)*

Marriage: Protestantism and, 494; in early modern Europe, 504; Henry VIII and, 507; in colonial Latin America, 523; Aro alliances, 567; Hindu-Muslim, 596; Ottoman women and, 733; Victorian Age, 796; working-class women and, 797; and abortion, in Soviet Union, 883; polygamy, 863, 919

Marshall, George, 897

Marshall Plan, 940

Martí, José, 838

Martin, P.-D., 511*(illus.)*

Martin de Porres, 525*(illus.)*

Martinique, 550, 552

Marx, Karl, 797, 854, 889; on global trade and bourgeoisie, 799, 800–801

Marxism, 854, 889

Mary, mother of Jesus, 526

Masonic lodges, 740–741

Massachusetts, 647, 685; colonial, 536–537, 543, 561, 645

Mass media (mass communications), 1008, 1013–1014. *See also* Film (motion pictures); Newspapers; Radio; Television; in Mussolini's Italy, 885–886

Mass production. *See also* Industrial Revolution; assembly-line, 609*(illus.),* 612, 613, 868, 872; interchangeable parts for, 676–677; of pottery, 674–675 *and illus.;* consumer goods, 792, 798

Mataram, 601

Mathematics, 497, 498, 749–750

Mau Mau movement (Kenya), 948–949

Mauritius, 774, 778, 839

Maximilian (Mexico), 707, 708*(illus.)*

Maximillian II (Bohemia), 606

Maya, 480, 526, 710; cotton textiles of, 798

May Fourth Movement (China), 862

Mazzini, Giuseppe, 802

Mbeki, Thabo, 1004

Mecca, 729; pilgrims in, 465, 570, 598, 728

Mechanization: of cotton industry, 675–676, 689; of tobacco industry, 529*(illus.);* tractors and, 873

Médecins Sans Frontières (Doctors without Borders), 1010

Medici family, 492

Medicine (physicians): *See also* Disease; Health care; in Africa, 477, 948; quinine, for malaria, 619, 821, 835 *and illus.;* Jesuit, in China, 619; Crimean War, 735; women and, 716, 735 *and illus.;* cult of cleanliness and, 872; antibiotics, 899; mortality rates and, 980; Doctors without Borders, 1010; Western *vs.* traditional, 1016

Medina, 598, 728, 729

Mediterranean region, 467, 500; Ottoman Empire and, 581, 582, 583, 734

Mehmed I, Sultan, 578

Mehmed II, Sultan, 581

Meiji Restoration (Japan), 806–808, 813, 860

Mein Kampf (Hitler), 886

Melanesia (Melanesians), 460, 462*(map),* 775

Melville, Herman, 777

Men: *See also* Gender differences; as slaves, on sugar plantations, 556; homosexuality in Islam and, 593; Victorian age, 795 *and illus.*

Mendoza, Antonio de, 522

Menelik (Ethiopia), 761, 828

Mensheviks, 854. *See also* Bolsheviks

Mercantilism, 559–561, 563, 686. *See also* Capitalism

Mercator (Gerhard Kremer), 501 *and illus.,* 785*(map)*

Merchants (traders). *See also* Business; Trade; Calicut, 478; Chinese, 464; Muslim, 463, 475, 598; Portuguese, 474, 582; peasant hatred of, 504; European, 500, 587, 598, 605, 612; monopoly trade and, 529, 560; North American, 537; African slave trade, 553, 566, 567, 568; in Iran, 591; Arab, 598, 764, 798; Japanese, 608, 611–612; in Chinese treaty ports, 620, 860; Russian, 627; Haitian, 658; Chinese opium trade and, 742, 743; African, 828; Egyptian, 825

Mercosur (Mercado Comun del Cono Sur), 1001, 1002*(map)*

Mercury, in silver mining, 526, 527

Mesopotamia, 853. *See also* Iraq; after World War I, 862

Mestizos (mixed race), 530–531, 533–534 *and illus.,* 920

Metternich, Klemens von, 660, 662

Mexican-American War (1846-1848), 707, 710

Mexican Revolution (1910-1940), 920–924; background to, 920–921; civil war (1911-1920), 921–923 *and map;* institutionalized (1920s-1940), 923–924

Mexican Revolutionary Party (PRM), 923

Mexico City, 707, 710, 721, 950; colonial, 523, 529(*illus.*); boom in (1876–1910), 921; future growth of, 985(*table*); garbage dumps in, 986

Mexico (Mexicans): Aztecs in, 479–481, 526, 532; colonial, 520, 522, 542, 920; Amerindians in, 520, 708, 710, 838; Catholic Church in, 526, 703, 707, 923, 924; chronology (1810–1867), 695; constitutionalism in, 699, 923; cotton in, 798; independence of, 696, 697(*map*), 698–699; abolition of slavery in, 707; Maximilian as emperor of, 707, 708(*illus.*); war with United States (1846-1848), 707, 710; territorial losses of, 707, 722; anti-Chinese prejudice in, 714; Caste War (1847), 710; labor movement in, 715; civil war in, 707, 921–923; mining in, 526, 528, 717, 721; mixed-descent groups in, 534, 920; oil industry in, 717, 922, 923–924, 950; Porfirio Diaz in, 694, 838, 921; railroads in, 692(*illus.*), 694, 921, 922(*map*), 923; immigration to United States, 715, 902, 986, 987, 1001; agricultural research in, 938; under Institutional Revolutionary Party (PRI), 950; economic nationalism in, 950; economic recovery of, 985; industries relocated to, 989; North American Free Trade Agreement and, 1001, 1002(*map*); population policy in, 979–980

Miao peoples, 727

Michigan, 721; native peoples in, 709

Middle class: *See also* Bourgeoisie; European, 619; Enlightenment and, 641; French Revolution and, 648, 651, 653, 656; Revolutions of 1848 and, 668; British industrialization, 668, 674; cult of domesticity and, 686; worker protest and, 687; consumer goods for, 792; Latin American, 694, 921, 925; Indian nationalism and, 772; Middle East, 863; urbanization and, 794, 872; Victorian, 795–796 *and illus.*; industrialized world, 868; liberalism and, 809; Indian independence and, 908; Mexican, 921, 922

Middle East: *See also* Islam; *and specific countries, empires, cultures, and regions;* Indian Ocean trade and, 463; immigrants from, 714; African slave trade and, 759; World War I in, 846; after World War I, 856, 862–868, 873; chronology (1909-1923), 847; oil and Arab-Israel conflict (1947-1973), 957–959 *and map;* nationalism in, 960–961; chronology (1979-1991), 967

Middle Passage, 561, 563–565. *See also* Slave trade, African

Midlands (England), 674, 680, 790, 794

Midnight's Children (Rushdie), 1017

Midway, Battle of (1942), 894

Mies van der Rohe, Ludwig, 872

Migrations (population movements): *See also* Immigrants; and drought, in East Africa, 600; rural-to-urban, 680; in China, 742; in nineteenth century Africa, 758(*map*); railroads and, 793; labor, British Empire and, 778–779; rural to urban, in Middle East, 863; African-American, 853; World War I refugees, 855; rural-to-urban, 918–919, 950, 984; World War II refugees, 901; unequal development and, 984–987; partition of India and, 915 *and illus.*; wealth inequality and, 984–985, 993; global, and English language, 1016

Militancy, Christian, 467, 470. *See also* Crusades

Military, the: *See also* Armed forces; Navy; War; Weapons and military technology; Amerindians and, 480, 710; French, under Napoleon, 656, 658(*illus.*), 660; Mexican independence, 699; Ottoman, 582, 732, 733(*illus.*); Americas, 703–704; United States, 707; Egyptian, 729; European, 728; Qing China, 746, 861; Russian, in Central Asia, 739–740; British India, 766; Ethiopian, 760(*illus.*); Japanese, 878, 884, 888; Chinese Red Guard, 956, 957(*illus.*); Cold War installations, 942(*map*); United States, 940, 998; Cuban, 951

Military dictatorships, in Latin America, 885, 927, 966, 967–968, 969

Military draft (conscription), 732, 808; in China, 891; in Egypt, 729; in Nazi Germany, 887

Military-industrial complex, 945

Military slaves. *See* Janissaries; Slave soldiery

Military technology. *See* Weapons and military technology

Millennium Summit (2000), 1003

"Milton" (Blake), 680

Minais Gerais, mining in, 721

Mines Act of 1842 (Great Britain), 687

Ming Empire (China), 612–614; Indian Ocean trade and, 463–465 *and illus.*; Jesuits in, 615; collapse of, 613–614

Mining (minerals). *See also* Coal, industrialization and; *and specific metals;* in Latin America, 526, 527, 923(*illus.*); environmental impact of, 526, 527, 721, 841; steam engines in, 676(*illus.*), 677–678; new technology in, 717 *and illus.*, 989; tin, 671, 792, 885; industrialization and, 820; in colonial Africa, 827, 841(*illus.*), 885, 903, 918

Missionaries, Christian. *See also* Jesuits; in Africa, 474; in Latin America, 525–526; in North America, 540; in Southeast Asia, 598, 600, 834; in Japan, 605; in Ottoman Empire, 733; Orthodox, in Siberia, 625, 628; in China, 615, 619, 743, 745, 747, 860; Protestant, 745, 761, 820; in India, 766; women as, 820; New Imperialism and, 820; in colonial Africa, 761, 763, 829, 832, 919, 948

Mississippi River, 639; steamboats on, 678

Mississippi River Valley, 675; native peoples in, 519–520, 709

Missouri, native peoples in, 709

Mit'a labor system, 528, 543

Mitsubishi, 861, 899, 989

Mitsui companies, 608, 861

Mixed race: *See also* Creoles; in colonial Latin America, 530–531, 533(*illus.*), 534; Haitian

gens de couleur, 658–659; discrimination against, in Americas, 716–717

Mobile, Alabama, 535

Mobutu, Joseph, 978

Moby Dick (Melville), 777

Moctezuma II (Aztec), 480–481 *and illus.*

Modernization, 907. *See also* Industrialization; Westernization; of Japan, 608, 807(*map*), 808; of Russia, 626, 635; in Egypt and Ethiopia, 759–760; national culture and, 715; in Argentina, 718; British India, 766; state power and, 782; technologies of, 869–872; in China, 862, 964(*illus.*), 965; in Turkey, 863 *and illus.*; in French Indochina, 916; in Soviet Union, 940

Mohawk peoples, 537, 538(*illus.*), 645

Moluccas (Spice Islands), 472, 475, 832

Mombasa, 600

Monarchy (emperors; kingship): *See also* Constitutional monarchy; *specific monarchs and emperors;* Spanish, 470, 482, 525; West African, 473, 474, 476–477, 567; Aztec, 480 *and illus.*; English, 507, 510 *and table;* European centralization, 505, 507; French, 510 *and table,* 647, 649, 656, 660; Portuguese, 525; Japanese, 606, 807; Qing China, 615, 618–619 *and illus.,* 640; Russian tzars, 625, 627; European nationalism and, 661(*illus.*); Revolutionary era, 638; Enlightenment and, 640; popular protest in Europe and, 642, 662; Congress of Vienna and, 660; Brazilian, 699, 703

Monasteries and convents, in England, 507

Monetary system, 717. *See also* Banks; Coinage; Currency; Finance; American silver and, 528; paper money, 613, 643, 651; Guomindang, in China, 897, 898(*illus.*); Ottoman, 733; capitalist *vs.* communist, 939

Mongols (Mongolia), 832; China and, 613, 618, 619, 742; destruction of Baghdad by, 590; Galdan in, 613, 618, 619, 623; cotton clothing in, 798

Monopolies, industrial, 719; in telecommunications, 1013

Monopoly, trading: Portuguese, 470, 473–474, 475, 478, 582, 826; chartered companies for, 502, 550, 573; in colonial Americas, 529, 537, 540, 541, 542, 543; royal, 560; Dutch, in Indian Ocean, 601; Russian fur trade, 627; Chinese government, 860; salt, in British India, 912

Monroe Doctrine, 838

Monsoons, 463; failure of, and famine, 908, 930

Montana, mining in, 721, 792

Monterrey, Mexico meeting (2002), 1003

Montgolfier brothers, 670

Moon landing (1969), 945

Morality, Victorian, 686, 795, 796

Morelos, José María, 699

Morelos (Mexico), 922(*map*), 923

Morocco, 569, 846, 865; Portugal and, 467, 468, 600

Moro Wars (Philippines), 598
Morse, Samuel, 680
Moscow, 622–623, 625; Napoleon in, 656, 738, 892; Nixon in, 939(illus.); fall of Communism in, 977
Moscow University, 741
Mosques, 581(illus.) 590, 591
Most-favored nation status, 743
Motion pictures (film), 870, 872, 1013; Indian, 1015, 1018
Mountain, the (France), 652
Mountbatten, Lord, 914
Mount Huanyaputina, 632
Movable type, 606. See also Printing
Mozambique, 600, 826; independence in, 949
MTV (Music Television), 1013
Mughal Empire (India), 478, 489, 580(map); chronology (1526-1739), 579; decay of, and regional challenges to, 597; East India Company and, 764, 765(map), 766, 767; Hindu-Muslim coexistence in, 596–597; political foundations of, 594–596; tobacco in, 588(illus.)
Muhammad Ali (Egypt), 730, 731, 734, 738, 756, 764; industrialization and, 688, 760; military of, 729, 732; modernization of, 759–760; reforms of, 740
Muhammad (prophet), 598
Muir, John, 721
Mulattos, in Latin America, 531, 534
Mules (spinning device), 675, 676
Munich Conference (1938), 887
Murdock, William, 683
Muscovy, 604(illus.), 623. See also Moscow
Music: in early modern Europe, 491; and immigrants in Americas, 715; twenty-first century, 987, 1013
Muskets, 565; rifle technology compared, 734, 743, 767, 821, 822(illus.)
Muslim Empires. See Mughal Empire (India); Ottoman Empire; Safavid Empire (Iran)
Muslim-Hindu relations, in India, 596–597, 908, 910–911, 914–915, 1004 and illus.
Muslim League, All-India, 911, 912, 914
Muslims (Muslim countries): See also Arabs; Islam; traders, 463, 475, 598; Chinese, 464; expelled from Spain, 471; in Southeast Asia, 598, 600; in Africa, 759; in British India, 766, 767; in Ottoman Empire, 737, 739; refugees from Russia, 740; Shi'ite, 584, 589, 591, 1006; expelled from Greece, 863; in West Africa, 826, 828; in Pakistan, 910(map), 914–915, 945; shrines in Jerusalem and, 958; population growth in, 982; in Bosnia-Herzegovina, 978; Kosovo crisis and, 978; in Europe, 987; global spread of, 1007(map); terrorists, 932, 1008–1009
Musqat, Portuguese fort in, 600, 601(illus.)
Mussolini, Benito, 885–886, 894
Mutsuhito (Japan), 806, 807
Myanmar (Burma), 615; British in, 769, 774, 834; Japanese conquest of, 914, 931; independence of, 947
Mysore, India, 755–756, 764, 766

Nadir Shah, 594, 597
NAFTA (North American Free Trade Agreement), 989, 1001, 1002(map)
Nagasaki, 609, 610; atomic bombing of, 895(map), 897
Nagoya earthquake (1944), 896
Naipaul, V. S., 1016
Nairobi (Kenya), 918, 1012
Namibia (Southwest Africa), 828, 852, 862
Nana Sahib, 767
Nanjing (Nanking), 861, 889, 897; Japanese in (1937-1938), 891; Taiping Rebellion and, 745(illus.), 746–747
Nanjing (Nanking), Treaty of (1842), 743, 747
Napoleon Bonaparte, 653, 662, 682; defeat of, 656; Europe of, 657(map); Haitian Revolution and, 658(illus.), 660; invasion of Egypt by, 728–729, 756, 759, 761; invasion of Russia by, 656, 738, 740, 892, 931; as personalist leader, 704
Napoleonic Civil Code, 656
Napoleonic Wars, 657(map), 847; end of, 719, 772, 774
Napoleon III (Louis Napoleon), 662, 707, 804
Narayan, R. K., 1017
Narodniki (Russian movement), 741
Nasir, Gamil Abd al-, 955, 958
Natal, 774, 778
Nation, Carrie, 868
National Assembly (France), 649–651, 949
National Colored Convention, 711
National Convention (France), 651, 653, 656, 659
National culture, immigration and, 715
Nationalism. See also Decolonization; Independence; German, 493, 505; in Revolutionary era (1775–1848), 638, 656; republicanism and, 656, 660; economic, in Latin America, 694, 785; Belgian, 661(illus.); personalist leaders and, 704; census and, 783; Hindu, in India, 767, 771–772, 808, 834, 911, 1004 and illus., 1015; liberalism and, 638, 663, 802; Austria-Hungary, 810; language and, 802, 987, 1014; Italian unification, 802–804 and map; European, 802–804, 805(map), 877; German unification, 804, 805(map); Great Depression and, 884; Japanese, 804–808, 888; Russian, 810; Zulu, 827; social Darwinism and, 808–809; Cuban, 838; World War I and, 847; World War II and, 785, 891, 960; Indonesian, 896; mandate system, 862–863; Vietnamese, 916–917, 943; in colonial Africa, 920; social justice and, 927; and decolonization, in Africa, 947–950; economic, in Mexico, 950; Palestinian, 958; in former Soviet Union, 977; in Middle East, 865, 873, 960–961; and religion, in Eastern Europe, 976; world trade and, 998–999
Nationalist China. See Guomindang (China)
Nationality, citizenship and, 987
Nationalization (expropriation): in Mexico, 923–924; in France and Great Britain, 940; in Chile and Nicaragua, 968; in Cuba, 951; in Iran, 972

National liberation movements, 947, 955, 969
National Light and Heat Company, 683
National parks (North America), 721
National Revolutionary Party (Mexico), 923
National self-determination: See also Independence; Self-government; Revolutions of 1848 and, 662; mandate system and, 862
National Socialist German Workers' Party (Nazis), 886. See also Nazi Germany
Nation building, 945, 954
Natives Land Act (South Africa, 1913), 827
Nativist political movements, 714
NATO. See North Atlantic Treaty Organization
Natural disasters: See also Environment, the; Floods; volcanic eruption, 632; Lisbon earthquake (1755), 496; in Ming China, 613; Japanese earthquakes (1923 and 1944), 860, 896; Sumatra earthquake and tsunami (2004), 1004
Natural law, 499, 686
Natural resources. See Raw materials
Natural rights, 640, 651. See also Rights
Natural selection, 808
Nature reserves, 721
Navajo people, 523, 709(illus.)
Navarino, Battle of (1829), 730
Navigation: astrolabe for, 467; compass for, 467, 515; Indian Ocean, 463; Polynesian, 461, 462; Portuguese, 467; Viking, 465
Navigation Acts (Great Britain), 543, 561
Navy (naval warfare; warships). See also British navy; Pirates; Chinese, 463–464 and illus.; Portuguese in Indian Ocean, 474, 475, 479, 482; Spanish Armada, 512(illus.), 529, 534, 541, 638, 838; European in Mughal India, 595–596; Ottoman, 581, 582, 583, 730, 731; Safavid Iran, 594; Russian, 626, 628, 731(map), 734, 811; Korean, 606, 608(illus.); steam-powered (gunboats), 689, 743, 786(illus.), 787, 821; Japanese, 813; New Imperialism and, 821; in Spanish-American War (1898), 838; in World War I, 850, 852, 855; British, in China, 897; United States, 894; United States, in Persian Gulf, 973; submarine warfare, 850, 855, 896, 900, 903, 944; in World War II, 888, 891, 896, 900, 903; aircraft carriers, 891, 894
Nawabs, 597, 764, 766
Nazi Germany, 886–888 and illus., 896. See also Germany, in World War II; Wehrmacht; economic and social policies, 886; Holocaust and, 899, 901 and illus.; Argentina and, 927
Nazi-Soviet Pact (1939), 888
Ndebele people, 827, 828
Nehru, Jawaharlal, 955 and illus., 1018; Indian independence and, 914, 945
Nemesis (gunboat), 689
Neo-liberalism, 969. See also Free trade; women's rights and, 970–971
Nepal, 615, 767
Nerchinsk, Treaty of (1689), 619, 623
Netherlands, the (the Dutch; Holland), 940. See also Dutch East India Company (VOC);

Netherlands *(Continued)*
  bourgeoisie in, 500; mapmaking by, 501
  and illus.; Spain and, 500, 514, 551; in
  North America, 537, 539; slave trade and,
  551–552, 553, 563, 639; South American
  colonies of, 559; West India Company, 500,
  502, 537, 551–552, 560; Atlantic economy
  and, 561, 562*(map)*; tulip mania in, 587;
  banking in, 500, 514, 560; wars with
  England, 502, 560; Cape Colony, 568,
  827; India trade and, 595–596; commercial
  power of, 606; China trade and, 615; Japan
  and, 610*(illus.)*, 611; as sea power, 638–639;
  in East Indies, 773*(map)*; slavery abolished
  in colonies of, 713, 778; colonies of,
  599*(map)*, 833*(map)* 840*(map)*;
  decolonization of, 945; in World War II,
  893, 903; oil embargo and, 958; English
  in, 1016
Nevada, mining in, 721
Newcomen engine, 676*(illus.)*, 677–678
New Deal (United States), 884
New Economic Policy (Soviet Union), 858, 880
New England: colonial, 536–537, 543, 643;
  cotton mills in, 676, 685, 797
Newfoundland, 465, 534, 538
New France, 538–541
New Granada, 524*(map)*
New Guinea, 460, 837
New Imperialism (1869–1914), 784, 812,
  816–842, 847; in Africa, 818, 823,
  824*(map)*, 825–832; in Asia, 832, 833*(map)*,
  834–836; chronology, 819; colonial
  administration, 821–823; colonial
  possessions of great powers, 840*(map)*;
  cultural motives, 820, 829, 832; economic
  motives, 818, 820–821, 837–838; global
  environment and, 839, 841; in Hawaii and
  Philippines, 836–837; in Latin America,
  837–839; motives and methods, 818–823;
  political motives, 818–820, 828–829; in
  Southeast Asia, 832, 834, 836; Suez canal
  and, 816*(illus.)*, 817–818; technology and
  tools of, 821; tropical ecology and, 835
  and illus.
New Jersey, voting rights in (to 1807), 647
New Lanark, 687
New Laws of 1542 (Spain), 526, 528
Newly industrialized economies (NIEs), 974
New Orleans, 535; Battle of (1813), 704
New Spain, 523, 524*(map)*, 525, 705. *See
  also* Latin America, colonial
Newspapers: Amerindians portrayed in, 710;
  Crimean War and, 734, 735; Ottoman,
  732; imperialism and, 820; nationalism
  and, 808
Newton, Isaac, 498, 499, 640, 869
New York City, 713, 721, 859; colonial, 537;
  electrification of, 791; growth of, 680,
  794, 795, 985*(table)*; skyscrapers in, 872;
  stock market crash (1929) in, 881; World
  Trade Center attack (2001), 996*(illus.)*,
  997–998
New Zealand, 461, 462*(map)*, 862; British
  colonization of, 756, 773*(map)*; European
  immigrants to, 601, 792, 822, 855; Maori

of, 775–776, 778; whaling off, 776,
  777*(illus.)*; women's rights in, 868
Nguni peoples, 756, 758*(map)*
Nguyen Thai Hoc, 916–197
Niagra Falls, power plant at, 791
Nian, rebellion in (1850s), 747
Nicaragua: Contras in, 969, 973; Sandanista
  revolution in, 968 *and illus.*, 969, 973;
  United States and, 838, 968–969, 973
Nicholas I (Russia), 738, 739 *and illus.*, 741
Nicholas II (Russia), 734, 810, 811, 854
Niger, 949
Niger Delta, 473, 761, 762, 828; guerrilla
  movement in, 1004
Nigeria, 839, 852, 985; colonial rule, 823,
  830; missionaries in, 820; economic and
  social change in, 915, 918–919; Ibadan in,
  918, 938; Biafran war in, 931; independ-
  ence of, 948; democracy in, 978, 1004; oil
  industry in, 1004; English in, 1016
Nightingale, Florence, 735 *and illus.*
Nile River: bridge across, 688*(illus.)*; explo-
  ration of, 761; Aswan dam on, 825, 955
Niña (ship), 472
Nitroglycerin, 790
Nixon, Richard M., 939*(illus.)*; Chile and,
  968; China policy of, 957
Nizam al-Mulk, 597
Nkrumah, Kwame, 948, 955
NKVD (Soviet secret police), 880, 881
Nobel, Alfred, 790
Nomadic peoples. *See also specific peoples;*
  Iranian (qizilbash), 589, 593; Kazakh,
  740, 832
Non-allied nations, in Cold War, 955
Nongovernmental organizations (NGOs), 1010
Nonindustrial world. *See also* Developing
  nations; Third world; industrialization and,
  688–689; global economy, 792; New
  Imperialism and, 820; Great Depression
  and, 884–885
Nonviolence *(ahimsa)*, Gandhi and, 912, 916
Noriega, Manuel, 969
Normandy, landing in (1944), 895
North Africa, 473. *See also specific country;*
  Portuguese in, 467; Islam in, 568; slave
  trade and, 759; World War II in, 893*(map)*,
  894; Maghrib, 865
North America. *See also* Americas; British
  North America; Canada; United States;
  Vikings in, 465; European claims in
  (1755–1763), 540*(map)*; French and Indian
  War (1756–1763), 541, 639, 649; Russian,
  624*(map)*, 627; forest products of, 681;
  immigration to, 685, 792–794; voting
  rights in, 799; world trade and, 792;
  chronology (1904–1927), 847; radio in,
  870; population in (1750–2050), 981*(table)*
North American Free Trade Agreement
  (NAFTA), 989, 1001, 1002*(map)*
North Atlantic Treaty Organization (NATO),
  937, 941, 942*(map)*; war against Serbs
  (1999), 978; in Afghanistan, 1006
Northern Rhodesia (Zambia), 827, 829, 885
North German Confederation, 804, 805*(map)*
North Korea, 941, 1005

North River (steamboat), 678
North Vietnam, 943. *See also* Vietnam; treaty
  with United States (1973), 944
Norway, 868; Nazi invasion of, 892
Novgorod, 623
Nuclear Non-Proliferation Treaty, 944–945
Nuclear power, 899, 960, 987
Nuclear weapons: atomic bombs, in World
  War II, 896–897 *and illus.*; Cuban missile
  crisis (1962), 936, 944, 954; proliferation
  of, 944; treaties to limit, 944–945; in Iran
  and North Korea, 1005
Nuns, 504, 505, 531
Nuremburg rallies, 887*(illus.)*
Nyamwezi traders, 758*(map)*, 764
Nyasaland (Malawi), 829, 852

Oath of the Tennis Court (Paris, 1789), 649
Obasanjo, Olusegun, 978, 1004
Obregón, Alvaro, 922, 923
Observatory, in Europe, 497 *and illus.*
O'Connor, Fergus, 687
October Revolution (1917, Russia), 854
Ogé, Vincent, 660
Oglethorpe, James, 572
Ohio River, steamboats on, 678
Ohio River Valley, 539; native peoples in, 709
Oil (oil industry), 978; in Mexico, 717, 922,
  923–924, 950; in World War II, 891, 892,
  894; in Algeria, 947; Arab-Israel war and
  (1973), 958 *and illus.*, 959*(map)*; in Iran,
  958, 959*(map)*, 1003; in Iraq, 853, 865,
  958, 959*(map)*; needs of American
  economy, 999; in Nigeria, 1004;
  Organization of Petroleum Exporting
  Countries (OPEC) and, 958, 959*(map)*,
  1001; price increases in, 958 *and illus.*,
  960, 973; Russian, 858, 1003; in Saudi
  Arabia, 958, 959*(map)*
Oil palms. *See* Palm oil
Okinawa, 611, 614, 896
Oligarchy: in Argentina *(oligarquía)*, 924, 926;
  in Japan (Meiji), 806–807, 813, 860
Oman, 600, 601*(illus.)*; Sultanate of,
  763, 764
Omdurman, Battle of (1898), 821, 822*(illus.)*
Oneida peoples, 537, 645
Onondaga peoples, 537, 645
On the Origin of Species (Darwin), 808
OPEC. *See* Organization of Petroleum Export-
  ing Countries
Opium trade, 736, 766, 812, 862, 1006
Opium War (1839–1842), 742–743, 744*(map)*
Opobo, 762, 763*(illus.)*
Orange Free State, 774, 827
Order of Christ, 470
Order of Knights Templar, 470
Organization of European Economic
  Cooperation (OEEC), 940
Organization of Petroleum Exporting
  Countries (OPEC), 958,
  959*(map)*, 1001
Orizaba, Mexico, train station at, 692*(illus.)*
Orozco, José Clemente, 924, *(illus.)*
Orthodox Christianity: in Balkans, 730, 734,
  978; Russian, 623, 626, 627, 628, 739, 740

Osaka, 608, 791
Osman, 578
Osmanli language, 582–583
Ostade, Adriaen van, 500(illus.)
Ottawa people, 643
Ottoman Empire, 492, 576–589, 728–734.
    See also Turkey; central institutions,
    582–583; chronology (1514–1730), 579;
    crisis in (1585–1650), 586; economic
    change and weakness in (1650–1750),
    586–587, 589; Egypt and, 474, 478, 582,
    688, 728–730; expansion of, 467, 568, 578,
    580(map), 581–582; Greek independence
    and, 660, 729, 730; Holy Roman Empire
    and, 505; Safavid Iran and, 578, 581, 583;
    Spain and, 514; tobacco in, 587, 588,
    590(illus.); trade, 467, 570, 582, 586, 587;
    women in, 577–578; Islamic law in,
    584–585; Istanbul (Constantinople) and,
    591–592, 593, 623; Janissaries in, 582,
    586, 587, 589, 730, 731; chronology
    (1805–1876), 729; Russia and, 587, 623,
    626, 627, 731(map), 737, 738, 739, 740;
    Tanzimat reforms, 731–733, 737(illus.),
    740, 741; European reform model for,
    634–635, 730–734; Crimean War and
    (1853–1856), 734, 736, 751; ethnic
    minorities in, 846, 847; military
    modernization in, 846; World War I
    and, 846, 853; Balkan crisis and, 846;
    division of, after World War I, 863,
    864(map), 873
Owen, Robert, 687
Oyo kingdom, 561

Pacific Islanders, 778. See also Melanesians;
    Polynesians
Pacific Ocean (Oceania). See also specific
    islands; exploration of (before 1500),
    460–462 and map; chronology, 461; Spanish
    exploration of, 459, 472; European
    possessions in, 773(map); whaling in,
    777(illus.); chronology (1865–1898), 819;
    chronology (1931–1949), 879; German
    colonies in, 837; World War II in, 894,
    895(map), 896; population (1750–2050),
    981(table)
Páez, José Antonio, 704, 722
Pago Pago, 836
Pahlavi, Muhammad Reza, Shah, 972
Paine, Thomas, 645
Paintings. See also Art and artists; Flemish,
    490(illus.), 491; of Versailles, 511(illus.);
    colonial Spanish, 533(illus.); Safavid Iran,
    590(illus.), 593; Mughal India, 595(illus.),
    596; Revolution of 1830, 661(illus.); of St.
    Petersburg, 811(illus.); Mexican Revolu-
    tion and, 923(illus.), 924
Pakistan, 973; cotton production in, 798;
    India and, 945, 947; Muslims in, 910(map),
    914–915, 945; partition of 1947 and,
    910(map), 914–915; secession of
    Bangladesh from, 947; population growth
    in, 982, 983(map), 984(figure)
Palestine. See also Israel; Arabs and, 863,
    865–866; Britain and, 865–866, 868; Jewish

homeland in, 853, 865–866 and illus., 867;
    partitioning of (1947), 939
Palestine Liberation Organization (PLO), 958
Palestinians (Palestinian Arabs), 1006. See also
    Arab-Israeli conflict; refugees from, 957–958;
    terrorism and, 958
Palmares, 533
Palm Island (Dubai), 1001(illus.)
Palm oil, 762, 763(illus.), 779, 834, 839, 918
Pampas, of Argentina, 523, 721, 924
Pan-African Congress, 856
Pan-Africanists, 920
Panama, 481; isthmus of, 471, 481, 789;
    railroad in, 789
Panama Canal, 838–839; returned to
    Panama, 968
Pan American Airways, 925
Pan-Indian nationalism, 771–772
Panipat, Battle of (1526), 595
Pankhurst, Emmeline, 796 and illus.
Pan o palo policy (Mexico), 921
Pan-Slavism, 739
Papacy (popes). See also individual popes;
    treaty negotiation by, 472; reformation
    and, 492–493, 494; Henry VIII and, 507
Papal states, 803 and map
Paper money: in Ming China, 613; in colonial
    Americas, 643; in France, 651
Paraguay, 722; independence of, 635(map),
    697(map), 699, 705; Mercosur (trade
    agreement) and, 1001, 1002(map)
Paraguayan War (1865–1870), 708, 712
Paris, 660; population of, 499; alcohol
    consumed in, 503; women's salons in, 641;
    Treaty of (1783), 646; French Revolution
    and, 648, 649–651, 650(illus.); Reign of
    Terror and, 651–652, 654–655; Revolution
    of 1848 and, 662; housing in, 681(illus.);
    as "City of Lights," 791(illus.), 794
Paris Peace Conference (1919), 856, 862
Parlement of Paris, 649
Parliament (Britain), 621, 675; House of
    Commons, 507, 537, 661; House of Lords,
    507, 912; sugar planters in, 558; American
    Revolution and, 644; enclosure movement
    and, 669; Chartism
    and, 687
Parsis (Zoroastrians), 772
Pastoral nomads, in Africa, 828
Patent system, British, 671
Patriarch of Alexandria, 475
Patriotism, immigrants and, 715
Paul, on faith, 492
Pawnee people, 710
Peace of Augsburg (1555), 505
Pearl Harbor (Hawaii), 836; Japanese attack
    on (1941), 894
Peasants (peasantry). See also Farmers; Rural
    societies (rural areas); European, 502–504,
    669; rebellion by, 504; Russian serfs, 625,
    629, 635, 738, 739, 741, 931; Chinese,
    621, 629; Indian, 689, 766, 767, 908;
    Egyptian, 760, 825; French Revolution
    and, 648, 650, 656; in colonial Africa,
    829; in Middle East, 863; in Soviet Union,
    858–859, 879, 880; Mexican, 922, 923 and

illus., 924, 950; Vietnamese, 916, 917;
    Brazilian, 926; Chinese Communists and,
    889, 891, 897, 956
Pedro I (Brazil), 699, 703
Pedro II (Brazil), 699, 712
Penal colonies, in Australia, 776
Penn, William, 537–538
Pennsylvania, 790, 998; colonial, 537–538;
    canals in, 678
Pentagon attack (2001), 998, 1009
Pepper trade, 465, 473, 478, 479, 598
Perestroika (Soviet reform), 976
Perkin, William, 790
Pernambuco, Brazil, 528
Perón, Eva Duarte, 926(illus.), 927
Perón, Isabel Martínez de, 968
Perón, Juan, 926(illus.), 927, 968
Perry, Matthew C., in Japan, 786(illus.),
    787–788, 804–805
Persian Gulf (Persian Gulf states), 478, 594;
    oil wealth in, 1001(illus.), 1006; United
    States Navy in, 973
Persian Gulf War (1990–1991), 978–979, 1013
Persian language, 588, 590, 591
Personal computers (PCs), 988, 1014
Personalist leaders, 703–705, 722
Peru, 462, 798, 838; colonial, 523,
    524(map), 528, 542; independence of,
    696, 697(map), 698; war with Chile, 708,
    722; Chinese immigration to, 713, 714;
    feminism in, 970–971; glacier shrinkage
    in, 993
Pesticides, 992
Peter the Great (Russia), 606, 625–627 and
    illus., 738
Petrograd, in Russian Revolution, 854
Petroleum industry. See Oil (oil industry)
Philadelphia, colonial, 538, 641, 645
Philip II (Spain), 507, 514
Philippine Islands (Filipinos), 985; Magellan's
    discovery of, 459, 472; Christianity in,
    600; Muslims in, 598; revolt against Spain
    in, 836–837 and illus.; Spanish and, 472,
    528, 598, 599(map), 615, 773(map);
    United States and, 707, 837, 838;
    independence of, 837; in World War II,
    894, 895(map); garbage pickers in,
    986(illus.)
Philip V (Spain), 541
Philosophy: See also Political thought; and
    specific philosophers; positivism, 687
Physics: Aristotelian, 497, 498; Newtonian,
    498, 869; twentieth century revolution
    in, 869
Piedmont-Sardinia, 802, 803 and map
Pilgrims (pilgrimages): Islamic, 465, 570,
    598, 728; Safavid Iran, 591; in India, 771
Pilgrims (Protestants), 536
Pin-makers' workshop, 672–673 and illus.
Pinochet, Augusto, 968, 969
Pinta (ship), 472
Pirates (piracy), 529, 587; China and, 614,
    621, 628; Japanese, 611, 804; Muslim
    corsairs, 600
Pittsburgh, first radio station in, 870
Pius IX, Pope, 802

Pizarro, Francisco, 481–482, 532
Pizza Hut, in India, 990(illus.)
Plague: bubonic, 503; pulmonary, 520–521
Planck, Max, 869
Plantations: See also Rubber plantations; Sugar plantations; indigo, 536, 658, 775, 790; rice, 536, 538; slave labor for, 523, 536; clove, 763; in colonial Africa, 918; in French Indochina, 916
Planter elite (plantocracy), 535, 536, 553, 555, 558; Haitian Revolution and, 658, 659; in United States, 705
Platt Amendment (United States), 838
Plows, steel, 721
Plymouth colony, 536
Poets and poetry: See also Literature; Safavid Iran, 590–591; English, 680; Italian futurist, 878
Pogroms (massacres of Jews), 810
Poland-Lithuania, 625
Poland (Polish), 940, 941; nationalism in, 661; immigration from, 714, 736, 792; rebellions in, 810; Russia and, 627, 810; after World War I, 856; independence of, 854, 858; Nazi invasion of, 888, 892; code-breakers in, 900; World War II casualties, 898, 901; Roman Catholicism of, 901, 976; fall of communism in, 976; life expectancy in, 982
Political corruption. See Corruption
Political institutions: colonial, 537; Enlightenment and, 640; French Revolution and, 650, 656; Japan
Political militarism, in Russia, 739, 741
Political reforms. See Reforms
Political rights. See Rights; Individual rights
Political thought (political ideology): Macchiavelli and, 508–509; Locke and, 510; Industrial Revolution and, 686–688; socialism, 798–799; Gandhi's nonviolence, 912, 916
Politics: See also Democracy; Political thought; European innovation in, 505–514; Ottoman, 586; chronology (1853–1910), 789; labor movement and, 799; New Imperialism and, 818–819; in colonial Africa, 828–829; appeasement of Nazi Germany and, 887; Indian independence and, 911; in sub-Saharan Africa, 919–920; of famine, 930–931; Arab-Israeli conflict and, 958; neoliberal, 970–971; chronology (2000-2006), 999; global economy and, 998–1006; religion and, 1006, 1008–1009
Pollution: in England, 666(illus.); Industrial Revolution and, 680; mining and, 721; in late nineteenth century, 791, 795; horses and, 795, 872; controls for, in late twentieth century, 992, 1010, 1011
Polygamy, 863, 919
Polynesians, 460–462 and map, 463(illus.), 776
Polytheism, in Africa, 759
Pombal reforms (Brazil), 543
Ponce de León, Juan, 479
Pondicherry, 597
Pontiac (Ottawa), 643
Poor countries. See also Developing nations; Poverty: abuse of labor and environment

in, 989; aid to, 938, 1003; immigration from, 984
Poor Richard's Almanac (Franklin), 641
Pope, Alexander, 499
Popular authoritarianism, of Napoleon, 656
Popular culture, 870. See also Folk culture; global, 1014–1015
Popular protest, in Europe, 642–643, 662
Popular sovereignty, 645, 650, 656, 696
Population (population growth). See also Birthrates; European cities, 499; colonial Americas, 528, 537, 541, 544; Columbian exchange and, 520–522; India, 595, 908; sub-Saharan Africa, 570; wages and, 686; Eurasia, 728; imperial China, 613, 621, 742, 860, 979; Japan, 611; Russia, 625; industrialized Europe, 668–669, 792, 979; Canada, 794; census and, 782–783; United States, 719, 794; urbanization and, 794–795; France, 809; Southeast Asia, 834; Cuba, 951; environmental stress and, 966, 979, 987, 989; demographic transition and, 979–980; developing nations, 979, 980, 982, 992, 993; industrialized nations, 980–982; age structure comparison, 982, 984 and figure; projected growth rate, 983(map); world and major areas (1750-2050), 981(table)
Porcelain: Japanese, 608, 609(illus.); mass production of, 609 and illus., 612, 674; Ming Chinese, 612–613
Port Said, 817
Portsmouth, Treaty of (1905), 813
Portugal (Portuguese), 818, 940; in Africa, 482; in China (Macao), 475, 615, 742; monopoly trade of, 470, 473–474, 475, 478, 582; slave trade and, 474, 476–477, 563, 567, 568(illus.); West African trade and, 473–474; in East Africa, 474–475, 600; Atlantic economy and, 562(map); Hormuz and, 475, 582, 594; Indian Ocean trade and, 471, 472, 475, 478–479, 582, 600, 601(illus.); Brazil and, 533, 699; Dutch and, 601; Napoleon's invasion of, 656, 657(map), 695
Portuguese colonies, 840(map). See also Brazil, colonial; African, 567, 568 and illus., 573, 600, 638, 824(map), 826, 949; coastal China (Macao), 475, 615; in Indian Ocean, 599(map), 601(illus.), 773(map)
Portuguese exploration, 459; in Atlantic, before 1500, 465, 467–470, 469(map); West Africa and, 468(illus.)
Positivism, 687
Potatoes, 488, 522; in Europe, 503, 669; Irish famine and, 685, 930
Potential support ratio (PSR), 982
Potosí, silver refinery at, 526–527and illus., 528, 543
Pottery, mass production of, 674–675 and illus.. See also Porcelain
Poverty (the poor): See also Poor countries; American crops and, 503; in Europe, 503–504; British, 661; disease and, 681; factory work and, 685; housing for, 680, 681(illus.); in Mexico, 698–699; laissez faire theory and, 686; French Revolution and,

648–649 and illus., 651; in Brazil, 722; in British India, 766, 771, 772; urbanization and, 795; nationalism and, 808; of industrial workers, 800; in Russia, 811(illus.); of Japanese farmers, 861; in China, 862, 965; in Great Depression, 884 and illus.; in India and Gandhi, 912; in Latin America, 925; neo-liberalism and, 971; garbage pickers, 986(illus.); global trends in, 966, 985; UN Conference (2000), 1003; women and, 971
Power. See Balance of power; Great powers
Power looms, 675, 676
Predestination, 494
Prices (price inflation): See also Inflation; in Europe, 514; in Ming China, 613; in French Revolution, 649, 650; boom and bust cycle, 719; oil embargo and (1973), 958 and illus., 960, 973; oil demand (1973–2000), 1001
Priestley, Joseph, 683
Priests. See Clergy
The Prince (Macchiavelli), 508–509
Princip, Gavrilo, 845
Printing press, 493, 515, 675
Printing technology: Dutch, 500; in colonial Latin America, 525; Japanese woodblock, 611(illus.); moveable type, 606; in Egypt, 759
Prisoners of war: as slaves, 474, 566–567, 568, 571, 596; Christian, in Ottoman Empire, 578, 582; in Nazi Germany, 901
Prisons and prisoners: penal colonies, in Australia, 776; reconcentration camps, in Philippines, 837; Russian (Soviet) in Siberia, 623, 931, 975; concentration camps, World War II, 886, 901 and illus., 902
Proclamation of 1763 (Britain), 643
Progress, belief in, 499, 869, 921; New Imperialism and, 820, 829, 839
Prohibition (1919–1923, United States), 868
Propaganda: anti-slavery, 711; Crimean War, 734; fascist, 885–886; in Soviet Russia, 880; Chinese Communist, 891; World War II, 920; al-Qaeda, 1009
Property, voting rights and, 647, 702
Property rights: in France, 656, 662; women and, 592, 733–734, 829; in colonial Africa, 829
Prophet (Tenskwatawa), 709
Prostitution, 503, 770, 829, 971, 986; in French cities, 648–649
Protestantism, 498, 802, 1008. See also specific denomination
Protestant missionaries, 745, 761, 820. See also Missionaries, Christian
Protestant Reformation, 505, 507, 534; Catholic Church and, 492–494, 495(map)
Protests (demonstrations): in colonial Americas, 644 and illus.; European folk culture and, 642–643, 662; industrialization and, 661; strikes, 613, 685, 799; Indian independence and, 912, 914; African nationalism and, 948–949, 950; student, 861, 862, 960, 975; Beijing, 975; Ukraine, 1003; against globalization, 1003, 1019

Proxy wars, in Cold War, 932, 945, 961, 966, 975, 993
Prussia, 626, 671; army of, 511, 512, 804, 808; railroads in, 679 and map; French Revolution and, 651, 656; Holy Alliance and, 660; conservatism in, 802; unification of Germany and, 662, 804, 805(map); war with France (1870-1871), 804, 808, 818–819, 847
Psychoanalysis, 869
Puerto Madero, 718 and illus.
Puerto Rico, 707, 838, 989; abolition of slavery in, 713; as Borinquen, 479
Pulmonary plague, 520–521
Punjab, 597, 930
Puritans, 507, 536, 543
Puyi (boy-emperor of China), 861
Pythagoras, 497

Qatar, 958, 1013
Qianlong (China), 615, 619, 627
Qing Empire (China), 605, 735, 741–751, 834; climate and diversity in, 622(map); Emperor Kangxi, 615, 618–619 and illus.; rise of, 606, 613–615; tea and diplomacy, 620–621; trading companies in, 615; Europeans and, 615, 619, 640; expansion (1644–1783), 614(map), 615, 628; Russia and, 618–619, 832; Yangzhou Massacre, 616–617; missionaries in, 615, 619, 743, 745; population and social stress, 621–622; reform in, 635; chronology (1794-1908), 729; corruption in, 727–728; economic and social disorder in, 742; conflicts in (1839–1870), 744(map); Great Britain and, 741–743, 744(map), 747–748, 766, 812; Opium War and aftermath, 742–744 and map; Taiping Rebellion in, 744–747; Western imperialism and, 749–750; decentralization at end of, 747–748, 751; end of, 861
Qizilbash nomads, 589, 591, 593
Quakers, 558; in Pennsylvania, 537
Quaque, Philip, 570
Quebec, colonial, 541, 643
Quinine, 619, 821, 835 and illus.
Quito (Ecuador), 530–531
Quran, 570. See also Islam
Quran schools, 732, 759, 832, 919 and illus.

Rabih, 828
Racism (racial discrimination), 979. See also Mixed race; and ethnicity in colonial Americas, 530–531, 533(illus.); African slavery and, 552; in Americas, 716–717, 722; anti-Asian, in Americas, 714; in Australia, 776 and illus.; lynching in United States, 712; census taking and, 783; New Imperialism and, 820, 823, 837; Hitler's Germany, 901; in colonial Africa, 828, 919; in India under British rule, 909; in South Africa, 949–950, 952–953
Radio, 870, 1013; in Latin America, 871, 925
Raffles, Thomas Stamford, 774
Railroads: bridges for, 682, 688(illus.); in Britain, 671(map), 678, 679, 680, 788; in Canada, 719, 788, 839; telegraph and,

680; in United States, 678–679 and illus., 693, 719, 720(map), 788; in Egypt, 688(illus.), 738, 760; in Europe, 679(map); in India, 689, 754(illus.), 755, 771, 789, 833(map), 839, 930; in Japan, 789, 833(map); environmental impact of, 680–681, 841; in Latin America, 693, 837–838, 839; in Mexico, 692(illus.), 694, 719, 921, 922(map), 923; in Russia, 738, 741, 788, 811, 832, 833(map), 839; in Argentina, 719, 837, 924; urbanization and, 794; immigration and, 793; world economy and, 788–789, 839; World War I mobilization and, 848; Manchurian Incident (1931) and, 888; in Africa, 918, 948; famine and, 930
Rainfall: See also Drought; Monsoons; in China, 622(map); in Sub-Saharan Africa, 632
Rain forest. See Tropical (rain) forests
Rajputs, 596
Raleigh, Walter, 534
Rangoon, 774
Rao, Dinkur, 769
Raw materials (natural resources), 954; cottage industry and, 670; Indian export of, 689; industrialization and, 682; export of, from Americas, 711, 719, 920; New Imperialism and, 818, 820, 837; United States' economy and, 999; world economy and, 792, 801; World War II, 892, 894, 903; Africa and, 918
Reagan, Ronald, 975; Nicaragua and, 968–969, 973
Rebellions (revolts). See also Revolution(s); Aztec, 480–481; Dutch, 514; in Scotland, 507; peasant, 504, 650; slave, 532, 536, 556, 558, 711; slave, in St. Domingue, 636(illus.), 637–638, 659, 712, 762; Amerindian, 543, 698; in Arabia, 600; in China, 606, 613–614, 621, 629, 742; in Ottoman Empire, 586, 589, 730, 731; by war veterans, in United States, 647; Decembrist, in Russia, 741; Taiping (1850-1864), 744–747, 744(map), 745(illus.); in British India, 767, 779; Polish, 810; Arab (1916), 853, 865; Hungarian (1956), 941
Recession, 792. See also Depression
Reconcentration camps, in Philippines, 837
Red Army (Soviet Union), 858 and illus., 881; in Korean War, 941; in World War II, 876(illus.), 892 and illus., 894, 895, 898, 902
Red Guard (China), 956, 957(illus.)
Red Sea area, 478, 581, 582, 600
Red Shoes (Shulush Homa), 519–520
Reforms: Enlightenment, 498–499, 640, 641, 642–643; colonial Americas, 526, 528, 543; Russian, 626–627, 628, 738; popular protest and, 642–643; industrialization and, 681, 687; democratic, in Europe, 662; French Revolution, 649–650, 653; in Americas, 711; Islamic, in West Africa, 757, 759, 779; in British India, 766, 767, 772; Ottoman Empire, 634–635, 730–734, 737–738 and illus., 846; Turkish

modernization, 863 and illus.; women and, 868–869; in Brazil and Argentina, 925, 927; Mexican Revolution, 923, 924; in Cuba, 935, 936; Great Society, in United States, 944; Guatemalan, 950; socialist, in Chile, 968; Soviet, under Gorbachev, 976; economic, in China, 965, 974–975
Regionalism, in Americas, 705, 707, 722
Regional trade associations, 1001–1003 and map
Reichstag (Germany), 799, 809
Reign of Terror (France, 1793-1794), 651–653, 654–655, 656
Religion. See also Buddhism; Christianity; Clergy; Islam; Hindus; and statecraft, early modern Europe, 507; in colonial North America, 536; on Caribbean plantations, 558; Enlightenment and, 640; abolition of slavery and, 711; Heavenly Kingdom of Great Peace, 745–746, 747; in British India, 767, 911; in Egypt, and Suez Canal, 818; Eastern European nationalism and, 976; global, 1007(map); politics and, 1006, 1008–1009
Religious reformation, 492–494, 495(map), 505
Renaissance: art of, 490(illus.), 491, 492; Italian, 467; science of, 497
Republican institutions, 646–647. See also Democracy; Voting rights
Republicanism, nationalism and, 656, 660
Republican Party (United States), 711
Resources. See Raw materials; specific resources
Réunion, 774
Revolutionary Alliance (China), 861
Revolutionary era (1750–1850), 636–664; colonial wars and fiscal crises, 638–639; Congress of Vienna and, 660; eighteenth century crisis, 638–643; Enlightenment and old order, 640–642, 663; folk cultures and popular protest, 642–643; in France, 647–656 (See also French Revolution); Haitian Revolution (1789–1804), 658–660, 659(map), 662, 663; Napoleonic Europe, 657(map); nationalism and reform (1821–1850), 660–662; in North America, 643–647, 662; popular sovereignty in, 645, 650, 656; Conservative response (1789-1850), 656–662, 663
Revolution(s): See also Rebellions; Revolutionary era; scientific, 497–498, 640, 641; Belgium (1830), 661(illus.); Europe (1848), 662, 802; India (1857), 767; Philippines (1899), 836 and illus., 837; Russia (1905), 811; Russia (1917), 854; Mexico, 920–922 and map; Cuba (1959), 934(illus.), 935–936, 967; Cultural (China, 1966), 956, 957(illus.); Soviet promotion of, 936; agricultural, 933, 938 and illus.; Nicaragua and El Salvador, 968–969 and
illus.; computer, 987–989; Islamic, 966, 969, 972–973, 1008
Rhineland, 804, 856, 887
Rhode Island, 561
Rhodes, Cecil, 827, 949
Ricardo, David, 686

Ricci, Matteo, 499, 501, 615
Rice and rice cultivation, 774; in North America, 536, 538; in Caribbean, 554; in India, 596–597; in Japan, 608, 611; Green Revolution and, 938 *and illus.*
Rifles, 623, 790, 832, 861; breech-loading, 736, 821; Enfield, 767; percussion-cap, 734, 743; repeating, 821, 822*(illus.)*
Righteous Fists (Boxers) in China, 812 *and illus.*, 813, 861
Rights: *See also* Individual rights; Voting rights; Women's rights; Napoleonic France, 656; natural, 640, 651; for African colonials, 852–853; human rights, 968, 1009–1010
Rio de Janeiro, 529, 699, 721, 924, 926, 985*(table)*; market in, 542*(illus.)*; rush hour in, 906*(illus.)*; street children in, 986; Earth Summit in (1992), 1011
Rio de la Plata region, 523, 524*(map)*, 542
Ritual: Amerindian, 526; Chinese kowtow, 615, 620
Rivera, Diego, 923*(illus.)*, 924
Rizal, José, 836
Roads: Inca, 481; in Japan, 607; in France and England, 682; in Russia, 738; automobiles and, 872
Roanoke Island, 534
Robespierre, Maximilien, 652–653, 654–655
Rockefeller Foundation, 938
Rocket (locomotive), 678
Roman Catholics. *See* Catholic Church
Romance languages, 583
Romania, 734, 846, 941, 1001; fall of Communism in, 976
Romanov, Mikhail, 625
Rome, 492, 662
Romero, Oscar, 969
Rommel, Erwin, 900
Roosevelt, Franklin D., 884, 895, 899
Roosevelt, Theodore, 721, 838
Rosas, Juan Manuel de, 705
Rousseau, Jean-Jacques, 640, 641, 652
Roy, Arundhati, 1016
Roy, Rammohun, 771–772 *and illus.*
Royal African Company (RAC), 560, 563, 565, 572
Royal Air Force (Great Britain), 892
Royal Botanic Gardens (Kew), 620*(illus.)*, 839
Royal charter, colonial, 536
Royal monopolies, 560
Royal Society (London), 498, 674
Rubber, synthetic, 899
Rubber plantations, 820; in Brazil, 839, 924, 925, 926; in Congo, 826–827; in Southeast Asia, 834 *and illus.*, 835, 839
Ruhr (Germany), 671, 679*(map)*, 680, 790, 794, 859
Rum, 553, 565, 951
Rural areas: poverty in, 503; Ottoman, 587; folk custom in, 598; French Revolution and, 650; industrialization and, 670, 681–682; urban expansion and, 794; technological advances in, 872–873
Rushdie, Salman, 1017
Russia Federation (Russia), 979, 985, 1015; end of Soviet Union and, 977–978*(map)*;

HIV/AIDS in, 980; declining birthrates in, 982; oil wealth of, 1001, 1003; in Shanghai Cooperative Organization, 1001, 1003
Russian language, 625, 628, 810, 1015
Russian Orthodox Church, 623, 626, 627, 739, 740; Siberian missions of, 625, 628
Russian Revolutions (1914–1918), 854; women and family values in, 882–883
Russia (Russian Empire), 605, 738–741, 840*(map)*. *See also* Russian Federation; Soviet Union (USSR); Armenians in, 500; forest resources of, 503, 623, 682; society and politics, 623–625; war with Sweden (1700–1721), 512, 626; Central Asia and, 625, 739–740, 832; China and, 618–619; chronology (1533–1799), 607; consolidation of, 627–628; diplomats to Holland, 604*(illus.)*, 606; Holy Alliance and, 660; Europe and, 626, 738–739, 751; expansion of, 489, 606, 618, 622–623, 624*(map)*, 626, 628, 629, 731*(map)*, 734, 736, 739–740; North American claims of (Alaska), 540*(map)*, 624*(map)*, 627; Ottoman Empire and, 587, 626, 627, 660, 731*(map)*, 737, 738, 739, 740; Peter the Great and, 606, 625–627 *and illus.*, 738; westernization of, 625–627, 628, 739, 740; Crimean War and, 734, 738; cultural trends, 740–741; Napoleon's invasion of, 656, 738, 740, 892, 931; immigrants from, 740, 793; industrialization in, 738, 788; chronology (1801–1861), 729; Qing China and, 743; railroads in, 738, 741, 788, 811, 832, 839, 848; as great power, 788; conservative regime in, 802, 808, 810; war with Japan (1904–1905), 811, 813, 834, 846; Balkans and, 846; ethnic minorities in, 810, 847; in World War I, 849*(map)*, 850, 851*(map)*, 854; double Revolution in, 854; civil war in, 856–858, 931; after World War I, 857*(map)*, 873
Russo-Japanese War (1904–1905), 811, 813, 834, 846
Rwanda, genocide in, 978

Sa'adi family, 600
Saarinen, Eero, 872
Saar region, 856
Sabah, 577–578
Sacrifice, Aztec, 480
Sa'di (poet), 590
Safavid Empire (Iran), 489, 580*(map)*, 589–594, 623; chronology (1502–1747), 579; economic crisis and collapse of, 593–594; Isfahan in, 591–592, 593; Ottomans and, 578, 581, 583, 587; rise of, 589; Shi'ite Islam in, 584, 589, 591; society and religion in, 589–591; tobacco and waterpipes in, 588*(illus.)*, 590*(illus.)*; women and family in, 592
Sagres, 467
Sahel, 828
Sailing ships, 775, 792. *See also* Ships and shipping
St. Domingue (Haiti): sugar plantations in, 553–554, 558, 573; social classes in, 558, 658–659; slave rebellion in, 636*(illus.)*,

637–638, 712; revolution in (1789–1804), 658–660, 658*(illus.)*, 659*(map)*, 662, 663, 712; United States and, 838
St. Lawrence River, 539
St. Petersburg, 626, 627 *and illus.*, 738, 739*(illus.)*, 811*(illus.)*; Revolution in (1917), 854; as Leningrad, 892
Saint-Exupéry, Antoine de, 817
Saint George of the Mine (Elmina), 473, 474
Saint-Germaine, Treaty of (1920), 856
Saint Peter's Basilica, 492
Saint-Simon, duke of, 510, 687
Saipan, 896
Sakhalin (Karafutu), 807*(map)*
Salé, 600
Salt monopoly, in British India, 912
Salvador, Brazil, 525, 529
Salvation, Protestant, 493, 494
Samarkand, 595, 832
Samoa, 836, 837
Samori Toure, 828
Samurai, 606, 608, 611–612, 786*(illus.)*, 806
Sandinistas (Nicaragua), 968*(illus.)*, 973
Sandino, Augusto César, 968
San Francisco, 747
Sanger, Margaret, 869
Sanitation: in British India, 771; disease and, 735, 771, 821; sewage treatment, 771, 794, 872; urbanization and, 794
San Martín, José de, 698
Santa Maria (ship), 472
Santo Domingo, 659
Santos-Dumont, Alberto, 925
São Paulo, Brazil, 528, 543, 713, 926, 985*(table)*
São Tomé, 470, 474, 528
Saratoga, Battle of (1777), 645, 646*(map)*
Sardinia-Piedmont, 734
Satellites, 945, 1013; mapping by, 933*(illus.)*
Sati (widow burning), 772, 820, 908
Satsuma (Japan), 804, 806
Saud family, 728, 729
Saudi Arabia, 973, 978, 998, 1009; oil wealth of, 958, 959*(map)*, 1001; women's rights in, 1012
Savannah (steamship), 678
Scandinavia, 494. *See also* Denmark; Finland; Norway; Sweden; immigration from, 792; English in, 1016
Schools and scholars, 808. *See also* Education; Literacy; in colonial Latin America, 525, 526; Quranic (Muslim), 732, 759, 832, 919 *and illus.*; women and, 505, 716; Confucian, 618*(illus.)*; Islamic ulama, 591, 730, 731; immigrants and, 714–715; woman as teachers, 716, 796, 820; in Egypt, 724; in India, 772; in Russia, 741; Ottoman, 737; in Africa, 763; mission, in China, 860; mission, in colonial Africa, 828, 829, 919, 948
Science: *See also* Mathematics; Technology; European revolution in, 497–498, 640, 641, 869; economic botany and, 835 *and illus.*, 839; of World War II, 899; global culture and, 1016
Scotland (Scots), 512, 534, 810; rebellion in, 507

Seacole, Mary, 735
Seal hunting, off New Zealand, 776
"Seasoning" of slaves, 557
Second Estate (France), 648, 649
Second Treatise on Civil Government (Locke), 510
Second World War. *See* World War II
Security Council, United Nations: China on, 937, 957, 974; Korean War and, 941
Seko, Moduto Sese, 936, 949
Sékou Touré, 949
Selassie, Haile, 920
Self-government (self-determination), 638, 660, 662, 755. *See also* Independence; Nationalism; in British colonies, 776, 778, 912; League of Nations and, 856, 862; in sub-Saharan Africa, 949
Selim I, Sultan, 581, 591
Selim II, Sultan, 584
Selim III, Sultan, 728, 730, 741
Seminole peoples, 704
Senate (United States), 647, 705
Seneca Falls (New York), Women's Rights Convention in (1848), 716
Seneca people, 537, 645
Senegal, 825, 852, 918, 919
Senior, Nassau, 667–668
Separate spheres, Victorian age, 795 *and illus.*
Sepoys (India), 765, 766; Rebellion of, 767
Seppuku (ritual suicide), 612
September 11 terrorist attacks (9/11/2001), 932, 996*(illus.)*, 997–998, 1005, 1009, 1019
Serbia, 845, 848; Ottoman Empire and, 578, 730, 734, 846; independence of, 734, 847; NATO war against (1999), 978
Serfs (serfdom), 502–503; Russian, 625, 629, 738; freeing of Russian, 635, 739, 741, 810
Sevastopol, 734
Seven Years War (1756-1763), 541, 639, 649, 766
Sèvres, 674; Treaty of (1920), 863
Sewage treatment, 771, 794, 872
Sewing machine, 798 *and illus.*
Sexuality: *See also* Prostitution; celibacy, 494; women and rape, 504; homosexuality in Islam, 593; in folk festivals, 643
Sexual liberation, 1012
Sexually-transmitted disease, 829; AIDS/HIV, 980, 1012*(figure)*
Shaka (Zulu), 756–757
Shakespeare, William, 491
Shanghai, 743, 747, 862; Bund in, 860 *and illus.*; Japan and, 888, 889; sale of gold in, 898*(photo)*; old meets new in, 964*(illus.)*; future growth of, 985*(table)*
Shanghai Cooperative Organization (SCO), 1001, 1003
Sharecroppers (tenant farmers), 669, 670, 797; Irish famine and, 930
Shari'a (Islamic law), 591, 598, 757; in Mughal India, 596; in Ottoman Empire, 583, 584–585, 732; women and, 577–578, 592
Sharpeville massacre (1960), 950
Shawnee people, 709
Sheep: in Americas, 522–523, 532; in New Zealand, 778; in Argentina, 924

Shifting (swidden) agriculture, 834
Shi'ite Islam: in Iran, 584, 589, 591, 972; in Iraq, 1006
Ships and shipping (merchant marine): *See also* Canals; Navy; Pirates; Steamships; Chinese junks, 463–464 *and illus.*, 468; Indian dhows, 463, 475; Polynesian canoes, 461–462, 463*(illus.)*; Portuguese caravels, 468, 471 *and illus.*; African, 465, 762; lateen sails, 468, 471 *and illus.*, 472; canoes, in Canadian fur trade, 539*(illus.)*; Dutch, 500, 502 *and illus.*, 514; English, 502, 514; European, in Istanbul, 591; European, in Mughal India, 595–596; slave trade, 549–550, 559, 563, 564 *and illus.*; port construction for, 718 *and illus.*; British merchant, 670, 772, 774, 775; shipping lines, 790; major routes (1913), 840*(map)*; New Imperialism and, 821; Japanese, 956
Shipyard Diary of a Woman Welder (Clawson), 902
Shoa kingdom, 668, 761
Shoguns, in Japan, 606, 804. *See also specific shogunate*
Shona peoples, 758, 827
Shrines, Islamic, 958
Shulush Homa (Red Shoes), 519–520
Siam (Thailand), 774, 834, 894, 985
Siberia, 619, 623, 629; Orthodox missionaries in, 625, 628
Sibir Khanate, 623
Sicily, 803 *and map*
Sierra Leone, 468 *and map*, 565, 762–763; Christianity in, 763, 829
Sikhism (Sikhs), 597, 767
Silesia, 671
Silk industry: in China, 613; Iranian, 587, 593, 594
Silver: Mexican, 698; from colonial Latin America, 482, 525, 526, 527–528 *and illus.*, 543, 559, 613; from Americas, 514, 561, 586, 594, 733; in China trade, 621, 742
Sinai Peninsula, 958
Singapore, 839, 894, 947; British in, 774, 775; bubonic plague in, 747; economic growth in, 974, 975, 1019
Singer, Isaac, 798
Sino-Japanese War (1894), 812–813, 837
Sino-Japanese War (1937–1945), 889–891 *and map*
Sioux people, 523, 540, 710
Sirius (steamship), 677*(illus.)*, 678
Skyscrapers, 872, 964*(illus.)*
Slave Coast, 565–567, 568
Slave rebellions, 532, 536, 556, 558, 711; St. Domingue, 636*(illus.)*, 637–638, 659, 712, 762
Slave soldiery, 532, 569, 582, 594, 728, 764. *See also* Janissaries
Slaves (slavery): Amerindians as, 479, 528, 535, 552; prisoners of war as, 474, 596; and serfdom compared, 625; on sugar plantations, 582, 670
Slaves (slavery), African, 470, 503, 758*(map)*; in Brazil, 528, 533, 543, 699, 700–701, 722; in colonial North America, 535, 536;

disease and, 528, 550, 552, 557; freedom for, 532, 533, 558–559; Haitian Revolution and, 658–660; in Latin America, 532, 535, 696; in North America, 663; punishment for, 556, 557*(illus.)*; in West Africa and Americas compared, 571–572; rebellions, 532, 536, 556, 558; on sugar plantations, 532, 549, 551–558, 573, 685, 711; in United States, 647, 705
Slave trade, African, 503; Portuguese and, 470, 474, 476–477; Amerindian food crops and, 555; disease and, 521, 564; sugar plantations and, 551–552, 553, 557; in colonial Latin America, 523, 532, 534; (1551–1850), 552*(figure)*, 563*(map)*; Dutch and, 551–552, 553, 639; Atlantic system and, 559, 561, 562*(map)*; Middle Passage, 561, 563–565; prisoners of war and, 566–567, 568, 571; Islam and, 569–570, 763; trans-Saharan, 470, 563*(map)*, 566, 569–570, 759; Americas and, 647, 713; Brazil and, 699, 700; in Eastern Africa, 600; Great Britain and, 699, 700, 712, 713; Sokoto Caliphate and, 759; in Zanzibar, 764; end of, 634, 685, 711, 712, 762–763, 764, 830
Slavophiles, 739, 741
Slavs, 810. *See also* Eastern Europe; *specific Slavic countries;* Russian, 623, 625, 892; Balkan, 846, 847
Slessor, Mary, 820
Slovakia, 977*(map)*
Slovenia, 977*(map)*, 978
Smallpox, 550, 681, 918; Amerindians and, 479, 481, 520, 522; African slave trade and, 564
Smith, Adam, 672–673, 686
Smoot-Hawley tariff (United States; 1930), 881
Smyrna (Izmir), 587
Social classes (social stratification). *See also specific class;* Europe (1500-1750), 499–500, 502–504; colonial Latin America, 523, 533; colonial North America, 536, 537; in slave plantations, 555, 558; Industrial Revolution and, 670; in India, 464, 766, 772, 908, 912; Parisian housing and, 681*(illus.)*; urbanization and, 795; Marxism and, 854; and gender, in industrialized world, 868–869; in China, 860
The Social Contract (Rousseau), 640
Social Darwinism, 808–809
Social Democratic Party (Germany), 799
Socialism, 797, 799, 852, 868. *See also* Marx, Karl; utopian, 687; in Chile, 968
Social reform. *See* Reforms
Social revolution: in China, 889; in Mexico, 921, 927; in Russia, 854
Social sciences, 869
Social welfare: dismantling of, in Soviet bloc, 982; for elderly, 981–982, 984
Society (social conditions): in colonial Latin America, 529, 532–534 *and illus.*; Safavid Iran, 589–591; Enlightenment thinkers and, 640; in Qing China, 621; population and migrations (1850–1914), 792, 794; in Argentina; urbanization and, 794–795;

Society (Continued)
Victorian Age women, 795–797; in colonial Africa, 828–829, 918–919; in Mexico, 920; Meiji Japan, 860–861; chronology (2001–2004), 999
Soil erosion, 553–554, 720–721, 989, 993; in Brazil, 992(illus.)
Sokoto Caliphate, 756, 758(map), 759
Solano López, Francisco, 708
Solidarity (Poland), 976
Solzhenitzen, Alexander, 975
Somaliland, 894
Somme River, Battle of (1916), 850, 851(map)
Somoza, Anastasio, 968(illus.)
Song China, iron industry in, 676
Songhai Empire, 566(map), 569
Sons of Liberty, 644
Sophia (Russia), 626
South African War (1899–1902), 827
South America: See also Latin America, and specific countries; Amerindian exploration, 465, 466(map); exploration of, 459, 461, 472; cattle in, 523; colonial, 520; disease in, 520; in 1820s, 635(map); chronology (1808-1888), 695
South Asia, 568. See also Sri Lanka; India; decolonization in, 945
South Carolina, 663, 675, 720; colonial, 535, 536, 538
Southeast Asia. See East Indies (maritime Southeast Asia) and specific country; Chinese immigration to, 614, 774, 794, 834; deforestation in, 775; New Imperialism in, 832, 833(map), 834–836; Japan and, 894, 956; rubber in, 834 and illus., 835, 839; decolonization in, 946; miracle rice in, 938 (illus.)
Southern Africa, 792, 822, 915, 918, 985; Cape Colony, 568, 772, 774, 827; Zulu of, 756–757, 774, 779, 827, 828; mining boom (1930s) in, 885; diamond mining in, 827, 841(illus.); railroads in; native landownership in, 827, 829; education in, 919; gold in, 827; race and struggle for justice in, 949–950, 952–953; democracy in, 978; English language in, 1016; trade agreement (SADC), 1001, 1002(map)
Southern Rhodesia (Zimbabwe), 756, 827, 949
South Korea, 941, 954. See also Korea; economic growth in, 974, 975, 1018; age distribution in, 982, 984(figure)
South Vietnam, 943–944. See also Vietnam
Southwest Africa (Namibia), 828, 852, 862
Southwest Asia, Empires in (1500-1750). See Ottoman Empire; Safavid Empire
Soviet-Japanese Neutrality Pact (1941), 891
Soviet Union (USSR). See also Russia (Russian Empire); bureaucracy in, 859, 940, 956; chronology (1928–1944), 879; collectivization of agriculture in, 879–880 and illus., 931; Communist Party in, 878, 880, 881; famine in, 880, 931; five-year plans in, 878–879, 880; industrialization in, 785, 858–859, 878, 880, 881; New Economic Policy (N.E.P.) in, 858, 880; pact with Germany, 859, 888;

pact with Japan (1941), 891; peasants in, 858–859, 879, 880; terror and opportunities in, 880–881; in World War II, 892–894, 893(map), 902; World War II casualties, 898
Soviet Union (USSR), Cold War era, 949, 950. See also Cold War (Bipolar world); China and, 956, 957, 961; Cuba and, 951, 954; economy of, 939–941; Egypt and, 955; Korean War, 941; missile installations of, 936, 942(map); nuclear supremacy and, 944–945; rivalry with United States, 966; Third World and, 954–955; Warsaw Pact and, 937, 941, 942(map); collapse of, 977–978 and map, 993, 998, 1019; environmental damage in, 989; war in Afghanistan, 969, 973, 975, 976, 1006; Gorbachev's reforms in, 975–976
Soyinka, Wole, 1016
Space exploration, 933(illus.), 945, 1015
Spain, 660, 704, 940. See also Spanish exploration; Armada (navy) of, 512(illus.), 529, 534, 541, 638, 838; economic decline in, 514, 543; Habsburgs and, 505, 506(map), 510(table); Netherlands and, 500, 514, 551; royal dynasties in, 510(table); immigration from, 542, 698, 714, 792; War of Spanish Succession and, 512, 639; Atlantic economy and, 562(map); Jews expulsed from, 583; popular protest in, 642; Napoleon and, 656, 657(map), 695; Junta Central in, 695; war with United States (1898–1899), 707, 836–837, 838; Mexico and, 707, 920
Spanish-American War (1898–1899), 707, 836–837, 838
Spanish Armada (navy), 512(illus.), 529, 534, 541, 638, 838
Spanish colonies, 840(map). See also Latin America, colonial; abolition of slavery in, 712–713; in Africa, 824(map); in Caribbean, 553, 558, 559, 573, 643, 660, 712–713; Dutch assault on, 638; in North America, 540(map), 541, 563; popular protest in, 642; Philippines and, 472, 528, 598, 599(map), 615, 773(map)
Spanish exploration, 469(map), 470–472, 479; Magellan, 458(illus.), 459–460, 461, 472
Spanish Inquisition, 507
Spanish language, 808
Spear, Percival, 912
Spencer, Herbert, 808
Spice Islands (Moluccas), 472, 475, 832
Spice trade, 472, 475, 587, 601; pepper, 465, 473, 478, 479, 598
Spinning jenny, 675, 676, 798
Spinning wheel, Gandhi and, 913 and illus.
Sputnik satellite (1957), 945
Sri Lanka (Ceylon), 772, 774; coffee in, 766; English in, 1015; tea in, 835, 839, 885
Staffordshire pottery, 674 and illus.
Stalin, Joseph, 859, 878–881, 888, 891, 895; famine and, 880, 931; Hitler and, 887, 888; on women and abortion, 883
Stalingrad (Volgagrad), 892 and illus., 894
Stamp Act (1765), 644
Standard Oil corporation, 719
Stanley, Henry Morton, 761, 764, 825

Stanton, Elizabeth Cady, 796
The Starry Messenger (Galileo), 498
State power, census and, 782–783
Steam engines, 675, 676 and illus.; coal and, 676(illus.), 677–678, 792; pollution from, 666(illus.); railroads and, 678(illus.); electric power compared, 791; tractors, 873
Steamships, 677(illus.), 678, 818; for Congo River, 826(illus.); railroads and, 719; in Russia, 738; sailing ships compared, 792; in British India, 771; global economy and, 789–790, 839; warships (gunboats), 689, 743, 786(illus.), 787, 821
Steel production (steel mills). See also Iron industry; in Japan, 608, 891, 894; pollution from, 791; in shipbuilding, 789; steel plows, 721; in United States, 719, 790; in India, 911; in Brazil, 926
Steel swords, 479, 480, 482
Stephenson, George and Robert, 678
Steppe, in Eurasia, 623, 832
Stimson, Henry, 897
Stock exchanges, 502, 560, 985, 989
Stock market crash (1929), 881
Stono Rebellion (1739), 536
Straits Settlements, 774. See also Singapore
Streetcars and subways, 791, 794, 795, 906(illus.)
Strikes, 799; in Ming China, 613; by millworkers, 685
Strogonov family (Russia), 623, 625
Stuart dynasty (England), 507, 510(table)
Student protests: in China, 861, 862; Earth Day, 960
Submarine telegraph cables, 680, 790, 821
Submarine warfare, 850, 855, 944; World War II U-boats, 896, 900, 903
Sub-Saharan Africa. See also specific countries; slave trade and, 503; European trade and, 568; Islam in, 568, 570; population of, 570, 982; rainfall in, 632; Muslims in, 832, 919 and illus.; economic and social changes, 915, 918–919; nationalism, 920; religious and political changes in, 915, 918–920; independence in, 947–950; cities in, 918–919, 986; democracy in, 978, 1004; HIV/AIDS in, 980, 1012(figure)
Suburbs, 681, 870(illus.), 872
Subway trains. See Streetcars and subways
Sudan, 569, 570, 764, 828, 865; Battle of Ondurman in, 821, 822(illus.); famine and drought in, 600, 931; refugees from Darfur, 1008(illus.)
Suez Canal, 767, 790, 865, 887; opening of (1869), 737, 816(illus.), 817–818; New Imperialism and, 821, 825, 839; Arab-Israeli tensions and, 955, 957, 958
Suffrage. See Voting rights (enfranchisement)
Sufism, 589, 591, 596, 598
Sugar consumption, in Europe, 561
Sugar plantations, 820, 834; abolition of slavery in, 713, 778; in Africa, 470, 474; in colonial Brazil, 525, 526, 528, 529, 532, 533, 551, 573, 778; deforestation and, 553–554, 775; indentured labor on, 778, 794; in Jamaica, 553, 556(table), 558; in

Mexico, 710; planters and plantocracy, 535, 536, 553, 555, 558; slave labor for, 551, 552–557, 563, 670, 685, 711; technology and environment for, 553–554; Venetian, 582; in West Indies, 549, 551–557, 558, 573, 643, 658; windmills on, 548(*illus.*), 553; in Cuba, 573, 720, 778, 792, 838, 950–951

Sukarno, Achmad, 896, 954, 955

Suleiman the Magnificent, 581, 583, 584, 587; funeral procession of, 576(*illus.*)

Sulu Empire (Philippines), 598

Sumatra, 598, 601, 834

Sun-god (Aztec), 481

Sunni Islam, 589, 596, 1006

Sun Yat-sen (Sun Zhongshan), 861, 862, 916

Supernatural, European witchcraft and, 496

Superpowers, Cold War, 954, 957. *See also* Cold War; Soviet Union; United States; environment and, 960; Islamic Revolutions and, 969, 972–973; non-aligned nations and, 936, 955–956; nuclear non-proliferation and, 944–945; proxy wars of, 945, 961, 966, 975, 993

Surat, 595

Surinam (Dutch Guiana), 559, 713, 774, 945

Survival of the fittest, 808

Sustainable development, 1003

Swahili Coast, 464–465, 475, 568, Islam in, 570, 600; secondary empires in, 763, 764

Swahili language, 600, 764

Swazi kingdom, 756–757

Sweden, 714, 940; army of, 511; deforestation in, 503, 682; war with Russia (1700-1721), 512, 626; aging population in, 981, 982, 984(*figure*)

Sweet potatoes, 461, 479, 621

Switzerland, 985

Swords, steel, 479, 480, 482

Sybil; or, The Two Nations (Disraeli), 685

Syrian Congress (1919), 867

Syria (Syrians), 734, 958, 1006; Mamluks in, 578, 582, 590; Ibrahim of Egypt and, 729–730, 731, 734; Ottoman Empire and, 582, 728, 853; after World War I, 863, 864(*map*), 867; in West Africa, 918; independence of, 957

Tacky (slave rebel), 558

Taft, William, 838

Tahiti, 461, 462(*map*)

Tahmasp, Shah, 589

Taino (Arawak) peoples, 465, 479, 550, 554

Taiping Rebellion (1850-1864), 744–747, 744(*map*); Nanjing in, 745(*illus.*), 746–747

Taiwan, 611, 614, 615; Japan and, 807(*map*), 813, 837, 888; Guomindang (nationalists) in, 897–898, 957; economic growth in, 974, 1018

Tajikistan, 1001

Taliban (Afghanistan), 1005, 1006

Tanzania, 1009

Tanzimat reforms (Ottoman Empire), 731–733, 737 *and illus.*, 740, 741

Tariffs, 561, 687, 717, 792; Ottoman, 736; in British India, 914; Japanese and, 973; protections for farmers, 1003

Tashkent, 740, 832

Tasman, Abel, 601

Tata, Jamsetji and Dorabji, 911

Taxation (taxes), 512; Portuguese, 478; French nobility and, 502, 510, 514, 649; peasant revolts against, 504; in colonial Americas, 479, 525, 541, 561, 639, 644; Enlightenment reforms and, 640; in England, 507; in Mughal India, 596; Ottoman Empire, 583, 586–587; reform of, in France, 514; Safavid Iran, 594; American Revolution and, 643–644; French Revolution and, 649; Ottoman Empire, 730, 732; in African Caliphate, 759; in British India, 766; in colonial Africa, 826, 829; in Egypt, 825; in China, 862, 891, 897; in United States, 985

Tax farming, 586–587, 732

Teachers, women as, 716, 796, 820

Tea trade, 561, 670, 685, 775, 820, 834; American Revolution and, 644; in British India, 766, 770, 835, 839; China and, 620, 674, 742

Technology: *See also* Construction and building techniques; Engineering; Manufacturing; Science; Ships and shipping; Technology, Industrial Revolution and; Weapons and military technology; of early modern Europe, 515; Columbian exchange and, 522; colonial sugar plantation, 553; Enlightenment, 640; in Americas, 719; mining in United States, 717(*illus.*); European, in Ottoman Empire, 732; and modernization in Egypt, 759; whaling, 777 *and illus.*; in British India, 771, 909; in middle class homes, 796; shipbuilding, 775; world economy and, 788–792; Japanese adoption of, 788, 808; accelerating rate of, 846; New Imperialism and, 821; of modernity, 869–872; Pacific Rim economies and, 974; Gandhi's rejection of, 913 *and illus.*; computers, 987–989, 1014; environmental change and, 987–993; industrial robots, 989; resource conservation, 989, 992; world economy and, 987, 989; cultural globalization and, 1012–1014, 1016

Technology, Industrial Revolution and, 670, 672–680, 788. *See also* Railroads; chronology (1759-1851), 669; division of labor, 672–673 *and illus.*; iron industry, 676–677, 682; mass production and, 674–675; mechanization in cotton industry, 675–676; steam engine and, 676(*illus.*), 677–678; telegraph, 670, 679–680

Tecumseh, 709

Teheran, Iran: meeting (1943), 895; hostage crisis in (1979), 972

Telecommunications, 1013–1014

Telegraph, 670, 679–680, 689, 719, 735, 771, 921; radio and, 925; submarine cables for, 680, 790, 821

Television, 1013, 1014

Tenant farmers. *See* Sharecroppers

Tennyson, Alfred Lord, 736

Tenochtitlan, 481

Tenskwatawa (Prophet), 709

Terror (terrorism): France (1793–1794), 651–653, 654–655, 656, 662; Soviet purges, 880–881; Palestinian, 958; in Argentina, 968; September 11 attacks (2001), 932, 996(*illus.*), 997–998, 1005, 1009, 1019; al-Qaeda sponsorship of, 998, 1005, 1008–1009; in Bali (2004), 1004; global war on, 932, 1009, 1010

Tet Offensive (1968), 944

Téwodros II (Ethiopia), 760 *and illus.*, 761

Texas, 676, 705, 706(*map*), 710; cattle in, 523; independence of, 707

Textile industry. *See also* Clothing; Cotton; Silk; Netherlands, 500; piecework in, 503; African trade and, 565; child labor in, 668, 675, 684 *and illus.*; women in, 644, 684, 685, 797, 889; British, 675, 684; in Russia, 738; Japanese, 797; in China, 989

Thailand (Siam), 774, 834, 894, 985

Tharoor, Shashi, 1017–1018

Theology, reformation and, 492–493, 494

Third Estate (France), 648, 649

Third Geneva Convention (1950), 1010

Third Reich, 886. *See also* Nazi Germany

Third World, 979, 985. *See also* Developing nations; Nonindustrial countries; *and specific countries;* Cold War and, 954–955; garbage pickers in, 986(*illus.*)

Thirty Years War (1618–1648), 511

Tiananmen Square massacre (1989), 975

Tibet, 743; Buddhism in, 613

Timber and Stone Act of 1878 (U.S.), 721

Timbuktu, 569(*illus.*)

Timor, 601

Timur, 578, 594–595, 832

Timurids, 589, 593, 594

Tin mining, 671, 792, 885

Tippu Tip, 764

Tipu Sultan, 755–756, 766, 772

Tlaxcalans, 480, 481

Tobacco, 479, 500, 522, 561, 565, 820, 834; in Caribbean colonies, 550–551, 552, 554, 573; in colonial Virginia, 535, 551; in Mexico City, 529(*illus.*); in Ottoman Empire, 587, 588, 590(*illus.*), 730, 736; in Cuba, 838

Tocqueville, Alexis de, 812

Togo, 852

Tokugawa Ieyasu, 605

Tokugawa shogunate (Japan), 605, 607–612, 628; decentralization in, 607; elite decline and social crisis in, 611–612; Europeans and, 610–611; porcelain

Tokugawa shogunate *(Continued)* production in, 608, 609 *and illus.*; civil war ending, 806

Tokyo (Edo), 607, 608, 611, 804, 860; industrialization in, 790; Perry in, 786(*illus.*), 787; population growth in, 794, 985(*table*); bombing of, World War II, 894, 899

Tolstoy, Leo, 741

Tonkin Gulf Incident (1964), 943

Tordesillas, Treaty of (1494), 469(*map*), 472, 599(*map*)

Torture and cruelty: of witches, 496; Inquisition, 498; in colonial Latin America,

Torture and cruelty *(Continued)*
526; African slavery and, 558, 564; tarring and feathering, 644*(illus.)*; Nazi German, 901 *and illus.*; in Latin America, 967, 968, 969

Toussaint L'Ouverture, François Dominique, 638, 659–660

Toyoda Sakichi, 808

Toyota Motor Company, 973; origins of, 808

Tractors, 873, 879–880*(illus.)*

Trade, with Africa. *See* Gold (gold trade); Slave trade, African; Trans-Saharan trade

Trade associations, 1001–1003 *and map*

Trade barriers, 792, 820. *See also* Tariffs

Trade (commerce): *See also* Free trade; Merchants; Monopolies, trade *and specific commodities;* bourgeoisie and, 499; Dutch, 514; Anglo-Dutch rivalry in, 514; West African, 561; French colonial, 658; North American colonies and, 518*(illus.)*, 519, 537, 541, 643, 647; Qing China, 615, 742; Ottoman, 467, 570, 582, 586, 587; Japanese, 607, 861; Russian, 626, 628; English with China, 620–621; Industrial Revolution, 638, 670, 671; protective tariffs and, 561, 687, 717, 736; British Empire and, 502, 529, 719, 772, 774, 779; in nineteenth century Africa, 758*(map)*; legitimate, with Africa, 762; in British India, 770, 775; industrialized nations and, 792; Opium war and, 742–743; global, 861; tropical products and, 834, 835 *and illus.*; West African, 826, 918; Great Depression and, 884–885; colonial Africa, 918; Cuban, 950; Japanese surplus, 973; e-commerce (Internet), 1014; regional associations, 1001–1003 *and map*

Trade networks. *See* Atlantic trading system; Indian Ocean trade

Trade unions. *See* Labor unions

Trading companies, 550, 560, 563, 686. *See also specific companies;* European, in China, 615; European, in India, 765

Trading monopolies. *See* Monopolies, trading

Traditions, in British India, 766, 767. *See also* Folk cultures

Trafalgar, Battle of (1805), 656, 657*(map)*

Transnational corporations, 717, 933, 989

Transportation: *See also* Automobiles; Canals; Railroads; Roads; Ships and shipping; green-house gas emissions from, 1011; Industrial Revolution, 670–671, 679, 682; urban streetcars and subways, 791, 794, 795, 906*(illus.)*; world economy and, 839, 987; famine and, 930, 931

Trans-Saharan trade, 473, 569; slave trade and, 470, 563*(map)*, 566, 569–570, 759

Trans-Siberian Railway, 811, 833*(map)*, 839, 857

Transvaal, 774, 827

Travel (travelers): Chinese (Zheng He), 462*(map)*, 464 *and illus.*, 465, 468, 471; Amerindians in Europe, 504

Treaty ports, in China, 743, 812, 860, 862. *See also* Hong Kong; Shanghai

Trench warfare, World War I, 844*(illus.)*, 850, 855

Trent, Council of (1545-1563), 494

Trevithick, Richard, 678

Triangular trade, in Atlantic system, 561

Tribute system, Chinese, 607, 615

Trinidad, 774, 778

Trinidad (ship), 460, 461

Trinidad Tobago, 845, 1016

Triple Alliance (World War I), 848

Trivedi, Harish, 1017

Tropics (tropical ecology), 792. *See also specific tropical countries and regions;* New Imperialism and, 835 *and illus.*, 839; rain forests, 775, 835 *and illus.*, 839, 924, 926, 992 *and illus.*; agriculture, 938 *and illus.*

Trotsky, Leon, 858, 859, 878

Truman, Harry S, 941

Truman Doctrine (1947), 941

Truth and Reconciliation Commission (South Africa), 953

Tsars, of Russia, 625. *See also specific* tsar

Tsirinana, Philibert, 949

Tsushima Strait, Battle of (1905), 811

Tuberculosis, 681, 918

Tudor dynasty (England), 510*(table)*

Tulip Period, 587, 589

Tunisia, 581, 865

Tupac Amaru II, 543, 698

Turkestan, 740

Turkey, 867, 941, 944, 1001. *See also* Anatolia; Ottoman Empire; rise of, 784, 863 *and illus.*, 864*(map)*; women's rights in, 863, 868; immigrants in Germany, 987

Turkic peoples: of Central Asia, 589, 625; Uzbeks, 594, 740, 1003

Turkish language, 590–591, 732

Tuscarora peoples, 645

Tutsi-Hutu rivalry (Rwanda), 978

Tutu, Desmond, 953

Twenty-One Demands (Japan), 861

Typhus, 520, 930

Uganda, 764

Ukraine, 892; Orange Revolution in (2004), 1003; Russia and, 625, 740, 810; Soviet Republic of, 858

Ulama (Islamic scholars), 591, 730, 731

Ulloa, Antonio de, 530, 531

Underdevelopment, 717, 719–720. *See also* Developing nations; in Cuba, 935

Union of South Africa, 827–828. *See also* South Africa

Union of Soviet Socialist Republics. *See* Soviet Union (USSR)

United Arab Emirates, 1001*(illus.)*

United Fruit Company, 950

United Nations (UN), 974, 1019; Arab-Israeli conflict and, 957; Cold War and, 936, 937, 939; decolonization and, 939, 954; General Assembly, 936, 937, 957, 1009, 1010; genocide tribunal and, 978; Iraq and, 979; Persian Gulf War and, 979; Security Council, 937, 941, 957, 974; peacekeeping efforts of, 939; human rights and, 1009–1010; Millenium Summit, 1003; women's rights and, 1010, 1012; English language and, 1016

United Nations (World War II alliance), 894, 895

United Provinces of the Free Netherlands. *See* Netherlands

United Provinces of the Río de la Plata, 635*(map)*, 697*(map)*, 698. *See also* Argentina; Paraguay; Uruguay

USS Cole (destroyer), 1009

United States. *See also* United States, Industrial Revolution in; American Revolution, 643–647; voting rights in, 661; slavery debate in, 685; chronology (1789–1890s), 695; constitutional experiment in, 702; personalist leaders in, 703–704; war with Britain (1812), 661, 707, 709; war with Mexico (1846–1848), 707, 710; Amerindians in, 708–710 *and illus.*; abolition of slavery in, 707, 711–712; expansion of, 705, 706*(map)*, 720*(map)*, 820; civil war (1861–1865) in, 702, 707, 710, 711–712, 737; immigration to, 669, 670, 705, 715, 719, 722, 792–794 *and illus.*; labor movement in, 715; Latin America and, 694, 720; environmental degration in, 720–721; racial discrimination in, 714; railroads in, 678–679 *and illus.*, 693, 719, 720*(map)*; technology and development in, 719, 810; mining technology in, 717*(illus.)*, 721; national parks in, 721; end of slave trade and, 762; north-south division in, 802; opening of Japan and, 786*(illus.)*787–788; steel production in, 719, 790; Qing China and, 742, 748; shipping and shipbuilding in, 775, 792; census in, 783; Chinese immigration banned, 714, 747; as great power, 788, 812; British investment in, 792; population growth in, 792; European immigrants in, 792; universal male suffrage in, 799; urban growth in, 794, 795; immigrants and English in, 808; imperialism of, 836, 840*(map)*; intervention in Central America, 838–839; opening of Japan and, 804–805; Hawaii and, 836; Philippines and, 833*(map)*, 837, 838; war with Spain (1898–1899), 707, 836–837, 838; World War I and, 846, 850, 853, 854–855; World War I reparations and, 859; technologies of modernity in, 869–870 *and illus.*, 872; Great Depression in, 884 *and illus.*; isolationism in, before World War II, 856, 873, 887; Japanese and, 891; Guomindang and, 897–898; in World War II, 894–895 *and map*, 896–897, 903; World War II casualties, 898; homefront in, World War II, 902; Latin America and, 837, 920, 925; Mexican Revolution and, 921, 923–924; neoliberalism and, 970; Persian Gulf War (1990–1991), 978–979; fertility and immigration to, 981; wealth in, 985, 1000*(illus.)*; consumption patterns in, 989; immigration to, 986, 987; industrial robots in, 989; genocide convention and, 1010; Kyoto Protocol and, 1010, 1011; rising oil demand in, 1001; environmental legislation in, 992; cultural imperialism of, 1013; invasion of Iraq and Afghanistan by, 1004–1006; death penalty in, 1012; terrorist attacks in (9/11), 996*(illus.)*, 997–998, 1008, 1019